MW00608043

Messenger of the Lord

The Prophetic Ministry of Ellen G. White

"Early in my youth I was
asked several times,
Are you a prophet?
I have ever responded,
I am the Lord's messenger. . . .
My Saviour declared me to
be His messenger."

—Selected Messages,
book 1, page 32.

Herbert E. Douglass

Pacific Press® Publishing Association
Nampa, Idaho
Oshawa, Ontario, Canada

Edited by Kenneth H. Wood
Designed by Bryan Gray/Genesis Design
Cover Illustration by Gary Holland

Except where indicated otherwise, Bible quotations throughout this book are from the New King James Version (NKJV) of the Bible.

Douglass, Herbert E.
Messenger of the Lord : the prophetic ministry of Ellen G. White / Herbert E. Douglass.
p. cm.
Includes bibliographic references and index.
ISBN 0-8163-1657-0 (pbk. : alk paper)
1. White, Ellen Gould Harmon, 1827-1915. I. Title.
BX6193.W5D68 1998
286.7'092—dc21 98-15574
CIP

00 01 02 03 04 • 5 4 3 2 1

Dedication

To Kenneth H. Wood

Elder Statesman
Consummate Editor
Keen Observer and Thinker
Skilled Chairman
Loyal and Tested Friend
Model Husband, Gallant and Caring

Table of Contents

SECTION IV

CHAPTER

The Voice of a Movement

SECTION V

Nurturer of Inspired Concepts

SECTION VI

How to Listen to the Messenger

SECTION VII

CHAPTER

How to Evaluate Criticism

SECTION VIII

Continuing Relevancy of God's Messenger

Preface

In the mid-nineteen-fifties T. Housel Jemison, an associate director of the White Estate, wrote a book entitled, *A Prophet Among You.* This comprehensive work on the gift of prophecy focused specifically on the life and ministry of Ellen G. White. For many years it was used in Seventh-day Adventist colleges as the standard textbook on the gift of prophecy.

But in recent decades, much has been learned regarding inspiration/revelation, hence in 1989 the Board of Trustees of the Ellen G. White Estate authorized production of a new book. Sponsors included not only the White Estate but the General Conference Department of Education and the Board of Higher Education.

Herbert E. Douglass was selected as the author. Dr. Douglass, who taught Spirit of prophecy courses in college, had also served as a college president, associate editor of the *Adventist Review*, and book editor of the Pacific Press. He immediately began work on the project, researching the subject thoroughly.

Exposure to a galaxy of scholars and ideas is reflected in the footnotes throughout the book, but the fact that an author is quoted on a particular point should not be taken as an endorsement either of the person or of all the ideas and positions held by that person.

We believe that this book presents the prophetic ministry of Ellen G. White in a way that makes it appealing to both young and old. Instead of approaching the subject from the abstract to the personal, it leads from the personal to the abstract. As a result, readers will become acquainted with the gift of prophecy by becoming personally acquainted with Mrs. White. Further, they will be drawn closer to the personal God whom she served; they will admire the wise and careful way in which He communicated His messages to His messenger; and they will be awe-struck as they observe the way He led her through the theological, medical, and social mine fields of her day.

Readers will find at the end of each chapter a series of study questions that will lead into further, deeper study of the subject covered by the chapter. The questions may function as a review of the chapter, and may encourage research that will enlarge readers' understanding of the topic presented in the chapter.

We believe that everyone who reads this book will understand better how God works through His prophets, and will be deeply convicted that Ellen White was divinely called to the prophetic office. They also will face the future with new confidence and strengthened faith, exclaiming with God's messenger: "We have nothing to fear for the future, except as we shall forget the way the Lord has led us, and His teaching in our past history" *(Life Sketches*, p. 196).

The Board of Trustees of the Ellen G. White Estate, Inc.
Silver Spring, Maryland

Acknowledgments

Books do not arise in a vacuum. A lifetime of influences pour into an author's mind, and all those people, books, and teachers in one's past fill the cerebral omnibus that the author drives in the development of his manuscript. To acknowledge all those contributions would be impossible because they have become faceless thoughts—but this author is acutely aware of this immense reservoir that others have filled for him.

But in the specific task of responding to the request of the church's Board of Higher Education and the Ellen G. White Estate, this author wants to give credit to those who have made this somewhat technical book possible.

Without the enormous vision and editorial skills of Kenneth H. Wood, this book would not have been conceptualized nor completed in its present state. His empathetic encouragement and insights for more than three years during the research and writing provided the environment to think in areas that have been cloudy for many.

The two directors of the Ellen G. White Estate under which this book was commissioned and then finished, Paul Gordon and Juan Carlos Viera, have provided not only encouragement but special insights at crucial points. Norma Collins, the tireless and efficient associate director, courageously entered the many suggestions and the often-revised author's comments into the final computer copy.

The White Estate is fortunate to have two proven scholars in their particular specialties—Jim Nix in Adventist history and lore, and Tim Poirier, archivist and technical craftsman of Ellen White materials. Although they are not responsible for any errors or omissions, they contributed much to the level of accuracy in this book. Besides these two scholars, I owe much to Drs. Robert Olson and Roger Coon, who in past years had done careful research on many topics dealt with in the book.

Among many others who provided timely help and suggestions are my brother Melvyn who served as my browser in the mysterious world of Internet, finding, on many occasions, most elusive information almost immediately; Drs. John Scharffenberg and Gary Fraser, who patiently read and contributed to the chapters on health; Dr. Richard Schwarz, who used his historiographical micrometer in reviewing final pages; and Francis Wernick, Neal Wilson, and Rowena Rick, members of the Ellen G. White Board, who read and critiqued the manuscript.

Special appreciation also must go to skilled scholars and specialists such as P. Gerard Damsteegt, Fritz Guy, Bert Haloviak, Roland Hegstad, Robert Johnston, Mervyn Maxwell, and Alden Thompson, who shared thoughtful insights at certain points.

No author can go far without an understanding, encouraging publishing house. Robert Kyte and Russell Holt provided the needed touch at the right times that kept the window on the future open and bright; they were determined that the product of their hands would be worthy of the subject of this book.

And to all this I add the input of my understanding soulmate, dear Norma, who continually refocused priorities for three and one-half years, as she sensed the dimensions of this assignment. To God be the glory!

Herbert E. Douglass

An Overview by the Author

This book was written with two purposes in mind: (1) to provide Seventh-day Adventists with a fresh look at the life and witness of Ellen G. White, and (2) to provide resource material for college and seminary courses on the gift of prophecy, especially as manifested in the life and ministry of this inspired messenger of God.

Some people, lacking a clear understanding of how revelation/inspiration works, have permitted "problems" and criticisms to weaken or destroy their confidence in Mrs. White's unique seventy-year ministry. Yet, millions of people around the world consider her an inspired, epoch-making religious leader. They have found their love for Jesus deepened as she directed their minds to the Bible, her chief source of enlightenment and joy. They have discovered that her writings provide clear, highly motivating and accurate insights for healthy, disciplined living. Most important, they have found in her writings coherent insights into the Biblical story of salvation.

Thus, in addition to the twin purposes mentioned above, this book is written for at least two groups: (1) those who are immensely grateful for the pen of Ellen White and want to learn more about her, and (2) those with unresolved questions about certain aspects of her long ministry. This book sets forth abundant reasons for affirming her claim to be God's messenger; it provides ample evidence to satisfy the most discerning mind.

Certainty, Authority, and Trust

This book is concerned with how young and old find certainty. Is there any "authority" anywhere that can speak with clarity, satisfying the head as well as the heart?

Seventh-day Adventists answer "Yes! there is an Authority." We point to the One who made us, and call Him God—the God who communicates. Further, He made us capable of responding to Him. Wonderful thought; we were made to listen to our friendly Maker! And when we listen, we hear the truth about who we are, why we exist, and what kind of unending future He has planned for us—if we keep listening.

How does God "speak" to human beings? "Many times and in many ways," Paul wrote in Hebrews 1:1 (TEV). For example:

- Through His created works, which we call "nature."
- Through the Holy Spirit, who makes contact with each person's conscience.
- Through Jesus Christ, who was God Himself.

But God did even more. He knew that thousands of years *before* Jesus would come as man, men and women needed to hear His side of the story of the great controversy between good and evil.

God's Communication System

Even after God became man, He could not be everywhere at once. Nor could Jesus be physically present everywhere after His ascension. So, to get His message across, God added to His Self-communicating system a very humanly oriented plan—He spoke in "many times and in many ways through the prophets" (Heb. 1:1-3, TEV).

This communication system "through the prophets" was well-recognized throughout Biblical times. God's people learned by experience that they were at their best when they listened to the prophets: "Believe in the Lord your God, and you shall be established; believe His prophets, and you shall prosper" (2 Chron. 20:20). Further, they knew through experience that God would not let them go blindly into the future. "Surely the Lord God does nothing, unless He reveals His secret to His servants the prophets" (Amos 3:7).

Divine communication through prophets was not confined to Old Testament times. During our Lord's last hours on earth, He promised that this line of communication between heaven and earth would always be kept open—through the Holy Spirit, the Spirit of Truth, His personal representative. Today, even as in Old Testament times, the Holy Spirit continues to speak, not only to each person's conscience, but through prophets: "I will give you another Helper, that He may abide with you forever, even the Spirit of truth" (John 14:16). "And He Himself gave some to be apostles, some prophets" (Eph. 4:11; see also 1 Cor. 12:28).

The Spirit of Truth is also the Spirit of prophecy! That means that these specially selected men and women would be "under control of the Holy Spirit as they spoke the message that came from God" (2 Pet. 1:21, TEV). The church was told to expect this truth-communication system to function until Jesus returns.

This Biblical overview teaches that God never wanted men and women to be without certainty regarding the purpose of life. Especially during the unparalleled stress of the last days, He made certain that we could know the truth about the future. Whenever men and women carefully listen to God's prophets, they "know" they are listening to the "truth." Truth carries its own authority because truth appeals to and satisfies our concern for objective certainty and subjective certitude—the linking of the head and heart.

This book will help answer the following questions: Does Ellen White fulfill the Biblical qualifications of a prophet? On what basis can one regard her as authority in her role as God's messenger? In reviewing her seventy-year active ministry, what difference did her counsel make in determining the course and development of the church? What was the effect of her counsel to individuals? Did she manifest the marks of coherence and reliability and, thus, the test of authority?

We will consider "the weight of evidence." Her long ministry and the fruitage of her labors is an open book. No *contrived* "evidence" or "argument" is needed to support her claim to be God's messenger.

Ellen White's own abiding principle will govern our journey together: "The subjects which we present to the world must be to us a living reality. It is important that in defending the doctrines which we consider fundamental articles of faith, we should never allow ourselves to employ arguments that are not wholly sound. These may avail to silence an opposer, but they do not honor the truth. We should present sound arguments, that will not only silence our opponents, but will bear the closest and most searching scrutiny" (*Gospel Workers*, p. 299).

At the heart of the great controversy between God and Satan, between good and evil, is the conflict over truth, that is, who is right about how to run the universe, God or Satan? God's position is that truth needs no defense, it simply needs to be seen and demonstrated. Satan, "a liar and the father of it" (John 8:44), makes his points by deception.

Clever debater, slick insinuator, Satan appeals to the self-centered "heart" to be the final arbiter of "truth." One of his most effective tools is to raise doubt, causing hesitancy and postponement of a spiritual commitment. For this reason, tampering with truth in any way, casting unwarranted shadows over what may not be totally clear, is an immoral act. It is part of a cosmic attempt to obscure truth and thwart God.

Ellen White could not be clearer than when she appeals for openness and the rejection of fear when separating facts from opinions. She knew that faith is in jeopardy if one sets limits to research, fearing that new discoveries may unsettle faith. But she often made clear that one's faith also is in jeopardy when human reason or feelings are permitted to set the limits of faith. For her, truth must be honored at all costs.

How the Book Is Organized

This book is divided into eight sections:

I. God's Communication System (chapters 1 to 3).

II. The Real Ellen White (chapters 4 to 12).

III. The Listening Messenger (chapters 13 to 16).

IV. The Voice of a Movement (chapters 17 to 21).

V. Nurturer of Inspired Concepts (chapters 22 to 31).

VI. How to Listen to the Messenger (chapters 32 to 40).

VII. How to Evaluate Criticism (chapters 41 to 44).

VIII. Continuing Relevancy of God's Messenger (chapters 45 to 47).

Chapters 1 to 3 will explore briefly the Biblical teaching about *how* God has been revealing the "good news" (the gospel) of salvation to men and women. The "good news" is the truth about God and His way of running the universe—a picture in sharp contrast to Satan's lies and libels. God is revealed through Jesus Christ, the Revealer. The Holy Spirit passes on, through the "gift of prophecy," the truth as revealed in Jesus.

Chapters 4 to 12 will focus first on Ellen Harmon's childhood and teen-age experiences. Then, her role as Mrs. Ellen G. White—wife, mother, neighbor, soul winner, and public personality—by examining her life from her own writings as well as from the viewpoint of those who knew her best. Because one's thought as well as temperament are largely determined by contemporary social, economic, and philosophical influences, we will briefly note the circumstances prevailing in northeastern United States, and later national factors that most probably touched her as she developed under her divine assignment. Her fascinating blend of Victorian woman and rugged American pioneer will be studied.

Chapters 13 to 16 will observe how the prophetic gift functioned in the ministry of Ellen White. The historical background of the 1840s and 1850s will help us to understand the unfavorable climate that existed for anyone claiming to have visions. Nevertheless, the vision phenomena of Ellen White brought clarity and assurance to those who wanted a Biblical explanation for the 1844 experience.

We will study Ellen White as a writer and speaker, by:

• noting her development in style and content as she responded to changing circumstances and deepening enlightenment during her seventy-year ministry;

• tracing how she, as any writer would and does, employed research materials to amplify and make more specific the core message she was commissioned to bear;

• noting the remarkable reception to her spoken and written words by non-Adventists;

• recalling her unusual speaking abilities, often with physical circumstances that would overwhelm her contemporaries, or even anyone today.

Chapters 17 to 21 will explore the phenomenal relationship between Ellen G. White and the church with which she became so intimately involved for seventy years. No other person has so directly affected the growth and shaping of the Seventh-day Adventist Church, theologically and institutionally. She had much to do with its strategic planning. Her counsel was sought from Australia to Europe and across North America regarding the establishment of schools, health institutions, and publishing houses. Her writings became beacons of enlightenment to be avidly studied in later generations.

Chapters 22 to 31 will examine Ellen White's role as conceptual nurturer. She had a unique ability to synthesize the clear prophetic message with human experience and the insights of others. Out of this synthesis developed a distinctively integrated and coherent body of thought, firmly and consistently Biblically based. This integration unified her vast contribution to practical principles of education, evangelism, organization, and health, for which Seventh-day Adventists have become well known.

The Great Controversy Theme

We will note how she used certain principles of investigation as she processed and conveyed truth. Her introduction to *The Great Controversy* is instructive: "The great events which have marked the progress of reform in past ages, are matters of history, well known and universally acknowledged by the Protestant world; they are facts which none can gainsay. This history I have presented briefly, in accordance with the scope of the book, and the brevity which must necessarily be observed, the facts having been condensed into as little space as seemed consistent with a proper understanding of their application.

"In some cases where a historian has so grouped together events as to afford, in brief, a comprehensive view of the subject, or has summarized details in a convenient manner, his words have been quoted; but in some instances no specific credit has been given, since the quotations are not given for the purpose of citing that writer as authority, but because his statement affords a ready and forcible presentation of the subject. In narrating the experience and views of those carrying forward the work of reform in our own time, similar use has been made of their published works."

The organizing principle that gathered this material like a magnet into her synthesis is the Great Controversy Theme. Seeing the Bible as a whole and the relation of its parts, Ellen White clearly illuminated the basic issues regarding the character of God, the nature of man, the rise of sin, and how God plans ultimately to deal with this rebel planet.

Ellen White's understanding of the Great Controversy Theme provided remarkable stability and harmony as the Adventist Church developed its theology and denominational structure. It established the thought center for her to provide personal comfort and theological correction at those junctures where other religious bodies usually have splintered.

Under Section 6, "How to Listen to the Messenger," chapters 32 to 38 emphasize *how* men and women should "hear" the message of Ellen G. White. Any study of written documents, whether they be Shakespearean sonnets or Holy Scripture, involves "hermeneutics," that is, using principles of interpretation that will assist the reader in understanding the author. We will examine rules of interpretation that help us determine what Ellen White meant to those who heard her, and what these same writings mean in modern times. For example, one rule is to consider time, place, and circumstances when we apply her counsel today. Principles remain, but the application of principle may be different as we follow this hermeneutical rule.

Fundamental to understanding Ellen White is our larger need to understand how God gives His messages through His messengers to His people. In past years, those who have believed that words themselves are inspired have been greatly troubled by what appear to be Biblical "errors" and "contradictions." This same confusion between mechanical or dictation inspiration (each word being just the way God spoke it to the prophet) and thought inspiration (God inspired the prophets, not their words) has troubled many when reading the writings of Ellen White. We shall note how this misunderstanding of the revelation/inspiration process has created doubt and unwarranted criticism of Ellen White.

An equally important issue is the relationship between Ellen White's writings and the Bible. We will seek to understand such terms as "levels of inspiration," "progressive revelation," "canonical authority," and "lesser light, greater light."

Chapters 39 and 40 will review how Ellen White wrote her books. We will note how she related to her editorial assistants, and their role in producing *Steps to Christ, The Desire of Ages,* and *The Great Controversy.*

In chapters 41 to 43 we will evaluate criticisms of Ellen White. Inevitably, prophets will be criticized by contemporaries, primarily because they are far out in front in God's controversy with evil. No Biblical prophet had an easy time fulfilling his or her assignment. This sad fact has led to the observation that one generation kills its prophets, only to have the next build monuments in their honor.

Some criticism finds its source in the perennial reaction of those who object to truth that cuts across personal inclination or pride of opinion. Examples of such rejection are found in the criticism of Jesus, Jeremiah, Paul and Ellen White.

These chapters do not attempt to answer every allegation or criticism that has been leveled at Ellen White, but we will note several general types. After evaluating these criticisms, the reader will be able to differentiate between the humanness of the earthly container and the authority of the message carried by the container. (See 2 Cor. 4:7.)

Chapter 44 is a case study of the "shut-door" issue, a major source of contention for more than a century.

How Ellen White Measures Up

In the final section, "Continuing Relevancy of the Messenger," we will ask: Does Ellen White measure up as a messenger bearing God's message in modern times? Does her seventy-year ministry establish her credentials as a divine messenger? We will note how she did her work, both privately and publicly, and review the virtually seamless relationship between her ministry and the development of the Seventh-day Adventist Church.

Seventh-day Adventists have generally believed that Ellen G. White was God's messenger. Why did Adventists in her day come to that conclusion, and why have Adventists since her death also arrived at this conclusion?

In our closing pages we will ask: How relevant is Ellen White today? She died in 1915. Can she speak in any meaningful way to a transistorized global village where information by the Internet is instantaneous to computer operators throughout the planet, where science always seems to have one more solution to the world's needs "in the nick of time"? Though circumstances have changed drastically, and the socio-political world is sharply different, we will note that Ellen White's writings speak pointedly to our day, and are increasingly relevant in this end-time.

SECTION I

God's Communication System

CHAPTER

CHAPTER 1

The Revealer and the Revealed

"The Helper will come—the Spirit, who reveals the truth about God and who comes from the Father. I will send him to you from the Father, and he will speak about me" (John 15:26, TEV).

The Gospel is not *about* Jesus; the Gospel *is* Jesus and what He taught. Teachings *about* Jesus provide the framework for proclaiming the "good news," but Jesus Himself is the "good news." Jesus and His teachings are not the prelude to the gospel, they are the gospel![1]

The "good news" is that in the wonderfull mind of God, One of the Godhead chose to come to this rebel planet with hands outstretched, inviting men and women everywhere to return to the family of God. The "good news" is that the God-who-became-man "gave" Himself to the human family forever, forever limited to time and space. For what purpose? To show us what God is like! (John 14:7.)

As we will see, the Revealer we call "Jesus"; the Revealed we call "God"; and the Person through whom the Godhead chose to "reveal" the Revealer to the human race is the Holy Spirit.

Jesus made this clear a few hours before Gethsemane: "I will ask the Father, and he will give you another Helper, who will stay with you forever. He is the Spirit, who reveals the truth about God" (John 14:16, 17, TEV). Further, "The Helper, the Holy Spirit, whom the Father will send in my name, will teach you everything and make you remember all that I have told you" (John 14:26, TEV).

And to make sure that the point was clear: "The Helper will come—the Spirit, who reveals the truth about God and who comes from the Father. I will send him to you from the Father, and he will speak about me" (John 15:26, TEV).

Jesus said further: "When, however, the Spirit comes, who reveals the truth about God, he will lead you into all the truth. He will not speak on his own authority, but he will speak of what he hears and will tell you of things to come. He will give me glory, because he will take what I say and tell it to you. All that my Father has is mine; that is why I said that the Spirit will take what I give him and tell it to you" (John 16:13-15, TEV).

The Holy Spirit is our Lord's counterpart. The Spirit will say and do exactly what Jesus would say and do if He were present today!

How does all this work? The Holy Spirit gives to each Christian some special gift: "There are different kinds of spiritual gifts, but the same Spirit gives them. . . . The Spirit's presence is shown in some way in each person for the good of all" (1 Cor. 12:4, 7, TEV).

The Gift of Prophecy

One of those special gifts is the gift of "prophecy" (1 Cor. 12:10; Eph. 4:11). Through the gift of prophecy the Holy Spirit links Himself with certain men and women who then convey to others the truth about Jesus. That is the Spirit's job description—to "speak about" Jesus through gifted men and women called "prophets." Knowing Jesus and what He can tell us about God is the most essential information needed by the human family, for "to know [Jesus] is life eternal" (John 17:3, KJV).

In the book of Revelation, the prophet John wrote how this gift was working in his own life: "The revelation of Jesus Christ, which God gave him to show to . . . his servant John, who bore witness to the word of God and to the testimony of Jesus Christ" (Rev. 1:1, 2, RSV).

Here we see the divine communication system at work: The Revealer working through the Spirit to reveal the truth about God through His prophet. In chapter 19, the angel who visited John reminded him that the "testimony of Jesus is the spirit of prophecy" (vs. 10, RSV).

The purpose of the gift of prophecy is to tell the story of Jesus. The prompting Agent who inspires the human prophet to tell the truth about Jesus is the Holy Spirit. In Biblical shorthand, the Spirit of prophecy is "the testimony of Jesus."

Peter understood this divine system of communication: "You love him, although you have not seen him, and you believe in him, although you do not now see him. So you rejoice with a great and glorious joy which words cannot express, because you are receiving the salvation of your souls, which is the purpose of your faith in him. It was concerning this salvation that the prophets made careful search and investigation, and they prophesied about this gift which God would give you. They tried to find out when the time would be and how it would come. This was the time to which Christ's Spirit in them was pointing, in predicting the sufferings that Christ would have to endure and the glory that would follow. God revealed to these prophets that their work was not for their own benefit, but for yours, as they spoke about those things which you have now heard from the messengers who announced the Good News by the power of the Holy Spirit sent from heaven. These are things which even the angels would like to understand" (1 Peter 1:8-12, TEV).

Genuine prophets are not motivated by personal whim or reward but by the direct moving of the Spirit of Christ, the "Holy Spirit sent from heaven." In one sense, the "Spirit of prophecy" *is* the Spirit of Christ through His Divine Helper, the Holy Spirit—made known to men and women through the human prophet. In another sense, "the Spirit of prophecy" is also the testimony *about* Christ, the chief purpose for the gift of prophecy.

Since Jesus returned to heaven, this simple, double-edged formula is one of the clearest, safest tests as to the genuineness of a "prophet's" claim: Does he or she tell the truth about Jesus? In the spirit of Jesus?

Why has the very name of Jesus, through the years, softened the voice and calmed the heart of people on all continents? Because men and women remember the courage recovered, the hope revived, and the surge of strength they received to pick up life's challenge anew—when they remembered how much they matter to Jesus who said through the Spirit of prophecy, "Fear not, for I am with you" (Isa. 41:10, RSV); "I will never fail you nor forsake you" (Heb. 13:5, RSV). They have learned through experience what He meant when He said, "I will not leave you desolate; I will come to you" (John 14:18, RSV).

Telling the Truth About God

Why such confidence in a Man called Jesus who lived for only thirty-three years in old Palestine? Because men and women came to know Him as their Creator who became man. Why? Because He was the only One in the universe who could convincingly tell the truth about God—the One who had been sorely misrepresented by the great rebel and by many of the world's greatest thinkers. God was not severe, arbitrary, and unforgiving, as He had been portrayed. When He asked men and women for willing allegiance, He also showed them that He too, by nature, was self-denying, and that love means doing for others what they cannot do for themselves, or even do not deserve.

How was that revealed? Paul contemplated Christ's magnificent revelation as an "emptying" of His divine prerogatives when He entered the human family (Phil. 2). Not suddenly as a valiant prince wielding the sword of justice, but slowly in the womb of a woman. Not to be honored as a special guest, but to be misunderstood and maligned because of His unambiguous integrity and focus.

How can it be that earth's only hope became this planet's target of humiliating abuse? "He came unto his own, and his own received him not" (John 1:11, KJV). Christians are not only awed by this monstrous ingratitude, they are strangely moved with regret and determined that He will find a hearty welcome in their lives. Christians are amazed at the God-man's condescension, and this wonder becomes part of a daily reason to honor Him in all they do.

Both Sacrifice and High Priest

When they look at Jesus they see Him both as Sacrifice and High Priest.[2] On Calvary, He did something about the crushing "wages of sin" that forever changed our relationship with God: He died! He is the only Person who has ever truly died! All other men and women who have "passed on" are now *sleeping,*[3] except for those few who have been resurrected or translated and are now in heaven.[4] Jesus alone has tasted "death," so that all who make Him Lord of their lives will never have to "die." "For the wages of sin is death, but the free gift of God is eternal life in Christ Jesus our Lord" (Rom. 6:23, RSV). What a gift! Through Him we escape what we deserve!

But there is even more! He now lives as our High Priest. What does this mean? He stands before the heavenly beings and the unfallen worlds as a Man whose cheerful obedience proved that God had not been unfair in asking for willing compliance from His created beings. Satan was wrong! And they see this heroic Overcomer who went through the unspeakable anguish of being "God-forsaken" on Calvary, proving that God Himself did care about His creation, that He was unselfish and the essence of genuine love. The whole universe (beyond the confines of earth) sees Jesus standing in heaven's Most Holy Place as God's answer to Satan's lies about Him.

What do *we* see when we think of Jesus as our High Priest? We see Him as the Mediator between God and sinful humanity. We see Him as our Advocate who joins justice and mercy, stopping all charges against God and believers (1 John 2:1). He is our Intercessor, not only representing us before the Father but also interceding between us and the evil one (Heb. 4:16).[5]

The apostle Paul put it this way: "Since then we have a great high priest who has passed through the heavens, Jesus, the Son of God, let us hold fast our confession. For we have not a high priest who is unable to sympathize with our weaknesses, but one who in every respect has been tempted as we are, yet without sinning. Let us then with confidence draw near to the throne of grace, that we may receive mercy and grace to help in time of need" (Heb. 4:14-16, RSV).

This kind of intercession every person needs every day: the peace of pardon and the power of interceding grace. Christ's powerful presence, through the Holy Spirit and angels, reaches out to every person committed to Him. He breaks through the power with which Satan has held each person captive. He reaches into their neural pathways. He strengthens the believer's will power. He is ever ready to assist human beings in resisting sin, both from within and without. Jesus simply shares with us the defense system by which He overcame temptation (Rev. 3:21).

Too often, after contemplating Christ's condescension as a hounded and finally crucified Man, believers consider His "gift" to earth finished. But God did not *give* "his only Son" (John 3:16, RSV) on a kind of temporary lend-lease basis. The Creator of hundreds of billions of island galaxies, who walked among the stars and whirled universes into orbit, imprisoned Himself within His own creation, not for just nine months, nor for only thirty-three years, but forever!

This kind of love awakens love. And heart-appreciation. And towering commitment to this great Lover, above any of this world's most alluring appeals.

Before the prophet can tell the truth about God, as known through Jesus, the prophet must know Jesus personally. Theological talk is cheap; personal experience comes with a price.

Ellen G. White's Devotion to Jesus

Ellen White responded wholeheartedly to this love, and made it a major theme of her writings. Wherever one turns in her voluminous books and letters to family, friends, and co-workers, one sees evidences of her deep love for the Saviour. Many whose first contact with Seventh-day Adventists was through the writings of Ellen White have expressed amazement at her awareness of, and deep appreciation for, the dimensions of our God's "Gift" to this rebel planet.

Her spiritual insights began early. In her early teen years, deeply affected by William Miller's preaching, she longed for a deeper religious experience: "As I prayed, the burden and agony of soul that I had so long felt left me, and the blessing of God came upon me like the gentle dew. I gave glory to God for what I felt, but I longed for more. I could not be satisfied till I was filled with the fullness of God. Inexpressible love for Jesus filled my soul."[6]

Ellen White was, above all, a spiritual person, full of appreciation for her Saviour and Lord. This personal sense of God's presence put her on-line with God, enabling Him to reveal much more of Himself and His plans for this world. Her personal experience in responding to the simple gospel preceded theology—Jesus was the core and center of all her theological thought.

Here is one example of her pervasive theme of extolling Jesus: "It will be profitable to contemplate the divine condescension, the sacrifice, the self-denial, the humiliation, the resistance the Son of God encountered in doing His work for fallen men. Well may we come forth from contemplation of His sufferings exclaiming, Amazing condescension! Angels marvel, as with intense interest they watch the Son of God descending step by step the path of humiliation. It is the mystery of godliness. It is the glory of God to conceal Himself and His ways, not by keeping men in ignorance of heavenly light and knowledge, but by surpassing the utmost capacity of men to know. Humanity can comprehend in part, but that is all that man can bear. The love of Christ passes knowledge. The mystery of redemption will continue to be the mystery, the unexhausted science and everlasting song of eternity. Well may humanity exclaim, Who can know God? We may, as did Elijah, wrap our mantles about us, and listen to hear the still, small voice of God."[7]

Ellen White walked with Jesus, through sunshine and shadow. Writing to son William and his young bride, Mary, she spoke of her husband James's companionship and their common walk: "We are trying to humbly follow in the footprints of our dear Saviour. We need His Spirit and His grace every hour, or we shall make blunders and shall do harm."[8]

A few weeks later, during a very strenuous covered-wagon trip from Texas to Kansas, she wrote again to Mary: "I am worn and feel as though I was about 100 years old. . . . My ambition is gone; my strength is gone, but this will not last. . . . I hope that by the cheering light of the countenance of my Saviour, I shall have the springback power."[9]

Contemplating Christmas in 1880, now 53, she wrote to a friend, "Christmas will be spent in seeking Jesus to be a welcome guest in my heart. His presence will drive all the shadows away."[10]

Ellen White wrote hundreds of articles for both the *Review and Herald* and the *Signs of the Times.* Almost every article contained some reference to her Lord, who had become not only her strength but the joy of her life. At 69, she wrote: "I love to speak of Jesus and His matchless love. . . . I know that He is able to save to the uttermost all that come unto Him. His precious love is a reality to me, and the doubts expressed by those who know not the Lord Jesus Christ, have no effect upon me. . . . Do you believe that Jesus is your Saviour, and that He has manifested His love for you in giving His precious life for your salvation? Take Jesus as your personal Saviour. Come to Him just as you are; give yourself to Him; grasp His promise by living faith, and He will be to you all that you desire."[11]

Ellen White considered Jesus her Saviour and best Friend.[12] But more than that, He was her Lord. In Europe she was told that people would be more receptive to the advent message, "if we dwell on the love of Jesus." They warned that there was "danger of losing our congregations if we dwell on the sterner questions of duty and the law of God."

Having heard that kind of talk before, she wrote in her travel notes, "There is a spurious experience prevailing everywhere. Many are continually saying, 'All that we have to do is to believe in Christ.' They claim that faith is all we need. In its fullest sense, this is true; but they do not take it in the fullest sense. To believe in Jesus is to take Him as our redeemer and our pattern. If we abide in Him and He abides in us, we are partakers of His divine nature, and are doers of His word. The love of Jesus in the heart will lead to obedience to all His commandments. But the love that goes no farther than the lips is a delusion; it will not save any soul. Many reject the truths of the Bible, while they profess great love for Jesus; but the apostle John declares, 'He that saith, I know him, and keepeth not his commandments, is a liar, and the truth is not in him.' While Jesus has done all in the way of merit, we ourselves have something to do in the way of complying with the conditions."[13]

The Great Controversy Theme

In her theological instruction, Ellen White's insight into the prevailing theme of the Bible, the Great Controversy Theme,[14] illuminated the reason why Jesus became man. This core understanding permeated all her writings. For example: "In order to grow in grace and in the knowledge of Christ, it is essential that you meditate much upon the great themes of redemption. You should ask yourself why Christ has taken humanity upon Himself, why He suffered upon the cross, why He bore the sins of men, why He was made sin and righteousness for us. You should study to know why He ascended to heaven in the nature of man, and what is His work for us today. . . . We think that we are familiar with the character of Christ, and we do not realize how much is to be gained by the study of our glorious Pattern. We take it for granted that we know all about Him, and yet we do not comprehend His character or mission."[15]

"Listening" to Ellen White is like hearing Handel's Messiah, page after page. "The Spirit of Christ" pervades her ministry. Consistency, clarity, and coherency mark her devotion to her best Friend. More than all else, it seems, Ellen White helps to satisfy our human craving for grace. In personal letters, in magazine articles, and speaking to large audiences, her grace-oriented messages enlarged

God's embrace of grace to needy, weary hearts. For those who listen, Ellen White has the surest mark of the "Spirit of prophecy"—she bore witness to Jesus.

Endnotes

1. "The gospel is glorious because it is made up of His righteousness. It is Christ unfolded, and Christ is the gospel embodied. . . .We are not to praise the gospel, but praise Christ. We are not to worship the gospel, but the Lord of the gospel."—Manuscript 44, 1898, cited in *Seventh-day Adventist Bible Commentary (SDABC)*, vol. 7, p. 907.
2. *The Acts of the Apostles,* p. 33.
3. The Bible speaks of the first death as a "sleep." See John 11:11-14; 1 Thess. 4:13-16; 5:10. The second death is reserved for sinners who reject the gospel's invitation. See Rev. 20:6, 14; 21:8.
4. Enoch (Gen. 5:24), Elijah (2 Kings 2:11), Moses (Jude 9), those raised with Jesus (Matt. 27:52, 53).
5. "Everyone who will break from the slavery and service of Satan, and will stand under the blood-stained banner of Prince Immanuel will be kept by Christ's intercession. Christ, as our Mediator, at the right hand of the Father, ever keeps us in view, for it is as necessary that He should keep us by His intercession as that He should redeem us with His blood. If He lets go His hold of us for one moment, Satan stands ready to destroy. Those purchased by His blood, He now keeps by His intercession." (Manuscript 73, 1893, in *SDABC,* vol. 6, comments on Romans 8:34, p. 1078; also *Manuscript Releases (MR),* vol. 15, p. 104.
6. *Early Writings,* p. 12.
7. *Bible Echo,* April 30, 1894.
8. Letter 18, 1879, cited in Arthur White, *Ellen G. White Biography,* vol. 3, (Washington, D.C.: Review and Herald Publishing Association, 1984), p. 105. Hereafter, references to Arthur White's biography of Ellen White, six volumes, will be *Bio.,* followed by volume number and pages.
9. Letter 20, 1879, cited in *Ibid.,* p. 117.
10. Letter 51, 1880, cited in *Ibid.,* p. 149.
11. *Review and Herald,* June 23, 1896.
12. See James Nix, "Oh, Jesus, How I Love You!" *Adventist Review*, May 30, 1996, pp. 10-14.
13. *Historical Sketches of the Foreign Missions of the Seventh-day Adventists,* (Basle, Switzerland: Imprimerie Polyglotte, 1886), p. 188; see also *Bio.*, vol. 3, p. 320.
14. See pp. 256-263.
15. *Signs of the Times,* Dec. 1, 1890.

Study Questions

1. Why is it a mistake to distinguish between Jesus and the gospel?
2. If the Holy Spirit is the Person who "reveals" God's messages to prophets, why is Jesus spoken of as the Revealer?
3. What is the primary purpose of the "gift of prophecy"?
4. What New Testament texts teach that God continues to speak in post-apostolic times?
5. What twin roles does Christ fill as our High Priest?
6. Select a chapter from either *Steps to Christ* or *The Desire of Ages*, and list some things it tells you about Jesus.

CHAPTER

God Speaks Through Prophets

"God, who at various times and in different ways spoke in time past to the fathers by the prophets . . ." (Heb. 1:1). "If there is a prophet among you, I, the Lord, make Myself known to him in a vision, and I speak to him in a dream" (Num. 12:6).

God has been communicating with human beings ever since He created Adam and Eve.[1] Human beings were created as God's counterparts, made "in his own image" (Gen. 1:27). He made them responsible—that is, able-to-respond to Him and to other persons. God provided everything imaginable for our first parents' happiness. He "planted a garden" (Gen. 2:8) already in blossom, full of plants suitable for food. Our first couple did not have to scratch out an existence, using trial and error, in order to survive.

Further, God made men and women with the ability to produce children in *their* image, even as Adam and Eve were created in *His* image. Nothing was left out; everything that men and women needed was in place—the right kind of food, the joy of work, a dazzling flower-and-garden show daily, no rain or rust, perfect companionship with each other and with God Himself. God's plan for our first parents remains a workable blueprint for us today as we seek peace and health amidst a sad breakdown of what the Lord intended for the human family.

Communication Before Sin

Before our first parents sinned, they were in constant communication with God and His angels. In this way they learned how to care for all living creatures and to provide for their own needs as stewards of this fantastic paradise called Planet Earth. Perhaps every day they had sundown worship with God "in the cool of the day" (Gen. 3:8). And they learned that not all was safe, even in Eden! Evil lurked in the shadow of the "tree of the knowledge of good and evil" (Gen. 2:17).

But terrible changes took place when Adam and Eve sinned. They no longer could speak with God face-to-face. Not because God had changed, but the first couple had—sin reconfigured their mind and emotions. Isaiah starkly described this new situation: "Your iniquities have separated you from your God; and your sins have hidden His face from you" (Isa. 59:2).

Sin damages the neural paths. No one is ever the same after he or she sins—new boutons in the neural pathways are formed that make sinning easier to repeat. To think clearly again requires special help from God. Thus, when our first parents sinned, God had to change His communication system with human beings. Not all the deplorable results of sin happened to Adam and Eve immediately, but the sad degeneracy of the human race began that day when they yielded to "the lust of the flesh, the lust of the eyes, and the pride of life" (1 John 2:16).

How God Bridged the Gap of Sin

How could the sin-gulf be bridged? God always has a solution. He knows how to adapt to changing circumstances. For example, instead of face-to-face communication He "speaks" to everyone through "conscience" (see John 1:9; Rom. 2:15). In some meaningful way, the Holy Spirit calls reasoning people to choose right over wrong, whatever their situation. Further, for those who specifically call for divine help, even though not much may be known about God, the promise is open to all: "In all your ways acknowledge Him, and He shall direct your paths" (Prov. 3:6).[2]

He also reveals Himself through angels: "Are they not all ministering spirits sent forth to minister for those who will inherit salvation?" (Heb. 1:14).[3]

Though marred by the results of sin, the physical world still reveals much about the nature and character of God: "For since the creation of the world His invisible attributes are clearly seen, being understood by the things that are made, even His eternal power and Godhead, so that they are without excuse" (Rom. 1:20). People on all continents and throughout history have associated God with such "attributes" as order, beauty, predictability, and design that they have seen in the heavenly bodies or the wonders of earth, both animate and inanimate.[4]

Before Moses led the Israelites out of Egypt God had been communicating with men and women through such patriarchs as Noah (Gen. 5-9), Abraham (Gen. 12-24), Isaac (Gen. 26:2-5), and Jacob (Gen. 32:24-30). Moses was the shining example of a human being with whom God conversed (Ex. 3, etc.).

In relating to the nation of Israel in its early years, God "spoke" through the Urim and Thummim, two precious stones set in the breastplate (the ephod) of Israel's high priest. When the nation's leaders wanted to know the will of God, the high priest asked specific questions that were answered by light resting on either the Urim or Thummin.[5] For a young nation so soon out of slavery and before the establishment of the written Word, this dramatic communication method was decisive and affirming.

God also spoke through dreams. Think of Joseph's dream that had prophetic significance (Gen. 37), the dreams of Pharaoh's butler and baker (Gen. 40), Pharaoh's dream (Gen. 41), the dream of the Midianite soldier (Judges 7), and Nebuchadnezzar's dreams (Dan. 2, 4).

Beyond question, the clearest revelation of God and His will for men and women has been through Jesus Christ: "God, who at various times and in various ways spoke in time past to the fathers by the prophets, has in these last days spoken to us by His Son" (Heb. 1:1, 2). Jesus was explicit: "He who has seen Me has seen the Father" (John 14:9). But Christ did not point to God as all prophets had been doing; He was the One to whom they had been pointing.

Prophets—the Most Recognized Form of Divine Disclosure

Although God used many methods, the "prophet" was the most recognized form of divine communication. Priests in Israel were the people's representatives before God; the prophets were God's official representatives before His people. The priest's calling was hereditary; the prophet was specifically called by God.[6]

Prophets have been the most visible channel in God's communication system. "Surely the Lord God does nothing, unless He reveals His secret to His servants the prophets" (Amos 3:7). "The Lord God of their fathers sent warnings to them by His messengers, rising up early and sending them, because He had compassion on His people" (2 Chron. 36:15).

God said very clearly that if people would not listen to His prophets, He had no other remedy to help them in their personal or national problems: "But they mocked the messengers of God, despised His words, and scoffed at His prophets. . . till there was no remedy" (2 Chron. 36:16).

In *A Prophet Among You,*[7] T. Housel Jemison listed eight reasons why God used prophets rather than some dramatic attention-getting device such as writing on the clouds or thundering out His will every morning at dawn:

1. Prophets prepared the way for Christ's first advent.
2. As representatives of the Lord, prophets showed the people that God valued human beings enough to choose from among them men and women to represent Him.
3. Prophets were a continual reminder of the nearness and availability of God's instruction.
4. Messages through the prophets accomplished the same purposes as a personal communication from the Creator.
5. Prophets were a demonstration of what fellowship with God and the transforming grace of the Holy Spirit could accomplish in a human life.
6. The presence of the prophets tested the people as to their attitude toward God.
7. Prophets assisted in the plan of salvation, for God has consistently used a combination of the human and the divine as His most effective means for reaching lost humankind.
8. The prophets' outstanding product is their contribution to the Written Word.

The Prophet's Work

The prophet's work was twofold: to *receive* the divine message and to *deliver* that message faithfully. These aspects are reflected in the three Hebrew words for "prophet." To emphasize their role in listening to God's will as it was revealed to them, the Hebrew writer used *chozeh* or *ro'eh*, translated as "seer." The Hebrew word *nabi,* (the most frequently used Hebrew word for prophet) describes prophets as they convey their message through speech or in writing.

In 1 Samuel 9:9, both roles are noted: "Formerly in Israel, when a man went to inquire of God, he spoke thus: 'Come, let us go to the seer' [*ro'eh*]; for he who is now called a prophet [*nabi*] was formerly called a seer [*ro'eh*]."

Chozeh, derived from the same Hebrew root word from which we get the English word *vision*, emphasizes that the prophet receives messages through divinely initiated visions.

Each of the three Hebrew terms for "prophet" underscores the prophetic office as the human side of the divine communication plan.

In the New Testament, the Greek word *prophetes,* corresponding to the Old Testament *nabi,* is transliterated in English as "prophet." Its basic meaning is "to speak forth." The genuine "prophet" speaks for God.

Long Line of Splendor

The first (so far as we know) of this amazing line of brave, faithful, and luminous prophets through whom God spoke His mind was "Enoch, the seventh from Adam" (Jude 14). Later there were Abraham (Gen. 20:7), and Moses (Deut. 18:15). Miriam was the first woman designated as a prophet (Ex. 15:20).

As time passed, the nation of Israel lost its spiritual focus and became like its neighbors in the worship of other gods. During the long and dreary period of the Judges, Israel was oppressed and humiliated by its neighbors. When Samuel was called to his prophetic role, the Philistines harshly controlled Israel. Eli, the high priest, was aged and ineffective. His two sons, Hophni and Phineas, though entrusted with the leadership both of government and the priesthood, "were corrupt; they did not know the Lord" (1 Sam. 2:12). Not surprisingly, "the word of the Lord was rare in those days; there was no widespread revelation" (1 Sam. 3:1).[8]

The "word of the Lord was rare" in Israel because rare were the men or women who could be entrusted with Heaven's messages. God was willing to guide His people, but He lacked men and women through whom He could safely impart His word. When visions were rare, Israel's spiritual and political circumstances were at low ebb. Israel's well-being was restored only when the prophetic office was restored.

For example, Israel's restoration as a free and blessed nation coincided with Samuel's prophetic ministry. Samuel's long life is an amazing record of how one man can change the course of a whole nation. His early years, after his mother had given him to the Lord, are well known: "And the child Samuel grew in stature, and in favor both with the Lord and men" (1 Sam. 2:26). As he matured, his spiritual leadership became evident: "So Samuel grew, and the Lord was with him and let none of his words fall to the ground. And all Israel from Dan to Beersheba knew that Samuel had been established as a prophet of the Lord" (1 Sam. 3:19, 20). Eventually, "the Lord revealed Himself to Samuel in Shiloh. . . . And the word of Samuel came to all Israel" (1 Sam. 3:21-4:1).

Samuel's faithfulness as God's messenger made it possible for God to reverse Israel's misery. The prophet's spiritual example, exhortation, and national leadership were so effective that the record states: "So the Philistines were subdued, and they did not come anymore into the territory of Israel. And the hand of the Lord was against the Philistines all the days of Samuel" (1 Sam. 7:13).

The life of Samuel is a clear and profound illustration of how effective the Spirit of prophecy can be in the establishment of God's program on earth. Who can imagine what can be accomplished in these last days by heeding the Spirit of prophecy!

When Samuel was old, something almost inexplicable occurred. Israelite leaders came to him and asked him to appoint "a king to judge us like all the nations" (1 Sam. 8:4). They forgot that their restored sovereignty and pleasant circumstances were due to Samuel's *prophetic* leadership.

God warned the leaders that a king would bring trials and troubles to their land—but they persisted, "that we also may be like all the nations, and that our king may judge us and go out before us and fight our battles" (vs. 20).

But, though Israel rejected God's plan for leading His people (theocracy), God did not reject Israel. He did not withdraw the prophetic gift. From the time of Saul, Israel's first king, to the bleak days when both Israel and Judah were taken captive by Assyria and Babylon, thirty prophets are mentioned by name in the Bible. In addition, there were unnamed prophets, along with "sons of the prophets."

Low Success Rate

How successful were the prophets? Only minimally, much to the detriment of those national leaders who rejected them. Note Jehoiakim (Jer. 36) to whom the prophet Jeremiah was bidden by God to write out words of condemnation and hope. Baruch, Jeremiah's editorial assistant, read the message "in the hearing of all the people" (vs. 10). The scroll was soon in the hands of court advisers who also were greatly impressed. They urged King Jehoiakim also to read Jeremiah's message. The king asked Jehudi to read it aloud.

But, by the time the king's trusted minister had read only "three or four columns. . . the king cut it with the scribe's knife and cast it into the fire that was on the hearth, until all the scroll was consumed in the fire. . . . Yet they were not afraid, nor did they tear their garments" (Jer. 36:23, 24).

Unfortunately, Jehoiakim was typical of many spiritual leaders, even Christian leaders in our time, who would utterly destroy God's message and His messengers if they could. Many have tried through the years, whether with a "scribe's knife" or by "benign neglect," to nullify a prophet's effectiveness, but

God's message survives for those who seek to know His will.

David is another example of an Israelite leader who received a message of reproof from a prophet. But the result was the opposite of Jehoiakim's experience. After King David had Uriah killed so that he could marry Bathsheba, Uriah's wife, God told the prophet Nathan to confront the king. Without trying to hedge his words with "sympathy" or favor, Nathan pointed his finger at David and delivered God's word of condemnation: "You are the man!" (2 Sam. 12:7). David accepted the word of the Lord—and capitulated: "I have sinned" (2 Sam. 12:13; see also Ps. 51). David is one of the finest examples of those who have heeded the condemning words of the Lord, thus changing their future for good. His example has been replicated many times in the history of the church.

Names Applied to the Prophetic Messages

Various terms are used in the Bible to describe the messages given by the prophets: counsel (Isa. 44:26); Lord's message (Hag. 1:13); prophecy, or prophecies (2 Chron. 9:29; 15:8; 1 Cor. 13:8); testimonies (1 Kings 2:3; 2 Kings 11:12; 17:15; 23:3; also many verses in Ps. 119); and Word of God (1 Sam. 9:27; 1 Kings 12:22).

Each term, though easily interchangeable, emphasizes a particular aspect of God's communication system. "Testimonies," for example, suggests "messages." The thought included in "the testimony of Jesus" (Rev. 12:17 and 19:10) is that the messages or will of Jesus are revealed when a prophet speaks or writes.

How God and Prophets Interact

Prophets clearly recognize the presence and power of the Holy Spirit in their role as God's messengers. Peter well understood this relationship: "Prophecy never came by the will of man, but holy men of God spoke as they were moved by the Holy Spirit" (2 Pet. 1:21).

Note Saul's experience: "When they came there to the hill, there was a group of prophets to meet him; then the Spirit of God came upon him [Saul], and he prophesied among them" (1 Sam. 10:10).

Ezekiel often referred to the Holy Spirit's presence: "Then the Spirit entered me when He spoke to me, and set me on my feet; and I heard Him who spoke to me" (Eze. 2:2; see also 3:12, 14, 24; 8:3; 11:5; 37:1).

How did the prophet recognize the presence and power of the Spirit? By out-of-the-ordinary visions and dreams—and by the accompanying physical phenomena. Many have been the fulfillments of God's promise that "If there is a prophet among you, I, the Lord, make Myself known to him in a vision, and I speak to him in a dream" (Num. 12:6). (The Biblical record does not make a clear distinction between a prophetic vision and a prophetic dream, the terms often being used interchangeably.)

In Daniel 10, the prophet described some of the physical phenomena accompanying "this great vision" (vs. 8). Although he "was in a deep sleep on my face. . . to the ground," he was able to hear "the sound of his words" (vs. 9). Others were with Daniel when he was in vision but he "alone saw the vision" (vs. 7).

Daniel was physically changed while in vision: "No strength remained in me; for my vigor was turned to frailty in me, and I retained no strength" (vs. 8).

Whatever may have been the particular phenomena accompanying a vision or dream, prophets knew that God was speaking to them.

What we know about the prophets' messages and how they delivered them is recorded in the Bible. Originally, not all the messages as we have them today were in written form. Some were public sermons, some were letters to friends or to church groups, some were official announcements by kings to their people. Some of the inspired prophetic writings were not even original with the prophets.

Out of the plentiful prophetic messages presented over several thousand years, God has supervised a compilation that we call the Bible. This sampling has been preserved for one purpose: "Now all these things happened to them as examples, and they were written for our admonition, upon whom the ends of the ages have come" (1 Cor. 10:11).

How Prophets Delivered Their Messages

Throughout history the Spirit of prophecy has used three methods of delivering God's messages: Oral, Written, Dramatized.

Oral. The regular, sermon-type of presentation is perhaps the best known form of a prophet's work. We think immediately of Jesus giving His sermon on the Mount of Blessing (Matt. 5-7) or Peter's sermon on the Day of Pentecost (Acts 2). The entire book of Deuteronomy was an oral discourse in which Moses reviewed the previous forty years of Israelite history. Many of the Minor Prophets first delivered their messages orally.

In addition to these more formal presentations, the prophets recorded in writing their counsel given earlier to individual leaders or groups. Isaiah wrote down his interview with Hezekiah (Isa. 37). Most of the book of Jeremiah is a written summary of his public messages. Ezekiel transcribed his earlier conversations with the leaders of Israel. For example: "And it came to pass in the sixth year, in the sixth month, on the fifth day of the month, as I sat in my house with the elders of Judah sitting before me, that the hand of the Lord God fell upon me there" (Eze. 8:1; see 20:1).

Those private interviews such as Nathan with David (2 Sam. 12:1-7); Jeremiah with Zedekiah (Jer. 38:14-19); and Jesus with Nicodemus (John 3) were also considered worthy by the Spirit of prophecy for wider application.

In addition to their more official and public duties, prophets wrote personal letters to people who had special needs.

Written. Written messages have advantages over other forms of communication. They can be read and reread. Compared to an oral presentation, they are less subject to misunderstanding. The Lord told Jeremiah to write a book containing the words He would give him. Jeremiah asked Baruch to be his editorial assistant, and the book eventually was read to the people of Jerusalem and to the king. Years later, the prophet Daniel (9:2) tells of his reading Jeremiah's messages and how Jeremiah had promised deliverance for God's people after the seventy-years' captivity. Daniel himself was told to write a book especially for those living at "the time of the end" (12:4).

The apostle Paul wrote fourteen books of the New Testament, all but one book being letters to various churches or their pastors. Some of his letters were not included in the Bible, such as the letter to the church at Laodicea (Col. 4:16).

Peter also wrote letters to various church groups: "Beloved, I now write to you this second epistle (in both of which I stir up your pure minds by way of reminder)" (2 Pet. 3:1). He also wrote private letters, such as to Silvanus (1 Pet. 5:12).

John wrote at least three letters in addition to his Gospel and the Book of Revelation: "And these things we write to you that your joy may be full" (1 John 1:4).

Letters Carry Authority

Prophets' letters carried the same weight of authority as their formal sermons. In some cases, letters would be more helpful than a sermon because they were written to specific people with specific problems. Letters written to one person or to a church became equally beneficial to others as these letters (and sermons) were copied and widely distributed. People everywhere down through time have identified with these inspired, practical applications of divine principles to the details of life.

Dramatization. Parables in words or actions are frequently-used teaching devices throughout the Bible. Jesus made generous use of parables to make clear the value of divine principles.

Jeremiah's ministry often used the parable of action and example. God asked him not to take a wife (16:1, 2) so that he would be a living reminder to the Jews of the approaching ordeal during the destruction of Jerusalem. Think of the teaching aids in the "potter's earthen flask" (Jer. 19) that was to be broken as a sign of Jerusalem's fall; or the "bonds and yokes" (Jer. 27) portending the coming yoke of Babylon.

Like Jeremiah, Ezekiel often expressed his prophetic messages in the form of parables. Examples include the scroll that he was asked to eat (Eze. 3:1-3); the razor to cut the hair and beard (Eze. 5:1); the cooking pot (Eze. 24:3, 4); and the valley of dry bones (Eze. 37). Messages through parables got attention and were easily remembered.

In reviewing these various methods of getting attention, one is impressed that God selected any method that would best fit the occasion. God is adaptable and persistent. All methods are authentic, for they come from the same Source. Moses' Deuteronomic sermon, Isaiah's personal interviews, Jeremiah's transcribed sermons, Paul's letters, Ezekiel's parabolic dramatizations, Daniel's books, Peter's sermon at Pentecost, Jesus's interview with Nicodemus—all were inspired by the Spirit. "Holy men of God spoke as they were moved by the Holy Spirit" (2 Pet. 1:21).

Literary Assistants

We know very little about how most Biblical authors prepared their materials. We know only what they have told us. Jeremiah explained how he used Baruch as his literary assistant: "Then Jeremiah called Baruch the son of Neriah; and Baruch wrote on a scroll of a book, at the instruction of Jeremiah, all the words of the Lord which He had spoken to him" (36:4). When the king's officials heard Baruch read these messages, they asked: "Tell us now, how did you write all these words—at his instruction?" Baruch answered them, "He proclaimed with his mouth all these words to me, and I wrote them with ink in the book" (36:17, 18).

Baruch, known as a scribe (36:26), apparently was well educated. Jeremiah employed the literary skills of this man to prepare in written form his messages given orally: "Then Jeremiah took another scroll and gave it to Baruch the scribe, the son of Neriah, who wrote on it at the instruction of Jeremiah all the words of the book which Jehoiakim king of Judah had burned in the fire. And besides, there were added to them many similar words" (36:32).

Paul's Several Assistants

In the New Testament, Paul employed several editorial assistants. Tertius helped prepare the Romans manuscript (16:22). Apparently Sosthenes assisted in writing the first letter to the Corinthians (1:1). Paul, in the Roman prison, dictated his second letter to Timothy, and Luke, his physician, prepared it in written form.[9]

Paul was a consummate Greek scholar, well-recognized by Jewish leaders. But there were plausible reasons why he would employ literary assistants. In prison, his writing capabilities would be severely reduced, but assistants could take his thoughts and write them down much more conveniently. Some feel that his "thorn in the flesh" was poor eyesight (2 Cor. 12:7-9; Gal. 4:15). Whatever method Paul used in writing his Epistles, those who read these letters (or heard them read) knew they were listening to inspired messages.

The significant difference in the Greek style (not necessarily in content) of each of his letters suggests strongly that Paul used different literary assistants with varying abilities to place his messages in written form.[10]

Peter referred to his literary assistant by name, Silvanus [Silas], "our faithful brother" (1 Pet. 5:12). Why would Peter need editorial help? For several reasons: In addition to not being academically trained, Peter had the same prison restrictions as Paul; and since his mother tongue was Aramaic, he probably was not skilled in Greek. Peter's first epistle is high-grade polished Greek, the mark of an educated mind, reflecting Silvanus's assistance. However, Peter's second epistle is written in a crude literary style, though truth shines through brightly. Obviously, Silvanus was not available on short notice, and Peter either wrote it himself or employed another scribe without Silvanus's literary skill.[11]

Obvious Difference Between 1 and 2 Peter

The difference between First and Second Peter is so obvious that Peter's authorship of one or even both has been questioned. Allan A. McRae observed: "Nor can we rule out the idea that on occasion a writer may have given an assistant a general idea of what he wanted, telling him to put it into written form.[12] In such a case, he would have checked it over to be sure it represented what he wanted to say, and therefore he could truly be called its author. The Holy Spirit would have guided the entire process so that what was finally written expressed the ideas God desired His people to have.

"Probably Paul seldom followed this latter procedure, since he was highly educated and must have had confidence in his ability to express himself in Greek. But the situation may have been different in the case of Peter and John. The style of First and Second Peter differ so considerably that some critics have suggested one is a fraud. Yet Peter could well have written one book in Greek himself (2 Peter?) and, for the other, expressed his thought in Aramaic to an associate who was more experienced in writing Greek (1 Peter). This associate could then have written Peter's ideas in his own style, afterward making alterations Peter might have suggested. The two letters would thus differ in style; yet, under the direction of the Holy Spirit both would express Peter's thought as truly as if Peter had dictated every word. John Calvin held such a view, but had no doubt that both presented Peter's thought accurately."[13]

Comparing the Gospel of John with the book of Revelation we see again a strikingly different literary style. Evidence is compelling that the apostle John wrote both books even though the literary styles are very different. The book of Revelation is generally loose Greek construction while John's Gospel conforms to acceptable literary standards—a clear indication of different scribes.[14] Part of the difference, of course, could be attributed to the fact that John was an old man when he wrote Revelation.

How Luke Was Written

Another way to look at editorial assistance in the preparation of Biblical material is provided by noting how and why the book of Luke was prepared. Luke was not an eyewitness of Christ's ministry. Probably he never heard Jesus speak. Yet, Luke's Gospel has been comparable to Matthew's, Mark's, and John's in reporting faithfully the words and deeds of Jesus.

How did Luke do it? By collecting the most valid accounts from eyewitnesses and presenting them in a coherent manner.[15]

Luke put it this way: "Inasmuch as many have taken in hand to set in order a narrative of those things which are most surely believed among us, just as those who from the beginning were eyewitnesses and ministers of the word delivered them to us, it seemed good to me also, having had perfect understanding of all things from the very first, to write to you an orderly account, most excellent Theophilus, that you may know the certainty of those things in which you were instructed" (1:1-4).

God communicated His messages not through mechanical dictation but through acts and words that men and women could understand. The prophets who heard God speak directly to them conveyed these messages through the thought processes of their day, and through the idioms and analogies that their hearers could understand.

Understanding the revelation/inspiration process correctly prevents distressful concern when people see in the Gospels clear differences between reports of the same event, even the same messages of Jesus. Nothing disturbs some sincere students more than to observe the different ways Bible writers describe the same event, "quote" the same conversation, or report the parables of Jesus. Even having two versions of the Lord's Prayer, as recorded in Matthew 6 and Luke 11, upsets those who mistakenly believe that the Bible writers wrote, word for word, as the Holy Spirit dictated.

Verbal Inspiration or Thought Inspiration

Verbal, inerrant inspiration implies that the prophet is a recording machine, transmitting mechanically and unerringly God's message. Belief in mechanical inspiration forbids differences in reporting a message or event. Verbal inspiration requires prophets to transmit the exact words supplied by the heavenly Guide even as a court stenographer types what is being said by the witnesses. No room is given to prophets to use their own individuality (and limitations) in expressing the truths revealed to them.

One of the obvious problems for those who believe in verbal inspiration is what to do in translating the Bible, either from Old Testament Hebrew/Aramaic or New Testament Greek, into other languages.

Another problem is Matthew 27:9, 10 where Matthew refers to Jeremiah rather than Zechariah (11:12) as the Old Testament source for a messianic prophecy. This might be a copyist's mistake. But if it is Matthew's, it is a human mistake any teacher or minister might make, a mistake that will cause no problem for thought inspirationists. Why? Because thought inspirationists know what Matthew *meant!*

Or, what did Pilate actually write on the sign placed on Christ's cross? Matthew 27:37; Mark 15:26, Luke 23:38, and John 19:19 report the sign differently. To thought inspirationists, the message is clear; to verbal inspirationists, a problem!

Prophets, Not Words, Are Inspired

For thought inspirationists, God inspires the prophet, not his or her words.[16] Thought inspirationists read the Bible and see God working through human beings with their individual characteristics. God provides the thoughts, and prophets, in relaying the divine message, use whatever literary capacity they possess.[17] Trained scholars will report a message or describe an event much differently than will a sheepherder. But if both are inspired by God, the truth will be heard by the educated and unlearned alike. This is the way the Bible was written, all writers using their best words to express faithfully the message they had received from the Lord.

Revelation in the revelation/inspiration process emphasizes the divine act that discloses information. Seventh-day Adventists believe that this divinely revealed message, or content, is infallible and authoritative. "Your word is a lamp to my feet and a light to my path" (Ps. 119:105).[18]

Inspiration refers to the process by which God fits a person to be His messenger. This kind of inspiration is different from the colloquial use of the word when we describe some insightful poet or gifted singer as being "inspired."

Paul wrote to young Timothy that "all

scripture is given by inspiration of God" (2 Tim. 3:16). The Greek word that Paul used, translated as "inspiration," is *theopneustos*, a contraction of two words, "God-breathed." This is more descriptive than a mere poetic touch. When Daniel, for example, was in vision he did not breathe, literally (Dan. 10:17)!

Peter said that prophets were "moved by the Holy Spirit" (2 Pet. 1:21). The Greek word for "moved" is *pheromeni*, the same word that Luke used (Acts 27:17, 27) to describe being "driven" across the Mediterranean Sea in a terrifying storm. Prophets did not mistake the "moving" of the Spirit for normal emotional promptings. They knew when the Lord was speaking to them—they were inspired!

Another word that is used often in describing God's communication system is *illumination*. When prophets deliver their messages, how do men and women recognize the messages as authentic? The same Holy Spirit that spoke through the prophets speaks to those who hear or read the prophet's message. The listener or reader is "illuminated" (but not inspired). Further, the Holy Spirit enables the sincere believer to understand the message and to apply it personally.[19]

How the revelation/inspiration process worked in the ministry of Ellen White will be discussed in Chapter 13. Fortunately, Mrs. White spoke forcefully and lucidly on how this process worked both in Bible times and in her own ministry.

Some Prophetic Messages Not Preserved

The Bible does not contain all that prophets have said or written. For example, we do not have all that Jesus said or did.[20]

Does that mean that the messages that were not preserved were less important, less inspired, than those we have in the Bible? No! Everything God says is important and inspired. But some messages were of local interest. Some were covered by other messages that were preserved. Beyond question, the greater amount of prophetic messages, including the words of Jesus, were not preserved.

Biblical prophets can be classified into four groups:[21]

1. Prophets who wrote some of the Bible, such as Moses, Jeremiah, Paul, and John.

2. Prophets who wrote none of the Bible, but whose messages and ministries are amply preserved in the Bible, such as Enoch, Elijah, and Elisha.

3. Prophets who gave oral testimonies (perhaps even written messages) but whose words were not preserved. Throughout the Old Testament, many unnamed prophets are noted, including the seventy elders who received the Holy Spirit and prophesied (Num. 11:24, 25), the group that joined Saul after he became king (1 Sam. 10:5, 6, 10), and those who were hidden in caves by Obadiah (1 Kings 18:4, 13). In the New Testament, for example, the four daughters of Philip prophesied, but their messages were not recorded (Acts 21:9).

4. Prophets who wrote books that have not been preserved, including Nathan (1 Chron. 29:29), Gad (1 Chron. 29:29), Shemaiah (2 Chron. 12:15), Jasher (Josh. 10:13; 2 Sam. 1:18), Iddo (2 Chron. 12:15; 9:29), Oded (2 Chron. 15:8), Ahijah (2 Chron. 9:29), and Jehu (2 Chron. 20:34).

What has been preserved in the Bible is the distillation of the glorious line of splendor through which God has spoken to men and women, "at various times and in various ways" (Heb. 1:1). The purpose of Biblical writings was not to produce a complete history of all that happened to God's people in both Old and New Testament times. The primary purpose of the Bible is to give later readers a clear understanding of the plan of salvation and the highlights exposing the great controversy between Christ and Satan. In addition, Paul wrote that the Bible provides "examples" of right and wrong, of truth and error, alerting readers to "take heed lest [they] fall" (1 Cor. 10:12).

God Is Gender Impartial

The Bible refers to a number of prophetesses. Moses considered his sister Miriam a prophetess (Ex. 15:20, 21). Standing by his side from his earliest years, she was a faithful spokesperson for God. Through the centuries, Israel highly regarded her and included her as one of the three "sent before you" in the founding of the Israelite nation after the Exodus (Micah 6:4). At one point her humanness led her to rebel against Moses (Num. 12), but this sad act did not jeopardize her standing as a true prophetess.

Deborah was a judge during a long, dismal period in Israel's history. Note how bleak this era was: "When all that generation had been gathered to their fathers, another generation arose after them who did not know the Lord nor the work which He had done for Israel. Then the children of Israel did evil in the sight of the Lord, and served the Baals; and they forsook the Lord God of their fathers. . . . And the anger of the Lord was hot against Israel. So He delivered them into the hands of plunderers who despoiled them; and He sold them into the hands of their enemies all around, so that they could no longer stand before their enemies. . . . Then the Lord raised up judges who delivered them out of the hand of those who plundered them. . . . And when the Lord raised up judges for them, the Lord was with the judge and delivered them out of the hand of their enemies all the days of the judge" (Judges 2:10-18).

Deborah More Than a Judge

Deborah was not only a judge, she was the only judge who was also called a prophetess (Judges 4:4). She was so compelling a spiritual leader that when Barak, her general, was asked to lead an army against the oppressive Canaanites, he would not go without her. Israel had recognized her spiritual leadership, and Barak wanted the nation to know that what he had been asked to do was a call from their spiritual leader, not an ambitious, personal plot. After all, how could he get 10,000 men to go against a trained army with "nine hundred chariots of iron" (Judges 4:3) unless they too were convinced that God had directed the plan? Deborah's record as a faithful judge was so convincing that her counsel regarding what appeared to be an impossible venture was accepted as the will of God. She spoke the word of the Lord with authority, and put her own life on the line as she led her countrymen by voice and example into the future.

Other women throughout history have carried the heavy weight of prophetic responsibility. Clearly, gender is not an issue when God selects a person to speak for Him.

Huldah was a prophetess during a great day of change as the young king Josiah committed himself and his nation to profound spiritual reformation. In the process of "cleaning up" the temple, the workers found a copy of what may have been Deuteronomy—a book that had been strangely neglected by the nation's religious leaders.

Josiah, sensing that he needed to know more about this discovery, commanded his counselors: "Go, inquire of the Lord for me, for the people and for all Judah, concerning the words of this book that has been found" (2 Kings 22:13). So where did the priest and chief counselors go? To "Huldah the prophetess, the wife of Shallum" (vs. 14). Jeremiah had been living in Jerusalem for five years (compare 2 Kings 22:3 and Jer. 1:2), but it was to Huldah they went for spiritual guidance!

Whatever the reason, Huldah had earned the respect and confidence of her contemporaries. When they wanted a word from the Lord, they turned to her. She helped them to understand more clearly the meaning of the writings of

Moses. She illuminated the written Word and made specific predictions. Her Biblical insights and predictions were accepted as divinely inspired.

Isaiah referred to his wife as "the prophetess" (8:3) on the occasion of their son's birth, but at no other time.

When Joseph and Mary took the infant Jesus to the Temple for dedication, they met two interesting people besides the priest who performed the service (see Luke 2). Simeon, "just and devout," had been waiting for Israel's Deliverer, and he made several poignant predictions regarding the Saviour's ministry. Also in the temple that day was Anna, a prophetess (vs. 36) who also recognized the baby Jesus as the Messiah. Because of her clear understanding of the Scriptures, she understood the importance of this child; thus, she "spoke of Him to all those who looked for redemption in Jerusalem" (vs. 38).

More than thirty-three years later, the young Christian church was exploding in numbers and influence. The presence of godly men and women through whom God revealed His counsel was one of the reasons for this religious phenomenon.[22]

The Biblical picture of God's communication system includes men and women. Though mentioned less often than men, women prophetesses were recognized by their contemporaries as genuine messengers of the Lord. They illuminated the Scriptures, counseled leaders, and made significant predictions.

Dreary Gap Between Malachi and John the Baptist

The Old Testament record of the illustrious line of prophets and prophetesses ends with Malachi who lived in the last half of the fifth century B.C. Did God's communication system shut down for more than four centuries?

It does seem that Israel no longer had the benefit of national prophets during this period. At the same time, the Scriptures (the prophetic record) were greatly valued. They became the focus of worship in the synagogues, newly constructed throughout Israel by the returning exiles from Babylon.

But did God withdraw the "gift of prophecy" during this period? Ellen White makes an interesting comment on this long interval between Biblical prophets: "Outside of the Jewish nation there were men who foretold the appearance of a divine instructor. . . and to them the Spirit of Inspiration was imparted."[23]

During this intertestamental period (between the time of Malachi and Matthew) "heathen" scholars studied the Hebrew Scriptures (perhaps translated into their own languages). To them God spoke as they sought truth.[24]

The "wise men from the East" (Matt. 2:1) no doubt were examples of those in Gentile lands who "foretold the appearance of a divine instructor" to whom "the Spirit of Inspiration was imparted." They knew the time of Messiah's birth and where He would be born. God spoke directly to these earnest men, urging them to return to their eastern home without further contact with the evil Herod.

We should ponder well this incident and the general truth: "God shows no partiality" (Acts 10:34). Every generation has had men and women somewhere, Jew or Gentile, who were God's inspired witnesses. Their names may not be writ large in Holy Scripture but their witness exists and the flame of truth survived.

Malachi, the last prophet of the Old Testament, closed his messages with the prediction: "Behold, I will send you Elijah the prophet before the coming of the great and dreadful day of the Lord" (Mal. 4:5).

The First Century, A.D.[25]

Speaking of John the Baptist, Jesus said, "But what did you go out to see? A prophet? Yes, I say to you, and more than a prophet. For this is he of whom it is written: 'Behold, I send My messenger before Your face, who will prepare

Your way before You'" (Matt. 11:9, 10).

Even before his birth, John the Baptist was destined to be God's spokesman. The angel spoke to his father Zacharias: "Do not be afraid, Zacharias, for your prayer is heard; and your wife Elizabeth will bear you a son, and you shall call his name John. . . . He will be great in the sight of the Lord. . . . And he will turn many of the children of Israel to the Lord their God. He will also go before Him in the spirit and power of Elijah. . . to make ready a people prepared for the Lord" (Luke 1:13-17).

John turned men and women Godward; he did not make himself a spiritual guru around whom his followers would gather. More than all other prophets, before or since, John had the honor of personally pointing to the living Christ. His highest moment was when he said, "He must increase, but I must decrease" (John 3:30).

Not everyone thinks of Jesus as a prophet. But such He was: "So the multitudes said, 'This is Jesus, the prophet from Nazareth of Galilee'" (Matt. 21:11; Luke 7:16).

The Prophet Jesus

The twelve disciples saw Him as a prophet. One wrote: "The things concerning Jesus of Nazareth, who was a Prophet mighty in deed and word before God and all the people. . . ." (Luke 24:19).[26]

Jesus referred to Himself as a prophet: "So they were offended at Him. But Jesus said to them, 'A prophet is not without honor except in his own country and in his own house.' And He did not do many mighty works there because of their unbelief" (Matt. 13:57, 58).

Jesus felt it all—He experienced the hot knife of ingratitude and rejection that most all prophets and prophetesses have endured. No one had better personal credentials, or a more impeccable and consistent life, but prophets are not generally welcome because they speak for God and not to gratify the desires of the human heart.[27]

For the first time in the history of the world, a prophet came who would not point to another. The Prophet Jesus said of Himself: "This is the work of God, that you believe in Him whom He sent. . . . Most assuredly, I say to you, Moses did not give you the bread from heaven, but My Father gives you the true bread from heaven. For the bread of God is He who comes down from heaven and gives life to the world. . . . I am the bread of life" (John 6:29-35).

As all genuine prophets and prophetesses, Christ's chief focus was to tell the truth about God and how men and women can rejoin the celestial family: "And this is eternal life, that they may know You, the only true God, and Jesus Christ whom You have sent. I have glorified You on the earth. I have finished the work which You have given Me to do" (John 17:3, 4).

Before Jesus returned to heaven, He made provision for the prophetic office to continue until His return. The same good news about God would be needed until His return. The same good news about how rebels could be transformed into happy, obedient believers would be needed. This prophetic provision would be one of the primary responsibilities of the Holy Spirit who would give "gifts to men" (Eph. 4:8).

The beginning of the Christian church coincides with the renewal of these spiritual gifts: "He Himself [Jesus] gave some to be apostles, some prophets, some evangelists, and some pastors and teachers" (vss. 11, 12).

These gifts were not only to launch the Christian church, they were to remain in the church until the end: "Till we all come to the unity of the faith and the knowledge of the Son of God, to a perfect man, to the measure of the stature of the fullness of Christ; that we should no longer be children, tossed to and fro and carried about with every wind of doctrine. . ." (vss. 13, 14). How long? As long as the church exists; as long as imperfect and immature men and women need time to "grow up" to the "measure of. . . Christ," apostles, prophets, evangelists, pastors, and teachers will be needed.

Paul reminded his Corinthian friends that they were "enriched in everything by Him in all utterance and all knowledge, even as the testimony of Christ was confirmed in you" (1 Cor. 1:5, 6). That is, they have grown spiritually and will continue to mature to the extent they continue to listen closely to the messages of the prophets which are signified as "the testimony of Christ." As we noted on page 3, "the testimony of Jesus [or Christ]" (Rev. 12:17) is the "spirit of prophecy" (Rev. 19:10).

Further, Paul declared that the church would "come short in no gift, eagerly waiting for the revelation of our Lord Jesus Christ" (1 Cor. 1:7). It may be significant that Paul singled out the "gift of prophecy" when he emphasized that the church would not be lacking any of the gifts until Jesus returned. Probably no gift would be more needed in the end-time than the gift of prophecy.

Later, in the same letter, Paul elaborated on how the gifts would function in the work of the church (1 Cor. 12). Although each gift would have its own special work, all the gifts would serve the common purpose of helping men and women "grow up."

Clearly, the gifts of the Spirit are "given" by the Spirit (1 Cor. 12:7). They are not abilities earned by training or an honor conferred by human beings. The "fruit of the Spirit" (Gal. 5:22) is to be sought by everyone, but the "gifts of the Spirit" are distributed "to each one individually as He wills" (1 Cor. 12:11). Whether one possesses a particular gift is not to be made a test of Christian fellowship, because no one has all the gifts.

The permanence of these spiritual gifts, especially the gift of prophecy, is assumed in the apostolic instruction. Remembering Christ's counsel that "false prophets" would arise in the end-time (Matt. 24:24), Paul cautioned: "Do not quench the Spirit. Do not despise prophecies. Test all things; hold fast what is good" (1 Thess. 5:19-21). The well-being of church members awaiting the Advent will depend on how they accept the counsel of true prophets—especially in being able to discern the false from the true.

Since Apostolic Times

In the last chapter we noted that New Testament writers expected the prophetic gift to continue to the Second Advent. We also saw that the prophetic gift will be especially prominent in the end-time (Rev. 12:17; 19:10). But why the apparent silence, the absence of the prophetic voice, soon after the death of John?

Historians are divided regarding the prophetic presence during the past 2,000 years. Generally speaking, most writers believe that prophetic illumination ended soon after the second century A.D. Paul K. Jewett wrote: "With the death of the apostles, who had no successors, gradually those with the gift of prophecy also disappeared, so that from the third century onward, of the original triad of apostles, prophets, and teachers, there remained only the teachers. . . . With the rise of Montanism in the second century claiming new prophetic insights which did not correspond with the tradition received from the apostles, the church began to distinguish such prophecies from the true prophecies contained in Scripture. From this time on, the prophetic gift appears here and there, but increasingly it gives place to teaching. By the time of Hippolytus (235) and Origen (250), the word 'prophecy' is limited to the prophetic portions of Scripture. In the place of the prophet one finds the teacher, specifically the catechist and apologist, who oppose all false doctrine and seek to support their exposition of true doctrine by appealing to the authoritative word of Scripture."[28]

Justin Martyr, a well-educated second-century pagan philosopher, united with the Christians after studying the life of

Jesus. One of his defenses and appeals to his non-Christian friends is known today as "Dialogue With Trypho, a Jew." Included in this lengthy interchange is this reference to spiritual gifts, especially the gift of prophecy:

"Daily some (of you) are becoming disciples in the name of Christ, and quitting the path of error; who are also receiving gifts, each as he is worthy, illumined through the name of this Christ. For one receives the spirit of understanding, another of counsel, another of strength, another of healing, another of foreknowledge, another of teaching, and another of the fear of God.

"To this Trypho said to me, 'I wish you knew that you are beside yourself, talking these sentiments.'

"And I said to him, 'Listen, O friend, for I am not mad or beside myself; but it was prophesied that, after the ascent of Christ to heaven, He would deliver us from error and give us gifts. The words are these: 'He ascended up on high; He led captivity captive; He gave gifts to men.' Accordingly, we who have received gifts from Christ, who has ascended on high, prove from the words of prophecy that you, 'the wise in yourselves, and the men of understanding in your own eyes,' are foolish, and honor God and His Christ by lip only. But we, who are instructed in the whole truth, honor them both in acts, and in knowledge, and in heart, even unto death."[29]

Later in the dialogue, Justin Martyr continued: "For the prophetic gifts remain with us, even to the present time. And hence you ought to understand that (the gifts) formerly among your nation have been transferred to us. And just as there were false prophets contemporaneous with your holy prophets, so are there now many false teachers amongst us, of whom our Lord forewarned us to beware; so that in no respect are we deficient, since we know that He foreknew all that would happen to us after His resurrection from the dead and ascension to heaven."[30]

After reviewing with Trypho that after Christ "no prophet has arisen among you" (that is, the Jewish nation), Justin Martyr explains why. Spiritual gifts would again be given "by the grace of His Spirit's power . . . to those who believe in Him, according as He deems each man worthy thereof. . . . Now, it is possible to see amongst us women and men who possess gifts of the Spirit of God."[31]

All the apostles were dead. Christ was in heaven. The Holy Spirit was doing His promised work of giving "gifts" to men and women whenever He deemed it wise for the proclamation of the gospel. Eusebius, bishop of the church in Caesarea (Palestine), is recognized as a reputable source of Christian history in the second and third centuries. In his *Ecclesiastical History* he records the names of a number of Christian leaders who, he says, were endowed with spiritual gifts, including the gift of prophecy. He concluded: "We hear many of the brethren in the church who have prophetic gifts, and who speak in all tongues through the Spirit, and who also bring to light the secret things of men for their benefit, and who expound the mysteries of God."[32]

Were there any factors developing in the Christian church that may help explain why the "gift of prophecy" was no longer a prominent factor? We noted earlier that teaching took the place of prophecy, but why?

Teaching Replaced Prophecy

At least two reasonable responses may be offered:

(1) The excesses of the Montanists in the last half of the second century A.D. who started out well in upbraiding the churches for their laxity and lack of zeal but who became "wild" in their prophetic interpretations: "Soon Christian prophets ceased to exist as a distinct class in the Church's organization."[33]

(2) The rise of sacerdotalism (the rise of the priesthood as the prime mediators between God and the human race) and the

institutionalizing of canonized "saints" supplanted the voice of the prophet as a visible element in the life of the church.[34]

But, though the institutional church slipped into the dark ages, spiritual gifts were present wherever the gospel was faithfully proclaimed. They did not cease altogether. One of the reasons why we know so little about this relatively silent period for the gift of prophecy may simply be that the writers in the institutionalized church rejected spiritual gifts and persecuted their recipients. But the record of that long period does exist: "The history of God's people during the ages of darkness that followed upon Rome's supremacy, is written in heaven, but they have little place in human records."[35]

Endnotes

1. For a more extended review of prophets and prophetesses from patriarchal times through the New Testament, read A. G. Daniells, *The Abiding Gift of Prophecy* (Mountain View, CA: Pacific Press Publishing Association, 1936), pp. 36-172.
2. See also Isa. 30:21; Matt. 10:19, 20.
3. See also Gen. 19:15; Judges 6:11-14; Ps. 34:7; Matt. 1:18-25.
4. See also Acts 14:17 and Ps. 19:1, 2.
5. See Ex. 28:30; Lev. 8:8; Num. 27:21; 1 Sam. 22:10; 28:6.
6. Note the difference between the duties of the priest and prophet: "The priest was concerned largely with the ceremony and ritual of the sanctuary, which centered in public worship, in the mediation of forgiveness of sins, and in the ritual maintenance of right relations between God and His people. The prophet was chiefly a teacher of righteousness, spirituality, and ethical conduct, a moral reformer bearing messages of instruction, counsel, admonition, warning, whose work often included the prediction of future events."—Siegfried Horn, *Seventh-day Adventist Bible Dictionary (SDABD Revised edition),* (Washington, D.C.: Review and Herald Publishing Association, 1979) , p. 903.
7. T. Housel Jemison, *A Prophet Among You* (Mountain View, CA: Pacific Press Publishing Association, 1955), pp. 24-28.
8. "Widespread revelation" is translated from two Hebrew words *paras* ("to burst forth") and *chazon* ("vision"). As far as the Israelite nation was concerned, no "word of the Lord" was "bursting forth." This is the first use of *chazon* in the Old Testament. The more frequently used word for "vision" is *mar'ah,* messages from God either in dreams or by personal encounters. The root meaning of *chazon* is "to perceive with inner vision," whereas *mar'ah* is derived from a root meaning "to see visually."
9. *Testimonies,* vol. 4, p. 353.
10. Comparing Paul's various letters, we note a substantial difference in literary style. For example, the pastoral letters (First and Second Timothy and Titus) use a vocabulary considerably different from Paul's other letters. There are 902 different words used in the pastoral letters; of these 206 do not occur in the other Pauline letters. Of the 112 untranslatable particles (enclitics) in the other Pauline letters, not one is found in the pastoral epistles. See William Barclay, *The Letters to Timothy, Titus, and Philemon* (Philadelphia: The Westminster Press, 1975, revised edition), pp. 8, 9.
11. "Either he [Silvanus] corrected and polished Peter's necessarily inadequate Greek, or, since Silvanus was a man of such eminence, it may well have been that Peter told him what he wanted said, and left him to say it, and then approved the result, and added the last personal paragraphs to it. . . . When Peter says that Silvanus was his instrument or agent in the writing of this letter, it gives us the solution to excellence of the Greek. The thought is the thought of Peter; but the style is the style of Sylvanus."—William Barclay, *The Letters of James and Peter* (Philadelphia: The Westminster Press, revised edition, 1976), p. 144.
12. On one occasion when Ellen White was ill, she outlined her thoughts to Marion Davis who then wrote them out in a letter to Uriah Smith and George Tenney. Mrs. White signed the letter (Letter 96, 1896, June 8, 1896). See *1888 Materials*, p. 1574 and *Selected Messages*, book 1, pp. 254, 255.
13. "The Ups and Downs of Higher Criticism," *Christianity Today,* Oct. 10, 1980, p. 34. McRae's scenerio does not describle how Ellen White did her writing. See pp. 108-121.
14. "It is not difficult to account for the linguistic and literary differences that exist between the Revelation, written probably when John was alone on Patmos, and the Gospel, written with the help of one or more fellow believers at Ephesus."—*SDABC,* vol. 7, p. 720.
15. See George E. Rice, *Luke, a Plagiarist?* (Mountain View, California: Pacific Press Publishing Association, 1983).
16. "The Bible is written by inspired men, but it is not God's mode of thought and expression. It is that of humanity. God, as a writer, is not represented. Men will often say such an expression is not like God. But God has not put Himself in words, in logic, in rhetoric, on trial in the Bible. The writers of the Bible were God's penmen, not His pen. Look at the different writers.

    "It is not the words of the Bible that are inspired, but the men that were inspired. Inspiration acts not on the man's words or his expressions but on the man himself, who, under the influence of the Holy Ghost, is imbued with thoughts. But the words receive the impress of the individual mind. The divine mind is diffused. The divine mind and will is combined with the human mind and will; thus the utterances of the man are the word of God."— *Selected Messages,* book 1, p. 21. In other words, God inspires prophets, not words. Compare Matthew's digest of the Sermon on the Mount (Matt. 5-7) and Luke's further abridgment in Luke 6.
17. Commenting on Genesis 9:11-16 where God is quoted as saying (in reference to the rainbow of promise): "I will look upon it, that I may remember the everlasting covenant between God and every living creature," Ellen White wrote that God is not implying "that He would ever forget, but He speaks to us in our own lan-

guage, that we may better understand Him." *Patriarchs and Prophets*, p. 106.

18. See Raoul Dederen, "The Revelation-inspiration Phenomenon According to the Bible Writers," Frank Holbrook and Leo Van Dolson, *Issues in Revelation and Inspiration* (Berrien Springs, MI: Adventist Theological Society Publications, 1992), pp. 9-29.
19. John 14:26; John 16:13; 1 John 3:24; 4:6, 13; 5:6.
20. "And there are also many other things that Jesus did, which if they were written one by one, I suppose that even the world itself could not contain the books that would be written" (John 21:25).
21. See Jemison, *A Prophet Among You*, p. 73. "Not all prophets were given the same mission, nor did they do the same kind of work, but all spoke for God; all communicated Heaven-inspired messages. Some prophets set forth divine standards for human conduct, some revealed God's purposes for individuals and for nations, some protested against prevailing evils, some encouraged the people to faithfulness, some strengthened and guided national rulers, some directed building and other kinds of activities, some served as teachers. In the course of their work, some performed miracles, some wrote books. In every case, true prophets served a body of people as God's spokespersons; they were not merely instructed of God at the personal or family level."—Kenneth H. Wood, "Toward an Understanding of the Prophetic Office."—*Journal of the Adventist Theological Society*, Spring, 1991, p. 24.
22. Luke notes the four daughters of Philip "who prophesied" (Acts 21:9).
23. *The Desire of Ages*, p. 33.
24. *Ibid.*
25. Although the time designation of B.C.E. (Before the Common Era) and C.E. are now popular, B.C. and A.D. are used throughout this book because of their long-time use.
26. See also Jaroslav Pelikan, *Jesus Through the Centuries* (New Haven, CT: Yale University Press, 1985), pp. 14-17.
27. "The whole public ministry of our Lord was that of a prophet. He was much more than this. But it was as a prophet that He acted and spoke. It was this which gave Him His hold on the mind of the nation. He entered, as it were naturally, on an office vacant but already existing. His discourses were all, in the highest sense of the word, 'prophecies.'"—Dean Arthur P. Stanley, *History of the Jewish Church,* volume III, (New York: Charles Scribner's Sons, 1880) p. 379.
28. Article on "Prophecy" in *The New International Dictionary of the Christian Church,* J. D. Douglas, general editor, (Grand Rapids, MI: Zondervan Publishing House, 1974) pp. 806-807.
29. *The Ante-Nicene Fathers* (Grand Rapids, MI: William B. Eerdmans Publishing Company, 1981) Vol. I, chap. 39, p. 214.
30. *Ibid.,* chap. 82, p. 240.
31. *Ibid.,* chaps. 87 and 78, p. 243.
32. *The Ecclesiastical History of Eusebius Pamphilus,* translated from the Greek by C. F. Cruse, A.M., (London: George Bell and Sons, 1879) Book III, chap. 38, pp. 111, 112; Book V, chap. 7, p. 175.
33. Article, "Prophet" in *Encyclopedia Britannica,* 14th edition, Vol. XVIII.
34. Article, "Prophet" in *Encyclopedia Britannica,* 11th edition, Vol. XXII. Article, "Prophecy" in *The Westminster Dictionary of Christian Theology*, edited by Alan Richardson and John Bowden (Philadelphia: The Westminster Press, 1983), p. 474.
35. *The Great Controversy*, p. 61.

Study Questions

1. What are some of the ways (Heb. 1:1) God uses in communicating with human beings?

2. Why did God choose prophets and prophetesses as His chief method of communicating His messages?

3. In what three general ways did prophets or prophetesses convey their messages?

4. What evidence do we have that Bible writers used editorial assistants?

5. What is the essential difference between verbal and thought inspiration?

6. Why do you think the gift of prophecy is God's most effective method for communicating with the human family?

7. What are some of the risks God takes in speaking through prophets and prophetesses?

CHAPTER 3

Characteristics of the Prophets

"Beware of false prophets, who come to you in sheep's clothing, but inwardly they are ravenous wolves. You will know them by their fruits" (Matt. 7:15). "Do not quench the Spirit. Do not despise prophecies. Test all things; hold fast what is good" (I Thess. 5:19-21).

For many reasons each prophet is "one-of-a-kind." Life experiences and their own specific mission at a specific time in history shape products into an unrepeatable configuration of physical, mental, emotional, and spiritual capabilities. Thus, even prophets may look at their prophetic calling in a different sense than other prophets would. Kenneth H. Wood pictured it well: "Making two cookies exactly alike is one thing; making two prophets just alike is quite another. In making a prophet, God must take the entire person—body, soul, spirit, intelligence, personality, weaknesses, strengths, education, idiosyncrasies—then endeavor through that person to proclaim His message and accomplish a special mission."[1]

Because of these individual differences and because each prophet was called to address a particular audience at a specific time in history (much of which is difficult, if not impossible, to reconstruct), the reader of the Bible as well as the writings of Ellen G. White could not do better than to focus on the message rather than on the messenger.

The authority of revelation is in the message, not in the messenger. This is not to minimize the value of studying the prophet's life. The more we know, the better we will understand the prophet's message. But the priority of concern should be on the content of the prophet's contribution, not on the container in which the message is carried.

Prophets Share Common Characteristics

Prophets assume their prophetic duties with a unique mix of life experiences coupled with an individualized personality shaped by their physical and mental limitations. Yet when in vision they are all in an "unnatural" state. What do we know about the changed characteristics of a prophet or prophetess in vision?

Balaam, though he had grave spiritual difficulties, was still used by God in Israel's behalf. His experience in vision is enlightening: "And Balaam raised his eyes, and saw Israel encamped according to their tribes; and the Spirit of God came upon him. Then he took up his oracle and said:

"'The utterance of Balaam
the son of Beor,
The utterance of the man
whose eyes are opened,
The utterance of him
who hears the words of God,
Who sees the vision of the
Almighty,
Who falls down
with eyes opened wide'"
(Num. 24:2-4).

Daniel's experience, too, is instructive. First, his public visions: "I, Daniel, alone saw the vision, for the men who were with me did not see the vision [Others did not see what Daniel saw]; but a great terror fell upon them, so that they fled to hide themselves.

"Therefore I was left alone when I saw this great vision, and no strength remained in me; for my vigor was turned to frailty in me, and I retained no strength [Others could see how the phenomenon affected Daniel].

"Yet I heard the sound of his words; and while I heard the sound of his words I was in a deep sleep on my face, with my face to the ground [Daniel experienced what appeared to be a deep sleep while lying on the ground].

"Then, suddenly, a hand touched me, which made me tremble on my knees and on the palms of my hands. And he said to me, 'O Daniel, man greatly beloved, understand the words that I speak to you, and stand upright, for I have now been sent to you.' While he was speaking this word to me, I stood tremblingly [Daniel was aware of a Divine Presence speaking to him]. . . .

"When he had spoken such words to me, I turned my face toward the ground and became speechless. And suddenly, one having the likeness of the sons of men touched my lips; then I opened my mouth and spoke, saying to him who stood before me, 'My lord, because of the vision my sorrows have overwhelmed me, and I have retained no strength. For how can this servant of my lord talk with you, my lord? [Daniel spoke with the Divine Presence.]

"As for me, no strength remains in me now, nor is any breath left in me.' [Daniel could not breathe.]

"Then again, the one having the likeness of a man touched me and strengthened me" (Dan. 10:7-11, 15-18). [Daniel was given extra physical strength.]

Daniel also had night visions or dreams: "In the first year of Belshazzar king of Babylon, Daniel had a dream and visions of his head while on his bed. Then he wrote down the dream, telling the main facts" (chap. 7:1). [Daniel received divine communication during his sleep.]

We do not know why prophets/prophetesses had both public (or open) visions and night visions or dreams. But we do know that the prophet/prophetess made no distinction between them as to their significance and authority.[2]

Ezekiel probably provides more information regarding how visions affect prophets and prophetesses than any other Biblical writer. At times he was taken to distant places in vision although his physical body did not "travel." While in vision in faraway places, what he saw was as vivid and real as if he were physically present.

Though Ezekiel remained in Babylon, God showed him the woeful conditions in Jerusalem: "The hand of the Lord God fell upon me there. . . . He stretched out the form of a hand, and took me by a lock of my hair; and the Spirit lifted me up between earth and heaven, and brought me in visions of God to Jerusalem, to the door of the north gate of the inner court, where the seat of the image of jealousy was, which provokes to jealousy. And behold, the glory of the God of Israel was there, like the vision that I saw in the plain" (chap. 8:1-4).

Further in the chapter, Ezekiel graphically described the corrupt conditions prevailing in the temple system in Jerusalem. Though still in Babylon, he walked in vision through the temple court, dug into the temple wall, heard conversations, and saw various groups in abominable idolatry. In chapter nine, he even saw future events, especially the coming destruction of Jerusalem.

Zacharias, father of John the Baptist, was given a vision that provides further insight into the condition of a prophet in vision: "An angel of the Lord appeared to him, standing on the right side of the altar of incense. And when Zacharias saw him, he was troubled, and fear fell upon him. But the angel said to him, 'Do not be afraid, Zacharias, for your prayer is heard; and your wife Elizabeth will bear you a son, and you shall call his name John. . . . And Zacharias said to the angel, 'How shall I know this? For I am an old man, and my wife is well advanced in years.' [Zacharias conversed with the heavenly Presence.] "And the angel answered and said to him, 'I am Gabriel, who stands in the presence of God, and was sent to speak to you and bring you these glad tidings. But behold, you will be mute and not able to speak until the day these things take place, because you did not believe my words which will be fulfilled in their own time. And the people waited for Zacharias, and marveled that he lingered so long in the temple. But when he came out, he could not speak to them; and they perceived that he had seen a vision in the temple, for he beckoned to them and remained speechless" (Luke 1:11-13, 18-22). [Zacharias was physically affected by his vision experience.]

When Saul met the Lord on the Damascus road, his whole life was changed as well as his name. Note the circumstances involved in this roadside vision: "And as he journeyed he came near Damascus, and suddenly a light shone around him from heaven. Then he fell to the ground, and heard a voice saying to him, 'Saul, Saul, why are you persecuting Me?' And he said, 'Who are You, Lord?' And the Lord said, 'I am Jesus, whom you are persecuting. It is hard for you to kick against the goads.' So he, trembling and astonished, said, 'Lord, what do You want me to do?' And the Lord said to him, 'Arise and go into the city, and you will be told what you must do.' And the men who journeyed with him stood speechless, hearing a voice but seeing no one" (Acts 9:3-7). [Saul, too, after conversing with the divine Presence, was physically affected by his vision experience.]

Later, he spoke of being "caught up to the third heaven . . . into Paradise and heard inexpressible words" (2 Cor. 12:2-4).

The apostle John recorded one of his visions and how it affected him physically: "When I saw Him [Jesus], I fell at His feet as dead" (Rev. 1:17).

What do these examples teach us about prophets during their vision experiences?

1. Prophets are very aware of a supernatural Person communicating with them; they have a sense of worthlessness.
2. Prophets often lose their strength.
3. Prophets at times fall to the ground in a deep sleep.
4. Prophets hear and see events in faraway places, as if they are actually present.
5. Prophets at times are unable to speak, but when their lips are touched, they are able to speak.
6. Prophets often do not breathe.
7. Prophets are oblivious to their surroundings though often their eyes are open.
8. Prophets at times are given extra strength while in vision.
9. Prophets receive renewed strength and breath when the vision is over.
10. Prophets occasionally experience temporary physical trauma following the vision.

Not all of these physical characteristics accompany each vision. Thus, physical phenomena should not be used as the sole test of whether a prophet is genuine. Moreover, they can be easily counterfeited. The Scriptures do not present them as tests. However, the presence of such characteristics should be considered normal for anyone who indeed claims to "speak for God." Though physical aspects are helpful in considering a prophet's credentials, other criteria are much more reliable, as we shall now observe.

Tests of a Genuine Prophet

In applying "tests" as Paul admonishes us (1 Thess. 5:20), we should remember Christ's warning: "Beware of false prophets, who come to you in sheep's clothing, but inwardly they are ravenous wolves. You will know them by their fruits" (Matt. 7:15).

When testing the claims of a prophet, it is much easier to make a judgment after sufficient time has passed for the fruit of his or her ministry to ripen. This may have been the reason Josiah's counselors went to the mature Huldah rather than to young Jeremiah (see pages 31, 32). One can only imagine the carefulness of trust required by contemporaries during the time prophets were establishing their prophetic role. Consequently, the affirmation of contemporaries who knew the prophet and his or her ministry should be prime witnesses to the prophet's credibility or lack of it.

But which contemporaries should one believe? Consider Christ's experience. How many church leaders and scholars accepted Him? Some said that His miracles were caused by "Beelzebub, the ruler of the demons" (Matthew 12:24). His brothers, who lived closely with Him for many years, did not, at first, believe in Him (John 7:5). His disciples "murmured" often regarding His teachings (John 6:61), and forsook Him after Gethsemane (Mark 14:50).

Jesus warned His contemporaries that they were in danger of repeating the mistakes of earlier generations: "How terrible for you! You make fine tombs for the prophets—the very prophets your ancestors murdered. You yourselves admit, then, that you approve of what your ancestors did; they murdered the prophets, and you build their tombs. For this reason the Wisdom of God said, 'I will send them prophets and messengers; they will kill some of them and persecute others.' So the people of this time will be punished for the murder of all the prophets killed since the creation of the world. . . .

"When Jesus left that place, the teachers of the Law and the Pharisees began to criticize him bitterly and ask him questions about many things, trying to lay traps for him and catch him saying something wrong" (Luke 11:47-54, TEV).

If Jesus, the unimpeachable Man, the paradigm of virtue, faced this kind of reception, what should lesser men or women with the prophetic gift expect? One wonders why anyone would accept the responsibility when getting a fair hearing is so difficult!

But some did believe! Why? On what rational basis did some contemporaries of Jeremiah gradually become convinced that he was a genuine prophet? A few definite guidelines were needed because many self-styled prophets in his day claimed the same authority. Listen to the Lord describe this strange situation: "The prophets prophesy lies in My name. I have not sent them, commanded them, nor spoken to them; they prophesy to you a false vision, divination, a worthless thing, and the deceit of their heart" (Jer. 14:14; see also 5:13, 31; 14:18; 23:21).

Every age has had the same responsibility: "Do not quench the Spirit. Do not despise prophecies. Test all things; hold fast that which is good" (1 Thess. 5:19-21).

1. The Test of Fulfilled Predictions[3]

Jeremiah's contemporaries were instructed to use the benchmark of "fulfilled predictions" as one of the tests of a genuine prophet: "As for the prophet who prophesies of peace, when the word of the prophet comes to pass, the prophet will be known as one whom the Lord has truly sent" (Jer. 28:9).[4]

Making predictions, or foretelling, is only one aspect of a prophet's work. In fact, it may be only a minor phase. We often think of Daniel and John the Revelator in terms of their prophecies. However, their work as God's "forth-tellers" was even more important than being God's "fore-tellers." Both John the Baptist and Moses were "great" prophets, but for reasons other than their fulfilled prophecies.

In contemplating "fulfilled predictions" we also must understand the principle of conditional prophecy. Jeremiah helps us to understand this principle, as he reports the Lord's conversation with him:

"The instant I speak concerning a nation and concerning a kingdom, to pluck up, to pull down, and to destroy it, if that nation against whom I have spoken turns from its evil, I will relent of the disaster that I thought to bring upon it. And the instant I speak concerning a nation and concerning a kingdom, to build and to plant it, if it does evil in My sight so that it does not obey My voice, then I will relent concerning the good with which I said I would benefit it" (Jer. 18:7-10).

Conditional prophecy, or controlled uncertainty, is a Biblical principle applied to statements of a predictive nature that concern or involve the responses of human beings. Whenever an unfolding of events depends upon human choice, certain aspects of prophetic fulfillment are necessarily conditional.

An unnamed prophet emphasized this principle to aging Eli: "Therefore the Lord God of Israel says: 'I said indeed that your house and the house of your father would walk before Me forever.' But now the Lord says: 'Far be it from Me; for those who honor Me I will honor, and those who despise Me shall be lightly esteemed. Behold, the days are coming that I will cut off your arm and the arm of your father's house, so that there will not be an old man in your house'" (1 Sam. 2:30, 31).

Jonah had to learn this lesson of conditionality the hard way: "Then God saw their works, that they turned from their evil way; and God relented from the disaster that He had said He would bring upon them, and He did not do it" (Jonah 3:10).

The experience of young king Josiah, though sad, is another example of conditional prophecy. He had led his people in a remarkable reformation (2 Chron. 34). Because of his faithfulness, the Lord promised, "I will gather you to your fathers, and you shall be gathered to your grave in peace" (vs. 28). But Josiah did not die in peace, he died in battle! What went wrong? He did not obey God's instruction. God did not give him orders to attack Egypt. In fact, the king of Egypt sent a special message to Josiah, emphasizing that Josiah's God was directing Egypt in battle against Babylon: "God is on my side, so don't oppose me, or he will destroy you" (2 Chron. 35:21, TEV).

Young Josiah should have obeyed God and listened to the confirming voice of Egypt's king. But no, he disguised himself, led his army into the Battle of Carchemish (605 B.C.), and was killed. God's promise that Josiah would die a peaceful death was conditional upon continual obedience. When faithful leaders go against God's counsel, choosing to follow personal inclination, God does not save the headstrong from the consequences of their actions.

2. Agreement With the Bible

Obviously, God does not put conceptual contradictions within His communication system. Neither does He give later prophets an "erase" or "delete" button. The unchangeableness of God will be reflected in His revelations to men and women.[5]

Isaiah notes that genuine prophets will be tested by their faithfulness to previously written revelations: "To the law and to the testimony! If they do not speak according to this word, it is because there is no light in them" (chap. 8:20).

Many are the attempts in every generation to define the "truth" about man's origin and destiny. Plentiful are the intellectual ventures that try to spell out the "rights" and "wrongs" for human conduct. But the Bible has endured the centuries as the great test for men and women everywhere, under all conditions, as to the truth about human origin and morality. The Bible is not only inspired truth, it is the final standard of any claim to inspiration.

Every successive prophet, in Old or New Testament times, has made all previous prophetic writings the benchmark for his or her own ministry. Each, in a sense, was a lesser light that pointed to the greater light. Paul succinctly summed up this relationship: "All Scripture is given by inspiration of God, and is profitable for doctrine, for reproof, for correction, for instruction in righteousness, that the man of God may be complete, thoroughly equipped for every good work" (2 Tim. 3:16, 17).

This second test of a prophet's authenticity is clear and inescapable. Though later prophets reveal additional insights as to God's thoughts regarding the plan of salvation, they will not contradict the basic concepts already given.

3. *The Orchard Test*

The setting for the test of fruitage is found in the Sermon on the Mount, as it deals specifically with "false prophets": "Beware of false prophets, who come to you in sheep's clothing, but inwardly they are ravenous wolves. You will know them by their fruits. Do men gather grapes from thornbushes or figs from thistles? Even so, every good tree bears good fruit, but a bad tree bears bad fruit. A good tree cannot bear bad fruit, nor can a bad tree bear good fruit. . . . Therefore by their fruits you will know them" (Matt. 7:15-20).

What kind of person do the prophet's contemporaries see and hear? What is the general tenor of his or her life? Reliable or inconsistent? Worldly or godly? Faithful to commitments or unfaithful? Do his or her teachings exalt the written Word, or do they create new and exotic paths that do not find their basis in the Word? Above all else, Does the prophet reflect accurately the clear, consistent Biblical message? What is the result of the prophet's leadership? Under his/her guidance, does the work of God prosper in ways that best fulfill the gospel mission? Do others see the prophet's walk with the Lord as consistent? Do sinners find the Lord through his or her writings?

Unfortunately, through the years many have followed ecstatic, charismatic men and women who have assumed the credentials of a prophet. Great money-chests have been collected and massive religious empires have been created. But we must ask, Does the leader reflect the simple life style exemplified by Biblical prophets and by the Lord Himself? Most times, this test quickly categorizes self-promoted "prophets" as pretenders.

Unlike the first two tests, the orchard test often takes time; "fruit" develops slowly. But careful evaluation of results flowing from the "prophet's" ministry is as necessary as the first two tests. What may *appear* to be Biblical, and what may be argued as "fulfilled predictions," may, in the long run, prove to be otherwise. The most valid test for authentic prophets is seen in the consequences of their teachings. Do they turn minds and conduct Godward so that the life pattern reflects the spirit and practice of Jesus? Do their theological teachings show simplicity while maintaining the fullness of the written Word? Or, do their teachings create "new" doctrines not rooted in Scripture?

Prophets, of course, are human. Moses was a prophet who spoke with God "face to face" (Ex. 33:11), but his prophetic gift did not guarantee that he would not make mistakes. Because of his lack of patience, he was not permitted to enter the Promised Land, a prize worthy of his long and courageous leadership.

Many other Biblical examples could be noted to show that the prophetic container, at times, has been subject to the weaknesses of humanity. But the content transcends the container. The prophetic *message* is self-authenticating; the *messenger* is appreciated but not canonized.

Further, even though the prophet's message is precisely what God wants communicated, his/her own ministry may not appear to make a positive impact. Think of the heroic but "unsuccessful" ministries of Jeremiah and Isaiah. When these men lived, they seemed to be "failures." But not so today!

Think of Ezekiel's predicament: "As for you, son of man, the children of your people are talking about you beside the walls and in the doors of the houses; and they speak to one another, everyone saying to his brother, 'Please come and hear what the word is that comes from the Lord.' So they come to you as people do, they sit before you as My people, and they hear your words, but they do not do them; for with their mouth they show much love, but their hearts pursue their own gain. Indeed you are to them as a very lovely song of one who has a pleasant voice and can play well on an instrument; for they hear your words, but they do not do them. And when this comes to pass—surely it will come—then they will know that a prophet has been among them" (Eze. 33:30-33).

Ezekiel was saluted and lauded, but rarely was he followed. Because his contemporaries did not join him in genuine reformation, was that the prophet's fault? Does this "failure" show that the consequences of his ministry were negative and unfruitful? What might have been the fruit of his ministry if his listeners had followed his counsel?

Many godly men and women, consistent and faithful to their calling and to the highest Biblical standards, have been church leaders through the centuries. But their fruitful lives did not prove that they were prophets. The tests of a prophet are cumulative in the sense that all the tests must apply; but without the test of "good fruit," all the other tests should be suspect.

4. Unequivocal Witness to the Divine-human Nature of Jesus Christ

John offered one further test of a genuine prophet: "Beloved, do not believe every spirit, but test the spirits, whether they are of God; because many false prophets have gone out into the world. By this you know the Spirit of God: Every spirit that confesses that Jesus Christ has come in the flesh is of God, and every spirit that does not confess that Jesus Christ has come in the flesh is not of God" (1 John 4:1-3).

As we said in chapter 1, the Gospel is not *about* Jesus, the Gospel *is* Jesus. But during the last twenty centuries the world has rarely heard the truth about Jesus. Hence, a muddled and vague gospel.

John's test is not that the prophet should merely agree that Jesus of Nazareth once lived on earth. Most Christians believe that, even though many do not believe that He is God incarnate. Many others believe that He is indeed God in the flesh but that He did not become truly man, as man is "in the flesh."

John saw the problem in his day, and his warning is even more relevant today. The whole truth about why Jesus came, why He became our Saviour and Example, why He died and now serves as our High Priest—all this is involved in this test of a genuine prophet. This acknowledgment of Jesus "in the flesh" is more than an intellectual assent. Jesus is not our Lord if we do not submit to His Lordship. Jesus is not our Saviour if we do not let Him *save us from our sins* (Matt. 1:21). Actions reveal the genuineness of personal commitment. And correct knowledge helps us to make quality commitments that enable us to produce actions that honor God.

So the test: Does the prophet teach the whole truth about the purpose of Christ's coming "in the flesh"?

Physical Manifestations

As we noted earlier (page 28), certain physical phenomena are associated with Biblical prophets while in vision. Although these manifestations can be duplicated by the wrong "spirit," when combined with the preceding tests they add to the coercive evidence that a prophet is genuine.

Timeliness of the Prophet's Messages

We have already seen that the "fruit" of the prophet's ministry often takes time to "ripen." However, many were the occasions when the prophet changed the course of history by being the right person for the right time in the right place with the right message.

Think of Elisha and the king of Syria as recorded in 2 Kings 6. The Syrian king was determined to invade Israel. He set up ambushes here and there. But Elisha kept the king of Israel informed regarding these ambushes, and the record says that Israel's king "was watchful there, not just once or twice" (vs. 10).

The Syrian king was exasperated and was confident that he had spies among his counselors—after all, his most secret strategies were known almost immediately by his enemy. But one of his counselors knew what was happening: "Elisha, the prophet who is in Israel, tells the king of Israel the words that you speak in your bedroom" (vs. 12).

For a prophet's contemporaries, the prophet's prompt and precise intervention by personal presence or written communication is compelling affirmation of his or her divine credentials.

Heroic and Unequivocal Witnessing

Numerous are the Biblical examples of fearless witnessing by faithful, authentic prophets. Nathan gave heavy-duty condemnation to David, his king (2 Sam. 12).

Elijah confronted Ahab, his king (not easy work). Note his response to Ahab's question: "Is that you, O troubler of Israel?" (1 Kings 18:17). Answer: "I have not troubled Israel, but you and your father's house have, in that you have forsaken the commandments of the Lord and have followed the Baals" (vs. 18). Timely and fearless!

Coupled with the other tests, unequivocal witnessing is an essential part of a genuine prophet's ministry.

Practical Counsel, Not Abstractions, Characterize Their Ministry

The writings of genuine prophets are known for their intense practicality. Note Christ's Sermon on the Mount or any of Paul's letters to young churches. Compared to religious writings generally, the Bible is in a class by itself. Not merely because of the subject matter, but because the Biblical prophets speak to the human condition. Not theory but practical admonition, even when talking about theological aspects of who Jesus is, why He came, and what He is now doing!

One characteristic of many false prophets is their appeal to the mysterious, to the lure for novelty. For some reason, people are inclined to follow religious leaders who attract them with fanciful prophetic interpretations or with involved theological fantasies.

But the genuine prophet speaks to "common" people, to people with practical problems who need practical solutions and comfort. Without this emphasis, the "prophet" lacks divine credentials.

Weight of Evidence

In summary, when a person has all the above characteristics and meets the above tests, the "weight of evidence" seems compelling, adequate, and coercive. Undergirding all these observable tests, however, the highest test of a prophet's credentials is his or her message: Does it square with all previous prophetic messages as it speaks in perhaps fuller terms to the urgency of the prophet's day?

Can All Be Prophets?

The prophetic calling is not a career that one may study for, such as elementary school teaching or the practice of law. Prophets are chosen by God. Men and women should seek the fruits of the Spirit, but the gifts of the Spirit are just that—gifts.[6]

But the Bible also refers to the "sons of the prophets" and the "company of prophets," especially in the days of Samuel, Elijah, and Elisha.[7] It seems that Samuel inaugurated the "school of the prophets" to educate teachers to assist parents in the training of their children for lifelong usefulness and service. Though not directly inspired as was Samuel, the young men in these schools were "divinely called to instruct the people in the works and ways of God."[8]

The question as to whether all can be prophets becomes exceedingly practical.

On one occasion Ellen White was asked: "Do you think we must understand the truth for ourselves? Why can we not take the truths that others have gathered together, and believe them because they have investigated the subjects, and then we shall be free to go on . . . ? Do you not think that these men who have brought out the truth in the past were inspired of God?"

Her answer is instructive: "I dare not say they were not led of God, for Christ leads into all truth; but when it comes to inspiration in the fullest sense of the word, I answer, No."[9]

The issue is not concerning the personal guidance of the Holy Spirit that all committed believers should experience daily. Paul faced a similar issue in 1 Corinthians 12, and he asked: "Are all apostles? Are all prophets? Are all teachers?" (vs. 29). The answer implied was "No."

In modern times, "prophetic preaching" is often understood in terms of anyone who seeks to interpret and proclaim the Word of God, especially in terms of social issues. If that preaching or writing is done with special earnestness and drama, the effort is described as a prophetic tone. However, to assert that such proclamation is evidence that one has the gift of the Spirit of prophecy would be wrong. All the tests of the genuine prophet must be applied.

Jack Provonsha, long-time professor of Christian Ethics at Loma Linda University, pointed out three ways in which prophets differ from others of God's people: (1) Prophets are chosen, "not because their comprehension and transmission would be flawless, but because they are the best vehicle" available; for example, their perceptions are "less skewed by character and experience than others." (2) Prophets are given a voice because they "command attention"; their contemporaries "see in them someone special, someone different from the ordinary." (3) Prophets are given "special communications" from God, sometimes in "extraordinary ways," and other times "in rather ordinary ways, such as thoughts, impressions, and intuitions, which were perceived by the prophet as the prompting of the Spirit."[10]

Some have advocated the view that all believers have the gift of prophecy in the sense that each believer has the ability to distinguish between inspired and uninspired writings—that is, their own judgment determines what is inspired and what is not when reading the claims of a genuine prophet. This position is not taught in the Bible.

Prophets Not Always Aware of the Full Meaning

Peter noted that prophets did not always understand the full meaning of their own writings, especially those that related to future events: "Of this salvation the prophets have inquired and searched carefully, who prophesied of the grace that would come to you, searching what, or what manner of time, the Spirit of Christ who was in them was indicating when He testified beforehand the sufferings of Christ and the glories that would follow. To them it was revealed that, not to themselves, but to us they were ministering the things which now have been reported to you through those who have preached the gospel to you by the Holy Spirit sent from heaven—things which angels desire to look into" (1 Pet. 1:10-12).

Prophets are not omniscient. Their understanding of truth and duty may develop as more is revealed to them. But, unless they are given special divine aid, even that which is revealed will be understood only within the limited context of their own circumstances and experience.

The principle of progressive, or unfolding, revelation (see page 422) works out in the life of each prophet even as it does from one generation to another. Elijah continued to learn about the character of God as he lived from the experience on Mount Carmel to Horeb's cave (1 Kings 18, 19). Isaiah had only a faint idea of how and when the dreadful days he foretold would overtake Israel and Judah. Jeremiah saw much more clearly what Isaiah wrote about.

Not being omniscient, at times prophets make mistakes in judgment and have to change their counsel. King David consulted with the prophet Nathan about building an appropriate Temple in Jerusalem, and Nathan replied, "Do all that is in your heart, for God is with you" (1 Chron. 17:2). But Nathan had to change his testimony: "It happened that night that the word of God came to Nathan, saying, 'Go and tell My servant David, "'Thus says the Lord: 'You shall not build Me a house to dwell in'"'" (vss. 3, 4). The fact that a prophet may change his or her mind regarding a testimony from the Lord makes clear that one who truly seeks God's will must look at the big picture, and not reject a message because of the humanness of the prophet.

A Contrast Between the True and False

In view of the great controversy between Christ and Satan, one might expect that Satan would use his brilliant mind to undermine God's communication system with men and women. This he has done. And false prophets will become even more plentiful in the last days of the final crisis.[11]

An incident in 1 Kings 22 illustrates certain strategies that Satan uses in trying to subvert the work of true prophets. Ahab, king of Israel, had asked King Jehoshaphat, of the southern kingdom, to join forces with him against the king of Syria. Enthusiastically Jehoshaphat agreed, but then had second thoughts. Feeling the need for confirmation from the Lord, he asked Ahab where a prophet could be asked about the venture. Ahab was prepared with his own prophets, "about four hundred men, and said to them, 'Shall I go against Ramoth Gilead to fight, or shall I refrain?' So they said, 'Go up, for the Lord will deliver it into the hand of the king'" (vs. 6).

But Jehoshaphat sensed something was not right. He could see that these 400 were court prophets. So he asked, "Is there not still a prophet of the Lord here, that we may inquire of Him?" (vs. 7).

Ahab replied: "There is still one man, Micaiah . . . but I hate him, because he does not prophesy good concerning me, but evil" (vs. 8).

When they brought Micaiah to join the 400 who had continued to emphasize that the Lord would deliver the Syrians into their hands, he replied, "As the Lord lives, whatever the Lord says to me, that I will speak" (vs. 14).

Ahab asked Micaiah whether they should go to war against the king of Syria. In veiled irony, he replied: "Go and prosper, for the Lord will deliver it into the hand of the king!" (vs. 15).

Ahab picked up the derisive tone and replied, "How many times shall I make you swear that you tell me nothing but the truth in the name of the Lord?" (vs. 16).

The rest of the story (vss. 24-28) is a paradigm of how genuine prophets are attacked and ridiculed by those who do not want to hear the truth. Soon after, Ahab was killed in battle, even as Micaiah had predicted.

It is apparent from this incident that lying and deceit are tools of Satan's trade. He ascertains the desires of men and women, then produces what appears to be religious confirmation for those desires. In other words, men and women usually find the "prophetic" message that their hearts want. One way or another, they will get some kind of "spiritual" affirmation for what they really want to do. If one's desires cannot be easily affirmed by those who speak for God, self-centered, determined men and women will ridicule and/or attack the genuine prophet.

Jehoshaphat sincerely wanted to hear the message from the true prophet amidst all the other religious voices of his day. Micaiah suffered the abuse of the prison rather than change his testimony. But events proved him right.

Like Jehoshaphat, Christians today must detect the air of deceit and illegitimacy as they listen to the message of those who falsely claim to speak for God. They must quickly know how to apply the tests of a genuine prophet. No one should be confused as to how he or she can determine whether a prophet is false or true.[12]

Physical Phenomena Often Provide Coercive Evidence

Before enough time had passed to be judged by the "fruit" of His ministry, Jesus pointed John the Baptist to the physical manifestations that accompanied His ministry. John, in prison, was on the edge of doubt, and sent word to his cousin, Jesus: "Are You the Coming One, or do we look for another?" (Matt. 11:3).

Jesus did not send back a simple, "I am." The Baptist needed more than words. Jesus instructed John's disciples to "tell John the things which you hear and see: The blind receive their sight and the lame walk; the lepers are cleansed and the deaf hear; the dead are raised up and the poor have the gospel preached to them. And blessed is he who is not offended because of Me" (vss. 4-6).

A few years later, after Christ's ascension, another pivotal moment in God's plan arrived: How could the good news of Jesus Christ get fair and favorable attention? Could it be done by sheer debate or would it take more? God decided it would take more.

On the day of Pentecost, the disciples gathered for prayer as their custom had been since Christ ascended to heaven (Acts 1:14; 2:1). Though they were not aware of it, the Lord was ready to launch the Christian church. How would He do it? By sending physical phenomena with the prophetic word. "And suddenly there came a sound from heaven, as of a rushing mighty wind, and it filled the whole house where they were sitting. Then there appeared to them divided tongues, as of fire, and one sat upon each of them. And they were all filled with the Holy Spirit and began to speak with other tongues, as the Spirit gave them utterance" (Acts 2:2-4).

As time passed, physical phenomena became less and less common because the point had been made—the Christian church had been given a dramatic start. These marvelous displays had provided validation to those who saw and heard. The public phenomena ceased when enough time had passed for the fruit of the Christian message to be established.

In many ways the early days of the Advent movement replicated the early days of the Christian church. How else could a relatively few believers get the attention of enough people to launch a movement destined to encircle the world? How else could a prophet get the notice that his or her message deserved unless God accompanied visions with physical phenomena?

The physical phenomena that attracted attention on the Day of Pentecost were not the Christian message, but they did lead people to listen attentively to that message. In the same way, the visible phenomena (divine healings, phenomena associated with public visions, etc.) associated with the early ministry of Ellen White were not, and are not, her message. Nor are they necessarily proof of her divine credentials. But the physical phenomena did get the attention of her contemporaries—and she held that attention until many were convinced that her message was a word from God. As time passed, after thousands were convinced of the fruit of her messages, public visions, accompanied by physical phenomena, became less frequent. Yet God continued to speak to His prophet through night visions. The quality of counsel remained the same, but without the physical phenomena.[13]

The 1840s a Turbulent Period for Prophetic Claims

One of the most prominent features of

the religious churning of the "restless [eighteen] thirties and forties" is that much of the interest "lay outside the bounds of conventional religion."[14]

One of the more striking voices of this religious ferment was that of millennial expectation.[15]

For a decade or more, North America had been listening to many voices, in the pulpit and in the public press, that the Second Advent was near. But most of the Christian world believed that Jesus would return only after the world had been converted to Christianity. Called post-millenialists (the Second Advent occurs *after* the 1,000 years of Revelation 20), these Christian leaders looked with disdain on the pre-millenialists (Second Advent occurs *before* the 1,000-year period) who predicted that Jesus would return in 1843-1844.[16]

Also, among the many fascinating happenings of the 1840s was the emergence of a number of persons who claimed the prophetic gift. Not all these claimants were pre-millenialists; some were developers of "new" religions; some focused on social experiments. Because bizarre happenings often accompanied these experiments, religious or social, many contemporaries were hostile to charismatic phenomena.[17]

Looking at this period from Satan's standpoint, in the light of the Great Controversy Theme (see pages 256-263), would it not be expected that he would muddle events in order to make the acceptance of a genuine prophet more difficult? The book of Revelation makes plain that Satan is aware of the prophetic time-line and the projected end of his own time in the universe. As events continued to take place as divinely predicted, "the devil" will have "great wrath, because he knows that he has a short time" (chap. 12:12).

Extreme fanaticism and outlandish manifestations associated with false prophets caused sober men and women to look with disgust at *anyone* who claimed to speak for God. Both post-millennialists and pre-millennialists looked with disdain on the manifestation of the gift of prophecy.[18]

J. V. Himes, at the 1845 Albany Conference of Millerite leaders, said, "The seventh month movement produced mesmerism seven feet deep."[19] Millerite leaders, at the same conference, voted the following resolution, as reported in *The Advent Herald,* May 21, 1845: "*Resolved,* That we have no confidence in any new messages, visions, dreams, tongues, miracles, extraordinary gifts, revelations, impressions, discerning of spirits, or teachings, etc., etc., not in accordance with the unadulterated word of God."

Furthermore, largely paralleling the rise of the Seventh-day Adventist Church, was the development of the Shakers, the Mormon Church, the Christian Scientists, and the emergence of Spiritualism.[20]

It is notable that each of these modern religious movements was generated by charismatic leaders who claimed the gift of prophecy. Jemina Wilkinson and Ann Lee were early American prophetesses. Lee, best known for "mothering" the Shakers, experienced what appeared to be "trances and visions in which it was revealed to her that the root and foundation of human depravity and the source of all evil was sexual intercourse. . . . During the final four years of her life, 'Mother Ann' was reported to have performed miracles which convinced her followers that she was Christ in his 'second coming.'"[21]

Young Joseph Smith became very disturbed by the smorgasbord display of religious choices: "'In the midst of this war of words and tumult of opinions,' I often said to myself, 'what is to be done? Who of all these parties are right? Or are they all wrong together?'"

Soon his prayer was answered by the "appearance" of both the Father and the Son. According to him, they told him that he should not join any denomination, that all were corrupt. After a period of further study, he reported that the angel Moroni had appeared to him and led him to "long-buried gold plates which told the story of a lost tribe of Israel that had inhabited the American continent centuries before." Later, Smith published the *Book of Mormon* in 1830.

This new scripture became the Mormons' authority on most every issue. It declared that "anyone who denies 'the revelations of God' and says 'that they are done away, that there are no revelations, nor prophecies, nor gifts, nor speaking with tongues and interpretation of tongues' betrays his ignorance and denies 'the gospel of Christ.'"[22]

Spiritism, or spiritualism, found its theological roots in the prevailing Christian doctrine of the conscious state of the dead—in hell or heaven. The modern resurrection of this age-old paganism is attributed to Andrew Jackson Davis (1826-1910), the "Poughkeepsie Seer," and to the audible phenomena at the home of the Fox sisters, near Rochester, N.Y., in 1848. Davis is referred to as the one who introduced *"intellectual* Spiritualism," and Katie Fox as the introducer of *"phenomenal* Spiritualism."[23]

William Foy and Hazen Foss

More relevant to early Seventh-day Adventists are the experiences of William Foy and Hazen Foss. Both had visions similar to the first vision given to Ellen Harmon.

William Ellis Foy (c. 1818-1893), a black American in his early twenties, received several dramatic visions in 1842, several years prior to those received by Hazen Foss and Ellen Harmon. The first one (January 18) lasted two and one-half hours, and the second one (February 4), twelve and one-half hours! His physical condition during the visions resembled Daniel's trancelike state.[24]

Sometime before October 22, 1844, Ellen Harmon heard Foy speak in Beethoven Hall in Portland, Maine. A few weeks later, shortly after her first vision in December 1844, Foy was present in a meeting held near Cape Elizabeth, Maine, during which she spoke of her first vision. "As she began, Foy became engrossed in what she was saying; he was caught up in the enthusiasm and pathos that accompanied her presentation. She talked of heavenly things—of guides, of lights, of imagery—things familiar to Foy. . . . Caught up in the jubilance of the moment, he could hold back no longer. All of a sudden, right in the middle of Ellen's presentation, Foy let out a shout of joy, rose to his feet, and excitedly 'jumped right up and down.' As Ellen remembered, 'Oh, he praised the Lord, praised the Lord.'

"He repeated again and again that her vision was just what he had seen. He knew there was no way to falsify such an experience—hers was legitimate."[25]

In 1906 Ellen White recalled her conversations with William Foy. She remembered that he had four visions, all before her first vision: "They were written out and published, and it is . . . [odd] that I cannot find them in any of my books. But we have moved so many times." And then she gave Foy a very meaningful compliment: "It was remarkable testimonies that he bore."[26]

Hazen Foss met Ellen Harmon in January, 1845, at a meeting in Poland, Maine. Here Ellen had been invited by Mary Foss, her sister, to relate her first vision of a month earlier.[27]

Hazen, Mary's brother-in-law [Mary was the wife of Samuel Foss], is remembered "as a man of fine appearance, pleasing address, and education." Prior to October 22, 1844, he had a vision depicting the journey of the Adventists (Millerites) to the city of God. He was instructed to make known this vision along with specific messages of warning, but he declined.

After October 22 he felt that he had been misled by his earlier vision. In his second vision, he was warned that if he was not faithful in relating the first vision, the vision and the responsibility would be taken from him and given to one with much fewer qualifications. He continued to dread the potential ridicule and rejection of his fellow Millerites. Finally he believed he heard a voice saying, "You have grieved away the Spirit of the Lord."

Frightened by this prospect, he called a meeting to relate the vision. But, after making several unsuccessful attempts to recall it, he declared: "It is gone from me; I can say nothing, the Spirit of the Lord has left me." Some in attendance reported the meeting as "the most terrible meeting they were ever in."

After this experience, Hazen met Ellen in Poland, Maine. Though invited into the meeting, he remained outside the closed door, though close enough to hear her message. The next day, he told Ellen: "'The Lord gave me a message to bear to His people. And I refused after being told the consequences; I was proud; I was unreconciled to the disappointment. . . . I heard you talk last night. I believe the visions are taken from me, and given to you. Do not refuse to obey God, for it will be at the peril of your soul. I am a lost man. You are chosen of God; be faithful in doing your work, and the crown I might have had, you will receive.'"[28]

God Reveals Himself Through Prophets in Times of Crisis

God is very compassionate, very caring for His people—especially when He makes Himself known in periods of crisis. The appearance of His prophets is often linked with major crises. Thus, when a prophet appears we should examine the nature of the crisis. And when we study the crisis, we should look for the prophet's message. Think of the Flood and Noah comes to mind. Israel in Egyptian bondage—Moses. Dire oppression—Deborah, and later Samuel. Dark apostasy—Elijah. Tragic national decline—Isaiah and Jeremiah. Dismal captivity—Daniel and Ezekiel. Birth of the Christian church—Peter and Paul. Restoration of special truth in the last days—Ellen White.

This same kind of divine thoughtfulness was evident on Resurrection Sunday. Two defeated disciples were shuffling off to Emmaus, walking in the dark shadow of a crucifixion (see Luke 24). But the Lord knew their despair and came close to them. He knew that He had allowed their gloom. He would not leave them in their grief and bewilderment.

How did Jesus reveal Himself? First, by leading their minds back to the Scriptures. He helped them to trace the truth that they had only hazily understood. This kind of Bible study provided those early disciples with more stability and Biblical insight than even a miracle could have supplied.

In the 1840s another epochal moment in God's salvation plan occurred. The end of the longest time prophecy in the Bible was at hand (Dan. 8:14). The occasion was awesome—the Advent was near. But, though much of the world had been hearing the authentic message of the Second Advent, the time of the Advent was based on a wrong interpretation of Daniel's prophecy.

During the confusion and despair following October 22, 1844, God came close to His people. Through a teenager He encouraged them to restudy the Bible[29] and instructed them to hear His comfort and affirmation. Through young Ellen Harmon the perplexity and gloom surrounding the Great Disappointment of October 22 soon changed to hope and courage. Even as the two Emmaus-bound disciples returned to Jerusalem with the joy of present truth, so those early Adventists faced the world again with the joy of present truth.

Ellen White Appeared at the Time of Greatest Distress

Ellen White had to contend with the prevailing sentiment among Millerite leaders that all charismatic phenomena, such as visions and trances, were to be rejected.[30]

Equally troubling were the widening divisions and fearsome fanaticisms within the Millerites after October 22, 1844.[31]

Perhaps even more oppressive was the ridicule of those who had rejected the

Millerites before the Disappointment as they observed the humiliation of the disappointed.[32]

In addition, young Ellen was only a teenager, a very sick girl who could barely speak above a whisper. But in December 1844, God gave her a vision. Who would listen to her, the "weakest of the weak"?

As time went by, the reluctant, self-effacing, unswerving fidelity of Ellen Harmon to be God's messenger in most forbidding times became the rallying center for earnest Bible students who wanted to know what was right and wrong about October 22, 1844. Even as on the road to Emmaus, Jesus came very close to earnest but puzzled believers in the months following the "magnificent disappointment."[33]

Note

At times, a comparison is made between both the life history and visions of William Foy and Ellen Harmon. Both experienced unsettling spiritual conflicts prior to their visions, both experienced great aversion to relating their visions publicly. Occasionally, both used common phrases of the day, such as "comfort the saints."

Although a few verbal parallels exist between Foy's visions and those of Ellen Harmon, there are important dissimilarities in content. In describing the journey of one who had just died as going to heaven in a chariot, Foy makes no mention of the resurrection at the Second Advent, due to his belief in the immortality of the soul. Foy sees a mountain on which were printed in gold letters, "The Father and the Son," providing a backdrop for the judgment scene. Nothing similar is found in the records of Ellen Harmon's visions.

Foy and Harmon (White) both describe the tree of life, using common words such as "the fruit looked like clusters of grapes in pictures of pure gold" (Foy), and "the fruit was glorious; it looked like gold mixed with silver" (White). Speaking of eating the fruit, Foy recalled, "the guide then spoke to me and said, 'Those who eat of the fruit of this tree, return to earth no more.'" White wrote: "I asked Jesus to let me eat of the fruit. He said, 'Not now. Those who eat of the fruit of this land go back to earth no more.'" In the context, dissimilarities are apparent.

Both refer to a large group of the redeemed, standing in a "perfect square." Foy wrote that they were "the size of children 10 years of age" and that they sang a "song which the saints and angels could not sing." For Ellen White, "Here on the sea of glass the 144,000 stood in a perfect square."

However, if Foy's visions were authentic and faithfully disclosed, should we not expect similarities and parallels, at least to some extent? But the general conceptual content of Foy's published visions do not parallel those of Ellen White.[34]

Some questions exist regarding the Pearsons (John Pearson, Jr., and C. H. Pearson) who published Foy's pamphlet, *The Christian Experience,* and "Father" Pearson, who is referred to in *Life Sketches,* pages 70, 71, and in *Testimonies for the Church,* volume 1, page 64.

"Father Pearson," an older leader of the small group of believers in Portland, Maine, opposed those who claimed they were "prostrated" by the Spirit of God—until he and his family had the "experience."[35] James White had worked with "Father" Pearson's son, John Pearson, Jr., in 1843 and after. John, the son, with Joseph Turner, edited *Hope of Israel,* an Advent paper, and published William Foy's pamphlet early in 1845.

It seems clear that if Ellen Harmon's visions were mere duplications of Foy's earlier visions, the Pearsons would have been the first to perceive the fraud, especially when Father Pearson had been so sensitive and suspicious regarding visions and other so-called manifestations of the Spirit. Father Pearson believed in the genuineness of William Foy and went on to solidly endorse Ellen Harmon.

Endnotes

1. Kenneth H. Wood, "Toward an Understanding of the Prophetic Office"—*Journal of the Adventist Theological Society*, Spring, 1991, p. 21.
2. Moses recorded God's words regarding the prophetic system, using visions and dreams interchangeably: "If there is a prophet among you, I, the Lord, make Myself known to him in a vision; I speak to him in a dream" (Num. 12:6).
3. T. H. Jemison was one of the first to categorize these four tests in *A Prophet Among You,* (Mountain View, CA: Pacific Press Publishing Association, 1955), pages 100-112.
4. In this instance Jeremiah was using irony in speaking to the false prophet Hananiah. The principle, however, stands.
5. See Mal. 3:6; James 1:17. Progressive revelation (see page 422) is a term that describes God's "continuing education" plan. It builds on previous revelation; it does not displace or contradict previous revelation.
6. See pages 2, 3.
7. See 1 Sam. 10:5, 10; 1 Kings 20:35; 2 Kings 2:3, 5; 4:38; 5:22; 6:1.
8. *Education,* p. 46.
9. *Review and Herald,* March 25, 1890. See also *Selected Messages,* book 3, p. 341, wherein Ellen White had another occasion to clarify the role of a gifted prophet: "These ideas in relation to prophesying, I do not hesitate to say, might better never have been expressed. Such statements prepare the way for a state of things that Satan will surely take advantage of to bring in spurious exercises. There is danger, not only that unbalanced minds will be led into fanaticism, but that designing persons will take advantage of this excitement to further their own selfish purposes."
10. Jack Provonsha, *A Remnant in Crisis* (Hagerstown, MD: Review and Herald Publishing Association, 1993), pp. 57, 58. Applying these principles to Ellen White, Provonsha writes: "Ellen White apparently often 'heard' the voice of God speaking to her as she read books in her library. A person who had spent a lifetime as God's messenger would surely develop unusual sensitivity to such intuitions and might even quite understandably employ, at times, the very words of the authors through which they were presented to her mind—with or without quotation marks."—*Ibid.,* pp. 58, 59.
11. See Christ's predictions in Matt. 24:11.
12. Jeremiah records what the Lord has said about "false prophets": "The prophets and the priests are godless; I have caught them doing evil in the Temple itself. . . . I have seen the prophets in Jerusalem . . . : they commit adultery and tell lies, they help people to do wrong, so that no one stops doing what is evil. . . . ; they are filling you with false hopes. They tell you what they have imagined and not what I have said. . . . None of these prophets has ever known the Lord's secret thoughts. None of them has ever heard or understood his message, or ever listened or paid attention to what he said. . . . I did not send these prophets, but even so they went. I did not give them any message, but still they spoke in my name. . . . I know what those prophets have said who speak lies in my name and claim that I have given them my messages in their dreams. How much longer will those prophets mislead my people with the lies they have invented? . . . The prophet who has had a dream should say it is only a dream, but the prophet who has heard my message should proclaim that message faithfully. . . . I am against those prophets who take each other's words and proclaim them as my message. I am also against those prophets who speak their own words and claim they came from me. Listen to what I, the Lord, say! I am against the prophets who tell their dreams that are full of lies. . . . I did not send them or order them to go, and they are of no help at all to the people. I, the Lord, have spoken" (chap. 23:11-32, TEV); see also chap. 28; 29:8, 15-19, 31.
13. Writing later, Ellen White referred to the physical phenomena that played an important part in connection with her early ministry: "Some of the instruction found in these pages was given under circumstances so remarkable as to evidence the wonder-working power of God in behalf of His truth. . . . These messages were thus given to substantiate the faith of all, that in these last days we might have confidence in the Spirit of prophecy."—*Review and Herald,* June 14, 1906. See p. 28
14. Winthrop S. Hudson, "A Time of Religious Ferment," *The Rise of Adventism,* ed. Edwin S. Gaustad, (New York: Harper & Row, 1974) p. 8.
15. Ernest R. Sandeen wrote that America "was drunk on the millennium." Cited by Ernest Dick, "The Millerite Movement," *Adventism in America,* ed. Gary Land, (Grand Rapids: William B. Eerdmans Publishing Company, 1986) p. 3; See also Ernest R. Sandeen, "Millennialism," in *The Rise of Adventism,* ed. Edwin S. Gaustad (New York: Harper & Row, 1974), pp. 104-118; George R. Knight, *Millennial Fever* (Boise, Idaho: Pacific Press Publishing Association, 1993), pp. 1-384.
16. Most all Christians were "post-millennialists," who believed that Jesus would return after the 1,000-year period of Revelation 20. Their main rationale was that Satan would be bound on this earth by the advance of Christianity throughout the world, that good would overcome evil as the world became more enlightened by the gospel. See Ernest R. Sandeen, "Millennialism," Gaustad, *The Rise of Adventism,* pp. 10-118.
17. Harold Bloom, *The American Religion* (New York: Simon & Schuster, 1993), pp. 21-75; Hudson, "A Time of Religious Ferment," in Gaustad, *The Rise of Adventism,* pp. 1-17; William G. McLoughlin, "Revivalism," in Gaustad, *The Rise of Adventism,* pp. 119-150.
18. "Declaration of Principles" in Charles Fitch's periodical, *The Second Advent of Christ* (Cleveland, Ohio, June 21, 1843): "We have no confidence whatever in visions, dreams, or private revelations. 'What is the chaff to the wheat? saith the Lord.' We repudiate all fanaticism, and everything which may tend to extravagance, excess, and immorality, that shall cause our good to be evil spoken of."
19. James White, "The Gifts of the Gospel Church," in *Review and Herald,* April 21, 1851.
20. Hudson, "A Time of Religious Ferment," in Gaustad, *The Rise of Adventism,* pp. 9-17.
21. *Ibid.,* p. 10.
22. *Ibid.,* p. 13; H. Shelton Smith, Robert T. Handy, Lefferts A. Loetscher, *American Christianity: An Historical Interpretation With Documents* (New York: Charles Scribner's Sons, 1963), pp. 80-84.
23. Cited in LeRoy Edwin Froom, *The Conditionalist Faith of Our Fathers,* vol. II (Washington, D.C.: Review and Herald Publishing Association, 1965), p. 1069.

24. It is reported that he did not breathe, had significant loss of strength, was not able to speak, etc. Additional background on William Foy may be found in Delbert W. Baker's *The Unknown Prophet* (Washington, D.C.: Review and Herald Publishing Association, 1987). A Freewill Baptist minister of exceptional abilities, his first vision was related to a Methodist congregation. After this vision, his strong, earnest preaching focused on the nearness of the Advent and preparation for the event. Baker does not agree with the popular opinion that Ellen Harmon later filled the responsibility first given to Foy.

    "William Foy served as a spokesman for God to the Advent movement in the pre-Disappointment period, whereas Ellen White became a post-Disappointment prophet. Foy spoke to the early Adventists, assuring them of God's personal interest, encouraging them on to greater revival and reformation. He brought timely truths to view that would later, if understood, have spared His people the Great Disappointment, or at least prepared them for it. Foy received a limited number of visions with a set objective. He never suggested that his prophetic role would extend past 1844, or that he would receive more visions.

    "A misleading generalization that is often made is that if Foy is accepted as a genuine prophet to the Advent movement (pre-Seventh-day Adventist), he must also be a prophet to the Seventh-day Adventist movement for all time remaining. This belief, though understandable, finds no real support."—Delbert Baker, "William Foy, Messenger to the Advent Believers," *Adventist Review,* Jan. 14, 1988.
25. Baker, *The Unknown Prophet,* pp. 143, 144. See note at end of chapter.
26. Ellen White, "William Foy," Ellen G. White Estate, Document File 231. Only two of Foy's visions were published in his *The Christian Experience of William E. Foy Together With the Two Visions He Received in the Months of January and February 1842* (Portland, Me.: The Pearson Brothers, 1845). The third is summarized by J. N. Loughborough in *Rise and Progress of the Seventh-day Adventists (RPSDA)* (Reprinted by Payson, AZ: Leaves-of-Autumn Books, Inc., 1988), p. 71. No information is available as to the contents of the fourth vision.
27. See Robinson, *James White*, p. 28; see also *Bio.*, vol. 1, p. 71.
28. "Hazen Foss," in *Seventh-day Adventist Encyclopedia, (SDAE),* ed. Don F. Neufeld, second revised edition (Washington, D.C.: Review and Herald Publishing Association, 1996), vol, 2, p. 562.
29. Note the Biblical studies of Hiram Edson, O. R. L. Crozier, and F. B. Hahn in late 1844 and early 1845. See Schwarz, *Light Bearers*, pp. 60-63.
30. Knight, *Millennial Fever,* p. 273.
31. Everett N. Dick, "The Millerite Movement, 1830-1845," in *Adventism in America,* ed. Gary Land (Grand Rapids, MI: William B. Eerdmans Publishing Company, 1986), pp. 31-35; Knight, *Millennial Fever,* pp. 245-293; R. W. Schwarz, *Light Bearers to the Remnant* (Boise, ID: Pacific Press Publishing Association, 1979), pp. 56-58.
32. Land, *Adventism in America,* pp. 29-30; Schwarz, *Light Bearers,* p. 53; *Bio.,* vol. 1, p. 54.
33. See C. Mervyn Maxwell, *Magnificent Disappointment* (Boise, ID: Pacific Press Publishing Association, 1994).
34. Foy continued to preach for the Freewill Baptists. In the 1860s he settled near East Sullivan, Maine, where he pastored a church and worked his small farm. "'Elder Foy,' as he was called, was greatly esteemed and loved in that area; verbal tradition has it that he was friendly and kind, yet of strong convictions. The local history declared Foy an excellent preacher and a skilled pastor."—Baker, *The Unknown Prophet,* p. 158. He died at 75 years of age, and was buried near Ellsworth, Maine, where his tombstone may be found in Birch Tree Cemetery.
35. *Testimonies,* vol. 1, pp. 47, 64.

Study Questions

1. What Biblical examples illustrate the principle of conditional prophecy?
2. Why don't all believers possess the gift of prophecy?
3. What are some of the common characteristics shared by prophets in their vision experiences?
4. What are the best tests of a genuine prophet or prophetess?
5. What were some of the contemporary circumstances that made it difficult for Ellen Harmon to gain a hearing in 1845?
6. Why is our attitude toward prophets an indication of our attitude toward God?
7. Why do you think physical phenomena are more associated with visions at certain times than at other times?

SECTION II

The Real Ellen White

CHAPTER

CHAPTER 4

The Person and Her Times

"Remember your leaders, those who spoke to you the word of God; consider the outcome of their life, and imitate their faith" (Heb.13:7, RSV).

How can a person get to know the *real* Abraham Lincoln or Florence Nightingale or Booker T. Washington? In part, by reading their writings. But to get objectivity one should listen to what others say about them. One must turn to their contemporaries and note how they were affected or influenced by these exceptional people.

When Lincoln died, note the mourning of a nation. As his funeral train slowly wound itself west to his resting place in Springfield, Illinois, thousands of mourners lined the track, tears flowing freely. Rich and poor, black and white, educated and unschooled—the grief throbbed across a union of States now nearly at peace. After his death, even his enemies applauded his greatness of spirit and transparent unselfishness.[1] For the millions who called him "Father Abraham," his premature death was as if a parent had died. When the United States built its first transcontinental highway from Jersey City, New Jersey, to San Francisco, California, President Taft felt that naming the new road the "Lincoln Highway" would further national unity.[2]

However, when President Lincoln was alive, he was the target of immense ridicule and scathing rejection by many national leaders, their followers, and by the public press. But after he died, a stunned nation began to appreciate what he stood for. A sad but grateful nation soon treasured his profound speeches and writings, such as the Gettysburg Address and his Second Inaugural Address. The enormous contribution of Abraham Lincoln could be seen in true perspective only with the passing of time and after calm reflection.

Looking forward to Ellen White's visit to Australia in 1891, G. C. Tenney, first president of the Australian Conference, wrote in the church paper: "I need hardly say that this event is anticipated by us all with great interest. I believe it is most opportune. The position that Sister White and her work occupy in connection with our cause renders it imperative that our people should become personally acquainted with her, so far as possible.

"The evidences, from a Bible standpoint, of the authenticity of the work of the Spirit of Prophecy in connection with the last church are all-sufficient, but a closer acquaintance with the work of Sister White seems to be demanded, in order to satisfy the honest inquirer that it fills the requirements of God's Word."[3]

Like Lincoln, Ellen White was often maligned. She faced lies of "sheer malice and enmity" and "pure fabrications of iniquity." Writing from Greenville, Michigan, when she was 41, she contemplated: "I do not doubt for a moment but the Lord had sent me that the honest souls who had been deceived might have an opportunity to see and hear for themselves what manner of spirit the woman possessed who had been presented to the public in such a false light in order to make the truth of God of none effect. . . ."[4]

Later in that letter she wrote: "None are compelled to believe. God gives sufficient evidence that all may decide upon the weight of evidence, but He never has nor never will remove all chance [opportunity] for doubt, never will force faith."

Quoting an old woodsmen's proverb, Carl Sandburg entitled the next-to-the-last chapter in his six-volume biography of Abraham Lincoln, "A tree is best measured when it's down."[5] While alive, no man or woman can be fully measured. Never was this more true than with the life of Christ. Only with the passing of time can anyone's life be properly evaluated. The gushing praise of flatterers and the derisive contempt of adversaries alike are best gauged and reappraised against the lasting results of a person's words and deeds.

To a large extent, we are all children of our time. On November 26, 1827, Ellen Harmon was born into a world of enormous ferment and rapid change. To help us understand the subjects she talked or wrote about, even the phrases she used, as well as the kind of daily life she lived, we shall briefly note geographical, political, economic, social, and religious factors that may have influenced her maturing ministry.

Geographical Environment

Portland, Maine, the largest city nearest Ellen during her first twenty years, was also the largest in Maine in 1840, with a population of 15,218. Though that number seems small today, in the 1840s Portland exceeded the size of New Haven and Hartford, Connecticut; and Savannah, Georgia. Portland, a busy seaport, placed Maine third behind only Massachusetts and New York in total shipping. Regular steamship connections with Boston often experienced price wars, once dropping fares as low as 50 cents each way in 1841.[6]

In Ellen White's time, as today, the summers were proverbially pleasant, winters harsh, with temperatures often below zero, even to a record 24 degrees Fahrenheit below zero (February 1, 1826). The harbor was often frozen for days, even weeks, while the countryside, usually covered with snow, made travel by sleigh ideal.[7]

Portland had a "progressive school system" for students between 4 and 21 years of age. Following primary school, a student could enter grammar school after a public examination. However, free education for girls ended with grammar school, while boys could go on to the English high school, after passing another public examination.[8]

Because Portland did not have a hospital until 1855, the sick were cared for at home or in the physician's office. An M.D. degree could be attained at Bowdoin College at Brunswick (about 26 miles from Portland) after three months of lectures, a written thesis, and a final examination before the faculty of medicine (equivalent to the best American medical schools of that day).[9]

City statistics list a wide array of causes for death, "from an extensive variety of fevers (typhoid and typhus to 'putrid fever') and common diseases of the age (cholera and measles) to some designations that are now quaint or archaic (scrofula, 'sudden,' and gravel). By far the most common cause of death was consumption (tuberculosis), followed by 'fevers,' dropsy, 'bowel complaints,' or other diseases that had reached epidemic proportions (such as measles in 1835 and scarlet fever in 1842).

"Heavily hit were the young; those under 10 often constituted close to 50 percent of deaths in a year (not counting the many stillborn). Stated differently, the average age at death during 1840 was 22.6 years, which the *Advertiser* claimed demonstrated 'the superior degree of health enjoyed in Portland.'"[10]

Frederick Hoyt, Adventist historian, summarized the impact of growing up in the vicinity of Portland, Maine, in the 1830s and 1840s: "This then was the environment that nurtured the body, mind, and soul of young Ellen Gould Harmon. In many ways it was a harsh environment that could only toughen the character of those it did not break. In the words of American historian James Truslow Adams, in this setting 'the gristle of conscience, work, thrift, shrewdness, duty, became bone.' Other words could well be used to characterize Down-Easterners: religious fervor, a passionate search for truth, stubborn independence, Spartan toughness, resourcefulness, frugality, sturdy individualism, and a propensity to adopt and fight for unpopular causes."[11]

Political Environment

Perhaps no two decades in the nineteenth century saw more rapid growth and momentous events than the 1830s and 1840s. The United States became united from coast to coast. During these two decades seven States joined the union, with California, in 1850, becoming the thirty-first. War with Mexico ended with large territorial annexations. The population of the United States soared from about 5 million in 1800 to more than 20 million in 1850.

Increasing waves of immigrants changed the texture of cities, from a "tiny trickle of 150,000 immigrants in the 1820s . . . to a powerful stream of two and one-half million in the 1850s." Though they brought "vigor and variety," they also aroused "fear, suspicion, and hostility." Roman Catholics from Ireland, Italy, and other European countries were especially resented because their sheer numbers flooded the market with cheap labor; in addition, their religious homogeneity threatened the previous uniformity of a Protestant America.[12]

Race relations, though a social phenomenon, affected many of the political issues even in States "free" from slavery. The slavery issue escalated inexorably through the first half of the nineteenth century, culminating in a polarized nation and the Civil War that shook and drained the Union. As the young country lurched toward its dark night of civil conflict, many white abolitionists risked their lives, speaking out against slavery and for its immediate elimination.[13]

Social Environment

The mid-nineteenth century rocked with the dynamics of social change, mainly driven by the flush of individualism. The presidency of Andrew Jackson opened the door to freeing the "common man" from the status quo. It seemed that every conceivable reform issue was inaugurated.

Lyceums, and later the Chautauqua circuit, attracted millions to hear lectures on such diverse topics as slavery, Fourierism (small, cooperative communities), non-resistance, land reform, perfectionism, mesmerism (hypnotism), whole-wheat bread, and all aspects of health. And the publications of these "reforms" flooded the market. "There are temperance papers. . . . There have been numerous journals devoted to Spiritualism, Socialism, Phrenology, Homeopathy, Hydrotherapy, Anti-Rent, Bloomerism, Women's Rights, Odd Fellowship, Masonry, Anti-masonry, and all the notions, movements, and sensations of a very active-minded community."[14]

Young America was also a cauldron of social polarizations. Race relations haunted most communities in every State. Ethnic groups, including certain Europeans, Orientals, Hispanics, Negroes, and Native Americans, had to face blind prejudice affecting the work place as well as the neighborhood.[15]

The consumption of alcoholic beverages was also a national concern. One historian described the United States as an "alcoholic republic." Annual per capita consumption of alcohol increased from three gallons in 1800 to four gallons in 1830.[16]

By 1839, the American Temperance Society, through its more than 8,000 local societies, had convinced 350,000 to sign the total abstinence pledge—the "total" pledge becoming a great step even for temperance advocates. The Woman's Christian Temperance Union, organized on November 18, 1874, was especially effective on the local level.[17]

The last half of Ellen White's ministry coincided with the phenomenal rise of urban-industrial cities. A nation born on the farm had moved to the cities. "The number of Americans living in centers with more than 2,500 inhabitants had grown from 19 percent in 1860 to 39 percent in 1900 and to 52 percent in 1920."[18]

The change of pace from the time-honored natural pace of the farm to the artificial life of the city forced many new and difficult adjustments. "Rural America had its vices, but none seemed as blatant as those of the metropolis." For most Protestants, the city was a symbol of everything wrong— "an alien and hostile world hopelessly steeped in rum and Romanism."[19]

Another factor that polarized the cities was class conflict—conspicuous rich being envied by those working the factories, most of them the stereotyped immigrants with their unconventional, insular ways. For the first time America heard the term, "organized labor."[20]

Ellen White's ministry paralleled a turbulent time of great social changes. She wrote much about the dark years of the Civil War and the plight of the slave, the shakeup of the move from the farm to the city, the obvious implications of extravagant alcoholic consumption, and the class struggle between the rich and the poor.

Religious Environment

It would be difficult to find any period in U.S. history that would come close to the religious ferment of the mid-nineteenth century.[21]

"Revivalists and millennialists, communitarians and utopians, spiritualists and prophesiers, celibates and polygamists, perfectionists and transcendentalists"—all were adding spice to the religious scene previously dominated by the conventional denominations.[22]

Established churches were torn by controversy, especially the Old and New School Calvinists. The Wesleyan emphasis on free grace produced an astounding rise in the "primacy of religious experience." New religious groups were springing up with astonishing success, but "nowhere were they produced in greater variety than in the heated seedplot of upstate New York."[23]

Camp meetings, primarily Methodist, were spiritual hothouses where various stages of exuberance merged with the sense of "fresh revelation," the possibility of holiness here and now, and the consciousness of participating in fulfilling "ancient millennial hopes."[24] The shouts of the distressed mingled with the shouts of praise and glory. The falling, the jerking, the barking, even the crawling on the ground, the rolling, the heavenly dancing, the laughing and the shouting of thousands at once, "creating such a volume of noise that the sound carried for miles"—all became remarkable characteristics of those "slain by the Spirit."[25]

The camp meeting "spirit" carried over into the weekly church services and city gospel tabernacles. Professional evangelists carried on the camp meeting legacy with high-voltage preaching; respect for the "old-time religion" was reflected in camp meeting songs that are still effective today.

As one would expect, early Adventists (many of them former Methodists) often expressed their spiritual feelings as did other evangelical Protestants. "Shouting," for a short while, was probably the most characteristic mode of public expression.[26]

The remarkable coincidence of the emergence of Mormonism, Christian Science, and modern Spiritualism with the rise of the Seventh-day Adventist Church in the first half of the nineteenth century was noted in the previous chapter.

Family Tree

A resourceful farmer and hatmaker, Ellen's father, Robert F. Harmon, Sr., (1786-1866) was disfellowshipped in 1843 from Portland's Methodist Episcopal church for embracing the Millerite message.[27]

Eunice Gould Harmon (1787-1863) mothered two sons and six daughters, of whom Ellen and her twin, Elizabeth, were the last. The record notes that she was a school teacher prior to her marriage; afterwards she was an industrious homemaker at the time of whale-oil lamps and wood-burning stoves—and unpredictable family income. Her parents descended from resourceful ancestors. They fought in the earlier wars, beginning with King Philips's War (1675). Some were entrepreneurs. Ellen's great-great-grandfather built a mill on the river at Scarboro, Maine, known as "Harmon's Mill."[28]

Four of the eight Harmon children became Sabbath keepers—Ellen and her sisters Mary and Sarah (six and five years older, respectively, than Ellen) and Robert. Caroline's (1811-1883) daughter Mary worked briefly as Ellen's literary assistant (1876-77). Robert, Jr. died at 27 of consumption in 1853. Both of Ellen White's parents became Sabbath keeping Adventists in later life.

Shortly before their father died (and after Ellen had visited her sisters once more) she wrote: "Although we were not practically agreed on all points of religious duty, yet our hearts were one."[29]

Ellen's marriage to James White, August 30, 1846, produced four children, only two of whom survived to adulthood.

Their first born, Henry Nichols (1847-1863), a happy young man, died of pneumonia at 16.[30] James Edson (1849-1928) learned the printer's trade from his father at 14. He became a popular Adventist writer and composer. His tenacious work for Blacks in the southern States was unparalleled. His printing establishment became the foundation of the former Southern Publishing Association.[31]

Early in life the managerial skills of William Clarence (1854-1937) were recognized; he was elected to a variety of heavy responsibilities in church leadership. After his father died, he became a traveling companion and trusted counselor to his mother. Soon after his mother died in 1915, he was appointed secretary of the Ellen G. White Estate, supervising its work for more than two decades.

John Herbert, born in 1860, died after three months, from erysipelas.[32]

Early Life Prior to 1845[33]

Three major events or circumstances occurred in Ellen White's early years that directly affected and focused the rest of her life—her physical trauma at age nine; the preaching of William Miller; and her profound religious experience.

In 1836 while young Ellen was walking with a group of schoolmates, an older girl followed them with threats. Just as Ellen turned, the older girl threw a rock that smashed her face, knocking her unconscious. For three weeks she lay in a virtual coma.

Some days later, when her father returned home from a business trip, Ellen was crushed further—her father did not recognize her. "Every feature" of her face was changed. More than that, the loss of blood had severely affected her respiratory system—a weakness she bore for the rest of her life. In addition, because her hand "trembled," Ellen could make "no progress in writing."[34] Looking back after nearly fifty years, she wrote, "The cruel blow which blighted the joys of earth, was the means of turning my eyes to heaven. I might never have known Jesus, had not the sorrow that clouded my early years led me to seek comfort in Him."[35]

Schooling became impossible. The letters of the alphabet in her books would run together, her eyes could not focus properly, perspiration flowed, and she would become dizzy and faint. And so, at the age of nine, this bright student left her academic preparation in great disappointment, never to return to formal schooling—the first of two great disappointments in her early life. Her mother became her teacher, and the fields around Portland, her laboratory.[36]

But fresh hope came to Ellen in 1840 when William Miller held his Portland, Maine, audience spellbound as he traced the prophecies that seemed to indicate that the return of Jesus was near. This new understanding, fresh (and thus controversial) to most of her religious contemporaries, profoundly affected the rest of her life.

Spiritual matters were always important to young Ellen. But her primary motivation was fear—fear of not being ready when Jesus would come, fear of failure because of her limited schooling and weakened body, and fear that in some way God had afflicted her with her horrid, physical burden. All this became her "secret agony" that she locked in her lonely heart. Years of listening to "hell-fire" sermons had etched a false picture of God into her soul. God was Ellen's heavenly Ruler, but was He her Friend?

Two dreams and some timely pastoral counseling became the third of those turning points in young Ellen's life that set the course for the rest of her life. For the next 75 years, her most compelling mission was to tell the truth about the character of God.

One of the two dreams portrayed a visit to the heavenly temple; the other, a meeting with Jesus. With a smile, Jesus seemed to touch her head, saying, "Fear not." He gave her a green cord, representing faith, leading her to declare: "The beauty and simplicity of trusting in God began to dawn upon my soul." Ellen now felt free to discuss her fears with her mother. With quick insight and encouragement, her mother suggested a visit with young Levi Stockman, in his late thirties.

After Elder Stockman heard her story of the two dreams as well as her deep fears, he said: "Ellen, you are only a child. Yours is a most singular experience for one of your tender age. Jesus must be preparing you for some special work."

Then the perceptive pastor gave her a clearer picture of God as seen in Jesus. Writing later, Ellen wrote: "During the few minutes in which I received instruction from Elder Stockman, I had obtained more knowledge on the subject of God's love and pitying tenderness, than from all the sermons and exhortations to which I had ever listened."[37]

Her new-found understanding—that God is like Jesus, her best Friend—prompted her to share her insights and gratitude with others: "While relating my experience, I felt that no one could resist the evidence of God's pardoning love that had wrought so wonderful a change in me. The reality of true conversion seemed so plain to me that I felt like helping my young friends into the light, and at every opportunity exerted my influence toward this end."[38]

New Picture of God

This new picture of God, coupled with her deep conviction that Jesus was soon to come, was shared by her brother Robert. He reflected with her about what these fresh insights had done for them: "'A tree is known by its fruits. What has this belief done for us? It has convinced us that we were not ready for the coming of the Lord; that we must become pure in heart, or we cannot meet our Saviour in peace. It has aroused us to seek for new strength and grace from God.

"'What has it done for you, Ellen? Would you be what you are now if you had never heard the doctrine of Christ's soon coming? What hope has it inspired in your heart; what peace, joy, and love has it given you? And for me it has done everything. I love Jesus, and all Christians. I love the prayer meeting. I find great joy in reading my Bible and in prayer.'"[39]

Most probably, if Ellen had not had this self-authenticating relationship with her Lord, she would not have been prepared for the profound disappointment on October 22, 1844. She recalled: "It was a bitter disappointment that fell upon the little flock whose faith had been so strong and whose hope had been so high. But we were surprised that we felt so free in the Lord, and were so strongly sustained by His strength and grace. . . . We were disappointed, but not disheartened."[40]

Thus, in late 1844 Ellen was prepared for her unforeseen future. Fully mindful of her frail physical condition, captured by her new and compelling picture of God as her heavenly Friend, and focused on the consuming truth that Jesus was still coming soon, she was ready for her first vision. She had just turned 17.

But not all the Millerites thought alike after the Great Disappointment. Not all could say they were "disappointed but not disheartened." On one hand, radical ideas generated radical behavior. Some former leaders, believing that Christ had indeed come spiritually, espoused "spiritual wifery," whereby they renounced marriage and formed "spiritual" unions, devoid of sex, with new partners. Others, believing that the 1,000-year Sabbath had now begun, and to show their faith in what they believed, would do no more secular work.[41]

On the other hand, doctrinal differences began to separate Miller's followers.[42] They soon divided into at least four groups: (1) Those known as Evangelical Adventists eventually abandoned Miller's prophetic teachings and were absorbed into other Protestant groups when it became evident that very little divided them; (2) Another group believed that the millennium was in the past, that the dead were now "sleeping," awaiting the resurrection, and that the wicked would be annihilated. Eventually they became known as the Advent Christian Church, now the largest non-Sabbath keeping remnant of Millerite adventism; (3) Centered around Rochester, N.Y., another group saw the millennium as yet future wherein the Jews would return to Palestine. Firmly opposed to formal church organization, these "Age-to-Come" adventists never became strong and united.

(4) The fourth group became known as the "Sabbath and Shut-door" Adventists. Through prayer, Bible study, and divine confirmation they developed a rationale for the events that centered on October 22, 1844. This scattered group eventually found their unity and mission and went on to become Seventh-day Adventists, the largest of the Millerite bodies today. They believed that something had happened on October 22, but what?[43]

God understood their pain and confusion, just as He understood those two dejected disciples trudging to Emmaus with "sad faces" (Luke 24:17) after the crucifixion. Jesus did not let His disheartened disciples sink without an explanation 2,000 years ago—and He did not forget His believers in late 1844.

And so He made His presence felt that December morning in 1844, when a small group of Adventist women in Portland, Maine joined themselves in prayer and Bible study—reaching out to God and to each other for encouragement and understanding. The emaciated Ellen had been staying at the Haines home for a few days, giving her mother some much needed rest. Her physician and friends had given her up to die of consumption. While they were praying, this seventeen-year-old teenager became lost to her surroundings, and God gave her the kind of encouragement that those troubled believers desperately needed. Thus began a seventy-year ministry that became more significant as the years went by.[44]

Endnotes

1. See Carl Sandburg, *Abraham Lincoln* (New York: Charles Scribner's Sons, 1939), vol. 6, pp. 387-413.
2. "Lincoln, Abraham," *The World Book Encyclopedia* (Chicago: Field Enterprises Educational Corporation, 1960), p. 287.
3. *Review and Herald*, Nov. 17, 1891.

4. *Bio.*, vol. 2, 276.
5. Sandburg, *Abraham Lincoln,* pp. 387-413.
6. Frederick Hoyt, "Ellen White's Hometown: Portland, Maine, 1827-1846," ed. Gary Land, *The World of Ellen G. White* (Hagerstown, MD: Review and Herald Publishing Association: 1987), pp. 14, 15, 30, 31.
7. *Ibid.*, p. 14.
8. *Ibid.*, p. 16.
9. *Ibid.*, pp. 26, 27.
10. *Ibid.*, p. 27.
11. *Ibid.*, p. 31.
12. *Ibid.*, p. xii; Ronald E. Osborn, *The Spirit of American Christianity* (New York: Harper & Brothers, 1958), pp. 18-21.
13. H. Shelton Smith, et al., *American Christianity: An Historical Interpretation with Documents,* pp. 167-212.
14. Thomas Low Nichols, *Forty Years of American Life: 1821-1861* (New York: Stackpole Sons, 1937), p. 208.
15. "Within the framework of American history, the nineteenth century was probably the most crucial period with regard to race relations. Racial issues headlined the newspapers as white Americans found themselves in positions of conflict and compromise with ethnic groups such as Blacks, Native Americans (Indians), Hispanics, Orientals, and European ethnics. In each encounter the Caucasian majority had to face its own fears of, and prejudices toward, the minority groups. Often sheer, blind prejudice dictated the ways in which minority people were treated until greater contact modified the more extreme views. . . . Contact and exposure between the races did little to modify stereotypes held about the minority group. In such situations complex relationships both sociological and psychological mitigated against any real racial harmony or understanding. This was especially true in the case of Afro-Americans."—Norman K. Miles, "Tension Between the Races," in Land, *The World of Ellen G. White,* p. 47.
16. Jerome L. Clark, "The Crusade Against Alcohol," in Land, *World of Ellen G. White,* p. 131.
17. *Ibid.*, pp. 132, 138.
18. Carlos A. Schwantes, "The Rise of Urban-Industrial America," in Land, *World of Ellen G. White,* p. 80.
19. Land, *World of Ellen G. White,* pp. 84, 85; Osborn, *The Spirit of American Christianity,* pp. 16-18; Winthrop S. Hudson, *The Great Tradition of the American Churches* (New York: Harper & Row, [Torchbooks] 1963), pp. 110-136.
20. "In the late nineteenth century people often referred to corporations as 'trusts,' 'monopolies,' 'soulless machines,' or 'octopuses' whose grasping tentacles reached everywhere; labor unions were referred to as 'communistic' or 'un-American.' Of the two forms of organization, labor usually seemed the greater threat. . . . As the nineteenth century wound to a close, it became ever more evident that Protestantism was losing its working-class members. The close alliance between Protestantism and wealth, and the attitude of Protestant clergymen toward labor's struggle, had not gone unnoticed by workers. . . . For many working-class worshipers, it was increasingly difficult to find even a Protestant church to attend. As the church adopted an increasingly middle-class stance, it not only alienated many workers but also discovered compelling reasons to abandon physically the working-class neighborhoods of the metropolis in order to flee to suburban or rural environments."—Land, *World of Ellen G. White,* pp. 91-93.
21. K. S. Latourette, *A History of the Expansion of Christianity,* (New York: Harper & Brothers, 1941) vol. VI, pp. 442, 443, 450; VII, p. 450.
22. Edwin S. Gaustad, "Introduction," Gaustad, *The Rise of Adventism,* p. xv.
23. Winthrop S. Hudson, "A Time of Religious Ferment," Gaustad, *The Rise of Adventism,* p. 7.
24. *Ibid.*, p. 9.
25. Charles A. Johnson, *The Frontier Camp Meeting* (Dallas: Southern Methodist University Press, 1955), pp. 52-64. See Appendix A for an eye-witness's description of a camp meeting in the early 1800s.
26. Malcolm Bull and Keith Lockhart, *Seeking a Sanctuary* (San Francisco: Harper & Row, 1989), p. 152.
27. *Bio.*, vol. 1, pp. 43, 44.
28. See Ellen Harmon's family tree in *Bio.*, vol. 1, p. 487.
29. *Review and Herald,* April 21, 1868.
30. *Bio.*, vol. 2, pp. 70-72.
31. *SDAE,* vol. 11, p. 888.
32. *Bio.*, vol. 1, p. 430.
33. The most complete review of Ellen Harmon's early years is found in Arthur L. White's *Ellen G. White: The Early Years,* the first volume of his six-volume biography, Vol. 1: 1827-1862 (Washington, D.C.: Review and Herald Publishing Association, 1985), pp. 15-71.
34. Ellen White, *Spiritual Gifts,* vol. 2, pp. 7-11, cited in *Bio.*, vol. 1, pp. 28-31.
35. *Review and Herald,* Nov. 25, 1884.
36. Charles Dickens and Mark Twain, among other authors, did not reach the equivalent of secondary school.—Anthony Smith, *The Mind* (New York: The Viking Press, 1984), p. 208.
37. *Life Sketches,* p. 37; Maxwell, *Tell It to the World,* p. 56; see also *Bio.*, vol. 1, pp. 38-49.
38. *Life Sketches,* p. 41.
39. *Ibid.*, p. 45.
40. *Ibid.*, p. 61.
41. Schwarz, *Light Bearers,* p. 56. See p. 559.
42. See p. 134.
43. *Ibid.*, pp. 56-58.
44. *Ibid.*, pp. 55, 56; Maxwell, *Tell It to the World,* p. 58.; *Spiritual Gifts,* vol. 2, pp. 30, 31; J. N. Loughborough, *The Great Second Advent Movement (GSAM)* (Washington, D.C.: Review and Herald Publishing Association, 1905), p. 202.

Study Questions

1. How do we know that Ellen Harmon was a religiously oriented young person prior to 1844?
2. What misunderstanding of Bible truth led Ellen Harmon to have a wrong understanding of the character of God?
3. What fears burdened young Ellen and how were they relieved?

CHAPTER 5

Messenger, Wife, and Mother

"Who can find a virtuous wife? . . . The heart of her husband safely trusts her; . . . Strength and honor are her clothing; she shall rejoice in time to come. . . . Her children rise up and call her blessed; her husband also, and he praises her: 'Many daughters have done well, but you excel them all'" (Prov. 31:10, 11, 25, 28, 29).

During 1845, Ellen Harmon was invited to share her early visions with adventist groups in Maine, New Hampshire, and Massachusetts. A young preacher, six years older than Ellen, became convinced that her visions were genuine and that her message of encouragement was needed. And so James White entered young Ellen's life, but not with romantic thoughts—at first.

In fact, for a few months after October 22 he and most others in the fourth group of Millerites mentioned in the last chapter, viewed marriage as a denial of their faith in the soon-coming of Christ. In the *Day Star,* James condemned a couple who, in announcing their approaching wedding, had "denied their faith in being published for marriage, and we all look upon this as a wile of the Devil. The firm brethren in Maine who are waiting for Christ to come have no fellowship with such a move."[1]

But reality and common sense prevailed. James discovered that love was becoming more than a principle! After realizing that his joint ministry with young Ellen, though always chaperoned by her sister Sarah or other faithful friends, was activating gossip, he proposed marriage. Ellen accepted his proposal and they were married by a justice of the peace in Portland, Maine, on August 30, 1846.[2]

Ellen recalled after James's death: "It was not over a year before James White talked it over with me. He said something had come up, and he should have to go away and leave me to go with whomsoever I would, or we must be married. He said something had got to be done. So we were married, and have been married ever since. Although he is dead, I feel that he is the best man that ever trod shoe leather."[3]

James viewed Ellen as his "crown of rejoicing."[4]

L. H. Christian, long-time church leader, recalled a conversation with a woman who, in her early youth, had played together with young Ellen and remembered her sad accident. When Christian asked her what she remembered about Ellen as a young woman, she responded with a smile, "Well, that is an interesting story which I delight to tell. James was older than Ellen by about six years. We were young people there together. Their friendship was a model and an inspiration to us all, and their marriage a most beautiful and happy event."[5]

Thus began a remarkable 35-year marriage founded on their mutual love and conviction that Ellen's visions were of divine origin. Ellen Gould Harmon became Mrs. Ellen G. White, the name by which she is known as the prophetess/messenger of the Seventh-day Adventist Church.

The public saw Ellen as the revivalist and James as the organizer. "As man and wife they were a unique and strong gospel team. Their method and division of the work were perfect. Adventists have never had their equal."[6]

Even before their marriage James recognized Ellen's exceptional preaching skills: "Although but sixteen, she was a laborer in the cause of Christ in public and from house to house. She was a decided Adventist, and yet her experience was so rich and her testimony so powerful that ministers and leading men of different churches sought her labors as an exhorter in their several congregations. But at that time she was very timid, and little thought that she was to be brought before the public to speak to thousands."[7]

Known for his persistence and sound judgment, James was considered a trusted leader by fellow Seventh-day Adventists. He was not only a strategist, he fought like a warrior in the field. He started the church's publishing work with nothing, fostered church organization, and developed an educational system when others saw only a dream. His rugged faith and contagious cheer moved audiences. Funds and support emerged. His remarkable business skills saved the denomination from many embarrassments.[8]

When James White died, the editor of the *Battle Creek Journal* (who had lived very close to most of White's enterprises) wrote: "He was a man of the patriarchal pattern, and his character was cast in the heroic mold. If the logical clearness to formulate a creed; if the power to infect others with one's own zeal, and impress them with one's own convictions; if the executive ability to establish a sect and to give it form and stability; if the genius to shape and direct the destiny of great communities, be a mark of true greatness, Elder White is certainly entitled to the appellation, for he possessed not one of these qualities only, but all of them in a marked degree."[9]

Probably, however, James White would not be admired and remembered today so vividly if he had not been teamed with one who possessed the Spirit of prophecy. L. H. Christian wrote: "Great as was the leadership service of Elder White to the advent cause, his greatest service was his abiding faith in and defense of the Spirit of prophecy. That he—a strong businessman of broad good sense and balanced judgment, absolutely free from fanaticism, always against counterfeit manifestations of religion, and knowing the messenger intimately as his wife—should always stand so staunchly for her calling and work as a messenger from God, gave our members great confidence in her testimonies. . . . He thought of his life mission as an instrument to make known to the church the visions of the Lord given to his companion. These testimonies instructed and reproved him as they did others, but he accepted and followed them implicitly as light from heaven."[10]

Messenger and master builder, prophet and apostle, "James and Ellen White were an invaluable team. Ellen shared with James her wisdom based on her revelations; he acted vigorously to implement what she advised and what to him seemed common sense."[11]

Ellen White's role as a loving, loyal wife is well documented. In 1876, while making their home in Oakland, California, Ellen, then 48 years old, felt the need to focus on finishing the second volume of *The Spirit of Prophecy,* which emphasized the life and work of Christ. James departed alone for Battle Creek to attend a special session of the General Conference.

In a typical note two days after his departure, she wrote (March 24): "We are all well as usual. It takes a little time to get settled down from the excitement of your going. You may be assured we miss you. Especially do we feel the loss of your society when we gather about the fireside evenings. We feel your absence when we sit around the social board [dining table]. But we shall get more used to this after a while. We have been writing today."[12]

A few weeks later she wrote a letter that revealed more of her humor as well as her warm relationship with James. Part of the letter reads: "I had written you quite a lengthy letter last night, but the ink was spilled upon it, making an unsightly blotch, and I will not send it. We received your few words last night on a postal card— 'Battle Creek, April 11. No letters from you for two days. James White.'

"This lengthy letter was written by yourself. Thank you, for we know you are living. No letter from James White previous to this since April 6, 1876. We were very thankful to receive a few lines in reference to yourself from Sister Hall, April 9. I have been anxiously waiting for something to answer."

Then followed an extensive description of the previous day's activities sailing in San Francisco Bay, the high waves reminding her of the disciples on stormy Galilee. A few lines later, "I will write every morning. . . . Will you do the same?"[13]

Several days later, she penned her affection for James and her loneliness when he was away: "We are all quite well and cheerful. We feel every day a most earnest desire for a more sacred nearness to God. This is my prayer, when I lie down, when I awake in the night, and when I arise in the morning, Nearer my God to Thee, nearer to Thee."[14]

As most maturing spouses learn sooner or later, stress times do come. In 1876, James, 55, was carrying extremely heavy responsibilities as president of the General Conference as well as being the firm counselor to the publishing work. Often his greatest concern was that few of his colleagues were as intense and as courageous regarding challenges as he was. Being a man of action, James tended to become dictatorial and demanding. At times he felt unappreciated. In experiencing the effects of several strokes and advancing age, thoughts of discouragement and resentment assailed him. Bleak thoughts seeped into his letters to his wife.

On May 12, 1876, Ellen, at 48, replied to one of his letters: "In regard to my independence, I have had no more than I should have in the matter under the circumstances. I do not receive [accept] your views or interpretation of my feelings on this matter. I understand myself much better than you understand me. But so it must be, and I will say no more in reference to the matter. I am glad you are free and happy, and I rejoice that God has blessed me with freedom, with peace, and cheerfulness and courage. . . . I shall look to God for guidance and shall try to move as He shall lead the way."[15]

Four days later she wrote: "It grieves me that I have said or written anything to grieve you. Forgive me, and I will be cautious not to start any subject to annoy and distress you. We are living in a most solemn time and we cannot afford to have in our old age differences to separate our feelings. I may not view all things as you do, but I do not think it would be my place or duty to try to make you see as I see and feel as I feel. Wherein I have done this, I am sorry.

"I want an humble heart, a meek and quiet spirit. Wherein my feelings have been permitted to arise in any instance, it was wrong. . . .

"I wish that self should be hid in Jesus. I wish self to be crucified. I do not claim infallibility, or even perfection of Christian character. I am not free from mistakes and errors in my life. Had I followed my Saviour more closely, I should not have to mourn so much my unlikeness to His dear image. . . . No more shall a line be traced by me or expression made in my letters to distress you. Again, I say, forgive me, every word or act that has grieved you."[16]

James and Ellen wrote their personal, touching letters without any thought that they would be read by others some day. In these letters we gain uncommon insights into how committed Christians handled marital stress, and through them other husbands and wives have taken heart and learned how to handle their own tensions and conflicts. These letters have become sources of hope and strength to many modern marriages.[17]

Did their faithfulness to each other override lonely moments of misunderstanding? Indeed. The years to come revealed their consistent, tenacious love. One year later, James's health began to fail again. In late October 1877, Ellen wrote to her son William, and Mary his wife, in Battle Creek:

"Dear Children: I am tired tonight. I have been trying to get a piece for the *[Health] Reformer*. It is hard to write much, for Father is so lonesome I have to ride out with him and devote considerable time to keep him company. Father is quite cheerful but talks but little. We have some very precious seasons of prayer. We believe that God will raise him to health. We are of good courage."[18]

Ellen White's Fiftieth Birthday

James could still write, even though he spoke little in public. To honor Ellen's fiftieth birthday, he wrote these words in the *Signs of the Times*:

"Today, November 26, Mrs. White is 50 years old. She became a devoted Christian at the tender age of 12 years, and immediately became a laborer for other youth, and was very successful in winning them to Christ.

"At the early age of 17 years she became a powerful public speaker, and was able to hold large audiences an hour or more. She has traveled and spoken to large audiences, some of them reaching as far as twenty thousands [sic], from the Atlantic to the Pacific, in eighteen States, besides the Canadas. She has now labored publicly thirty-three years.

"Besides this great labor she has written an immense amount. Her books now in print amount to not less than five thousand pages, besides thousands of pages of epistolary matter addressed to churches and individuals.

"And notwithstanding this great work, Mrs. White is, at the age of 50 years, as active as at any former time in her life, and more efficient in her labors. Her health is excellent, and during the last season's camp meetings she was able to perform as much labor in speaking, exhorting, and praying as two of our ablest ministers. . . .

"Mrs. White enters upon the second half-century of her life, with the confident expectation of spending most of it over on the evergreen shore."[19]

These are words of a loving, grateful husband.

Ellen's caring, dedicated service as James's helpmeet, especially in times of sickness and discouragement, is legendary. But, on one occasion in 1878, James, now 58 years old, though attempting to maintain a rigorous writing program, made little physical improvement. Ellen wrote to Mary, William's wife: "I am his constant companion in riding and by the fireside. Should I go, shut myself in a room, and leave him sitting alone, he would become nervous and restless. . . . He depends on me and I shall not leave him in his feebleness."[20]

On the night of April 4, Ellen was given a vision of her husband's true condition, the details of which she wrote out the next day:

"Dear Husband: I dreamed last night that a celebrated physician came into the room while we were engaged in prayer for you. Said he, 'Prayer is well, but living out your prayers is still more essential. Your faith must be sustained by your works, else it is dead faith. . . .

"'You are not brave in God. If there is any inconvenience, instead of accommodating yourself to circumstances, you will keep the matter, be it ever so small, in your mind until it suits you; therefore, you do not work out your faith. You have no real faith yet. You yearn but for victory. When your faith is made perfect by works, you will cease studying yourself and rest your case in the hands of God, bearing something, enduring something, not exactly in accordance with your feelings.

"'All the powers on earth could not help you unless you work in harmony, exercising your reason and your judgment and setting aside your feelings and your inclination. You are in a critical condition.'"

Then the "celebrated physician" became specific: "'Your own depraved habits are keeping not only you but your wife from the work to which God has called you. . . .

"'You have felt so fearful you would be reduced in strength that you have eaten more than was necessary, placed in your stomach a greater amount of food than the system could take care of well. . . . Your food should be taken dry and [you should] take a longer time to masticate it. Eat slowly and much less in quantity. Two or three articles at one meal is all that should be placed in the stomach. . . . You are dying of notions and yet you do not make sufficient efforts to produce a radical change. . . . Your life would be more secure in self-forgetfulness. God has a work for you and your wife to do. Satan says, "you shall not accomplish the work if I have power to control the mind. I can control everything and bind both as with fetters of iron." . . . You can arise. You can throw off this invalidism.'"[21]

The counsel worked. He felt cheered by the promise that "You can arise. You can throw off this invalidism." The stressed-out General Conference president agreed to go to Battle Creek and place himself under the care of Dr. John Harvey Kellogg. On June 24, James wrote to Ellen, "I report myself very much improved." Part of his cheer was the result of finding a man who could take shorthand, thus enabling him to do in "two days . . . what would take a whole week alone."[22]

In early July, James left for their Colorado cabin with Dudley Canright and Mary White (William went later). When Ellen met them in August, she wrote: "I find Father every way improved. It is cool here all the time. . . . Father is himself again in almost all things. He is always cheerful."[23]

Because of appointments in the east, Ellen White did not stay long in Colorado. Reporting back to James and her children regarding happenings in Battle Creek, she wrote with wifely and motherly zest and wisdom: "Do not regard this time of recreation as a drudgery or a task. Lay aside your work; let the writings go. Go over into the park and see all that you can. . . . Throw off every burden, and be a carefree boy again. . . . Father needs to be a boy again. Roam all around. Climb the mountain steeps. Ride horseback. Find something new each day to see and enjoy. This will be for Father's health. Do not spend any anxious thought on me. You will see how well I will appear after the camp meetings are over. . . . Strive to make each other happy."[24]

By 1880 James's tired body pleaded for rest even though his head kept planning new campaigns. Others were now to take over his chief responsibilities—but retreat for the general was not easy. In a letter to Ellen on April 18, he wrote: "I am considering these things with great care. Whatever the Lord has shown you respecting my duty, take time to write it out carefully and give me the complete idea. . . . We both see a great deal to do in the line of writing, and our brethren are constantly urging us into the field to speak. In the fear of God, we must take this matter in our own hands, and be our own judges of what we should do and how much."[25]

On August 6, 1881, "the tired warrior" died. The news stunned Adventists from the Atlantic to the Pacific. No one could review the development of the Adventist Church without thinking of James White. The eulogies, even from those with whom he differed, put the valiant church leader in proper perspective.[26]

Though extremely ill herself, Ellen White rose from her sickbed to laud her "strong, brave, noble-hearted husband." The messenger wife summed up their life journey together: "And now he upon whose large affections I have leaned, with whom I have labored—and we have been united in labor for thirty-six years—is taken away; but I can lay my hands upon his eyes and say, I commit my treasure to Thee until the morning of the resurrection."[27]

A few days after the funeral, Ellen White wrote to close friends: "The light of my home had gone and henceforth I should love it [their home] for his [James's] sake who thought so much of it. It just met his taste. . . . But how can I ever regard it as I could if he had lived?"[28]

Anyone reviewing the record of their marriage must conclude that this was an extraordinary relationship of two exceptional people. Each had a public life, yet their affection flowed through their messages and actions one toward the other. Though living through the "Victorian Period," Ellen's warm and persevering devotion to James was far more than platonic. His appreciation for her was well-known, the depth of which any wife would be glad to experience.

After being released from wifely responsibilities, she traveled even more extensively. Her literary output became even more productive, not only in quantity but also in the depth of her larger books. James had been her helpful editor; he never was the source of her messages.

Messenger Mother

Deborah is perhaps the best known of the Biblical prophetesses. Her reputation was so great, her judgment and counsel so respected, that even her residence was named "the palm tree of Deborah between Ramah and Bethel" (Judges 4:5). But she was more than a wise judge. Her contemporaries trusted her as "a mother in Israel" (Judges 5:7; see p. 18).

Likewise, Ellen White's contemporaries regarded her as a "mother in Israel."[29] They knew her as an incredibly busy wife and mother, a homemaker who proverbially opened her home to the needy, the orphans, and whoever needed a bed for the night. Reviewing how she earned the respect of her contemporaries as she combined motherhood with her public duties helps us to appreciate more fully her counsel for today's mothers and fathers.

But how did her children fare as they shared their busy mother with others who were making ever increasing demands on her time and energies?

As previously mentioned, James and Ellen had four children, all boys: Henry, born August 26, 1847; Edson, born July 28, 1849; William, born August 29, 1854; and John Herbert, September 20, 1860.

Herbert died after living only three months, a victim of erysipelas. The 33-year-old mother recalled this heartbreaking experience: "My dear babe was a great sufferer. Twenty-four days and nights we anxiously watched over him, using all the remedies we could for his recovery, and earnestly presenting his case to the Lord. At times I could not control my feelings as I witnessed his sufferings. Much of my time was spent in tears, and humble supplication to God."[30]

She described the infant's final hours: "My babe was worse. I listened to his labored breathing, and felt his pulseless wrist. I knew that he must die. That was an hour of anguish for me. The icy hand of death was already upon him. We watched his feeble, gasping breath, until it ceased, and we felt thankful that his sufferings were ended. When my child was dying, I could not weep. I fainted at the funeral. My heart ached as though it would break, yet I could not shed a tear. . . . After we returned from the funeral, my home seemed lonely. I felt reconciled to the will of God, yet despondency and gloom settled upon me."[31]

Ellen White's first-born, Henry, died at the age of sixteen. He had become the delight of his parents as well as of a host of friends. His noble voice in song was well-known among fellow workers at the Review publishing house. In late November 1863, He caught a cold which turned into pneumonia. He was treated with poisonous drugs—the wisdom of conventional medicine. Ellen and James had used hydrotherapy earlier that year to help two of their sons battle diphtheria, but they were not yet aware of its value in treating pneumonia.

Predictably, Henry failed rapidly. He and his parents talked openly about death. He confessed freely his sins; his faith grew stronger and his confidence in eternal life ever brighter. One morning he said to his mother: "Promise me, Mother, that if I die I may be taken to Battle Creek, and laid by the side of my little brother, John Herbert, that we may come up together in the morning of the resurrection."[32]

Later, he said to his father, "Father, you are losing your son. You will miss me, but don't mourn. It is better for me. I shall escape being drafted [Civil War], and shall not witness the seven last plagues. To die so happy is a privilege."[33]

During his last hours, he dictated messages of admonition and assurance to his young friends in Battle Creek. Adelia Patten, a close family friend and one of Ellen White's helpers, recorded his last moments: "'Mother, I shall meet you in heaven in the morning of the resurrection, for I know you will be there.' He then beckoned to his brothers, parents, and friends, and gave them all a parting kiss, after which he pointed upward and whispered, 'Heaven is sweet.' These were his last words."[34]

After the death of Henry, a small book was published that included Uriah Smith's funeral sermon, a brief biography, and many of Ellen White's frequent letters sent to him and his brothers, especially when she was away on church responsibilities. These letters make clear why Henry could die with such peace and confidence in Jesus.

Adelia Patten, who had lived in the White home for nearly two years, helped to assemble this small book, *An Appeal to the Youth*. She wrote: "They [Mrs. White's letters to her sons] were written hastily for her children only, without a thought that they would be made public. This makes them still more worthy of publication, as in them is more clearly seen the real feelings and sentiments of a godly mother."[35]

In reading these private, intimate family letters, we are reading the heart of a young mother, and later, a seasoned mother, as seldom revealed to others.

As might be expected, the White children developed as all children do. They had to learn through experience and parental counsel as all children should. Further, James and Ellen White had to learn how to be parents as their children developed.

Counsel Given Through a Vision

In 1862, Ellen, 35, and James, 41, were busily trying to balance their church responsibilities with care for their three children, then 15, 13, and 8. In a vision God stepped in to give the parents some needed advice: "I was shown in regard to our family that we had failed in our duty; we had not restrained them. We had indulged them too much, suffered them to follow their own inclinations and desires, and suffered them to indulge in folly. . . . We are separated from them so much that when we are with them we should perseveringly labor to knit their hearts to us that when we are absent we can have influence over them. I saw that we should instruct them with sobriety and yet with kindness and patience; take an even course. Satan is busy to tempt our children and lead them to be forgetful and to indulge in folly that we may be disheartened and grieved and then take a course to censure and find fault with them in a spirit which will only injure and discourage them instead of helping them.

"I saw that there had been a wrong in laughing at their sayings and doings and then when they err, bearing down upon them with much severity, even before others, which destroys their fine and sensitive feelings and makes it a common thing to be censured for trifles and mistakes, and places accidents and mistakes upon the same level with sins and actual wrong. Their dispositions will become soured and we shall sever the cord which unites them to us and gives us influence with them. . . . We have been in danger of expecting our children to have a more perfect experience than their age warrants us to expect. . . .

"Our children love us and will yield to reason, and kindness will have a more powerful influence than harsh reproof. The spirit and influence which have surrounded our children require us to restrain them and draw them from young company and deny them privileges that children commonly have enjoyed. If we take the course in these things which it is our duty to take, we should ever have our words and acts perfectly reasonable to our children, that their reflection may not be embittered with harsh words or words spoken in a severe manner. It leaves a wound or sting upon their spirits which destroys their love for their parents and the influence of their parents over them."[36]

For Ellen White, her children were high priority.[37] Her diary entries, letters to others and to her sons, all indicate her unending concern for them, especially their spiritual growth.[38] She took their shortcomings as well as her own very seriously. After a difficult encounter with young Edson, she wrote in her diary: "Had an interview with Edson. Felt distressed beyond measure, feeling that it was not conducted wisely."[39]

A few have wondered about certain expressions Ellen White used in some letters to her children in the early 1860s. In her tender love, she appealed to their soul in many ways. In 1860, she was speaking to children between ages 6 and 13. Trying to make the big picture clear in simple language, this 33-year-old mother used language at times that was more like theological shorthand, especially when she wrote that the Lord loves children "who try to do right" but "wicked children God does not love."[40]

Just as we must consider some difficult Biblical texts within the total Biblical context, we must do the same with Ellen White. For example, in Deuteronomy 7:9, 10, we note that God "repays those who hate Him to their face, to destroy them. He will not be slack with him who hates Him; He will repay him to his face. Therefore you shall keep the commandment, the statutes, and the judgments which I command you today, to observe them." By itself this sounds harsh, but when placed in the context of the whole Bible (such as Isa. 1:18-20; Jer. 31:3; John 3:16, 17; John 14-17) its true meaning becomes clear.

Note the larger context of Ellen White's counsel to parents (1892): "Jesus would have the fathers and mothers teach their children . . . that God loves them, that their natures may be changed, and brought into harmony with God. Do not teach your children that God does not love them when they do wrong; teach them that He loves them so that it grieves His tender Spirit to see them in transgression, because He knows they are doing injury to their souls. Do not terrify your children by telling them of the wrath of God, but rather seek to impress them with His unspeakable love and goodness, and thus let the glory of the Lord be revealed before them."[41]

In other circumstances, she clearly made a difference between God's loving a person and endorsing what that person may be doing.[42]

In clear theological terms, she set forth the fact that character determines destiny. Even a loving God will not refashion people's character after their death in order to redeem them.[43]

Yet, how much theology can a six-year-old understand? God had the same challenge when He instructed the recently freed Israelites after their exodus from Egypt. He used kindergarten language and methods—including the sandbox illustration of the desert sanctuary service—for that was the only language level they could understand. Sometimes the threat of disapproval and punishment can get the attention of six-year-olds and recently delivered Israelites when "love talk" would have no impact.

Ellen White used both methods when dealing with her boys, apparently with good effect.[44] The record contains numerous instances in which she talked to her sons about a friendly God, on many occasions praying with them about their spiritual growth. If young Ellen was to be confronted with a possible misunderstanding of her words, she would quickly say what, in substance, she later wrote out more completely: What I meant—and I believe what the boys understood—was that God will not condone disobedience, even though He always loves little boys and girls, good or bad. Disobedience has tough consequences, and God, in love, doesn't want them to experience the costs of disobedience.[45]

A large portion of Ellen White's counsel to the church focuses on the importance of the home and the positive atmosphere in which children should develop. The two books, *Adventist Home* and *Child Guidance* (compilations from hundreds of her diaries, manuscripts, and sermons), have been gratefully studied by thousands of men and women. One would have difficulty finding any other writer who has focused so clearly or graphically on the high calling of the Christian mother and father. Her lucid summons for all parents to realize their enormous responsibility in leading their children heavenward is legendary.

Ellen White gave counsel only after she had first practiced it. For instance: "'Oh,' say some mothers, 'my children bother me when they try to help me.' So did mine, but do you think I let them know it? Praise your children. Teach them, line upon line, precept upon precept. This is better than reading novels, better than making calls, better than following the fashions of the world."[46]

Although Mrs. White is best known as a remarkable public figure, for those who knew her best she was a consistent Christian mother and wife who maintained a close and tender relationship with her husband and children.

Endnotes

1. October 11, 1845, cited in Charles W. Teel, Jr., ed. *Remnant & Republic* (Loma Linda, CA.: Center for Christian Bioethics, 1995), p. 148. See also *The Day Star*, Oct. 11, 1845, p. 47.
2. Ronald Graybill, "The Courtship of Ellen Harmon," *Insight* (Washington, D.C.: Review and Herald Publishing Association), Jan. 23, 1973, pp. 4-7; Virgil Robinson, *James White* (Washington, D.C.: Review and Herald Publishing Association, 1976), pp. 33-39; Schwarz, *Light Bearers*, p. 66; *Bio.*, vol. 1, pp. 110-112.
3. Ellen G. White Estate Document File 733-c, cited in *Bio.*, vol. 1, p. 84.
4. *Life Sketches, Ancestry, Early Life, Christian Experience, and Extensive Labors of Elder James White, and his wife, Mrs. Ellen G. White* (Battle Creek, MI: Seventh-day Adventist Publishing Association, 1888), pp. 131, 132.
5. Lewis Harrison Christian, *The Fruitage of Spiritual Gifts* (Washington, D.C.: Review and Herald Publishing Association, 1947), p. 50.
6. *Ibid.*, p. 98.
7. James White, *Life Sketches*, p. 126.
8. Christian, *The Fruitage of Spiritual Gifts*, p. 99; Robinson, *James White*, pp. 111-115, 151-163, 207-218, 226-231; Spalding, *Origin and History*, vol. 1, pp. 43-55.
9. George Willard, *In Memoriam, A Sketch of the Last Sickness and Death of Elder J. White* (Battle Creek, Mich.: Review and Herald Press, 1881), p. 10, cited in Robinson, *James White*, p. 302.
10. Christian, *The Fruitage of Spiritual Gifts*, p. 111.
11. Emmett K. VandeVere, "Years of Expansion, 1865-1885," Land, *The World of Ellen G. White*, p. 67.
12. Letter 1a, 1876, cited in *Bio.*, vol. 3, p. 23.
13. Letter 5, 1876, cited in *Ibid.*, p. 26.
14. Letter 6, 1876, cited in *Ibid.*, pp. 27, 28.
15. Letter 25, 1876, cited in *Ibid.*, p. 34.
16. *Ibid.*
17. See Appendix B for an exchange of letters in 1874 that reveal marital tensions they both worked through on the basis of their love for each other and their trust in God.
18. Letter 25, 1877, cited in *Bio.*, vol. 3, p. 73.
19. *Signs of the Times*, Dec. 6, 1877, cited in *Ibid.*, p. 76.
20. Letter 4d, 1878 cited in *Ibid*, p. 81.
21. Letter 22, 1878, cited in *Ibid.*, pp. 82, 83.
22. *Ibid.*, p. 90.
23. *Ibid.*, p. 93.
24. Letter 1, 1878, *Ibid.*, pp. 94, 95.
25. *Ibid.*, p. 139.
26. See Uriah Smith's funeral address, cited in *Ibid.*, pp. 174, 175.

27. *Ibid.*
28. Letter 9, 1881, cited in *Ibid.*, p. 177.
29. A letter from Norwegian Adventists to Ellen White on her eighty-fifth birthday began: "Dear Mother in Israel and Servant of the Lord!"—D. A. Delafield, *Ellen G. White in Europe* (Washington, D.C.: Review and Herald Publishing Association, 1975) p. 319.
30. *Spiritual Gifts,* vol. 2, p. 296, cited in *Bio.,* vol. 1, p. 430.
31. *Ibid.*
32. *An Appeal to the Youth*, p. 26, cited in *Ibid.*, vol. 2, p. 71.
33. *Appeal,* p. 29, cited in *Ibid.*, p. 72.
34. *Appeal,* p. 31, cited in *Ibid.*, p. 72.
35. *Appeal,* p. 19, cited in *Ibid.*, p. 62.
36. Manuscript 8, 1862.
37. "Although the cares that came upon us in connection with the publishing work and other branches of the cause involved much perplexity, the greatest sacrifice which I was called to make in connection with the work was to leave my children frequently to the care of others."—*Life Sketches,* p. 165.
38. See Jerry Allen Moon, *W. C. White and Ellen G. White* (Berrien Springs, MI: Andrews University Press, 1993), pp. 34-42.
39. Manuscript 12, 1868.
40. An example of letters from Ellen White to young, six-year-old Willie revealed her motherly attempts to keep him focused on cheerful obedience: "You must be a good, sweet, little boy, and love to obey Jenny [Fraser] and Lucinda [Hall]. Give up your will, and when you wish to do anything very much, inquire, Is it not selfish? You must learn to yield your will and your way. It will be a hard lesson for my little boy to learn, but it will in the end be worth more to him than gold."* "Learn, my dear Willie, to be patient, to wait others' time and convenience; then you will not get impatient and irritable. The Lord loves those little children who try to do right, and He has promised that they shall be in His kingdom. But wicked children God does not love. He will not take them to the beautiful City, for He only admits the good, obedient, and patient children there. One fretful, disobedient child, would spoil all the harmony of heaven. When you feel tempted to speak impatient and fretful, remember the Lord sees you, and will not love you if you do wrong. When you do right and overcome wrong feelings, the Lord smiles upon you.

    "Although He is in heaven, and you cannot see Him, yet He loves you when you do right, and writes it down in His book; and when you do wrong, He puts a black mark against you. Now, dear Willie, try to do right always, and then no black mark will be set down against you; and when Jesus comes He will call for that good boy Willie White, and will put upon your head a wreath of gold, and put in your hand a little harp that you can play upon, and it will send forth beautiful music, and you will never be sick, never be tempted then to do wrong; but will be happy always, and will eat of rich fruit, and will pluck beautiful flowers. Try, try, dear boy, to be good. Your affectionate Mother." [*"By the blessing of God and his mother's instruction, Willie has overcome the impatient spirit which he sometimes manifested when quite young, and he now possesses a most affectionate, amiable, and obedient disposition."—A.P.P.]—Ellen White, *An Appeal*, pp. 62-63. A careful look at the whole letter (and her total writings on child guidance) suggests strongly that when Ellen White wrote that "wicked children God does not love," she meant that ultimately children who continue to be "wicked" will not be taken to heaven.
41. *Signs of the Times,* February 15, 1892; "His [Jesus] heart is drawn out, not only to the best behaved children, but to those who have by inheritance objectionable traits of character. Many parents do not understand how much they are responsible for these traits in their children. . . . But Jesus looks upon these children with pity. He traces from cause to effect."—*The Desire of Ages,* p. 517.
42. See *Testimonies,* vol. 2, pp. 558-565, for a sensitive letter to an indulged teenager.
43. *Christ's Object Lessons,* pp. 74, 84, 123; *Testimonies,* vol. 2, pp. 355, 356.
44. Note her first-born son's attitude toward his parents and his imminent death—page 58.
45. See previous footnotes, citing *Signs*, Feb. 15, 1892, and *The Desire of Ages,* p. 517.
46. *The Adventist Home,* p. 289.

Study Questions

1. What evidence do we have that Ellen White was a devoted wife, ever loyal to her husband, James?
2. What circumstances may have led to James White's struggles with discouragement in later life?
3. What obvious tensions would arise today in a family if the wife was expected to fulfill many public responsibilities, and was more popular than her husband?
4. What role, if any, did James White have in helping to prepare his wife's books for publication?
5. List some experiences that demonstrate the close working relationship between James and Ellen White.
6. What can be learned from Ellen White's rearing her children as a working mother?

CHAPTER 6

Physical Health

"I sought the Lord, and He heard me, and delivered me from all my fears" (Ps. 34:4).

Ellen White was not a superwoman although her schedule and achievements would seem to indicate that she was. Imagine anyone crossing the United States twenty-four times by 1885, only sixteen years after the Union Pacific and Central Pacific railroads joined up near Ogden, Utah, in 1869![1] Then remember that this traveling church leader was speaking to groups large and small wherever she went. And writing! When she died she left behind about 100,000 pages of published and unpublished materials, all once handwritten. She is thought to be "the third most translated author in the history of literature, its most translated woman writer, and the most translated American author of either sex."[2]

But those who knew her saw more than a 5-foot-2-inch public speaker and prodigious writer, tireless in her lifelong dedication to noble causes. As we have already noted, she was an active homemaker, staunchly loyal wife, and warm, affectionate mother.

How could all this be when, at age nine, physicians gave her only months to live after the complications that followed her fateful blow in the face?[3]

Some have suggested that her trauma early in life damaged the temporal lobe of her brain. This blow, they speculate, caused her to have a type of epilepsy known as complex-partial seizures. In turn, they allege that Ellen White's visions were due to temporal lobe epilepsy, not divine revelation.

In response to the charge that she had temporal lobe epilepsy, eight professors in the Loma Linda University School of Medicine and Nursing, including three neurologists, plus a psychiatrist in northern California, studied the evidence available. In 1984 they wrote their report entitled, "Did Ellen White Have Complex-Partial Seizures?"[4]

The report stated: "The diagnosis of a complex-partial seizure disorder (temporal-lobe or psychomotor epilepsy) is often difficult even with the help of modern techniques such as electroencephalography and video recording. Thus, the establishment of such a diagnosis retrospectively in a person who died almost 70 years ago, and concerning whom no medical records exist, can only be, at best, speculative, tenuous, and controversial.

"The recent articles and presentations, which suggest that Ellen White's visions and writings were the result of a complex-partial seizure disorder, contain many inaccuracies. Ambiguous reasoning and misapplication of facts have resulted in misleading conclusions.

"This committee was appointed to evaluate the hypothesis that Ellen G.

White had complex-partial seizures. After a careful review of the autobiographical and biographical material available, considered in the light of the present knowledge of this type of seizure, it is our opinion that: (1) There is no convincing evidence that Ellen G. White suffered from any type of epilepsy. (2) There is no possibility that complex-partial seizures could account for Mrs. White's visions or for her role in the development of the Seventh-day Adventist Church."[5]

Donald I. Peterson, M.D., professor of neurology at Loma Linda University's School of Medicine and chief of neurology at Riverside General Hospital, California (author of more than sixty articles in the field of neurology in scientific magazines), gave a more extended response. In *Visions or Seizures: Was Ellen White the Victim of Epilepsy?*[6] he reviewed certain allegations that Ellen Harmon sustained severe brain damage, that her "visions" were characteristic of complex-partial seizures, that her physical features during "visions" were characteristic of complex-partial seizure disorder ("automatisms"), etc.

No Form of Mental Incompetence

After examining the technical aspects of the allegations in the light of the latest medical knowledge, Dr. Peterson forthrightly denied any correlation between Ellen White's condition during visions or her prolific writing capacity (hypergraphia) with any indication of any kind that would suggest brain damage and a resulting complex-partial seizure disorder. He concluded: "A careful examination of [these] theories in the light of the historical record shows that they have failed to establish that Ellen White's 'sickness' consisted of serious temporal lobe injury or that the phenomena associated with her visions were consistent with partial seizure disorder. . . . It is the conviction of this researcher that it was a manifestation of the true prophetic gift—not some form of epilepsy."[7]

After the accident at nine years of age, she was plagued with headaches, eye inflammation, and respiratory weakness. Tuberculosis drained her, and physicians offered no hope, only an early death. Dropsy, a heart condition, affected her for most of her life. When she received her first vision, in December 1844, she had to be transported in a wheel chair to Elizabeth Haines's home; she could not talk above a whisper.[8]

When she was invited to share her December vision at Poland, Maine, in late January 1845, she had no voice. However, when she began to speak, all the promises that God had given her regarding His abiding strength were fulfilled. She spoke with a clear, audible voice for nearly two hours, without fatigue.[9] This experience of restored strength in the pulpit before the eyes of those who saw the amazing transformation from weakness to power was repeated many times in her long ministry.

In early summer 1845, a physically-weakened young Ellen had a remarkable vision: "Up to this time I could not write. My trembling hand was unable to hold my pen steadily. While in vision I was commanded by an angel to write the vision. I attempted, and wrote readily. My nerves were strengthened, and my hand became steady."[10]

In 1854, while pregnant with her third child, Ellen White at 26 was battling with health problems. She recalled: "It was difficult for me to breathe lying down, and I could not sleep unless raised in nearly a sitting posture. I had upon my left eyelid a swelling which appeared to be a cancer. It had been gradually increasing for more than a year, until it had become quite painful, and affected my sight."[11]

A "celebrated physician in Rochester" provided her with "eyewash" after telling her that he thought the swelling would prove to be cancerous. But after feeling her pulse, he told her that she would die of apoplexy before the cancer developed!

He said, "You are in a dangerous condition with disease of the heart."

Within a few weeks she suffered a stroke, making her left arm and side helpless, her tongue numb. Prayers were offered everywhere, but healing did not come. Yet she maintained her assurance in God's love. She whispered to James: "'I believe that I shall recover.' He answered, 'I wish I could believe it.' I retired that night without relief, yet relying with firm confidence upon the promises of God. I could not sleep, but continued my silent prayer to God. Just before day I slept."

When she awakened, her husband could "scarcely comprehend it at first; but when I arose and dressed and walked around the house, and he witnessed the change in my countenance, he could praise God with me. My afflicted eye was free from pain. In a few days the cancer was gone, and my eyesight was fully restored. The work was complete."

Her physician declared later that a "complete" change had taken place—a mystery beyond his ability to understand.[12]

Rheumatism in Both Ankles

Two years later, Ellen White slipped on ice, badly wrenching her ankle, and had to struggle with crutches for six weeks. Rheumatism eventually affected both ankles and bothered her severely till her death.

When three months pregnant in March 1860, she, with James, was heading west to Iowa. James's report in the *Review* (March 6) was graphic: "We left Battle Creek at 3:00 P.M., changed cars at midnight at Chicago, reached the Mississippi River at 7:00 A.M., crossed the ice on foot, walking behind the baggage drawn on a sleigh by four men, the ice being too weak to bear up horses; and felt relief when we stepped upon Iowa soil."

The first night in Iowa, Ellen White became very ill, vomiting and raising blood. But on she went, through the mud of springtime in Iowa, speaking often in the meetings.

After the birth of John Herbert, she slowly regained strength. Six weeks after delivery, she commented in a letter to Lucinda Hall that she was so weak that she crawled up stairs on her knees, that she had "a good cry now and then," and found that "it does me good." Barely three months after his birth, the baby died.

Ellen White's Australian years were most productive, not only in helping to establish a sound educational and evangelistic program in that young country, but in authoring *The Desire of Ages* plus thousands of pages of timely letters. But not without cost! Her illnesses in Australia were devastating: "I made the long journey and attended the conference held in Melbourne. . . . Just before the conference closed I was stricken with a severe illness. For eleven months I suffered from malarial fever and inflammatory rheumatism. During the period I experienced the most terrible suffering of my whole life. I was unable to lift my feet from the floor without suffering great pain. My right arm, from the elbow down, was the only part of my body that was free from pain. My hips and my spine were in constant pain. I could not lie on my cot for more than two hours at a time, though I had rubber cushions under me. I would drag myself to a similar bed to change my position. Thus the nights passed. . . . Physicians said I would never be able to walk again, and I had fears that my life was to be a perpetual conflict with suffering."[13]

How did she manage? Those who stood by could gratefully validate her further reflections: "But in all this there was a cheerful side. My Saviour seemed to be close beside me. I felt His sacred presence in my heart, and I was thankful. These months of suffering were the happiest months of my life, because of the companionship of my Saviour. He was my hope and crown of rejoicing. I am so thankful that I had this experience, because I am better acquainted with my precious Lord and Saviour. . . .

"I felt at first that I could not bear this inactivity. I think I fretted in spirit over it, and at times darkness gathered about me. This unreconciliation was at the beginning of my suffering and helplessness, but it was not long before I saw that the affliction was a part of God's plan. I carefully reviewed the history of the past few years, and the work the Lord had given me to do. Not once had He failed me. Often He had manifested Himself in a marked manner, and I saw nothing in the past of which to complain. I realized that, like threads of gold, precious things had run through all this severe experience.

"Then I prayed earnestly and realized continually sweet comfort in the promises of God: 'Draw nigh to God, and he will draw nigh to you.' 'When the enemy shall come in like a flood, the Spirit of the Lord shall lift up a standard against him.'"[14]

For reasons that God alone can explain, Ellen White suffered much in her life. Yet, she was a remarkably productive, active woman, and out of her suffering came a philosophy of suffering that has been a solid rock for millions. Her book, *The Ministry of Healing,* plus many hundreds of letters to others who also were under great affliction, might never have been written without her own experience providing the human setting for basic divine principles.

One thing is certain: Ellen White never used her physical afflictions as a means of gaining the pity of others. To the contrary, when others saw her cheery spirit and determined resolve under intense physical adversities, they took courage.[15]

Her life of literary production and personal ministry, plus her extensive public travels, strongly argues for an awareness of how the human will can triumph over physical hardships in the pursuit of God's plan for one's life. In 1915, reaching the age of 87 was not common! Her last known writing, a letter (June 14, 1914), overflowed with hope and Christian joy.[16] The cause of her death, on July 16, 1915, as recorded on both her death certificate and the cemetery sexton's records, was: "Chronic myocarditis; (Contributory) Asthenia resulting from intracapsular fracture of the left femur (Feb. 13, 1915); (Secondary contributory) arterio-sclerosis."

Endnotes

1. Manuscript 16, 1885, cited in D. A. Delafield, *Ellen G. White In Europe,* p. 25. See pp. 104, 105.
2. Roger Coon, *A Gift of Light* (Washington, D.C.: Review and Herald Publishing Association, 1983), p. 21.
3. In dealing with her broken nose and loss of blood, Ellen White reported: "Physicians thought that a silver wire could be put in my nose to hold it in shape [without anesthesia, of course], but said that it would be of little use; that I had lost so much blood my recovery was doubtful; that if I should get better, I could not live long. I was reduced to almost a skeleton."—*Spiritual Gifts,* vol. 2, p. 9. In late 1840, she was no better: "My health failed rapidly. I could only talk in a whisper, or broken tone of voice. One physician said my disease was dropsical consumption; that my right lung was gone, and my left affected. He thought I could not live long, might die very suddenly. It was very difficult for me to breathe lying down, and nights was bolstered almost in a sitting posture, and would often awake with my mouth full of blood."—*Ibid.,* p. 30.
4. *Ministry,* August, 1984, and referred to in *Adventist Review,* August 16, 1984.
5. *Ibid.*
6. Boise, Idaho: Pacific Press Publishing Association, 1988.
7. *Ibid.,* pp. 26, 27.
8. *Spiritual Gifts,* vol. 2 , p. 30; Document File, No. 230 (Ellen G. White Estate), J. N. Loughborough, "Some Individual Experiences," p. 44.
9. *Ibid.,* p. 38.
10. *Ibid.,* p. 60. Years later, she reflected: "The Lord has said, 'Write out the things which I shall give you.' And I commenced when very young to do this work. My hand that was feeble and trembling because of infirmities became steady as soon as I took the pen in my hand, and since those first writings I have been able to write. . . . That right hand scarcely ever has a disagreeable sensation. It never wearies."—Ellen White, Ms. 88a, 1900, cited in *Bio.,* vol. 1, pp. 91, 92.
11. *Life Sketches,* p. 151.
12. *Bio.,* vol. 1, pp. 292, 293.
13. *Bio.,* vol. 4, pp. 31, 32.
14. Manuscript 75, 1893, cited in *Bio.,* vol. 4, p. 33.
15. Numerous occasions could be cited pointing out the varied physical stress Ellen White endured without complaining. For example, while in New Zealand in

1893, she had trouble with abscessed teeth. She knew from experience that she was allergic to pain medication. We pick up the story in her diary for July 5: "Sister Caro [a dentist] came in the night; is in the house. I met her in the morning at the breakfast table. She said, 'Are you sorry to see me?' I answered, 'I am pleased to meet Sister Caro, certainly. Not so certain whether I am pleased to meet Mrs. Dr. Caro, dentist.'

"At ten o'clock I was in the chair, and in a short time eight teeth were drawn. I was glad the job was over. I did not wince or groan. . . . I had asked the Lord to strengthen me and give me grace to endure the painful process, and I know the Lord heard my prayer.

"After the teeth were extracted, Sister Caro shook like an aspen leaf. Her hands were shaking, and she was suffering pain. . . . She dreaded to give pain to Sister White. . . . But she knew she must perform the operation, and went through with it."

The diary concludes with the patient turning attendant as Ellen White led Dr. Caro to a chair and found something to refresh her.—Manuscript 81, 1893, cited in *Bio.,* vol. 4, p. 98.

16. *Testimonies to Ministers,* pp. 516-520.

Study Questions

1. What long-term damage did Ellen White experience from her facial injury at the age of nine?

2. How do you answer the question: If Ellen White was called of God to be His special messenger, why would He allow her to pass through numerous physical and emotional hardships?

3. From the 1984 medical report on Ellen White, what are the strongest evidences to you that dispute the charge she suffered from complex-partial seizures?

4. Describe Ellen Harmon's physical condition at the end of 1844.

CHAPTER 7

Personal Characteristics

"Trust in the Lord, and do good; dwell in the land, and feed on His faithfulness. Delight yourself also in the Lord, and He shall give you the desires of your heart" (Ps. 37:3, 4).

Ellen White's primary emphasis in life, born out of her own experience and amplified in her visions, was to obtain and portray an accurate picture of God's character. She saw correctly that the great religious divisions throughout time and especially those within Christendom developed out of an inadequate understanding of God.

Spiritual Awareness

In her early life, she was a victim of prevailing errors that permeated various churches within Protestantism. For example, misunderstanding the character of God—and thus the plan of salvation—was at the bottom of her teen-age confusion "concerning justification and sanctification."[1]

Further, because she had been taught that God's sovereignty and justice were Christianity's central themes, she had little peace and almost a total unawareness of a friendly God.[2]

The doctrine of eternal punishment, a central aspect of Calvinistic thinking that focused on God's sovereignty at the expense of human responsibility, unloaded a profound anguish on young Ellen, as it does on anyone who wonders about a God who would punish sinners forever.[3]

A clearly focused theology. When divine light helped her to read the Bible without being driven by the prevailing misconceptions that dominated contemporary churches, the truth about God became increasingly clear. Her writings soon focused on the main question in the great controversy between God and Satan—what is God really like?[4] Who can be trusted—God or Satan?

A clear picture of God's character. Along with a focused theology that captured the main theme of the Bible came a fresh, captivating picture of God that charmed her into a deep, dynamic relationship with her loving and gracious friendly Lord.[5]

During the third European Missionary Council in Basel, Switzerland, September 22, 1885, she gave one of her typical talks to workers: "I feel so thankful this morning that we can commit the keeping of our souls to God as unto a faithful Creator. Sometimes the enemy presses me the hardest with his temptations and darkness when I am about to speak to the people. I have such a sense of weakness that it seems like an impossibility to stand before the congregation. But if I should give up to feelings, and say that I could not speak, the enemy would gain the victory. I dare not do this. I move right forward, take my place in the desk, and say, 'Jesus, I hang my helpless soul on Thee; Thou wilt not suffer me to be brought to confusion,' and the Lord gives me the victory. . . . Oh, that I could impress upon all the importance of exercising faith moment by moment, and hour by hour! . . . If we believe in God, we are armed with the righteousness of Christ; we have taken hold of His strength. . . . We want to talk with our Saviour as though He were right by our side."[6]

Grand subjects such as righteousness by faith, the importance of calm, unimpassioned reason in the Christian's response to the gospel, and the responsibility of a "prepared people" in completing the gospel commission in the last days were clearly defined in print and realized in her own daily need for pardon and power.[7]

Trust when the future was unclear. Ellen White was an example of one who trusted God even when outward circumstances seemed forbidding. Typical of hundreds of letters and of her many books is a passage in a letter to James, her husband, from Washington, Iowa, July 2, 1874: "We are justified to walk by sight as long as we can, but when we can no longer see the way clearly, then we need to put our hand in our heavenly Father's and let Him lead. There are emergencies in the life of all in which we can neither follow sight nor trust in memory or experience. All we can do is simply to trust and wait. We shall honor God to trust Him because He is our heavenly Father."[8]

Love her motivating principle. Ellen White's clear understanding of love set her apart from most other religious writers, before her time or since. Love (agape) as a principle, not a feeling burdened by hope of reward or favor, permeated her writings. For example: "Love is an active principle; it keeps the good of others continually before us, thus restraining us from inconsiderate actions lest we fail of our object in winning souls to Christ. Love seeks not her own. It will not prompt men to seek their own ease and indulgence of self. It is the respect we render to *I* that so often hinders the growth of love."[9]

Practical religion, (applied theology). Practical religion was another all-pervasive theme in Ellen White's sermons and writings. For her, religion was more than a fountain of feeling. If religion does not motivate a person to reach out to help others without hope of gain, it is worthless. If religion does not change a person so that he or she bears the "fruit of the Spirit" (Gal. 5:22, RSV) and reflects the character of Jesus, one's professed Christianity is meaningless.

For Ellen White, practical Christianity was not optional; it had everything to do with one's preparation for eternal life. Writing to a woman who had serious shortcomings, she declared: "Unless this is overcome now, it never will be, and Sister King will have no part with God's people, no home in His heavenly kingdom. God cannot take you to heaven as you are. You would mar that peaceful, happy place.

"What can be done for you? Do you design to wait until Jesus comes in the clouds of heaven? Will He make you all over new when He comes? Oh, no. This will not be done then. The fitting up must be done here; all the hewing and squaring must take place here upon earth, in the hours of probation. You must be fitted up here; the last blow must be given here."[10]

Relation between religion and health. Ellen White understood well the relationship between religion and the health of mind and body, that the well-being of one directly affects the health of the other. Her particular insights on this topic were much ahead of conventional thinking. For example: "Pure and undefiled religion is not a sentiment, but the doing of works of mercy and love. This religion is necessary to health and happiness. It enters the polluted soul temple and with a scourge drives out the sinful intruders. . . . With it comes serenity and composure. Physical, mental, and moral strength increase because the atmosphere of heaven as a living, active agency fills the soul."[11]

The chapter, "Mind-Cure," in *The*

Ministry of Healing is recognized by many as breaking new ground. It opens with this paragraph: "The relation that exists between the mind and the body is very intimate. When one is affected, the other sympathizes. The condition of the mind affects the health to a far greater degree than many realize. Many of the diseases from which men [people] suffer are the result of mental depression. Grief, anxiety, discontent, remorse, guilt, distrust, all tend to break down the life forces, and to invite decay and death."[12]

Her understanding of the cause of suffering and death. Ellen White's counsels regarding the cause of suffering and death were not only profound, they have stood the test of a century as a faithful reflection of the mind of God. She maintained that "sickness, suffering, and death are [the] work of an antagonistic power. Satan is the destroyer; God is the restorer."[13]

What then is the cause of sickness? One answer was: God's laws have been violated, either by one's ancestors or by oneself. She was unequivocal: "When Christ healed disease, He warned many of the afflicted ones, 'Sin no more, lest a worse thing come unto thee' (John 5:14). Thus He taught that they had brought disease upon themselves by transgressing the laws of God, and that health could be preserved only by obedience."[14]

Suffering, other than sickness due to neglect of physical laws, is also caused by Satan and not the deliberate intervention of God. On many occasions she reinforced the teaching of Jesus on this point. In 1883 she wrote concerning a small group of new believers in Ukiah, California: "Our hearts are made glad as we see this little center of converts to the truth advancing step by step, growing stronger amid opposition. They are becoming better acquainted with the suffering part of religion. Our Saviour instructed His disciples that they should be despised for His name's sake. 'Blessed are ye when men shall revile you, and persecute you, and shall say all manner of evil against you falsely, for my sake.'"[15]

Her teachings regarding the cause of death, as well as suffering, flowed from the big picture of the great controversy between God and Satan: "It is true that all suffering results from the transgression of God's law, but this truth had become perverted. Satan, the author of sin and all its results, had led men to look upon disease and death as proceeding from God—as punishment arbitrarily inflicted on account of sin."[16]

Quick to see her own mistakes. Ellen White was quick to confess her mistakes and seek forgiveness. She knew well the peace of forgiveness and was quick to release others from the weight of remorse and guilt. Out of her own experience and reflecting divine instruction, she offered this counsel: "It is not praiseworthy to talk of our weakness and discouragement. Let each one say, 'I am grieved that I yield to temptation, that my prayers are so feeble, my faith so weak. I have no excuse to plead for being dwarfed in my religious life. But I am seeking to obtain completeness of character in Christ. I have sinned, and yet I love Jesus. I have fallen many times, and yet He has reached out His hand to save me. I have told Him all about my mistakes. I have confessed with shame and sorrow that I have dishonored Him. I have looked to the cross and have said, All this He suffered for me. The Holy Spirit has shown me my ingratitude, my sin in putting Christ to open shame. He who knows no sin has forgiven my sin. He calls me to a higher, nobler life, and I press on to the things that are before.'"[17]

Tireless soul winner. Her contemporaries knew Ellen White to be a tireless soul winner. They observed her daily life; they received her earnest letters. Her neighbors and companions in travel were blessed by her helpful initiatives. In fact, her constant, cheerful concern for the spiritual welfare of others became a defining characteristic of her life. She never saw herself as the "ivory-tower author" far removed from the world of spiritual warfare that she wrote about.

Throughout her life, young and old found Jesus through her personal ministry. One of her contemporaries wrote late in life: "My recollection of Sister White is that never in my life have I known a woman who seemed so completely devoted to the Lord Jesus. He seemed to be to her a personal friend whom she knew and loved and trusted. She found great joy in talking about Jesus; and all of the younger people agreed that there, at least, was a young lady who lived very near to the Lord and who in her sincere, practical way tried with all her heart to follow Jesus."[18]

A trip to Vergennes, Michigan, in June 1853, is remembered for more than becoming "lost" on a road very familiar to the driver of their wagon. Toward evening after a long day of wandering, without food and water, James and Ellen White were delighted to find a lonely log cabin and the housewife at home. While being refreshed, Mrs. White talked to her hospitable hostess about Jesus and gave her a copy of her first book, *Experience and Views.* For years the events of that day seemed not only exhausting but meaningless. But in 1876, at a camp meeting in Lansing, Michigan, the housewife in that log cabin more than twenty years before, grasped Ellen White's hand and recalled their first meeting. Further, she introduced Mrs. White to a group of Seventh-day Adventists, all of whom began their new fellowship with the Lord after reading *Experience and Views.* The housewife had told her scattered neighbors of this traveling lady who "talked to her of Jesus and the beauties of heaven, and that the words were spoken with such fervor that she was charmed, and had never forgotten them."[19]

Camp Meeting Appeals

Ellen White's camp meeting appeals, from coast to coast, became legendary. For example, in 1884, at the age of 56, she spoke at four camp meetings. Of the Jackson, Michigan, meeting, Uriah Smith, editor of the church paper, reported in the *Review* that on several occasions between 200 and 350 people responded to her appeals by going forward for prayers. "There was deep feeling and though no excitement or fanaticism, the manifest movings of the Spirit of God upon the heart," Smith wrote.[20]

During her visit to England in 1885, Ellen White was invited to speak to an audience of 1,200 in the town hall at Grimsby. Her topic was "The Love of God." Later she wrote: "I tried to present the precious things of God in such a way as to draw their minds from earth to heaven. But I could only warn and entreat, and hold up Jesus as the center of attraction, and a heaven of bliss as the eternal reward of the overcomer."[21]

In 1885, Cecile Dahl, a Norwegian, translated for Mrs. White as they made a six-week tour of Germany and the Scandinavian countries. Miss Dahl was one of many that the speaker had led to the Lord.

Ellen White was ever ready to share the truth about God and salvation, even when it required an aggressive response. On an ocean voyage up the coast from San Francisco to Portland, in June, 1878, she overheard a fellow-passenger, a minister, stating that "it was impossible for any man to keep the law of God; that man never did keep it, and never can keep it. . . . No man will get to heaven by keeping the law. Mrs. White is all law, law; she believes that we must be saved by the law, and no one can be saved unless they keep the law."

Feeling the injustice of the charge, Ellen White felt that the group listening to this minister should hear the necessary corrections. Finding an appropriate moment, she spoke to the minister: "That is a false statement. Mrs. White has never occupied that position."

She then developed the Bible story of

the law as mirroring sin and Jesus as our pardoning Advocate. "Elder Brown, please never again make the misstatement that we do not rely on Jesus Christ for salvation, but trust in the law to be saved. We have never written one word to that effect, nor taught such a theory in any manner. We believe that no sinner can be saved in his sins (and sin is the transgression of the law), while you teach that the sinner may be saved while knowingly transgressing the law of God."

Recalling this incident for a *Signs* article, Ellen White referred to Christ's words in His Sermon on the Mount: "Christ here shows the object of His mission: To show man by His example, that he could be entirely obedient to the moral law, and regulate his life by its precepts. That law was exalted and made honorable by Jesus Christ."[22]

Two days after her sixty-eighth birthday, in 1895, Ellen White was speaking to a camp meeting audience in Hobart, Tasmania, finishing one of her sermons with an altar call. A large share of the audience came forward. But she wasn't satisfied. She was hunting souls. She left the platform, and went to the back seats where five young people sat. In her quiet way, she invited them to give their hearts to the Lord. All five did, and several other young people joined them, as they went forward in their decision to make Jesus their Master.[23]

Clear priorities. People can be judged by their "wants." Ellen White reiterated often her "want list": "I want to be like Him. I want to practice His virtues."[24] "I want to be among that number who shall have their names written in the book, who shall be delivered. I want the overcomer's reward."[25] "I want my treasure in heaven."[26] "I want to be like Him; I want to be with Him through the ceaseless ages of eternity."[27] "I want to know more and more of God's word and of His works."[28] "I want to have a home with the blessed, and I want you to have a home there."[29]

Abiding trust. In her late eighties (not a common achievement in the early 1900s), Ellen White was still taking an active part in book development. She moved freely in her Elmshaven home, able to go unassisted up and down the stairs. Often she could be heard singing an old Advent hymn, "The Better Land," penned by William H. Hyde, words that were composed after Hyde had heard her describe a vision given in the spring of 1845. She often lingered on the last part:

"We'll be there, we'll be there in a little while,

We'll join the pure and the blest;

We'll have the palm, the robe, the crown,

And forever be at rest."[30]

On February 13, Ellen White tripped in her hallway. X-rays revealed an "intracapsular fracture of the left femur at the junction of the head and the neck," a most painful injury, especially without modern alleviating medication. When asked about pain, she said: "It is not so painful as it might be, but I cannot say that it is comfortable." Weeks later, when she was asked again about her comfort, she replied: "A good day—in spots." Her long habit of walking with the Lord was making all the difference.[31]

Last Vision

Ellen White had her last vision on March 3, 1915. Summarizing the vision, she said to her son W. C. White: "There are books that are of vital importance that are not looked at by our young people. They are neglected because they are not so interesting to them as some lighter reading. . . . We should select for them books that will encourage them to sincerity of life, and lead them to the opening of the Word. . . . I do not expect to live long. My work is nearly done. Tell our young people that I want my words to encourage them in that manner of life that will be most attractive to the heavenly intelligences, and that their influence upon others may be most ennobling.

"I have no assurance that my life will

last long, but I feel that I am accepted of the Lord. . . . I have felt that it was imperative that the truth should be seen in my life, and that my testimony should go to the people. I want that you should do all you can to have my writings placed in the hands of the people in foreign lands. . . . I am impressed that it is my special duty to say these things."[32]

A few days before her death, a friend noted her cheeriness. Her reply: "I am glad that you find me thus. I have not had many mournful days. . . . The Lord has arranged and led in all these things for me, and I am trusting in Him. He knows when it will all end."

The visitor said, "Yes, it will soon end and we shall meet you in the kingdom of God, and we will 'talk it all over there together,' as you wrote in one of your last letters."

To which she replied, "Oh, yes, it seems almost too good to be true, but it is true!"

Her last words to her son and Sara, her nurse were: "I know in whom I have believed."[33]

Mental Capabilities

Although not a formally educated woman, Ellen White utilized every opportunity to increase her bank of information and insights. We noted earlier the trauma of the scarred face (pp. 48, 62, 63) which, she said later, "was to affect my whole life."[34] She was never able again to attend school, yet her innate quest for knowledge led her to amass a personal and office library that, by the time of her death, totaled more than 800 volumes.[35] When she lived in Battle Creek, she freely used the Review and Herald Publishing Company's library.

As a mother and wife, she and her husband read substantive books to each other and to their children, books such as D'Aubigne's *History of the Reformation of the Sixteenth Century.*[36]

She was an avid reader of religious journals. After Uriah Smith, long-time editor of the *Review and Herald,* had completed reading the periodicals that came to his office, he would pass them on to her to keep her current regarding religious and political developments.[37]

The sheer magnitude of her literary production, coupled with her hundreds of sermons that were transcribed, indicate remarkable mental powers. Though she was often under extreme time constraints, as well as unfavorable circumstances, she was still able to present in person or in manuscript form cogent and appealing messages.

Emotional Experiences

Ellen White was an exceptionally sensitive woman, open to all the human emotions. Her ability to verbalize her various experiences indicates an uncommon capacity for empathy, whether the experience was sad or elevating.

Always a lover of the beautiful, her emotional response to the spectacular Alps, Colorado Rockies, a Norway sunset, or the Milan Cathedral reveals a depth of appreciation for beauty that pervades her writings.

For example, in the summer of 1873, the Whites were seeking much overdue relaxation in Colorado. She reflected: "I love the hills and mountains and forests of flourishing evergreens. I love the brooks, the swift-running streams of softest water which come bubbling over the rocks, through ravines, by the side of the mountains, as if singing the joyful praise of God. . . .

"We have here in the mountains a view of the most rich and glorious sunset it was ever our privilege to look upon. The beautiful picture of the sunset, painted upon the shifting, changing canvas of the heavens by the great Master Artist, awakens in our hearts love and deepest reverence for God."[38]

After an early winter sunset in Norway, she wrote: "We were favored with a sight of the most glorious sunset it was ever my privilege to behold.

Language is inadequate to picture its beauty. The last beams of the setting sun, silver and gold, purple, amber, and crimson, shed their glories athwart the sky, growing brighter and brighter, rising higher and higher in the heavens, until it seemed that the gates of the city of God had been left ajar, and gleams of the inner glory were flashing through." This glorious experience required two pages to record.[39]

Knew Discouragement

Ellen White knew the bleakness of discouragement as she fulfilled her role as God's messenger. Throughout her life, discouragement, at times, flirted with temporary depression. No doubt her physical weaknesses, her heart condition and respiratory problems, made her susceptible to discouragement. And being a messenger for the Lord, striking out ahead of her contemporaries on the battlefield of the cosmic conflict, also invited Satan's constant attacks. How did she relate to this black shadow that so many people from the beginning of time have experienced? Her counsels to others who are discouraged, even in depression, come bathed in her own personal trials.

Throughout her ministry Ellen White faced both the fire of fanaticism and the ice of indifference.[40] Her words of counsel, often reproof, frequently were countered with gossip and slander. This affected her physically. Of her experience when she was only 18 and still greatly diminished physically, she reported: "Discouragements pressed heavily upon me and the condition of God's people so filled me with anguish that for two weeks I was prostrated with sickness."[41]

Those reading her letters and diary entries have the privilege of almost "listening" to her heart beat as she recorded her responses to those moments of discouragement from various causes. How she beat back the "hellish shadow" of the evil one may be just the insight some reader needs today!

Although eight months pregnant in 1847, she wrote a cheery letter to Joseph Bates, noting that "my health is quite good for me." Then she bared her heart: "I have had many trials of late, discouragement at times has laid so fast hold upon me it seemed impossible to shake it off. But thank God, Satan has not got the victory over me yet, and by the grace of God he never shall. I know and feel my weakness, but I have laid hold upon the strong arm of Jehovah, and I can say today I know that my Redeemer liveth, and if He lives I shall live also."[42]

Trials? Not many people have known the kind of hard times faced by the Whites. These servant-leaders had been given a divine commission, and they dared not turn to a life of ordinary pursuits.

But think, here was a young family in the winter of 1847-1848 (Henry was born on August 26, 1847) trying to speak and write as God opened the way, yet determined to be financially independent. James, at 26, hauled stone at a railroad cut near Brunswick, Maine, until his hands were bloody, and he cut cord wood, working long hours for 50 cents a day. On a limited "budget," Ellen, now 20, could afford only a pint of milk per day for herself and Henry. Then she had to eliminate the milk supply for three days so that she could buy a piece of cloth to make Henry a simple garment.

The day came when "their provisions were gone." James walked three miles and back in the rain to his employer for either his wages or needed supplies. When he returned with a bag of provisions, Ellen recalled: "As he entered the house very weary my heart sank within me. My first feelings were that God had forsaken us. I said to my husband, 'Have we come to this? Has the Lord left us?' I could not restrain my tears, and wept aloud for hours until I fainted."

In other words, "Lord, why is life so hard when we have committed ourselves unreservedly to Your cause?"

Through her account of this experience we get a glimpse of how she climbed out of this deep pit of discouragement. She regretted that she had sunk so low; she reminded herself that her first desire was to "follow Christ and be like Him; but we sometimes faint beneath trials and remain at a distance from Him. Suffering and trials bring us nigh to Jesus. The furnace consumes the dross and brightens the gold."[43]

In Rochester, New York, late June, 1854, Mrs. White was seven months pregnant with her third son. But other problems faced her daily. Key workers in Rochester were dying of consumption (tuberculosis). Husband James appeared to be sinking also, not only with the signs of consumption but with the lack of sympathy from fellow workers, plus the strain of his usual traveling, speaking, and writing. Try to imagine the full range of concerns facing the young wife and mother!

"Trials thickened around us. We had much care. The office hands boarded with us, and our family numbered from fifteen to twenty. The large conferences and Sabbath meetings were held at our house. We had no quiet Sabbaths; for some of the sisters usually tarried all day with their children. Our brethren and sisters generally did not consider the inconvenience and additional care and expense brought upon us. As one after another of the office hands would come home sick, needing extra attention, I was fearful that we should sink beneath the anxiety and care. I often thought that we could endure no more; yet trials increased."

What does a young mother of two, seven months pregnant, do under such conditions? "With surprise I found that we were not overwhelmed. We learned the lesson that much more suffering and trial could be borne than we had once thought possible. The watchful eye of the Lord was upon us, to see we were not destroyed. . . . If the cause of God had been ours alone, we might have trembled; but it was in the hands of Him who could say, No one is able to pluck it out of My hands. Jesus lives and reigns."[44]

In the weeks preceding the Minneapolis General Conference of 1888, Ellen White was burdened with the "unbelief and resistance to reproof" that prevailed against her ministry, much of it developing while she was in Europe, 1885-1887: "The brethren did not seem to see beyond the instrument. . . . I had also been told [in vision] that the testimony God had given me would not be received, because the hearts of those who had been reproved were not in such a state of humility that they could be corrected and receive reproof."

Discouragement seemed to overwhelm her, and she became very ill. Recalling the event, she wrote: "I felt no desire to recover. I had no power even to pray, and no desire to live. Rest, only rest, was my desire, quiet and rest. As I lay for two weeks in nervous prostration, I had hope that no one would beseech the throne of grace in my behalf. When the crisis came, it was the impression that I would die. This was my thought. But it was not the will of my heavenly Father. My work was not yet done."

Responding to Discouragement

How did Ellen White respond to weighty discouragement? As she had done many times in the past: "To walk out by faith against all appearances was the very thing that the Lord required me to do."[45]

"To walk out by faith against all appearances." Such was the counsel she gave herself throughout her life and often expressed in her counsel to others. In a morning talk at the Minneapolis Conference, October 19, 1888, she spoke out of tested experience: "You say, 'How can I talk faith, how can I have faith, when clouds and darkness and despondency come over my mind? I do not feel as though I could talk faith; I do not feel that I have any faith to talk.' But why do you feel in this way? It is because you have permitted Satan to cast his dark shadow across your pathway, and you cannot see the light that Jesus sheds upon your pathway. But another says: 'I am very frank; I say just what I feel, I talk just as I think.' Is that the best way to do?—No; God wants us to educate ourselves so that we shall speak right words—words that will be a blessing to others, that will shed rays of light upon their souls."[46]

One may wonder whether, after long years of service and trusting God, Christians grow beyond dark moments when they see clouds rather than the sun. Think about Jesus in Gethsemane. Or the lives of saintly people. What they learned through the years is how to battle the devil's hellish shadows. In Ellen White's eighty-seventh year, C. C. Crisler, one of her secretaries, wrote to William, her son: "She says she does not wish to make any great noise about having courage continually, although she has; and she adds that the very fact that members of the household are waked up at times hearing her repeating the promises of God and claiming them as her own is proof that she still has battles of her own to fight against Satan."[47]

A Lonely Path

Loneliness, however, not discouragement, was a frequent companion, a lonesomeness not often or necessarily clothed in discouragement. The nature of her divine assignment seemed to necessitate that Ellen White would walk her path alone. The marvel is that she was not known as a dreary recluse. Her family knew her to be the sunshine of the home; her neighbors and co-workers remember her as their source of encouragement.

Prophets, by the nature of their task, deliver more reproofs than praise. This was true with Mrs. White. And not all recipients relate well to messages of correction or rebuke. Misunderstanding and resentment are to be expected.

In addition, being out front in almost every church enterprise from the beginning required an enormous emotional strength such as few people possess. Leading a group of strong-willed men and women into new paths of church organization, developing substantial medical and educational institutions, and helping to navigate a whole denomination through difficult theological controversies—all this invited misunderstanding and estrangement.

Thus, we can understand Ellen White when she wrote in 1902: "I have been alone in this matter, severely alone with all the difficulties and all the trials connected with the work. God alone could help me."[48]

In Europe at 59, her husband dead for five years, she was actively trying to put the European program on a solid and united footing. Here was a challenge that would, and did, daunt the strongest of leaders. In a letter to the General Conference president, she penned: "I tell you, these hard spots in my experience make me desire the climate of California, and the refuge of *home.* Have I any home? Where is it?"[49]

In the aftermath of the 1888 Minneapolis General Conference, probably Ellen White went through her deepest loneliness. Writing earnestly to Uriah Smith, she declared: "My brethren have trifled and caviled and criticized and commented and demerited, and picked and chosen a little and refused much until the testimonies mean nothing to them. They put whatever interpretation upon them that they choose in their own finite judgment and are satisfied. I would, if I had dared, [have] given up this field of conflict long ago, but something has held me. But I leave all this in the hands of God. I feel cut loose from many of my brethren; they do not understand me or my mission or my work, for if they did they could never have pursued the course they have done."[50]

Through it all, Ellen White knew inward joy and happiness. She urged others by word and example to pick the roses and ignore the thorns.[51] In the church paper she wrote: "Let us represent the Christian life as it really is; let us make the way cheerful, inviting, interesting. We can do this if we will. We may fill our own minds with vivid pictures of spiritual and eternal things, and in so doing help to make them a reality to other minds."[52]

Loneliness, even frustration and discouragement, need not shut down a cheery Christian. During a troubling time in the 1860s, when the Whites were in Dansville, New York, seeking help for James's physical problems, Ellen captured in her diary an earlier conversation: "It is the want of genuine religion that produces gloom, despondency, and sadness. . . . A half service, loving the world, loving self, loving frivolous amusements, make a timid, cowardly servant. Such follow Christ a great way off. A hearty, willing service to Jesus produces a sunny religion. Those who follow Christ the most closely have not been gloomy."[53]

People can be happy though lonely. Ellen White's ability to manifest this truth permeates the historical record and vouches for her declaration in Great Grimsby, England, in 1886:

"I do not look to the end for all the happiness; I get happiness as I go along. Notwithstanding I have trials and afflictions, I look away to Jesus. It is in the strait, hard places that He is right by our side, and we can commune with Him, and lay all our burdens upon the Burden Bearer, and say, 'Here, Lord, I cannot carry these burdens any longer.'"[54]

Endnotes

1. "My ideas concerning justification and sanctification were confused. These two states were presented to my mind as separate and distinct from each other; yet I failed to comprehend the difference or understand the meaning of the terms, and all the explanations of the preachers increased my difficulties. I was unable to claim the blessing for myself, and wondered if it was to be found only among the Methodists, and if, in attending the advent meetings, I was not shutting myself away from that which I desired above all else—the sanctifying Spirit of God. Still, I observed that some of those who claimed to be sanctified, manifested a bitter spirit when the subject of the soon coming of Christ was introduced. This did not seem to me a manifestation of the holiness which they professed."—*Life Sketches,* pp. 28, 29.
2. "They taught that God proposed to save none but the sanctified; that the eye of God was upon us always; that God Himself was keeping the books with the exactness of infinite wisdom; and that every sin we committed was faithfully registered against us, and would meet its just punishment. . . . If the love of God had been dwelt upon more, and His stern justice less, the beauty and glory of His character would have inspired me with a deep and earnest love for my Creator."—*Ibid.,* pp. 30, 31.
3. "In my mind the justice of God eclipsed His mercy and love. The mental anguish I passed through at this time was very great. I had been taught to believe in an eternally burning hell; and as I thought of the wretched state of the sinner without God, without hope, I was in deep despair. I feared that I should be lost, and that I should live throughout eternity suffering a living death. The horrifying thought was ever before me, that my sins were too great to be forgiven, and that I should be forever lost."—*Ibid.,* p. 29.
4. In many ways Ellen White developed the central focus of the Biblical theme of the great controversy. See pp. 256-266. For example: "From the opening of the great controversy it has been Satan's purpose to misrepresent God's character, and to excite rebellion against His law, and this work appears to be crowned with success. The multitudes give ear to Satan's deceptions, and set themselves against God. But amid the working of evil, God's purposes move steadily forward to their accomplishment; to all created intelligences He is making manifest His justice and benevolence."—*Patriarchs and Prophets,* p. 338.

   "Satan's efforts to misrepresent the character of God, to cause men to cherish a false conception of the Creator, and thus to regard Him with fear and hate rather than with love; his endeavors to set aside the divine law, leading the people to think themselves free from its requirements; and his persecution of those who dare to resist his deceptions, have been steadfastly pursued in all ages. They may be traced in the history of patriarchs, prophets, and apostles, of martyrs and reformers."—*The Great Controversy,* p. x.

   "God desires from all His creatures the service of love—homage that springs from an intelligent appreciation of His character."—*Ibid.,* p. 493.

   "The enemy of good blinded the minds of men, so that they looked upon God with fear; they thought of Him as severe and unforgiving. Satan led men to conceive of God as a being whose chief attribute is stern justice—one who is a severe judge, a harsh, exacting creditor. He pictured the Creator as a being who is watching with jealous eye to discern the errors and mistakes of men, that He may visit judgments upon them. It was to remove this dark shadow, by revealing to the world the infinite love of God, that Jesus came to live among men."—*Steps to Christ,* pp. 10, 11.

   Thus, Ellen White made clear that the main theme, the driving, organizing principle of the church's everlasting gospel message in the last days would be a recognition of the main focus of the Great Controversy Theme: "It is the darkness of misapprehension of God that is enshrouding the world. Men are losing their knowledge of His character. It has been misunderstood and misinterpreted. At this time a message from God is to be proclaimed, a message illuminating in its influence and saving in its power. His character is to be made known. Into the darkness of the world is to be shed the light of His glory, the light of His goodness, mercy, and truth. . . . Those who wait for the Bridegroom's coming are to say to the people, 'Behold your God.' The last rays of merciful light, the last message of mercy to be given to the world, is a revelation of His character of love."—*Christ's Object Lessons,* p. 415.

5. See p. 5.
6. *Historical Sketches,* pp. 130-133.
7. For a typical review of Ellen White's understanding of "righteousness by faith," see *Faith and Works,* pp. 15-122; *Selected Messages,* book 1, pp. 350-400; *Christ's Object Lessons,* pp. 307-319. For her insights into a dynamic religious experience, see *The Great Controversy,* pp. 461-478. For her teaching regarding a "prepared people," see *Christ's Object Lessons,* pp. 405-421; *The Great Controversy,* pp. 582-634.
8. *Bio.,* vol. 2, pp. 432, 433. See *Steps to Christ,* pp. 96, 104.
9. *Testimonies,* vol. 5, p. 124. "Love is power. Intellectual and moral strength are involved in this principle, and cannot be separated from it. The power of wealth has a tendency to corrupt and destroy; the power of force is strong to do hurt; but the excellence and value of pure love consist in its efficiency to do good, and to do nothing else than good. Whatsoever is done out of pure love, be it ever so little or contemptible in the sight of men, is wholly fruitful; for God regards more with how much love one worketh, than the amount he doeth. Love is of God. The unconverted heart cannot originate nor produce this plant of heavenly growth, which lives and flourishes only where Christ reigns.

   "Love cannot live without action, and every act increases, strengthens, and extends it. Love will gain the victory when argument and authority are powerless. Love works not for profit nor reward; yet God has ordained that great gain shall be the certain result of every labor of love. . . . Pure love is simple in its operations, and is distinct from any other principle of action. The love of influence and the desire for the esteem of others may produce a well-ordered life and frequently a blameless conversation. Self-respect may lead us to avoid the appearance of evil. A selfish heart may perform generous actions, acknowledge the present truth, and express humility and affection in an outward manner, yet the motives may be deceptive and impure; the actions that flow from such a heart may be destitute of the savor of life and the fruits of true holiness, being destitute of the principles of pure love."—*Testimonies,* vol. 2, pp. 135, 136.
10. Letter 3, 1863, cited in *Bio.,* vol. 2, p. 95. See also *Testimonies,* vol. 2, p. 355: "When He comes, He is not to cleanse us of our sins, to remove from us the defects in our characters, or to cure us of the infirmities of our tempers and dispositions. If wrought for us at all, this work will all be accomplished before that time. When the Lord comes, those who are holy will be holy still. Those who have preserved their bodies and spirits in holiness, in sanctification and honor, will then receive the finishing touch of immortality. . . . No work will then be done for them to remove their defects, and give them holy characters. The Refiner does not then sit to pursue His refining process, and remove their sins and their corruption. This is all to be done in these hours of probation. It is *now* that this work is to be accomplished for us.

    "We embrace the truth of God with our different faculties, and as we come under the influence of that truth, it will accomplish the work for us which is necessary to give us a moral fitness for the kingdom of glory and for the society of the heavenly angels. We are now in God's workshop. Many of us are rough stones from the quarry. But as we lay hold upon the truth of God, its influence affects us. It elevates us and removes from us every imperfection and sin, of whatever nature. Thus we are prepared to see the King in His beauty, and finally to unite with the pure and heavenly angels in the kingdom of glory."
11. *Mind, Character, and Personality,* vol. 1, p. 27. "Health of body depends largely upon health of soul; therefore whether you eat or drink, or whatsoever you do, do all to the glory of God. Personal religion is revealed by the deportment, the words, and the actions. It causes growth, till at last perfection claims the commendation of the Lord, 'Ye are complete in Him' (Col. 2:10)."—*Ibid.* See also pp. 291-294.
12. *The Ministry of Healing,* p. 241.
13. *Ibid.,* p. 113.
14. *Ibid.*
15. Manuscript 5, 1882, cited in *Bio.,* vol. 3, p. 220.
16. *The Desire of Ages,* p. 471.
17. *Mind, Character, and Personality,* vol. 2, p. 777.
18. Christian, *Fruitage of Spiritual Gifts,* p. 50.
19. *Bio.,* vol. 1, pp. 278, 279.
20. *Review and Herald,* Oct. 7, 1884.
21. *Historical Sketches,* pp. 162, 163.
22. *Signs of the Times,* July 18, 1878; see also *Ibid.,* Sept. 23, 1889.
23. *Bio.,* vol. 4, p. 235.
24. Manuscript 12, 1894, cited in *Sermons and Talks,* vol. 1, p. 246.
25. *Review and Herald,* Mar. 26, 1889.
26. *Signs of the Times,* Oct. 14, 1889.
27. *Review and Herald,* July 16, 1889.
28. *Review and Herald,* Sept. 27, 1892.
29. *General Conference Bulletin,* April 3, 1901.
30. James Nix, *Early Advent Singing,* (Hagerstown, MD: Review and Herald Publishing Association, 1994), pp. 141-144. William H. Hyde was only 17 when he wrote this hymn. His father, William Hyde, was a prominent publisher in Portland, Maine.
31. *Bio.,* vol. 6, pp. 423, 424.
32. *Fundamentals of Christian Education,* pp. 547-549, and in *Messages to Young People,* pp. 287, 289.
33. *Bio.,* vol. 6, pp. 430, 431.
34. *Life Sketches,* p. 72.
35. See *Libraries, a Bibliography of E. G. White's Private and Office Libraries* (at the time of her death in 1915). This document is available at any E. G. White-SDA Research Center.
36. *Selected Messages,* book 3, p. 437.
37. *Ibid.,* p. 463.
38. *Health Reformer,* Aug. 1873.
39. *Historical Sketches,* p. 220. For Ellen White's description of her visit to the Milan Cathedral and of her trip

through the magnificent Alps in 1886, see Arthur Delafield, *Ellen G. White in Europe,* pp. 175, 176 and 181-183.
40. *Testimonies,* vol. 5, p. 644; *Ibid.,* vol. 1, p. 502; *Review and Herald,* Feb. 12, 1901.
41. *Bio.*, vol. 1, p. 88. Later she came to realize that the suffering of the mind directly affects the health of the body—see pp. 330-332.
42. *Ibid.,* p. 131.
43. *Ibid.,* pp. 134, 135.
44. *Ibid.,* pp. 304-306.
45. *Ibid.,* vol. 3, pp. 385, 386.
46. *Signs of the Times,* Nov. 11, 1889. A few months later, at a camp meeting in Ottawa, Kansas, she said: "You have to talk faith, you have to live faith, you have to act faith, that you may have an increase of faith. Exercising that living faith, you will grow to strong men and women in Christ Jesus."—*Faith and Works,* p. 78. Note other times when, physically and emotionally exhausted, Ellen White moved out in faith, talking faith and bringing this insight to others; for example, in Australia, 1895, cited in *Bio.*, vol. 4, p. 228.
47. *Bio.*, vol. 6, pp. 413, 414.
48. *Selected Messages,* book 3, p. 67.
49. *Bio.*, vol. 3, p. 354.
50. *Ibid.,* p. 471.
51. *Steps to Christ,* p. 117.
52. *Review and Herald,* Jan. 29, 1884.
53. *Bio.*, vol. 2, p. 122.
54. *Life Sketches,* p. 292.

Study Questions

1. What were the steps in Ellen White's thinking that led her to a correct picture of God as her friend?
2. How did Ellen White connect theological belief with a believer's personal life?
3. How would you express Ellen White's understanding of the relationship between health and one's spiritual life?
4. What insights did Ellen White have regarding the cause of suffering and death?
5. How do you account for Ellen White's remarkable writing career, noting that her formal education ended at the age of nine?

CHAPTER 8

As Others Knew Her

"Let love be without hypocrisy. Abhor what is evil. Cling to what is good. Be kindly affectionate to one another with brotherly love, in honor giving preference to one another; not lagging in diligence, fervent in spirit, serving the Lord; rejoicing in hope, patient in tribulation, continuing steadfastly in prayer; distributing to the needs of the saints, given to hospitality. . . . If it is possible, as much as depends on you, live peaceably with all men" (Rom. 12:9-13, 18).

Did Ellen White practice what she preached? Yes. Others knew her as a well-rounded, exceptional Christian leader. Though subject to human weaknesses, she was respected as one who practiced the forward-looking, all-embracing, ever-expanding insights that were constantly being revealed to her.

Frugality

She learned how to endure and triumph over financial hardships. Her prudent habits are well known.

The Whites began housekeeping in poverty. In 1848 they left the Howland family, in Topsham, Maine, where they had lived in the upstairs rooms, to attend a conference of Sabbath keeping Adventists in Rocky Hill, Connecticut, the first of many conferences to come. How did they plan to pay their way? James had earned ten dollars for cutting wood; half was spent on preparing the young family of three for the trip, and the other half was for transportation to Boston and the Otis Nichols home. Although they had not said a word about their financial circumstances, Mrs. Mary Nichols gave them five dollars. After they bought their train tickets to Middletown, Connecticut, they had 50 cents to spare. They had to face similar economic challenges many times in the years that followed.[1]

Midwinter 1851 the Whites were invited to speak at a conference in Waterbury, Vermont. They had already lent Charlie, their faithful horse, and carriage to S. W. Rhodes and J. N. Andrews so these two preachers could meet appointments in Canada and northern Vermont. Along the way the Whites met a poor believer whom they encouraged to attend the conference. To make it possible, they gave him their train fare to help buy a horse—so that all three could ride in a sleigh together. Soon they met another believer and gave him five dollars to pay his fare on the train. The Whites continued in an open sleigh without blanket or buffalo robe in Vermont cold. Ellen wrote: "We suffered much."[2]

In the summer of 1852 the publishing office was established in Rochester, New York. All the printing equipment plus the meager household furniture was sent west from Maine on borrowed money. The Whites set up the publishing house in their own home—not only the printing equipment but living quarters for all the workers. No one except the non-Adventist press foreman received wages beyond a small allowance for clothing and other expenses that "were deemed absolutely necessary."[3]

James brought home six old chairs, no two alike. He soon added four more, each without seating. Ellen made the seats.

Potatoes and butter cost too much; their first meals were served on a board placed upon two flour barrels. Ellen noted: "We are willing to endure privations if the work of God can be advanced."[4]

Home circumstances did improve as the years went by. Both James and Ellen White were specialists in making do, or doing without. However, James knew that many times Ellen would sacrifice too much. In 1874, he wrote to son William who was with his mother in Battle Creek: "I was very glad to learn that you were with your mother. Take the tenderest care of your dear mother. And if she wishes to attend the eastern camp meetings, please go with her. Get a tent that will suit you; get everything good in the shape of satchels, blankets, portable chair for Mother, and do not consent to her economical ideas, leading you to pinch along."[5]

Ellen White taught by example in Europe. After landing at Calais, France, she and her traveling companions discovered that a sleeping compartment on the train to Basel would cost $11 apiece. Ever frugal, they decided to make do in the seats. She commented: "A bed was made for me between the seats on the top of the satchels and telescope boxes. I rested some, but slept little. . . . We were not sorry to have the night pass."[6]

From Dansville, New York, in 1865, Mrs. White wrote to her children regarding clothing for Edson: "If a man tailor makes these coats they must cost too much for making. If you can obtain a good woman tailor whom you can trust, engage her to make both coats, if she does not ask too much."[7]

"Down under" in 1894, Ellen White was now 66. Australia was having economic struggles, with even worse times to come. And Mrs. White was tired for many reasons. While in Melbourne she wrote: "I am tired, tired all the time, and must ere long get a restful place in the country. . . . I want this year to write and to exercise prudently out of doors in the open air."

Later she wrote: "I am getting to be very tired of moving. It worries me out, settling and unsettling, gathering manuscripts and scattering them, to be gathered up again."

Soon she moved to a Sydney suburb. "We find there are many ways we can spend money and many ways we can save money. We have a skeleton wardrobe of two upright standards, and crosspieces nailed to these, and a shelf put on the top. A very simple cheap lace over blue or red cheap cambric is fastened to the top and back of the shelf. This back is neatly arranged, lifted up and fastened securely to the posts of the head of the bedstead." Most of the rest of the furniture was bought at auctions.[8]

On a trip from Melbourne to Geelong, forty miles southwest, the party took the slow boat for eighteen pence round-trip each, rather than the train for eight shillings each. Writing later, Mrs. White wrote: "A penny saved is as good as a penny earned."[9]

Generosity

Ellen White was frugal because she wanted to contribute as much as she could to hard-pressed people as well as to the growing needs of the young Seventh-day Adventist Church.[10]

"Sharing" seems to have been her middle name. Her sharing of her home with co-workers and traveling ministers, many times not knowing how many would appear at meal time, reveals a prevailing generous spirit. After inspiring and challenging others to build churches, publishing houses, health facilities, and schools, she would lead the way with substantial donations, often loans from others that she managed to repay—with interest. In 1888 at an Oakland, California, gathering, she may have raised astonished eyebrows when she noted that she and her husband, out of frugal savings and wise investments, had contributed $30,000 "in the cause of God."[11]

In a sermon delivered at the 1891

General Conference session, after James had been dead for ten years, she wrote: "For years we received no wages, except barely enough to furnish us with the plainest food and clothing. We were glad to wear second-hand clothes, and sometimes we had hardly food enough to sustain our strength. Everything else was put into the work."[12]

Her unselfishness with her time and scant resources became a model for all. John O. Corliss (1845-1923), who lived in the White home for several years prior to his baptism in 1868,[13] wrote of his close connection with Mrs. White through the years: "She was most careful to carry out in her own course the things she taught to others. For instance, she frequently dwelt in her public talks upon the duty of caring for widows and orphans, citing her hearers to Isaiah 58:7-10, and she exemplified her exhortations by taking the needy to her own home for shelter, food, and raiment. I well remember her having at one time, as members of her family, a boy and a girl and a widow and her two daughters. I have, moreover, known her to distribute to poor people hundreds of dollars' worth of new clothes, which she bought for that purpose."[14]

One cannot review the history of the Adventist Church in Australia without noting that Ellen White was generous, to a fault. In 1892 Australia was sinking into an economic depression. Adventist believers were fewer than 1,000. Yet Mrs. White's constant motto was "Advance," which, at first, meant a school near Melbourne. Funds were nonexistent, but she decided to use $1,000 from the royalty of foreign books sold in America, funds that were already committed elsewhere.[15]

While funds were being raised in Parramatta for the first church building owned by Seventh-day Adventists in continental Australia, a gift of $45 from California was sent to Ellen White. Her friends wanted her to have a comfortable chair during her painful illness. But she promptly put it into the Parramatta building fund, explaining to her thoughtful friends that she wished them to feel that they too had something invested in Australia.[16]

Ellen White remained at the center of the Adventist world in Australia, not only for encouragement but also for raising funds. A letter to Dr. J. H. Kellogg in 1896 provides a glimpse of the ongoing, year by year, struggle in Australia: "I have to stand as a bank to uphold, borrow, and advance money. I turn and twist every way to do the work. Others will take hold and do something when they see that I have faith to lead out and donate. Here are all our workers that must be paid. I am heavily in debt in this country to those in other countries. Eighteen hundred dollars from one person; this money has been used up. Five hundred dollars from one in Africa, which is a loan and has been applied in different ways that demanded means to forward the work. I moved by faith."[17]

In 1899 G. A. Irwin, General Conference president, invited Mrs. White to return to America and attend the next session of the General Conference at South Lancaster, Massachusetts. She replied: "I was 71 years old the twenty-sixth of November. But this is not the reason I plead for not attending your conference. . . . We have advanced slowly, planting the standard of truth in every place possible. But the dearth of means has been a serious hindrance. . . . We dare not show one particle of unbelief. We advance just as far as we can see, and then go far ahead of sight, moving by faith. . . .

"We strip ourselves of everything we can possibly spare in the line of money, for the openings are so many and the necessities so great. We have hired [borrowed] money until I have been compelled to say, I cannot donate more. My workers are the best, most faithful and devoted girls I ever expect to find. In order to advance the work I have donated the wages that should have been paid them. When the last call was made, my name was not on the list for the first time. . . . There is nothing for me to do but to remain here until the work is placed on a solid foundation."[18]

As the last decade of the nineteenth century closed, the denomination was heavily in debt largely because of ignoring the counsel of Ellen White. Although she made her position very clear to church leaders as to the reasons for avoiding the huge debts, she did not criticize and complain. Instead, she had a plan. She proposed to give her royalties on *Christ's Object Lessons* (a book soon to be published in 1900) to help clear the debts on denominational schools. With the cooperation of church members throughout North America, that gift yielded more than $300,000.

When church funds were low in 1906, she donated royalties from her book *The Ministry of Healing* (sold in the eastern United States) for construction of the Washington Sanitarium (now Washington Adventist Hospital) in Takoma Park, Maryland.[19] All of the royalties from *Ministry of Healing* went to relieve the indebtedness of the church's medical institutions.

From 1914 to 1918 L. H. Christian was president of the Lake Union Conference, comprising Wisconsin, Illinois, Indiana, and Michigan. He was impressed by the many older Adventists in these states who treasured their memories of James and Ellen White. They reported how kind and helpful the Whites were to the poor at a time when early settlers often lacked food and shelter. The men liked to recall the compelling leadership of James and how he would say to his wife, "Ellen, talk is cheap; but the thing that counts is what you and I can give. It is good to sympathize with these folk, but the result of our sympathy is determined by how deep we dig into our pocketbooks."

In his book, *The Fruitage of Spiritual Gifts*, Christian reported: "What she writes in such books as *Ministry of Healing* and many of the *Testimonies* concerning our duty to the needy and sick was exemplified most beautifully in her own life. This chapter would become much too long if I should recount all the things that these old acquaintances said of Sister White. I never heard one of them find fault with her in any way."[20]

Commitment to Duty

Many noble virtues characterized Ellen White's remarkable life, but commitment to duty seems to tower over all others. Wherever we look in her long life, commitment to her divine assignment carried the highest priority.

When only 22, with a young child, she wrote this letter on February 10, 1850: "We should have written you before but we have no certain abiding place, but have traveled in rain, snow, and blow with the child from place to place. I could not get time to answer any letters and it took all James's time to write for the paper and get out the hymn book. We do not have many idle moments."[21]

At Battle Creek in 1865, Ellen White was feeling the coldness even of her friends. Being a faithful messenger for God is always difficult, but living close to those who received the personal testimonies made life even more difficult. God had given her a special vision of the wilted vine that received special support; it represented the strength she should expect from God as she continued to do her duty: "From this time I was settled as to my duty and never more free in bearing my testimony to the people."[22]

How did she understand her duty? In 1873 James White was suffering the consequences of several strokes when the work in Battle Creek required his steady administrative vision. Wife Ellen, knowing that immediate decisions were needed, called the leading workers together for prayer. In her July 5 diary entry, she wrote: "My husband had an ill turn. We had a season of prayer in our chamber. We called the brethren together and had a season of prayer for more clear understanding of duty. I felt that it was my duty to go to the Iowa camp meeting. We had two praying seasons. We finally decided to go on the morning train."

At the Iowa campground, which was near their Washington, Iowa, hideaway home, James spoke four times and Ellen five times. They both were refreshed, yet further drained. The four far-west camp meetings were expecting them. What to do now?

They went out into the orchard and prayed. In her account of this experience, Mrs. White continued: "We feel very anxious to know our duty. We do not want to make any wrong move. We need sanctified judgment and heavenly wisdom to move in the counsel of God. We cry unto God for light and grace. We must have help from God or we perish. Our earnest cry is for the direction of God's Holy Spirit. We dare not move in any direction without clear light."[23]

At South Lancaster, Massachusetts, in 1889, topics of immense importance needed to be addressed, especially in understanding how men and women become right and remain right with God. In a report to the *Review and Herald,* she wrote: "It is the privilege of everyone to say, 'I will carry out my Captain's orders to the very letter, feeling or no feeling. I will not wait for a happy sensation, for a mysterious impulse.' I will say, 'What are my orders? What is the line of my duty? What says the Master to me? Is the line of communication open between God and my soul? What is my position before God?' Just as soon as we come into right relations to God, we shall understand our duty and do it; and we shall not think the good things we do entitle us to salvation."[24]

In most situations prophets learn their duty as every other child of God must. Even Jesus learned His duty "when He had offered up prayers and supplications, with vehement cries and tears to Him who was able to save Him from death, and was heard because of His godly fear" (Heb. 5:7, 8).

Decisions made in the line of duty are often endorsed in ways that are convincing. In the humid July heat in Battle Creek, 1881, Ellen White felt the need to spend some time in Colorado where she could write under better conditions. But the needs of Battle Creek, especially of the youth, overwhelmed her, and she decided to remain there. Uriah Smith wrote of this incident: "On making this decision, she felt at once a marked return of bodily and mental vigor, giving good evidence that this determination was in the line of duty."[25]

Some of her last words to an assembled General Conference session (1913) summed up her own life of commitment to duty: "When the Lord sets His hand to prepare the way before His ministers, it is their duty to follow where He directs. He will never forsake or leave in uncertainty those who follow His leadings with full purpose of heart."[26]

Strenuous Schedules

Her taxing schedules were arduous even for strong men. We have already noted her exhausting travel arrangements under terrible weather conditions. In those early years, Ellen and James White would stay up past midnight, reading proof sheets and folding papers, then face each new day's unending duties.[27]

For an example of her church duties that lapped over Ellen White like shingles on a roof, we can point to June 23, 1854. Now seven months pregnant, she and James returned to their Rochester home from a busy seven-week journey through Ohio, Michigan, and Wisconsin. The trip included many speaking appointments, counseling with evangelists regarding better methods, traveling nights by train, and a train wreck that involved a premonition to change cars (their first car was "much broken").

But they returned in time for a four-day conference in their home, representatives coming from western New York, Pennsylvania, and Canada. Ellen White sighed, "We returned . . . much worn, desiring rest. . . . Without rest we were obliged to engage in the meeting."[28]

Throughout her vigorous schedule of speaking, traveling, and writing continually, Ellen White supervised a busy home schedule. As we noted earlier (p. 75) she generally had more boarders than her immediate family. A diary entry for January 28, 1868, written at their Greenville, Michigan, home, is typical: "Brother [J. O.] Corliss (a young convert) helped me to prepare breakfast. Everything we touched was frozen. All things in our cellar were frozen. We prepared frozen turnips and potatoes. After prayer, Brother Corliss went into the woods near Thomas Wilson's to get wood. James, accompanied by Brother [J. N.] Andrews, went to Orleans, expecting to return to dinner.

"I baked eight pans of gems, swept rooms, washed dishes, helped Willie [age 13] put snow in boiler, which requires many tubsful. We have no well water or cistern. Arranged my clothes press [closet]. Felt weary; rested a few minutes. Got dinner for Willie and me. Just as we got through, my husband and Brother Andrews drove up. Had had no dinner. I started cooking again. Soon got them something to eat. Nearly all day has thus been spent—not a line written. I feel sad about this. Am exceedingly weary. My head is tired."[29]

While their new Battle Creek home was being constructed in late 1868, the Whites were meeting appointments in the eastern states. James shared with readers of the *Review and Herald* the relief he felt after returning home on December 30, 1868: "We found a convenient and pleasant house built at Battle Creek for us, and partly furnished with goods moved from our [Greenville] home in Montcalm County. This place seems like home. Here we find rest in several senses of the word. We had become tired of meetings, tired of traveling, tired of speaking, tired of visiting, and tired of the business cares incident to an absence from home, living, as it were, in our trunks nearly one-third of the year. Here we find quiet for the present." Later in the article he noted that sixty letters awaited them, all to be opened and answered![30]

Back-to-Back Camp Meetings

Camp meetings seemed to be pressed together, almost seamlessly, for James and Ellen White. For instance, the Kansas camp meeting, late May, 1876, where Ellen was to meet James. She was coming from the west coast, all the while busy writing the first volume on the life of Christ. Her train, instead of arriving on Friday after six days of endurance, was delayed. She arrived on the campgrounds early Sabbath morning, after a twenty-mile, farm-wagon trip over rough roads. James wrote in the *Signs of the Times*: "Weary, of course, short of sleep, and trembling with nervous headache, she takes the speaker's stand at half past ten and is wonderfully sustained in her effort."

Ellen White spoke several times in the evening meetings and on Tuesday morning was up at 4 o'clock for a "precious social parting meeting."[31]

By July 4 the Whites had spoken many times at six camp meetings! Before going on to the Ohio camp meeting, they dashed home to Battle Creek to catch their breath. Ellen wrote to William and Mary (married early that year) describing the Fourth of July celebration: "Some things were really interesting and some ridiculous, but I cannot write. I have kept on the strain so long I am now finding my level and I am not very intelligent. We cannot, Father, Mary [Clough], or myself, do anything now. We are debilitated and run down like an old clock."[32]

A few days later they headed east for the next series of camp meetings. At Norwalk, Ohio, 2,500 people; at Groveland, Massachusetts, an estimated 20,000 (the largest audience Ellen White addressed). Writing to William during this tour, she commented like a mother: "Your father and your mother are worked down. I am looking old and poor [sic] for the very reason that there is no rest for us. We work hard. Your father does the work of three men at all these meetings. I never saw a man work so energetically, so constantly, as your father. God does give him more than mortal energy. If there is any place that is hard, your father takes it."[33]

This 1876 program was not unusual. Typical also was the preaching schedule in 1880. James was not well; overwork had led to several strokes. Growing old gracefully was his wish, but easier said than done. Circumstances seemed to awaken harsh, insensitive thoughts and words. The old warrior charged on, wishing that others would carry the load more efficiently.

While Ellen White was meeting west coast camp meeting appointments, she received a telegram from James that urged her to join him in meeting the calls "from Maine to Dakota, and from Michigan to Kentucky." In spite of her heavy writing program, she and Lucinda Hall took the "slow train" east on July 26. The "slow train" cost less but it took nine days! They arrived in Battle Creek at noon Wednesday. At 8:00 P.M. she and James caught the train for a two-hour trip to Jackson. After spending the night with friends, they left the next day for Alma, arriving just before dark, just in time for her to speak at the evening meeting.

From Alma they spent the next two months traveling week by week to camp meetings. These included Maine, Massachusetts, Vermont, New York, Ohio, Indiana, and the national camp meeting at Battle Creek, Michigan, October 2 and 9. At most of them they stayed three to five days, but always Sabbath and Sunday. All this, not in automobiles over paved highways, but on those early trains and other tiresome conveyances—a feat that would weary the hardiest traveler today riding in the most comfortable cars or buses.[34]

Throughout these busy years Ellen White was supplying the *Review and Herald* and *Signs of the Times* with scores of articles annually. The writing of volume 4 of the *Spirit of Prophecy, (The Great Controversy Between Christ and Satan)* though slowed down by her many speaking appointments, was always on her mind.

Early in 1884, however, she determined to finish this pressing manuscript: "I am writing every day. Mean to get my book finished next month, and can scarcely write a letter, I am so intent on this matter."[35]

Writing to Harriet Smith, Uriah's wife, she penned this personal touch: "As I write upon my book I feel intensely moved. I want to get it out as soon as possible, for our people need it so much. I shall complete it next month if the Lord gives me health as He has done. I have been unable to sleep nights, thinking of the important things to take place. Three hours' sleep, and sometimes five, is the most I get. My mind is stirred so deeply I cannot rest. Write, write, write, I feel that I must, and not delay."

Before she could finish, she met three camp meeting appointments. During the final few weeks, she wrote to William to bring her "another good fountain pen."[36]

Only profound dedication to duty and divinely provided energy, year after year, can explain seventy years of amazing accomplishments under the most strenuous conditions.[37]

Mindful of Personal Example

While in Europe (1885) someone gave a gold watch to Ellen White. However, it became a topic for conversation; so, rather than be misunderstood or become a stumbling block, she sold it.[38]

Courage and Perseverance

God can give messages to a person but prophets must have courage and perseverance to fulfill their assignments. Think of this 17-year-old girl, frail and emaciated, poor and gravely ill, but faced with a divine call to speak for God. The idea appeared preposterous to most of her adult contemporaries! In the years to come, she fulfilled well the role of a mother and wife, yet, above all else, she threw herself into the path of duty, often far in advance of even her closest friends. No wonder she wrote: "I coveted death as a release from the responsibilities that were crowding upon me."[39] Only a person with courage and perseverance could have plunged into such a life assignment—and succeeded.

Ellen White's care for her husband, James, with his nervous exhaustion during 1866/1867 is astounding. Taking her worn-out, 45-year-old husband to northern Michigan in mid-winter seemed foolhardy to all, even to their physician and to James's father and mother who now lived in Battle Creek. They all felt that she at nearly 39 was sacrificing her life, that for the sake of her children and the cause of God she should let nature take its course. They all believed that James would never recover.[40]

But courage and perseverance moved her to respond: "As long as life is left in him and me, I *will* [sic] make every exertion for him. That brain, that noble, masterly mind, shall not be left in ruins. God will care for him, for me, for my children. . . . You will yet see us standing side by side in the sacred desk, speaking the words of truth unto eternal life."[41]

Ellen White's awesome strategy and effort to restore health of mind and body to her husband have become a model for many thousands since. Courage, perseverance, and undying love won the day and James returned to lead out in perhaps his greatest achievements for the growing church. Throughout this extraordinary period as her husband's nurse, confidante, physical therapist, and dietitian, Mrs. White kept up a heavy schedule of speaking appointments and writing. On this courageous woman in northern Michigan the future of the Seventh-day Adventist Church (as we now know it) rested.

But at the same time, swirling, unfounded charges were being circulated in Battle Creek, allegations that would have smothered almost anyone else. The Whites, especially Ellen, courageously faced them all down. In so doing, she and James earned deep respect and gratitude from most of those involved.[42] Very few public persons have had to endure slander as often as James and Ellen White.

More than once, charges were made that the Whites unduly profited from their many business dealings. How quickly forgotten was their unparalleled channeling of funds to new projects, ranging from church buildings, health institutions, and publishing houses, to the newest educational institution! For much of her ministry, Ellen White did not receive a salary. For many years, the Whites covered their own travel expenses. They bore all the costs for household helpers who assisted in caring for their many boarders and visitors. In addition, they paid editorial assistants from personal funds.[43]

Frequent references have already been made to the physical challenges that Ellen White faced almost continually throughout her life. One example of her courage under trying conditions occurred in Basel, Switzerland, on June 15, 1886 as she prepared to leave for Sweden. She was painfully struggling with pleurisy. In a *Review and Herald* article she commented: "Every breath was painful. It seemed impossible for me to travel, especially at night. To take a sleeping car, for one night only, would involve an extra expense of ten or twelve dollars, and this was out of the question. Yet it was necessary for us to leave Basel that night in order to reach Orebro [Sweden] before the Sabbath." But leave they did in a coach seat, arriving in Sweden Friday morning.

This kind of courage and perseverance demonstrated the truth of her words written several months earlier: "I can, when I have to, do most anything."[44]

An interesting example of Ellen White's perseverance occurred when her son Willie was twenty months old. Young Willie was playing with a "boat" in the kitchen near a large pail of mop water. His caretaker left the room momentarily to get wood for the fire. When she returned she saw only one little foot sticking out of the dirty water. She pulled the child out of the pail, then screamed to his mother that her son had drowned.

James was called for, as well as a physician. But Ellen was busy rolling Willie on the grass, forcing the water from his body. A neighbor urged James: "Take that dead baby out of that woman's hands."

"No," he replied, "it is her child, and no one shall take it away from her." Twenty minutes went by. Then Ellen White saw a flick of the eyelid and a little pucker in his lips. Soon he was in his crib, wrapped with heated cloths. The mother did not give up. Years later, she said of Willie that God had shown her that he was born to be her helper after her husband died. And so he was.[45]

Courage When Standing Alone

In 1881 James White was in rapid decline. More than four strokes had left him physically and emotionally weak, and overwork depleted what strength he had left. Mrs. White wrote on January 6 that she was perplexed as to how to help her husband: "Father has been in such a state of mind I feared he would lose his reason. But he is concluding to lay off the burdens of office matters and go to writing. I hope he will do so. . . . I am at times in such perplexity and distress of mind I covet retirement or death, but then I gather courage again."[46]

But her real test of strength came from a surprising development. By May, she was so criticized in Battle Creek that even her closest friends grew cool toward her. The criticism? Her word could not be trusted because she was manipulated by others! How could this be? Soon she became aware of the tension between her husband and Dr. Kellogg.

In his dark moments of depression and paranoia, James was using her writings to undermine the president and secretary of the General Conference (G. I. Butler and S. N. Haskell, respectively). From another direction, J. H. Kellogg was attacking James White and James was retaliating. How were all these unpleasant assaults carried out? By each quoting the words of Ellen White to substantiate their allegations against one another—and by charging that the "quotes" used by their opponents were not valid words "from the Lord"! Each man was trying to destroy the influence of the others, but the real damage was being done to Ellen White.

On June 14 she wrote to Willie and Mary at the Pacific Press in Oakland, California: "This lack of harmony is killing me. I have to keep my own counsel and have confidence in no one [in Battle Creek] . . . . Now, Willie, I have written freely and confidentially. I hope the Lord will preserve you well balanced. I hope you will not go to extremes in anything . . . and be molded by no one's influence except it be the Spirit of God."[47]

By Sabbath, July 16, Ellen White, with courage and candor, was ready to clear the air. She asked for her husband and Dr. Kellogg to meet with her privately. She read to them "a large number of pages." The following Tuesday evening she called together the denominational leaders in Battle Creek and read to them the same pages she had read to James and Dr. Kellogg.

The results were most positive. Her next letter to Willie and Mary was cheerful, illuminating, and helpful to others who have experienced similar circumstances: "Why do men always carry things to extremes? They cannot stop when they have gone far enough, but they will, if the course of one is questioned, not feel content till they crush him. . . .

"The very men who would condemn him [James White] for sharpness in words and for dictating and being overbearing are tenfold more so when they dare to be, than he has ever been. . . . I have felt crushed and heartbroken for months, but I have laid my burden on my Saviour and I shall no longer be like a bruised reed. In the strength of Jesus I assert my freedom . . . ."

The letter continued, noting that her deepest concern was that the in-fighting among key leaders would cast a shadow over the validity of her prophetic ministry: "I had been in continual fear that my husband's mistakes and errors would be classed with the testimonies of the Spirit of God and my influence greatly injured. If I bore a plain testimony against existing wrongs they would say, 'She is molded by her husband's views and feelings.' If I reproved my husband he would feel I was severe and others had prejudiced me against him."

Then she summed up her appraisal of these two meetings: "I was crippled [in spirit], but I should be so no longer. I should act perfectly free. They might think of me as they pleased. I would give them reproof, warning, or encouragement as the Lord should give me. The burden of their questioning and doubts should no longer grieve me and close my lips. I should do my duty in the fear of God and if they would be tempted [by doubts about "influence"] I should not be responsible for this. I would cut my way through in the fear of God."[48]

Uriah Smith, a co-worker of James White for thirty years, summed up the remarkable occasion with an upbeat report: "Oh, that all might be enabled to heed the good words of counsel and admonition! Then would the spirit of religion revive in all our hearts, and the cause of Christ would flourish in our midst."[49]

Only those who are confident of their life mission and transparent enough for all contemporaries to trust their motives could face dilemmas as courageously as Ellen White did in Battle Creek, July 1881.

Tact

Mary and John Loughborough were close friends of the Whites, both families fully committed to the Adventist assignment. Both had lost a child in the early 1860s. The two young mothers often exchanged thoughts and feelings. In June 1861, Mary (in her twenties) had written Ellen (now 33), asking her opinion regarding the latest fashion—wearing hoops. After sharing her counsel, Ellen used the opportunity to say something not easy to say: "Dear Mary, let your influence tell for God. You must take a position to exert an influence over others to bring them up in spirituality. . . .

"And Mary, suffer me a little upon this point. I wish in all sisterly and motherly kindness to kindly warn you upon another point: I have often noticed before others a manner you have in speaking to John in rather a dictating manner, the tone of your voice sounding impatient. Mary, others notice this and have spoken of it to me. It hurts your influence. . . .

"I have said more perhaps upon this point than necessary. Please watch this point. I am not reproving you, remember, but merely cautioning you. Never talk to John as though he were a little boy. You reverence him, and others will take an elevated position, Mary, and you will elevate others.

"Seek to be spiritually minded. We are doing work for eternity. Mary, be an example. We love you as one of our children, and I wish so much that you and John may prosper. . . . Please write me, Mary, fully. Tell me all your joys, trials, disappointments, et cetera. In much love, Ellen G. White."[50]

We observe a beautiful example of Mrs. White's enduring tactfulness while she was caring for her husband in northern Michigan in 1866/1867. James was in deep depression following serious nervous exhaustion due to overwork. He felt he had no future. Ellen, contrary to the opinions of all others including physicians, believed that trust in God, exercise, and a proper diet would offer her husband his best chance to recover. Each day they took a long walk until the first heavy snow came. James used the snowflakes as an excuse to stop walking!

Not for long. Ellen went to Brother Root, with whom they were staying, and asked to borrow a spare pair of boots. Then she trudged a quarter of a mile in the deep snow. Returning, she asked her husband to take their usual walk. He replied that no one could walk in that weather.

"Oh, yes, you can," Ellen replied. "Surely you can step in my tracks."

James, a man who had great respect for women, saw her tracks—and that morning "he took his usual walk."[51]

Ellen White perceived that her husband also needed to exercise his brain. But he did not want to speak to anyone outside of the home. So she worked out a tactful plan. When a visitor would come with troubling questions, she would quickly invite him in before James could excuse himself. Then she would say, "Husband, here is a brother who has come to ask a question, and as you can answer it much better than I can, I have brought him to you."

James remained in the room long enough to answer the question. Such ploys kept him exercising his mind and he slowly improved. When special spiritual leadership was required in Wright, Michigan, the Whites' local church, Ellen provided much counsel, but "she was careful to see that her husband led out."[52]

Later in 1867, the White family moved to their Greenville, Michigan, farm, again to help James recover his health. In preparing their garden, Mrs. White asked young Willie to buy three hoes and three rakes. James objected to his rake and hoe, but she took hers and began to work, blistering her hands. Reluctantly James followed, going through the motions. But soon he was harnessing the horses and buying house materials. He reported that he was beginning to sleep well at night and to awaken each morning refreshed. The faithful wife's planning, perseverance, and tact were working, though slowly.

When July came, the hay was ready for cutting. James arranged with the neighbors to cut the hay and expected them to return later to stack it for winter. But his wife had a better plan. She went to these same neighbors and told them to excuse themselves, which they resisted at first.

When James's call for help went out, all the neighbors excused themselves as being too busy. James was very disappointed, but Ellen, with typical cheerfulness, suggested that she and Willie would rake the hay and pitch it on the wagon if James would load it and drive the horses. But how would the stack be built?

The neighbors were astonished to see that little five-foot-two woman stamping the hay and building the stack while her husband pitched hay from the wagon.

What was happening to James? He reported to *Review* readers: "I have worked from six to twelve hours each day, and have enjoyed blessed sleep from six to nine hours each night. . . . My work has been haying, plowing, grading about the house, hoeing, and putting down carpets."[53] Ellen's tact and courageous, resolute spirit prodded James into recovering his health.

Kindness

Many were the occasions when Ellen White showed her deep interest in young people. For example, she met a new Adventist family at the Oregon camp meeting in late June, 1878. Their teen-age daughter, Edith Donaldson, was eager for a Christian education at Battle Creek College. Mrs. White promptly suggested that Edith return with her to California and then on to Michigan. In a letter to her husband James, she manifested her kind heart. Describing Edith as a "girl of rare promise," she wrote: "I want her to board at our house and receive all the attention she needs."[54]

Ellen White received many letters from those who were suffering from disease or were mourning the death of loved ones. When the General Conference sent J. N. Andrews to Europe as the denomination's first official missionary, they sent a man who had already lost his wife and two infant children to disease. He left America with Mary, his 12-year-old daughter, and Charles, age 16. Four years later, in 1878, Mary died of tuberculosis. Coupled with his wife's early death and now Mary, Andrews felt that he was holding on to God "with a numb hand."[55]

One of Her Kindest Letters

Ellen White wrote to her long-time friend one of her kindest letters, which included the following words: "We have drunk at the same cup of sorrow, but it was mingled with joy and rest and peace in Jesus. [Ellen had lost two sons to disease.] . . . The cloud of mercy is hovering over your head even in the darkest hour. God's benefits to us are numerous as the drops of rain falling from the clouds upon the parched earth. . . . The mercy of God is over you.

"Mary, dear precious child, is at rest. She was the companion of your sorrows and disappointed hopes. She will no more have grief or want or distress. Through faith's discerning eye you may anticipate, amid your sorrows and griefs and perplexities, your Mary with her mother and other members of your family answering the call of the Life-giver and coming forth from their prison house triumphing over death and the grave. . . . You with them erelong, if faithful, will be walking in the streets of the New Jerusalem. . . . Could your eyes be opened, you would see your heavenly Father bending over you in love; and could you hear His voice it would be in tones of compassion to you who are prostrate with suffering and affliction. Stand fast in His strength; there is rest *for you*."[56]

Dr. John Harvey Kellogg grew up like a son to Ellen White. The Whites assisted him financially in his medical training and strongly supported him in developing the health work in Battle Creek.[57] But in 1904 Dr. Kellogg had charted a course that could potentially divide the church. In a message to be given at the Lake Union constituency meeting in late May, 1904, Ellen White spoke of her sympathy for her old friend but that "unless he changes his course, and takes an entirely different course, he will be lost to the cause of God. . . . I have lain awake night after night, studying how I could help Dr. Kellogg. . . . I have spent nearly whole nights in prayer for him."

She would do her best to stand in the breach between Dr. Kellogg and church leaders. She wrote to Elders [A. G.] Daniells and [W. W.] Prescott, informing them that through a vision she knew that "now is our time to save Dr. Kellogg."

She pressed her point, born out of a kind heart: "Not one of us is above temptation. There is a work that Dr. Kellogg is educated to perform as no other man in our ranks can perform. . . . We are to draw with all our power, not making accusations, not prescribing what he must do, but letting him see that we are not willing that any should perish." Then she asked, "Is it not worth the trial?"[58]

Matters did not develop as Ellen White had hoped. Prospects of unity were bleak. Yet she wrote to Elder Daniells: "If we can do him [Kellogg] good in any way, let us show that we do not want to hurt him, but to help him. Let us avoid everything that would provoke retaliation. Let us give no occasion for contention."[59]

Earlier, during the dark days of the Civil War, Adventists were feeling their way along regarding noncombatancy. Though the various State governments, as well as the Federal, had granted recognition to Seventh-day Adventists as noncombatants, the issue was far from clear among field commanders, as well as among many young Adventists.

Enoch Hayes, who had joined the army, was disfellowshipped from the "membership of the Battle Creek church, by a unanimous vote of the church, March 4, 1865." When Ellen White heard of this action she responded with that touch of kindness that characterized her ministry. She expressed her conviction that the young man should not be disfellowshipped for following his conscience and answering the call of his country. The result: The action was rescinded and the young man remained a member in "good and regular standing." Kindness overruled.[60]

Endnotes

1. James cut hay in the summer of 1848 and earned $40, part of the money going to clothing and the rest for travel to meet speaking appointments—*Bio.*, vol. 1, p. 140.
2. *Ibid.*, p. 205.
3. Virgil Robinson, *James White* (Washington, D.C.: Review and Herald Publishing Association, 1976), pp. 81-87; W. C. White, "Sketches and Memories of James and Ellen G. White, XXIV—Settling in Battle Creek," *Review and Herald,* Aug. 22, 1935.
4. *Bio.*, vol. 1, p. 230.
5. *Ibid.*, vol. 2, pp. 439, 440.
6. *Ibid.*, vol. 3, p. 293. At the Minneapolis Conference, 1888, the officers had rented two elegant rooms, richly furnished. Ellen White demurred and found another room in the boardinghouse, plainly furnished.—*Ibid.*, p. 390.
7. *Manuscript Releases,* vol. 10, p. 27 (Hereafter, *MR*).
8. *Bio.*, vol. 4, pp. 138-140.
9. *Ibid.*, p. 343.
10. Emmett K. VandeVere, "Years of Expansion, 1865-1885," in Land, *Adventism in America*, p. 67.
11. Manuscript 3, 1888, cited in Arthur White, *Ellen G. White, Messenger to the Remnant,* Ellen G. White Publications, 1956, p. 123.
12. *General Conference Bulletin,* March 20, 1891, p. 184.
13. *SDAE,* vol. 10, 1996, p. 410.
14. *Review and Herald,* August 30, 1923. See also *Ibid.*, July 26, 1906, for Ellen White's account of her ministry to orphans and others in her home.
15. *Bio.*, vol. 4, p. 44.
16. *Ibid.*, p. 69.
17. *Ibid.*, p. 266.
18. *Ibid.*, p. 371.
19. Schwarz, *Light Bearers,* p. 311.
20. Christian, *Fruitage of Spiritual Gifts*, p. 49.
21. Letter 4, 1850, *MR,* vol. 1, p. 31.
22. For background on this experience and how Ellen White related to her specific duty in delivering divine messages, see *Testimonies,* vol. 1, pp. 583-585.
23. *Bio.*, vol. 2, pp. 383, 384.
24. *Ibid.*, vol. 3, pp. 425, 426.
25. *Ibid.*, p. 164.
26. *Ibid.*, vol. 6, p. 389.
27. *Ibid.*, vol. 1, p. 205.
28. *Ibid.*, pp. 295, 301.
29. *Ibid.*, vol. 2, pp. 225, 226.
30. *Ibid.*, p. 252.
31. *Ibid.*, vol. 3, pp. 36, 37.
32. *Ibid.*, p. 42.
33. *Ibid.*, p. 44.
34. *Ibid.*, pp. 142, 143. See also p. 104.
35. *Ibid.*, p. 241.
36. *Ibid.*, p. 242.
37. Ellen White's two years in Europe seemed to surpass even her North American schedule for prodigious activity in writing, speaking, and traveling, often under most severe conditions. See Delafield, *Ellen G. White in Europe.*
38. *Historical Sketches,* p. 123.
39. *Life Sketches,* p. 70.
40. See pp. 89, 90.
41. *Bio.*, vol. 2, pp. 157, 159.
42. *Ibid.*, pp. 160-170.
43. See *Ibid.*, pp. 277-284 for how these allegations were handled in Battle Creek in 1870.
44. *Ibid.*, vol. 3, pp. 344, 345.
45. *Ibid.*, vol. 1, p. 337.
46. Letter 1a, 1881.
47. Letter 5a, 1881.
48. Letter 8a, 1881.
49. *Review and Herald,* July 19, 1881.
50. *Bio.*, vol. 1, pp. 468, 469.
51. *Ibid.*, vol. 2, p. 161.
52. *Ibid.*, pp. 162, 165.
53. *Ibid.*, pp. 188, 189.
54. *Bio.*, vol. 3, pp. 88, 89.
55. Maxwell, *Tell It to the World,* pp. 171-173.
56. *In Heavenly Places,* p. 272.
57. Richard W. Schwarz, *John Harvey Kellogg, M. D.* (Nashville, TN: Southern Publishing Association, 1970), p. 30.
58. *Bio.*, vol. 5, pp. 331-333.
59. *Ibid.*, p. 339.
60. George R. Knight, "1862-1865: Adventists at War," *Adventist Review,* April 4, 1991.

Study Questions

1. How do you account for the remarkable confidence that strong-minded men had so early in the ministry of Ellen White?

2. How would you respond to the suggestion that Ellen White did not live what she advocated?

3. Review the events that prompted Ellen White's remarkable generosity and frugality.

4. What examples would you give that illustrate Ellen White's courage and perseverance?

5. How did Ellen White use courage and common sense in rehabilitating her husband James in the winter of 1866-1867?

CHAPTER 9

Humor, Common Sense, and a Practical Counselor

"Let us pursue the things that make for peace and the things by which one may edify another" (Rom. 14:19).

Ellen White has been stereotyped by the uninformed as a grim, severe kill-joy. Far from the truth! L. H. Christian reported the memories of his wife's mother who lived in the White home while she was Ellen White's secretary. She remembered especially "the sunny spirit of the home" and Ellen White's "kindly humor and good sense."[1]

Humor

Often Mrs. White's writings reveal a touch of humor. In 1882 she had just moved from Oakland to Healdsburg. At 55 she enjoyed buying grain and hay, a cow with its calf, and horses for farm work and transportation. One of her horses she named Dolly—a horse that seemed allergic to work. Ellen White wrote, "She stares at the mountains and hills as if she was a tourist viewing the scenery."[2]

In 1885 she was sailing for Europe on the *S.S. Cephalonia,* which was to depart on Sabbath. Her party made arrangements to embark on Friday afternoon in order to be settled for the Sabbath. She noted in her diary, "We accomplished this nearly."[3]

While in Italy, 1886, she was writing about the ministerial personnel in Torre Pellice. The minister in charge was great on planning, but was accomplishing little. Ellen White depicted his efforts as "the array of Quaker guns."[4]

A few months later, still in Italy, she was enjoying some sunny days after a stretch of rain, and wrote in her diary: "We drove very slowly, for the horse, although strong, had no idea of hurting his constitution."[5]

After a boat trip, she penned, "When I got off the boat, when I walked up through the streets, it seemed to me as though I was still on the boat, and I would step so high that people must have thought I was drunk."[6]

Ellen White's oldest brother, John, apparently was a poor correspondent. In a January 21, 1873, letter to him, Ellen gently chided him with humor: "Dear Brother John: I have written you several letters but have not heard one word from you. We concluded you must be dead, but then again we thought if this was the case, your children would write us."[7]

She showed her humor as well as her practical bent when she wrote about the careless dress of certain women: "Their clothing often looks as if it flew and lit upon their persons."[8] Or, "Sisters when about their work should not put on clothing which would make them look like images to frighten the crows from the corn."[9]

At the time when Ellen White was issuing warnings to safeguard the ownership of the Battle Creek Tabernacle[10] she received a letter from A. T. Jones challenging her to provide the names of those involved in the effort to take control of the property. Realizing the true intent of his request, Ellen White responded to her secretary, Dores Robinson, that "if she should write to Brother Jones at all, she would tell him that everything is written in the books of heaven, but she does not have these books at her disposal to send him."[11]

Mrs. White knew how to handle potentially embarrassing public moments. Son Willie frequently assisted his mother in her speaking tours. During a Sabbath sermon in St. Helena, California, Willie sat on the platform while his mother spoke. Noticing a ripple of suppressed laughter in the audience, Mrs. White turned to find him taking a nap. She apologized with a touch of humor: "When Willie was a baby, I used to take him into the pulpit and let him sleep in a basket beneath the pulpit, and he has never gotten over the habit."[12]

In her late years at Elmshaven, Ellen White was given cold-mitten friction treatments. That meant standing in a tub while someone applied cold water and then rubbed her with mittens to increase circulation. Twice a week she was given a salt rub ("salt glow").

One day, sensing a difference in the liquid, she wet her finger and tasted it. The worker had used sugar by mistake! With good humor, Ellen White observed: "Just trying to sweeten me up, huh?"[13]

Common-Sense Interpreter of Truth

One of the soundest principles for getting a picture of Ellen White (as well as the intent of her writings) is to study the *time, place*, and *circumstance* that governed what she wrote.[14]

In other words, Ellen White's plea throughout her ministry was for common sense. For example, the constituency for the church school at St. Helena, California, in 1904, had a problem. Some strongly felt that no provision should be made for children under the age of ten. Why? Because Mrs. White had counseled some years earlier that "parents should be the only teachers of their children until they have reached eight or ten years of age."[15] Others felt that some children would be better off in school than roaming the village while their parents either worked at the hospital or for other reasons were unable to supervise their children.

The problem was not confined to St. Helena; church schools were being established throughout the world wherever Adventists planted churches. So the question everywhere was: What shall we do with Mrs. White's counsel regarding when to start children in school?

Ellen White was at that St. Helena school board meeting (it was held in her home at Elmshaven) and took the initiative in resolving the impasse. She reviewed her frequently emphasized counsel regarding parental responsibilities and firm discipline in the home. Then she indicated that she too had observed parental neglect, with certain children running loose (especially on the sanitarium grounds), "sharp-eyed, lynx-eyed, wandering about with nothing to do . . . getting into mischief"—not the best recommendation of Adventist decorum before the sanitarium guests!

Under the circumstances, she said: "The very best thing that can be done is to have a school . . . for those who [should] have the restraining influence upon them which a schoolteacher should exert."

Then she explained her earlier statements about holding children out of school until they are ten —a teaching that some were faithfully trying to implement. She spoke clearly: "I wanted to tell you that there was not a Sabbath keeping school when the light was given to me that the children should not attend school until they were old enough to be instructed. They should be taught at home to know what proper manners were when they went to school, and not be led astray. The wickedness carried on in the common schools is almost beyond conception. That is how it is."

She went further, expressing her concern about those who make an unreasonable application of her writings: "My mind has been greatly stirred in regard to the idea, 'Why, Sister White has said so and so, . . . and therefore we are going right up to it.' God wants us all to have common sense, and He wants us to reason from common sense. Circumstances alter conditions. Circumstances change the relation of things."[16]

Along with key words that best describe the real Ellen White, we must include "common sense." The principles she disclosed were clear, timely, and timeless. But applying them required sanctified common sense.

Ellen White understood well the ellipse of truth.[17] She knew that theology without common sense and a corresponding life style could create prejudice against the gospel. Throughout her writings she emphasized that word and deed, doctrine and life, should never be separated.[18]

Common sense is not to negate Bible counsel; sanctified common sense applies immutable truths to the human situation, taking all circumstances into account. Common sense does not lower God's instructions regarding human thought and behavior; it lifts people up to them, within the capabilities and possibilities of time, place, and circumstance. Principles are timeless; applying them requires common sense. On one occasion when asked about certain Sabbath school practices, Ellen White answered: "Exactly; it is not the place for it. That is to be done; but it has its time and place."[19]

For example, she wrote extensively about health principles. She stated clearly certain health practices that were far in advance of the conventional thinking of her day. But these principles must be understood and applied through common sense.

Regarding eating two meals a day, she wrote: "Some eat three meals a day, when two would be more conducive to physical and spiritual health."[20] But she also wrote: "The practice of eating but two meals a day is generally found a benefit to health; yet under some circumstances persons may require a third meal."[21]

Further revealing her common sense, she wrote in 1903: "I eat only two meals a day. But I do not think that the number of meals should be made a test. If there are those who are better in health when eating three meals, it is their privilege to have three."[22]

Whatever Is Best

The principle of what is *best* under all circumstances, not merely what is *good*, should be the Christian's benchmark. Too often, the good is the enemy of the best.

In other areas of healthful living also, Ellen White's counsel has been beneficial for millions. Why? Because of her principle of common sense—for example, in the area of food combinations[23] or recommending the same health practices for everyone.[24] Beyond most people of her time she saw the close connection between vitality, good health generally, and exercise. Not only exercise but having the right attitude when one exercises! It was all a matter of common sense.[25]

In conducting public work, especially in our health institutions, Ellen White admonished: "Act so that the patients will see that Seventh-day Adventists are a people who have common sense."[26]

Further, Adventist ministerial and medical workers must not create the impression, as some other Christian groups were doing, that the sick could be healed by prayer alone. Again, Ellen White appealed to common sense.[27]

In every area, it seemed, she had common-sense counsel. Some ministers were falling victim to the prevailing elocution fashion of preaching in an unnatural voice pitch, far from a conversational style that would best reflect calm reason. She appealed to ministers to study the "wisest manner" of using their vocal organs "by the exercise of a little common sense."[28]

Ellen White was concerned about how the youth were educated for the real world. No one seemed to be more optimistic about the possibilities open to industrious, dedicated young people. At the same time, she was troubled with those who "are merely useless creatures, only good to breathe, eat, wear, chat, and talk nonsense. . . . But few of the youth show real sound judgment and good common sense. They lead a butterfly life with no special object in view."[29]

She often wrote that manual training as a practical preparation for life must be part of Christian education. Such training would make a person preparing for the various scientific and academic professions even more fit for his or her duties: "An education derived chiefly from books leads to superficial thinking. Practical work encourages close observation and independent thought. Rightly performed, it tends to develop that practical wisdom which we call common sense."[30]

After seeing worship services in some churches, Mrs. White observed: "It is sometimes more difficult to discipline the singers and keep them in working order, than to improve the habits of praying and exhorting. Many want to do things after their own style; they object to consultation, and are impatient under leadership. Well-matured plans are needed in the service of God. Common sense is an excellent thing in the worship of the Lord."[31]

This principle of common sense should be applied in all areas of Christian living, such as in the kind of clothing one wears.[32]

From time to time, people would push the dress question into a church controversy. Here again, Ellen White used common sense and gave practical advice: "The dress question is not to be our present truth. . . . Follow the customs in dress so far as they conform to health principles. Let our sisters dress plainly, as many do, having the dress of good, durable material, appropriate for this age, and let not the dress question fill the mind."[33]

At Christiana (Oslo), Norway, in 1885, Ellen White counseled about 120 new Adventists, some needing guidance pertaining to children attending public schools on Sabbath, and Sabbath business operations. Some, however, were overconscientious "in making the matter of dress of first importance, criticizing articles of dress worn by others, and standing ready to condemn everyone who did not exactly meet their ideas. A few condemned pictures, urging that they are prohibited by the second commandment, and that everything of this kind should be destroyed."[34]

What problem did she see? She feared that "unbelievers" would get the impression that Adventists "were a set of fanatics and extremists, and that their peculiar faith rendered them unkind, uncourteous, and really unchristian in character." Further, "one fanatic, with his strong spirit and radical ideas, who will oppress the conscience of those who want to do right, will do great harm."[35] As time went on, she was pleased that common sense prevailed.

In her sermons and in many letters to young people she knew well, Mrs. White emphasized the need for common sense in choosing a life mate.[36]

Her far-ranging counsel included direct and candid guidance to married church members. She pointed out that home tensions often were caused by spousal irresponsibility and the lack of common sense.[37]

Practical Counselor

Practical religion seemed to be the harmonizing theme throughout Ellen White's writings. She saw a direct connection between doing church work and properly representing the character of God. When the young Australian publishing house was near bankruptcy, she pointed out the problems: Job estimates were bid too low, cost-control management was lacking, office overhead was too high. Then she wrote: "I was shown that this was not the way to do business. It is not the will of our heavenly Father that His work should be so conducted as to be a continual embarrassment. . . . Some of the workers were not willing to help and instruct their fellow workmen. . . . The workers in the Echo office had very little insight into the right methods of obtaining success."

She ended her counsel with these words: "Brethren and sisters connected with the work of the Echo office, these words I have written were spoken to you by my guide."[38]

During those difficult days, when the future of a college in Australia seemed uncertain, Ellen White was confident that the land purchased at such a "cheap price" would indeed fulfill all the needs of a future school. But none of the committee members were convinced regarding what she had been shown. She was distressed at their "unsanctified caution."[39]

In a letter to Marian Davis, her confidante and efficient helper in bookmaking, Mrs. White used her practical imagination regarding Avondale, and, based on the counsel of her Guide, wrote: "I have planned what can be raised in different places. I have said, 'Here can be a crop of alfalfa; there can be strawberries; here can be sweet corn and common corn; and this ground will raise good potatoes, while that will raise good fruit of all kinds.'"[40]

Part of the problem in the early days in Australia was that not much had been done along the lines of scientific farming. Ellen White knew that if Avondale would show the way in proper soil management, more than just the college would benefit. She knew that poverty in that area of Australia would be greatly reduced when people saw how successfully they could raise their own food. In a letter to Edson, she emphasized what she had been exemplifying in the development of orchards at the school and on her own two acres: "The cultivation of our land requires the exercise of all the brainpower and tact we possess. The lands around us testify to the indolence of men. . . . We hope to see intelligent farmers, who will be rewarded for their earnest labor. . . . If we accomplish this, we shall have done good missionary work."[41]

Healing of Herbert Lacey

Practical counsel was often needed in the treatment of the sick. Professor Herbert Lacey, leading out in the school program at Avondale early in 1897, was quickly devastated by typhoid fever. He lost twenty pounds in one week; his vitality was low and his fever high. Convinced of Dr. Kellogg's success with hydrotherapy, the medical team applied ice to reduce the fever and to restore circulation in "his bowels." Hearing of this, Ellen White dashed off a telegram to the medical workers: "Use no ice, but hot applications."

Why did she do this, and do it with dispatch? She saw too many dying of typhoid, largely because of conventional drugs that wasted the patient's ability to overcome the enervation brought on by the drugs. But she also knew that hydrotherapy should be used wisely. With Lacey's low vitality, ice on his head and body would further weaken him.

Mrs. White later wrote of this serious event: "I was not going to be so delicate in regard to the physician as to permit Herbert Lacey's life to be put out. . . . There might be cases where the ice applications would work well. But books with prescriptions that are followed to the letter in regard to ice applications should have further explanations, that persons with low vitality should use hot in the place of cold. . . . To go just as the book of Dr. Kellogg shall direct without considering the subject is simply wild."[42]

Of Ellen White's practicality, as well as her common sense, her granddaughter Grace White Jacques once said: "I recall a young nurse who had only a few clothes, and so Grandmother gave her three dress lengths of material, one of red, one blue, one a golden color. She told this young lady, as she did several young women, that she should have at least one red dress."[43] Ellen White never lost her ability to relate to people in practical ways.

Endnotes

1. Christian, *Fruitage of Spiritual Gifts,* p. 48.
2. *Bio.,* vol. 3, p. 195.
3. *Ibid.,* p. 290.
4. Delafield, *Ellen G. White in Europe,* p. 174.
5. *Ibid.,* p. 177.
6. Manuscript 4, 1878, cited in *MR,* vol. 5, p. 178.
7. Glen Baker, "The Humor of Ellen White," *Adventist Review,* April 30, 1987.
8. *Child Guidance,* p. 415.
9. *Testimonies,* vol. 1, p. 464.
10. *Bio.,* vol. 6, pp. 124-129.
11. D. E. Robinson to W. C. White, Sept. 30, 1906.
12. Baker, *op. cit.*
13. *Ibid.*
14. See p. 395. "Regarding the testimonies, nothing is ignored; nothing is cast aside; but time and place must be considered. Nothing must be done untimely. Some matters must be withheld because some persons would make an improper use of the light given. Every jot and tittle is essential and must appear at an opportune time. In the past, the testimonies were carefully prepared before they were sent out for publication. And all matter is still carefully studied after the first writing." —*Selected Messages,* book 1, p. 57.
15. *Testimonies,* vol. 3, p. 137.
16. *Bio.,* vol. 5, pp. 312-315. Read the whole section, pages 315-317, for additional comments that display Ellen White's clear principles regarding early education, for whom and how it should be provided.
17. See Appendix P.
18. "We are to be guided by true theology and common sense. Our souls are to be surrounded by the atmosphere of heaven. Men and women are to watch themselves; they are to be constantly on guard, allowing no word or act that would cause their good to be evil spoken of. He who professes to be a follower of Christ is to watch himself, keeping himself pure and undefiled in thought, word, and deed. His influence upon others is to be uplifting. His life is to reflect the bright beams of the Sun of Righteousness."—*Counsels to Parents, Teachers, and Students,* p. 257. See pp. 305-307, 311, 326, 400-402, 436 for further examples of Ellen White's appeal for common sense.
19. *Counsels on Sabbath School Work,* p. 186.
20. *Testimonies,* vol. 4, pp. 416, 417.
21. *The Ministry of Healing,* p. 321. See also *Education,* p. 205.
22. *Counsels on Diet and Foods,* p. 178.
23. "In the use of foods we should exercise good judgment, and sound sense. When we find that something does not agree with us, we need not write letters of inquiry [to Ellen White] to learn the cause of the disturbance. We are to use our reason. Change the diet; use less of some of the foods; try other preparations. Soon we shall know the effect that certain combinations have on us. We are not machines; we are intelligent human beings; and we are to exercise our common sense. We can experiment with different combinations of foods." —*The Kress Collection,* p. 144.
24. "There is real common sense in dietetic reform. The subject should be studied broadly and deeply, and no one should criticize others because their practice is not, in all things, in harmony with his own. It is impossible to make an unvarying rule to regulate everyone's habits, and no one should think himself a criterion for all. Not all can eat the same things. Foods that are palatable and wholesome to one person may be distasteful, and even harmful, to another. Some cannot use milk, while others thrive on it. Some persons cannot digest peas and beans; others find them wholesome. For some the coarser grain preparations are good food, while others cannot use them."—*The Ministry of Healing,* p. 319.

    "We don't make the health reform an iron bedstead, cutting people off or stretching them out to fit it. One person cannot be a standard for everybody else. What we want is a little sprinkling of good common sense. Don't be extremists. If you err, it would be better to err on the side of the people than on the side where you cannot reach them. Do not be peculiar for the sake of being peculiar. Away with cake. Persons may kill themselves with sweets. More harm is done to children by sweets than by anything else."—*Sermons and Talks,* vol. 1, p. 12.
25. "The world is full of women with but little vitality and less common sense. Society is in great need of healthful, sensible young women who are not afraid to work and soil their hands. God gave them hands to employ in useful labor. God did not give us the wonderful human machinery of the body to become paralyzed by inaction. The living machinery God designed should be in daily activity, and in this activity or motion of the machinery is its preserving power. Manual labor quickens the circulation of the blood. The more active the circulation the more free will be the blood from obstructions and impurities. The blood nourishes the body. The health of the body depends upon the healthful circulation of the blood. If work is performed without the heart being in it, it is simply drudgery, and the benefit which should result from the exercise is not gained."—*Signs of the Times,* April 29, 1885.
26. *Evangelism,* p. 540.
27. "Do not let the idea prevail that the Health Retreat is a place where the sick are healed by the prayer of faith. There are instances when this will be done, and we need to have faith in God constantly. Let no one think that those who have abused themselves and taken no intelligent care of themselves can come to the Health Retreat and be healed by the prayer of faith, for this is presumption. I see so little wisdom, so little common sense exercised by some of our brethren, that my heart is sick, sore, and distressed. They do not have sensible ideas and do not honor God. They have need of a divine touch. If the idea should once prevail that the sick can come to the Institute to be cured by the prayer of faith, you will have such a state of things there that you

cannot now discern even if I should point it out to you in the best English language I could command." —*MR,* vol. 7, p. 370 (1886).

28. "I was shown that our ministers were doing themselves great injury by carelessness in the use of their vocal organs. Their attention was called to this important matter, and cautions and instructions were given them by the Spirit of God. It was their duty to learn the wisest manner of using these organs. The voice, this gift of heaven, is a powerful faculty for good, and if not perverted, would glorify God. All that was essential was to study and conscientiously follow a few simple rules. But instead of educating themselves, as they might have done by the exercise of a little common sense, they employed a professor of elocution."—*Testimonies for the Church,* vol. 4, p. 604. See also *Medical Ministry,* pp. 264, 265.
29. *Testimonies,* vol. 1, p. 394.
30. *Education,* p. 220.
31. *Evangelism,* p. 505.
32. "Christians should not take pains to make themselves a gazing stock by dressing differently from the world. But if, when following out their convictions of duty in respect to dressing modestly and healthfully, they find themselves out of fashion, they should not change their dress in order to be like the world; but they should manifest a noble independence and moral courage to be right, if all the world differ from them. If the world introduce a modest, convenient, and healthful mode of dress, which is in accordance with the Bible, it will not change our relation to God or to the world to adopt such a style of dress. Christians should follow Christ and make their dress conform to God's Word. They should shun extremes. They should humbly pursue a straightforward course, irrespective of applause or of censure, and should cling to the right because of its own merits." —*Testimonies,* vol. 1, pp. 458, 459 (1864).
33. *Ibid.,* p. 333. For the full Manuscript 167, 1897 wherein Ellen White stated guiding principles in dress reform, see the Appendix in D. E. Robinson, *The Story of Our Health Message* (Nashville: Southern Publishing Association, 1965, Third edition), pp. 441-445.
34. *Selected Messages,* book 2, p. 319.
35. *Ibid.,* pp. 318.
36. "The youth trust altogether too much to impulse. They should not give themselves away too easily nor be captivated too readily by the winning exterior of the lover. . . . Common sense is needed here if anywhere; but the fact is, it has little to do in the matter."—*Review and Herald,* Jan. 26, 1886. See *Messages to Young People,* p. 450.
37. In appealing to a self-centered wife, Ellen White wrote: "Do you think it is no disappointment to your husband that he finds you what God has shown me you are? Did he marry you with the expectation that you would bear no burdens, share no perplexities, exercise no self-denial? Did he think that you would feel under no obligation to control self, to be cheerful, kind, and forbearing, and to exercise common sense?"—*MR,* vol. 16, p. 310.
38. *Bio.,* vol. 4, pp. 26, 27.
39. *Ibid.,* p. 215.
40. *Ibid.,* p. 154. For further reading on the divinely guided development of Avondale College, see p. 355.
41. *Ibid.,* p. 224.
42. *Ibid.,* pp. 292, 293.
43. "My 'Special' Grandmother," *The Youth's Instructor,* Dec. 5, 1961.

Study Questions

1. If you were to explain the value of "common sense," how would you begin in the light of the fact that God's Word, not our personal opinion, is the test of truth?

2. How would you counter the charge that Ellen White was a "kill-joy" and a cranky "saint"?

3. What is the main principle that determines how to apply common sense in all aspects of life?

CHAPTER 10

The American Pioneer and the Victorian Woman

"She lifted herself from a sickbed and took her first, feeble, tentative steps toward becoming both a Victorian woman and an Adventist prophet."[1]

Of all the female leaders of social or religious groups in the nineteenth century, Ellen White was virtually unique. She combined the rugged characteristics of the American pioneer with the virtues of the typical Victorian woman.

At Ease With Horses

Here was a once-frail, five-foot-two woman who could harness and ride horses as well as most men.[2] Further, based on her own experience, she strongly urged that boys should learn, either at home or in school, how "to make a bed and put a room in order, to wash dishes, to prepare a meal, to wash and repair his own clothing." Girls should "learn to harness and drive a horse, and to use the saw and hammer, as well as the rake and hoe."[3]

Familiar With Hardships

Ellen White is most often remembered as a powerful speaker and a prolific writer, but her contemporaries knew her also as a competent homemaker and cheerful mother. All this was not easy in a day without electricity or running water. Not easy, either, when neither she nor her husband received any regular income for years. And not having a "fixed place of abode" made life downright difficult.[4]

Skillful at Sewing

But the Whites, with two of their children, survived, as did most other families with the pioneer spirit of the nineteenth century. Throughout most of her long life Ellen White did her own sewing. At one time she wrote: "sheets and pillowcases and my clothes are in good order."[5]

On a late November day, 1865, in Rochester, New York, she penned a note to James: "Last night was a cold night. I dreaded sleeping alone in a cold room, but my nice warm nightdress was finished and I put it on and it was real comfortable. . . . My sewing is going off bravely without my taxing myself at all."[6]

A Typical Day

One gets some insight into Ellen White's daily life by reading her diaries and letters. In an 1873 letter to Elder and Mrs. D. M. Canright, she wrote, in part: "I have felt for some time that I ought to write you, but have not found the time. I have arisen at half past five o'clock in the morning, helped Lucinda wash dishes, have written until dark, then done necessary sewing, sitting up until near midnight; yet we have not gotten sick. I have done the washings for the family after my day's writing was done. I have frequently been so weary as to stagger like an intoxicated person, but, praise the Lord, I have been sustained."[7]

Keen Purchaser

At one point in her busy European schedule, Ellen White needed relief from her unrelenting writing and speaking appointments. For diversion, she and Sara McEnterfer, her traveling companion, sewed for themselves and for others. Some women, noticing that she bought with thrift and taste, often wanted her to help with their shopping.[8]

But with everything, even sewing, she cautioned balance and urged maintaining right priorities. Speaking of mothers, she wrote: "Let her keep cheerful and buoyant. Instead of spending every moment in endless sewing, make the evening a pleasant social season, a family reunion, after the day's duties."[9]

Enthusiastic Gardener

Ellen White was an avid gardener, not only to satisfy household needs for vegetables and fruit, but also to beautify the home with fresh flowers. Springtime in Battle Creek (1859) stirred the gardening blood of this busy, 31-year-old mother of three. On a cold, windy March 24, her diary reads: "Arose early. Assisted my husband and Brother Richard [Godsmark] in taking up a currant bush to plant in our garden."

The weather was warmer on March 30 and she "set out the raspberries. Went to Manchesters' for strawberry plants. Got some currant bushes. . . . Sent off three letters."

The next day she planted "a patch of strawberries." Two weeks later she wrote: "Spent most of the day making a garden for my children. Feel willing to make home as pleasant for them as I can, that home may be the pleasantest place of any to them."[10]

From their small home in Washington, Iowa, she wrote to Edson: "We are in the midst of flowers of almost every description, but the most beautiful of all is to be surrounded with roses on every hand, of every color and so fragrant. The prairie queen is just opening, also the Baltimore bell. Peonies have been very lovely and fragrant, but now they are fast going to decay. We have had strawberries for several days."[11]

Gardening for Ellen White meant work, pleasant work. Writing from Oakland, California, to her husband at Battle Creek, she told of a new friend who shared plants for her garden: "I set out my things in my garden of the new house by moonlight and by the aid of lamplight. The two Marys tried to have me wait until morning, but I would not listen to them. We had a beautiful shower last night. I was glad then I persevered in setting out my plants."[12]

In 1881, the Whites were living again in Battle Creek. This time, writing to Mary, her daughter-in-law, Ellen White wanted items from her Oakland garden: "I have a favor to ask of you. Will you get a small box and put in it small pink roots and slips, a few choice rose cuttings, fuchsia, and geraniums, and send [it to] me?"

A few days later she wrote again: "We have the most beautiful situation in Michigan. . . . I have been gathering up shrubs and flowers until we have quite a garden. Peonies, I have a large number of them; hope to get California pinks. I want to get some of that green bordering we get from Sister Rollin. . . . I wish I had some seeds from California."[13]

This long and avid interest in the garden and orchard prepared her for the challenge in Australia during the 1890s. When she noticed that most of her encouragement for expanding agriculture development fell on pessimistic ears, she declared boldly that the men of the area were wrong. In fact, she said, they were bearing "false witness" concerning the land.

She led the way, by example and by visionary exhortation. The result was reviewed in a letter written on February 3, 1896: "We have the testimony that with care taken of the trees and vegetables in the dry season, we shall have good results. Our trees are doing well. . . . I can testify by experience that false witness has been borne of this land. On the school ground, they have tomatoes, squashes, potatoes, and melons. . . . We know the land will do well with proper care."

A few days later, she wrote in her diary that she arose at 4:30, and was in the garden by 5:00, "spading up the ground and preparing to set out my flowers." Then, with two helpers, she set out twenty-eight tomato plants. The next morning she was in the orchard, "tying up the trees. A tuft of grass is put between the stake and the trees so that the tree shall not be marred."[14]

Intrepid Traveler

Ellen White's pioneer spirit was probably best manifested in her remarkable travel itinerary. By 1885 she had crossed the United States from California to Michigan about twenty-four times by train, only sixteen years after the transcontinental connection had been made at Promintory, Utah! Obviously, these trips were nothing like what people today can even remember, nothing resembling the "romance" that people attached to rail travel in the first half of the twentieth century.[15]

Wooden passenger cars, hazardous in accidents, were the order of the day, not being replaced by all-steel cars until 1907. "Seats were straight backed and thinly cushioned, if at all. A coal stove furnished the only heat; candles and oil lamps provided the light. Open platform vestibules offered little protection from the weather when walking from one car to another."[16] The engineer "could be identified by his aroma of bourbon as readily as a drummer by his sample case."[17]

The first forty years of rail travel to the West were the "heyday of the miner, the cowboy, the train robber, and the bad man, any and all of whom you might find riding the plush or the wooden slats of the steam cars." The country going west "was bare and harsh, buffeted by cruel winters, baked by torrid summers. Rain, when it came, was a destructive torrent. Droughts occurred at regular intervals. . . . In 1874, with most railroad construction halted by the financial panic of 1873, the grasshoppers struck, eating every growing thing from the Canadian border to northern Texas. A Union Pacific train at Kearney [Nebraska] was stalled in a three-foot drift of 'hoppers.'"[18]

In 1876 the conventional travel time between the Pacific coast and New York was seven days and nights, with changes of cars at Omaha and Chicago.[19]

Three times Ellen White took the hazardous ocean trip to Oregon (1878, 1880, 1884) when facilities were still primitive. Of her visit in 1878 when she was 50, a worker's wife reported: "Sister White was so ambitious when here, when contemplating work that was to be done, that it really seemed that she forgot her years. Her visit to Oregon was of the most valuable benefit to the work of Present Truth [sic] here."[20]

In 1852, the Whites left Rochester, New York, for a two-month trip to New England by horse and carriage. James arranged the itinerary and informed Adventists through the church paper as to the time and place they could expect the Whites. The schedule was grueling; one leg of 100 miles was allotted only two days! But with good weather and no breakdowns, they managed to meet their appointments. While they bumped along in an open carriage, James thought of what he would write to the *Review* and *Youth's Instructor*. When they stopped to let Charlie, their horse, eat, he would write the articles "on the cover of our dinner box, or the top of his hat."[21]

Ellen White's experience trying to get to a camp meeting appointment in Williamsport, Pennsylvania, early in June, 1889, well illustrates her persevering, pioneering spirit. This was the year of the heavy rain and the Johnstown Flood. Many roads and bridges were washed away enroute. The train moved slowly from Battle Creek. When they reached Elmira, New York, they were advised to return home. But Mrs. White (now 61) and Sara McEnterfer forged ahead. When the train could go no further, these two women hired a carriage. When the carriage was forced to stop, the women walked—

completing the last 40 miles in four days.

The phenomenal journey is described in Ellen White's report in the *Review and Herald*, July 30, 1889. In that report she wrote: "We were obliged to walk miles on this journey, and it seemed marvelous that I could endure to travel as I did. Both of my ankles were broken years ago, and ever since they have been weak. Before leaving Battle Creek for Kansas, I sprained one of my ankles, and was confined to crutches for some time; but in this emergency I felt no weakness or inconvenience, and traveled safely over the rough, sliding rocks."[22] At the Williamsport camp meeting, she spoke thirteen times, including all the early-morning meetings—and that without a public address system!

This persevering, cheerful, pioneer spirit was evident, as usual, when the Whites crossed the Mississippi River in December 1857. A foot of water flowed over the ice, other teams with wagons had broken through—but the White party pressed on. In Iowa, through fierce, cold winds, with their horses breaking paths through high snow, they finally reached their destination.[23]

The Victorian Lady

Yet, though a hardy example of the rugged pioneer woman of the nineteenth century, Ellen White displayed the characteristics of the Victorian lady. Researcher Kathleen Joyce noted a widely quoted passage by Barbara Welter who listed four virtues by which the Victorian woman was judged: ". . . piety, purity, submissiveness, and domesticity. Put them all together and they spell mother, daughter, sister, wife—woman. Without them, no matter whether there was fame, achievement, or wealth, all was ashes. With them she was promised happiness and power."[24]

Joyce added the area of "women's health and medical care" as another special characteristic of the Victorian woman. She noted that Ellen White's career was a constant balance between fulfilling her Victorian obligations (marriage, motherhood, homemaker) and responding to her prophetic calling. "Her frailty, the visions over which she had no control, her unwillingness, particularly in the early years, to accept a leadership position that required her to be more than God's amanuensis, reveal a particularly feminine pattern of religious prophecy. It was a pattern that accommodated the need for women to be servants rather than masters, and served to reinforce the comforting perception of women as passive vessels through whom God and men achieve great works. By adhering to this pattern, Ellen White became the type of female prophet that Victorian America was able to tolerate."[25]

Mrs. White manifested one of the many characteristics of the Victorian model by her frequent use of euphemisms. For example, in referring to sexual intercourse, she used phrases such as "privilege of the marriage relation,"[26] "marriage privileges,"[27] and "privacy and privileges of the family relation."[28]

Her Victorian euphemisms were not mere prudery. She was a loving, devoted wife who won and held the admiration of her husband until the day he died. But she understood mental health and how marital priorities should be established. Her frequent counsel to others regarding marriage relations was generated not only through divine inspiration but articulated out of personal experience. She not only verbally advocated civility and Christian modesty, but practiced it with a husband who adored her.

For example, note her wedding-night tip to Daniel T. Bourdeau, a nervous young man of 26. Bourdeau, ordained at age 23, looked for a wife for three years. In 1861 he was married to Marion Saxby in Bakersfield, Vermont, with James White officiating in a private home. James was 40 and Ellen was 33, still a young woman.

Because the service was late in the day, the newlyweds accepted the invitation of their host to spend the night in his home. The Whites also stayed as house guests.

When Ellen White went upstairs to

retire, she saw a very nervous young man pacing back and forth in front of a closed bedroom door. She suspected a problem. Gently she said to the young bridegroom (as the bride later quoted her husband's recital of the incident): "Daniel, inside that room is a frightened young woman in bed petrified with fear. Now you go in to her right now, and you love her, and you comfort her. And, Daniel, you treat her gently, and you treat her tenderly, and you treat her lovingly. It will do her good."

Then she added, "Daniel, it will do you good, too!"[29] Here is a Victorian woman who had her priorities straight—and that young couple were ever grateful.

In some other respects, Ellen White was distinctively different from the typical Victorian woman. She did not use her frailty for personal advantage or special attention, but rose above it to the astonishment of her contemporaries. Though respectful of James, she was not typical of Victorian submission to one's husband, nor did she cater to social expectations (merely to gain male approval) or to Victorian domesticity (to enhance standing among other women). In fulfilling her prophetic role, these Victorian "virtues" took on new meaning. Physical frailty became a challenge to conquer weaknesses by the grace of God, an achievement that gave her increasing strength and endurance as she grew older.

Although submission to her husband and meeting her family's needs were important, Ellen White's prophetic responsibilities were paramount in her life. She showed everyone that religious responsibilities do not minimize home responsibilities. Life, for her, was not compartmentalized, as either prophet or homemaker. She saw life as a whole—to fulfill her religious responsibilities she would not diminish her responsibilities as a wife, mother, and neighbor.

Endnotes

1. Jonathan Butler, "Prophecy, Gender and Culture: Ellen Gould Harmon [White] and the Roots of Seventh-day Adventism," *Religion and American Culture: A Journal of Interpretation*, vol. 1, (Winter 1991), pp. 3-29.
2. A number of references describe her horseback riding in the Colorado mountains, for pleasure as well as for travel. See *MR*, vol. 3, pp. 158, 163, 170; vol. 8, p. 121; vol. 20, p. 208.
3. *Education*, p. 216.
4. *Life Sketches*, p. 105. See p. 80.
5. *MR*, vol. 5, p. 430 (1874).
6. *Ibid.*, vol. 10, p. 27.
7. *Ibid.*, vol. 15, p. 231.
8. Delafield, *Ellen G. White in Europe*, p. 200. Willie, traveling with his mother, wrote to his wife Mary in Basel: "Mother and Sara have carried on quite a stroke of dressmaking. If you will rent a store I think they will be able to stock it with a good line of dress goods."
9. *The Ministry of Healing*, p. 294.
10. *Bio.*, vol. 1, p. 400.
11. *Ibid.*, vol. 2, p. 340.
12. *Ibid.*, vol. 3, p. 24.
13. *Ibid.*, p. 158.
14. *Ibid.*, vol. 4, pp. 261-262.
15. See pp. 84-86.
16. *Overland Route* (No. Highlands, California: History West, 1981), p. 17.
17. Lucius Beebe and Charles Clegg, *The Age of Steam* (New York: Rinehart & Company, Inc., n.d.), p. 17. A drummer was a traveling salesman.
18. Oliver O. Jensen, *The American Heritage History of Railroads in America* (New York: American Heritage Publishing Company, 1975), p. 123. See Appendix C for selections from Robert Louis Stevenson's account of his train ride west in 1879.
19. Lucius Beebe, *The Age of Steam*, p. 161. In 1848 no one had yet traveled a mile in sixty seconds in any conveyance. President Washington was told by leading physicians "that a stage-coach speed of fifteen miles an hour would invariably result in the death of anyone attempting it by causing all the blood in the body to run to the head."—Lucius Beebe, *High Iron* (New York: D. Appleton-Century Company, 1938), p. 55. In his chapter, "Overland by Rail, 1869-1890," in Gary Land, *The World of Ellen G. White*, pp. 63-76, Randall R. Butler II wrote that before 1880 the Union Pacific and the Central Pacific trains averaged about twenty-two miles per hour. After 1880 average speeds doubled but with stops at more than two hundred stations and water tanks, the total hours spent crossing the country remained the same. Concluding this chapter, Butler wrote: "By midmorning, westbound trains arrived at the Oakland terminal. The tired, weary passengers rejoiced universally with the conclusion of the journey. It was a long, hard four-and-a-half days from Omaha, and most passengers had begun their trip from one to three days further east or south. After a week of noise, dust, and tobacco and locomotive smoke, the disembarking passengers looked forward to a warm bath and quiet rest."
20. Cited in Land, *The World of Ellen G. White*, p. 83. For insights into the hardships that early Adventist workers endured, see *Ibid.*, pp. 74-80.
21. *Bio.*, vol. 1, pp. 232-234.
22. L. H. Christian recalled that "this article in the *Review* was read and discussed and used as an example to fol-

low, but never thought of as something out of the ordinary."—*The Fruitage of Spiritual Gifts,* p. 152.
23. *Bio.,* vol. 1, pp. 346-349. See also p. 431. For another example of exciting but rigorous pioneer living, review the months spent in Texas during the winter of 1878-79 and the wagon train ordeal in the spring of 1879.—*Ibid.*, pp. 98-120.
24. "The Cult of True Womanhood: 1820-1860," *American Quarterly,* vol. 8 (1966), p. 151, cited in Kathleen Joyce's "An Ambiguous Woman: Victorian Womanhood and Religious Prophecy in the Life of Ellen Gould White," 1991, an unpublished manuscript.
25. Joyce, *Ibid.*, p. 24.
26. *Testimonies*, vol. 2, p. 380.
27. *Ibid.*, p. 391.
28. *Ibid.*, p. 90.
29. Roger W. Coon, "Counsel to a Nervous Bridegroom," *Adventist Heritage,* Summer, 1990, pp. 17-22.

Study Questions

1. What are the distinguishing characteristics of the "Victorian" woman?
2. In what interesting ways was Ellen White an exemplary pioneer woman?
3. How do you think that Ellen White's gardening skills helped her in her writing? Give some examples.
4. Could a woman in today's world be both "Victorian" and an American pioneer?

CHAPTER 11

The Prolific Writer

"My heart is overflowing with a good theme; I write my composition concerning the King; my tongue is the pen of a ready writer" (Ps. 45:1).

Ellen White is thought to be the third most translated author in history and the most translated American author, male or female. So far as we know, she wrote and published more books, and in more languages, which circulate to a greater extent than the written works of any other woman in history. By the close of her seventy-year ministry, her literary productions totaled approximately 100,000 pages, or the equivalent of 25 million words, including letters, diaries, periodical articles, pamphlets, and books.[1]

At the time of Mrs. White's death (1915), twenty-four books were currently in print and two more were at the publishers awaiting publication. In the 1990s, 128 titles were in print bearing Ellen White's name, including books that are compilations of her thoughts on various subjects.[2]

How did it all begin? Not a brilliant student, college-trained! Not a skilled and published writer! It would be difficult to say that Ellen White's remarkable literary production was merely a product of human genius and invention. Her contemporaries, knowing her background and minimal education, also knew that more than human wisdom was responsible for her incisive, commanding eloquence in print as well as in the pulpit.

In late spring 1845, Ellen Harmon's hand, trembling in weakness, was unable to write. But in a vision she was told to write what she saw. For the first time, her "hand became steady." Many years later she recalled this experience: "The Lord has said, 'Write out the things which I shall give you.' And I commenced when very young to do this work. My hand that was feeble and trembling because of infirmities became steady as soon as I took the pen in my hand, and since those first writings I have been able to write. God has given me the ability to write. . . . The right hand scarcely ever has a disagreeable sensation. It never wearies. It seldom ever trembles (1900)."[3]

Ellen White wrote on note paper, large sheets, and in bound, ruled copybooks, almost always with a pen. Her assistants copied her manuscripts on the typewriter after the mid-1880s.[4]

She wrote at all times, day and night, and under circumstances that would intimidate others. Her son, W. C. White, recalled a typical schedule when the Whites were at home in Battle Creek: "With but little variation, the daily program of the White family was something like this: At six o'clock all were up. Often Mother had been writing for two or three hours, and the cook had been busy in the kitchen since five o'clock. By six-thirty breakfast was ready. Mother would frequently mention at the breakfast table that she had written six, eight, or more pages, and sometimes she would relate to the family some interesting portions of what she had written.

"Father would sometimes tell us of the work in which he was engaged, or relate interesting incidents regarding the progress of the cause, east and west. At seven o'clock all assembled in the parlor for morning worship. . .

"After Father had left the house, Mother enjoyed spending half an hour in her flower garden during those portions of the year when flowers could be cultivated. In this her children were encouraged to work with her. Then she would devote three or four hours to her writing. Her afternoons were usually occupied with a variety of activities, sewing, mending, knitting, darning, and working in her flower garden, with occasional shopping trips to town or visits to the sick."[5]

Often she would be writing while traveling. In her August 18, 1859, diary entry, she noted: "Awoke a little past two A.M. Take cars [train] at four. Feel very miserable. Write all day. . . . Our journey on the cars ended at six P.M."[6]

On that same trip, in her diary entry for October 10, she spoke of her crowded schedule while staying at the home of a church member: "The house is full of company. . . . Had no time to visit. Shut myself in the chamber to write."[7]

After a three-month tour of the eastern states in 1891, just prior to leaving for Australia, she wrote that she had "spoken fifty-five times, and have written three hundred pages. . . . The Lord it is who has strengthened and blessed me and upheld me by His Spirit."[8]

Insight into how her assistants helped her is found in a letter Ellen White wrote to G. W. Amadon in 1906: "The evening after the Sabbath I retired, and rested well without ache or pain until half past ten. I was unable to sleep. I had received instruction [by heavenly Guide], and I seldom lie in bed after such instruction comes. There was a company assembled in ____, and instruction was given by One in our midst that I was to repeat and repeat with pen and voice. I left my bed, and wrote for five hours as fast as my pen could trace the lines. Then I rested on the bed for an hour, and slept part of the time.

"I placed the matter in the hands of my copyist, and on Monday morning it was waiting for me, placed inside my office door on Sunday evening. There were four articles ready for me to read over and make any corrections needed. The matter is now prepared, and some of it will go in the mail today.

"This is the line of work that I am carrying on. I do most of my writing while the other members of the family are asleep. I build my fire, and then write uninterruptedly, sometimes for hours."[9]

Editorial Assistants

In order to keep up with the incessant demand for articles and books, Ellen White eventually developed an efficient organization of paid and unpaid editorial assistants. In the early years, James was her keen and ready helper in preparing material for publication.[10]

The very idea of a prophet's needing editorial "assistance" has come as a new thought to some in recent years. But those who were Ellen White's contemporaries knew how necessary literary helpers were, considering the volume of writing to which she was committed.[11]

Often those who are troubled by a prophet's use of assistants have a faulty understanding of how God speaks to human beings. They believe that inspired persons, including Mrs. White, mechanically wrote out exactly what God had spoken or revealed word for word.[12] Some expect inerrancy from Ellen White, even as they do from the Bible writers. Mrs. White's own understanding of how revelation/inspiration works will be discussed on page 421.

Ellen White employed literary assistants for the same reasons that Biblical writers did. She recognized her own limitations of time and literary skills. In 1873, she wrote in her diary: "My mind is coming to strange conclusions. I am thinking I must lay aside my writing I have taken so much pleasure in, and see if I cannot become a scholar. I am not a grammarian. I will try, if the Lord will help me, at forty-five years old to become a scholar in the science. God will help me. I believe He will."[13]

She was often interrupted while writing and this left tangled copy. Commenting on this need for editorial assistance, she wrote: "Doing as much writing as I do, it is not surprising if there are many sentences left unfinished."[14]

In a letter to G. A. Irwin, General Conference president, Willie White noted that his mother sought literary assistance because she recognized the varying quality in her writings: "Sometimes when Mother's mind is rested, and free, the thoughts are presented in language that is not only clear and strong, but beautiful and correct; and at times when she is weary and oppressed with heavy burdens of anxiety, or when the subject is difficult to portray, there are repetitions and ungrammatical sentences."

He further described the guidelines that his mother set for her literary assistants: "Mother's copyists are entrusted with the work of correcting grammatical errors, of eliminating unnecessary repetitions, and of grouping paragraphs and sections in their best order. . . . Mother's workers of experience, such as Sisters Davis, Burnham, Bolton, Peck, and Hare, who are very familiar with her writings, are authorized to take a sentence, paragraph, or section from one manuscript and incorporate it with another manuscript where the same thought was expressed but not so clearly. But none of Mother's workers are authorized to add to the manuscripts by introducing thoughts of their own."[15]

By 1881 Willie served as the editorial coordinator for his mother's literary assistants.[16] Because Ellen White was either traveling or writing new material most of the time, she chose not to be involved in editorial details. She knew that she would review all documents before they would be published unless she gave, on occasion, specific permission to a periodical editor to abridge to fit space. The record shows that they made few changes.

A "hierarchy of responsibility" developed. For example, for minor editorial work, Marian Davis was authorized to decide matters herself; larger questions were to be submitted to W. C. White. Ellen White would make the final decisions as to editorial changes after both William and Marian had done their work.[17]

Marian Davis had occasions to describe her work as she saw it: "I have tried to begin both chapters and paragraphs with short sentences, and indeed to simplify wherever possible, to drop out every needless word, and to make the work, as I have said, more compact and vigorous."[18]

The publishers hoped to keep Ellen White on *their* schedule, which was not easy during her heavy duties in Australia. Marian wrote to Willie: "Sister White is constantly harassed with the thought that the manuscript should be sent to the printers at once. . . . Sister White seems inclined to write, and I have no doubt she will bring out many precious things. I hope it will be possible to get them into the book. There is one thing, however, that not even the most competent editor could do—that is prepare a manuscript before it is written."[19]

At times Ellen White reached out beyond her immediate helpers for assistance. She explained this procedure to W. H. Littlejohn in 1894: "I have all my publications closely examined. I desire that nothing shall appear in print without careful investigation. Of course I would not want men who have not a Christian experience or are lacking in ability to appreciate literary merit to be placed as judges of what is essential to come before the people, as pure provender thoroughly winnowed from the chaff. I laid out all my manuscript on *Patriarchs and Prophets* and on [*Spirit of Prophecy*] Vol. IV before the book committee for examination and criticism. I also placed these manuscripts in the hands of some of our ministers for examination. The more criticism of them the better for the work."[20]

When she wrote of medical matters, her office helpers asked medical specialists to review the manuscripts with care: "I wish that in all your reading you would note those places where the thought is expressed in a way to be especially criticized by medical men and kindly give us the benefit of your knowledge as to how to express the same thought in a more accurate way."[21]

Regardless of wherever she received editorial help, Ellen White read everything in final form: "I find under my door in the morning several copied articles from Sister Peck, Maggie Hare, and Minnie Hawkins. All must be read critically by me . . . . Every article I prepare to be edited by my workers, I always have to read myself before it is sent for publication."[22]

A 19th Century Accent

Like the prophets who wrote the Bible, Ellen White wrote from within the literary, historical, social, and religious context of her time. She not only wrote with a human accent, she wrote with the accent and the thought-forms of the 19th century.

As with the prophets of old, contemporary issues often determined the emphasis and frequency of what she wrote about. For example, she saw profound implications for understanding last-day events as she noted Sunday-law activity.[23] Both Biblical prophets and Ellen White, though speaking to contemporary issues in their day, provided us with ageless principles that apply to us today.

Wide Reading Habits

Ellen White's wide reading habits helped to fill in her broad conceptual framework with historical background and fresh ways to state her insightful perceptions.

When the White children were young, their mother read broadly in religious magazines looking for stories with moral lessons that would be suitable especially for Sabbath reading. She clipped the desirable articles and pasted them in scrapbooks.[24]

In the 1870s many of these articles were sorted out into books for different age groups. The first of these collections, *Sabbath Readings, Moral and Religious Lessons for Youth and Children*, contained 154 individually-paged stories.[25] Later, *Sabbath Readings for the Home Circle*, a four-volume set of stories, appeared in numerous editions.[26] At the turn of the century, *Golden Grains*, a series of ten pamphlets, each containing 72 pages, was published by the Pacific Press Publishing Association.[27] An undated collection of children's stories, *Sunshine Series*, was also published; the first had ten pamphlets of 16 pages, and the second had 20 pamphlets of 16 pages each.[28]

Early in 1900, while in Australia, Ellen White wrote to her son, Edson, asking him to send certain books from her library: "I have sent for four or five large volumes of Barnes' notes on the Bible. I think they are in Battle Creek in my house now sold, somewhere with my books. I hope you will see that my property, if I have any, is cared for and not scattered as common property everywhere. I may never visit America again, and my best books should come to me when it is convenient."[29]

In 1920, E. E. Andross, president of the North American Division, made a plea for clarification on Mrs. White's use of materials found in her reading. W. C. White responded: "In the early days of her work, Mother was promised wisdom in the selection from the writings of others, that would enable her to select the gems of truth from the rubbish of error. We have all seen this fulfilled, and yet when she told me of this, she admonished me not to tell it to others. Why thus restricted I never knew, but now am inclined to believe that she saw how this might lead some of her brethren to claim too much for her writings as a standard with which to correct historians."[30]

W. C. White wrote to the Publication Committee of the Pacific Press in 1911: "It is generally admitted that in Sister White's discourses, spoken to the people, she uses great freedom and wisdom in the selection of proofs and illustrations, to make plain and forcible her presentation of the truths revealed to her in vision. Also, that she selects such facts and arguments as are adapted to the audience to which she is speaking. This is essential to the attainment of the best results from her discourses. And she has always felt and taught that it was her duty to use the same wisdom in the selection of matter for her books, that she does in the selection of matter for her discourses."[31]

With her mind and heart overflowing with the love of God, Ellen White had been given the big picture of God's plan for resolving the sin problem; it was her duty to find the best way to convey this picture to others. In the introduction to *The Great Teacher* (a volume Ellen White valued highly), John Harris wrote: "Suppose, for example, an inspired prophet were now to appear in the church, to add a supplement to the canonical books—what a Babel of opinions would he find existing on almost every theological subject! And how highly probable it is that his ministry would consist, or seem to consist, in a mere selection and ratification of such of these opinions as accorded with the mind of God. Absolute originality would seem to be almost impossible. The inventive mind of man has already bodied forth speculative opinions in almost every conceivable form, forestalling and robbing the future of its fair proportion of novelties and leaving little more, even to a divine messenger, than the office of taking some of these opinions and impressing them with the seal of heaven."[32]

These words could be applied to Ellen White. Her ability to read voluminously and to select carefully provided her with the tools that her prophetic mission required. Mentally armed with the inspired outline of truth, her extensive reading frequently helped her to fill in the details with pertinent historical background and with literary adaptations that make her writings forceful, delightful, and creative.

Writing for the General Public

When her books were to be published later for non-Adventists, she authorized revisions that would eliminate possible misunderstandings. More than merely authorized, she actively encouraged such revisions.

For example, her chapter on "Proper Education," now found in *Testimonies,* volume 3, pages 131-138, was also submitted to the *Health Reformer*, September, 1872; however, certain differences in wording appear in the *Health Reformer* because it was prepared especially for the general public.

Sarah Peck, an education specialist, joined Ellen White's staff at the turn of the century. One of her assignments was to assemble Mrs. White's writings on the principles of education. Miss Peck soon saw that these materials divided themselves into two groups. Those most appropriate for the church now appear in certain sections of the *Testimonies*, volume 6 (1900) and *Counsels to Parents and Teachers* (1913); those suitable for the general public are in *Education* (1903).

While helping his mother prepare the 1911 edition of *The Great Controversy,* W. C. White wrote to the Publication Committee: "In *Great Controversy*, Volume IV, published in 1885, in the chapter 'Snares of Satan,' there are three pages or more of matter that were not used in the later editions, which were prepared to be sold to the multitudes by our canvassers. It is most excellent and interesting reading for Sabbathkeepers, as it points out the work that Satan will do in persuading popular ministers and church members to elevate the Sunday sabbath, and to persecute Sabbathkeepers.[33]

"It was not left out because it was less true in 1888 than in 1885, but because Mother thought it was not wisdom to say these things to the multitudes to whom the book would be sold in future years. . . .

"With reference to this, and to other passages in her writings which have been omitted in later editions, she has often said: 'These statements are true, and they are useful to our people; but to the general public, for whom this book is now being prepared, they are out of place. Christ said, even to His disciples, "I have many things to say unto you, but ye cannot bear them now." And Christ taught His disciples to be "wise as serpents, and harmless as doves."' Therefore, as it is probable that more souls will be won to Christ by the book without this passage than with it, let it be omitted.

"Regarding changes in forms of expression, Mother has often said: 'Essential truths must be plainly told; but so far as possible they should be told in language that will win, rather than offend.'"[34]

Ellen White's sermons were often published as articles in the *Signs of the Times* or the *Review and Herald*. However, preparing them for the *Review* was much easier than preparing articles for the *Signs*. Why? Because readers of the *Review* were mainly Seventh-day Adventists, and those of the *Signs,* primarily the general public.

Personal Experiences Enriched Her Writing

Creative preachers have a "homiletical bias," that is, in whatever they read, in whatever their personal experiences, they "pick up" information for sermons to come. Such experiences enrich their sacred subjects, enhancing the interest for their hearers. No one at any time begins to think with a blank mind. On the minds of creative thinkers is the sum total of all that they have ever read, all that they have ever experienced.

In addition to all that Ellen White was reading, her many travel experiences added to the wealth of her thought. For instance, after spending a day on a sailboat in San Francisco Bay (1876), she was writing on the life of Christ. Her subject that day was Christ walking on the Sea of Galilee, and in her mind she saw the disciples toiling through the stormy night. She continued in her letter to her husband: "Can you wonder that I was silent and happy with these grand themes of contemplation? I am glad I went upon the water. I can write better than before."[35]

In 1886 while holding meetings in Valence, France, she visited the Cathedral of Saint Apollinaire where she observed the impressiveness of a Catholic worship service. The priests officiated with their white robes, overlaid with a black velvet surplice trimmed with gold braid. This kind of experience helped her when later, in *The Great Controversy*, she described the grandeur of Catholic worship.[36]

While in Zurich, Switzerland, she visited the Gross Munster, the church where Zwingli preached during the Protestant Reformation. She was intensely interested in viewing Zwingli's Bible, and his life-size statue where "one hand rests upon the handle of his sword, while in the other hand he clasps a Bible."[37]

In view of the fact that she was then enlarging *The Great Controversy,* especially the part dealing with the Protestant Reformation era, Ellen White's comments on this city tour are understandable: "We gathered many items of interest which we will use."[38]

Variety of Personal Letters

Ellen White never expected that her private letters would be made public, except for those portions that she later used in developing a periodical article or for those letters that she thought would be of general interest. How would people today feel about having their private correspondence suddenly become public property? Especially correspondence written forty years before? Especially confidential letters to family members?

Or letters of reproof to leading church leaders or to their wives?

But today we must face reality. Much of Ellen White's private, confidential correspondence (letters she never published) has become public. How has this happened? Let us note several ways.

Because of her unique standing within the church, her letters became treasured correspondence by recipients. Older members passed them on to their children or to trusted pastors or students. Soon they took on a life of their own, usually without the background of time, place, or circumstance that would have provided the context for each letter's meaning and purpose.

This lack of context, of course, did not matter to those who believed in some form of verbal inspiration![39] For many, each word of these letters often became the "final word" on any question. The appeal to "Sister White says . . . ," on the basis of these many private letters, frequently closed further thought, bringing in unnecessary perplexity in church discussions. In the chapters on "Hermeneutics" (32-34) we will discuss the problems that arise when Ellen White's writings, especially her letters, are misused.

Another way her letters have become published is by the White Estate releasing them to researchers. After researchers have used these letters, the White Estate has made most of them available in the 21 *Manuscript Releases* volumes. Other complete letters are available in the four volumes of the *1888 Materials.* All of these letters are available on CD-ROM.

Many of Ellen White's letters were sent to her own family members, including close associates. Affectionate letters to James and her sons are numerous. As noted earlier,[40] some of these letters may appear abrupt and defensive. Considering time, place, and circumstance, the reader today can easily empathize with a busy, intensely committed, and sometimes tired, wife and mother. The real test of an occasional family letter that seems stiff and insensitive today is the response of her sons and her husband to these letters through the years. The sons loved their mother dearly and profited by her counsel. James adored his wife, even during his dark days of sickness and depression.[41]

In 1876 James White was preparing a biography of his wife. Because her letters were seen as the most "fruitful source" for tracing her unique ministry, he noted on the back page of the February 10 issue of the *Signs* that her friends should "forward all letters that remain in their hands."

Typical of hundreds of encouraging letters is the one Ellen White sent to two young families, the Robinsons and Boyds, when they left the Fifth European Council at Moss, Norway, in June, 1887, to open mission work in South Africa. During this meeting, Mrs. White had preached evangelistic sermons to the general public, pastoral sermons to church members, provided counsel in business meetings, and shared pioneer experiences with other workers. But when Sabbath afternoon came, she knew her work was not yet finished. She and Mrs. Ings walked into the forest, spread a blanket, and instead of resting, she wrote a ten-page letter of counsel and encouragement to the young, mission-field-bound workers. That letter, now known as Letter 14, 1887, has been quoted and published often; its rich insights have guided many workers throughout the years.[42]

At times, Ellen White talked lucidly and candidly in confidential letters to her sons as well as co-workers. Her private letters to son Edson appear frank, even sharp, especially if the historical context is ignored. Not until Edson was forty-four years of age did he emerge as a committed preacher and educator. In later years, he pioneered Adventist work in the post-Civil-War American South. But in his younger years he was reluctant to assume responsibility for financial decisions as well as for his conduct.[43]

When Edson was considering marriage at the age of twenty, his mother wrote one of her frank letters. She noted his intellectual brilliance, "capable of filling a position as a physician or business man," but he was a "spendthrift." He lacked self-control. "Father weeps over your case. But we are both at a loss to know what to say or do in your case. We view it just alike. You are at present not fitted to have a family, for in judgment you are a child—in self-control a child. You have no strength to resist temptation although by yielding you would disgrace us and yourself and dishonor God. You would not bear the yoke in your youth. You love ease and to be free from care."[44]

During Edson's youth, he clashed with his father. Mother Ellen often tried to keep the peace, which may not have been fully appreciated by either. James believed that his wife favored Edson during breakdowns in communication. If so, perhaps it was because she understood best the special circumstances surrounding Edson during his early life, such as her own stressful pregnancy with him and unfavorable prenatal influences; his extreme ill health as a baby; and the early and frequent separation from parents while they traveled from state to state uniting early Seventh-day Adventists. These circumstances she (now 50) referred to when she wrote to William in 1878: "The circumstances of his birth [in 1849] were altogether different than yours. His mother knows, but everyone does not."[45]

During her children's formative years, Ellen White believed that she and James had "failed" to restrain their children from following "their own inclinations and desires," but at the same time had censured them and found fault "with them in a spirit which will only injure and discourage them instead of helping them."[46] James and Ellen White were experiencing the "growing pains" that most serious and committed parents make in their high goal of being responsible under God. Further, she had been given divine enlightenment regarding the curse that came upon Eli and his sons because of the father's indulgence of their sins—and she did not want to make a similar mistake.[47]

With this background, one can better understand her letters to Edson like the following (which was marked *"Read this alone, Private"*): "My dear Son Edson [at 15]: When we went to Monterey last summer, for instance, you went into the river four times and not only disobeyed us yourself but led Willie to disobedience. A thorn has been planted in my heart from that time, when I became convinced that you could not be trusted. . . . A gloom which I cannot express shrouds our minds in regard to your influence upon Willie. You lead him into habits of disobedience and concealment and prevarication. This influence, we have seen, has affected our noble-hearted, truthful Willie. . . . You reason and talk and make things appear all smooth to him, when he cannot see through the matter. He adopts your view of it and he is in danger of losing his candor, his frankness. . . . You had so little sense of the true value of character. You seemed as much pleased in the society of Marcus Ashley as with your own innocent brother Willie. You never prized him as he deserved to be prized. He is a treasure, beloved of God, but I fear your influence will ruin him."[48]

In this letter we have the typical candor of the mother who prized candor in her children. In her attempt to awaken the conscience of Edson and ease him into fulfilling parental expectations, she used young Willie (five years younger) as Edson's model. Years later she was able to see that this kind of comparison among siblings was not the best approach, even though both children had abundant evidence of their mother's love. She had their eternal interests in mind at all times, and simply did not want her love confused with indulgence.

How Categories of Literary Production Were Developed

During her most productive years, especially after 1881, Ellen White maintained a steady stream of letters, sermons, periodical articles, and books. These materials were further processed by her literary assistants into other forms for publication. Sermons became periodical articles, and letters, sermons, and articles were often reassembled into book form. The output was prodigious as the pages of the *Review* and *Signs* attest, plus the books that came forth from her pen during the last thirty-five years of her life.

Diaries. The White Estate has some 60 diary/journals belonging to Ellen White that trace back to 1859. Some record daily events, much as we would think of a diary today, while others are simply ruled blank books that she used for writing letters or manuscripts of a general nature. It is not uncommon to find a range of several years' writing in a single journal, years that might overlap with writing in other journals. This is due to the fact that she regularly passed these books to her secretaries for copying. Thus several books might be in use at the same time, some being in the copyists' hands, while she continued her writing in another available journal.

Letters. Editing Ellen White's letters before mailing involved more than typing her handwritten manuscripts. W. C. White noted the process in a letter to his mother after receiving a long one from her to A. C. Bourdeau (4,000 words). He said that Mary, his wife, "will try to fix it as she has strength."[49] "Fix it" meant that grammatical corrections were expected. This kind of editorial assistance can easily be seen when one compares hastily written hand copies with the typewritten edited copies.

Sermons and Periodical Articles. Many of Ellen White's sermons were stenographically recorded. Mary K. White and Mary Clough, as well as others, often prepared sermons for publication. Both church papers sought these articles on a regular basis. This schedule was not easy to maintain because of travel interruptions and other pressing writing goals. To make it easier for all concerned, especially for her hard-pressed assistants, Ellen White gave permission to the editors of the *Review* and *Signs* to take the typewritten manuscripts and prepare them for their particular needs. In doing so, they were to "drop out the personal matter and make it general, and put it to whatever use you may think best for the interests of the cause of God."[50]

Although the editors had earned this trust, they changed the fewest possible words and sentences to fit their needs. This accounts for the slight differences between the periodical article and the same material used later in a book.

Books (other than the Testimonies). During the 1890s, several books were in process simultaneously, including *Gospel Workers, Steps to Christ,*[51] and *The Desire of Ages*[52]—the first, a complete compilation, and the last two, largely compilations and rearrangements of previously written material.

Marian Davis "My Bookmaker"

In a 1900 letter to G. A. Irwin, Ellen White called Marian Davis "my bookmaker." In that same letter, she described how Marian did her work: "She takes my articles which are published in the papers, and pastes them in blank books. She also has a copy of all the letters I write. In preparing a chapter for a book, Marian remembers that I have written something on that special point, which may make the matter more forcible. She begins to search for this, and if when she finds it, she sees that it will make the chapter more clear, she adds it.

"The books are not Marian's productions, but my own, gathered from all my writings. Marian has a large field from which to draw, and her ability to arrange the matter is of great value to me. It saves my poring over a mass of matter, which I have no time to do."[53]

Marian wrote to Willie reflecting the weight of her work: "Perhaps you can imagine the difficulty of trying to bring together points relating to any subject, when these must be gleaned from thirty scrapbooks, a half-dozen bound [E. G. White] volumes, and fifty manuscripts, all covering thousands of pages."[54]

But Marian did none of the writing. When Marian died in 1904, Ellen White looked back over their close association with great appreciation: "We have stood side by side in the work, and in perfect harmony in that work. And when she would be gathering up the precious jots and tittles that had come in papers and books and present it to me, 'Now,' she would say, 'there is something wanted [needed]. I cannot supply it.' I would look it over, and in one moment I could trace the line right out. We worked together, just worked together in perfect harmony all the time."[55] Others, including Mary White, J. H. Waggoner, W. W. Prescott, and J. H. Kellogg, also helped W. C. White and Marian Davis in book production.

Dr. Kellogg helped in the publication of *Christian Temperance and Bible Hygiene.* He wrote the introduction in which he noted how the book was developed: "This book is not a new presentation . . . but is simply a compilation, and in some sense an abstract, of the various writings of Mrs. White upon this subject, to which have been added several articles by Elder James White, elucidating the same principles, and the personal experience of Elders J. N. Andrews and Joseph Bates, two of the pioneers in the health movement among Seventh-day Adventists. The work of compilation has been done under the supervision of Mrs. White, by a committee appointed by her for the purpose, and the manuscript has been carefully examined by her."[56]

Testimonies. "Testimonies" early became a term well known among Seventh-day Adventists for three reasons: (1) Adventists who formerly were Methodists were familiar with the "social" meetings, or "testimony" meetings, wherein members would share personal experiences and their faith commitments; (2) communications from Ellen White to others, either oral or written, became known as "testimonies"; (3) the published compilations of letters, manuscripts, and previously published periodical articles were eventually assembled into nine volumes known as *Testimonies for the Church.*

These "testimonies" were written whenever Ellen White had the time and occasion to write out the revelations given to her, either through night dreams or day visions. One interesting occasion took place at Adams Center, New York, in early November, 1863. Nearly a whole Seventh Day Baptist church had been converted to the Adventist message. James and Ellen White spoke several times, as did J. N. Andrews.

On Sunday afternoon, Andrews preached while Mrs. White wrote six pages during the sermon, writing only four feet away from the pulpit, using her Bible as a writing prop. When the sermon ended, she arose and addressed the congregation. One church member reported in the *Review* that "her words were enough to melt a heart of stone." Her ability to concentrate is well illustrated by her reaction that same day when someone asked her what she thought of Andrews as a speaker. She replied that "she could not say, as it had been so long since she had heard him."[57]

Many of the original, personal communications from Ellen White were later recognized to be of value for others as well. In response to requests, the Whites arranged to have them printed in brochure form. The first ten of these *Testimonies*, between 1855-1864, contained from 16 to 240 pages each in pocket-size pamphlets. In 1874 the first ten were reprinted in book form. (No doubt after ten years the originals, not in permanent form, were not easily available.)

However, the 1881-1883 revision of the previously published *Testimonies*, 1-28, became a major project. The fact that a messenger's public writings could or should be "revised" brought new focus on how God worked through His messenger.

For many people, it appeared to be a fresh insight.

The 1878 General Conference voted that all previous *Testimonies* should be reprinted in permanent form. Reprinting involved a complete resetting of type, creating a new page format and providing consecutive paging.

Ellen White and her close assistants (W. C. and Mary White, Marian Davis, Eliza Burnham, and J. H. Waggoner) saw this request as an opportunity to improve imperfect grammar and clarity of expression. Her aim continued to be to present truth in the clearest manner possible.

Why Revisions Were Necessary

The 1883 General Conference resolution endorsed the 1878 vote, noting the circumstances under which the *Testimonies* had been written: "Many of these testimonies were written under the most unfavorable circumstances, the writer being too heavily pressed with anxiety and labor to devote critical thought to the grammatical perfection of the writings, and they were printed in such haste as to allow these imperfections to pass uncorrected; etc."[58]

The editors took this task of revision seriously. Mary wrote to her husband, W. C. White: "With regard to changes, we will try to profit by your suggestions. The fear that we may make too many changes or in some way change the sense haunts me day and night."[59]

But not everyone was enthusiastic about the revision of the published *Testimonies.* Dark fears arose at the heart of church leadership. W. C. White wrote to his wife Mary from the General Conference session in 1882, alerting her to the resistance: "Butler and Haskell do not find serious fault with Testimony proofs, but say they see no good in about one-third of the changes. They wish you could go with them into meetings and see such men as Mooney [an anti-Adventist polemicist] bring forward one edition and then another and show changes and try to make a point of it. I argue that there is no salvation in bad grammar, etc. A thought grammatically expressed is just as good to reach the hard and sinful heart as if badly expressed."[60]

Fears came from two directions: Leaders knew (1) that critics of the denomination would jump at the opportunity to show that the Adventist "prophet" was unreliable, that she was manipulated by circumstances and other people; (2) that changes in published writings would unsettle some Adventists, causing them to feel they had been misled and that Ellen White was not a safe guide.

Were these fears justified? Yes and No. Fears were justified when leaders observed that many people, both Adventists and non-Adventists, held an inadequate view of how God speaks to His human messengers; they believed that God dictated the exact words that prophets used in revealing divine messages. However, fears were unnecessary whenever people understood that God inspired the messenger with thoughts, not words.

The 1883 General Conference resolution did its best to clarify the truth about the nature of revelation/inspiration: "We believe the light given by God to His servants is by the enlightenment of the mind, thus imparting the thoughts, and not (except in rare cases) the very words in which the ideas should be expressed; therefore—

"*Resolved,* That in the republication of these volumes such verbal changes be made as to remove the above-named imperfections, as far as possible, without in any measure changing the thought."[61]

This General Conference resolution became a benchmark for the Adventist understanding of revelation/inspiration.[62]

Opposition to Revisions

However, the fears did not abate. Uriah Smith, editor of the church paper, as well as many others, opposed the revision—even after the resolution was passed. Three months after the Conference, Ellen White wrote to Smith, defending the revision project that was nearing completion: "Information has been received from Battle Creek that the work upon the *Testimonies* is not accepted. I wish to state some matters, which you can do what you please with. These statements you have heard me make before—that I was shown years ago that we should not delay publishing the important light given me because I could not prepare the matter perfectly. My husband was at times very sick, unable to give me the help that I should have had and that he could have given me had he been in health. On this account I delayed putting before the people that which has been given me in vision.

"But I was shown that I should present before the people in the best manner possible the light received; then as I received greater light, and as I used the talent God had given me, I should have increased ability to use in writing and in speaking. I was to improve everything, as far as possible bringing it to perfection, that it might be accepted by intelligent minds.

"As far as possible every defect should be removed from all our publications. As the truth should unfold and become widespread, every care should be exercised to perfect the works published.

"I saw in regard to Brother Andrews' *History of the Sabbath,* that he delayed the work too long. Other erroneous works were taking the field and blocking the way, so that minds would be prejudiced by the opposing elements. I saw that thus much would be lost. After the first edition was exhausted, then he could make improvements; but he was seeking too hard to arrive at perfection. This delay was not as God would have it.

"Now, Brother Smith, I have been making a careful, critical examination of the work that has been done on the *Testimonies*, and I see a few things that I think should be corrected in the matter brought before you and others at the General Conference [November, 1883]. But as I examine the matter more carefully I see less and less that is objectionable. Where the language used is not the best, I want it made correct and grammatical, as I believe it should be in every case where it can be without destroying the sense. This work is delayed, which does not please me. . . .

"My mind has been exercised upon the question of the *Testimonies* that have been revised. We have looked them over more critically. I cannot see the matter as my brethren see it. I think the changes will improve the book. If our enemies handle it, let them do so. . . .

"I think that anything that shall go forth will be criticized, twisted, turned, and boggled, but we are to go forward with a clear conscience, doing what we can and leaving the result with God. We must not be long in delaying the work.

"Now, my brethren, what do you propose to do? I do not want this work dragging any longer. I want something done, and done now."[63]

But Ellen White's letter to Uriah Smith was not strong enough. Fears prevailed that the changes would undermine confidence in her writings. "Uriah Smith ran into a hailstorm of opposition from believers in Battle Creek. Nobody was going to touch their *Testimonies!*"[64] But Mrs. White, with her good judgment and common sense, conceded to leadership fears, and had her assistants "re-revise" the project so that only the most glaring imperfections were changed. William explained all this to O. A. Olsen: "We have reset many pages of that which was criticized at Battle Creek, and have made hundreds of changes in the plates so as to bring the phraseology of the new edition as nearly as possible to that of the old without making the statements awkward and the grammar positively incorrect."[65]

The first four volumes of the *Testimonies*, as we have them today, retain the corrections of the 1885 printing.

Revision Experience Teaches Lessons

What do we learn from this revision experience? (1) We have an "official" understanding of what Adventists believe about revelation/inspiration. Adventists are thought inspirationists, not verbal inspirationists.

(2) We have an example of the problems created when people have a wrong concept of the revelation/inspiration process. Misunderstanding how God's thoughts become the words of an inspired messenger directly affects how a person reads the Bible as well as the writings of Ellen White. Misunderstanding this subject creates problems in understanding truth, and eventually could destroy confidence in both the Bible and the writings of Mrs. White when imperfections of language are discovered.

(3) Publication of the *Testimonies* as revised in 1885 was used by Adventist critics to attack the inspiration of Ellen White. Because many critics believe that genuine prophetic messages are verbally inspired, they are greatly disturbed when those words are changed or challenged. Thus, for them, changes in the writings of Mrs. White are clear evidence that those writings were not inspired by God.

In her letter to Uriah Smith, Ellen White wrote that she knew that "enemies" would use the revision to mock Adventists, but she said, "Let them do so." She would not mute the truth just to avoid unfair, unprincipled attacks based on a mistaken understanding of how inspiration works.

Not much time passed before D. M. Canright did "handle" it! In 1889 this former Adventist preacher, who had been in and out of the ministry at least four times, wrote in his scathing book, *Seventh-day Adventism Renounced:* "In 1885 all her 'testimonies' were republished in four volumes, under the eye of her own son and a critical editor. Opening haphazard to four different pages in Vol. 1, I read and compared them with the original publication which I have. I found on an average *twenty-four changes of the words on each page!* Her words were thrown out and other words put in and other changes made, in some cases so many that it was difficult to read the two together. At the same rate in the four volumes, there would be 63,720 changes.

"Taking, then, the words which were put in by her husband, by her copyist, by her son, by her editors, and those copied from other authors, probably they comprise from one-tenth to one quarter of all her books. Fine inspiration that is!"[66]

Canright greatly exaggerated the revisions made, but he was not alone in his distress over revisions of Ellen White's published works. Leaders such as W. W. Prescott, S. N. Haskell, and Milton Wilcox (editor, *Signs of the Times*) maintained some form of verbal inspiration that, in turn, affected their attitudes on certain doctrinal issues to come. Prescott, especially, seems to have been influenced by Louis Gaussen's widely circulated *Theopneustia* (1841) which was a clear defense for Biblical inerrancy.[67]

Gaussen and, later, Prescott, lived in a time of great theological upheaval. English rationalists, German mystics, and budding American liberals combined higher critical methods in their frontal assault on the integrity of the Bible. Gaussen and others were leaders in upholding basic Christian fundamentals, but much of this defense was behind the moat of Biblical inerrancy, which, for them, meant some form of verbal inspiration. They believed that it was an either/or warfare: either higher criticism or verbal inspiration. For the sake of defending the high view of Scripture, they employed an indefensible view of inspiration. Gaussen, for example, believed that the prophet's words were inspired, not the prophet: "If the words of the book are dictated by God, of what consequence to me are the thoughts of the writer?"[68]

Through the years Prescott's earlier confusion, along with that of other leaders, contributed to unnecessary and unachievable expectations regarding the writings of Ellen White. This confusion erupted from time to time, especially in the 1919 Bible Conference, and, later, in the 1970s.[69]

Many ministers and laymen, because

they had not been clearly instructed, continued to feel more secure with some form of verbal inspiration. Careful leadership instruction, such as that which W. C. White tried to convey, generally fell on deaf ears.[70]

Endnotes

1. Roger Coon's research (as of 1983) at the Library of Congress, Washington, D.C., revealed the following top ten most-translated modern authors: "1. Vladimir I. Lenin, Russian communist leader—222 languages; 2. Georges Simenon, Franco-Belgian detective-story writer—143; 3. Leo Tolstoy, Russian novelist—122; 4. Ellen G. White, American cofounder of SDA—117 [more than 140, as of 1996, possibly making Ellen White the second most translated author of all time]; 5. Karl Marx, German socialist philosopher—114; 6. William Shakespeare, English playwright—111; 7. Agatha Christie, English mystery writer—99; 8. Jakob and Wilhelm Grimm, German fairy-tale collaborators—97; 9. Ian Fleming, British creator of James Bond thrillers—95; 10. Ernest Hemingway, American novelist—91."—*A Gift of Light* (Washington, D.C.: Review and Herald Publishing Association, 1983), pp. 30, 31. Of course, Biblical writers have been translated more than any other writers in history.
2. A complete list of all published Ellen G. White books and pamphlets may be obtained from the Ellen G. White Estate, 12501 Old Columbia Pike, Silver Spring, Maryland 20904-6600, USA.
3. *Bio.,* vol. 1, pp. 91, 92.
4. "We used the calligraph [typewriter] with good effect."—Manuscript 16a, 1885, cited in *Bio.,* vol. 3, p. 291. The typewriter, though invented in 1843, received numerous improvements until 1883, when Remington sold 3,000 machines with the upper/lower case shift capability. In 1894, Underwood produced a typewriter that enabled the typist to see what was being typed.—James Trager, *The People's Chronology* (New York: Henry Holt and Company, 1992), pp. 435, 548, 566, 612.
5. William C. White, "Sketches and Memories of James and Ellen White," *Review and Herald,* Feb. 13, 1936.
6. Cited in Arthur White, *Ellen G. White, Messenger to the Remnant,* (Washington, D.C.: Ellen G. White Publications, 1954), p. 109.
7. *Ibid.*
8. Manuscript 4, 1891, cited in *Ibid.*
9. Letter 28, 1906, cited in *Ibid.*
10. "While my husband lived, he acted as a helper and counselor in the sending out of the messages that were given to me. We traveled extensively. Sometimes light would be given to me in the night season, sometimes in the daytime before large congregations. The instruction I received in vision was faithfully written out by me, as I had time and strength for the work. Afterward we examined the matter together, my husband correcting grammatical errors and eliminating needless repetition. Then it was carefully copied for the persons addressed, or for the printer. As the work grew, others assisted me in the preparation of matter for publication. After my husband's death, faithful helpers joined me, who labored untiringly in the work of copying the testimonies and preparing articles for publication. But the reports that are circulated, that any of my helpers are permitted to add matter or change the meaning of the messages I write out, are not true." —*Selected Messages,* book 3, p. 89.
11. Pages 14-16 discuss the literary helpers of Biblical writers.
12. Pages 16, 120, 173, 375, 376, 421 discuss the difference between verbal inspiration and thought inspiration.
13. *Selected Messages,* book 3, p. 90.
14. Letter 103, 1895, to Marian Davis, cited in "The Fannie Bolton Story" (Washington, D.C.: Ellen G. White Estate, 1982), p. 49.
15. W. C. White to G. A. Irwin, May 7, 1900. Poirier cited in Moon, *W. C. White and Ellen G. White,* p. 115. Tim Poirier describes "two levels" of editing between Ellen White's original, handwritten documents and their present forms, as referred to in the May 7, 1900, letter to G. A. Irwin. Level One refers to "correcting grammatical errors, of eliminating unnecessary repetitions, etc." More experienced assistants in Level Two move beyond the level of presenting the material in the desired grammatical form; they rearrange, assemble, and compile the Level One typewritten material into a new literary document ("incorporate it with another manuscript"), such as a periodical article or a book (e.g., *Steps to Christ,* or *The Desire of Ages*). Photocopies of how these two levels developed in various stages of Ellen White materials are in Tim Poirier's "Exhibits Regarding the Work of Ellen White's Literary Assistants," 1990, available at Ellen G. White-SDA Research Centers.
16. At first, Mary K. White and Marian Davis were the chief assistants. "Among those who helped Ellen White in preparing her writings for publication over the years were James White, Mary Kelsey-White, Lucinda Abbey-Hall, Adelia Patten-Van Horn, Anna Driscol-Loughborough, Addie Howe-Cogshall, Annie Hale-Royce, Emma Sturgess-Prescott, Mary Clough-Watson, Mrs. J. I. Ings, Mrs. B. L. Whitney, Eliza Burnham, Fannie Bolton, Marian Davis, C. C. Crisler, Minnie Hawkins-Crisler, Maggie Hare, Sarah Peck, and D. E. Robinson."—Robert W. Olson, *One Hundred and One Questions* (Washington, D.C.: Ellen G. White Estate, 1981), p. 87.
17. Moon, *W. C. White and Ellen G. White,* p. 114.
18. Letter from Marian Davis to W. C. White, April 11, 1897. In a letter from Marian Davis to G. A. Irwin: "For more than 20 years I have been connected with Sister White's work. During this time I have never been asked either to write out a testimony from oral instruction, or to fill out the points in matters already written." — Enclosed with Ellen White's Letter 61a, 1900, to G. A. Irwin.
19. Marian Davis to W. C. White, Aug. 9, 1897, cited in Robert W. Olson, "How *The Desire of Ages* Was Written," p. 34.
20. *MR,* vol. 10, p. 12. While James White remained on the West Coast launching the first issues of *Signs of the Times* (1874), his wife wrote from Battle Creek: "We have just finished 'Sufferings of Christ.' Willie has helped me, and now we take it to the office for Uriah [Smith] to criticize it. It will, I think, make a thirty-two page tract."—Letters, July 11 and 17, 1874.
21. W. C. White to David Paulson, concerning the manu-

script for *The Ministry of Healing,* Feb. 15, 1905. (WEDF 140-a.)

22. Letter 84, 1898; "I read over all that is copied, to see that everything is as it should be. I read all the book manuscript before it is sent to the printer. So you can see that my time must be fully occupied."—Letter 133, 1902, cited in *Selected Messages*, book 3, p. 90. "I wish to write words that shall remove from the minds of any of my brethren the impression that I did not, before their publication, read the pages in *Testimony for the Church,* volume 9, relating to Sunday labor. I read the matter before it went to the printer, and have read it several times from the book, and I can see nothing in it to give one reason to say that Sunday-keeping is there taught. Neither does the counsel there given contradict the Bible, nor former testimonies."—Letter 94, 1910, cited in *MR,* vol. 8, p. 21.
23. *Last Day Events*, pp. 123-142.
24. These scrapbooks are on display at the E. G. White Estate office, Silver Spring, Maryland.
25. Battle Creek, MI: Steam Press of the Seventh-day Adventist Publishing Association, 1863.
26. Oakland, CA: The Pacific Press, 1877, 1878, 1881; Nashville, TN: M. A. Vroman, publisher, 1905.
27. Unknown date.
28. In 1881, James White wrote: "Mrs. White has ever been a great reader, and in our extensive travels she has gathered juvenile books and papers in great quantities, from which she selected moral and religious lessons to read to her own dear children. This work commenced about thirty years since. We purchased every series of books for children and youth printed in America and in Europe in the English language, which came to our notice, and bought, borrowed, and begged miscellaneous books of this class, almost without number. . . . And there we published the Sunshine Series of little books for the little ones, from 5 to 10 years old, the series of Golden Grains, for children from 10 to 15 years, and the volumes for the *Sabbath Readings for the Home Circle* for still more advanced readers. . . . Precious books! The compilers have spent years in reading and rejecting, ninety-nine parts, and accepted one. Precious books, indeed, for the precious youth."—*Review and Herald,* June 21, 1881.
29. Letter 189, 1900, cited in *Bio.,* vol. 4, p. 448.
30. White Estate Correspondence File, cited by Robert W. Olson, "Ellen G. White's Use of Historical Sources in *The Great Controversy,*" *Adventist Review,* Feb. 23, 1984.
31. *Selected Messages,* book 3, p. 441.
32. Pages xxxiii, xxxiv.
33. These pages are in *Testimonies to Ministers,* pp. 472-475.
34. *Selected Messages,* book 3, pp. 443, 444. In a statement made by W. C. White to the General Conference Council, October 30, 1911, he said (in reference to the changes made in the 1911 edition of *The Great Controversy*): "In several places, forms of expression have been changed to avoid giving unnecessary offense. An example of this will be found in the change of the word 'Romish' to 'Roman' or 'Roman Catholic.' In two places the phrase 'divinity of Christ' is changed to 'deity of Christ.' And the words 'religious toleration' have been changed to 'religious liberty.'. . . Mother's contact with European people had brought to her mind scores of things that had been presented to her in vision during past years, some of them two or three times, and other scenes many times. Her seeing of historic places and her contact with the people refreshed her memory with reference to these things, and so she desired to add much material to the book. . . . After our return to America, a new edition was brought out much enlarged. In this edition some of the matter used in the first English edition was left out. The reason for these changes was found in the fact that the new edition was intended for worldwide circulation."—*Ibid.,* pp. 435-438.
35. Letter 5, 1876, cited in *Bio.,* vol. 3, p. 27.
36. *Ibid.,* pp. 566, 567.
37. Manuscript 29, 1887, cited in Delafield, *Ellen G. White in Europe,* p. 273.
38. Manuscript 29, 1887, cited in *Bio.,* vol. 3, p. 363. Note W. C. White's comment regarding his mother's Basel visit: "During her two years' residence in Basel, she visited many places where events of special importance occurred in the Reformation days. This refreshed her memory as to what she had been shown and this led to important enlargement in those portions of the book dealing with Reformation days."—*Selected Messages,* book 3, p. 465.
39. See pp. 16, 20, 173, 375, 376, 421.
40. See p. 54
41. When Mrs. White was still recovering from the birth of her fourth son, John Herbert, September 20, 1860, James had to be away for about six weeks. He wrote a note to her that closed with these words: "I do not ask you to weary yourself with long letters. Your care for me is great. May God help you and the children."—Cited in *Bio.,* vol. 1, p. 429. Later, a few months before James died, he sensed that the time had come to lay off the heavy burdens of church leadership—but it was hard. A few days before he was stricken, he wrote to son Willie: "Where I have erred, help me to be right. I see my mistakes and am trying to rally. I need the help of yourself, Mother, and Haskell."—*Ibid.,* vol. 3, p. 145.
42. See *Evangelism,* pp. 89-91, 94, 97, 132, 142, 248, 553.
43. For general background on Edson White, see Alta Robinson, "James Edson White: Innovator," in *Early Adventist Educators,* ed. George R. Knight (Berrien Springs, MI: Andrews University, 1983), pp. 137-158; Virgil Robinson, *James White* (Nashville, TN: Southern Publishing Association, 1959), pp. 135-44; Jerry Allen Moon, *W. C. White and Ellen G. White* (Berrien Springs, MI: Andrews University Press, 1993) pp. 42-54.
44. Letter 6, 1869.
45. Letter 12, 1878. In 1899, when Edson was fifty years of age, Ellen White wrote to W. C.: "I . . . am more sympathetic for Edson than for you because before his birth circumstances were particularly unfavorable in regard to his stamp of character. My association while carrying him, the peculiar experience I was forced to have, was most objectionable and severely trying. After his birth it was no less so for years. It was altogether different in your case."—E. G. White to W. C. White, Letter 12, 1899. This letter to Willie was as candid and forthright as any letter she sent to Edson.
46. Manuscript 8, 1862.
47. *Testimonies,* vol. 1, pp. 118-120, 216-220.
48. Letter 4, 1865, from E. G. White to Edson.
49. W. C. White to E. G. White, Nov. 22, 1886, cited in Moon, *W. C. White and Ellen G. White,* p. 116.
50. E. G. White to Uriah Smith, Sept. 19, 1892, cited in Moon, *ibid.,* p. 118.

51. See pp. 444, 445.
52. See p. 450.
53. *Selected Messages,* book 3, pp. 91, 92. "I feel very thankful for the help of Sister Marian Davis in getting out my books. She gathers materials from my diaries, from my letters, and from the articles published in the papers. I greatly prize her faithful service. She has been with me for twenty-five years, and has constantly been gaining increasing ability for the work of classifying and grouping my writings."—*Ibid.*, p. 93.
54. Marian Davis to W. C. White, March 29, 1893, cited in *Bio.,* vol. 4, p. 383.
55. Manuscript 95, 1904, cited in *Ibid.*
56. *Bio.*, vol. 3, pp. 446-447. See J. H. Kellogg, preface to *Christian Temperance and Bible Hygiene,* by E. G. White and James White (Battle Creek, MI: *Good Health,* 1890), p. iv.
57. *Bio.,* vol. 2, pp. 68, 69.
58. *Review and Herald,* Nov. 27, 1883, Resolution #33, 741.
59. *Bio.,* vol. 3, p. 218.
60. W. C. White to M. K. White, Dec. 31, 1882, cited in Moon, *W. C. White and Ellen G. White*, p. 124.
61. *Bio.*, vol. 3, p. 219.
62. This statement on revelation/inspiration was not breaking new ground for Seventh-day Adventists. In a letter to L. E. Froom, W. C. White wrote: "This statement made by the General Conference of 1883 was in perfect harmony with the beliefs and positions of the pioneers in this cause, and it was, I think, the only position taken by any of our ministers and teachers until Prof. [W. W.] Prescott, president of Battle Creek College, presented in a very forceful way another view—the view held and presented by Professor Gausen [Gaussen]. The acceptance of that view by the students in the Battle Creek College and many others, including Elder Haskell, has resulted in bringing into our work questions and perplexities without end, and always increasing."—*Selected Messages,* book 3, p. 454.
63. Letter 11, 1884, cited in *Selected Messages,* book 3, pp. 96-98.
64. Alden Thompson, "Improving the *Testimonies,* Through Revisions," *Adventist Review,* Sept. 12, 1985, p. 14.
65. July 11, 1885, cited in Moon, *W. C. White and Ellen G. White,* p. 128.
66. D. M. Canright, *Seventh-day Adventism Renounced* (New York, N. Y.: Fleming H. Revell Company, 1889), p. 141. W. H. Branson wrote a 395-page reply to Canright, *In Defense of the Faith* (Washington, D. C.: Review and Herald, 1933).
67. Francois Samuel Louis Gaussen (1790-1863), a Swiss Reformed pastor, was the author of many Calvinistic works but best known for *Theopneustia.*—J. D. Douglas, editor, *The New International Dictionary of the Christian Church* (Grand Rapids, MI: Zondervan Publishing House, 1974), p. 402.
68. F. S. L. Gaussen, *The Plenary Inspiration of the Holy Scriptures* (London: Samuel Bagster, English translation, 1841), p. 304.
69. See pp. 439, 440.
70. See Alden Thompson's four-part series on "Adventists and Inspiration," *Adventist Review,* Sept. 5, 12, 19, 26, 1985.

Study Questions

1. What was the difference between Marian Davis's responsibility and that of Ellen White's other editorial assistants?

2. What is meant by writing with "a human accent"?

3. Why do you think a prophet would read widely?

4. Why did Ellen White write differently to the general public than she did to Adventists? Give examples.

5. What underlying problem caused controversy in the 1880s when the earlier *Testimonies* were to be edited?

CHAPTER 12

The Sought-for Speaker

"They read distinctly from the book, in the Law of God; and they gave the sense, and helped them to understand the reading" (Neh. 8:8). "Encourage all to use simple, pure, elevated language. Speech, pronunciation, and voice—cultivate these talents, not under any great elocutionist of the world, but under the power of the Holy Spirit of God."[1]

Probably no public speaker had a more unlikely beginning than Ellen Harmon, but late in 1844 she heard the invitation: "Make known to others what I have revealed to you." Nothing caused her more despair. She prayed to be released from this burden; she even "coveted death."[2]

Was she merely being modest? Was her reluctance prompted by Christian humility? In a way, Yes, to both questions, but she was also a realist, along with anyone else who knew this eighty-pound, "frail," seventeen-year-old. Contemporaries did not expect her to live; her respiratory problems appeared terminal. In her own words, "[I] was unused to society, and naturally so timid and retiring that it was painful for me to meet strangers."[3]

What happened when Ellen Harmon accepted her first invitation to relate her vision in Poland, Maine? Driven by a sense of duty, able to speak only in a whisper, she began "to make known to others" what God had revealed to her. After five minutes her "voice became clear and strong," and she spoke for nearly two hours "with perfect ease."[4] When she finished, her vocal problems returned—until the next time she stood in public to share her message. With each repeated "restoration" of vocal strength and ease, she became more certain that she was following in the path of duty.

From that unlikely beginning, Ellen White's seventy years of public service reveals an astonishing and unforeseen record. She became a sought-after speaker by Adventists and non-Adventists alike. For many decades she was one of the major speakers at General Conference sessions and possibly the most wanted speaker at camp meetings from coast to coast. Non-Adventists by the thousands (audiences ranging from 20 to 20,000) listened to her evangelistic sermons with great appreciation, long before there were public address systems.[5]

How did she do it? No doubt God gave her special help when she stepped out in faith in 1845. Other experiences were similar to the following at the Healdsburg, California, camp meeting, in October, 1882. During the summer she exhausted herself in heavy traveling, much preaching, and writing vigorously.[6] Though confined to her bed, she asked that she be taken to the large tent to rest on a sofa. After J. H. Waggoner finished his sermon, she asked her son to help her to the pulpit.

Recalling later, she wrote: "For five minutes I stood there trying to speak, and thinking that it was the last speech I should ever make—my farewell address. . . . All at once I felt a power come upon me, like a shock of electricity.

It passed through my body and up to my head. The people said that they plainly saw the blood mounting to my lips, my ears, my cheeks, my forehead."

A businessman from town, standing to his feet, exclaimed: "We are seeing a miracle performed before our eyes; Mrs. White is healed!"

Elder Waggoner, the previous speaker that day, wrote in his *Signs* report: "Her voice and appearance changed, and she spoke for some time with clearness and energy. She then invited those who wished to make a start in the service of God, and those who were far backslidden, to come forward, and a goodly number answered to the call."[7]

Speaking Style

Ellen White's vocal characteristics were considered unusually pleasing and powerful. A minister, reporting on his experience at the 1874 Biblical Institute in Battle Creek, wrote about James and Ellen White: "I venture the assertion that no fine-minded person can listen to either of them and not feel assured that God is with them. Sister White's style and language is altogether solemn and impressive, and sways a congregation beyond description, and in a direction always heavenward."[8]

L. H. Christian heard Ellen White for the first time in Minneapolis in 1888. Of this experience he wrote: "She began to talk in her low, pleasing, melodious voice . . . so beautifully natural. One would think she was talking to people within four or five feet of where she was standing. I wondered whether the other folks could hear. Later, at the 1905 conference in Takoma Park, Washington, D.C., after I had entered the ministry, I had a chance to test her voice. She was standing on the large platform in front addressing an audience of five thousand people, some of them in the very back of a large tent. I sat in front, and I said to myself, They never can hear in the rear so as to know what she is saying. Slipping out, I walked outside the tent to the rear, and when I came in and stood behind the great crowd I could hear every word and almost every syllable of every word just as plainly as I could up in the front.

"With her magnificent gift of speaking and her ability to control an audience and to move them either to solid thinking or to the deepest emotion, she seemed quietly sure of herself as a messenger of God; yet she did nothing to call attention to herself or exalt her authority. She merely stood there as a mouthpiece for the Lord, thinking only of His Word and seeking only to lift up Jesus, so that we might see Him alone."[9]

For students of speech and persuasion, Ellen White's speaking style is a treasure house for sustained examples of clarity, forcefulness, and beauty. "She achieved clearness by choosing uncomplicated words and sentences that were marked with directness and not likely to be misunderstood. She gained force by means of reiteration, repetitive linking, climax, anaphora, challenge, and command. She attained the higher peaks of beauty in her descriptive imagery through tropes and figures that, though familiar and common, were in balance with her themes. There was often a pleasing cadence in her prose rhythm that echoed a familiarity with the language of Scripture."[10]

S. P. S. Edwards, a physician, remembered how Ellen White had both a "conversational voice" and a "public speaking voice." In conversation, she was a "mezzo soprano," a "sweet tone, not monotonous, but especially noticeable because of the sweet smile and the personal touch she put into what she said."

"Stomach Voice"

Ellen White's speaking voice, her "stomach voice," as Edwards described it, was a "deep contralto with a wonderful carrying power. . . . We could always hear her. . . . I am not sure whether it was her voice that carried or the power of the words she spoke. . . . Everyone could hear always . . . whether it was 10,000 outdoors or a lonely heart in the privacy of her own room."[11]

In 1957-1959, Horace Shaw, long-time professor of speech at Emmanuel Missionary College (Andrews University), developed a list of 366 people who had heard Ellen White speak. He asked them to recall her platform manner, whether the event was public or private, what impressed them most, and what they remembered about her message. He also asked them to describe the influence of her speaking on the audience.[12]

Since these "hearers" were interviewed late in life, obviously they observed Mrs. White in her later years. Typical phrases included, "at 82, bent with age," "little and frail," "structurally short. . . . rather stockily built but not over obese."

Of her physical features, her face seemed to be remembered the longest—"features round and full," "sweetest smile broke out occasionally," "noticed her nose, but soon forgot it—thinking she was really pretty, dignified," and "face seemed to light up."

Eye Language

Her eyes—"beautiful brown eyes and far-away look," "truthful eye," "earnest look that seemed to penetrate," "her eyes were large and became larger if she was in earnest or excited, and grew smaller when she smiled."

There was general agreement regarding Ellen White's hair: "wore a net over neat hair," "plain hair style," "hair dark and always parted and combed back simply to a braided knot in the back of her neck."

Twenty-nine referred to her dress material, describing it as "black velvet or silk," "two-piece garment," "dress did not seem to adorn her, she seemed to adorn the dress." As an accent to the black, Mrs. White often wore white cuffs and collar. Other accessories mentioned were a "gold watch chain" with a "silver watch in her pocket, and a simple brooch."

The hundreds of respondents alike recalled that Mrs. White used few gestures, no swinging of her arms and hands—"natural poise and gentle and easy manner."

She most often preached without notes, though on some occasions she read from a manuscript. With her Bible open, she spoke with force and logic that enthralled her audiences.[13] A *Detroit Post* reporter described observing one of Mrs. White's sermons as a "remarkable and thrilling" experience: "Although her eloquence and persuasive powers were well-known by the audience, still they were unprepared for the powerful and unanswerable appeal which she made. She seemed indeed almost inspired as she implored sinners to flee from their sins. The effect of her magnetic speech and manner was most remarkable."[14]

Obviously, Mrs. White heard and saw these comments on her remarkable speaking ability. She gave God the glory but she did not always call the phenomenon a miracle. She learned how to speak by studying the fundamentals of voice projection. Further, she wrote much general counsel on effective vocal communication, and many times, specifically, to ministers who were ruining not only their voices but their health by improper speech habits.

She advocated support by the diaphragm, plus deep breathing: "Speaking from the throat, letting the words come out from the upper extremity of the vocal organs, all the time fretting and irritating them, is not the best way to preserve health or to increase the efficiency of those organs . . . . If you let your words come from deep down, exercising the abdominal muscles, you can speak to thousands with just as much ease as you can speak to ten."[15]

Ellen White's instruction on public speaking involved more than the ability to speak to thousands. Above all else, it was a spiritual matter, especially for the gospel minister: "Those who consider it a little thing to speak with an imperfect utterance dishonor God."[16] "Let the students in training for the Master's service make determined efforts to learn to speak correctly and forcibly, in order that when conversing with others in regard to the truth, or when engaged in public ministry, they may properly present the truths of heavenly origin."[17]

For Ellen White, wrong methods of speaking directly affect the speaker's health. She wrote: "Their excessive use [vocal organs] . . . will, if often repeated, not only injure the organs of speech, but will bring an undue strain upon the whole nervous system. . . . The training of the voice has an important place in physical culture, since it tends to expand and strengthen the lungs, and thus to ward off disease."[18]

Through the years, serious students of all ages have been grateful for Ellen White's counsel on public speaking. Her own experience, beginning with a hoarse whisper and developing into an often-sought-after speaker, provided profound authenticity to her principles. These principles expressed in topics such as "Christian Attitudes in Speaking," "Voice Culture," "Effective Methods of Public Speaking," "Content of Our Discourses," and "Use of the Voice in Singing," have been brought together in the volume entitled, *The Voice in Speech and Song.*[19]

General Topics

What were Mrs. White's general topics? Her public messages, according to listeners, focused on joy, on lifting the downcast, and presenting the charm of a loving Lord. A typical sermon closing would be: "This life is a conflict, and we have a foe who never sleeps, who is watching constantly to destroy our minds and lure us away from our precious Saviour, who has given His life for us. Shall we lift the cross given to us? or shall we go on in selfish gratification, and lose the eternity of bliss? . . ."[20]

Ellen White preached most often from Isaiah in the Old Testament, and the Gospel of John in the New. The New Testament chapters that she used most often were John 15 ("I am the Vine . . ."), 2 Peter 1 (ladder of Christian growth), and 1 John 3 ("What manner of love. . .").[21]

Ministers noted that her messages on the simplest of Bible topics, such as conversion, the work of the Holy Spirit, and the love of God, became unusually heart-searching moments that lifted their spirits with courage and deeper insights. At the last General Conference session she attended (1909), now 81, she asked to speak to the ministers. The ministers could think of many subjects on which they wanted her opinion.

L. H. Christian reported that she chose John 3:1-5 as her text, focusing on "Ye must be born again." The ministers were disappointed, feeling that the topic was not appropriate; they wanted something more solid.

However, after two minutes Christian was saying to himself, "That is something new. That is deeper and higher and grander than anything I have ever read or heard on the topic of the new birth, and the new birth as a daily experience for the preacher."

Then he recorded his further thoughts: "I had never before, nor have I since, heard such a heart-searching and yet kind and beautiful presentation of the work of the Holy Spirit in transforming human lives into the glorious likeness of Christ as she presented to us. . . . When her talk was finished (it lasted less than thirty minutes), we preachers said, 'That is the best for our own souls we have ever heard.' It was not critical; it was not discouraging; it did not condemn us; but it did give us a glimpse of the heights of spiritual excellence to which we might attain and to which we ought to attain if we were really servants of Christ to lead people on to a living faith in the Lord Jesus."[22]

Interesting phenomena often occurred

when Ellen White was in the pulpit. Occasionally she would stop her prepared message and recognize people in the audience that she had not seen before except in vision. At Bushnell, Michigan, on July 20, 1867, Ellen and James White found a spiritually bleak group outside under the trees. James reported that shortly after his wife began to speak, she laid aside her Bible and began to address those who recently had been baptized. Because she had not seen them before, except in vision, she "designated each brother and sister by his or her position, as the one by that tree, or the one sitting by that brother or sister of the Greenville or Orleans church, with whom she was personally acquainted, and whom she called by name."

For the next hour, she reviewed the cases, one by one, stating that the Lord had shown her their condition two years before, that while she was reading her text from the Bible their individual needs were illuminated "like sudden lightning in a dark night distinctly revealing every object around."

What was the response? Each person, when addressed, arose and "testified that their cases had been described better than they could have done it themselves." Wrongs were righted and a reformation unfolded that led to a strong church.[23]

Sometimes Ellen White was taken off in vision while preaching. At Lovett's Grove, Ohio, mid-March, 1858, after her husband preached a funeral sermon, she was bearing her testimony on the cheery hope of the Second Advent. Then, she wrote later, "I was wrapt in a vision of God's glory." For the next two hours she remained in vision as those in that crowded schoolhouse watched with avid interest. That Lovett's Grove vision has come to be known as "the great controversy vision."[24]

Non-Adventist Audiences

Non-Adventist audiences listened to her messages, often lasting more than an hour, in rapt and grateful appreciation. A newspaper reporter covered a lecture that she gave in Battle Creek, Michigan, in 1887:

"There was a good attendance including a large number of our most prominent people, at the lecture of Mrs. Ellen G. White, at the Tabernacle, last evening. This lady gave her audience a most eloquent discourse, which was listened to with marked interest and attention. Her talk was interspersed with instructive facts which she had gathered in her recent visit to foreign lands, and demonstrated that this gifted lady has, in addition to her many other rare qualifications, a great faculty for attentive careful observation and a remarkable memory of details; this together with her fine delivery and her faculty of clothing her ideas in choice, beautiful and appropriate language, made her lecture one of the best that has ever been delivered by any lady in our city. That she may soon favor our community with another address, is the earnest wish of all who attended last evening, and should she do so, there will be a large attendance."[25]

At times some have asserted that the beauty, force, and power of Ellen White's writings are due to her editorial assistants. But who were the editorial assistants who interposed between her and her audiences? No literary assistant stood by her side, "polishing up" her grammar, "correcting" her details, etc., as she used "choice, beautiful and appropriate language."

This "gifted lady" with a "remarkable memory of details" demonstrated, as is true for many other public persons, that speaking skills are often different from one's writing techniques. Writing habits often reveal that the author's mind is racing faster than the pen can write; regardless, the author knows that the end product is what really matters, not the hasty techniques the author uses to get thought on paper.

Clifton L. Taylor, a long-time college Bible teacher, reflected on an occasion when he heard Ellen White for the first time: "All my life I had heard of this woman, and had wished to hear and see for myself. . . . I had heard her critics declare that her writings were largely the work of her secretaries. Now I observed that in her extemporaneous speech her statements were filled with expressions exactly like those I had read so many times in her writings. . . . As she related her various experiences . . . she impressed me as one who was glad to share with others the richness and blessing she had received."[26]

Comments by the journalistic world were not limited to Ellen White's "gifted" platform skills. They also included her straightforward message: "I would that all other religious beliefs in Battle Creek were as true to morality as Mrs. White and her adherents. Then we would have no infamous dens of vice, no grog shops, no tobacco stores, no gambling hells, no air polluted with the fumes of rum and that fell destroyer of man, tobacco."[27]

Mrs. White enjoyed responding to invitations from non-Adventist churches. In 1880, after she had spoken at the Salem, Oregon, camp meeting (which was held in the town square), some Methodists were impressed. Church leaders requested that she speak to them on the following Sunday. In a letter to James, she described the event: "Sunday evening the Methodist church, a grand building, was well filled. I spoke to about seven hundred people who listened with deep interest. The Methodist minister thanked me for the discourse. The Methodist minister's wife and all seemed much pleased."[28]

In that remarkable wagon-train trail ride in 1879, James and Ellen White preached most every evening to those "on the ride" and to those along the way. Writing of one experience, she said: "Last night I spoke to one hundred people assembled in a respectable meetinghouse. We find here an excellent class of people. . . . I had great freedom in presenting before them the love of God evidenced to man in the gift of His Son. All listened with the deepest interest. The Baptist minister arose and said we had heard the gospel that night and he hoped all would heed the words spoken."[29]

Adventist leaders realized the unique contribution of the Whites to their various meetings. Uriah Smith reported on the Sparta, Wisconsin, camp meeting in 1876: "Here, as in Iowa, the presence of Brother and Sister White constituted, in a large measure, the life of the meeting, their counsel and labors giving tone to the exercises and progress of the work. Sister White, especially, was at times called out in powerful appeals, and most forcible descriptions of scenes in the life of Christ from which lessons can be drawn applicable to everyday Christian experience. These were of absorbing interest to all the congregation. These servants of the church, though now of so long and large experience, and notwithstanding all their wearing labors, are still growing in mental and spiritual strength."[30]

One of the Ablest Platform Speakers

When James died in 1881, his contributions were recorded in several newspapers. Included in these life sketches and eulogies were comments on Mrs. White and her public work: "He has been admirably aided in his ministerial and educational labors by his wife, Ellen G. White, one of the ablest platform speakers and writers in the west."[31]

"In 1846 he married Ellen G. Harmon, a woman of extraordinary endowments, who has been a co-laborer in all his work and contributed largely to his success by her gifts as a writer and especially her power as a public speaker."[32]

In 1878, at the age of 50, Ellen White was included in the reference book, *American Biographical History of Eminent and Self-Made Men of the State of Michigan, Third Congressional District,* page 108: "Mrs. White is a woman of singularly well-balanced mental organization. Benevolence, spirituality, conscientiousness, and ideality are the predominating traits. Her personal qualities are such as to win for her the warmest fellowship of all with whom she comes in contact, and to inspire them with the utmost confidence in her sincerity. . . . Notwithstanding her many years of public labor, she has retained all the simplicity and honesty which characterized her early life.

"As a speaker, Mrs. White is one of the most successful of the few ladies who have become noteworthy as lecturers, in this country, during the last twenty years. Constant use has so strengthened her vocal organs as to give her voice rare depth and power. Her clearness and strength of articulation are so great that, when speaking in the open air, she has frequently been distinctly heard at the distance of a mile. Her language, though simple, is always forcible and elegant. When inspired with her subject, she is often marvelously eloquent, holding the largest audiences spellbound for hours without a sign of impatience or weariness.

"The subject matter of her discourses is always of a practical character, bearing chiefly on fireside duties, the religious education of children, temperance, and kindred topics. On revival occasions, she is always the most effective speaker. She has frequently spoken to immense audiences, in the large cities, on her favorite themes, and has always been received with great favor."[33]

Endnotes

1. *The Voice in Speech and Song*, p. 15.
2. *Testimonies,* vol. 1, p. 63; *Life Sketches,* p. 70.
3. *Life Sketches,* pp. 69, 70.
4. *Ibid.,* p. 72.
5. The attendance of about 20,000 at the Groveland camp meeting, Groveland, Massachusetts, August 25-30, 1876, reached an all-time high in Adventist camp meetings. Many more were denied access to the meetings because all transportation services, including trains, river steamers, barges, etc., were taxed beyond their capacity to accommodate all who wished to attend, according to a local news reporter. —*Review and Herald,* Sept. 7, 1876, p. 84. As soon as she finished, Ellen White was invited by the Haverhill Temperance Reform Club to speak the next evening. She reported: "The Queen of England could not have been more honored. . . . One thousand people were before me of the finest and most select of the city. I was stopped several times with clapping of hands and stomping of feet. . . . Never did I witness such enthusiasm as these noble men leading out in temperance reform manifested over my talk upon temperance. It was new to them. I spoke of Christ's fast in the wilderness and its object. I spoke against tobacco. I was besieged after the meeting and commended, and I was urged, if I came to Haverhill, to speak to them again."—Letter 42, 1876, cited in *Bio.,* vol. 3, p. 46; see Uriah Smith, "Grand Rally in New England," *Review and Herald,* Sept. 7, 1876, p. 84.
6. In July she had written five hundred manuscript pages. See *Bio.,* vol. 3, p. 202.
7. *Bio.,* vol. 3, p. 204; see also p. 158. Reflecting on this phenomenon that happened often, Mervyn Maxwell suggests that "God could have healed her outright, but evidently He preferred to provide this proof of His nearness when she stood up to speak." —Maxwell, *Tell It to the World,* p. 197.
8. *Review and Herald,* Jan. 8, 1875, p. 14. On another occasion, J. N. Loughborough observed: "Sister White gave two searching and powerful, practical discourses."—*Signs of the Times,* Jan. 11, 1877, p. 24. D. M. Canright, then president of the Ohio Conference, wrote: "Sister White spoke for a little while on the great importance of the Sabbath school work, in her usually forcible and eloquent manner." —*Review and Herald,* Sept. 4, 1879, p. 85.
9. Christian, *Fruitage of Spiritual Gifts,* pp. 45, 46.
10. Horace Shaw, "A Rhetorical Analysis of the Speaking of Mrs. Ellen G. White, A Pioneer Leader and Spokeswoman of the Seventh-day Adventist Church" (Michigan State University, 1959, a doctoral dissertation), p. 282.
11. *Ibid.,* p. 514.
12. *Ibid.*, pp. 502-510, 606-644.
13. "When I am speaking to the people, I say much that I have not premeditated. The Spirit of the Lord frequently comes upon me. I seem to be carried out of, and away from myself; the life and character of different persons are clearly presented before my mind. I see their errors and dangers, and feel compelled to speak of what is thus brought before me."—*Testimonies,* vol. 5, p. 678.
14. Cited in *Review and Herald,* Aug. 18, 1874, p. 68.
15. *Testimonies,* vol. 2, p. 616. "The right use of the abdominal muscles in reading and speaking will prove a remedy for many voice and chest difficulties, and the means of prolonging life."—*Counsels to Parents and Teachers,* p. 297.
16. *Evangelism*, p. 665.
17. *Ibid.,* p. 666.
18. *Ibid.,* pp. 667, 669.
19. Pacific Press Publishing Association, 1988.
20. *Life Sketches*, pp. 291, 292.
21. Shaw, "A Rhetorical Analysis of the Speaking of

Mrs. Ellen G. White," p. 355.

22. Christian, *Fruitage of Spiritual Gifts,* p. 47.
23. *Signs of the Times,* Aug. 29, 1878, p. 260.
24. See Chapter 22; *Bio.*, vol. 1, pp. 368-375.
25. "Mrs. Ellen G. White's Able Address. A Characteristic and Eloquent Discourse by This Remarkable Lady," Battle Creek *Daily Journal*, Oct. 5, 1887. The editor and publisher of the Newton (Iowa) *Free Press* gave extended space to the Adventist camp meeting in early June, 1875. Among his remarks, he said: "Mrs. White is a preacher of great ability and force, much called for as a speaker at the camp meetings of the denomination all over the Union, and a large share of her time is given to this work."
26. *Review and Herald,* Sept. 25, 1958, p. 3.
27. *Lansing* [Michigan] *Republican*, Jan. 7, 1880, cited in *Bio.*, vol. 3, p. 131.
28. Letter 33a, 1880, cited in *Bio.*, vol. 3, p. 142; later in the letter she mentioned: "One of the Methodist ministers said to Brother Levitt that he regretted Mrs. White was not a staunch Methodist, for they would make her a bishop at once; she could do justice to the office." See also *Ibid.*, p. 88.
29. Letter 36, 1879, cited in *Ibid.,* p. 111. In October, 1886, Ellen White presented twelve consecutive evangelistic messages, ten of which are available today. Her sermon texts and topics reveal the Christ-centered emphasis of her sermons. See also Delafield, *Ellen G. White in Europe,* pp. 239, 240.
30. *Review and Herald,* June 29, 1876, p. 4.
31. *Lansing* [Michigan] *Republican,* Aug. 9, 1881, cited in Nichol, *Ellen G. White and Her Critics,* p. 475.
32. *The Echo* [Detroit], Aug. 10, 1881, cited in Nichol, *Ibid.,* p. 475.
33. Cited in Shaw, "A Rhetorical Analysis of the Speaking of Mrs. Ellen G. White," pp. 28, 29, and in Arthur White, *Messenger to the Remnant,* pp. 114-115.

Study Questions

1. What were the chief characteristics of Ellen White's speaking style?

2. How does correct speaking aid physical health?

3. What Bible passages did Ellen White quote most often?

4. What was Ellen White's favorite theme, the one that she emphasized throughout her ministry? Check the CD-ROM containing Ellen White's published writings for clues.

5. From the standpoint of persuasion, how did Ellen White use language to gain fair, favorable attention? Think of examples that reflect simplicity, force of well-chosen words, illustrations, etc.

The Listening Messenger

CHAPTER

CHAPTER 13

Delivering God's Message

"Then the Spirit entered me when He spoke to me, and set me on my feet; and I heard Him who spoke to me" (Ezekiel 2:2).

The Millerites, in the early 1840s, with their millennial expectations, were "predisposed . . . to the powerful outpouring of charismatic prophesyings, tongues, healings, and other 'signs and wonders,' which fulfilled the Biblical promise for the 'last days.'. . . Their gatherings convulsed with shouts, praises, weeping, and 'melting seasons of prayer.'"

Though Millerite leaders, such as Miller himself, Charles Fitch, and Joshua V. Himes, opposed "charismatic phenomena," the movement was "commonly criticized". . . for such "fanaticism" as healings, speaking in tongues, visions, and prophesyings . . . . Several Millerite women received press coverage for their "visions."[1]

After October 22, 1844, for most Millerites and the scoffing religious world generally, charismatic phenomena such as visions were highly suspect. Millerites, stung by being labeled as fanatics, were especially wary of anyone claiming to have visions.[2]

Two other "Millerites" (William Foy and Hazen Foss) had felt the opposition to visions. Foy had four visions but received none after 1844. He shared them with people whenever he found interested hearers.

Foss never revealed his visions to others but recognized the authenticity of Ellen Harmon when he heard her visions explained.[3]

Disappointed Millerites fell into several major groups in the late 1840s over their beliefs in what happened in 1844: (1) Those who continued to believe that Christ's return was imminent, that their mistake was in fixing on the wrong date. This group included the main Millerite leaders (Miller, Bliss, Hale, and Himes); (2) those who believed that Christ had indeed come, but not as a physical event; the spiritual experience of the believers became the "second coming" to them, thus they were labeled "spiritualizers"; and (3) those who believed that the date was correct but that the event occurred in heaven with the commencement of Christ's High Priestly ministration in the "most holy place"—the emerging Seventh-day Adventist Church.[4]

Ellen White became the one clear voice that rallied the third group who believed that the October 22, 1844, date had important cosmic significance.[5] She helped to steer the emerging group of Bible students between the fanaticisms of the "spiritualizers" on the left and the "First-day Adventists" on the right, who repudiated both the significance of October 22 and "spiritual gifts." Confusion and rejection reigned on both sides of the early Sabbatarian Adventists. The visions of Ellen Harmon (before her marriage, 1844-1846; Ellen White after 1846) became the confirming, correcting, comforting center for the emergence of the third group's integrated Biblical platform.[6]

Purpose of the Visions

No one can read very far into the writings of Mrs. White without becoming aware of her profound veneration for the Bible. She was a champion of Bible study, and in the strongest words urged consistent and thorough Bible study.[7]

In fact, one of the signs of false prophets is their attempt to make of none effect the work of former prophets (Isaiah 8:20). One of the prime signs of genuine prophets is their constant reference to former prophets. The coherency and unity of the Bible rest on this simple fact borne out through the years. One of the common observations made regarding Ellen White is that she made extensive use of Scripture in her sermons and in her voluminous writings.

But if the Bible is "the only true guide in all matters of faith and practice,"[8] why were the messages of Ellen White necessary? What is the purpose of her prophetic role?

She explained why her messages were needed: "I took the precious Bible and surrounded it with the several *Testimonies for the Church*, given for the people of God. Here, said I, the cases of nearly all are met. The sins they are to shun are pointed out. The counsel that they desire can be found here, given for other cases situated similarly to themselves. God has been pleased to give you line upon line and precept upon precept. But there are not many of you that really know what is contained in the *Testimonies*. You are not familiar with the Scriptures. If you had made God's Word your study, with a desire to reach the Bible standard and attain to Christian perfection, you would not have needed the *Testimonies*. It is because you have neglected to acquaint yourselves with God's inspired Book that He has sought to reach you by simple, direct testimonies."[9]

Only when their purpose is clearly understood will Ellen White's writings be properly appreciated. She explained why God saw the need to speak through her: "To bring the minds of His people to His Word"[10]; to simplify "the great truths already given"[11]; to call attention to "Biblical principles for the formation of correct habits of living"[12]; to specify "man's duty to God and to his fellow man"[13]; and "to encourage the desponding."[14]

In essence, the messages of Ellen White were given not "for a new rule of faith, but for the comfort of His people, and to correct those who err from Bible truth."[15]

Vision Phenomena

Ellen Harmon/White shared with the Biblical prophets similar physical characteristics while in open, or public, vision.[16] In 1868 James White gave the following comprehensive description of his wife in vision:

"1. She is utterly unconscious of everything transpiring around her, as has been proved by the most rigid tests, but views herself as removed from this world, and in the presence of heavenly beings.

"2. She does not breathe. During the entire period of her continuance in vision, which has at different times ranged from fifteen minutes to three hours, there is no breath, as has been repeatedly proved by pressing upon the chest, and by closing the mouth and nostrils.

"3. Immediately on entering vision, her muscles become rigid, and joints fixed, so far as any external force can influence them. At the same time her movements and gestures, which are frequent, are free and graceful, and cannot be hindered nor controlled by the strongest person.

"4. On coming out of vision, whether in the day-time or a well-lighted room at night, all is total darkness. Her power to distinguish even the most brilliant objects, held within a few inches of the eyes, returns but gradually, sometimes not being fully established for three hours. This has continued for the past twenty years; yet her eyesight is not in the least impaired, few persons having better than she now possesses.

"She has probably had, during the past twenty-three years, between one and two hundred visions. These have been given under almost every variety of circumstances, yet maintaining a wonderful similarity; the most apparent change being, that of late years they have grown less frequent, but more comprehensive. She has been taken off in vision most frequently when bowed in prayer.

"Several times, while earnestly addressing the congregation, unexpectedly to herself and to all around her, she has been instantly prostrated in vision. This was the case June 12, 1868, in the presence of not less than two hundred Sabbathkeepers, in the house of worship, in Battle Creek, Mich. On receiving baptism at my hands, at an early period of her experience, as I raised her up out of the water, immediately she was in vision. Several times, when prostrated by sickness, she has been relieved in answer to the prayer of faith and taken off in vision. At such times her restoration to usual health has been wonderful.

"At another time, when walking with friends, in conversation upon the glories of the kingdom of God, as she was passing through the gate before her father's house, the Spirit of God came upon her, and she was instantly taken off in vision. And what may be important to those who think the visions the result of mesmerism, she has a number of times been taken off in vision when in prayer alone in the grove or in the closet.

"It may be well to speak as to the effect of the visions upon her constitution and strength. When she had her first vision, she was an emaciated invalid, given up by her friends and physicians to die of consumption. She then weighed but eighty pounds. Her nervous condition was such that she could not write, and was dependent on one sitting near her at the table to even pour her drink from the cup to the saucer. And notwithstanding her anxieties and mental agonies, in consequence of her duty to bring her views before the public, her labors in public speaking, and in church matters generally, her wearisome travels, and home labors and cares, her health and physical and mental strength have improved from the day she had her first vision."[17]

But visions cannot be explained or authenticated by physical characteristics only. Many times, especially during night visions/dreams, Ellen White did not exhibit the typical physical characteristics. Physical phenomena were not the proof of her divine credentials.[18]

Further, as Arthur G. Daniells wrote: "Those who would accept such physical phenomena as the determining evidence may be deceived, for the enemy of righteousness may produce similar conditions in persons subject to his control."[19] Ellen White warned: "There will be those who will claim to have visions. When God gives you clear evidence that the vision is from Him, you may accept it, but do not accept it on any other evidence; for people are going to be led more and more astray in foreign countries and in America. The Lord wants His people to act like men and women of sense."[20]

Why, then, did physical phenomena accompany the visions given to Biblical prophets? Why were physical manifestations so extraordinary and so widely documented during the public visions of Ellen White? Apparently, as in Biblical times, God used the miraculous to capture attention and hold it long enough for people to hear the message of the prophet. The message itself bore the divine credentials; the physical phenomena demonstrated the presence of the supernatural.[21]

Ellen White received messages from God in different ways. Messages received during waking hours are called open visions, those during sleep, dreams. The duration of visions extended from less than a minute to more than an hour, and on one occasion, about four hours. At times visions occurred as "an almost instantaneous flashlight view given of certain situations or conditions. At such times the vision usually related to only one subject or one phase of a subject, while the longer views might take in many, many subjects, or deal with events occurring over a long period of time."[22]

Open visions could be expected on almost any occasion. At times, while writing out the day's events in her diary, pertinent thoughts would come "like a flash of lightning . . . so sharply [that] I wrote on and on."[23]

While a group of believers were united in family prayer on a Sabbath morning, Ellen White gave that ringing shout of "Glory! Glory! Glory!" (to which audiences through the years had become accustomed), and her husband James arose, informing the audience that his wife was in vision.[24]

Frequently she had a vision in a church service. The Parkville, Michigan, vision, on January 12, 1861, which depicted some of the facts and terrors of the coming Civil War, was received in church after she finished her powerful exhortation and had sat down. The vision lasted for approximately twenty minutes. After she began breathing again, she spoke briefly about what had been revealed to her, especially certain items that related directly to that intensely interested audience.

Ellen White's last public vision, for which we have detailed information, occurred in Battle Creek on January 3, 1875. J. N. Loughborough, however, (who personally witnessed "about fifty" visions) attested that her last public vision was at the 1884 Oregon camp meeting.[25]

Night visions, or dreams, occurred in various ways, such as "at the beginning of the Sabbath I fell asleep, and some things were clearly presented before me."[26] Hundreds of letters contained the phrase, "in the night season," wherein she heard or saw a message that had to be communicated to some particular person or group, such as a church, camp meeting, or official meeting. At times that phrase may have been absent but the occasion was obvious: "I cannot sleep. I was awakened at one o'clock. I was hearing a message borne to you."[27]

Night visions or dreams became more customary even as open visions became less frequent.

Recognizing that questions would arise concerning the private nature of "dreams" and their authenticity as revelations, Ellen White wrote: "The multitude of dreams [ordinary dreams] arise from the common things of life, with which the Spirit of God has nothing to do. There are also false dreams, as well as false visions, which are inspired by the spirit of Satan. But dreams from the Lord are classed in the Word of God with visions, and are as truly the fruits of the Spirit of prophecy as visions. Such dreams, taking into the account the persons who have them, and the circumstances under which they are given, contain their own proofs of their genuineness."[28]

Messages Received in Different Ways

Variety best describes the manner in which Mrs. White received visions and dreams, and the way she conveyed the messages to others was as varied as the manner in which she received the visions.

Ellen White was involved in her visions and dreams in at least nine ways.[29] The visions referred to in this book can be classified under these nine categories:

1. At times, she was seemingly present and participating in the events of the vision.[30]

2. Some visions were panoramic, with

sweeping views of the past, present, and future.[31]

3. An angel (or some other heavenly person, such as "my Guide," etc.) would observe the event with her and provide an interpretation.[32]

4. Occasionally she saw buildings yet to be constructed and was given instruction as to her role in instructing those who were to work in that future building.[33]

5. Her Guide either explained symbolic representations or their meaning was self-evident.[34]

6. Often she "visited" various institutions, committee meetings, families in their homes, and persons who thought they were observed by "no one."[35]

7. Sometimes, she was given contrasting developments: one would be the consequences of not following inspired instruction, the other, the results of following her counsel.[36]

8. Frequently, she had specific information for the benefit of her husband, for themselves as parents, and for fellow leaders of the church and its institutions.[37]

9. Often, she was shown sweeping principles that would integrate some advanced opinions of her day with additional insights on such subjects as health, education, and temperance.[38]

Messages Were Diverse and Broad

Ellen White received messages for individuals and groups that covered a broad array of subjects. Men and women received admonition, encouragement, and reproof regarding their personal lives and their Christian influence. Individuals and groups received insights, caution, and direction in general ideas, including education, health, administrative policy, evangelistic and publishing principles, and church finance.[39]

Manner of Delivering Messages Varied

The manner of giving the information received in vision was varied and never predictable. At times, Ellen White was instructed to "go public" with private testimonies. How could this be?

She saw people and events in vision that others could not see in their true light. When these people resisted counsel, ignoring the privately sent reproof, she saw her duty to the whole church. She was told by her heavenly Guide that the church must not continue to languish because of those who refused correction: "I was taken off in vision [December 23, 1860], and was shown the wrongs of individuals which have affected the cause. I dare not withhold the testimony from the church to spare the feelings of individuals."[40]

What happened after she went public in print, often identifying her co-workers with their initials? In the *Review and Herald* for the next few months, most of those who were identified in her testimonies acknowledged the truth of these testimonies and confessed their errors. Ten years later, when these testimonies were reprinted, she substituted blanks for the initials. References to personalities were removed, but the principles remained.

On other occasions, she reproved men and women openly, in public meetings. For example, in her diary describing a Sabbath meeting in 1868 at Tuscola, Michigan, she noted that she had spoken one hour, reproving individual wrongs: "Some felt exceedingly bad because I brought out these cases before others. I was sorry to see this spirit."[41] In a letter to Edson, her son, she explained that these public testimonies focused on "the sin of hasty speaking, jesting, joking, and laughing"—all very public manifestations.

But one couple was seriously offended. The wife, with her husband, came crying: "You have killed me, you have killed me clean off." In her letter to Edson, Ellen White continued: "I found their greatest difficulty was that the testimony was given before others and that if I had sent it to them alone, it would have been received all right. Pride was hurt, pride was wounded terribly. We talked awhile, and they both cooled down wonderfully and said they felt differently."[42]

Visions were often directed to specific events that would convince non-Adventists that Ellen White was a genuine messenger of the Lord. In 1850 the Whites were in Oswego, New York, doing their usual work of writing and preaching. The county treasurer, who was also the local Methodist lay preacher, had developed a lively interest among the town people. Two young people, Hiram Patch and his fiancee, had attended both the Methodist meetings and the Adventist meetings and were undecided as to which group they should join. The couple witnessed Ellen White in vision, after which they asked, "What do you think of Brother M [county treasurer]?" Mrs. White answered (as Mr. Patch recalled), after noting Hosea 5:6, 7: "I was told [in vision] to say to you that in this case the statement of the text will be literally fulfilled. Wait a month, and you will know for yourself the character of the persons who are engaged in this revival, and who profess to have such a great burden for sinners."[43]

Shortly after this conversation, the county treasurer broke a blood vessel and remained at home in a "feeble condition." The sheriff and a deputy, after taking over the county finances, found a deficit of $1,000. When confronted at his home, the treasurer pleaded ignorance. But the deputy brought into the house the missing $1,000 in a bag that the treasurer's wife had tried to hide in a snowbank.

The treasurer's evangelistic meetings terminated, and the two young people made their choice to join the Adventists—they had witnessed clear evidence of the genuineness and helpfulness of Ellen White's visions.[44]

A vision (or a dream) often turned a group from hasty decisions to the right course of action to be seen better as time went by. In the summer of 1881 James and Ellen White were tired. She was ill. However, she had a "deep impression" that they should leave the Michigan camp meeting and go to the Iowa camp meeting, which was to open in two days. When they arrived in Des Moines, she said to a minister, "Well, we are here at the Lord's bidding, for what special purpose we do not know, but we shall doubtless know as the meeting progresses."

The Whites did much of the preaching. On Sunday evening, after Mrs. White had retired, the constituency was conducting a business meeting on the subject of voting, especially in regard to temperance and prohibition. After a short time the message came that the group wanted her counsel. G. B. Starr recalled later that Ellen White related a dream that described the Iowa circumstance and that the heavenly spokesman had said: "God designs to help the people in a great movement on this subject. He also designed that you, as a people, should be the head and not the tail in the movement; but now the position you have taken will place you at the tail."

In the meeting, Mrs. White was asked whether the Iowa Adventists should vote for prohibition. Her answer was swift: "Yes, to a man everywhere and perhaps I shall shock some of you if I say, If necessary, vote on the Sabbath day for prohibition if you cannot at any other time."

Writing later, Starr emphasized: "I can testify that the effect of the relation of that dream was electrical upon the whole conference. A convincing power attended it, and I saw for the first time the unifying power of the gift of prophecy in the church."[45]

Sometimes delivering a testimony was unusually dramatic. In May 1853, at Vergennes, Michigan, an incident happened that greatly increased confidence in Ellen White's visions. The matter concerned Mrs. Alcott, a woman who had professed great holiness and now was ingratiating herself among the new believers. Mrs. White had a vision earlier in

Tyrone, Michigan, regarding this woman's real spiritual state and wrote out some of the details. Two ministers, M. E. Cornell and J. N. Loughborough, knew of the written details and said, "Now we will watch, and see how the case comes out."[46]

Finally arriving at Vergennes, with Loughborough and Cornell present, Mrs. White said to her husband in front of the house where they were to stay, that they must find the church where "that woman lives whom I saw in the Tyrone vision." She also noted that the couple who were entertaining them knew this woman. The wife had no confidence in Mrs. Alcott but her husband "thinks she is all right." (No conversation had yet taken place between this couple and the Whites.)

Soon a carriage drove up and Ellen White said that none in that load had any confidence in "that woman's pretensions." When the next carriage drove up, she said that load was divided. The third load were "all under the woman's influence." Then she said: "This must be the church where that woman lives; for I have seen all these persons in connection with that affair."

On Sabbath, while James White was preaching, an old man, a young man, and a woman came in, the woman remaining near the door. When James finished his sermon, Ellen White rose to say a few words about the care ministers must take in their work. She said that God did not call a woman to travel with any man other than her husband. To make her point, she referred to "that woman who just sat down near the door. . . . God has showed me that she and this young man have violated the seventh commandment." Loughborough commented: "All in that barn knew that Sister White had never personally seen these individuals until they came into that barn. Her picking out of the persons and her delineation of the case had weight in favor of her vision."

What was Mrs. Alcott's response? Loughborough wrote: "She slowly arose to her feet, put on a sanctimonious look, and said, 'God—knows—my—heart.' That was all she said, and sat down. Here was just what the Lord showed (May 28) that the woman would say. On June 11 she did just as it was said she would do, and said the identical words predicted she would say when reproved, and no more."

What about the young man? A few weeks later, before he returned to Canada, he was asked regarding Ellen White's vision, and he replied, "That vision was too true."[47]

Another experience, perhaps even more dramatic, and even more of a misfortune if Ellen White's visions were not accurate, happened at the Wisconsin camp meeting in the early 1870s. The speaker had already begun when the Whites arrived. Ellen and James paused as she said something to James, not heard by those who watched. But those closest heard James say, "All right!" Down the center aisle they went but Ellen White did not sit down. She looked up at the preacher, pointed her finger at him and said, "Brother, I have heard your voice in vision, and when I entered this tent this morning, I recognized that voice, and the Lord told me when I heard that voice, to look straight up and deliver the message that He gave me for you and I will have to do it."

The preacher stopped. Ellen White continued: "Brother, I know a woman in Pennsylvania with two little children. That woman calls you husband and those children call you father and they are hunting everywhere for you and they can't find you. They don't know where you are. Right over there is another woman with six children hanging to her skirts and she calls you husband and they call you father. Brother, you have no business in that desk."

The preacher made one lunge for the tent flap and vanished. His brother, who was sitting in the audience, sprang to his feet, telling the stunned audience, "Brethren, the worst of it is, it is all true."[48]

Many were the life experiences of

most every kind that Ellen White addressed, always counseling, reproving, encouraging, whatever the need. In every instance, recipients and observers alike noted that no one could possibly have known the facts of the situation unless the Spirit of God had prompted His human messenger.[49]

Endnotes

1. Jonathan Butler, "The Making of a New Order," in Ronald L. Numbers and Jonathan M. Butler, editors, *The Disappointed* (Bloomington, IN: Indiana University Press, 1987), p. 196.
2. See pp. 36, 37. Winthrop S. Hudson, "A Time of Religious Ferment," in the *Rise of Adventism*, pp. 8-10; Knight, *Millennial Fever*, pp. 267-293, 303.
3. See pp. 38-40; Baker, *The Unknown Prophet*, p. 130.
4. See Knight, *Millennial Fever*, pp. 245-300; Schwarz, *Light Bearers*, pp. 56-58.
5. See pp. 40, 41.
6. See pp. 182-238 for the contribution of Ellen White to the development of Seventh-day Adventist doctrine and thus to the stability of the Seventh-day Adventist Church.
7. See *Christ's Object Lessons*, pp. 109-114; *Counsels to Parents*, pp. 138, 139; *Education*, pp. 185-192; *Fundamentals of Christian Education*, p. 187; *Selected Messages*, book 1, pp. 15-18, 242-245; *Testimonies*, vol. 2, p. 694; *Testimonies to Ministers*, pp. 105-111, etc.
8. *Review and Herald*, Jan. 4, 1881, p. 3.
9. *Testimonies*, vol. 5, pp. 664, 665.
10. *Ibid*., p. 663.
11. *Ibid*., p. 665.
12. *Ibid*., pp. 663, 664.
13. *Ibid*., p. 665.
14. *Review and Herald*, Jan. 10, 1856, p. 118. Read *Testimonies*, vol. 5, pp. 654-696, for full context.
15. *Early Writings*, p. 78; see pp. 170-172.
16. See pp. 26-40
17. James White, *Life Incidents, in Connection With the Great Advent Movement*, pp. 272, 273, cited in F. D. Nichol, *Ellen G. White and Her Critics* (Washington D.C.: Review and Herald Publishing Association, 1951), pp. 52, 53. Present at the Parkville, Mich., vision on January 12, 1861, was a spiritualist physician who had boasted earlier that he could bring Ellen White out of her "hypnotic" trances in a minute. Being reminded of his boast, he went forward to begin his examination. Suddenly "he turned deathly pale, and shook like an aspen leaf. Elder White said, 'Will the doctor report her condition?' He replied, 'She does not breathe,' and rapidly made his way to the door. Those at the door who knew of his boasting spirit said, 'Go back, and do as you said you would do; bring that woman out of the vision.' In great agitation he grasped the knob of the door, but was not permitted to open it until inquiry was made by those near the door, 'Doctor, what is it?' He replied, 'God only knows; let me out of this house.'"—J. N. Loughborough, *GSAM*, pp. 210-211. On June 26, 1854, three people recalled how two physicians examined Ellen White while in vision. One brought a mirror close to her mouth and reported, "She doesn't breathe." After examining her sides as she spoke, he still could not find evidence for breathing. Later, after placing a lighted candle close to her lips without the slightest flicker, the physician reported, "That settles it forever, there is no breath in her body." —*Bio*., vol. 1, pp. 302, 303; see also p. 351 for an incident at Hillsdale, Michigan, on Feb. 12-15, 1857.
18. See pp. 28, 32.
19. *The Abiding Gift of Prophecy*, p. 273. "Let none cherish the idea that special providences or miraculous manifestations are to be the proof of the genuineness of their work or of the ideas they advocate. If we keep these things before the people, they will produce an evil effect, an unhealthful emotion. . . . We shall encounter false claims; false prophets will arise; there will be false dreams and false visions; but preach the Word, be not drawn away from the voice of God in His Word. Let nothing divert the mind. The wonderful, the marvelous, will be represented and presented. Through satanic delusions, wonderful miracles, the claims of human agents will be urged. Beware of all this." —*Selected Messages*, book 2, pp. 48, 49.
20. *Evangelism*, p. 610.
21. See "Physical Phenomena Often Provide Coercive Evidence," p. 36.
22. Arthur White, *Ellen G. White, Messenger to the Remnant*, p. 8.
23. *Bio*., vol. 4, p. 359.
24. *Ibid*., vol. 1, p. 275.
25. *Ibid*., vol. 2, p. 462.
26. *Ibid*., vol. 4, p. 424.
27. Letter 21a, 1895, cited in *Bio*., vol. 4, p. 251.
28. *Testimonies*, vol. 1, pp. 569, 570 (1867); repeated in *Ibid*., vol. 5, p. 658.
29. Arthur White, *Ellen G. White, Messenger to the Remnant*, pp. 9-11.
30. *Early Writings*, p. 14.
31. *The Great Controversy*, pp. x, xi. Two Civil War visions are reviewed in Roger Coon, *The Great Visions of Ellen G. White* (Hagerstown, MD: Review and Herald Publishing Association, 1992), pp. 76-89.
32. *Testimonies*, vol. 9, pp. 92, 93.
33. Letter 135, 1903, cited in *Bio*., vol. 6, pp. 96, 97.
34. "Push a long car up a steep ascent"—*MR*, vol. 1, p. 26; "Satan . . . conductor of the train"—*Early Writings*, pp. 88, 89; "gigantic iceberg . . . . 'meet it!'"—*Selected Messages*, book 1, p. 205.
35. Letter 1, 1893, in *MR*, vol. 20, pp. 51, 52.
36. *Testimonies*, vol. 9, pp. 28, 29.
37. See pp. 114, 115.
38. See pp. 278-369.
39. For a sample of some of these diverse testimonies, note: "November 5, 1862, I was shown the condition of Brother Hull. He was in an alarming state."—*Testimonies*, vol. 1, p. 426. "June 5, 1863, I was shown that Satan is ever at work to dishearten and lead astray ministers. . . . The most effectual way in which he [Satan] can work is through home influences, through unconsecrated companions."—*Ibid*., p. 449. I was shown that Sabbathkeepers as a people labor too hard without allowing themselves change or periods of rest."—*Ibid*., p. 514. "In the vision given me in Rochester, New

York, December 25, 1865, I was shown that our Sabbathkeeping people have been negligent . . . in regard to health reform."—*Ibid.*, p. 485.

40. *Testimonies*, vol. 1, p. 210. "Individuals were presented before me who had shunned the pointed testimony. I saw the influence of their teachings upon God's people."—*Ibid.*, p. 248. See *Testimonies*, vol. 1, pp. 210-252, for an overview of how Ellen White made public the previously given private communications. In an earlier message she wrote: "My course is now clear to wrong the church no longer. If reproofs are given, I dare not commit them alone to the individuals to be buried up by them, but shall read what the Lord has seen fit to give me, to those of experience in the church, and if the case demands, bring it before the whole church."—*Spiritual Gifts*, vol. 2, pp. 293, 294. In 1868 she continued to instruct others regarding making private testimonies public: "In rebuking the wrongs of one, He designs to correct many. But if they fail to take the reproof to themselves, and flatter themselves that God passes over their errors because He does not especially single them out, they deceive their own souls and will be shut up in darkness and be left to their own ways to follow the imagination of their own hearts."—*Testimonies*, vol. 2, pp. 112, 113.
41. Manuscript 13, 1868, cited in *Bio.*, vol. 2, p. 228.
42. Letter 6, 1868, cited in *Bio.*, vol. 2, pp. 228, 229. Later in her diary of that date, she concluded, "We did not lighten the burden, for all this development only showed how much she needed the reproof."—*Ibid.*, p. 229.
43. Loughborough, *GSAM*, p. 231, cited in *Bio.*, vol. 1, p. 175.
44. *Ibid.*, pp. 175, 176.
45. *Bio.*, vol. 3, pp. 158-160. Ellen White endorsed G. B. Starr's report.
46. *Ibid.*, vol. 1, p. 277. Loughborough wrote: "In Sister White's written description of the woman she not only told her mode of procedure, but that when she should reprove her, she would 'put on a sanctimonious look, and say, God—knows—my—heart.' She said this woman was traveling about the country with a young man, while her own husband, an older man, was at home working to support them in their course. Sister White said the Lord had shown her that 'with all this woman's pretensions to holiness, she was guilty of violating the seventh commandment.'"—Loughborough, *Review and Herald*, May 6, 1884, p. 299.
47. *Ibid.*, pp. 279-281
48. Elder Armitage told this story in the Redlands, California, church in early 1931, where G. B. Starr was pastor. Later that year, at the Oakland, California, camp meeting on June 30, Starr retold the story. The interesting fact accompanying this story is that when Elder Armitage told it in Redlands he also said that when his mother died, his father married the sister of that Wisconsin woman with the six children. All of the six were church members, one of them "occupying a very important place in the Loma Linda Sanitarium." Then, to make the story even more dramatic, he pointed to the mother who had been deceived by her bigamist husband—she was in the church that day visiting her daughter, one of the six children.—DF 496-d.
49. For a partial list of additional events in which the prophetic eye and finger of Ellen White led people heavenward, note the following: (1) The business manager at the St. Helena Sanitarium (1887) whose moral infidelity was revealed to Ellen White while she was in Europe and brought to his attention by her letters, finally was thankful for Ellen White's persistent confrontation and her manner of dealing with him.—Roger Coon, *A Gift of Light* (Hagerstown, MD: Review and Herald Publishing Association), 1983, pp. 34, 35. (2) Elbe (Sam) Hamilton, a dying young man who was diagnosed by Ellen White as suffering from trichinosis, learned how to cook and eat properly in her own kitchen. A few years later, she brought Sam to Paradise Valley Sanitarium where he witnessed the famous well-dig and her amazing predictions.—*Ibid.*, pp. 35-38. (3) Nathaniel Davis, editor of the *Signs of the Times* in Australia who had severe problems with money, spiritualism, and morals, was exposed in a public meeting but later was exceedingly grateful for Ellen White's persistence.—*Ibid.*, pp. 38-41. (4) Late 1851, in Johnson, Vermont, Brother Baker and others were having doctrinal disagreements that led to highly spirited discussions. Ellen White's visions during a period of several days brought clarity and calmness. Baker came full circle, confessing that "every word of the vision related in the forenoon concerning him was, every word of it, truth, just exactly as it was."—*Bio.*, vol. 1, pp. 220, 221. (5) In Vergennes, Vermont, shortly after Baker's experience in 1851, Ellen White, through a vision, helped a church member who was confused with the "age to come" error. "After I had the vision and told it, Brother Everts began to confess and break down before God. He gave up his 'age to come' and felt the necessity of keeping the minds of all on the third angel's message."—*Ibid.*, pp. 222-223. (6) Ellen White related a vision that included a preacher (whom she did not know) who was away from home on a preaching itinerary—yet violating the seventh commandment. Six weeks later, she met the man in the presence of others, and said, "Thou art the man." He fully confessed immediately, verifying a vision given more than five hundred miles away—Loughborough, *Review and Herald*, Mar. 4, 1884. See also Loughborough, *GSAM*, pp. 319, 320. (7) In June 1853, an Ellen White vision helped end a raucous dispute over "who said what" that was dividing the Jackson, Michigan, church. But the incident also gave background to the first dissident movement among Sabbath keeping Adventists, known as the *Messenger Party*. —*Bio.*, vol. 1, pp. 276, 277. (8) Victor Jones, a young man in Monterey, Michigan, had a struggle with appetite. Ellen White wrote him a testimony based on a vision—an eloquent appeal.—Letter 1, 1861, cited in *Bio.*, vol. 1, p. 465.

Study Questions

1. What was Ellen White's understanding of her job description as the Lord's messenger?

2. How would you describe the characteristics of an open vision?

3. What were the various ways that Ellen White delivered vision-messages to others?

4. What were the different ways that Ellen White received visions and dreams?

5. What did Ellen White mean when she said that her testimonies would not have been needed if church members had been diligent Bible students?

6. Can Satan cause confusion by duplicating the physical characteristics of a prophet's open visions? What is the danger of building confidence in a person merely because of the remarkable characteristics of a public vision?

CHAPTER 14

Confirming the Confidence

"And they went out and preached everywhere, the Lord working with them and confirming the word through the accompanying signs" (Mark 16:20).

Visions were not always involved in dramatic exposures or in spectacular instruction during church deliberations. Some visions were about everyday matters.

In 1850, church members in Sutton, Vermont, realized that the Whites were wearing themselves out, traveling on common stagecoaches or wagons. They contributed $175 to help buy a horse and carriage, and left it up to the Whites to choose the horse. This important decision did not take long. During the night, Mrs. White had a vision in which she would have the choice of three horses. The next day, she knew that the beautiful dapple chestnut, named Charlie, was the one to be trusted for many years—because the angel had said in the vision, "This is the one for you."[1]

Open Visions Often Changed Skeptics Into Believers

For several decades, contemporaries observed Ellen White in vision and wrote out their descriptions of these impressive events. Open visions often changed skeptical people, even adversaries, into believers.

One of the earliest, most prominent, skeptic-turned-believer was Joseph Bates.[2] Along with others who knew only by rumor of Ellen White's early visions, Bates was not convinced that her visions "were of God."[3] Visions at that time were confused with spiritualistic seances or mesmerism. Bates thought they were nothing "more than what was produced by a protracted debilitated state of her body."[4] But he changed his mind after observing her in several vision experiences.

One vision, in particular, impressed him. In November 1846, at the Stockbridge Howland home in Topsham, Maine, a small company of Sabbath keepers had convened. Among them were Joseph Bates and the Whites. Ellen White was taken in vision and "for the first time had a view of other planets." After the vision she related what she had seen.

Bates, an amateur astronomer, asked her if she had ever studied astronomy. He was astonished at what he had heard, saying, "This is of the Lord." Later, after observing several other visions, he wrote in a small tract, "I thank God for the opportunity I have had with others to witness these things. . . . I believe the work is of God, and is given to comfort and strengthen His scattered, torn, and pealed people."[5]

Ellen White never wrote out this "astronomy vision." She never identified by name the planets she saw, nor did she mention the number of moons any planet may have. But Bates attached the planets' names *to what he thought* Ellen White was describing, and others, including James White, reported what Bates seemed to have understood from her brief comments. Telescopes today reveal much more about the planets, the number of their moons, and other heavenly phenomena than Bates would ever have dreamed of. What really astounded him was not the description of "planets," but Mrs. White's description of the "opening heavens," a reference to the so-called "open space in Orion." He was reported to have said that her description "far surpassed any account of the opening heavens he had ever read from any author."[6]

Not An Astronomy Lesson

The point seems clear: the vision was not a lesson on astronomy that was intended to be verified by modern telescopes. Rather, it provided enough information, by a young woman totally uninformed on astronomy, that conformed to the limited information that Bates, an amateur astronomer, had in 1847.[7] If Ellen White had given a preview of what the Hubble telescope revealed in the 1990s, Joseph Bates would certainly have been convinced that Ellen White was a fraud, a misguided zealot. His doubts would have been confirmed. Probably he would not have identified himself further with Seventh-day Adventists.

Bates's confidence in Mrs. White's visions was tested two years later. The Whites were desperately in need of funds to continue publishing the *Present Truth*. Unfortunately, Bates was highly critical of the periodical approach to disseminating the message. He favored the pamphlet approach. At the most critical point of disagreement and lack of funds, Ellen White had a vision that the periodical "was needed . . . . that the paper should go . . . that it would go where God's servants cannot go."

When Bates heard of Mrs. White's endorsement, he dropped his opposition and lent his influence to the developing publishing work.[8]

Young Daniel Bourdeau, at the age of twenty, was doing missionary work for the Baptist Church in Canada when he heard that his parents and older brother (Augustin C.) had joined the Sabbatarian Adventists in northern Vermont. In his attempt to dissuade them, he discovered that they had persuaded him regarding the Sabbath and other doctrines.

But Daniel was still an "unbeliever in the visions" until Sunday morning, June 21, 1857, when he observed Ellen White in vision at Buck's Bridge, New York. He was told that he could examine her during the vision. In his words, "to satisfy my mind as to whether she breathed or not, I first put my hand on her chest sufficiently long to know that there was no more heaving of the lungs than there would have been had she been a corpse. I then took my hand and placed it over her mouth, pinching her nostrils between my thumb and forefinger, so that it was impossible for her to exhale or inhale air, even if she had desired to do so. I held her thus with my hand about ten minutes, long enough for her to suffocate under ordinary circumstances. She was not in the least affected by this ordeal. . . . Since witnessing this wonderful phenomenon, I have not once been inclined to doubt the divine origin of her visions."[9]

Ellen White's longest vision (four hours) occurred in 1845 before her marriage to James. One of the allegations against her was that she could not have a vision if James White and her sister, Sarah (both persons accompanied Ellen on her early travels) were not present. Otis Nichols, hoping to expose the charge, invited Ellen and Sarah to his home, leaving James in Portland. Among those in the Boston area who contested the validity of Ellen Harmon's experience were fanatical leaders, including Sargent and Robbins, who were also advocating that it was a sin to work.[10]

Sargent and Robbins were invited and came to Nichols' home, but when they learned that Ellen Harmon was present, they quickly withdrew, warning Nichols that her visions were "of the devil." Before they left, Nichols told them that Ellen Harmon would like to attend their next meeting in Boston, to which they gave their approval.

But the night before the proposed meeting, Ellen was shown in vision that these men had no plan to meet with her; they had alerted their followers to gather in Randolph, thirteen miles south of Boston. In that vision she also was told that she should meet with this group in Randolph, that God would give her a message that would convince "the honest, the unprejudiced ones, whether her visions were of the Lord or from Satan."[11]

When Ellen Harmon and her party arrived, Sargent and Robbins groaned in surprise. Robbins told Sarah, Ellen's sister, that Ellen could not have a vision if he were present! In the afternoon meeting, according to the report of Otis Nichols, Ellen was "taken off in vision with extraordinary manifestations and continued talking in vision with a shrill voice which could be distinctly understood by all present, until about sundown [about four hours]."

What did Sargent and Robbins do during this time? "They exhausted all their influence and bodily strength to destroy the effect of the vision. They would unite in singing very loud, and then alternately would talk and read from the Bible in a loud voice in order that Ellen might not be heard, until their strength was exhausted and their hands would shake, so they could not read from the Bible."

Heavy Family Bible

Mr. Thayer, the owner of the house, was not convinced that Ellen Harmon was of the devil. He had heard that one test of whether the visions were from Satan was to lay an open Bible on the person in vision. He asked Sargent to do so, but he refused.

Being a man of action, Thayer took his heavy family Bible, opened it, and laid it on Ellen Harmon's chest (who was inclined against the wall). She arose immediately and walked to the middle of the room, holding the Bible high with one hand. With her free hand, her eyes looking upward and not on the Bible, she began to turn the pages of the Bible, placing her finger on certain texts.

Many in the room who were able to look at the passages where her finger was pointing while her eyes were looking upward, noted that she was quoting them correctly. But Sargent and Robbins, though now silent, continued to steel themselves against the dramatic refutation of all they had said.

Nichols reported later that this "No-work Party" became even more fanatical, declaring themselves free from all sinning. About a year later, the group was scattered amidst the revelations of "shameful acts of their lives."[12]

In 1852 a very personal event convinced Marion Stowell that Ellen White's visions were genuine. On one of their itineraries through northern and western New York, the Whites found Marion exhausted after two-and-a-half years of caring for Mrs. David Arnold. They asked her to join them in their sleigh as they continued their journey.

Marion Stowell recalled later in a letter to Mrs. White: "We had not gone many more miles when you said, 'James, everything that was shown me about this trip has transpired but one. We had a little meeting in a private family. You spoke with great freedom on your favorite theme, the near coming of Christ."

James responded: "It is impossible [for this] to transpire on this trip as there is not an Adventist family between here and Saratoga. We will put up at a hotel tonight, and we surely wouldn't have a meeting there, and tomorrow afternoon will reach home. It must occur on our next trip. . . ."

Ellen replied: "No, James, it was surely on this, as nothing has been shown me of the next one, and it is three months before we take another. It was shown me on this trip, yet I can't see how it can come to pass."

Near sundown the Whites, recalling that a recently married friend lived nearby, stopped for a visit and were happily welcomed.

Marion Stowell continued the story: "Supper over, Emily said, 'Brother White, would you mind speaking to my neighbors on the near coming of Christ? I can soon fill both rooms. They have heard me tell so much about you both, they will come.'"

And they came. Not until the traveling party were on their way to the next stopping place, Saratoga Springs, did anyone remember the connection between the earlier vision and that evening meeting. Marion confided to Ellen White: "Not once from that time to this has Satan ever tempted me to doubt your visions."[13]

Many are the stories, each unique, that reveal how men and women became convinced regarding the genuineness of Mrs. White's visions. The experience of Stephen Smith is typical. Reports in the *Review and Herald* indicated that Smith had a series of experiences in the 1850s that led to his being disfellowshipped. During this period, Mrs. White wrote him a testimony. When he received it, he thrust it, unopened, deep within a trunk for twenty-eight years!

During these years Mrs. Matilda Smith remained faithful and received the *Review and Herald* weekly. Eventually her husband picked up the copies, read them, and was softened by articles written by Ellen White, whom he remembered from the 1850s. Then he attended a revival meeting in the Washington, New Hampshire church, a church that he had been ridiculing for nearly three decades. After making a public confession one Sabbath of how wrong he had been, the following Thursday he remembered that unopened testimony in the bottom of his trunk. The following Sabbath he returned to the Washington church and gave his story:

"Brethren, every word of the testimony for me is true, and I accept it. And I have come to that place where I finally believe they [the testimonies] all are of God, and if I had heeded the one God sent to me, as well as the rest, it would have changed the whole course of my life, and I should have been a very different man. . . .

"The testimonies said there was to be no more 'definite time' preached after the '44 movement, but I thought that I knew as much as an old woman's visions, as I used to term it. May God forgive me! But to my sorrow, I found the visions were right, and the man who thought he knew it all was all wrong, for I preached the time in 1854, and spent all I had when if I had heeded them, I should have saved myself all that and much more. The testimonies are right and I am wrong. . . . I want to tell our people everywhere that another rebel has surrendered."[14]

How Visions Were Remembered

Most of Ellen White's visions or dreams probably were written down in broad outline soon after she received them. As time went on, she would fill in the details.[15]

The vision given on Christmas Day 1865, at Rochester, New York, was especially comprehensive. By 1868, according to James White, Ellen White had written "several thousand pages" based upon that one vision.[16] The many concerns in that vision became an important part of her agenda for the next three years.

Mrs. White did not remember at any one time all elements of the vision. When she visited churches and families on her eastern tour in late 1867 and in northern Michigan in 1868, she saw many faces that instantly brought back the messages for them which she then delivered orally or in writing.[17]

Many times, those who had special testimonies given to them orally wanted a written copy. Obviously these were serious believers who wanted to bring their lives into harmony with the prophet's admonition. In reference to this practice, James White wrote in 1868: "We wished to say to those friends who have requested Mrs. White to write out personal testimonies, that in this branch of her labor she has about two months' work on hand."[18]

This practice of not writing out the whole vision at once was not uncommon. In 1860 Ellen White reflected: "After I come out of vision I do not at once remember all that I have seen, and the matter is not so clear before me until I write, then the scene rises before me as was presented in vision, and I can write with freedom.

"Sometimes the things which I have seen are hid from me after I come out of vision, and I cannot call them to mind until I am brought before a company where that vision applies, then the things which I have seen come to my mind with force. I am just as dependent upon the Spirit of the Lord in relating or writing a vision, as in having the vision. It is impossible for me to call up things which have been shown me unless the Lord brings them before me at the time that He is pleased to have me relate or write them."[19]

Not All Visions Written Out

Occasionally Ellen White did not write out the specifics of a vision; what we know about the vision has come from observers. For example, her first health vision in 1848 was reported by her husband James twenty-two years later in the *Review and Herald*, November 8, 1870.

Her first vision on the Civil War, received at Parkville, Michigan, January 12, 1861, does not seem to have been recorded. However, after coming out of the twenty-minute vision she related to the audience soon-to-be-enacted events. J. N. Loughborough was present and took copious notes.[20]

Endnotes

1. *Bio.*, vol. 1, p. 178.
2. For a biography of Joseph Bates, read Godfrey T. Anderson, *Outrider of the Apocalypse: Life and Times of Joseph Bates* (Mountain View, CA: Pacific Press Publishing Association, 1972); Schwarz, *Light Bearers*, pp. 59-70; Spalding, *Origin and History*, vol. 1, pp. 25-41; see also Joseph Bates, *Autobiography* (Battle Creek, MI: Seventh-day Adventist Publishing Association, 1868, facsimile reproduction, Southern Publishing Association, Nashville, TN, 1970) for a review of his life up to 1858. Bates, a converted sea captain, spent his fortune promoting the Millerite message. He became one of the first Sabbatarian Adventists (1845), the first to print a tract, *The Seventh-day Sabbath a Perpetual Sign* (1846), on the seventh-day Sabbath. This tract became the convincing confirmation for James and Ellen White that Saturday, not Sunday, is the Christian Sabbath.—Schwarz, *Light Bearers*, pp. 59, 60; *Bio.*, vol. 1, pp. 116, 117.
3. *Life Sketches*, p. 97.
4. *Ibid.*
5. *A Word to the Little Flock*, p. 21, in Knight, *1844 and The Rise of Sabbatarian Adventism*, p. 175 ; see J. N. Loughborough, *Rise and Progress of the Seventh-day Adventists* (Battle Creek, MI: General Conference Association of the Seventh-day Adventists, 1892, reprinted by Payson, AZ: Leaves of Autumn Books, Inc., 1988), pp. 125-128; Schwarz, *Light Bearers*, p. 67; *Bio.*, vol. 1, pp. 113, 114.
6. Loughborough, *GSAM*, pp. 258, 259.
7. Some may wonder why God did not give Ellen White "the whole truth" about planets, open spaces, etc. Experience shows that He has never given "the whole truth" to any prophet in one sitting. Paul, for instance, had much to say about how Christian slave holders should treat their slaves, but he did not see "the whole truth" about how slavery as a system should be dismantled. The Lord emphasized this principle: "I still have many things to say to you, but you cannot bear them now" (John 16:12); see also, Mark. 4:33 and 1 Cor. 3:2
8. *Bio.*, vol. 1, pp. 171, 172.
9. Loughborough, *GSAM*, p. 210.
10. See p. 50.
11. *Bio.*, vol. 1, pp. 100-102.
12. *Ibid.*, pp. 103-105.
13. Letter to Ellen White from Marion Stowell Crawford, Oct. 9, 1908, cited in *Bio.*, vol. 1, pp. 225, 226.
14. *Ibid.*, pp. 490-492.
15. See the story of the 1890 Salamanca, New York, vision in *Bio.*, vol. 3, pp. 464-467, 478-483. See also p. 188.
16. *Review and Herald*, June 16, 1868, p. 409.
17. See the Bushnell experience, pp. 127, 128.
18. *Review and Herald*, March 3, 1868, p. 192.
19. *Spiritual Gifts*, vol. 2, pp. 292, 293.
20. See pp. 159, 160. Loughborough, *RPSDA*, pp. 236, 237. In his preface, Loughborough wrote: "Since November 1853 I have kept a diary of daily occurrences." The narrative [in *RPSDA*] from that date is from the record of this diary.

Study Questions

1. What circumstances changed Joseph Bates's skepticism into calm confidence?
2. Why didn't God give Ellen White a picture of Orion such as a modern Hubble telescope would provide?
3. How did Ellen White's longest vision provide confidence to the observers?
4. How did the 1852 vision in eastern New York bring confidence to others?

CHAPTER 15

Timely Instruction and Predictions[1]

"As for the prophet who prophesies of peace, when the word of the prophet comes to pass, the prophet will be known as one whom the Lord has truly sent" (Jeremiah 28:9).

Prophets are not always aware of the time to which visions apply. While in Australia Ellen White wrote to a minister, reproving him for violating the seventh commandment. The minister, perplexed by the testimony because he had not committed adulterous acts, went to W. C. White for an explanation. Elder White reminded him that men may draw fine distinctions in this area but God looks at the heart. Within six months, this minister was dismissed from the ministry for the problem for which Mrs. White had reproved him.[2]

Also while in Australia she was "shown a large building in Chicago . . . elaborately furnished." She was perplexed when told that "no such building was erected in Chicago." But she knew what she had seen in vision: "The Lord showed me what men were planning to do. I knew that the testimony was true, but not until recently was the matter explained."[3]

How was she enlightened? Judge Jesse Arthur, long-time attorney connected with the Battle Creek Sanitarium, visited with her in the summer of 1902. Judge Arthur told her that her testimony regarding "a large building in Chicago" was plain to him "because he knew that preparations were being made to erect in Chicago a building corresponding to the one shown . . . in vision."

Later the judge confirmed his conversation with a letter written on August 27, 1902. He was the chairman of the building committee of three: "The committee met [on June 26, 1899] and immediately formulated plans for the purchase of a site and the erection of such a building. I was instructed as chairman of the committee to open negotiations . . . and otherwise take steps to raise the necessary funds to purchase the site, and erect the building contemplated."[4]

Ellen White wrote to Kellogg on October 28, 1903: "If this view had not been given me, and if I had not written to you about the matter, an effort would have been made to erect such a building in Chicago, a place in which the Lord has said that we are not to put up large buildings. At the time when the vision was given, influences were working for the erection of such a building. The message was received in time to prevent the development of the plans and the carrying out of the project."

After receiving these messages, Kellogg turned away from the Chicago project.[5] Thus the reason for Ellen White's vision was made clear.

Timeliness of Delivering Visions Often Crucial

Often a letter from Ellen White would arrive in a distant committee meeting or a crucial church meeting on exactly the day when needed, even when she would be thousands of miles away.

Other times, not a letter but her presence would alter the direction of a meeting, chiefly because of being instructed by a vision. In 1887 at Vohwinkel, Prussia, she was to speak on Sabbath morning, May 28. During Friday night, she had a dream of what she would be facing Sabbath morning. In the dream the elder of the church "seemed to be trying to hurt someone . . . . the assembling together had not been refreshing to anyone." A Stranger, who had earlier seated Himself in the assembly, arose to speak at the end of the service, pointing to Jesus as their example in all things.

After Ellen White concluded the sermon (that she had entitled, "The Prayer of Christ, that His disciples may be one as He was one with the Father") in which she described the dream, confessions and weeping and rejoicing swept through the congregation. The church service continued for three hours as the "mellow light of heaven" filled the room.[6]

General Conference sessions were frequent occasions for Ellen White's direct intervention. While the 1879 session was in progress, she had a vision, of which she wrote: "November 23, 1879, some things were shown me in reference to institutions among us and the duties and dangers of those who occupy a leading position in connection with them." Seventy pages followed, filled with counsel, reproof, and encouragement—all of which provided the substance for several talks she gave to the assembly.

Before the session concluded, the following action was voted: "*Whereas*, God has again most mercifully and graciously spoken to us as ministers, in words of admonition and reproof through the gift of the Spirit of Prophecy; and

"*Whereas*, These instructions are just and timely, and of the utmost importance in their relation to our future labors and usefulness; therefore

"*Resolved*, That we hereby express our sincere and devout thanksgiving to God that He has not left us in our blindness, as He might justly have done, but has given us another opportunity to overcome, by faithfully pointing out our sins and errors, and teaching us how we may please God and become useful in His cause.

"*Resolved*, That, while it is right and proper that we express our thankfulness to God and His servants in this manner, yet the best manner of expressing our gratitude is to faithfully heed the testimony that has been borne to us; and we hereby pledge ourselves to make a most earnest effort to reform on those points wherein we have been shown to be deficient, and to be obedient to the will of God thus graciously made known to us."[7]

Salamanca Vision

The crucial presence of Ellen White during the March 1891 General Conference in Battle Creek, Michigan, kept the leadership from making a serious mistake regarding the church's religious liberty program and other publishing policies.[8] The usefulness of the vision's purpose and relevancy is highlighted in the timing of its presentation in public. Although given to Mrs. White in November 1890, in Salamanca, New York, and though she found many opportunities to apply much of the vision's message to current conditions, the central feature of the vision was held from her memory until the exact moment when it would be most effective.

If she had reported the whole vision (as she tried to do on several occasions) at any other time than after that famous Saturday night secret meeting, it would have been considered patently false information.[9]

But it was not only with General Conference matters that denominational leaders recognized the timely counsel provided through the Spirit of prophecy. Those involved in crises such as the proposed sale of the Boulder (Colorado) Sanitarium would never forget the prompt, propitious, and lucid direction that the situation demanded—wisdom that leadership could not see without the inspired witness of Ellen White.

The Boulder Sanitarium crisis in the closing months of 1905 is a case study in how "reasonable" certain business plans may appear, even when higher principles and purposes are neglected. At that time conference leadership and leading laymen believed that they were doing the denomination a favor by selling the institution. However, Ellen White made clear that it was not in God's purpose that another sanitarium should be built in Boulder or in Canon City, one hundred miles south of Boulder—at least not by Adventists. Her unambiguous counsel written to the key players turned the tide although such admonition came as a heavy blow to the leaders.[10]

Foreign Language Tensions

Also in 1905 another festering problem was coming to a head. The leaders in foreign-language work in North America were striving hard to have separate printing establishments for work in the German, Danish-Norwegian, and Swedish languages. Further, these leaders wanted separate conferences for the three ethnic groups. At the Foreign Department Council of the General Conference held at College View, Nebraska, on September 5, 1905, church leaders gathered with great apprehension.

Ellen White, residing in California, was asked for counsel. In addition to gathering previous relevant materials, she wrote three new testimonies. The central theme of her counsel, clearly stated in her two years in Europe where the subject was always in front of her, was: "According to the light given me of God, separate organizations, instead of bringing about unity, will create discord. . . . I must write plainly regarding the building up of partition walls in the work of God. Such an action has been revealed to me as a fallacy of human invention."[11]

G. A. Irwin, vice-president of the General Conference who was present at the College View meeting, wrote after the council: "I am glad to tell you that the Lord has given the victory here just as signally as He did in Colorado [Boulder Sanitarium crisis, same year]. The communications from Sister White came in just the right time, and answered the most important questions before us. They made the matter so clear and plain that even the most extreme agitators of a separation were led to accept them."[12]

During the 1905 controversy with John Harvey Kellogg, many people in Battle Creek were convinced that he had been abused, or, at least, misunderstood. Kellogg's usual response to Mrs. White's interventions in the early1900s had been: "Somebody has told Sister White!"

The Kellogg crisis was perhaps more severe than any previous denominational conflict. Ellen White, on December 21, 1905, had sent a telegram to A. G. Daniells, president of the General Conference, that she had special counsel for him and others at that critical time. The package of manuscripts arrived on December 26 and were read to an overflow audience in the Battle Creek Tabernacle. What proved to be astonishing to all was that two of the manuscripts were written much earlier (August 1903 and June 1, 1904) but were not copied out until she was impressed to do so on the previous Thursday when she had sent her telegram.

The effect of the manuscripts, read without comment, was stunning. Several men who had been captivated by Kellogg's arguments approached Daniells immediately, saying that the notable meeting held with Kellogg the night before was clearly described by Ellen White in the manuscripts written many months before and copied only days before. They also said that "if there had been a doubt in their minds regarding the source of the testimonies, it would have been swept away by their own statements [as set forth by Ellen G. White] in the testimonies."[13]

Shortest Testimony

The shortest testimony Ellen White ever gave was a telegram received by M. N. Campbell, pastor of the Battle Creek church (Tabernacle), during the 1906-1907 struggle over the ownership of the Tabernacle. The Sanitarium group was determined to secure the property. Most of the church trustees were inclined to support the Sanitarium group's wishes.

But the young pastor, equally determined that the property would remain in denominational hands, called together a few of the leading members for special prayer before the last, and most crucial, meeting. Campbell recorded the event:

"They were all good, faithful men but I don't know that I ever saw a set of men more scared. Old Brother Amadon,[14] one of the finest Christians that ever lived, moaned, 'If only Sister White were here, if only Sister White were here.'"

Everyone knew that Ellen White was in California, but Amadon continued, "Oh, if only Sister White were here."

A few minutes later, ten minutes before the opening of the tense meeting, a telegram arrived for Campbell. It contained this message: "Philippians 1:27, 28. (Signed) Ellen G. White."

That text and her intended message braced the men for what had to be done. Campbell wrote: "That settled the question. That was a communication from Sister White that we needed right at that moment. God knew we were holding that meeting, and that we had a group of scared men, and that we needed help from Him, and so He gave us the message that came straight to us in the nick of time. It sounded pretty good to us."[15]

At times, Ellen White would plead with individuals prior to a serious and life-changing decision, warning them of their own impending crisis. Her concern for her long-time friend, D. M. Canright, while he was going through his final defection, is one example of many.

Canright had asked that his name be dropped from the church books in Otsego, Michigan—a request that was granted on February 17, 1887.[16]

Although in Europe, Ellen White was not surprised at these sad developments. In vision she had seen Canright going through "rough waters." She pleaded with him to "Wait, and God will help you. Be patient, and the clear light will appear. If you yield to impressions you will lose your soul. . . ." This letter was later printed in *Testimonies*, vol. 5, pp. 571-573, with "Brother M" referring to Canright. But Canright did not wait, and Mrs. White's prediction that his "sun will surely set in obscurity" was tragically fulfilled.[17]

In 1900 Daniel H. Kress, an Adventist physician, was appointed to head up the medical work in Australia. He zealously advocated dispensing with all animal products. But in his frequent travels at the turn of the century he found it difficult to get suitable foods for a balanced diet. As a result, he developed pernicious anemia at the age of forty. When Ellen White saw him in vision, he was at death's door.

In her usual straightforward manner she instructed him to "make changes, and at once. Put into your diet something you have left out. . . . Get eggs of healthy fowls. Use these eggs cooked or raw. Drop them uncooked into the best unfermented wine [grape juice] you can find. This will supply that which is necessary to your system."[18]

Her counsel, prompted by the vision regarding Kress's dire physical condition, was exactly what the ill physician needed. He fully recovered, and lived fifty-two years longer in a life of medical service and administration.[19]

Visions, at Times, Changed Mrs. White's Habits and Opinions

At times, Ellen White experienced how Nathan felt when he discovered that he had given King David wrong counsel.[20] In 1902 she had an opportunity to reverse counsel that she had given to the leading officers of the General Conference.

At the turn of the century, Edson White was leading out in working for the Blacks in the South, especially through publishing literature in the South for the South. His mother had strongly endorsed his work, primarily because it was the only significant work being done. As Edson's work developed, plans were made to establish a denominational publishing house in Nashville, Tennessee. But Edson's strength rested not in finance but in promotion, printing, and writing literature to fit the needs of the South. Debts were mounting dangerously at a time when denominational leaders were trying to stabilize the severe financial crisis that had overtaken the church. And leaders were hesitant to close down the budding Nashville publishing house because Ellen White had been supporting her son generally for his pioneering work.[21]

At a special meeting called at Elmshaven on October 19, 1902, church leaders needed counsel regarding denominational debt and the work at Nashville in particular. After Mrs. White heard the facts, she said: "God's cause must not be left to reproach, no matter who is made sore by arranging matters on a right basis. Edson should give himself to the ministry and to writing, and leave alone the things that he has been forbidden by the Lord to do. Finance is not his forte at all. I want the brethren . . . to act just as they would act if my son were not there. . . . I do not want anyone to feel that I am sustaining Edson in a wrong."

A. G. Daniells, General Conference president, satisfied with the interview, returned to Battle Creek with a copy of the interview in his pocket. Leadership was now assured that closing the Nashville establishment was the right thing to do.

But within twenty-four hours of the Elmshaven interview, Mrs. White wrote a letter that would change the whole picture. Prompted by a vision of the night (or night dream), she saw that closing the Nashville press was not necessary, that consolidation of the denominational publishing interests was not God's plan, and that "the Southern field [must] have its own home-published books."[22]

Vision Changes Prophet's Counsel

A few weeks later, she explained to denominational leadership: "During the night following our interview in my house and out on the lawn under the trees, October 19, 1902, in regard to the work in the Southern field, the Lord instructed me that I had taken a wrong position."

Further, she wrote words of encouragement, that "from this center light will shine forth in the ministry of the word, in the publication of books large and small," that "we have as yet merely touched the Southern field with the tips of our fingers."[23]

All those involved realized that they were experiencing the same emotions that stirred Nathan and David three millennia before. The Lord was very close to His people who wanted to listen to the Spirit of prophecy.

In 1849, the Adventist people gathered into various nuclei across New England and upper New York State. S. W. Rhodes, a discouraged former leader in the Millerite movement, refused social interchange. But his friends kept up their attention, though often rebuffed. The Whites did not feel that any further special effort in Rhodes's behalf was warranted. However, while a group of Adventists were praying, Ellen White had a vision "which was contrary to her former opinion and feeling relating to our going after Brother Rhodes, up to the time that the Spirit took her off in vision."[24]

In planning for the first church building at Avondale in 1897, discouragement prevailed. The depressed financial situation throughout Australia directly affected the development of the church's educational and medical work. Ellen

White knew that building the church was essential to the general spirit that should prevail in the further growth of the struggling college. Yet, she was willing to listen to the caution of the local leaders. She knew that they carried heavy burdens and that the financial picture was bleak. One day, in human sympathy, she mentioned to one of the leaders, "We will not hasten the building of the meeting-house."

But that night she had a vision that changed her "ideas materially." In a letter to the person she had agreed with a few hours earlier, she said: "I received instruction to speak to the people, and tell them that we are not to leave the house of the Lord until the last consideration. . . . Build a house for God without delay. Secure the most favorable location. Prepare seats that will be proper for a house of God."[25]

Visions, at Times, Modified Ellen White's Theological Opinions

Prophets grow in grace and knowledge as do other believers. In choosing His prophets and prophetesses, God has always selected the best for His purposes—but only the best at that time! He has chosen polygamists and doubters, even some who lied (e.g., Abraham and David).

No prophet saw the whole picture from start to finish. All prophets went through "on-the-job-training." If we knew all the facts about each prophet, we would discover that each one kept learning more and more about his or her assignment, more and more about God's plan for them and for His people. They had much to learn, much to unlearn. As a result, their messages became more precise as time continued.

Think of John the Baptist whom Jesus declared to be "more than a prophet. . . . Among those born of women there has not risen one greater than John the Baptist" (Matt. 11:9, 11). Yet John "did not understand the nature of Christ's kingdom."[26] In his dramatic ministry, he misapplied Isaiah's prophecies and, to some extent, misunderstood the character of God. In prison, he was "bitterly disappointed in his mission" and considered himself a failure. John, with all of his Bible study and prophetic mission, "had not fully comprehended the future, immortal life through the Saviour."[27] Later, he even doubted the experience at the Jordan, the day he baptized Jesus: "Are You the Coming One, or do we look for another?" (Matt. 11:3).

Yet, Jesus applied to John Malachi's term, "My Messenger." Messenger, yes, but a "lesser light, which was to be followed by a greater."[28]

Think of Peter whom God chose to be the gospel link to Cornelius, the Gentile centurion (Acts 10). Peter, blessed by Pentecost, still believed that the gospel of Christ was meant only for the Jews. He needed his theology changed, and a vision did it. Every step to the home of Cornelius was taken reluctantly.[29] His "shut-door" theology was changed into a wide open door into the Gentile world and finally to Rome and his own crucifixion.

Ellen White was the first to recognize that her judgment and perception had greatly broadened and deepened through the years. She was a human messenger who, with all the human baggage common to prophets, constantly followed the Light. She spoke of this lifelong development process: "With the light communicated through the study of His word, with the special knowledge given of individual cases among His people under all circumstances and in every phase of experience, can I now be in the same ignorance, the same mental uncertainty and spiritual blindness, as at the beginning of this experience? Will my brethren say that Sister White has been so dull a scholar that her judgment in this direction is no better than before she entered Christ's school, to be trained and disciplined for a special work? Am I no more intelligent in regard to the duties and perils of God's people than are those before whom these things have never been presented? I would not dishonor my Maker by admitting that all this light, all the display of His mighty power in my work and experience, has been valueless, that it has not educated my judgment or better fitted me for His work."[30]

Ellen White did grow, led along by the Spirit of God. Most Millerites who did not reject the 1844 experience believed that the "door was shut" (Matt. 25:10) to those who had rejected their "midnight cry" message as well as to the general population.[31] The developing group that came to be known as Sabbatarian Adventists, of which James and Ellen White were a part, also retained this belief for a few years.

But Mrs. White's first visions showed her the significance of October 22, 1844, and that the door was shut only to those who had consciously rejected the light of truth. Most probably, without the visionary leadership of Ellen White, the Sabbatarian Adventists would not have seen the larger picture of heavenly events relating to October 22. Her encouraging and instructive development of thought as to the role of Seventh-day Adventists in completing God's last-day invitation to the world, became the church's central, unifying element.

Corrected By a Vision

When to begin the weekly Sabbath was another doctrinal issue on which Mrs. White was corrected by a vision—an instructive story of how God gently leads His people along through His messengers. On Friday, November 16, 1855, the General Conference in session ushered in the Sabbath at 6:00 P.M., although the sun had set an hour before. They ended the Sabbath, the next day, at sunset! What happened?

For years Adventists had been generally following the reasoning of Joseph Bates—that sunset at the equator (6:00 P. M.) would be the most uniform way to handle the Sabbath on a round world, no matter what the time of year.[32] (Beginning and ending the Sabbath at sunrise or midnight were other options.)

But other believers raised the question of Leviticus 23:32, "from evening unto evening, you shall celebrate your sabbath." Trying to bring unity, James White had asked John N. Andrews to make a Biblical study of the issue and prepare a paper. When this paper was read on Sabbath morning at the 1855 General Conference, the matter was settled for James White and the rest of the delegates—all except Joseph Bates and Ellen White!

A few days later, November 20, Mrs. White had a vision that dealt with many matters, including validation of Andrews's Bible study. Both she and Joseph Bates capitulated wholeheartedly. Bible study, confirmed by vision, continued as the general rule in the development of Adventist theology.[33]

Commenting later, Uriah Smith wrote: "Lest any should say that Sister White, having changed her sentiments, had a vision accordingly, we will state that which was shown her in vision concerning the commencement of the Sabbath was contrary to her own sentiment at the time the vision was given."[34]

Ellen White's attitude toward eating pork was another example of how advancing light changed her personal interpretation of Scripture. In 1858 she wrote to the Haskells (Bro. and Sister A.) on a number of items, rebuking him for insisting that pork-eating was a violation of Leviticus 11:7: "I saw that your views concerning swine's flesh would prove no injury if you have them to yourselves; but in your judgment and opinion you have made this question a test. . . . If God requires His people to abstain from swine's flesh, He will convict them on the matter."[35]

Why didn't God tell Ellen White that Haskell's Bible study on Leviticus was correct, following her general pattern of confirming Bible study by the light revealed in vision?

Part of the answer may be found in the note written by James White in the second printing of this testimony to Haskell: "This remarkable testimony was written October 21, 1858, nearly five years before the great vision in 1863, in which the light upon health reform was given. When the right time came, the subject was given in a manner to move all our people. How wonderful are the wisdom and goodness of God! It might be as wrong to crowd the milk, salt, and sugar question now, as the pork question in 1858."[36]

In the health reform vision of June 6, 1863, a broad array of health principles was revealed.[37] In 1864 Ellen White made her first published presentation of that vision, a fifty-page chapter entitled "Health," in *Spiritual Gifts,* volume 4. In reference to swine's flesh she said: "God never designed the swine to be eaten under any circumstances."[38]

In 1865 she prepared a series of six articles under the title *Health, or How to Live.*[39] Here she amplified the injurious consequences of eating swine's flesh, a fact that she continued to emphasize in her later books.[40]

Lessons Learned

What can we learn from this experience wherein Ellen White changed her mind between 1858 and 1863? (1) She had received no light from God on swine's flesh before 1863. (2) She didn't think it should create division among Adventists; it was not a test question. (3) When God makes His will known, it will be revealed to more "than two or three. He will teach his *church* their duty."[41] (4) The test of the logic involved in her change of opinion on eating swine's flesh is that when the vision did come, the whole church saw the issue clearly and never again was there division regarding this issue.[42]

Delivering Reproof—a "Cross"

Ellen White was a timid, frail teenager when she was told by God to relate the visions to others. As we have seen, not all her visions or dreams were theological in content. Some contained reproof and counsel for individuals. At times the reproof was severe and not always appreciated. Mrs. White shrank from her prophetic duties.[43]

Describing her experience in 1845, when she was eighteen years old, Ellen White wrote: "It was a great cross for me to relate to the erring what had been shown me concerning them. It caused me great distress to see others troubled or grieved. And when obliged to declare the messages, I would often soften them down, and make them appear as favorable for the individual as I could, and then would go by myself and weep in agony of spirit."[44]

In a letter written in 1874, she recalled the past thirty years: "I have felt for years that if I could have my choice and please God as well, I would rather die than have a vision, for every vision places me under great responsibility to bear testimonies of reproof and of warning, which has ever been against my feelings, causing me affliction of soul that is inexpressible. Never have I coveted my position, and yet I dare not resist the Spirit of God and seek an easier position."[45]

In 1880, now fifty-two, Ellen White was at the Vermont camp meeting where she had several testimonies to deliver. She referred to these personal burdens: "I have had many individual testimonies to write which has been quite a heavy burden on me in addition to my labors in talking the truth." ("Talking the truth" involved her daily sermons, altar calls, and her usual Sunday afternoon talk on temperance to Vermont audiences of from 1,000 to 4,000 people.) In reference to one couple, she wrote: "I had some very bad, bad jobs to perform. I took Brother Bean and wife and talked to them very plain. They did not rise up against it. I cried myself, could not help it."[46]

Some Visions Contained Predictions

As noted earlier on page 29, a prophet's responsibility covers far more than predicting the future. Prophets are primarily God's messengers, His forth-tellers, not necessarily His fore-tellers. However, prophets, at times, are given information and instruction that indeed predicts the future.

Ellen White predicted specific events and general developments or trends:

Food for Worms

The May 27, 1856, Battle Creek conference is remembered especially for an unusual vision regarding some of the members in attendance.[47] In the midst of the report is this prediction: "I was shown the company present at the conference. Said the angel, 'Some food for worms, some subjects of the seven last plagues, some will be alive and remain upon the earth to be translated at the coming of Jesus.'"

What could this mean? Three days after the conference, Clarissa Bonfoey died. (Clarissa Bonfoey was a close friend of the Whites to whom they had entrusted Edson during his early years before they were able to set up their own home.) She seemed to be in good health at the time of the conference. As death approached, she expressed her conviction that she was one of those represented in the vision who would be "food for worms."[48]

For years, some people kept lists of those present at that conference, believing that Jesus would come before all had died. But Ellen White had been given a picture of what might have been if God's people had aroused themselves to their divine assignment. Mrs. White should not be held to a higher, tighter standard than we apply to Bible prophets.[49] In 1883 she had to write: "It is true that time has continued longer than we expected in the early days of this message. Our Saviour did not appear as soon as we hoped. But has the word of the Lord failed? Never! It should be remembered that the promises and threatenings of God are alike conditional. . . .

"Had Adventists, after the great disappointment in 1844, held fast their faith, and followed on unitedly in the opening providence of God, receiving the message of the third angel and in the power of the Holy Spirit proclaiming it to the world, they would have seen the salvation of God, the Lord would have wrought mightily with their efforts, the work would have been completed, and Christ would have come ere this to receive His people to their reward."[50]

Civil War

Ellen White received her first Civil War vision on Sabbath afternoon, January 12, 1861, in Parkville, Michigan. For about twenty minutes the congregation watched with intense interest this 33-year-old woman. The vision over, she shared briefly what had been revealed to her.

Her words made a lasting impression (as reported by J. N. Loughborough, an eye-witness): "Men are making light of the secession ordinance that has been passed by South Carolina [Dec. 20, 1860]. They have little idea of the trouble that is coming on our land. No one in this house has even dreamed of the trouble that is coming. I have just been shown in vision that a number of States are going to join South Carolina in this secession, and a terrible war will be the result. In the vision I saw large armies raised by both the North and the South. I was shown the battle raging."

Then, looking over the congregation, she continued: "There are men in this house who will lose sons in that war."[51]

On August 3, 1861, at Roosevelt, New York, Ellen White had her second Civil War vision. It focused on the evil of slavery—the North was to blame for the continuing extension of slavery, and the South for the sin of slavery. She was given a "view of the disastrous battle at

Manassas, Virginia" (First Battle of Bull Run, July 21, 1861), and observed the mysterious confusion in the advance of the Northern army.[52]

Further, she wrote; "I was shown that many do not realize the extent of the evil which has come upon us. They have flattered themselves that the national difficulties would soon be settled, and confusion and war end; but all will be convinced that there is more reality in the matter than was anticipated. Many looked for the North to strike a blow and end the controversy."[53]

What shall we make of these Civil War visions? The Parkville vision occurred three months *before* the guns fired on Fort Sumter, April 12, 1861. At that time many people believed that there would be no war, but should war begin, it would be short and the North would win in a brief fight.[54] (For an extended review of contemporary viewpoints that were in sharp contrast with the predictions of Ellen White, see Appendix O.)

Ellen White saw it differently. She predicted that war would come and that other States would join South Carolina in seceding from the Union. She saw large armies in brutal combat, and widespread carnage over a long period wherein men would waste away in prison.[55]

Regarding her solemn prediction that some families in her Parkville audience would "lose sons" in the war, Loughborough spoke some time later with the local elder of the Parkville church who had presided over that memorable Sabbath service. The elder identified five families, with a possible five additional families, who had lost loved ones.

Further, in these visions Mrs. White saw clearly that the main issue was slavery, and that God would permit both the North and the South to be punished until they confronted this issue. Many political and religious leaders saw this only after years of terrible struggle had killed and injured millions. The politics of Washington, interlocked with Southern sympathizers in Northern leadership, had kept the purposes of the war muddied. The Fugitive Slave Acts,[56] requiring Northerners to return runaway slaves to their masters, is a good example of the political and moral confusion. Note how long it took President Lincoln to decide that it was time to issue the Emancipation Proclamation (on September 22, 1862, effective January 1, 1863).[57]

Contrary to Contemporary Optimism

Ellen White's general predictions made in the waning years of the nineteenth century seem like a review of modern newspapers. Some could say that she was simply using the same sagacity that other thoughtful people were using when contemplating the future. But what she wrote and what thought leaders in her day were projecting were light-years apart.

The period between 1890 and 1914 is noted for "millennial" predictions, a time when the future looked bright with promise. In most all areas of Western society, whether in medicine, economics, technology, or scientific inventions, the picture of peace, prosperity, and a golden future was a prevailing sentiment.[58]

Some of the predictions Ellen White made contrary to the spirit of her age focused on the social world: "Step by step, the world is reaching the conditions that existed in the days of Noah. Every conceivable crime is committed. The lust of the flesh, the pride of the eyes, the display of selfishness, the misuse of power, the cruelty, and the force used to cause men to unite with confederacies and unions . . . all these are the working of Satanic agencies. . . . The whole world appears to be in the march to death."[59]

"I am bidden to declare the message that cities full of transgression, and sinful in the extreme, will be destroyed by earthquakes, by fire, by flood."[60]

"I have been shown that the Spirit of the Lord is being withdrawn from the earth. God's keeping power will soon be refused to all who continue to disregard His commandments. The reports of fraudulent transactions, murders, and crimes of every kind are coming to us daily. Iniquity is becoming so common a thing that it no longer shocks the senses as it once did."[61]

She turned to the development of international tensions and war: "The tempest is coming, and we must get ready for its fury. . . . We shall see troubles on all sides. Thousands of ships will be hurled into the depths of the sea. Navies will go down, and human lives will be sacrificed by millions. Fires will break out unexpectedly, and no human effort will be able to quench them. The palaces of earth will be swept away in the fury of the flames. Disasters by rail will become more and more frequent; confusion, collision, and death without a moment's warning will occur on the great lines of travel."[62]

"Last Friday morning, just before I awoke, a very impressive scene was presented before me. I seemed to awake from sleep but was not in my home. From the windows I could behold a terrible conflagration. Great balls of fire were falling upon houses, and from these balls fiery arrows were flying in every direction. It was impossible to check the fires that were kindled, and many places were being destroyed. The terror of the people was indescribable. After a time I awoke and found myself at home."[63]

"Soon great trouble will arise among the nations—trouble that will not cease until Jesus comes."[64]

Another perceptive insight ran cross-grained with the phenomenal optimism prevailing in 1909, the year of the following prediction regarding increasing economic and social impasses: "There are not many, even among educators and statesmen, who comprehend the causes that underlie the present state of society. Those who hold the reins of government are not able to solve the problem of moral corruption, poverty, pauperism, and increasing crime. They are struggling in vain to place business operations on a more secure basis."[65]

Modern Spiritualism

Ellen White's previews of the rise of modern spiritualism were given when spiritistic manifestations were local, isolated, and more of a curiosity than anything else. Those 1848 displays of strange rappings involving the Fox sisters in Hydesville, New York, were shown to her as the revival of spiritualism in modern times. In reporting a vision seen March 24, 1849, she wrote: "I saw that the mysterious knocking in New York and other places was the power of Satan, and that such things would be more and more common, clothed in a religious garb so as to lull the deceived to greater security."[66] Spiritualism probably has never been more prominent in the history of the world than it is today. Adherents include people on all levels of society and in every economic class. Politicians and heads of government freely admit their reliance on spiritualist mediums. Who, other than Ellen White in 1849, had the insight to label the Fox-sisters-phenomenon as the beginning of a worldwide, sophisticated movement with tremendous implications for events in the last days?

Rise of Papal Influence

Another predictive area involves the astounding rise of papal influence, from virtual innocuousness in the nineteenth century to its current worldwide power and influence. In 1888, during the dark days of the papacy, Ellen White wrote: "Let the principle once be established in the United States, that the church may employ or control the power of the state; that religious observances may be enforced by secular laws; in short, that the authority of church and state is to dominate the conscience, and the triumph of Rome in this country [the U.S.A.] is assured.

"God's word has given warning of the impending danger; let this be unheeded, and the Protestant world will learn what the purposes of Rome really are, only when it is too late to escape the snare. She is silently growing into power. Her doctrines are exerting their influence in legislative halls, in the churches, and in the hearts of men. . . . Stealthily and unsuspectedly she is strengthening her forces to further her own ends when the time shall come for her to strike. All that she desires is vantage ground, and this is already being given her. We shall soon see and shall feel what the purpose of the Roman element is."[67]

The 1980s and 1990s witnessed a dramatic recovery of world stature by the Pope of Rome, a far cry from those decades between 1870 and 1929 when the pope was the "prisoner of the Vatican."[68] The world was stunned to see the President of the United States and the Pope on the cover of *Time* magazine, February 24, 1992, under the words, "The Holy Alliance." The feature article unfolded the story behind the collapse of communism. President Reagan and Pope John Paul II had been in close, highly secret, consultation for years as they worked together to destabilize the communist network. "They regarded the U.S.–Vatican relationship as a holy alliance; the moral force of their church combined with their fierce anticommunism and their notion of American democracy." Without this close cooperation between the Catholic Church and the United States, world developments in recent decades probably would have been vastly different.

Further, as if to single-handedly endorse Ellen White's 1888 predictions, *Time* magazine's cover for December 26, 1994, featured Pope John Paul II as "Man of the Year." In that cover story, the Pope presented himself as the "moral compass for believers and nonbelievers alike." Even Billy Graham, symbol of evangelical Protestantism, said of the Pope: "He's been the strong conscience of the whole Christian world."[69]

Union of Catholics and Protestants

But Ellen White saw more than the resurgence of papal adoration worldwide. She also saw what no person even a few years ago would have dreamed—the astonishing rapprochement between Catholics and Protestants, even evangelical Protestants! In 1885 she wrote: "When Protestantism shall stretch her hand across the gulf to grasp the hand of the Roman power, when she shall reach over the abyss to clasp hands with spiritualism, when, under the influence of this threefold union, our country shall repudiate every principle of its Constitution as a Protestant and republican government and shall make provision for the propagation of papal falsehoods and delusions, then we may know that the time has come for the marvelous working of Satan and that the end is near."[70]

A landmark document that no one could have foreseen even in the 1980s was signed in joint declaration on March 29, 1994, by leading evangelical Protestants and Roman Catholics. Perhaps the most significant event in the last 500 years of church history, the signing of this amazing statement entitled "Evangelicals and Catholics Together: The Christian Mission in the 3rd Millennium," (ECT), substantially overturns the Protestant Reformation as it fulfills Bible prophecy—and Ellen White's predictions.[71]

One prediction yet to be completely fulfilled involves the threefold union of Protestantism, Catholicism, and Spiritualism (New Agers, etc.) in the concerted effort to enforce Sunday worship. With the stunning rapidity of recent Protestant-Catholic joint efforts, unified at the center by their common theological thread of the immortality of the soul, their further union with modern Spiritualism (New Agers) is not difficult to foresee—now. But not in the 1880s![72]

All the above illustrations of Ellen

White's predictive ministry are interesting and, to a degree, coercive.

Health and Medicine

What has amazed thoughtful people throughout the world is that her general comments on health, science, or environment have stood the test of the years—something that probably cannot be said about any other writer in the nineteenth century. That in itself is a remarkable achievement. More than that, her writings contain certain principles and developments that were not common in her day but today are well-validated.

For example, note her profound emphasis on how the mind affects the body in producing sickness;[73] her warm concern for prenatal influences, including drugs and alcohol;[74] and her monumental, interactive system of dietary principles that are increasingly supported by nutritional research.[75]

Worldwide Expansion of Adventists

Equally interesting are the predictions Ellen White made regarding the worldwide expansion of Seventh-day Adventists, long before her colleagues could see any evidence for her optimism:

• November, 1848, Dorchester, Massachusetts: At a time of great financial stress, and appealing to no more than one hundred Sabbatarian Adventists, she predicted that the periodical her husband was starting would be "small at first," but eventually its "streams of light" would go "clear round the world."[76]

In 1995, Seventh-day Adventists had worldwide 56 publishing houses, 7,485 full-time literature evangelists, with worldwide sales of $99,253,123 (U.S. dollars), with literature being published in 229 languages (including oral evangelism. Adventists are working in 717 languages worldwide).[77]

• Speaking from a chair (mostly bedridden for eleven months) at the opening of the Melbourne Bible School (predecessor of Avondale College), August 24, 1892, Mrs. White said: "The missionary work in Australia and New Zealand is yet in its infancy, but the same work must be accomplished in Australia, New Zealand, in Africa, India, China, and the islands of the sea, as has been accomplished in the home field [USA]."[78]

Young A. G. Daniells, one of the first American expatriate workers in Australia, heard this prediction with astonishment and wrote later of the sense of being "overwhelmed." All present felt that this prediction "seemed like the wildest kind of speculation. . . . But some who were present have lived to see these staggering predictions strikingly fulfilled."[79]

• In 1894 Ellen White urged the Australian Adventist constituency of fewer than one thousand to plan immediately for a college to train workers for the Adventist mission to the South Pacific. Further, she envisioned a college that would break new ground after learning lessons from the difficult experiences at Battle Creek College. Few, even of her closest advisers, saw wisdom in her counsel, but without her visionary understanding of what the South Pacific needed and her tenacity to see the project through, neither Avondale College, nor much else in Australia and New Zealand, would be standing under the Adventist name today.

• In November, 1901, Ellen White wrote a severe warning to the board of trustees of the Review and Herald Publishing Association, "the best equipped printing office in the state of Michigan."[80] They had problems: about ninety percent of their work was commercial, some of it clearly inappropriate for Adventist publishers. Other problems revolved around interpersonal relationships.

After many previous warnings, Mrs. White made what amounted to a divine threat: "I have been almost afraid to open the *Review,* fearing to see that God has cleansed the publishing house by fire. . . . Unless there is a reformation, calamity will overtake the publishing house, and the world will know the reason."[81]

Thirteen months later, December 30, 1902, a fire of "unknown origin" destroyed the complex. Nothing of value was saved. When leaders wanted to rebuild in Battle Creek, Ellen White objected, saying, "Never lay a stone or a brick in Battle Creek to rebuild the Review office there. God has a better place for it."[82]

• On at least three occasions Ellen White urged her stunned colleagues to buy property in southern California for medical centers.[83] On October 13, 1902, she wrote that properties with buildings "especially suited to sanitarium work" could be bought "at much less than their original cost."[84] Without this insight into God's plan for southern California, Paradise Valley Hospital, Glendale Adventist Medical Center, and Loma Linda University would not be centers for Adventist outreach.[85]

• Before church leaders could get their breath after purchasing the Loma Linda property, Ellen White was painting the future of Loma Linda as the principal center for educating medical personnel. Far beyond any human dream, she was calmly adamant: "This will be."[86]

Since Ellen White's awesome prediction, Loma Linda University has graduated many thousands in various fields of advanced education. It is internationally known for some of its medical achievements.

Some Visions Directed to Secret Problems

Ellen White had many experiences dealing with people's secret problems. In 1858 she wrote about a farm family (father, mother, and grown daughter) who had moved to Illinois from New England three years earlier. Ostensibly the reason for the move was to "introduce the work in the West. The husband went with one intention, his wife with another. His intention was to proclaim the truth, her intention was to have all their means laid out in house and lands."

As time went on, the husband "disobeyed the call of God to gratify his wife and daughter, and was too willing to excuse or cover up his love of the world under a show of duty to his family. . . . I saw that unless she got out of her husband's way . . . the Lord would visit the family with judgment, and move her out of the way."

Soon disease came and the wife died. While the Whites visited the bereaved husband and father, Mrs. White had a vision of the spiritual struggle he was going through and "was astonished at what was shown me." She was shown how the father was snared by the deceitfulness of riches and that the daughter was "wrapped up in selfishness."

But time went on. In 1857 Ellen White had another vision regarding this Illinois family. She saw "that he was not moving fast enough, that he was not using his means to advance the cause of God as fast as he should." Soon after that vision, she heard that this very prosperous father had died at the age of 51.

Why did Mrs. White report this private story in the church paper? She closed her article with these words: "As I have seen that the reward of covetousness thus far upon this family should be a warning to the church, I cannot withhold from the people of God what has been shown me respecting them."[87]

Always the soul winner, she recognized a young watchmaker in Nimes, France, whom she had seen in vision. Once a believer, Abel Bieder had become discouraged and was, at the time, working on the Sabbath while he perfected his watchmaking trade. After meeting him at his shop, she invited him to meetings where she was to speak. She spoke privately with Abel, telling him that she knew the history of his life and his youthful errors.

"I then entreated him with tears to turn square about, to leave the service of Satan and of sin, for he had become a thorough backslider, and return like the prodigal to his Father's house. . . . I told him that I dared not have him cross the threshold of the door until he would before God and angels and those present say, 'I will from this day be a Christian.'"

The next day Abel resigned from his promising career, happy in the Lord. Soon Ellen White paid his fare to Basel so he could assist L. R. Conradi and James Erzberger in their evangelistic work.[88]

The N. D. Faulkhead experience in 1892 is a classic illustration of Ellen White's prophetic ministry for the early Australian Adventists. When she went to Australia in 1891, Faulkhead was treasurer of the publishing house; he also held the highest positions in several secret organizations. As time went on, he became increasingly involved in his lodge work, and his church interests waned.

On the boat trip to Australia and soon after arrival, Ellen White had a comprehensive vision involving the publishing house generally and several personal testimonies, including one for the Faulkheads. When she went to mail the message, she felt strongly restrained: "When I enclosed the communication all ready to mail, it seemed that a voice spoke to me saying, 'Not yet, not yet, they will not receive your testimony.'" She held the testimony for almost twelve months.[89]

During that time Faulkhead's co-workers noticed his fading interest in his work and pleaded with him to reconsider his infatuation with the lodges. Ellen White saw in vision that he was "a man about to lose his balance and fall over a precipice."[90]

One of the Australian Adventists asked Faulkhead what he would do if Mrs. White had a testimony for him in regard to his lodge affiliations. To this he responded, "It would have to be mighty strong." That she indeed had a message for Faulkhead almost a year old, no one yet knew.[91]

Shortly after Faulkhead's defiance, he had a dream that Ellen White had a message for him! In a few days, he met her and asked if she had something for him. Replying that she had, she proposed an early meeting in the future. But Faulkhead was eager: "Why not give me the message now?"

She told him that several times she had been ready to send the message but she was "forbidden by the Spirit of the Lord to do so" because the time was not ripe. But now was the time. She began to read the fifty-page manuscript, especially the portion dealing with his involvement with Freemasonry. She went on to reveal how he dropped small coins into offerings on the Sabbath but large coins into the treasury of the lodges. She heard him addressed as "Worshipful Master."

Later, Faulkhead recalled: "I thought this was getting pretty close home when she started to talk to me in reference to what I was doing in the lodges."[92]

Then it happened. After giving a certain movement of her hand, she said: "I cannot relate all that was given to me."[93]

Faulkhead turned pale, recounting later: "Immediately she gave me this sign. I touched her on the shoulder and asked her if she knew what she had done. She looked up surprised and said she did not do anything unusual. I told her that she had given me the sign of a Knight Templar. Well, she did not know anything about it."

Ellen White went on about how impossible it is to be a committed Christian and a Freemason. Then she made another secret sign, which she said "my attending angel made to me." Faulkhead knew that this particular sign was known only to the highest order of Masons, and said later: "This convinced me that her testimony was from God. . . . Immediately the statement that I had made to Brother Stockton, that it would have to be mighty strong before I could believe that she had a message for me from the Lord, flashed through my mind."

Faulkhead's response to the interview was immediate. He told his co-workers the next day how God had spoken to him through Ellen White. His first work of the day was to dictate his resignation to his various lodges. But his lodge friends did not give up easily, insisting that he was honor-bound to serve out his term for the next nine months. The struggle was severe and fellow church members trembled for him.

At the end of those nine months Faulkhead wrote to God's messenger: "How thankful I am to Him for sending me a warning that I was traveling on the wrong road. . . . I can see now very clearly that to continue with them would have been my downfall, as I must confess that my interest for the truth was growing cold."

Faulkhead continued to serve the publishing house for many years and remained a strong spiritual leader in Australia.[94]

Endnotes

1. For a partial list of Ellen White's visions, see Appendix D.
2. *Bio.,* vol. 6, pp. 98, 99.
3. *Ibid.,* p. 96.
4. DF 481, Jesse Arthur to WCW, Aug. 27, 1902, cited in *Bio.,* vol. 6, p. 97.
5. *Ibid.,* pp. 97, 98. The Salamanca vision and the 1891 General Conference Session experience provide other examples of how a prophet is not always aware of the timing when the vision is to be presented to others. See pp. 149, 188. On another occasion, when Ellen White visited the Swiss publishing house in 1885, she recognized the press room as one that she had seen in vision. She shook hands with two young workers and then asked for the third worker. B. L. Whitney, president of the Swiss Mission, was puzzled until Mrs. White said, "There is an older man here and I have a message for him." The other worker was in the city on business. Ten years before, she had seen this particular worker in vision and now she was reminded that she had a special message for him. This incident brought immense encouragement to all the workers in Basel. (Story in *Bio.*, vol. 3, pp. 293, 294.
6. *Bio.*, vol. 3, pp. 363-365.
7. *Bio.*, vol. 3, pp. 128, 129; *Review and Herald*, Dec. 11, 1879. p. 190.
8. See p. 188.
9. The Salamanca Vision episode reveals how a prophet is led by the Lord not to reveal and use all the contents of a vision at once. The central message is to be given at the exact time when needed most. After the dramatic events in Battle Creek that followed Ellen White's public testimony, O. A. Olsen, General Conference president, wrote: "Sister White had had no opportunity to have any knowledge of what had gone on in that room during the night in the Review office. . . . The Lord had shown it to her before the thing took place; and now, the very morning in which it took place, she had been, in a special manner, called by the Lord to present what had been shown her. It is needless to say not only that it brought relief to many minds, but that it gave cause for great thankfulness that at such a critical moment the Lord stepped in and saved us from the perplexity and confusion that seemed to be coming up on important questions."—DF 107b, O. A. Olsen account, cited in *Bio.*, vol. 3, pp. 477-481. Six prominent ministers signed a statement that included these words: "The relation [telling] of this vision made a profound and solemn impression upon that large congregation of Seventh-day Adventist ministers present at that early-morning meeting. When they heard those who had been reproved for the wrong course taken in that council confess that all Mrs. White had said about them was true in every particular, they saw the seal of divine inspiration had been set upon that vision and testimony. The power and solemnity of that meeting made an impression upon the minds of those present not soon to be forgotten."—DF 107b, joint statements, cited in *Ibid.*, p. 482.
10. In order that all concerned throughout the denomination might profit by the Boulder Sanitarium experience, the history of the crisis and testimonies from Ellen White were incorporated in a pamphlet of eighty pages under the title "Record of Progress and an Earnest Appeal in Behalf of the Boulder, Colorado, Sanitarium." This pamphlet is known today as *Special Testimonies*, Series B, No. 5. See also *Bio.*, vol. 6, pp. 33-43.
11. *Bio.*, vol. 6, p. 48.
12. *Ibid.*, p. 49.
13. *Bio.*, vol. 6, pp. 67-72. For a similar experience, occurring in 1903, see Schwarz, *Light Bearers*, p. 292. See pp. 200-204 for further discussion of the Kellogg/Pantheism controversy and another timely message from Ellen White.
14. George Amadon joined the Review and Herald Publishing Association in 1853 as a young printer. After the Press fire and the move to Washington, D.C., he remained in Battle Creek and served the Battle Creek church as a visiting pastor. *SDAE*, vol. 10, p. 58.
15. *Bio.*, vol. 6, pp. 126-129.
16. The church clerk, in that church business meeting, summarized Canright's public statement wherein he stated "that he had come to a point where he no longer believed that the Ten Commandments were binding upon Christians and had given up the law, the Sabbath, the messages, the sanctuary, our position upon [the] United States in prophecy, the testimonies, health reform, the ordinances of humility. He also said that he did not believe the Papacy had changed the Sabbath. And though he did not directly state it, his language intimated that he would probably keep Sunday. He thinks that Seventh-day Adventists are too narrow in their ideas."—Cited in Carrie Johnson, *I Was Canright's Secretary* (Washington, D.C.: Review and Herald Publishing Association, 1971), p. 82.
17. *Ibid.*, pp. 168, 169.

18. D. H. Kress, M.D., "The Testimonies and a Balanced Diet," in George K. Abbott, M.D., *The Witness of Science to the Testimonies of the Spirit of Prophecy* (revised edition) (Mountain View, CA: Pacific Press Publishing Association, 1948), pp. 138-141. Portions of Ellen White's letter to Dr. Kress are found in *Counsels on Diet and Foods*, pp. 202-207.
19. *SDAE*, vol. 10, p. 886. For a sample of scores of similar occasions wherein Ellen White, in the most timely manner and because of the facts given to her in vision, intervened to counsel, reprove, encourage someone, note the following: (1) A minister in the young San Francisco church was saved from an embarrassing, potentially disastrous, church investigation on Sunday, January 28, 1872, because of a letter he received from Ellen White on Saturday evening.—Loughborough, *GSAM*, pp. 387, 388, cited in *Bio.*, vol. 2, pp. 363, 364. (2) W. W. Prescott, president of Battle Creek College, had become a forceful advocate of Anna Phillips, a self-proclaimed "prophet." One of his purposes for traveling to Walla Walla College in early 1894 was to read one of Anna Phillips's testimonies. Elder Haskell was also at Walla Walla and reported to Ellen White: "Your testimony came just in season to save some trouble at College Place. I have heard of something of the kind before when your letters or testimony would come just at the time when a meeting was in progress and it just reached the people in time to save trouble, but [I] never experienced it before. . . . Brother Prescott was going to read the testimony of Anna Phillips, although we had had some talk over the matter. But the day just in season your letter came and then he of course had opportunity to read it. This settled the question with him. He said, 'Then that is all there is to it. Now I will take some of the same medicine that I have given other people.' . . . But God in His providence had that testimony come on the very train it should have come and it reached me just in season."—Letter from S. N. Haskell to Ellen White, March 9, 1894, cited in Glen Baker, "Anna Phillips—Not Another Prophet," *Adventist Review*, Feb. 20, 1986, p. 9. (3) The famous Waukon-trip dash across the "frozen" Mississippi in December 1857 was prompted by a vision wherein Ellen White saw the early Adventist leaders from New England in need of immediate spiritual counsel. Against all recommendations, the White party pushed through the snowstorms and the breathtaking experience on the river, suffering frostbite and little food—only to find that their old friends, including the Andrewses, Loughboroughs, and Stevenses, were "sorry that we had come." But the Spirit of God prevailed.—*Bio.*, vol. 1, pp. 345-349; Maxwell, *Tell It to the World*, pp.139-141; Spalding, *Origin and History*, vol. 1, pp. 279-289. See also p. 202.
20. 1 Chron. 17:1-15. See p. 35.
21. See "Appeal for the Southern Field," cited in Daniells, *AGP*, p. 322.
22. *Bio.*, vol. 5, pp. 187-193; Daniells, *Ibid.*, pp. 323-327.
23. Daniells, *AGP*, pp. 327-329.
24. Hiram Edson's report in *Present Truth* (*PT*), Dec. 1849, cited in *Bio.*, vol. 1, pp. 196-198. In the same issue of *PT*, Ellen White reported: "While in vision the angel pointed to the earth, where I saw Brother Rhodes in thick darkness; but he still bore the image of Jesus. I saw it was the will of God that Brethren Edson and Ralph should go."
25. *Bio.*, vol. 4, pp. 315-317.
26. *The Desire of Ages*, p. 215.
27. *Ibid.*, p. 220.
28. *Ibid.*
29. *The Acts of the Apostles*, p. 137.
30. *Testimonies*, vol. 5, p. 686.
31. For a discussion of the "Shut-Door" issue, see chapter 44.
32. *The Review and Herald*, Apr. 21, 1851, pp. 71, 72.
33. See p. 170, 171.
34. *Review and Herald*, Aug. 30, 1864, p. 109.
35. *Testimonies*, vol. 1, pp. 206, 207.
36. *Ibid.*
37. See pp. 281-284 for an analysis of this vision.
38. The text continued: "Swine were useful. In a fruitful country, where there was much to decay upon the ground, which would poison the atmosphere, herds of swine were permitted to run free, and devoured the decaying substances, which was a means of preserving health. Other animals were forbidden to be eaten by the Israelites, because they were not the best articles of food."—Page 124.
39. Available today in *Selected Messages*, book 2, pp. 411-479.
40. *Selected Messages*, book 2, p. 417. See *Counsels on Diet and Foods*, p. 392, and *The Ministry of Healing*, p. 314.
41. *Testimonies*, vol. 1, p. 207.
42. Ellen White never changed her position regarding eating pork as to making the issue a test question, even though she emphasized in her writings that God declared swine as an unclean food because of its unhealthy nature: "If you are a Bible doer as well as a Bible reader, you must understand from the Scriptures that swine's flesh was prohibited by Jesus Christ enshrouded in the billowy cloud. This is not a test question. Directions have been given to families that such articles as butter and the eating largely of flesh meats is not the best for physical and mental health. . . . I advise every Sabbathkeeping canvasser [literature evangelist] to avoid eating meat, not because it is regarded as a sin to eat meat, but because it is not healthful."— *MR*, vol. 16, p. 173.
43. *Bio.*, vol. 1, p. 61. Giving reproof never became easier.
44. *Life Sketches*, p. 90.
45. *Selected Messages*, book 3, pp. 36, 37.
46. *Bio.*, vol. 3, p. 146. In a nearly thirteen-page testimony that was read at the Michigan camp meeting in 1881, she wrote near the close: "Let none entertain the thought that I regret or take back any plain testimony I have borne to individuals or to the people. If I have erred anywhere, it is in not rebuking sin more decidedly and firmly. Some of the brethren have taken the responsibility of criticizing my work and proposing an easier way to correct wrongs. To these persons I would say: I take God's way and not yours. What I have said or written in testimony or reproof has not been too plainly expressed. God has given me my work, and I must meet it at the judgment. . . . All through my life it has been terribly hard for me to hurt the feelings of any, or disturb their self-deception, as I deliver the testimonies given me of God. It is contrary to my nature. It costs me great pain and many sleepless nights."—*Ibid.*, pp. 184, 185.
47. The vision is reported in two parts: the powerful description of "The Two Ways," and "Conformity to the World."—*Testimonies*, vol. 1, pp. 127-137.
48. *Ibid.*, p. 132, footnote.

49. *Ibid.*.
50. Manuscript 4, 1883, cited in *Selected Messages,* book 1, pp. 67, 68. This sad recognition of reality was reflected in her writings at least thirty times as recorded in Herbert E. Douglass, *The End* (Mountain View, Calif.: Pacific Press Publishing Association, 1979), pp. 161-167. This fact should not be obscured—the delay in the Advent is not God's fault or His arbitrary plan: "We may have to remain here in this world because of insubordination many more years, as did the children of Israel; but for Christ's sake, His people should not add sin to sin by charging God with the consequence of their own wrong course of action."—*Evangelism,* p. 696.
51. *Bio.,* vol. 1, p. 463.
52. *Ibid.*
53. *Testimonies,* vol. 1, p. 264.
54. How shortsighted most everyone was: A few days before the Parkville vision, on December 22, 1860, William H. Seward, secretary-of-state-elect to the Lincoln cabinet, predicted a peaceful settlement of the national crisis within the next sixty days.—Cited in Henry S. Commager, ed., *Documents of American History* (New York: Appleton-Century-Crofts, Inc., 1863, 2 vols., 7th ed), I, pp. 366, 369. In mid-February 1861 Thomas R. R. Cobb, Georgia secessionist and committee member preparing the Confederate constitution, wrote: "The almost universal belief here [Montgomery] is that we shall not have war."—Cited in Edward Channing, *History of the United States* (New York: Macmillan Co., 1905-1925, 6 volumes), Vol. VI, p. 264. Two days before his Inaugural Address of March 4, 1861, Lincoln declared in Philadelphia: "I have felt all the while justified in concluding that the crisis, the panic, the anxiety of the country at this time is artificial."—Cited in *Harper's Weekly,* March 2, 1861, p. 135.

    The *Encyclopedia Britannica* estimated that the Civil War cost "a total of some $11,450,500,000 for the North alone. But the cost to the South was enormous; $4,000,000,000 cannot be exaggeration. It follows that, up to 1909, the cost of the war to the nation had approximated the tremendous total of $15,500,000,000 . . . and the death of probably 300,000 men on each side."—11th ed., vol. XXVII, p. 710.
55. Loughborough, *RPSDA,* pp. 236, 237.
56. Fugitive Slave Acts of 1793, 1850, and upheld by Supreme Court in 1859: In the Rochester vision Ellen White wrote: "The fugitive slave law was calculated to crush out of man every noble, generous feeling of sympathy that should arise in his heart for the oppressed and suffering slave."—*Testimonies,* vol. 1, p. 264. "The officers of the Southern army are constantly receiving information in regard to the plans of the Northern army. . . . Rebels know they have sympathizers all through the Northern army. . . . The spirits of devils, professing to be dead warriors and skillful generals, communicate with men in authority, and control many of their movements. . . . Many professed Union men, holding important positions, are disloyal at heart. Their only object in taking up arms was to preserve the Union as it was, and slavery with it. They would heartily chain down the slave to his life of galling bondage, had they the privilege. Such have a strong degree of sympathy with the South. . . . I saw that both the South and the North were being punished."—*Ibid.,* pp. 363-368.
57. In an August 22, 1862, letter to Horace Greeley, editor of the *New York Tribune,* President Lincoln wrote: "My paramount object in this struggle is to save the Union and is not either to save or to destroy slavery. If I could save the Union without freeing any slave, I would do it; and if I could do it by freeing all the slaves, I would do it; and if I could save it by freeing some and leaving others alone, I would also do that."—Carl Sandburg, *Abraham Lincoln: The War Years* (New York: Charles Scribner's Sons, 1937), vol. 3, p. 567.
58. For a sampling of turn-of-the-century "peace and prosperity" sentiment, note the following: "Since the Exhibition [London, 1851], western civilization has advanced steadily, and in some respects more rapidly than any sober mind could have predicted—civilization, at least, in the conventional sense, which has been not badly defined as 'the development of material ease, of education, of equality, and of aspirations to rise and succeed in life.' The most striking advance has been in the technical conveniences of life—that is, in the control over natural forces. It would be superfluous to enumerate the discoveries and inventions since 1850 which have abridged space, economized time, eased bodily suffering, and reduced in some ways the friction of life, though they have increased it in others. This uninterrupted series of technical inventions, proceeding concurrently with immense enlargements of all branches of knowledge, has gradually accustomed the least speculative mind to the conception that civilization is naturally progressive, and that continuous improvement is part of the order of things. . . .

    "In the seventies and eighties of the last century [19th] the idea of progress was becoming a general article of faith. Some might hold it in the fatalistic form that humanity moves in a desirable direction, whatever men do or may leave undone; others might believe that the future will depend largely on our own conscious efforts, but that there is nothing in the nature of things to disappoint the prospect of steady and indefinite advance. The majority did not inquire too curiously into such points of doctrine, but received it in a vague sense as a comfortable addition to their convictions. But it became a part of the general mental outlook of educated people. . . .

    "Within the last forty years every civilized country has produced a large literature on social science, in which indefinite progress is generally assumed as an axiom."—J. B. Bury, *The Idea of Progress* (New York, N.Y.: Dover Publications, Inc. 1955), pp. 331, 332, 346, 348.

    The spirit of optimism at the turn of the century is reflected in church historian Arthur Cushman Giffert's sermon entitled, "The Kingdom of God," delivered several times during 1909: "The modern age is marked by a vast confidence in the powers of man. For many centuries it was the custom to think of man as a weak and puny thing. Humility and self-distrust were the cardinal virtues, pride and self-reliance and independence the root of all vice. The change is not the fruit of speculation, a mere philosophical theory as to man's relation to the universe, but the result of the actual and growing conquest of the world in which we live. . . . Characteristic of the present time is its faith in the future, based upon its solid experiences of the past. . . . The great task of the Christian church of the twentieth century is ready to its hand. Upon the church devolves the chief responsibility for the bringing of the kingdom. . . . We are on the eve of great happenings. No one familiar with history and able to read the signs of the times can for a moment doubt it."—Cited in H. Shelton Smith, Robert T. Handy, Lefferts A. Loetscher, *American Christianity, An Historical Interpretation With Representative Documents* (New York: Charles Scribner's Sons, 1963), pp. 286, 290.

59. Manuscript 139, 1903, cited in *Evangelism,* p. 26.
60. *Ibid.*
61. Letter 258, 1907, cited in *Last Day Events,* p. 27.
62. *Signs of the Times,* April 21, 1890, p. 242.
63. Letter 278, 1906, cited in *Last Day Events,* pp. 24, 25.
64. *Review and Herald,* Feb. 11, 1904, p. 8.
65. *Testimonies,* vol. 9, p. 13. Current books, magazines, and TV programs seem in concert in their lament regarding worldwide economic problems inherent in various degrees of government socialism, job dislocations caused by "the information age," the moral corruption connected with drugs and alcohol and their contribution to the astonishing rise in crime worldwide, the stunning rise in teen-age pregnancies, etc. All these problems have contributed to rising government costs and increased taxation.
66. *Early Writings,* p. 43. A year later, Aug. 24, 1850, she wrote: "I saw that the 'mysterious rapping' was the power of Satan; some of it was directly from him, and some indirectly, through his agents, but it all proceeded from Satan. . . . I was shown that by the rapping and mesmerism these modern magicians would yet account for all the miracles wrought by our Lord Jesus Christ, and that many would believe that all the mighty works of the Son of God when on earth were accomplished by this same power."—*Ibid.,* p. 59.
67. *The Great Controversy,* p. 581. See also *Last Day Events,* p. 132.
68. No pope since 1870, when the unified Kingdom of Italy took over the papal territories, had stepped outside of the Vatican grounds until the 1929 Concordat with Mussolini's government.
69. *Time*, Dec. 26, 1994, p. 54.
70. *Testimonies*, vol. 5, p. 451. See *The Great Controversy*, pp. 445, 448, 449.
71. Revelation 13:3 foretold the day when "all the world marveled and followed the beast [Papal Rome]." The essence of this declaration set forth by prominent evangelical and Catholic leaders is: "Those who love the Lord must stand together"; that which unites us is far more than that which divides. One of the signers, J. I. Packer, defended his endorsement in "Why I Signed It" (*Christianity Today,* Dec. 12, 1994): "The plot-line of its 8,000 words is simply summarized. After stating that its concern is with 'the relationship between evangelicals and Catholics, who constitute the growing edge of missionary expansion at present and, most likely, in the century ahead,' it announces its composers' agreement on the Apostles' Creed and on the proposition that 'we are justified by grace through faith because of Jesus Christ'; it affirms a commitment to seek more love, . . . it sketches out a purpose of non-proselytizing joint action for the conversion and nurture of outsiders. . . . The drafters of ECT declare that they . . . understand the Christian life from first to last as personal conversion to Jesus Christ and communion with him, know that they must 'teach and live in obedience to the divinely inspired Scriptures, which are the infallible Word of God,' and on this basis are 'brothers and sisters in Christ.'"

    Charles Colson, another prominent signer, defended the ECT document in "Why Catholics Are Our Allies," wherein he advocated: "When confronting the non-Christian world—whether in evangelism or political activism—we should present a united front. This is the goal of ECT . . . . Let's be certain that we are firing our polemical rifles against the enemy, not against those [Roman Catholics] fighting in the trenches alongside us [Protestants] in defense of the Truth."—*Christianity Today,* Nov. 14, 1994.
72. "Through the two great errors, the immortality of the soul and Sunday sacredness, Satan will bring the people under his deceptions. While the former lays the foundation of Spiritualism, the latter creates a bond of sympathy with Rome. The Protestants of the United States will be foremost in stretching their hands across the gulf to grasp the hand of spiritualism; they will reach over the abyss to clasp hands with the Roman power; and under the influence of this threefold union, this country will follow in the steps of Rome in trampling on the rights of conscience."—*The Great Controversy,* p. 588.
73. *Testimonies,* vol. 1, p. 566 (1867); *Testimonies,* vol. 3, p. 184 (1872); *The Ministry of Healing,* p. 241 (1905).
74. *Selected Messages,* book 2, p. 442 (1865); *Patriarchs and Prophets,* p. 561 (1890).
75. See on pp. 320-336 her insights on the dangers of the free use of sugar and animal fats, the problems of obesity and irregularity of eating, the towering value of exercise, the challenge of childhood diet patterns, the dangers in flesh food, tea, and coffee, etc., in *Counsels on Diet and Foods* (Washington, D.C.: Review and Herald Publishing Association, 1938).
76. *Life Sketches,* p. 125.
77. 133rd *Annual Statistical Report—1995.* (Published by General Conference of Seventh-day Adventists.)
78. *Life Sketches,* p. 338.
79. *The Abiding Gift of Prophecy,* p. 309 (1936). Imagine how delighted and amazed those present in 1892 would be if they could see the remarkable outreach of Adventists throughout the South Pacific today.
80. James White, *Life Sketches* (Battle Creek, Mich.: Steam Press of the Seventh-day Adventist Publishing Assn., 1880), pp. 353-355.
81. *Testimonies,* vol. 8, pp. 91, 96.
82. *General Conference Bulletin,* 1903, p. 85.
83. See p. 189.
84. Letter 157, 1902, cited in *MR* vol. 4, p. 280.
85. D. E. Robinson, *The Story of Our Health Message* (Nashville, Tenn.: Southern Publishing Association, 1965), pp. 337-361.
86. *Ibid.,* pp. 351, 352.
87. *Review and Herald,* April 15, 1858, p. 174. Ellen White's first letter to this family is dated July 12, 1856.
88. Delafield, *Ellen G. White in Europe,* pp. 233-234, 236.
89. Letter 39, 1893, cited in *Bio.,* vol. 4. pp. 49, 50.
90. Manuscript 4, 1893, cited in *Ibid.,* pp. 50, 51.
91. DF 522a, N. D. Faulkhead to EGW, Feb. 20, 1908, cited in *Bio.,* vol. 4, p. 51.
92. N. D. Faulkhead letter, Oct. 5, 1908, cited in *Ibid.,* pp. 51, 52.
93. Letter 46, 1892, cited in *Ibid.*
94. Letter 46, 1892, cited in *Ibid.*, p. 55.

Study Questions

1. On what occasions did the remarkable timeliness of a vision cause much rejoicing and added confidence?

2. How did Ellen White's visions help Doctor Kress in a practical way?

3. List some of Ellen White's beliefs and opinions that were modified after receiving a vision.

4. Why do you think that God did not reveal all the truth that He wanted His messengers to know at the beginning of their ministry?

5. What Ellen White predictions have you observed being fulfilled in the last twenty years?

6. How would you have reacted to Ellen White's insight if you had been N. D. Faulkhead?

7. List and discuss visions given in the following categories: Predictions; Direct counsel to individuals; An end-time vision.

8. Consider some times when Ellen White's "listening to God" prompted her to communicate to others at precisely the right time the message that was needed.

CHAPTER 16

Ellen White's Self-awareness as a Messenger

"For half a century I have been the Lord's messenger, and as long as my life shall last I shall continue to bear the messages that God gives me for His people."[1]

Ellen White's self-perception of her mission determined how she set priorities in her personal life and how determined she would be in getting her message before the world. She understood herself to be a "frail instrument . . . a channel for the communication of light."[2] In a statement before 2,500 people (not all church members) in the Battle Creek Tabernacle on Sunday, October 2, 1904, she said: "I am not, as I said yesterday [a Sabbath meeting], a prophet. I do not claim to be a leader; I claim to be simply a messenger of God, and that is all I have ever claimed."[3]

Naturally this was picked up by some and heralded as a confession that the Adventist leader was not a prophet after all. But Ellen White wanted to clarify a common misunderstanding of what a prophet is and does. If prophets primarily predict events, she wanted people to understand that definition did not apply to her role as God's messenger.[4]

She answered the concerns of both Adventists and non-Adventists when she said: "To claim to be a prophetess is something that I have never done. If others call me by that name, I have no controversy with them. But my work has covered so many lines that I cannot call myself other than a messenger, sent to bear a message from the Lord to His people, and to take up work in any line that He points out."[5]

She was conscious that she was in the historical stream of God's communication system through prophets and prophetesses: "In ancient times God spoke to men by the mouth of prophets and apostles. In these days He speaks to them by the testimonies of His Spirit. There was never a time when God instructed His people more earnestly than He instructs them now concerning His will and the course that He would have them pursue."[6]

Clarifying Biblical Truth

Ellen White never claimed that her writings were to supersede the Bible.[7] She saw that her "first duty" was "to present Bible principles" and if there was no "decided, conscientious reform" she would "appeal to them personally."[8] In fact, her "Testimonies" would not have been needed "if you had made God's Word your study with a desire to reach the Bible standard and attain Christian perfection."[9]

Further, she never claimed infallibility, always emphasizing that "God alone is infallible."[10] She was always open to the unfolding of truth. Progressive truth, for her, would not contradict previously revealed truths but expand it.[11]

Correcting contemporary errors in

Christian thought became an essential part of setting forth Biblical principles. Ellen White would say: "It has been given to me to correct specious errors and to specify what is truth."[12]

In her primary concern that the Bible be seen as the Christian's only rule of faith and practice, she felt compelled to emphasize that, in some instances, what had been understood for centuries to be "Bible truth" might be merely "floating germs" and the "rubbish of error."[13]

In addition to correcting these "floating" theological germs that permeated conventional Christianity in the nineteenth century, she was shown that some basic Christian truths had lain dormant from the first century. These truths were to be recovered and placed within the larger framework of the "everlasting gospel" that was to be preached in its fullness at the end of time.[14]

Because of these self-perceptions as God's messenger to assist in clarifying Biblical truth, Ellen White and her contemporaries understood that her counsel was on a higher level than that of other Bible students. Her involvement in the formation of Seventh-day Adventist doctrine was perceived as normative.

Visions Defined Truth and Created Unity After Bible Study

In the formative days Sabbatarian Adventists gathered on various occasions to establish their core beliefs and to bring harmony into their ranks.[15] With their Bibles open, sometimes they devoted entire days and nights to study. When the group became locked in an impasse with varying viewpoints firmly defended, Ellen White would be granted a vision in which the correct Biblical interpretation would be indicated. Hence, she was able to affirm the results of Brother C's Biblical study, rather than that of Brethren A, B, or D.

Here is how Ellen White described these occasions: "At that time [after the 1844 disappointment] one error after another pressed in upon us; ministers and doctors brought in new doctrines. We would search the Scriptures with much prayer, and the Holy Spirit would bring the truth to our minds. Sometimes whole nights would be devoted to searching the Scriptures and earnestly asking God for guidance. Companies of devoted men and women assembled for this purpose. The power of God would come upon me, and I was enabled clearly to define what is truth and what is error.

"As the points of our faith were thus established, our feet were placed upon a solid foundation. We accepted the truth point by point, under the demonstration of the Holy Spirit. I would be taken off in vision, and explanations would be given me. I was given illustrations of heavenly things, and of the sanctuary, so that we were placed where light was shining on us in clear, distinct rays."[16]

These experiences, wherein Ellen White brought clarity and harmony to their Biblical studies, conveyed validity and certitude to early Seventh-day Adventists. From time to time, when basic doctrines were being attacked from within the church, she would appeal to these earlier experiences: "Let none seek to tear away the foundations of our faith—the foundations that were laid at the beginning of our work by prayerful study of the word and revelation. Upon these foundations we have been building for the last fifty years."[17]

For later Adventists to deny these historical happenings—these Bible study/Spirit affirming experiences—would be to throw themselves back into the confusion when Brethren A, B, C, or D endeavored to convince others that each one's particular Biblical position was "the truth." Throughout her long life, Ellen White helped others to become "first-generation," early-Adventist "disciples." She knew that only by helping later Adventists to relive the "experience" (Bible study plus Spirit affirmation) would they see the coherency and urgency of the Adventist message.[18]

It follows, then, that to reject Ellen White's writings is to insult the Spirit of God, not her. In many instances throughout her ministry, she expressed anguish that those who slighted or rejected her messages were rejecting far more than a mere human being. For example: "The testimonies I have borne you have in truth been presented to me by the Lord. I am sorry that you rejected the light given. . . . It is not I whom you are betraying. It is not I against whom you are so embittered. It is the Lord, who has given me a message to bear to you."[19]

Tragic Consequences

She frequently warned of sad, sometimes tragic, personal consequences that would follow rejection of her writings.[20] Because she knew her visions were from the Lord and especially for preparing a people for the return of Jesus, she did not respond casually to those who treated her counsel with indifference. She saw the end of it all in the unfolding of that person's life, and she was alarmed.

The following is a sample of her insights regarding those who trifle with her messages: "It is Satan's plan to weaken the faith of God's people in the *Testimonies*. Satan knows how to make his attacks. He works upon minds to excite jealousy and dissatisfaction toward those at the head of the work. The gifts are next questioned; then, of course, they have but little weight, and instruction given through vision is disregarded. Next follows skepticism in regard to the vital points of our faith, the pillars of our position, then doubt as to the Holy Scriptures, and then the downward march to perdition. When the *Testimonies* which were once believed, are doubted and given up, Satan knows the deceived ones will not stop at this; and he redoubles his efforts till he launches them into open rebellion, which becomes incurable, and ends in destruction. . . . They rise up with bitter feelings against the ones who dare to speak of their errors and reprove their sins."[21]

Ellen White understood what motivated people to reject her writings. Some accepted the parts with which they agreed, and rejected "those portions which condemn their favorite indulgences."[22]

Some who did not "understand" her writings "had the light but have not walked in it. What I might say in private conversations would be so repeated as to make it mean exactly opposite to what it would have meant had the hearers been sanctified in mind and spirit."[23]

Others "made of none effect the counsel of God" because her writings did not agree with preconceived opinions or particular ideas. . . . Everything that sustains their cherished ideas is divine, and the testimonies to correct their errors are human—Sister White's opinions."[24]

One threat to faith that Ellen White hit without compromise was the practice of some to "dissect" her writings: "Do not feel that you can dissect them [Testimonies] to suit your own ideas, claiming that God has given you ability to discern what is light from heaven and what is the expression of mere human wisdom. If the *Testimonies* speak not according to the Word of God, reject them."[25]

She believed her writings to be consistent and harmonious from beginning to end—"a straight line of truth." That is a remarkable statement for any author to make, especially one who had been writing for more than sixty years.[26] The defining principle that kept her writings coherent and harmonious was her "great controversy theme."[27]

Twin Roles

Because she firmly believed that God was using her as His last-day messenger, she saw herself as having twin roles: To the general public, an evangel of appeal and warning, and to the Adventists, a counselor-teacher.[28]

Realizing the distinct difference in this dual responsibility, she emphatically declared that her writings were not to be used as doctrinal authority for the general public: "The first number of the *Testimonies* ever published contains a warning against the injudicious use of the light which is thus given to God's people. I stated that some had taken an unwise course; when they had talked their faith to unbelievers, and the proof had been asked for, they had read from my writings, instead of going to the Bible for proof. It was shown me that this course was inconsistent and would prejudice unbelievers against the truth. The *Testimonies* can have no weight with those who know nothing of their spirit. They should not be referred to in such cases."[29]

But to church members, it was different. Knowing that her writings were in harmony with the Bible and that God had given her special light for Adventists with a distinctive last-day assignment, she urged church members to accept her writings as truth from God: "As the end draws near and the work of giving the last warning to the world extends, it becomes more important for those who accept present truth to have a clear understanding of the nature and influence of the *Testimonies*, which God in His providence has linked with the work of the third angel's message from its very rise."[30]

Ellen White made it clear that she did not receive a specific vision for each testimony. Some people were taking the position that if she did not have a special vision for each individual case, her warnings or reproof "should have no more weight than counsels and warnings from other sources."[31]

She then used Paul's experience as an analogy. Even as Paul did not have a special vision before writing his first letter to the Corinthians but received background information from the household of Chloe (1 Cor. 1:11), so she had been moved to write out general principles that would be appropriate for the special need of the moment. The Corinthians did not take Paul's letter less seriously because he revealed the source of his concern. They knew that the apostle was speaking the truth about their condition, and they listened carefully to his admonitions. So, in her experience, "God has shown me that a certain course, if followed, or certain traits of character, if indulged, would produce certain results. He has thus been training and disciplining me in order that I might see the dangers which threaten souls, and instruct and warn His people, line upon line . . . that they might not be ignorant of Satan's devices, and might escape his snares. . . . Shall I hold my peace because each individual case has not been pointed out to me in direct vision?"[32]

From her earliest visions to her death, Ellen White knew the Source of her insights. "I saw" was a very frequent phrase as she spoke to church members. Other expressions that emphasized her sense of authority and mission include, "I am talking of what I know"[33]; "from the instruction that the Lord has given me, . . . If ever the Lord has spoken to me."[34]

Though she wanted her readers to "hear" the voice of God through her writings, she clearly taught that God did not dictate each word. She believed that her words were not God's words (even as the words of Biblical authors were not); she conveyed God's thoughts with the best words she could employ.[35]

In 1867 she wrote the following within an article involving appropriate female attire when in public, at a time when long, flowing dresses were in fashion: "Although I am as dependent upon the Spirit of the Lord in writing my views as I am in receiving them, yet the words I employ in describing what I have seen are my own, unless they be those spoken to me by an angel, which I always enclose in marks of quotation."[36] Here she is making a distinction between exact words divinely spoken and her words used in conveying the message of the vision. The distinction is between divine words and her words, not between her words and the words of other human beings that she, at times, used in bringing precision and historical color to her writings.

Ellen White appealed to the reader's common sense even as we must use common sense when studying the Bible. Principles do not change; but policies and applications of principles to a particular time and place may change due to changing times and circumstances.[37]

Common sense is needed when discerning the difference between the common and the sacred. A classic example of confusing the common and the sacred occurred in 1909. A church member believed Mrs. White was in error when she stated in a letter that the Paradise Valley Sanitarium had forty rooms when it had only thirty-eight. To help those confused, she explained:

"The information given concerning the number of rooms in the Paradise Valley Sanitarium was given, not as a revelation from the Lord, but simply as a human opinion. There has never been revealed to me the exact number of rooms in any of our sanitariums; and the knowledge I have obtained of such things I have gained by inquiring of those who were supposed to know. In my words, when speaking upon these common subjects, there is nothing to lead minds to believe that I receive my knowledge in a vision from the Lord and am stating it as such. . . . For one to mix the sacred with the common is a great mistake. . . .

"There are times when common things must be stated, common thoughts must occupy the mind, common letters must be written and information given that has passed from one to another of the workers. Such words, such information, are not given under the special inspiration of the Spirit of God. Questions are asked at times that are not upon religious subjects at all, and these questions must be answered. We converse about houses and lands, trades to be made, and locations for our institutions, their advantages and disadvantages. I receive letters asking for advice on many strange subjects, and I advise according to the light that has been given me."[38]

Extrinsic Sources in Relating Visions

Occasionally Ellen White used either material she had been reading or interesting incidents in the recent past to add force to the message she sought to convey. Recent events obviously were on her mind even as they are on the minds of uninspired people. They are a part of the mental process and all use them to connect the known to the unknown. At times God could get the prophet's attention and make His message most forceful in a vision by linking it to some recent event.

An example of this event-linkage is the tragedy of a New Zealand undertow that swept three swimmers to their death and a heart-wrenching appeal she made to her son, Edson.[39] Another example took place in 1903 when the denomination was involved in the serious pantheism crisis. Not long before she was given a vision that would prove enormously helpful, she had read in the newspaper about a ship meeting an iceberg in a fog. In the vision, the iceberg analogy was instructive: "Well I knew the meaning of this representation. I had my orders. I had heard the words, like a living voice from our Captain, 'Meet it!' I knew what my duty was, and that there was not a moment to lose. . . . This is why you received the testimonies when you did."[40]

Obviously the Lord, in giving His visions, might use knowledge and ideas that prophets had earlier discovered through reading or experience.[41] Otherwise, God would be making a fax machine out of the prophet's mind.

We should have no doubt regarding the inspiration of the Bible. It has survived intense scrutiny and skepticism for centuries. When we study how Biblical authors did their work, we find that they occasionally borrowed from other writers, without informing their readers about the practice.[42]

Several examples can be cited to show that Ellen White also borrowed language from other authors when she related her visions. This practice is what we would expect when prophets use their own experience and frame of reference in describing what they have seen in visions or dreams.

Through the years, Mrs. White used the phrase, "I saw" and "I was shown" when relating her visions or dreams.[43] In her earlier ministry, she used these phrases frequently because she was primarily speaking or writing for believers. But in later years, when some of these visions were republished for the general public, these phrases were deleted—for obvious reasons.

Two Ways to Understand

These two phrases may be understood in two ways: Prophets either actually saw with their own eyes or heard with their own ears what they later related; or, prophets "were led by the Holy Spirit to understand that certain concepts were true even apart from a vision. In any case, the expression always means that what was written was written under the inspiration of the Spirit of God."[44]

Everyone has had the experience of quoting another person, whether in a letter or a conversation. To hold the interest of hearers or readers, one quotes "the main points" in order to avoid a tedious recitation.

But often the person quoted will appeal: "That isn't what I meant!" Or, "That is not the way I said it!" The excerpt, the condensed quotation, may be exactly what was said—but without the setting and context of the original comment it may take on a life of its own without conveying the original intent.

Our own personal experiences help us as we try to understand Mrs. White more accurately, more fairly. For the sake of space and time, we sometimes quote only a portion of an Ellen White letter, diary entry, or manuscript. The quotation may be clearly understood, but often it lacks her warmth, affection, earnestness, and generous spirit because the surrounding context is missing. In fact, sometimes she may appear abrupt, even harsh, in partially quoted letters or sermons. Only when the entire letter is read do we get her full mood and purpose.[45]

The safest method for understanding oft-quoted authors is to relive their circumstances and feel their concern when they wrote. *To best understand Ellen White's messages, we must remember how her contemporaries understood her.* They were assured of her honest candor, her generous spirit, her warmheartedness, and her overarching commitment to conveying the messages from God undiluted by human sympathies. Most received her admonitions—sometimes cutting reproof—with the confidence that she was an earnest "mother" as well as a correct disciplinarian. Those who rejected her messages lived either to regret their stubbornness or to watch her predictions come true in their lives.

Visions Not a Substitute for Bible Study

In the 1850s, opponents of Seventh-day Adventists ridiculed their doctrines as "vision views." James White responded by pointing to the fact that every doctrine is Bible based and sustained by Biblical arguments: "The revival of any, or of all the gifts, will never supersede the necessity of searching the Word to learn the truth. . . . It is not God's plan to lead out His people into the broad field of truth by the gifts. But after His people have searched the Word, if then individuals err from Bible truth, or through strife urge erroneous views upon the honest seekers for truth, then is God's opportunity to correct them by the gifts. This is in harmony with our entire experience on this subject."[46]

In 1874 Uriah Smith, editor of the church paper, responded to a charge by a

Sunday-observing Adventist that Seventh-day Adventists base their sanctuary teachings on the visions of Ellen G. White. In his reply, Smith wrote that "works upon the sanctuary are among our standard publications. . . . But in no one of these are the visions referred to as any authority on this subject, or the source from whence any view we hold has been derived. . . . The appeal is invariably to the Bible, where there is abundant evidence for the views we hold on this subject."[47]

Throughout her ministry, Ellen White maintained the primacy of the Bible. In 1851 she appealed: "I recommend to you, dear reader, the Word of God as the rule of your faith and practice. By that Word we are to be judged."[48] In 1901: "The Lord desires you to study your Bibles. He has not given any additional light to take the place of His Word. This light [the gift of prophecy] is to bring confused minds to His Word."[49]

Ellen White's Writings Primarily for the Church

On page 112 we noted how Ellen White and her designated editorial assistants modified her writings when they were printed for the general public. Why? So that no cause for offense would be given to those hearing the distinctive truths of the gospel for the first time. It reflected Paul's principle of reaching people where they are (1 Cor. 9:21-23). References to visions were removed from her earlier writings when republished for the general public. When it became obvious that a book like *The Great Controversy* should be sold to the general public, and especially in Europe, modifications were made. In the 1888 edition of *The Great Controversy*, for example, certain references that assumed a knowledge of Millerite history were expanded for a worldwide readership.

Another caution Ellen White gave her co-workers was that ministers should not use her writings in evangelistic meetings to "sustain your positions." For her, as well as for all Adventists, the Bible must remain "up front" in establishing the main points of the "everlasting gospel" (Rev. 14:6): "Let none be educated to look to Sister White, but to the mighty God, who gives instruction to Sister White."[50]

In the first of the *Testimonies*, Ellen White admonished fellow believers not to take "an injudicious course" when they talked to unbelievers by reading from a vision "instead of going to the Bible for proof." Why? Mrs. White saw that "this course was inconsistent, and prejudiced unbelievers against the truth. The visions can have no weight with those who have never seen them, and know nothing of their spirit. They should not be referred to in such cases."[51]

This principle of accommodation[52] to the experience level of one's hearers or readers is illustrated in the ministry of Jesus and of Paul. Many times the Saviour wanted to tell the world, even His disciples, the "whole" truth, but they were not ready for it; premature instruction can arouse resistance and prejudice unnecessarily. Even in His parable instruction to His disciples—to those who knew Him best—Jesus taught them only up to a point, "as they were able to bear it" (Mark 4:33). And only hours before His death, Jesus reminded His disciples that they needed to learn much more but they were not ready: "I have yet many things to say to you, but you cannot bear them now" (John 16:12).

In proclaiming the gospel to the general public, Jesus was even more restrained. Above all, He avoided offense wherever possible. He did not want to prejudice anyone by saying something that would unnecessarily arouse a negative response. He led them from the known to the unknown by beginning with the authorities they already relied on, even to the witness of nature itself. For these reasons, Jesus withheld much of the meaning in His parables when talking to the general public but, when alone with His disciples, He explained the parables more thoroughly (Matt. 13).

Paul had a full head and heart to share with the world. With unbelievers, he would think like a Jew or a Greek or a Lystrian, and talk to them in some winsome, unprejudicial way—holding back many things he was able to share with believers (1 Cor. 9:19-22). But even with believers who were still growing in their experience, Paul said: "I fed you with milk and not with solid food; for until now you were not able to receive it, and even now you are still not able" (1 Cor. 3:2).

In his letter to the Hebrews, Paul was developing certain aspects of the Incarnation and why Jesus became man. This information had much to do with a deeper understanding of Christ's ministry in the heavenly sanctuary. But Paul knew, for some reason of which we are not aware, that his readers were not ready for the larger implications of further truth about Jesus "of whom we have much to say, and hard to explain, since you have become dull of hearing. You . . . need milk and not solid food. . . . Solid food belongs to those who are of full age, that is, those who by reason of use have their senses exercised to discern both good and evil" (Heb. 5:11-14).

Ellen White's experience was the same as that of Christ and Paul: She had the truth, so much so that it burned within her soul, but she could not release it all at once. Teachers can go only as far as their listeners can share basic assumptions. Prophets must be astute and wise in how they present unfolding truth. Even for believers who know something of the working of the Spirit of God, teachers and prophets must use Paul's careful respect for the hearers' level of experience—only as they were "able to receive it."

Endnotes

1. Letter 84, 1909, cited in *Selected Messages*, book 3, p. 71.
2. Letter 86, 1906, to George Butler, cited in *MR*, vol. 10, p. 343. See p. 182.
3. *Bio*., vol. 5, p. 355; "It is not right for you to suppose I am striving to be first, striving for leadership. . . . I want it to be understood that I have no ambition to have the name of leader, or any other name that may be given to me, except that of a messenger of God. I claim no other name or position. My life and works speak for themselves."—Letter 320, 1905 to J. H. Kellogg, in *MR*, vol. 5, p. 439.
4. "Why have I not claimed to be a prophet? Because in these days many who boldly claim that they are prophets are a reproach to the cause of Christ; and because my work includes much more than the word prophet signifies."—*Review and Herald*, July 26, 1906, cited in *Selected Messages*, book 1, p. 32.
5. *Selected Messages*, book 1, p. 34.
6. *Testimonies*, vol. 5, p. 661. "The Holy Ghost is the author of the Scriptures and of the Spirit of Prophecy." —Letter 92, 1900, cited in *Selected Messages*, book 3, p. 30.
7. *The Great Controversy*, p. vii.
8. Letter 69, 1896, cited in *Selected Messages*, book 3, p. 30.
9. *Testimonies*, vol. 5, p. 665. See *Selected Messages*, book 3, pp. 29-33
10. Letter 10, 1895, cited in *Selected Messages*, book 1, p. 37. See p. 376.
11. "The truths of redemption are capable of constant development and expansion. Though old, they are ever new, constantly revealing to the seeker for truth a greater glory and a mightier power. In every age there is a new development of truth, a message of God to the people of that generation. The old truths are all essential; new truth is not independent of the old, but an unfolding of it. It is only as the old truths are understood that we can comprehend the new. . . . He who rejects or neglects the new, does not really possess the old."—*Christ's Object Lessons*, pp. 127, 128.
12. Letter 117, 1910, cited in *Selected Messages*, book 3, p. 32. "God has . . . promised to give visions in the 'last days'; not for a new rule of faith, but . . . to correct those who err from Bible truth."—*Ibid*., p. 29. "Besides the instruction in His Word, the Lord has given special testimonies to His people, not as a new revelation, but that He may set before us the plain lessons of His Word, that errors may be corrected, that the right way may be pointed out, that every soul may be without excuse."—Letter 63, 1893, cited in *Ibid*., p. 31. See also *Early Writings*, p. 78. *Review and Herald*, Aug. 5, 1893.
13. "Error could not stand alone, and soon would become extinct, if it did not fashion itself like a parasite upon the tree of truth. The traditions of men, like floating germs, attach themselves to the truth of God, and men regard them as part of the truth. . . . And as traditions pass on from age to age, they acquire a power over the human mind. But age does not make error truth." —Letter 43, 1895, cited in *SDABC*, vol. 5, p. 1094.
14. "Great truths that have lain unheeded and unseen since the days of Pentecost are to shine from God's Word in their native purity. To those who truly love God the Holy Spirit will reveal truths that have faded from the mind, and will also reveal truths that are entirely new."

—*Review and Herald*, Aug. 17, 1897.

"As the end approaches, the testimonies of God's servants will become more decided and more powerful, flashing the light of truth upon the systems of error and oppression that have so long held the supremacy. The Lord has sent messages for this time to establish Christianity upon an eternal basis, and all who believe present truth must stand, not in their own wisdom, but in God, and raise up the foundations of many generations."—Letter 1f, 1890, cited in *Selected Messages*, book 3, p. 407.

"Gems of thought are to be gathered up and redeemed from their companionship with error; for by their misplacement in the association of error, the Author of truth has been dishonored. The precious gems of the righteousness of Christ, the truths of divine origin, are to be carefully searched out and placed in their proper setting, to shine with heavenly brilliancy amid the moral darkness of the world. Let the bright jewels of truth which God gave to man, to adorn and exalt His name, be carefully rescued from the rubbish of error, where they have been claimed by those who have been transgressors of the law, and have served the purpose of the great deceiver on account of their connection with error. Let the gems of divine light be reset in the framework of the gospel."—*Review and Herald*, Oct. 23, 1894, p. 1.

"If we do our very best to present the truth in its stirring character, crossing the opinions and ideas of others, it will be misinterpreted, misapplied, and misstated, to those who are entertaining error, in order to make it appear in an objectionable light. There are few to whom you bring the truth, who have not been drinking of the wine of Babylon. It is hard for them to comprehend the truth, therefore the necessity of teaching it as it is in Jesus."—*Ibid.*, June 3, 1890, p. 338.

15. *Bio.*, vol. 1, pp. 137-151, 187-194, 208, 264, 265.
16. *Selected Messages*, book 3, pp. 31, 32. An illustration of this Bible study/Spirit-affirming development of doctrine is found in *Testimonies*, vol. 1, p. 86: "Our first conference in New York was held at Volney, in a brother's barn. About thirty-five were present—all that could be collected in that part of the state. But of this number, hardly two were agreed. Some were holding serious errors, and each strenuously urged his own views, declaring that they were according to the Scriptures.

    "These strange differences of opinion brought a heavy weight upon me, as it seemed to me that God was dishonored; and I fainted under the burden. Some feared that I was dying; but the Lord heard the prayers of His servants, and I revived. The light of heaven rested upon me, and I was soon lost to earthly things. My accompanying angel presented before me some of the errors of those present, and also the truth in contrast with their errors. These discordant views which they claimed to be according to the Bible were only according to their opinion of the Bible, and they must yield their errors and unite upon the third angel's message. Our meeting closed triumphantly. Truth gained the victory. The brethren renounced their errors, and united upon the third angel's message, and God greatly blessed them and added to their numbers."
17. *Testimonies*, vol. 8, p. 297.
18. "In the early days of the message, when our numbers were few, we studied diligently to understand the meaning of many Scriptures. At times it seemed as if no explanation could be given. My mind seemed to be locked to an understanding of the Word; but when our brethren who had assembled for study came to a point where they could go no farther, and had recourse to earnest prayer, the Spirit of God would rest upon me, and I would be taken off in vision, and be instructed in regard to the relation of Scripture to Scripture. These experiences were repeated over and over and over again. Thus many truths of the third angel's message were established, point by point. Think you that my faith in this message will ever waver? Think you that I can remain silent, when I see an effort being made to sweep away the foundation pillars of our faith? I am as thoroughly established in these truths as it is possible for a person to be. I can never forget the experience I have passed through. God has confirmed my belief by many evidences of His power."—*Review and Herald*, June 14, 1906, p. 8. At least six accounts of these Sabbath-Sanctuary Conferences exist: *Spiritual Gifts*, Vol. II, pp. 47-49; *Testimonies*, vol. 1, pp. 75-87; *Testimonies to Ministers*, pp. 24-26; *Selected Messages*, book 1, pp. 206, 207; *MR*, vol. 3, pp. 412-414; *Sermons and Talks*, vol. 1, pp. 340-348.
19. Letter 66, 1897, cited in *Selected Messages*, book 3, p. 84; see also *Testimonies*, vol. 7, p. 136. Such have "insulted God"—*Testimonies*, vol. 5, p. 64; are "fighting against God"—*Testimonies*, vol. 5, p. 234; and "are doing as the children of Israel did again and again." —*Selected Messages*, book 3, p. 70.
20. For examples, think of Stephen Smith (*Bio.*, vol. 1, pp. 490-492); B. F. Snook and W. H. Brinkerhoff, *Ibid.*, vol. 1, pp. 416, 473; vol. 2, pp. 23, 44, 146-151; J. M. Stephenson and D. P. Hall, *Ibid.*, vol. 1, pp. 310-315, 323, 332, 336; Moses Hull, *Ibid.*, vol. 2, pp. 53-58, 63, 65, 67, 74; Dudley Canright, *Ibid.*, vol. 3, pp. 152, 153, 263-267, 290, 360; S. McCullagh, *Ibid.*, vol. 4, pp. 275-286, 453.
21. *Testimonies*, vol. 5, p. 672.
22. *Testimonies,* vol. 9, p. 154. "I realize that some are watching keenly for some words which have been traced by my pen and upon which they can place their human interpretations in order to sustain their positions and to justify a wrong course of action—when I think of these things, it is not very encouraging to continue writing."—*Selected Messages*, book 3, pp. 82, 83. "Sinful indulgences are cherished, the *Testimonies* are rejected, and many excuses which are untrue are offered to others as the reason for refusing to receive them. The *true* reason is not given. It is a lack of moral courage—a will, strengthened and controlled by the Spirit of God, to renounce hurtful habits."—*Testimonies*, vol. 5, p. 675; see also vol. 4. p. 32.
23. *Selected Messages*, book 3, p. 82.
24. *Ibid.*, p. 68.
25. *Testimonies*, vol. 5, p. 691. "My Instructor said to me, Tell these men that God has not committed to them the work of measuring, classifying, and defining the character of the testimonies. Those who attempt this are sure to err in their conclusions."—*Selected Messages*, book 1, p. 49.
26. "The light that I have received, I have written out, and much of it is now shining forth from the printed page. There is, throughout my printed works, a harmony with my present teaching."—*Review and Herald*, June 14, 1906, p. 8. "While I am able to do this work, the people must have things to revive past history, that they may see that there is one straight chain of truth, with-

out one heretical sentence, in that which I have written." —Letter 329a, 1905, cited in *Selected Messages*, book 3, p. 52.

27. See p. 256.
28. See p. 112 regarding the magazine articles (primarily the *Signs of the Times*) that she prepared for the general public.
29. *Testimonies,* vol. 5, p. 669; also *Review and Herald*, Aug. 22, 1893.
30. *Ibid.*, p. 654. "Through His Holy Spirit the voice of God has come to us continually in warning and instruction, to confirm the faith of the believers in the Spirit of prophecy. Repeatedly the word has come, Write the things that I have given you to confirm the faith of my people in the position they have taken. . . . The instruction that was given in the early days of the message is to be held as safe instruction to follow in these its closing days. Those who are indifferent to this light and instruction must not expect to escape the snares which we have been plainly told will cause the rejecters of light to stumble, and fall, and be snared, and be taken." —*Review and Herald*, July 18, 1907, p. 8.
31. *Testimonies*, vol. 5, p. 683.
32. *Ibid.*, pp. 686, 687.
33. *Australian Union Conference Record*, July 28, 1899, p. 8.
34. *General Conference Bulletin*, June 3, 1909, p. 292.
35. See pp. 16, 120, 173, 375, 376, 421 for a discussion on the difference between verbal and thought inspiration; see *Selected Messages*, book 1, pp. 15-26.
36. *Review and Herald*, Oct. 8, 1867, p. 260.
37. "Regarding the testimonies, nothing is ignored; nothing is cast aside; but time and place must be considered. Nothing must be done untimely."—*Selected Messages*, book 1, p. 57. See pp. 395-397.
38. *Ibid.*, pp. 38, 39.
39. *Bio.*, vol. 4, pp. 94-97.
40. *Ibid.*, vol. 5, p. 301.
41. Ronald Graybill, "The 'I saw' Parallels in Ellen White's Writings," *Adventist Review*, July 29, 1982, p. 4.
42. *Ibid.* See p. 378 for further discussion about inspired authors who "borrow" language from non-canonical writers.
43. Ronald Graybill, "The 'I saw' Parallels," *Adventist Review*, July 29, 1982, p. 5.
44. "It is important to recognize that although Mrs. White sometimes recorded the exact words of her angel-guide in quotation marks, often she merely reported the gist of what was said to her in vision, reconstructing the words of the angel as best she could recall them, placing them in the form of direct address and enclosing them in quotation marks."—*Ibid.*, p. 5.
45. See p. 394.
46. *Review and Herald*, Feb. 26, 1856, p. 172.
47. *Review and Herald*, Dec. 22, 1874. "Though Ellen White received confirming visions at the time of the doctrinal discussions and following . . . Adventists consistently made their final appeal to Scripture."—Paul A. Gordon, *The Sanctuary, 1844, and the Pioneers* (Hagerstown, MD: Review and Herald Publishing Association, 1983), p. 29.
48. *Early Writings*, p. 78.
49. Letter 130, 1901, cited in *Selected Messages*, book 3, p. 29; see *Testimonies*, vol. 2, pp. 604-609.
50. Letter 11, 1894, cited in *Selected Messages*, book 3, p. 30.
51. *Testimonies*, vol. 1, pp. 119, 120.
52. See George Reid, "Is the Bible Our Final Authority?" —*Ministry*, Nov., 1991, p. 9.

Study Questions

1. What significance do you see in Ellen White's choice of the term "messenger" rather than "prophet" to describe her ministry?

2. What are some of the "floating" theological germs of conventional Christianity that Ellen White felt compelled to reject?

3. With what doctrines does the Seventh-day Adventist Church replace those "germs" ?

4. Why did Ellen White say that her writings, especially the *Testimonies*, were written primarily for church members?

5. How could the apostle Paul and Ellen White write letters of counsel without a vision prompting such letters?

6. How do some, even today, make of "none effect" the writings of Ellen White? What is the safest barrier that we can erect to keep from "rejecting" the authority of Ellen White?

The Voice of a Movement

CHAPTER

CHAPTER 17

Organization, Unity, and Institutional Development

"We have nothing to fear for the future, except as we shall forget the way the Lord has led us, and His teaching in our past history."[1]

The ministry of Ellen White and the emergence of the Seventh-day Adventist Church are inseparable. To try to understand one without the other would make each unintelligible and undiscoverable. Ellen White and the history of the Seventh-day Adventist Church, in thought and structure, are as integrated as the union of Anglo-Saxon languages in the formation of English speech.[2]

Ellen and James White were the rallying center for those Millerites who later became the Sabbatarian (Saturday-sabbath) Adventists. James White, a remarkably resilient organizer, embraced simultaneously many aspects of a growing movement as few others could. By his side, emboldened with a holy candor and unwavering commitment, Ellen White encouraged the growing "little flock" with visions bold. This administrator/prophet team within a few decades led a New England group into an international mission. Though they were the human center of a worldwide movement, neither claimed recognition, reward, or even earthly comforts.[3]

On one hand, the Whites fearlessly denounced the evils of the social order; on the other, they led tens of thousands in their day to catch a picture of how the gospel brings spiritual, social, and physical restoration *in this life*—all in fulfilling the divine command to prepare a people to meet the soon-coming Lord. Out of this twin emphasis, a turning from the distracting customs of worldly practices and the commitment to tell the world of the principles of the kingdom of God, emerged an international network of medical and educational institutions, supported by scores of publishing houses and a worldwide mission network.[4]

The indisputable guiding force behind this impulse was Ellen White. Her unifying, motivating "voice" continues to provide light and compelling dynamics long after her death in 1915.[5] Yet, one of the unique factors that distinguishes her from others who claimed the prophetic gift in the nineteenth century[6] is that she never perceived herself as a leader of a new movement. She never swerved from her simple self-perception that she was only God's messenger to the Advent movement.

Mrs. White kept one eye on the divine commission as set forth in Revelation 14, an assignment that would ultimately unite all who seek truth, from every continent and from every ethnic, social, and economic background; her other eye was on the core group that was to make credible this good news of God's last-day invitation to a judgment-bound world. She knew that without the gospel principles working in the lives of those who proclaimed the gospel, results would be minimal. For her, the church's highest priority was to reflect the Christlike life that would make Christ's gospel appealing and convincing.[7]

Organization and Unity

Being the messenger, however, meant that she was often ahead of the church's leaders, not only in theological insights and their practical applications, but also in her continual insistence on unity and organization. In comparing other contemporary millenarians such as the Mormons and the Jehovah's Witnesses, historians and sociologists consider "remarkable" the rapid transition from the post-Millerite instability to the "largely stable, uniform organization" achieved by the Seventh-day Adventist Church.

Five reasons are suggested for this phenomenon in the development of Sabbatarian Adventists: (1) they separated themselves from other post-Millerite groups and millenarians "after the reformulation of ideas"; (2) they "not only preached the Advent but the conditions for it"; (3) "these conditions were validated by divine inspiration, whereby the group acquired an independent source of inspiration, apart from the Scriptures"; (4) they "established a professional ministry which opened the way to other specialized agencies"; and (5) they developed an "accretion of concerns for education, diet, medical care, religious liberty, and Sabbatarianism [that] further advanced its denominationalization both ideologically and institutionally."[8]

None of these five components would have resulted in a worldwide religious movement without Ellen White's presence and messages. Her messages to the church were far-reaching. On one hand, she covered the whole range of the salvation story; on the other, she dealt with civil government, the home, and questions of race relations, health, and education. The striking point is that all this instruction was creative: whenever followed faithfully, schools and hospitals, publishing houses and ministerial institutes, temperance and welfare societies sprang up worldwide. Even more striking is that this woman, without a church office and without formal training in any one of the many areas of her profound instruction, was the leading inspiration in molding all these various interests into a united organization.

The Seventh-day Adventist Church did not develop out of a crisis in some previous church wherein a charismatic leader arose to lead his/her followers into a new organization, such as John Wesley and the Methodists. Nor did it arise because of a doctrinal quarrel, similar to the beginnings of the various Lutheran or Presbyterian churches existing today.

The Seventh-day Adventist Church was born in a profound spiritual awakening known as the Millerite movement. Fellowship created by belief in the "blessed hope" (Titus 2:13), one of the central New Testament themes, held the young group together. This fellowship, this sense of "family," is the open secret of the church's worldwide cohesiveness. With its leaders and members under conviction that the movement was raised up to prepare the way for the return of Jesus (Rev. 14), sinners were rescued, backsliders were reclaimed, and young and old were motivated to realize their potential as they joined in a worldwide evangelistic movement.

Beneath all this motivation and the sense of belonging to a worldwide "family" has been the inspiring challenge and clear direction of Ellen White. She and her husband knew early that motivation and fellowship had to be unified and organized. Without a unifying organization, the warmest feelings soon fray out into frustration and tangled relationships. Throughout her writings, Ellen White made clear that personal religion and organized religion are the two sides of a coin that we call "the church."[9]

In the early years of the Adventist

experience, the lack of organization led to various problems and disillusionment. Self-appointed ministers preached what they pleased; even the "appointed" traveled without salary or paid expenses. Divisions arose in the scattered groups of believers, and no method for dealing with divisive heresies existed.[10] Whatever church properties they used were held in the name of some individual member; when the member died, the property passed to relatives, some of whom were not church members. By 1853, James and Ellen White were urging church organization to eliminate "uncredentialed" ministers and to establish a stable basis for owning church property.

But this plea for organization was met with strong resistance. Organization for many was a "return to Babylon."[11] Opposers to organization still felt the sting of the organized churches that refused the Millerite call. The religious freedom that Adventists had been enjoying for a few years, they did not want to exchange for the cold blanket of an organized church. Organization, for them, was inconsistent with the freedom of the gospel.[12]

In 1853, James White, the "father of our present church order,"[13] wrote five editorials in the *Review and Herald*[14] on organization, with little or no positive response. But Ellen White's quiet, firm, counsel eventually caught the attention of church leaders and they were led to see the common sense and urgency of her husband's call for organization.[15]

Many meetings were held as leaders studied the need and method of organization. One of the first considerations was a name for this new body of Adventist believers. On October 1, 1860, the name finally chosen was, "Seventh-day Adventists."[16]

But that act appeared to be the most that could be decided on at the time. Now that they had a name, the leaders found it easier to incorporate the Seventh-day Adventist Publishing Association on May 3, 1861, than to organize churches! However, the manner in which local churches would organize and unite in some kind of federation was finally settled on October 4 and 5, 1861, at least for Battle Creek and the newly formed Michigan Conference, the first conference to be organized. In 1862 six other state conferences followed. One year later the General Conference was organized, on May 20-23, 1863.[17]

Centralization of Power

In 1892 plans were being formulated that would foster a greater centralization of power in Battle Creek leadership. On December 19 Ellen White wrote a fifteen-page message from Australia to the leadership in Battle Creek. She reviewed the blessings of organization "that God gave us special light upon. . . . The system of organization proved a grand success." But she also pointed out the dangers of bureaucratic machinery—that some of the present procedures that seemed burdensome were not caused by organization, but by its abuse. She further noted: "In reviewing our past history, having traveled over every step of advance to our present standing, I can say, 'Praise God!' As I see what the Lord has wrought, I am filled with astonishment and with confidence in Christ our Leader. We have nothing to fear for the future, except as we shall forget the way the Lord has led us, and His teaching in our past history."[18]

Ellen White's warnings and suggestions from Australia were neglected, setting the stage for the General Conference Session in 1901. The 1901 reorganization of denominational structure was radical and explosive, but practical. The formation of union territories between the General Conference Committee and the local conferences decentralized much of the denomination's decision making. The enlargement of the General Conference Committee from a few to twenty-five, with all union presidents members *ex officio,* broadened the base of decision making. Policies were established that would guarantee the flow of funds from prosperous conferences to those with limited resources. Departmental organization, such as the Sabbath School Department, would function not only at the General Conference but on the union and local conference levels. Perhaps the greatest disappointment in 1901 was the inability to bring into the church structure the International Medical Missionary and Benevolent Association headed by Dr. J. H. Kellogg—a problem that would become the denomination's most critical crisis up to that time.

Without the counsel and perseverance of Ellen White the much needed reorganization might not have been accomplished. The dramatics of the event cannot be overstated. As soon as the General Conference president had concluded his opening address on April 2, Mrs. White, absent in Australia for nine years, moved quickly to the platform and came at once to her point. After describing briefly how the Lord had signally led through the years, she told church leaders: "You have no right to manage unless you manage in God's order. . . . What we want now is a reorganization. We want to begin at the foundation, and to build upon a different principle. . . . There are to be more than one or two or three men to consider the whole vast field. The work is great, and there is no one human mind that can plan for the work which needs to be done. . . . According to the light that has been given me—and just how it is to be accomplished I cannot say—greater strength must be brought into the managing force of the Conference. . . . There must be a renovation, a reorganization; a power and strength must be brought into the committees that are necessary."[19]

The response was immediate. During the deliberations when impasses occurred, Ellen White would perceive the issues involved and make suggestions; in turn, the delegates would move forward with added insights and unanimous votes. Within three weeks, the breathtaking reorganization was accomplished, except for the meshing of the medical work with that of the General Conference.[20]

Those who compare Mrs. White's candid directions at the beginning of the conference with the organization that was adopted and then followed can fully appreciate the new life and benefits felt the world over almost immediately—all because of the Lord's messenger. These changes were intricate, fundamental, and far-reaching; in some respects, novel and untested. For a person who never studied ecclesiastical structure or who had never held a high-level office, her contribution to the Adventist Church in church government remains astounding.

L. H. Christian, long-time General Conference officer, wrote: "Many have asked whether the Adventist worldwide church organization is congregational, presbyterian, or episcopal. . . . While it has similarities with other churches, it is really different, and an organism by itself. It came as a fruitage of the creative ideas of the advent message guided by God through the Spirit of prophecy. The Adventist Church is a church with a task, and the Lord gave it a body to fit the task."[21]

"Get Out of Battle Creek!"

Ellen White referred to the move from Rochester, New York, to Battle Creek, Michigan, in 1855, as the time when "the Lord began to turn our captivity."[22] Soon, along with the growth of the publishing house, the Health Reform Institute was established, and eventually Battle Creek College. The three institutions were largely the result of Mrs. White's visions and James White's organizational skills.[23]

However, as time passed and the need for people to operate these institutions grew, all the problems associated with an Adventist ghetto emerged. With worldly success came the human traits of jealousy, gossip, and complacency. Many of the members came from poor communities in New England and the Midwest, hoping to place their children in church schools; the dissension regarding the policies of these early schools contributed to the general unrest. Through the years Mrs. White had written and spoken much regarding the declining spiritual condition of the Battle Creek church members.

The year 1902 was anchored on both ends with stunning disasters. On February 18 the internationally famous Battle Creek Sanitarium burned to the ground. During the night of December 30, the Review and Herald Publishing Association also was reduced to ashes.

At the General Conference Session, on April 3, 1903, the unpopular motion before the delegates was: "That the General Conference offices or headquarters be moved from Battle Creek, Mich., to some place favorable for its work on the Atlantic Coast." Ellen White arose and said: "Some seemed to think that when they reached Battle Creek, they would be near heaven, that in Battle Creek they would not have many temptations." They didn't realize that "in Battle Creek . . . the enemy was working the hardest."[24]

She reminded the church leaders that God had been warning for years to "Get out of Battle Creek." She reviewed her reply to two young educators (P. T. Magan and E. A. Sutherland) who had asked for counsel regarding the future of Battle Creek College: "Take the school out of Battle Creek, if you can possibly do so." The move, she said, was a "success."

Then she turned to the future of the publishing house: "The very worst thing that could now be done would be for the Review and Herald office to be once more built up in Battle Creek."

But she wasn't finished. She included the church leadership: "Let the General Conference offices and the publishing work be moved from Battle Creek. I know not where the place will be, whether on the Atlantic Coast or elsewhere."

Without doubt, her direction at this meeting stopped the hesitation. Search committees were formed and properties from Connecticut to New Jersey were investigated. The hope was to find something near New York City.

Then letters began to come from Ellen White in response to fervent urging from the president of the General Conference. From the light she had, she was not in favor of New York. Rather, Washington, D. C., seemed to have special advantages. The formula still worked: God will not remove the task of decision-making from human beings. Men and women must do their part, while God does His. God encourages people with sufficient light to make right choices, always providing, when asked, the wisdom to make the right choice and the power to act. When correct decisions are made, God has His special way of endorsing those decisions.

This was not an easy time for church leaders. Constituents of the publishing house corporation were promising a legal battle. The publishing house employees and other church members had invested heavily in their Battle Creek properties and now feared they would suffer personal financial disaster.

A. G. Daniells, president of the General Conference, wrote in July, 1903: "We are in a dreadful place. God must help us. We are helpless. . . . I want to tell you that I realize as I never have in all my life the need, and the value to the church, of the Spirit of Prophecy. The working of Satan at this present time is surely with all power, and signs, and lying wonders. And it is so intense and cunning that only God can meet it successfully. We who accept the high and sacred responsibilities of this work must let God teach us, and we must listen to His voice."[25]

After preliminary investigation church leaders were satisfied that Takoma Park, on the northern edge of Washington, D.C., should be the new home for the

Review and Herald Publishing Association and the headquarters for the General Conference. Then a letter came from Ellen White: "The Lord has opened this matter to me decidedly. The publishing work that has been carried on in Battle Creek should for the present be carried on near Washington. If after a time the Lord says, Move away from Washington, we are to move."[26]

In reflecting on this moment, Daniells wrote: "No one but those who passed through this very trying experience can appreciate the relief brought to us by that word of certainty."[27]

Warnings Against Consolidation of Institutions

For many in business, "consolidation" suggests cost-savings and greater efficiency. Yet, many in business have discovered that bigger is not always better. Great international corporations have learned to their dismay by lost sales that consolidation can also mean the inefficiency of centralization and loss of touch with the potential buyer.

In the church, the plea for unity must be understood in terms of the church's purpose. Decision-making must never be far from the people who must implement decisions and live with the consequences. Unity in goals, as history has demonstrated, need not be defined in terms of decision-making by the few.

The Seventh-day Adventist Church has learned through experience the perversion of unity when overcentralization, without appropriate checks and balances, produces "kingly power" and the ominous potential of error overwhelming the church body. The early Adventists, fearful of "Babylonian" power in church organization, kept their institutions legally separate from each other and from the General Conference. For example, in the late 1890s the Health Institute founded in the mid-1860s had grown into a chain of twenty-seven sanitariums—all administered by the International Medical Missionary and Benevolent Association, an entity independent from the General Conference. At the beginning of the twentieth century, other more integral departments of the church, such as the International Sabbath School Association, the International Religious Liberty Association, and the International Tract and Missionary Society, also were administered by boards distinct from the General Conference.

Was this decentralization good or bad? Not good, when the various departments of the church were spending unnecessary funds to operate their programs, often in competition with one another. Yet, there was something positive in that each organization was pursuing its goals without another level of decision-makers above them that would possibly slow progress and thwart the plans that were devised by people closer to the problem or challenge.

But all of the major associations and departments had their own problem of overcentralization. Most were headquartered at Battle Creek, some later in Philadelphia and New York. Decisions were made at these head offices with very little freedom by local conferences or churches to meet their immediate needs. The problem with the Adventist Church in the 1890s and early 1900s can be understood in terms of rapid growth and of long-time leaders who were not used to a multiplicity of challenges, not only in numbers but in variety. The charges of "kingly power" and sluggish decision-making were all too accurate.[28]

Throughout this period Ellen White sounded the alarm regarding the problems caused by the consolidation of top decision-makers in Battle Creek. She had reason to be even more alarmed when the publishing leaders planned to merge the Pacific Press Publishing Association with the Review and Herald Publishing Association, as well as all other publishing houses of the future.[29]

Her clear voice against consolidation of publishing houses, medical institutions, and educational institutions rested on the principle, enunciated in 1896, that consolidation "shows that men are seeking to grasp the scepter of power, and hold control over human minds."[30] In the consolidation of the church's work in one place and in the hands of a few men, she wrote, "Mistakes have been made in this line. Individuality and personal responsibility are thus repressed and weakened."[31] Further, she foresaw the danger in terms of bad policy that would diffuse everywhere under consolidated management: "When so great power is placed in the hands of a few persons, Satan will make determined efforts to pervert the judgment, to insinuate wrong principles of action, to bring in a wrong policy; in so doing he cannot only pervert one institution, but through this can gain control of others and give a wrong mold to the work in distant parts."[32]

Counsel from Ellen White eventually quelled the surge for consolidation. Publishing houses and schools remained sovereign with their own boards.[33] Only the medical work resisted the messages, and this led eventually to the separation of the Battle Creek Sanitarium from denominational control.[34] The radical and innovative reorganizing of the church structure in the 1901 General Conference session further decentralized decision-making; union conferences worldwide could now make many decisions that hitherto had to wait for Battle Creek permission.

Danger in Muting the Adventist Identification

One of the chief concerns addressed in the Salamanca vision, November 4, 1890,[35] and visions in the weeks to follow was the pending danger of muting Adventist distinctiveness, especially in denominational periodicals. The immediate focus evoking Ellen White's admonition was the plan put forth by "influential men to the effect that if *The American Sentinel* would drop the words 'Seventh-day Adventist' from its columns, and would say nothing about the Sabbath, the great men of the world would patronize it. . . . This policy is the first step in a succession of wrong steps."[36]

As reported by Uriah Smith, Ellen White spoke at the General Conference session in Battle Creek, Michigan, March 7, 1891, on "the danger of covering up, and keeping in the background, the distinctive features of our faith, under the impression that prejudice will thereby be avoided. If there is committed to us a special message, as we believe, that message must go, without reference to the customs or prejudices of the world, not governed by a policy of fear or favor. . . . The discourse was a timely one, and made a profound impression upon the large congregation."[37]

The argument set forth by the National Religious Liberty Association (not yet under the umbrella of the General Conference) seemed plausible: (1) religious liberty was a vital part of the third angel's message; (2) current religious liberty issues opened many doors before large audiences; (3) these principles would get a much broader and more favorable response if they were not associated with such doctrines as the Sabbath and the Second Coming; (4) if the *Sentinel's* policies could not be changed, another journal would be established to further their interests.[38]

After Ellen White's early Sunday morning exposé of their late Saturday night deliberations, the Association leaders, including A. F. Ballenger, freely acknowledged the error of their thinking. That Sunday morning saw the reversal of a strong course of action, voted only hours before.[39]

However, those committed to a nonsectarian religious liberty magazine eventually had their way. In "seeking 'a wider sphere of influence,' the *Sentinel* lost . . . its vitality, its circulation, and at last, its life. It ceased publication . . . in 1904."[40]

But the need for a religious liberty journal remained, a magazine committed to the full-orbed message of the Seventh-day Adventist Church. In 1906, the *Sentinel* was reincarnated as *Liberty.* But strange as it may seem, the same philosophy that energized the *Sentinel* eventually molded the new *Liberty!* By the 1950s, the editors of *Liberty* were working under the policy that the journal "has only one basic teaching, that of soul liberty. . . . It is nonsectarian in scope and subject matter."[41]

With the change of editors in 1959, a decided shift was eventually made so that the principles advocated by Ellen White in 1891 would again distinguish the church's journal of religious liberty. The wisdom of divine counsel and the courage of its new editor were validated in that the subscription list jumped from 160,000 in 1959 as a quarterly to more than half a million as a bi-monthly! "The Salamanca vision has now become part of the preamble to the editorial policy."[42]

Establishing Educational and Medical Institutions

Health Reform Institute. Health Reform Institute in Battle Creek, Michigan, the denomination's first health institution, was a direct response to Ellen White's urging as she communicated the light given her. Reporting the Rochester, New York, vision, December 25, 1865, among many other health principles and admonitions, she advocated a health institution with two objectives: (1) for the benefit of the diseased and suffering among Adventists who needed the added advantages that could not be found "in a popular water cure"; and (2) for "the means of bringing our views before many whom it would be impossible for us to reach by the common course of advocating the truth."[43]

The prospect of establishing a medical institution in the mid-1860s seemed daunting, perhaps impossible, from a human point of view. But J. N. Loughborough, president of the Michigan Conference, gathered together his committee leaders and said: "We will pledge to the enterprise, venturing out on what is said in the testimony, though it looks to us like a heavy load for us to hold up."[44]

Four months later, Uriah Smith, editor of the *Review and Herald*, wrote about this struggling infant: "We have only to look back . . . four short months. Now we behold an elegant site secured, buildings ready for operation . . . and operations actually commenced. In no enterprise ever undertaken by this people has the hand of the Lord been more evidently manifested than in this thing."[45]

Other medical institutions owe their existence to Ellen White's visionary insight, courage, and personal sacrifice. In 1902 she wrote to the General Conference president: "Constantly the Lord is keeping southern California before me as a place where we must establish medical institutions. . . . Sanitariums must be established in this section of the State." A few days later she said: "For months the Lord has given me instruction that He is preparing the way for our people to obtain possession, at little cost, of properties on which there are buildings that can be utilized in our work."[46]

Paradise Valley Sanitarium. Ellen White borrowed $2,000 from a bank (in 1904) and encouraged Mrs. Josephine Gotzian to donate $2,000 so that the Paradise Valley Sanitarium property could be bought—in spite of understandable reluctance on the part of conference leadership—on property that had cost the original owners $25,000.[47]

Glendale Sanitarium. As soon as Paradise Valley Sanitarium had been secured, Mrs. White urged leadership to find property for a sanitarium "near Los Angeles." Under her prodding a search was made in the Los Angeles suburbs. In Glendale a desirable property worth $60,000 was bought for $12,500.[48]

Loma Linda Sanitarium. The church leadership thought that surely they had fulfilled their responsibilities as they struggled to develop the Paradise Valley and Glendale sanitariums. But Ellen White was not finished. She had been instructed that the Redlands-Riverside area was pointed out as a place where the next sanitarium should be located—and soon. She told the conference leadership that they "could find it if they wanted to."[49]

When the description of the Loma Linda resort hotel was presented to her while she was attending the 1905 General Conference session in Washington, D. C., she replied that the place answered in every particular to the instruction seen in vision. Great was the tension regarding the necessary finances; the local conference was heavily in debt, chiefly because of the recent acquisitions urged by Ellen White! But time was of the essence. Mrs. White sent a telegram to faithful John Burden: "Secure the property!" The events of the next few months in finding the necessary funds to complete the sale and the rapid development of the medical educational center at Loma Linda provide reason for amazement and gratitude. The final purchase price was $38,900 on an initial investment of more than $150,000 by the original owners. Except for divine guidance through His messenger from Elmshaven, Loma Linda University would not exist today.[50]

Avondale College. The establishment of Avondale College by fewer than 1,000 believers in the 1890s, during one of Australia's worst economic depressions, is one more awesome example of the success that comes by following the counsel of God's messenger. Less than four months after Ellen White arrived in Australia, and with her urging, church leadership voted in December 1891 "that it is our duty to take immediate steps toward the establishment of a school in Australia."[51]

In 1893 the search committee located a 1,450-acre site seventy-five miles north of Sydney, near Cooranbong. Though the land was very cheap, church leadership felt that it would not support a farm, a conviction endorsed by the state agricultural service. Ellen White remained unmoved while others vacillated. To show her faith in the Lord's guidance, she borrowed $5,000 so that building materials could be bought.

For years, Avondale College was considered by many to be closer to the educational principles set forth by Ellen White than any other denominational school. It became a showcase for the benefits of a work-study program; the value of school industries as a source for student labor as well as for cash-flow to help the budget; the benefit to student, school, and community of student-sponsored community welfare activities, projects that reduced the need for extensive sports programs; the long-term investment in young people who would become denominational workers, and, above all else, a demonstration school for the common sense practicality of Ellen White's counsels on education.

Avondale College, after several other colleges had been established in America, was actually a new start in Adventist education. It developed relatively free from the conventional educational wisdom that influenced the American colleges. In 1897, Ellen White reflected on Avondale as "the best school in every respect that we have ever seen, outside our people, or among Seventh-day Adventists."[52]

Endnotes

1. *Life Sketches*, p. 196.
2. "During a long life span, she exerted the most powerful single influence on Seventh-day Adventist believers." —*Dictionary of American Biography,* Vol. XX, p. 99. "Mrs. White was the acknowledged inspiration of the movement. . . . Her ideas established the world of Adventism in its medical, educational, and missionary work around the world."—Hartzell Spence, "The Story of Religions in America—Seventh-day Adventists," *Look,* XXII (June 24, 1958), p. 79.
3. In the Bible Conference of 1919, A. G. Daniells, president of the General Conference, reflected on how he would teach young people about the relationship of Ellen White to the thought and structure of the Seventh-day Adventist Church: "I would want to begin with the beginning of this movement. At that time here was a gift given to this person; and with that gift to that individual, at the same time, came this movement of the three-fold message. They came right together in the same year. That gift was exercised steadily and powerfully in the development of this movement. The two were inseparably connected, and there was instruction given regarding this movement in all its phases through this gift, clear through for seventy years."—"The Use of the Spirit of Prophecy in Our Teaching of Bible and History," *Spectrum,* vol. 10, no. 1, p. 29.
4. See VandeVere, in *Adventism in America,* pp. 66, 67.
5. "Since her death [in 1915] there has been constant recourse to EGW's thoughts and positions on each and every issue which faced the Seventh-day Adventist Church . . . so that in every discussion her approval was either assumed or subsumed. Still today her voluminous writings are read, quoted and discussed by both ministry and laity of the SDA church to a much greater degree than are the writings of John Wesley in Methodism, and perhaps more than the works of Martin Luther in the various Lutheran churches."—Roy Graham, *Ellen G. White, Co-founder of the Seventh-day Adventist Church* (New York: Peter Lang, 1985), p. 1.
6. Joseph Smith of the Mormons, Mary Baker Eddy of the Christian Scientists, etc., see p. 37.
7. "The gospel is to be presented not as a lifeless theory, but as a living force to change the life. God would have His servants bear testimony to the fact that through His grace men may possess Christlikeness of character and may rejoice in the assurance of His great love. . . . We are witnesses for God as we reveal in ourselves the working of a power that is divine. . . . These precious acknowledgments to the praise of the glory of His grace, when supported by a Christlike life, have an irresistible power that works for the salvation of souls." —*The Ministry of Healing,* pp. 99, 100; see p. 470. See also *The Desire of Ages,* p. 826.
8. Jonathan Butler, "The Making of a New Order," in *The Disappointed,* pp. 199, 200.
9. "In all this period the testimonies to the church which came through Mrs. White deal often, very understandably, with this unstable state in men and movements. Without this gift of the Holy Spirit, as was proved over and over, the ties of brotherhood would not have sufficed to bind the movement together. . . . The fact stands out to us now, that in that early time, when there was no church organization and no ecclesiastical authority among the Sabbathkeeping Adventists, the Spirit of prophecy in Ellen G. White and the faith of the believers in her divine commission constituted the sole disciplinary agent of the body, the one rallying point of the faithful, the final court of appeal. Yet how modestly, with what godly fear, in what travail of soul, did she bear her testimony! No other agency could have so united while purifying. The outcome was a nuclear body comparatively clean, disciplined, and directed, for which later generations have every reason to be grateful."—Spalding, *Origin and History,* vol. 1, p. 293.
10. Errors included time-setting for the return of Jesus, perfectionism (fully sanctified and could not sin), spiritual union (violators of the seventh commandment), saints have yet to go to old Jerusalem before Jesus returned, etc.—See James White, *Review and Herald Extra,* July 21, 1851, Aug. 19, 1851, Nov. 25, 1851; Ellen White, *Early Writings,* p. 101; *Bio.,* vol. 1, pp. 216, 217.
11. George Storrs wrote in 1844: "Take care that you do not seek to manufacture another church. No church can be organized by man's invention but what it becomes Babylon *the moment it is organized."—The Midnight Cry,* Feb. 15, 1844, cited in David Arthur, "Millerism," in Gaustad, *Rise of Adventism,* p. 168.
12. Godfrey T. Anderson, "Sectarianism and Organization, 1846-1864," in Land, *Adventism in America,* pp. 36, 46, 47; Jonathan Butler, "Adventism and the American Experience," in Gaustad, *Rise of Adventism,* pp. 177, 179.
13. Christian, *Fruitage of Spiritual Gifts,* p. 119.
14. *Review and Herald,* Dec. 6, 13, 20, and 27, 1853.
15. In Sept., 1852, Ellen White had a vision that prompted an article that was published in late 1853, in which she said, "The Lord has shown that gospel order has been too much feared and neglected. Formality should be shunned; but, in so doing, order should not be neglected. . . . Men whose lives are not holy and who are unqualified to teach the present truth enter the field without being acknowledged by the church or the brethren generally, and confusion and disunion are the result. . . . These self-sent messengers are a curse to the cause. . . . I saw that this door at which the enemy comes in to perplex and trouble the flock can be shut. I inquired of the angel how it could be closed. He said, 'The church must flee to God's Word and become established upon gospel order, which has been overlooked and neglected.' This is indispensably necessary in order to bring the church into the unity of the faith."—*Early Writings,* pp. 97-100; "As our numbers increased, it was evident that without some form of organization there would be great confusion, and the work would not be carried forward successfully. To provide for the support of the ministry, for carrying the work in new fields, for protecting both the churches and the ministry from unworthy members, for holding church property, for the publication of the truth through the press, and for many other objects, organization was indispensable."—*Testimonies to Ministers and Gospel Workers,* p. 26; see *Testimonies,* vol. 1, pp. 210-216.
16. Throughout the meetings Ellen White stayed in the background, but as soon as the name was chosen she sent out the following endorsement: "No name which we can take will be appropriate but that which accords with our profession and expresses our faith and marks us a peculiar people. The name Seventh-day Adventist is a standing rebuke to the Protestant world. . . . The name Seventh-day Adventist carries the true features of our faith in front, and will convict the inquiring mind.

Like an arrow from the Lord's quiver, it will wound the transgressors of God's law, and will lead to repentance toward God and faith in our Lord Jesus Christ." —*Testimonies,* vol. 1, pp. 223, 224. Another name considered was "The Church of God."—See Damsteegt, *Foundations,* pp. 254, 255.

17. Godfrey T. Anderson, "Make Us a Name," *Adventist Heritage,* July, 1974, pp. 28-34. C. Mervyn Maxwell, *Tell It to the World,* pp. 125- 146; Spalding, *Origin and History,* vol. 1, pp. 291-311; Schwarz, *Light Bearers,* pp. 86-103; *Bio.,* vol. 1, pp. 420-431, 445-461; *SDAE,* vol. 10, pp. 880, 1046.
18. *Life Sketches,* p. 196.
19. *General Conference Bulletin,* April 3, 1901, pp. 23-26.
20. Maxwell, *Tell It to the World,* pp. 254-258; R. W. Schwarz, *Light Bearers,* pp. 267-281; R. W. Schwarz, "The Perils of Growth, 1886-1905," in Land, *Adventism in America,* pp. 128, 129; A. W. Spalding, *Origin and History,* vol. 3 (Washington, D.C.: Review and Herald Publishing Association, 1962), pp. 19-46; *Bio.,* vol. 5, pp. 70-96.
21. Christian, *Fruitage of Spiritual Gifts,* p. 125.
22. *Life Sketches,* p. 159.
23. See pp. 52, 53.
24. *Review and Herald,* April 14, 1903, p. 17.
25. A. G. Daniells to Ellen G. White, July 6, 1903, cited in *Bio.,* vol. 5, pp. 275, 276.
26. Letter 140, 1903, cited in Daniells, *Abiding Gift,* p. 349.
27. *Ibid.* For additional background, see A. G. Daniells, *Abiding Gift,* pp. 343-352; Schwarz, *Light Bearers,* pp. 299-313; Schwarz, "The Perils of Growth, 1886-1905," in Land, *Adventism in America.,* pp. 131-133; A. W. Spalding, *Origin and History,*vol. 3, pp. 66-81; *Bio.,* vol. 5, pp. 271-279.
28. *Testimonies,* vol. 8, p. 233; Schwarz, "The Perils of Growth, 1886-1905," in Land, *Adventism in America,* pp. 123-125.
29. "Notwithstanding frequent counsels to the contrary, men continued to plan for centralization of power, for the binding of many interests under one control. This work was first started in the Review and Herald office. Things were swayed first one way and then another. It was the enemy of our work who prompted the call for the consolidation of the publishing work under one controlling power in Battle Creek."—*Testimonies,* vol. 8, pp. 216, 217.
30. *Testimonies to Ministers and Gospel Workers,* p. 291.
31. *The Publishing Ministry,* p. 157.
32. *Testimonies,* vol. 7, p. 173; *Testimonies,* vol. 8, pp. 217, 218; *The Publishing Ministry,* pp. 131-158; Schwarz, *Light Bearers,* p. 272; *Bio.,* vol. 3, pp. 449-452.
33. In the mid-1870s, Mrs. White had been shown that the west-coast publishing house "was ever to remain independent of all other institutions; that it was to be controlled by no other institution."—Letter 81, 1896, cited in *The Publishing Ministry,* p. 141.
34. See pp. 200-204 regarding the Battle Creek Sanitarium crisis.
35. See p. 149.
36. Manuscript 29a, 1890, cited in *Bio.,* vol. 3, p. 469.
37. *Review and Herald,* March 10, 1891, p. 160.
38. *Life Sketches,* pp. 312, 313.
39. A. T. Robinson reported that "men of strong iron wills, who the night before manifested a spirit of unyielding stubbornness, confessed with tears and brokenness of voice. Elder Dan Jones said, 'Sister White, I thought I was right. Now I know I was wrong.'"—*Bio.,* vol. 3, p. 482.
40. Roland R. Hegstad, "*Liberty* Learns a Lesson," *Adventist Review,* May 15, 1986.
41. *Ibid.*
42. *Ibid.* Present *Liberty* policy reflects Ellen White's counsel regarding denominational publications: Adventists do not have a message "that men need to cringe to declare. They are not to seek to cover it, to conceal its origin and purpose. . . . We are not to make less prominent the special truths that have separated us from the world and made us what we are. . . . We are to proclaim the truth to the world, not in a tame, spiritless way, but in demonstration of the Spirit and power of God."—*Life Sketches,* p. 329.
43. *Testimonies,* vol. 1, pp. 485-495.
44. "Sketches of the Past," No. 133 in *Pacific Union Recorder,* January 2, 1913, as cited in Dores Eugene Robinson, *The Story of Our Health Message* (Nashville, Tenn.: Southern Publishing Association, 1965), p. 150.
45. *Review and Herald,* Sept. 11, 1866, p. 116.
46. Letters 138, 153, 1902, cited in Robinson, *Health Message,* p. 335.
47. Robinson, *Health Message,* pp. 337-339; Schwarz, *Light Bearers,* pp. 314, 315; Spalding, *Origin and History,* vol. 2, pp. 145-167; *Bio.,* vol. 5, pp. 361-371.
48. Robinson, *Health Message,* pp. 340, 341; Schwarz, *Light Bearers,* pp. 315, 316; Spalding, *Origin and History,* vol. 2, pp. 145-167; *Bio.,* vol. 5, pp. 372-376; *SDAE,* vol. 10, p. 613.
49. *Bio.,* vol. 6, p. 11.
50. Robinson, *Health Message,* pp. 343-402; Schwarz, *Light Bearers,* pp. 316, 317; Spalding, *Origin and History,* vol. 3, pp. 145-167; *Bio.,* vol. 6, pp. 11-32.
51. *Bio.,* vol. 4, pp. 24, 25.
52. Schwarz, *Light Bearers,* pp. 202, 203; *Bio.,* vol. 4, pp. 24, 25; 146-161; 287-322.

Study Questions

1. Why did many prominent Seventh-day Adventists resist church organization?

2. What conditions prevailed in church organization prior to 1901 that caused Ellen White to plead for a radical reorganization of how the Adventist Church conducted its world mission?

3. Why was Ellen White so insistent that the publishing house and the General Conference headquarters leave Battle Creek?

4. What were some of the negative aspects of consolidation of denominational enterprises at the turn of the century?

5. What was the real issue in the debate over the publishing policies of the National Religious Liberty Association in 1891?

6. How might Ellen White's counsel regarding the principles of consolidation apply today? Are there occasions when consolidation (of conferences, publishing houses, departments within organizations, etc.) would be appropriate?

7. Review Ellen White's contribution to the establishment of health institutions in California and show how these particular institutions would probably not exist today without her dramatic insistence and perseverance.

CHAPTER 18

Theological Crises

"[God has given me light] to correct specious errors and to specify what is truth."[1]

Throughout history since Cain and Abel, as Ellen White has wisely noted, Satan has done well in his attempt "to deceive and destroy the people by palming off upon them a counterfeit in place of the true work."[2] Every reformatory movement has experienced this phenomenon. The apostle Paul had to contend with wily counterfeits in his day.[3] During the Protestant Reformation, counterfeit religious movements and theologies plagued Martin Luther, as they did John Wesley two centuries later. The very nature of counterfeits requires immediate response; if left unchecked, truth comes close to shipwreck until a clear voice arises to reveal the error.

Such has been Ellen White's role in the Seventh-day Adventist Church from the beginning of her ministry to this day through her published works. In reviewing the fanaticism and counterfeit views of the 1840s and 1850s, we are reminded that these same errors will be faced repeatedly until the close of time.[4]

Counterfeits in the 1840s and 1850s

In 1845, before her marriage to James White, Ellen Harmon and others confronted a group in New Hampshire who appeared to be assured in the Lord. She soon learned that "they claimed perfect sanctification, declaring that they were above the possibility of sin." The leaders told her: "All that we have to do is to believe, and whatever we ask of God will be given us." This kind of thinking leads to the belief that "the affections and desires of the sanctified ones were always right, and never in danger of leading them into sin." In many cases, this thinking led to free love with all of its worst consequences.[5]

The "no-work" group, strange as it may seem today, attracted followers, especially those who cared for their leader's needs! First in Paris, Maine, and then in Randolph, Massachusetts, Ellen Harmon had to give reproof, reminding all concerned that "reason and judgment" were not to give way to impressions: "God ordained that the beings He created should work. Upon this their happiness depends."[6]

False humility, accompanied with boisterous excitement of some in Maine, brought disrepute to early Adventists prior to 1846. Young Ellen reported: "Some seemed to think that religion consisted in great excitement and noise. They would talk in a manner that would irritate unbelievers. . . . They would rejoice that they suffered persecution. . . . Some . . . professed great humility, and advocated creeping on the floor like children, as an evidence of their humility. . . . I told them plainly that . . . the humility which God looked for in His people was to be shown by a Christlike life, not by creeping on the floor."[7]

Frequent time-setting became a spiritual disaster for those who indulged in it and rejected the admonition from Ellen White. She wrote: "Different times were set for the Lord to come, and were urged upon the brethren. But the Lord showed me that they would pass by, for the time of trouble must take place before the coming of Christ, and that every time that was set, and passed, would weaken the faith of God's people. For this I was charged with being the evil servant that said, 'My Lord delayeth his coming.'"[8]

On the back page of the *Review,* July 21, 1851, Ellen White reported on a vision given her on June 21: "The Lord has shown me that the message of the third angel must go, and be proclaimed to the scattered children of the Lord, and that it should not be hung on time; for time never will be a test again. I saw that some were getting a false excitement arising from preaching time; that the third angel's message was stronger than time can be."

Salvation by Faith—1888

Nearly eight years after the notable 1888 General Conference session in Minneapolis, Minnesota, Ellen White summed up the crucial theological issues involved in the messages that she, E. J. Waggoner, and A. T. Jones presented at that time. In a candid testimony to the membership of the Battle Creek church, she wrote that many still "despised" the essence of the third angel's message because they "hated the light."

In this testimony and many others, Mrs. White uplifted the presentations made by Waggoner and Jones as a "most precious message" that "the Lord in His great mercy sent" to His people. She succinctly summarized this "precious message": "It presented justification through faith in the Surety; it invited the people to receive the righteousness of Christ, which is made manifest in obedience to all the commandments of God. Many had lost sight of Jesus. They needed to have their eyes directed to His divine person, His merits, and His changeless love for the human family. All power is given into His hands, that He may dispense rich gifts unto men, imparting the priceless gift of His own righteousness to the helpless human agent. This is the message that God commanded to be given to the world. It is the third angel's message, which is to be proclaimed with a loud voice, and attended with the outpouring of His Spirit in a large measure.

"The message of the gospel of His grace was to be given to the church in clear and distinct lines, that the world should no longer say that Seventh-day Adventists talk the law, the law, but do not teach or believe Christ. . . .

"This is the testimony that must go throughout the length and breadth of the world. It presents the law and the gospel, binding up the two in a perfect whole. . . . These ["the sons of God"] have not a mere nominal faith, a theory of truth, a legal religion, but they believe to a purpose, appropriating to themselves the richest gifts of God. . . ."

Ellen White closed her forceful testimony with these graphic words: "I have no smooth message to bear to those who have been so long as false guideposts, pointing the wrong way. If you reject Christ's delegated messengers, you reject Christ."[9]

What was the problem in Battle Creek generally? With all the personal sacrifices they had made for the cause that was closest to their hearts, the stalwart, hardworking leaders of the church generally did not yet fully understand the gospel! She told them that there was little if any hope for them if they continued to despise the "glorious offer of justification through the blood of Christ, and sanctification through the cleansing power of the Holy Spirit."[10]

Without Ellen White the messages of Jones and Waggoner would have been crushed and the history of the Seventh-day Adventist Church would have been drastically different after the 1888 Conference than what we now know it to be. That Conference was one of the most difficult times of her long and strenuous ministry, "the hardest and most incomprehensible tug of war we have ever had among our people."[11]

"Rebuffed at headquarters," Mrs. White, together with Waggoner and Jones, took the refreshing view of a full-orbed understanding of righteousness by faith to the churches throughout North America, first on the camp meeting circuit and later in institutional centers. The experiences at Ottawa, Kansas, and South Lancaster, Massachusetts, were especially memorable, and her messages on those occasions remain instructive today.[12]

What were the major issues and the main problems? The issues were theological, the problems were attitudes. In 1890 at the time of the ministerial institute in Battle Creek, Ellen White summarized the theological issues in what we now know as Manuscript 36, 1890. In this document she freely used the ellipse of truth as she threaded her way through deep theological waters.[13]

To emphasize a basic gospel principle she said: "Let this point be fully settled in every mind: If we accept Christ as a Redeemer, we must accept Him as a Ruler." Christian assurance can be claimed only when we "acknowledge Him as our King and are obedient to His commandments."

She clearly outlined the weaknesses in the contemporary religious world regarding basic gospel principles: "While one class perverts the doctrine of justification by faith and neglect to comply with the conditions laid down in the Word of God—*'If ye love Me,* keep My commandments'—there is fully as great an error on the part of those who claim to believe and obey the commandments of God but who place themselves in opposition to the precious rays of light—new to them—reflected from the cross of Calvary. The first class do not see the wondrous things in the law of God for all who are doers of His Word. The others cavil over trivialities and neglect the weightier matters, mercy and the love of God. . . .

"On the one hand, religionists generally have divorced the law and the gospel, while we have, on the other hand, almost done the same thing from another standpoint. We have not held up before the people the righteousness of Christ and the full significance of His great plan of redemption. We have left out Christ and His matchless love, brought in theories and reasonings, and preached argumentative discourses."[14]

The basic issue in 1888 was how to understand the fullness of gospel truth as reflected in John's words that God's people at the end of time would "keep the commandments of God and the faith of Jesus" (Rev. 14:12).[15]

Orthodox Adventists clearly understood the claims of God's commandments as especially highlighted in the Sabbath commandment. But, as happens often in Christian history, right thinking may not always be joined with a clear faith-commitment to Christ who alone can save one from the guilt and power of sin. Adventists, generally, in their earnestness to proclaim the neglected law of God, tended to leave Christ out of His law. Many preached Christless sermons, thus misrepresenting what it meant to have "the faith of Jesus" (Rev. 14:12).[16]

Part of the problem arose because Adventists saw in the general religious world the danger of antinomianism (the belief that faith, as mental assent, is sufficient and that obedience to law is legalism).[17] Spurious concepts of justification and sanctification permeated various denominations. Many Adventists thought that Jones and Waggoner represented a crack in the door that would lead to these prevalent errors.

Ellen White, however, transcended the fears of both sides of the conflict by making it clear that the gospel is the joining of law (including the seventh-day Sabbath) and grace, of pardon and power, of forgiveness and cleansing. She moved the theological argument above the conventional "either/or impasse" to the "both/and level" (that is, both law *and* grace, etc). She placed this strong Biblical understanding within the messages of the three angels of Revelation 14. By focusing on this Adventist recovery of the "everlasting gospel" (Rev. 14:6), she clarified the unambiguous message of the Adventist Church. This profound uniting of what had been dividing the religious world for centuries and the Adventist Church specifically, was her remarkable contribution to the 1888 crisis over salvation by faith. Further, her messages clearly demonstrated that this "precious message" was not a mere recovery of a sixteenth-century emphasis, nor a borrowing of a nineteenth-century Methodist accent, such as represented by Hannah Whitall Smith's, *The Christian's Secret of a Happy Life.*

Were these presentations by Waggoner and Jones new light for Ellen White? Generally, no, as one can discover by reading her messages prior to 1888.[18] She stated on several occasions that these great truths had been "imprinted indelibly on my mind by the Spirit God" and that they had been "presented in the testimonies again and again."[19]

But she saw certain aspects of the "precious message" as fresh, timely, and part of the increasing light she called "present truth": "The peculiar work of the third angel has not been seen in its importance. God meant that His people should be far in advance of the position which they occupy today. . . . It is not in the order of God that light has been kept from our people—the very present truth which they needed for this time. Not all our ministers who are giving the third angel's message, really understand what constitutes that message."[20]

During this difficult period it could have been argued that if Mrs. White had been more specific regarding, for example, the precise meaning of Galatians 3, the conflict would have been resolved quickly. In fact, she searched in vain for more than a year for materials that she had written on the subject. She even raised the question in a sermon at the 1888 Session: "Why was it that I lost the manuscript and for two years could not find it? God has a purpose in this. He wants us to go to the Bible and get the Scripture evidence."[21]

Here again, the 1888 delegates saw the principle prevail, as it had from the very beginning of Ellen White's ministry: first, Bible study, then confirmation through divine revelation. At Minneapolis she urged careful Bible study to be done in a courteous spirit, calling for "both sides of the question, for all we wanted was the truth, Bible truth, to be brought before the people."[22] Further, she said: "I cannot take my position on either side until I have studied the question [the law in Galatians]."[23]

Light Was Resisted

In a profound statement to Uriah Smith in 1896, Ellen White put her finger on the open sore that would continue to affect denominational plans and crises until the sore was healed. After reaffirming that the "schoolmaster" in Galatians 3 was the moral law, she wrote: "An unwillingness to yield up preconceived opinions, and to accept this truth, lay at the foundation of a large share of the opposition manifested at Minneapolis [1888] against the Lord's message through Brethren Waggoner and Jones. By exciting that opposition, Satan succeeded in shutting away from our people, in a great measure, the special power of the Holy Spirit that God longed to impart to them. The enemy prevented them from obtaining that efficiency which might have been theirs in carrying the truth to the world, as the apostles proclaimed it after the day of Pentecost. The light that is to lighten the whole earth with its glory was resisted, and by the action of our own brethren has been in a great degree kept away from the world."[24]

For Mrs. White, the emphasis on salvation by faith during the 1888-1895 period embodied the "third angel's message," especially as this message related to Christ's work in the Most Holy Place of the heavenly sanctuary. It was more than a mere recovery of "righteousness by faith" as proclaimed by the Reformers.

The increased light that Bible study had presented to the 1888 Minneapolis General Conference confirmed the linkage between the commandments of God and the faith of Jesus in an inseparable union, a union as efficient and interdependent as two poles of a battery, in the dynamic transformation of human lives.

In the 1888 emphasis, linkage was further made between the results of a personal application of salvation by faith and the closing work of Christ in the Most Holy Place. For Ellen White, the church will languish until its members understand and experience the truth that seeing Christ in the law enables men and women to be obedient to that law. When people see how Christ truly removes the guilt the law condemns, they will see how He truly enables men and women to become what the law describes. In so doing, such people become what John predicted would exist in the generation that proclaims the third angel's message (Rev. 14:12). Thus, "Christ Our Righteousness" becomes that "one subject that will swallow up" all others.[25]

Some of Ellen White's pivotal contributions to the 1888 Minneapolis General Conference and thus to us today, include:

• Conflicting points of view should be discussed with a proper attitude; improper attitudes may be a sign that the views are deficient.

• Wise students of the Bible do not emphasize minor points that distract from the primary issues, such as details on prophetic interpretation.

• The essence of the gospel embraces the law and a genuine faith response so that by the grace of Christ, imputed and imparted, the intent of the law and gospel will be fulfilled.

• Church leaders should be examples of openness so that "new light" is not kept from the church.

• The 1888 "revelation of the righteousness of Christ" was only "the beginning of the light of the angel whose glory shall fill the whole earth" (Rev. 18:1).

• Clarifying and restating the principles of the "precious message" that was the beginning of the "loud cry" (Rev. 14:18) will become "the one subject that will swallow up" all others.

This profound endowment to the Adventist Church is on record today in the many documents of that period. It can be strongly argued that, without Ellen White's prophetic leadership at that time, the Seventh-day Adventist Church would have been mortally wounded. Without her insistence that only a full understanding of what she and others were emphasizing in 1888 and the years soon following, the church today would not know what it means to fulfill its role in proclaiming the "everlasting gospel."

The urgency of the messages of this period, 1888-1896, persists today. To be truly informed, a person must re-read the actual messages, not through the eyes of another but directly as if the present reader were an eyewitness hearing Jones, Waggoner, and Ellen White for the first time.[26]

Holy Flesh Movement

An interesting trail runs from the continuing discussions on righteousness by faith following the 1888 Minneapolis Conference to the "cleansing message" proclaimed in the Indiana Conference at the turn of the century. By 1900 the entire Indiana Conference executive committee and almost all of its ministers were enthusiastically proclaiming that, in order to be translated, church members must go through the "garden experience," receive the "holy flesh" that Jesus had, and thus be prepared for translation. After this experience, the church members could no longer be tempted "from within" and would not see death; they would be translated!

How was this to happen? They believed that the Holy Spirit, when He comes in His fullness, will cleanse church members (in the "garden experience") from all sin. A cleansed church would then be prepared to warn the world of Christ's return, with the "loud-cry power" of Revelation 18:4.

At the Indiana camp meeting in 1900, Stephen Haskell did his best to reverse this conference-wide heresy. In his report to Ellen White who was still in Australia, he wrote: "When we stated that we believed that Christ was born in fallen humanity, they would represent us as believing that Christ sinned, notwithstanding the fact that we would state our position so clearly that it would seem as though no one could misunderstand us.

"Their point of theology in this particular respect seems to be this: They believe that Christ took Adam's nature before he fell; so He took humanity as it was in the garden of Eden, and thus humanity was holy, and this is the humanity which Christ had; and now, they say, the particular time has come for us to become holy in that sense, and then we will have 'translation faith' and never die."[27]

Further false doctrines that Haskell and others exposed included: (1) the impartation of the Holy Spirit was primarily for physical manifestations and miracles rather than character preparation for service; (2) perfectionism (understood as "holy flesh") in the sense of not being able to sin because no temptation now arises from within; (3) Jesus was born with "sinless flesh;" (4) the Holy Spirit insulated Jesus at conception from the law of heredity; (5) sealed people will not die; and (6) sealed people are healed physically as well as spiritually.

Of these doctrines Ellen White declared at the Indiana Conference constituency meeting, in Indianapolis, May 5, 1901, "there is not a thread of truth in the whole fabric."[28]

At the 1901 General Conference session in Battle Creek she met openly the holy flesh heresy and its conference leaders. In her prepared manuscript she said, in part: "The teaching given in regard to what is termed 'holy flesh' is an error. All may now obtain holy hearts, but it is not correct to claim in this life to have holy flesh. . . . Not a soul of you has holy flesh now. . . . It is an impossibility. If those who speak so freely of perfection in the flesh could see things in the true light, they would recoil with horror from their presumptuous ideas. . . . Let this phase of doctrine be carried a little further, and it will lead to the claim that its advocates cannot sin, that since they have holy flesh, their actions are all holy. What a door of temptation would thus be opened! . . .

"The manner in which the meetings in Indiana have been carried on, with noise and confusion, does not commend them to thoughtful, intelligent minds. There is nothing in these demonstrations which will convince the world that we have the truth. Mere noise and shouting are no evidence of sanctification, or of the descent of the Holy Spirit. . . . Fanaticism, once started and left unchecked, is as hard to quench as a fire which has obtained hold of a building. . . . We need to contemplate Christ and become assimilated to His image through the transforming power of the Holy Spirit. This is our only safeguard against being entangled in Satan's delusive snares."[29]

After reading her prepared statement for an hour, Ellen White spoke impromptu, recalling lessons learned from similar fanaticism with which she and fellow pioneers contended in the 1840s and 1850s.

The result? The next day the Indiana Conference president made a candid confession, saying, in part: "When I found this people, I was more than glad to know that there was a prophet among them, and from the first I have been a firm believer in, and a warm advocate of, the Testimonies and the Spirit of Prophecy. It has been suggested to me at times in the past, that the test on this point of faith comes when the testimony comes directly to us. As nearly all of you know, in the testimony of yesterday morning, the test came to me. But, brethren, I can thank God this morning that my faith in the Spirit of Prophecy remains unshaken. God has spoken. He says I was wrong, and I answer, God is right, and I am wrong."[30]

Other Indiana Conference officials also made open and full confession of their errors—all pointing to God's messenger as the reason for their enlightenment. A few weeks later, the Indiana Conference constituency voted a new conference committee and a change of key pastorates. With these confessions, the Holy Flesh Movement was broken.[31]

Pantheism Crisis

"Pantheism" is derived from two Greek words—*pan*, "all," and *theos*, "God." In pantheism, everything manifests the presence of God; nature and God are identical. By misunderstanding the role of the Holy Spirit the Christian church for two thousand years has lapsed into various heresies that border on pantheism; some have been direct incursions into pantheistic territory. That same misunderstanding created a crisis in the Seventh-day Adventist Church in the early 1900s.

In the 1840s and 1850s ex-Millerite "spiritualizers" not only emphasized that Jesus had indeed "come" in 1844 to the "believers," they were also "highly introverted" in their ecstatic worship practices. In addition, many groups were allied with the growing influence of modern spiritualism, first with the Shakers and then with the Fox-sisters movement in Hydesville, New York. But underneath the "spiritualizer" movement was the reduction of Jesus to that of a "spirit" rather than a material Person.[32]

When pantheistic ideas developed half a century later among Seventh-day Adventists, Ellen White recognized the similarities with the "spiritualizers" that she had firmly confronted in the 1840s and early 1850s.[33]

Before the death of James White in 1881 J. H. Kellogg shared with the Whites some theories of "new light" in understanding God. Ellen White responded forthrightly that she had "met them before" and that he should "never teach such theories in our institutions."[34]

But by 1897 Kellogg was introducing his pantheistic concepts at a ministerial institute preceding the General Conference session. His presentations were recorded in the 1897 *General Conference Bulletin.* Expressions such as the following were enthusiastically received by those who were not able to see where such thoughts would lead: "What a wonderful thought, that this mighty God that keeps the whole universe in order, is in us! . . . What an amazing thing that this almighty, all-powerful, and all-wise God should make Himself a servant of man by giving man a free will—power to direct the energy within his body!"[35]

In the late 1890s E. J. Waggoner also developed similar concepts. Because of his reputation as a Bible student and previous support from Ellen White for his salvation-by-faith teachings in 1888-1892, Waggoner's linkage with Dr. Kellogg brought plausibility to the teachings of both men. At the General Conference of 1899 he taught that men and women should be able to overcome their diseases and live forever, that every breath taken is "a direct breathing of God" in the nostrils, and that God is in pure water and good food, because "God is in everything."[36]

From these General Conference sessions and the *Bulletins,* these "new" and intriguing thoughts, pantheistic to the core, soon circled the Adventist world. That this age-old error in modern dress, often misusing Ellen White statements in sermons and articles, was not confronted early and head-on, seems astonishing today.[37]

But Ellen White in Australia was aroused. Letters had been written many weeks prior to the 1899 General Conference in order to arrive in time to be read to the delegates. On March 1 the first letter was entitled: "The True Relation of God and Nature." In part, she wrote: "Nature is not God and never was God. ... As God's created work, it but bears a testimony of His power. . . . We need carefully to consider this; for in their human wisdom, the wise men of the world, knowing not God, foolishly deify nature and the laws of nature."[38]

This communication should have been enough to eliminate further pantheistic teaching by denominational spokesmen. But these clear statements were ignored. Pantheistic theories seemed to pick up additional supporters among physicians at the Battle Creek Sanitarium as well as ministers in the field.

When A. G. Daniells returned from Australia to assume leadership of the General Conference, he was astounded to hear expressions such as "a tree maker in the tree," and God in flowers, trees, and all mankind. W. A. Spicer, newly appointed secretary of the Foreign Mission Board, had just spent several years as a missionary in India where pantheism permeated Hinduism. He quickly recognized the popularized American concepts for what they were.

On February 1, 1902, the world-renowned Battle Creek Sanitarium burned to the ground. Within hours Dr. Kellogg was laying plans to rebuild. Within days he was asking the General Conference for financial assistance. (The denomination at that time was heavily in debt—much of the debt due to expansive medical facilities.) Daniells, remembering that funds were being raised to reduce the debts on educational facilities by selling Ellen White's book, *Christ's Object Lessons,* suggested that Dr. Kellogg write a laymen's book on physiology and health care as promoted in the Battle Creek Sanitarium. He thought that 500,000 copies could be sold by Adventists to their friends, and all the proceeds would go to help reconstruct the sanitarium.[39]

But in the discussion over the proposed book, Daniells made it plain to Kellogg that none of his "new theory" must be in the book because, if it were, many church members would not cooperate in the venture. The doctor quickly agreed and immediately began to dictate the manuscript for *The Living Temple.*

However, as soon as the galley proofs were read by W. W. Prescott and W. A. Spicer, controversy over its contents began.[40] Kellogg saw that the General Conference Committee intended to withdraw support for publication of the book, so he withdrew it from further consideration as a church venture. Nevertheless, he placed a personal order for 5,000 copies with the Review and Herald Publishing Association.[41] About a month later, December 30, 1902, fire destroyed the publishing house with the plates for the book then ready for the press.

At the General Conference of 1903 other issues besides *The Living Temple* dominated the agenda. Management decisions regarding the Battle Creek Sanitarium and denominational health work in general became a struggle of leadership, Kellogg against Daniells. The doctor was determined to reopen Battle Creek College (the faculty and student body under Sutherland and Magan had already moved to Berrien Springs, Michigan). Prescott, as editor of the *Review*, used its pages to resist Kellogg's "ill-advised" venture and to expose the errors of his pantheism.

Not Clear on the Personality of God

During that period, Ellen White wrote to Dr. Kellogg: "You are not definitely clear on the personality of God, which is everything to us as a people. You have virtually destroyed the Lord God Himself."

A few days later she continued: "Your ideas are so mystical that they are destructive to the real substance, and the minds of some are becoming confused in regard to the foundation of our faith. If you allow your mind to become thus diverted, you will give a wrong mold to the work that has made us what we are."[42]

But Mrs. White did not openly confront the doctor at the session. In vision she was told that she "must not say anything that would stir up confusion and strife in the conference." The whole controversy must play out further so that all concerned would see the issues more clearly.[43]

Disregarding her counsel, Dr. Kellogg had 5,000 copies of *The Living Temple* produced by a commercial printer. Now more of the general public could see for themselves why church leaders had been concerned. Opposing sides developed; those in favor saw this "new light" to be conducive to a deeper religious experience; those opposed saw it as contributing to the dismantlement of the sanctuary doctrine, creating confusion regarding the function of the Holy Spirit, and blurring the truth concerning the distinct personalities of the Godhead. Throughout the summer Ellen White remained silent.

When the Autumn Council of the General Conference opened in Washington, D. C., on October 7, everyone knew that the Kellogg controversy and *The Living Temple* would have to be addressed. Among those supporting Kellogg were E. J. Waggoner, A. T. Jones, and David Paulson, a young physician.[44]

After a spirited all-day and late-evening meeting, Daniells returned home to find a group of people waiting. Their first greeting was: "Deliverance has come! Here are two messages from Mrs. White."

The messages were clear, concise, and unambiguous: "These sentiments [*The Living Temple*] do not bear the endorsement of God. They are a snare that the enemy has prepared for these last days. . . . The track of truth lies close beside the track of error, and both tracks may seem to be one to minds which are not worked by the Holy Spirit, and which, therefore, are not quick to discern the difference between truth and error."[45]

Read at the Council the next day, these messages settled the issue for most of the waverers. Daniells wrote immediately to Ellen White, saying, in part: "Never were messages from God more needed than at this very time; and never were messages sent from Him to His people more to the point than those you have sent to us. They have been exactly what we have needed, and have come at just the right time. . . . The conflict was severe, and we knew not how things would turn. But your clear, clean-cut, beautiful message came and settled the controversy. I do not say that all parties came into perfect harmony, but it gave those who stood on the right side strength to stand, and hold their ground."

Again in the letter, Daniells emphasized the remarkable timing: "Dr. Kellogg had been with us two or three days. His attitude had brought more or less confusion in the minds of a number of our ministers—men who do not really know where they stand. Your message came on just the right day—a day earlier would have been too soon."[46]

"Meet It!"

After receiving this letter from the General Conference president, Mrs. White wrote back, explaining the circumstances that prompted her timely messages. In this reply she revealed the vision in which she saw the iceberg and the captain's order, "Meet it!" She knew immediately what her duty was. Beginning at 1:00 A.M., she wrote as fast as she could. When her office help arrived, they had pages to edit. She wrote throughout the day, and the secretaries worked throughout the next night so that the material could be sent on the early-morning train.

They worked until they heard the sound of the train whistle. D. E. Robinson, one of the secretaries, rode his bicycle as fast as he could for almost two miles to catch the mail car. Days later, these timely messages arrived in Washington, D. C., *not a day too early, nor a day late!* [47]

Ellen White wrote personally to E. J. Waggoner, one of the foremost supporters of *The Living Temple*, urging him to change his ways: "I have seen the results of these fanciful views of God, in apostasy, spiritualism, free loveism. The free love tendencies of these teachings were so concealed that it was difficult to present them in their real character. Until the Lord presented it to me, I knew not what to call it, but I was instructed to call it unholy spiritual love."[48]

With these public messages now before the denomination and *The Living Temple* available for all to see the issues involved, the struggle at Battle Creek especially, was intense. More than the issue of pantheism was involved, of course. A number who felt identified with Dr. Kellogg's position on the control of the sanitarium also felt inclined to support his "new light." The big picture was not clear for many.

Two Definite Camps

At the Lake Union Conference session in May 1904, the deepening cleavage between two definite camps continued. Each camp was composed of strong, well-known church leaders. Each group looked differently and deeply at various denominational issues. According to E. K. VandeVere, long-time head of the history department at Emmanuel Missionary College (E.M.C.), the polarities at the 1904 session included:

Centralization vs decentralization of authority

Orthodoxy vs the new theology (pantheism, etc.)

Organization vs independence

Paid ministry vs a self-supporting ministry

Validity of Ellen White's "testimonies" vs her being questioned and/or ignored

Medical work as "arm" vs medical work as "body"

Emmanuel Missionary College's success vs the reopening of Battle Creek College

Battle Creek regarded as "punished" vs Battle Creek's fires as accidental

Move to Washington vs the value of Battle Creek label

Educational orthodoxy vs experimental education

Board control of E.M.C. vs E.M.C. administrators being led by the Spirit

"Reformers" Kellogg, Sutherland, Magan, E. J. Waggoner, A. T. Jones vs top-level church administrators Daniells, Spicer, Prescott, Morrison.[49]

Into this ferment came Ellen White with sermons each morning at eleven o'clock, including "The Foundation of Our Faith," "Lessons From Revelation 3," "A Plea for Unity," "Take Heed to Thyself," and "A Change of Feeling Needed."[50]

In these sermons Mrs. White emphasized the principles that each side was trying to uphold. She hoped that both sides would see the big picture. But she also saw what prevented both groups from understanding each other. Attitudes on both sides of various issues were the chief obstacle to resolving the apparent dilemmas: "Angels from heaven, sent to minister wisdom and grace, were disappointed to see self pressing its way in, to make things appear in a wrong light. Men were talking and discussing, and conjectures were brought in that should have had no place in the meeting."[51]

Near the end of the meetings, Ellen White had a vision. She wrote an account of it and gave it to W. C. White to read to the delegates on the last day: "Last night matters were presented to me, showing that strange things would mark the conclusion of the conference . . . unless the Holy Spirit of God should change the hearts and minds of many of the workers. The medical missionaries especially should seek to have their souls transformed by the grace of God."[52]

Tensions continued building. To provide as much help as possible to those who still wavered, Mrs. White rushed the printing of *Testimonies,* volume 8, with its section entitled, "The Essential Knowledge."[53] Further, she was fast developing her next health book especially for the general public, *The Ministry of Healing.* In this book she incorporated the same principles regarding the personality of God and His involvement in the healing of disease, especially in the section also entitled, "The Essential Knowledge."[54]

The Ballenger/Sanctuary Crisis, 1905

The sanctuary-doctrine crisis in 1905 was one more result of misunderstanding the role of the Holy Spirit in the salvation process. Whenever one neglects the work of the Holy Spirit in the relationship between the commandments of God and the faith of Jesus (Rev. 14:12), the tendency is either toward cold legalism or hot feelings and fervent individualism. Or error arises when the work of the Holy Spirit is de-emphasized when focusing on the substitutionary death of Christ; or, when one focuses on the "indwelling Spirit" to the neglect of Christ as Sacrifice and High Priest.[55] Misunderstanding Christ's double role[56] as Sacrifice and enabling High Priest set the stage for the Holy Flesh Movement, the pantheistic crisis, and, later, the sanctuary challenge.

Unfortunately for the Seventh-day Adventist Church, it seemed difficult for many in the 1890s, including E. J. Waggoner, John Harvey Kellogg, A. F. Ballenger, and, for a time, W. W. Prescott, to keep in balance the 1888 messages that Christ was "as ready to impart victory over future sins as to forgive those that were past."[57] Their attention focused on the "imparting victory" and the manifestation of the Spirit, overlooking the Holy Spirit's primary role in character transformation that precedes the promised "latter rain" and "loud cry" experiences.[58] After "accepting" the 1888 Minneapolis messages, these leaders believed that God would follow through quickly by sending His Spirit in a marked manner, enabling the church to "finish the work" and thus hasten the return of Jesus. For some, this focus on the work of the Spirit would lead them to believe that each person "filled with the Spirit" would also receive the gift of the Spirit of prophecy. Further, such church members would not need strong denominational organization because they would be Spirit-led.[59]

Ever since Ellen White returned from Australia in 1900, she had been sending scores of letters, private and public, warning of the deceptions and errors developing among leading spokesmen who were missing the point of sanctification, even as many leaders had been missing the point of commandment-keeping prior to 1888. In 1903 she wrote to Daniells: "I have often been warned against overstrained ideas of sanctification. They lead to an objectionable feature of experience that will swamp us unless we are wide-awake. . . . During the General Conference of 1901, the Lord warned me against sentiments that were being gathered and then held by Brethren Prescott and [E. J.] Waggoner. Instruction was given me that these sentiments received have been as leaven put into meal. Many minds have received them. The ideas of some regarding a great experience, called and supposed to be, sanctification have been the alpha of a train of deception which will deceive and ruin the souls of those who receive them. Because of some overdrawn expressions frequently used by Brother E. J. Waggoner at the conference, I was led to speak words intended to counteract their influence. . . . Satan is surely presenting some false theories which you must not receive. Elders Waggoner and Prescott are out of the way."[60]

A. F. Ballenger wrongly believed with many others that the Holy Flesh Movement was the logical extension of the 1888 messages. What he did see clearly was that, since the 1888 messages on righteousness by faith had been circulated through the denomination, "we are in the time of the latter rain, but the outpouring of the Spirit is withheld because of our sins."[61] He rightly saw the connection between the character of God's people and finishing their assignment as God's last-day witnesses. That had been a strong emphasis in Ellen White's messages for many years.[62] But he was wrong as to how the Holy Spirit was to prepare people for latter-rain witnessing: he held that believers could claim and receive sanctification as they could claim and receive justification. Further, for him, believers could claim the promise of the Spirit through faith even as they could claim the gift of healing by faith.[63]

Reports of physical healings followed Ballenger's preaching, which, for many, added special credence to his theology. What was the basis for Ballenger's connection between receiving the Spirit and physical healing? He believed that because Jesus "'took our infirmities, and bare our sicknesses,'"[64] Scripture "proves that the Gospel includes salvation from sickness as well as salvation from sin."[65]

What was Mrs. White's response to these "new ideas"? Writing to J. H. Kellogg in 1898, she said that some read the Bible without thorough study and then, "full of ardor and zeal, present theories which, if received, will counterwork" that which had been received since 1844 as "a connected chain of truth. . . . These crave for new ideas and suppositions, which mar the symmetrical development of character. . . . Let such a one put his whole mind upon some idea which is not correct, and deformity rather than symmetry is developed."[66]

At the 1905 General Conference session in Washington, Ballenger presented three one-hour studies on his "new" light on the sanctuary doctrine. His main thrust was that Jesus, on ascending to heaven, entered the second apartment of the heavenly sanctuary, the Most Holy Place. Prior to the cross, He had been functioning in the first apartment, the Holy Place. Ballenger did not convince the committee members. The committee responded with a Biblical exegesis that had been worked out decades before and confirmed by revelation to Ellen White. The response seemed to have led to a stalemate.

Misunderstanding the Role of the Holy Spirit

A decade or more of misconstruing the role of the Holy Spirit in salvation by faith weakened Ballenger's understanding regarding Christ's role in the atonement. Focusing his attention on the immediacy of the cleansed experience through claiming the Holy Spirit, he took his theological eyes off Christ's function as High Priest, both in His first phase of ministry in the Holy Place and then in the Most Holy. Refusing to accept the correcting ministry of Ellen White, Ballenger began a course of attacking her credibility on theological matters as well as other areas.

In one of her public responses during this period, Mrs. White said: "In the future, deception of every kind is to arise, and we want solid ground for our feet. . . . Not one pin is to be removed from that which the Lord has established. The enemy will bring in false theories, such as the doctrine that there is no sanctuary. This is one of the points on which there will be a departing from the faith. . . . I am praying that the power of the Saviour will be exerted in behalf of those who have entered into the temptations of the enemy. They are not standing under the broad shield of Omnipotence."[67]

Later she wrote: "He [Ballenger] was gathering together a mass of scriptures such as would confuse minds because of his assertions and his misapplication of these scriptures, for the application was misleading and had not the bearing upon the subject at all which he claimed justified his position. Anyone can do this, and will follow his example to testify to a false position; but it was his own."[68]

After noting how Ballenger reacted to her counsel in 1891, Mrs. White continued: "Now again our Brother Ballenger is presenting theories that cannot be substantiated by the Word of God. It will be one of the great evils that will come to our people to have the Scriptures taken out of their true place and so interpreted as to substantiate error that contradicts the light and the Testimonies that God has been giving us for the past half century. . . . I declare in the name of the Lord that the most dangerous heresies are seeking to find entrance among us as a people, and Elder Ballenger is making spoil of his own soul. The Lord has strengthened me to come the long journey to Washington to this meeting to bear my testimony in vindication of the truth of God's Word, and the manifestation of the Holy Spirit in confirmation of Bible truth. The Word is sure and steadfast, and will stand the test."

She continued: "There is not truth in the explanations of Scripture that Elder Ballenger and those associated with him are presenting. The words are right, but misapplied to vindicate error. We must not give countenance to his reasoning. He is not led of God. . . . I am instructed to say to Elder Ballenger, Your theories which have multitudes of fine threads, and need so many explanations, are not truth, and are not to be brought to the flock of God."[69]

In one of the public sessions Ellen White was led to recount early experiences. As she had done on several earlier occasions,[70] she described how, in the early years, intense Bible study preceded the "clear explanation of the passages we had been studying" that would be revealed to her in vision. None of this was done in secret. "The brethren knew that, when not in vision, I could not understand these matters, and they accepted, as light directly from heaven, the revelations given."[71]

She presented several other messages to various groups at the 1905 session, each one warning both Ballenger and church leaders "not to mingle erroneous theories with the truth of God." She emphasized that he had "been allowing his mind to receive and believe specious error." If his theories were accepted, they "would undermine the pillars of our faith." One of the problems was that in removing "the old landmarks," they were "working as blind men."[72]

Under God's illumination, Ellen White's clarifying and unifying leadership in these four theological crises—Salvation by Faith encounter at Minneapolis in 1888; Holy Flesh Movement in 1901 at Battle Creek; Pantheism crisis in 1903 at Washington, D. C.; and the Sanctuary challenge in 1905—was remarkably timely as well as determinative. No other person involved in these four potentially divisive crises was able to unify and set the course for the future. As noted often by many, "It was she who played a key role in resolving these issues. . . . Without Ellen White's authoritative voice, the outcome may have been very different."[73]

Ellen White was indeed the voice of the Advent movement, but not by spelling out each theological detail and settling each crisis with Sinai thunder. She worked to build up the best thinking of the moment, waiting at times until that best thinking ripened so that she did not break the equation initiated many years before: sound Bible study + confirmation by divine revelation = present truth.

It seems that Mrs. White's highest, greatest contribution was to keep the big picture in view, sensing always the harmful consequences of false theories. Clear in her mind was the full-orbed understanding of the gospel, and any theory that blurred any aspect of the gospel got her careful and concerned attention. She steered the church away from legalism on the right and romantic fanaticism on the left, always concerned with unity and with the distinctive mission of the Adventist Church.

Endnotes

1. Letter 117, 1910, cited in *Selected Messages*, book 3, p. 32.
2. *The Great Controversy*, p. 186.
3. Acts 20:28-31; Col. 2:8, 16-23; 2 Tim. 4:3-5; Titus 1:9-16.
4. "In later years I have been shown that the false theories advanced in the past have by no means been given up. As favorable opportunities come, they will have a resurrection. Let us not forget that everything is to be shaken that can be shaken."—*Life Sketches*, pp. 92, 93; see *Selected Messages*, book 2, pp. 25-30.
5. *Life Sketches*, p. 83.
6. *Ibid.*, p. 87. See also pp. 50, 559.
7. *Ibid.*, pp. 85, 86.
8. *Testimonies*, vol. 1, p. 72.
9. *Testimonies to Ministers and Gospel Workers*, pp. 91-97.
10. *Ibid.*, p. 97. In her writings, Ellen White referred to A. T. Jones and E. J. Waggoner more than 200 times. The emphasis given to "righteousness by faith" at Minneapolis in 1888 was distinctively different from the understanding prevailing in Protestantism during the nineteenth century, a fact that has not always been understood by those who have written of that important period.
11. Letter 82, 1888, in *The Ellen G. White 1888 Materials*, vol. 1, p. 182; "Brethren . . . I must tell you plainly that the course pursued toward me and my work since the Gen. Conf. at Minneapolis—your resistance of the light and warnings that God has given through me—has made my labor fifty times harder than it would otherwise have."—Letter 1, 1890, *Ibid.*, vol. 2, pp. 659; "the most grievous trial of my life."—Manuscript 30, 1889, *Ibid.*, vol. 1, p. 354; "one of the saddest chapters in the history of the believers in present truth."—*Ibid.*, vol. 4, p. 1796. See p. 234.
12. *1888 Materials*, vol. 1, p. 152; Schwarz, *Light Bearers*, pp. 187-192; *Faith and Works*, pp. 59-84; *Bio.*, vol. 3, pp. 416-418.
13. For a discussion of the ellipse of truth, see p. 260 and Appendix P.
14. *Faith and Works*, pp. 15, 16.
15. Manuscript 24, 1888, *The Ellen G. White 1888 Materials (1888 Materials)*, vol. 1, pp. 217, 218.
16. *Review and Herald*, Mar. 11, 1890, pp. 1, 2; *Christ's Object Lessons*, p. 48; "You may say that you believe in Jesus, when you have an appreciation of the cost of salvation. You may make this claim, when you feel that Jesus died for you on the cruel cross of Calvary; when you have an intelligent, understanding faith that His death makes it possible for you to cease from sin, and to perfect a righteous character through the grace of God, bestowed upon you as the purchase of Christ's blood."—*Review and Herald*, July 24, 1888.
17. Schwarz, *Light Bearers.*, p. 192.
18. *Faith and Works*, pp. 29-58.
19. Manuscript 24, 1888, *1888 Materials*, vol. 1, pp. 217-218; see also pp. 211, 212; "I have had the question asked, What do you think of this light that these men are presenting? Why, I have been presenting it to you for the last forty-five years—the matchless charms of Christ. This is what [I] have been trying to present before your minds. When Brother Waggoner brought out these ideas in Minneapolis, it was the first clear teaching on this subject from any human lips I had heard, excepting the conversations between myself and my husband. . . . When another presented it, every fiber of my heart said, Amen."—Sermon at Rome, N.Y., June 19, 1889, *Ibid.*, pp. 348, 349.
20. *Testimonies*, vol. 5, pp. 714, 715; "That which God gives His servants to speak today would not perhaps have been present truth twenty years ago, but it is God's message for this time."—Manuscript 8a, 1888, quoted in Olson, *op. cit.*, p. 274; "We want the past message and the fresh message."—*Review and Herald*, Mar. 18, 1890; "We are in the day of atonement, and we are to work in harmony with Christ's work of cleansing the sanctuary. . . . We must now set before the people the work which by faith we see our great High Priest accomplishing in the heavenly sanctuary." —*Review and Herald*, Jan. 21, 1890; "The mediatorial work of Christ, the grand and holy mysteries of redemption, are not studied or comprehended by the people who claim to have light in advance of every other people on the face of the earth. Were Jesus personally upon earth, He would address a large number who claim to believe present truth with the words He addressed to the Pharisees: 'Ye do err, not knowing the Scriptures, or the power of God.' . . .

    "There are old, yet new truths still to be added to the treasures of our knowledge. We do not understand or exercise faith as we should. . . . We are not called to worship and serve God by the use of the means employed in former years. God requires higher service now than ever before. He requires the improvement of the heavenly gifts. He has brought us into a position where we need higher and better things than ever have been needed before."—*Ibid.*, Feb. 25, 1890; "We have been hearing His voice more distinctly in the message that has been going for the last two years. . . . We have only just begun to get a little glimmering of what faith is."—*Ibid.*, Mar. 11, 1890.
21. *1888 Materials*, vol. 1, p. 153; A. V. Olson, *Thirteen Crisis Years* (Washington, D.C.: Review and Herald, 1966), p. 302.
22. *1888 Materials*, p. 221.
23. *Ibid.*, p. 153; also in Olson, *Thirteen Crisis Years*, p. 30.
24. *Ibid.*, p. 1575; see also *Selected Messages*, book 1, pp. 234, 235. This letter was first published in *Review and Herald*, Feb. 13, 1952.
25. *Review and Herald Extra*, Dec. 23, 1890, p. 2; A. G. Daniells, *Christ Our Righteousness* (Washington, D.C.: Review and Herald Publishing Association, 1941) 128 pages.
26. *Review and Herald*, "Repentance the Gift of God," Apr. 1, 1890; Nov. 22, 1892, "The Perils and Privileges of the Last Days; Maxwell, *Tell It to the World*, pp. 231-241; Olson, op. cit., pp. 1-320; Schwarz, *Light Bearers.*, pp. 183-197; Spalding, *Origin and History*, vol. 2, pp. 281- 303; Arnold V. Wallenkampf, *What Every Adventist Should Know About 1888* (Washington, D.C.: Review and Herald Publishing Association, 1988), pp. 1-92; Robert J. Wieland, *The 1888 Message, An Introduction* (Nashville, Tenn.: Southern Publishing Association, 1980), (Paris, Ohio: Glad Tidings Publishers, 1997). pp. 1-158; Robert J. Wieland and Donald K. Short, *1888 Re-examined, Revised and Updated* (Leominster, MA: The Eusey Press, 1987), pp. 1-213; *Bio.*, vol. 3, pp. 385-433. George R. Knight, *From 1888 to Apostasy* (Hagerstown, MD: Review and

Herald Publishing Association, 1987). See George Knight, *Angry Saints.*

27. Letter to Ellen G. White, Sept. 25, 1900, E. G. White Estate Document File 190.
28. G. A. Roberts, "The Holy Flesh Fanaticism," E. G. White Estate Document File 190.
29. *General Conference Bulletin*, Apr. 23, 1901, pp. 419-421; for a shortened version, see *Selected Messages,* book 2, pp. 31-35.
30. *Ibid.,* p. 422.
31. William H. Grotheer, *The Holy Flesh Movement* (Florence, MS: Adventist Laymen's Foundation of Mississippi, Inc., n.d.) pp. 1-65; Ella M. Robinson, *S. N. Haskell, Man of Action* (Washington, D. C.: Review and Herald Publishing Association, 1967), pp. 168-176; Schwarz, *Light Bearers.*, pp. 446-448; *Bio.*, vol. 5, pp. 39, 99, 100-107, 112, 113.
32. Bull and Lockhart, *Seeking a Sanctuary,* pp. 56-62.
33. "Before I was 17 years old, I had to bear my testimony against them [sentiments regarding God such as are found in *The Living Temple*] before large companies." —Letter 217, 1903, cited in *Bio.*, vol. 5, p. 304.
34. Manuscript 70, 1905, cited in *Bio.*, vol. 5, p. 281.
35. *General Conference Daily Bulletin* 1897, p. 83.
36. *General Conference Daily Bulletin* 1899, pp. 57, 58, 119.
37. Ellen White's frequent emphasis on the "Christ in you" theme, coupled with her equally strong emphasis on the impartation of the Holy Spirit in fulfilling Peter's appeal that Christians "may be partakers of the divine nature" (2 Pet. 1:4), were taken out of context. Her statements were extrapolated into a teaching that an immanental God pervaded all humanity, both the converted and unconverted; in obeying the laws of life, a person could become like the divine, leaving no need for divine power to help, no need for Christ's substitutionary death, etc. Behind both the Holy Flesh Movement and the pantheistic development was the shift, in the minds of some, from the sanctifying process that would prepare people for fuller service (latter rain and loud cry motifs) to the Sanctifier who would manifest Himself in some extraordinary, physical manner. For example, well-known Adventist leaders were teaching that receiving the Spirit meant also healing the body as well as the soul, that gray hair would be restored to its natural color, that truly Spirit-led people would not die!—See *General Conference Daily Bulletin* 1899, pp. 53-58, 119, 120; Gilbert M. Valentine, *The Shaping of Adventism* (Berrien Springs, MI: Andrews University, 1992), pp. 159-163,
38. *General Conference Daily Bulletin*, p. 157.
39. Some research indicates that Dr. Kellogg may have suggested the idea. The clear facts are that both Daniells and Kellogg thought the book idea was a positive solution to raising funds.
40. Prescott listed three major areas where he and Kellogg were in profound disagreement: (1) "a wrong view of God and His dwelling place"; (2) a religion "which set aside any need of atonement and the work of Christ as our High Priest in the Sanctuary above"; and (3) "a breaking down of the distinction between the sinner and the Christian by teaching that every man is a temple of God regardless of his faith in Christ."—Valentine, *The Shaping of Adventism,* p. 162.
41. Valentine, *The Shaping of Adventism,* p. 151.
42. Letter 300, 1903 and Letter 52, 1903, cited in *Bio.*, vol. 5, p. 292.
43. *Bio.*, vol. 5, p. 293.
44. Young Dr. Paulson had been especially befriended by Kellogg and now was strongly supporting Kellogg's "new light." As he and Daniells walked home after a long evening discussion, he shook his finger at Daniells, saying: "You are making the mistake of your life. After all this turmoil, some of these days you will wake up to find yourself rolled in the dust, and another will be leading the forces." Daniells straightened up and replied, "I do not believe your prophecy. At any rate, I would rather be rolled in the dust doing what I believe in my soul to be right than to walk with princes, doing what my conscience tells me is wrong." —Daniells, *Abiding Gift of Prophecy,* pp. 336, 337. The next day Dr. Paulson was thoroughly impressed with Ellen White's messages read in the Council, and acknowledged that they were from God. He and his wife founded Hinsdale Sanitarium. Dr. Paulson became a striking example of living faith and a strong supporter of the ministry of Ellen White.
45. *Review and Herald,* Oct. 22, 1903; see also Letter 216, 1903, cited in *Bio.*, vol. 5, pp. 298, 299.
46. *Bio.*, vol. 5, p. 300. For other examples of the timeliness of Ellen White's visions, see chapter 15.
47. *Ibid.,* pp. 299-302.
48. Letter 230, 1903, cited in *Bio.*, vol. 5, p. 303. See also *Testimonies,* vol. 8, pp. 290-304.
49. Shaw, "A Rhetorical Analysis of the Speaking of Mrs. Ellen G. White," pp. 315, 316. Although aligned with some on certain positions, many leaders were not aligned with those same persons on other points. Although Kellogg, Sutherland, Magan, Jones, and Waggoner were "reformers," Sutherland and Magan did not support Kellogg and others in their pantheistic ideas.
50. *Bio.*, vol. 5, p. 336.
51. *Ibid.*, p. 334.
52. *Ibid.*, p. 338.
53. Pages 255-335.
54. Pages 409-466. For a fuller background of the pantheistic crisis, see A. G. Daniells, *The Abiding Gift of Prophecy*, pp. 330-342; Maxwell, *Tell It to the World.*, pp. 214-216; Schwarz, *Light Bearers,* pp. 288-292; Schwarz, "The Perils of Growth," in Land, *Adventism in America*, pp. 133- 138; Spalding, *Origin and History,* vol. 3, pp. 130-144; Valentine, *The Shaping of Adventism,* pp. 145-166; *Bio.*, vol. 5, pp. 402-404.
55. See p. 262. See also the "Ellipse of Truth," pp. 260, 573.
56. See *The Great Controversy,* p. 488.
57. Schwarz, *Light Bearers,* p. 188.
58. *The Desire of Ages*, p. 805.
59. A. T. Jones, *Review* editor, regularly closed his editorials with the words, "Receive ye the Holy Ghost." The camp meeting speakers of the late 1890s generally represented this Spirit-centered focus. Probably the most eloquent of these speakers was A. F. Ballenger, a highly sought speaker for church revivals. His influence in Indiana was reflected in the Holy Flesh Movement.
60. Letter 269, 1903 cited in *MR,* vol. 10, pp. 356, 357.
61. *Review and Herald,* Oct. 5, 1897, p. 629; see related articles on pp. 411, 523, 624; also *General Conference Daily Bulletin*, 1899, p. 96.
62. *Evangelism,* pp. 695, 696; *Testimonies,* vol. 6, pp. 9-13. See also *Christ's Object Lessons,* pp. 69, 414-416; *Review and Herald,* Mar. 31, 1910, pp. 3, 4.
63. *Review and Herald,* May 3, 1898, p. 288; "Physical

healing is *now present truth* to Seventh-day Adventists."—*Ibid.*, Oct. 4, 1898 p. 637; "The gift of healing . . . will appear when we receive the Holy Spirit, and not before."—*Ibid.*, Nov. 15, 1898 p. 740.
64. Matt. 8:17, KJV, quoting Isa. 53:4, "Surely he hath borne our griefs, and carried our sorrows."
65. *Signs of the Times*, June 13, 1900, p. 371.
66. *MR*, vol. 21, pp. 57, 58.
67. *Review and Herald*, May 25, 1905, p. 17.
68. Manuscript 59, 1905, cited in *Bio.*, vol. 5, p. 408. In 1891, A. F. Ballenger, the chief spokesman who contended for a shift in direction for the *American Sentinel*, was one of the leaders at the General Conference in Battle Creek who publicly confessed his error and reaffirmed his confidence in the integrity of Ellen White's ministry—see p. 188.
69. *Ibid.*
70. See pp. 170, 171.
71. *Review and Herald*, May 25, 1905, p. 17.
72. Manuscript 62, 1905, cited, in part, in *Bio.*, vol. 5, p. 411, 412. More than fifty pages of letters and manuscripts were written by Ellen White during this critical period. See Manuscript 75, 1905, cited, in part, in *Bio.*, vol. 5, pp. 425, 426; Letter 329, 1905 (*Selected Messages*, book 1, pp. 160-162), cited, in part, in *Bio.*, vol. 5, pp. 426, 427; Letter 50, 1906, cited in *Bio.*, vol. 5, pp. 427, 428; and Manuscript 125, 1907, cited, in part, in *Bio.*, vol. 5, p. 428, in which Ellen White wrote: "Any man who seeks to present theories which would lead us from the light that has come to us on the ministration in the heavenly sanctuary should not be accepted as a teacher." For a Biblical study of the texts in the book of Hebrews that Ballenger used for his position that Jesus entered the Most Holy Place in the heavenly sanctuary and for a refutation of his main argument, see William G. Johnsson, "Day of Atonement Allusions," F. B. Holbrook, ed., *Issues in the Book of Hebrews* (Silver Spring, MD: Biblical Research Institute, 1989), pp. 105-120.
73. Schwarz, in Land, *Adventism in America.*, p. 109. "The dimensions of the crisis faced by the church between 1897 and 1911 indicate that the church either would have lost its special message or would have hopelessly fractured without the guidance of the Lord through the Spirit of Prophecy."—Bert Haloviak, "Pioneers, Pantheists, and Progressives: A. F. Ballenger and Divergent Paths to the Sanctuary," p. 52, an unpublished manuscript, June 1980.

Study Questions

1. What were the basic issues that divided the delegates at the Minneapolis General Conference in 1888?

2. What were the basic issues at stake in the Holy Flesh Movement, and how did Stephen Haskell and Ellen White defuse the problem?

3. What were the basic issues involved in the pantheism crisis of the early 1900s?

4. What was the basic error that linked J. H. Kellogg, A. F. Ballenger, and, later, E. J. Waggoner?

5. Why did Ellen White consider the presentations of Elders Jones and Waggoner in 1888 to be a "precious message," a "fresh message," that presented God's "voice more distinctly"?

CHAPTER 19

Evangelism, Local and Global, and Race Relations

"Your conception of the work needs to be greatly enlarged."[1]

Sabbatarian Adventists in the 1840s were largely devoted to helping their little band understand better the meaning of the Disappointment of 1844.[2] Early leaders encouraged other Millerites not to deny their past Advent experience. They energetically set forth their new understanding regarding Christ's ministry in the heavenly sanctuary and the connection of the seventh-day Sabbath within the larger context of the messages of the three angels in Revelation 14. Understandably, their sense of mission was frustrated by hostile reactions from both the general public after the "embarrassment" of October 22, 1844, and by Sunday-keeping Millerites who bitterly rejected the new Saturday-Sabbath emphasis. It seemed that an ice curtain now isolated early Sabbatarian Adventists, leading to the conviction that, in some way, the door of mercy had been closed to those who had rejected the deeper implications of the Millerite message of 1844.[3]

But the sense of mission involving Adventist responsibility to share their message with the world soon changed. The force and clarity of young Ellen White was the primary reason for the shift from the "shut door" mentality of early Sabbatarian Adventists to that of responsibility for the completion of the gospel commission. In fact, "the views of E. G. White had a profound influence on the new theological interpretations as well as the emerging missionary consciousness, making doubtful that without her influence the early Sabbatarian Adventists would have survived this period of turmoil."[4]

The developing Adventist sense (theology) of mission moved on from (but not forsaking) (1) reaffirming the Advent experience of 1844, to (2) restoring certain neglected Bible doctrines that needed to be reset in "the everlasting gospel," to (3) recognizing that this restored gospel was to be preached to all the world before Jesus returned.[5]

Coupled with Adventism's consistent proclamation of the nearness of the Advent was its motivating and driving principle of restoration.[6] This principle involved more than a theological integration of restored Biblical teachings; it included "the context of man's spiritual and physical restoration as necessary preparation for Christ's return."[7] Ellen White was the foremost spokesperson for the restoration principle shaping Adventist eschatology.[8]

This theological emphasis on restoration differentiates Seventh-day Adventists from other religious groups that emphasize the nearness, or even imminence, of the Second Coming. Adventist theology of the Advent continues to attract those who want "to make sense of their own lives." In an Institute of Church Ministry (Andrews University) research study, "seventy percent of new believers in the Georgia-Cumberland Conference survey said that they were most attracted to the church by 'the truth and beauty of its teachings.' . . . Few people are attracted to churches in which theology is hedged around by qualifications. Adventism's evident ideological appeal may also be a function of the church's apparent theological certainty."[9]

In the early years, Adventists took their "world" assignment seriously but interpreted it less than globally. At first they believed that "if the third angel's message were preached throughout the United States, it would thus have been preached to all the world."[10]

How could this be? Uriah Smith, struggling with the concept, concluded that, though "we have no information that the Third Message is at present being proclaimed in any country besides our own . . . our own land is composed of people from almost every nation."[11] Even until 1872 Adventists generally believed that Matthew 24:14 was being fulfilled in the rapid expansion of Protestant missions generally.[12]

But Ellen White was being used by God to lift the vision of the emerging Adventist denomination. In her 1848 Dorchester, Massachusetts, vision she told her husband James that he should start a paper and "from this small beginning it was shown to me to be like streams of light that went clear round the world."[13] Such a concept seemed preposterous to contemporaries.[14]

During the 1850s Adventists with European family or friends were sending literature to them, and soon pockets of Sabbath keepers could be found in the "old" world. In 1864 M. B. Czechowski, an Adventist since 1858, left for Europe with his new-found convictions. This eventually led to a company of Sabbath keeping believers in Tramelan, Switzerland.[15]

Prompted by this European interest, the 1874 General Conference sent the J. N. Andrews family, the denomination's first official foreign missionaries, to Switzerland. Ellen White later commented that Andrews was "the ablest man in our ranks."[16] Three years later the John G. Matteson family was sent to Scandinavia to follow the literature that had been developing interest in the messages of the three angels.[17] By 1890 Adventist missionaries were in about 18 countries, including various European nations, Africa, Russia, Australia, India, and South Africa.

During this time Ellen White had been educating the church. In 1871, in a message based on a December 10 vision, she appealed: "Young men should be qualifying themselves by becoming familiar with other languages, that God may use them as mediums to communicate His saving truth to those of other nations. . . . Missionaries are needed to go to other nations to preach the truth in a guarded, careful manner."[18]

In 1874 she had "an impressive dream" of "giving the third angel's message to the world." In the dream she was told that Adventists were "entertaining too limited ideas of the work for this time. You are trying to plan the work so that you can embrace it in your arms. . . . Many countries are waiting for the advanced light the Lord has for them. . . . Your conception of the work needs to be greatly enlarged."[19]

Driven by her own sense of mission, Ellen White spent two years in Europe, 1885-1887. These years are well chronicled in *Ellen G. White in Europe, 1885-1887.*[20] Just as she was closely involved in the development of the Advent movement in North America, she now had much to do with establishing the work in Europe on firm principles. Not easy, working with many nationalities and languages, but her instruction at that time in bringing unity and good will has been most salutary for international and intercultural relationships since that time.[21]

L. H. Christian, an administrator in Europe, 1922-1936, wrote: "The advent movement in Europe would never have been the same if it had not been for her visit."[22]

Ellen White was a globalist. The "how" of fulfilling Matthew 24:14 she left up to God: "God will do the work if we will furnish Him the instruments."[23] She who saw the "streams of light" going "clear round the world" in 1848 when there were fewer than one hundred Sabbatarian Adventists, never gave up that vision of a world enlightened with the messages of the three angels. She prompted the church to develop its message, and prodded it to reach out to fulfill its staggering mission.[24]

Dynamic Advocate of Public Evangelism

Training must precede practice. In the two years that Mrs. White was in Europe (1885-1887) she gave those who were breaking new ground in evangelism clear and proven suggestions as to how to be most effective. One of the first lessons learned in the United States was that unprepared, untrained workers, no matter how earnest, did not honor God with ineffective methods. At the fifth session of the European Council (1887), in Moss, Norway, she counseled: "Much greater work could have been done if our brethren had taken greater pains, even at large expense, to educate the licentiates before they were sent into the field for labor. They were allowed to go and try their gift. They did not go with experienced workmen who could help them and educate them, but went out alone. . . . They did not grow, and were not taxing their powers to become able men in the Scriptures."[25]

Mrs. White would not substitute enthusiasm for proper ministerial preparation: "If young men would enter the field [public ministry], in nowise discourage them; but first let them learn the trade."[26] As James White stated, it was always "a disgrace to Seventh-day Adventists to do a second-class job in anything."[27]

Importance of starting right. First impressions were important to Ellen White. Those representing the Adventist Church in public must be prepared spiritually as well as professionally—or else their work would not be permanent: "There is the greatest need of the work in new fields starting right, bearing the impress of the divine. Many in these new fields will be in danger of accepting the truth or assenting to it, who have not a genuine conversion of heart. When tested by storm and tempest, it will be found that their house is not built upon a rock but upon sliding sand. Practical godliness must be possessed by the minister and developed in his daily life and character. His discourses should not be exclusively theoretical."[28]

"Starting right" also meant the impressions made by the choice of meeting places,[29] by avoiding "theatrical performances" and "startling notices . . . [that] create an alarm,"[30] by appropriate articles in "the secular papers,"[31] by becoming "acquainted with the pastors of the several churches,"[32] by being "abreast of the times" in messages,[33] by the ministers' dressing "in a manner befitting the dignity of their position,"[34] and by ministers avoiding anything that might be considered "uncouth" in any attitude or deportment that would "strike the beholder with disgust."[35]

Public presentations should reflect the spirit and manner of Jesus. One of the marks of the Spirit of prophecy is that Jesus is exalted and reflected in all soulwinning ventures. Whatever the subject Ellen White discusses, the reader is impressed with the prevailing sentiment that Christ is not only our Saviour but also our Example—in all things. His soul winning, whether in leading individuals to salvation or in directing multitudes heavenward, provide clear, proven methods of evangelistic effectiveness.

In the chapter "Our Example," in *The Ministry of Healing,* Ellen White depicted how Jesus would "meet men where they were." She wrote: "He sought access to the people by the pathway of their most familiar associations."[36] Often she emphasized that it is "essential that we understand and follow right methods of teaching and follow the example of Christ."[37]

Christ's example included avoiding "controversies,"[38] identifying with each person's "interest and happiness,"[39] watching "the faces of His hearers . . . which told that truth had reached the soul,"[40] speaking with "simplicity" by not bringing "many things before them at once, lest He might confuse their minds [making] every point clear and distinct," appealing to all intellectual and social levels by clothing His messages "with such beauty that they interested and charmed the greatest intellects,"[41] by measuring His instruction as His audience was ready to receive it, keeping back "many things in regard to which His wisdom kept Him silent."[42]

Bringing the gospel to the general public, including many who have been burned over with previous religious experiences, requires tact in selecting the sequence of subjects. Ellen White led the way by example and by persistent instruction. In emphasizing tact, she wrote: "When you meet those, who, like Nathaniel, are prejudiced against the truth, do not urge your peculiar views too strongly. Talk with them at first of subjects upon which you can agree. . . . Both you and they will be brought into a closer connection with heaven, prejudice will be weakened, and it will be easier to reach the heart."[43]

She commended church members who mingled with the Woman's Christian Temperance Union, urging them to be noted for the "light of life" on "subjects where you can all agree."[44]

Ellen White was invited to speak to the general public on scores of occasions throughout North America. Generally she chose the subjects of Christian temperance and practical godliness, developing the subjects in a way that deeply stirred her audiences. She knew that by starting with a neutral, contemporary subject she would gain a favorable hearing, thus setting the stage for more distinctive messages. She knew the principles of good public relations.[45]

Leading advocate of city evangelism. Some may wonder how and why a woman as busy as Ellen White would get involved in evangelistic techniques. Yet, many are the messages written to denominational leaders and leading evangelists, focusing on soul-winning methods for urban areas.[46] Her counsel on public evangelism, for example, especially in the world's large cities, prompted new moves toward city evangelism: "We stand rebuked by God because the large cities right within our sight are unworked and unwarned. . . . We have done none too much for foreign fields, but we have done comparatively nothing for the great cities right beside our own doors."[47]

Stephen and Hetty Haskell were perhaps the leading proponents of Ellen White's program for reaching the masses. Door-to-door selling of books, personal Bible studies, workers' meetings to teach personal evangelism, utilization of health education to arouse public interest, printed Bible studies, evangelistic journals, contacting business and professional leaders, finding suitable sites for public meetings—all came together in the Haskells' program for New York in the early 1900s.[48]

Denominational leadership, preoccupied with various crises at that time, neglected Ellen White's repeated emphasis on city evangelism. But she would not be deterred. For her, not only were many millions going to their graves unwarned, the preaching of the three angels' messages of Revelation 14 was seriously frustrated.[49]

In 1909 she met the issue head-on: the

church's top leaders, including A. G. Daniells, General Conference president, and W. W. Prescott, editor of the *Review*, should lead the way in public evangelism! She wrote sharply to both men in 1910 after she believed that her counsel in 1909 had produced only a token response: "I am charged with a message to you both that you need to humble your hearts before God. Neither Elder Prescott nor Elder Daniells is prepared to direct the work of the General Conference, for in some things they have dishonored the Lord God of Israel. . . . Some things were clearly opened before me during the last meeting I attended in Washington, D. C. . . . The work in the cities has not yet been carried forward as it should be. . . . Had the president of the General Conference been thoroughly aroused, he might have seen the situation. But he has not understood the message that God has given. . . . I can no longer hold my peace."[50]

Prescott made plans for evangelistic work but a combination of family tragedies overwhelmed him. His health suffered seriously. As time went on, new responsibilities in editorial work eventually occupied his time.[51]

Daniells had some difficulty in arranging his leadership responsibilities. During these months, Ellen White wrote him: "Redeem the lost time of the past nine years by going ahead now with the work in our cities, and the Lord will bless and sustain you."[52]

This constant urging on the president of the General Conference and others resulted in an explosion of Adventist city evangelism in the years that followed.[53]

Setting the Tone on Race Relations

As with many other major denominational issues, Ellen White was foremost in charting the moral dimensions involved in race relations as well as in suggesting pragmatic approaches to resolving problems during difficult times. Richard Schwarz wrote that it "took an earnest admonition from Ellen White to jolt Adventists into realizing their duty to share their faith with Afro-Americans."[54]

Prior to leaving for Australia, at the 1891 General Conference session in Battle Creek, Mrs. White made her first major public appeal for evangelistic work among American Blacks.[55] Understanding the growing restrictions being applied to Blacks throughout the southern states, she recognized that she was plunging into an explosive topic, "but I do not mean to live a coward or die a coward."[56]

She pointed out that "the black man's name is written in the book of life beside the white man's. . . . Birth, station, nationality, or color cannot elevate or degrade men." Further, those who "slight a brother because of his color are slighting Christ."

Then she turned to the church's neglect, acknowledging with regret that "we have not made a greater effort for the salvation of souls among the colored people." She recognized that she was referring to "perplexing questions," that both White and Black Adventists were needed to educate millions who had been "downtrodden" for so long, and that church workers in the South "must not carry things to extremes and run into fanaticism on this question."[57]

One of the first to sense the challenge was James Edson White, Ellen White's son.[58] Creative, energetic, a trained printer and songwriter, Edson joined with Will Palmer in producing *The Gospel Primer,* which they used (1) to raise funds, (2) to teach illiterates how to read, and (3) to teach Bible truths in simple language.

Knowing that they would not be welcome among Southern Whites, especially if they lived with Blacks, they had a river steamboat built (named the *Morning Star*), which for several years became their housing, printing plant, and chapel. This concerted effort to help fulfill the goals of Ellen White's 1891 appeal moved forward with little support from denominational sources. But Edson's tenacity, coupled with his mother's encouragement, paid off with the establishment of a Seventh-day Adventist presence along the Yazoo River, at Nashville, Tennessee, and Vicksburg, Mississippi.[59]

Mrs. White saw the color-line issue in broader dimensions than most of her contemporaries. In a series of ten articles in the *Review and Herald,*[60] after Edson had begun his work, she appealed to church members: "No human mind should seek to draw the line between the colored and the white people. Let circumstances indicate what shall be done, for the Lord has His hand on the lever of circumstances. As the truth is brought to bear upon the minds of both colored and white people, as souls are thoroughly converted, they will become new men and women. . . . Those who are converted among the white people will experience a change in their sentiments. The prejudice which they have inherited and cultivated toward the colored race will die away."[61]

Ellen White closed the first of the ten-article series with an appeal and caution: "As a people we should do more for the colored race in America than we have yet done. In the work we shall need to move with carefulness, being endowed with wisdom from above."[62] The remaining nine articles reemphasized the general concepts of the first article with several suggestions as to how White families should move to the southern states to share with the Blacks their knowledge of agriculture and other trades. The goal was to lead Blacks into their own self-help programs.

But time and circumstances soon changed. The closing years of the nineteenth century and the first decade of the twentieth saw whatever gains the Blacks enjoyed since emancipation reversed with a vengeance. The shameful, rigid, system of segregation emerged during this period, beginning what has been called the "betrayal of the Negro." Some refer to this period as "the long dark night," lasting to 1923.[63] In 1913, the President of the United States was still segregating federal office buildings in the nation's capital. In 1890 Mississippi led the way in eliminating the Blacks' right to vote; seven states soon followed. Lynching became a Southern racial phenomenon; some Blacks were burned at the stake. Major race riots occurred in both North and South.

Did Ellen White contradict herself? Did she set her sails depending on how the wind was blowing when she told church members, White and Black, in 1908 that Blacks should not expect or demand social equality and that Blacks and Whites should worship in segregated buildings? That surely sounds like a different Ellen White from the bold, clear-eyed leader in the first-half of the 1890s!

The answer to such criticism of Ellen White lies in observing several facts: (1) Her son, Edson, during this period, was demonstrating the principles that his mother had encouraged. He and his associates were working during the darkening shadows when "Jim Crow" racial segregation was sweeping the South. Edson's mother kept close contact with him and from this correspondence we can understand where her heart was. Almost single-handedly, mother and son, during the most difficult times showed the Adventist Church how to begin work in the southern states.

(2) The rapidly changing circumstances in the southern states required timely, unambiguous counsel from the messenger of God who was able to see the big picture developing. Ellen White never advocated inviting the time of trouble before its time.[64] She recognized that the dawn of a better day would eventually brighten that dark night of shameful Black oppression but that "for this time" they must be "'wise as serpents, and harmless as doves.'" The cautionary measures Ellen White advocated were "to be followed until the Lord shows us a better way."[65] She proclaimed courage because "God is laying bare His arm to do a

mighty work in this mission field within the borders of our own land."[66]

(3) Ellen White's counsel during this appalling period in the history of the United States reflects more than human wisdom. Flexibility is a mark of wisdom when time and circumstances change. Living in Australia prevented her from reading the daily newspapers of that period. Yet, she saw clearly the implications of the new oppression of Blacks. Evangelistic work for Whites was in jeopardy if "wrong" moves in working for the Blacks were adversely interpreted by the Whites. And Blacks would be in greater jeopardy if unsympathetic Whites thought Blacks were stepping "outside" of their social sphere in responding to White evangelists.[67] The larger picture that Ellen White always kept before the church was to honor God by steady progress in reaching honest seekers, White or Black, even though the pace, at times, slowed to allow for immediate circumstances. Her prediction that times would change certainly gave hope to those struggling during the dark night.

(4) Ellen White's instruction to the church, by counsel and example, paved the way for Adventists to work in the southern states when circumstances would change: (a) She believed in the equality of all races; (b) She clearly did not foster the prevailing belief on the part of many in her day that the Black race was genetically inferior. Often she would point out: "You will meet with deplorable ignorance. Why? Because the souls that were kept in bondage were taught to do exactly the will of those who call them their property, and held them as slaves. . . . Now, there are those who are intelligent. Many have had no chance who might have manifested decided ability if they had been blessed with opportunities such as their more favored brethren, the White people, have had."[68] In other words, remove the bondage and inevitable results of slavery, give Blacks the same opportunities as Whites, and so-called ignorance would vanish as a consequence.

Ellen White would have been better understood on race relations through the years if the totality of her statements had been studied in the context of their time. Adventist racial tensions would have been greatly reduced if her lucid principles had molded personal and organizational decisions. Otis B. Edwards, a longtime Black educator, may have said it best: "Perhaps the greatest stimulus to missionary efforts for the Negro came . . . from Mrs. Ellen G. White."[69]

Endnotes

1. *Life Sketches of Ellen G. White*, p. 289.
2. Probably the Sabbatarian Adventists numbered no more than 100 in 1849. By 1852, numbers increased to 250; by 1863, when the Seventh- day Adventist Church was organized, members numbered 3,500.—Bull and Lockhart, *Seeking a Sanctuary*, pp. 111, 112.
3. Damsteegt, *Foundations*, pp. 163, 164.
4. See Chapter 44, "The Shut Door—a Case Study."
5. Damsteegt, *Foundations*, p. 295.
6. *Ibid.*, p. 295.
7. *Ibid.*, p. 296. "In this mission of restoration the concept of God's mission was recognized while man's function was placed in the context of a divine-human cooperation."—*Ibid.*
8. *Ibid.*, p. 270.
9. Bull and Lockhart, *Seeking a Sanctuary*, p. 117.
10. Spalding, *Origin and History*, vol. 2, p. 194; Gottfried Oosterwal, "Continuity and Change in Adventist Mission," in Vern Carner and Gary Stanhiser, *The Stature of Christ* (Privately published, Loma Linda, CA, 1970), pp. 45-57.
11. *Review and Herald*, Feb. 3, 1859, p. 87.
12. *Review and Herald*, April 16, 1872, p. 138; July 16, 1872, p. 36.
13. *Life Sketches*, p. 125.
14. Spalding, *Origin and History*, vol. 2, p. 195; Loughborough, *GSAM*, p. 275.
15. Maxwell, *Tell It to the World*, pp. 158-164; Schwarz, *Light Bearers*, pp. 142-144; *SDAE*, vol. 10, p. 428.
16. Maxwell, *Tell It to the World*, pp. 165-173; Schwarz, *Light Bearers*, pp. 144-147.
17. Schwarz, *Light Bearers*, pp. 147-148.
18. *Life Sketches*, p. 204.
19. *Ibid.*, pp. 208-209.
20. D. A. Delafield, *Ellen G. White in Europe, 1885-1887* (Washington, D.C.: Review and Herald Publishing Association, 1975).
21. "Some who have entered these missionary fields have said: 'You do not understand the French people; you do not understand the Germans. They have to be met in just such a way. But I inquire, Does not God understand them? Is it not He who gives His servants a message for

the people? . . . Though some are decidedly French, others decidedly German, and others decidedly American, they will be just as decidedly Christlike. . . . Let no one think that there need not be a stroke placed upon him. There is no person, no nation, that is perfect in every habit and thought. One must learn of another. Therefore God wants the different nationalities to mingle together, to be one in judgment, one in purpose. Then the union that there is in Christ will be exemplified. . . . Look to Jesus, brethren; copy His manners and spirit, and you will have no trouble in reaching these different classes. We have not six patterns to follow, nor five; we have only one, and that is Christ Jesus. . . . I warn you, brethren and sisters, not to build up a wall of partition between different nationalities. On the contrary, seek to break it down wherever it exists." —*Testimonies,* vol. 9, pp. 179-181.

22. Christian, *Fruitage of Spiritual Gifts,* pp. 161, 162. "For many, many years, our members and their children in England, Switzerland, Norway, Denmark, and Sweden, never tired of telling about Mrs. White. And when now and then in later years a few disloyal ones ridiculed and belittled the gift of prophecy and the servant of God, our people said: 'We know better. We heard her speak. We have seen her humble, godly, inspiring life. We have her books, and they agree with the Bible and deepen our love for Jesus.'"
23. *Testimonies,* vol. 9, p. 107.
24. Maxwell, *Tell It to the World,* pp. 174-183; Emmet K. VandeVere, "Years of Expansion, 1865-1885," in Land, *Adventism in America,* pp 87-94; Schwarz, "The Perils of Growth, 1886-1905," in Land, *Ibid.,* pp. 116-119; Spalding, *Origin and History,* vol. 2, pp. 191-212.
25. Manuscript 34, 1887, cited in *Bio.,* vol. 3, p. 369.
26. *Testimonies,* vol. 4, p. 437-448. Students at Battle Creek College should "reach a higher standard of intellectual and moral culture" than could be found in "any other institution of the kind in our land."—*Testimonies,* vol. 4, p. 425.
27. *Review and Herald,* May 24, 1877, p. 164.
28. *Testimonies,* vol. 4, p. 321.
29. *Evangelism,* p. 126; Delafield, *Ellen G. White in Europe,* p. 99.
30. *Evangelism,* pp. 136-139.
31. *Ibid.,* p. 129.
32. *Ibid.,* p. 143.
33. *Ibid.,* p. 151.
34. *Ibid.,* pp. 145, 673.
35. *Ibid.,* p. 145.
36. *The Ministry of Healing,* p. 23.
37. *Evangelism,* p. 53. "Learn His ways. We shall gain much instruction for our work from a study of Christ's methods of labor and His manner of meeting the people. . . . The words of the Master were clear and distinct, and were spoken in sympathy and tenderness. They carried with them the assurance that here was truth. It was the simplicity and earnestness with which Christ labored and spoke that drew so many to Him." —*Ibid.,* p. 53.
38. *Ibid.,* pp. 59, 172, 339, 340, 162, 304; *The Desire of Ages,* p. 253.
39. *The Ministry of Healing,* pp. 22-24.
40. *Evangelism,* p. 55.
41. *Ibid.,* p. 56.
42. *Ibid.,* p. 57.
43. *Ibid.,* p. 446; "Present Jesus because you know Him as your personal Saviour. Let His melting love, His rich grace, flow forth from human lips. You need not present doctrinal points unless questioned."—*Ibid.,* p. 442.
44. *Welfare Ministry,* p. 164.
45. Temperance/health sermons "will be an agency through which the truth can be presented to the attention of unbelievers. They will reason that if we have such sound ideas in regard to health and temperance, there must be something in our religious belief that is worth investigation."—*Evangelism,* p. 514.
46. *Evangelism,* pp. 384-428; see Howard B. Weeks, *Adventist Evangelism in the Twentieth Century* (Washington, D.C.: Review and Herald Publishing Association, 1969).
47. *Ibid.,* pp. 401, 402.
48. Robinson, Ella M., *S. N. Haskell, Man of Action,* (Washington, D.C.: Review and Herald Publishing Association, 1967), pp. 177-195. One of Ellen White's evangelistic principles that the Haskells took seriously was: "If one half of the sermonizing were done, and double the amount of personal labor given to souls in their homes and in the congregations, a result would be seen that would be surprising."—*Evangelism,* p. 430.
49. *Testimonies,* vol. 9, pp. 97-108; *Review and Herald,* July 1, 1909.
50. Letter 58, 1910, cited in *Bio.,* vol. 6, p. 225; *MR,* vol. 6, pp. 73-77; vol. 10, pp. 362-364.
51. Valentine, *The Shaping of Adventism,* pp. 197-214.
52. Letter 68, 1910, cited in *Bio.,* vol. 6, p. 229; pp. 219-230; *MR,* vol. 19, pp. 123, 124.
53. Schwarz, *Light Bearers,* pp. 336-341.
54. Schwarz, *Ibid.,* p. 235.
55. For consistency, in this volume we refer to African-Americans as Blacks, even as we refer to Caucasians as Whites. In his illuminating 1970 book on Adventist race relations, Ron Graybill discussed the various terms that designate the two major races in the United States: "Ellen White generally used the term 'colored' in reference to those of African descent, but also 'black' and 'Negro.' Sometimes she even referred to them as the 'Southern race' or the 'Southern people,' just as she used 'Southern work' and 'Southern field' for 'the work for the colored people' in the South."—*E. G. White and Church Race Relations* (Washington, D. C.: Review and Herald Publishing Association, 1970), p. 11.
56. *The Southern Work* (Washington, D.C.: Review and Herald Publishing Association, 1966), p. 10.
57. *Ibid.,* pp. 12-18.
58. Schwarz, *Light Bearers,* p. 236.
59. *Ibid.,* pp. 237-242.
60. *Review and Herald,* Apr. 2, 1895, Nov. 26 to Dec. 24, 1895, Jan. 14 to Feb. 4, 1896; also found in *The Southern Work,* pp. 19-65.
61. *Review and Herald,* April 2, 1895, p. 210.
62. *Ibid.*
63. Graybill, *Ellen G. White and Church Race Relations,* p. 18. During this darkening night for the southern Blacks, in 1908 Ellen White wrote admonitions that have alarmed some people who read them in later years without understanding the frightening changes that had occurred subsequent to her strong, positive statements of 1895. For example, she reminded leaders that, from Australia years before, she had warned of the erupting color line crisis and how it would soon affect evangelistic work in the southern states. She cautioned: "Workers were to make no political speeches, and that the mingling of whites and blacks in social equality was by no means to be encouraged. . . . I said plainly

that the work done for the colored people would have to be carried on along lines different from those followed in some sections of the country in former years. Let as little as possible be said about the color line, and let the colored people work chiefly for those of their own race. In regard to white and colored people worshiping in the same building, this cannot be followed as a general custom with profit to either party—especially in the South. . . . This is particularly necessary in the South, in order that the work for the white people may be carried on without serious hindrance. Let the colored believers be provided with neat, tasteful houses of worship. Let them be shown that this is done not to exclude them from worshiping with white people, because they are black, but in order that the progress of the truth may be advanced. Let them understand that this plan is to be followed until the Lord shows us a better way. . . . As time advances, and race prejudices increase, it will become almost impossible, in many places for white workers to labor for the colored people. . . . White ministers and colored ministers will make false statements, arousing in the minds of the people such a feeling of antagonism that they will be ready to destroy and to kill. . . . Let us follow the course of wisdom. . . . The time has not come for us to work as if there were no prejudice. . . . If you see that by doing certain things which you have a perfect right to do, you hinder the advancement of God's work, refrain from doing these things. . . . All things may be lawful, but all things are not expedient."—*Testimonies*, vol. 9, pp. 199-215.

64. "Let our workers be careful to speak guardedly at all times and under all circumstances. Let all beware lest by reckless expressions they bring on a time of trouble before the great crisis which is to try men's souls." —*Testimonies*, vol. 6, p. 395.
65. *Testimonies*, vol. 9, pp. 214, 215, 207.
66. *Ibid.*, p. 225.
67. The experiences of Edson White became a living (and frightful) experiment in testing the White hostility toward "outsiders" who were urging the improvement of the Blacks. See Graybill, *Ellen G. White and Church Race Relations*, pp. 53-69.
68. Letter 80-a, 1895, cited in Graybill, *Ellen G. White and Church Race Relations*, pp. 108, 109.
69. "Origin and Development of the SDA Work Among Negroes in the Alabama-Mississippi Conference," unpublished M. A. thesis, Andrews University, August 1942, p. 21.

Study Questions

1. What were some of the immediate concerns of early Sabbatarian Adventists that superseded any sense of a world mission?
2. In what significant ways did Ellen White prod her colleagues into thinking globally?
3. What two families were the first officially designated missionaries by the General Conference?
4. What three dynamic principles of evangelism were advocated by Ellen White?
5. Why is it said that Ellen White was the "greatest stimulus" in helping Seventh-day Adventists to reach out in missionary efforts to Blacks in the United States?
6. How do you explain Ellen White's seeming reversal of counsel regarding how to work with the Blacks in the southern states of America between 1895 and 1908?
7. What were Ellen White's high expectations for quality preparation before ministers and evangelists were formally assigned public responsibilities?
8. Name some of the "perplexing problems" that faced those who wanted to evangelize North American Blacks in the late nineteenth century and into the twentieth.

CHAPTER 20

Stewardship, Government Relations, and Humanitarian Involvement

"We need not sacrifice one principle of truth while taking advantage of every opportunity to advance the cause of God."[1]

A pressing question during the 1850s was how to support the ministry. Ministers with families had a most difficult challenge when they had to rely on the liberality of believers, especially when few church groups were organized. Many could preach only on a part-time basis. The Whites sold Bibles and other books to supplement the little income they received from friends. Furthermore, the barter system often prevailed, for money was scarce, especially in a largely agrarian society.

In late 1858 Ellen White told her husband that the Lord had shown her that J. N. Andrews should come to Battle Creek, hold a Bible class, and in the study they would develop a Biblical plan for sustaining the ministry. In that Bible class held in January 1859, the leaders agreed that the tithing system is still binding, and they suggested calling the program, "Systematic Benevolence on the tithing principle." On January 29 the Battle Creek congregation voted unanimously to adopt the program and publish the plan in the *Review and Herald.* The example of the Battle Creek church set the pace for other churches to follow.[2]

By June Mrs. White was writing that "the plan of systematic benevolence is pleasing to God."[3] In the early days of implementation, the "plan" did not separate tithes from offerings and all was devoted to supporting the ministry. In January 1861 Mrs. White wrote a candid message that more clearly defined the tithing principle, applying Malachi 3:8-11 to present-day obligations to the Lord. She delineated how the tithing principle was fair to all, the poor as well as to the wealthy, and that "in the arrangement of systematic benevolence, hearts will be tested and proved. . . . Here is a test for the naturally selfish and covetous."[4]

Ellen White said often that the "tithe is sacred, reserved by God for Himself. It is to be brought into His treasury to be used to sustain the gospel laborers in their work."[5] Gospel laborers are defined as ministers and Bible instructors, Bible teachers in our educational institutions, minister-physicians, retired gospel workers, and workers in needy mission fields in North America and abroad.[6] God has blessed the tithing system. Tithe alone for the members of the North American Division for 1996 amounted to $507,406,823.[7]

The Church's Changed Policy Towards Government Aid

As was true in other matters, the intervention of Ellen White changed the course of Seventh-day Adventist policy in regard to the church's relationship to government aid. In fact, her counsel reversed an action taken by the General Conference session in 1895.

In late 1893 A. T. Robinson, the church's leader in establishing new work in South Africa, approached Cecil Rhodes who was both Premier of the Cape Colony and head of the British South Africa Company. At that time, the Company was offering large grants to various mission bodies to cultivate the land and educate the nationals. Robinson needed land and Rhodes was the only person who could provide it. In reply, Rhodes wrote a sealed letter to his representative in Bulawayo, instructing him to give the Adventists all the land they needed.

A 12,000-acre tract was selected and became the site of Solusi College, the first Seventh-day Adventist educational institution among non-Christian people. The small group of Adventists in South Africa regarded this event as clear providential intervention.

But this gift of land was not viewed with rejoicing in Battle Creek. Religious liberty leaders, including A. T. Jones, declared the transaction to be a blatant violation of the principle of separation of church and state. They rushed into battle, often with injudicious words.

Steamy Crisis

The issue came to a steamy head at the 1895 General Conference session. In fact, two so-called religious liberty items were on the agenda: (1) the South Africa land grant and (2) tax exemption on church property. The session voted to refuse tax exemption for American churches and to instruct South African leaders that the church must pay for any land provided.

Experienced leader Stephen Haskell was in South Africa at the time the General Conference decision arrived. Immediately he sent off letters of protest to the president of the General Conference and to W. C. White, Ellen White's son. Mrs. White wrote back a fourteen-page letter, sending copies to leading workers in Battle Creek, in which she strongly protested those two General Conference actions.

Six Basic Principles Reflected in Letter From Ellen White

The portion of her letter that dealt especially with accepting government aid, about three and one-half typewritten pages, was later published in *Testimonies to Ministers.*[8] In it six basic principles[9] are reflected:

• *Denominational decisions must be based on "correct principles."* "Let these men [Religious Liberty leaders] read the book of Nehemiah with humble hearts touched by the Holy Spirit, and their false ideas will be modified, and correct principles will be seen, and the present order of things will be changed."[10]

• *Applying these "principles" should be done by leaders nearest to the problem.* "Let the Lord work with the men who are on the ground, and let those who are not on the ground walk humbly with God, lest they get out of their place, and lose their bearings."[11]

• *"True principles" must be differentiated from false principles.* Although Ellen White strongly advocated the principle of religious liberty, she never used the phrase "separation of church and state." She urged church leaders not to "build up a wall of separation between themselves and the world, by advancing their own ideas and notions."[12] To not think clearly would "move . . . workers to make them take a course which will bring on the time of trouble before the time." Wrong thinking would "cut off any favors" by withdrawing "from the help that God has moved men to give, for the advancement of His cause."[13]

False principles do not originate with the Holy Spirit. In Old Testament times the Lord "moved upon heathen kings to come to [Nehemiah's] help . . . which they so much needed." Refusing government aid was "zeal . . . not according to knowledge." In reference to Battle Creek leaders, Ellen White was clear: "The movement they have made to pay taxes on the property of the Sanitarium and Tabernacle have manifested a zeal and conscientiousness that in all respects is not wise nor correct. Their ideas of religious liberty are being woven with suggestions that do not come from the Holy Spirit, and the religious liberty cause is sickening."[14]

• *Correct concepts of stewardship undergird correct religious liberty principles.* God "owns the world" and "has placed His goods in the hands of unbelievers, but they are to be used in favor of doing the works that must be done for a fallen world."[15]

Throughout history God has moved "upon hearts of kings and rulers in behalf of His people." He used Cyrus and Darius of Persia, to help Nehemiah. "Proper persons . . . [should] set before those who have means and influence, the needs of the work of God. . . . They should seek to bring the truth before the men in high places, and give them a fair chance to receive and weigh evidence. . . . What they would give we should be privileged to receive." Further, with false principles of stewardship and religious liberty the church has "put away from us privileges and advantages that we might have had the benefit of, because we chose to stand independent of the world."[16]

• *Seventh-day Adventists must use wisdom in deciding what and when to implement the "correct principles" in the area of government aid.* Adventists are told that "we need not sacrifice one principle of truth while taking advantage of every opportunity to advance the cause of God."[17] Twice in her counsel on government aid, Ellen White admonished that leaders should exercise "the wisdom of the serpent, and the harmlessness of the dove [that] we might obtain advantage from them [men in high places], for God would move upon their minds to do many things in behalf of His people."[18] Further, leaders should avoid "taking extreme positions, and burdening themselves over matters that should not be taken up or worried over."[19]

Wisdom in avoiding "extreme positions" would also advise caution in accepting government aid with latent strings attached that would compromise or restrict church programs or principles, then or in the future. Government aid should be rejected if it compromises the church's purpose, but it should not be rejected because of reasoning based on false principles.

• *Government aid, or aid from anyone willing to give it, should be gratefully accepted if, in the taking, "truth is to have a standing place and . . . uplifted in many places in regions beyond."*[20] Solusi Mission and College was the beginning of scores, perhaps hundreds, of Seventh-day Adventist educational and medical institutions on most all continents where "truth" has "a standing place" because of government assistance. Most European and African countries require church-related schools to be licensed by the government. After being licensed, government funding follows. The record shows that truth need not be compromised because of this connection; without the connection, there would be no "standing place" for truth in those countries.

Champion of Christian Unity

The Seventh-day Adventist Church is an international body with various components that interact constantly with other churches and national governments. The Adventist Church is not a member of the World Council of Churches,[21] yet, it is very concerned about the unity of Christians. Perhaps Ellen White has been foremost in emphasizing this towering Biblical concern. She removed all questions regarding whether the only genuine Christians in the world are Seventh-Adventists when she wrote: "Notwithstanding the spiritual darkness and alienation from God that exist in the churches which constitute Babylon, the great body of Christ's true followers are still to be found in their communion."[22]

The attitude of the Adventist Church toward religious ecumenism is based not on a sense of superiority but on a self-understanding of the church's history and its teachings. The early beginning of the Adventist Church, emerging out of the Millerite movement in the early 1840s, had much to do with the church's attitude toward other denominations. For years, early Adventists understood themselves as a prophetic movement with a specific message regarding the return of Jesus and the preparation of a people to be translated at His coming. In contrast to post-millennialism which prevailed in the nineteenth century, Seventh-day Adventists emphasized an Advent that was near.

In contrast to social progress and natural selection to explain the process of evolution, Adventists reasserted the Creation story as the basis for human worth and responsibility. The Sabbath became the core focus in emphasizing the seven-day Creation week of Genesis 1 and 2. Because these distinctive doctrines defined the Seventh-day Adventist Church, harmony with the stated positions of the World Council of Churches is virtually impossible.[23]

Yet, Ellen White emphasized unity in the Christian body probably as much as any other theme. Her ecclesiology (understanding of the church) traces God's "church" through the Old and New Testaments, extending through the centuries until the return of Jesus. The church is "God's fortress" that has existed "from the beginning" with "faithful souls . . . in every age."[24] For her, church membership on earth is not automatically equated with being enrolled in the "Lamb's book of life. They may be joined to the church [a denomination], but they are not united to the Lord."[25]

Mrs. White's frequent appeals for unity among Christians are primarily addressed to fellow church members whom she believes were called into existence "to restore the principles that are the foundation of the kingdom of God."[26] In the context of the nineteenth century she appealed to fellow Adventists: "If there was ever a time when the people of God should press together, it is now. God has committed to us the special truths for this time, to make known to the world. . . . We cannot afford now to give place to Satan by cherishing disunion, discord, and strife. . . . Divisions in the church dishonor the religion of Christ before the world, and give occasion to the enemies of truth to justify their course. . . . What are we doing to preserve unity in the bonds of peace?"[27]

What does she mean when she pleads for unity within the church? First, she saw the unity of love in an international church as a magnificent witness to Christ's prayer for unity in John 17.[28] This same sentiment governs her solemn concern for unity among "different nationalities"[29] and among different races.[30]

Further, she urged that Seventh-day Adventist ministers should "come near to the ministers of other denominations. Pray for and with these men, for whom Christ is interceding. . . . As Christ's messengers, we should manifest a deep, earnest interest in these shepherds of the flock."[31]

But underlying her unrelenting emphasis on unity as it fulfills Christ's prayer in John 17 is this simple concept: Truth must not be sacrificed to achieve unity. After quoting Christ's prayer that through the unity of His people the world may be drawn to Him, she wrote: "While we are not to sacrifice one principle of truth, it should be our constant aim to reach this state of unity."[32]

Promoter for Helping the Disadvantaged

With great emphasis for more than seven decades Ellen White provided the church with a vast reservoir of tender and specific instruction regarding the

Christian's responsibility to the sick, to the physically impaired, and to the economically disadvantaged. Her written counsel reflected her personal practice.

Her diaries are full of concern for the poor and suffering. For example, her diary for 1859, when she was a 31-year-old mother with three active boys, contains not only references to her many letters but also many jottings as to what she did with her family, etc: "January 2—Gave Sister Irving a warm cloak and dress and a few other things to make over for her." "January 3—Paid Sister Bognes $1.00 for making a coat. She was unwilling to take it, but I felt it duty to hand it to her. She is poor and sickly. May the Lord pity and care for her. Said Jesus, 'The poor always ye have with you.' May the Lord rid us of selfishness and help us to care for others' woes and relieve them." "January 6—Gave Agnes a half-worn dress for her mother. They are poor. The husband and father is sick. Their crops have failed. Have breadstuff to buy and nothing to buy with. Agnes is their main support. She is only seventeen. There are four children now at home. They must suffer unless the church interests themselves in their behalf. May the Lord have mercy upon the needy, and put it in His children's hearts to dispense to them with a liberal hand." On and on the diaries go through the years.[33]

Her personal example added power to her words as she enlisted others in welfare ministry. In 1860 she wrote the following lines in the church paper: "The treasury in the Poor Fund, consisting of clothes, et cetera, for those in need, is nearly exhausted. And as there are cases of destitution continually arising, and one new one has arisen recently, I thought it would be well for those who have clothing, bedding, or money to spare to send it on here immediately. We hope there will be no delay, for we are going to assist some that are needy as soon as we get things together. Send your donations to Sr. Uriah Smith or myself."[34]

The dignity of the person being helped always was considered. Ellen White made it clear that used clothing was most appropriate to give to the needy only if it were suitable to be worn without embarrassment: "Some of our people say to me, 'Give away your old clothes, and that will help the poor.' Should I give away the garments that I patch and enlarge, the people would not be able to see anything of which they could make use. I buy for them new, strong, durable material. I have visited the factories where they make tweed cloth and have bought a number of remnants that perhaps have a flaw but can be purchased cheap, and will do some good to those to whom we give. I can afford to wear the old garments until they are beyond repair. I have purchased your uncle excellent cloth for pants and vests, and he is now supplied with good respectable clothing. In this way I can supply large families of children with durable garments."[35]

Throughout Ellen White's diary or letter files are requests to someone, on behalf of others, such as this needy student: "Will you please inquire of Brother _______ in regard to the clothing that he requires, and what he needs please furnish to him, and charge the same to my account."[36]

Of course, Ellen White realized that her family and a few others could not provide for all the desperate needs of those around her, including the needy in the church. While in Australia, she organized a "Dorcas Society" to relieve to some extent the burden that she carried for the disadvantaged. She wrote of one meeting of the Society that met in her home: "Last evening we had a Dorcas Society in our home, and my workers who help in the preparation of my articles for the papers and do the cooking and sewing, five of them, sat up until midnight, cutting out clothing. They made three pairs of pants for the children of one family. Two sewing machines were running until midnight. I think there was never a happier set of workers than were these girls last evening."[37]

In her own home, which often was filled with sick relatives and co-workers, the Whites worked in "medical missionary lines." They took in the sick who had been given up by the physicians, and had many recoveries under the "mighty Healer": "We used the simple water treatments, and then tried to fasten the eyes of the patients on the great Healer."[38]

As a general pattern of life, Ellen White would give ample sums to those who needed financial help. At times she would encourage others to "match" her gifts. She often made clear that in the main she gave for the purpose of helping the needy to become self-sufficient. One such occasion occurred in 1889 when she asked C. H. Jones to "match" her $100 to help Nellie L., a struggling widow with three children, who was trying to educate herself to do kindergarten work so "that she may keep her children with her." She wrote: "I will help Nellie one hundred dollars if you will do the same. . . .Will you encourage others to help her to get a start in life? It would be far better to do this than to wait and let Nellie be worn out with anxiety and care and fall in the struggle, leaving her children helpless, motherless, to be cared for by others. . . . I know she will struggle with all her powers to be self-supporting."[39]

Removing Prejudice

In developing the work in Australia, when Adventists were numbered only in the hundreds, Ellen White showed how prejudice would be broken down "by the medical missionary work": "We made a hospital of our home. My nurse [Sara McEnterfer, Mrs. White's personal secretary] treated successfully some most difficult cases that the physicians had pronounced incurable. This labor was not without its reward. Suspicion and prejudice were removed. The hearts of the people were won, and many accepted the truth."[40]

Through the years Mrs. White gave specific instruction regarding how individuals, and, at times, the church as a body, should care for the "unfortunate, the blind, the lame, the afflicted, the widows, the orphans, and the needy." She said that Christians who have pity on those people are represented by Christ "as commandment keepers, who shall have eternal life."[41]

But she kept this ministry to the unfortunate in perspective. She was insistent that struggling church members should not be overlooked in "the wholesale business of feeding the wretched class who are in poverty": "If you knew the circumstances of this brother, and did not make earnest efforts to relieve him, and change his oppression to freedom, you are not working the works of Christ, and are guilty before God. I write plainly, for, from the light given me of God, there is a class of work that is neglected." She called it "misdirected zeal" to pass by those in "the household of faith and let their cry of distress come up to God because of suffering which we might alleviate."[42]

Ellen White was specific regarding the Christian's responsibility to widows with children,[43] to orphans and foster parents,[44] to the aged,[45] and to the blind.[46]

In the 1890s, Dr. Kellogg was reaching out to the social outcasts in Chicago. Ellen White had joined him through the years on similar projects. In 1898, however, she wrote him seventeen letters, many of them concerning the unbalanced focus in the welfare missions that the Medical Missionary and Benevolent Association was sponsoring "in a dozen large American cities scattered from New York to San Francisco."[47] "Constant work is to be done for the outcasts, but this work is not to be made all-absorbing. . . . All the means must not be bound up in the work, for the highways have not yet received the message. . . . No one should now visit our churches, and claim from them means to sustain the work of rescuing outcasts. The means to sustain that work should come . . . from those not of our faith."[48]

Though Ellen White continually held up the challenge of taking the gospel to those "however fallen, however dishonored and debased,"[49] she clearly strove for perspective: "The Lord has marked out our way of working. As a people we are not to imitate and fall in with Salvation Army methods. This is not the work that the Lord has given us to do. Neither is it our work to condemn them and speak harsh words against them. There are precious, self-sacrificing souls in the Salvation Army. . . . The Salvation Army workers are trying to save the neglected, downtrodden ones. Discourage them not. Let them do that class of work by their own methods and in their own way. But the Lord has plainly pointed out the work that Seventh-day Adventists are to do."[50]

These cautions were aimed at the misdirection of city mission work; it needed correction, not dismantling. Ellen White was most explicit regarding the work to be done in the cities, strongly supporting the evangelistic centers with their restaurants, literature distribution centers, and, in some cases, lodging for the workers involved in the centers.[51]

Whenever her counsel was heeded, "Seventh-day Adventist urban involvement maintained equilibrium. It was not trapped in the social gospel movement (bottom-heavy with humanitarianism) developing in this period; but neither was it like the conservative Evangelicalism (top-heavy with evangelism) that developed after World War I."[52]

Endnotes

1. *Testimonies to Ministers*, p. 198.
2. *Bio.*, vol. 1, pp. 387-393. The Biblical argument was based primarily on the New Testament call for gospel order; at that time they were not sure how to detach the tithing plan from the ceremonial laws that were done away at the cross. The tithing "principle" was considered operative and had much to do with their final conclusions. The concept of "systematic benevolence" was made practical with the following suggestions: (1) Men 18-60 should give 5 to 25 cents weekly; (2) Women from 18-60, 2 to 10 cents weekly; (3) In addition, all should "lay aside" weekly 1 to 5 cents "on each and every $100 of property they possess."
3. *Testimonies,* vol. 1, p. 190. The plan was known for many years as "Sister Betsy."
4. *Ibid.*, pp. 220-223.
5. *Testimonies,* vol. 9, p. 249.
6. *Evangelism,* p. 492; *Testimonies,* vol. 6, p. 215; *MR* vol. 1, pp. 189, 192; *Medical Ministry,* p. 245.
7. *North American Division Statistical Report*, Fourth Quarter, 1996.
8. *Testimonies to Ministers*, pp. 197-203.
9. Roger Coon led the author to think of the first five principles through his unpublished manuscript, "Ellen White and the Issue of the Reception of State Aid."
10. *Testimonies to Ministers*, pp. 200, 201.
11. *Ibid.*, pp. 201, 202.
12. *Ibid.*, p. 202.
13. *Ibid.*
14. *Ibid.*, pp. 200, 201.
15. *Ibid.*, p. 203.
16. *Ibid.*, pp. 197.
17. *Ibid.*, p. 198.
18. *Ibid.*, pp. 197, 203.
19. *Ibid.*, p. 201.
20. *Ibid.*
21. For many years, the Seventh-day Adventist Church has sent reporters and, later, observers who have participated in various study committees sponsored by the World Council. As individuals, a few Adventists also have served as members of committees.
22. *The Great Controversy,* p. 390.
23. For an overview of Ellen White's influence on the Adventist church's approaches to ecumenism, see Graham, *Ellen G. White, Co-founder,* pp. 297-354.
24. *The Acts of the Apostles,* p. 11; "All of God's people upon the earth are one body, from the beginning to the end of time. They have one Head that directs and governs the body."—*Testimonies,* vol. 1, p. 283.
25. *Review and Herald,* Jan. 17, 1893, p. 33.
26. *Prophets and Kings,* pp. 677, 678.
27. *Testimonies,* vol. 5, pp. 236-239; see also *Ibid.*, pp. 179-183; *Selected Messages,* book 2, pp. 158-161.
28. *Testimonies,* vol. 9, p. 188.
29. *Ibid.*, p. 181.
30. *Review and Herald,* Dec. 17, 1895; *Ibid.*, Oct. 24, 1899; *Testimonies,* vol. 9, p. 209.
31. *Testimonies,* vol. 6, p. 78; *Evangelism,* pp. 143, 144, 562.
32. *Patriarchs and Prophets,* p. 520. Compromise of truth for the sake of unity must be avoided: "One object must be kept in view constantly; that is, harmony and cooperation must be maintained without compromising one principle of truth."—Letter 37, 1887, cited in *Counsels to Writers and Editors,* p. 79; see also *The Great Controversy,* p. 45.
33. *Welfare Ministry,* pp. 322, 323.
34. *Review and Herald*, Oct. 30, 1860, p. 192.
35. Letter 89a, 1894, cited in *Welfare Ministry,* pp. 328, 329.
36. *Ibid.*, p. 329.
37. *Ibid.*, p. 334.

38. *Ibid.*, p. 326, 327.
39. *Ibid.*, p. 327. Frequently Ellen White emphasized that the goal in helping others is to assist them in becoming self-reliant. See *Testimonies*, vol. 1, pp. 480, 481; *Ibid.*, vol. 6, pp. 188, 189, 278, 279; *The Ministry of Healing*, pp. 183-195; *Historical Sketches*, p. 293; *Review and Herald*, April 18, 1871; Jan. 3, 1899.
40. *Ibid.*, pp. 327, 328.
41. *Testimonies*, vol. 3, p. 512.
42. *Welfare Ministry*, pp. 210, 211; see also *Testimonies*, vol. 2, pp. 27-29; vol. 3, pp. 517, 518.
43. *Ibid.*, pp. 214-219.
44. *Ibid.*, pp. 220-231.
45. *Ibid.*, pp. 237, 238.
46. *Ibid.*, pp. 239-242.
47. Schwarz, *Light Bearers*, p. 208.
48. Letter 138, 1898, cited in *Bio.*, vol. 4, p. 397.
49. *Welfare Ministry*, p. 246.
50. *Testimonies*, vol. 8, pp. 184, 185. Cautions concerning glamorizing slum work, and the danger to young men and women who become involved with working with the socially marginalized are found in *Welfare Ministry*, pp. 253-255. Jonathan Butler lists four reasons for Ellen White's alarm and sharp counsel to Dr. Kellogg. The Chicago program, especially, was (1) "overcentralized in relation to missions work in the world field"; (2) "was overspecialized in its service for one class of people"; (3) "threatened imbalance with one kind of ministry—medical ministry"; (4) and "lacked church distinctiveness."—"Ellen G. White and the Chicago Mission," *Spectrum*, Winter 1970, pp. 41-51.
51. *Testimonies*, vol. 5, pp. 368-385; vol. 7, pp. 37-39, 95-98, 110-114; vol. 9, pp. 89-149; *Counsels on Health*, pp. 493, 494, 554-556; *Medical Ministry*, p. 303; *Review and Herald*, Jan. 18, 1912.
52. Butler, "Chicago Mission," *Spectrum*, Winter, 1970, p. 49.

Study Questions

1. What six principles should guide Adventists when relating to government aid?

2. How do you explain the principles involved in systematic benevolence?

3. How do you defend the concept that Seventh-day Adventists are truly ecumenical?

4. How did Ellen White set an example in welfare work?

5. What principles guided Ellen White in her personal humanitarian program?

6. What are the advantages of an active welfare program in a local church? What guidelines would determine the distribution of cash and goods? List worthwhile goals of welfare work.

7. Review Ellen White's counsel to Dr. Kellogg regarding his Chicago mission. Discuss her view that our work is not to parallel the good work done by the Salvation Army.

CHAPTER 21

Dissidents, Within and Without

"When Simon saw that through the laying on of the apostles' hands the Holy Spirit was given, he offered them money, saying 'Give me this power also, that anyone on whom I lay hands may receive the Holy Spirit.' But Peter said to him, 'Your money perish with you . . . Your heart is not right in the sight of God. Repent therefore'" (Acts 8:18, 19, 20-22).

Dealing with motives is a thankless task, even for a prophet. Most often in church-related activities a conflict of motives arises either over the misuse of power or over the allocation of funds. The Battle Creek situation in the 1890s provides a textbook case for dealing with both problem areas.

Denominational debt had increased dramatically due to the rapid expansion of the sanitarium, the college, and the publishing house. Further, the development of Dr. Kellogg's enterprises, including the medical school, the orphanage, and an old people's home, drew heavily on Adventist resources.

Leaders With Secular Motives

Down under in Australia, in 1896, Ellen White was appalled by the overcentralization of power and the huge increase of debt that all this expansion reflected. For her, adding building to building did not give the right "character to the work." What was needed was not more power and buildings in Battle Creek but for church leaders to realize that "their own characters needed the transforming grace of Christ,"[1] which would enable them to represent Christ. Two leaders, A. R. Henry, treasurer of the Review and Herald Publishing Association, and Harmon Lindsay, treasurer of the General Conference, were her chief concern. Both were highly influential in making denominational decisions.

Henry, a banker before he became a Seventh-day Adventist, was invited to Battle Creek in 1882 to assist in the development of the publishing house. In 1883 he also was asked to be the treasurer of the General Conference, a post he held until 1888 when Lindsay became treasurer. Simultaneously during this period, in addition to these two major responsibilities, Henry was a member of the governing boards of nearly all the denomination's medical and educational institutions in the central and western states.[2]

Lindsay, though shrewd in business matters, had a less forceful personality than Henry. O. A. Olsen, General Conference president, described him as one who "says but little openly but mutters a great deal." However, he had been treasurer of the General Conference as early as 1874-1875. His unbroken years of involvement in developing both the sanitarium and the college, as well as control of denominational finances while other General Conference personnel came and went, gave him an understandable reason for sensing his power.[3]

When new presidents assumed office, it was only natural for them to turn to the "experienced" treasurers for counsel. Elder Olsen, a forbearing, gentle spirit, tried to alleviate the "unChristian speeches" and hard bargaining that characterized denominational business. Not until some very forceful statements from Ellen White arrived did he separate himself from Henry and Lindsay and call other men to take their places. Many letters to Olsen from Mrs. White in Australia emphasized and warned against the secular principles that dominated the business affairs in Battle Creek institutions. She wrote: "I fear and tremble for the souls of men who are in responsible places in Battle Creek. . . . If their works had no further influence than simply upon themselves, I could breathe more freely; but I know that the enemy is using men who are in positions of trust, and who are not consecrated to the work and who know not what manner of spirit they are of. When I realize that men who are connected with them are also in blindness, and will not see the harm that is being done by the precept and example of these unconsecrated agents, it seems to me that I cannot hold my peace. I have to write, for I know that the mold that these men are giving to the work is not after God's order."[4]

Although Ellen White's sympathies were with Elder Olsen, she did not spare words: "I felt that you were being bound hand and foot, and were tamely submitting to it." Because God was illuminating her mind, she saw what others could not see clearly: "Things are being swayed in wrong lines." She saw, behind the surface reasonings, that leading men were acting "as though they were in God's place, . . . deal[ing] with their fellow men as if they were machines. I cannot respect their wisdom or have faith in their Christianity."

Then, writing specifically: "The Lord has presented to me his [Henry's] dangers. I expect nothing else but he will say, as he has always done, 'Somebody has been telling Sister White.' This shows that he has no faith in my mission or testimony, and yet Brother Olsen has made him his right-hand man."[5]

In 1896 Elder Olsen made a serious effort to change the widespread secularism prevailing among Adventist workers in Battle Creek. In the publishing house were A. R. Henry, Clement Eldridge, and Frank Belden, and others who pressed their secular ideas. Along with the secularism, Olsen was "exercised" over the "disbelief, skepticism, and indifference that are manifested by our people with reference to the gift of prophecy."[6]

Swayed in Wrong Lines

Some of the particular matters that were "swayed in wrong lines" were the disproportionate salaries being paid to publishing house executives (and more being sought), the persistent refusal to provide merit increases to workers, the feeling of mistrust between workers and management over piecework rates, failure to maintain a systematic training program for apprentices, failure to advance persons within the organization, the appointment of supervisors without spiritual qualifications, failure to conduct evangelistic work among the substantial number of non-Adventist workers, the reluctance to reduce the amount of commercial work or even monitor the offensive jobs, and failure to provide sanitary premises.[7]

One other important example of the two-faced, high-handed actions of the publishing house's executives was their relationship to authors. Ellen White was specific: "In the past, publishers have placed themselves as God, to dictate, to control, to manage as they pleased, and to lord it over God's heritage. They have done a deceptive work in dealing with authors. I have been taken into private councils, and have heard the plans laid down. Men have managed to make an author believe that his work is naught, and that they do not want to have anything to do with the book. The author has no means. He feels that his hands are tied. Men talk and think over the whole process, and succeed in bringing him to their terms, to take the royalty that they offer on the book.

"The dealing with Frank Belden was not true and righteous in all its points. Justice was not done to him. The effort made to grind down Brother Bell and to obtain possession of books, has made a most miserable showing, driving him to an opposite extreme. Men's brains have been bought and sold."[8]

Mrs. White counseled: "Let not authors be urged to either give away or to sell their right to the books they have written. Let them receive a just share of the profits of their work; then let them regard their means as a trust from God, to be administered according to the wisdom that He shall impart."[9]

Her counsel regarding sound business principles that reflect the Christlike pattern have become a rich reservoir for Seventh-day Adventists. The difference between the Christlike spirit and the secular, selfish spirit is clearly delineated in her writings.[10]

Clear Response to Dissidents

Case and Russell. In 1853 H. S. Case and C. P. Russell, the first dissenters to arise from the emerging Seventh-day Adventist Church (seven years before the first local conference was organized in Michigan, 1861), made two charges against the Whites: (1) that they were getting rich off the church paper, and (2) that Ellen White was being placed above the Bible. Offended at Mrs. White's counsel directed at them, they launched a new paper, *Messenger of Truth,* in 1854, to supplant the *Review and Herald.* In that paper they printed their allegations against Mrs. White's reliability. They also charged James with using donations for private enterprises and for profiting on church members because he sold Bibles at a higher price than he had paid for them (after buying them wholesale and having them shipped from New York City!). Case and Russell were soon joined by other critical church members.

In June of 1855, Ellen White had a public vision in Oswego, New York. She told members at the meeting that they should no longer be distracted by the *Messenger* party, that soon the dissidents would be fighting among themselves, and that in a short while our own membership would double.[11]

Stephenson and Hall. Concurrent with the *Messenger* party in Michigan, another dissident group was developing in Wisconsin under the leadership of J. M. Stephenson and D. P. Hall, former ministers of the Millerite Movement. These two men had revived a doctrinal position held by some Millerites that Christ, at His second advent, would reign for a thousand years on earth, during which time probation would continue while the Jews played a leading role in the conversion of the nations.

Because James White would not print their views in the church paper, Stephenson and Hall allied themselves with the Michigan-based *Messenger* party in October, 1854—a great disappointment for James because he thought he had their confidence. In November 1855, at the first conference held in Battle Creek, Michigan after the move from Rochester, New York, Mrs. White had a vision that encouraged those who were troubled by the Age-to-Come group led by Stephenson and Hall. In that vision she revealed how these two men had earlier been convinced of the integrity of her visions, but on further examination they discovered that their Age-to-Come theology did not agree with certain visions. She saw behind their "smooth" words and their deception. Her advice to the growing church: "The church of God should move straight along, as though there were not such a people in the world."[12]

What happened to these dissenters? By 1858, after internal arguments, all had gone their separate ways. Stephenson adopted further strange doctrines, involved himself in "an unsavory divorce," and ended up in the "poorhouse," an imbecile at death. Hall went into real estate investments and eventual bankruptcy that terminated in insanity.[13]

Moses Hull. The tragic case of Moses Hull reveals how kindly warnings given by Ellen White can be disregarded only to one's hurt. Hull joined the church in 1858, and soon became an influential Adventist preacher, often appearing in the general councils of the church. But within a few weeks after preaching an evangelistic sermon on September 20, 1863, he joined the Spiritualists. What happened?

For two years prior to his defection, Ellen White had been warning him regarding his selfishness, covetousness, lack of management skills, and overweening trust in his own abilities.[14] In 1862 he had been debating publicly with Spiritualists, enjoying his success as he turned some of his hearers into espousing Christianity. But on one occasion, with no Adventists to accompany him, he debated in Paw Paw, Michigan, a strong Spiritualist center. Overconfident of his own ability, he soon found (in his own words) his "tongue . . . seemingly as thick as my hand, and what I had often used before as an argument seemed to me like nonsense. I was defeated."[15]

Two weeks later, November 5, 1862, Hull sensed his problem and asked for the Whites and M. E. Cornell to come to his Battle Creek home to pray for him. During the prayer session, Ellen White was given a vision. Of it she wrote: "I was shown the condition of Bro. Hull. He was in an alarming state. His lack of consecration and vital piety left him subject to Satan's suggestions. . . . He is asleep to his own danger. . . . He was presented to me as standing upon the brink of an awful gulf, ready to leap. If he takes the leap, it will be final; his eternal destiny will be fixed. . . . Never should one man be sent forth alone to combat with a Spiritualist."[16]

The Whites then took Hull with them on a preaching circuit in Michigan, hoping that close companionship would help him throw off his bondage.

On June 6, 1863, Ellen White sent another message to Moses Hull. She analyzed part of his problem: "When you should be studying your own heart, you are engaged in reading books. When you should by faith be drawing near to Christ, you are studying books. I saw that all your study will be useless unless you faithfully study yourself. . . . You lack sobriety and gravity out of the pulpit. . . .When treating upon the most solemn subjects, you often bring in something comical to create a smile, and this frequently destroys the force of your whole discourse. . . . Be not flattered by remarks which unwise and foolish brethren may make concerning your efforts. If they praise your preaching, let it not elate you."[17]

But three months later, Hull did leap into that "awful gulf." He became a lecturer and writer for the Spiritualists.[18]

Stanton in Montana. While Ellen White was in Australia, A. W. Stanton, a worried Montana layman, published a compilation of Mrs. White's statements that seemed to support his position that the Adventist Church had apostatized and become Babylon. He concluded that it was time to stop supporting the organized church financially and to "come out of her."[19]

Further, Stanton had sent an intermediary to Ellen White in Australia, hoping to enlist her support. He could have saved his money, because she had already written her comments to Stanton on March 23, 1893. Her review of the Biblical teaching regarding what John the Revelator meant by "Babylon" was simple and cogent. Forthrightly, she wrote: "If you are teaching that the Seventh-day Adventist Church is Babylon, you are wrong. God has not given you any such message to bear. . . . I presume that some may be deceived by your message, because they are full of curiosity and desire for some new thing."[20]

In addition, she wrote four articles for

the *Review* entitled, "The Remnant Church Not Babylon." These were later republished in *Testimonies to Ministers.*[21]

In this series of articles Mrs. White made clear her distress with those who took selections from her writings, making them appear to endorse the particular position of the compiler. She wrote: "Through making unwarrantable liberties, they have presented to the people a theory that is of a character to deceive and destroy. In times past many others have done this same thing, and have made it appear that the Testimonies sustained positions that were untenable and false." (See hermeneutical principles, pp. 389-391.)

Then she reminded her fellow church members: "There are matters in the Testimonies that are written, not for the world at large, but for the believing children of God." (See pp. 176, 177.)

She agreed that evils exist in the church and will continue until the end, yet "the church in these last days is to be the light of the world that is polluted and demoralized by sin. The church, enfeebled and defective, needing to be reproved, warned, and counseled, is the only object upon earth upon which Christ bestows His supreme regard."[22]

Ellen White's published counsel stopped the movement about as fast as it had developed. Earlier, in the late 1880s, she had analyzed the anatomy of apostasy and Satan's strategies:

- "He works upon minds to excite jealousy and dissatisfaction toward those at the head of the work,
- "The gifts are next questioned; then, of course, they have but little weight, and instruction given through vision is disregarded,
- "Next follows skepticism in regard to the vital points of our faith, the pillars of our position,
- "Then doubt as to the Holy Scriptures, and
- "Then the downward march to perdition."

Mrs. White continued her probe: "When the Testimonies which were once believed, are doubted and given up, Satan knows the deceived ones will not stop at this; and he redoubles his efforts till he launches them into open rebellion, which becomes incurable, and ends in destruction."[23]

The Voice—Not Always Welcome

It would be rewriting history to assert that Ellen White's detractors were only the dissidents, the charismatic leaders who revived once-forsaken theological errors, or the preachers in the popular churches. Counsel, and, at times, reproof, are not always welcome, no matter to whom given. If she had offered praise only, she would have been acclaimed as the bearer of singular good judgment. But she shared the burden of Scripture's genuine prophets.

From the earliest days of her prophetic ministry she had to contend with strong-willed men and women whose self-centered motives and unBiblical views needed to be exposed.[24]

In 1869, Ellen White at 41 again had to contend with slander, rumor, and disinformation. Looking back after the camp meeting itineraries, she wrote: "The lies of sheer malice and enmity, the pure fabrication of iniquity uttered and circulated to defeat the proclamation of truth, were powerless to affect the minds of those who were really desirous to know what is truth. I did not doubt for a moment but the Lord had sent me that the honest souls who had been deceived might have an opportunity to see and hear for themselves what manner of spirit the woman possessed who had been presented to the public in such a false light in order to make the truth of God of none effect."

In that letter she emphasized a point that is always relevant: "None are compelled to believe. God gives sufficient evidence that all may decide upon the weight of evidence, but He never has nor never will remove all chance [opportunity] for doubt, never will force faith."[25]

Later, in October 1869, the malicious attacks were so prominent that a leadership committee of J. N. Andrews, G. H. Bell, and Uriah Smith was appointed to investigate the charges leveled against James and Ellen White. The committee called for all the evidence that could be gathered that would substantiate the allegations.

Following the committee's open invitation a few weeks later, the Whites also requested on the back page of the *Review*: "Will those who know of things in the general course of Mrs. White and myself, during the period of our public labors, worthy of exposure, or unworthy of Christians, and teachers of the people, be so kind as to make them known to the office immediately."[26]

On April 26, 1870, the report in pamphlet form was ready for distribution. Church members everywhere now had in their hands the evidence proving that the slanders, rumors, and disinformation were without foundation. The report was not challenged.

In the *Review*, beginning at the end of 1869 and running well into 1870, James White wrote twenty-five front-page articles on "Our Faith and Hope, or Reasons Why We Believe as We Do." J. N. Andrews, then *Review* editor, followed with an editorial of twenty propositions regarding the use of Ellen White's visions.

Of using Ellen White's writings as a "test," Andrews penned: "There is such a thing . . . as men having in the providence of God an opportunity to become acquainted with the special work of the Spirit of God, so that they shall acknowledge that their light is clear, convincing, and satisfactory. To such persons, we consider the gifts of the Spirit are clearly a test."[27]

In 1880 *Testimony* No. 29 was published.[28] Much of the counsel was directed at the developing Adventist "ghetto" in Battle Creek. Some of the Battle Creek church members, not ready for the reproofs and challenge, turned to the local newspapers to express their feelings. The editors of the newspapers in Battle Creek, as well as in Lansing, Chicago, and Detroit, along with the citizens of Battle Creek, were also able to read Ellen White's searching messages. And newspapers love conflict.

Uriah Smith asked the Battle Creek *Journal* for the courtesy of printing a rejoinder, which was granted, exposing some of the lies. A few days later, correspondent Henry Willis wrote in the *Journal:* "I would that all other religious beliefs in Battle Creek were as true to morality as Mrs. White and her adherents. Then we would have no infamous dens of vice, no grogshops, no tobacco stores, no gambling hells, no air polluted with the fumes of rum and that fell deadly destroyer of man, tobacco."[29]

In 1883, noting that Uriah Smith and others seemed cool to her work, Ellen White asked for a meeting with the publishing house employees.[30]

Later she reported, in part, her remarks made at that August 20 meeting: "The most extravagant, inconsistent reports in regard to my position, my work, and my writings will be put in circulation. But those who have had an experience in this message, and have become acquainted with the character of my work, will not be affected by those things unless they themselves backslide from God, and become corrupted by the spirit of the world. Some will be deceived because of their own unfaithfulness. They want to believe a lie. Some have betrayed sacred, important trusts, and this is why they wander in the mazes of doubt. . . . There are some, even connected with our institutions, who are in great danger of making shipwreck of faith. Satan will work in disguise, in his most deceptive manner, in these branches of God's work. . . .

"For forty years, Satan has made the most determined efforts to cut off this testimony from the church; but it has continued from year to year to warn the erring, to unmask the deceiver, to encourage the desponding. My trust is in God."[31]

Ellen White's Counsels and Appeals to D. M. Canright

Ellen White's experience with D. M. Canright illustrates well her concern for people as well as the sad result when they rejected her counsel. Both of the Whites recognized early Canright's above average qualifications for the ministry. He soon became an outstanding evangelist and debater. But he was often discouraged and required close personal labors from the Whites and other leaders to keep focused.[32]

In 1882 Canright gave up preaching and went to farming. In a letter to a friend in 1884 he said that he no longer had confidence in the visions of Ellen White. "I have no feelings against any of them [leading church workers], excepting Mrs. White. I dislike her very much indeed. . . . But they are good men for all that, and I never shall willingly oppose them."[33]

Responding to the urging of his friends, Canright attended the Jackson, Michigan, camp meeting in September, 1884. Here he once again confessed his error before a thousand people, declaring that the clouds of darkness had rolled away. He humbly sought Ellen White's forgiveness. In the October 7, 1884, *Review,* he published the whole story that led up to his rejection of Ellen White, reciting one testimony after another that he thought too severe or inaccurate. But now his mind had changed. He wrote: "I want to say to all my friends everywhere, that now I not only accept, but believe the testimonies to be from God. Knowing the opposition I have felt to them, this change in my feelings is more amazing to myself than it can be to others."[34]

During 1885 and the early months of 1886, almost every issue of the church paper had strong, cogent articles by Canright. His article, "To Those in Doubting Castle," was perhaps his strongest as he went over his own experience, driving in stake after stake with the evidences for the doctrines of the Adventist Church and the validity of Ellen White's ministry.[35] He spent the summer in aggressive evangelism, he wrote friendly letters to Mrs. White in Europe, and was well thought of throughout the denomination.

However, key leaders knew his weaknesses as well as his strengths. When G. I. Butler, not Canright, was elected president of the Michigan Conference in 1886, Canright apparently made his next decision. In January 1887 he advised Butler that he no longer would be a Seventh-day Adventist. By March, now preaching for the Baptists, he began his campaign to recant all of his many confessions and affirmations for the Adventist faith that he had made time after time for years.[36] Canright could not take counsel. The voice of the Lord through His messenger was not welcome, though often publicly affirmed.

Spurned in 1888

Earlier, we noted that Ellen White was spurned by many at the 1888 General Conference in Minneapolis.[37] Her appeal to lift eyes higher than the legalism that so many had unconsciously slipped into fell on many deaf ears. A few days after the conference she wrote: "I have not had a very easy time since I left the Pacific Coast. Our first meeting was not like any other General Conference I ever attended. . . . My testimony was ignored, and never in my life experience was I treated as at the [1888] conference."[38]

In 1890 she penned: "Brethren, you are urging me to come to your camp meetings. I must tell you plainly that the course pursued toward me and my work since the General Conference at Minneapolis—your resistance of the light and warnings that God has given through me—has made my labor fifty times harder than it would otherwise have. . . . It seems to me that you have cast aside the word of the Lord as unworthy of your notice. . . . My experience since the conference at Minneapolis has not been very assuring. I have asked the Lord for wisdom daily, and that I may not be utterly disheartened, and go down to the grave brokenhearted as did my husband."[39]

Though unwelcome in Minneapolis, Ellen White remained undaunted. Her writings in the 1890s drilled into the church, to whoever would listen, the voice of God making clear the fullness of the everlasting gospel (Rev. 14:6, 7).[40]

We can now see what lay behind the leadership's strong desire for Ellen White to leave America for Australia. The earthquake aftershocks into the 1890s prompted by her strong support of A. T. Jones and E. J. Waggoner, her equally strong disapproval of attitudes among many church leaders, plus the deep insights and clear messages involving the policies of the financial men running the General Conference and the publishing house, had much to do with the "urging" that she be sent to Australia.

In 1896 she wrote to the General Conference president: "The Lord was not in our leaving America. He did not reveal that it was His will that I should leave Battle Creek. The Lord did not plan this, but He let you all move after your own imaginings. . . . We were needed at the heart of the work, and had your spiritual perception discerned the true situation, you would never have consented to the movements made. But the Lord read the hearts of all. There was so great a willingness to have us leave, that the Lord permitted this thing to take place. Those who were weary of the testimonies borne were left without the persons who bore them. Our separation from Battle Creek was to let men have their own will and way, which they thought superior to the way of the Lord. . . . When the Lord presented this matter to me as it really was, I opened my lips to no one, because I knew that no one would discern the matter in all its bearings."[41]

Earlier she had written in her diary on August 5, 1891: "This morning my mind is anxious and troubled in regard to my duty. Can it be the will of God that I go to Australia? This involves a great deal with me. I have not special light to leave America for this *far-off country*. Nevertheless, if I knew it was the voice of God, I would go. But I cannot understand this matter. Some who are bearing responsibilities in America seem to be very persistent that my special work should be to go to Europe and to Australia."[42]

But go she did, setting a good example for all to follow in responding to the decisions of church leadership. As time went on, she discovered, as did Joseph, that "it was not you who sent me here, but God" (Gen. 45:8). In spite of not being welcomed by men at the heart of denominational leadership, once more Ellen White set her face like flint to duty.

But with each crisis, it seems that some forget the way they had been led in the past. For example, during the critical year 1903, when all Battle Creek—Adventists and the general public—were in consternation regarding proposals and plans to move the General Conference and the publishing house, Ellen White's counsel was unambiguous, as clear as the noon sun on a cloudless day: "Move!" But the chaplain of the Sanitarium, Lycurgus McCoy, led the multitude who resisted the moves. He did not think the denominational leadership had enough business acumen to make such heavy decisions. Further, though McCoy considered Ellen White sincere, he did not "believe that the Lord has spoken to her on this question, although she believes it."[43]

McCoy's faint praise has often been repeated through the years. Those who have faced challenges, thinking that each new occasion is "different" from past problems, may or may not have had time to see clearly the relevancy of Ellen White.

It is apparent from Biblical history that prophets do not hold an elective position; they are not "called" to their office by the group they are to serve. In a special way the prophet stands outside the bureaucratic or institutional door. Hebrew prophets understood this unique role, much to their distress at times. When the institutionalized church is confronted by the prophet, certain human dynamics are in motion that often treat the prophet as "unwelcome."

The prophet perceives the possible inhumanities of bureaucracy and the inherent rigidities and possible irregularities in institutionalism. For those within the institutional structure, the prophet is often perceived as exasperating with his/her vigorous challenges, searching counsel, or frank reproof. For those within who are motivated by other than the purest principles, the prophet is always unwelcome.

Throughout Ellen White's seventy-year ministry, many listened to her voice gladly. Her counsel proved self-authenticating. When the prophet's disturbing voice ruffled unconsecrated feelings, relatively few leaders and members found excuses to turn away. When church leaders listened to the voice, the Advent movement prospered.[44]

Endnotes

1. *Testimonies to Ministers,* p. 319.
2. *SDAE,* vol. 10, pp. 690, 691.
3. Schwarz, *Light Bearers,* p. 262.
4. Letter 59, 1895, cited in *Bio.,* vol. 4, pp. 253, 254.
5. *Ibid.,* p. 255.
6. Schwarz, *Light Bearers,* pp. 262, 263.
7. *Ibid.,* p. 263. See also *The Publishing Ministry,* pp. 114-178, 205-249.
8. Letter 43, 1899, cited in *The Publishing Ministry,* p. 232.
9. *Testimonies,* vol. 7, pp. 176-178. See also *The Publishing Ministry,* pp. 230-238.
10. *Testimonies to Ministers,* pp. 279-423, 457-484. In the *Comprehensive Index to the Writings of Ellen G. White,* vol. 1, pages 344-352 are devoted to an enormous amount of counsel on subjects such as management principles, necessary competencies required, entanglements, causes of failure, personal integrity, Christlike principles that should mold transactions, secular attitudes that mar Christian business management, and the danger of speculation.
11. Loughborough, *GSAM,* pp. 325, 326. In the Jan. 14, 1858, issue of the *Review and Herald,* the editor wrote in reference to the disbanded *Messenger* party: "At the time of the disaffection, when the effort was made to break down the *Review,* the church property at the office was valued at only $700. Since then it has increased to $5,000. Then there were about one thousand paying subscribers, now there are about two thousand, besides quite a free list."—See *Testimonies,* vol. 1, pp. 122-123; *Bio.,* vol. 1, pp. 306-310.
12. *Testimonies,* vol. 1, pp. 116-118.
13. Schwarz, *Light Bearers,* p. 446; *Bio.,* vol. 1, pp. 308-315.
14. *Testimonies,* vol. 1, pp. 411-442; vol. 2, p. 625; vol. 3, p. 212.
15. *Bio.,* vol. 2, p. 55.
16. *Testimonies,* vol. 1, pp. 426-430; see *Bio.,* vol. 2, pp. 56, 57.
17. *Testimonies,* vol. 1, pp. 435, 436.
18. *SDAE,* vol. 10, p. 718. See also James R. Nix, *The Life and Work of Moses Hull,* unpublished Seminary paper, 1971, 81 pp.
19. Schwarz, *Light Bearers,* p. 446.
20. The complete letter was printed in the *Review and Herald,* Sept. 12, 1893.
21. *Review and Herald,* Aug. 22, 29, Sept. 5, 12, 1893; *Testimonies to Ministers,* pp. 32-62.
22. *Testimonies to Ministers,* pp. 34, 49. See also pp. 176, 177.
23. *Testimonies,* vol. 5, p. 672. Here Ellen White recalls portions of testimonies first given in *Testimonies,* vol. 1, p. 236; vol. 3, p. 328; and vol. 4, p. 211. In the early 1880s, she wrote: "A prevailing skepticism is continually increasing in reference to the Testimonies of the Spirit of God; and these youth encourage questionings and doubts instead of removing them, because they are ignorant of the spirit and power and force of the Testimonies."—*Testimonies,* vol. 4, p. 437.
24. Note the 1851 conferences at Washington, NH; Bethel, VT; Johnson, VT, cited in *Bio.,* vol. 1, pp. 217-223.
25. Letter 12, 1869, cited in *Bio.,* vol. 2, p. 276.
26. *Ibid.,* pp. 277-279. In this same Jan. 11, 1870 issue, James White wrote: "The position and work of Mrs. White and myself, for more than twenty years, have exposed us to the jealousies of the jealous, the rage of the passionate, and the slanders of the slanderer. Having consciences void of offense toward God and toward men, we have kept at our work. But from our almost utter silence in the line of defense, accusers have grown impudent and bold, so that it has been thought best, for the good of the cause with which we hold so intimate connections, to meet their slanders with a plain statement of facts, which will probably appear in pamphlet form for very extensive circulation."
27. *Review and Herald,* Feb. 15, 1870. Proposition 14 stated: "The object of spiritual gifts is to maintain the living work of God in the church. They enable the Spirit of God to speak in the correction of wrongs, and in the exposure of iniquity. They are the means whereby God teaches His people when they are in danger of making wrong steps. They are the means by which the Spirit of God sheds light upon church difficulties, when otherwise their adjustment would be impossible. They also constitute the means whereby God preserves His people from confusion by

pointing out errors, by correcting false interpretations of the Scriptures, and causing light to shine out upon that which is in danger of being wrongly understood, and therefore of being the cause of evil and division to the people of God.

"In short, their work is to unite the people of God in the same mind and in the same judgment upon the meaning of the Scriptures. Mere human judgment, with no direct instruction from Heaven, can never search out hidden iniquity, nor adjust dark and complicated church difficulties, nor prevent different and conflicting interpretations of the Scriptures. It would be sad indeed if God could not still converse with His people."

28. *Testimonies,* vol. 4, pp. 384-522.
29. *Bio.,* vol. 3, pp. 130, 131. In a special message to the Battle Creek church, *Testimony for the Battle Creek Church,* July, 1881, p. 80, Ellen White wrote: "I have been shown there are unruly tongues among the church members at Battle Creek. There are false tongues that feed on mischief. There are sly, whispering tongues. There is tattling, impertinent meddling, adroit quizzing. Among the lovers of gossip, some are actuated by curiosity, others by jealousy, many by hatred against those through whom God has spoken to reprove them. All these discordant elements are at work. Some conceal their sentiments, while others are eager to publish all they know, or even suspect, of evil against another. I saw that the very spirit of perjury that would turn truth into falsehood, good into evil, and innocence into crime is now active, doing a work which savors of hell rather than of heaven. . . . All have defects of character, and it is not hard to find something that jealousy can interpret to his injury."—Cited in *Bio.,* vol. 3, p. 189.
30. Uriah Smith had taken sides in the Battle Creek College crisis against Goodloe Bell, the former head of the English Department at the college. See *Bio.,* vol. 3, p. 196. The deeper issue, however, was Uriah Smith's refusal to read a testimony that Ellen White had given him to read to the church during the college crisis. He withheld it for several weeks because he was not in agreement with her counsel. Learning of this attitude, she wrote another, more candid, letter to the Battle Creek church wherein she wrote that "you might say it was only a letter. Yes, it was a letter, but prompted by the Spirit of God, to bring before your minds things that had been shown me." —*Ibid.,* pp. 198-201.
31. *Review and Herald,* Oct. 16, 1883. Several weeks after that August 20 meeting, Uriah Smith reported in the church paper the activities of the autumn Michigan camp meeting. His account at that time showed that he had a definite change of mind and heart regarding Ellen White. See *Ibid.,* Oct. 9, 1883. In the *Review Extra* of Dec. 1887, Uriah Smith wrote an extended review of his period of doubt in 1883 regarding some aspects of Mrs. White's ministry. The full statement, entitled "The Weight of Evidence," may also be found in *Bio.,* vol. 3, pp. 493-496.
32. *Bio.,* vol. 2, pp. 455-456; vol. 3, pp. 152, 153.
33. Carrie Johnson, *I Was Canright's Secretary* (Washington, D.C.: Review and Herald Publishing Association, 1971), p. 65.
34. *Ibid.,* pp. 65-72; *Bio.,* vol. 3, pp. 263-267. Published testimonies to the Canrights appear in *Testimonies,* vol. 3, pp. 304-329 (1873); *Selected Messages,* book 2, pp. 162-170 (1880); *Testimonies,* vol. 5, pp. 516-520 (1886).
35. *Review and Herald,* Feb. 10, 1885.
36. Johnson, *I Was Canright's Secretary*, pp. 74-80.
37. See p. 195.
38. Letter 7, 1888, in *1888 Materials*, pp. 186-189.
39. Letter 1, 1890, in *1888 Materials,* pp. 659, 660, 664.
40. See p. 198.
41. Letter 127, 1896, in *1888 Materials,* pp. 1622, 1623.
42. *Bio.,* vol. 4, p. 15.
43. Schwarz, *Light Bearers,* p. 308.
44. General Conference president G. I. Butler lived through the growing pains of the young Seventh-day Adventist Church. He saw and heard the voice of God's messenger as she counseled, reproved, guided, and taught her contemporaries. Ellen White was not an historical footnote to Butler, she was a living voice who saw clearly when others stumbled. Out of a living experience with her and her testimonies, Butler wrote the following: "We have tested them as a people for nearly a quarter of a century, and we find we prosper spiritually when we heed them, and suffer a great loss when we neglect them. We have found their guidance to be our safety. They never have led us into fanaticism in a single instance, but they have ever rebuked fanatical and unreasonable men. . . . We admit that their influence upon Seventh-day Adventists during their past history has been weighty, but it has always been for good, and always had a tendency to make us a better people."—*Review and Herald*, June 9, 1874.

Study Questions

1. In what ways did Ellen White use the term "character" in describing the work in Battle Creek at the beginning of the twentieth century?
2. What is meant by "secular" leadership?
3. When people become acquainted with the writings of Ellen White, in what ways are the writings a test?
4. What are the personality features that characterized D. M. Canright in his leadership role as an Adventist minister? What was the flaw that motivated him during his various defections and final break with the church?
5. Who were some of the prominent dissidents of the nineteenth century? What were their chief complaints? Were these complaints justified? What happened to the defectors?
6. What is the basic problem in apostasy?

Who's Who in the Adventist World of Ellen G. White

(Photos arranged alphabetically)

ANDREWS, J. N. (1829-1883). *In 1874 he was sent as the first Seventh-day Adventist missionary to countries outside of North America. A capable theologian, he made significant contributions to the development of various doctrines of the church, including the time to begin and end the Sabbath. He was the third president of the General Conference (1867-1869).*

AVONDALE COLLEGE campus, near Cooranbong, Australia. *Covering 1,450 acres (585 hectares), the college was founded in 1897 as a result of Ellen White's insistence that Australia have an educational institution patterned according to the light given her in vision. This 1997 picture shows the Sanitarium Health Food Company next to Dora Creek, on the left. The College Church is to the right of the Ellen G. White Administration Building, near the center of the picture.*

BATES, Joseph (1792-1872). *Mariner, reformer, Advent preacher, he was one of the founders of the Seventh-day Adventist Church. As captain of a ship, he forbade the use of intoxicants and profanity. In 1839 he accepted William Miller's views on the Second Advent and became active in preaching. One of the first to accept the Sabbath truth, he wrote and circulated a pamphlet on the subject. He also was an early advocate of health reform, discontinuing the use of flesh foods, tea, and coffee.*

BATTLE CREEK SANITARIUM. 1866-1993. *Young Dr. J. H. Kellogg renamed the Health Reform Institute after becoming its superintendent in 1876. Under his dynamic leadership the Battle Creek Sanitarium became world famous. When the Adventist Church and Dr. Kellogg parted company in 1907, the sanitarium was lost to the denomination. Dr. Kellogg remained its medical director until his death in 1943.*

BELL, G. H. (1832-1899). *An educator and author, he taught at Battle Creek College, and later became principal of South Lancaster Academy. When the General Conference Sabbath School Association was formed in 1878, he was made the first recording secretary, and later the president.*

BOLTON, Frances (Fannie) E. Bolton (1859-1926). *Baptized when she was 28, she joined the staff of Ellen White in 1889. Though talented, she had an exaggerated view of her abilities. Emotionally unstable, she even claimed to have authored* Steps to Christ. *In 1901 she wrote to "Brethren in the truth," acknowledging that she misunderstood Mrs. White's prophetic ministry and regretted the results of her criticisms.*

BOURDEAU, D.T. (1835-1905). *Ordained to the Adventist ministry in 1858, he, with his brother, A. C. Bourdeau, spent many years in evangelism in New England and Canada. He opened work in California, and organized French-speaking churches in Wisconsin and Illinois. Later he engaged in evangelism in Europe, and for a short time was associated with J. N. Andrews in editorial work.*

BURDEN, JOHN (1862-1942). *Administrator who was closely associated with Ellen G. White in the development of sanitariums. He became manager of the St. Helena Sanitarium in 1891, then engaged in sanitarium work in Australia for three years. Back in the United States, he helped purchase the Glendale Sanitarium and played an important part in obtaining the Loma Linda property. He began the medical missionary school that is now the Loma Linda University School of Medicine.*

BUTLER, George I. (1834-1918). *Minister and administrator, he was a two-term president of the General Conference. During his first term (1871-1874) he was active in raising funds to establish Battle Creek College and the Pacific Press Publishing Company. On a visit to Europe in 1884 he laid the groundwork for publishing houses in Norway and England. Later he served as president of the Florida Conference, the Southern Union Conference, and the Southern Publishing Association.*

BYINGTON, John (1798-1887). *First president of the General Conference, elected in 1863, and served for two one-year terms. Before becoming a Seventh-day Adventist he had been active in other denominations. He is said to have maintained a station of the Underground Railroad at Buck's Bridge, New York, where he lived on a farm. In 1852, after reading a copy of the* Review and Herald, *he began to keep the Sabbath. At the request of James White in 1858, he moved to Michigan, and for 15 years traveled throughout the State aggressively planning for the growing church.*

CANRIGHT, D. M. (1840-1919). *A onetime Seventh-day Adventist minister and writer who renounced his church affiliation, wrote extensively against the ministry of Ellen G. White, and became a champion of those who opposed Seventh-day Adventist beliefs. He predicted that the Adventist Church would soon disappear.*

DANIELLS, A. G. (1858-1935). *Minister, administrator, and author, he attended Battle Creek College for one year, entered the ministry in 1878, and was secretary to James and Ellen White for one year. In 1886 he was called to do pioneer missionary work in New Zealand, and later became president of the New Zealand Conference, the Australian Conference, and the Australasian Union Conference. He was closely associated with Ellen White during her ten years "down under." In 1901 he became president of the General Conference, served until 1922, then led in the formation of the Ministerial Association.*

DAVIS, Marian (1847-1904). *A valued literary assistant to Ellen White, accompanying her on her travels throughout the United States, Europe, and Australia. Before joining Mrs. White's staff she taught a country school for a short time and worked as a proofreader in the Review and Herald printing office for several years.*

ELMSHAVEN. *Ellen White's home near St. Helena, California, early in 1915. Mrs. White is in a wheelchair on the porch, attended by May Walling. W. C. White and Tessie Woodbury are on the steps below.*

ELLEN WHITE with her office and household staff at Elmshaven in 1913. *Seated, left to right: Dores E. Robinson, Ralph W. Munson, Mrs. White, William C. White, Clarence C. Crisler; standing, Harold Bree, Maggie Hare-Bree, Mary Steward, Paul Mason, Arthur W. Spalding, Helen Graham, Tessie Woodbury, Alfred Carter, May Walling, Effie James.*

ELLEN G. WHITE giving the dedicatory address at Loma Linda, April 15, 1906.

FAULKHEAD, N. D. (1860-1923). *Treasurer of the Echo Publishing House in Australia in the early 1890s. For a while after accepting the three angels' messages, he continued as a leader in the Masonic Lodge, but separated from it after Mrs. White relayed to him a message given her in vision regarding his spiritual peril.*

FOSS, Hazen (d. 1893). *A young Millerite in Poland, Maine, to whom the Lord gave visions similar to those received later by Ellen Harmon. Foss was told to relate the visions, but when he refused to do so, the gift of prophecy was removed from him. He later lost interest in religious matters.*

HANDWRITTEN PAGE OF ELLEN G. WHITE LETTER.
Portion of an E. G. White letter written to her son Edson and his wife.

Sunnyside Cooranbong N.S.W. Jan 1 1900
Children Edson and Emma
I wish you a happy new year
I am very grateful to my heavenly Father that through our Lord and Saviour Jesus Christ, that he has spared my life and given me all spiritual blessings and I praise his holy name I am as active as at any period in my life in walking and how thankful I should be for this short [illegible] and a short distance with Willie but there can be no presumption on my part. If I go a little further than I should I have to bear the penalty of in suffering with my hips, We see a great work to be done only twenty seven miles from here and twenty five miles several have decided to obey the truth and some of the most precious are now keeping the Sabbath and in the settlement called [illegible] that is four miles distant, twenty came from this place walked both men and women to an evening meeting this is a mining district and all the chance they have is holidays and Sundays and evenings Bro Hilcoxe is doing good work in that place, Himself and wife ~~the~~ she is a good trained singer and this is her talent, as well a good Bible worker she is welcomed any where and every where they go
I have still another request to make to you will you see if Mrs Walling is in Battle Creek if she is tell her I will be pleased to see her in Australia I would write direct to these girls but I do not know where to address my letter If May would come to Australia to do ~~nurse~~ work as a nurse she will find plenty to do, Bro Rand opens a ~~sanitar~~ little treatment building not so small but small in comparison with the large institutions, but it is in Hamilton is six miles from New Castle toward Maitland, and every place is to be worked New Castle to Maitland these are places similar but on a very infant scale

HASKELL, S. N. (1833-1922).
Evangelist and administrator. He organized the first Tract and Missionary Society, was simultaneously president of the California and Maine conferences, and helped open denominational work in Australia. His written works include The Cross and Its Shadow *and* The Story of Daniel the Prophet.

HOWELL, W. E. (1869-1943).
Seventh-day Adventist educator, editor, and missionary. At various times he was connected with Healdsburg College, Emmanuel Missionary College, and the College of Medical Evangelists. For twelve years he was secretary of the General Conference Department of Education.

JAMES AND ELLEN WHITE with their two sons, "Willie" (left) and Edson, about 1865.

JONES, Alonzo T. (1850-1923). *Minister, editor, and author, he and E. J. Waggoner stirred the 1888 General Conference session in Minneapolis with their messages on righteousness by faith. From 1897 to 1901 he was editor of the* Review and Herald. *Later, being disaffected by church administrative policies, he left denominational employ and eventually was disfellowshipped.*

KELLOGG, John Harvey (1852-1943). *Surgeon, inventor of surgical instruments, and pioneer in physiotherapy and nutrition. In 1873, encouraged by James and Ellen White, he enrolled at Bellevue Hospital Medical College in New York. Soon after completing a two-year medical course he was appointed superintendent of the Health Reform Institute in Battle Creek, Michigan, which developed into the Battle Creek Sanitarium. He became world famous as a surgeon and inventor of vegetarian foods such as cornflakes and meat substitutes. In time he came into conflict with church leaders over administrative and theological issues, and was disfellowshipped in 1907.*

KRESS, D. H. (1862-1956). *A physician who specialized in health education and internal medicine. With his wife, Lauretta, who also was a physician, he served for a time at the Battle Creek Sanitarium. In 1898 they went to England to establish medical work there. From 1900 to 1907 they worked in Australia and New Zealand. Upon returning to the United States, he became the first medical superintendent of the newly established Washington (D.C.) Sanitarium and Hospital; she was staff physician.*

LACEY, H. C. (1871-1950). *Educator. Born in England, he moved with his family to India and Tasmania where they became Seventh-day Adventists in 1887. After graduation from Healdsburg College and Battle Creek College, he joined the first faculty of the Avondale school in Australia. Later he taught in several colleges in the United States, including what is now Loma Linda University.*

LAY, H. S. (1828-1900). *Pioneer Seventh-day Adventist physician and editor of the* Health Reformer. *After graduating from medical school, he practiced in Allegan, Michigan, and joined the Adventist Church about 1856. For a time he served on the staff of Dr. J. C. Jackson's "Home" in Dansville, New York, and in 1866 was called to head the Health Reform Institute in Battle Creek, Michigan.*

LINDSAY, Harmon (1835-1919). *He was treasurer of the General Conference from 1874 to 1875 and from 1888 to 1893, and helped establish and develop Battle Creek College and Oakwood College. He also served as treasurer of several other church institutions in the 1890s. Late in life he joined the Christian Scientists.*

LOMA LINDA UNIVERSITY TODAY. *In response to Ellen White's urgent testimonies, Loma Linda Sanitarium was purchased and opened in southern California in 1905. Two years later a school of nursing was started, followed by a medical school in 1909. Today Loma Linda University continues to train Christian health professionals in a variety of specialities for service around the world.*

LOUGHBOROUGH, J. N. (1832-1924). *Pioneer evangelist and church administrator. In 1852 he accepted the Sabbath under the preaching of J. N. Andrews. For several years he conducted evangelistic meetings in Pennsylvania, New York, and the Midwest. In 1868 he pioneered work in California, and in 1878 went to England for five years. He was the first president of the California Conference, and published a number of books, including* The Rise and Progress of Seventh-day Adventists.

MAGAN, P.T. (1867-1947). *Minister, physician, and administrator. He served as a licensed minister in Nebraska in 1887, and the next year enrolled in Battle Creek College. After graduating, he became secretary to S. N. Haskell, and, in succeeding years, associate secretary of the Foreign Mission Board, teacher at Battle Creek College, and dean of Emmanuel Missionary College. After taking the medical course at the University of Tennessee, he was elected dean of the College of Medical Evangelists, and later served as its president (1928-1942).*

MILLER, William (1782-1849). *American farmer and Baptist preacher from Low Hampton, New York, who, after studying the prophecies of Daniel, announced that Christ's second advent would take place in 1843 or 1844. His preaching attracted a large following, including ministers of various Christian bodies. Though the Millerite movement disintegrated when Christ did not come on October 22, 1844, several denominations rose from the ashes, including the Seventh-day Adventist Church.*

OLSEN, O. A. (1845-1915). *Administrator, General Conference president. About 1870 he began work among the Scandinavians of Wisconsin, and in 1873 was ordained. From 1880 to 1885 he served as president, successively, of the Wisconsin, Dakota, Minnesota, and Iowa conferences. In 1886 the General Conference sent him to the Scandinavian countries of Europe to supervise the growing work there. He was elected president of the General Conference in 1888, and served in that post for nine years.*

PRESCOTT, W. W. (1855-1944). *Educator and administrator. Became president of Battle Creek College in 1885, and for a time (1891-1892) was simultaneously president of two other colleges–Union and Walla Walla. He helped found what is today Avondale College in Australia. Later he served as editor of the* Review and Herald. *As a scholar and administrator he had a strong influence on the worldwide educational work of the denomination.*

REVIEW AND HERALD PUBLISHING HOUSE. *This building was constructed in Battle Creek in 1861. Officially organized in 1860, and legally incorporated the following year, the Seventh-day Adventist Publishing Association was the denomination's first institution. From our first Washington Hand Press purchased in 1852, to today's high speed printing presses, the Review and Herald Publishing Association is the direct successor of this early publishing house.*

ROBINSON, A. T. (1850-1949). *Minister and administrator. In 1891 he went to South Africa, where he organized the first conference. Three years later he and Pieter Wessels obtained from Cecil Rhodes a 12,000-acre (4,850-hectare) tract of land on which Solusi Mission was established. After spending six years in Australia, he returned to the United States, and during the next 18 years served as conference president in Nebraska, Colorado, and Southern New England.*

SMITH, Uriah (1832-1903). *Minister, writer, and editor. He became a Sabbathkeeping Adventist in 1852, and joined the* Review *staff the next year. From that time until his death his name was listed on the masthead, most of the time as editor. He was the first Bible instructor in Battle Creek College, was secretary of the General Conference, and wrote a number of books, the best known of which is* Thoughts on Daniel and the Revelation.

THE WHITE HOME ON WOOD STREET IN BATTLE CREEK. *James and Ellen White built this home in Battle Creek, Michigan in 1856. It was here, in the large upstairs bedroom, that Ellen White wrote out her "Great Controversy" vision.*

WAGGONER, E. J. (1855-1916). *Editor, minister, physician. He attended Battle Creek College and obtained a medical degree from Bellevue Medical College, New York. In 1886 he and A. T. Jones became editors of the* Signs of the Times. *At the 1888 General Conference session in Minneapolis, he and Jones gave a memorable series of sermons on righteousness by faith. In 1892 he moved to England to edit* Present Truth, *and in 1902 became the first president of the South England Conference. Some time after his return from England, he left denominational employment.*

WAGGONER, J. H. (1820-1889). *Evangelist, editor, author. In 1860 he was a member of the conference called to consider forming a legal association for the church, and was one of a committee of three that recommended the name "Seventh-day Adventist" for the church. He was one of the speakers at the first camp meeting, held in Wright, Michigan, in 1868. In 1881 he succeeded James White as editor of the* Signs of the Times, *and in 1886 helped establish the work in Europe. He edited the German and French papers, and wrote* From Eden to Eden.

HEALTH REFORM INSTITUTE. Established 1866. *Three years after Ellen White's 1863 health reform vision, the church's first medical facility was opened in Battle Creek, Michigan. Originally called the Western Health Reform Institute, by the time it was incorporated in 1867 the name had been shortened to Health Reform Institute. Later still it was designated as the Battle Creek Sanitarium, a name that became recognized around the world.*

WHITE, Ellen Gould (1827-1915). *With her husband and Joseph Bates, she was one of the co-founders of the Seventh-day Adventist Church. Converted in 1840, she at once felt a burden for soul winning, a burden that she carried throughout her long life. Possessing the prophetic gift as described in the Bible, she became a distinguished writer and speaker, and worked tirelessly and successfully to build up and extend the advent movement. To this end she traveled and preached extensively in the United States, Europe, and Australia. At meetings in Groveland, Massachusetts (1876 and 1877) she spoke to audiences estimated at 20,000. She contributed more than 5,000 articles to journals of the church, many of which were later published in book form. Her five-volume* Conflict of the Ages *series has been the means of leading many thousands to Christ.*

WHITE, James Springer (1821-1881). *One of three co-founders of the Seventh-day Adventist Church, the other two being his wife, Ellen, and Joseph Bates. He taught school for two years, but when scarcely 21 joined the Millerite movement, and, with chart in hand, began to preach. It is reported that during the winter months of 1842-1843 he led more than 1,000 persons to Christ. After the disappointment of October 22, 1844, he joined other Christians in Bible study, seeking further light. In 1846 he accepted the Sabbath truth, and in 1849 began publishing* Present Truth. *As the number of Sabbathkeeping Adventists increased, he urged that they develop an organization. This resulted in the formation of the General Conference in 1863. He was a leader in developing the church's publishing, educational, and medical work. For many years he was editor of the* Review and Herald, *and served three terms as president of the General Conference (1865-1867; 1868-1871; 1874-1880).*

WHITE, James Edson (1849-1928). *The second son of James and Ellen White, he is best known for his evangelistic endeavors for Black Americans in the South. In 1894 he had a riverboat constructed in Michigan for $3,700, and, naming it the Morning Star, sailed it down the Mississippi River to Yazoo City. He and his missionary-minded company of workers held gospel meetings on board ship, and offered schoolwork to both children and adults. Within a few years 50 small schools and churches were erected. Many Black ministers and teachers trace their first contacts with Seventh-day Adventists to these schools and the Morning Star that gave them birth.*

WHITE, William (Willie) Clarence (1854-1937). *The third son of James and Ellen White, he served as editorial assistant and publishing manager for his mother after the death of his father. In 1874 he began denominational work at the age of 20, helping with the* Signs of the Times *in Oakland, California. One year later he was elected business manager of the Pacific SDA Publishing Association, and president of the Board. In 1877 he was sent to Battle Creek College to prepare for service in Europe with J. N. Andrews. While still a student, he was made a member of the college board of trustees, and also became involved in the publishing, Sabbath school, and health work in Battle Creek. From 1880 to 1885 he helped develop the educational and medical work on the Pacific coast. He went to Europe to assist his mother for two years beginning in 1885, and went to Australia in 1891. For approximately ten years he served in that field, for three years being president of the Australian Union Conference. Upon returning to the United States in mid-1900, he chaired the committee on reorganization at the 1901 General Conference session, continued to assist his mother with her publishing endeavors, and after her death helped carry out the provisions of her will. Except for four years (1897-1901), when he asked to be relieved of the responsibility, he served on the General Conference committee from 1883 until his death in 1937.*

WILLIAM MILLER HOME. *Built by William Miller in 1815, this home is now owned by Adventist Heritage Ministry. A Baptist farmer-turned-preacher, Miller emphasized the soon return of Christ, based upon his study of Bible prophecy. Seventh-day Adventists trace their origins to the Millerite movement of the 1840s. The house is open for tours during the spring and summer months.*

SECTION V

Nurturer of Inspired Concepts

CHAPTER

CHAPTER 22

The Organizing Theme

"Seventh-day Adventism is one of the most subtly differentiated, systematically developed and institutionally successful of all alternatives to the American way of life. . . . The central figure in Adventism has remained largely out of public view. Ellen White . . . her life and thought shaped the characteristic features of Adventism. To understand how and why Adventism has impinged on the public consciousness, a detailed analysis of Adventist theology and Ellen White's writings is necessary."[1]

In the preceding chapters we have observed that Ellen White and the history of the Adventist movement are as interconnected as the warp and woof of a beautiful rug. The same can be said about the close relationship between Ellen White and the Adventist mind as expressed in its distinctive theological contribution, its educational and health principles, its sense of social responsibilities, and its missiology.[2] Without Ellen White, the Adventist mind in all these areas, as historically understood, would be as porous as a window screen.[3]

The uniqueness of Ellen White's contribution lies not in total originality of thought but in her synthesis of divinely revealed insights and the results of her own reading and observation. While selecting specific expressions from her contemporaries that helped her to depict more fully the broad principles of truth that were revealed to her, she avoided notions from those same authors that were not consonant with those principles.

The Great Controversy Theme

All significant theologies have an organizing principle.[4] Many scholars have identified Ellen White's unifying principle as the Great Controversy Theme. This provided a coherent framework for her theological thought as well as for her principles in education, health, missiology, social issues, and environmental topics.[5] Not that she single-handedly devised these interacting thought patterns, but she was the conceptual nurturer, urging study, noting errors, always exhorting freshness, not novelty. Along with nurturing, her own writings helped to form a core of Biblical understanding that provided integrity to the development of Adventist thought.[6]

George Knight, church historian, suggests that by focusing on the Great Controversy Theme "we can tell when we are on center or chasing stray geese near the edges of what is really important." In pointing to what Ellen White calls the "grand central theme" of the Bible, Knight wrote that "in such passages we find our marching orders for the reading of both the Bible and the writings of Ellen White. . . . All our reading takes place within that context, and those issues closest to the grand central theme are obviously of more importance than those near its edges."[7]

The conceptual key. Ellen White defined the Great Controversy Theme as the conceptual "key" to understanding humanity's greatest questions: How did life begin? Why good and evil, and how does one know the difference? What happens after death? Why suffering and death? The Great Controversy Theme provides the background for the development of evil—the story of Lucifer's (Satan's) rebellion against the government of God. The thrust of Satan's argument is that God cannot be trusted, that His law is severe and unfair, and thus the Lawgiver is unfair, severe, and arbitrary.[8]

Satan's initial success in winning the allegiance of one-third of the angels in heaven was followed by his deceiving Adam and Eve (Rev. 12:4, 7-9; Gen. 3:1-16). By so doing, this earth has experienced all the bitter fruit of distrusting God and spurning His will.

God's response has been, not to destroy Satan, but to expose him. God's long-term interest is to demonstrate how wrong Satan has been to charge Him with being supremely selfish, arbitrary, and unfair. Primarily through the life and death of Jesus, and through His designated people on earth, God has been revealing and demonstrating His side of the story.[9]

The controversy ends on this earth only after God's people give glory to Him (Rev. 14:7) in such a way that all earthly inhabitants can make an intelligent decision as to whether God's program is something they should choose for themselves. All must decide whether they would be eternally comfortable in keeping "the commandments of God and the faith of Jesus" (Rev. 14:12). After ushering in the return of Jesus, the controversy is reviewed during the millennium and finally settled when the chorus echoes from world to world, "'Hallelujah! Salvation and glory and power belong to our God, for His judgments are true and just.' . . . 'Hallelujah! For the Lord our God the Almighty reigns, Let us rejoice and exult and give Him the glory'" (Rev. 19:1-7). The rebellion is over.

The Purpose of God's Strategy in the Great Controversy

God's purpose in the Controversy is twofold: (1) To demonstrate before all the universe "the nature of rebellion" and, in so doing, "vindicate . . . [His] character,"[10] and (2) to restore in men and women "the image of God." More than forgiveness, the goal of the gospel is restoration.[11]

The new earth will be populated with those who have let God fulfill His plan for restoring His image in them. *Thus, the goal of redemption is not forgiveness but restoration; the purpose of the gospel is to restore all that was harmed by sin, to bring men and women back to their original state, step by step.*[12] Only by redeeming overcomers (Rev. 3:5, 12, 21) will God be able to "place things on an eternal basis of security."[13]

The vindication of God's fairness and trustworthiness, coupled with the concept of restoration as being the purpose of the gospel brought a Biblical freshness to Ellen White's theological system and provided coherence to all other aspects of her teachings.

Unfolding the Theme

How does the Great Controversy Theme inform and determine those principles of theology, education, health, and all the other topics that Ellen White has unified into a coherent, interconnected, distinctively Adventist way of life? What are those theological principles that undergird and permeate all these various aspects of Adventist thought?

Each of the following foundation principles not only unfolds the Theme but also exposes some error in contemporary Christian thought:

• God is not the kind of person that Satan has made Him out to be. God is not severe, unforgiving, harsh, arbitrary, or unfair.[14] Although God revealed Himself in His law and other revelations through His prophets, Jesus is God's clearest revelation.[15]

• What we need to know about God can be understood by observing the actions of Jesus and listening to His counsel while on earth. In revealing the truth about God, Jesus revealed God's image.[16] In revealing the truth about human beings, Jesus manifested humanity's lost image, the image He has promised to restore in all who trust Him and obey His will.[17]

(a) Jesus proved that God was not unfair—that is, He did not make laws that created beings cannot keep.[18]

(b) Jesus proved that God was not selfish by demanding submission and sacrifice from His created intelligences without manifesting the same willingness to sacrifice for others. His own life and death, an eternal gift to humanity, revealed God's unselfishness toward His created beings.[19]

(c) Jesus proved that God was not "severe, exacting, and harsh," by revealing God's tact, thoughtfulness, self-denial, forbearance, and love under rejection.[20]

• Because God is fair, loving, and respectful of His created intelligences, He does not coerce, force, intimidate, or deceive them in order to obtain their loyalty, submission, or compliance.[21]

(a) He does not use peer pressure, or compel a person to make a decision against his or her will, or attempt to bypass reason—all of which are techniques employed by the forces of evil.[22]

(b) He appeals to reason and waits for each person to decide on the basis of the weight of evidence and the constraint of love.[23]

(c) Thus, His people are to be known for their defense of liberty for others and the absence of oppressive methods among themselves.[24]

• Because God is willing to wait until all the evidence is in regarding Satan's charges, and because He will not force compliance, the principle of conditionality permeates His relationship with His created intelligences—He waits for people to respond.[25]

(a) The process of salvation by faith requires certain human conditions more than mere mental assent and appreciation for what Christ has done. Saved people are transformed rebels (the degree of change subject to the time and opportunities available), and transformation involves human decisions at every step.[26]

(b) The timing of the Second Advent depends, in part, on certain human conditions. The Advent is delayed, depending on the preparedness of God's people to receive the latter rain and thus be equipped to help implement the "loud cry" that brings the world to decision.[27]

(c) The incarnation of Jesus Christ involved a conditionality that beggars the human imagination—the possibility that Jesus might fail.[28]

(d) Character development determines destiny—the human response to God's gifts of destiny—pardon and power.[29]

• Human beings were created to be God's counterparts, "in His own image." They were created to communicate with God and with freedom to choose. Thus, they are responsible (able-to-respond) beings; human beings can be *ir*responsible, but never *un*responsible—they were, and are, free moral agents.[30]

(a) Since men and women are responsible beings, it is evident that they are not totally depraved; their destiny is not determined by a sovereign God who "elects" some to be saved and others to be lost.[31]

(b) Because human beings are responsible beings, God must communicate with them in human terms, in thought patterns that humans can understand. For this reason, the principle of the incarnation explains why Jesus "took humanity with all its liabilities" in order that His followers would know that He identified with them in every way.[32]

(c) The principle of the incarnation explains why God used the thought patterns and vocabulary of human beings when He revealed Himself in the Bible.[33]

• Human beings were created as an indivisible whole wherein such components as the physical body, mind, soul, spirit, emotions, and the will interact, influencing each of the other components. Components are interdependent and all are needed for human beings to survive in a healthy state.[34]

(a) Thus, people do not possess immortal souls that live in physical bodies for a short space of time. When they physically die, they do not continue to live somewhere in a spiritual, disembodied state. They "sleep" (in Biblical terms) awaiting the call of the Life Giver.[35]

(b) Because human beings are not composed of three units (body, spirit, soul) separate from one another, the well being of the physical body directly affects the health of the mind (including the emotions and spiritual values), and vice versa. Each person's health depends on the optimal interacting of all that contributes to a healthy body and to a healthy mind.[36]

- Because God is love He yearns for a loving response from human beings. He has promised eternal life to those who freely appreciate His love and who choose to obey His loving will for them.[37]

(a) Thus, eternal life is promised to those who cheerfully forsake their sins and gladly cooperate with His Spirit in reconstructing their habit patterns so that they will spontaneously love others—the ultimate will of their loving Lord.[38]

(b) Thus, God will not play word games and "save" those who mentally say the right words but whose lives do not reflect, in some maturing fashion, the profession of their lips.[39]

(c) Therefore, God has permitted the law of cause and effect to play out so that created intelligences throughout the universe, as well as human beings, can see the results of both obedience and disobedience to God's expressed will.[40]

(d) The redeemed will be composed of those who have cooperated with God in developing a habitual attitude of loving trust and cheerful obedience to His will; they have demonstrated that they can be trusted with eternal life, never again to put the security of the universe in jeopardy.[41]

One Thread Unravels the Fabric

As one studies the history of the Christian church it is interesting to note the results of unraveling even one thread (one doctrine) of the coherent fabric of truth. The cohesiveness and inner coherence of truth is one mark of its authenticity. When a person takes one doctrine—for instance, the nature of man—and imposes on it an unscriptural definition such as the immortal soul notion, other doctrines are affected in some way. When one removes conditionality from the plan of salvation, human responsibility is diminished and the sovereignty of God is exaggerated or misunderstood.

The unifying and synoptic range of Ellen White's contribution to the development of the Adventist movement is the result of her lucid understanding of the principles inherent in the Great Controversy Theme. Ellen White's theological concepts were not "divinely" transmitted through her as water passes through a pipe. Nor was she a systematic theologian. She was primarily a communicator, guided by heavenly counsel. Her mission was to comfort where people needed encouragement and to correct those errors that either misrepresent God or incorrectly define how men and women are finally saved.[42]

Her understanding of theology, though grounded in vision experiences, grew through the years as she listened to her Adventist colleagues cross-pollinate each other with their Biblical studies.[43]

The Key That Unlocked Mysteries

Ellen White's theological plumb line, as governed by the Great Controversy Theme and affirmed by revelation, remained the same, even as her insights deepened. Her theological discernment provided a unifying center that helped church members to share with others, in a lucid and convincing manner, the coherent message. Her written understanding of the sanctuary doctrine, for example, became the microcosm of the plan of salvation. This teaching not only was the "key" that unlocked the mystery of the 1844 disappointment, "it opened to view a complete system of truth, connected and harmonious, showing that God's hand had directed the great Advent Movement, and revealing present duty as it brought to light the position and work of His people. . . . Light from the sanctuary illumined the past, the present, and the future."[44]

From the earliest days of her prophetic ministry, Ellen White saw in the three angels' messages (Rev. 14:1-12) "the perfect chain of truth." Flowing from within this "chain" was the sanctuary doctrine. These Biblical messages "were represented to [her] as an anchor to hold the body."[45]

The "Theme" Transcends Modern Errors

The Great Controversy Theme transcends the tensions, paradoxes, and antinomies of conventional philosophy and theology. Tensions between all groups have roots that go back to the earliest "falling away" predicted by the apostle Paul.[46] Each particular church with its distinctive theology is emphasizing some aspect of truth that it holds precious. Yet, its leaders and members see their opponents as heretics, and the best they will settle for is a cease-fire, not a truce. Contending church groups are like two circles of partial truth, neither circle knowing how to bring the two together into a coherent, elliptical whole.

The Ellipse of Truth

The Great Controversy Theme, however, changes those opposing circles into an ellipse. By using the principle of the ellipse,[47] each circle finds its treasured truths (for which its adherents have been willing to die) safely preserved, even greatly enhanced. In the ellipse, truth is united in such a way that its fundamental components are not seen as antithetical, but as correlates.[48]

Truth is not the sum of paradoxes. Truth is the union of components in such a way that when one component is not connected to the other, something serious happens to even that portion of truth each group holds precious. For example, H_2O is another way of saying "water." Hydrogen and oxygen by themselves are very important, but without their proper union, water does not exist. The question of whether hydrogen or oxygen is more important becomes meaningless when one needs water to drink. The truth about water is that water does not exist unless both hydrogen and oxygen are in proper relationship to each other. The same is true with components in the ellipse of truth.[49]

Another way to illustrate the usefulness of the ellipse analogy is to observe how Ellen White speaks of law and gospel, not as antithetical but as correlates. It thus follows that the law does not forbid what the gospel permits, and the gospel does not permit what the law forbids. Further, to emphasize the law in the Christian's experience is not a journey into legalism. Ellen White highlighted how Jesus rejected the legalism of the Pharisees which led to bondage and pride while emphasizing that the law will guide the Christian "till heaven and earth pass away."[50] The Christian obeys God's law, not to impress Him but to honor Him, not in fearful compliance but in grateful submission and joyful loyalty.

In philosophy and theology, the two circles, representing the usual "two sides" of almost every argument, are generally known as "objectivism" and "subjectivism." Towering theological and philosophical thinkers can be catalogued in one or the other of the two circles. The various churches within Christianity can also be catalogued as being either "objectivist" or "subjectivist." The history of theology is the story of which circle is predominant at the moment—and the recurring oscillation, the persistent pendulum swing between the two foci of the ellipse, is as predictable as the rising of the sun.[51]

Conservatives and Liberals

In typical religious language, conservatives form the "objectivist" circle and liberals are in the "subjectivist" circle, although these labels are far from satisfactory. Each circle is emphasizing something correct, timely, and needed. Even as water is not formed until the circles of hydrogen and oxygen are reformed as an ellipse, so the partial truths represented by conservatives and liberals do not set forth the full picture of truth until they are both cast within the ellipse of truth.

Key words for conservatives (for which they will fight to the death) are: transcendence, authority, orthodoxy, rootage, law, structure, security, and grace—*all good words to hold on to.* But the historic weakness of conservatives is often a misunderstanding of the character of the transcendent God. They often emphasize authority at the expense of human responsibility and freedom. Because of these misunderstandings, faith becomes mainly a mental assent to doctrine. Some form of "only believe" is stressed. The result too often is human passivity in the salvation process.

Key words for liberals (for which they also will fight to the death) are: immanence, freedom, responsibility, reason, flexibility, meaning, relevance, and personal faith—*also good words to hold on to.* The historic weakness of liberalism is rooted in its subjectivity. Pietists, mystics, rationalists, charismatics (and whoever else puts human autonomy "in front" of divinely revealed truths) base their security either on reason, feeling, intuition, or historical research. Absolutes are rarely appealed to. "It must make sense to me" is often heard—a wish not to be overlooked.

In modern times, both conservatives and liberals cross lines when they no longer ask, "Is it true?" but rather, "Does it work?" Pragmatic experientialism puts the question, "What is there in it for me?" rather than the more Biblical "What am I going to do about it?"

Ellen White puts these questions into proper perspective as she appeals to both the traditional conservatives and liberals to see the answers within the Great Controversy Theme. She understood well this historic standoff between these two circles and how both conservatives and liberals alike will fail to see the whole picture without the ellipse of truth that transcends the weakness of both conservatives and liberals. She wrote: "The progress of reform depends upon a clear recognition of fundamental truth. While, on the one hand, danger lurks in a narrow philosophy and a hard, cold orthodoxy, on the other hand there is great danger in a careless liberalism. The foundation of all enduring reform is the law of God. We are to present in clear, distinct lines the need of obeying this law."[52]

"Hard, cold orthodoxy" and "careless liberalism" are the end results of placing truth in two circles rather than letting truth be truth in its elliptical form. Ellen White transcends these two circles by uniting authority and responsibility, doctrinal security and heart assurance, so that the Seventh-day Adventist Church does not need to fall back into the theological arguments that divide all other churches.

Most every Biblical argument, traditionally, presents the observer with an either/or choice. The ellipse of truth shows how important positions are to be joined by the indispensable *and,* either spoken or implied.

Twin Truths are Joined

The following examples show where Ellen White has transcended the either/or arguments in crucial theological areas wherein Christians have been divided for centuries. In these examples, note the ellipse of truth joining twin components as securely as hydrogen bonds with oxygen to make water:

1. *The relationship between Christ's work on the cross and the work of the Holy Spirit:* "The Spirit was to be given as a regenerating agent, and without this the sacrifice of Christ would have been of no avail. . . . It is the Spirit that makes effectual what has been wrought out by the world's Redeemer."[53]

2. *The relationship between the law and the gospel:* "No man can rightly present the law of God without the gospel, or the gospel without the law. The law is the gospel embodied, and the gospel is the law unfolded. The law is the root, the gospel is the fragrant blossom and fruit which it bears."[54]

3. *The relationship between Christ as Redeemer and as Ruler:* "Let this point be fully settled in every mind: If we accept Christ as a Redeemer, we must accept Him as a Ruler. We cannot have the assurance and perfect confiding trust in Christ as our Saviour until we acknowledge Him as our King and are obedient to His commandments. Thus we evidence our allegiance to God. We have the genuine ring in our faith, for it is a working faith. It works by love."[55]

4. *The relationship between objective authority and subjective responsibility in the faith experience:* "Faith in Christ as the world's Redeemer calls for an acknowledgment of the enlightened intellect, controlled by a heart that can discern and appreciate the heavenly treasure. This faith is inseparable from repentance and transformation of character. To have faith means to find and accept the gospel treasure, with all the obligations which it imposes."[56]

5. *The relationship between God's work and man's work in the salvation process:* "God works and cooperates with the gifts He has imparted to man, and man, by being a partaker of the divine nature and doing the work of Christ, may be an overcomer and win eternal life. The Lord does not propose to do the work He has given man powers to do. Man's part must be done. He must be a laborer together with God, yoking up with Christ. . . . God is the all-controlling power. He bestows the gifts; man receives them and acts with the power of the grace of Christ as a living agent. . . . Divine power and the human agency combined will be a complete success, for Christ's righteousness accomplishes everything."[57]

6. *The relationship between imputed and imparted righteousness:* "Our only ground of hope is in the righteousness of Christ imputed to us, and in that wrought out by His Spirit working in and through us."[58]

7. *The relationship between forgiveness of sin and a transformed life in defining genuine Christianity:* "The religion of Christ means more than the forgiveness of sin; it means taking away our sins, and filling the vacuum with the graces of the Holy Spirit. It means divine illumination, rejoicing in God. It means a heart emptied of self, and blessed with the abiding presence of Christ. When Christ reigns in the soul, there is purity, freedom from sin. The glory, the fullness, the completeness of the gospel plan is fulfilled in the life. The acceptance of the Saviour brings a glow of perfect peace, perfect love, perfect assurance. The beauty and fragrance of the character of Christ revealed in the life testifies that God has indeed sent His Son into the world to be its Saviour."[59]

8. *The relationship between the prayer for pardon and the prayer for divine help to resist sin:* To show how simple theology, rightly put, can be understood by the general public, note Ellen White's report of a sermon she preached in Basel, Switzerland: "All listened with the deepest interest, and at the close of the discourse an invitation was given for all who desired to be Christians, and all who felt that they had not a living connection with God, to come forward, and we would unite our prayers with theirs for the pardon of sin, and for grace to resist temptation."[60]

9. *The relationship between Christ's role as Sacrifice/Saviour and as High Priest/Mediator:* "Satan invents unnum-

bered schemes to occupy our minds, that they may not dwell upon the very work with which we ought to be best acquainted. The archdeceiver hates the great truths that bring to view an atoning sacrifice and an all-powerful mediator. He knows that with him everything depends on his diverting minds from Jesus and His truth."[61]

10. *The relationship between the new birth and obedience to God's law:* "In the new birth the heart is brought into harmony with God, as it is brought into accord with His law. When this mighty change has taken place in the sinner, he has passed from death unto life, from sin unto holiness, from transgression and rebellion to obedience and loyalty."[62]

11. *The relationship between repentance and reformation:* "No repentance is genuine that does not work reformation. The righteousness of Christ is not a cloak to cover unconfessed and unforsaken sin; it is a principle of life that transforms the character and controls the conduct. Holiness is wholeness for God; it is the entire surrender of heart and life to the indwelling of the principles of heaven."[63]

12. *The relationship between the work of Christ without and the work of the Spirit within:* "I call upon every one who claims to be a son of God, never to forget this great truth, that we need the Spirit of God within us in order to reach heaven, and the work of Christ without us in order to give us a title to the immortal inheritance."[64]

13. *The relationship between faith and works:* "Abraham's faith was made manifest by his works. . . . There are many who fail to understand the relation of faith and works. They say, 'Only believe in Christ and you are safe. You have nothing to do with keeping the law.' But genuine faith will be manifest in obedience."[65]

14. *The relationship between the old and new covenants:* "As the Bible presents two laws, one changeless and eternal, the other provisional and temporary, so there are two covenants. The covenant of grace was first made with man in Eden. . . . To all men this covenant offered pardon, and the assisting grace of God for future obedience through faith in Christ. It also promised them eternal life on condition of fidelity to God's law. . . . The law of God was the basis of this covenant, which was simply an arrangement for bringing men again into harmony with the divine will, placing them where they could obey God's law. . . . Another compact—called in Scripture the 'old' covenant—was formed between God and Israel at Sinai, and was then ratified by the blood of a sacrifice. . . . But if the Abrahamic covenant contained the promise of redemption, why was another covenant formed at Sinai? . . . Living in the midst of idolatry and corruption, they had no true conception of the holiness of God, of the exceeding sinfulness of their own hearts, their utter inability, in themselves, to render obedience to God's law, and their need of a Saviour. All this they must be taught. . . . The same law that was engraved upon the tables of stone, is written by the Holy Spirit upon the tables of the heart. . . . Through the grace of Christ we shall live in obedience to the law of God written upon our hearts."[66]

15. *The relationship between believing in Christ and abiding in Him:* "It is not enough that the sinner *believe* in Christ for the pardon of sin; he must, by faith and obedience, *abide* in Him."[67]

16. *The relationship between Christ's free gift of remission of sins and His free gift of His attributes in the development of the Christian's character:* "His life stands for the life of men. Thus they have remission of sins that are past, through the forbearance of God. More than this, Christ imbues men with the attributes of God. He builds up the human character after the similitude of the divine character, a goodly fabric of spiritual strength and beauty. Thus the very righteousness of the law is fulfilled in the believer in Christ. God can 'be just, and the justifier of him which believeth in Jesus' (Rom. 3:26)."[68]

Endnotes

1. Malcolm Bull and Keith Lockhart, *Seeking a Sanctuary* (San Francisco, Calif.: Harper & Row Publishers, 1989), pp. ix, 14. For another viewpoint, see George Knight, *Meeting Ellen White*, chapter 6.
2. Russell L. Staples emphasized this relationship in his chapter, "Adventism," in *The Variety of American Evangelicalism:* "The Seventh-day Adventist movement cannot be understood apart from its history. Of course, the theological positions on which the movement is grounded can be spelled out; but even though these may be explicated in terms of mutually accepted principles of interpretation and theological argument, only part of the meaning of its movement is thus revealed. And what is revealed may fail to explain its inner consciousness or its ordering of priorities. Some such matters lie beneath the surface and may be better accounted for by historical experience than by exposition of belief. This may be truer of the Adventist Church than of some others, on two counts. First, it grew out of the Millerite movement, and the events and meaning of that experience have been indelibly engraved on its corporate memory and serve as one of the beacons lighting its course. Second, the function of the inner Adventist conviction that it was accorded supernatural guidance in the ministry of Ellen White must be seen in historical perspective in order to be understood."—Donald W. Dayton and Robert K. Johnston, eds. (Downers Grove, IL: InterVarsity Press, 1991) p. 57.
3. "Adventist doctrine does not derive from the Ellen White writings, although she did much to confirm Adventists in the doctrinal way worked out by the pioneers; but much that is distinctively Adventist derives directly from her writings and influence. Included are: the Adventist life of Bible study and piety; the Christian values that have engendered a distinctive lifestyle; ideas regarding the relationship between physical health and spirituality, which have resulted in a healthful way of living and eventually in a worldwide network of medical institutions; and ideas regarding Christian education, which led to the establishment of thousands of schools. These institutions, both medical and educational, have served to transmit and foster the complex of belief, value, and lifestyle that informs what it means to be an Adventist—and these institutions in turn have exerted a reciprocal influence on the church. In addition to all of this, Ellen White constantly encouraged the church to break out of its narrow circuit and establish institutions and outreach programs of many kinds."—*Ibid.*, p. 66.
4. John Cobb, among others, recognized "that any developed position is understood best when it is grasped in terms of its essential structure. This structure in turn can be understood only as the immediate embodiment of the controlling principles of a man's thoughts." After reviewing several seminal thinkers of the twentieth century, he wrote: "In each case we have seen that the philosophy employed profoundly affected the content as well as the form of the affirmation of faith. Furthermore, the implication of the whole program is that Christian faith depends for its intelligibility and acceptance upon the prior acceptance of a particular philosophy. In our day, when no one philosophy has general acceptance among philosophers, and when all ontology and metaphysics are widely suspect, the precariousness of this procedure is apparent."—*Living Options in Protestant Theology* (Philadelphia: The Westminster Press, 1962), pp. 12, 121.
5. In 1858, H. L. Hastings wrote a book entitled, *The Great Controversy Between God and Man, Its Origin, Progress, and End.* His theme was to trace the worldwide implications of Jeremiah's announcement that the "Lord has a controversy with the nations" (Jer. 25:31.) Hastings revealed no concept of a cosmic controversy between Satan and Christ with supernatural implications involving the security of the universe. Nor did he depict how the controversy affects the conflict between various theories of salvation and how these theories directly affect their proponents. He reviewed the bleak history of humanity, noting that "reason, philosophy and history can give us no proper solution" to "earth's long continued rage—its ceaseless din of war, commotion, and strife." The cause of earth's prolonged troubles is that humanity has "refused their allegiance to the king of heaven. They set at naught his high authority. Hence he had a controversy with them. Sin was the cause of it. . . . We are then to regard this controversy as a controversy between *right* and *wrong,* between good and evil . . . between a just and Almighty ruler and his frail and rebellious subjects."—(Rochester, NY: H. L. Hastings, 1858), pp. 14-17.

   Joseph Battistone was one of the first in print to recognize the centrality of the Great Controversy Theme in the writings of Ellen G. White. He emphasized how this central theme directly affected her religious teachings in theology, health, education, history, and science. His method was to demonstrate how the five volumes in the Conflict of the Ages series reveal how "the great controversy" engages men and women from Eden to the Second Advent. If Battistone had continued, he probably would have not only described the conflict but also analyzed the theological issues at stake and how this theme contributed to the distinctiveness of Seventh-day Adventist doctrines. This book is a prime source of homiletical gems for those who want the Great Controversy Theme to inform their preaching and teaching.—*The Great Controversy Theme* (Berrien Springs, Mich.: Andrews University Press, 1978).
6. See pp. 170, 171 for the typical way Ellen White entered into the process of developing core Adventist beliefs: Bible study + confirmation by vision = present truth.
7. Knight, *Reading Ellen White,* pp. 48, 49.
8. "The central theme of the Bible, the theme about which every other in the whole book clusters, is the redemption plan, the restoration in the human soul of the image of God. From the first intimation of hope in the sentence pronounced in Eden to that last glorious promise in the Revelation, 'They shall see His face; and His name shall be in their foreheads,' the burden of every book and every passage of the Bible is the unfolding of this wondrous theme—man's uplifting, the power of God, 'which giveth us the victory through our Lord Jesus Christ.' He who grasps this thought has before him an infinite field of study. He has the key that will unlock to him the whole treasure-house of God's word."—*Education,* pp. 125, 126.

   "The Bible is its own expositor. Scripture is to be compared with Scripture. The student should learn to view the word as a whole, and to see the relation of its parts. He should gain a knowledge of its grand central theme, God's original purpose for the world, of the rise of the great controversy, and of the work of redemption. He should understand the nature of the two principles that are contending for supremacy, and should learn to trace their workings. . . . He should see how this controversy enters into every phase of human experience; how in every act of life he himself reveals the one or the other of the two antagonistic motives; and how, whether he will or not, he is even now deciding upon which side of the controversy he will be found."—*Ibid.*, p. 190.

"From the opening of the great controversy it has been Satan's purpose to misrepresent God's character, and to excite rebellion against His law; and this work appears to be crowned with success. The multitudes give ear to Satan's deceptions, and set themselves against God. But amid the working of evil, God's purposes move steadily forward to their accomplishment; to all created intelligences He is making manifest His justice and benevolence. Through Satan's temptations the whole human race have become transgressors of God's law; but by the sacrifice of His Son a way is opened whereby they may return to God. Through the grace of Christ they may be enabled to render obedience to the Father's law. Thus in every age, from the midst of apostasy and rebellion, God gathers out a people that are true to Him—a people 'in whose heart is His law' (Isa. 51:7)."—*Patriarchs and Prophets*, p. 338; see also pp. 69, 331, 596; *Signs of the Times*, Dec. 1, 1890; *Steps to Christ*, pp. 10, 11, 116; *Prophets and Kings*, p. 311; *The Great Controversy*, pp. x, 193; *Selected Messages*, book 1, p. 341; *Testimonies*, vol. 5, p. 738. See George Knight, *Meeting Ellen White*, (Hagerstown, Md.: Review and Herald Publishing Association, 1996), pp. 111-113.

9. *Patriarchs and Prophets*, pp. 39-42, 68, 78, 79; *Signs of the Times*, Dec. 22, 1914.
10. *Patriarchs and Prophets*, pp. 78, 68.
11. *Education*, p. 125. "The very essence of the gospel is restoration."—*The Desire of Ages*, p. 824.
12. "There are many who will be lost because they depend on legal religion, or mere repentance for sin. But repentance for sin alone cannot work the salvation of any soul . . . for this would place all heaven in jeopardy, and make possible a second rebellion."—*Signs of the Times*, Dec. 30, 1889.
13. *The Desire of Ages*, p. 759.
14. *Steps to Christ*, pp. 10, 11; *Patriarchs and Prophets*, pp. 38, 78; *The Great Controversy*, pp. 519, 536, 569; *The Desire of Ages*, p. 22; *Christ's Object Lessons*, p. 204; *Testimonies*, vol. 5, p. 738.
15 *The Ministry of Healing*, pp. 418, 419. "God was represented as severe, exacting, revengeful, and arbitrary. He was pictured as one who could take pleasure in the sufferings of His creatures. The very attributes that belonged to the character of Satan, the evil one represented as belonging to the character of God. Jesus came to teach men of the Father, to correctly represent Him before the fallen children of earth. Angels could not fully portray the character of God, but Christ, who was a living impersonation of God, could not fail to accomplish the work. The only way in which He could set and keep men right was to make Himself visible and familiar to their eyes. . . . The Father was revealed in Christ as altogether a different being from that which Satan had represented Him to be. . . . The whole purpose of His own mission on earth [was] to set men right through the revelation of God. . . . When the object of His mission was attained—the revelation of God to the world—the Son of God announced that His work was accomplished, and that the character of the Father was made manifest to men."—*Signs of the Times*, Jan. 20, 1890.
16 *The Desire of Ages*, p. 19.
17. *The Desire of Ages*, pp. 37, 38; *Education*, pp. 73, 74; *Testimonies*, vol. 5, p. 537; *Mind, Character, and Personality*, vol. 1, p. 249; *Signs of the Times*, Apr. 21, 1887; Dec. 22, 1887; *Selected Messages*, book 3, pp. 135, 136.
18. *Christ's Object Lessons*, p. 314; *The Desire of Ages*, p. 762; *The Faith I Live By*, p. 114.
19. *Patriarchs and Prophets*, p. 70; *Selected Messages*, book 1, p. 341; *Education*, p. 154.
20. *Steps to Christ*, pp. 11, 12.
21. *The Desire of Ages*, pp. 22, 487, 759; *Christ's Object Lessons*, pp. 74, 77, 101, 235; *Review and Herald*, June 4, 1901; *The Great Controversy*, p. 541.
22. *Steps to Christ*, p. 34; *Thoughts From the Mount of Blessing*, p. 142; *My Life Today*, p. 340; *Early Writings*, p. 221; *Testimonies*, vol. 1, p. 345; *Counsels to Parents and Teachers*, p. 116; *The Desire of Ages*, pp. 466, 759.
23. *Steps to Christ*, pp. 43-47; *The Desire of Ages*, p. 458; *Testimonies*, vol. 3, p. 255; vol. 4, pp. 583, 584.
24. *The Great Controversy*, pp. 45, 441, 443, 591; *Testimonies to Ministers*, pp. 200, 206, 219, 359-373.
25. *Selected Messages*, book 1, p. 378; *Patriarchs and Prophets*, pp. 42, 535, 579.
26. *Thoughts From the Mount of Blessing*, p. 76; *Selected Messages*, book 1, pp. 377, 378.
27. *Selected Messages*, book 1, p. 67; *The Desire of Ages*, pp. 297, 633, 634; *Early Writings*, p. 71; *Testimonies*, vol. 5, p. 214; *Christ's Object Lessons*, pp. 69, 121.
28. *The Desire of Ages*, pp. 49, 131.
29. *Christ's Object Lessons*, pp. 74, 84, 123, 260, 310, 356, 378, 388; *Testimonies to Ministers*, pp. 379, 430, 440, 441.
30. *Education*, pp. 15-19; *Patriarchs and Prophets*, pp. 44, 48-51.
31. *Patriarchs and Prophets*, pp. 207, 208.
32. *The Desire of Ages*, pp. 19, 24, 49, 117, 119; *The Ministry of Healing*, pp. 418, 419; *Selected Messages*, book 3, pp. 135, 136; Manuscript 1, 1892, cited in *Review and Herald*, June 17, 1976.
33. *Selected Messages*, book 1, pp. 19-22; *The Great Controversy*, pp. v-vii.
34. *Mind, Character, and Personality*, vol. 2, pp. 373-412.
35. *The Great Controversy*, pp. 531-562.
36. *Mind, Character, and Personality*, vol. 2, pp. 380-412; *The Ministry of Healing*, pp. 295-335.
37. *The Desire of Ages*, p. 668; *Christ's Object Lessons*, pp. 100-102, 112, 116-121.
38. *The Desire of Ages*, pp. 672, 675, 678; *Testimonies*, vol. 5, p. 206; *God's Amazing Grace*, p. 235; *Christ's Object Lessons*, p. 384; *The Ministry of Healing*, p. 491.
39. *Christ's Object Lessons*, pp. 97, 272, 316, 410-420; *Signs of the Times*, Feb. 25, 1897.
40. *Patriarchs and Prophets*, pp. 78, 79; *Christ's Object Lessons*, p. 84; *The Great Controversy*, pp. 28, 35-37, 589, 614; *Signs of the Times*, Dec. 22, 1914.
41. *Christ's Object Lessons*, pp. 96, 280, 315, 317.
42. See pp. 171, 172.
43. For a detailed account of the theological interchanges

between Adventist authors during the period of 1850-1874, see Damsteegt, *Foundations,* pp. 165-270. Ellen White did not assume pride of ownership for Adventist doctrine. She and her husband often made it clear that Bible study was "in front" of her vision-based confirmations. In referring to her Adventist colleagues she wrote: "These zealous searchers after truth risked their capital of strength and their all in the work of defending the truth and spreading the light. Link after link of the precious chain of truth has been searched out, until it stands forth in beautiful harmony, uniting in a perfect chain. These men of beautiful minds have brought out arguments and made them so plain that a schoolboy may understand them."—*Testimonies,* vol. 2, p. 651.

44. *The Great Controversy,* p. 423. For a Biblical study of Daniel 8-9 as these chapters related to the heavenly sanctuary, see Angel Manuel Rodriguez, "The Sanctuary and Its Cleansing," *Adventist Review,* September, 1994 (North American Edition).
45. "The third angel was pointing them to the Most Holy Place, and those who had an experience in the past messages were pointing them the way to the heavenly sanctuary. Many saw the perfect chain of truth in the angels' messages, and gladly received it. They embraced them in their order, and followed Jesus by faith into the heavenly sanctuary. These messages were represented to me as an anchor to hold the body. And as individuals receive and understand them, they are shielded against the many delusions of Satan." —*Spiritual Gifts,* vol. 1, pp. 165, 166. For an analysis of the historical understanding of the message of the three angels, see Damsteegt, *Foundations,* pp. 268-270.
46. 2 Thess. 2:3.
47. The ellipse with its two foci instead of the circle's one focus (center) is a geometric form that is used in many ways in the mechanical world. If one of the ellipse's foci is overemphasized, ignoring or out of proportion to the other focus, the form is altered and mechanically the machine will no longer function. Truth is radically altered when one focus of the ellipse of truth is overemphasized at the expense of the other.
48. See Appendix P, The Ellipse of Salvation-Truth.
49. For example, when the ellipse of truth is understood, arguments over the relative importance of justification and sanctification in the salvation process are as irrelevant as the relative importance of hydrogen and oxygen in the making of water.
50. Matt. 5:18. "By His own obedience to the law, Christ testified to its immutable character and proved that through His grace it could be perfectly obeyed by every son and daughter of Adam. . . . The disciples of Christ must obtain righteousness of a different character from that of the Pharisees, if they would enter the kingdom of heaven. God offered them in His Son, the perfect righteousness of the law. If they would open their hearts fully to receive Christ, then the very life of God, His love, would dwell in them, transforming them into His own likeness; and thus through God's free gift they would possess the righteousness which the law requires." —*Thoughts From the Mount of Blessing*, pp. 49, 55.
51. Stanley J. Grenz and Roger E. Olson, *20th-Century Theology*, (Downers Grove, IL: Inter-Varsity Press, 1992), pp. 11-13, 310-315.
52. *The Ministry of Healing,* p. 129.
53. *The Desire of Ages,* p. 671.
54. *Christ's Object Lessons,* p. 128. "There is perfect harmony between the law of God and the gospel of Jesus Christ. 'I and My Father are one,' says the Great Teacher. The gospel of Christ is the good news of grace, or favor, by which man may be released from the condemnation of sin, and enabled to render obedience to the law of God. The gospel points to the moral code as a rule of life. That law, by its demands for undeviating obedience, is continually pointing the sinner to the gospel for pardon and peace. . . . God has given a complete rule of life in His law. Obeyed, he shall live by it, through the merits of Christ. Transgressed, it has power to condemn. The law sends men to Christ, and Christ points them back to the law."—*Review and Herald,* Sept. 27, 1881.
55. *Faith and Works,* p. 16.
56. *Christ's Object Lessons,* p. 112. "A nominal faith in Christ, which accepts Him merely as the Saviour of the world, can never bring healing to the soul. The faith that is unto salvation is not a mere intellectual assent to the truth. He who waits for entire knowledge before he will exercise faith cannot receive blessing from God. It is not enough to believe *about* Christ; we must believe *in* Him. The only faith that will benefit us is that which embraces Him as a personal Saviour; which appropriates His merits to ourselves. Many hold faith as an opinion. Saving faith is a transaction by which those who receive Christ join themselves in covenant relation with God. Genuine faith is life. A living faith means an increase of vigor, a confiding trust, by which the soul becomes a conquering power."—*The Desire of Ages,* p. 347.
57. *Faith and Works,* pp. 26, 27. "Though Ellen White spoke of making strenuous efforts in the life of sanctification, the effort was always conceived of as being empowered by God's grace. This grace was primarily ministered through the Word and the Spirit, working in intimate concert. This combined ministry would bring spiritual truth home to the individual heart in such a way that character transformation takes place." —Woodrow W. Whidden, II, *Ellen White on Salvation* (Hagerstown, Md.: Review and Herald Publishing Association, 1995), pp. 128, 129.
58. *Steps to Christ,* p. 63.
59. *Christ's Object Lessons,* pp. 419, 420. "The atonement of Christ is not a mere skillful way to have our sins pardoned; it is a divine remedy for the cure of transgression and the restoration of spiritual health. It is the Heaven-ordained means by which the righteousness of Christ may be not only upon us but in our hearts and characters."—Letter 406, 1906 cited in *Seventh-day Adventist Bible Commentary (SDABC),* vol. 6, p. 1074.
60. *Review and Herald,* Nov. 3, 1885.
61. *The Great Controversy,* p. 488.
62. *Ibid.*, p. 468.
63. *The Desire of Ages,* pp. 555, 556; see also *Patriarchs and Prophets,* p. 92.
64. *Testimonies to Ministers,* p. 442; "The righteousness by which we are justified is imputed; the righteousness by which we are sanctified is imparted. The first is our title to heaven, the second is our fitness for heaven." —*Messages to Young People,* p. 35; see also *Review and Herald,* June 4, 1895.
65. *Patriarchs and Prophets,* pp. 153, 154.
66. *Ibid.,* pp. 370-372.
67. *Ibid.,* p. 517.
68. *The Desire of Ages,* p. 762.

Study Questions

1. In what sense is originality not a test of a prophet's authority? Give examples to support your answers.

2. What are the differences between Hastings' book entitled, *The Great Controversy Between God and Man*, and Ellen White's understanding of the "Great Controversy Theme"?

3. How would you describe the essential concepts that highlight the concerns of both conservatives and liberals generally, and theological concerns specifically?

4. In what way does the Great Controversy Theme provide the organizing principle for Ellen White's distinctive development of other areas of thought besides theology, such as education, health, church government, etc.?

5. What are the theological principles that unfold from the Great Controversy Theme?

6. What are the basic elements in the Great Controversy Theme and how do they interrelate? Ask first the three basic questions: What kind of God is running the universe? What is God's purpose in redeeming sinners? How does this purpose ultimately affect the universe?

CHAPTER 23

Clarification of Major Doctrines

"All Scripture is given by inspiration of God, and is profitable for doctrine, for reproof, for correction, for instruction in righteousness, that the man of God may be complete, thoroughly equipped for every good work" (2 Tim. 3:16).

Because of the Great Controversy Theme as expressed in the ellipse principle, Ellen White was able to transcend the objectivists (undue emphasis on doctrinal correctness) and the subjectivists (undue emphasis on feeling or human autonomy) of her time. This ability was very evident in the 1888 Minneapolis doctrinal crisis. Note how she transcended the tensions in contemporary theologies: "While one class pervert the doctrine of justification by faith and neglect to comply with the conditions laid down in the Word of God—'If ye love Me, keep My commandments'—there is fully as great an error on the part of those who claim to believe and obey the commandments of God but who place themselves in opposition to the precious rays of light— new to them—reflected from the cross of Calvary. The first class do not see the wondrous things in the law of God for all who are doers of His Word. The others cavil over trivialities and neglect the weightier matters, mercy and the love of God.

"Many have lost very much in that they have not opened the eyes of their understanding to discern the wondrous things in the law of God. On the other hand, religionists generally have divorced the law and the gospel, while we have, on the other hand, almost done the same from another standpoint. We have not held up before the people the righteousness of Christ and the full significance of His great plan of redemption. We have left out Christ and His matchless love, brought in theories and reasonings, and preached argumentative discourses."[1]

Limited ideas of the character and purposes of God lead to limited ideas of the atonement. Monumental arguments have arisen throughout Christian history because the disputants did not understand the truths involved in the Great Controversy.[2]

Larger View of the Plan of Salvation

Ellen White was led to see the results of "limited views of the atonement."[3] Some of these results included:

(1) A limited sense of what Christ suffered on Calvary, linking His agony to physical pain only.[4]

(2) A limited sense of how the Father was involved in the agony of Calvary, not comprehending that God's wrath expressed in His withdrawal of His immediate presence was the ultimate "price of redemption."[5]

(3) A limited sense of how Christ's life and death together "were earning the right" for Jesus to become humanity's High Priest.[6]

(4) A limited sense of how far-reaching Christ's atonement was in that it

embraced everyone who has ever lived, this limited sense caused by the presupposition that God's sovereignty has chosen both the special "elect" and those predestined to burn in an eternal hell-fire.[7]

(5) A limited sense of the "cost" of what God "gave" (John 3:16) in the death of Jesus by not recognizing that Jesus did not resume all of His former prerogatives, that He indeed "gave" Himself to the human race, to forever identify as a human with the human race—He was forever limited to time and space.[8]

(6) A limited sense of what Christ "satisfied" on Calvary in not recognizing that He died to give sinners a "second probation . . . that they might return to their loyalty and keep God's commandments," not that He died so that obedience to God's law was unnecessary.[9]

(7) A limited sense of the "atonement" by confining the benefits to justification only, not grasping that the atonement was a "divine remedy for the cure of transgression and the restoration of spiritual health," not sensing that it provided the means "by which the righteousness of Christ may be not only upon us but in our hearts and characters."[10]

(8) A limited sense of the depth in Jesus's cry, "My God, my God, why? . . ." whenever a person believes in the immortal soul error, not realizing that His hour of death was that which all sinners will experience in their "second" death after the judgment. Nobody on this planet except Christ has really died, those who have "passed on" are only sleeping, awaiting the Life Giver's call; Jesus felt the final agony of sinners who realize what they have rejected.[11] Further, Jesus experienced the unspeakable "wages of sin" (Rom. 6:23), thus proving that Satan was wrong when he said, "You will not surely die" (Gen. 3:4).

(9) A limited sense of sin in that most Christians have no idea of the universal implication of sin on this earth and how it affects the well-being of the universe.[12]

(10) A limited sense of how God plans, because of the atonement, to "place things on an eternal basis of security," a plan that involves an executive review including angels prior to the Second Advent of all people who have ever lived, and then a peer review conducted by the redeemed between the two resurrections (John 5:29).[13]

Sickness, Suffering, and Death

Because of Ellen White's understanding of the Great Controversy Theme, she could clearly teach why suffering existed, who caused it, and when it would end. Amidst a mountain of speculative books written since the dawn of history on the problem of suffering, she lucidly explained that "sickness, suffering, and death are [the] work of an antagonistic power. Satan is the destroyer; God is the restorer."[14]

Throughout Christian history the notion has prevailed that God punishes sinners and that a suffering sinner must accept his or her plight as the will of God. An incorrect picture of God's character produces this kind of thinking. Because of Ellen White's understanding of the Great Controversy as it unfolds in the Biblical story, she was able to transcend the prevailing view: "It is true that all suffering results from the transgression of God's law, but this truth had become perverted. Satan, the author of sin and all its results, had led men to look upon disease and death as proceeding from God—as punishment arbitrarily inflicted on account of sin. . . . The history of Job had shown that suffering is inflicted by Satan, and is overruled by God for purposes of mercy. But Israel did not understand the lesson. The same error for which God had reproved the friends of Job was repeated by the Jews in their rejection of Christ."[15]

Ellen White did not lay the blame for all suffering on Satan's direct intervention. She recognized that whenever men and women accept Satan's philosophy of self-indulgence they open the door to sad consequences. Jesus "taught that they had brought disease upon themselves by transgressing the laws of God, and that health could be preserved only by obedience."[16]

Yet, she saw even more in the big picture regarding suffering. She saw how God would use (not cause) human troubles as a means of helping human beings to "be partakers of His holiness" (Heb. 12:10). Though the suffering has been caused either by satanic intervention or by wrong human choices, God will intervene and help the sufferers find a blessing amidst the misery. She asked: "How many there are who would never have known Jesus had not sorrow led them to seek comfort in Him! The trials of life are God's workmen, to remove the impurities and roughness from our character. . . . The Lord will work for all who put their trust in Him. Precious victories will be gained by the faithful. Precious lessons will be learned. Precious experiences will be realized."[17] "The trials of life" that could destroy all hope are turned around by God, if He is asked, and made His "workmen" for each person's spiritual growth.

Jesus spoke of another kind of suffering not caused by human disobedience to the laws of life—the frequent fallout of serving righteousness (Matt. 5:10). Paul referred to this kind of suffering: "Yes, and all who desire to live godly in Christ Jesus will suffer persecution" (2 Tim. 3:12). In many comforting and ennobling ways, Ellen White put suffering for truth's sake in its proper perspective: "God never leads His children otherwise than they would choose to be led, if they could see the end from the beginning, and discern the glory of the purpose which they are fulfilling as coworkers with Him. Not Enoch, who was translated to heaven, not Elijah, who ascended in a chariot of fire, was greater or more honored than John the Baptist, who perished alone in the dungeon. . . . And of all the gifts that Heaven can bestow upon men, fellowship with Christ in His sufferings is the most weighty trust and the highest honor."[18]

Light for the Heathen

In providing the big picture, the Great Controversy Theme helps us to understand the plight of the heathen (at all times, in all places on earth, in all social and economic strata). God is the waiting Father who chooses to have all His children return home; in fact, He is persistently seeking them with wooing invitations that vary from person to person because of varying capabilities and circumstances. He knows where everyone lives, He knows their names.

Everyone, in some way, receives some light from our heavenly Father's front door (John 1:9). Everyone has enough light to make a moral decision. Ellen White caught this higher view that has not often been present in the Christian world: "Wherever there is an impulse of love and sympathy, wherever the heart reaches out to bless and uplift others, there is revealed the working of God's Holy Spirit. In the depths of heathenism, men who have had no knowledge of the written law of God, who have never even heard the name of Christ, have been kind to His servants, protecting them at the risk of their own lives. Their acts show the working of a divine power. The Holy Spirit has implanted the grace of Christ in the heart of the savage, quickening his sympathies contrary to his nature, contrary to his education. The 'Light which lighteth every man that cometh into the world' (John 1:9), is shining in his soul; and this light, if heeded, will guide his feet to the kingdom of God."[19]

Eschatology

The study of the end-time (the end of the world as we now know it and the events that precede the return of Jesus) is a subject that has been given much attention in recent times, especially in the evangelical churches. The Second Advent of Christ is one of the defining doctrines of the Seventh-day Adventist Church.

However, no other church looks at the Second Advent the same way as do Adventists.[20] The distinctly Adventist view is formed by a "mutually supportive cluster" of ideas. This "cluster" includes "conditional immortality, seventh-day Sabbatarianism, a premillennial historicist eschatology that emphasizes the imminence [nearness] of the Second Coming, acceptance of the gift of prophecy in the ministry of Ellen White, and teachings about the priestly work of Christ in the heavenly sanctuary. These doctrines coalesce into a distinctive eschatological theme, which lies at the heart of Adventism."[21]

"Conflict of the Ages" Series

This "mutually supportive cluster" of ideas that marks Adventist eschatology exists today because of the writings of Ellen White. Each book in the five-volume Conflict of the Ages series presents a particular aspect of the Great Controversy Theme. The first, *Patriarchs and Prophets*, reveals the origin and nature of sin and how it affects the universe as well as planet earth. *Prophets and Kings* traces the controversy as truth survives even during Israel's defeats, backslidings, captivity, and reformations; it shows that God's side of the conflict can still be given during apparent defeat and captivity. *The Desire of Ages* focuses on the purpose of Christ's incarnation and why His life and death were the supreme display of God's love and justice. *The Acts of the Apostles* unfolds the marvelous manifestation of God's Spirit in the life of men and women who found in the life and death of Jesus a new power that regenerated and ennobled those who gladly followed His "way."

The last book in the series, *The Great Controversy Between Christ and Satan,* answers the great questions of how long the controversy will last, how it will end, and why the questions that started the controversy will be settled forever. The latter part of this volume focuses on the "end-times" and how the destiny of all will be affected by each person's response to Bible truth. In no book by any other author can be found Ellen White's "mutually supportive cluster" of ideas, all interdependent. Note how interdependent, unambiguous, relevant, and totally reflective of actual events (excepting those yet to take place on the time-sequence line) are the chapters, "Modern Revivals," "The Investigative Judgment," "Snares of Satan," "Spiritualism," "Aims of the Papacy," "The Impending Conflict," "The Scriptures a Safeguard," "The Final Warning," and "The Time of Trouble."

This eschatologically focused volume draws together Ellen White's first forty years of comment on last-day events. In 1851 she wrote: "Such subjects as the sanctuary, in connection with the 2300 days, the commandments of God and the faith of Jesus, are perfectly calculated to explain the past Advent movement and show what our present position is, establish the faith of the doubting, and give certainty to the glorious future. These, I have frequently seen, were the principal subjects on which the messengers [Adventist preachers] should dwell."[22]

But the Adventist emphasis was not to be on mere prophetic interpretation. Ellen White strongly affirmed that the third angel's message was "the soul-purifying truth for this time."[23]

The Laodicean Message

In the early years after the 1844 experience, Sabbatarian Adventists identified themselves as the church of Philadelphia, other Adventists as Laodiceans, and non-Adventists as Sardis.[24] However, by 1854 Ellen White was led to point out that "the remnant were not prepared for what is coming upon the earth. Stupidity, like lethargy, seemed to hang upon the minds of most of those who profess to believe that we are having the last message. . . . Ye suffer your minds to be diverted too readily from the work of preparation and the all-important truths for these last days."[25]

By 1856 James White, Uriah Smith, and J. H. Waggoner were clearly telling the young Adventist groups that the Laodicean message applied to Sabbatarian Adventists as well as others who were "lukewarm" in their Christian experience. They, too, needed thorough repentance. Further, they combined in their conclusion that the third angel's message was the final message to the "rebellious world," and the Laodicean message was the final message to a "lukewarm church."[26]

Anti-Triumphal Self-Understanding

This anti-triumphal self-understanding stirred Sabbatarian Adventists to renewed missionary activity, hoping thus to hasten the Advent. However, most church members heard the mission emphasis without the deeper implication: "The heart must be purified from sins which have so long shut out Jesus . . . . But as they failed to see the powerful work accomplished in a short time, many lost the effect of the [Laodicean] message. . . . It is designed to arouse the people of God, to discover to them their backslidings, and to lead to zealous repentance, that they may be favored with the presence of Jesus, and be fitted for the loud cry of the third angel."[27]

One of Ellen White's consistent themes is that character preparation is needed before God can endorse the church's missionary efforts with the latter rain experience and the resulting "loud-cry" world-shaking interventions just before the Advent: "If the message had been of as short duration as many of us supposed, there would have been no time for them to develop character. Many moved from feeling, not from principle and faith. . . . It wrought upon their feelings, and excited their fears, but did not accomplish the work which God designed that it should."[28]

In this same chapter, "The Laodicean Church," Mrs. White gave candid counsel regarding what the Laodicean message needed to accomplish if members of the last-day church were to complete their assignment as the proclaimers of the three angels' messages. She emphasized that those who apply the message to their lives will be "purified through obeying the truth"; they will have stood "every test, and overcome, be the price what it may"; they will "have heeded the counsel of the True Witness [Laodicean message]."

When God's people have fully cooperated with the Lord who stands at the door, when, by the enabling power of the "indwelling Christ," God's people will "overcome . . . as I also overcame and sat down with my Father on His throne" (Rev. 3:21), then "they will receive the latter rain, and thus be fitted for translation."[29] "This antitriumphalism in the Laodicean context has continued to be an important factor in the Adventist theology of mission up till the present. It has not only improved the spiritual climate for mission work but has also provided a rationale for the delay of the parousia [Second Advent]."[30]

Because of Ellen White's eschatological teachings, Adventists think differently about the return of Jesus than do other Christians. They know that "certain events in the history of salvation" must yet occur.[31] Using the Elijah motif,[32] a special emphasis was placed on the work of restoration as a specific burden of the third angel's message. One of these specific burdens was the place that health reform would serve in preparing a people for fulfilling their spiritual responsibilities.[33]

Sanctification Interacting With Last-day Events

Another emphasis embedded in the third angel's message is the principle that "the Christian is in the world as a representative of Christ, for the salvation of other souls." The purpose of character development is to prepare Christians for the latter rain and the "loud cry" (Rev. 18:4) when God steps in to greatly enhance the impact and credibility of the third angel's message. Ellen White graphically depicts the Christian's primary privilege: "Christ is seeking to reproduce Himself in the hearts of men; and He does this through those who believe in Him. The object of the Christian life is fruit-bearing—the reproduction of Christ's character in the believer, that it may be reproduced in others."[34]

The Great Controversy Theme informs all areas of Ellen White's thought. Every area, because it unfolds out of this organizing principle, is coherent and interactive with all other areas. For example, her understanding of sanctification is thoroughly interactive with last-day events. As we will note later, her profound emphasis on the Adventist health message interacts with both sanctification and last-day events.[35]

Sanctification relates to eschatology not only in terms of each person's moment of death but also in terms of the generation alive when Jesus returns. Sanctification prepares the Christian to be "safe" to save,[36] for the latter rain,[37] and for translation.[38] The principle is transparent throughout her writings: "Character cannot be changed when Christ comes, nor just as a man is about to die. Character building must be done in this life."[39]

Key to Perception of Truth

The Great Controversy Theme provides the conceptual framework for an understanding of epistemology—how we learn, the process of knowing. Along with the knowledge that human beings are free moral agents comes the awareness that two loyalties are in conflict—allegiance to God, or loyalty to self and Satan's kingdom of evil.

Since Plato and Aristotle, men and women have proposed a variety of suggestions as to how knowledge is acquired, most of them contradictory. In reference to salvation truth, Ellen White lucidly taught that "the perception and appreciation of truth . . . depends less upon the mind than upon the heart."[40] She based her insights on Christ's teaching: "If anyone wants to do His will, he shall know concerning the doctrine, whether it is from God or whether I speak on My own authority" (John 7:17).

What does this mean—the heart determines the perception of truth? The conflict of loyalties in the Great Controversy directly affects how people perceive truth! The Reformers grasped this concept when they distinguished three aspects of faith: cognition, assent, and trust. Without assent and trust, theology would be a mere intellectual exercise; without cognition, feelings would be the master and the door would be open to individual whim. Ellen White would agree with Calvin when he wrote that "all right knowledge of God is born of obedience."[41] Defining this thought further, she wrote that the reception of truth "depends upon the renunciation of every sin that the Spirit of God reveals."[42] A mind using the scientific method alone, for example, will fail "to understand the things of God. . . . Only the mind and heart cleansed by the sanctification of the Spirit can discern heavenly things."[43]

Thus, not by reason or historical research alone can salvation truth be discovered. Ellen White emphasized: "A knowledge of the truth depends not so much upon strength of intellect as upon pureness of purpose, the simplicity of an earnest, dependent faith."[44]

A spinoff of the practical aspect of this "knowing" principle occurred in the 1888-1901 period. Helping the church to come to a peaceful and constructive agreement regarding the "two laws" in Galatians, she maintained that "it is not so essential to understand the precise particulars in regard to the relation of the two laws. It is of far greater consequence that we know whether we are transgressing the law of God, whether we stand in obedience or disobedience before the holy precepts."[45]

Rebellion Rarely Curable

Closely connected to the principle that the heart [human desire] determines the way the head perceives "truth," is the phenomenon of rebellion. Rebellion means that a person who once knew truth, to some degree, chooses no longer to perceive it as "truth." Some personal, internal conflict has arisen that is in conflict with the obligations of "truth." In terms of the Great Controversy, such persons have made their own judgment the "lord" of their lives.

For all of us, we must move on from the limited knowledge of the past to the fuller knowledge of unfolding truth. At those moments we should abide by our consciences and move on, with head and heart united, in responding to the higher demand of truth. The committed Christian makes a habit of responding to "known duty."[46]

Rebellion, however, is a turning away from "known duty," from that advancing light—rebelling at the increasing demand of the lordship of truth. No one other than the person involved knows when that first rebellious thought arises. Neither does one know when someone else crosses the line in letting thoughtful reflection become rationalization. But rationalizers who seek reasons to justify their reluctance to accept all the implications of truth know when that intoxicating spirit of rebellion takes over. It then becomes a slippery slope.

In reflecting on the experience of Australian Pastor Stephen McCullagh[47] in the 1890s, Ellen White wrote: "I question whether genuine rebellion is ever curable."[48]

The issue in rebellion is primarily attitude—an attitude that determines and governs the way a person looks at information. Rebellion happens when a person changes allegiance—a change that he or she may not recognize intellectually. Mrs. White used Korah's rebellion against Moses as an example of an incurable rebellion, even as she did Satan's rebellion in heaven.[49]

The anatomy of rebellion is this: "jealousy [gives] rise to envy, and envy to rebellion."[50] The heart of rebellion is self-will set against the expressed will of God. The appeal of a rebellion is that people have "been deprived of their liberty and independence," and that relief will be found by joining the rebellion.[51] The methodology of rebellion is to whisper half-truths and to dissemble when confronted; those whom the rebels oppose are vilified and "represented in the blackest character."[52]

Why is it that rebellion is not easily cured by the light of truth? Because incurable rebellion rests on a refusal to submit to divine authority. Pride of opinion rises up to shade the light of truth. In Korah's rebellion, his followers "fondly cherished the hope that a new order of things was about to be established, in which praise would be substituted for reproof, and ease for anxiety and conflict. . . . It is hardly possible for men to offer greater insult to God than to despise and reject the instrumentalities He would use for their salvation."[53]

After the death of the rebel leaders, God gave those who had been deceived by their dead leaders time to think and to come to their senses. How did they spend the night? By "devising some way to resist the evidences which showed them to be the greatest of sinners. They still cherished hatred of the men of God's appointment, and braced themselves to resist their authority."[54] Again, the rebels selected from the evidences of truth those notions that pleased their hearts.

Ellen White saw how the rebellion of Korah was a repeat of Satan's ambition for position and honor in heaven. But she saw more: "All through the history of the church, God's servants have had the same spirit to meet."

How does this "spirit" take hold of a

person? Ellen White was unequivocal: "By sinful indulgence . . . men give Satan access to their minds. . . . The rejection of light darkens the mind and hardens the heart, so that it is easier for them to take the next step in sin and to reject still clearer light, until at last their habits of wrongdoing become fixed."[55]

What are the first signals of a rebel spirit? "They [rebels] are ready to pervert the truth, falsifying and misrepresenting the Lord's servants, and even charging them with the base and selfish motives that inspire their own hearts. By persistently reiterating falsehood, and that against all evidence, they at last come to believe it to be truth. While endeavoring to destroy the confidence of the people in the men of God's appointment, they really believe that they are engaged in good work, verily doing God service."[56]

Ellen White recognized that one thing that helps create the rebel heart is unwillingness "to endure the pain and sacrifice necessary to reform." Thus, one of the rebel's key motives is to soothe the conscience by "turn[ing] upon the Lord's servant, and [denouncing] his reproofs as uncalled for and severe."

Mrs. White saw the thread of rebellion from Moses' day through the Reformation to our day: "Every advance made by those whom God has called to lead in His work, has excited suspicion; every act has been misrepresented by the jealous and fault-finding. Thus it was in the time of Luther, of the Wesleys, and other reformers. Thus it is today."[57]

Rebellion becomes incurable when the "weight of evidence" is continually rejected, when habits of self-justification are so deeply etched in the neural pathways that light and darkness change places. Ellen White wrote that closing the mind to the light because of heart preferences is to sin against the Holy Spirit, "a sin by which man's heart is effectually hardened against the influence of divine grace." The Spirit does not leave principally because He feels offended, although that is a factor (Eph. 4:30; 1 Thess. 5:19); He leaves because He no longer can break through the rebel's defenses against the truth. God has no more "reserve power."[58]

The principle of the Great Controversy is working itself out: God does not coerce anyone to believe against his/her will. God will provide "the most convincing evidence"[59] but He will leave the decision finally up to men and women. Rebels supplant the Lordship of God with the kingship of their own desires. Because His character is opposed to coercion God respects freedom, even for created beings who choose to rebel.

Endnotes

1. *Faith and Works*, pp. 15, 16.
2. "Through the plan of salvation a larger purpose is to be wrought out even than the salvation of man and the redemption of the earth. Through the revelation of the character of God in Christ, the beneficence of the divine government would be manifested before the universe, the charge of Satan refuted, the nature and results of sin made plain, and the perpetuity of the law fully demonstrated. Satan had declared that the law of God was faulty, and that the good of the universe demanded a change in its requirement. . . . But through the plan of salvation the precepts of the law were to be proved perfect and immutable, that at last one glory and love might rise to God throughout the universe. . . ."—*Signs of the Times*. Feb. 13. 1893.
3. "In order to fully realize the value of salvation, it is necessary to understand what it cost. In consequence of limited ideas of the sufferings of Christ, many place a low estimate upon the great work of the atonement. . . . Some have limited views of the atonement. They think that Christ suffered only a small portion of the penalty of the law of God; they suppose that, while the wrath of God was felt by His dear Son, He had, through all His painful sufferings, the evidence of His Father's love and acceptance; that the portals of the tomb before Him were illuminated with bright hope, and that He had the abiding evidence of His future glory. Here is a great mistake. . . . We should take broader and deeper views of the life, sufferings, and death of God's dear Son. When the atonement is viewed correctly, the salvation of souls will be felt to be of infinite value." —*Testimonies*, vol. 2, pp. 200, 213, 215.
4. *Ibid.*, pp. 200-215.
5. *Steps to Christ*, p. 13.
6. *The Desire of Ages*, p. 745.
7. *Ibid.* "Variously described as the decline of Calvinism, the rise of Arminianism, and the defeat of deism. . . . it may be summed up by saying that Americans ceased to believe, between 1800-1860, in the doctrines of predestination and election preached by Edwards and

Whitefield; they could no longer accept the notion that men were too depraved to play any part in their own salvation. Instead they decided that God had given man the ability, the freedom of the will, to understand his fallen state, to repent of his sins, and to turn to Christ for help and salvation."—William G. McLoughlin, "Revivalism," Gaustad, ed., *Rise of Adventism,* p. 142; see also p. 131.

8. *Review and Herald,* Dec. 22, 1891; *SDABC,* vol. 7, p. 925; *Testimonies to Ministers,* p. 19.
9. *Testimonies to Ministers,* p. 134; *Review and Herald,* Jan. 25, 1898, Sept. 17, 1901. "Christ came to this earth to show the human race how to obey God. He might have remained in heaven, and from there given exact rules for man's guidance. But He did not do this. In order that we might make no mistake, He took our nature, and in it lived a life of perfect obedience. He obeyed in humanity, ennobling and elevating humanity by obedience.... By so doing, he not only declared that we ought to obey, but showed us how to obey. . . . We need to keep ever before us the reality of Christ's humanity. . . . He came to show what God is willing to do and what he has done that we might be made partakers of the divine nature. . . . The obedience that Christ rendered is exactly the obedience that God requires from human beings today."—*Signs of the Times,* Jan. 25, 1899.
10. Letter 406, 1906, cited in *SDABC,* vol. 6, p. 1074.
11. *SDABC,* vol. 5, p. 1149; *The Desire of Ages,* pp. 752, 753; *The Great Controversy,* pp. 668, 671; *Fundamentals of Christian Education,* p. 429; *Selected Messages,* book 1, p. 340.
12. *Patriarchs and Prophets,* pp. 68, 78, 79; *Signs of the Times,* Dec. 22, 1914.
13. *The Desire of Ages,* p. 759; *Selected Messages,* book 1, p. 341; *Signs of the Times,* Dec. 30, 1889 (*SDABC,* vol. 5, p. 1132).
14. *The Ministry of Healing,* p. 113. See *Steps to Christ,* p. 46.
15. *The Desire of Ages,* p. 471; *Selected Messages,* book 2, p. 411; *Welfare Ministry,* p. 16.
16. *Ibid.* See *Patriarchs and Prophets,* p. 461; see also *Testimonies for the Church,* vol. 6, p. 224; *The Ministry of Healing,* p. 113.
17. *Thoughts From the Mount of Blessing,* pp. 10, 11.
18. *The Desire of Ages,* pp. 224, 225. See also *Testimonies,* vol. 5, p. 71.
19. *Christ's Object Lessons,* p. 385. "God's test of the heathen, who have not the light, and of those living where the knowledge of truth and light has been abundant, is altogether different. He accepts from those in heathen lands a phase of righteousness which does not satisfy Him when offered by those of Christian lands. He does not require much where much has not been bestowed." —Manuscript 130, 1899, cited in *SDABC,* vol. 5, p. 1121.
20. Douglass, *The End,* pp. 21-55.
21. Staples, "Adventism" in *Variety of American Evangelicalism,* p. 65.
22. *Early Writings,* p. 63.
23. Letter 13, 1859 and Letter 18, 1861, cited in Damsteegt, *Foundations,* p. 216.
24. References to the churches mentioned in Revelation 2-3; see Damsteegt, *Foundations,* p. 244.
25. *Early Writings,* p. 119.
26. Damsteegt, *Foundations,* p. 246.
27. *Testimonies,* vol. 1, p. 186.
28. *Ibid.,* pp. 186, 187.
29. *Testimonies,* vol. 1, pp. 186-188.
30. Damsteegt, *Foundations,* p. 248.
31. *Ibid.,* p. 270.
32. A reference to Mal. 4:5 and Luke 1:17—that God will raise up a people before the Second Advent "in the spirit and power of Elijah."
33. *Testimonies,* vol. 3, pp. 62, 63.
34. *Christ's Object Lessons,* p. 67. "Therefore, since all these things will be dissolved, what manner of persons ought you to be in holy conduct and godliness, looking for and hastening the coming of the day of God, because of which the heavens will be dissolved being on fire, and the elements will melt with fervent heat?" —2 Pet. 3:11, 12. *Ibid.* "By giving the gospel to the world it is in our power to hasten our Lord's return. We are not only to look for but to hasten the coming of the day of God. 2 Peter 3:12, margin. Had the church of Christ done her appointed work as the Lord ordained, the whole world would before this have been warned, and the Lord Jesus would have come to our earth in power and great glory."—*The Desire of Ages,* pp. 633, 634.
35. See pp. 292, 293.
36. *Christ's Object Lessons,* p. 280.
37. *Testimonies,* vol. 1, pp. 187, 188.
38. See *Testimonies,* vol. 2, pp. 355, 505; *Ibid.,* p. 705; *Signs of the Times,* Sept. 29, 1887; *Last Day Events,* p. 295.
39. *Testimonies to Ministers,* p. 430. See also *Review and Herald,* July 20, 1897.
40. *The Desire of Ages,* p. 455.
41. John Calvin, *Institutes of the Christian Religion,* book 1, chapter 6, section 2.
42. *The Desire of Ages,* p. 455.
43. *Testimonies,* vol. 8, p. 301.
44. *Christ's Object Lessons,* p. 59. "Human theories and speculations will never lead to an understanding of God's word. Those who suppose that they understand philosophy think that their explanations are necessary to unlock the treasures of knowledge and to prevent heresies from coming into the church. But it is these explanations that have brought in false theories and heresies."—*Ibid.,* p. 110.
45. Letter 165, 1901, cited in *SDABC,* vol. 6, p. 1110.
46. *Selected Messages,* book 1, p. 396.
47. The McCullagh family had received many letters from Ellen White between 1893-1901. During that time, Pastor McCullagh had been a successful evangelist. But he and his wife resented Mrs. White's counsel, though his expressions of devotion to her are memorable. He eventually made wild allegations against her, only later to repent publicly. Returning to evangelism he became restless again, and in the midst of an evangelistic meeting he abruptly left the ministry, declaring the church to be "a machine of the devil for the manufacture of hypocrites."—*Bio.,* vol. 4, p. 286.
48. Letter 1, 1897, cited in *SDABC,* vol. 1, p. 1114; also *Selected Messages,* book 2, p. 393.
49. Korah, a cousin of Moses and a man of ability and influence, wanted the status of a priest. Because Moses had set apart his brother Aaron and his family to the priestly office, Korah, though a Levite, allowed jealousy and dissatisfaction to grow in his heart. His insinuations and dissemblings attracted the sympathies of other leaders who also grumbled at the wilderness hardships. They forgot they were being led by God, not Moses; yet, they looked for every pretext to believe

that Moses was masterminding their wanderings which led to their disappointments. The small group of leaders knew well how to arouse the sympathy and praise of the people; they knew how to incite people by planting thoughts that Moses was an overbearing ruler and by urging them to fight for "their rights."—See *Patriarchs and Prophets*, pp. 395-405.

50. *Patriarchs and Prophets*, p. 397.
51. *Ibid.*, p. 398.
52. *Ibid.*, p. 399.
53. *Ibid.*, pp. 401, 402.
54. *Ibid.*, p. 402.
55. *Ibid.*, p. 404.
56. *Ibid.*, p. 404.
57. *Ibid.*
58. *Ibid.*, p. 405; see also pp. 268, 269, 635; *Testimonies*, vol. 5, p. 66.
59. *Ibid.*

Study Questions

1. What are the theological concepts and emphases that divide other churches but which can be either clarified or united by the Great Controversy Theme?

2. How did Ellen White harmonize two concepts that have divided Christianity for centuries—the sovereignty of God and human responsibility?

3. How did the Great Controversy Theme inform Ellen White's understanding of why suffering exists and when it will end?

4. How does the Great Controversy Theme help us to understand the plight of the heathen who have never heard about Jesus?

5. Why is character preparation a core issue in end-time events?

6. How did Ellen White transcend the limited concepts of the atonement that prevailed in her day with her fuller view of salvation provided by the Great Controversy Theme?

7. How does the Great Controversy Theme clarify certain elements in the way we understand truth?

CHAPTER 24

Health Principles/1
Emergence of a Health Message

"Through it all [the development and history of Seventh-day Adventist health principles and medical practice] we see the guidance of God as projected by the little lady from Elmshaven. At strategic moments in the development of our medical work, this remarkable woman gave the encouragement and wise counsel needed to keep the program balanced and moving forward."[1]

Because of her understanding of the Great Controversy Theme, Ellen White saw the implications involved in humanity's indivisible unity of body, mind, and spirit. Not only were human beings "free moral agents,"[2] the interacting, integrating components of body, mind, and spirit required the health of each component so that all the components would function effectively. Without the well-being of this synergy, the human being would soon suffer and hasten the slide to death.[3]

Interaction a Spiritual Matter

In 1875 Ellen White called this interaction between mind and body "a mysterious and wonderful relation. They react upon each other." Further, she made this profound concept intensely practical: "It cannot be to the glory of God for His children to have sickly bodies or dwarfed minds."[4]

One may ask, why do "sickly bodies or dwarfed minds," as a general rule, have anything to do with "the glory of God"? Ellen White is consistent and wholistic: "Anything that lessens physical strength enfeebles the mind, and makes it less capable of discriminating between right and wrong. We become less capable of choosing the good, and have less strength of will to do that which we know to be right."[5]

The question is: How did Mrs. White develop her expansive, wholistic contribution to health awareness, an emphasis that has become more relevant as the years pass? Was her distinctive formulation of health principles developed in a mind hermetically sealed from the world around her and penetrated by the Spirit alone? No, that is not how God works.[6] Her theological understanding of the Great Controversy Theme provided the mental grid whereby she was able to recognize in the area of health and disease the fundamental and enduring wisdom of her age, and to reject that which would soon prove worthless.

Emanating from this theological sense of wholeness flowed a distinctive and eventually coherent philosophy of health. This philosophy, in addition to clear insights by which millions of church members have ordered their personal lives, has spanned the earth with a singular system of health institutions.

Nineteenth-Century Health Notions

To better appreciate the distinctiveness of Ellen White's philosophy of health, let us review some of the prevailing health notions of the nineteenth century. At the beginning of the century, a remarkably standardized pattern for the treatment of disease relied "mostly on bleeding, purging, and polypharmacy."[7]

The cause of disease was a matter of widely diverse conjecture. The Christian world generally believed that illness and suffering were divinely inflicted because of sin. Healing, if possible, was the result of prayer and faith.

But new ideas were surfacing in the early 1800s. Horace Mann, in his famous 1842 report to the Massachusetts school authorities, wrote that suffering was "no part of the ordination of a merciful Providence, but to be directly chargeable to human ignorance and error." Further, if people would obey "the physical laws of God, they would no more suffer pain than they would suffer remorse, or moral pain, if in all things they would obey the moral laws of God."[8]

But changing the source of disease from heaven to earth did not automatically explain its cause. Mann, for example, rejected the idea of an invading, foreign body. Contemporaries blamed various causes, including variations in body fluids, filth and odors as found in garbage and sewage, and stimuli, either too much or too little. For many medical specialists, health was an intermediate state of excitement, and the physician's task was to adjust the excitement level. Whenever people occasionally raised the possibility that nature itself contained healing powers, as Hippocrates long before had believed, they were "confronted with the almost uniform opposition of the regular medical practitioners, who labeled them as empiric rustics attempting to restore a discredited element of primitive medicine."[9]

The "stimuli" theory, probably the prevailing treatment of disease, became known as "heroic" medicine. Benjamin Rush (1745?-1813), dean of American physicians, actively promoted this popular treatment wherein the sick had to resign themselves to "massive bloodletting, considered a panacea for almost every problem, and to submit to the violent purgatives and emetics which the medical doctors administered." The physician's task was to "conquer nature" with a special drug, the more violent the better, for each disease. George Washington became a well-known victim of deadly conventional medicine during the first half of the nineteenth century.[10]

In 1860 Dr. Oliver Wendell Holmes, professor of anatomy at Harvard University, wrote that "if the whole materia medica, as now used, could be sunk to the bottom of the sea, it would be all the better for mankind—and all the worse for the fishes."[11]

The second quarter of the nineteenth century, often known as the Jacksonian era, was swamped with innovation and change in most all areas of American life. Emotional, human-centered ideas overtook the rational, classical order of the preceding century. Fresh optimism and the sense of equality of all human beings inspired "reforms" in such areas as education, prisons, abolition of slavery, women's rights, politics, and health.[12]

This new focus on the individual and away from traditional theories was thoroughly evident in the remarkably fresh concern for personal health.[13] Distrust of traditional medicine with its "heroic" treatments and pitiful results turned the minds of many in all classes to what could be done with common sense.[14]

In this exhilarating era of optimism and its new focus on the "common man," such health reform movements as the following sprang up everywhere: The temperance movement,[15] promotion of vegetarianism,[16] public renunciation of "all evil habits," (tobacco, alcoholic beverages, tea, coffee, etc.),[17] development of "physiological" societies,[18] emphasis on public health, including sanitation and hospitals,[19] new attention to fashion,[20] and the emergence of "water" treatments.[21]

Physical Afflictions of Early Adventists

Early Adventists were as physically afflicted as their contemporaries. Many of them, fearful of the prevailing medical practice, turned to prayer as their best hope. In 1846 Otis Nichols wrote to William Miller about young Ellen White: "The Spirit of God is with her and has been in a remarkable manner in healing the sick through the answer of her prayers; some cases are as remarkable as any that are recorded in the New Testament."[22]

Dramatic Healings

Ellen and James White participated in many dramatic healings within their own family. But they did not consider the use of natural remedies to indicate lack of faith. From her early years to her last, Mrs. White clearly warned against fanaticism: "We believe in the prayer of faith; but some have carried this matter too far . . . . Some have taken the strong ground that it was wrong to use simple remedies. We have never taken this position, but have opposed it. We believe it to be perfectly right to use the remedies God has placed in our reach, and if these fail, apply to the great Physician, and in some cases the counsel of an earthly physician is very necessary. This position we have always held."[23]

In 1854 she visited a "celebrated physician in Rochester" for a painful swelling on her left eyelid that was diagnosed as cancer. But the physician told her that she would die of apoplexy before the cancer would kill her! About a month later, after much trust and prayer, she suddenly was healed of both the cancerous eyelid and the oppressive heart condition that had made breathing difficult.[24]

First Health-minded Adventist

Joseph Bates, that indefatigable former sea captain, seemed to be the first and, for some time, the only Adventist leader who had come to terms with health principles and the cause of disease. On the basis of observation and personal experience, he had decided in 1824 (at the age of 32) to abstain "from all intoxicating drinks." Earlier, he had given up tobacco in all forms. After another seven years, he determined not to drink tea or coffee. Probably the lectures of Sylvester Graham, who had written that "both tea and coffee are among the most powerful poisons of the vegetable kingdom," confirmed his observations.[25] By 1843 Bates had given up flesh food.[26]

However, though a staunch Millerite and later an energetic apostle of the seventh-day Sabbath, Bates apparently was not a health-reforming evangelist. He did not write out his strong health-reform beliefs nor personally try to persuade his associates.[27] But he was very successful, through his Sabbath pamphlet, in convincing James and Ellen White in 1846 that the seventh day is the Sabbath of the fourth commandment. Thereafter, Bates and the Whites were intrepid leaders of the "scattered flock."

Ellen White's Early Awareness of Health Principles

As early as 1848 Ellen White was shown the harmful effects of tobacco, tea, and coffee.[28] Some church members were not easily convinced regarding tobacco. In an 1851 letter she responded to the question as to whether she had seen "in vision" that it was wrong to use tobacco: "I have seen in vision that tobacco was a filthy weed, and that it must be laid aside or given up." She wrote encouraging letters to those who struggled to break the tobacco habit.[29]

But diet was another matter for the Whites. Many lifestyle changes had already been made within a few short years. The introduction of further change, such as self-denial in dietary habits, would have been enormously distracting and a source of much division among these early Sabbath keeping church members. Achieving doctrinal unity was more important for early Sabbatarian Adventists. Such unity established the spiritual climate for the more personal tests that would be introduced later.[30]

The issue of eating swine's flesh is a good example of an important Biblical concept that had to wait until a church was ready for its significance. Some had contended as early as 1850 that the Bible definitely forbids eating swine's flesh, but James White thought that some of the Biblical reasoning was inappropriate: "We do object to a misapplication of the Holy Scriptures in sustaining a position which will only distract the flock of God, and lead the minds of the brethren from the importance of the present work of God among the remnant."[31]

By 1858 the issue was being zealously pushed by the Haskells, to whom Ellen White wrote this interesting counsel: "I saw that your views concerning swine's flesh would prove no injury if you have them to yourselves; but in your judgment and opinion you have made this question a test, and your actions have plainly shown your faith in this matter. . . . If it is the duty of the church to abstain from swine's flesh, God will discover it to more than two or three. He will teach His *church* their duty. . . . I saw that the angels of God would lead His people no faster than they could receive and act upon the important truths that are communicated to them."[32]

The Whites were not ready to take positions unless they had the clearest Biblical evidence or a clear word from the Lord through a vision. Up to the health vision of June 6, 1863, they believed that the dietary restrictions set forth in Leviticus 11 as part of the Jewish ceremonial laws, were no longer applicable since the Cross. During the 1850s, Adventists freely ate pork. After the June 6 vision, the issue of eating swine's flesh was settled among Seventh-day Adventists. Why? Ellen White now wrote with vision-certainty: "God never designed the swine to be eaten under any circumstances. . . . The eating of pork has produced scrofula [derived from the Latin word for a breeding sow, a term for tuberculosis of the lymph nodes], leprosy, and cancerous humors [blood or lymph fluids]. Pork-eating is still causing the most intense suffering to the human race."[33]

Ellen White had been suggesting for a decade other aspects of healthful living that cut across the general habits of almost everyone. In 1854, at a time when modern conveniences were not even thought of, she called for cleanliness among those professing Christianity: "I saw that the houses of the saints should be kept tidy and neat, free from dirt and filth and all uncleanness." Turning to maintaining health, especially in dietary matters, she wrote that we must "take special care of the health that God has given us. . . . Deny the unhealthy appetite, eat less fine food, eat coarse food free from grease. Then as you sit at the table to eat you can from the heart ask God's blessing upon the food and can derive strength from coarse, wholesome food."[34]

The Health Vision of 1863

On May 21, 1863, at Battle Creek, Seventh-day Adventists organized themselves under a General Conference that unified their scattered churches. For the first time they had a center that promised unity and efficiency in their missionary outreach. About two weeks later, on June 6, 1863, Ellen White was given the epochal health vision in Otsego, Michigan.[35] It seems that God waited until the church had completed its organizational struggles before giving them the next step in their assignment—a responsibility that required unity of spirit and a general sense of harmony in doctrinal matters.

James White may have said it best when he reflected in 1870 on how the Lord had been leading the "scattered flock" into becoming a transcontinental movement. Although his sentiments could be applied as well to their doctrinal development in the earlier years, he contemplated the growing unity around the health messages: "The Lord also knew how to introduce to His waiting people the great subject of health reform, step by step, so they could bear it, and make a good use of it, without souring the public mind. It was twenty-two years ago [1848] the present autumn, that our minds were called to the injurious effects of tobacco, tea, and coffee, through the testimony of Mrs. White. God has wonderfully blessed the effort to put these things away from us, so that we as a denomination can rejoice in victory, with very few exceptions, over these pernicious indulgences of appetite. . . . When we had gained a good victory over these things, and when the Lord saw that we were able to bear it, light was given relative to food and dress."[36]

Led Step by Step

Psychologically, it could not have been otherwise. It was the method of Jesus: "I still have many things to say to you, but you cannot bear them now" (John 16:12). People cannot relate to too much change at once. Early Adventists proclaimed the seventh-day Sabbath at a time when a six-day work week was common, and to get Sabbath privileges was virtually impossible. Their enthusiastic announcement of a very near Second Coming seemed far-fetched to their neighbors who remembered the Millerite embarrassment in 1844. To declare further, in those early years, that Adventist Christians should not smoke tobacco, drink alcoholic beverages, use tea and coffee, or eat swine's flesh—would have been too much to contemplate. Change takes time, even today.

And now the Otsego health vision. Many items in it were extremely relevant to the Whites themselves as to how they could improve their health by setting better priorities for their time and energies, by a more "cheerful, hopeful, peaceful frame of mind," and by not leaving their own health care to God "to take care of that which He has left for us to watch and care for."

Further, the Lord instructed the Whites and others to speak out "against intemperance of every kind . . . in working, in eating, in drinking, and in drugging." But they were not to have only a negative message. They were to guide Seventh-day Adventists and others to a life style that harmonized with the laws of the spiritual and natural world. The sweep of the vision "astonished" Ellen White. She wrote: "Many things came directly across my own ideas."[37]

In May 1866, she visited Dr. H. S. Lay, an Adventist physician in Allegan, Michigan. Fascinated with her vision summary, he wanted a full interview. Mrs. White responded reluctantly because she "was not familiar with medical language," and because "much of the matter presented to her was so different from the commonly accepted views that she feared she could not relate it so that it would be understood."[38]

Dr. Lay was impressed. Her insights were accurate and the overall coherency profound. He knew that the interacting nature of these principles did not come from human sources. He often related to others what he learned that day.

One of his medical friends with whom he much later shared this special information was Dr. John Harvey Kellogg. In 1897 Dr. Kellogg said: "It is a very interesting fact that the Lord began giving us this light thirty years ago. Just before I came to the Conference I had a talk with Dr. Lay, and he told me of how he heard the first instruction about health reform away back in 1860 and especially in 1863. While he was riding in a carriage with Brother and Sister White, she related what had been presented to her upon the subject of health reform, and laid out the principles which have stood the test of all these years—a whole generation."[39]

Speaking to the assembled delegates at the 1897 General Conference, Dr. Kellogg added: "It is impossible for any man who has not made a special study of medicine to appreciate the wonderful character of the instruction that has been received in these writings. It is wonderful, brethren, when you look back over the writings that were given us thirty years ago, and then perhaps the next day pick up a scientific journal and find some new discovery that the microscope has made, or that has been brought to light in the chemical laboratory—I say, it is perfectly wonderful how correctly they agree in fact.... There is not a single principle in relation to the healthful development of our bodies and minds that is advocated in these writings from Sister White, which I am not prepared to demonstrate conclusively from scientific evidence."[40]

While traveling on a brutal schedule, still mourning the sad death of Henry, their firstborn, Ellen White rushed to completion *Spiritual Gifts,* volumes 3 and 4. Volume 4 contained a section called "Health," which contained the first comprehensive statement on health principles since the Otsego vision.

Were Adventists ready for this next call for personal reform? So many orders were received that an announcement was made in the *Review and Herald,* August 23, 1864: "The call for *Spiritual Gifts* is so great that we are unable to fill orders as soon as they are received. We have two binders at work, but today have not a single copy in the office."

Reports of immediate and beneficial results began to pour into the *Review and Herald*, the Adventist clearing house for information. Pastor Isaac Sanborn wrote that for ten years he had tried many remedies for his inflammatory rheumatism. Then, in the spring of 1864 he gave up pork, and a few months later he adopted a two-meal-a-day program, without meat of any kind. He joyfully reported: "I enjoy as perfect health as probably can be enjoyed in this mortal state. I would not return to my old habits of eating for any consideration. . . . I thank God for the light He has given upon this subject."[41] M. E. Cornell recounted how his wife lay at the point of death with typhoid: "We knew that to take the drugs of physicians would be in this case certain death." They applied hydrotherapy treatments, giving "nature a chance to throw off the disease." In a short while, as they united in prayer, Mrs. Cornell was out of danger.[42]

Ellen White was forthright about the changes that had come to her as she applied the counsel she passed on to others, counsel that "came directly across my own ideas." In her "Health" article, one year after the vision, she wrote: "Since the Lord presented before me, in June, 1863, the subject of meat-eating in relation to health, I have left the use of meat. For a while it was rather difficult to bring my appetite to bread, for which, formerly, I have had but little relish. But by persevering, I have been able to do this. I have lived for nearly one year without meat. For about six months most of the bread upon our table has been unleavened cakes, made of unbolted wheat meal and water, and a very little salt. We use fruits and vegetables liberally. I have lived for eight months upon two meals a day."[43]

Ingredients of the Otsego Health Vision

What was so electrifying, so sweeping, so full of promise in the Otsego health vision?[44] The core principles were:

• Those who do not control their appetite in eating are guilty of intemperance.

• Swine's flesh is not to be eaten under any circumstance.

• Tobacco in any form is a slow poison.

• Strict cleanliness of the body and home premises is important.

• Tea and coffee, similar to tobacco, are slow poisons.

• Rich cake, pies, and puddings are injurious.

• Eating between meals injures the stomach and digestive process.

• Adequate time must be allowed between meals, giving the stomach time to rest.

• If a third meal is taken, it should be

light and several hours before bedtime.

• People used to meat, gravies, and pastries do not immediately relish a plain, wholesome diet.

• Gluttonous appetite contributes to indulgence of corrupt passions.

• Turning to a plain, nutritious diet may overcome the physical damage caused by a wrong diet.

• Reforms in eating will save expense and labor.

• Children eating flesh meat and spicy foods have strong tendencies toward sexual indulgences.

• Poisonous drugs used as medical prescriptions kill more people than all other causes of death combined.

• Pure water should be used freely in maintaining health and curing illnesses.

• Nature alone has curative powers.

• Common medicines, such as strychnine, opium, calomel, mercury, and quinine, are poisons.

• Parents transmit their weaknesses to their children; prenatal influences are enormous.

• Obeying the laws of health will prevent many illnesses.

• God is too often blamed for deaths caused by violation of nature's laws.

• Light and pure air are required, especially in the sleeping quarters.

• Bathing, even a sponge bath, will be beneficial on rising in the morning.

• God will not work healing miracles for those who continually violate the laws of health.

• Many invalids have no physical cause for their illness; they have a diseased imagination.

• Cheerful, physical labor will help to create a healthy, cheerful disposition.

• Willpower has much to do with resisting disease and soothing nerves.

• Outdoor exercise is very important to health of mind and body.

• Overwork breaks down both mind and body; routine daily rest is necessary.

• Many die of disease caused wholly by eating flesh food.

• Caring for health is a spiritual matter, reflecting a person's commitment to God.

• A healthy mind and body directly affects one's morals and one's ability to discern truth.

• All God's promises are given on condition of obedience.

Adventist Life Style

These fundamental principles became the clear, sensible, practical outline of what has become known worldwide as the Seventh-day Adventist life style.[45] Ellen White often amplified these core principles, probably most clearly in her 1905 volume, *The Ministry of Healing.* One of her graphic statements that has galvanized millions is: "Pure air, sunlight, abstemiousness, rest, exercise, proper diet, the use of water, trust in divine power—these are the true remedies."[46]

For Adventists living in 1864, these health principles were indeed electrifying. Adventists had read and heard some of these principles before but not within Ellen White's spiritual context. Furthermore, Adventists now had a concise, coherent outline of health laws separated from the excesses and frivolities of others who were promoting life style changes.

The Whites knew that Adventists would need all the help possible in educating themselves and others concerning the laws of life. James White used the church paper to draw attention to books and lecturers then available that would support his wife's first article on "Health": "Our people are generally waking up to the subject of health. . . . And they should have publications on the subject to meet their present wants, at prices within the reach of the poorest."[47]

He was referring to books by Mann, Jackson, Trall, Coles, Lewis, Shew, Graham, Alcott, and others.[48] For years these writers had been trying to get the attention of their world. Each of them emphasized certain aspects of healthful living that Ellen White recommended.

But their books were often technical, voluminous, costly, and, at times, merely personal opinion floating in oceans of verbiage. And none of them had placed healthful living within the context of the Third Angel's Message, preparing a people to meet the Lord.

So innovative James White moved ahead with his usual enthusiasm. He announced that since Adventists had an urgent need for health literature "to meet their present wants" and "at prices within the reach of the poorest," six pamphlets were being prepared and would be published under the title, *Health, or How to Live*. Mrs. White would "furnish a liberal chapter in each number on health, happiness, and miseries of domestic life, and the bearing which these have upon the prospects of obtaining the life to come."[49] The six "chapters" unfolded the basic message of her earlier message, "Health." In addition, in the second article Ellen White wrote specific counsel regarding the relationship between husbands and wives and the proper care of infants and young children. In article four she gave added counsel to those who cared for the sick.

New material on the subject of dress for women and children appeared in the fifth and sixth articles.[50]

Endnotes

1. Godfrey T. Anderson, long-time president of Loma Linda University, cited in Warren L. Johns, Richard H. Utt, editors, *The Vision Bold* (Washington, D.C.: Review and Herald Publishing Association, 1977), p. vii.
2. *Patriarchs and Prophets,* pp. 49, 331.
3. "Since 1863, Seventh-day Adventists have promulgated a wholistic view of the human person. The view that the body, mind, and spirit are all integrated and interrelated constituent elements that together form a single being is the very cornerstone on which much of our work as a church has been built. Believing that these three are interdependent and constantly interacting, we have adopted a 'systems' approach in our anthropology: the whole person cannot be understood merely as the sum of separate, constituent parts. Each variable in the system is so enmeshed in its interaction with the other parts as to make the relationship the key to understanding each individual component. . . . From this vantage point, the spiritual enterprise addresses a sentient being with the capacity to monitor the universe and respond to it (both consciously and unconsciously) on the basis of information gleaned from physical, rational-emotive, and spiritual radar. Thus, each of these spheres provides the total person with methods of learning and wisdom distinctly its own, and may be the appropriate starting point for spiritual education or discernment, just as distortion or distress in any one of these spheres will serve to undermine the survival or well-being of the person."—Ginger Hanks-Harwood, "Wholeness," Charles W. Teel, Jr. ed., *Remnant and Republic: Adventist Themes for Personal and Social Ethics* (Loma Linda, Calif.: Center for Christian Bioethics, 1995), pp. 127, 128.
4. *Testimonies,* vol. 3, pp. 485, 486.
5. *Christ's Object Lessons,* p. 346. "The moral powers are weakened, because men and women will not live in obedience to the laws of health and make this great subject a personal duty."—*Testimonies,* vol. 3, p. 140.
6. See p. 111.
7. George W. Reid, *A Sound of Trumpets* (Washington, D.C.: Review and Herald Publishing Association, 1982), p. 21.
8. Horace Mann, "The Study of Physiology in the Schools," Educational Annual Report for 1842, *Annual Reports on Education,* ed. Mary Tyler Mann, vol. 3, *Life and Works of Horace Mann* (Boston: Horace B. Fuller, 1868), p. 227, cited in Reid, *A Sound of Trumpets,* p. 25.
9. Reid, *A Sound of Trumpets,* pp. 25-28.
10. *Ibid.,* pp. 29-31; D. E. Robinson, *The Story of Our Health Message* (Nashville, Tenn.: Southern Publishing Association, 1965), pp. 13-27.
11. Ronald L. Numbers, *Prophetess of Health* (New York: Harper & Row, Publishers, 1976), p. 49.
12. Reid, *A Sound of Trumpets,* pp. 31-48.
13. Malcolm Bull and Keith Lockhart, *Seeking a Sanctuary,* p. 128.
14. Rennie B. Schoepflin, "Health and Health Care," Land, *World of E. G. White,* pp. 143-158.
15. Jerome L. Clark, "The Crusade Against Alcohol," Land, *World of E. G. White,* pp. 131-140; Stephen Nissenbaum, *Sex, Diet, and Debility in Jacksonian America* (Chicago: The Dorsey Press, 1980)), pp. 69-85; Robinson, *Our Health Message,* pp. 38-42.
16. Nissenbaum, *Sex. Diet, and Debility,* pp. 39-52; Reid, *A Sound of Trumpets,* p. 85; Robinson, *Our Health Message,* pp. 42-47.
17. Reid, *A Sound of Trumpets,* pp. 42, 43.
18. *Ibid.,* p. 37; Robinson, *Our Health Message,* pp. 47, 48.
19. Schoepflin, in Land, *World of E. G. White,* pp. 151-157.
20. *Ibid.,* p. 155.
21. *Ibid.,* pp. 146-148; Reid, *A Sound of Trumpets,* pp. 79-81; Robinson, *Our Health Message,* pp. 28-37. See also Ronald L. Numbers, *Prophetess of Health,* pp. 48-76.
22. Otis Nichols Letter, Apr. 20, 1846, cited in *Bio.,* vol. 1, pp. 76, 77. Several instances of divine healing include Mrs. Penfield—Letter 1, 1848 in *MR,* vol. 5, pp. 248, 249; Frances Howland—*Spiritual Gifts,* vol. 2, p. 42; William Hyde—*Ibid.,* p. 44; Clarissa Bonfoey—Letter 14, 1850 in *MR,* vol. 7, pp. 352; vol. 8, pp. 221, 222; Lumen Masten—*Review and Herald,* Sept. 30, 1852. J. N. Loughborough reported on these experiences in 1909, noting that in the 1850s Adventists "had not the light on the treatment of disease by the use of nature's remedies, but were requested to bring our sick ones to

the Lord in prayer, following the rule in the fifth chapter of James. . . . This led some to conclude that every case thus presented to the Lord would be healed. For this conclusion we had not, however, had any such instruction from either Brother or Sister White." When some were troubled after prayed-for people died, Loughborough pointed to Ellen White's counsel in *Testimonies,* vol. 1, pp. 120, 121, where she made clear that every sincere prayer is answered in God's wisdom. In some cases, death may be the most compassionate way for a prayer to be answered. See J. N. Loughborough, "Sketches From the Past—77," *Pacific Union Recorder,* Sept. 16, 1909, p. 1.

23. *Spiritual Gifts,* vol. 2, p. 135 (1860). In *The Ministry of Healing* (1905), Ellen White wrote: "Those who seek healing by prayer should not neglect to make use of the remedial agencies within their reach. It is not a denial of faith to use such remedies as God has provided to alleviate pain and to aid nature in her work of restoration."—Pages 231, 232.
24. *Bio.,* vol. 1, p. 292. Some people are puzzled by a statement Ellen White made in a January 31, 1849 broadside (a one-sheet publication) that said: "If any among us are sick, let us not dishonor God by applying to earthly physicians, but apply to the God of Israel. If we follow His directions (James 5:14, 15), the sick will be healed." This broadside was edited and reproduced in *Experience and Views* and again in *Early Writings,* pp. 56-58. This particular reference to physicians was one of the sentences deleted in later printings. Ellen White often edited her own material, sometimes several times, before publication and before reprints. Any wise author does the same for the sake of clearer communication and to avoid misunderstanding. As time passed for this material to be republished, Mrs. White could see how it could be misunderstood in view of her own practice of consulting physicians when it seemed appropriate. When we think of the limited medical knowledge of the mid-nineteenth century, we can understand well her agreement with Oliver Wendell Holmes's assessment of contemporary medicine (see p. 279) when she wrote in the early 1860s: "I was shown that more deaths have been caused by drug-taking than from all other causes combined. If there was in the land one physician in the place of thousands, a vast amount of premature mortality would be prevented"—*Spiritual Gifts,* vol. 4, p. 133. But there was more behind that 1849 statement. Adventists in the late 1840s experienced many dramatic divine healings (see *Life Sketches,* pp. 121-124, and *Bio.,* vol. 1, pp. 88, 89, 115, 158, 159, 232, 371), from illnesses that often defied medical knowledge at that time. They threw themselves on James 5:14, 15 and rejoiced with the promise fulfilled, over and over again. They saw too many of their contemporaries being bled, purged, and drugged to an early death. In later writings, Mrs. White made very plain the proper balance between faith and working with God in employing the best of medical knowledge.
25. Joseph Bates, *The Autobiography of Elder Joseph Bates* (Battle Creek, Mich.: Steam Press of the Seventh-Adventist Publishing Association, 1868), pp. 168, 234.
26. *The Health Reformer,* July 1871.
27. "Regarding the minor points of [dietary] reform, he [Bates] exerted a silent influence, but did not urge his practices upon others. Sometimes his friends would ask him why he did not partake of flesh meat, or grease, or highly spiced foods; and he would quietly reply, 'I have eaten my share of them.' He did not make prominent in public or in private his views of proper diet unless asked about them."—Robinson, *Our Health Message,* p. 59.
28. *Review and Herald,* Nov. 8, 1870.
29. *Bio.,* vol. 1, p. 224. Tobacco was tolerated for some time among Sabbath-keeping Adventists. The church paper published various articles with both scientific and scriptural arguments against tobacco in the 1850s. The first disfellowshipping of tobacco users occurred in Morristown, Vermont, in 1855.—Robinson, *Our Health Message,* pp. 66-70.
30. James White wrote in 1857: "In those days [referring to the late 1840s and early 1850s] there were trials, and these trials generally arose in consequence of a disposition to draw off from the great truths connected with the Third Message, to points of no vital importance. It has been impossible to make some see that present truth is *present* truth, and not future truth, and that the Word as a lamp shines brightly where we stand, and not so plainly on the path in the distance."—*Review and Herald,* Dec. 31, 1857.
31. *Present Truth,* Nov. 1850.
32. *Testimonies for the Church,* vol. 1, pp. 206, 207. See p. 34.
33. *Spiritual Gifts,* vol. 4, pp. 124, 146.
34. Manuscript 3, 1854, cited in *Selected Messages,* book 3, p. 274. Careful examination of Ellen White's writings indicates that by "grease" she meant animal fat, such as lard and suet, very common cooking ingredients in her day. "Coarse" was a word that could have at least two meanings, such as "coarse" in a healthy sense (unrefined bread) and "coarse" in an unfavorable sense (certain vegetables not properly cooked).— *Education,* p. 204.
35. Background for this important vision may be found in *Bio.,* vol. 2, pp. 16-22; Robinson, *Our Health Message,* pp. 75-85. It was actually Friday evening, June 5. Since the Sabbath had already started, Ellen White refers to the date as June 6.
36. *Review and Herald,* Nov. 8, 1870; also cited in *Counsels on Diet and Foods,* pp. 495, 496.
37. Manuscript 149, undated, cited in Robinson, *Our Health Message,* p. 81.
38. Robinson, *Our Health Message,* p. 83.
39. *General Conference Daily Bulletin,* March 8, 1897, p. 309; cited in Robinson, *Our Health Message,* pp. 83, 84.
40. *Ibid.,* p. 84.
41. *Review and Herald,* April 11, 1865.
42. Robinson, *Our Health Message,* p. 96.
43. *Spiritual Gifts,* vol. 4, p. 153, cited in Robinson, *Our Health Message,* p. 94. For a continuing record of Ellen White's experience with health reform principles, plus her principles of common sense, see *Testimonies,* vol. 2, pp. 362-390. For a discussion of her dietary record and personal growth, see p. 311.
44. *Spiritual Gifts,* vol. 4, pp. 120-151. See *Counsels on Diet and Foods,* pp. 481-494.
45. *Time,* Oct. 28, 1966, referred to the astounding health and mortality statistical differences between California Adventist men and the general population as "The Adventist Advantage."
46. *The Ministry of Healing,* p. 127. See also *Testimonies,* vol. 5, p. 443.
47. *Review and Herald,* Dec. 13, 1864.

48. Horace Mann "Report for 1842," *Life and Works of Horace Mann* (Boston: Lee and Shepard, 1891); James C. Jackson, *American Womanhood: Its Peculiarities and Necessities* (Dansville, N.Y.: Austin, Jackson & Co., Publishers); Russell T. Trall, *Drug Medicines; their Nature, Consequences, and Modus Operandi; with an Exposition of the False Doctrines on which their Employment is Predicated* (New York: Davies & Kent, 1862); Larkin B. Coles, *Philosophy of Health: Natural Principles of Health and Cure* (Boston, Ticknor and Fields, 1855); Larkin B. Coles, *The Beauties and Deformities of Tobacco-Using* (Boston: Ticknor and Fields, 1855); Dio Lewis, *Weak Lungs and How to Make Them Strong* (Boston: Ticknor and Fields, 1863); Joel Shew, *Tobacco: Its History, Nature, and Effects on the Body and Mind* (New York: Fowler and Wells, 1850); Joel Shew, *The Hydropathic Family Physician; a Ready Prescriber and Hygienic Advisor with Reference to the Nature, Causes, Prevention, and Treatment of Disease, Accidents, and Casualties of Every Kind* (New York: Fowlers & Wells, 1854); Mrs. M. L. Shew, *Water-Cure for Ladies: a Popular Work on the Health, Diet, and Regimen for Females and Children, and the Prevention and Cure of Diseases; With a Full Account of the Processes of Water-Cure; Illustrated With Various Cases* (New York: Wiley and Putnam, 1844); Sylvester Graham, *Lectures on the Science of Human Life*—People's Edition (London: Horsell, Aldine, Chambers, 1849); Sylvester Graham, *A Lecture to Young Men on Chastity* (Boston: Charles H. Pierce, 1848); William A. Alcott, *The Physiology of Marriage* (Boston: Dinsmoor and Co., 1866); William A. Alcott, *Forty Years in the Wilderness of Pill and Powders* (Boston: John P. Jewett and Co., 1859); William A. Alcott, *The Library of Health, and Teacher on the Human Constitution* (Boston: George W. Light, 1837).
49. These "chapters" have been republished in *Selected Messages,* book 2, pp. 410-479. In this material Ellen White utilized some information from contemporary writers that she could endorse.
50. When discussing Ellen White's admonitions on dress today, knowledge of dress customs in the 1860s and her common-sense principles need to be seen in perspective. One of her basic principles appeared in the sixth article: "Christians should not take pains to make themselves gazing-stocks by dressing differently from the world. But if, in accordance with their faith and duty in respect to their dressing modestly and healthfully, they find themselves out of fashion, they should not change their dress in order to be like the world."—*Selected Messages,* book 2, pp. 476. See also *Selected Messages* book 3, pp. 241-255.

Study Questions

1. In what integrating way did the Great Controversy Theme contribute to Ellen White's health message?
2. How did the Whites maintain common sense in their practice of healing themselves and others, when ill?
3. How did the Adventist Church arrive at a position against the eating of swine?
4. What was the essential contribution of the Otsego health vision of 1863 that transcended any particular aspect of the health reform message?
5. What was the significance of including the writings of well-known health reformers in the Seventh-day Adventist magazine, *The Health Reformer*?
6. Review some of the elements of conventional medicine in the nineteenth century.
7. Why were dramatic healings apparently more prevalent among Adventists in the middle nineteenth century than now?
8. Explain Ellen White's rebuke to Stephen Haskell in 1858 regarding swine's flesh and her later condemnation of the practice. What principle can explain each event?

CHAPTER 25

Health Principles/2
Relationship of Health to a Spiritual Mission

"Do not be wise in your own eyes; fear the Lord and depart from evil. It will be health to your flesh, and strength to your bones" (Prov. 3:7, 8).

In their six pamphlets on health, the Whites deliberately included the writings of "able and experienced health reformers in addition to Ellen White's articles."[1] Writing a few years later, James White said that the pamphlets were "made up chiefly from the most spirited and valuable articles and extracts from Trall, Jackson, Graham, Dio Lewis, Coles, Horace Mann, Gunn, and many others. . . . This work was readable and well adapted to the wants of the people. It has also had a wide circulation outside of Seventh-day Adventists, and its influence for good in calling the attention of the people to the subject of health reform can hardly be estimated."[2]

In the first pamphlet, James White wrote the lead article, entitled, "Sanctification." He set the tone for the six-pamphlet set in connecting physical health with spiritual health. Toward the end of this article he said: "To those who are active yet suffering from failing health we urgently recommend health publications, a good assortment of which we design to keep on hand. . . . To those who call themselves well, we would say: As you value the blessings of health, and would honor the Author of your being, learn to live in obedience to those laws established in your being by High Heaven."[3]

The articles written by other health reformers were used to buttress Ellen White's straightforward counsel. At the same time, she urged caution regarding certain notions or suggestions in those other articles included in these six pamphlets, such as a warning that not all sick people may be strong enough for the heroics of cold-water therapy and heavy exercise for long periods of time.

Ellen White avoided the notions of contemporary health reformers that were in conflict with the principles she had received in vision, such as the condemnation of salt, not only as wholly lacking in nutrition but also as indigestible.

How many of these fundamental health principles had Adventists known and implemented in their lives prior to the Otsego vision? What was the result of this additional orbit of reform that those 3,500 Adventists now began to understand more clearly? Apart from Joseph Bates, who decided to be only a silent evangelist for health (see p. 280), very few had adopted any of these principles. Although these principles were discussed here and there, they surely did not represent the medical world in the mid-nineteenth century. And it seems just as certain that few Seventh-day Adventists had taken these reforms seriously prior to 1863.

Several Adventist families (including Annie Smith, J. N. Loughborough, the

J. P. Kellogg family, and the J. N. Andrews family) seemed to have had some acquaintance with one or two of the contemporary advances, but the concept of total health eluded them until they got the coherent, spiritually motivated picture depicted by Ellen White. Some had tried hydrotherapy and used Graham bread. But their general life style, including the way they related to diet, exercise, cleanliness, and fresh air, was generally the same as that of other Americans.[4]

Young Annie Smith

While working at the publishing house in Rochester, New York, as one of James White's editorial assistants, Annie Smith contracted tuberculosis (a very common disease). Although, according to her mother, she made use of hydrotherapy treatments, the disease progressed rapidly, and she was dead in eight months. Very gifted and almost indispensable, she died in 1855 at the age of 27.[5]

J. N. Loughborough's Experience

When J. N. Loughborough was 16, his uncle introduced him to "Graham bread" and a certain kind of hydrotherapy that consisted of bathing in ice-cold water followed by vigorous exercise. His lungs were hemorrhaging and the remedy advised was to smoke tobacco! Writing about the incident years later, Loughborough added: "This resort to cigar smoking shows how vague were our ideas of healthful living."[6]

As a layman, Loughborough preached the doctrines of the First Day Adventists from 1849 to 1852. In 1852, when he was 20, he became a Seventh-day Adventist. In 1864, at age 32, he accompanied the Whites on a New England itinerary. He later wrote of this experience: "I have been greatly benefited in this trip, not only by their instruction in spiritual things, but also by the excellent information they imparted on health, diet, etc.

"And here I would say, that the instruction I have received on health, I am trying to practice. For the short time I have been striving to live strictly in accordance with the laws of life, I have been greatly benefited. It is, however, about one year since I commenced a reform in relation to meat-eating. As I had been in the habit of using meat three times a day when I could get it, for the first two months I only ate meat twice a week. Then for a month, once a week. Then for three months once a month. And for the last four months no meat has passed my lips. And for the last two months I have eaten but two meals a day. Never was sleep sweeter, or health better, or my mind more cheerful, since I first started in the service of God at the age of 17 years, than for the last two months.

"With the short experience I have had, I would not, for any consideration, go back to the meat, spice, pepper, sweet cake, pickles, mustard, headache, stomachache and gloom, and give up the good wholesome fruit, grain, and vegetable diet, with pure cold water as a drink, no headaches, cheerfulness, happiness, vigor and health.

"But I do not urge these things upon others, or judge them about their meat. But I do esteem it a privilege to tell them what a temporal blessing I have found in this direction."[7]

The Andrews Family

Angeline Andrews, scholarly John's wife, kept a diary for the years 1859-1864. An early entry noted the butchering of a pig. She referred to the death of a neighbor child who had a sore throat. The physician lanced it and gave him a dose of morphine, all of which contributed to his sudden death.

In the fall of 1862, daughter Mary had whooping cough. Angeline wrapped the baby in wet sheets, attempting to reduce the fever. The local physician on several occasions administered an assortment of poisons such as ipecac, nitre, and quinine. The worried mother, still reaching out for help, received a recipe for syrup from her sister. After giving the dose to Mary, she wrote: "Mary has never been sicker than this afternoon. Medicine has no effect to vomit her as I supposed it would."[8]

After an article on healing diphtheria with simple water treatments that James White had reprinted in the church paper,[9] it seems that the Andrews family became more interested in "warm baths" in the treatment of illness. But other health reform notions were not evident in the Andrews family life.

In July 1869, J. N. Andrews wrote: "The subject of health reform has engaged my earnest attention for more than five years. During this entire period of time I have endeavored, as a matter of conscience, strictly to regard and live out the principles of this noble reform. As its effects upon myself have been very marked, and such that all with whom I have been associated for this period have observed them, I take pleasure in briefly stating my own experience."[10]

In February 1872, he noted that the beginning of health reform for the Andrews family happened in March 1864.[11] A month later, he wrote specifically about his family's 1864 commitment when they put away "spice, pepper, vinegar . . . butter, meat, fish, and substituted graham flour for fine floor." In their place, they now ate "plenty of good fruit, vegetables, grains," and "used some milk and a very little salt."[12]

The Kellogg Family

The John P. Kellogg family eagerly followed truth as fast as they discovered it. By 1852 they were observing the seventh-day Sabbath through the efforts of Joseph Bates. In 1852 Kellogg had joined three other Adventist stalwarts in proposing to James White that they would underwrite the move of the printing establishment from Rochester, New York, to Battle Creek, Michigan, with a donation of $300 apiece—a heavy sum from their meager assets. Later, Kellogg headed the list of subscribers for the first health institution of the Adventist Church. He fathered sixteen children, including Dr. Merritt Kellogg, Dr. John Harvey Kellogg, and Will K. Kellogg, the cornflake king. The Kellogg family was at the heart of the growing Adventist work in the midwest.

Family records indicate that the Kelloggs made good use of hydropathic methods. But apparently other aspects of health reform were either unknown or, if they were, their importance made no impact. Son John Harvey, born in 1852, recalled that two foods were his favorites in his childhood—ox tails nicely browned in the oven and the candy his father sold in the family store. In the Kellogg family cellar rested a keg of ale to be used "for a weak stomach."[13]

Dr. Kellogg put the question of "who told Ellen White about health reform?" into sharp perspective when he wrote in 1890 in his preface to the book, *Christian Temperance and Bible Hygiene:* "Nearly thirty years ago there appeared in print the first of a series of remarkable and important articles on the subject of health, by Mrs. E. G. White. . . . Thousands were led to change life-long habits, and to renounce practices thoroughly fixed by heredity as well as by long indulgence. So great a revolution could not be wrought in a body of people, without the aid of some powerful incentive, which in this case was undoubtedly the belief that the writings referred to not only bore the stamp of truth, but were endorsed as such by a higher than human authority. . . .

"At the time of the writings referred to first appeared, the subject of health was almost wholly ignored, not only by the people to whom they were addressed, but by the world at large. The few advocating the necessity of a reform in physical habits, propagated in connection with the advocacy of genuine reformatory principles the most patent and in some instances disgusting errors.

"Nowhere, and by no one, was there

presented a systematic and harmonious body of hygienic truths, free from patent errors, and consistent with the Bible and the principles of the Christian religion.

"Many of the principles taught have come to be so generally adopted and practiced that they are no longer recognized as reforms, and may, in fact, be regarded as prevalent customs among the more intelligent classes. The principles which a quarter of a century ago were either entirely ignored or made the butt of ridicule, have quietly won their way into public confidence and esteem, until the world has quite forgotten that they have not always been thus accepted. . . .

"It certainly must be regarded as a thing remarkable, and evincing unmistakable evidence of divine insight and direction, that in the midst of confused and conflicting teachings claiming the authority of science and experience, but warped by ultra notions and rendered impotent for good by the great admixture of error—it must be admitted to be something extraordinary, that a person making no claims to scientific knowledge or erudition should have been able to organize, from the confused and error-tainted mass of ideas advanced by a few writers and thinkers on health subjects, a body of hygienic principles so harmonious, so consistent, and so genuine that the discussions, the researches, the discoveries, and the experience of a quarter of a century have not resulted in the overthrow of a single principle, but have only served to establish the doctrines taught.

"The guidance of infinite wisdom is as much needed in the discerning between truth and error as in the evolution of new truths. Novelty is by no means a distinguishing characteristic of true principles, and the principle holds good as regards the truths of hygienic reform, as well as those of other reformatory movements. . . ."[14]

What should we make of Dr. Kellogg's unqualified endorsement of the impact of Ellen White's seminal health messages derived from her Otsego vision in 1863?

Dr. Kellogg's Endorsement

- In 1863 health reform was "almost totally ignored" by Adventists and "the world at large."
- The few who were advocating "reform" included with their insights "the most patent and . . . disgusting errors."
- No one before Ellen White's messages had presented "a systematic and harmonious body of hygienic truths, free from patent errors, and consistent with the Bible and the principles of the Christian religion."
- Thousands changed lifelong habits after reading these messages because they recognized not only the inherent harmony of these truths, but also their divine endorsement.
- Ellen White's principles have stood "the test of time and experience."
- Many of those principles, ridiculed or ignored in 1863, had become accepted in 1890.
- Remarkable scientific discoveries since 1863 had only strongly fortified those principles, without "the overthrow of a single principle."
- Divine guidance is "as much needed" in distinguishing truth from error as "in the evolution of new truths."
- This nearly thirty-year record gives "unmistakable evidence of divine insight and direction"; in the midst of "confused and conflicting teachings" whereby a person "making no claims to scientific knowledge . . . should organize, from the confused and error-tainted mass of ideas a body of hygienic principles so harmonious, so consistent, and so genuine."

Linkage of the Health Message With the Gospel Commission

Ellen White consistently linked the health emphasis with the "third angel's message"—as close as the "hand is with the body."[15] That is to say, the health message constituted a very important aspect of the "everlasting gospel" (Rev. 14:6). This fundamental linkage is based on three principles:

• *The Humanitarian principle.* In many ways, by example and teaching, Ellen White emphasized that the "work of health reform is the Lord's means for lessening suffering in our world."[16]

• *The Evangelical principle.* Ellen White was instructed (and her own experience validated the principle) that health reform is to be the bridge over which the gospel will meet people where they are. She called the health message a "great entering wedge . . . the door through which the truth for this time is to find entrance to many homes . . . [It] will do much toward removing prejudice against our evangelical work."[17]

Specifically, in regard to Adventist health-care institutions, she wrote: "The great object of receiving unbelievers into the institution [the sanitarium] is to lead them to embrace the truth."[18]

• *The Soteriological principle.* This third principle supplied the Adventist distinctive to nineteenth-century health reform: the Adventist emphasis on health was to help "fit a people for the coming of the Lord." "He who cherishes the light which God has given upon health reform, has an important aid in the work of becoming sanctified through the truth, and fitted for immortality."[19]

This threefold linkage has not always been understood. Some made the health message an end in itself in developing a worldwide network of hospitals and clinics; others made the health message into a compelling public relations stratagem whereby non-Adventists would become interested enough to sit through an evangelistic sermon. Both were worthy uses of Adventist health principles—but short of the primary purpose that made Ellen White's health emphasis distinctive. The primary purpose was to join the spiritual and the physical on the practical, daily level of the average person.

Health Principles and Spiritual Goals

Ellen White was specific and practical as she applied the principles of the Great Controversy Theme to joining the spiritual with the physical and mental. Placing health matters within the intent of the Three Angels' Messages of Revelation 14 raised the health issue from personal opinion to the level of spiritual commitment and character development. Health principles were linked with spiritual goals:

• *First duty to God and man is self-development.* The following creative statement by Mrs. White has inspired many young people: "Our first duty to God and our fellow beings is that of self-development. . . . Hence that time is spent to good account which is used in the establishment and preservation of physical and mental health. We cannot afford to dwarf or cripple any function of body or mind."[20]

• *Heart reform before health reform.* Ellen White kept priorities straight—preserving health is primarily a spiritual challenge: "Men will never be truly temperate until the grace of Christ is an abiding principle in the heart. . . . No mere restriction of your diet will cure your diseased appetite. . . . What Christ works within, will be worked out under the dictation of a converted intellect. The plan of beginning outside and trying to work inward has always failed, and always will fail."[21]

• *Preparation for the latter rain and the loud cry.* This application of health principles is profound and distinctively an Adventist insight. Ellen White wrote in 1867: "God's people are not prepared for the loud cry of the third angel. They have a work to do for themselves which they should not leave for God to do for them. . . . Lustful appetite makes slaves of men and women, and beclouds their intellects and stupefies their moral sensibilities to such a degree that the sacred, elevated truths of God's Word are not appreciated. . . . In order to be fitted for translation, the people of God must know themselves. . . . They should ever have the appetite in subjection to the moral and intellectual organs."[22]

• *Health closely linked with sanctification.* Ellen White was not hesitant in pointing to the direct relationship between daily habits and character development: "A diseased body and disordered intellect, because of continual indulgence in hurtful lust, make sanctification of the body and spirit impossible."[23] Further, for "those who have received instruction regarding the evils of the use of "flesh foods, tea, and coffee, and rich and unhealthful food preparations, . . . God demands that the appetite be cleansed, and that self-denial be practiced. . . . This is a work that will have to be done before His people can stand before Him a perfected people."[24]

Adventist leaders such as J. H. Waggoner saw the distinctive difference between contemporary voices appealing for health reform and the "advanced principle" of Ellen White. Waggoner wrote: "We do not profess to be pioneers in the general principles of the health reform. The facts on which this movement is based have been elaborated, in a great measure, by reformers, physicians, and writers on physiology and hygiene, and so may be found scattered through the land. But we do claim that by the method of God's choice it has been more clearly and powerfully unfolded, and is thereby producing an effect which we could not have looked for from any other means.

"As mere physiological and hygienic truths, they might be studied by some at their leisure, and by others laid aside as of little consequence; but when placed on a level with the great truths of the third angel's message by the sanction and authority of God's Spirit, and so declared to be the means whereby a weak people may be made strong to overcome, and our diseased bodies cleansed and fitted for translation, then it comes to us as an essential part of present truth, to be received with the blessing of God, or rejected at our peril."[25]

• *Health directly affects moral judgment.* Probably Ellen White's linking health with moral judgment has been one of the most compelling concepts for unnumbered thousands: "Anything that lessens physical strength enfeebles the mind, and makes it less capable of discriminating between right and wrong. We become less capable of choosing the good and have less strength of will to do that which we know to be right."[26]

Many early Adventists conceded that eliminating pork and alcoholic beverages was in one's best interest. Some further conceded that flesh foods were not beneficial. But the connection between temperance (self-control) and spiritual discernment, did not come quickly. Most, at first, saw no link between preaching the gospel or their own spiritual growth and what they ate. Ellen White maintained her course, often against many who thought she was advocating extremes. She resolutely led her colleagues into thinking more clearly: "Some have sneered at this work of reform, and have said it was all unnecessary; that it was an excitement to divert minds from present truth. They have said that matters were being carried to extremes. Such do not know what they are talking about. While men and women professing godliness are diseased from the crown of their head to the soles of their feet, while their physical, mental, and moral energies are enfeebled through gratification of depraved appetite and excessive labor, how can they weigh the evidences of truth, and comprehend the requirements of God?"[27]

• *Commitment to health reveals one's depth of caring for others.* Ellen White was intensely practical. Her counsel was easy to understand. In those days before the services of the modern hospital and the latest antibiotics, the extended family often lived under one roof. The elderly and the sick were the burdens of whoever happened to be healthy at the moment.

Mrs. White, observing how heavy that burden fell on young busy mothers and other members of the family, wrote: "Many by their actions have said, 'It is nobody's business whether I eat this or that. Whatever we do, we are to bear the consequences ourselves.' Dear friends, you are greatly mistaken. You are not the only sufferers from a wrong course. The society you are in bears the consequences of your wrongs, in a great degree, as well as yourselves. If you suffer from your intemperance in eating or drinking, we that are around you or associated with you are also affected by your infirmities. We have to suffer on account of your wrong course. . . . If, instead of having a buoyancy of spirit, you are gloomy, you cast a shadow upon the spirits of all around you. . . . We may have a good degree of confidence in our own judgment, yet we want to have counselors; for 'in the multitude of counselors there is safety'. . . . But what care we for your judgment, if your brain nerve power has been taxed to the utmost, and the vitality withdrawn from the brain to take care of the improper food placed in your stomachs, or of an enormous quantity of even healthful food? . . . Therefore your course of living affects us. It is impossible for you to pursue any wrong course without causing others to suffer."[28]

• *Commitment to health is best motivated by a desire to glorify God in helping others.* Paul made it clear that living for the glory of God is the Christian's highest goal: "Therefore, whether you eat or drink, or whatever you do, do all to the glory of God" (1 Cor. 10:31). Ellen White frequently focused on this motivation as the "glory of self-sacrificing love. In the light from Calvary it will be seen that the law of self-renouncing love is the law of life for earth and heaven; that the love which 'seeketh not her own' has its source in the heart of God."[29]

Side benefits of this highest motivation include longer life and less disease, etc. But if the higher motivation is eclipsed, much of health reform may be self-centered to the neglect of the well-being of others. Caring for one's health is a spiritual matter, not merely a physical concern.

• *Commitment to health among the factors relating to a prepared people.* Ellen White directly linked a person's commitment to physical and spiritual health with his or her readiness for eternal life. Here again "restoration"[30]—the goal of The Great Controversy Theme—determined the philosophy of health.

Regarding the kind of people prepared for Jesus's return, Mrs. White wrote: "We believe without a doubt that Christ is soon coming. . . . When He comes He is not to cleanse us of our sins, to remove from us the defects in our characters, or to cure us of the infirmities of our tempers and dispositions. If wrought for us at all, this work will all be accomplished before that time. When the Lord comes, those who are holy will be holy still. Those who have preserved their bodies and spirits in holiness, in sanctification and honor, will then receive the finishing touch of immortality."[31]

Not Merely a Difference of Opinion

Uniting or separating the physical from the spiritual is not merely a philosophical issue, nor a matter of only interpersonal differences of opinion. The Kellogg crisis of the late 1890s and early 1900s may have ended up as a power struggle but it rested on issues far deeper than personal opinion. It centered on the future direction of Adventist thought and practice. At the turn of the century the denomination was struggling with the growing strength of the "right arm."[32] The health-message proponents and its growing political (denominational) power seemed to be directing the worldwide program of the church.[33] Complicating the confrontation were the aberrant theological views of Dr. Kellogg. At stake was not only the clarity of Adventist theology but also the direction of denominational finances.

Underlying the power struggle was the

conviction of the medical leadership, with considerable evidence, that the ministerial leadership accepted only a part of the health message. Some denominational leaders actually resented Kellogg's enthusiastic endorsement of Mrs. White's larger view of healthful living—especially in her condemnation of flesh foods. Kellogg found it difficult to accept criticism of his book, *The Living Temple,* from meat-eating denominational leaders.[34]

Though wrong, from Kellogg's point of view Ellen White's support of the denomination's "spiritual" leadership in 1901 (in the reorganization that would also limit the health arm) and in her attack on *The Living Temple* meant that she had been misled and strongly influenced by his enemies. The subsequent rupture between the health emphasis and the ministerial-theological leadership has separated many through the years and unnecessarily complicated the unified voice of the Seventh-day Adventist Church.

The administrative "surgery" in the 1900s that reduced the "right arm" to its proper relationship to the body only deepened the wound. Divorcing the spiritual from the physical created an even more serious illness. Reducing the "right arm's" political power to its proper relationship to denominational organization crippled the deeper issues of how physical habits directly affect mental and spiritual health.

Some say that the "right arm" of the gospel of health has been living in virtual isolation from the spiritual body—a sign that the spiritual body has misunderstood its own gospel. For some strange reason, for the most part, neither spiritual leaders nor health leaders saw that physical habits could not be separated from spiritual growth if the integrity of the Adventist message was to be maintained. Ellen White called this separation between gospel ministers and medical missionary workers "the worst evil" that could be placed on the Adventist Church.[35]

This rupture is not a mere theoretical disagreement. Not including the principles of the health message within the fullness of the "everlasting gospel" directly affects the preparation of the church to fulfill its gospel commission. Further, it hinders growth in grace.[36]

This divorce between what God Himself had joined together has limited the potential of the Adventist witness and blunted the full impact of the "everlasting gospel." (1) Denominational health-care institutions may not fully sense their original purpose of (a) instructing the world in the application of "natural remedial agencies" to prevent as well as cure disease and (b) to make their institutions an unequivocal witness to the principles of the gospel as developed in the third angel's message.[37] (2) At the same time, some spiritual leaders have either discredited or ignored the health principles that Dr. Kellogg and Ellen White strongly endorsed. Trying to promote the distinctive message of Revelation 14 with the right arm paralyzed is virtually self-defeating.

Both medical and ministerial leadership have often forgotten that one of the principles of the Great Controversy Theme is that men and women are responsible and that God will not work "miracles" that bypass obedience to known duty.[38] When both health leaders and spiritual leaders encourage "healing" methods that bypass human responsibility for choices, the principles of life are violated. For example, when the sick are encouraged to receive health care without adherence to the natural laws that caused the sickness, the gospel is not understood.[39] Or, when the sinner is encouraged to believe that God forgives when commitment to known duty is ignored, clearly the gospel is misrepresented.[40]

Ellen White boldly encouraged church members who sense "the dead level into which they have fallen" to reconnect the health message to the theological message: "Send into the churches workers who will set the principles of health reform in their connection with the third angel's message before every family and individual. Encourage all to take a part in work for their fellow men, and see if the breath of life will not quickly return to these churches."[41]

Linkage of the Minister and the Physician

The Great Controversy Theme seeks "restoration" as the goal of salvation. Whatever subject Ellen White focuses on, this goal integrates all of its aspects. Thus the Great Controversy Theme informs the basis and purpose of health reform. It naturally follows, then, that the physician and the minister are to "work in tandem. Like harnessed horses, they . . . [are] to pull the Adventist carriage at the same speed."[42]

In the developing years of Adventist health work, Ellen White riveted her contemporaries on the importance of joining health reform with the completion of the gospel commission.[43] For her, the gospel evangelist/minister and the gospel healer were to work together with mutual aims and joint evangelistic efforts.[44]

Dr. John Harvey Kellogg was one of the few leaders who took Mrs. White's counsel on health seriously. Few gospel ministers saw the same connection between the health message and spiritual development.[45] And her support of Dr. Kellogg was never in doubt, until—until Dr. Kellogg's fertile mind began to misunderstand the purpose of his own health message.

In 1896 he was instrumental in changing the name of his health network from the Seventh-day Adventist Medical Missionary and Benevolent Association to the International Medical Missionary and Benevolent Association. Two years later he explained that this organization was developed "to carry forward medical and philanthropic work independent of any sectarian or denominational control, in home and foreign lands."[46] In 1898 he declared at a convention of the association that the delegates gathered "'here as Christians, and not as Seventh-day Adventists.'"[47]

Ellen White had been exceedingly patient with Dr. Kellogg, whom she and her husband had personally sponsored in getting his medical degree.[48] She knew well the resentment and unpleasantries that some of the ministers had directed at him. And she knew also his untactful sharpness. But when he openly defied the denomination, which through the years had supplied the money for the development of his famous Battle Creek Sanitarium, she felt compelled to speak openly: "It has been stated that the Battle Creek Sanitarium is not denominational. But if ever an institution was established to be denominational in every sense of the word, this sanitarium was."[49]

Dr. Kellogg was permitting health reform to eclipse theological principles. The situation came to a head, symbolized by the "iceberg" analogy.[50] Though Ellen White groaned under the pending rupture between the ministers and the physicians, she was deeply sympathetic for her friend, Dr. Kellogg. In 1904 she wrote of her frustration and her empathy for him. But in that same letter she also wrote: "My brethren, the Lord calls for unity, for oneness. We are to be one in the faith. I want to tell you that when the gospel ministers and the medical missionary workers are not united, there is placed on our churches the worst evil that can be placed there. . . . It is time that we stood upon a united platform. But we cannot unite with Dr. Kellogg until he stands where he can be a safe leader of the flock of God."[51]

The challenge ever since 1904 has been to address "the worst evil" that could rest on the Seventh-day Adventist Church. If the challenge is to be met, both ministers and physicians must restudy the counsel of Ellen White regarding the purpose of church health-care institutions, rethink the purpose of the "everlasting gospel" that must be proclaimed credibly before Jesus returns, and make a new commitment to the inspired principles set forth by Ellen White.

Endnotes

1. *Review and Herald,* Dec. 13, 1864.
2. *The Health Reformer,* Feb., 1871.
3. *Health, or How to Live*, No. 1, p. 18.
4. A specialist in the history of medicine graphically describes nineteenth-century habits: "For all its apparent vitality, America in the early nineteenth century was a sick and dirty nation. Public sanitation was grossly inadequate, and personal hygiene virtually nonexistent. The great majority of Americans seldom, if ever, bathed. Their eating habits, including the consumption of gargantuan amounts of meat, were enough to keep most stomachs continually upset. Fruits and green and leafy vegetables seldom appeared on the table, and the food that did appear was often saturated with butter or lard. A 'common' breakfast consisted of 'Hot bread, made with lard and strong alkalies, and soaked with butter; hot griddle cakes, covered with butter and syrup; meats fried in fat or baked in it; potatoes dripping with grease; ham and eggs fried in grease into a leathery indigestibility—all washed down with many cups of strong Brazil coffee.' It is no wonder that one writer called dyspepsia 'the great endemic of the northern states.'"—Numbers, *Prophetess of Health,* p. 48.
5. Rebekah Smith (mother) *Poems With a Brief Sketch of the Life and Experience of Annie R. Smith* (Manchester, N.H.: John B. Clarke, Printer, 1871).
6. *Medical Missionary and Gospel of Health,* Dec. 1899.
7. *Review and Herald,* Dec. 6, 1864.
8. Diary for August 25, 1862, in Heritage Room, Del E. Webb Memorial Library, Loma Linda University.
9. James C. Jackson, "Diphtheria, Its Causes, Treatment and Cure," *Review and Herald,* Feb. 17, 1863.
10. *Health Reformer*, July 1869. Andrews died in 1883 at the age of 54, a victim of tuberculosis.
11. *Ibid.,* Feb., 1872.
12. *Ibid.,* Mar., 1872.
13. Richard Schwarz, *John Harvey Kellogg,* **M.D.**, (Nashville: Southern Publishing Association, 1970), p. 25. Schwarz, *John Harvey Kellogg: American Health Reformer* (Ph.D. dissertation, University of Michigan, Ann Arbor, 1964), p. 10.
14. *Christian Temperance and Bible Hygiene* (Battle Creek: Good Health Publication Company, 1890.) The preface does not name its author as Dr. J. H. Kellogg, however in his presentation to the General Conference session on March 3, 1897, Dr. Kellogg said: "Now in the preface to *Christian Temperance* you will find a statement which I presume not very many of you have read. There is no name signed to the preface, but I wrote it. But if you will read it, you will find a statement to the effect that every single statement with reference to healthful living, and the general principles that underlie the subject, have been verified by scientific discovery. I sometimes see some of our brethren appear to be a little shaky on the testimonies; they do not know whether these things come from the Lord or not; but to those I invariably say that if you will study the subject of health reform from the testimonies, and then from the light of scientific discovery—compare it with what science teaches at the present time—you will be amazed; you will see what a flood of light was given us thirty years ago. There is, however, a more amazing thing than that, and it is that this light which was given to us at that time, confirmed as it is by scientific discovery—I say the most amazing thing of all is that we as a people have turned our backs upon this, and have not accepted it, and believed in it as we should. I want to repeat it that there is not a single principle in relation to the healthful development of our bodies and minds that is advocated in these writings from Sister White, which I am not prepared to demonstrate conclusively from scientific evidence." Ellen White wrote the part of the book called "Christian Temperance," and "Bible Hygiene" was written by James White.
15. *Testimonies,* vol. 3, p. 62.
16. *Ibid.,* vol. 9, p. 112.
17. *Evangelism*, pp. 513, 514
18. *Testimonies,* vol. 1, p. 560.
19. *Testimonies,* vol. 3, pp. 161; *Christian Temperance and Bible Hygiene*, p. 10
20. *Counsels on Diet and Foods,* p. 15; see also *Christ's Object Lessons,* p. 329.
21. *Ibid.,* p. 35.
22. *Ibid.,* pp. 32, 33.
23. *Ibid.,* p. 44.
24. *Ibid.,* p. 381.
25. *Review and Herald*, Aug. 7, 1866.
26. *Christ's Object Lessons,* p. 346.
27. *Counsels on Diet and Foods,* pp. 50, 51. "What a pity it is that often, when the greatest self-denial should be exercised, the stomach is crowded with a mass of unhealthful food, which lies there to decompose. The affliction of the stomach affects the brain. The imprudent eater does not realize that he is disqualifying himself for laying plans for the best advancement of the work of God."—*Ibid.,* p. 53.
28. *Testimonies,* vol. 2, pp. 356, 357.
29. *The Desire of Ages,* p. 20; *Ibid.,* p. 824; *Education,* p. 125.
30. *The Desire of Ages,* p. 824; *Education*, p. 125. See p. 257.
31. *Testimonies,* vol. 2, p. 355.
32. *Ibid.,* see vol. 6, p. 327.
33. In 1901 John Harvey Kellogg's Medical Missionary and Benevolent Association employed about 2,000 workers compared to only 1,500 under the direction of the General Conference.—Schwarz, *Light Bearers,* p. 278.
34. "To Kellogg, the chief villains responsible for denominational backsliding in regard to health principles were the Adventist ministry. They, the doctor charged, tended to 'discourage the people by their example.'" —Schwarz, *John Harvey Kellogg,* p. 175.
35. *Medical Ministry,* p. 241.
36. *Review and Herald,* May 27, 1902.
37. *The Ministry of Healing,* p. 127. "The purpose of our health institutions is not first and foremost to be that of hospitals. The health institutions connected with the closing work of the gospel in the earth stand for the great principles of the gospel in all its fullness. . . . If a sanitarium connected with this closing message fails to lift up Christ and the principles of the gospel as developed in the third angel's message, it fails in its most important feature, and contradicts the very object of its existence."—*Medical Ministry,* pp. 27, 28.
38. See pp. 274, 310.
39. *Testimonies,* vol. 6, p. 441.
40. *Selected Messages,* book 1, p. 396; *Steps to Christ,* pp. 23-33.
41. *Testimonies to Ministers,* p. 416. "Make regular, organized efforts to lift the church members out of the dead

level in which they have been for years. Send out into the churches workers who will live the principles of health reform. Let those be sent who can see the necessity of self-denial in appetite, or they will be a snare to the church. See if the breath of life will not then come into our churches. A new element needs to be brought into the work."—*Testimonies*, vol. 6, p. 267.

42. Bull and Lockhart, *Seeking a Sanctuary*, p. 219.
43. See pp. 285, 292.
44. "I wish to speak about the relation existing between the medical missionary work and the gospel ministry. It has been presented to me that every department of the work is to be united in one great whole. The work of God is to prepare a people to stand before the Son of man at His coming, and this work should be a unit. The work that is to fit a people to stand firm in the last great day must not be a divided work. . . .

    "Gospel workers are to minister on the right hand and on the left, doing their work intelligently and solidly. There is to be no division between the ministry and the medical work. The physician should labor equally with the minister, and with as much earnestness and thoroughness for the salvation of the soul, as well as for the restoration of the body."—*Medical Ministry*, p. 237. "The Holy Spirit never has, and never will in the future, divorce the medical missionary work from the gospel ministry. They cannot be divorced. Bound up with Jesus Christ, the ministry of the word and the healing of the sick are one."—Manuscript 21, 1906, cited in *Special Testimonies*, Series B, No. 7.
45. Bull and Lockhart, *Seeking a Sanctuary*, p. 219.
46. *Medical Missionary*, Jan. 1898, cited in *Bio.*, vol. 5, p. 160.
47. *Medical Missionary Conference Bulletin*, May, 1899, *Extra*, cited in *Bio.*, *Ibid.*
48. Schwarz, *John Harvey Kellogg: American Health Reformer*, *op. cit.*, p. 29.
49. Letter 128, 1902, to "The GC Committee and the Medical Missionary Board," cited in *Bio.*, vol. 5, p. 160. Later in that letter she wrote: "Why are sanitariums established if it is not that they may be the right hand of the gospel in calling the attention of men and women to the truth that we are living amid the perils of the last days? And yet, in one sense, it is true that the Battle Creek Sanitarium is undenominational, in that it receives as patients people of all classes and all denominations. . . . We are not to take pains to declare that the Battle Creek Sanitarium is not a Seventh-day Adventist institution; for this it certainly is. As a Seventh-day Adventist institution it was established to represent the various features of gospel missionary work, thus to prepare the way for the coming of the Lord."
50. See *Bio.*, vol 5, p. 160.
51. Manuscript 46, 1904, an address to the union conference session at Battle Creek, cited in *Bio.*, vol. 5, p. 332.

Study Questions

1. Why do you think Dr. Kellogg's introduction to *Christian Temperance and Bible Hygiene* is significant?
2. What are the three basic principles that link the health message with the mission of the Seventh-day Adventist Church? How have they developed in the work of Seventh-day Adventists?
3. Do you agree that "restoration" is a good one-word description of the plan of salvation? How does this concept relate to health principles?
4. What is the essential message in the "iceberg" analogy involving Dr. Kellogg?
5. In what way is the Christian's "first duty toward God" and our fellow human beings that of self-development and yet the opposite of self-centeredness?
6. How do health principles directly affect spiritual goals, and how does the health of God's people relate to end-time events?

CHAPTER 26

Health Principles/3
Quality Improvement in Adventist Health

"You need not go into the water, or into the fire, but take the middle road, avoiding all extremes."[1]

Across the Adventist world in the 1860s went the broad message of health reform. Not all joined the march forward. But many did and their hearty gratitude was reported in the church paper.

R. M. Kilgore, former army captain and long-time evangelist-administrator, described the new life of better health shared by many: "As they advanced, they felt their diseases, aches, and pains leaving them, and in return buoyancy of spirit, and glow of health, the greatest earthly blessings. Thus, those in front accepted the offered mercies, not given by commandment or way of urging, but to obtain the blessing resulting from such a course of life and habits; by obeying the laws of their being which God implanted, and cleansing the temple for the indwelling of His Holy Spirit; which will be poured more copiously upon those who are ready to receive it."[2]

M. E. Cornell, pioneer evangelist in Michigan and California, penned his gratitude: "I believe the reform came up just in time to save me from becoming a complete wreck. Fourteen years of incessant labor, with all kinds of unhealthy diet and but little attention to the laws of life, had nearly used up a strong constitution. Now I hope to recover, by the blessing of God, and endure to the end. My whole being cries out, Praise God for the health reform. Let those who have adopted the reform hold on. And I exhort all others to take hold of it in earnest."[3]

At 68, John Byington, the church's first General Conference president, wrote that after making "proper changes in diet" he no longer had a severe cough that threatened his survival. Further, he had "gained in flesh, have more warmth in my system, and feel better prepared to endure another cold winter."[4]

J. H. Waggoner affirmed: "I thank God for the health reform. It is no cross; it is no hardship; it brings pleasure in pain and gives strength in weakness. . . . When bearing heavy burdens of body and mind, when all looked dark and cheerless in this world, it has come as a messenger of mercy, strengthening the body, cheering the mind, and refreshing the spirits, and bringing the peace of the Saviour to the sorrowing soul."[5]

Joseph Clark, a layman, wrote enthusiastically: "Since adopting the health reform, my own health has been so much benefited that I have been at a loss to know whether it was duty to tell others of it, lest they might consider me an enthusiast; but over two years have passed away since we commenced to live out the health reform, and it is proving to be even better than I had imagined at first."[6]

Looking back over the previous twenty years, Dr. J. H. Kellogg stated:

"Numerous reforms in diet and dress were introduced and quite generally adopted. These reforms were of such a character that, when conscientiously carried out, they invariably produced a decided change for the better on the part of those adopting them. Hundreds who had for years suffered from various chronic ailments were soon relieved of the distressing symptoms which had been endured so long. Many whose cases had been pronounced hopeless were restored to excellent health. Others who seemed to be just on the brink of the grave received a new lease of life and ability for eminent usefulness. The most extraordinary evidences of good resulting from the adoption of health reform principles—results which in many instances seemed little short of miracles—were to be met on every hand. In every community of Sabbathkeepers were to be found those who freely acknowledged that they owed their lives to the light which they had received upon this question."[7]

James White, the Highly Visible Exception

As we noted earlier, pages 54-56, James White since 1844 had been doing the work of several men. By the time he was 44 he was worn out. He had carried the burden of financial accountability when others were slow to contribute; he had almost single-handedly led a "scattered flock" into becoming an organized church with doctrinal unity and a common goal; his pen had become a remarkable expositor of clear gospel teachings; and he was a constant source of encouragement and vision for others. But he did not know how to rest, nor was he temperate in his eating habits.

On August 16, 1865, he suffered his first stroke after a week of unusual stress and little sleep. He was mentally and physically exhausted, virtually incapacitated. Realizing that emergency procedures were needed when he failed to respond to home rest, Ellen White remembered that her health reform principles included a special emphasis on hydrotherapy. But she did not know how this principle would work out in practice, especially for such a serious problem as her husband's. So, in late September, 1865, she took James to "Our Home," a health institution at Dansville, New York, that emphasized hydropathic treatments and other medical practices that involved natural methods rather than conventional drug therapy.[8]

In reflecting on this decision, especially when some church members thought they were not truly trusting James to God in prayer, Ellen White wrote: "While we did not feel like despising the means God had placed in our reach for the recovery of health, we felt that God was above all, and He who had provided water as His agent would have us use it to assist abused Nature to recover her exhausted energies. We believed that God would bless the efforts we were making in the direction of health.

"We did not doubt that God could work a miracle, and in a moment restore to health and vigor. But should He do this, would we not be in danger of again transgressing—abusing our strength by prolonged, intemperate labor, and bringing upon ourselves even a worse condition of things?"[9]

The Gospel Sieve

The Whites remained at Dansville for three months although Dr. Jackson strongly advocated six to eight months.[10] What did they learn? By late November, Ellen White, convinced that James was not getting better, decided to return to their Battle Creek home.

However, she "did not feel that the three months . . . was in vain." They had gathered "many things of value from those who had obtained an experience in health reform." But she concluded that there was no further "necessity of gathering the chaff with the wheat."[11] Here, in a practical setting, her vision-driven understanding of health reform was able to separate worthy principles of her day from the ill-advised. For example:

• Discarding salt at Dansville was not in everyone's best interest. Because of an emerging digestive problem, Dr. Jackson suggested that Ellen White eat in her room where she could use salt in moderation without raising questions in the minds of others.[12]

• Overheated lecture halls seriously affected James's head. Fresh air was needed at all times for clear thinking as well as for physical comfort.[13]

• Though they considered Dr. Jackson to be a "clear and impressive speaker" and "decidedly thorough,"[14] he and the other physicians believed that the Whites were "too intensely religious, and that is the reason why we are invalids."[15] The Dansville program emphasized "amusements and pleasure, dancing, card-playing, theater going, etc.," which the Whites could not harmonize with the "teachings of Christ recorded in the New Testament."[16] While experiencing severe mood swings and sinking hope, many prayer sessions through the days and nights provided James with the peace of mind that led to sleep.

• Believing that overwork caused James's physical and mental breakdown, the Dansville physicians strongly promoted complete physical and mental inaction. But Ellen White realized that this dictum was "one of the most serious obstacles to his recovery. Because of her vision-driven insights, she knew that for him "to sink down in aimless inactivity was to foster disease and to become the prey of despondency."[17]

Though she often stated that the Dansville "water-cure establishment" was the best institution of its kind in the United States, she soon saw that those accompanying her and James would have to "carry along with them at all times the gospel sieve, and sift everything they hear, that they may choose the good and refuse the bad."[18]

Early in December, Mrs. White was convinced that further time at Dansville would not help James recover. She saw his courage and buoyancy of spirit slipping rapidly. Weeks of inaction had brought him to the place where he himself feared physical exercise. Furthermore, she knew that trust in God was the pathway to courage and hope and that Dansville was not the environment to encourage such faith. And so to Rochester, New York, forty miles (64 km) from Dansville, the White party went where they would be surrounded by men and women of faith.

The Rochester Vision of Hope and New Territory to Conquer

While in family worship Christmas day, December 25, 1865, Ellen White was taken off in vision. This vision ranks with the Otsego vision of June 6, 1863, in unfolding the significance of health reform within the third angel's message.

The Otsego vision opened up the integrated system of health principles that the Lord wanted the Adventist Church to adopt. The Rochester vision emphasized how feeble had been the response of most church members and gave even more explicit information as to how the church was to coordinate health reform with the gospel message. Ellen White wrote out the vision the next day and gave the document to James. For months they had been wondering why they had seen no progress in his recovery. They now knew why and what they must do about it.

The key points of the vision were:

• It was God's will that they went to Dansville, for otherwise they could not have learned what had to be known "in so short a time."

• The Dansville home is the "best health institution in the United States . . . yet, the leaders there are but men, and their judgment is not always correct."

• When people who have suffered much "are relieved by an intelligent system of treatment . . . they are often led to conclude" that their physicians who treat them are also "right in matters of religious faith, or at least cannot greatly err from the truth."

• God could not glorify His name by answering the prayers of His people for the Whites while at Dansville, for "the physicians there would have taken the glory which should be given to God."

• Through this experience God was "fitting up" James to be a stronger leader in health reform, in that he and others could speak more effectively regarding the "relation which eating, working, resting, and dressing sustain to health."

• "God requires all . . . to place themselves in the best possible condition of bodily health" to attain a "healthy religious experience," and that the Lord will not "do for them that which He requires them to do for themselves."

• James had let fear and anxiety overwhelm his faith and that, by the power of his will and trusting in God's power, he would regain his health.

• Church members had been "negligent in acting upon the light which God has given in regard to the health reform"; that such work "had scarcely" begun.

• "Few . . . understand how much their habits of diet have to do with their health, their characters, their usefulness in this world, and their eternal destiny."

• "God's people are not prepared for the loud cry of the third angel. They have a work to do for themselves which they should not leave for God to do for them."

• Seventh-day Adventists must develop their own health institution. This institution would be "the means of introducing our faith in new places and raising the standard of truth where it would have been impossible to gain access had not prejudice been first removed."

• This health institution should provide a home for (1) "the afflicted," and (2) for those "who wish to learn how to take care of their bodies that they may prevent sickness."

• This institution must be financially independent, not to be "embarrassed by a constant expenditure of means without realizing any returns."

• "The great object" of this institution "is not only health, but perfection and the spirit of holiness, which cannot be attained with diseased bodies and minds."

• The sick are to be taught that "it is wrong to suspend all physical labor in order to regain health."

• "The greatest danger" would be for the managers to depart "from the spirit of the present truth, and from that simplicity which should ever characterize the disciples of Christ . . . in order to help the feelings of unbelievers, and thus secure their patronage."[19]

The Beginning of Adventist Health Institutions

The implications of this Rochester vision were broad; the principles set forth are still valid. In practice, this vision provided Ellen White with a course of action to help her feeble husband in his slow recovery, a plan to spend the winter of 1866-1867 in northern Michigan.[20] Further, this vision became an electrifying call to the young church to advance and establish an Adventist health institution. On one hand, such a thought seemed preposterous; on the other, it was the next logical step in fulfilling God's plan through the Adventist Church.

Ellen White's Sabbath sermon at the General Conference session in Battle Creek, May 19, 1866, emphasized, perhaps for the first time publicly, the instruction given her in the Rochester health reform vision. Within days, the leadership responded to the call for a health institution, though with trepidation. J. N. Loughborough, president of the Michigan Conference, recalled: "When this testimony was read to our people, the question arose, 'How can we, in our condition of limited means, obtain and control a health institution? . . . The committee . . . prayed over the matter, and said, 'We will pledge to the enterprise, venturing out on what is said in the testimony, though it looks to us like a heavy load for us to hold up.'"[21]

Within days, property was bought and tanks installed on the roof for hydrotherapy treatments. By September 5 the Western Health Reform Institute was ready for patients under the medical care of Drs. H. S. Lay and Phoebe Lamson.[22] Yet, many were the perils that lay ahead. The counsel of Ellen White saved the institutional management from making serious errors, especially in regard to the purpose of the institution: (1) The object is not primarily for "gain," although it must be financially independent, not drawing on other denominational funds; (2) Standards must not be lowered in order to "patronize unbelievers"; (3) The institution, though not to be a place for "diversion or amusement," will create an environment free from "diseased imaginations," "dissatisfied feelings," and "discontented repinings"; (4) The institution is established to "improve the health of the body that the afflicted may more highly appreciate eternal things"; (5) The institution should not expand any faster than adequate "skill, experience, and finance could be provided."[23]

Even more amazing, in addition to establishing a medical institution, was the decision to publish *Health Reformer,* a periodical that Dr. H. S. Lay would edit. Shortly after its introduction, Ellen White wrote: "The *Health Reformer* is the medium through which rays of light are to shine upon the people. It should be the best health journal in our country. It must be adapted to the wants of the common people, ready to answer all proper questions and fully explain the first principles of the laws of life and how to obey them and preserve health."[24]

Fifth Health Vision

The fifth of the health vision series occurred in Bordoville, Vermont, on December 10, 1871.[25] Visions were not given frivolously or merely to repeat the message of previous visions. God dispenses wisdom as fast as men and women can appreciate it, especially after they have obeyed known duty. Prophets also learn step by step, even as church groups advance step by step in joining divine instruction with practice.[26]

By 1871 the Western Health Reform Institute had been operating for five years. The leaders were working in untried territory and mistakes were made, even to the point of failure. Without the Whites, the Institute would have died under a load of debt and extremist policies.[27]

In the Bordoville vision Ellen White again reiterated the primary purpose of Adventist health institutions—a purpose that had become fuzzy in the interim: Adventist health work is as "closely connected with the third angel's message as the hand is with the body."[28] Further, Adventist health work was not to be done in some quiet corner: Adventist health principles should "be agitated, and the public mind deeply stirred to investigate."[29] Mrs. White reiterated that Adventist institutions are "established upon different principles" from health centers that are "conservative, making it their object to meet the popular class half way . . . that they will receive the greatest patronage and the most money."[30]

Other explicit principles relating to Adventist health institutions included:

• Adventist health institutions are to unite Biblical principles with the care of the sick. But Adventist distinctives "should not be discussed with patients," even in the weekly prayer meetings. "Silent witness will do more than open controversy. . . . We must meet people where they are."[31]

• Wise health-care workers realize that many sufferers have more than physical pain. "Many carry a violated conscience, and can be reached only by the principles of Bible religion."[32]

• The home church at Battle Creek must live up to its "greatest responsibility," and when church members do not live up to the light that health-care workers are giving to the patients, confusion and discouragement are the result.[33]

By the early 1870s Adventist interest in health reform, with its first medical institution and health journal plus its emphasis on training quality physicians, had now become highly visible and effective in reaching out to all classes of society.[34]

The Principle of Moderation Avoids Extremes

The credentials of a prophet are seen often in the common sense of his or her message. God is not unreasonable, neither are His prophets. Ellen White provides a classic example of common sense[35] in her relation to health reform. After she had emphasized the need for health reform through her writings for a few years, after the first few years of the Battle Creek health institution, and after a few years of the *Health Reformer*, she recognized that some caution was needed: "In reforms, we would better come one step short of the mark than to go one step beyond it. And if there is error at all, let it be on the side next to the people."[36]

One of the problems that had developed in Battle Creek was the extremism fostered by Dr. Russell T. Trall and advocated by William Gage, resident editor of the *Health Reformer.* Dr. Trall advocated absolute discontinuance of salt, sugar, milk, butter, and eggs. This extremism caused confusion and a loss of subscriptions. When Ellen White returned from her west-coast camp meeting assignments, she saw why the *Health Reformer* was about dead: "The position to entirely discontinue the use of these things [salt, sugar, milk, butter, and eggs] may be right in its order; but the time had not come to take a general stand upon these points."[37]

Worse! The editor of the *Health Reformer* was ill. Why? Because he and those who were supporting these extreme positions for that time *were not following a balanced program in their own homes!* The confusion and subsequent despair among church members in their attempts to meet these extreme positions opened the door to much backsliding in the whole area of health reform. So Ellen White set forth several points for her fellow church members to consider:

- Meet people "where they are."[38]
- Allow others "as much time as we have required" to reach our present understanding.
- We must not "advocate positions" that are not put to "a practical test" in our own homes.
- "A free use" of items such as salt, sugar, and milk is "positively injurious to health" and "if they were not used at all, a much better state of health would be enjoyed."
- But, for the present, "our burden is not upon these things [salt, sugar, milk, butter]."[39]
- Because so many people were so far behind on health reform, they were advised to "bear positive testimony against" the most "injurious indulgences and stimulating narcotics . . . [such as] tobacco, spirituous liquors, snuff, tea, coffee, flesh meats, butter, spices, rich cakes, mince pies, a large amount of salt, and all exciting substances used as articles of food."[40]

James Becomes Editor

Because the editor of the *Health Reformer* was ill, and because the paper needed resuscitating, James White took over as editor. In his first editorial, he wrote: "the *Reformer* proposes to reach the people with all their prejudices, and their ignorance of the laws of life, where they are. It will avoid extreme positions, and come as near those who need reforming as possible, and yet be true to the principles of health reform."[41]

Under his leadership, confidence was restored in the magazine and in the broad health principles that Ellen White advocated. Within the first year, subscriptions increased from 3,000 to more than 10,000.[42]

Every reform movement since New Testament times has had to contend with extremists. Their message may contain truth, but their timing, methods, and ensuing consequences do much to weaken the impact of their message. At a New York conference in 1868 Ellen White wrote that some who were health reform advocates "were extremists, and would run the health reform into the ground. . . . Their influence would disgust believers and unbelievers."[43]

Before pointing out some of the inconsistencies of these "extremists," Mrs. White insightfully analyzed typical reactions to a health reform message: "The masses will reject any theory, however reasonable it may be, if it lays a restriction upon the appetite. The taste is consulted instead of reason and health. All who leave the common track of custom, and advocate reform, will be opposed, accounted mad, insane, radical, . . . [even if they] pursue ever so consistent a course."[44]

Then she spoke plainly to several of these extremist spokesmen. One man, "aided by items gathered from books," had demanded that his family come up immediately to his "high" standards, but in so doing he "failed to bring himself to the mark, and to keep his body under."

His marital relations were more like the unleashing of "animal propensities" than those of a considerate husband. His wife was not in a condition to give birth "to healthy children." Why? Because "he did not provide the quality and quantity of food that was necessary to nourish two lives instead of one." Her children were born with "feeble digestive powers and impoverished blood."

Applying Common Sense

Note how Ellen White applied her principle of common sense and moderation: "Her system craved material to convert into blood; but he would not provide it. A moderate amount of milk and sugar, a little salt, white bread raised with yeast for a change, graham flour prepared in a variety of ways by other hands than her own, plain cake with raisins, occasionally, and many other dishes I might mention, would have answered the demand of appetite. If he could not obtain some of these things, a little domestic wine [for medicinal purposes] would have done her no injury; it would have been better for her to have it than to do without it. In some cases, even a small amount of the least hurtful meat would do less injury than to suffer strong cravings for it."[45]

She then turned to another family who had lost a loved one because of a physician guilty of "maltreatment" under the guise of health reform. Apparently a young man had died after a severe fever. After recognizing that "abstinence from food for a short time will lessen the fever," she noted that when the fever is broken, "nourishment should be given in a careful, judicious manner." However, each person should be treated on an individual basis. "If there is a great desire expressed for food, even during the fever, to gratify that desire with a moderate amount of simple food would be less injurious than for the patient to be denied."[46]

In the case of this young man, Ellen White specifically pointed to mismanagement that led to his unnecessary death: "A little good wine and food would have brought him back to his family." The father also would have died if it had not been for the "presence and timely counsel of a doctor from the Health Institute." Doing the best possible under the circumstances was a basic health principle with Ellen White.[47]

She warned concerning extremists: "It is impossible for the best qualified advocates of health reform to fully relieve the minds of the public from the prejudice received through the wrong course of these extremists, and to place the great subject of health reform upon a right basis in the community where these men have figured. The door is also closed in a great measure, so that unbelievers cannot be reached by the present truth upon the Sabbath and the soon coming of our Saviour."[48]

In 1868 James White wrote an editorial pointing out that extremists made the work of Mrs. White unnecessarily difficult: "While Satan tempts the many to be too slow, he always tempts these [some with more zeal than caution] to be too fast. Mrs. W.'s labors are made very hard, and, sometimes perplexing, by reason of the course of extremists, who think the only safe position is to take the extreme view of every expression she has written or spoken upon points where different views may be taken."[49]

Both James and Ellen White recognized individual differences.[50] They were patient with others because they knew how long it had taken them to see the logic and beauty in health principles that were affirmed by vision.[51]

They further knew that they could not be conscience for anyone else. They could lead only by example and clear teaching.

Endnotes

1. *Counsels on Diet and Foods,* p. 211.
2. *Review and Herald,* Sept. 10, 1867.
3. *Ibid.,* Jan. 15, 1867.
4. *Health Reformer,* Dec. 1866.
5. *Review and Herald,* Jan. 1, 1867.
6. *Health Reformer,* Feb. 1867.
7. *Review and Herald,* Jan. 5, 1886.
8. One year earlier, in September, 1864, James and Ellen White had spent three weeks at Dansville, after she had completed Volumes III and IV of *Spiritual Gifts.* Volume IV contained the unfolding of her Otsego health vision of June 6, 1863. The principles contained in this Otsego vision were clear and the times were urgent; how to assimilate them and incorporate them into practical living would take time and experience.

   A timely article by Dr. James C. Jackson, "Our Home's" administrator, on the treatment of diphtheria was reprinted in the church paper in February, 1863, and greatly impressed the Whites. At a time when terrified parents watched their children die without medical hope, the Whites employed the water treatment method advocated by Jackson, and three children, Moses Hull's boy and the Whites' Edson and Willie, survived diphtheria. Yet, later in November 1863, Henry's cold became pneumonia and was treated with conventional drug therapy with no positive results. Although the Whites understood the principle of hydrotherapy when it applied to diphtheria, they had not yet seen its application to other diseases. The theory needed time and experience before it became a compelling principle in practice.

   The Whites sensed this need for a practical understanding of the full application of the Otsego health vision. Certain dietary changes were immediately made in regard to meat-eating, butter, healthier bread, less salt, and two meals a day, but other changes were yet to be made as the principles became clearer over time. Thus, off to Dansville in September 1864, not only for their health after so much stress of travel and publication, but "to see what we could see and hear, so as to be able to give to many inquiring friends a somewhat definite report."—James White, in *How to Live,* cited in *Bio.*, vol. 2, p. 83.
9. *Review and Herald,* Feb. 20, 1866.
10. *Review and Herald,* Oct. 3, 1865.
11. Manuscript 1, 1867, cited in Robinson, *Our Health Message,* p. 135.
12. "A moderate use of salt is necessary to you; without it you will become a dyspeptic."—Letter 19a, 1891, cited in Robinson, *op. cit.,* p. 136; "From the light given me by God, this article [salt], in the place of being deleterious, is actually essential for the blood. The whys and wherefores of this I know not, but I give you the instruction as it is given me."—*Counsels on Diet and Foods,* p. 344. Obviously, at times certain medical conditions (such as high blood pressure) may indicate that the use of salt should be reduced until good health is recovered. Ellen White is here speaking of a moderate use of salt in a healthful, maintenance diet. In modern times, because salt is frequently present in packaged foods, this should be taken into consideration when assessing one's daily need of a "moderate" use of salt.
13. *Bio.,* vol. 2, p. 121.
14. *Ibid.,* vol. 2, p. 86.
15. Manuscript 1, 1867, cited in *Bio.*, vol. 2, p. 122.
16. *Review and Herald,* Feb. 20, 1866.
17. *Life Sketches of Elder James White and Mrs. Ellen G. White* (1888), pp. 353, 354, cited in Robinson, *Our Health Message,* p. 138.
18. *Testimonies,* vol. 1, p. 490.
19. *Testimonies,* vol. 1, pp. 485-495, 553-564, 612-620.
20. *Bio.,* vol. 2, pp. 157-175.
21. *Bio.,* vol. 2, p. 141.
22. Robinson, *Our Health Message,* pp. 145-155; *Bio.,* vol. 2, pp. 139-142, 174, 176.
23. *Testimonies,* vol. 1, pp. 564-567; *Bio.,* vol. 2, pp. 192-204; Robinson, *Our Health Message,* pp. 172-190.
24. *Testimonies*, vol. 1, pp. 552, 553.
25. Prior to the vision in Bordoville were the visions of 1848 and 1854; Otsego, Michigan, June 6, 1863, and Rochester, New York, Dec. 25, 1865.
26. See pp. 34, 282, 304, 311, 422.
27. *Bio.,* vol. 2, pp. 301-311.
28. *Testimonies,* vol. 3, p. 161.
29. *Ibid.,* p. 162.
30. *Ibid.,* p. 165.
31. *Ibid.,* pp. 166, 167.
32. *Ibid.,* p. 168.

33. *Ibid.*, pp. 170, 171.
34. Robinson, *Our Health Message*, pp. 203-212.
35. See pp. 95-97, 306, 311, 326, 400-402, 436.
36. *Testimonies*, vol. 3, p. 21. But no real erring is necessary: "You need not go into the water, or into the fire, but take the middle path, avoiding all extremes." —*Counsels on Diet and Foods*, p. 211.
37. *Testimonies*, vol. 3, p. 19. "We know that a free use of these things is positively injurious to health, and in many cases we think that if they were not used at all, a much better state of health would be enjoyed. But at present our burden is not upon these things. The people are so far behind that we see it is all they can bear to have us draw the line upon their injurious indulgences and stimulating narcotics."—*Ibid.*, p. 21. Ellen White saw that Dr. Trall's counsel in the *Health Reformer* was too extreme when he wrote: "Salt, being a poison, should not be used at all."—July, 1869. Her position is best stated in *The Ministry of Healing*, p. 305: "Do not eat largely of salt." Recent research strongly indicates that unexplained high blood pressure is often found in persons who use too much salt. See p. 334.
38. For many in the nineteenth century, hygienic standards, "balanced" meals, and refrigerated food were not even thought of. "The masses were forced to subsist on a crude and scanty diet of which tea and bread were staples, supplemented now and then by a soup or stew of questionable origin. . . . Nostalgia even for the food of most rural Americans cannot survive the light of truth. While to a degree substantial, their diet was very simple, monotonous and often far from healthful. . . . *Harper's Weekly* complained in 1869: 'The city people are in constant danger of buying unwholesome meat; the dealers are unscrupulous, the public uneducated.' . . . In the absence of electric refrigeration, perishable goods were subject to the whims of the weather. . . . One is tempted to believe that with meat and fish so unreliable the urban Victorians sustained themselves by consuming an abundance of fruit. But that was not the case. They had a lingering suspicion of fruit—and vegetables—that had its origins in a cholera epidemic of 1832 which was believed to have been caused by fruit. In fact, following the epidemic, the New York City Council had forbidden the sale of all fruits, and though the ban had been lifted some years later the mistrust was to remain."—Otto Bettmann, *The Good Old Days—They Were Terrible!* (New York: Random House, Inc., 1974), pp. 109, 110, 113.
39. This advice was primarily to Ellen White's agrarian readers. For those who had to buy milk, it was a hazardous undertaking. "It was common knowledge to New Yorkers that their milk was diluted. And the dealers were neither subtle nor timid about it; all they required was a water pump to boost two quarts of milk to a gallon. Nor was that the end of the mischief: to improve the color of milk from diseased cattle they frequently added molasses, chalk, or plaster of Paris. No wonder, that in 1889 New York's public health commissioner reported seeing in certain districts a 'decidedly suspicious-looking fluid bearing the name of milk.'

    "Bacteria-infected milk held lethal possibilities of which people were unaware. The root of this problem was in the dairy farms, invariably dirty, where the milch cows were improperly fed and housed.

    "It was not unusual for a city administration to sell its garbage to a farmer, who promptly fed it to his cows. Or for a distillery to keep cows and feed them distillery wastes, producing what was called 'swill milk.' This particular liquid, which purportedly made babies tipsy, caused a scandal in the New York of 1870 when it was revealed that some of the cows cooped up for years in filthy stables were so enfeebled from tuberculosis that they had to be raised on cranes to remain 'milkable' until they died.

    "When in 1902 the city's Health Commission tested 3,970 milk samples, it was found that 2,095, or 52.77 percent, were adulterated."—Bettmann, *The Good Old Days*, pp. 114, 115.
40. *Testimonies*, vol. 3, pp. 20, 21. The phrase "excessive use of butter" might well have been used in this statement to express her view more precisely, because a few paragraphs earlier, she indicated that part of the confusion and distress brought about by the extreme view of the *Reformer* editors was their position advocating the "entire disuse of milk, butter, and sugar."
41. *Health Reformer*, March, 1871.
42. Robinson, *Our Health Message*, p. 202; see *Bio.*, vol. 2. pp. 306-309.
43. *Testimonies*, vol. 2, p. 377. See *Counsels on Diet and Foods*, pp. 195-213.
44. *Ibid.*
45. *Ibid.*, p. 384. See also pp. 95-97, 305, 306, 311, 326, 400-402, 436.
46. *Ibid.*, pp. 384, 385.
47. See p. 310.
48. *Ibid.*, pp. 386, 387.
49. *Review and Herald*, Mar. 17, 1868. James White continued regarding his wife's challenge: "She works to this disadvantage, namely: she makes strong appeals to the people, which a few feel deeply, and take strong positions, and go to extremes. Then to save the cause from ruin in consequence of these extremes, she is obliged to come out with reproofs for extremists in a public manner. This is better than to have things go to pieces; but the influence of both the extremes and the reproofs are terrible on the cause, and brings upon Mrs. W. a three-fold burden. Here is the difficulty: What she may say to urge the tardy, is taken by the prompt to urge them over the mark. And what she may say to caution the prompt, zealous, incautious ones, is taken by the tardy as an excuse to remain too far behind."

    In 1871, James White again set forth his wife's balanced counsel as they both led church members step by step, even as they themselves were advancing step by step in their adjustments to advancing light: "While she [Ellen White] does not regard milk, taken in large quantities, as customarily eaten with bread, the best article of food, her mind, as yet, has only been called to the importance of the best and most healthful condition of the cow possible where milk is used. . . . She cannot unite in circulating publications broadcast which take an extreme position on the important question of milk, with her present light upon the subject. . . . Mrs. W. thinks that a change from the simplest kinds of flesh meats, to an abundant use of sugar, is going from 'bad to worse.' She would recommend a very sparing use of both sugar and salt. The appetite can, and should be, brought to a very moderate use of both."—*Review and Herald*, Nov. 8, 1870.
50. "Our diet should be suited to the season, to the climate in which we live, and to the occupation we follow." —*The Ministry of Healing*, p. 297; "There is a wide difference in constitutions and temperaments, and the demands of the system differ greatly in different per-

sons. What would be food for one, might be poison for another; so precise rules cannot be laid down to fit every case. I cannot eat beans, for they are poison to me; but for me to say that for this reason no one must eat them would be simply ridiculous."—*Counsels on Diet and Foods,* p. 494.

51. "Some of us have been years in arriving at our present position in health reform. It is slow work to obtain a reform in diet. . . . If we should allow the people as much time as we have required to come up to the present advanced state in reform, we would be very patient with them and allow them to advance step by step, as we have done, until their feet are firmly established upon the health reform platform. But we should be very cautious not to advance too fast, lest we be obliged to retrace our steps."—*Testimonies,* vol. 3, pp. 20, 21.

Study Questions

1. What did Ellen White mean by the "gospel sieve"?

2. What practices at the Dansville "Home" were incompatible with the broad principles of healthful living that Ellen White was beginning to see more clearly?

3. In her counsel to those launching the church's first medical institution, what fundamental principles did Ellen White advocate that could apply to all later institutions?

4. What common-sense principles were reemphasized when the *Health Reformer* needed rescuing?

5. Review some of the obvious improvements in health that Adventists in the 1860s soon enjoyed when they incorporated health principles into their daily program. How do those principles apply today?

CHAPTER 27

Health Principles/4
Principles and Policies

"Let it ever be kept before the mind that the great object of hygienic reform is to secure the highest possible development of mind and soul and body. All the laws of nature—which are the laws of God— are designed for our good. Obedience to them will promote our happiness in this life, and will aid us in a preparation for the life to come."[1]

Ellen White set forth certain guidelines that would help everyone to make positive and progressive decisions, especially in health reform. The *first principle*, which applies to all areas of Christian responsibilities, is that everyone knows for himself what "known duty" is. "Known duty" at any given moment may not be the same for any two people. Yet, to balk at "known duty," little or much, reveals the heart of a rebel—a deeper problem than a matter of diet.[2]

In 1893 Ellen White wrote: "No one can believe with the heart unto righteousness, and obtain justification by faith, while continuing the practice of those things which the Word of God forbids, or while neglecting any known duty."[3]

Neglecting "known duty" will cause "weakness and darkness, and subject us to fierce temptation."[4] In other words, to hear instruction that God validated through Ellen White but not to incorporate it into one's life, opens the door to other temptations and spiritual darkness.

The *second principle* is that we should do the best we can under all circumstances. For example, in the days when nutritional supplements were not available, or when various vegetables and fruit were not easily obtainable, Ellen White suggested that grape juice in the best form available was appropriate as a food supplement for *medicinal* purposes.[5] Obviously she was not suggesting that wine be used as a recreational beverage or as a feature of one's regular diet.

When she advised "domestic wine" for medicinal purposes, she knew that the sick person needed the nutritional properties of the grape, nutrients that could be assimilated quickly by the body. Under the circumstances, if the domestic wine contained a little alcohol, it still would have provided more benefit than not taking it. In 1868, in one of his question/answer articles, James White wrote: "During the past year, Mrs. W. has, at three or four times, had feelings of great debility and faintness in the morning. . . . To prevent distressing faintness at these times, she, immediately after rising, had taken an egg in a little pure, domestic, grape wine, perhaps a spoonful at a time, and never thought that this had to do with drugs, as she uses the term in her writings, more than with the man in the moon. During the past year, she may have used one pint of wine. It is only in extreme cases that the use of wine is justifiable, and then let it be a 'little wine,' to gently stimulate those in a sinking condition."[6]

In Australia during the 1890s, finding a quality diet was difficult and meat was the cheapest food available. On one occasion when sickness was in a neighbor's home, Mrs. White recalled that "there was nothing in the house suitable to eat. And they refused to eat anything that we took them. They had been accustomed to having meat. We felt that something must be done. I said to Sara [McEnterfer], 'Take chickens from my place, and prepare them some broth.' . . . They soon recovered."

The lesson? "Although we did not use flesh foods ourselves, when we thought it essential for that family in their time of sickness, we gave them what we felt they needed. There are occasions when we must meet the people where they are."[7]

Here again, however, common sense is needed: the first and second principle taken together should give wisdom to the health-care provider and to the ill.

The *third principle* is to avoid "everything hurtful," and the *fourth* is "to use judiciously that which is healthful."[8]

The *fifth principle* focuses on self-control. "Excessive indulgence in eating, drinking, sleeping, or seeing is sin."[9] Self-indulgence is often displayed in "dressing" and "overwork," thus indicating that the mind is not under the "control of reason and conscience."[10]

The *sixth principle* is that we should "not mark out any precise line to be followed in diet."[11] Obviously, clear and precise warnings were given on certain unhealthful foods. But in turning to the diet that should take the place of injurious foods, Ellen White stroked out broad lines, such as "grains, fruits, nuts and vegetables."[12] Why the broad strokes without "precise lines"? Because she recognized that a healthful diet must recognize individual differences in climate, occupation, and physical characteristics.[13]

The *seventh principle* reveals caring and compassion: a non-flesh diet should not be urged until appropriate substitutes for protein are available and the reasons for the replacement understood.[14]

The *eighth principle* focuses on the motivation behind health reform: health reform is not a set of duties by which we impress God and earn His love (legalism). Rather, it is one more revelation from a loving Lord as to how best to avoid sorry circumstances that result from bad decisions. Health reform contains those insights that will hasten character development and a life of service—the object of redemption and the purpose of living. Health reform embodies a system of choices that is understood progressively through experience. For this reason, meat eating, for example, has never been a "test of fellowship" in the Seventh-day Adventist Church.[15]

The *ninth principle* is best expressed in Ellen White's simple formula: "I make myself a criterion for no one else." She did not attempt to be conscience for others; neither did she make "a raid" on the tables of those who were slower to follow advancing light.[16]

The *tenth principle* permeates the previous nine: We must reason from cause to effect, perhaps best expressed in Paul's counsel: "God is not mocked; for whatever a man sows, that he will also reap" (Gal. 6:7).[17]

Ellen White's Journey, Step by Step

Both James and Ellen White realized that it took time for them to respond "step by step" to advancing truth.[18] Experience, common sense, and divine insight prompted her often-repeated principle: "The diet reform should be progressive."[19] God has always used this principle in revealing truth.[20]

Visions in 1848 and 1854 emphasized the injurious effects of tobacco, coffee, and tea. In the second vision such health-related issues as lack of bodily cleanliness, and the need for appetite control were noted.[21] Ellen White stated that in 1863 "the Lord presented a general plan before me," including the concept that caring for one's health is a spiritual duty.[22] Six months later she wrote: "Our plain food, eaten twice a day, is enjoyed with a keen relish. We have no meat, cake, or any rich food upon our table. We use no lard, but in its place, milk, cream, and some butter. We have our food prepared with but little salt, and have dispensed with spices of all kinds. We breakfast at seven, and take our dinner at one. . . . My food is eaten with a greater relish than ever before."[23]

In 1870 Mrs. White revealed further how health principles were working in her home. She referred to her "well-set table on all occasions." Visitors, expected and unexpected, came frequently. She set before everybody "simple, healthful food" and "if any want more than this, they are at liberty to find it elsewhere. No butter or flesh meats of any kind come on my table. Cake is seldom there. I generally have an ample supply of fruits, good bread, and vegetables." Sugar was not placed on the table although sometimes it was used in kitchen preparation.[24]

When traveling on the railroad in 1870 the Whites ate at their usual hour, 1:00 P.M., "of graham bread without butter, and a generous supply of fruit."[25]

The Best Food Available

Did Ellen White eat meat after 1863? Yes, but not as a regular part of her diet. She practiced the general principles she taught others, such as that one must use the best food available under the circumstances. When away from home, either while traveling or camping in austere conditions, decades before frozen foods were invented, finding an adequate diet was often difficult. Not always able to obtain the best, for whatever reason, she at times settled for the good—the best under the circumstances.

In 1873 while on a working vacation high in the Rocky Mountains, the White party had no choice but to hunt and fish for food. She wrote in her diary: "Our provisions have been very low for some days. Many of our supplies have gone. . . . We expected supplies three days ago certainly, but none have come. Willie went to the lake for water. We heard his gun and found he had shot two ducks. This is really a blessing, for we need something to live upon."[26]

A few weeks later, after arriving in California, she reported that they no longer ate meat, although they "bought meat once for May Walling while she was sick, but not a penny have we expended for meat since."[27]

During the rainy, foggy January of 1884, Ellen White spent some time at the St. Helena Health Retreat where there was more sunshine and warmth. But the physician, manager, and cook did not favor a vegetarian cuisine. She wrote of her experience: "When I came to the Retreat, I determined not to taste meat, but I could get scarcely anything else to eat, and therefore ate a little meat. It caused unnatural action of the heart. It was not the right kind of food. . . .

"The use of meat while at the Retreat awakened the old appetite, and after I returned home, it clamored for indulgence. Then I resolved to change entirely, and not under any circumstances eat meat, and thus encourage this appetite. Not a morsel of meat or butter has been on my table since I returned. We have milk, fruit, grains, and vegetables.

"For a time I lost all desire for food. Like the children of Israel, I hankered after flesh meats. But I firmly refused to have meat bought or cooked. I was weak and trembling, as everyone who subsists on meat will be when deprived of the stimulus. But now my appetite has returned. I enjoy bread and fruit, my head is generally clear, and my strength firmer. I have none of the goneness so common with meat eaters. I have had my lesson, and, I hope, learned it well."[28]

In 1888 Mrs. White wrote that she had not bought "a penny's worth of tea for years." However, she would use some tea "as a medicine" for "severe vomiting."[29]

In 1890, after two years of traveling in Europe, she observed: "Where plenty of good milk and fruit can be obtained there is rarely any excuse for eating animal food. . . . In certain cases of illness or exhaustion it may be thought best to use some meat, but great care should be taken to secure the flesh of healthy animals. . . . When I could not obtain the food I needed, I have sometimes eaten a little meat; but I am becoming more and more afraid of it."[30]

Ellen White, with her heavy writing program and frequent public appearances, needed the help of a cook to care for her extended family. She was not always able to secure the services of a cook trained in health reform principles. In Australia during the 1890s, where fruit, vegetables, grains, and nuts were not easy to obtain or affordable, meat was the standby for most people. Two weeks after arriving in Australia, she penned her plea: "I am suffering more now for want of someone who is experienced in the cooking line, to prepare things I can eat. The cooking in this country is in every way deficient. Take out the meat, which we seldom use—and I dare not use it here at all—and sit at their tables, and if you can sustain your strength, you have an excellent constitution. . . . I would pay a higher price for a cook than for any other part of my work."[31]

While in Australia, she came to the place where she "absolutely banished meat from my table." For a time, she had allowed some meat to be served to workers and family members. From that time on [January, 1894] it was understood "that whether I am at home or abroad, nothing of this kind is to be used in my family, or come upon my table. I have had much representation before my mind in the night season on this subject."[32]

Ellen White's Dietary Practice After 1900

What was her dietary practice at Elmshaven after her return to America in 1900? A number of letters reveal the daily routine of that busy home with many workers and members of the family eating together. Among the dietary features of the White home were:[33]

• Breakfast at 7:30 A.M. and dinner at 1:00 P.M., the most convenient time decided by the extended family;

• No meat, no butter, no cheese, no "greasy mixtures of food"; "all are satisfied" with the cream from their two cows;

• Ellen White preferred vermicelli and canned tomatoes cooked together, which she ate with zwieback; stewed fruit of various kinds augmented her main meal. Other items used occasionally included dried corn cooked with milk, and lemon pie;

• All members of the extended family ate items that best served their needs. (Ellen White said that she did not hold herself up as a criterion for them);

• Anyone desiring to eat in the evening was free to do so;

• A variety of food—simple, wholesome, and palatable—was always provided.

What shall we make of this "step-by-step" journey?

• Ellen White's major health visions of 1863 and 1865 encompassed all features of the health reform message that she emphasized until her death. Changes in certain emphases through the years only refined those principles, they did not add or subtract from them. As time passes, even prophets must take time to assimilate revealed principles—time for theory to become practice in their own lives. She constantly advocated the principle, in practice as well as in teaching, that everyone who is committed to truth will move from the bad to the good, from the good to the better, from the better to the best. Such was her experience.

• Ellen White saw the difference between patently injurious substances (alcoholic beverages, pork, tobacco, tea, and coffee) and those items of diet that were not healthful in immoderate amounts (clean meat, milk, eggs, salt, and sugar). Some of this divine insight, especially regarding pork, came as a surprise to her. Other items were being discussed in the nineteenth century, but nowhere else were all the principles she advanced integrated into a practical program. Nowhere else were these principles put in terms of preparing a people for the coming of the Lord.

• What may appear to be lapses in her journey from the good to the best (in incorporating into her life-practice divinely-revealed health principles), can well be understood by those who remember their own journey from the good to the best. Circumstances beyond one's control and the absence of the best often dictate selections that are not always one's preferred choice. Those who understand the gospel, those who realize that God asks only for our best under the circumstances that prevail, those who realize that obedience to known duty is not done to impress God (legalism) but to honor Him—such people will understand why on rare occasions and unusual circumstances Ellen White ate some meat.

• Ellen White followed the principle of the Great Controversy Theme that was reflected in Christ's example—truth should never be coerced. She conveyed to others, whenever she had an appropriate opportunity, the principles of health reform as she had received them—an integrated, coordinated system of principles that promises health of mind and body and soul. She was clear and forceful regarding the relationship of health to one's spiritual growth and eternal destiny. But she did not compel, threaten, or coerce others to do what she knew they should do—she would not be conscience or criterion for others. That fact, in itself, reveals the truth about God and our responsibility for each other.[34]

We are now better able to understand what Ellen White meant when she said at the General Conference session of 1909: "It is reported by some that I have not followed the principles of health reform as I have advocated them with my pen; but I can say that I have been a faithful health reformer. Those who have been members of my family know that this is true."[35]

In modern attempts to understand history, too frequently we judge the past by the present, most often unknowingly. Individuals of the past must be judged in the context of their circumstances, not ours. In a day without refrigeration, when obtaining fresh fruit and vegetables depended on where one lived and the time of the year, when meat substitutes were rarely obtainable before the introduction of peanut butter and dry-cereals (mid-1890s),[36] on some occasions one either ate meat or nothing at all. In our day, at least in developed countries, meat eating is rarely a necessity.

Rumors and Allegations

What should we make of the rumors and charges that have been circulated through the years regarding Ellen White's own dietary choices?

Ham on the White table. D. M. Canright, a hostile ex-Adventist preacher, is reported to have said that he saw the Whites eat ham in their own home. He probably was right since he "embraced the Sabbath" under James White's preaching in 1859. Early Adventists did not understand the distinction between clean and unclean meats. In the late 1850s, the Whites were still eating swine's flesh.[37] Not until after the Otsego vision of June, 1863, did they cease eating it.[38] Between 1859 and 1863, Canright would have had many opportunities to see the Whites eating swine's flesh.

Ellen White was a backslider on meat eating all her life. Ellen White did not claim that after the 1863 Otsego health vision she never again ate meat. Prior to the vision, she believed that she "was dependent upon a meat diet for strength." Because of her weak physical condition, especially for her tendency to faint when weak and dizzy, she thought that meat was "indispensable."[39] In fact, at that time she was "a great meat eater"; flesh meat was her "principal article of diet."[40]

But she complied with advancing light. She cut meat out of her "bill of fare" immediately, along with butter and three meals a day. What was the result? "My former faint and dizzy feelings have left me." Years later, at eighty-two years of age, she could write: "I have better health today, notwithstanding my age, than I had in my younger days."[41]

Yet, as we studied earlier (see p. 312), Ellen White did eat meat occasionally, noting in 1901 that there were times in the past when she "was compelled to eat a little meat."[42] Difficult travel conditions, new cooks, and medical emergencies demanded reasonable adjustments. In other words, she was not a fanatic regarding meat eating, especially in her counsel to others: "I have never felt that it was my duty to say that no one should taste of meat under any circumstances. To say this . . . would be carrying matters to extremes. I have never felt that it was my duty to make sweeping assertions. What I have said I have said under a sense of duty, but I have been guarded in my statements, because I did not want to give occasion for anyone to be conscience for another."[43]

It is also important to note that Ellen White distinguished between "meat" and "fish." In 1876 she wrote her traveling husband: "We have not had a particle of meat in the house since you left and long before you left. We have had salmon a few times. It has been rather high [in price]."[44]

In poverty-stricken Australia during the mid-1890s, she recognized that fish would be an appropriate part of the diet of the workmen who were building Avondale College. In a letter to her son Willie, she wrote: "We cannot feed them all, but will you please get us dried codfish and dried fish of any description—nothing canned? This will give a good relish to the food."[45]

Two years after her personal no-meat pledge at the Brighton (Australia) camp meeting, Mrs. White wrote to her non-Adventist niece, Mary Clough Watson: "Two years ago I came to the conclusion that there was danger in using the flesh of dead animals, and since then I have not used meat at all. It is never placed on my table. I use fish when I can get it. We get beautiful fish from the salt water lake near here. I use neither tea nor coffee. As I labor against these things, I cannot but practice that which I know to be best for my health, and my family are in perfect harmony with me. You see, my dear niece, that I am telling you matters just as they are."[46]

Oysters. Fannie Bolton,[47] a former literary assistant, wrote that Ellen White, at a rail depot, ate "big white raw oysters with vinegar, pepper and salt. . . . I was overwhelmed with this inconsistency and dumb with horror. Elder Starr hurried me out and made all sorts of excuses and justifications of Sister White's action; yet I kept thinking in my heart, 'What does it mean? What has God said? How does she dare eat these abominations?'"[48]

When G. B. Starr heard of this letter he was astounded. He responded to W. C. White: "I can only say that I regard it as the most absurdly, untruthful lot of rubbish that I have ever seen or read regarding our dear Sister White.

"The event simply never occurred. I never saw your mother eat oysters or meat of any kind either in a restaurant or at her own table. Fannie Bolton's statement . . . is a lie of the first order. I never had such an experience and it is too absurd for anyone who ever knew your mother to believe. . . .

"I think this entire letter was written by Fannie Bolton in one of her most insane moments.[49] . . .

"When we visited Florida in 1928, Mrs. Starr and I were told that at a camp meeting, Fannie Bolton made a public statement that she had lied about Sister White, and that she repented of it."[50]

Though Fannie Bolton's report was false, Ellen White did request oysters in 1882 in a letter to Mary, her daughter-in-law: "If you can get me a good box of herrings, fresh ones, please do so. These last ones that Willie got are bitter and old.

If you can buy . . . half a dozen cans of good tomatoes, please do so. We shall need them. If you can get a few cans of good oysters, get them."[51]

What shall we make of this request for oysters? Aren't oysters considered unclean according to Leviticus 11? The answer to that question was not clear to Seventh-day Adventists in the 1880s any more than their attitude toward pork was clear in the 1850s.[52]

In 1883 W. H. Littlejohn, pastor of the Battle Creek Tabernacle, conducted a question/answer column in the church paper. In answering whether oysters are included among the unclean foods of Leviticus 11, Littlejohn said: "It is difficult to decide with certainty whether oysters would properly come under the prohibition of Leviticus 11:9-12. . . . It would, however, seem from the language, as if they might."[53]

Where no direct vision insight was given, Adventists like anybody else had to work their way through such dietary matters.

Ellen White was a hypocrite. This charge is based on the fact that Ellen White was lucid and forthright regarding the danger of meat eating but occasionally ate flesh foods.

Her son W. C., wrote to G. B. Starr in 1933 that the White family had been vegetarians but not always "teetotalers" (total abstainers from flesh foods).

In 1894, Ellen White wrote to a non-Adventist active in the temperance cause in Australia who had asked about the Adventist position on being "total abstainers": "I am happy to assure you that as a denomination we are in the fullest sense total abstainers from the use of spirituous liquors, wine, beer, [fermented] cider, and also tobacco and all other narcotics. . . . All are vegetarians, many abstaining from the use of flesh food, while others use it in only the most moderate degree."[54] Many of Ellen White's strongest statements against meat were written after she had renewed her commitment to total abstinence in 1894.

Here we note that for Ellen White a vegetarian was not necessarily a "teetotaler," that is, a total abstainer, but one who did not eat flesh foods as a habit. Here we have a clear example of the difference between a principle and a policy. Vegetarianism was a policy based upon principle: we should eat the best food obtainable under the circumstances. Principles are clear statements, always true under all circumstances. Policies may change, due to time, place, and circumstances. Policies work out the principles by always doing the best possible under the circumstances. Only the individual's conscience knows when those decisions of doing "one's best" have been made.

Applying the Principles

For Ellen White, the two basic principles in health reform are to "preserve the best health,"[55] and "to eat the food which is most nourishing" in any given set of circumstances.[56]

In applying these principles, she said on many occasions: "In countries where there are fruits, grains, and nuts in abundance, flesh food is not the right food for God's people."[57]

She frequently used the term, "principle," when stating her views on health reform. She credited her much improved personal health to "the principles of health reform."[58] She noted that her instruction on health reform dwelt "upon general principles."[59]

Toward the end of her life, reflecting back on the years since 1863, she penned: "It is reported by some that I have not lived up to the principles of health reform, as I have advocated them with my pen. But I can say that so far as my knowledge goes, I have not departed from those principles."[60]

For this reason Ellen White counseled church members "to avoid meat eating, not because it is regarded as a sin to eat meat, [that is, not a principle] but because it is not healthful [but a good policy]."[61]

She understood clearly the difference between unchangeable principles and the conditionality of policies. Note this wisdom: "Those who understand the laws of health and who are governed by principle, will shun the extremes, both of indulgence and of restrictions. Their diet is chosen, not for the mere gratification of appetite, but for the upbuilding of the body. They seek to preserve every power in the best condition for the highest service to God and man. . . . There is real common sense in dietetic reform. The subject should be studied broadly and deeply, and no one should criticize others because their practice is not, in all things, in harmony with his own. It is impossible [in matters of diet] to make an unvarying rule to regulate everyone's habits, and no one should think himself a criterion for all."[62]

Prior to the 1901 General Conference session, a few leaders met with Ellen White concerning dietary practices. Her remarks were recorded by C. C. Crisler, her secretary: "Oh, how it has hurt me to have the [road] blocks thrown in the way in regard to this subject. Some have said, 'Sister White eats cheese, and therefore we are at liberty to eat cheese.' I have tasted cheese once or twice, but that is a different thing from making it a diet. Once when at Minneapolis, I sat down at a table on which there was some cheese. I was quite sick at the time, and some of my brethren told me that they thought if I ate a little cheese, it might do me good. I ate a small piece, and from then it has been reported in large assemblies that Sister White eats cheese.

"I have not had meat in my house for years. But do not give up the use of meat because Sister White does not eat it. I would not give a farthing for your health reform if that is what it is based upon. I want you to stand in your individual dignity and in your individual consecration before God, the whole being dedicated to Him. . . . I want you to think of these things. Do not make any human being your criterion."[63]

Ellen White understood clearly the difference between principle and policy. Her common sense in regard to health reform made her a physically stronger, more productive person as she became older—not a common experience for many in her day. Far from being a hypocrite, she led the way in assimilating principle into practice. Dietary practices were not a form of penance, nor a ritual by which to earn salvation.[64]

Endnotes

1. *Counsels on Diet and Foods,* p. 23. See also pp. 273, 274, 310.
2. *Selected Messages,* book 1, p. 396. See also pp. 274, 295, 310.
3. *Ibid.*
4. *Selected Messages,* book 2, p. 58. See also *Patriarchs and Prophets,* p. 256.
5. *Testimonies,* vol. 2, pp. 384, 386. In the nineteenth century, no method had been devised to keep grape juice from fermenting, excepting with ice (which was not a practical alternative). When the Whites used the term "domestic wine," they referred to grape juice as free from fermentation *as possible.* In reference to communion services, James White counseled in 1867: "This objecting to a few drops of domestic wine with which to only wet the lips at the Lord's supper, is carrying total abstinence principles to great length. . . . Know what you use. Let the deacons obtain the cultivated grape, see the wine made, and secured from the air to keep it from fermenting as much as possible." —*Review and Herald,* April 16, 1867. See p. 153 for Dr. Kress's experience.
6. *Review and Herald,* March 17, 1868.
7. Letter 363, 1907, cited in *Counsels on Diet and Foods,* p. 466.
8. *Patriarchs and Prophets,* p. 562.
9. *Testimonies,* vol. 4, p. 417; "Every violation of principle in eating and drinking blunts the perceptive faculties, making it impossible for them to appreciate or place the right value upon eternal things. It is of the greatest importance that mankind should not be ignorant in regard to the consequences of excess. Temperance in all things is necessary to health and the development and growth of a good Christian character." —*Counsels on Health,* p. 38.
10. *Temperance,* pp. 139, 146.
11. *Testimonies,* vol. 9, p. 159.
12. *The Ministry of Healing,* p. 296.
13. See pp. 95-97. Ellen White's sound judgment was reflected in her admonition against extremism in diet matters: "Those who desire to be co-workers with God must consider carefully before they specify just what foods should and should not be eaten. We are to be brought into connection with the masses. Should health

reform in its most extreme form be taught to those whose circumstances forbid its adoption, more harm than good would be done. As I preach the gospel to the poor, I am instructed to tell them to eat that food which is most nourishing. . . . The gospel must be preached to the poor, but the time has not yet come to prescribe the strictest diet."—*General Conference Bulletin,* June 2, 1909, p. 270.

14. "None should be urged to make the change abruptly. The place of meat should be supplied with wholesome foods that are inexpensive. . . . In all cases, educate the conscience, enlist the will, supply good, wholesome food, and the change will be readily made, and the demand for flesh will soon cease."—*The Ministry of Healing,* p. 317.
15. "We are not to make the use of flesh food a test of fellowship, but we should consider the influence that professed believers who use flesh foods have over others. . . . Will those who are supported by the tithe from God's storehouse permit themselves by self-indulgence to poison the life-giving current flowing through their veins?"—*Testimonies,* vol. 9, pp. 159, 160; "While we do not make the use of flesh meat a test, while we do not want to force anyone to give up its use, yet it is our duty to request that no minister of the conference shall make light of or oppose the message of reform on this point."—Letter 48, 1902, cited in *Counsels on Diet and Foods,* p. 401.
16. *Counsels on Diet and Foods,* p. 493; *MR,* vol. 1, p. 223. Note Christ's example: "While Christ accepted invitations to feasts and gatherings, He did not partake of all the food offered Him, but quietly ate of that which was appropriate for His physical necessities, avoiding the many things that He did not need. His disciples were frequently invited with Him, and His conduct was a lesson to them, teaching them not to indulge appetite by overeating or by eating improper food."—*MR,* vol. 7, p. 412.
17. "I consider that one reason why I have been able to do so much work both in speaking and in writing, is because I am strictly temperate in my eating. If several varieties of food are placed before me, I endeavor to choose only those that I know will agree. Thus I am enabled to preserve clear mental faculties. I refuse to place in my stomach knowingly anything that will set up fermentation. This is the duty of all health reformers. We must reason from cause to effect." —*Counsels on Diet and Foods,* p. 493.
18. *Testimonies,* vol. 3, pp. 20, 21.
19. *The Ministry of Healing,* p. 320. See also pp. 282, 304, 311.
20. See pp. 34, 274, 304, 422.
21. James White, *Review and Herald,* Nov. 8, 1870; Manuscript 1, 1854 in *MR,* vol. 6, pp. 217-219.
22. *Counsels on Diet and Foods,* p. 481; Manuscript 1, 1863 in *Selected Messages,* book 3, pp. 279, 280.
23. *Spiritual Gifts,* vol. 4, p. 154, cited in *Counsels on Diet and Foods,* pp. 482, 483; see also *Testimonies,* vol. 2, pp. 371, 372.
24. *Counsels on Diet and Foods,* pp. 330, 486.
25. *Ibid,* p. 486.
26. Manuscript 12, 1873, cited in *MR,* vol. 7, p. 346.
27. Letter 12, 1874, cited in *MR,* vol. 7, pp. 346, 347.
28. Letter 2, 1884, cited in *Bio.,* vol. 3, p. 245.
29. Letter 12, 1888, cited in *Counsels on Diet and Foods,* p. 490.
30. *Counsels on Diet and Foods,* p. 394.
31. Letter 19c, 1892, cited in *MR,* vol. 7, p. 346.
32. Letter 76, 1895, cited in *Counsels on Diet and Foods,* p. 488.
33. *Bio.,* vol. 6, pp. 393-396.
34. Mrs. White divided her nutritional principles into three major categories: (1) Foods to be used freely, such as fruits, grains, and vegetables; (2) Foods to be used moderately, such as salt, nuts, and certain non-animal fats; (3) Foods injurious to health (some worse than others), such as animal products, coffee, tea, alcohol, etc. Letters 45, 1903; 62, 1903; 127, 1904; 50, 1908, as cited in *Counsels on Diet and Foods,* pp. 490-492.
35. *Testimonies,* vol. 9, p. 159.
36. Except for beans, which not everyone could eat: "I cannot eat beans, for they are poison to me."—Letter 19a, 1891, cited in *Counsels on Diet and Foods,* p. 494.
37. *Testimonies,* vol. 1, pp. 206, 207.
38. *Spiritual Gifts,* vol. 4, pp. 124, 146.
39. *Spiritual Gifts,* vol. 4, pp. 153, 154.
40. *Testimonies,* vol. 2, pp. 371, 372; *Counsels on Diet and Foods,* p. 487.
41. Manuscript 50, 1904, cited in *Counsels on Diet and Foods,* p. 482; Letter 83, 1901, cited in *Ibid.,* p. 487; *Testimonies,* vol. 2, p. 371; *Spiritual Gifts,* vol. 4, p. 154; *Testimonies,* vol. 9, p. 150.
42. Letter 83, 1901, cited in *Counsels on Diet and Foods,* p. 487.
43. Letter 76, 1895, cited in *Counsels on Diet and Foods,* pp. 462, 463.
44. Letter 13, 1876, cited in *MR,* vol. 14, p. 336.
45. Letter 149, 1895, cited in Roger Coon, *Ellen White and Vegetarianism* (Boise, Idaho: Pacific Press Publishing Association, 1986), pp. 20, 21.
46. Letter 128, 1896, cited in *MR,* vol. 14, p. 330.
47. See pp. 479-482.
48. Letter of Frances E. Bolton to Mrs. E. C. Slauson, Dec. 30, 1914, cited in *The Fannie Bolton Story: A Collection of Source Documents* (Ellen G. White Estate, April 1982), pp. 108, 109.
49. Fannie Bolton spent thirteen months as a mental patient in the Kalamazoo State Hospital, 1911-1912, and another three-and-a-half months in the same institution in 1924-25; she died in 1926.
50. Letter of G. B. Starr to W. C. White, Aug. 30, 1933, cited in *Ibid.,* pp. 118, 119.
51. Letter 16, 1882, cited in Coon, *Ellen White and Vegetarianism,* p. 19.
52. In a document entitled, "The Development of Adventist Thinking on Clean and Unclean Meats," Ron Graybill stated that "nineteenth-century Adventists . . . did not generally accept this distinction [between clean and unclean meats] based on Levitical law, even though they clearly condemned pork [eventually]. . . . While Adventists argued vigorously against pork, the weight of their argument continued to be carried by physiological criteria. Uriah Smith explicitly rejected the applicability of the Mosaic distinction: 'We believe there is better ground on which to rest [the prohibition on pork] than the ceremonial law of the former dispensation, for if we take the position that the law is still binding, we must accept it all, and then we shall have more on our hands than we can easily dispose of.'. . .

   "Ellen White's own understanding of the clean-unclean distinction seems to have grown stronger over time. In 1864 she did note in passing that Noah was allowed to eat 'clean' beasts after the Flood. And in 1890, when *Patriarchs and Prophets* was published, she noted that Samson's parents had been instructed to withhold from him 'every unclean thing.' This distinction 'between articles of food as clean and unclean' was not, she said, 'a merely ceremonial and arbitrary regulation, but was based upon sanitary principles.' Furthermore, the 'marvelous vitality' of the Jewish people for thousands of years could be traced to this distinction.

"Probably more familiar to early Adventists were James C. Jackson's comments on oysters, included along with his other criticisms of flesh foods in an article James and Ellen White reprinted in *Health: or How to Live.* Jackson objected to the oysters because they were scavengers." Graybill noted that S. N. Haskell was probably the most explicit in using Leviticus 11 as a clear Biblical prohibition on all unclean meats. He concluded his research with this perspective: "Compared with the amount of material in the [Adventist] literature against pork, however, the objections to oysters and other 'unclean' meats is so minuscule as to hardly be noticed."—Ron Graybill, "The Development in Adventist Thinking on Clean and Unclean Meats," available from the Ellen G. White Estate.

53. *Review and Herald,* Aug. 14, 1883.
54. Letter 99, 1894, cited in *Bio.,* vol. 4, p. 119.
55. *The Youth's Instructor,* May 31, 1894, cited in *Counsels on Diet and Foods,* p. 395.
56. *Testimonies,* vol. 9, p. 163.
57. *Ibid.,* p. 159.
58. *Counsels on Diet and Foods,* p. 482.
59. *Ibid.,* p. 493; *Testimonies,* vol. 2, p. 372.
60. *Ibid.,* pp. 491, 492.
61. Manuscript 15, 1889, cited in *MR,* vol. 5, pp. 400, 401; vol. 16, p. 173.
62. *The Ministry of Healing,* p. 319.
63. Manuscript 43, 1901, cited in *MR,* vol. 13, pp. 202-203.
64. "I saw that you had mistaken [dietary] notions about afflicting your bodies, depriving yourselves of nourishing food. These things led some of the church to think that God is surely with you, or you would not deny self, and sacrifice thus. But I saw that none of these things will make you more holy. The heathen do all this, but receive no reward for it."—*Testimonies,* vol. 1, p. 205; (See whole testimony, pp. 204-209).

Study Questions

1. What are Ellen White's ten guidelines for keeping health reform positive and progressive?
2. What is the difference between being a "teetotaler" and a practicing vegetarian?
3. In regard to health reform, how does one distinguish between principles and policies?
4. Why is the practice of ignoring "known duty" a symptom of rebellion?
5. How do we explain Ellen White's "step-by-step" journey into incorporating her own health principles into her daily practice?
6. How can serious health reformers distinguish between principles and policies? What possible circumstances alter policies, but not principles?

CHAPTER 28

Health Principles/5
Reviewing a Century of Health Reform Principles

"The health and lifespan advantages of the Seventh-day Adventist Church have been traced to the way they live and eat. Since the 1800s, Seventh-day Adventists have practiced eight secrets of health that reduce their risk of heart disease and cancer . . . the two leading causes of premature death. By keeping these two killers at bay, Seventh-day Adventists enjoy greater health and a longer life than the general population. . . . The scientific confirmation has just been available in recent years, so how did they know before the scientists? From a woman named Ellen G. White. This visionary said God did not want people to suffer unnecessary illness and death and He inspired her to tell people how they could enjoy maximum wellness. Ellen G. White wrote with amazing simplicity and accuracy what has since been proved to be the best formula for health and longevity."[1]

In reviewing Ellen White's health reform principles, readers should first place themselves in the middle of the nineteenth century. Without any more information about the future than the prevailing notions that governed medical practice at that time, think of how strange the unfolding, synthesizing, integrating health principles of Ellen White must have seemed. Of course, some of these principles had been promoted by contemporaries, but in no place were they so complete or so integrated. No other writers were so free from those errors that subsequent research contradicted.[2]

For the average person, even for physicians, in the middle of the nineteenth century, the germ theory was unheard of. Physicians were still using opium, calomel, mercury, arsenic, and strychnine to "heal" disease. Aspirin was unknown, along with the X-ray machine, antibiotics, pasteurization, immunizations, and blood transfusions.

People generally saw no connection between their life style and disease. Fresh air in the home, night or day, aroused qualms for fear of catching a cold or being bitten by an invasion of flies or mosquitoes.[3] People seldom bathed.[4]

Headlines shouting the deteriorating impact of high-fat, low-fiber diets and the sheer necessity of exercise were a century away.[5] The profound linkage between the mind and body seemed far-fetched. Birth defects due to drugs and alcohol were not to be understood for another hundred years. The concept of cancer germs was a thought that was cross-grain with the medical world. Prenatal influences were considered of little importance.

In many of these areas, as recently as a few decades ago, Ellen White seemed not only extreme but even fanatical. Imagine how she could have been viewed in 1863! The record is in, however. Those who believed in her role as God's messenger, those who faithfully put her health principles into practice, became healthier, stronger, more productive people. To the extent that people picked and chose which principles they would incorporate into their life style, to that extent they fell short of reaching their full potential.

Dietary Aspects of Health Reform

Has anyone ever become sick or sicker by following these health principles? Have the health reform principles advocated by Ellen White proved to be unfounded or dangerous?

Yeast germ in bread. Ellen White

penned that bread should be "thoroughly baked that, so far as possible, the yeast germs shall be destroyed." She was scoffed at for this statement, even as late as the 1940s. For years popular magazines advocated eating a cake of live yeast daily! We now know that live yeast cells "take up B vitamins from the food material in the intestine, thus making them unavailable for the body."[6]

Butter. In 1870 Ellen White wrote that "from principle" she had discarded the use of meat, butter, mince pies, spices, and lard.[7] In 1903 she stated that "as for myself, I have settled the butter question. I do not use it."[8] Health principles, for Ellen White, guided one's plan of life in determining what the best choice should be under all circumstances. At times, in the absence of the best, we must settle for the good.

Here again we see her principle of "progressive" diet reform: "Let the people be taught how to prepare food without the use of milk or butter."[9] Further suggestions included: "Butter is less harmful when eaten on cold bread than when used in cooking."[10] "When properly prepared, olives, like nuts, supply the place of butter and flesh meats."[11]

What's bad about butter? Two basic problems: disease and health factors relating to fat and cholesterol in the diet. Regarding disease, in the late 1800s butter "was often rancid . . . a mixture of casein and water, or of calcium, gypsum, gelatin fat [sic] and mashed potatoes."[12]

Referring to the future, Ellen White wrote: "Tell them that the time will soon come when there will be no safety in using eggs, milk, cream, or butter, because disease in animals is increasing."[13]

Apart from the danger of disease, butter is almost pure fat. It has many of the long-chained saturated fatty acids that tend to increase serum cholesterol (as well as short-chained fatty acids which do not cause the problem). One tablespoon of butter contains 33 mg. of saturated fats and cholesterol.

The American Heart Association stated on May 13, 1994: "Because butter is rich in both saturated fat and cholesterol, it is potentially a highly atherogenic food [causing hardening of the arteries]. Most margarine is made from vegetable fat and provides no dietary cholesterol. The more liquid the margarine, i.e., tub or liquid forms, the less hydrogenated it is and the less trans fatty acids it contains. Therefore, though still high in fat, margarine is a preferable substitute for butter, and soft margarines are better than hard ones."[14]

Dietary fiber. Ellen White warned that "fine-flour bread cannot impart to the system the nourishment that you will find in the unbolted-wheat bread. The common use of bolted-wheat bread cannot keep the system in a healthy condition."[15]

The body needs two major types of fiber in the diet. Soluble fiber helps to lower serum cholesterol and triglyceride levels. The best sources are oats, beans, apples, barley, and buckwheat: thus these foods help reduce the risk of a heart attack. Insoluble fiber can be found in wheat bran, which reduces the risk of colon cancer. Foods high in fiber help to reduce the risk of carcinogenic agents in the intestines. The fiber attaches to the cholesterol and bile acids that have been secreted by the gallbladder, and removes them from the intestinal tract rapidly.

Animal products have little or *no fiber. Refined* grains and other refined products have *very little.* In an Adventist Health Study,[16] men who often ate whole wheat bread had only 56 percent of the expected non-fatal heart attack rate and 89 percent of the expected fatal heart attack rate.

Numerous recent studies relate the risk of colon cancer to the lack of fiber in the diet. Gastro-intestinal transit time is seventy-seven hours when on a refined diet, but thirty-five hours on an unrefined diet.[17] Populations on a refined diet have a higher incidence of colon cancer than in countries where most are on an unrefined diet.[18] Colon-cancer risk *decreases* as the fiber in the diet *increases.* Experts such as Dr. D. P. Burkitt, world-renowned British surgeon and medical researcher, state that a lack of dietary fiber is a major cause of appendicitis, varicose veins, diverticulosis, colon cancer, hiatal hernias, constipation, and other health problems.[19]

Flesh foods. In 1866 Ellen White wrote that "the liability to take disease is increased tenfold by meat eating."[20] Further, in 1869 she said that "meat should not be placed before our children."[21]

Why was she so explicit? Because the practice of meat eating is detrimental to physical, mental, and spiritual health.

• Physical impact: Ellen White wrote that meat eating increases the "liability to disease . . . tenfold." Further, it causes obesity,[22] sudden death (heart attack or stroke),[23] "unwholesome condition" of bones (probably osteoporosis),[24] and cancer.[25] Contrary to conventional thinking, she called it "a mistake to suppose that muscular strength depends on the use of animal food. The needs of the system can be better supplied, and more vigorous health can be enjoyed, without its use."[26] In addition, "the use of the flesh of animals tends to cause a grossness [obesity] of body."[27]

• Mental impact: She cautioned that "students would accomplish much more in their studies if they never tasted meat. When the animal part of the human agent is strengthened by meat eating, the intellectual powers diminish proportionately."[28]

• Spiritual impact: Even more important than the physical and mental liabilities of meat eating is the fact that the "religious life can be more successfully gained and maintained if meat is discarded, for this diet stimulates into intense activity lustful propensities, and enfeebles the moral and spiritual nature."[29]

For Ellen White, "diet reform is progressive."[30] For this reason, she said frequently that she never felt it her "duty to say that no one should taste of meat under any circumstances. To say this when the people have been educated to live on flesh to so great an extent, would be carrying matters to extreme."[31]

At the same time, she did not soften her words when eternal issues were at stake. In the context of those who were proclaiming the messages of the three angels (Rev. 14) and thus were preparing for Christ's return, she said: "Among those who are waiting for the coming of the Lord, meat eating will eventually be done away; flesh will cease to form a part of their diet."[32] Meat eating will be eliminated "before His people can stand before Him a perfected people."[33]

Ellen White spoke directly to church leaders regarding meat eating: No one should be a "teacher of the people" who, by teaching or example, "contradicts" the principles of health reform.[34] Physicians "who use flesh meat and prescribe it for their patients, should not be employed in our institutions."[35] Ministers who eat meat "set an evil example," and make it difficult for others to have "confidence" in them.[36]

What Scientific Research Indicates Regarding a Meat Diet

• Meat and obesity: It is difficult to become obese when following humanity's original diet (Genesis 1-3—fruits, grains, nuts, and vegetables). Recent studies indicate that those who eat a meat diet are much more likely to be obese. In the Adventist Mortality Study 16 percent of vegetarian women and 8 percent of men were obese whereas in the non-vegetarian Adventist group 32 percent of the women and 20 percent of the men were obese.[37] Because meat is high in fat, it contains many calories in a small space and is thus a high-caloric-density food.

• Meat, obesity, and cancer: But obesity leads to further liabilities. Obesity increases the risk of coronary heart disease by 50-100 percent, and the correlation with the risk of cancer increases dramatically. Obesity increases the risk of cancers such as breast cancer,[38] endometrial cancer,[39] prostate cancer, colon cancer,[40] and other cancers. "People who eat high-fat diets tend to be heavier and to eat more meat and fewer fruits and vegetables, so their risk of cancer also is increasing."[41]

In Hiroshima, Japan, breast cancer was 3.8 times greater in people consuming meat daily compared to vegetarians. Daily users of eggs had 2.8 times greater risk, and butter and cheese users 2-3 times greater risk than non-consumers of these items.[42] In a study of 265,118 Japanese, meat eaters had 2.5 times greater risk of pancreatic cancer.[43]

• Immune system: The human immune system is directly affected by what one eats, and thus the body's resistance to cancer may be the most important factor in preventing cancer. Excesses or deficiencies of any nutrient adversely affects the immune system. For example, a high protein diet depresses T-lymphocyte cells,[44] and an unreasonably low protein diet, as in Kwashiorkor, depresses the immune system. Obesity depresses the immune system, as does starvation. A high serum cholesterol depresses the immune system, as do excess doses of vitamins C or E.[45]

• Meat and cancer: The mortality ratio involving ovarian cancer is distinctly different between (a) Adventist lacto-ovo-vegetarians (15.9/100,000), (b) those using meat one to three times a week (18/100,000), (c) the general population of California (24/100,000), and (d) Adventists using meat four or more times weekly (26.4/100,000).[46]

In that same study comparing the three groups, the mortality ratios for breast cancer were: (a) 64/100,000; (b) 73.3/100,000; and (c) 81.6/100,000.[47]

Animal Products Increase Death Risk

Heavy consumers of animal products (meat, milk, eggs, cheese) had a 3.6 times greater risk of death from prostate cancer compared to low consumers.[48] The study also reported that those who eat meat more than three times a week increase their risk of fatal or near-fatal bladder cancer.[49] Eating meat five or more times a week may triple the risk of coronary heart disease for a 40-year-old male.[50]

The American Cancer Society's 1996 report emphasized that "diets high in foods from plant sources [vegetables, fruits, whole gains, beans] have been associated with a decreased risk, whereas diets high in fat and red meat have been associated with an increased risk of colorectal cancer." Further, "intake of animal fat, red meats, and dairy products has been found to be associated with an increase in the risk of prostate cancer."[51]

Dietary patterns in fifteen countries were compared with lymphoma death rates. A positive correlation existed between beef and all animal protein (fish being an exception). Vegetable protein foods were negatively correlated.[52]

Seventh-day Adventists in the United States consume as much fat as the general population.[53] Yet, Adventists have only half as many cancers, even cancers not related to tobacco and alcohol. The explanation apparently lies in the difference in the kind of fat consumed. The National Research Council stated that cancer is most closely related to total fat *and saturated fat*.[54]

• Meat and cancer germs: When Ellen White wrote that "tuberculosis, cancer, and other fatal diseases" are caused by "tuberculosis and cancerous germs," the medical world scoffed, and continued to do so for many decades. *But not today.*[55] In 1974, milk from leukemic cows was fed to six chimpanzees. Two died with leukemia at nine months of age, demonstrating that cancer viruses can be transmitted, even between different species.[56] The chicken leukosis virus can be found in five to ten percent of all eggs.[57]

• Meat and diabetes: In the Adventist Health Study, those who consumed meat six or more days a week had a 3.8 times greater risk than vegetarians of dying of diabetes.[58]

• Meat and endurance: A three-day, high-carbohydrate diet (such as the original diet, (Gen.1-3) produced almost three times the endurance (167 minutes) as the three-day, high-protein, fat diet (57 minutes) in a study of Swedish athletes.[59]

• Meat and essential fatty acids: God's original diet (Gen.1-3) contained no animal fat but had sufficient essential polyunsaturated fatty acids from plant sources. Adequate linoleic acid, found in grains, reduces hypertension (high blood pressure)[60] and platelet stickiness, and the aggregation of red blood cells[61] lowers blood cholesterol[62] and reduces the risk of heart attacks[63] and ventricular fibrillation.[64]

• Meat and longevity: Non-meat-eaters have an increased life expectancy beyond eighty years although there does not appear to be an increase in maximal life-span.[65]

Salt. Although Ellen White stated that salt was "essential for the blood,"[66] she also advised against using "an undue amount of salt."[67] Further, "a free use of" salt (as well as sugar and milk) "is positively injurious."[68]

Tea and coffee. For Ellen White, using tea and coffee as a beverage "is a sin, an injurious indulgence."[69] After the immediate stimulating effect "a feeling of depression" sets in.[70] With continual use, the abuser of the nervous system will experience "headaches, wakefulness, palpitation of the heart, indigestion, trembling, and many other evils, for they [tea, coffee, and "many other popular drinks"] wear away the life forces."[71] Both tea and coffee are "poisonous," and "Christians should let it [them] alone,"[72] a position validated in current research.[73]

Caffeine, a major culprit in tea and coffee, is easily available in many popular drinks (cola drinks) and over-the-counter medications. Physiological effects of caffeine are apparent in adults at doses of only 100-200 mg.—the equivalent of one to three cups of coffee. But for a child (age 1-5) one can of caffeinated soda is equal to four cups of coffee!

The Adventist Health Study found that the use of even one cup of coffee daily was associated with a 33 percent increase in the risk of fatal heart disease in men. Adventists who use two or more cups of coffee daily are reported to have a greater risk of fatal colon and bladder cancer.[74]

The caffeine syndrome is recognized by aggressiveness, hyperactivity, and sometimes psychotic behavior. Caffeine and the excess ingestion of xanthine alkaloids (found in coffee, tea, cocoa, and some popular beverages) affect people differently, usually observed in the abnormal stimulation of the nervous system and the inflammation of the gastrointestinal tract.[75]

Humanity's Original Diet

Original Diet. Ellen White's simple, positive statement regarding the best diet for human beings has stood the test of time and research: "In order to know what are the best foods, we must study God's original plan for man's diet. . . . Grains, fruits, nuts and vegetables constitute the diet chosen for us by our Creator."[76] The affirming research is voluminous and growing yearly.

Nuts. Although the scientific community has long ignored nuts, or thought them too high in fat to be recommended, evidence now substantiates Ellen White's teachings. She included them in the "diet chosen for us by our Creator."[77] Further, she said that "some nuts are not as wholesome as others. Almonds are preferable to peanuts."[78]

Aware of some of the dangers of too many nuts in the diet (because of their high fat content), she warned that "too large a quantity of nut food is an injury . . . but . . . all can eat freely of fruit."[79]

In the Adventist Health Study men who ate nuts 4-5 times a week had only half as many fatal heart attacks as those who rarely ate nuts.[80] Walnuts and almonds have been shown to lower serum lipids (reducing risk of atherosclerosis).[81]

Fruits and vegetables. Recent research has focused on the health benefits of a diet rich in vegetables and fruits. "Vegetables and fruits are complex foods containing more than 100 beneficial vitamins, minerals, fiber, and other substances. Scientists do not yet know which of the nutrients or other substances in fruits and vegetables may be protective against cancer. The principal possibilities include specific vitamins and minerals, fiber, and phytochemicals—carotenoids, flavonoids, terpenes, sterols, indoles, and phenols—that are present in foods of plant origin. . . . Until more is known about specific food components, the best advice is to eat five or more servings of fruits and vegetables each day."[82]

The Adventist Health Study indicated that vegetarians consume twice as much vitamin A and four times as much vitamin C as people in the general population. The antioxidant vitamins A, C, and E may lower the risk of cancer and coronary heart disease. Eating four servings of legumes per week decreases risk of pancreatic cancer much more than eating legumes only once a week.[83]

Where does one find these antioxidants? In carrots, squash, tomatoes, leafy vegetables, dried fruits, fresh strawberries, melons, broccoli, cauliflower, Brussell sprouts, etc. In a study of elderly people, high consumers of these foods had only 30 percent of the cancer mortality as that of low consumers.[84] In the 1996 American Cancer Society's Report, reference was made to the "oxygen-induced damage to tissues that occurs constantly as a result of normal metabolism. Because such damage is associated with increased cancer risk, antioxidant nutrients are thought to protect against cancer. Antioxidant nutrients include vitamin C, vitamin E, selenium, and carotenoids. Studies suggest that people who eat more fruits and vegetables containing these antioxidants have a lower risk for cancer."[85]

Those eating cabbage once a week had only one-third the risk of colon cancer compared to those who ate it once a month.[86] Those getting adequate vitamin A had only one-third the risk of lung cancer compared to those with low intake of vitamin A.[87] Oral and pharyngeal cancer were reduced by half in those consuming high quantities of fruits and vegetables.[88]

Adequate amounts of the antioxidant vitamins A, C, and E have been shown to reduce the risk of cataracts. Those who consumed fewer than 3.5 servings of fruit or vegetables daily had a five to ten times increased risk of cataracts![89]

Foods high in potassium . . . like oranges, bananas, potatoes, and milk . . . reduce risk of stroke by as much as 40 percent.[90]

Fruits and vegetables at the same meal. Ellen White counseled that "we should avoid eating vegetables and fruit at the same meal."[91] "At one meal use bread and fruit, at the next bread and vegetables."[92]

Whenever possible, Mrs. White followed this practice: "I eat the most simple foods, prepared in the most simple way. For months my principal diet has been vermicelli and canned tomatoes, cooked together. This I eat with zwieback. Then I have also stewed fruit of some kind and sometimes lemon pie. Dried corn, cooked with milk or a little cream, is another dish that I sometimes use."[93]

What are the problems when fruit and vegetables are combined? For many with a "feeble" digestion, the mix will cause "distress," and "inability to put forth mental effort."[94] Some children "become fretful and peevish."[95]

Ellen White saw in vision the cause of a minister's sickness: "I took notice of your diet. You eat too great a variety at one meal. Fruit and vegetables taken at one meal produce acidity of the stomach; then impurity of the blood results, and the mind is not clear because the digestion is imperfect."[96]

Mrs. White advised students to eat fruit and grains rather than vegetables for supper: "Let the students have the third meal prepared without vegetables, but with simple, wholesome food, such as fruit and bread."[97]

The White family considered vegetables to include peas, beans, potatoes, turnips, parsnips, onions, cabbages, and squashes (although some of these would be classified as fruits botanically). Fruits included tomatoes, apples, pears, peaches, strawberries, raspberries, blackberries, huckleberries, grapes, cranberries, and raisins. Grains (or seeds) included wheat, corn, rye, barley, oatmeal, rice, farina, cornstarch, "and the like."[98]

Some have wondered about Ellen White's inclusion of tomatoes within the fruit group, but that she did, according to common usage.[99]

Olives were an item that could be safely eaten at any meal.[100]

Milk. Ellen White's counsel regarding milk has often been misunderstood both by those who freely use it and those who avoid it. On one hand, she clearly says that the time will come when "milk of the cows will also be excluded from the diet of God's commandment-keeping people."[101]

However, again demonstrating Ellen White's common sense as well as enlightened counsel, she also said that, in her day, "as the situation now is,"[102] the time to "discard" or "exclude" milk had not come. She gave two reasons: (1) The poor were not able to make the dietary adjustment immediately: "I cannot say to them, 'You must not eat eggs or milk or cream. You must use no butter in the preparation of food.' The gospel must be preached to the poor, and the time has not yet come to prescribe the strictest diet."[103] Common sense indicated that "until we can teach them how to prepare health reform foods that are palatable, nourishing, and yet inexpensive, we are not at liberty to present the most advanced propositions regarding health reform diet."[104]

(2) Disease in animals was increasing, and for "safety" reasons it would be wise to discard milk from the diet.[105]

But while counseling that we should prepare for the day when milk will not be "safe," she emphasized that milk, or its "equivalent,"[106] is still part of "the most healthful diet."[107] Milk seems to be the most available source of Vitamin B-12; without milk, for most people, supplements of B-12 may be necessary.

Ellen White's common sense also warns against *extreme* positions. For some, prematurely discarding milk without providing its equivalent may cause sickness, even death.[108] For others, it would be an unwarranted financial hardship to find an equivalent for milk.[109]

Her common sense urged her to warn against premature proscriptions that would make some people the arbiters as to what others should be putting on their tables, thus "creating a time of trouble beforehand."[110] Above all, "we should not allow differences of opinion to create disunion."[111]

So, the question remains: When should we "discard" milk from the diet? In 1901 the time had "not yet come."[112] When the time does come, "God will reveal it."[113] We should wait, using our best judgment, always with the principle of "known duty"[114] leading us individually, "waiting until the circumstances demand it, and the Lord prepares the way for it."[115]

Grains. Ellen White's emphasis on grains as an essential component of an adequate diet has been unequivocally validated in recent research. "Grains such as wheat, rice, oats, barley, and the foods made from them constitute the base of healthful diets as illustrated in the Food Guide Pyramid. Healthful diets contain six to 11 standard servings of foods from this group each day. . . . Grains are an important source of many vitamins and minerals such as folate, calcium, and selenium, all of which have been associated with a lower risk of colon cancer."[116]

Alcohol affects brain cells. When Ellen White wrote in 1885 that alcoholic beverages destroy "reason and life," and in 1905 that such drinking "destroys the sensitive nerves of the brain," she sounded like an overzealous temperance orator.[117] But in 1970 research indicated that "even the moderate imbiber may incur some loss of irreplaceable brain cells—every time he drinks. . . . The only real difference between his loss of brain tissue and that of the heavy drinker is one of degree."[118] The ability to make decisions concerning moral issues begins to slip at very low alcohol intake levels (much below what is considered adequate to lower heart attack risk).[119]

Caffeine affects spirituality. Ellen White may not have known that she was many decades ahead of scientific confirmation when she warned that "all such stimulants and narcotics as tea, coffee, tobacco, alcohol, and morphine . . . exert a pernicious influence upon moral character. The earlier these hurtful habits are formed, the more firmly will they hold their victim in slavery to lust, and the more certainly will they lower the standard of spirituality."[120] But this truth is reflected in current studies. Researchers, among other findings, note that as coffee drinkers grow older, their coffee consumption increases. On a spiritual plane, this increase in consumption accompanies a decrease in religious involvement.[121]

Faulty diet and poor scholarship. In 1884 Ellen White stated that "nine tenths of the wickedness among the children of today is caused by intemperance in eating and drinking." Six years later she wrote that "the diet materially affects the mind and disposition."[122] Today widespread evidence indicates that there is a correlation between poor diet habits and poor scholarship. Better-fed children get better grades in school. When students with poor grades and poor diets are given nutritionally enriched meals, their grades and other scholastic indicators improve.[123]

Non-dietary Features of Health Reform

Objectionable aspects of city living. In 1890 Ellen White spoke of Satan at work "poisoning the atmosphere." In 1902 she predicted that city life "will grow more and more objectionable," and "a peril of health," with the "prevalence of foul air, impure water, impure food," including "poisonous gases." She looked to the day when many will move to the country, "for wickedness and corruption will increase to such a degree that the very atmosphere of the cities will seem to be polluted."[124] Modern research validates this warning.

Beneficial effect of sunlight. Ellen White wrote in 1865 that the atmosphere of rooms that are not exposed to light and air "is poisonous, because it has not been purified by light and air." Why? "Death-producing germs abound in dark, neglected corners, in decaying refuse . . . . Perfect cleanliness, plenty of sunlight, careful attention to sanitation in every detail of the home life, are essential to freedom from disease and to the cheerfulness and vigor of the inmates of the home."[125]

Exercise and physical health. Exercise directly affects the circulation of the blood. Contrary to conventional medicine in the nineteenth century, exercise is vital to recovery from most diseases as well as to the prevention of disease. In 1872 Ellen White wrote that "no exercise . . . can take the place of walking. By it the circulation of the blood is greatly involved."

Two years earlier she urged that "all who can possibly do so ought to walk in the open air every day, summer and winter." Why? "The muscles and veins are enabled better to perform their work. There will be increased vitality, which is so necessary to health." In 1905 she gave several reasons why "inactivity is a fruitful cause of disease": (1) slow circulation of the blood; (2) impurities are not expelled through the skin; (3) lungs are not fed with fresh air; (4) a double burden rests on the excretory organs.[126]

Exercise reduces risk of heart disease.[127] Sedentary people have twice as much risk of heart disease and high blood pressure as physically active people.[128] Even medium levels of physical activity in men protects against strokes.[129] The relative risk of mortality for women ages 50-74 was one-third less in the most active quartile compared to the least active.[130]

Exercise may also reduce the risk of

cancer of the colon, prostate, and breast, as well as diabetes.[131] After emphasizing that a person should be moderately active for 30 minutes or more on most days of the week, the American Cancer Society's 1996 report noted that "physical activity can help protect against some cancers, either by balancing caloric intake with energy expenditures or by other mechanisms. An imbalance of caloric intake and output can lead to overweight, obesity, and increased risk for cancers at several sites: colon and rectum, prostate, endometrium, breast (among postmenopausal women), and kidney."[132]

Exercise may boost the immune system.[133]

Exercise and mental ability. Ellen White wrote that "physical inaction lessens not only mental but moral power."[134] Exercise linked with the ability to think was noted in a study of twenty persons who exercised three times a week for six months. Conclusion: they were not only twenty percent fitter, they also were seventy percent better at making decisions than before beginning their exercise regimen.[135]

A walk after meals. Mrs. White clearly stated that we should not "engage in brain labor immediately after a meal." Further, we should not consider this counsel "a matter of trifling importance." "To engage in deep study or violent exercise immediately after eating, hinders the digestive process. . . . A short walk after a meal, with the head erect and the shoulders back, exercising moderately, is a great benefit."[136]

In 1964 Gerhard Volkheimer, M. D., a cardiovascular researcher in Berlin, reported that he had found that "physical inactivity can lead to the accumulation of chyle (fat) in the thoracic duct. And any sudden movement can apparently propel enough chyle into the blood to produce a coronary embolism."[137] Because of his research, Dr. Volkheimer strongly advised an after-meal walk to avoid the risk of a coronary attack.

Adequate sleep. Mrs. White included a program of adequate sleep as part of her eight natural remedies.[138] After linking mental vigor with physical health, she wrote: "Proper periods of sleep and rest and an abundance of physical exercise are essential to health of body and mind. To rob nature of her hours for rest and recuperation, by allowing one man to do the work of four, or of three, or even of two, will result in irreparable loss."[139]

In the Belloc-Breslow study it was noted that sleeping seven to eight hours nightly is one of the health factors that extends life by as much as eleven years.[140]

Trust in God. Long before many had linked health with spiritual values, Mrs. White wrote: "Courage, hope, faith, sympathy, love, promote health and prolong life."[141] A strong correlation exists between the mind and the body in physical recovery, even in the program of reversing heart disease.[142] Mrs. White was equally clear about how spiritual values not only help in curing disease, but are perhaps "health's greatest safeguard."[143]

Literature is abundant that documents how faith and social support from family and friends encourage mental and spiritual well-being.[144] People who attend church regularly have fewer illnesses than non-churchgoers. Non-religious Jews are twice as likely to have a coronary attack as synagogue-attending Jews.[145]

Cancer, a Virus

On page 322 we discussed Ellen White's instruction regarding dietary factors that may cause cancer. At the time she wrote, eminent men and women of science emphatically declared that cancer was not infectious, that there was no cancer germ.

Decades later, in 1956, Wendell Stanley, a Ph.D. virologist and Nobel Prize winner at the University of California, asserted his belief that "viruses cause most or all human cancers." He described viruses as "midget germs" that "lurk in the human body for years, even a lifetime;

some cause trouble, some do not. . . . In some cases, the cancer viruses might become active by aging, dietary indiscretions, hormonal imbalance, chemicals, radiation, or a combination of these stresses, and malignancies may follow."[146] Much cancer research has been done since, lending support to Ellen White's reference to "cancerous germs,* but currently it is believed that there are other, more common, causes of cancer as well.

Dr. Robert J. Huebner, chief of the Laboratory of Infectious Diseases at the National Institutes of Health at Bethesda, Maryland, reported in 1961 that "there isn't the slightest doubt in our minds that human cancers are caused by viruses. To this extent, they are simply infectious diseases."[147]

Contributing Causes of Cancer

• Associated factors with aging*:* Note Ellen White's interesting comment in 1864 regarding how aging may affect certain factors that stimulate latent cancer germs: "Cancerous humor [bodily fluid] which would lay [lie] dormant in the system [throughout] their life-time, is inflamed, and commences its eating, destructive work."[148]

• Drugs*:* Referring to a popular treatment for disease in the nineteenth century, Ellen White declared: "This is the effect of calomel . . . . It inflames the joints, and often sends rottenness into the bones. It frequently manifests itself in tumors, ulcers, and cancers, years after it has been introduced into the system."[149]

• Tobacco**:** In 1864 Mrs. White added her voice to the few in her day who had recognized that tobacco is a "poison of the most deceitful and malignant kind . . . a slow poison."[150]

Among the many cancers caused by smoking, lung cancer among ex-servicemen became prevalent in the mid-1930s in the United States as a direct result of heavy smoking during World War I. It takes about twenty years for cancer-producing results to become obvious. Before the 1930s, cancer of the lung was an extremely rare disease. In 1995, in the United States alone, 418,000 deaths were caused by smoking.[151] Unless the present trend is reversed, it is expected that by the year 2025, ten million people will die annually as a consequence of smoking tobacco.[152]

**The Ministry of Healing*, p. 313. "Proof that viruses cause various forms of malignant diseases in a variety of animals has been obtained by direct experimentation; thus, purified viruses inoculated into susceptible animals can induce malignant cells, and the cells of the malignancy can be shown to contain virus or virus-induced products. . . . Similar investigations cannot be carried out in man . . . due to the ethical constraints. . . . The viruses now thought to be possibly aetiologically associated with human cancers are shown in Table 11-5. In all cases association is based on circumstantial evidence, but the weight of evidence in some cases is now heavy."

Table 11-5: Virus implicated in various cancers

Agent	*"Cancer"*	*Predisposing Conditions*
Epstein-Barr virus	Burkitt's lymphoma Nasopharyngeal carcinoma	Possibly malaria
Herpes hominis	Carcinoma cervix	Promiscuity/venereal infection
Papovaviruses (SV 40; JC, BK)	Progressive multifocal encephalopathy	Immunosuppression
Unknown virus	Kaposi's sarcoma	Acquired immunodeficiency syndromes
Hepatitis B	Primary hepatocellular carcinoma	Chronic hepatitis B infection
Human Papillomaviruses	Genital tumors	Venereal infection
T-cell leukemia virus	1. Sezary syndrome 2. Mycosis fungoids	— —

—C. W. Potter and R. C. Rees, "Viruses, Immunity, and Cancer," in B. W. Hancock, and A. M. Ward, editors, *Immunological Aspects of Cancer* (Boston: Martinus Nijhoff Publishing, 1985), pp. 225-229.

But tobacco smokers also show high death rates from coronary artery disease.[153] Indeed, "those who acquire and indulge the unnatural appetite for tobacco, do this at the expense of health."[154]

Although the major risk factor for lung cancer is tobacco, diet also affects risk. But a "greater consumption of vegetables, fruits, or both together has also been associated with a lower risk of lung cancer. . . . Fruits and vegetables reduce cancer risk whether or not people smoke."[155]

Parental smoking is a significant factor in their children's health, even their death. Researchers at the University of Wisconsin, Madison, Wisconsin, say that "more young children are killed by parental smoking than by all unintentional injuries combined." They attribute 2,800 deaths to low birth weight caused by mothers who smoke during pregnancy. Another 2,000 deaths are due to sudden infant death syndrome (SIDS) caused by secondhand smoke; another 1,000 are caused by asthma. The same research said that an additional 5.4 million children suffer nonfatal asthma and ear infections triggered by parents' smoking, costing an estimated $4.6 billion annually to treat.[156]

Further research indicates that pregnant women who smoke more than ten cigarettes a day run the risk of giving birth to a child who will develop "conduct disorder," defined as "serious" antisocial behavior, for six months or more. Boys whose mothers smoked during pregnancy were 4.4 times more likely to engage in antisocial activities, including lying, stealing, arson, vandalism, or cruelty than boys whose mothers did not smoke or smoked fewer than ten cigarettes a day. Studies suggest that smoking causes changes in a child's brain functioning.[157]

Drugs and birth defects. In 1865 Mrs. White linked birth defects with poisonous drugs administered by physicians. In 1890 she warned that thousands "born deaf, blind, diseased, or idiotic" were casualties of their parents' indulgences in alcoholic beverages.[158] Scientific research beginning in the 1950s has validated this warning, including the negative effects of smoking and caffeine consumption on the fetus.[159] During pregnancy even "aspirin should be taken only in small amounts and not over long periods of time."[160]

Physical activity for the sick and the convalescent. In the 1860s, bed-rest and the rest-cure were standard recuperative procedures and remained so into the mid-twentieth century. Contrary to conventional medical practice, Ellen White declared in 1867 that she had been frequently "shown that the sick should be taught that it is wrong to suspend all physical labor in order to regain health. . . . To suspend activity in order to regain health, is a great error." Three years later: "If invalids would recover health, they should not discontinue physical exercise; for they will thus increase muscular weakness and general debility." Further, "the blood is not enabled to expel the impurities as it would if active circulation were induced by exercise."[161]

Mervyn G. Hardinge, M.D., one-time Dean, School of Health, Loma Linda University, reviewed this amazing 180-degree turn in medical practice."The 'rest cures' of the recent past have today given way to programs of occupational and educational therapy."[162]

Hypnosis and medical practice. Ellen White's condemnation of hypnotism has been supported by many modern psychiatric practitioners—and ridiculed by others. In speaking to a physician in 1901, she said: "No man or woman should exercise his or her will to control the senses or reason of another, so that the mind of the person is rendered passively subject to the will of the one who is exercising the control. This science [hypnotherapy] may appear to be something beautiful, but it is a science which you are in no case to handle. . . . Temporary relief may be felt, but the mind of the one thus controlled is never again so strong and reliable."[163]

In reference to the use of hypnotism in dentistry, two dentists authored an article entitled, "Psychological Evaluation of Hypnosis in Dentistry," in which they concluded: "In [a] study of the personality characteristics of dentists who employ hypnosis in their practice, the subjects consisted of 34 dentists. . . . The results indicated that most well-adjusted dentists do not tend to use hypnosis. . . .

"The vast majority of practicing dentists feel it is possible to render adequate service without employing hypnosis. . . . Hypnosis, in general, is not held in high esteem by the dental profession. . . .

"Dentists who are well-adjusted, who are relatively satisfied with themselves, and who obtain satisfaction from the conventional practice of their profession do not tend to use hypnosis or to become interested in its use. It is as if they do not need such an additional and unusual source of gratification."[164]

Mind-body relationships. In 1867 Ellen White linked the "sickness of body and mind to nearly all its dissatisfied feelings and discontented repinings."[165] In 1872 she urged physicians to "cure the body through the mind," because "a great deal of the sickness which afflicts humanity has its origin in the mind and can only be cured by restoring the mind to health. . . . Heart sickness makes many dyspeptics, for mental trouble has a paralyzing influence upon the digestive organs."[166]

In 1905 Mrs. White expanded these psychosomatic concepts in noting that "disease is sometimes produced, and is often greatly aggravated, by the imagination. . . . Many die of disease, the cause of which is wholly imaginary."[167]

Ancient medical science attested that the mind and body cannot be separated. But this truth has not always been translated into medical practice. In the latter half of the twentieth century, medical research generally affirmed not only that health and happiness are intertwined but that faulty emotional patterns can actually cause disease.[168]

In 1993 psychiatrist George F. Solomon, of the University of California at Los Angeles, said: "The mind and body cannot be separated. The mind is the brain, and the brain is part of the body. The brain regulates and influences many physiological functions, including immunity. Mental and physical well-being are inextricably intertwined." Dr. Solomon coined the term "psychoimmunology" in 1964 (a term that was expanded to "psychoneuroimmunology" [PNI] by Robert Ader). After twenty-five years of studying the biological mechanisms by which emotions and attitudes affect one's resistance to disease, Solomon said, "We have studied people with a variety of illnesses, and people with very good coping skills tend to have a greater speed of recovery."[169]

In 1995, *Healing and The Mind*, a remarkable book by Bill Moyers based on the television series with the same title, was devoted to two important questions: "How do thoughts and feelings influence health? How is healing related to the mind?" Author Bill Moyers and his team directed these questions to physicians in large public hospitals and small community clinics. They talked with people in stress reduction clinics and therapeutic support groups. They explored these questions with scientists on the frontier of mind/body research. Their answers were remarkably consistent: the mind controls the body for good or ill. Moyers concluded that "talking with different doctors during this journey, I realize that we do need a new medical paradigm that goes beyond 'body parts' medicine, and not only for the patient's sake. At a time when the cost of health care is skyrocketing, the potential economic impact of mind/body medicine is considerable." Moyer quoted Eric J. Cassell approvingly when Cassell wrote that healing powers "consist only in and no more than in allowing, causing, or bringing to bear those things or forces for getting better (whatever they may be) that already exist in the patient."[170]

Dean Ornish, in an extended interview that flowed from Ornish's ground-breaking research on reversing arteriosclerosis through non-invasive methods such as diet, exercise, and stress-reduction, said: "Taking into account cholesterol, blood pressure, smoking, genetics, and all of the other known risk factors still explains only about half of the heart disease we see. Clearly, something else is going on. My clinical experience, as well as what we're showing in our research, suggests that psychological, emotional, and even spiritual factors are important, not only in terms of how they affect our behaviors, like diet and exercise, but also in more direct ways."[171]

Electrical currents in brain and nervous system. In 1934 members of the Mayo Clinic staff in Rochester, Minnesota, were discussing the electrical action of the brain. In 1962 Dr. Ernest Weber, president of Polytechnic Institute, Brooklyn, New York, wrote that he knew of no greater modern wonder than the discovery of "electromagnetic waves."

In 1954 an article in *The Scientific American* reviewed the developing science of electromagnetic waves: "Twenty-five years ago [1929] Hans Berger, a German psychiatrist, . . . began to publish some strange little pictures consisting of nothing but wavy lines. They should have caused great excitement among his colleagues, because he claimed that they showed the electrical activity of the human brain. But in fact no one took them seriously. For several years no one even bothered to repeat his experiments. . . . In the quarter of a century since then the study of his little wavy lines has grown into a new department of science called electroencephalography. Today several hundred laboratories in the United States and a similar number in Europe are recording and interpreting charts of the electrical discharges of human brains. Their total annual output of charts would girdle the earth."[172]

Ellen White wrote in 1869: "Whatever disturbs the circulation of the electric currents in the nervous system lessens the strength of the vital powers; and the result is a deadening of the sensibilities of the mind." Three years later she declared: "This class [physical laborers who use the brain powers very little] fall more readily if attacked by disease; the system is vitalized by the electrical force of the brain to resist disease."[173]

In 1903 she added: "The influence of the mind on the body, as well as of the body on the mind, should be emphasized. The electric power of the brain, promoted by mental activity, vitalizes the whole system, and is thus an invaluable aid in resisting disease. This should be made plain. The power of the will and the importance of self-control, both in the preservation and in the recovery of health, the depressing and even ruinous effect of anger, discontent, selfishness, or impurity, and, on the other hand, the marvelous life-giving power to be found in cheerfulness, unselfishness, gratitude, should also be shown."[174]

Caution in the use of the X-ray. Ellen White not only endorsed the proper use of the X-ray, she permitted X-ray treatment for a black spot on her forehead.[175]

But she sounded an early warning about overexposure in X-ray therapy. Speaking in regard to new "electrical appliances" being installed in the Paradise Valley Sanitarium, she said: "I was instructed that some connected with the institution were introducing things for the treatment of the sick that were not safe. The application of some of these electrical treatments would involve the patient in serious difficulties, imperiling life. . . . I have been instructed that the X-ray is not the great blessing that some suppose it to be. If used unwisely it may do much harm. The results of some of the electrical treatments are similar to the results of using stimulants. There is a weakness that follows."[176]

Through the years, the effects of

excessive X-ray radiation in the treatment of disease have become well known—tissue breakdown with the potential risk of anemia, leukemia, cataract formation, and shortening of life. But when used wisely, the positive results of X-ray diagnostics and treatment are incalculable.

Prenatal influences. From 1865 to her last years, Ellen White emphasized the various facets of prenatal influences. Yet, not until the 1950s was this concept given credibility in scientific circles. Since then, a tidal wave of concurrence has flooded the medical world.

In 1865 Mrs. White wrote: "The irritability, nervousness, and despondency, manifested by the mother, will mark the character of her child. In past generations, if mothers had informed themselves in regard to the laws of their being, they would have understood that their constitutional strength, as well as the tone of their morals, and their mental faculties, would in a great measure be represented in their offspring."[177]

In 1954 Ashley Montagu wrote: "There is now sufficient evidence from many sources to indicate that the unborn child can be variously affected by physical changes in the mother, and that although a woman cannot 'mark' her baby by seeing something unpleasant before he is born, nor make him a poet by reading Keats and Shelley during her pregnancy, there are ways in which she definitely can influence his behavior pattern. It is largely up to her, and to those surrounding her during her pregnancy, whether her infant will be born a happy, healthy, sweet-tempered individual or an ill-adjusted neurotic."[178]

Corroborating the research of many, Leland H. Scott wrote in 1967: "There is a growing evidence that chemical irregularities in the mother's blood brought about by endocrine imbalance, dietary deficiencies, or ill health may have serious effects. Maternal malnutrition often results in the unborn child being deprived of essential vitamins or nutrients necessary for its normal growth and health. Childhood abnormalities, such as rickets, nervous instability, epilepsy, and cerebral palsy, have been found to result from serious malnutrition in the mother at certain points during the period of pregnancy."[179]

First years of a child's life. Tightly connected with the concept of prenatal influences is the belief that the first few years of a child's life set the life course. In 1881 Ellen White wrote that the "parents' work must begin with the child in its infancy."[180]

More precisely, parents should "properly discipline . . . children during the first three years of their lives. Do not allow them to form their wishes and desires. The mother must be mind for her child. The first three years is the time in which to bend the tiny twig."[181]

In the overall training of the child, in areas beyond discipline, Ellen White is emphatic: "Too much importance cannot be placed on the early training of children. The lessons that the child learns during the first seven years of life have more to do with forming his character than all that it learns in future years."[182]

The importance of a child's first three years of learning was stressed in 1997 by a White House panel of experts, as reported in *The Washington Post.* The scientists and child development specialists presented "compelling new research showing that a child's language, thinking and emotional health are largely formed before age 3. . . . Not only are most brain synapses—connections between brain cells—formed before age 3, the report said, 'those synapses that have been activated many times by repeated early experience tend to become permanent; the synapses that are not used tend to become eliminated.'"[183]

Modern Research Confirms Health Principles

Clive McCay. The late Dr. Clive M. McCay, professor of nutrition at Cornell's New York State College of Agriculture and Life Sciences (where he taught for thirty-seven years—1925-1962), was recognized worldwide as a pioneer and authority in nutritional theory, research, and history.[184]

After coming into contact with the health principles of Ellen White through Helen Chen, a 20-year-old Seventh-day Adventist graduate student, he wanted to know more about her church and its health teachings. Eventually he received *Counsels on Diet and Foods* at his request. This book, a compilation of Ellen White materials on a healthful diet and its relation to physical, mental, and spiritual health, also dates and lists the source of the various extracts. Since McCay believed that anything written before 1900 was unscientific, he urgently asked Helen: "Where did she [Ellen White] get her information?"[185]

Later, Dr. McCay talked to F. D. Nichol, editor of the *Review and Herald,* about his new interest in Adventist health principles as set forth by Ellen White. Nichol, knowing that the Unitarian scientist probably would not understand the Biblical doctrine of spiritual gifts, parried his questions about Ellen White. He told McCay that her critics dismissed her as a plagiarist, copying from contemporaries.

"Nonsense!" McCay responded. "I simply cannot accept that explanation: it creates a much bigger problem than it resolves! If she merely copied her contemporaries, how did she know which ideas to borrow and which to reject, out of the bewildering array of theories and health teachings current in the 19th century? Most were quite irrational and have now been repudiated! She would have had to be a most amazing person, with knowledge beyond her times, in order to do this successfully."[186]

In the years following, McCay gave lectures featuring Ellen White's writings on nutrition to various groups, including scientific bodies. A summation of his findings was published in the *Review and Herald.*[187]

U. S. Department of Agriculture and Health, Education, and Welfare. In July 1980, USDA and HEW issued jointly their "Dietary Guidelines for Americans": (1) Eat a variety of foods. (2) Maintain ideal weight. (3) Avoid too much fat, saturated fat, and cholesterol. (4) Eat foods with adequate starch and fiber. (5) Avoid too much sugar. (6) Avoid too much sodium. (7) If you drink alcohol, do so in moderation.[188] This report served as a ringing wakeup call to health workers as it was to the general population. But if this report had been issued in 1863, it would have been as startling as Ellen White's instructions were at that time!

In 1995 the same offices issued their updated "Dietary Guidelines," emphasizing that "vegetarian diets are consistent with the Dietary Guidelines for Americans and can meet Recommended Dietary Allowances for nutrients.[189] This 1995 update placed greater emphasis on the plant foods consistent with the Food Guide Pyramid. "The revised guideline also acknowledges that grains are associated with 'a substantially lowered risk of many chronic diseases, including certain types of cancer,' that antioxidant nutrients have a 'potentially beneficial role in reducing the risk of cancer and certain other chronic diseases,' and that folate 'reduces the risk of a serious type of birth defect.'" Further, the revised guideline emphasized that foods, not the salt shaker, are the source of most dietary sodium, continuing to note "the link between sodium and hypertension" and that sodium "is an essential nutrient substantially overconsumed by the American public in general."[190]

National Academy of Sciences (National Research Council). This research-oriented body gave a joint report in June 1982, entitled "Diet, Nutrition, and Cancer." Focusing on the connection between diet and cancer, this report was essentially the same as the government report of 1980.

Their research indicated that by making

changes in one's diet, cancer risk can be greatly reduced. Specifically they urged eating largely of fruits, whole grains, and vegetables, and reducing consumption of fats, sugar, salt, and alcohol.[191]

American Cancer Society. In February 1983 the editor of the Society's journal, *Cancer News,* published an article entitled, "At Last, An Anti-Cancer Diet." The first paragraph pointed to California Seventh-day Adventists as having a much lower rate of colon/rectal cancer than other Americans.

Later in the article, studies were noted that indicated breast, colon, and prostate cancer "is significantly lower among people who eat lots of vegetables. This 'startling finding,' says Walter Troll, professor of environmental medicine at New York University, suggests that vegetables contain substances 'capable of inhibiting cancer in man.'"[192]

Surgeon General of the U.S.A. In July 1988 C. Everett Koop, M.D., released the first nutrition report by a U. S. Surgeon General. Based on more than 2,500 scientific articles, his prescription for America was: "Less fat, more vegetables and fruit."[193]

Preventive Medicine Research Institute at the School of Medicine, University of California. In 1990 Dean Ornish, president of this research institute at the University of California, published his findings that arterial blockage built up by cholesterol can be *reversed* by a largely vegetarian diet plus exercise and stress reduction. His conclusions were backed up by four-color slides of computer-analyzed coronary angiograms and PET (Positron Emission Tomography) scans.

After a dramatic study of 6,500 persons at Cornell University in 1990, Ornish wrote a parody on the slogan used by the American Beef Association: "Meat. Real food for real death [of people]."[194]

Authority on high blood pressure. Norman M. Kaplan, professor of internal medicine and head of the hypertension section of the Southwestern Medical School (University of Texas) in Dallas, speaking at Loma Linda University to more than 1,000 health-care professionals, said: "You as Adventists may have espoused a certain dietary lifestyle on the basis of faith, in the past; but now you can practice it on the basis of scientific evidence. Hopefully you will not [go back and re-] join the midstream, but [rather] adhere to your health heritage."[195]

Adventist Mortality Study, 1958, and a joint study with the American Cancer Society, 1960. These California studies compared the cause of death for a large group of Seventh-day Adventist men with a similar number of non-Seventh-day Adventist men. The research *does not differentiate* between Adventists who eat meat daily, weekly, monthly, or none at all. *Neither does it distinguish* between lacto-ovo-vegetarians and total vegetarians. Compared with non-Seventh-day Adventist men, Adventist men can expect fewer deaths caused by some form of cancer. For example, according to the results of the Mortality Study listed below, Adventist men have 20 percent fewer deaths caused by lung cancer compared to the general population's death rate from lung cancer. Note the percent of fewer deaths expected among all Adventists for other kinds of cancer:

- 20 percent, lung cancer
- 5 percent, mouth, throat, and larynx cancer
- 32 percent, bronchitis and emphysema
- 28 percent, bladder cancer
- 34 percent, esophageal cancer
- 13 percent, cirrhosis of the liver
- 72 percent, breast cancer
- 65 percent, digestive tract cancer
- 62 percent, leukemia
- 61 percent, ovarian cancer
- 54 percent, uterine cancer
- 66 percent, other cancer
- 53 percent, strokes
- 55 percent, diabetes
- 42 percent, peptic ulcer
- 31 percent, suicides

• 59 percent, deaths attributed to all medical causes[196]

The Adventist Incidence Study in 1974. Sent to 63,350 Adventist households in California, this questionnaire enumerated "348 variables covering demographic, socioeconomic, and religious belief and practice characteristics; family and personal medical histories; and nutritional, drug use, and exercise patterns."[197] The results continue to bear out the positive health benefits of the Adventist health message set forth by Ellen White a century ago.[198]

European studies confirm these two Adventist studies. A Norwegian seventeen-year study covering all Adventists in that country concluded in 1981 that Norwegian Adventists enjoyed about the same benefits as California Adventists. The study confirmed the observation "that neither social groups nor geographic selection explains the health advantage observed among Norwegian Seventh-day Adventists" and that "the total life style generally advocated and followed by Seventh-day Adventists explains the observed results."[199]

In 1982 Denmark's Cancer Registration Office in Copenhagen reported, after a thirty-five-year study, that only one in ten Adventists developed cancer, whereas the rate for the Danish population was one in four during the same period. The Cancer Registration's chief medical director said "that, without doubt, the Adventists studied in the investigation sustained far less risk of developing cancer than the average person. Their risk was 70 to 80 percent less than that of the general Danish population."[200]

In 1983 a Dutch study reported an 8.9-year life expectancy advantage for Adventist men and a 3.7-year advantage for Adventist women.[201]

A Polish study reported in 1985 that Adventist men had an advantage of 9.5 years, and Adventist women a difference of 4.5 years.[202]

American Cancer Society Guidelines on Diet, Nutrition, and Cancer Prevention, 1996. Their four basic guidelines were: 1. Choose most of the foods you eat from plant sources. Eat five or more servings of fruit and vegetables each day. Eat other foods from plant sources, such as breads, cereals, grain products, rice, pasta, or beans several times each day. 2. Limit your intake of high-fat foods, particularly from animal sources. Choose foods low in fat. Limit consumption of meats, especially high-fat meats. 3. Be physically active: Achieve and maintain a healthy weight. Be at least moderately active for 30 minutes or more on most days of the week. Stay within your healthy weight range. 4. Limit consumption of alcoholic beverages, if you drink at all.[203]

Summary of Ellen White's Principles of Health Reform

Ellen White's contribution to an advanced understanding of health and disease may be attributed to these factors: (1) insights received through visions; (2) her Spirit-directed ability to perceive what was in harmony with those insights from the maze of current opinion, and (3) her governing principle of the Great Controversy Theme that placed health matters within the context of a person's spiritual motivation, commitment, and preparation for the Advent.

The record stands: Compared to the relatively few "health reformers" in her day, Ellen White was unique. When compared to or contrasted with conventional medical wisdom and practice, she was decades ahead of her time.

In what way was Ellen White unique? Contemporary health reformers were prescient in some areas, but gravely wrong in others. Many held extreme positions on "discarding milk, sugar, and salt," etc.[204] Others believed that rest, not physical exercise, was indicated for those recuperating from illness.[205]

What if Ellen White had held these and other extreme positions? Her credibility would have been severely damaged in the ensuing years. More than that, if she had endorsed contemporary medical knowledge, her credibility would have been demolished. Further, her appeal that she was directed by divine guidance eventually would have been seen as a temporary ploy for self-serving purposes.[206]

But the health principles found in her nineteenth-century writings, distinctively coherent, have stood the test of time. Her principles relating to disease prevention as well as health restoration are not today viewed as fads. They were not the result of a "shotgun" approach.[207] All of the principles are integrally related; specifics are seen relating to the whole person's total health. The lifestyle of Seventh-day Adventists "is reflected in the phenomenal accumulation of published research papers concerning the Adventist lifestyle. . . . It seems probable that no other religious group has attracted so much recent interest from scientists."[208]

Endnotes

1. Stoy and Leilani Proctor, "Searching for the Fountain of Youth" (Hagerstown, Md.: The Health Connection, 1991).
2. See Dr. J. H. Kellogg's introduction to Ellen White's *Christian Temperance and Bible Hygiene.* See pp. 290, 291.
3. "In summer if they opened their windows to avoid suffocation they were eaten alive by insects. And in winter if they closed the windows to avoid freezing they choked on smoky air."—Bettmann, *The Good Old Days,* p. 53.
4. "In one area of personal care, the Victorians appeared untroubled. They seldom bathed. Glorification of the bathroom is a modern fetish. In 1882 only 2 percent of New York's homes had water connections. . . . Bathing was considered harmful by some doctors, and one, C. E. Sargent, described it as a 'needless waste of time.'"—Bettmann, *Ibid.,* p. 35.
5. In 1996 it was said that "about one-third of the 500,000 cancer deaths that occur in the United States each year is due to dietary factors." *CA*—A Cancer Journal for Clinicians, 46:6, November/December 1996. Hereafter, cited as *CA*/1996.
6. L. Jean Bogert, in *Nutrition and Physical Fitness* (Philadelphia: W. B. Saunders, 7th ed., 1962), p. 406.
7. *Testimonies,* vol. 2, p. 367.
8. *Counsels on Diet and Foods,* p. 357.
9. *Testimonies*, vol. 7, p. 135.
10. *The Ministry of Healing,* p. 302.
11. *Ibid.,* p. 298.
12. "The alternative was 'bogus butter,' and the ingredients of this concoction were so wildly incongruous as to generate several investigations by city and state. Fat from hogs along with every conceivable animal part that the slaughterhouses could not turn to cash were picked up . . . and processed in filthy work sheds. Bleaches were blended into the mix to give the product the appearance of real butter.

    "A margarine [not vegetable oil margarine] factory employee in 1889 told New York State investigators that his work had made 'his hands so sore . . . his nails came off, his hair dropped out and he had to be confined to Bellevue Hospital for general debility.' That customers frequently bought this pestilent muck and fed it to their families was due to the artfulness of the grocers, who scraped off the real labels and relettered the boxes 'Western butter' or 'best creamery butter.'"—Bettmann, *The Good Old Days,* p. 117.
13. *Testimonies,* vol. 7, p. 135 (1902).
14. American Heart Association News Release, May 13, 1994.
15. *Counsels on Diet and Foods,* p. 320 (two statements, 1868 and 1905).
16. G. E. Fraser, J. Sabaté, W. L. Beeson, T. Strahan, *Archives of Internal Medicine* (1992), 152:1416-1424.
17. D. P. Burkitt, *British Medical Journal* (1972), 2:556-561.
18. H. S. Page and A. J. Asire, *Cancer Rates and Risk,* 3rd edition, NIH Publication 85:691 (Bethesda, Md.: National Cancer Institute, April, 1985).
19. D. P. Burkitt, A. R. P. Walker, and N. S. Painter, *Journal of the American Medical Association* (1974), 229:1068-74.
20. *Counsels on Diet and Foods*, p. 386.
21. *Ibid.,* pp. 389, 390.
22. *Ibid.*, pp. 386, 387.
23. *Ibid.,* p. 387.
24. *Ibid.,* p. 387.
25. "Cancers, tumors, and pulmonary diseases are largely caused by meat eating."—*Ibid.,* p. 383.
26. *Ibid.,* p. 396.
27. *Testimonies,* vol. 2, p. 63.
28. *Counsels on Diet and Foods,* p. 389.
29. *Ibid.*
30. *The Ministry of Healing,* p. 320. See also pp. 282, 304, 311. For everyone, including prophets, "the path of the just is like the shining sun, that shines ever brighter unto the perfect day" (Prov. 4:18). Those who follow known duty, follow truth "step by step." (See pp. 274, 310.)
31. *Counsels on Diet and Foods,* pp. 462, 463.
32. *Ibid.,* pp. 380, 381.
33. *Ibid.,* p. 381.
34. *Ibid.,* pp. 453, 454.
35. *Ibid.,* p. 290.
36. *Ibid.*, pp. 399, 402, 404.
37. R. L. Phillips, F. R. Lemon, W. L. Beeson, J. W. Kuzma, *American Journal of Clinical Nutrition* (1978) 31:S191-S198.
38. T. Hirayama, *Preventive Medicine* (1978), 7:173-195.
39. E. L. Winder, G. C. Ersher, and N. Mantel, *Cancer* (1966), 19:489-520. (Some studies in the United States, however, have not directly linked diets heavy in fat or meat to breast cancer.)

40. Regina Ziegler, lecturer from the National Cancer Institute in Atlanta, Ga., at the Diet and Cancer Symposium, April, 1991. See also D. A. Snowden, R. L. Phillips, W. Choi, *American Journal of Epidemiology* (1984), 120:224-250; R. L. Phillips and D. A. Snowdon, *Journal of the National Cancer Institute* (1985), 74:307-317.
41. *CA*/1996, p. 329.
42. T. Hirayama, *Preventive Medicine* 7:173-195, (1978). "Egg yolk consumption should be discouraged. The yolk is the highest source of cholesterol in the average American diet. Ingestion of two eggs a day—in visible and/or invisible form (i.e., in prepared foods)—virtually negates dietary programs aimed at reducing serum cholesterol. Consequently, the public should be encouraged to avoid egg yolk in commercially prepared foods. Food manufacturers have recently developed low cholesterol and low saturated fat egg substitutes that may be used successfully in quantity cookery and for scrambled eggs, waffles, pancakes, omelettes, and the like. These developments should be encouraged, but with a lower salt content."—"Special Report: Inter-Society Commission for Heart Disease Resources," *Circulation*, July 1984, 70:188A.
43. "Diet, Nutrition, and Cancer," p. 6-3, Committee on Diet, Nutrition, and Cancer (Washington, D.C.: National Academy Press, 1982).
44. E. H. Krick, *Life and Health Special Cancer Prevention Issue*, pp. 12-14, (1978).
45. J. Vitale, *Oncology Times*, Jan. 1980.
46. R. L. Phillips, D. A. Snowden, B. N. Brin, in E. L. Wynder, G. A. Leveille, J. H. Weisburger, G. E. Livingston, editors, *Environmental Aspects of Cancer—The Role of Macro and Micro Components of Foods* (Westport, Conn.: Food and Nutrition Press, 1983), pp. 53-72. No distinction was made between lacto-ovo-vegetarians and total vegetarians—which could lead to the conjecture that an even lower ratio would have been indicated for total vegetarians.
47. These percentages may not be statistically significant and await further substantiation in later studies.
48. D. A. Snowden, R. L. Phillips, and W. Choi, *American Journal of Epidemiology*, 120:244-250, (1984).
49. P. K. Mills, W. L. Beeson, R. L. Phillips, and Gary E. Fraser, *American Journal of Epidemiology*, 133:230-239 (1991).
50. D. A. Snowden, R. L. Phillips, and Gary E. Fraser, *Preventive Medicine*, 1984, 13:490-500 (1984).
51. *CA*/1996, pp. 332, 333.
52. A. S. Cunningham, *The Lancet*, 2:1184-1186, (1976).
53. B. M. Calkins, D. J. Whittaker, P. P. Nair, A. A. Rider, and N. Turjman, *American Journal of Clinical Nutrition*, 40:896-905, October, 1984.
54. "Diet, Nutrition, and Cancer," *Cancer Research*, June, 1983, 43:3018-3023.
55. See p. 329.
56. M. F. Stanton, *CA.—A Cancer Journal for Clinicians*, (1974), 24:189.
57. Personal communication from the Director of the Michigan Department of Agriculture Regional Poultry Laboratory, East Lansing, Mich., to John Scharffenberg, M.D., (1982).
58. D. A. Snowden and R. L. Phillips, *American Journal of Public Health* 75:507-512, 1985.
59. *Nutrition Today*, 3:9-11, 1968. A high animal-fat diet reduces diphosphoglycerate (DPG) in the red blood cells which indicates less oxygen is available for the tissue cells, whereas plant fats do not reduce the DPG.
60. *Preventive Medicine*, 12:60-69, (1983).
61. A. J. Vergroesen, "Physiological Effects of Dietary Linoleic Acid," *Nutrition Review*, 335:1-5, (1977).
62. *Journal of Nutrition*, 62:421-424.
63. *CVD Epidemiology Newsletter*, 27:81, (1979).
64. *Journal of Cardiovascular Pharmacology*, 3:847-853, 1981; *Lancet*, 2:285, July 30, 1988.
65. K. D. Linsted., S. Tonstad, and J. W. Kuzma, *Journal of Clinical Epidemiology*, 44:363.
66. *Counsels on Diet and Foods*, p. 207.
67. *Ibid.*, p. 340.
68. *Ibid.*, p. 468. See T. Antonios and G. A. MacGregor, "Salt—more adverse effects," *Lancet*, 1996, 348:250, 251.
69. *Counsels on Diet and Foods*, p. 425.
70. *Ibid.*, p. 425.
71. *Ibid.*, p. 424.
72. *Ibid.*, p. 421.
73. *Ibid.*, p. 421. Coffee has been positively associated with factors that promote coronary heart disease (*Preventive Medicine* 1994), 23:377- 384); cholesterol increased with even one cup of regular coffee daily (*Journal of Clinical Epidemiology* [1995], 48:1189-1196); the risk of myocardial infarction (*American Journal of Epidemiology* [1995] 14:724-731); accelerated bone loss from the spine and total body in women with calcium intakes below recommended dietary allowance of 800 mg. (*American Journal of Clinical Nutrition* [1994] 60:573-578); the risk of ovarian cancer (*International Journal of Cancer* [1981] 28:691-693); and "exhibits the features of a typical psychoactive substance of dependence."—*Journal of the American Medical Association* (1994) 272:1043-1048.
74. D. A. Snowden, R. L. Phillips, *American Journal of Public Health*, 74:820-823, August, 1984; K. D. Lindsted, J. W. Kuzma, J. E. Anderson, *Journal of Clinical Epidemiology*, 1992, 45:733-742.
75. H. A. Reimann, "Caffeinism," *Journal of the American Medical Association*, Dec. 18, 1967, 202:12, pp. 131, 132.
76. *Counsels on Diet and Foods*, p. 81.
77. *Ibid.*, p. 363.
78. *Ibid.*, p. 364.
79. *MR*, vol. 21, p. 285 (1901).
80. G. E. Fraser, J. Sabaté, W. L. Beeson, and T. M. Strahan, *Archives of Internal Medicine*, July 1992, 152:1416-1424.
81. J. Sabaté, et al., *New England Journal of Medicine*, 1993, 328:603-607; G. A. Spiller, et al., *Journal of American College of Nutrition*, 1992, 11:126-130; J. Sabaté, G. E. Fraser, "The Probable Role of Nuts in Preventing Coronary Heart Disease," *Primary Cardiology*, 1993, 19:65-72.
82. *CA*/1996, p. 327.
83. "Increasing consumption of vegetarian protein products, beans, lentils, and peas as well as dried fruit was associated with highly significant protective relationships to pancreas cancer risk."—P. K. Mills, W. L. Beeson, D. E. Abbey, G. E. Fraser, and R. L. Phillips, *Cancer*, 1988, 61:2578; "Diets rich in animal fat appear to be associated with increased risk for prostatic cancer."—P. K. Mills, W. L. Beeson, R. L. Phillips, G. E. Fraser, *Cancer*, 1989, 64:598. "Beans are especially rich in nutrients that may protect against cancer and can be a useful low-fat but high-protein alternative to meat."—CA/1996, p. 329.

84. Colditz, et al., *American Journal of Clinical Nutrition*, 1985, 41:32-36.
85. *CA*/1996, p. 333.
86. S. Graham and C. Mettlin in G. R. Newell, N. H. Ellison, editors, *Progress in Cancer Research and Therapy*, vol. 17, *Nutrition and Cancer Etiology and Treatment* (New York: Raven Press, 1981), pp. 189-215; "Of the many scientific studies on this subject, the great majority show that eating fruits and vegetables (especially green and dark yellow vegetables and those in the cabbage family, soy products, and legumes) protects against colon cancer."—*CA*/1996, p. 326.
87. E. Bjelke, *International Journal of Cancer*, 15:561-565, 1975.
88. D. M. Winn, R. G. Ziegler, L. W. Pickle, et al., *Cancer Research*, 44:1216-1222, 1984.
89. P. F. Jacques and L. T. Chylack, Jr., *American Journal of Clinical Nutrition*, 53:335S-355S, 1991.
90. *New England Journal of Medicine*, 1987, vol. 316, 5:235-240.
91. *The Youth's Instructor*, May 31, 1894; *Counsels on Diet and Foods*, p. 112; *The Ministry of Healing*, pp. 299, 300.
92. *Signs of the Times*, Sept. 23, 1897.
93. *Counsels on Diet and Foods*, p. 491.
94. *Ibid.*, p. 112; *The Ministry of Healing*, pp. 299, 300.
95. *MR*, vol. 18, p. 84.
96. *Ibid.*, pp. 112, 113.
97. *Ibid.*, p. 178.
98. *Christian Temperance and Bible Hygiene*, pp. 218, 219; *Counsels on Diet and Foods*, pp. 94, 95, 309; *The Ministry of Healing*, p. 299; *MR*, vol. 3, p. 408.
99. *MR*, vol. 8, pp. 252, 253; vol. 14, p. 332, *Bio.*, vol. 2, pp. 298, 299, 357; vol. 4, p. 271.
100. *Counsels on Diet and Foods*, p. 349.
101. *Counsels on Diet and Foods*, p. 411 (1898); *Ibid.*, p. 357 (1899); *Ibid.*, p. 356 (1902); *MR*, vol. 21, p. 286 (1901).
102. *Counsels on Diet and Foods*, p. 352 (1901).
103. *Ibid.*, p. 358 (1901).
104. *Ibid.*, p. 351 (1902); p. 470 (1905).
105. *Ibid.*, p. 411 (1898); p. 210 (1901); p. 359 (1901); p. 356 (1902).
106. *Ibid.*, p. 207 (1909).
107. *Ibid.*, p. 92 (1890).
108. *Ibid.*, p. 358 (1901), p. 204 (1901). See also pp. 95-97, 306.
109. *Ibid.*, p. 351 (1902); p. 358 (1901).
110. *Ibid.*, p. 359 (1901); p. 210 (1901).
111. *Ibid.*, p. 352 (1904).
112. *Ibid.*, p. 358.
113. *Ibid.*, p. 359 (1901).
114. See pp. 274, 295, 304, 310.
115. *Ibid.*, pp. 355, 356 (1909).
116. *CA*/1996, p. 328.
117. *Testimonies*, vol. 5, p. 441; *Temperance*, p. 59; see also *The Ministry of Healing*, p. 344.
118. Albert Q. Maisel, "Alcohol and Your Brain," *Reader's Digest*, June, 1970; "Alcohol impairs mental and physical functions. Even at the lowest measurable level, alcohol affects perception, information processing, learning, judgment, reaction time, sound processing, and peripheral vision. Most seriously, it reduces the individual's awareness of being impaired."—Herbert Moskowitz, *Alcohol Health and Resource World*, Summer, 1995, 9:4, pp. 11-15; CAT indicated that there is shrinkage of the brain even in light to moderate drinkers.—*Recent Developments in Alcoholism*, vol. 3, pp. 253-264 (1985). "Another important chronic effect of alcohol consumption is brain damage, entailing mood disorder. . . . alcohol appears to accelerate aging processes that interfere with the ability to reason and solve the problems of everyday living."—World Health Organization Technical Series 797: *Diet, Nutrition, and the Prevention of Chronic Disease*, Report of a WHO Study Group, Geneva, 1990, pp. 62-65, 83-84, 101, 111.
119. *Journal of Genetic Psychology*, 1979, 31:540-543.
120. *The Sanctified Life*, p. 28.
121. As cited in Galen C. Bosley, "Is Adventist Health Reform Scientific?" *Ministry*, April, 1987: J. F. Greden, R. Fontaine, M. Lubetsky, and K. Chamberlin, "Anxiety and Depression Associated with Caffeinism Among Psychiatric Patients," *American Journal of Psychiatry* 135, No. 8 (1978), pp. 963-966; B. S. Victor, M. Lubetsky, and F. Greden, "Somatic Manifestations of Caffeinism," *Journal of Clinical Psychiatry* 42, No. 5 (1981), pp. 185-188.
122. *The Adventist Home*, p. 252.
123. "The Link Between Nutrition and Cognitive Development in Children," Center on Hunger, Poverty, and Nutrition Policy, Tufts University School of Nutrition, Medford, Mass., 1995.
124. *Selected Messages*, book 2, p. 52; *Testimonies*, vol. 7, p. 82; *The Ministry of Healing*, pp. 262, 365; *Country Living*, pp. 28, 29. According to the May, 1996, report, "Guide to Mortality and Pollution Tables," by the National Resources Defense Council, New York, (NRDC), about 64,000 people are thought to die prematurely annually from cardiopulmonary causes linked to particulate air pollution. The same report estimates that in heavily populated cities, lives are shortened by an average of about one to two years.
125. *Selected Messages*, book 2, p. 462; *The Ministry of Healing*, pp. 274, 276. "Women living in areas of high concentrations of 'total suspended particles' in the air had a 37 percent higher risk of developing cancer than women in less polluted areas."—Report released in October, 1991, by investigative team headed by D. E. Abbey, Loma Linda University, after a 20-year, $8.4 million investigation into the health effects of air pollution—"Recent Adventist Health Study Findings Link Air Pollution and Cancer in Women," *Pacific Union Recorder*, March 16, 1992.
126. *Testimonies*, vol. 3, p. 78; vol. 2, p. 529; *The Ministry of Healing*, p. 238.
127. G. E. Fraser, T. M. Strahan, J. Sabaté, W. L. Beesen, D. Kissinger, "Effects of Traditional Coronary Risk Factors as Rates of Incident Coronary Events in a Low Risk Population: The Adventist Health Study," *Circulation*, 1992, 86:406-13.
128. K. E. Powell, P. D. Thompson, C. J. Caspersen, and J. S. Kendrick, *Annual Reviews of Public Health*, 1987, 8:253-287. "Special Report: Inter-Society Commission for Heart Disease Resources," *Circulation*, July, 1986, pp. 177A, 178A. *Heart Disease and Stroke*, 1993, 2:183-187. David Krtichevsky, "Diet and Nutrition," *Cancer Journal for Clinicians*, 1991, pp. 328-333.
129. *American Journal of Epidemiology*, 1994, 140:608-620.
130. *American Heart Journal*, 1994, 128:965-972.
131. *Epidemiology*, 1995, 6:602-606.
132. *CA*/1996, p. 330.

133. University of California at Berkeley *Wellness Letter,* Oct. 1994.
134. *Education,* p. 209.
135. "Decision-making: A Boost for Thought," *American Health,* Nov/Dec, 1983. Thirty people aged 65-72 were divided into three groups—walking, weight-training, and control (without specific exercise). At sixteen weeks, the walking group not only increased their aerobic capacity but also improved their cognitive function test scores. The other two groups showed no improvement.—*Health After 50,* Nov. 1995.
136. *Counsels on Health,* pp. 565, 566; *Counsels on Diet and Foods,* pp. 103, 104.
137. *Medical World News,* Sept. 24, 1964. For a review of the chief benefits of walking in maintaining health and preventing disease, see David C. Nieman, *The Adventist Health Style* (Hagerstown, Md.: Review and Herald Publishing Association, 1990), pp. 52-56.
138. *The Ministry of Healing,* p. 127.
139. *Testimonies,* vol. 7, p. 247.
140. N. B. Belloc and L. Breslow, "Relationship of Physical Health Status and Health Practices," *Preventive Medicine,* 1972, 1:409-421. Dr. Lester Breslow, dean of the School of Public Health, University of California at Los Angeles, led out in a study of 7,000 adult residents of Alameda County, California, in 1965. Dr. Breslow has continued to check his statistics and the results are always the same. (See "Persistence of Health Habits and Their Relationship to Mortality," *Preventive Medicine,* 9:469-483 (1980). Breslow's studies startled the scientific community with his conclusion that Americans could add eleven years to their lives by following seven common-sense health habits: (1) Don't smoke; (2) Use little or no alcohol; (3) Start the day with a good breakfast; (4) Avoid eating between meals; (5) Sleep seven to eight hours each night; (6) Engage in frequent, regular exercise; (7) Maintain ideal weight and avoid overweight. The statistics further suggested that the health benefit is cumulative and that the absence of any one of the seven habits decreases life expectancy markedly.
141. *The Ministry of Healing,* p. 241.
142. See p. 331.
143. "'A merry [rejoicing] heart doeth good like a medicine' (Prov. 17:22). Gratitude, rejoicing, benevolence, trust in God's love and care—these are health's greatest safeguard."—*The Ministry of Healing,* p. 281.
144. "The Second 50 Years Promoting Health and Preventing Disease," National Academy of Science, 1990; "The comparatively robust and substantial 'main' effects of divine relations . . . suggest that whatever the mediating processes prove to be, they are as potent as virtually any that affect well-being."—Melvin Pollner, "Divine Relations, Social Relations, and Well Being," *Journal of Health and Social Behavior*, 1989, vol. 30, p. 102.
145. G. W. Comstock and K. B. Partridge, "Church Attendance and Health," *Journal of Chronic Diseases,* 1972, vol. 25, pp. 665-672.
146. Third National Cancer Conference, as reported by World Wide Medical News Service, Chicago, 1956. See also *Review and Herald*, May 2, 1957, p. 12.
147. *Newsweek,* March 27, 1961.
148. *Appeal to Mothers,* p. 27.
149. *Selected Messages,* book 2, p. 449.
150. *The Ministry of Healing,* pp. 327, 328.
151. Statistics compiled by the Centers for Disease Control and Prevention, cited in *USA Today*, Oct. 29, 1996.
152. *Health Benefits of Smoking Cessation, A Report of the Surgeon General,* U.S. Department of Health and Human Services, 1990.
153. "Deaths from coronary heart disease related to cigarette smoking exceed those for lung cancer threefold. . . . The evidence linking cigarette smoking to CHD [coronary heart disease] is formidable and meets the criteria for an etiological relationship. . . . Heavy smoking nearly doubles cardiovascular and total mortality under 65. In men, cigarette smoking is significantly related to cardiovascular coronary and total mortality even beyond age 65."—"Special Report: Inter-Society Commission for Heart Disease Resources," *Circulation*, July, 1984, 70:176A, 177A.
154. *Signs of the Times,* Jan. 6, 1876.
155. *CA*/1996, p. 326.
156. *Archives of Pediatrics and Adolescent Medicine*, July, 1997.
157. *Archives of General Psychiatry,* July, 1997.
158. *Health or How to Live,* No. 3, p. 51; *Patriarchs and Prophets,* p. 561.
159. *Time,* Oct. 27, 1958; *Saturday Evening Post,* Aug. 12, 1967. Fetal alcohol syndrome rises with the risk of alcohol from less than one ounce in any one day with little risk to 1-2 ounces—10%, five ounces—50%, more than five ounces, 75% risk.—*Journal of Health Education,* Jan./Feb. 1993, pp. 22-26. Moderate alcohol consumption (3 drinks per week) in women showed an odds ratio of low birth weight to be 2.6 which represented a 143 gram decrease in birth weight.—*Epidemiology,* 1995, 6:591-597.
160. Robert F. Chinnock, M. D., *Life and Health,* Dec., 1964.
161. *Testimonies,* vol. 1, p. 555; vol. 2, p. 529.
162. *Review and Herald,* Nov. 3, 1960.
163. *Medical Ministry,* pp. 111-116; *Selected Messages,* book 2, pp. 349-350.
164. Loren R. Borland, D.D.S., and Sidney Epstein, D.D.S., *Journal of the American Dental Association,* Jan., 1961, pp. 54-64.
165. *Testimonies,* vol. 1, p. 566.
166. *Ibid.,* vol. 3, p. 184.
167. *The Ministry of Healing,* p. 241.
168. "The pathways along which the human mind makes its registrations on physiology are being probed more deeply then ever before. A biology of the emotions is coming into view. . . . These facts fit in with the last article written by the late Franz Ingelfinger as editor of *The New England Journal of Medicine,* in which physicians were reminded that 85 percent of human illnesses are within the reach of the body's own healing system. Hence the importance of the expanding knowledge about the way mind and body can collaborate in meeting serious challenges."—Norman Cousins, *Head First: The Biology of Hope,* (New York: E. P. Dutton, 1989), pp. 37, 38. Other books by Norman Cousins that set forth the relationship between the mind and physical healing are: *The Healing Heart* (New York: Avon Books, 1984) and *Anatomy of an Illness* (New York: W. W. Norton, 1979).
169. Beth Baker, "Scientists finding more evidence of link between mind and health," *AARP Bulletin,* Oct. 1993. See "Faith and Healing," *Time*, June 24, 1996, pp. 58-68.
170. Bill Moyers, *Healing and The Mind* (New York: Doubleday, 1995), p. 5.

171. *Ibid.,* p. 102. Ornish reviewed his landmark research findings in *Hospital Practice*, May 15, 1991: "By combining a strict low-fat vegetarian diet, moderate aerobic exercise, abstinence from smoking, and stress management training," his study group showed "measurable regression of disease in patients with severe coronary atherosclerosis (with less than 12 mg a day of dietary cholesterol 82% of the patients showed regression of coronary atherosclerosis)."—Pages 123-132.
172. *Scientific American,* June, 1954, p. 54.
173. *Testimonies,* vol. 2, p. 347; vol. 3, p. 157. "The brain is the capital of the body, the seat of all the nervous forces and of mental action. The nerves proceeding from the brain control the body. By the brain nerves, mental impressions are conveyed to all the nerves of the body as by telegraph wires; and they control the vital action of every part of the system. All the organs of motion are governed by the communications they receive from the brain."—*Testimonies,* vol. 3, p. 69.
174. *Education,* p. 197. "The brain nerves that connect with the whole system are the medium through which heaven communicates with man, and affects the inmost life. Whatever hinders the circulation of the electric current in the nervous system, thus weakening the vital powers and lessening mental susceptibility, makes it more difficult to arouse the moral nature." —*Education.,* p. 209.
175. *Selected Messages,* book 2, p. 303.
176. *Loma Linda Messages*, p. 177.
177. *Selected Messages,* book 2, p. 431. "The idea that women, because of their special condition, may let the appetite run riot is a mistake based on custom, but not on sound sense. . . . If ever there is need of simplicity of diet and special care as to the quality of food eaten, it is in this important period. Women who possess principle, and who are well instructed, will not depart from simplicity of diet at this time of all others. . . . If she chooses to eat as she pleases and what she may fancy, irrespective of consequences, she will bear the penalty, but not alone. Her innocent child must suffer because of her indiscretion."—*The Adventist Home,* pp. 257, 258 (1870); see also *The Ministry of Healing,* pp. 372, 373.
178. *Ladies Home Journal,* Feb., 1954, p. 43.
179. *Child Development: An Individual Longitudinal Approach* (New York: Holt, Rinehard and Winston, Inc., 1967), pp. 371, 372.
180. *Child Guidance,* p. 193; "It is during the first years of a child's life that his mind is most susceptible to impressions either good or evil. During these years decided progress is made in either a right direction or a wrong one."—*Counsels to Parents, Teachers, and Students,* p. 132.
181. *Child Guidance,* p. 194.
182. *Ibid.,* p. 193.
183. *The Washington Post,* April 18, 1997, p. 3.
184. Dr. McCay authored or coauthored more than 150 scientific publications; cofounded (1942) the *Archives of Biochemistry* and served as its early editor; served as editor of the Swiss journal, *Gerontologia;* served one year, each, as president of the American Gerontological Society (1949) and the American Institute of Nutrition (1951).
185. Roger Coon, "E. G. White, M.D.," in *Dialogue,* vol. III, No. 1, 1991, p. 11.
186. Francis D. Nichol, *Why I Believe in Mrs. E. G. White* (Washington, D.C.: Review and Herald Publishing Association, 1964), pp. 57-59. In a letter to Helen Chen-Chung, Dec. 18, 1958, McCay wrote: "If I were to start life again I would like to be an Adventist. I believe their philosophy has the best solution of the problems of living amidst the strains of the American culture. I have only made a slight beginning of discovering the wisdom of Mrs. White."
187. See Roger W. Coon, *A Gift of Light* (Washington, D.C.: Review and Herald Publishing Association, 1983), pp. 43-51; a series of three articles in the *Review and Herald,* "A Nutritional Authority Discusses Mrs. E. G. White" (Feb. 12, 19, and 26, 1959; reprinted in *Ibid.,* with slight abridgment, Jan. 8, 15, 1981).
188. Home & Garden Bulletin, No. 231, 1980, p. 1.
189. Nutrition and Your Health: Dietary Guidelines for Americans, 4th edition, Dec. 1995, United States Department of Agriculture & United States Department of Health and Human Services.
190. "Report of the Dietary Guidelines Advisory Committee, *Dietary Guidelines for Americans, 1995, Nutrition Review,* vol. 53:376-379, Dec., 1995.
191. Washington, D.C.: National Academy Press, 1982.
192. *Reader's Digest,* Feb. 1983, pp. 78-82.
193. "A Call to Get the Fat Out," *U. S. News and World Report* (Aug. 8, 1988), pp. 59-61.
194. "A New Menu to Heal the Heart," *Newsweek,* July 30, 1990, pp. 58-59; "For a Better Life, Don't Eat Any Beef," *USA Today* (int. ed.), Dec. 19, 1990.
195. Cited in Far Eastern Division *Outlook* (August 1983), p. 12.
196. "Summary of Results of Adventist Mortality Study—1958-65," unpublished report, Loma Linda University School of Health, undated, 2 pp. based on R. L. Phillips and J. W. Kuzma, "Rationale and Method for an Epidemiologic Study of Cancer Among Seventh-day Adventists," *National Cancer Institute Monographs,* 1977, 47:107-112. (These statistics relate to deaths caused by the designated cancers.) For a later review of the Adventist Mortality Study, see Gary E. Fraser, "Epidemiological Studies of Adventists," *Scope*, July-Sept., 1991, cited in full in DeWitt S. Williams, Kay Kuzma, and Leo Van Dolson, compilers, *Ministries of Health and Healing*; (Lincoln, Nebr.: Advent *Source*, 1997), pp. 305-320. See also Roland L. Phillips, "Cancer Among Seventh-day Adventists," *Journal of Environmental Pathology and Toxicology,* 3:157; Frank R. Lemon, M.D., and Richard T. Walden, M.D., "Death From Cancer Among Seventh-day Adventists," *Review and Herald,* July 9, 1964; Frank R. Lemon, M.D., and Richard T. Walden, M.D., "Death From Respiratory System Disease Among Seventh-day Adventist Men," *Journal of the American Medical Association,* vol. 198, no. 2, Oct. 10, 1966; Ernest L. Wynder, M.D., Frank R. Lemon, M.D., and Irwin J. Bross, Ph.D., "Cancer and Coronary Artery Disease Among Seventh-day Adventists," *Cancer,* vol. 12, no. 5, Sept.-Oct., 1959.
197. Martin Strahan, Harley Stanton, and Gary Fraser, "Adventist Health Studies," in P. William and Yvonne M. Dysinger, eds. *Adventist International Medical Society: Health Evangelism Study Guide* (Siloam Springs, Ark.: Creation Enterprises International, 1991), chapter 8, p. 4.
198. Adventist men live 8.9 years longer than the general population; women, 7.5 years longer. Vegetarian Seventh-day Adventist men live 3.7 years longer than

non-vegetarian SDA men.—*Ministry,* Sept. 1989, pp. 24-27. Note also F. R. Lemon, J. W. Kuzma, "A Biologic Cost of Smoking: Decreased Life Expectancy, *Archives of Environmental Health,* 1969, 18:950-955.

199. *Ibid.,* June 25, 1981.
200. *Adventist Review,* Dec. 2, 1982.
201. J. Berkel and F. de Waard, "Mortality Pattern and Life Expectancy of Seventh-day Adventists in the Netherlands," *International Journal of Epidemiology* 12: (1983), pp. 455-459.
202. W. Jedrychowski, A. Olma, B. Tobiassz-Adamczyk, and P. Gradzikiewicz, "Survival Rates Among Seventh-day Adventists Compared With the General Population in Poland," *Scandinavian Journal of Social Medicine,* (1985), 13:49-52. (This study was small, analyzing statistics from only one city church.)
203. *CA*/1996, pp. 326, 327.
204. *Testimonies,* vol. 3, p. 19.
205. See p. 330.
206. See pp. 290, 291 for Dr. Kellogg's unqualified opinion of Ellen White's divine guidance in the development of Adventist health principles.
207. Seventh-day Adventists are described as "the healthiest group of people in the country."—John Cook, "A Church Whose Members Have Less Cancer," *Saturday Evening Post,* Mar. 1984, pp. 42, 108.
208. Strahan, Stanton, and Fraser, "Adventist Health Studies," p. 8-1.

Study Questions

1. For what reasons did Ellen White discourage meat eating?
2. What eschatological reasons are involved in regard to meat eating today?
3. What are the chief benefits of a vegetarian diet?
4. What are the advantages of a regular exercise program?
5. In what way can we be certain that the mind affects physical health and vice versa?
6. What has been Ellen White's distinctive contribution to the understanding of health principles?
7. What health problems are posed by coffee drinking?
8. List and discuss Ellen White's suggested life style program.
9. List the contributions to medical science made by the two Adventist Health Studies. How does this research corroborate the fundamental principles enunciated by Ellen White?
10. Ellen White made a distinctive contribution to disease prevention and to the restoration of health. In what way was she original and distinctive? In what way was she reflecting the views of her own time?

CHAPTER 29

Education/1
Principles and Philosophy

Ellen White's "able articulation of the role of Christian education as a prime vehicle for the transmission of religious values and purpose constitutes a profound theology of Christian education."[1]

Ellen G. White was recognized as the "prophetic thought leader of Adventist education from its inception until her death in 1915. . . . It is impossible to comprehend Adventist education either currently or historically without understanding the role and impact of Ellen White upon its development. She was not only a central figure in its development, but she was the only Adventist leader who was in constant prominence from its beginnings up through the end of its formative period (about 1910)."[2]

Nowhere in the writings of Ellen White do we find the principles of the Great Controversy Theme more explicitly unfolded than in her writings on educational principles. Her understanding of redemption as "restoration" lies at the heart of her educational philosophy.[3] These educational principles were developed, on one hand, within the context of nineteenth century attempts to reform education, and, on the other, within the denominational context of "comparative indifference to education reform."[4]

Voices that attempted to reform educational systems in the nineteenth century sounded like lonely cries in the wilderness. The nineteenth century was a transition era from centuries of traditional thinking. In almost every area of American life—including theology, philosophy, medicine, industrialization, and education—the nineteenth century was in ferment.

In education, the struggle focused on the old wineskins of classical education that focused on the words (ancient languages) and ideas (philosophies) of Western civilization.[5] The educated person, as a common denominator, was expected to read and discuss the ancient poets and philosophers in Greek and Latin. However, the question was being asked: With the emergence of democratic ideas, more leisure time, and changing work conditions and expectations, was this elitist, bookish education meeting the needs of "modern" times? John Locke, Jean Jacques Rousseau, Heinrich Pestalozzi, and others had been saying "no" for several centuries, but their efforts made little "dent" in traditional education.[6]

However, two influences in the nineteenth century were significant and made some impact on Adventist educational reform. Horace Mann (1796-1859) was perhaps the leader in establishing the need for the public school elementary system in the United States.[7] He also wrote extensively on the early need for children to understand physiology and to get a practical education.[8]

The other major influence centered in educational experiments with manual labor coupled with the emphasis on Biblical instruction rather than the traditional classics at certain academic institutions. Oberlin College (Ohio), the best known of these centers, promoted the Bible as "a textbook in all the departments of education," integrated a manual labor program for all students, required physiology, and fostered a campus environment of non-competition in areas usually associated with prizes and honors. Its president/founder announced: "The system of education in this Institute will provide for the body and heart as well as the intellect: for it aims at the best education of the whole man." But by the late 1850s these remarkable educational reforms had lost their initial enthusiasm and their programs soon conformed to the prevailing pattern of other American colleges.[9]

Though Oberlin faded as a reforming institution, probably because it did not maintain a compelling spiritual context, other voices arose that emphasized a more practical education (progressive education) in unseating the classics with more "useful" subjects and in promoting manual education. The president of Johns Hopkins University in 1888 declared that manual training not only improved physical health but also "increased mental vigor."[10] But these voices were not mainstream.

The similarity between Ellen White's educational reform message and that of a few, clear voices of her time rests on the obvious fact that all those involved in educational reform were contending with the same problems: classic curricula rather than a more practical education; poorly ventilated, poorly lighted classrooms; direct relationship between manual training/exercise with mental vigor, even spiritual values; and education as an important factor in character development. Especially when Bible-oriented reformers attempted educational reform, one would expect general agreement on principles and practice. Ellen White understood this when in her book *Education* she wrote this remarkable summation of educational principles: "We can trace the line of the world's teachers as far back as human records extend; but the Light was before them. As the moon and the stars of our solar system shine by the reflected light of the sun, so, as far as their teaching is true, do the world's great thinkers reflect the rays of the Sun of Righteousness. Every gleam of thought, every flash of the intellect, is from the Light of the world."[11]

Is there anything unique about Ellen White's principles of education? Her special contribution lies in the unity and clarity of her educational philosophy, unencumbered with the fads and "false leads" of nineteenth century contemporaries.[12] Although a few contemporaries also saw the religious purpose of education, Mrs. White placed education within the Great Controversy Theme, including its vital role in eschatology (the study of last-day events). Originality is not the test of a prophet; dynamic freshness, coherence and unity that harmonize with the Bible are.[13]

Educational Principles

• *"Fatal errors" of prevailing educational philosophies focus either on intellectual attainment, temporal success, or even correct behavior, hoping to "develop the good that exists in man by nature."*[14] Ellen White drove past these flattering, self-serving purposes of education with the simple clarity that "redemption . . . is the object of education."[15]

Not wanting to leave this definition in an undefinable generality, she explained the Biblical framework for connecting education with redemption (note the four cornerstones): "In order to understand what is comprehended in the work of education, we need to consider both the nature of man and the purpose of God in creating him. We need to consider also the change in man's condition through the coming in of a knowledge of evil, and God's plan for still fulfilling His glorious purpose in the education of the human race."[16] This educational strategy can be understood only within the framework of the Great Controversy Theme.

• *First and constant aim of Christian education.* Thus, for Christian teachers on whatever level, their "first effort and . . . constant aim" should be (1) to aid "the student in comprehending these principles," and (2) to enter "into that relation with Christ which will make [these principles] a controlling power in the life."[17] Ellen White reiterated often that the "all-important thing" in education "should be the conversion" of students.[18] "It is upon the foundation of the new birth experience that Christian education can proceed with its other aims and purposes. If it fails at the foundational and primary point, it has failed entirely."[19]

• *Fundamental aim sets agenda.* This fundamental aim of education—to restore the broken relationship between God and the student—sets the educational agenda and curriculum. All the other purposes of education are enlightened and molded by this primary purpose. Christian teachers know that character education (not personality change in order to add to one's self-esteem or to assist in climbing the career ladder) seeks "to restore the image of Christ in those placed under their care."[20]

• *Towering motivation for reaching one's full potential.* The Great Controversy Theme leaves its mark on all phases of the Christian's life. "Restoration" is its key thought. The full development of all human capabilities is the goal before every Christian. The Energy of heaven is promised to those who permit the heavenly current to flow. But that Energy flows only in the direction of loving service. That is why Ellen White wrote that astounding sentence: "The development of all our powers is the first duty we owe to God and to our fellow men."[21]

Self-development, yes. But not to become Number One! The pursuit of excellence? Yes! "We should cultivate every faculty to the highest degree of perfection, that we may do the greatest amount of good of which we are capable. . . . God will accept only those who are determined to aim high. . . . And those who would be workers together with God must strive for perfection of every organ of the body and quality of the mind. True education is the preparation of the physical, mental, and moral powers for the performance of every duty; it is the training of body, mind, and soul for divine service."[22]

• *The pursuit of intellectual greatness if. . . .* Students are challenged "to reach to the highest point of intellectual greatness . . . if balanced by religious principle."[23] "Dullness and ignorance are no virtue."[24] "The highest culture of the mind, if sanctified through the love and the fear of God, receives His fullest approval."[25] "All who engage in the acquisition of knowledge should strive to reach the highest round of the ladder. Let students advance as fast and as far as they can; let the field of their study be as broad as their powers can compass; but let them make God their wisdom."[26]

• *Occupational skills imperative.* Further, each student is to join intellectual pursuits with "a knowledge of some trade or occupation by which, if need be, he may earn a livelihood."[27]

Learning an occupational skill was urged not merely to be prepared to earn a living if circumstances required such, but also to add vigor to mental studies[28] and to provide a special opportunity for character growth. Learning a trade would help produce "a more elevated class of youth . . . with stability of character. They would have perseverance, fortitude, and courage to surmount obstacles." In fact, if students had to make a choice between a knowledge of the sciences or a "knowledge of labor for practical life," Mrs. White would "unhesitatingly answer, The latter. If one must be neglected, let it be the study of books."[29]

• *School curriculum must be organized to fulfill education's highest aim.* The contrast between secular and Bible-centered curricula is seen most clearly in how the nature of human beings is perceived. Are we products of an evolutionary ascent, or are we created beings, made in the image of our Creator? Is education a matter of "getting ahead" and "succeeding" in a secular career, or is it a process of allowing our Creator to work out His original plan for human beings?

Ellen White's many references to making the Bible "a textbook in our schools" meant that the Bible should be the "basis of all education." The Bible should not be inserted into the curriculum "sandwiched in between infidelity," to merely "flavor" other studies.[30]

Further, making the Bible "the basis of education" does not mean that it is to be the only textbook for classes such as arithmetic, languages, and geography. The Bible was not given to the human family to be its best encyclopedia, but it does give a worldview that helps to interpret and apply information. Ellen White noted that all academic disciplines, every area of thought, take on "new significance" when seen in the light of the Great Controversy Theme. She meant that all classes must be taught within the framework of the Biblical worldview, that every class should reflect the grand purpose of Christian education—"to restore in man the image of his Maker."[31]

• *Essential courses of study.* In addition to her emphasis on the Biblical context for all classes,[32] Ellen White asserted that physiology should be "the first study" in the educational program in order "to preserve health."[33]

Vocal training would greatly increase the usefulness of every student. Speaking to both men and women, Ellen White wrote: "However imperfect may be your manner of utterance, you may correct your faults, and refuse to allow yourself to have a nasal tone, or to speak in a thick, indistinct way. If your articulation is distinct and intelligible, your usefulness will be greatly increased. Then do not leave one defective habit of speech uncorrected."[34]

• *Role of the parents as educators.* Educational psychologists and sociologists are alarmed at what many call the most critical issue facing modern civilization—the disintegration of the family.[35]

Ellen White wrote much about the influence of the home for good or ill in the education of children. Neither parent should shift the responsibilities of educating the children to the other: "Only by working in unison, can the father and mother accomplish the work which God has committed to their hands."[36]

But the mother has a unique role: "No other work can equal hers in importance."[37] A surrogate mother is a poor substitute for a biological mother who pursues other goals.[38]

Why does the responsibility of educating children rest so heavily on parents, especially the mother? Why cannot outside-the-home services such as day-care centers and early kindergartens take the place of parents? Because "lessons learned, the habits formed, during the years of infancy and childhood, have more to do with the formation of character and the direction of the life than have all the instruction and training of after years."[39]

In fact, Mrs. White wrote: "The first six or seven years of a child's life" should be "given to its physical training, rather than the intellect. . . . Parents, especially mothers, should be the only teachers of such infant minds."[40] However, circumstances may require earlier schooling, as Ellen White made clear at St. Helena, California, in 1904.[41]

One of the startling misconceptions of modern times is that children need parents less after they start school, even after becoming adolescents.[42]

• *Higher education more than information.* When Ellen White spoke of "higher education" she meant more than schooling beyond the twelfth grade. In fact, "higher education" had more to do with a religious experience than with advanced information: "Higher education calls for something greater, something more divine, than the knowledge to be obtained merely from books. It means a personal, experimental knowledge of Christ; it means emancipation from ideas, from habits and practices, that have been gained in the school of the prince of darkness."[43]

Mrs. White often emphasized that one should excel in literary and science studies but must not accomplish this to the neglect of religious experience. She wrote: "An intellectual religion will not satisfy the soul. Intellectual training must not be neglected, but it is not sufficient. Students must be taught that they are in this world to do service for God. They must be taught to place the will on the side of God's will."[44] To her, both strict intellectualism, even theological understanding, without Christian commitment, are to be avoided.

One of her frequent themes was that "ignorance will not increase the humility or spirituality of any professed follower of Christ." Further, "the truths of the divine word can be best appreciated by an intellectual Christian. Christ can be best glorified by those who serve Him intelligently. The great object of education is to enable us to use the powers which God has given us in such a manner as will best represent the religion of the Bible and promote the glory of God."[45]

• *Teacher credibility.* Mrs. White called for teachers who are able to bridge the gap between religion and theology, between experience and knowledge: "The teacher of truth can impart effectively only that which he himself knows by experience."[46] In fact, the teacher's personal habits and spiritual experience should be "considered of even greater importance than his literary qualifications."[47]

• *Recreation as necessary as study and labor.* A frequent theme in Ellen White's writings is her call for balance and moderation in most any activity of the Christian. For some who have heard only her call to diligence and perseverance in pursuing excellence, her emphasis on recreation may come as a shock. She wrote early in her ministry: "Recreation is needful to those who are engaged in physical labor, and is still more essential for those whose labor is principally mental. It is not essential to our salvation, nor for the glory of God, to keep the mind laboring constantly and excessively, even upon religious themes."[48]

Mrs. White used the word "recreation" in its best sense. She focused on the "re-creating" purpose of withdrawing from the busy program of either mental or physical activity. She suggested, for example, that several families unite and "make an excursion into the country" with tasty and wholesome food in their baskets. What would these families do? She continued: "Parents and children should feel free from care, labor, and perplexity. Parents should become children with their children, making everything as pleasant for them as possible. Let the whole day be given to recreation."[49]

But, for Ellen White recreation was not to be a spiritual vacation from Christian commitment. In her landmark book on education, *Education*, she devoted a chapter to "Recreation." In that chapter she differentiated between recreation and amusement: "Recreation, when true to its name, re-creation, tends to strengthen and build up. Calling us aside from our ordinary cares and occupations, it affords refreshment for mind and body, and thus enables us to return with new vigor to the earnest work of life. Amusement, on the other hand, is sought for the sake of pleasure, and is often carried to excess; it absorbs the energies that are required for useful work, and thus proves a hindrance to life's true success."[50]

Compared to the pace of life in the nineteenth century, modern families live under much greater stress. One of the paradoxes is that today's families, though having more "labor-saving devices," also live more tension-filled, schedule-driven lives than their forebears. Furthermore, very few professions in the Western world require physical activity. The need for recreation today is substantial, not only to "take the mind off" the business at hand but to provide the physical exercise that good health requires. In other words, no people in history have ever needed planned recreation more. At the same time, perhaps no other people in history have ever been confronted with so much pseudo-recreation in the form of spectator sports, passive entertainment, and sedentary amusements.

Ellen White laid out clear principles regarding recreation:

- Students must have vigorous exercise, but it should be done, whenever possible, in the open air.
- Sports of violence, as well as athletic games carried to excess, in addition to promoting the "love of domination [and] the pride in mere brute force . . . stimulate the love of pleasure and excitement, thus fostering a distaste for useful labor, a disposition to shun practical duties and responsibilities."
- Parents and teachers "can do much to supply diversions wholesome and life-giving" instead of "frivolous associations, habits of extravagance, or pleasure-seeking."
- The highest form of recreation, filled with blessings to students, are those activities "which make them helpful to others."
- "The preoccupation of the mind with good is worth more than unnumbered barriers of law and discipline."[51]

Train Students to Be Thinkers, Not Mere Reflectors

Thinkers do more than accept passively the thinking of others; they endeavor to master what others have said or discovered. Thinkers "contemplate the great facts of duty and destiny"; they are "masters and not slaves of circumstances [possessing] breadth of mind, clearness of thought, and the courage of their convictions."[52]

How does one fulfill this lofty goal? Ellen White expressed certain principles that "thinkers" should understand:

Thinkers understand the perils of competition. Why one wants to excel is the defining question.

One of her constant themes is the call to excellence, to reach the highest level possible in whatever field of study or lifework one is engaged.[53]

But a core problem of prevailing educational systems is that it urges excellence for the wrong reasons and its attainment by the wrong methods. Mrs. White asked the question, "What is the trend of the education given?" Then she answered, "To self-seeking." She described the goals of "true education" as the antithesis of "selfish ambition, the greed for power, and . . . selfish rivalry." She observed that traditional educational methods "appeal to emulation and rivalry . . . [and] foster selfishness, the root of all evil."[54]

"Strife for supremacy" encourages "the system of 'cramming'" and often "leads to dishonesty." By driving students to compete, "discontent . . . embitters the life" and "helps to fill the world with . . . restless, turbulent spirits."[55]

What feeds this spirit of rivalry and the desire for supremacy? Ellen White pointed to the content of much literature: Students "drink . . . from the wells of paganism . . . fed by the corruptions of ancient heathendom. . . . And of how many modern authors also might the same be said!" In the sciences she saw the effects of "evolution and its kindred errors" that tend "to infidelity." Further, she saw that the "work of 'higher criticism' . . . is destroying faith in the Bible as a divine revelation . . . robbing God's word of power to control, uplift, and inspire human lives."

Ellen White saw that when "youth go out into the world" motivated by the assumptions of non-Biblical thought, they have no barriers to meet the prevailing sentiments that "desire is the highest law, that license is liberty, and that man is accountable only to himself." Youth catch the spirit of society flawed by rivalry and competition and, unless made aware of the price of competition, they have no safeguards to maintain "individual integrity. . . purity of the home, the well-being of society, or the stability of the nation."[56]

For Ellen White a world of difference separates excellence and competition. This distinction rests on the purpose of education: to "restore the image of God in the soul."[57] Men and women are to "reach the highest possible degree of excellence," but this goal cannot be reached by a "selfish and exclusive culture; for the character of God, whose likeness we are to receive, is benevolence and love."[58]

To reach the Biblical goal of education, Mrs. White observed, would require a "radical change in some of the current methods of education. Instead of appealing to pride and selfish ambition, kindling a spirit of emulation, teachers would endeavor to awaken the love of goodness and truth and beauty—to arouse the desire for excellence. The student would seek the development of God's gifts in himself, not to excel others, but to fulfill the purpose of the Creator and to receive His likeness."[59]

The inherent flaw in using the spirit of competition to motivate students in the classroom or on the playing field, (or to arouse pastors to reach certain goals and congregations to raise funds, etc.) is that competition is not a principle of God's kingdom of love—cooperation is.[60] To fulfill the purpose of education, to restore in men and women the image of their Maker, "the temptation to be first would be quenched in the lessons daily learned in the school of Christ."[61]

Modern educational psychologists have recognized that competition is not a valid motivator. They point out three basic flaws. Flaw One: That young people need competitive experiences in order to enter a competitive society. Flaw Two: That competition is an effective motivator. Granted, they say, competition is "valuable as a motivator only for those people who believe that they can win." But those who do not believe that they can win are not so motivated; they are further "discouraged and disillusioned." Flaw Three: The stress on competition leads to morality breakdown and to the compelling rule that the end justifies the means.[62]

Thinkers (both students and teachers) have learned that mere memorization is insufficient. Thinking is a learned event. Learning to think is a joint effort by thinking teachers and eager students. Ellen White urged Bible teachers especially "to make the students understand their lessons, not by explaining everything to them, but by requiring them to explain clearly every passage they read. Let these teachers remember that little good is accomplished by skimming over the surface."[63]

Dynamic discussion with students repeating the teacher's explanations "in their own language" so that it can be determined that "they clearly comprehend" their lessons may be "a slow process," but it is of "ten times more value than rushing over important subjects." Not only will students better understand the subject, they will be better prepared to explain the material to others.[64]

Thinkers will appreciate a "moral taste in love of work." To modern minds, this hardly seems to be a factor in developing thinkers, but it lies close to the root of Ellen White's philosophy of education. In the establishment of the Avondale school in the late 1890s, she urged a principle that she had been emphasizing for at least twenty years—that students must be educated to be *masters* of labor, and not *slaves* of labor. She wanted students to see the "science in the humblest kind of work," to see "nobility in labor."

As we have shown on page 346, "manual occupation . . . is essential" in order to balance and strengthen mental activity. Minds are "abused" when the physical powers are not "equally taxed."

Further, "habits of industry will be . . . an important aid to the youth in resisting temptation." "Pent-up energies . . . if not expended in useful employment, will be a continual source of trial to themselves, and to their teachers."

For these reasons, Ellen White declared that those whose goal is to obtain a "transformed mind and character" will develop "a new moral taste in love of work."[65]

Thinkers understand that perseverance and commitment are the price of excellence. To excel in any line of work requires an eye not easily distracted by "the voice of pleasure" and other diversions. Ellen White pleaded with parents and teachers to instruct young people that good intentions "will not avail," that "no excellence is gained without great labor." Furthermore, no great achievement is reached quickly or by ignoring "present opportunities." Those who reach the "height in moral and intellectual attainments . . . must possess a brave and resolute spirit."[66]

Endnotes

1. George H. Akers, "The Role of SDA Education in the Formation of Adventist Lifestyle," *Journal of the Adventist Theological Society,* Spring, 1993, p. 3.
2. George Knight, *Early Adventist Educators* (Berrien Springs, Mich.: Andrews University Press, 1983), p. 26; "Under the guidance of Ellen White, Seventh-day Adventists have always been committed to quality education. . . . The quality of Adventist education was virtually assured by the active role that Ellen White played in establishing the system."—Provonsha, *Remnant in Crisis,* p. 27. "Ellen White . . . the denomination's first and major writer on educational theory." —SDAE, vol. 1, p. 497; "Mrs. White's educational thinking forms the philosophical base for the Seventh-day Adventist program of education."—Richard Lesher's conclusion in his doctoral dissertation, "Ellen G. White's Concept of Sanctification," New York University, 1970; "How did we get into this system of Christian education that is distinctive in all the world, and that has brought such fruitage in training workers for gospel service? You know how we were led into this thing. You know the years in which that gift of the Spirit of prophecy continually warned us and exhorted us and drew us and marked the way for us to follow. All through these books by the Spirit of prophecy the true educational idea is emphasized."—W. A. Spicer, "The Spirit of Prophecy in the Advent Movement," *Report of the Blue Ridge Educational Convention* (Washington, D.C.: General Conference of Seventh-day Adventists, 1937), p. 79.
3. "To restore in man the image of his Maker, to bring him back to the perfection in which he was created, to promote the development of body, mind, and soul, that the divine purpose in his creation might be realized—this was to be the work of redemption. This is the object of education, the great object of life."—*Education,* pp. 15, 16. See p. 257.
4. Graham, *Ellen G. White, Co-founder,* p. 91.
5. The aims and purposes of education have been a major concern of all societies and great thinkers, at least from the time of Aristotle: "That education should be regulated by law and should be an affair of state is not to be denied, but what should be the character of this public education, and how young persons should be educated, are questions which remain to be considered. As things are, there is disagreement about the subjects. For mankind are by no means agreed about the things to be taught, whether we look to virtue or the best life. Neither is it clear whether education is more concerned with intellectual or with moral virtue. The existing practice is perplexing; no one knows on what principle we should proceed—should the useful in life, or should virtue, or should the higher knowledge, be the aim of our teaching; all three opinions have been entertained. Again, about the means there is no agreement; for different persons, starting with different ideas about the nature of virtue, naturally disagree about the practice of it."—Richard McKeon, ed., *The Basic Works of Aristotle* (New York: Random House, 1941), "Politica," book VIII, ch. 2, pp. 1305, 1306.
6. See Knight, *Early Adventist Educators,* pp. 4, 5.
7. *Ibid.,* pp. 5, 6.
8. James and Ellen White published excerpts from Mann's writings in *Health: Or How to Live* (V:19-25; VI:25-47). Writing from Australia, Mrs. White asked her son, Edson, who was contemplating the journey, to bring with him certain books that Mann had authored.
9. Knight, *Early Educators*, pp. 5, 6.
10. *Ibid.*
11. *Education,* pp. 13, 14.
12. George R. Knight, *Myths in Adventism* (Washington, D.C.: Review and Herald Publishing Association, 1985), p. 36.
13. *Ibid.* See George H. Akers, "The Role of SDA Education in the Formation of Adventist Lifestyle," *Journal of the Adventist Theological Society,* Spring, 1993, p. 3: "Because Seventh-day Adventists believe that the *work of redemption and the work of Christian education are one and the same,* we have in that very belief the conceptual construct for a theology of educa-

tion: the Christian Gospel—in theory and application."

14. *Counsels to Parents, Teachers and Students,* p. 49; *Steps to Christ,* pp. 18, 19.
15. *Education,* p. 16.
16. *Ibid.,* pp. 14, 15.
17. *Ibid.,* p. 30. In the mid-nineties, world leader of the Adventist educational system, Humberto Rasi, summarized the objectives of Adventist education: "1. To educate Seventh-day Adventist youth for a useful life, in the context of Christian faith and Biblical values, keeping in balance their intellectual, spiritual, physical, and social development. 2. To train future Adventist leaders and denominational workers, encouraging them to devote their talents to accomplishing the church's mission until Jesus comes. 3. To deepen the commitment of Adventist youth to Christ, and to attract to His church non-Adventist youth of high ideals, helping all of them to develop Christlike characters. 4. To exert an uplifting influence on society, the nation, and the world through service, evangelism, research, and discoveries carried out by Adventist educators, students, and alumni. 5. To cooperate with church leaders and members in discovering new truths, developing mission strategies, and providing Adventist answers to the ethical issues faced by society."—"A Matter of Mission," *The Journal of Adventist Education,* Summer, 1994.
18. *Fundamentals of Christian Education,* p. 436.
19. Knight, *Myths,* p. 51.
20. *Counsels to Parents, Teachers, and Students,* p. 61.
21. *Christ's Object Lessons,* p. 329. See *Counsels on Diet and Foods,* p. 15.
22. *Ibid.,* p. 330.
23. *Fundamentals of Christian Education,* p. 48.
24. *Ibid.,* p. 316.
25. *Ibid.,* p. 47.
26. *Counsels to Parents, Teachers, and Students,* p. 394.
27. *Education,* p. 218.
28. "Students will realize elasticity of spirit and vigor of thought, and will be able to accomplish more mental labor in a given time than they could by study alone." —*Fundamentals of Christian Education,* p. 44.
29. *Ibid.,* pp. 40, 41.
30. *Fundamentals of Christian Education,* pp. 131, 395, 474; *Testimonies,* vol. 6, p. 131. "The Bible constitutes the basis and reference point of school endeavors. The entire curricular and co-curricular program reflects the world view and the principles revealed in the Scriptures. Teachers and students believe that the same Holy Spirit that inspired the Bible writers will guide those who approach it with a teachable attitude."—Humberto Rasi, "Back to the Real Basics," *The Journal of Adventist Education,* October/November, 1995.
31. *Education,* p. 125; "Religion and business are not two separate things; they are one. Bible religion is to be interwoven with all we do or say."—*Christ's Object Lessons,* p. 349. "If I, as a Christian teacher, am teaching the same material in the same way that it is presented in a public institution, then what right do I have to take the hard-earned money of my constituents? . . . Christian education that does not provide a Christian understanding of the arts, sciences, humanities, and the world of work is not Christian. One major aim of Christian education must be to help students think Christianly."—Knight, *Myths,* pp. 139-151.
32. See *Fundamentals of Christian Education,* pp. 123-137.
33. *Ibid.,* p. 26; "Physical health lies at the very foundation of all the student's ambitions and his hopes. Hence the preeminent importance of gaining a knowledge of those laws by which health is secured and preserved. Every youth should learn how to regulate his dietetic habits—what to eat, when to eat, and how to eat. He should learn how many hours to give to study and how much time to spend in physical exercise. . . . The proper regulation of his habits of eating, sleeping, study, and exercise, is a duty which every student owes to himself, to society, and to God."—*Ibid.,* p. 72; "The relation of the physical organism to the spiritual life is one of the most important branches of education. . . . He who remains in willing ignorance of the laws of his physical being, and who violates them through ignorance, is sinning against God."—*Christ's Object Lessons,* p. 348; "The importance of caring for the health should be taught as a Bible requirement."—*Counsels to Parents, Teachers, and Students,* p. 295.
34. *Fundamentals of Christian Education,* p. 215; see *Christ's Object Lessons,* pp. 335-339; *The Voice in Speech and Song,* pp. 178, 179.
35. Knight, *Myths,* pp. 71-87; Akers, "Role of SDA Education . . . ," *Journal of Adventist Theological Society,* Spring, 1993, p. 15.
36. *Fundamentals of Christian Education,* p. 69.
37. *The Ministry of Healing,* p. 378.
38. Circumstances, notably death or some other uncontrollable event, often alter the best of intentions. The wise father will do all he can to fill the void in some way so that his child's need for security and loving direction is met.
39. *Ibid.,* p. 380; see "The Child," *The Ministry of Healing,* pp. 379-387.
40. *Selected Messages,* book 2, p. 437; *Fundamentals of Christian Education,* p. 21.
41. See pp. 95-97.
42. *The Ministry of Healing,* p. 394. Urie Bronfenbrenner, a recognized child psychologist, wrote: "If there's any reliable predictor of trouble, it probably begins with children coming home to an empty house, whether the problem is reading difficulties, truancy, dropping out, drug addiction, or childhood depression."—"Nobody Home: The Erosion of the American Family," *Psychology Today,* May 1977, p. 41.
43. *Counsels to Parents, Teachers, and Students,* pp. 11, 12. "It is necessary that both teachers and students not only assent to truth, but have a deep, practical knowledge of the operations of the Spirit."—*Fundamentals of Christian Education,* p. 435.
44. *Ibid.,* p. 540.
45. *Fundamentals of Christian Education,* p. 45.
46. *Counsels to Parents, Teachers, and Students,* p. 435.
47. *Ibid.,* p. 19. "The over-arching purpose of our schools, the macro effect, when it's all said and done, is to give our youth a *Christian world view—to see everything from God's point of view,* as revealed in His inspired word. It's giving our students a 'Christian mind.' . . . The integration of faith and learning is not some special teaching method; *it's general teacher behavior (modeling!).* Presuppositional thinking . . . must . . . bear on every study in the Christian critique. Students . . . must practice it together under the example and coaching of a benign Christian teacher. If there is a secret driving force that gives true Christian education its peculiar potency, it is this. Have no doubt about it, this natural, unfeigned, pervasive integration of faith and learning is *the* distinguishing mark of a truly Christian school, at whatever level. . . . The credibility of such

teacher life-style, absorbed at close range and for prolonged exposure, is indisputably authentic and has a tremendous molding power on impressionable young minds."—Akers, "Role of SDA Education . . . ," *Journal of Adventist Theological Society*, Spring, 1993, p. 11.

48. *Testimonies,* vol. 1, p. 514.
49. *Ibid.,* p. 515.
50. *Education,* p. 207.
51. *Ibid.,* pp. 210-213. "Satan would lead [students] to believe that amusements are necessary to physical health; but the Lord has declared that the better way is for them to get physical exercise through manual training, and by letting useful employment take the place of selfish pleasure. The desire for amusement, if indulged, soon develops a dislike for useful, healthful exercise of body and mind, such as will make students efficient in helping themselves and others."—*Counsels to Parents, Teachers, and Students,* p. 354. See pages 321-355.
52. *Ibid.,* pp. 17, 18.
53. "[God] designs that His servants shall possess more intelligence and clearer discernment than the worldling, and He is displeased with those who are too careless or too indolent to become efficient, well-informed workers. . . . This lays upon us the obligation of developing the intellect to its fullest capacity, that with all the mind we may know and love our Creator." —*Christ's Object Lessons,* p. 333; see *Counsels to Parents, Teachers, and Students,* p. 499.
54. *Education,* pp. 225, 226. "In our institutions of learning there was to be exerted an influence that would counteract the influence of the world, and give no encouragement to indulgence in appetite, in selfish gratification of the senses, in pride, ambition, love of dress and display, love of praise and flattery, and strife for high rewards and honors as a recompense for good scholarship. All this was to be discouraged in our schools." —*Fundamentals of Christian Education,* p. 286.
55. *Education,* p. 226.
56. *Ibid.,* pp. 226-229.
57. *Patriarchs and Prophets,* p. 595.
58. *Ibid.,* p. 595.
59. *Ibid.* The teacher who understands the purpose of education "will allow nothing to stand in the way of earnest endeavor for self-improvement. He will spare no pains to reach the highest standard of excellence. All that he desires his pupils to become, he will himself strive to be."—*Counsels on Sabbath School Work,* p. 103.
60. "Cooperation should be the spirit of the schoolroom, the law of its life."—*Ibid.,* p. 285.
61. *Counsels to Parents, Teachers, and Students,* p. 372.
62. Knight, *Myths,* pp. 225-229. Alfie Kohn, in the book *No Contest,* argues that competition is inherently destructive, analyzes the prevailing notion that competition is a prod to productivity, a builder of character, and an unavoidable part of "human nature." The author assembles an enormous collection of psychological and sociological studies that show that competition causes anxiety, selfishness, self-doubt, and poor communication in the workplace, in the classroom, and between individuals.—(Boston: Houghton Mifflin Company, 1986), 257 pages.
63. *Counsels to Parents, Teachers, and Students,* p. 483.
64. *Ibid.,* p. 434.
65. *Life Sketches,* pp. 352-355.
66. *Sons and Daughters of God,* p. 333.

Study Questions

1. How does the Great Controversy Theme permeate Ellen White's philosophy of education?
2. What were the two major influences in the nineteenth century that set the tone for educational reform?
3. What were the "fatal errors" that prevailed in educational philosophies in the nineteenth century and perhaps today?
4. What did Ellen White mean by the term "higher education"?
5. How did Ellen White incorporate recreation in her philosophy of education?
6. Analyze the positive and negative aspects of competition.
7. Explain how Ellen White's emphasis on "intellectual greatness" and "self-development" fits her primary aim of education as "restoring in man the image of his Maker."

CHAPTER 30

Education/2
Establishing Educational Institutions

"The truths of the divine word can be best appreciated by an intellectual Christian. Christ can be best glorified by those who serve Him intelligently."[1]

B*attle Creek College.* A Battle Creek school for Adventist youth, locally supported, had been successfully conducted by G. H. Bell beginning in 1868. In April 1872 James and Ellen White called for an upgrading of this school into an advanced educational facility, the first attempt to have a school supported by the denomination. The primary purpose of this proposal was to educate teachers and preachers "to proclaim the third angel's message."[2]

As guidance for this school, Mrs. White wrote *Testimony for the Church,* No. *22*, entitled, "Proper Education."[3] This document has been studied for more than a century by Adventist educators as a clear charter for Adventist education. Here she developed one of her fundamental principles of Christian education: the correlation between "the physical, mental, moral, and religious" aspects of education.[4]

The early years of Battle Creek College were turbulent. The principles of this 1872 testimony may have been understood in theory but neither administrators nor teachers seemed to know how to implement certain of the key themes. Among these were how to include a manual labor program in the school curriculum, how to make the curriculum Bible-oriented and not merely include Bible as an elective subject, and how to frame the curriculum with practical subjects, eliminating the classics as the main thrust.[5]

This false start led Ellen White to address the denominational leaders in December 1881. She opened her remarks with a clear message of concern: "There is danger that our college will be turned away from its original design." Later she warned: "Our college stands today in a position that God does not approve." She noted the "effort to mold our school after other colleges. When this is done, we can give no encouragement to parents to send their children to Battle Creek College." To teach students only a knowledge of books could be done at any college. "A more comprehensive education is needed" that would include emphasis on character development, a daily reminder to give students a "sense of their obligation to God," and a program to "unite physical with mental taxation."

Mrs. White went on to spotlight the importance of right motivation in the work of both teachers and students: "The evils of self-esteem, and an unsanctified independence, which most impair our usefulness, and which will prove our ruin, if not overcome, spring from selfishness."[6]

Dark days came when the college closed on August 10, 1882. Problems included personnel clashes as well as the perceived crisis that the young college had not met the purposes for which it had been established. One year later it was reopened with the clear statement that the college would "in all respects" harmonize with the instruction provided through the Spirit of prophecy.[7]

However, again it was easier to publish the school's goals than to implement them. The turning point in the development of Adventist education came at the Harbor Springs, Michigan, educational convention in the summer of 1891. Ellen White made at least six presentations in addition to rereading her 1872 testimony on "Proper Education." She renewed her previous emphasis on eliminating from the curriculum pagan and infidel authors and the courses in Latin and Greek classics. In addition, her emphasis on Bible teaching and history from the standpoint of prophecy as well as the spiritual qualifications of teachers seemed to take hold among the leading educators.

After the Harbor Springs educational conference, Mrs. White wrote six articles in the church paper reinforcing the strong positions she had taken at the conference. The battle of the curriculum was changing in her favor but it did not come immediately. The knife edge of educational reform was the defining difference between conventional classical education and the perspective of Christian education in the light of the Great Controversy Theme.[8]

Healdsburg College/Pacific Union College

In 1881 the California Conference recognized the need for a west coast college. By April 1882 property was purchased in Healdsburg with Sidney Brownsberger, former president of Battle Creek College, as its first president. The school did not become financially secure, largely because of low charges to students. Ellen White counseled schools against attempting to attract higher enrollment by lowering fees, because of the "detrimental" effect this would have.[9]

Mrs. White's involvement in acquiring the Angwin, California, property when the Healdsburg site proved to be inadequate revealed again how human effort plus divine affirmation leads to sound decisions. The circumstances that led from one possible location to another provide a textbook lesson on divine guidance. Ellen White wrote of the experience: "Now this lesson given us at this time of our great necessity was one of the most remarkable adventures in our experience."[10]

Avondale College

When Ellen White went to Australia in 1891, little did anyone foresee how great the impact of its new institution of higher learning would have on the denomination's worldwide educational philosophy. No other Adventist school has been more favored by the presence and counsel of God's messenger to the church. Behind her were the struggling American schools, wobbling into the future trying to combine conventional education principles with the reforming principles of education driven by the Great Controversy Theme.[11]

Early in 1894 Mrs. White wrote the mandate for the new Australian school, entitled "Work and Education."[12] In the opening paragraph she raised the central questions regarding this and other schools: "How shall they be conducted? What shall be the education and training of the youth? Where shall our Australian Bible School be located?"

Then she proceeded to answer her questions. She reemphasized that the purpose of Christian education is to prepare students to meet the Lord. This kind of aim means students must rethink their recreational activities, that the school must be located "a wide distance from the cities," that useful work must be a part of the curriculum, that only the best workhabits are acceptable, that "dullness and ignorance are no virtue," that for Australia "there is hope in the soil," and that physiology must be in the curriculum for all.[13]

Ellen White was learning through experience as well as through visions. In 1898 she wrote that Adventist education must include "a different order of things," but that "it has taken much time to understand what changes should be made."[14] In September of 1898 she wrote that "our school must be a model school for others."[15] In 1899 she said that God had designed Avondale to be "an object lesson" and not "to pattern after any school that has been established in America, or after any school" in Australia.[16] In 1900 she penned that the Avondale school was "to be a pattern school."[17]

Ellen White never used the expression "educational blueprint."[18] Though using such words as "model," "object lesson," and "pattern," she did not mean that Avondale was to be rigidly copied in every detail: "The Lord has not designed any one, special, exact plan in education."[19] Regarding the new school at Madison, Tennessee (described below), she wrote that "no exact pattern can be given for the establishment of schools in new fields. The climate, the surroundings, the condition of the country, and the means at hand with which to work must all bear a part in shaping the work."[20] As with her counsel in other areas, such as health, she outlined basic principles, not inflexible rules.[21] Model schools, patterns, and object lessons are just that—they manifest basic principles that may require adaptation to local conditions.

To son Willie in 1897 she emphasized that "no breezes from Battle Creek are to be wafted in." Living adjacent to the campus, she still felt that she "must watch before and behind and on every side to permit nothing to find entrance that has been presented before me as injuring our schools in America."[22]

Madison College

Ellen White had much to do with locating the site for Madison College in 1904. She had been telling her colleagues that the school must be near Nashville, Tennessee. When a 400-acre property in Madison, seventeen miles from Nashville, became available for about $12,000, she asked to see it. Though some were not impressed, she reported that "it was a favorable location for the work" and must be purchased.[23]

Madison College was the only institution on which Mrs. White served as a member of the board of directors. She wanted to make sure that the bitter lessons learned at Battle Creek and the new school at Berrien Springs, Michigan, would not be repeated at Madison. One of the clear goals of the founders, Edward A. Sutherland and Percy T. Magan, was that "the more closely conditions in the school approximated the conditions students would face when they went out to teach, the more easily would they adjust to their vocations."[24]

Perhaps for the first time, student labor, rather than cash, was accepted for tuition. All the staff and faculty worked with the students in developing industries that would provide income. The vast majority of the student body expected to serve in some capacity in the rural South. By 1915, thirty-nine of these self-supporting schools had been developed by Madison College graduates.[25]

College of Medical Evangelists/ Loma Linda University

The establishment of this world-renowned medical institution would never have happened without the vision, courage, and continuing support of Ellen White. Richard Utt well said: "The rise of Loma Linda University was not so much fraught with the inevitable as with the impossible. That the feat was accomplished at all was due to a rare recipe of faith, works, and struggle, liberally laced with the improbable, the miraculous, and the heroic."[26]

In 1905 sunny southern California had two Adventist health centers—one at Paradise Valley, near San Diego, and another at Glendale, near Los Angeles, both of them founded on Ellen White's strong insistence and help in finding the initial funding.[27] Though popular, both institutions were deeply in debt.

But God was not finished with southern California. Through His promptings, Mrs. White called on John Burden,[28] the "founder" of the Glendale sanitarium, to look for property near Redlands. Incredible as it sounded to 1,400 church members in the local conference and their leaders who had been warned not to go further into debt, God's messenger had spoken again: "Redlands and Riverside have been presented to me as places that should be worked. . . . Please consider the advisability of establishing a sanitarium in the vicinity of these towns."[29] The story of the acquisition of the Loma Linda property, the remarkable faith of men like Burden, the sobering witness of funds that would arrive unexpectedly at the very moment needed, of men and women who mortgaged their homes and took out bank loans—all this is a matter of record.[30]

In the telling of this extraordinary story, the visible and invisible presence of Ellen White is as pervasive as sunshine at noonday. When all seemed bleak, she would counsel: "This is the very property that we ought to have. Do not delay; for it is just what is needed."[31] After seeing the buildings for the first time, she exclaimed: "I have been here before. . . . This is the place the Lord has shown me. . . . The Lord has not given us this property for any common purpose."[32]

A few weeks later when church leaders manifested little enthusiasm for her counsel, Ellen White wrote to Burden: "Do not be discouraged if in any wise there is some cutting across of your plans, and if you are somewhat hindered. . . . I have seen the hold-back principles followed, and I have seen the displeasure of the Lord because of this. If the same spirit is manifested, I shall not consent to keep silent as I have done."[33]

In fact, during conference business meetings that would have a significant bearing on the future of the struggling Loma Linda concept, Ellen White would sit on the platform so that she could hear the intent of each motion and ensuing discussion. She wrote that she was "old enough to be excused from such burdens" but "she feared that some action might be taken that would in the future bring about confusion."

One of the proposed motions sounded innocent enough but her years of experience helped her to see its danger: some wanted to change the constitution so that "every church member might become a delegate to the conference meetings." She spoke out: "Read that motion again, if you please." Then she commented, "Such a motion as that was made years ago, and the matter was distinctly opened before me. . . . The motion has never carried at any time, because it is not in harmony with the mind of the Lord." The resolution was withdrawn.[34]

After the land had been purchased, some church members thought that additional funds surely would be needed for developing the school. They urged that a portion of the seventy-six acres be sold for building sites. Immediately Mrs. White gave a resounding No! In fact, she urged the purchase of many more acres, another astounding challenge. With board members with her, she looked off into the valley toward the railroad and Colton Avenue. With a wave of her hand, she said, "The angel said, 'Get all of it.'" When others remonstrated, she said, "Well, we shall be thankful for what we have."

But the challenge seemed too much. Three years went by. Most of the land had doubled in price when steps finally were taken to acquire needed property. In 1911 further land became available. Again, there was hesitancy. In her eighty-fourth year Ellen White personally pledged $1,000 toward its purchase, and closed her appeal with these words: "I am highly gratified as I look upon the land we already have. This will be one of the greatest blessings to us in the future—one that we do not fully appreciate now, but which we shall appreciate by and by. I hope that you will get the other land that I have spoken of, and join it to that which you already have. It will pay you to do this. As I have carried the burden of this place from the very beginning, I wanted to say this much to you. Now I leave the matter with you; and let us work in harmony."

In a few days several board members took out personal bank loans to secure the property. Ellen White was delighted, writing to Burden that "the piece of land we must have, for it will never do to have buildings crowded in there. Do not fail to carry through the purchase of it. Do your best, and I will do my best."[35]

But she was also interested in the kind of institution to be established at Loma Linda. It should be more than a sanitarium. Earlier in 1905, she wrote: "This place will become an important educational center."[36] This was a new and lofty goal for Loma Linda—a school too! Yet the question remained, what kind of school?

A few weeks later she spelled out the new center's direction: "He [God] is opening ways whereby your children can be given an education in medical missionary lines without endangering their souls. . . . In a short time we shall have facilities for giving the necessary requirements." By December 10 she had written: "In regard to the school, I would say, Make it all you possibly can in the education of nurses and physicians."[37]

For a denomination to hear this challenge at the time when Battle Creek Sanitarium and the attached American Medical Missionary College was still an open wound, seemed too much. Perhaps a sanitarium at Loma Linda, but a medical school? All that most could think of was the financial burden that for years had overwhelmed Dr. Kellogg and the denomination.

But the Lord's messenger was courageous and compelling. Those who had learned to trust her in the past proceeded to do what seemed impossible for a small denomination of 91,531 members in 1906. The Lord was leading His people as fast as they were able to grasp what He had in mind for the institution at Loma Linda.

At the General Conference session in Washington, in June 1909, Ellen White addressed the delegates who had barely recovered their breath from the expense of moving two major institutions to the nation's capital. Among many topics was Loma Linda's destiny "to be not only a sanitarium, but an educational center," especially for the training of "gospel medical missionary evangelists," and that it was "very essential that a right beginning be made."

Step By Step

Later in her address she showed again that her own mind was being led step by step by the Lord. She declared that "we should not at this time seek to compete with worldly medical schools. Should we do this, our chances of success would be small. We are not now prepared to carry out successfully the work of establishing large medical institutions of learning. . . . At Loma Linda many can be educated to work as missionaries in the cause of health and temperance. Teachers are to be prepared for many lines of work."[38] Here she was painting, with broad strokes, not only a medical school but an educational facility that would prepare young people to meet the opportunities in "many lines of work."

The Lord is very kind, even to prophets; if He had revealed everything to Ellen White in 1905 that He would be helping her to grasp and communicate in 1909, perhaps she would have doubted her own mind and His instruction. As others made plans to develop a medical program for nurses and gospel medical missionary evangelists, they continually consulted her about questions along this untried path.

When asked whether medical students should get basic training at Loma Linda and get the "finishing touches . . . from some worldly institution," Mrs. White replied: "God forbid that such a plan would be followed." Responding to further questions, she said: "If the Lord gives you light, well and good, we will be glad to receive it; if not, then we will wait. . . . When we take hold upon God, and trust in Him, He will work in our behalf. But whatever the consequences may be, we are in regard to our faith to stand distinct and separate from the world."[39] She had learned well the painful lessons of Battle Creek.

Very clear on the purposes of the denomination's second medically-oriented school, she told the leaders that students at Loma Linda were to study under "carefully selected educators" who would teach them "to plow deep into the Word of God."[40]

In developing a State charter for a medical school, she gave further counsel: "If you can gain force and influence that will make your work more effective without tying yourselves to worldly men, that would be right. But we are not to exalt the human above the divine."

In November 1909 she wrote: "We cannot submit to regulations if the sacrifice of principles is involved, for this would imperil the soul's salvation. But whenever we can comply with the law of the land without putting ourselves in a false position, we should do so. Wise laws have been framed in order to safeguard the people against the imposition of unqualified physicians. These laws we should respect, for we are ourselves protected from presumptuous pretenders. Should we manifest opposition to these requirements, it would tend to restrict the influence of our medical missionaries." On December 9 a State charter was secured authorizing the College of Medical Evangelists to grant degrees in the liberal sciences, dentistry, and medicine.[41]

A few months later, perplexities still lingered. The school board faced enormous expenses and needed affirmation from Ellen White before they made any further commitments. Their concerns, addressed to her on January 26, 1910,[42] included these thoughts: "We are very anxious to preserve unity and harmony of action. In order to do this, we must have a clear understanding of what is to be done. Are we to understand, from what you have written concerning the establishment of a medical school at Loma Linda, that, according to the light you have received from the Lord, we are to establish a thoroughly equipped medical school, the graduates from which will be able to take State board examinations and become registered, qualified physicians?"[43]

Within twenty-four hours Ellen White responded, in part: "The light given me is, We must provide that which is essential to qualify our youth who desire to be physicians, so that they may intelligently fit themselves to be able to stand the examinations required to prove their efficiency as physicians."[44]

At that same meeting it was recommended that all North American unions plus the General Conference participate in sharing the expenses of the embryonic College of Medical Evangelists. This income would be in addition to that from tuition and private donations. Many speeches of renewed confidence followed.

I. H. Evans, a vice-president of the General Conference, summed up the unanimous mind of the large committee (this recommendation was voted without dissent): "When the statement from Sister White is read, I am sure that the majority of our brethren will feel as we feel tonight—that the Lord has spoken, and we will obey. . . . Past experiences should strengthen our faith at this time and help us to move forward courageously in heeding the words of counsel which the Lord has given to us through Sister White. We have before us tonight a plain, straightforward statement from Sister

White in regard to the establishment of a medical school. There is no guesswork about it; there is no equivocation; there is no false construction that need be put upon these words. The question is, Will we follow the counsel given?"[45]

Logical questions remained: Where would Adventists find qualified physicians to be teachers? Where would the enormous funds to operate a first-class medical institution, including nursing, medicine, dietetics, and years later dentistry, be found? But leaders had been learning how to lead as they broke new ground. Ellen White had been leading them into the untried many times before.

Here again, as we have seen often in the development of the Seventh-day Adventist Church, the principle of divine-human cooperation prevailed. Clearly, God does not plan to do for men and women what they can and should do for themselves. He leads, but people are to trust in His general principles and make their decisions accordingly. That is how believers grow and become prepared for future challenges. It is the parable of the talents operating on a larger scale. When the appointed head of the new school, W. E. Howell, asked Mrs. White for more details so that no mistakes would be made from the start, she replied: "We cannot mark out a precise line to be followed unconditionally. Circumstances and emergencies will arise for which the Lord must give special instruction. But if we begin to work, depending wholly upon the Lord, watching, praying, and walking in harmony with the light He sends us, we shall not be left to walk in darkness."[46]

In 1905 Ellen White's final book on health principles, *The Ministry of Healing*, appeared and was closely studied at Loma Linda. More material on gospel medical work was printed in volumes eight and nine of the *Testimonies*. In 1932, *Medical Ministry*, a compilation of many letters to physicians that focused on the divine purpose in health education and practice, was published.

Those men and women in 1910 should be paradigms and templates for all Seventh-day Adventists until the end of time. They listened to the messenger of God whom they had learned to trust. They knew that the only question that needed to be answered was I. H. Evans's question: "Will we follow the counsel given?"

Educational Leaders Learned to Listen to Ellen White

When one reviews the first fifty years after Ellen White published her first testimony on "Proper Education,"[47] in 1872, several common characteristics appear: (1) the closer a school followed inspired instruction, the more efficient and productive its program became; (2) the administrators who broke new ground in educational reform believed strongly in the inspiration of Ellen White; (3) when administrators and faculty taught these principles, by precept and example, the student body responded positively.

Whenever school staffs were ambivalent regarding educational reform, students would catch the ambiguity and express their frustration in some unconstructive way. The troublesome experiences of Battle Creek College would stand forever as an object lesson of the negative consequences of unsureness in responding to inspired counsel.[48]

Endnotes

1. *Fundamentals of Christian Education*, p. 45.
2. *Review and Herald*, May 20, 1873.
3. *Testimonies*, vol. 3, pp. 131-160; *Fundamentals of Christian Education*, pp. 15-46.
4. *Fundamentals of Christian Education*, p. 15; *Bio.*, vol. 2, p. 376.
5. *SDAE*, vol. 10, pp. 72, 73.
6. *Testimonies*, vol. 5, pp. 29, 30.
7. "Proceedings of the S.D.A. Educational Society: Eighth Annual Session," SDA Yearbook, 1883, p. 52; *Bio.*, vol. 3, pp. 187-191.
8. *Early Adventist Educators*, pp. 35-39.
9. "In some of our schools the price of tuition has been too low. This has in many ways been detrimental to the educational work. . . . The school should have a sufficient income not only to pay the necessary running expenses, but to be able to furnish the students during the school term with some things essential for their

work. . . . Properly increasing the tuition may cause a decrease in the attendance, but a large attendance should not be so much a matter of rejoicing as freedom from debt."—*Testimonies,* vol. 6, pp. 210-212; *Counsels to Parents, Teachers, and Students,* pp. 69, 70.
10. *Bio.,* vol. 6. pp. 176-188; see also W. C. Utt, *A Mountain, a Pickax, a College* (Angwin, Calif.: Alumni Association of Pacific Union College, 1968). Also, in the spring of 1882 South Lancaster Academy was founded, the precursor of Atlantic Union College, South Lancaster, Massachusetts.
11. See Schwarz, *Light Bearers,* pp. 202, 203; Milton Hook, "The Avondale School and Adventist Educational Goals, 1894-1900," (Ed. D. dissertation, Andrews University, Berrien Springs, MI, 1978). See pp. 256-263, 344.
12. *Fundamentals of Christian Education,* pp. 310-327.
13. *Ibid.*
14. Manuscript 56, 1898 (in *Testimonies,* vol. 6, p. 126).
15. Manuscript 186, 1898, cited in *Bio.,* vol. 4, p. 353.
16. *Life Sketches,* p. 374.
17. *Counsels to Parents, Teachers, and Students,* p. 349.
18. Knight, *Myths,* pp. 18, 19.
19. *Selected Messages,* book 3, p. 227.
20. *Counsels to Parents, Teachers, and Students,* p. 531.
21. See *Selected Messages,* book 3, pp. 285, 286.
22. Letter 138, 1897, in *MR,* vol. 20, p. 215.
23. *Bio.,* vol. 5, p. 345.
24. Schwarz, *Light Bearers,* p. 246. See Ira Gish and Harry Christman, *Madison: God's Beautiful Farm* (Mountain View, Calif.: Pacific Press Publishing Association, 1979).
25. Schwarz, *Light Bearers,* pp. 244-247.
26. Richard Utt, *From Vision to Reality* (Loma Linda, Calif.: Loma Linda University Press, 1980), p. 9.
27. See pp. 189, 190.
28. Ellen White described Burden as a man "of more than ordinary business acumen."—Utt, *The Vision Bold,* p. 179.
29. Letter 89, 1905, to J. A. Burden, manager of the Glendale Sanitarium, cited in *Bio.,* vol. 6, p. 11.
30. See *Bio.,* vol. 6, pp. 11-32, 78, 79, 345-349, 376, 377; Robinson, *Our Health Message,* pp. 363-413; Utt, *The Vision Bold,* (Washington, D.C.: Review and Herald Publishing Association, 1977), pp. 175-201.
31. Letter 139, 1904, cited in *Bio.,* vol. 6, p. 16.
32. *Bio.,* vol. 6, p. 18.
33. *Ibid.,* p. 22.
34. *Ibid.,* pp. 26, 27.
35. *Ibid.,* p. 349.
36. *Ibid.,* p. 273.
37. *Ibid.*
38. *Ibid.,* p. 275.
39. *Ibid.,* p. 276.
40. Schwarz, *Light Bearers,* p. 320.
41. *Bio.,* vol. 6, p. 275; Schwarz, *Light Bearers,* pp. 320-322.
42. Later published in *Review and Herald,* May 19, 1910.
43. *Bio.,* vol. 6, p. 279.
44. *Ibid.* See also, *Counsels to Parents, Teachers, and Students,* p. 480; *Medical Ministry,* pp. 57, 69.
45. *Ibid.,* p. 287.
46. Letter 192, 1906 to S. N. Haskell, cited in Robinson, *Our Health Message,* p. 368.
47. *Fundamentals of Christian Education,* pp. 15-49.
48. Schwarz, *Light Bearers,* pp. 199, 200, 328.

Study Questions

1. What were the fundamental problems that seemed to plague Battle Creek College until it was moved to Berrien Springs, Michigan?

2. How do you perceive the "evils of self-esteem and an unsanctified independence" to be especially destructive in an educational system?

3. Why did Ellen White counsel school leaders not to lower fees in order to attract a higher enrollment?

4. Why was Ellen White so insistent that Avondale College be located in a rural environment?

5. In what way was Avondale College to be a "pattern school"?

6. What was the larger vision that Ellen White had for the purpose and future of the educational center at Loma Linda, California?

7. Review the steps that led to the establishment of a medical school at Loma Linda, California. Note the extraordinary faith and courage that were needed at each step.

CHAPTER 31

Publishing, Temperance, and Social Principles

"Let none who profess godliness regard with indifference the health of the body, and flatter themselves that intemperance is no sin, and will not affect their spirituality. A close sympathy exists between the physical and the moral nature."[1]

Publishing pamphlets, tracts, and periodicals was the open secret of the success of the Millerite Second Advent movement. After the Disappointment (see pp. 39, 50), one of the Millerite papers, *The Hope of Israel*, published the first printed endorsement of the seventh-day Sabbath among Adventists.[2] After reading this article by T. M. Preble, Captain Joseph Bates became convinced that Saturday is the Biblical Sabbath. One year later, in August 1846, he published his own 48-page pamphlet entitled, *The Seventh Day Sabbath a Perpetual Sign From the Beginning to the Entering Into the Gates of the Holy City According to the Commandment*.[3]

James and Ellen White read a copy of Bates's pamphlet, became convinced that the seventh-day Sabbath is the day to keep holy, and began to teach it to the "scattered flock." Soon, about fifty Sabbath keepers could be counted in New England and New York State.[4]

Also in another Millerite paper, the *Day-Star* issue of January 24, 1846, Ellen Harmon's first vision, recounted in a personal letter to the editor, Enoch Jacobs, was printed. If she had known that Jacobs would publish her letter, no doubt she would have written out the vision in more detail. A description of her February 1845 vision was printed on March 14, 1846, one month after the *Day-Star* printed that momentous Bible study of Hiram Edson, F. B. Hahn, and O. R. L. Crosier setting forth the evidence for the two phases of ministry in both the earthly and heavenly sanctuaries. Later in 1846, James White and H. S. Gurney printed 250 copies of Ellen White's first vision, which they entitled, "To the Remnant Scattered Abroad."[5]

A Significant Vision

Printer's ink flowed through early Seventh-day Adventist veins. At Dorchester, Massachusetts, in November 1848, Ellen White had a significant vision outlining the power of the printed page. Speaking to her husband, she said: "I have a message for you. You must begin to print a little paper and send it out to the people. Let it be small at first; but as the people read, they will send you means with which to print, and it will be a success from the first. From this small beginning it was shown to me to be like streams of light that went clear round the world."[6]

This remarkable vision, at a time when the Whites were penniless, has been dramatically fulfilled.[7]

The story of the rapid development of Adventist publishing has been well-documented elsewhere.[8] But the point we make here is that at critical moments in this development, when the future was indeed bleak, Ellen White's messages kept her colleagues on course.[9]

When publication of *Present Truth* was in jeopardy in 1850, she received a vision, of which she wrote: "I saw the paper, and that it was needed. . . . I saw that the paper should go; and if they let it die they would weep in anguish soon. I saw that God did not want James to stop yet; but he must *write, write, write,* and speed the message and let it go. I saw that it would go where God's servants cannot go."[10]

In November 1850, the Whites saw wisdom in combining *Present Truth* and *Advent Review* into a new journal, *The Second Advent Review and Sabbath Herald,* now probably the longest regularly published religious journal in America. But those were difficult times. Ellen White wrote: "We suffered many privations. . . . We were willing to live cheaply that the paper might be sustained. . . . We had much care, and often sat up as late as midnight, and sometimes until two or three in the morning, to read proof-sheets. . . . Mental labor and privation reduced the strength of my husband very fast."[11] The Whites measured commitment by personal sacrifice and total concern for passing on the light of truth to others. This commitment was never more apparent than in their sacrifices setting up printing facilities in their home until others realized that a publishing house was necessary.[12]

Colporteur Ministry

A vision at the Rome, New York, camp meeting in September 1875 opened the eyes of the growing church toward the potential of literature evangelism. The "young man of noble appearance" who had often spoken to Ellen White in vision or dream noted the diligence of Adventists who were raising inquiry among the general public. But, he said, "more thorough effort" must be done to "fasten these impressions upon minds" or "your efforts now made will prove nearly fruitless." His suggestion was to supplement preaching with appropriate reading matter, which would result in a "hundredfold return to the treasury."

How was this supplemental work to be done? By literature evangelists (often called canvassers or colporteurs), "men of good address, who will not repulse others or be repulsed. . . . Those who distribute tracts gratuitously should take other publications to sell to all who will purchase them. Persevering efforts will result in great good."[13]

Thus began the worldwide program of literature evangelism wherein men and women carry the printed page door-to-door. This new evangelical approach was reviewed at the third session of the European Council of Seventh-day Adventist Missions, at Basel, Switzerland, September 14, 1885. But the literature evangelists were disheartened; they were convinced that Europeans would not buy books at their doors. It was a crisis moment. Ellen White was prepared. She already had received messages from God about the eventual success of the "colporteur" work in Europe.

After giving a review of these messages to the wavering delegates, she said: "God will soon do great things for us if we lie humble and believing at His feet. . . . More than one thousand will soon be converted in one day, most of whom will trace their first convictions to the reading of our publications."[14] Gradually the attractiveness of the literature was upgraded with illustrations, and the workers were better trained. Within a few years, the record shows that Adventist literature was being sold widely throughout Europe.

Publishing, a Sacred Ministry

Around the turn of the century Mrs. White was troubled by the fact that much of the financial success of the denomination's two publishing houses depended on commercial work, some of which was in conflict with teachings of the church.[15]

During the preceding decade she had been writing letters and speaking frequently on the growing problems at the Review and Herald, the church's largest publishing house. She spoke about the managers and their lack of fairness to workers and authors and their abdication of responsibility for checking the demoralizing literature they were printing. (The managers would reply that they were printers, not censors.) She admonished the Review board to keep the publishing house within its intended purpose.[16]

The sweeping fire of December 31, 1902, that destroyed the Review, seemed to alert most everybody that God had been warning them for ten years. The move to Washington, D. C. carried with it the decision to eliminate commercial work at the Review and Herald Publishing Company.[17]

Unfortunately, similar problems had been developing at the Pacific Press Publishing Company in Oakland, California. About half of the printed material was commercial work.[18] Because of warnings from Ellen White, especially those intensified after the Battle Creek fire, the management drastically reduced their commercial work and decided to locate at a more rural site. After the April 18, 1906, earthquake and a later fire, the management decided that no further commercial work would be accepted.

The decisions of both publishing houses to face the future without commercial work and to listen more closely to the counsel of Ellen White regarding management policies, were soon honored by an enormous increase in publishing business.[19]

Temperance Leadership

Ellen White had more than enough to do writing books, articles, letters, and manuscripts. In addition, she followed closely the development of Adventist educational and publishing institutions, and spoke at gatherings from coast to coast on an almost incredible schedule. But part of her great concern for proclaiming the gospel was her deep insights into the problem of intemperance. Intemperance, for her, was at the core of most all human problems.[20]

Mrs. White's approach to temperance/intemperance was unusual, compared with other temperance lecturers and organizations of the day. Whether in America or Europe, her unique approach captivated her listeners. On Sunday, November 8, 1886, at Christiana (Oslo), Norway, she spoke to 1,600 people in the largest hall in the city, at the invitation of the president of the local temperance society. Before her were many prominent people, including the bishop of the state church and a number of clergymen. Above her hung an American flag, which she "highly appreciated."

Instead of a rousing speech, full of dramatic stories and scary statistics, she delivered her typical temperance address based on Biblical principles and illustrations. In a report of the meeting, she wrote: "When they saw that the subject was to be argued from a Bible standpoint, they were at first astonished, then interested, and finally deeply moved."

The Religious Connection

At the close of her lecture the president of the local temperance society spoke, urging his audience to note that the success of the American temperance movement rested on religious zeal and Biblical principles. Mrs. White had requests to speak at local churches but she declined because her mission in Norway was to build up the Adventist churches.[21]

In reviewing the text of that Norway address, which was typical of her temperance talks to the general public, we can better understand what made her messages distinctive. She traced the subject of temperance in Bible history, especially emphasizing how closely Christ was connected to the work of temperance throughout His life on earth. The main points of her public talks on temperance were:

• Our first parents sinned by "the indulgence of appetite."

• Christ overcame the "indulgence of appetite" in the wilderness temptation, "showing that in His strength it is possible for us to overcome."

• Nadab and Abihu, men of holy office, suffered fearful judgment because they permitted their minds to become "beclouded" and thus incapable of distinguishing right from wrong.

• "Men of principle are needed" in legislative halls and in courts of justice, as well as in schools and churches—"men of self control, of keen perceptions and sound judgment." Intemperance will render them incapable of "just decisions" and the ability "to rise above motives of self-interest or the influence of partiality or prejudice."

• Parents must learn the lesson angels brought to Manoah, Samson's father, and to Zacharias, the father of John the Baptist. Children are affected "for good or evil, by the habits of the mother" and their early household training.

• Parents "transmit their own characteristics, mental and physical, their dispositions and appetites." "Children often lack physical strength and mental and moral power" because of parental intemperance (lack of self-control).

• "From babyhood" children should be taught the principles and habits of "self-denial and self-control."

• Daniel and his associates in the court of Babylon were used as forcible illustrations of true temperance. They were a "noble testimony" to the benefits of "strict temperance in the use of all His bounties, as well as total abstinence from every injurious and debasing indulgence."

• "Not only is the use of unnatural stimulants needless and pernicious, but it is also extravagant and wasteful. . . . Thousands of parents . . . spend their earnings in self-indulgence, robbing their children of food and clothing and the benefits of education."[22]

These principles are amplified, with more detail as to how they should be taught, in the Ellen G. White compilation entitled, *Temperance.* When most temperance leaders focused primarily on alcohol, largely ignoring tobacco and unnatural stimulants such as tea and coffee, Mrs. White went deeper—to the causes of drunkenness and debasement of morals.[23]

Temperance Begins at Home

In a January 3, 1873, vision, she was shown that temperance movements were limited in their effectiveness because they restricted their warfare against intemperance to the use of alcoholic beverages. She wrote: "Intemperance is increasing everywhere, notwithstanding the earnest efforts made during the past year to stay its progress. I was shown that the giant power of intemperance will not be controlled by any such efforts as have been made. The work of temperance must begin in our families, at our tables."[24]

Further, she wrote: "Intemperance commences at our tables. The appetite is indulged until its indulgence becomes second nature. By the use of tea and coffee an appetite is formed for tobacco, and this encourages the appetite for liquors."[25]

But intemperance is not only a matter of food and drink, it includes "excessive indulgence in eating, drinking, sleeping, or seeing."[26] Intemperance in certain dress habits is to be overcome.[27] Intemperance in overwork, in study, in seeking riches, is to be avoided.[28]

The only cure for intemperance is to regain self-control. Often Ellen White emphasized the principle that "passions are to be controlled by the will, which is itself to be under the control of God. The kingly power of reason, sanctified by divine grace, is to bear sway in our lives."[29]

She pointed out that when physical

habits are not right, "our mental and moral powers cannot be strong."[30]

She saw the direct connection between self-control and character development, between self-control in all areas of life and preparation for the coming of the Lord: "The controlling power of appetite will prove the ruin of thousands, when, if they had conquered on this point, they would have moral power to gain the victory over every other temptation of Satan. But those who are slaves to appetite will fail in perfecting Christian character."[31]

The challenge of self-control in every area of life is for all Christians, especially those who are proclaiming the "everlasting gospel" in the last days: "To make plain natural law, and urge the obedience of it, is the work that accompanies the third angel's message to prepare a people for the coming of the Lord."[32]

A Far-sighted Leader on Social Issues

Ellen White maintained inspired balance in her counsel to church members, notably in regard to social responsibilities. The primary purpose and motivation for all Christian service is to proclaim the gospel of restoration.[33] No single branch of Christian service is to become "all absorbing" so "that which should have the first place becomes a secondary consideration."[34]

The poor and disadvantaged. In reference to working for the disadvantaged she stated the principle of balance: "The great question of our duty to humanity is a serious one, and much of the grace of God is needed in deciding how to work so as to accomplish the greatest amount of good. . . . God does not require His workmen to obtain their education and training in order to devote themselves exclusively to these classes. The working of God is manifested in a way which will establish confidence that the work is of His devising, and that sound principles underlie every action."

Ellen White saw the danger of focusing on certain kinds of social work "which will amount to the least in strengthening all parts of the work by harmonious action."[35]

While emphasizing her concern for balance and priorities, she made it clear that the Christian's responsibility to the needs of others is as important as his or her duty to God. This may sound good in theory but more difficult to work out in practice. Too often Christians are more concerned with the first half of the Lord's command: "You shall love the Lord your God with all your heart. . . ." Compliance to the other half of Christ's command, "You shall love your neighbor as yourself" (Matt. 22:39), has been "left to caprice, subject to inclination or impulse."[36]

Genuine Christians realize that their religious profession has "little weight" before God or man if they "bend every energy toward some apparently great work, while neglect[ing] the needy or turn[ing] the stranger from his right."[37]

Christians also believe that when "self is merged in Christ, love springs forth spontaneously." How is this spontaneity revealed? Ellen White declared: "The completeness of Christian character is attained when the impulse to help and bless others springs constantly from within."[38]

To put the question of social issues in the sharpest focus, she wrote with unambiguous clarity that the judgment of all men and women rests on "one point. . . . When the nations are gathered before Him, there will be but two classes, and their eternal destiny will be determined by what they have done or have neglected to do for Him in the person of the poor and the suffering."[39]

How does this profound principle work? Note Ellen White's focus on Isaiah 58, the chapter on the Christian's responsibility for the needy and disadvantaged.[40] She frequently referred to the fifty-eighth chapter of Isaiah as the "message for this time, to be given over and over again," and "the whole chapter is of the highest importance."[41]

Three "arenas of service" are depicted in Mrs. White's voluminous counsel regarding the Christian's responsibility to others.[42] The first arena is the local church's responsibility for its own congregation: "It is the duty of each church to make careful, judicious arrangements for the care of its poor and sick."[43]

The local community is the second arena: "Wherever a church is established, its members are to do a faithful work for the needy believers. But they are not to stop here. They are also to aid others, irrespective of their faith."[44]

The third arena is the world community, outside of the local community: "Any human being who needs our sympathy and our kind offices is our neighbor. The suffering and destitute of all classes are our neighbors; and when their wants are brought to our knowledge, it is our duty to relieve them as far as possible. . . . Our neighbors are the whole human family."[45]

When Adventists today consider these three arenas, they think immediately of Dorcas societies, renamed in recent years as Community Services, and SAWS (Seventh-day Adventist World Service), also renamed in the 1980s as Adventist Development and Relief Agency (ADRA). For example, during the relief services needed at the end of World War II, between 1946 and 1949, the General Conference relief organizations "provided more than 3,300,000 pounds of food and 1,100,000 pounds of clothing" to Europe alone.[46]

In 1995, ADRA, working in 142 countries, administered humanitarian aid (including donated material) that was valued in excess of $120 million. The budget of ADRA's operations, based in Silver Spring, Maryland, exceeded $60 million.[47]

Importance of the Family

Perhaps Ellen White's most complete thoughts on the importance of the traditional family were summarized in *The Ministry of Healing*, published in 1905. Here she spoke prophetically. During the last half of the twentieth century, the traditional family came under attack with alternate attempts to supplement normal family nurture. In the last decade of the century, a renewal of concern for the health of the family has been observed.

In 1905 Mrs. White was clear and emphatic: "The restoration and uplifting of humanity begins in the home. The work of parents underlies every other. . . . The well-being of society, the success of the church, the prosperity of the nation, depend upon home influences."[48]

The home is not only the haven for children and parents in the midst of a troubled world, the Christian home is an "object lesson" that illustrates "the excellence of the true principles of life." Troubled youth from other homes should find in Christian homes "cheering, helpful influences."[49]

Relating Wisely to the Cities

Plight of the cities. The cities of the world have always been centers of corruption and vice. From early Bible times, cities were not the place for believers in Jehovah. In modern times, the phenomenal population increases have exponentially increased pollution and vice.[50]

At the 1903 General Conference session Ellen White warned that denominational institutions should "keep out of the cities." She urged church members to "get out of the cities into the country, where they can obtain a small piece of land, and make a home for themselves and their children." She predicted that "erelong there will be such strife and confusion in the cities that those who wish to leave them will not be able. We must be preparing for these issues."[51]

Although she urged church members to leave the cities for a number of reasons, she also counseled common sense: "Let there be nothing done in a disorderly manner that there shall be a great loss or sacrifice made upon property because of ardent, impulsive speeches which stir up an enthusiasm which is not after the order of God, that a victory that was essential to be gained, shall, for a lack of level-headed moderation and proper contemplation and sound principles and purposes, be turned into a defeat."[52]

Mrs. White recognized that the great cities of the world were not suitable places for Christians to live and raise families, but she carried a heavy burden for the unevangelized people in these crowded urban areas. In 1909 she urged: "The instruction has been given me, Work the cities; work the cities where the first and second angels' messages were proclaimed. The work of warning the cities has been kept before us for more than twenty years; but who has felt a burden for this work? Who has done real missionary work among them? We are bidden to go to those cities and preach the gospel and heal the sick."[53]

However, after warning of the increasing turmoil and corruption that would sweep over the world's cities, Ellen White repeatedly urged church leaders to place city evangelism high on their agenda. Indeed, without her insistence in the early years of the twentieth century, the Adventist presence in the large cities of North America would have been minimal. She specifically pointed to such centers as New York, Boston, Philadelphia, Baltimore, Washington, Nashville, St. Louis, New Orleans, Memphis, Detroit, Cincinnati, Cleveland, San Francisco, and Portland (Maine).

Many letters were sent to leading ministers, beginning with the president of the General Conference, to make city evangelism top priority.[54] In 1905 she wrote: "We stand rebuked by God because the large cities right within our sight are unworked and unwarned. A terrible charge of neglect is brought against those who have been long in the work, in this very America, and yet have not entered the large cities."[55]

Ellen White's urging created immediate results. In the greater New York area alone by 1915, fifteen evangelistic companies were at work, mostly in tents. Mrs. White strongly emphasized that "in our large cities the medical missionary work must go hand in hand with the gospel ministry. It will open doors for the entrance of truth."

Summary

We began this section on "The Nurturer of Inspired Concepts" by emphasizing that Ellen White was the "central figure" in the "most subtly differentiated, systematically developed and institutionally successful of all alternatives to the American way of life."[56]

We noted her unique contribution in the development of Adventism's distinctive principles of theology, education, health, church government, social responsibility, and missiology. She was the conceptual nurturer and the prodder of thought. Her exceptional freshness lies not in her total originality of thought but in her remarkable ability to synthesize the insights she received from God and the results of a keen perception in her research.

Without Ellen White's leadership in thought and personal courage, the Adventist Church most probably would not have survived. If it had, it would have been far different from what the world knows it to be today.

Endnotes

1. *Review and Herald*, Jan. 25, 1881, cited in *Temperance*, pp. 17, 18.
2. Feb. 28, 1845. See Joseph Bates, *The Seventh Day Sabbath, A Perpetual Sign*, 1846, p. 40.
3. *Bio.*, vol. 1, p. 116; see also Schwarz, *Light Bearers*, pp. 72-74.
4. *Ibid.*
5. Schwarz, *Light Bearers*, p. 72.
6. *Life Sketches*, p. 125.
7. See Schwarz, *Light Bearers*, pp. 72-85; Maxwell, *Tell It to the World*, pp. 95-105; Spalding, *Origin and History*, vol. 1, pp. 187-206. See M. Carol Hetzell, *The*

Undaunted (Mountain View, Calif.: Pacific Press Publishing Association, 1967).
8. *Ibid.*
9. "Almost singlehandedly [James White] had created a publishing business, against formidable obstacles. Several times it had been only his wife's vision-based encouragements that had kept him going."—Schwarz, *Light Bearers*, p. 84.
10. Manuscript 2, 1850, cited in *Bio.*, vol. 1, p. 172; Schwarz, *Light Bearers,* pp. 74-76.
11. *Life Sketches,* pp. 139, 140.
12. See *Bio.*, vol. 1, pp. 316-330 for the eventful move of the "publishing house" from Rochester, New York, to Battle Creek, Michigan.
13. *Bio.,* vol. 2, pp. 480, 481.
14. Reported by D. T. Bourdeau in *Review and Herald,* Nov. 10, 1885; *Evangelism*, p. 693.
15. "By 1899 the General Conference president estimated that 80 percent of the printing done at the Review [Battle Creek] was of a commercial nature. Not surprisingly, press workers began to think of their activities as a business operation for which they should be compensated more liberally. The evangelistic dedication shown by workers of an earlier era seemed to be fading away." —Schwarz, *Light Bearers,* p. 211.
16. "Presses poured forth fiction, Wild West stories, books promulgating Roman Catholic doctrines, sex literature, and books on hypnosis."—*Bio.*, vol. 5, pp. 227-234.
17. Schwarz, *Light Bearers,* pp. 306-311.
18. *Bio.,* vol. 5, pp. 164-168.
19. Schwarz, *Light Bearers,* p. 330.
20. "Intemperance, in the true sense of the word, is at the foundation of the larger share of the ills of life, and it annually destroys its tens of thousands."—*Signs of the Times,* Nov. 17, 1890.
21. *Historical Sketches,* pp. 207-211.
22. *Temperance,* pp. 267-273; *Historical Sketches of S. D. A. Foreign Missions,* pp. 207-211. Two other temperance addresses by Ellen White, one in 1891, the other at Sydney, Australia, in 1893, are also included in *Temperance,* pp. 273-292.
23. For a review of Adventist cooperation with temperance societies, see Robinson, *Our Health Message,* pp. 223-235. For an overview of anti-alcohol campaigns in the nineteenth century, see Jerome L. Clark, "The Crusade Against Alcohol," in Land, *World of E. G. White,* pp. 131-140.
24. *Testimonies,* vol. 3, p. 562.
25. *Ibid.,* p. 563.
26. *Ibid.,* vol. 4, p. 417; see also *Patriarchs and Prophets,* p. 562.
27. *Medical Ministry,* p. 275.
28. *Temperance,* pp. 139, 140.
29. *The Ministry of Healing,* p. 130.
30. *Testimonies,* vol. 3, p. 51. "The brain nerves that connect with the whole system are the medium through which heaven communicates with man, and affects the inmost life. Whatever hinders the circulation of the electric current in the nervous system, thus weakening the vital powers and lessening mental susceptibility, makes it more difficult to arouse the moral nature." —*Education,* p. 209. See *Ibid.*, p. 197.
31. *Testimonies,* vol. 3, pp. 491, 492.
32. *Ibid.,* vol. 3, p. 161.
33. See pp. 257, 344.
34. *Welfare Ministry,* p. 256.
35. *Ibid.,* p. 257.
36. *Christ's Object Lessons,* p. 382.
37. *Ibid.,* pp. 383-384.
38. *Ibid.* "Wherever there is an impulse of love and sympathy, wherever the heart reaches out to bless and uplift others, there is revealed the working of God's Holy Spirit."—*Ibid.,* p. 385.
39. *The Desire of Ages,* p. 637.
40. In the *Comprehensive Index to the Writings of Ellen G. White,* approximately 200 references involve Isaiah 58.
41. *Welfare Ministry,* pp. 29-34.
42. See Calvin B. Rock, "Did Ellen White Downplay Social Work?" *Adventist Review,* May 5, 1988.
43. *Welfare Ministry,* p. 29.
44. *Ibid.,* p. 180.
45. *Ibid.,* pp. 45, 46.
46. Land, *Adventism in America*, p. 178.
47. ADRA 1995 Annual Report. Adventist Development and Relief Agency, 12501 Old Columbia Pike, Silver Spring, MD 20904, USA.
48. *The Ministry of Healing,* p. 349.
49. *Ibid.,* pp. 352-354.
50. *Ibid.,* pp. 262, 263; see *Selected Messages,* book 2, pp. 355, 356.
51. *Bio.,* vol. 5, p. 250. See also *Testimonies,* vol. 7, p. 84.
52. *Selected Messages,* book 2, pp. 361-363.
53. *The General Conference Bulletin*, June 4, 1909.
54. Schwarz, *Light Bearers,* pp. 334-338.
55. *Evangelism*, p. 401.
56. Bull and Lockhart, *Seeking a Sanctuary,* pp. ix, 14.

Study Questions

1. How did the Whites, in their personal lives, affirm the vision-message that their exceedingly small group should begin a publishing program?

2. What problem in both American publishing houses at the turn of the century received Ellen White's focus and strong counsel to change course?

3. What were the chief points in most of Ellen White's public addresses on temperance?

4. Why is temperance a spiritual issue?

5. In view of the nineteenth century milieu, how can it be said Ellen White was a "far-sighted leader in social issues"?
6. Why did Ellen White paint a bleak future for the cities of the world?
7. How does Ellen White's concept of temperance (self-control) reflect New Testament teaching?
8. What are some of the dangers for Adventist publishing houses in accepting secular, commercial work?

SECTION VI

How to Listen to the Messenger

CHAPTER

CHAPTER 32

Hermeneutics/1
Basic Principles

"God has spoken! But what has He said? Every utterance, every written document, demands interpretation. And the need increases in proportion to the distance the text stands in time and culture from our own."[1]

Hermeneutics is the science of interpreting literary documents. We use this term when we attempt to understand the writings of secular writers such as Homer, Plato, and Shakespeare, as well as inspired writers such as Moses, Paul, and Ellen White. Hermeneutical rules help us understand what writers meant by what they said.

Ellen White noted the need for hermeneutics when she suggested, "Let us in imagination . . . sit with the disciples" on the Mount of Blessing (Matt. 5). "Understanding what the words of Jesus meant to those who heard them, we may discern in them a new vividness and beauty, and may also gather for ourselves their deeper lessons."[2]

What It Meant and What It Means

Here we are advised to study (1) what the words "meant" in 30 A.D., and (2) what we should understand them to "mean" to us today. That study must follow the rules of hermeneutics if two or more people are to agree on what a document originally "meant" and what it "means" today.[3] Further, the goal of hermeneutics is not only to understand what an author meant but to make sure that the author is not misunderstood.[4]

Here are some basic rules of hermeneutics:

- If a document is in a foreign language, a knowledge of that language is needed, including an understanding of that language's structure and idioms. Although especially true of the Bible with its Hebrew, Aramaic, and Greek documents, understanding the idioms and peculiarities of nineteenth-century American English is helpful in understanding Ellen White. Merely a dictionary knowledge is not sufficient.
- The type of literary form must be recognized—whether prose or poetry, prophecy or history, allegory or parable, etc. Both the Bible and the writings of Ellen White require this awareness.
- The historical context, including the precise time of writing, must be understood before correct deductions can be made, especially if the document deals with ethics, interrelationships with contemporary civil powers, and prevailing thought patterns. To understand the Bible and the writings of Ellen White, students must be aware of historical context.
- A knowledge of the climatic and geographical factors that influenced the writer is helpful. Much of the Bible, for example, would be obscure without a knowledge of Palestinian geographical conditions and the impact of its climate. Large parts of Ellen White's observations and counsel become more understandable when we recognize these factors.

• In order to think like the writer and to "hear" like his or her hearers, we today must try to "see" what they saw and "hear" what they heard. We must learn all we can about the character and personality of the author as well as the general personal interplay of the people referred to in the document being studied.

• Readers must discover what Bible statements meant to the prophet's contemporaries before focusing on what they should mean today. This will protect students from "seeing" in the Bible only what they are looking for.[5]

• In the study of the Bible, we accept the implicit Biblical understanding that the Old and New Testaments together form a canon that contains the record of God's unique revelation to human beings. Thus the Bible is its own best interpreter, providing a unifying theological context for understanding any particular chapter and verse. This same principle of unity and coherence will help students understand more clearly the totality of Ellen White's thoughts.[6]

The challenge to understand what the Bible means is not a modern phenomenon. Early in the New Testament the need for interpretation arose with Philip's question to the Ethiopian: "Do you understand what you are reading?"

And he (the Ethiopian) said, "How can I, unless someone guides me?" (Acts 8:30, 31). The role of guide is performed best by those who faithfully follow the principles of interpretation (hermeneutics).

Understanding Ellen White

We are in a better position to understand what Mrs. White meant than we are to understand many other writers, for we have massive amounts of material in the form of letters, diaries, interviews, sermons, general manuscripts, periodical articles, and published books.

In addition, we have a voluminous file of contemporary observations, written by people who knew Ellen White well. Hundreds had received direct, written "testimonies" from her and, in turn, expressed in writing their appreciation for her counsel. Men and women for more than seventy years watched her closely, heard her often, and waited eagerly for her next written testimony, article, or book. Their comments hold much legitimacy as we discuss her authority and relevance. Their understanding of what she said contributes much to our attempt today to determine what she meant.[7]

As noted earlier (see pp. 256-283, 344), Ellen White's contributions in areas such as health, education, and theology, are more fully understood if her prevailing Great Controversy Theme when recognized. That theme provides her coherent unity and helps to explain her use of historical sources and her application of Biblical passages.

Danger of Blind Obedience

However, it is one thing to acknowledge and accept this prevailing principle, it is another to answer the question as to how this principle is applied and understood in the breadth of her counsel in numerous areas of thought. Confidence in Ellen White is essential, but blind confidence should not be substituted for careful thinking when it comes to what she means today.

In understanding her writings it is helpful to note again how revelation-inspiration works as revealed in Biblical writings.[8] The comparison between one's understanding of Biblical writers and Ellen White can be seen in such areas as reader's attitude, thought or verbal inspiration, infallibility, the meaning of *sola scriptura,* the use of common sources, and the difference between the sacred and the common. What we know about how Bible writers were inspired is helpful to our study of Mrs. White's writings, and what we know about how God spoke through Ellen White can help us understand how God spoke through prophets in ancient times.

For Ellen White, the Bible is best understood by those who accept it as the Word of God: "I take the Bible just as it is, as the Inspired Word." When anyone finds it necessary to "define that which is inspired and that which is not, they have stepped before Jesus to show Him a better way than He has led us."[9] She believed that "the Bible was given for practical purposes"[10] and that "no one need be lost for want of knowledge, unless he is willfully blind."[11]

Attitudes Make a Difference

However, she recognized that there are problems in communication. "Minds of different education and thought receive different impressions of the same words." Thus, "it is difficult for one mind to give to one of a different temperament, education, and habits of thought by language exactly the same idea as that which is clear and distinct in his own mind. Yet to honest men, right-minded men, he [an author] can . . . convey his meaning for all practical purposes." But if the reader "is not honest and will not want to see and understand the truth, he will turn his words and language . . . to suit his own purposes."[12]

Ellen White lamented that some mistreated her writings as they did the Bible: "This is the way my writings are treated by those who wish to misunderstand and pervert them. . . . In the very same way that they treat the writings in my published articles and in my books, so do skeptics and infidels treat the Bible. They read it according to their desire to pervert, to misapply, to willfully wrest the utterances from their true meaning."[13]

One problem that Jesus had with the religious leaders of His day was that they misused and abused the Old Testament and thus did not recognize Him as their Messiah. Ellen White noted that these leaders were "unaccustomed to accept God's word exactly as it reads, or to allow it to be its own interpreter." The Jewish leaders read the Old Testament "in the light of their maxims and traditions. . . . They turned with aversion from the truth of God to the traditions of men."[14]

One's attitude in reading the Bible is fundamental to a correct understanding of what the Bible means. This is more important than trained scholarship. The Jewish leaders with their scholarship did not recognize Jesus. On many occasions Ellen White emphasized that "selfishness prevents us from beholding God. The self-seeking spirit judges of God as altogether such a one as itself. Until we have renounced this we cannot understand Him who is love."[15] She gave this promise: "Everyone who diligently and patiently searches the Scriptures that he may educate others, entering upon the work correctly and with an honest heart, laying his preconceived ideas, whatever they may have been, and his hereditary prejudice at the door of investigation, will gain true knowledge."[16]

In summary, Ellen White provided several suggestions as to how to study for truth:

• We should invite the Holy Spirit to help us in our study.[17]

• We must be willing to obey the truth.[18]

• We must be open-minded, even prepared to surrender previously held opinions.[19]

• We should expect to discover new truths.[20]

• We should expect "new" light to harmonize with old truth.[21]

• An interpretation may be wrong if it is accompanied by an unChristlike spirit. In the context of the 1888 General Conference session, Ellen White wrote to those who were still antagonistic to her and to Elders Jones and Waggoner: "These testimonies of the Spirit of God, the fruits of the Spirit of God, have no weight unless they are stamped with your ideas of the law in Galatians. I am afraid of you and I am afraid of your interpretation of any Scripture which has revealed itself in such an unChristlike spirit as you have manifested and has cost me so much unnecessary labor. . . . Let your caution be exercised in the line of fear lest you are committing the sin against the Holy Ghost. . . . I am afraid of any application of Scripture that needs such a spirit and bears such fruit as you have manifested."[22]

Thought or Verbal Inspiration

But Ellen White saw additional problems that could arise when one asks, How does the infinite, infallible God speak to finite, fallible men and women? How does a person, many years after the appearance of a prophet, understand his or her divinely inspired messages written hundreds, even thousands, of years before?

For some, it seems easier to believe that God dictated the words that the prophet faithfully recorded. For them, this method would avoid mistakes by eliminating human error.

For others, this dictation method not only ignores reality, it opens the door unnecessarily to an enormous list of problems that discredits what God has been trying to do.[23]

Ellen White identified with those who accepted the concept of thought inspiration rather than verbal inspiration. She recognized that "the writers of the Bible had to express their ideas in human language. It was written by human men. . . . The Bible is not given to us in grand superhuman language. . . . Everything that is human is imperfect. Different meanings are expressed by the same word; there is not one word for each distinct idea. . . . The Bible is written by inspired men, but it is not God's mode of thought and expression. . . . Inspiration acts not on the man's words or his expressions but on the man himself, who, under the influence of the Holy Ghost, is imbued with thoughts. But the words receive the impress of the individual mind. . . . The divine mind and will is combined with the human mind and will; thus the utterances of the man are the word of God."[24]

What shall we make of this recognition of enormous diversity of expression and logic, as diverse as there are writers? How can later readers of these prophets find coherence and unity in what all declare to be "the word of the Lord"? The unity of the message is guaranteed by the one Author who inspired them all. Ellen White wrote: "The Creator of all ideas may impress different minds with the same thought, but each may express it in a different way, yet without contradiction."[25]

Yet the unity of the Bible is not always apparent to the casual reader. "The illuminated soul sees a spiritual unity, one grand golden thread running through the whole, but it requires patience, thought, and prayer to trace out the precious golden thread."[26]

Biblical scholars have compared the divine-human union in Jesus Christ with the divine-human union in the writing of the Bible. Ellen White endorsed this comparison: "The Bible is not given to us in grand superhuman language. Jesus, in order to reach man where he is, took humanity."[27] "The Bible, with its God-given truths expressed in the language of men, presents a union of the divine and the human. Such a union existed in the nature of Christ, who was the Son of God and the Son of man. Thus it is true of the Bible, as it was of Christ, that 'the Word was made flesh, and dwelt among us'" (John 1:14).[28]

Jesus was born a Jew, not an African or a Norwegian. He probably was less than six feet tall. Humanly speaking, He was limited by the DNA of His genetic background. Nevertheless, He revealed the Word of God, His message, in its purest sense.[29]

The Bible as we know it today was written by limited "men who differed widely in rank and occupation, and in mental and spiritual endowments."[30] The Author of the Bible spoke to various men who all had varying insights, some more limited than others. Yet each writer would grasp "those points that harmonize[d] with his experience or with his power of perception and appreciation." When the written messages are finally put together, all these "different aspects of truth" are seen to be in "perfect harmony." Together, limited as each writer may be, they "form a perfect whole." These varied experiences and perceptions of its many writers present to later readers, in all places and in all times, the Word of the Lord "adapted to meet the wants of men in all the circumstances and experiences of life."[31]

In a significant letter to a young physician, David Paulson, Ellen White tried to steer him away from a verbal-inspiration viewpoint. Dr. Paulson, a remarkable man of faith, had much to do with establishing Hinsdale Sanitarium and Hospital, Hinsdale, Illinois. She wrote: "In your letter you speak of your early training to have implicit faith in the testimonies and say, 'I was led to conclude and most firmly believe that *every* word you ever spoke in public or private, that every letter you wrote under *any* and *all* circumstances, was as inspired as the Ten Commandments.'"

She continued: "My brother, you have studied my writings diligently, and you have never found that I have made any such claims, neither will you find that the pioneers in our cause ever made such claims.

"In my introduction to *The Great Controversy* you have no doubt read my statement regarding the Ten Commandments and the Bible, which should have helped you to a correct understanding of the matter under consideration." She then quoted substantially from her own introduction to *The Great Controversy* and from an earlier pertinent statement found in volume 5 of the *Testimonies.*[32]

In summary, to understand the Bible and the writings of Ellen White, the important difference between thought revelation and verbal inspiration must be clear. Although verbal inspirationists (whether students of the Bible or the writings of Mrs. White) claim to enjoy greater security in possessing the exact word from God, they have great difficulty trying to explain what appear as "errors," "contradictions," or "discrepancies." The false assumptions of verbal inspirationists have caused much of the confusion and loss of confidence among those who have tried to study inspired writings.

Those who believe in thought inspiration understand the prophet to be God's "penman," not His pen. God works through the mental processes of His messenger, inspiring the thoughts, but, under the guidance of the Spirit allowing the messenger to choose the way the thoughts are to be expressed.

Ellen White's introduction to *The Great Controversy* has given us clear insight as to how prophets work. Recognizing that discrepancies may exist in the Bible and that "perfect order or apparent unity" may not be present at times, she concluded: "All the mistakes will not cause trouble to one soul, or cause any feet to stumble that would not manufacture difficulties from the plainest revealed truth."[33]

Infallibility

Infallibility is a characteristic of God alone, not His messengers. Created beings cannot possibly be infallible; they are always dependent on their Creator, always short of ultimate perfection, always becoming what God intended them to be.

Although the message God reveals through His messengers is without error, the message is conveyed through error-prone, fallible messengers. That is why Ellen White called prophets God's penmen, not His pen. And that is why she said bluntly: "In regard to infallibility, I never claimed it; God alone is infallible."[34]

Therefore, infallibility is not "on trial" in the prophet's words, whether in the Bible or in the writings of Ellen White. What is at stake is the search for that infallible authority which God is communicating through His messengers. God's messages breathe with infallible authority. The search for accuracy in understanding God's infallible messages depends, in part, on a person's faithfulness to the rules of hermeneutics, uncontaminated by human philosophical presuppositions.

Sola Scriptura (Bible only)

"The Bible and the Bible only" was the fundamental premise of the Protestant reformers, whether Luther in Germany, Zwingli and Calvin in Switzerland, or Farel in France. In other words, for the Reformers the Bible replaced human authorities. But this heroic insistence on the "Bible only" as the Christian's rule of faith and practice calls for three observations: (1) the Reformers had difficulty accepting the entire Bible, (2) they did not understand fully the continuance of spiritual gifts that the Bible expressly teaches, and (3) they differed widely as to what the Bible meant. Clearly, the slogan was not sufficient in itself.

The first observation is supported by the fact that Luther had great difficulty with the books of James, Hebrews, and Revelation. Calvin virtually discarded the book of Revelation. Other Reformers rejected the Old Testament. In fact, later Reformers who tried to get the main Reformers like Luther to see the completeness of the entire Bible were themselves treated like heretics.[35]

The second and third observations, for our purposes, relate particularly to Ellen White. What was her understanding of that vital Protestant principle, "The Bible and the Bible only"?[36] She used the phrase often and with precision. She used it as the Reformers used it—as authority; that is, the Bible stood above and alone in contrast with papal dogmas, councils, and the writings of church fathers. For her, as with the Reformers, salvation truth is found in the Bible, not in papal decrees or the votes of church councils.

She wrote: "The grand principle maintained by these Reformers . . . was the infallible authority of the Holy Scriptures as a rule of faith and practice. They denied the right of popes, councils, Fathers, and kings, to control the conscience in matters of religion."[37]

She also used this "vital principle" in sharp contrast to the Zwickau enthusiasts in Luther's time who permitted themselves to be guided primarily by their feelings—which they assumed were the leading of the Holy Spirit. She wrote: "They rejected the great principle which was the very foundation of the Reformation—that the Word of God is the all-sufficient rule of faith and practice; and for that unerring guide they substituted the changeable, uncertain standard of their own feelings and impressions. By this act of setting aside the great detector of error and falsehood, the way was opened for Satan to control minds as best pleased himself."[38]

For Ellen White the Bible was always the test of truth. No other standard was either necessary or legitimate: "I recommend to you, dear reader, the Word of God as the rule of your faith and practice. By that Word we are to be judged."[39] In 1909, at her last public appearance in a General Conference session, after finishing her sermon she left the podium for her seat. But she returned, and, holding up the Bible she had been preaching from, opened it and held it out with hands trembling with age, saying, "Brethren and Sisters, I commend unto you this Book."[40]

She contrasted the phrase, "the Bible and the Bible only," with human views and any other way of expressing "unbiblical positions of religious traditions, experience, ecclesiastical position and human reason."[41]

Biblical prophets always pointed to the previously accepted Scriptures as the test of faith and practice. Long before the Old Testament was even envisioned, men such as King Josiah (2 Kings 22), Ezra and Nehemiah (Neh. 8), and Daniel (Dan. 9) referred to previous prophets as bearers of God's Word. It never even entered the minds of many of these prophets that their writings would eventually be classed with the writings of Moses. When Paul proclaimed the gospel, the Bible that he used as authority was the Old Testament. He had no idea that his letters would constitute a major part of what would be called the New Testament.

Each Bible writer was later judged to be authoritative because his writings met the test of Isaiah 8:20—"To the law and to the testimony! If they do not speak according to this word, it is because there is no light in them." Further, those who read these writings discovered the voice of God speaking to their souls. Truly, one of the primary tests of a prophet is his or her harmony with previous inspired messages.[42]

Thus *sola scriptura* means that all claims to divine authority must meet the standard of previously accepted prophetic messages. Appeals to personal feeling or to dramatic experiences, on one hand,[43] or appeals to human authorities such as church councils or respected theologians, on the other, are not, in themselves, evidence that God has spoken.

The slogan, "The Bible and the Bible only!" means that every later prophet would have his or her messages judged by their faithfulness to earlier messages. Further, this phrase means that all that the Bible has taught is to be honored, including its declaration that the "gift of prophecy" would continue to the end of time. Thus, *sola scriptura* does not mean that God does not intend to add information to men and women through the "gift of prophecy"—for that would be a non sequitur; it would deny a Biblical principle.[44]

Early Adventists knew that accepting Ellen White as a messenger of God would lead to misunderstandings with other Christian groups. Early in his wife's ministry James White made it clear that the Christian "should pray fervently to be aided by the Holy Spirit in searching the Scriptures for the whole truth, and for his whole duty. He is not at liberty to turn from them to learn his duty through any of the gifts. We say that the very moment he does, he places the gifts in a wrong place, and takes an extremely dangerous position. The Word should be in front, and the eye of the church should be placed upon it, as the rule to walk by, and the fountain of wisdom."[45]

Early Adventists also knew that other Christians would claim that the ministry of Ellen White violated the Protestant principle of "the Bible and the Bible only." But Adventists responded "that it was *because* of their confidence in the Scriptures that they accepted Ellen White's ministry as vital to them."[46]

Use of Common Sources of Information

When God speaks to prophets He does not install a dictionary or an encyclopedia in their minds. Prophets take the inspired message and do their best to convey that message in language and thought forms that will do justice to the message. Some (such as Peter) needed others to help them with their grammar;[47] others (such as Luke) gathered as much as they could from contemporary sources in order to set forth the truth that burned within them.[48] Paul used contemporary writers to better establish contact with his Grecian audiences.[49]

Old Testament writers often depended on oral reports or earlier documents in preparing their messages. Moses did not need visions to describe the story of his birth or to recount the historical narratives he placed in Genesis. The books of Joshua and Judges were probably compiled during David's monarchy, according to internal evidence. The authors of Kings and Chronicles obviously used sources that they often referenced. In fact, the authors at times quoted from other Old Testament books without crediting their sources: compare 2 Kings 19:1,

2 with Isaiah 37:1, 2, and 1 Chron. 10:1-3 with 1 Sam. 31:1-3.[50]

The New Testament presents many instances of borrowing from nonBiblical sources, such as the Wisdom of Solomon,[51] 1 Enoch,[52] *Testimonies of the Twelve Patriarchs,*[53] and the Palestinian Targums.[54]

Ellen White forthrightly explained why she used various historians as she traced "the history of the controversy in past ages." She wrote: "In pursuance of this purpose, I have endeavored to select and group together events in the history of the church in such a manner as to trace the unfolding of the great testing truths that at different periods have been given to the world."[55]

How did she use these historians? She noted: "In some cases where a historian has so grouped together events as to afford, in brief, a comprehensive view of the subject, or has summarized details in a convenient manner, his words have been quoted; but in some instances no specific credit has been given, since the quotations are not given for the purpose of citing that writer as authority, but because his statement affords a ready and forcible presentation of the subject. In narrating the experience and views of those carrying forward the work of reform in our own time, similar use has been made of their published works."[56]

As all prophets did, Ellen White had to supply the human language to convey the grand thoughts and arching panoramas that she either saw in vision or sensed in other times of divine communication. Her capacity to supply appropriate language and style matured as the years went by—as any study of her personal manuscripts and published writings will indicate. At times she recognized that others had written with beauty and precision on certain subjects that she wanted to make clearer in her writings. To better clothe those divinely revealed truths she utilized borrowed expressions. Speed truth along with as much human grace as possible was her compelling motivation.

Some have raised two questions regarding both Biblical writers and Ellen White: How does borrowing affect the authority of the writer? Does the borrowed material become inspired? The questions arise because inspiration is misunderstood as mechanical dictation (verbal inspiration).

Probably the two questions would not be asked if it were understood that prophets are permitted to find the best methods at their disposal to convey the thoughts God has given them.[57]

What, then, is the value of the borrowed material? It seems logical that if God revealed His message to prophets, He would also assist them in conveying the message in human language. Ellen White noted that God "guided the mind in the selection of what to speak and what to write. The treasure was entrusted to earthen vessels, yet it is, nonetheless, from Heaven."[58]

In a way, God did not expect the Biblical writer to "reinvent the wheel." He led Paul to borrow from the apocrypha in developing a substantial part of Romans 1. He led him to find useful material, at least to hearers in his day, in the Jewish Targums (Aramaic translation or paraphrase of a portion of the Old Testament) in developing 1 Corinthians 10:1-4 and 2 Timothy 3:8. He led John to find generous help from contemporary sources such as the Targums and 1 Enoch. If the language already available seemed to help the Biblical author to speed his message preparation along, he prudently borrowed for his purpose. No doubt many of his contemporaries recognized quickly from where the writer had borrowed his material. To the receivers of the prophet's message, such borrowing was no problem: they saw the big picture of the writer's message.

Likely many in Christ's day recognized His references to extraBiblical sources that He used to develop His messages—messages that were truly original.

But His use of sources had nothing to do with the authority or originality of His messages.[59]

Does borrowed material become inspired? Only in the sense that it assists the writer to state his message more clearly. This may lead to another question: Why did not Paul and John give credit to the authors of the borrowed material? Perhaps they believed, as did Ellen White, that "every gleam of thought, every flash of intellect, is from the Light of the world."[60] This conviction that God is the Author of all truth may have been one reason for not feeling the need to reference their frequent borrowings.

Distinguishing Between the Sacred and the Common

Prophets obviously mix common, everyday information with the divine message. When Paul referred to contemporaries with appreciation, that was not the divine message. When he asked Timothy to find the cloak and books that he had left at Troas and to "come before winter," that was common, everyday talk (2 Tim. 4:9-21). When we read the genealogy of the families of Israel since Adam, we are reading common historical information, not a message given by revelation. (1 Chron. 1-8).

Ellen White recognized this distinction between ordinary information and the divine message: "There are times when common things must be stated, common thoughts must occupy the mind, common letters must be written and information given that has passed from one to another of the workers. Such words, such information, are not given under the special inspiration of the Spirit of God. Questions are asked at times that are not upon religious subjects at all, and these questions must be answered. We converse about houses and lands, trades to be made, and locations for our institutions, their advantages and disadvantages."[61]

This distinction appeared in a 1909 letter where Ellen White was "troubled" about the former manager of the Paradise Valley Sanitarium, E. S. Ballenger. She wrote that Ballenger was "denying the testimonies as a whole because of what seems to him an inconsistency—a statement made by me in regard to the number of rooms in the Paradise Valley Sanitarium." In an earlier letter she had commented that the sanitarium had forty rooms, when it had only thirty-eight.

She continued: "The information given concerning the number of rooms in the Paradise Valley Sanitarium was given, not as a revelation from the Lord, but simply as a human opinion. There has never been revealed to me the exact number of rooms in any of our sanitariums; and the knowledge I have obtained of such things I have gained by inquiring of those who were supposed to know. . . . For one to mix the sacred with the common is a great mistake. In a tendency to do this we may see the working of the enemy to destroy souls."[62]

Students of prophetic writings should know how to separate the sacred from the common. Sometimes the question is asked in terms of what is inspired and what is not. (Obviously the distinction should not be based on whether we agree with a particular portion of a prophet's writings.) The 1909 incident regarding rooms at the Paradise Valley Sanitarium is one example of a "common" reference. Other examples are found in Mrs. White's hundreds of letters wherein she spoke of the weather, shopping lists, the garden, or her grandchildren. But sooner or later she would direct the reader's thought to his or her spiritual needs or some church activity. That shift would be a clear signal to readers that they were now listening to a message that went beyond "common" themes.

Only a small percentage of Ellen White's published writings deal with "common" topics, as anyone may readily see. She could write: "'In these letters which I write, in the testimonies I bear, I am presenting to you that which the Lord has presented to me. I do not write one article in the paper expressing merely my own ideas. They are what God has opened before me in vision—the precious rays of light shining from the throne.' It is true concerning the articles in our papers and in the many volumes of my books."[63]

Mrs. White makes no distinction between the inspiration of her books, articles, or letters when they are giving spiritual counsel. This eliminates the position some have made that only her books are inspired. Those taking that position forget that much in her books was first written in article form.[64]

Further, it is clearly the case that Bible writers "mixed" extraBiblical sources with their vision-based messages. One cannot then dismiss a prophet's work simply because some portion of the book contains material from sources other than divine revelation. If prophets include the writings of others to better express truth, that material is not understood as merely "common" in the sense we have been using the term.

Endnotes

1. Raoul Dederen, "Introduction to Hermeneutics," ed., Gordon M. Hyde, A Symposium on Biblical Hermeneutics (Washington, D. C.: Biblical Research Institute, 1974), pp. 1, 2.
2. *Thoughts From the Mount of Blessing,* p. 1.
3. For a study of the rules of hermeneutics, see Gerhard F. Hasel, "Principles of Biblical Interpretation," Gordon M. Hyde, editor, *A Symposium on Biblical Hermeneutics* (Washington D.C.: Biblical Research Institute, General Conference of Seventh-day Adventists, 1974), pp. 163-193; Miroslav M. Kis, "Biblical Interpretation and Moral Authority," *Journal of the Adventist Theological Society,* Autumn, 1995, pp. 52-62. George R. Knight, *Reading Ellen White: How to Understand and Apply Her Writings,* (Hagerstown, Md., Review and Herald Publishing Association, 1997).
4. First-century Quintilian, a master in the history of persuasive theory, wrote: "We must take care, not that it shall be possible for him [reader or hearer] to understand, but that it shall be utterly impossible for him not to understand!"—*The Institutio Oratorio of Quintilian,* book VIII, chap. 2, Nos. 23, 24 (translated by John A. Broadus, *On the Preparation of Sermons,* Revised Edition by Jesse Burton Weatherspoon (New York: Harper and Brothers, 1944), p. 241.
5. "This does not mean . . . that the original author or the original audience fully understood God's purpose in sharing the future with them. But what God would say to *us* about the end [of the world] will not contradict what He said to *them.* . . . To read these texts as though they were written *exclusively* for us is to launch ourselves into a bizarre journey that may appear Biblical, but will in fact lead us far from the truth."—Jon Paulien, *What the Bible Says About the End-Time* (Hagerstown, MD: Review and Herald Publishing Association, 1994), p. 36.
6. "Explaining Scripture by Scripture . . . was the great principle of the Reformation."—D'Aubigné, *History of the Reformation,* p. 501.
7. We can be thankful that Ellen White lived in an age prior to the extensive use of telephones, E-mail, and the delete button on a computer. What normally would be transmitted today by a short telephone call, required a written document.
8. See pp. 16, 120, 173, 421.
9. *Selected Messages,* book 1, p. 17.
10. *Ibid.,* p. 20.
11. *Ibid.,* p. 18.
12. *Ibid.,* p. 19.
13. *Ibid.*
14. Ms 24, 1891, cited in *MR,* vol. 19, p. 253.
15. *The Desire of Ages,* p. 302. "The perception and appreciation of truth, He said [John 7:17], depends less upon the mind than upon the heart. Truth must be received into the soul; it claims the homage of the will. If truth could be submitted to the reason alone, pride would be no hindrance in the way of its reception. But it is to be received through the work of grace in the heart; and its reception depends upon the renunciation of every sin that the Spirit of God reveals."—*Ibid.,* p. 455. See also pp. 312, 313.
16. Ms 4, 1896, cited in *MR,* vol. 4, p. 56. Jon Paulien, in beginning a list of hermeneutical principles, wrote: "*Pray earnestly for a learning attitude and an openness to the leading of the Holy Spirit whenever you pick up the Bible for deep study.* Without prayer and the enlightenment of the Holy Spirit, the work of even the finest scholar may go subtly astray. God's ideas are not naturally mastered by secular minds. I have found the following prayer helpful: 'Lord, help me find the truth on this subject, no matter what the cost.' Knowing the truth will cost you something, but it is well worth the sacrifice to understand God's mind."—*What the Bible Says About the End-Time,* p. 37. (See also Jon Paulien, "The Interpreter's Use of the Writings of Ellen G. White," Frank B. Holbrook, ed., *Symposium on Revelation,* Book 1, (Silver Spring, MD: Biblical Research Institute, General Conference of Seventh-day Adventists, 1992.)
17. "Without the enlightenment of the Spirit, men will not be able to distinguish truth from error, and they will fall under the masterful temptations of Satan."—*Christ's Object Lessons,* p. 411.
18. "Whenever men are not seeking, in word and deed to be in harmony with God, then however learned they may be, they are liable to err in their understanding of Scripture, and it is not safe to trust to their explanations." —*Testimonies,* vol. 5, p. 705. "Belief is not an intellectual act; belief is a moral act whereby I deliberately commit myself. . . . Belief must be the *will* to believe." —Chambers, *My Utmost for His Highest,* p. 265.
19. "We cannot hold that a position once taken, an idea

once advocated, is not, under any circumstances, to be relinquished. There is but One who is infallible." —*Testimonies to Ministers,* p. 105.

20. "In every age there is a new development of truth, a message of God to the people of that generation. The old truths are all essential; new truth is not independent of the old, but an unfolding of it. It is only as the old truths are understood that we can comprehend the new." —*Christ's Object Lessons,* p. 127; "Although great and talented authors have made known wonderful truths, and have presented increased light to the people, still in our day we shall find new ideas."—*Review and Herald,* June 3, 1890.
21. "One will arise, and still another, with new light, which contradicts the light that God has given under the demonstration of His Holy Spirit. . . . We are not to receive the words of those who come with a message that contradicts the special points of our faith. They gather together a mass of Scripture and pile it as proof around their asserted theories. This has been done over and over again during the past fifty years. And while the Scriptures are God's Word, and are to be respected, the application of them, if such application moves one pillar of the foundation that God has sustained these fifty years, is a great mistake."—*Selected Messages,* book 1, p. 161.
22. Letter 83, 1890, cited in *MR,* vol. 9, p. 330.
23. See pp. 16, 120, 173, 421.
24. *Selected Messages,* book 1, pp. 19-21. "Men will often say such an expression is not like God. But God has not put Himself in words, in logic, in rhetoric, on trial in the Bible. The writers of the Bible were God's penmen, not His pen."—*Ibid.,* p. 21.
25. *Ibid.,* p. 22.
26. *Ibid.,* p. 20. "Written in different ages, by men who differed widely in rank and occupation, and in mental and spiritual endowments, the books of the Bible present a wide contrast in style, as well as a diversity in the nature of the subjects unfolded. Different forms of expression are employed by different writers; often the same truth is more strikingly presented by one than by another. And as several writers present a subject under varied aspects and relations, there may appear, to the superficial, careless, or prejudiced reader, to be discrepancy or contradiction, where the thoughtful, reverent student, with clearer insight, discerns the underlying harmony."—*Ibid.,* p. 25. Gottfried Oosterwal noted: "Whenever God reveals Himself He does so in the cultural dress of the people who are the recipients of His message. . . . Though it takes on the diverse forms of human culture, God's truth itself comes from outside that culture. It sometimes stands above it, sometimes over against it. But whether in or above or over against culture, it always transcends it. Revelation and culture, integrated as they are, relate to each other as substance to shadow, meaning to form, content to the vessel that carries it."—"Gospel, Culture, and Mission," *Ministry,* October, 1989, p. 22. See also Niels-Erik Andreasen, "From Vision to Prophecy," *Adventist Review,* Jan. 28, 1982.
27. *Selected Messages,* book 1, p. 20.
28. *The Great Controversy,* p. vi.
29. Richard Rice wrote: "The divine-human character of Scripture is incompatible with the idea that the Bible is a mixture of the human and the divine. The Bible has a variegated texture. . . . The differences have led people to conclude that certain parts of the Bible are divinely inspired, while others are merely human, so we can get the pure Word of God by separating the two.

    "But the two aspects of Scripture, the divine and the human, are inseparable. The Bible is not a combination of the words of God and the words of men. It expresses the word of God *in* the words of men. Eliminate the human and you will also eliminate the divine.

    "The union of divine and human in the Bible is a little like the genetic combination of two parents in a child. Some things about a child remind you of its mother. In other ways, it resembles the father. But there is no way to separate the two without doing violence to the person involved."—*The Reign of God,* (Berrien Springs, Mich.: Andrews University Press, 1985), p. 26.
30. *The Great Controversy,* p. vi.
31. *Ibid.*
32. *Selected Messages,* book 1, pp. 24-31.
33. *Selected Messages,* book 1, pp. 16, 20. "Defining inspiration is like catching a rainbow. When we have put forth our best efforts, there will remain an elusive factor, an element of mystery. Inspired writings may be known, but never fully grasped. Instead, they grasp us—for through them God speaks to humanity."—William G. Johnsson, "How Does God Speak?" *Ministry,* October 1981.
34. *Selected Messages,* book 1, p. 37. "God and heaven alone are infallible."—*Ibid.*
35. Sabbatarian Anabaptists in the 1520s asserted that the Old and New Testaments were indivisible. "In this view they were far in advance of their time."—Gerhard Hasel, "Sabbatarian Anabaptists of the Sixteenth Century: Part II," *Andrews University Seminary Studies,* 6 (1968), p. 28.
36. *The Great Controversy,* p. 243.
37. *Ibid.,* p. 249; see also pp. 89, 291, 596. "[Luther] firmly declared that Christians should receive no other doctrines than those which rest on the authority of the Sacred Scriptures. These words struck at the very foundation of papal supremacy. They contained the vital principle of the Reformation."—*Ibid.,* p. 126.
38. *Ibid.,* p. 186.
39. *Early Writings,* p. 78 (1851).
40. *Bio.,* vol. 6, p. 197. In 1898, recounting the Newcastle evangelistic meetings in N.S.W., Australia, Ellen White wrote: "We do not conceal our banner of truth at all. We let them know that we are Seventh-day Adventists because we believe the Bible. The Bible and the Bible only is the foundation of our faith. Before these meetings close, the people will know from the Scriptures why we are a peculiar people. The Word is the foundation of our faith."—*Ibid.,* vol. 4, p. 374.
41. Damsteegt, "Ellen White on Theology," *Journal of the Adventist Theological Society,* Autumn, 1993, p. 129.
42. "The Bible must be your counselor. Study it and the testimonies God has given; for they never contradict His Word."—*Selected Messages,* book 3, p. 32; "If the *Testimonies* speak not according to this word of God, reject them. Christ and Belial cannot be united." —*Testimonies,* vol. 5, p. 691.
43. "Even the work of the Holy Spirit upon the heart is to be tested by the Word of God. The Spirit which inspired the Scriptures, always leads to the Scriptures." —*General Conference Daily Bulletin,* April 13, 1891, cited in *Selected Messages,* book 1, p. 43.
44. "In ancient times God spoke to men by the mouth of prophets and apostles. In these days He speaks to them by the testimonies of His Spirit. There was never

a time when God instructed His people more earnestly than He instructs them now concerning His will and the course that He would have them pursue."—*Testimonies*, vol. 5, p. 661.

45. *Review and Herald*, April 21, 1851; see also *Ibid.*, Feb. 28, 1856.
46. Roy Graham, "How the Gift of Prophecy Relates to God's Word," *Adventist Review*, Oct. 14, 1982. "During the ages while the Scriptures of both the Old and the New Testament were being given, the Holy Spirit did not cease to communicate light to individual minds, apart from the revelations to be embodied in the Sacred Canon. The Bible itself relates how, through the Holy Spirit, men received warning, reproof, counsel, and instruction, in matters in no way relating to the giving of the Scriptures. And mention is made of prophets in different ages, of whose utterances nothing is recorded. In like manner, after the close of the canon of the Scripture, the Holy Spirit was still to continue its work, to enlighten, warn, and comfort the children of God." —*The Great Controversy*, p. viii.
47. See pp. 14, 15. For Ellen White's use of copy editors, see p. 109.
48. Ellen White reached out to contemporaries to help her with dates and other information. At times she sent out a manuscript draft on autobiographical material to friends who "were present when the circumstances related occurred, for their examination before they were put in print." If they found "incorrect statements in this book, they will immediately inform me."—*Selected Messages*, book 3, p. 58. See p. 111.
49. For examples of Paul using extraBiblical sources, see comments on Acts 17:28; 1 Cor.15:32; and Titus 1:12, in *SDABC*, vol. 6.
50. For a careful review of extraBiblical sources, see Delmer A. Johnson, "The Sources of Inspired Writings," *Adventist Review*, Dec. 30, 1982.
51. Compare Romans 1:20-31; 9:20-22 and Wisdom of Solomon—C. H. Dodd, "The Epistle of Paul to the Romans," in *Moffatt's New Testament Commentary*. James Moffatt, ed. (London: Hodder and Stoughton, 1932), VI, p. 27; Bruce M. Metzger, *An Introduction to the Apocrypha* (New York: Oxford University Press, 1957), p. 160.
52. Compare many references in Rom., 2 Cor., Eph., Col., 1 and 2 Thess., 1 Tim., Heb., Jude, and Rev. with 1 Enoch—Leonard Rost, *Judaism Outside the Hebrew Canon* (Nashville, Tenn.: Abingdon, 1976), p. 200; R. H. Charles, *The Apocrypha and Pseudepigrapha of the Old Testament* (Oxford: Clarendon Press, 1913), II, p. 180.
53. R. H. Charles, *The Testaments of the Twelve Patriarchs*, (London: SPCK, 1925), p. 39.
54. William Barclay, *The Letters to the Corinthians* (Philadelphia: The Westminster Press, 1975), p. 88; Martin McNamara, *The New Testament and the Palestinian Targum to the Pentateuch* (Rome: Pontifical Biblical Institute, 1966), pp. 83, 85. Sylvester Q. Case provided a useful review of some of these extraBiblical sources in an unpublished paper, "When a Prophet Borrows From ExtraBiblical Sources: A Brief Survey of Biblical Evidence," Andrews University, 1982.
55. *The Great Controversy*, p. xi.
56. *Ibid.*, pp. xi, xii. References to those "in our own time" would include such works as those of J. N. Andrews and Uriah Smith.
57. See pp. 16, 120, 173, 375, 376, 421. Harold Lindsell wrote: "When we say the Bible is the Word of God, it makes no difference whether the writers of Scripture gained their information by direct revelation from God as in the case of the Book of Revelation, or whether they researched matters as Luke did, or whether they got their knowledge from extant sources, court records, or even by word of mouth. The question we must ask is whether what they wrote, wherever they may have secured their knowledge, can be trusted." —*The Battle for the Bible* (Grand Rapids, Mich.: Zondervan Publishing House, 1976), p. 20. Robert Nicole stated: "If God did not guide the sacred writers in the choice of the material that they decided to incorporate into their own text, then it will be forever impossible to distinguish between what is truly God's Word and what may be simply an accurate record of a fallible source. To the extent that any material appears endorsed by the sacred writer, it must be viewed as endorsed by God as well."—*Inerrancy and Common Sense*, (Grand Rapids, Mich.: Baker Book House, 1980), p. 89.
58. *The Great Controversy*, pp. vi, vii.
59. For a study of the relationship between Jewish rabbinic parables and Christ's parables, see Harvey K. McArthur & Robert M. Johnston, *They Also Taught in Parables*, (Grand Rapids, Mich.: Zondervan Publishing House, 1990). "The originality of Christ's teaching, which is abundantly clear from the Gospel records, did not prevent Him from incorporating into His teaching much that was good in what earlier teachers had taught."—W. D. E. Oesterley, *The Testament of the Twelve Patriarchs* (London: SPCK, 1925), p. xxi.
60. *Education*, p. 14.
61. *Selected Messages*, book 1, p. 39.
62. *Ibid.*, p. 38.
63. *Selected Messages*, book 1, p. 29.
64. In 1897 Ellen White wrote from Australia to John Wessels in South Africa, suggesting that he come to Australia to help in establishing the sanitarium work. The letter included matters that she had been shown regarding his family, but some things she had not been shown, and she made this clear: "I have not been given the message 'Send for Brother John Wessels to come to Australia.' No; therefore I do not say, I know that this is the place for you. But it is my privilege to express my wishes, even though I say, I speak not by commandment. But I do not want you to come because of any persuasion of mine. I want you to seek the Lord most earnestly, and then follow where He shall lead you. I want you to come when God says Come, not one moment before. Nevertheless, it is my privilege to present the wants of the cause of God in Australia. . . . A work is to be done here, and if you are not the one to do it, I shall feel perfectly resigned to hear that you have gone to some other locality. I have been shown that it were better for you and the other members of your mother's family to be in some other locality, because where they are, the companionship and associations are not the most favorable to their spiritual healthfulness."—Letter 129, 1897, parts of which may be found in *Selected Messages*, book 3, pp. 58, 59. Here we have a good example where Ellen White clearly differentiated between her opinion and revealed information, similar to Paul's experience as noted in 1 Cor. 7:6.

Study Questions

1. What is a simple definition for "hermeneutics"?

2. How do you distinguish between knowing what a writer "meant" and what his writings "mean" today?

3. What five suggestions did Ellen White give regarding the "right attitude" one must have when studying truth?

4. How would you define the difference between "verbal" and "thought" inspiration?

5. How is a reader to distinguish between "common/secular" and "inspired" material in a prophet's writings?

6. How did the Protestant Reformers use the phrase, "The Bible and the Bible only"? How did Ellen White use it?

7. How do the following terms differ: "infallibility," "inspired," "revelation," and "illumination"?

CHAPTER 33

Hermeneutics/2
Basic Rules of Interpretation—Internal

"The work of explaining the Bible by the Bible itself is the work that should be done by all our ministers who are fully awake to the times in which we live."[1]

In her personally written introduction to *The Great Controversy*, Ellen White recorded how "the scenes of the long-continued conflict between good and evil" had been revealed to her: "From time to time I have been permitted to behold the working, in different ages, of the great controversy between Christ . . . and Satan."[2]

How Prophets View History

How did she "behold" these mighty scenes? She continued: "As the Spirit of God has opened to my mind the great truths of His word, and the scenes of the past and the future, I have been bidden to make known to others that which has thus been revealed."[3]

How much detail did she see? The evidence is that she saw the great "scenes" but that the details involving dates, perhaps even geographical sites, she did not always "see." The same was true for Isaiah as he struggled for words to describe the throne of God (Isaiah 6) and for Daniel as he tried to describe the awesome visions of beasts and horns, etc. Ellen White saw the big picture, the basic concepts, the overall sweep of the forces of good and evil played out in human history. Her task was to "fill in" this big picture through research in the Biblical story and in common sources of historical information.

Just as God did not give Daniel words to describe the beasts of Daniel 7, so He did not give Ellen White the historical dates and events to fill in the great controversy story. Even as Luke searched out the best sources to complete his Life of Christ (Luke 1:1-4), so Mrs. White did what all prophets do when they had a message that had to be conveyed in human words and comprehended by historically oriented men and women. Thus, we look to Luke, not necessarily for historical accuracy for all statements made, but for his contribution to the big picture, the message about the ministry of Jesus.[4]

Possible Discrepancies

Would there be instances of possible errors? Probably. Henry Alford, the highly respected author of *New Testament for English Readers,* wrote: "Two men may be equally led by the Holy Spirit to record the events of our Lord's life for our edification, though one may believe, and record, that the visit to the Gadarenes took place before the calling of Matthew, while the other places it after that event; though one in narrating it speaks of two demoniacs—the other, only of one. . . .

"And not only of the *arrangement* of the Evangelic history are these remarks to be understood. There are certain minor points of accuracy or inaccuracy, of which human research suffices to inform men, and on which, from want of that research, it is often the practice to speak vaguely and inexactly. Such are sometimes the conventionally received distances from place to place; such are the common accounts of phenomena in natural history, etc. Now in matters of this kind, the Evangelists and Apostles were not supernaturally informed, but left, in common with others, to the guidance of their natural faculties. . . . The treasure is ours, in all its richness: but it is ours as only it can be ours—in the imperfections of human speech, in the limitations of human thought, in the variety incident first to individual character, and then to manifold transcription and the lapse of ages."[5]

In other words, the human phase of the divine-human communication system will be beset with occasional discrepancies—simply because of human finiteness. Stephen's eloquent sermon (Acts 7) contains an incidental reference to the number (75) of Jacob's family who went into Egypt to live with Joseph. However, the Genesis reference (46:27) states that 70 of Jacob's family went into Egypt. What shall we make of this difference? If we believe that Genesis is the only historical source that Jews in the first century had for this information, then we simply understand that the Holy Spirit (the Spirit of Prophecy) guided Stephen in reciting the big picture, but did not intervene on details. Prophets do not necessarily become "authorities" on historical data. Their inspirational value lies in their messages, not in some of the details that are incidental to the big picture.

W. C. White's 1911 Statement

Addressing a General Conference Council in 1911, W. C. White gave a "statement regarding the latest English edition of 'Great Controversy.'"[6] If this 1911 statement had been more fully studied and more broadly published, it might have prevented much misunderstanding through the years regarding how prophets work with historical materials.

This statement not only explains the changes in the 1911 edition of *The Great Controversy,* it also reveals the mind of Ellen White as to how she, and other prophets, did their work.

W. C. White said: "Mother has never claimed to be authority on history. The things which she has written out, are descriptions of flashlight pictures and other representations given her regarding the actions of men, and the influence of these actions upon the work of God for the salvation of men, with views of past, present, and future history in its relation to this work. In connection with the writing out of these views, she has made use of good and clear historical statements to help make plain to the reader the things which she is endeavoring to present. When I was a mere boy, I heard her read D'Aubigné's 'History of the Reformation' to my father. . . . She has read other histories of the Reformation. This has helped her to locate and describe many of the events and the movements presented to her in vision. This is somewhat similar to the way in which the study of the Bible helps her to locate and describe the many figurative representations given to her regarding the development of the great controversy in our day between truth and error.

No Claim to Verbal Inspiration

"Mother has never laid claim to verbal inspiration, and I do not find that my father, or Elder Bates, Andrews, Smith, or Waggoner put forth this claim. If there were verbal inspiration in writing her manuscripts, why should there be on her part the work of addition or adaptation? It is a fact that Mother often takes one of her manuscripts, and goes over it thoughtfully, making additions that develop the thought still further. . . .

"Mother's contact with European people had brought to her mind scores of things that had been presented to her in vision during past years, some of them two or three times, and other scenes many times. Her seeing of historic places and her contact with the people refreshed her memory with reference to these things, and so she desired to add much material to the book [*The Great Controversy*]."[7]

A few months later, W. C. White wrote to S. N. Haskell, a stalwart pioneer who leaned dangerously toward a verbal-inspiration viewpoint at that time: "Regarding Mother's writings, she has never wished our brethren to treat them as authority on the dates or details of history. When 'Great Controversy' was written, she oftentimes gave a partial description of some scene presented to her, and when Sister Davis made inquiry regarding time and place, Mother referred to what was already written in the books of [Uriah] Smith and in secular histories. When 'Controversy' was written, Mother never thought that the readers would take it as authority on historical dates and use it to settle controversies, and she does not now feel that it ought to be used in that way . . . .

Chronology

"It seems to me that there is a danger of placing altogether too much stress upon chronology. If it had been essential to the salvation of men that he [human beings] should have a clear and harmonious understanding of the chronology of the world, the Lord would not have permitted the disagreements and discrepancies which we find in the writings of the Bible historians, and it seems to me that in these last days there ought not to be so much controversy regarding dates. . . . I believe, Brother Haskell, that there is danger of our injuring Mother's work by claiming for it more than she claims for it, more than Father ever claimed for it, more than Elder [J. N.] Andrews, [J. H.] Waggoner, or [Uriah] Smith ever claimed for it."[8]

That same day, W. C. White wrote a virtually identical letter to W. W. Eastman, publishing director at the Southern Publishing Association. But in closing the letter, he added: "I have overwhelming evidence and conviction that they are the descriptions and delineation of what God has revealed to her in vision, and where she has followed the description[s] of historians or the expositions of Adventist writers, I believe that God has given her discernment to use that which is correct and in harmony with truth regarding all matters essential to salvation. If it should be found by faithful study that she has followed some exposition of prophecy which in some detail regarding dates we cannot harmonize with our understanding of secular history, it does not influence my confidence in her writings as a whole any more than my confidence in the Bible is influenced by the fact that I cannot harmonize many of the [Biblical] statements regarding chronology."[9]

In summary, for verbal inspirationists Ellen White's writings, unfortunately, have become an authority on historical dates and places. For thought inspirationists, that would be an unwarranted use of a prophet's work. Thought inspirationists focus on the big picture, the message; possible discrepancies in historical detail are considered incidental to the message, and of minor importance.

Basic Rules of Interpretation

Everyone wants to be understood. Often misunderstandings arise when a statement has been lifted out of context. Thus, everyone who has been misunderstood appeals to fairness and asks that the context be considered. Context includes both internal and external clues that will establish the truth about any statement under consideration.

Internally, we usually get a clear picture of "what" an author meant by reading the words, sentences, paragraphs, even chapters, surrounding a puzzling statement. Externally, we ask further questions that may help us to understand, such as when? where? why? and perhaps how? "Time," "place," and "circumstances" apply to the external context as we shall soon see.

Internal evidence:

• **Rule One:** *Recognize that the Bible and the writings of Ellen White are the product of thought inspiration, not verbal inspiration—as described in the previous chapter.*

• **Rule Two:** *Recognize that some word-definitions may change as time passes.* For example, hundreds of words in the King James Version (1611) of the Bible have changed in meaning or have acquired such new meanings that they no longer convey the meaning that the King James translators intended to convey. Casual readers would surely misunderstand certain Bible texts if they were not aware of these serious changes in word meanings.[10]

Word-change definitions have already occurred in the writings of Ellen White. How often have readers been confused with: "It is the *nicest* work ever assumed by men and women to deal with youthful minds"?[11] When Mrs. White used these words later in another setting, she saw the problem and elaborated: "This work is the nicest, the most difficult, ever committed to human beings."[12] What was going on? In the nineteenth century, "nice" was often used, as the dictionary indicates, to mean "exacting in requirements or standards . . . marked by, or demanding great or excessive precision and delicacy."[13]

Another word that has assumed a definition today that was not primary in the nineteenth century is "intercourse." For hundreds of years "intercourse" meant "dealings between people," or "the exchange of thoughts and feelings." Today it is most frequently used in reference to sexual contact, a use that was never meant in the hundreds of occasions Ellen White employed this word.[14]

• **Rule Three***: Understand the use of hyperbole.* Hyperbole is the use of obvious exaggeration to make a point. John used hyperbole when he said that if all the acts of Jesus were written, "the world itself could not contain the books" (John 21:25). Hyperbole is a literary device used throughout the Bible.[15]

Ellen White used the ratio 1 in 20 at least five times, and 1 in 100 at least twenty-one times. She did not say 1 in 13 or 1 in 99, etc. She may have used hyperbole when she wrote: "It is a solemn statement that I make to the church, that not one in twenty whose names are registered upon the church books are prepared to close their earthly history, and would be as verily without God and without hope in the world as the common sinner."[16]

• **Rule Four:** *Understand the meaning of the phrase in which a word is used.* In 1862 Ellen White wrote that Satan works through the channels of phrenology, psychology, and mesmerism.[17] But does this mean that *all* psychology is evil? Obviously not, because in 1897 she pointed out that "the true principles of psychology are found in the Holy Scriptures."[18] Similarly, we might note that television can be a channel through which Satan works, but Satan's use of television does not make television evil. Psychology, the study of the human mind and how it matures, is a proper study for Christians—if the presuppositions are Biblical and not humanistic.

• **Rule Five***: Recognize the possibility of imprecise expressions.* In 1861 Ellen White penned a thought that seems inconsistent with later statements on the same subject: "Phrenology and mesmerism are very much exalted. They are good in their place, but they are seized upon by Satan as his most powerful agents to deceive and destroy souls."[19] In an 1884 *Signs* article, she wrote: "The sciences which treat of the human mind are very much exalted. They are good in their place; but they are seized upon by Satan as his powerful agents to deceive and destroy souls."[20]

Obviously, in this 1884 statement we

have an editorial correction in the thought that Ellen White wanted conveyed regarding "the sciences which treat of the human mind." Possibly the 1861 statement referring to phrenology and mesmerism was a printer's error. More probably it was a general statement, corrected later, that reflected the commonly used terms for psychology in the mid-nineteenth century. Many books dealing with physical and mental health included chapters devoted to phrenology, psychology, and mesmerism, or advertised other works that focused on these modalities.

• **Rule Six**: *Look carefully at the immediate context* (that is, the same paragraph or page) for clarification of a statement that seems, at first glance, to be troublesome. For example, some people are confused about Ellen White's admonition that we "should never be taught to say, or feel, that they are saved."[21] This caution was meant to warn of the erroneous doctrine of "once saved, always saved" that was, and is, prevalent among most evangelical Christians.

But this warning was given within the larger context of explaining Peter's self-confidence that led to His tragic denial of his Lord on that Thursday night. She wrote: "Never can we safely put confidence in self, or feel, this side of heaven, that we are secure against temptation. [Then comes the often misunderstood statement] This is misleading. Everyone should be taught to cherish hope and faith; but even when we give ourselves to Christ and know that He accepts us, we are not beyond the reach of temptation. . . . Our only safety is in constant distrust of self, and dependence on Christ."[22]

Another example of the importance of context is found in Ellen White's assertion that "God's servants today could not work by means of miracles, because spurious works of healing, claiming to be divine, will be wrought."[23] This statement seems at variance with the Adventist position that "all" of the spiritual gifts given to the Christian church (1 Cor. 12 and Eph. 4) will continue to the end of time (1 Cor. 1:7). Further, this statement seems to contradict Ellen White's own comments that in the last days "miracles will be wrought, the sick will be healed, and signs and wonders will follow the believers."[24] How do we understand all this?

The seeming contradiction arises when one does not read the whole page carefully.[25] Ellen White made two points: First, she spoke to present conditions specifically: In referring to "miraculous works of healing," she said that "we cannot *now* work in this way" (emphasis supplied). Further, "God's servants *today* could not work by means of miracles" (emphasis supplied).

Secondly, she was setting forth the Lord's instruction *for the present time*: The "work of physical healing, combined with the teaching of the word" would be best done in the establishment of "sanitariums" where "workers . . . will carry forward genuine medical missionary work. . . . This is the provision the Lord has made whereby gospel medical missionary work is to be done for many souls."[26] In other words, *at the present time*, distinguished by many instances of false miracles of healing, God's work of healing can best be done within the sanitarium program of intelligent teaching regarding the cause and cure of disease.

Another "misquote" asserts that it is a "sin to laugh," using the quotation, "Christ often wept but never was known to laugh. . . . Imitate the divine, unerring Pattern." From what we know of Jesus in the Bible, that statement sounds strange. After all, why would children surround Him enthusiastically! Then we notice the ellipsis. Something is missing.

We check the passage and the context. Here Ellen White is counseling a church member who "has not seen the necessity of educating herself in carefulness of words and acts. . . . My sister, you talk too much. . . . your tongue has done much mischief. . . . Your tongue has kindled a fire, and you have enjoyed the conflagration. . . .You sport and joke and enter into hilarity and glee. . . . Christ is our example. . . . Christ often wept but never was known to laugh. I do not say it is a sin to laugh on any occasion, but we cannot go astray if we imitate the divine, unerring Pattern. . . . As we view the world bound in darkness and trammeled by Satan, how can we engage in levity, glee, careless, reckless words, speaking at random, laughing, jesting, and joking?. . . Christian cheerfulness is not condemned by the Scriptures, but reckless talking is censured."[27]

Here we note that the context puts a new cast on the misquote. "Laugh" in this context meant inappropriate recklessness of speech and behavior, a jesting and joking that had "shown a lack of wisdom in using the truth in a manner to raise opposition, arouse combativeness, and make war instead of possessing a spirit of peace and true humbleness of mind."[28] Ellen White was not condemning appropriate laughter, as she clearly noted, but she put her counsel in a balanced perspective.

• **Rule Seven**: *Recognize that the meaning of a word can change when it is used in a new context.* The term "shut door" meant several things to ex-Millerite Adventists. To Ellen White it meant something different. James White and Joseph Bates redefined their use of the term between 1844 and 1852.[29]

Other words that Ellen White used may seem obsolete today, such as "office," which most often referred to the administrative offices of the publishing house, but sometimes to the General Conference headquarters.[30]

• **Rule Eight**: *Recognize that the challenge of semantics resides in all communication.* Words mean different things to different people, because of personal differences such as education, age level, spiritual experiences, geographic location, and gender. Ellen White spoke to this problem: "There are many who interpret that which I write in the light of their own preconceived opinions. . . . A division in understanding and diverse opinions is the sure result. How to write in a way to be understood by those to whom I address important matter is a problem I cannot solve. When I see that I am misunderstood by my brethren who know me best, I am assured that I must take more time in carefully expressing my thoughts upon paper, for the Lord gives me light which I dare not do otherwise than communicate; and a great burden is upon me."[31] For a writer, the task of avoiding misunderstanding is more difficult than merely trying to be understood, because the writer must consciously be aware of semantic problems.

Endnotes

1. Letter 276, 1907, cited in *Lift Him Up*, p. 115.
2. *The Great Controversy*, p. x.
3. *Ibid.*, p. xi.
4. For a study of various differences between Luke's story of Christ's ministry and those of Matthew and Mark, see George Rice, *Luke, a Plagiarist?* (Mountain View, Calif.: Pacific Press Publishing Association, 1983.)
5. Henry Alford, *The New Testament for English Readers* (London: Rivingtons, 1863, vol. 1), pp. 23-27.
6. This lengthy statement is found as Appendix A of *Selected Messages*, book 3, pp. 433-440. The statement was approved by Ellen White as presenting "the matter correctly and well."—Letter to F. M. Wilcox, July 25, 1911, cited in Wilcox, *The Testimony of Jesus*, p. 115.
7. *Selected Messages*, book 3, pp. 437, 438.
8. Jerry Allen Moon, *W. C. White and Ellen G. White, The Relationship Between the Prophet and Her Son* (Berrien Springs, Mich.: Andrews University Press, 1993), pp. 431, 432. At the end of this letter Ellen White penned in her own handwriting, "I approve of the remarks made in this letter."
9. *Ibid.*, p. 433. In a 1915 letter to F. M. Wilcox, editor of the church paper, White clarified the issue regarding his mother's being a historian or theologian: "Sister White, as a teacher of sacred truth, has not been led to a technical treatment of theological questions, but has [been] given such views of the love of God and the plan of salvation, and of man's duty to God and to his fellow men, that when presented to the people, arouse the conscience, and impress upon the hearer the saving truths of the Word of God. She says, 'The written testimonies are not to give new light, but to impress vividly upon the heart the truths of inspiration already revealed.'

   "In the technical sense of the word, Sister White is not a historian. She has not been a systematic student of history and chronology, and she has never intended that her works should be used to settle controversies over historical dates. But as one who relates history, one 'in whose work the character and spirit of an age is exhibited in miniature' [Macauley's *Essays*], she is a historian whose works teach valuable lessons from the past for the present and the future."—*Ibid.*, p. 434.

10. Examples comparing KJV with NKJV include: abroad—outside (Deut. 24:11), allege—demonstrate (Acts 17:3), anon—immediately or at once (Mark 1:30), bowels—heart (Gen. 43:40), by and by—immediately (Mark 6:25), charity—love (1 Cor. 13), communicate—share (Gal. 6:6), conversation—conduct (1 Pet. 3:1, 2), feeble-minded—fainthearted (1 Thess. 5:14), forwardness—willingness (2 Cor. 9:2), let—hindered (Rom. 1:13), meat—food (Matt. 6:25), nephew—grandsons (Judges 12:14), outlandish women—pagan women (Neh. 13:26), peculiar—special (Tit. 2:14), reins—hearts (Ps. 7:9), suffer—let (Matt. 19:14), vain—worthless (Judges 9:4), virtue—power (Luke 6:19), witty inventions—discretion (Prov. 8:12).
11. *Counsels to Parents, Teachers, and Students,* p. 73, emphasis added.
12. *Education,* p. 292.
13. *Webster's Ninth New Collegiate Dictionary* (Springfield, MA: Merriam-Webster Inc., Publishers, 1983).
14. "The disciples prayed with intense earnestness for a fitness to meet men and in their daily intercourse to speak words that would lead sinners to Christ."— *The Acts of the Apostles,* p. 37. "By social intercourse acquaintances are formed and friendships contracted which result in a unity of heart and an atmosphere of love which is pleasing in the sight of heaven."—*Messages to Young People,* p. 405.
15. Compare Ex. 9:6 with Isa. 19. The frequent use of "all" is often an example of Hebrew hyperbole.
16. *Christian Service,* p. 41 (1893).
17. *Review and Herald,* Feb. 18, 1862.
18. *My Life Today,* p. 176.
19. *Testimonies,* vol. 1, p. 296.
20. *Signs of the Times,* Nov. 6, 1884.
21. *Christ's Object Lessons,* p. 155.
22. *Ibid.* See also *Selected Messages,* book 1, p. 314.
23. *Medical Ministry,* p. 14.
24. *The Great Controversy,* p. 612; see also *Early Writings,* p. 278; *Testimonies,* vol. 9, p. 126.
25. *Medical Ministry,* p. 14.
26. *Ibid.*
27. Ms 11, 1868, cited in *MR,* vol. 18, pp. 368-370.
28. *Ibid.,* p. 369.
29. See pp. 554-565 for a study of the "shut door" issue.
30. See Volume 3 of the *Comprehensive Index to the Writings of Ellen G. White,* pp. 3185-3188, for "Glossary of Obsolete and Little Used Words and Terms with Altered Meanings."
31. *Selected Messages,* book, 3, p. 79.

Study Questions

1. How do you account for discrepancies in prophetic writings, such as differences in numbers and dates, or misquotations?

2. What are eight rules of interpretation from the standpoint of internal evidence that will aid in understanding a prophet's message?

3. Compare how Biblical writers and Ellen White utilized information drawn from secular, non-vision sources.

4. What makes such writings with non-vision materials sacred?

CHAPTER 34

Hermeneutics/3
Rules of Interpretation—External

"Many men take the testimonies the Lord has given, and apply them as they suppose they should be applied, picking out a sentence here and there, taking it from its proper connection, and applying it according to their idea. Thus poor souls become bewildered, when could they read in order all that has been given, they would see the true application, and would not become confused."[1]

Eight basic rules of interpretation that embrace a document's wider context would include:

• **Rule One:** *Include **all** that the prophet has said on the subject under discussion before coming to a conclusion.*[2]

This rule seems obvious; yet, it probably is the first reason why confusion reigns when people disagree. The reason: most people see only what they want to see. This simple fact influences most all research, whether in astrophysics, medicine, politics, or theology. Unfortunately, few people will admit it. We call this phenomenon, the paradigm fixation or the problem of presuppositions.[3] Especially in studying the Bible, nothing seems more difficult for most people than to look at all the facts! This difficulty is not because a person's capability to think is deficient. The difficulty that separates thinkers looking at the same information is that their presuppositions are different, presuppositions not only of the head but of the heart.

Presuppositions most often steer students only to "see" what they want to see, thus they overlook the total range of what a writer has written on a particular subject. These paradigms control the mind in what it wants to see, and the heart in what it wants to believe. Earlier[4] we called this phenomenon "attitude." These deep, often unverbalized, attitudes most often determine one's conclusions.[5]

After recognizing this hovering cloud of presuppositions (paradigms or worldviews) that every student should recognize, the next challenge is to examine all that a person has said or written on the subject under discussion. Only in this way can the writer (or speaker) be treated fairly.

Many Biblical scholars through the centuries have accepted Isaiah's principle: "But the word of the Lord was to them, 'Precept upon precept, precept upon precept, Line upon line, line upon line, Here a little, there a little'" (28:13). Accepting this principle assumes that the Bible contains a unified, harmonious unfolding of God's messages to human beings. But this principle does not teach that all texts are equally clear, or that the meaning of a verse can be understood apart from that verse's context. The overarching message of the Bible (or any other book or author) provides the final context for the meaning of any particular "precept" or "line."

The same principle applies to the writings of Ellen White. She wrote often: "The testimonies themselves will be the key that will explain the messages given, as scripture is explained by scripture."[6]

She believed her writings to be consistent and harmonious from beginning to end, revealing "one straight line of truth, without one heretical sentence."[7] That is a remarkable statement for any author to make, especially one who had been writing for more than sixty years.[8]

On some subjects that many consider important today, Mrs. White wrote nothing. Movies, television and radio programs, abortion, cremation, organ transplants, etc., were not current topics in her day.

Little Said on Some Subjects

On some subjects she said very little. We have relatively few statements on life insurance,[9] and only one on the wedding ring.[10] Her comments on two "special resurrections" are brief—she mentions a special resurrection of some on Christ's resurrection morning[11] and another immediately prior to Christ's second coming.[12]

On some subjects she wrote abundantly—topics such as Jesus Christ, the Holy Spirit, faith, and divine-human cooperation.

Certain subjects have frequently caused unnecessary disagreements within the church because students did not apply this first rule of hermeneutics. For example, statements such as "eggs should not be placed upon your table" should be balanced, according to other statements Ellen White has written concerning eggs and her principle of "step-by-step" understanding of truth (see pp. 282, 310, 311).[13]

Other subjects in the writings of Ellen White that profit from a fair use of this first hermeneutical rule include appropriate clothing, Sabbath observance, and counseling. Theologically, one is wise to follow this first rule when studying such topics as the atonement, the nature of Christ, the nature of sin, how sin is punished, and the relation of the "latter rain" to the Second Coming. Several of these subjects have polarized Adventists because some put more weight on expressions in a private letter than on the general instruction of a book, or on a paragraph lifted out of context that seems to fly in the face of full chapters in a published book.[14]

• **Rule Two:** *Every statement must be understood within its historical context. Time, place, and circumstances under which that statement was made must be studied in order to understand its meaning.*

Although this rule seems obvious, it lies at the root of many deep disagreements. In the day of selective media bites, most anyone in the public eye has been misunderstood by having his/her statements taken out of context. How often a misquoted person is heard saying, "But that is not what I meant!" Or, "I said that, but they didn't include everything I said!"

If living today, Ellen White could often say, "But that is not what I meant!" "Yes, I said that, but they didn't include everything I said!" Let us note three times that she emphasized the importance of this second rule of hermeneutics.

In 1875 she pointed out that that "which may be said in truth of individuals at one time may not correctly be said of them at another time."[15] Why did she say this? Because she was being criticized for her endorsement of certain leaders who later fell from grace or apostatized.

In 1904 she appealed to the fact that God "wants us to reason from common sense. Circumstances alter conditions. Circumstances change the relation of things."[16]

In 1911 she emphasized that "regarding the testimonies, nothing is ignored; nothing is cast aside; but time and place must be considered."[17]

Here we have three fundamental categories: time, place, and circumstances—all of which must be considered when one seeks to understand the meaning of any statement. These categories are not synonymous.

Time. Some Ellen White statements need to be understood in terms of *when* she made them. For instance, on January 16, 1898, she wrote: "We are still in probationary time."[18] Will these words always be true? Obviously not. The time will come when probation will cease (Dan. 12:1; Rev. 22:11). At present we know that certain events still lie in the future, e.g., creation of the image to the beast (Rev. 13), Sunday-law enforcement, the great final earthquake, etc. Thus, at the moment, "we are still in probationary time."

What about the following statements? "The voice from Battle Creek, which has been regarded as authority in counseling how the work should be done, is no longer the voice of God."[19] "It has been some years since I have considered the General Conference as the voice of God."[20]

But in 1875 Ellen White wrote concerning the General Conference in session: "When the judgment of the General Conference, which is the highest authority that God has upon the earth, is exercised, private independence and private judgment must not be maintained, but be surrendered."[21]

Why the difference in her position? During the late 1880s and 1890s, as the record shows in her letters and sermons, some of the policies of the General Conference officers were not ones that Ellen White could endorse. On April 1, 1901, the day before the General Conference session opened, she spoke these words: "It is working upon wrong principles that has brought the cause of God into its present embarrassment. The people have lost confidence in those who have the management of the work. Yet we hear that the voice of the conference is the voice of God. Every time I have heard this, I have thought that it was almost blasphemy. The voice of the conference ought to be the voice of God, but it is not."[22] Obviously, times had changed and her observations changed accordingly.

But that 1901 General Conference session made significant changes in policies and personnel. Ellen White was pleased. Only two months after the changes, she became aware that her son Edson was quoting some of her pre-1901-session statements and applying them in the new, post-1901-session period. Times had changed—the statements of the 1890s no longer applied. She wrote to Edson: "Your course would have been the course to be pursued, if no changes had been made in the General Conference [1901]. But a change has been made, and many more changes will be made [in 1903, many more were made] and great developments will [yet] be seen. No issues are to be forced. . . . It hurts me to think that you are using words which I wrote prior to the Conference."[23]

In 1909 Ellen White was clearly in the post-1901 mode when she wrote: "God has ordained that the representatives of His church from all parts of the earth, when assembled in a General Conference [session], shall have authority."[24] In summary, when we speak of the authority of the General Conference and Ellen White's several statements, we should immediately determine *when* the statements were made, and under what conditions.

Place. Some statements may be true for one person or group while at the same time they may not be true for another person or group. James White spoke to this difficulty when two groups, in different places, would read his wife's admonitions: "She works to this disadvantage . . . she makes strong appeals to the people, which a few feel deeply, and take strong positions, and go to extremes. Then to save the cause from ruin in consequence of these extremes, she is obliged to come out with reproofs for extremists in a public manner. This is better than to have things go to pieces; but the influence of both the extremes and the reproofs are terrible on the cause, and brings upon Mrs. W. a three-fold burden. Here is the difficulty: What she may say to urge the tardy, is taken by the prompt to urge them over the mark. And what she may say to caution the prompt, zealous, incautious ones, is taken by the tardy as an excuse to remain too far behind."[25]

The "place" consideration will help those who have been confused about whether Ellen White's writings should be quoted in public. On one occasion Mrs. White wrote that "the words of the Bible, and the Bible alone should be heard from the pulpit."[26] The next two quotations speak to Seventh-day Adventist evangelists: "In public labor do not make prominent, and quote that which Sister White has written."[27] "The testimonies of Sister White should not be carried to the front. God's word is the unerring standard."[28]

Do these statements prohibit ministers from quoting the writings of Ellen White publicly, especially in a church service? The first quotation speaks to the Christian world generally, comparing "an imaginary religion, a religion of words and forms," with the "words of the Bible and the Bible alone [which] should be heard from the pulpit." The whole page (context) is emphasizing that "those who have heard only tradition and human theories and maxims [should] hear the voice of Him who can renew the soul unto eternal life."

Adventist evangelists should prove their doctrines from the Bible, not from the writings of Mrs. White. The second reason for this caution is obvious: those who are not acquainted with the authority of Ellen White would not be persuaded by her statements, and might react negatively.[29] In summary, Mrs. White never said that her writings should not be quoted in the Seventh-day Adventist church pulpit.

The *place* test is especially important when compilations are made of Ellen White's thoughts on selected subjects. An incident in the early 1890s demonstrates the problem of misapplying testimonies given to one person for a particular purpose. Mrs. White, writing from Australia, addressed a letter to A. W. Stanton in Battle Creek, a man who had taken the position that the Seventh-day Adventist Church is Babylon. She included that letter in articles printed in the church paper.[30]

In his fifty-page pamphlet, "The Loud Cry of the Third Angel's Message," Stanton quoted freely from Ellen White's reproofs to the church, concluding that these testimonies constituted God's rejection of the organized church. He stated that those who finish up God's work on earth must separate from the Adventist Church which had become Babylon. He made his case by stringing together misapplied Ellen White comments and by including a letter to a private party that was used out of context.

Mrs. White replied that Stanton had "misapplied [a private letter sent to another for a particular purpose], as many do the Scriptures, to the injury of his own soul and the souls of others. . . . In the use of a private letter sent to another, Brother S. has abused the kindly efforts of one who desired to help him."

Further, she acknowledged that her misapplied statements might "appear" to support Stanton's conclusions. However, "those who take them in parts, simply to support some theory or idea of their own, to vindicate themselves in a course of error, will not be blessed and benefited by what they teach."[31]

This Stanton incident and Ellen White's response (which settled the matter for church members) provides us with a historical example of how damaging and deceptive a compilation of worthy writings can be when time and place are not considered.[32]

• **Rule Three:** *The principle underlying each statement of counsel or instruction must be recognized in order to understand its relevance for those in different times or places.*

Whenever prophets speak they are either conveying truth as a principle or as a policy. Principles are universal, in the sense that they apply to men and women everywhere; they are eternal, in the sense that they are always relevant, always applicable.

Policies, however, are the timely applications of eternal, universal principles. Principles never change but policies do, depending on circumstances. Thus policies may apply a principle in a way that the prophet never envisioned.[33]

Ellen White was well aware of the difference between universal principles and policies that are determined by changing circumstances: "That which can be said of men under certain circumstances, cannot be said of them under other circumstances."[34] Her contemporaries recognized that Mrs. White appealed to the intelligence of her readers more often by citing principles than by spelling out the answers to local issues.[35]

Understanding the basic difference between principles and policies will help one avoid misusing either the Bible or the writings of Ellen White. The following topics illustrate the need to place Mrs. White's counsel in the context of time, place, and circumstances.

Teaching girls to harness and drive horses. In outlining a school curriculum, Ellen White wrote that "if girls . . . could learn to harness and drive a horse, and to use the saw and the hammer, as well as the rake and the hoe, they would be better fitted to meet the emergencies of life."[36] Is this a principle or a policy? Obviously, the principle is clear: girls should be "fitted to meet the emergencies of life."

When this counsel was given in the early years of the twentieth century, most Americans still lived on farms. For many practical reasons, including safety, this principle could be best applied by girls learning how to "harness and drive a horse" and not leave such things for boys only. Today, the principle would be best served in high school or college with courses in auto mechanics and driver's education.

School-entrance age. In 1872 Ellen White wrote her first major treatise on Christian education.[37] Regarding the age when students should begin school, she said: "Parents should be the only teachers of their children until they have reached eight or ten years of age. . . . The only schoolroom for children from eight to ten years of age should be in the open air amidst the opening flowers and nature's beautiful scenery."[38]

For thirty years this counsel was the rule for Adventist elementary schools generally. In 1904 the local school board of the St. Helena, California, church met, with Ellen White present, to discuss the issue of school-entrance age.[39] The principles quickly emerged: (1) children differ in their development; (2) ideally, parents should be their children's teachers for the early years, until they are 8-10 years old (thus recognizing differences in child development); (3) if parents are not able to teach and control their children properly, it would be better for the children to learn under a teacher who would teach discipline as well as the appropriate studies; (4) if both parents are employed outside the home, it would be better for their children to be placed in the controlled environment of the classroom rather than left in an empty house; (5) for the sake of the St. Helena Sanitarium's reputation, it would be beneficial to all if children were not observed throughout the day "wandering about, with nothing to do, getting into mischief, and all these things."

So, on the basis of principle, from the standpoint of what is best for children and for their influence on the reputation of the sanitarium, policy was changed and arrangements were made to accept younger students at the St. Helena church school.

The bicycle craze. At the beginning of the twentieth century, "the American people were swept with a consuming passion which left them with little time or money for anything else. . . . What was this big, new distraction? For an answer the merchants had only to look out the window and watch their erstwhile customers go whizzing by. America had discovered the bicycle, and everybody was making the most of the new freedom it brought. . . . The bicycle began as a rich man's toy. . . . The best early bicycle cost $150, an investment comparable to the cost of an automobile today. . . . Every member of the family wanted a 'wheel,' and entire family savings often were used up in supplying the demand."[40]

With that background we may be better able to understand Ellen White's counsel *at that time* when she wrote that "money expended in bicycles and dress and other needless things must be accounted for."[41] She went further than the principle of exorbitant cost; she cautioned regarding the spirit of "bewitching" competition and the desire to "be the greatest."[42]

Thus, her policy on bicycles (which, if placed within today's context, may seem odd, even ridiculous) was based on clear-cut Biblical principles. The wise and balanced expenditure of funds and the avoidance of the competitive spirit are principles that should impact on decisions in all ages. If Mrs. White were alive today, she might apply the principle of accountability to the way people spend money on luxury items, automobiles, sports equipment, electronic gadgets, or clothing.

Sports. Unfortunately some have excerpted some of Ellen White's statements on sports without maintaining her sense of balance. In 1895 she warned students that in "plunging into amusements, match games, pugilistic performances," they were declaring "to the world that Christ was not their leader. All this called forth the warning from God." However, the next sentence, often not quoted, reveals her common sense: "Now that which burdens me is the danger of going into extremes on the other side."[43]

For example, to rule out sports altogether would be missing Mrs. White's point. In the early 1870s she counseled parents and teachers that they should come close to their children and pupils and if they would "manifest an interest in all their efforts, and even in their sports, sometimes even being a child among children, they would make the children very happy, and would gain their love and win their confidence."[44]

On another occasion Ellen White wrote that she did not "condemn the simple exercise of playing ball." What did concern her was that ball-playing, and sports in general, "may be overdone." She followed this statement by explaining what she meant by being overdone.[45]

The lesson to be learned here, as in other subjects that often polarize readers of Ellen White's writings, is that the full range of her thoughts on a particular subject should be read in order to get her perspective.

Flesh food. Earlier we studied Ellen White's health principles and her application of these principles.[46] Here we will emphasize again how she, a dying consumptive at 17, went on to outlive her contemporaries after a remarkably rigorous life. One of her open secrets was to distinguish between principle and policy.

Out of the many examples available, let us note again how she related to flesh foods—the part of her diet in her younger years that she enjoyed most! In chapter 27 we saw how she embraced the health message as it came to her in 1863, some of which cut straight across her personal habits and delights. We also noted how she occasionally departed from her habitual practice of abstaining from flesh food. Yet, in 1870 she claimed that she had acted according to principle ever since receiving the health vision in 1863: "I have not changed my course a particle since I adopted the health reform. I have not taken one step back since the light from heaven upon this subject first shone upon my pathway. . . . I left off these things from principle. And since that time, brethren, you have not heard me advance an extreme view of health reform that I had to take back. I have advocated nothing but what I stand to today."[47]

What were the basic principles of health reform that Ellen White believed she had faithfully followed? (1) Do the best one can under circumstances that may be beyond one's control; (2) Avoid everything hurtful, such as alcohol, tobacco, and drugs; (3) Use judiciously that which is healthful—use self-control; (4) Do not mark out any precise line in diet that everyone must follow, because not everyone has the same physical needs or opportunities to find the best food; (5) Follow health practices to improve one's mind for spiritual purposes, not to earn God's acceptance (legalism); and (6) Reason from cause to effect.

Health reform policies are choices that flow from those principles. If vegetarianism were a principle, then we would have a problem with God's command for the Israelites to eat the Passover lamb. We also would wonder why He distinguished between clean and unclean meats. And what would we do with our Lord's practice of eating the Passover lamb, as well as fresh fish, with His disciples?

Vegetarianism is a policy, a wise policy, that is being reaffirmed constantly in the scientific laboratories of the world, as well as in the epidemiological studies showing the awesome difference in the incidence of disease between vegetarians and consumers of flesh foods.[48] The Christian's duty is to "eat that food which is most nourishing," leaving each person to apply this principle by making choices on the basis of "known duty."[49] Sometimes emergency situations arise and one is forced to choose the good rather than the best, or even a lesser evil to avoid a greater evil. Although the principle remains, the policy or application may change with circumstances.

Courting in school. Some people misunderstand Ellen White's counsel regarding dating or courting during the school years. They fail to note the age of the students involved. Part of the instruction was given especially for the Avondale campus where many of the students were still in high school: "We have labored hard to keep in check everything in the school like favoritism, attachment, and courting. We have told the students that we would not allow the first thread of this to be interwoven with their school work. On this point we are as firm as a rock."[50]

Some of her concern was directed to students at Battle Creek College, where also there was a mix of high-school and college students: "Students are not sent here to form attachments, to indulge in flirtation or courting, but to obtain an education. Should they be allowed to follow their own inclinations in this respect, the college would soon become demoralized. Several have used their precious school days in slyly flirting and courting, notwithstanding the vigilance of professors and teachers."[51]

Would Ellen White have given the same counsel regarding older, more mature students? Where would Christian young people find their life mates if not in the environment of a Christian campus committed to Adventist goals? On several occasions she set forth the principles that should guide young people and the school program in the area of Christian courtship. For example: "In all our dealings with students, age and character must be taken into account. We cannot treat the young and old just alike. There are circumstances under which men and women of sound experience and good standing may be granted some privileges not given to younger students. The age, the conditions, and the turn of mind must be taken into consideration. We must be wisely considerate in all our work. But we must not lessen our firmness and vigilance in dealing with students of all ages, nor our strictness in forbidding the unprofitable and unwise association of young and immature students."[52]

• **Rule Four:** W*e must use common sense and sanctified reason as we analyze the difference between principles and policies.*

During Ellen White's comments at the St. Helena school board meeting in 1904, she again emphasized a principle of hermeneutics that would help them and others when trying to apply principle to policy. She noted that church members were taking her words legalistically, unthinkingly: "Why, Sister White has said so and so, and Sister White has said so and so; and therefore we are going right up to it."

Her response: "God wants us all to have common sense, and He wants us to reason from common sense. Circumstances alter conditions. Circumstances change the relation of things."[53]

Christianity is a reasonable religion. God implanted within men and women not only the ability to respond to His grace (and the ability not to respond) but also the capacity to reason from cause to effect. On many occasions Ellen White said, "God has given us powers to be used, to be developed and strengthened by education. We should reason and reflect, carefully marking the relation between cause and effect. When this is practiced . . . they may fully answer the purpose of God in their creation."[54]

She did not make reason the final arbiter of right and wrong. Reason, for her, is the capacity to understand the reasonableness of God's counsel and the ability to reflect on the results of obeying or disobeying that counsel. She described this relationship between God's will and human reasoning powers: "We are to be guided by true theology and common sense."[55] For her, sanctified reason and common sense are virtually synonymous.

Reason and extremes. Every subject, whether it be in theology, law, ethics, music, graphic art, or constitutional law, is beset with those who tend to go to extremes. We call those groups Pharisees or Sadducees, conservatives or liberals, literalists or symbolists, indifferent (cool) or fanatics (hot), etc. In philosophy and religion, we call the one group objectivists, the other, subjectivists.[56]

Truth (as principle) is not some kind of balance between two errors. Truth transcends errors of both extremes by recognizing the truths that each extreme wants to guard.[57] But truth does not incorporate the spirit or the errors that each extreme holds to. When people recognize the element of truth in their opposition, a remarkable event happens—peace prevails, conciliation happens, and real unity develops. Real unity is not the result of administrative appeal or a committee vote; unity rests on commonly accepted principles of interpretation.

At the same time, matters dealing with policy (not principle) require a different approach. For example, dealing with dress Ellen White wrote: "There is a medium position in these things. Oh, that we all might wisely find that position and keep it." Speaking of diet, she counseled: "Take the middle path, avoiding all extremes."[58]

But avoiding extremes is more than an intellectual matter. Some people may understand intellectually the correct linkage between principle and policy, but emotionally they tend to extremes. Even when they promote correct policy, they may be either extremely hot or cold. Ellen White put her finger on their problem, even when their policy is correct: "We have found in our experience that if Satan cannot keep souls bound in the ice of indifference, he will try to push them into the fire of fanaticism."[59]

A respected Adventist theologian of an earlier generation recalls how he unintentionally exercised "the fire of fanaticism" in applying one of Ellen White's health principles. While selling religious books in his youth, M. L. Andreasen lived on granola. He carried it with him, mixed it with water, and ate it twice daily.

Then someone read from one of Ellen White's books that people "eat too much." He looked around and found sufficient verification of that statement. So, to be faithful to new light, he cut his daily ration in half. Some time later he read the statement himself in *Testimonies,* volume 2, page 374: "You eat too much." That caused him to think again. "Should he cut his daily ration in half again?"

Then it dawned on him. He was honest and wanted to do right but he now thanked God for "a little good sense."[60]

Because Ellen White said on several occasions that "two meals [daily] are better than three,"[61] some families made it a rule for everyone, including those in the sanitariums. In reference to sanitariums she showed how to link principle with policy and circumstances: "If, after dispensing with the third meal in the sanitarium, you see by the results that this is keeping people away from the institution, your duty is plain. We must remember that while there are some who are better for eating only two meals, there are others who eat lightly at each meal, and who feel that they need something in the evening. . . . [Eliminating the third meal may] do more harm than good."[62]

In 1867 Mrs. White answered some prevalent questions regarding health reform. One of the questions was: "Is there not danger of brethren and sisters taking extreme views of the health reform?" She answered: "This may be expected in all stirring reforms. . . . It is God's plan that persons who are suited to the work should prudently and earnestly set forth the health reform, then leave the people to settle the matter with God and their own souls. It is the duty of those every way qualified to teach it to make people believe and obey, and all others should be silent and be taught."[63]

In summary, this fourth principle of hermeneutics appeals to common sense in linking principle with policy. This requires both soundness in thought and emotional evenness. Ellen White well said: "There is a class of people who are always ready to go off on some tangent, who want to catch up something strange and wonderful and new; but God would have all move calmly, considerately, choosing our words in harmony with the solid truth for this time, which requires to be presented to the mind as free from that which is emotional as possible, while still bearing the intensity and solemnity that it is proper it should bear. We must guard against creating extremes, guard against encouraging those who would either be in the fire or in the water."[64]

• **Rule Five:** W*e must be certain that supposed quotations are indeed written by the author to whom they are attributed.*

Every public figure has had the problem of facing people who were adamant about what they "know" the speaker or author had said. The "belief" may be as wild as one's imagination, but still the speaker or author must try to defend himself against the error or distortion. Obviously, the contending person does not have the reference for what he is "quoting." Most of the time he/she got his information from a third or fourth party. We often call these distorted memories and flat errors "apocryphal statements."

This problem plagued Ellen White from the beginning of her early ministry, and even today. Included in statements that have been incorrectly attributed to her are topics such as: (1) Inhabitants of other planets are now gathering fruit for a Sabbath stopover of the redeemed on the way to heaven; (2) She saw an angel standing by Uriah Smith inspiring him as he wrote *Thoughts on Daniel and the Revelation*; (3) the Holy Spirit is, or was, Melchizedek; (4) She designated certain mountain spots as safe hideouts in the time of trouble; (5) She named specific cities, etc., that would be destroyed by coming earthquakes, fires, floods, etc.; (6) Christ will return at midnight; (7) Eggs should never be eaten (forgetting the immediate context and many other statements regarding varying circumstances); (8) She would be a member of the 144,000; (9) Literal darkness will cover the earth as a signal that probation has closed; (10) Christ's last mediatorial work before probation closes will be for children who have wandered away from the church; (11) We should live as though we had 1,000 years to live, and as we would if we were to die tomorrow; (12) Entire churches and conferences will apostatize, etc.[65]

• **Rule Six:** *Though not contradicting themselves, we must allow for the maturing experience of authors, even prophets, in that truth is unfolded to them only as fast as they are able to understand it.*

This rule helps students who are concerned about certain portions of a prophet's life or writings that fall into a category other than "time, place, and circumstances," addressed in Rule Three above.

Ellen White clearly taught that God leads His people along as fast as they are able to receive further truth. The history of Israel is a splendid example of how He works with people *where they are*, not where they will be in the future.[66] The prophets were also part of this divine plan to unfold truth as fast as people are ready for it. They themselves experienced the process. Paul not only knew more about the plan of salvation than did Joel or David, he experienced the "unfolding" in his own life.[67]

Some call this process "progressive truth." The term is helpful if it is describing a person's progressive awareness of spiritual truths. But it misses the mark if it is used in the context of an evolutionary development that proceeds out of the evolving of human understanding through trial and error, through thesis and antithesis into synthesis. God's method of teaching the human race involves both the recovery of lost truth and the unfolding of further truth, as fast as people are ready to receive it. Evolutionary progression is understood as humanity's growth from ignorance to knowledge, without any absolutes that would put universal value on knowledge.[68]

This process happens to individuals as well as to groups of people. Most people know how this process has been working in their own lives. If we have been growing in grace, what we knew about God's will for us individually ten years ago was much less than what each of us knows today. No doubt all of us wish we could adjust what we said to others ten years ago, even though we thought it wise at the time![69]

But some may say, "A prophet should be different. What prophets said when they were twenty years old should not need 'clarification' or 'expansion' when they are fifty-five!" This view arises out of a verbal-inspiration framework. We must not forget that God speaks to men and women who "differ widely in rank and occupation, and in mental and spiritual endowments."[70] This "wide" spread of individual differences includes the "wide" spread of a person's grasp of truth between his/her youth and the mature years.

Though the core of truth remains the same, one's insights are enlarged. Maturing skills of insight and communicating skills may express the core message differently in later years. In 1906 Ellen White reflected on her learning experience: "For sixty years I have been in communication with heavenly messengers, and I have been constantly learning in reference to divine things, and in reference to the way in which God is constantly working to bring souls from the error of their ways to the light in God's light."[71] Prophets are humble people who have seen, to some degree, the glory of the Lord. Humble prophets easily recognize indebtedness to God for their fresh perspective, "like the shining sun, that shines ever brighter unto the perfect day" (Prov. 4:18).[72]

The growth principle pervades all creation. It explains Paul's appeal to the Corinthians: "We all, with unveiled face, beholding as in a mirror the glory of the Lord, are being transformed into the same image from glory to glory, just as by the Spirit of the Lord" (2 Cor. 3:18). This text lies behind the rule: "It is a law of the human mind that by beholding we become changed."[73] Thus, the more young

Ellen Harmon studied her Bible and prayed for divine guidance as she faced life's choices, she became "transformed," and "changed"—she grew in knowledge of God's character and His ways.[74]

Consequently, letting the growth principle inform our study of Ellen White (or the Bible) we should expect deepening insights as she conveys God's messages to others. We can see the growth of her ability to convey deeper insights, especially when we compare her earliest descriptions of the origin of the great controversy in heaven with that in *Patriarchs and Prophets.*[75]

Thus, when readers sense a broader perspective in *Patriarchs and Prophets* (1890) than is found in *Spiritual Gifts* (1858), they are recognizing the hermeneutical rule that a prophet will grow, as anyone else, in spiritual perception. This increase in spiritual perception will help the prophet to state more clearly the message that God wants conveyed. This is the principle that best describes the experience of Jesus on earth. Luke described His growth and maturing ability to share spiritual things with others: "And Jesus increased in wisdom and stature, and in favor with God and men" (Luke 2:52).[76]

• **Rule Seven:** *In some instances, a person must understand the experience of an event, either directly or vicariously, before understanding the truth of the event.*

This rule may sound contrary to sound reasoning. But such was the situation when the apostles faced the unbelieving world after Christ's resurrection. Who would believe them unless the apostles had seen the empty tomb or had seen Jesus during the next forty days before His ascension? In a similar sense, early Adventists in the late 1840s and early 1850s "experienced" the growing connection between the supernatural visions of Ellen Harmon-White and the voice of authority for their growing community.[77]

In late 1896 while in Australia, Mrs. White had to respond to John Bell who was promoting a divisive message regarding the time when the three angels' messages of Revelation 14 would be fulfilled. In essence, he was placing it in the future. She wrote insightfully, in terms of this seventh rule of interpretation: "The peculiar views he holds are a mixture of truth and error. If he had passed through the experience of God's people as He has led them for the last forty years, he would be better prepared to make the correct application of Scripture. The great waymarks of truth, showing us our bearings in prophetic history, are to be carefully guarded, lest they be torn down, and replaced with theories that would bring confusion rather than genuine light."

She ended her five-page response by noting this seventh rule: "Many theories were advanced, bearing a semblance of truth, but so mingled with Scriptures misinterpreted and misapplied that they led to dangerous errors. Very well do we know how every point of truth was established, and the seal set upon it by the Holy Spirit of God. . . . The leadings of the Lord were marked, and most wonderful were His revelations of what is truth. Point after point was established by the Lord God of heaven. That which was truth *then,* is truth today."[78]

Later Ellen White wrote out a more extended response on this "futurism" that was being taught in Australia. Again she emphasized the role of experience that should be respected by Adventists: "The Lord will not lead minds now to set aside the truth that the Holy Spirit has moved upon His servants in the past to proclaim. . . . The Lord does not lay upon those who have not had an experience in His work the burden of making a new exposition of those prophecies which He has, by His Holy Spirit, moved upon His chosen servants to explain."[79]

Living through the experience when truth is revealed becomes a rock-solid foundation not only for those who first experience it but also for those who later want to "re-experience" it in their own truth system. Truth, whenever found, "fits" previous truth as a tree limb "fits" its trunk. Truth is coherent.

• **Rule Eight:** *Not everything in the Bible or in the writings of Ellen White can be understood at first glance, or even after years of study.*

This thought may sound strange to the inquiring mind. But think of astronomers and neurosurgeons (or genetic-code researchers, microchip specialists, etc.) who spend their entire lives expanding their knowledge—but feeling increasingly awed at what opens before them.

True Christians practice the principle of suspended judgment[80] when they and their colleagues reach the limit of understanding. Especially when they ponder the Biblical story (and Ellen White's writings) on such subjects as the nature of God (not His character, of which much has been revealed), why sin developed, how Christ could become a human being, how regeneration works—they acknowledge that these "are mysteries too deep for the human mind." They remember that we are not "to doubt His Word because we cannot understand all the mysteries of His providence."[81]

To *force* an interpretation because one feels everything *must* be understood is surely to lead to a misinterpretation. Or to dismiss or disregard any portion of the Bible or the writings of Ellen White simply because some passages are not easily understood also damages one's understanding of truth.

Endnotes

1. *Selected Messages*, book 1, p. 44.
2. See T. Housel Jemison, *A Prophet Among You* (Mountain View, Calif.: Pacific Press Publishing Association, 1955), pp. 438-450.
3. Note the kind of scientific thinking that prevailed before Copernicus changed the worldview of astronomers (and everyone else) with his paradigm shift, placing the sun instead of the earth at the center of the solar system. Consider the physicians who bled George Washington, America's first president, to death because their medical paradigm did not understand the germ theory nor even the strong possibility that hydrotherapy treatments might have reversed his chest infection. One of the chief responsibilities of those searching for truth is to examine the lens through which the researcher searches for truth. The lens (the paradigm or worldview) by which we look at information determines how we evaluate so-called "facts." Alfred North Whitehead said it well: "When you are criticizing [or, one may add, interpreting] the philosophy of an epoch, do not chiefly direct your attention to those intellectual positions which its exponents feel it necessary explicitly to defend. There will be some fundamental assumptions which adherents of all the variant systems within the epoch unconsciously presuppose. Such assumptions appear so obvious that people do not know what they are assuming because no other way of putting things has ever occurred to them. With these assumptions a certain limited number of types of philosophic systems are possible."—*Science and the Modern World* (New York: Mentor Editions, 1952), pp. 49, 50.
4. See p. 373.
5. Attitude determined how first-century Jews looked at Jesus as recorded in Matthew 16: If this young Galilean teacher did not fit their paradigm of what they thought the Messiah should be, they would look elsewhere—and they did. If one does not believe in miracles because of some kind of scientific paradigm, the Biblical story becomes folklore. If one does not believe that God speaks through men and women through visions, he/she then searches for reasons to explain away the vision phenomenon. And on it goes.
6. *Selected Messages*, book 1, p. 42.
7. *Selected Messages*, book 3, p. 52.
8. "The light that I have received, I have written out, and much of it is now shining forth from the printed page. There is, throughout my printed works, a harmony with my present teaching."—*Review and Herald*, June 14, 1906.
9. *Testimonies*, vol. 1, pp. 549-551 (1867). To understand this statement we must also employ "hermeneutic rule number two."
10. *Testimonies to Ministers*, pp. 180, 181 (1892).
11. *The Desire of Ages*, pp. 785-787, 833, 834; *Early Writings*, pp. 184, 185, 208; *The Great Controversy*, pp. 18, 667; *Selected Messages*, book 1, pp. 304-308.
12. *Early Writings*, p. 285; *The Great Controversy*, p. 637.
13. *Testimonies*, vol. 2, pp. 362, 400. Note some helpful statements in *Testimonies*, vol. 7, p. 135; vol. 9, p. 162; *The Ministry of Healing*, p. 320.
14. "If you desire to know what the Lord has revealed through her, read her published works."— *Testimonies*, vol. 5, p. 696. See George Knight, *Reading Ellen White*, pp. 121-123.
15. *Testimonies*, vol. 3, p. 471.
16. *Selected Messages*, book 3, p. 217. See p. 345.
17. *Ibid.*, book 1, p. 57.
18. *The Upward Look*, p. 30.
19. Letter 4, 1896, cited in *MR*, vol. 17, pp. 185, 186 (1896).
20. Letter 77, 1898, cited in *Ibid.*, p. 216 (1898).
21. *Testimonies*, vol. 3, p. 492.
22. Ms 37, 1901, cited in *Sermons and Talks*, vol. 2, pp. 159, 160. See also George E. Rice, "The Church: Voice of God?" *Ministry*, Dec., 1987, pp. 4-6.
23. Letter 54, 1901, cited in *MR*, vol. 19, pp. 146-148.
24. *Testimonies*, vol. 9, p. 261.
25. *Review and Herald*, Mar. 17, 1868.

26. *Prophets and Kings,* p. 626.
27. *Selected Messages,* book 3, p. 29.
28. *Evangelism,* p. 256.
29. In Ellen White's first testimony to the church, she wrote: "Some have taken an injudicious course; when they have talked their faith to unbelievers, and the proof has been asked for, they have read a vision, instead of going to the Bible for proof. I saw that this course was inconsistent, and prejudiced unbelievers against the truth. The visions can have no weight with those who have never seen them and know nothing of their spirit. They should not be referred to in such cases."—*Testimonies,* vol. 1, pp. 119, 120. See also *Ibid.,* vol. 5, p. 669.
30. *Review and Herald,* Aug. 22 to Sept. 12, 1893. See p. 231.
31. *Testimonies to Ministers,* pp. 32-62.
32. "I know that many men take the testimonies the Lord has given, and apply them as they suppose they should be applied, picking out a sentence here and there, taking it from its proper connection, and applying it according to their idea. Thus poor souls become bewildered, when could they read in order all that has been given, they would see the true application, and would not become confused. . . . Reports fly from one to another regarding what Sister White has said. Each time the report is repeated, it grows larger. If Sister White has anything to say, leave her to say it. No one is called upon to be a mouthpiece for Sister White. . . . Please let Sister White bear her own message."—*Selected Messages,* book 1, pp. 44, 45. "Those who are not walking in the light of the message, may gather up statements from my writings that happen to please them, and that agree with their human judgment, and, by separating these statements from their connection, and placing them beside human reasonings, make it appear that my writings uphold that which they condemn."—Letter 208, 1906, cited in Arthur White, *Messenger to the Remnant,* p. 86.
33. See p. 34.
34. *Testimonies,* vol. 3, p. 470.
35. In a private letter W. C. White reported to A. O. Tait on a union committee meeting to which his mother was invited. White noted how they hurried the discussion along in order to listen to Ellen White: "As you are well aware, Mother seldom answers such questions directly; but she endeavors to lay down principles and bring forward facts which have been presented to her that will aid us in giving intelligent study to the subject, and in arriving at a correct conclusion."—Cited in Arthur White, *The Ellen G. White Writings,* pp. 165, 166.
36. *Education,* pp. 216, 217.
37. *Testimonies,* vol. 3, pp. 131-160; *Fundamentals of Christian Education,* pp. 15-46.
38. *Ibid.,* p. 137.
39. A verbatim report of Ellen White's participation in the school board discussion is found in *Selected Messages,* book 3, pp. 214-226.
40. *Reader's Digest,* Dec. 1951. See George Knight, *Reading Ellen White,* pp. 100-102.
41. *Testimonies to Ministers,* p. 398.
42. *Testimonies,* vol. 8, pp. 51, 52.
43. *Fundamentals of Christian Education,* p. 378.
44. *Ibid.,* p. 18. See also *Testimonies,* vol. 3, pp. 134, 135.
45. *Adventist Home,* pp. 498, 499.
46. See pp. 310, 311.
47. *Testimonies,* vol. 2, pp. 371, 372. "I present these matters before the people, dwelling upon general principles."—*Counsels on Diet and Foods,* p. 493 (1897). In 1904, at the age of 76, she said that she was healthier than "in my younger days," attributing her improvement to the "principles of health reform."—*Ibid.,* p. 482. In 1908 she reacted to those who were stating that she had not been following the principles of health reform as she had "advocated them with my pen." Forthrightly she wrote: "As far as my knowledge goes, I have not departed from those principles."—*Ibid.,* pp. 491, 492, 494. See *Review and Herald,* Mar. 17, 1868, for an editorial by James White where he addressed those who were more rigid than they should have been with health principles. One of the problems that called forth the editorial was the virtual verbal-inspiration paradigm that drove some readers to their super-critical positions.
48. See pp. 322-324.
49. *Testimonies,* vol. 9, p. 163; *Selected Messages,* book 1, p. 396.
50. *MR,* vol. 8, p. 256.
51. *Testimonies,* vol. 4, p. 432; see also *Ibid.,* vol. 5, p. 109.
52. *Counsels to Parents, Teachers, and Students,* p. 101. See Moon, *W. C. White and Ellen G. White,* p. 359.
53. *Selected Messages,* book 3, p. 217. See p. 395.
54. *Mind, Character, and Personality,* vol. 2, p. 436.
55. *Ibid.,* vol. 1, p. 148.
56. *Testimonies,* vol. 1, p. 425.
57. See pp. 260, 261.
58. *Counsels on Diet and Foods,* p. 211. The ancient Greeks often spoke of moderation ("nothing in excess") as the search for the "golden mean."
59. *Testimonies,* vol. 5, p. 644.
60. Virginia Steinweg, *Without Fear or Favor* (Washington, D.C.: Review and Herald Publishing Association, 1979), pp. 53, 54.
61. *Counsels on Diet and Foods,* pp. 141, 173; *Testimonies,* vol. 4, pp. 416, 417.
62. *Ibid.,* p. 283. "The practice of eating but two meals a day is generally found a benefit to health; yet under some circumstances persons may require a third meal. This should, however, if taken at all, be very light, and of food most easily digested."—*The Ministry of Healing,* p. 321.
63. *Review and Herald,* Oct. 8, 1867.
64. *Testimonies to Ministers,* pp. 227, 228.
65. For further study of these and other illustrations of the Ellen White "apocrypha," see *Comprehensive Index to the Writings of Ellen G. White,* vol. 3, pp. 3189-3192.
66. For further study of the principle of accommodation, see pp. 34, 282, 304, 311, 422.
67. "The fact needs to be emphasized, and often repeated, that the mysteries of the Bible are not such because God has sought to conceal truth, but because our own weakness or ignorance makes us incapable of comprehending or appropriating truth. The limitation is not in its purpose, but in our capacity."—*Signs of the Times,* Apr. 25, 1906.
68. "In all ages, through the medium of communion with heaven, God has worked out His purpose for His children, by unfolding gradually to their minds the doctrines of grace. . . . He who places himself where God can enlighten him, advances, as it were, from the partial obscurity of dawn to the full radiance of noonday." —*The Acts of the Apostles,* p. 564.
69. "God intends that to the earnest seeker the truths of His Word shall be ever unfolding."—*Signs of the Times,*

Apr. 25, 1906; "He [Christ] promised that the Holy Spirit should enlighten the disciples, that the word of God should be ever unfolding to them. They would be able to present its truths in new beauty."—*Christ's Object Lessons*, p. 127.

70. *The Great Controversy*, p. vi.
71. *This Day With God*, p. 76.
72. "Whoever examines her written words—going from the childlike composition of her girlhood writings through the strenuous period of her young maturity to the gracious, eloquent, and deeply moving works of her later years—will perceive the steady progress in vision and expression, and may remember that she gained these abilities, under God's hand, not by supinely waiting for the outpouring of the Spirit, but by moving under the impulse of that Spirit in the exercise of every power of her being."—A. W. Spalding, *Origin and History*, vol. 1, p. 76.
73. *Patriarchs and Prophets*, p. 91.
74. "Looking unto Jesus we obtain brighter and more distinct views of God, and by beholding we become changed. Goodness, love for our fellow men, becomes our natural instinct."—*Christ's Object Lessons*, p. 355.
75. See Alden Thompson, "The Theology of Ellen White: The Great Controversy Story," *Adventist Review*, Dec. 31, 1981.
76. Ellen White spoke reverently about the development of Christ's spiritual and mental endowments: "The powers of mind and body developed gradually, in keeping with the laws of childhood. . . . Since He gained knowledge as we may do, His intimate acquaintance with the Scriptures shows how diligently His early years were given to the study of God's word. . . . Thus to Jesus the significance of the word and the works of God was unfolded, as He was trying to understand the reason of things. . . . From the first dawning of intelligence He was constantly growing in spiritual grace and knowledge of truth. . . . Communion with God through prayer develops the mental and moral faculties, and the spiritual powers strengthen as we cultivate thoughts upon spiritual things."—*The Desire of Ages*, pp. 69-71.
77. "Thus the process by which the mystical proclivities of a teenage girl were recognized as the revelations of an authoritative prophet was aided at every step by the underlying philosophical assumptions of the Adventist community. Unlike the Mormon prophet Joseph Smith, Ellen White did not proclaim her revelation and gather a following; rather, she had a particular kind of religious experience that came to be accepted as authoritative within an existing group. The prophetic ministry of Ellen White was an aspect of Adventist social experience, not just the psychological experience of a single individual."—Bull and Lockhart, *Seeking a Sanctuary*, p. 25.
78. *Selected Messages*, book 2, pp. 101-104.
79. *Ibid.*, pp. 110, 112; see *Ibid.*, book 1, p. 161.
80. See George Reid, *Ministry*, Nov. 1991.
81. *Testimonies*, vol. 5, p. 699. "The Bible is but dimly understood. A lifelong, prayerful study of its sacred revealings will leave much unexplained."—*Counsels to Writers*, p. 82; "Both in divine revelation and in nature, God has given to men mysteries to command their faith. This must be so. We may be ever searching, ever inquiring, ever learning, and yet there is an infinity beyond."—*Testimonies*, vol. 8, p. 261; "We can understand as much of His purposes as it is for our good to know; and beyond this we must still trust the might of the Omnipotent, the love and wisdom of the Father and Sovereign of all."—*Testimonies*, vol. 5, p. 699.

Study Questions

1. What are eight rules of external evidence that students should use in understanding the meaning of the Bible and Ellen White's writings?
2. Why is it essential that none of these rules be neglected?
3. How does the hermeneutical rule of "time, place and circumstances" explain many Ellen White references that seem difficult to understand or apply today?
4. For background in understanding hermeneutical principles in general, read Gerhard Hasel, *Understanding the Living Word of God* (Mountain View, Calif.: Pacific Press Publishing Association, 1980).

CHAPTER 35

Hermeneutics/4
Characteristics Shared by Biblical Writers and Ellen White

"Little heed is given to the Bible, and the Lord has given a lesser light to lead men and women to the greater light."[1]

In early 1903 Ellen White, burdened about the decline in colporteur work (literature evangelism), wrote an article for the *Review*. In that article she expressed appreciation for the successful promotion of *Christ's Object Lessons*.[2] She also wrote: "Sister White is not the originator of these books. . . . They contain the precious, comforting light that God has graciously given His servant to be given to the world. From their pages this light is to shine into the hearts of men and women, leading them to the Saviour."

Then she amplified this connection between God's light and her writings, and where her writings, as all other prophetic writings, would lead readers: "The Lord has sent His people much instruction, line upon line, precept upon precept, here a little, and there a little. Little heed is given to the Bible, and the Lord has given a lesser light to lead men and women to the greater light."[3]

In her larger context, Mrs. White seems to be referring to how all biblical prophets are lesser lights leading their people "to the Saviour"—the "Light of the world" (John 8:12; 9:5; 12:46)—even as John the Baptist "came . . . to bear witness of the Light" (John 1:7, 8). Because people in her day were giving "little heed . . . to the Bible" (which was to lead people to Christ, the Light of the world) the Lord spoke to her as a "lesser light" (even as John the Baptist and all other biblical prophets were lesser lights) to lead people to Christ, the "greater light."

From another point of view, no one can question that Ellen White regarded the Bible itself as a "greater light" with its centuries of inspired writings and its gold-standard acceptance as the Word of God.

Numerous are the references, from her earliest days to her last, that exalted the Bible, such as: "The Holy Scriptures are to be accepted as an authoritative, infallible revelation of His [God's] will. They are the standard of character, the revealer of doctrines, and the test of experience."[4]

She saw clearly the relationship of her writings to the Bible. They were not only to exalt the Bible, they were to "attract minds to it," to call "attention to the words of inspiration which you have neglected to obey," to "impress vividly upon the heart the truths . . . already revealed," "to awaken and impress the mind . . . that all may be left without excuse," "to bring out general principles," and to "come down to the minutiae of life, keeping the feeble faith from dying."[5]

Three Metaphors That Illustrate "Lesser Light"

What did she mean by saying her writings were a "lesser light"? Three metaphors have been used in past years:

• *The "testing instrument" and "that which is tested."* Displayed in the National Bureau of Standards at Gaithersburg, Maryland, is the National Prototype Meter No. 27 which was the national reference for line measurement from 1893 until 1960. It is made of 90 percent platinum and 10 percent iridium. Today the national standard is measured by an even more accurate method involving light emitted by electrically excited atoms of krypton-86. If anyone is unsure about his "yardstick," he or she may take it to the national standard for comparative analysis.

The application is obvious: the national standard is the "greater light." Copies of this national standard (called "working standards") or industrial tools requiring exact precision and accuracy that meet the standard of the "greater light," would be "lesser lights." Yet, for all practical purposes, these "copies" function as well as the standard. A prototype standard ("greater light") exists by which all other measures ("lesser lights") are tested—but the local hardware yardstick ("lesser light") is no less faithful to its task than the "greater light," if it has passed the "test." Thus, the reliability of the yardstick is, for all practical purposes, the same as the platinum-iridium bar in Gaithersburg, Maryland.[6]

• *The comparison of forty candles with one candle.* The analogy here is that the Bible was written by about forty authors—forty candles; Ellen White is one candle. Thus, the Bible is the "greater light."[7] Both the "greater light" and the "lesser light" give sufficient light to dispel darkness. The quality of light in the "greater light" is the same as that of the "lesser light."

• *National map and the state maps.* Many road atlases have a two-page map of the forty-eight contiguous states followed by the state maps. The national map with its coast-to-coast display of the Interstate highway system is the "greater light"; the state maps, though possessing more detail, are the "lesser light." Each has its special function. Both the "greater" and the "lesser" lights have equal authority in presenting truth.

The telescope analogy. Mrs. S. M. I. Henry, well-known in the late nineteenth century as a leader in the Woman's Christian Temperance Union, became a Seventh-day Adventist while a patient at the Battle Creek Sanitarium. She and Ellen White soon developed a close friendship, largely because of their common life experiences. One of Mrs. Henry's challenges was to present the Sabbath truth to her friends in the W.C.T.U., especially because they were often the leaders in promoting Sunday legislation.

However, accepting a prophet in the Adventist Church was not easy for Mrs. Henry. After close study, she saw the role of Ellen White to be akin to a telescope through which to look at the Bible. Mrs. Henry described her new insight in an article for the January 1898 issue of *Good Health*: "Everything depends upon our relation to it [telescope] and the use which we make of it. In itself it is only a glass through which to look; but in the hand of the divine Director, properly mounted, set at the right angle and adjusted to the eye of the observer, with a field, clear of clouds, it will reveal *truth* such as will quicken the blood, gladden the heart, and open a wide door of expectations. It will reduce nebulae to constellations; faraway points of light to planets of the first magnitude. . . . The failure has been in understanding what the Testimonies are and how to use them. They are not the heavens, palpitating with countless orbs of truth, but they do lead the eye and give it power to penetrate into the glories of the mysterious living word of God."

Ellen White saw this article and asked permission to have it republished in Australia. She thought that Mrs. Henry had captured the relationship between the Bible and her work "as clearly and as accurately as anyone could ever put into words."[8] For Mrs. White, the Bible was always the "greater" light from which she derived her theological principles.

No Difference in Degrees of Inspiration

At least eight prophets mentioned in the Bible wrote for their times but their works were not included in the canon.[9] The Biblical story not only does not hint of any difference in the quality of their inspiration, it describes their work as of equal authority with the canonical prophets. We find no difference in how they received their messages or in how they communicated them and how their contemporaries responded to them. Noncanonical prophets spoke for God and were regarded as God's spokesmen by their contemporaries.

With the suggestion that some prophets were granted a higher degree of revelation/inspiration than other prophets, comes the inescapable question: Who will decide? Can an uninspired person sit in judgment on a prophet's work and decide whether he or she is a first-, second-, or third-degree prophet? The gift of prophecy, as other spiritual gifts, is given to men and women "according to His own will" (Heb. 2:4), not man's will.

In 1884 the president of the General Conference, George I. Butler, attempted to contribute to a clearer understanding of this subject by authoring ten articles for the church paper. In these articles he discussed "differences in degrees" of inspiration.[10]

Ellen White waited five years to respond, hoping that he would catch his own mistake. But when others began to pick up on Butler's point of view and teach it in Battle Creek College, she wrote: "Both in the [Battle Creek] Tabernacle and in the college the subject of inspiration has been taught, and finite men have taken it upon themselves to say that some things in the Scriptures were inspired and some were not. I was shown that the Lord did not inspire the articles on inspiration published in the *Review*, neither did He approve their endorsement before our youth in the college. When men venture to criticize the Word of God, they venture on sacred, holy ground, and had better fear and tremble and hide their wisdom as foolishness. God sets no man to pronounce judgment on His Word, selecting some things as inspired and discrediting others as uninspired. The testimonies have been treated in the same way, but God is not in this."[11]

Writings are the product of inspiration or they are not. Prophets are genuine or they are impostors.[12] Other than the difference between the common and the sacred, which should be obvious to everyone, no one is able to divide a prophet's writings into the inspired and the less inspired. As soon as one tries, the final arbiter is human reason. Each person then believes that his own reason is more dependable than anyone else's.

Through the years some have suggested that Ellen White's articles in periodicals were not as inspired as her books. Or that her letters were not inspired, only her published books. In 1882 she wrote a candid letter on "slighting the Testimonies," to be read in the Battle Creek, Michigan, church: "Now when I send you a testimony of warning and reproof, many of you declare it to be merely the opinion of Sister White. You have thereby insulted the Spirit of God. You know how the Lord has manifested Himself through the Spirit of prophecy. . . . This has been my work for many years. A power has impelled me to reprove and rebuke wrongs that I had not thought of. Is this work of the last thirty-six years from above, or from beneath?

"When I went to Colorado, I was so burdened for you, that, in my weakness, I wrote many pages to be read at your camp meeting. Weak and trembling I arose at three o'clock in the morning to write to you. God was speaking through clay. You might say that this communication was only a letter. Yes, it was a letter, but prompted by the Spirit of God, to bring before your minds things that had been shown me. In these letters which I write, in the testimonies I bear, I am presenting to you that which the Lord has presented to me. I do not write one article in the paper expressing merely my own ideas. They are what God has opened before me in vision—the precious rays of light shining from the throne."[13]

No Differences in Authority Between Canonical and Noncanonical Prophets

The suggestion that prophets can be categorized by degrees of authority is similar to the previous discussion of differences in degrees of inspiration. Such appeals to categories of inspiration and authority would reduce some prophets to merely an inspirational, pastoral role or function, without divine authority.

Sometimes this proposed categorizing of prophets rests on the difference between canonical and noncanonical prophets: Noncanonical prophets are considered pastoral/inspirational; canonical prophets are considered authoritative.

Try out that reasoning in the Bible story. How much authority did David believe Nathan had? And how did Nathan understand his role—inspirational or authoritative? "The Lord sent Nathan to David. . ." (2 Sam. 12:1). Later David (a canonical prophet) had a similar experience with another noncanonical prophet —Gad, "David's seer" (1 Chron. 21:9). Again, the noncanonical prophet was conscious of his authority: "Gad came to David and said to him, 'Thus says the Lord . . .'" (1 Chron. 21:11). Further, "So David went up at the word of Gad, which he had spoken in the name of the Lord" (1 Chron. 21:19).[14]

In his last sermon, the late associate *Review* editor Don F. Neufeld said: "Through His witness to the New Testament prophets, Jesus predicted that prophetic activity, as one of many spiritual gifts, would continue in the church. In other words, the testimony of Jesus to His people was not to cease once the books that make up our present canon of Scripture would be written. Prophetic activity would continue beyond the close of the canon.

"This brings us to an important question. If in all prophetic activity it is Jesus who is speaking, whether in Old Testament times, in New Testament times, or in post-New Testament times, *can we logically draw a distinction and say that what Jesus said in any one period is more or less authoritative than what He said in any other period?. . .*

"For example, could something that Jesus said in the first century A.D. be more or less authoritative than what He said in the 19th century A.D.? The answer, I think, is obvious. It doesn't make any sense to argue for degrees of inspiration, as if what Jesus (through the Spirit of prophecy) said in one generation was more inspired than what He said in another."[15]

When Josiah (621 B.C.) recognized the long-lost Scriptures (probably Deuteronomy, see 2 Chron. 34:14), he trembled at the impending judgments foretold on God's people as a consequence of apostasy. He was perplexed as to whether he and his leaders had enough time to institute national reform. His loyal religious leaders—Shaphan, the scholar, Hilkiah, the high priest, and many teaching Levites—were equally troubled. They all wanted to know the meaning of the Scriptures that promised both doom and blessing. Where did they turn for counsel? To the prophetess, Huldah![16]

Josiah appreciated and respected his committed scholars and religious counselors. These trusted leaders were illuminated by the Spirit of God. But they, too, with Josiah, needed a higher authority to explain what these Scriptures had meant in Moses' day and what they should mean in their day. For that authority they turned to the prophetess.

Josiah and his counselors recognized that "the authority of a message is derived from its source." They perceived the "same divine Source in both the Bible . . . and in the message of a contemporary prophet." In comparing Huldah and Ellen White, we note that both "intensified" the importance of the written Word, both focused the Word on the current situation, both "exalted" the Scriptures, and both "attracted" the people to apply the Bible to their lives, leading to reform.[17]

Common Literary Characteristics—Errors of Facts and Grammar

All prophets use their own language, imperfect as all human language is and always will be. Prophets use the language of their own family, community, and time. As the years go by, through study and travel, they improve their ability to understand and present God's messages. This growth in perception and communicative skills makes their prophetic role even more effective.

But prophets are not perfect; they make mistakes. Sometimes they have faulty memories; sometimes they make a slip of the tongue (*lapsus linguae*); sometimes they misuse grammar. When Matthew wrote "Jeremiah" instead of "Zechariah" when he found an Old Testament analogy to Judas's thirty pieces of silver (Matt. 27:9, 10; Jer. 32:6-9; Zech. 11:12), he made a mistake of memory or lapse of thought. In a similar fashion, Ellen White attributed to Peter the words of Paul in 2 Corinthians 5:14: "'The love of Christ constraineth us,' the apostle Peter declared. This was the motive that impelled the zealous disciple in his arduous labors in the cause of the gospel."[18]

The Holy Spirit corrects the prophets when their counsel, for whatever reason, may adversely affect their work. Note how Nathan was told to change his counsel to David (2 Sam. 7) and when Ellen White changed her counsel regarding the closing of the Southern Publishing Association.[19]

But the Holy Spirit does not correct the prophets' human finiteness in the use of their communication skills.[20]

Biblical Models of Inspiration Correlate with Ellen White's Ministry

Revelation is the work of God as He "speaks" to the prophet. Inspiration describes the many ways God works through His prophets in conveying His message to people. Biblical prophets and Ellen White have used at least six "models"of inspiration.[21]

Visionary Model. Most often we connect prophets with visions and dreams.[22] But God also has revealed Himself in what we call "theophanies," in which the actual presence of a heavenly being is seen or heard. We think of Moses at the burning bush (Ex. 3:4) and Joshua before Jericho (Josh. 5:13-15). On another occasion, "the Lord opened the eyes of the young man [Elisha's associate] and he saw . . . the mountain was full of horses and chariots of fire" (2 Kings 6:15-17).

Often visions and dreams are so graphic that the prophet has difficulty distinguishing them from normal reality.[23] Isaiah confidently could say, "I saw the Lord. . . . I heard the voice of the Lord" (Isa. 6:1, 8).

Ellen White had many visions and dreams where the "reality" of the dream/vision experience overwhelmed her, as it did for Daniel or Ezekiel.[24]

Witness Model. God, at times, prompted certain Biblical writers to give their own account of what they had seen and heard. John exemplified this model when he wrote 1 John 1:1-3: "That which was from the beginning, which we have heard, which we have seen with our eyes, which we have looked upon, and our hands have handled. . . . These things we write to you that your joy may be full." The Gospels of Matthew and John are examples of the witness model—they did not need a vision to write out their messages. Here the Holy Spirit was using a different kind of model of inspiration, in addition to the vision/dream model.

Ellen White wrote many pages reflecting this witness model. Her words in such a mode are as qualitatively inspired as her writings that were prompted by a dream or vision.

Historian model. Luke and Mark did not write their Gospels after receiving dreams and visions. Neither were they witnesses to the revelation as Matthew and John. Mark, it is generally agreed, depended largely on Peter's "witness." But Mark was not an "eyewitness"; he was a faithful historian.

Luke candidly describes his method of telling the gospel story in his preface addressed to Theophilus: "Inasmuch as many have taken in hand to set in order a narrative of those things which are most surely believed among us, just as those who from the beginning were eyewitnesses and ministers of the word delivered them to us, it seemed good to me also, having had perfect understanding of all things from the very first, to write to you an orderly account, most excellent Theophilus, that you may know the certainty of those things in which you were instructed" (Luke 1:1-4.)

Thus, in the historian model God expects His messengers to use all pertinent historical records, oral or written, to fill out the message. God provides the message and helps the messengers find suitable material to make the message understandable to their readers. As we discovered in earlier pages,[25] certain parts of the New Testament were imported from extraBiblical sources. These secular and nonBiblical sources became part of the "inspired" message.

Ellen White, at times, reflected the historian model, especially in the Conflict of the Ages Series.[26]

Counselor model. Some of Paul's letters, such as those to Timothy, Titus, Philemon, and portions of the Corinthian letters, are classic letters of Christian counsel. None of these letters is solely theological. In 1 Corinthians 7 we find a mix of vision truth and inspired counsel. In verse 10 Paul said: "Now to the married I command, yet not I but the Lord: A wife is not to depart from her husband." In verse 25 he followed with his counsel: "Now concerning virgins: I have no commandment from the Lord; yet I give judgment as one whom the Lord in His mercy has made trustworthy." In verse 40 he reminded the church that the wife "is happier if she remains as she is, according to my judgment—and I think I also have the Spirit of God."

If someone would suggest that vision counsel is inspired and non-vision counsel is not, we would be dividing what Paul never did. What part of the Timothy letters is more inspired than other parts? Paul would say, "I have the Spirit of God."

A large part of Ellen White's *Testimonies* would be classified as counsel from one who had "the Spirit of God." Whoever she was writing to, whether parents, children, teachers, medical workers, administrators, or ministers, she used the words, "I saw." This does not always mean that she had a special vision for specific counsel. In her years of receiving visions, she had developed a keen sense of rightness and propriety. Her collected inspired wisdom gave her a rich store from which to draw, even as Paul would do in writing his counsel to individuals and to churches. Whether transmitting judgments derived from a vision or counsel based on years of listening to God, both communications came from one mind inspired by the same Spirit.

Epistolary Model. Letters to congregations and individuals was the most common method used by New Testament writers. Some of the letters were private; others were meant to be read publicly. It seems most probable that Paul never thought that his letters to Philemon, Timothy, and Titus would become public. But we are all thankful that they did. In these letters we see a mix of common matters with obviously spiritual counsel and instruction. These New Testament letters help us understand better how to relate to Ellen White's many letters that often were private and frequently mixed the common with the sacred.

If the Lord permitted Paul's private letters to be included in the canon for universal distribution, it would be appropriate to believe that the letters of His modern prophet might also bring encouragement and corrective counsel to those who do not have the benefit of her personal ministry.

Literary model. The Bible contains portions such as the Psalms, Proverbs, and Ecclesiastes where the writer expresses his most intimate feelings through poetry and prose. Again, it seems improbable that David or the other psalmists thought that their songs would eventually be in print and circulated the world over. Their deepest emotions, elation as well as anxiety, flow like an artesian well. In God's wisdom these human emotions were meant to be preserved for the benefit of all who struggle in their daily lives.

Although Ellen White was not a poet, she also expressed her keenest emotions in thousands of diary pages. We are reminded of the apostle's words in Hebrews 1:1 that God has "at various times and in different ways" spoken to us throughout human history. In listening to David or Ellen White, we often hear our own cries of anxiety, even discouragement, as well as our joy.

God has indeed spoken to us "in different ways." Through visions and dreams, through those who witness of their own account of things seen and heard, through those who are inspired by the Spirit to research the providences of God, through those who are gifted to counsel God's people regarding His will for them, through letters of instruction and correction, and through the vehicle of emotional expression of one's deepest thoughts—through these "different ways" God has spoken to the heads and hearts of men and women "at various times."

Thus, we can see that not all prophets had visions nor did all write letters. Some prophets laid their hearts bare to others while others were more objective in witnessing to what they had seen in the lives of others—or in recording the providences of God—as they did historical research. Some foretold the future, others were forth-tellers of God's will in their time.

In four ways Jesus is the best example of how true prophets perform their responsibilities:

1. He is the Messenger, the Revealer, of the mind of God.[27]
2. He amplified the meaning of previously written Scripture.[28]
3. He applied the Scripture to current circumstances.[29]
4. He clarified the meaning of previously written Scripture.[30]

Endnotes

1. *Selected Messages*, book 3, p. 30.
2. The royalties for that volume were donated by Ellen White to removing the debt on educational institutions. See *Bio.*, vol. 5, p. 92.
3. *Review and Herald,* Jan. 20, 1903. Here Mrs. White borrowed the language of Genesis 1:16 in her phrase "greater light ... lesser light."
4. *The Great Controversy,* p. vii.
5. *Testimonies,* vol. 5, pp. 654-691. See Jemison, *A Prophet Among You,* pp. 364-374.
6. Carlyle B. Haynes promoted this metaphor in many evangelistic meetings in the first half of the twentieth century. See Roger Coon, "Inspiration/Revelation: What It Is and How It Works," *The Journal of Adventist Education,* Feb-Mar, 1982.
7. M. L. Venden, Sr., popularized this illustration for many years in his evangelistic campaigns. See Coon, *Ibid.*
8. Arthur White, *Bio.,* vol. 4, pp. 346-348; Denton Rebok, *Believe His Prophets* (Washington, D.C.: Review and Herald Publishing Association, 1956), pp. 171-181.
9. Jasher (Joshua 10:13; 2 Sam. 1:18), Nathan (1 Chron. 29:29; 2 Chron. 9:29; 29:25), Gad (1 Chron. 21:9; 2 Chron. 29:25), Ahijah (1 Kings 11:29; 14:2-18; 2 Chron. 9:29), Shemaiah (2 Chron. 12:15), Iddo (2 Chron. 9:29; 12:15; 13:22), Jehu (1 Kings 16:1, 7; 2 Chron. 19:2; 20:34), Elijah (2 Chron. 21:12-15).
10. *Review and Herald,* Jan. 8-June 3, 1884.
11. *Selected Messages,* book 1, p. 23. "Men should let God take care of His own Book, His living oracles, as He has done for ages. They begin to question some parts of revelation, and pick flaws in the apparent inconsistencies of this statement and that statement. Beginning at Genesis, they give up that which they deem questionable, and their minds lead on, for Satan will lead to any length they may follow in their criticism, and they see something to doubt in the whole Scriptures. Their faculties of criticism become sharpened by exercise, and they can rest on nothing with a certainty. You try to reason with these men, but your time is lost. They will exercise their power of ridicule even upon the Bible. . . . Brethren, cling to your Bible, as it reads, and stop your criticisms in regard to its validity, and obey

the Word, and not one of you will be lost. . . . We thank God that the Bible is prepared for the poor man as well as for the learned man. It is fitted for all ages and all classes."—*Selected Messages,* book 1, pp. 17, 18.

12. Compare Matt. 12:22-32; "God is either teaching His church, reproving their wrongs and strengthening their faith, or He is not. This work is of God, or it is not. God does nothing in partnership with Satan. My work . . . bears the stamp of God or the stamp of the enemy. There is no halfway work in the matter. The Testimonies are of the Spirit of God, or of the devil."—*Testimonies,* vol. 5, p. 671.
13. *Testimonies,* vol. 5, pp. 64-67.
14. See Coon, "Inspiration/Revelation," *The Journal of Adventist Education,* Feb-Mar, 1982.
15. Sermon manuscript, "When Jesus Speaks," preached at the Takoma Park Seventh-day Adventist Church, Feb. 2, 1980. Italics supplied. See also Kenneth H. Wood, "Toward An Understanding of the Prophetic Office," *Journal of the Adventist Theological Society*, Spring, 1991, p. 28.
16. 2 Chron. 34:21, 22; Neh. 9:30.
17. Eric Livingston, "Inquire of the Lord," *Ministry,* April, 1981. Ellen White wrote of her own prophetic duty when she noted that she was "not to give new light, but to impress vividly upon the heart the truths of inspiration already revealed [intensification]. . . . God has through the *Testimonies* simplified the great truths already given [focused] . . . . The *Testimonies* are not to belittle the Word of God, but to exalt it and attract minds to it [exaltation and attraction]."—*Testimonies,* vol. 5, p. 665.
18. *Review and Herald,* Oct. 30, 1913.
19. *Bio.,* vol. 5, pp. 191-194.
20. "The treasure [God's message] was entrusted to earthen vessels, yet it is, none the less, from Heaven. The testimony is conveyed through the imperfect expression of human language, yet it is the testimony of God."—*Selected Messages,* book 1, p. 26.
21. Juan Carlos Viera, "The Dynamics of Inspiration," *Adventist Review,* May 30, 1996, pp. 22-28.
22. See pp. 9, 10.
23. 2 Cor. 12:1-4.
24. See *Selected Messages,* book 3, pp. 34-47 for descriptions of various occasions when Ellen White received a vision or a dream.
25. See p. 378.
26. "In some cases where a historian has so grouped together events as to afford, in brief, a comprehensive view of the subject, or has summarized details in a convenient manner, his words have been quoted; but in some instances no specific credit has been given, since the quotations are not given for the purpose of citing that writer as authority, but because his statement affords a ready and forcible presentation of the subject."—*The Great Controversy,* p. xii.
27. "Have I been with you so long, and yet you have not known Me, Philip? He who has seen Me has seen the Father; so how can you say, 'Show us the Father'? Do you not believe that I am in the Father, and the Father in Me? The words that I speak to you I do not speak on My own authority; but the Father who dwells in Me does the works" (John 14:9-10).
28. "You have heard that it was said to those of old, 'You shall not murder,' . . . But I say to you. . . ." (Matt. 5:21-48).
29. "And He was handed the book of the prophet Isaiah. . . . Then He closed the book and . . . began to say to them, 'Today this Scripture is fulfilled in your hearing'" (Luke 4:17-22).
30. "And He opened their understanding that they might comprehend the Scriptures" (Luke 24:45). Juan Carlos Viera set forth these four points in a 1995 presentation.

Study Questions

1. What are six Biblical models of how inspired writers do their work? Compare those models with Ellen White's ministry.
2. How would you answer someone who suggests that in using the phrase, "a lesser light to lead men and women to the greater light," Ellen White has less authoritative divine credentials than Biblical prophets?
3. How would you respond to someone who attempts to "grade" prophets as to the degree of their inspiration and authority, and dissect their writings into that which is inspired and that which is not inspired?
4. How was Jesus our best example of how true prophets perform their duties?
5. What is the error implicit in the thought that a prophet's ministry can be categorized or divided by differences in degrees of inspiration?
6. Think of other metaphors than the three in this chapter that help to explain the phrase "lesser light, greater light."

CHAPTER 36

Hermeneutics/5
Authority and Relationship to the Bible

"The Spirit of God rests upon me with power, and I cannot but speak the words given me. I dare not withhold one word of the testimony. . . . I speak the words given me by a power higher than human power, and I cannot, if I would, recall [retract] one sentence. In the night season the Lord gives me instruction in symbols, and then explains their meaning. He gives me the word, and I dare not refuse to give it to the people."[1]

Seventh-day Adventists have believed for more than a century that Ellen White was inspired in the same manner and to the same degree as Biblical prophets. At the same time, they do not make her writings another Bible—her writings differ in function and scope, not in authority.

But how did Ellen White understand her authority? From her teenage years to her final days, she was clear about her divine assignment. Hundreds of times she prefaced her messages with "I was shown," or "The Lord showed me." She reflected on those early moments: "When the Lord first gave me messages to deliver to His people, it was hard for me to declare them, and I often softened them down and made them as mild as possible for fear of grieving some. It was a great trial to declare the messages as the Lord gave them to me."[2]

The usual response to all prophets, even to Jesus Himself, has been to ask several basic questions: "By what authority are You doing these things? And who gave You this authority?"[3] What is your work? Who sent you?

Ellen White answered these questions often. The Lord sent her "for the comfort of His people and to correct those who err from Bible truth."[4]

Mrs. White often felt rejected. During the dark hours of Dr. Kellogg's 1902 confusion in theology, she wrote to her brother-in-law, S. T. Belden: "I am not to be depressed, but am to speak the words of the Lord with authority, and leave with Him all the consequences. I am instructed by the Great Physician to speak the word that the Lord gives me, whether men will hear or whether they will forbear."[5]

To her son, W. C. White, she wrote: "The awful sense of my responsibility takes such possession of me that I am weighted as a cart beneath sheaves. I do not desire to feel less keenly my obligation to the Higher Power. The Presence is ever with me, asserting supreme authority and taking account of the service that I render or withhold."[6]

During the Ballenger confrontation in the early 1900s, she reflected: "The question is asked, How does Sister White know in regard to the matters of which she speaks so decidedly, as if she had authority to say these things? I speak thus because they flash upon my mind when in perplexity like lightning out of a dark cloud in the fury of a storm. Some scenes presented before me years ago have not been retained in my memory, but when the instruction then given is needed, sometimes even when I am standing before the people, the remembrance comes sharp and clear, like a flash of lightning, bringing to mind distinctly that particular instruction. At such times I cannot refrain from saying the things that flash into my mind, not because I have had a new vision, but because that which was presented to me perhaps years in the past, has been recalled to my mind forcibly."[7]

To Evangelist W. W. Simpson, serving in southern California in 1906, she wrote: "I am thankful that the instruction contained in my books established present truth for this time. These books were written under the demonstration of the Holy Spirit."[8]

Ellen White's Relation to the Bible and to Bible Study

We have elsewhere noted Ellen White's undeniable submission to the Bible as the test of faith and practice.[9] She understood herself as "a lesser light to lead men and women to the greater light [Bible]."[10] She made it clear that her testimonies would not have been needed if people were studying earnestly to understand the Bible.[11] She urged people to "cling" to their Bibles, and stated that none who believe and obey the Bible would be lost.[12]

Not another Bible. Neither Ellen White nor the pioneers of the Advent movement ever considered her writings another Bible. No one made that clearer than she herself. No writer ever exalted the Bible more![13]

Bible study precedes inspired confirmation. A real life incident occurred in 1888 when thoughtful leaders were in conflict over the law in Galatians. Some remembered a position that Ellen White was supposed to have taken some years before—and they wanted to find that manuscript! Ellen White indeed tried to find the manuscript, but with all her many moves it could not be located. She was troubled by its absence.[14]

But in her last spoken message to the 1888 General Conference session she referred to the incident: "Why was it that I lost the manuscript [on the law in Galatians 3] and for two years could not find it? God has a purpose in this. He wants us to go to the Bible and get the Scripture evidence. . . .This investigation must go forward. All the object I had was that the light should be gathered up, and let the Saviour come in."[15]

In other words, even as in 1848 when Adventist Bible students grappled with salient Biblical teachings, Ellen White emphasized the Adventist principle of Bible study first, and then, when needed, the confirmation of prophetic revelation. In that order![16] No prophet since Enoch and Moses has had a complete understanding of truth. All prophets have had to wait for the Lord to reveal His mind, not only through visions but also through Bible study. When God wants truth confirmed, He makes His mind known to His messengers.

Biblical Principles Worthless Unless Internalized

Attitudes. One of the most important lessons to be learned from the 1888 experience is that Ellen White was more concerned with living the truth than in discussing it. She made that clear on many occasions. If an unChristlike spirit motivated a Bible student, that suggested for her that there might be something wrong with his/her theology![17]

Another emotionally laden event occurred the day before the 1901 General Conference session in Battle Creek. Many were the challenges that the delegates faced, but probably the greatest was the need to reorganize the General Conference which, for many years, involved only a few leaders with too much authority. Ellen White called it "a king-like, kingly ruling power."[18] Close to this root problem, the leaders had to face the enormous denominational debt, the amount and kind of commercial printing being done at the Review and Herald publishing house, and the growing contention with Dr. Kellogg.

Yet, underneath all these visible problems flowed a stream of inertia to change.

This inertia not only resisted improved policies of church governance, it also resisted openness to present truth and to a deepening of spiritual attitudes. Ellen White reminded the leaders of her counsel she had been giving them for years: "Enough has been said, over and over and over again, but it did not make any difference. The light shone upon them, just the same, professedly accepting it, but they did not make any change. That is what frightens me." The root of this spiritual problem was that Mrs. White's counsel, though often used, was misapplied to suit one's point of view, and the principles were ignored: "He [God] wants you to eat His principles: to live His principles;—but those that are there now [present church leaders] never will appreciate it. They have had their test, . . . they have had their warnings, and now there must be a change."[19]

Ellen White wanted no more lip service to her counsel: "Lay Sister White right to one side. . . . Do not you ever quote my words again as long as you live, until you can obey the Bible. When you take the Bible and make that your food . . . and make that the elements [sic] of your character, when you can do that you will know better how to receive some counsel from God. But here is the Word, exalted before you today. And do not you give a rap any more what 'Sister White said'—'Sister White said this,' and 'Sister White said that,' and 'Sister White said the other thing.' But say, 'Thus saith the Lord God of Israel,' and then you do just what the Lord God of Israel does, and what He says."[20]

She wanted the church leaders to live out the principles of the gospel—not to hide behind quotations from her as if meeting some of her counsel on church work could make up for their lack of Christian character. Her many testimonies regarding the seamless union of medical missionary work with the ministry had been generally ignored. Her counsel regarding the relationship of the mind and a healthy body had also been largely disregarded.[21]

In this 1901 setting at Battle Creek, Ellen White was *not* discussing the relationship of her writings in the development of doctrine when she said further: "Do not you quote Sister White. I do not want you ever to quote Sister White until you get your vantage ground where you know where you are. Quote the Bible. Talk the Bible. It is full of meat. . . . Carry it out in your life, and you will know more Bible than you know now. . . . And I ask you to put on the armor, every piece of it, and be sure that your feet are shod with the preparation of the gospel."[22] She was simply telling these church leaders that appeals to her writings for whatever purpose was missing the mark when they were not, generally speaking, internalizing the principles of the gospel found either in the Bible or in her writings. Living the gospel was more important than "playing church" no matter how many quotations about the gospel were in their heads.

"Gifts" Tested by the Bible, Not the Bible by the "Gifts"

In 1883 George I. Butler, president of the General Conference, spoke for his generation and for Adventists to this day: "We do not hold them [Ellen White's writings] to be superior to the Bible, or in one sense equal to it. The Scriptures are our rule to test everything by, the visions as well as all other things. That rule, therefore, is of the highest authority; the standard is higher than the thing tested by it. If the Bible should show the visions were not in harmony with it, the Bible would stand, and the visions would be given up. This shows plainly that we hold the Bible the highest, our enemies to the contrary, notwithstanding."[23]

Ellen White never swerved in her submission to the Bible: "The Word of God abounds in general principles for the formation of correct habits of living, and the testimonies, general and personal, have been calculated to call their attention more especially to these principles."[24]

Primarily a Commentator, Not an Exegete

Early in her ministry Mrs. White understood her role as "the Lord's messenger" and was told: "Strange things will arise, and in your youth I set you apart to bear the message to the erring ones, to carry the Word before unbelievers, and with pen and voice to reprove from the Word actions that are not right. Exhort from the Word. I will make My Word open to you. It shall not be a strange language."[25]

Throughout her writings, but primarily in her Conflict of the Ages series, Ellen White "commented" on the Biblical story from the entrance of sin in heaven to its final removal from the universe after the millennium. Her Great Controversy Theme is the integrating thread that ties all her thoughts together in a straight line of truth.[26] She opens the Word to her readers through typologies,[27] moralisms,[28] and character sketches.[29] The space she devotes to Biblical events and persons is not always proportional to the space given in the Bible. Her emphasis on certain events or persons depends on how she believes those events and persons contribute to the unfolding of the Great Controversy Theme.[30]

Many have discovered Ellen White to be a helpful commentator on Bible texts. W. W. Prescott recalled how, after studying the eighth chapter of Daniel for several years, he still felt the need for more clarity. He made his concern a matter of special prayer. Then the strong impression came to him, "Read what it says in *Patriarchs and Prophets.*" He reached for the book, turned to the appropriate chapter, and found it to be "exactly the thing I wanted to clarify my mind on that subject. It greatly helped me."[31]

Mrs. White quoted Bible verses thousands of times. In her sermons as well as letters, testimonies, and books she speaks to young and old by focusing the Biblical texts on human situations. This type of ministry is more pastoral and devotional than what we often think of as Biblical exegesis. Millions of readers have learned to appreciate the Biblical narrative by reading her commentary.

On other occasions Ellen White speaks with doctrinal emphasis. She gives a double application to Matthew 24:4-14 as New Testament writers did for Old Testament prophecies.[32] In tracing the prophecies of Daniel and Revelation, she makes specific applications, especially in reference to Daniel 7-9 and Revelation 6-17.

Mrs. White did not attempt to comment on every verse in the Bible. She focused only on those passages that had special significance in unfolding the working out of the Great Controversy Theme. On some passages she expressly said she had no special light, such as on the meaning of the "daily" in Daniel 8:11-13. Her only comment regarding the "daily" referred to the *timing* of that prophecy, not to the application of the "daily" itself.[33]

She did not identify the composition of the 144,000 (Rev. 14:1-5). Nor did she provide definite instruction regarding many other Biblical questions that are still discussed by sincere Bible students. She wrote on those texts that seemed to be most salient in the unfolding of the Great Controversy Theme.

When she commented on the Bible, how reliable was she? Understanding the limitations of finite human nature, one would expect some discrepancies.[34] Not to have made a few mistakes would have been a first for prophets! For that reason, she never expected anyone to consider her the Bible's infallible commentator or interpreter.[35]

Further, she wanted to wean Christians away from leaning on her for quick, mistake-free decisions regarding their personal lives. She encouraged her contemporaries to become secure in their relation to God as He spoke to them individually.[36]

On rare occasions Ellen White commented on a Bible text in a manner that may seem to be out of harmony with its context. Such was done also by Biblical writers.[37]

An interesting occasion developed at times when Ellen White would comment on a text in two ways—in harmony with the context, and then in a manner that would seem to be contrary to context but for a homiletical purpose. For example, commenting on John 5:39 in *The Desire of Ages* she focused on Jesus' accusers as rejecting the Word of God because they were rejecting Him, as the context would suggest.[38] But in a 1900 letter she made a homiletical point by using that text to encourage serious Bible study. It is interesting to note that the King James Version favors the homiletical approach but later versions translate the passage with the alternate meaning, "Ye search the scriptures," which seems to be in harmony with the context.

Additional Details to the Biblical Story

Every reader of the Conflict set, for example, knows the stimulation of reading further details of many Bible stories furnished by Ellen White. However, she wrote that her writings "are not to give new light," and that "additional truth is not brought out."[39] What should we make of these statements?

A big difference exists between "new light—additional truth" and additional details. If prophets do not provide additional details, what would be their purpose? "New light," in Ellen White's vocabulary, refers to the truths of salvation. "Additional truth" intimates that which is needed for a person's salvation. One of the prophet's functions throughout the Bible, and surely in the endtime, has been to give additional details about salvation truths and the character of God. In other words, Mrs. White does not introduce doctrines that are not already in the Bible. But she does add details and insights so that those truths are seen in greater clarity, with deeper understanding—such as we find in her understanding of the Great Controversy Theme.[40]

Practical Purpose of Bible Study

In her writings, Ellen White stated that the "Bible was given for practical purposes."[41] She urged her readers to join her in taking "the Bible just as it is, as the Inspired Word" and that in "obey[ing] the Word . . . not one of you will be lost."[42]

And what are those "practical purposes"? Mrs. White's ministry, from start to finish, continually focused on the place of the Bible in bringing salvation to its readers. Studying the Bible is not primarily an academic, intellectual venture; the Bible is a rich mine from which honest people discover the truth about God and how best to relate to Him. In respect to "higher education," she wrote: "The true higher education is gained by studying and obeying the Word of God. But when God's Word is laid aside for books that do not lead to God and the kingdom of heaven, the education acquired is a perversion of the name."[43]

The purpose of the Bible, in Ellen White's thinking, is to help honest seekers relate to the cosmic conflict in such a way that God's purpose to restore sinners will be achieved. For her, Bible study and character development are inseparable.

This conceptual consistency, this linkage between the Bible, character development, and the Great Controversy Theme, is one of the primary characteristics of Ellen White's writings. This threefold linkage defines the way her writings should be understood in relation to her use of the Bible. She never saw herself as an exegete. Or as a historical scholar. Thus her readers should not look to her, primarily, as an exegete or historian. Part of her job description was to serve as God's messenger in these last days to help prepare a people to meet the Lord. The Bible was her textbook in defining what that preparation means. It was her personal guide for her close walk with God. In her hands it became the textbook for others as she exhorted them to join her in this life-changing relationship.

Ellen White's Understanding of How Inspiration Works

No half-way inspiration. Ellen White was forthright: "God is either teaching His church . . . or He is not. This work is of God, or it is not. . . . There is no half-way work in the matter. The testimonies are of the Spirit of God or of the Devil."[44] Other than the obvious distinction between the common and the sacred, Mrs. White's work cannot be divided between the inspired and the less inspired: "The Holy Ghost is the author of the Scriptures and of the Spirit of Prophecy [a metonym for the writings of Ellen White]. . . . These are not to be twisted and turned to mean what man may want them to mean."[45]

This sense of divine direction kept Ellen White from commenting on matters on which she had no special light. In 1909 a minister felt he needed counsel. Mrs. White answered him, in part: "If the Lord gives me definite instruction concerning you, I will give it you; but I cannot take upon myself responsibilities that the Lord does not give me to bear."[46]

Often divinely helped in writing and speaking. In the oft-quoted introduction to *The Great Controversy,* Ellen White wrote regarding revelation: "One writer is more strongly impressed with one phase of the subject; he grasps those points that harmonize with his experience or with his power of perception and appreciation; another seizes upon a different phase; and each, under the guidance of the Holy Spirit, presents what is most forcibly impressed upon his own mind—a different aspect of the truth in each, but a perfect harmony through all."[47]

Ellen White recognized that the Holy Spirit "guided" her in the writing process even as He was "impressing" her in the revealing process, although in a different way. She explained: "Although I am as dependent upon the Spirit of the Lord in writing my views as I am in receiving them, yet the words I employ in describing what I have seen are my own, unless they be those spoken to me by an angel, which I always enclose in marks of quotation."[48]

Sometimes she struggled for the appropriate words. In a 1901 letter she shared her gratitude for her Lord's help: "He works at my right hand and at my left. While I am writing out important matter, He is beside me, helping me. He lays out my work before me, and when I am puzzled for a fit word with which to express my thought, He brings it clearly and distinctly to my mind. I feel that every time I ask, even while I am speaking, He responds, 'Here am I.'"[49]

The time to present the message is not always under the prophet's control. Ellen White wrote: "I cannot call [the vision] to mind until I am brought before a company where that vision applies, then the things which I have seen come to my mind with force. I am just as dependent upon the Spirit of the Lord in relating or writing a vision, as in having the vision. It is impossible for me to call up things which have been shown me unless the Lord brings them before me at the time that He is pleased to have me relate or write them."[50]

Interpreting symbols. The Bible frequently employs symbols to teach lessons that otherwise would not have been understood or remembered. The prophet usually explained the symbols in some literal fashion.[51]

Ellen White recalled how "in the night season the Lord gives me instruction in symbols, and then explains their meaning."[52] In describing the future of the publishing work (1894), she wrote that "the work has been presented to me as, at its beginning, a small, very small rivulet. The representation was given to the prophet Ezekiel of waters issuing 'from under the threshold of the house eastward . . . at the south side of the altar.' . . . This work was represented to me as extending to . . . all parts of the world."[53] The symbol conveyed the meaning that otherwise would have required many words.

On another occasion, she wrote to Dr. Kellogg during his crisis years that he was represented in a vision as "trying to push a long car up a steep ascent. But this car, instead of going up the hill, kept running down. This car represented the food business as a commercial enterprise."[54] Very graphic, saving her many words that otherwise would have been needed.

Most symbols were given, not to create mysteries, but to convey truth in a graphic manner, using an economy of words. To try to interpret most symbols literally would falsify or mystify truth. Some symbols in the Bible pointed to reality, to literal events or places. The sanctuary service given by God to Moses is an example of the literal symbol pointing to a literal place. Regarding the sanctuary lessons, Mrs. White wrote: "We all need to keep the subject of the sanctuary in mind. God forbid that the clatter of words coming from human lips should lessen the belief of our people in the truth that there is a sanctuary in heaven, and that a pattern of this sanctuary was once built on this earth. God desires His people to become familiar with this pattern, keeping ever before their minds the heavenly sanctuary, where God is all and in all."[55]

Harmony in a straight line of truth. In looking back over the years in 1905, Ellen White encouraged her readers to note that "there is one straight line of truth, without one heretical sentence" in her many pages of instruction.[56] The key to this harmony is the unfolding of the Great Controversy Theme, especially as developed in the sanctuary doctrine. She said that "the sanctuary was the key which unlocked the mystery of the disappointment of 1844. It opened to view a complete system of truth, connected and harmonious, showing that God's hand had directed the great Advent Movement, and revealing present duty as it brought to light the position and work of His people."[57]

Unfolding, or Progressive Revelation

On pp. 34, 282, 304, and 311 we noted that truth comes to prophets and others only as fast as it can be understood or desired.[58] Further, truth comes to prophets and others only as fast as it is obeyed.[59] These are fundamental facts of God's communication system.

Because of God's plan to unfold truth as fast as His people are able to understand it, each generation is blessed with additional truth. Thus, we know more today about God's will than did earlier generations. Not that truth is evolving in some kind of evolutionary scheme, but our perception of truth is continually progressing.[60]

Within the Bible story we find a built-in "capacity for self-correction of understanding." The Old Testament understanding of God's plan for this world and how He will intervene and create a "new world" was clarified in later revelations, in the New Testament. This is a practical example of how God always "meets people where they are, yet knows all along where He is going!"[61]

The Seventh-day Adventist Church is a forward-looking church. Its members and leaders have not let the past be the measure for the future. The primary value of the past has been in its unique ability to reveal the leading of God and His "big picture" that He is constantly unfolding.[62]

Through the years Ellen White "was consistently ahead of the leaders. She had the ideas and the energy to set them before the people." What was the reason? She understood by concept and experience that God is always leading His people into greater light, as fast as they are able to receive it, as fast as they are willing to obey it.[63]

Mrs. White was opposed to a creedal approach to Adventist doctrine. During the 1888 General Conference, resolutions were proposed that "nothing should be taught in the college contrary to what has been taught." She noted that she "felt deeply, for I knew whoever framed that resolution was not aware of what he was doing."[64] Such a resolution would not only perpetuate errors then taught (for example, verbal inspiration of the Bible), but would also slam the door against the Spirit of God who might have further light for honest truth-seekers.

In another letter Ellen White wrote: "I could not let the resolution pass, [that nothing should be "taught in the college but that which had been taught during the past year"], that there was to be special light for God's people as they neared the closing scenes of this earth's history. Another angel was to come from heaven with a message and the whole earth was to be lightened with his glory. It would be impossible for us to state just how this additional light would come. It might come in a very unexpected manner, in a way that would not agree with the ideas that many have conceived. It is not at all unlikely, or contrary to the ways and works of God to send light to His people in unexpected ways. Would it be right that every avenue should be closed in our school so that the students could not have the benefit of this light? The resolution was not called for."[65]

For Ellen White, "the best way to deal with error is to present the truth."[66] To paper over discussion with resolutions that often conceal opposition to truth and serious discord was not her way.

She spoke also to the present generation when she addressed the 1888 General Conference session: "No one must be permitted to close the avenues whereby the light of truth shall come to the people. As soon as this shall be attempted, God's Spirit will be quenched, for that Spirit is constantly at work to give fresh and increased light to His people through His Word."[67] Christians until the end of time, and throughout eternity, will be listening to the Spirit as He continues to build on the tree of truth with new branches that extend the broad outlines understood in the past.

Endnotes

1. *The 1888 Materials*, pp. 578, 579.
2. *Early Writings*, p. 76.
3. Matt. 21:23; Mark 11, Luke 20.
4. *Early Writings*, p. 78. See pp. 170, 171.
5. *The Upward Look*, p. 279.
6. Letter 197, 1902, cited in *MR*, vol. 5, p. 142.
7. Manuscript 33, 1911, cited in Arthur White, *Messenger to the Remnant*, p. 14.
8. Letter 50, 1906, cited in "The Integrity of the Sanctuary Truth," a shelf document available from the Ellen G. White Estate, March 12, 1981; "In ancient times God spoke to men by the mouth of prophets and apostles. In these days He speaks to them by the Testimonies of His Spirit. There was never a time when God instructed His people more earnestly than He instructs them now concerning His will, and the course that He would have them pursue. But will they profit by His teachings?"—*Testimonies*, vol. 4, p. 148.
9. See pp. 170, 175.
10. See pp. 408, 409.
11. *Testimonies*, vol. 2, p. 605.
12. *Selected Messages*, book 1, p. 18.
13. "However much one may advance in spiritual life, he will never come to a point where he will not need diligently to search the Scriptures; for therein are found the evidences of our faith. All points of doctrine, even though they have been accepted as truth, should be brought to the law and to the testimony; if they cannot stand this test, 'there is no light in them.'"—*Testimonies*, vol. 5, p. 575.
14. *Bio.*, vol. 3, p. 388. See p. 197.
15. Manuscript 9, 1888, cited in A V. Olson, *Thirteen Crisis Years* (Washington, D.C.: Review and Herald Publishing Association, 1981), pp. 300-303.
16. See pp. 170, 171.
17. "I am forced, by the attitude my brethren have taken and the spirit evidenced, to say, 'God deliver me from your ideas of the law in Galatians, if the receiving of these ideas would make me so unchristian in my spirit, words, and works as many who ought to know better have been.'. . . The constant dwelling upon the law in Galatians, and not presenting the gospel of Jesus Christ in distinct lines, is misleading souls. The preaching of Christ crucified has been strangely neglected by our people. Many who claim to believe the truth have no knowledge of faith in Christ by experience." —Manuscript 55, 1890, in *The Ellen G. White 1888 Materials*, pp. 841, 843. In a gathering of church leaders at her request in March 1890, she again pleaded: "If your views on the law in Galatians, and the fruits, are of the character I have seen in Minneapolis and ever since up to this time, my prayer is that I may be as far

from your understanding and interpretation of the Scriptures as it is possible for me to be. I am afraid of any application of Scripture that needs such a spirit and bears such fruit as you have manifested. One thing is certain, I shall never come into harmony with such spirit as long as God gives me reason."—Letter 83, 1890, *Ibid.*, p. 632. See pp. 373, 374.

18. Verbatim report of remarks by Ellen White at a meeting held in Battle Creek College library, on April 1, the day before the Conference officially opened —Manuscript 41, 1901, cited in Spalding and Magan's *Unpublished Manuscript Testimonies of Ellen White* (Graham, Wash.: Corner Stone Publishing, 1992), pp. 165-177.
19. *Ibid.*, p. 171.
20. *Ibid.*, p. 170.
21. In this same talk to the 1901 leaders, she said: "What you want is this: You have a body here, wonderfully made, and you want that body should be, oh, so carefully dealt with. . . . God did not make these precious organs to be swelled like a balloon. He never made them for that, and He wants every living soul to deal with this machinery as God's machinery; they must keep in perfect order to keep the brain power all right. The brain must work, and every burden you put upon your stomach will just becloud the brain. You go into a conference like this—you sit down and eat hearty meals and neglect to exercise, and then come into the conference meeting, and you are all sleepy; your ideas are not good for anything, and you really do not know what you are consenting to."—Spalding and Magan, *Unpublished Manuscript Testimonies of E. G. White,* p. 172.
22. *Ibid.*, pp. 176, 177.
23. *Review and Herald Supplement,* Aug. 14, 1883.
24. *Testimonies,* vol. 5, pp. 663, 664.
25. *Selected Messages,* book 1, p. 32.
26. "I believe that Ellen White's genius—that is, her divine inspiration—is revealed in her understanding and presentation of the great controversy between Christ and Satan. Here lies the uniqueness of her work. . . . It constitutes the basic perspective from which she interprets the Bible."—Joseph Battistone, "Ellen White's Authority as Bible Commentator," *Spectrum,* vol. 8, no. 2, pp. 37, 38. See pp. 256-263.
27. For example, Ellen White draws a typological significance between the prophet Elijah's experiences and the experiences of God's people in the last days.
28. Study Ellen White's comments on most any Bible character in *Patriarchs and Prophets.*
29. Note Ellen White's character sketch of Daniel in *Prophets and Kings,* pp. 479-548.
30. Joseph Battistone, *Great Controversy Theme,* provides an excellent review of how Ellen White commented on the Biblical story of the great controversy in her writings.
31. "The Bible Conference of 1919," *Spectrum,* vol. 10, no. 1, p. 32. Similar experiences of A. G. Daniells and W. E. Howell were also reported.
32. *The Desire of Ages,* p. 633.
33. *Early Writings,* pp. 74, 75; Moon, *W. C. White and E. G. White,* pp. 415-427; Schwarz, *Light Bearers,* pp. 397-399.
34. See pp. 379, 387 for a discussion on Ellen White's role as a historian and the possibility of occasional errors in dates or chronology. Compare *Selected Messages,* book 3, pp. 449, 450.
35. "In regard to infallibility, I never claimed it; God alone is infallible."—Letter 10, 1895, *1888 Materials,* vol. 4, p. 1393.
36. *Testimonies,* vol. 2, pp. 118, 119.
37. Compare Matt. 1:21-23 (where Matthew stated that Isa. 7:14 predicted the virgin birth of Christ) with Isaiah's context wherein the prophet told the Judean king that "the Lord Himself shall give you [Ahaz] a sign." The word that Isaiah used was not *bethulah* (virgin) but *almah* (young woman of marriageable age). Also compare Hosea 11:1 with Matt. 2:15—two different contexts. Or compare Paul's interesting use of Deut. 25:4 in 1 Cor. 9:9, 10. These rare instances that, at first glance, seem to misapply Scripture, do not invalidate the inspired writer's messages.
38. *The Desire of Ages,* p. 211.
39. *Testimonies,* vol. 5, p. 665.
40. Two examples among many wherein Ellen White expands the details and relationships between texts are the special resurrection that occurred simultaneously with our Lord's (Matt. 27:51-53 and Eph. 4:8), and the special resurrection prior to Christ's second coming (Dan. 12:1, 2; Matt. 26:64; Rev. 1:7; 14:13.)—Roger W. Coon, "Inspiration/Revelation: What It Is and How It Works," *The Journal of Adventist Education,* Feb-Mar. 1982, pp. 24, 25.
41. *Selected Messages,* book 1, p. 20.
42. *Ibid.*, pp. 17, 18.
43. *Christ's Object Lessons,* p. 107.
44. *Testimonies,* vol. 4, p. 230; p. 691. See p. 409 for a discussion of degrees of inspiration.
45. Letter 92, 1900, to J. H. Kellogg, in *MR,* vol. 2, p. 189.
46. *Selected Messages,* book 3, p. 51.
47. *The Great Controversy,* p. vi. See Index, Inspiration, Verbal vs. thought.
48. *Selected Messages,* book 1, p. 37.
49. Letter 201, 1902, cited in *MR,* vol. 2, pp. 156, 157. This is not a reference to verbal inspiration. God used the words in Ellen White's vocabulary, not in someone else's. Everyone doing work for God has experienced that gracious touch of the Spirit while seeking right words for the occasion, whether speaking or writing.
50. *Selected Messages,* book 1, pp. 36, 37.
51. "The Infinite One by His Holy Spirit has shed light into the minds and hearts of His servants. He has given dreams and visions, symbols and figures; and those to whom the truth was thus revealed, have themselves embodied the thought in human language."—*Selected Messages,* book 1, p. 25.
52. Ms 22, 1890, cited in *1888 Materials,* p. 578.
53. *The Publishing Work,* p. 157.
54. Letter 239, 1903, cited in *MR,* vol. 1, p. 26.
55. Letter 233, 1904, cited in *MR,* vol. 14, p. 217. See Spalding, *Origin and History,* vol. 1, pp. 108-111 for thoughts on how an earthly "diagrammatic pattern" interprets the truth of the heavenly sanctuary.
56. *Selected Messages,* book 3, p. 52. "There is, throughout my printed works, a harmony with my present teaching."—*Ibid.*, p. 38.
57. *The Great Controversy,* p. 423.
58. "I still have many things to say to you, but you cannot bear them now" (John 16:12). "Whenever the people of God are growing in grace, they will be constantly obtaining a clearer understanding of His Word. They will discern new light and beauty in its sacred truths. This has been true in the history of the church in all ages, and thus it will continue to the end. But as real

spiritual life declines, it has ever been the tendency to cease to advance in the knowledge of the truth." —*Testimonies,* vol. 5, p. 463.

59. See pp. 273, 274, 310.
60. "Greater light shines upon us than shone upon our fathers. We cannot be accepted or honored of God in rendering the same service, or doing the same works, that our fathers did. In order to be accepted and blessed of God as they were, we must imitate their faithfulness and zeal—improve our light as they improved theirs—and do as they would have done had they lived in our day."—*Testimonies,* vol. 1, p. 262. "Our responsibility is greater than was that of our ancestors. We are accountable for the light which they received, and which was handed down as an inheritance for us, and we are accountable also for the additional light which is now shining upon us from the Word of God."—*The Great Controversy,* p. 164. "The Word of God presents special truths for every age. The dealings of God with His people in the past should receive our careful attention. We should learn the lessons which they are designed to teach us. But we are not to rest content with them. God is leading out His people step by step. Truth is progressive. The earnest seeker will be constantly receiving light from heaven. What is truth? should ever be our inquiry."—*SDABC,* vol. 2, p. 1000.
61. Paulien, *What the Bible Says About the End-Time,* pp. 57, 58.
62. "We have nothing to fear for the future, except as we shall forget the way the Lord has led us, and His teaching in our past history."—*Life Sketches,* p. 196. See P. Gerard Damsteegt, "Seventh-day Adventist Doctrines and Progressive Revelation," *Journal of the Adventist Theological Society*, Spring, 1991.
63. Graham, *E. G. White, Co-founder,* pp. 414, 415.
64. Manuscript 16, 1889, cited in *The Ellen G. White 1888 Materials,* p. 258.
65. Letter 22, 1889, *Ibid.,* p. 239.
66. *Testimonies to Ministers,* p. 165.
67. *1888 Materials,* p. 171.

Study Questions

1. How do you set forth the truth that Ellen White was inspired as Biblical prophets were inspired, without making her writings another Bible?
2. What was Ellen White's understanding of her authority as God's messenger? How did she express that authority in her writings?
3. How did Ellen White urge her ministerial colleagues to use the Bible as well as her own counsel? What differences would there be?
4. How do you explain the phrase, "the 'gifts' are to be tested by the Bible, not the Bible by the 'gifts'"?
5. What was the open secret that kept Ellen White's message unfolding in a "straight line of truth" for so many decades?
6. Note some illustrations of how Ellen White related to the Bible both personally and in her public ministry.
7. Give examples of how the Bible is given for "practical purposes."
8. Summarize how Ellen White understood that inspiration works.

CHAPTER 37

Hermeneutics/6

How Contemporaries Understood Ellen White's Authority

"Our position on the Testimonies is like the keystone of the arch, take that out and there is no logical stopping-place till all the special truths of the message are gone. . . . Nothing is more sure than this, that this message and the visions belong together, and stand or fall together."[1]

In 1947 L. H. Christian, church administrator for decades, summarized the thinking of Adventists for a century: "Adventists have never regarded Mrs. White as infallible. They think she was inspired as Ezekiel and other prophets were inspired, and they accept her messages as counsels from the Lord. What our leaders and believers in earlier years thought of Mrs. White was well expressed in 1922 by O. A. Johnson, one of our respected Adventist college Bible teachers: 'While neither Mrs. White nor any of her most devoted followers ever claimed that she, as a human being, never erred, yet she claims that what she wrote under the direction of the Spirit of God was to be regarded as nearly perfect as could be given through human agency.'"[2]

Difference Between a Creed and Gifts of the Spirit

Although it may seem strange today, many Adventists in the early 1860s were resistant to plans for church organization. A contributing editor to the church paper declared that even selecting a name for the scattered Adventist groups would be "wrong" and that such an action "lies at the foundation of Babylon."[3]

At the bottom of this vocal and stiff resistance was the keen memory of how the Millerites were rejected by the Protestant churches in 1844. Adventists at that time called all church organizations "Babylon" and they experienced what it meant to "come out" of church organizations (Rev. 18:4). In 1860 some Adventists believed that church organization would again lead to Babylonian tactics.

After much discussion, however, Adventists in the early 1860s chose their name, organized conferences, and provided for a system to credential ministers. But there was another fear that some saw—with organization would come a creed!

In Battle Creek, October 5, 1861, when the Michigan Conference was organized, the wording of the resolution included "covenanting to keep the commandments of God, and the faith of Jesus Christ." Some felt strongly that even these words suggested a creed.

J. N. Loughborough declared that "the first step of apostasy is to get up a creed, telling us what we shall believe. The second is to make that creed a test of fellowship. The third is to try members by that creed. The fourth is to denounce as heretics those who do not believe that creed. And fifth, to commence persecution against such. I plead that we are not patterning after the churches in any unwarrantable sense in the step proposed."[4]

After others spoke, James White, in his inimitable fashion, made a comprehensive statement that had lasting significance. It included: "I take the ground that creeds stand in a direct opposition to the gifts. Let us suppose a case: We get up a creed, stating just what we shall do in reference to this thing and that, and say that we will believe the gifts too.

"But suppose the Lord, through the gifts, should give us some new light that did not harmonize with our creed; then, if we remain true to the gifts, it knocks our creed all over at once. Making a creed is setting the stakes, and barring up the way to all future advancement. God put the gifts into the church for a good and great object; but men who have got up their churches, have shut up the way or have marked out a course for the Almighty. They say virtually that the Lord must not do anything further than what has been marked out in the creed.

"A creed and the gifts thus stand in direct opposition to each other. Now what is our position as a people? The Bible is our creed. We reject everything in the form of a human creed. We take the Bible and the gifts of the Spirit; embracing the faith that thus the Lord will teach us from time to time. And in this we take a position against the formation of a creed. We are not taking one step, in what we are doing, toward becoming Babylon."[5]

Pre-1870 Attitudes Toward Gifts of the Spirit

From its inception in 1850 the *Review and Herald,*[6] the church paper, has served as the denomination's mirror of contemporary thought. Often the role of Ellen White was discussed in its pages, either in response to readers' questions or in rejoinder to opponents of "gifts" in the church.

Especially significant is the early affirmation of Joseph Bates. In 1849 he wrote: "More than two years are now past since I proved them [the visions] true. Therefore I profess myself a firm believer in her visions so far as I have witnessed, and I have seen her have many. In every instance they have been in accordance with God's Word: setting the promises of God, and the closing scenes around us in harmonious, Scriptural order, leaving the hearers the privilege of searching the Scriptures for the proof, and also in rebuking sins of omission and commission, without partiality to friend or foe, always causing the hearts of the righteous to rejoice, and the wicked to tremble: exactly the reverse of what God taught Ezekiel was false visions."[7]

In the April 21, 1851, *Review,* James White wrote a clear and forceful presentation of why the church should expect the "gifts of the Spirit" as set forth in Ephesians 4:11-14 and 1 Corinthians 12:28. He closed his article with the question: "Can we believe that the saints are to pass the perils of the last days, the time of trouble *such as never was,* unaided by the power of the Spirit?"[8]

A Troubling Editorial

In White's editorial, October 16, 1855, he tried to escape the charge that Adventist theology consisted of "vision views." In doing so, he made a few statements that greatly disturbed many Adventists, including other leaders.

To clear the air, a committee of three was delegated to report back to a gathering of leaders in Battle Creek on the topic of how the Seventh-day Adventist Church was to relate to the prophetic ministry of Ellen White. Their report, which was unanimously approved, said, in part: "Nor do we, as some contend, exalt these gifts . . . above the Bible; on the contrary, we test them by the Bible. . . . While we hold these views [Ellen White's messages] as emanating from the divine mind, we would confess the inconsistency (which we believe has been displeasing to God) of professedly regarding them as messages from God, and really putting them on a level with the inventions of men. We fear that this has resulted from an unwillingness to bear the reproach of Christ . . . and a desire to conciliate the feelings of our opponents; but the Word and our own experience have taught us that God is not honored, nor His cause advanced, by such a course.

". . .While we regard them as coming from God, and entirely harmonizing with His written Word, we must acknowledge ourselves under obligation to abide by their teaching, and be corrected by their admonitions. To say that they are of God, and yet we will not be tested by them, is to say that God's will is not a test or rule for Christians."[9]

The significance of this statement seems self-evident. Here were leaders who had witnessed the fruits of the Spirit flowing from the gift of the Spirit—the public witness of Ellen White. As the report said so clearly, "the Word and our own experience have taught us." This report proved to be a pivotal moment in the development of the Seventh-day Adventist Church: God's last-day revelations through Ellen White were formally recognized by the church as having theological authority.

Even more interesting and compelling, several days after this report was accepted, on November 20, 1855, Mrs. White had a significant vision on such subjects as the time to begin the Sabbath, how to deal with opposers to the truth, and preparation to meet the Lord.[10] When this vision was written out first for printing as a broadside, and then to be reprinted in a small pamphlet, the leaders of the emerging church expressed their affirmation in small type at its close: "We, the undersigned, being eyewitnesses when the above vision was given, deem it highly necessary that it should be published, for the benefit of the church, on account of the important truths and warnings which it contains. (Signed), Joseph Bates, J. H. Waggoner, J. Hart, G. W. Amadon, Uriah Smith."[11]

One year later David Arnold, one of the early Seventh-day Adventists from Volney, New York, reviewed the work of the Spirit of prophecy in Biblical times and applied those principles to these latter days. He closed with the exhortation: "O be intreated by one who from eight years' experience and close observation of this mode of teaching, believes it to be from God, to be careful how you reject these Gifts of the Church, lest haply you be found fighting against God."[12]

D. T. Bourdeau authored an article that answered some of the basic questions that people sometimes raise against women having visions as well as women speaking in church. He ended his study with this appeal: "We have these productions which we consider as sacred, and before we consent to reject them, our opponents will have to present palpable proofs that they are spurious."[13]

Harbor Pilot

In 1863 Uriah Smith wrote his oft-quoted editorial, entitled, "Do We Discard the Bible by Endorsing the Visions?" He focused on the meaning of the Protestant principle, "The Bible and Bible Alone," the same motto that James White presented in his October 16, 1855 editorial. He used the illustration of the ocean liner nearing port. The ship must stop for the harbor pilot to board, to insure a safe journey through the perilous waters nearing shore. His analogy was clear: "The gifts of the Spirit are given for our pilot through these perilous times, and wherever and in whomsoever we find genuine manifestations of these, we are bound to respect them, nor can we do otherwise without in so far rejecting the Word of God, which directs us to receive them. Who now stand upon the Bible, and the Bible alone?"[14]

J. N. Loughborough was asked to write out some of his observations after witnessing Ellen White in "about fifty visions." He reviewed two instances especially which demonstrated to all present that hidden information known to no one but those involved was fully revealed by

Mrs. White: "Works of sin and darkness were reproved, and it seemed to us indeed like the work of the Lord."[15]

A significant editorial over Uriah Smith's name appeared in 1868. The editor was responding to the charge that any clairvoyant could do what Ellen White did. Conceding that a clairvoyant might have ability to describe situations "one thousand miles away," Smith said that Mrs. White's visions had nothing in common with what clairvoyants claim to see in vision. Her "testimony is to reprove sin and correct wrong; and by their fruits, says the Saviour, we shall know them. . . . Nor have we yet to learn of the first instance in which a mesmerized subject, has brought to light hidden iniquity, and exposed sin and wrong. . . . This is just the difference between the two manifestations. . . . Ever bear in mind that the work of the visions is to correct error, restrain from sin, expose hidden evils, and tear self-deception from the sinner and the careless professor, and then say if you can that they are the work of mesmerism, or of demons."[16]

J. N. Andrews provided twenty points that have instructed the church since 1870 as to how Adventists understand their belief in "the doctrine of spiritual gifts, and particularly of the visions of Sister White." In this article he raised the question of making a "test" of the "gift," and made it plain that "the gifts of the Spirit pertain almost wholly to the household of faith. Men who have no acquaintance with them cannot be affected by them."

Further, he said, "We therefore do not test the world in any manner by these gifts. . . . Upon none of these persons do we urge these manifestations of the Spirit of God, nor test them by their teaching."

However, he believed that when men and women have the "opportunity to become acquainted with the special work of the Spirit of God, so that they shall acknowledge that their light is clear, convincing, and satisfactory. . . [to such] we consider the gifts of the Spirit are clearly a test."

In reference to "the reception of members . . . we desire . . . to know two things: 1. That they believe the Bible doctrine of Spiritual gifts; 2. That they will candidly acquaint themselves with the visions of Sr. White. . . . And those who occupy this ground, are never denied all the time they desire to decide in this matter."[17]

The General Conference session, March, 1870, voted a strong affirmation of Ellen White. This meeting, held in Battle Creek where wild allegations against the Whites had been carefully investigated and thoroughly rejected, signaled a clear advance in recognizing her authoritative counsel. It spelled out some of the reasons why Mrs. White's work had been wrongfully accused and why others would arise in the future attempting to diminish her authoritative voice.

The list of "facts" included the admission of "worldliness and selfishness" that pervaded those who professed "to believe the Testimonies," including a "licentious" and "deplorable case of depravity" in a particular minister. These leaders also acknowledged that, in spite of the warnings of the Testimonies against unacceptable policies in the publishing house, the house leaders continued "exactly the course against which they were warned, thereby contradicting their profession and wounding the cause." They also recognized that "those who disregard these Testimonies, whether in private or public life, have shown themselves to be lamentably weak in judgment, and have wounded themselves and the cause by their unfaithfulness."

In their resolutions they voted, "That we will humble ourselves before God for these things, and endeavor to so walk in harmony with the teachings of the Spirit, as no longer to present such inconsistency in our lives, and to grieve God's Spirit away from us."

Further, "That we recognize the wisdom of God in the 'Testimonies to the

Church,' and that it is dangerous and destructive to disregard or neglect their instructions; and we confess our weakness and inability to carry on this sacred work to divine acceptance, without their aid."[18]

1871-1888 Affirmations

Three years later, in 1873, at another General Conference session, it was voted "That our confidence is increasing in the gift of the Spirit of prophecy which God has so mercifully placed in the third angel's message; and that we will endeavor to maintain an affectionate regard for its presence and its teaching; and we hereby request our Executive Committee to prepare or cause to be prepared a work giving our reasons for believing the testimonies of Sister White to be the teachings of the Holy Spirit."[19]

Here were strong, hardy, resilient men and women, living in the swiftly changing turbulence of the nineteenth century, sensitively aware of those who challenged the presence of "prophets" in modern times—here were men and women fully aware of what they were voting, on the basis of their Bible study and their own experience. They knew of what they were professing.

One year later, in 1874, George I. Butler, president of the General Conference, wrote several powerful articles for the church paper, but written with the general public in mind. The lead sentence was: "Perhaps there is nothing in this age of the world that excites greater prejudice than the claim that visions and miraculous manifestations of God's Spirit are to be witnessed in our time." He than proceeded to examine the claims of contemporary prophets including Swedenborg, Ann Lee, Joseph Smith, and the Spiritualists. His argument for the legitimate claims of Seventh-day Adventists for Ellen White has rarely been surpassed.[20]

In 1883, Butler, as president of the General Conference, had an excerpt from Uriah Smith's book, *Objections to the Visions Answered,* printed in the church paper. The article began: "Every test which can be brought to bear upon such manifestations, proves these genuine. The evidence which supports them, internal and external, is conclusive. They agree with the Word of God, and with themselves."

After reviewing the various objections to Ellen White's writings, Smith concluded: "This covers the whole ground of the opposition; for we have never known any objection to arise which could not be traced to one or the other of these two sources. The opposer is always a person who has either been reproved for wrongs himself, or is in sympathy with those who have been so reproved, or he is a person who is openly hostile to the positions of S. D. Adventists as a whole. But neither of these positions is, in our mind, very well calculated to enlist the sympathy of any sincere lover of honesty and uprightness, or any true friend of the cause."[21]

Probably to firmly establish the truths expressed by Uriah Smith, in that same issue Butler wrote: "They [the visions] have exerted a leading influence among us from the start. They have first called attention to every important move we have made in advance. . . . We have found in a long, varied, and in some instances, sad experience, the value of their counsel. When we have heeded them, we have prospered; when we have slighted them, we have suffered a great loss. . . . The majority of our people believe these visions to be a genuine manifestation of spiritual gifts, and as such to be entitled to respect. . . . When we have Scripture and uniform experience in their favor, we have a strong case."[22]

Integrated Coherence

Ellen White's contemporaries saw an integrated conceptual coherence to her thinking, that the distinctive message of the Seventh-day Adventist Church was integrally connected to inspired counsel:

"Our position on the Testimonies is like the keystone of the arch, take that out and there is no logical stopping-place till all the special truths of the message are gone. . . . Nothing is more sure than this, that this message and the visions belong together, and stand or fall together."[23]

1888-1915 Affirmations

W. C. White's statement before the General Conference Council, October 30, 1911, reflects the respect Adventist leadership had for the authority of Ellen White. He presented to denominational leaders the guidelines used by Mrs. White and her associates in the 1911 revision of *The Great Controversy.* This revision provided one more occasion for all to note how the process of revelation and inspiration works. Improving language to avoid unnecessary misunderstanding or offense, updating historical references, replacing historical references with even "more forceful" ones—all was done with the participating approval of Ellen White.[24]

At the General Conference session, May 30, 1913, W. C. White again presented a significant contribution to the education of Adventists regarding his mother's prophetic ministry. Topics were dealt with such as what Ellen White thought about a possible successor, his own role as his mother's "helper and counselor," more information about his mother's editorial help through the years, examples of how his mother saw strangers in vision prior to giving much-needed counsel, background information on how *The Desire of Ages* was written, the reason for "rubber-stamp signatures," and the alertness of his mother during her last years as she worked closely with her associates.[25]

Later, in that same session, he was asked to give further background on his mother's ministry. The leaders had reached the time when they knew they would never again hear Ellen White's voice.[26] Responding to some questions that may have been asked earlier, White spoke to the charge that his mother had been influenced by others (notably the president of the General Conference and the editor of the church paper), and not by the Holy Spirit, in some of her testimonies. He spoke decisively, using Mrs. White's own comments, regarding whether all her articles were inspired and whether each of her words was divinely chosen.

It could be strongly argued that if denominational leaders in all areas, including schools and medical institutions, had listened closely to W. C. White in these public messages and read carefully his scores of letters on these subjects, later misunderstandings and crises regarding his mother's prophetic ministry would not have arisen. No doubt many ministers and laypeople generally did not have many, if any, of Ellen White's letters and manuscripts on how revelation and inspiration works. We have today an ample collection of her many comments on how she received and conveyed messages from the Lord. But her son, W. C. White, surely made the record clear on many occasions.

Post-1915 Reflections

F. M. Wilcox, editor of the church paper for more than three decades, and one of the five original trustees of the Ellen G. White Estate, Inc., wrote often on the contribution of Ellen White to the Adventist Church. An editorial in 1921 is typical of his consistent position: "As God has spoken to His church in past ages by prophets and special messengers, so to the remnant church He has sent by His own chosen servant many special messages of warning, reproof, instruction, and exhortation. These messages are contained in the writings of Mrs. E. G. White. . . . They do not constitute for the remnant church a new Bible, as our opponents sometime charge. . . . Rather, they constitute a spiritual commentary upon the Scriptures, a divine illumination of the Word, expressing in detail many of its great principles."[27]

Again, in 1928, Wilcox represented the thinking of the church: "The writings of Mrs. White were never designed to be an addition to the canon of Scripture. They are, nevertheless, the messages of God to the remnant church, and should be received as such, the same as were the messages of the prophets of old. As Samuel was a prophet to Israel in his day, as Jeremiah was a prophet to Israel in the day of the captivity, as John the Baptist came as a special messenger of the Lord to prepare the way for Christ's appearing, so we believe that Mrs. White was a prophet to the church of Christ today. And the same as the messages of the prophets were received in olden times, so her messages should be received at the present time."[28]

Kenneth H. Wood, *Adventist Review* editor for 16 years, observed in his September 15, 1977, editorial: Each succeeding generation "that lauds the ancient prophets and rejects contemporary ones becomes guiltier than the preceding one, since it has greater light and additional lessons from history. How great, then, is our guilt today if we fail to study and apply the counsels given to us by God through Ellen G. White." The editorial, entitled "Stoning God's Prophets," ended with this admonition, "This is no time to stone God's prophets. It is time to heed them."

In 1980 Neal C. Wilson, president of the General Conference, offered five points regarding the characteristics that are associated with the prophetic office, whether in Biblical times or in the ministry of Ellen White: "Originality is not a test of inspiration. . . . God inspires people, not words. . . . The Holy Spirit helps the messenger to select his material carefully. . . . The prophet's use of existing materials does not necessarily mean that the prophet is dependent upon these sources. . . . Whenever we recognize similarities we must also see the dissimilarities."[29]

Endnotes

1. G. I. Butler, president of the General Conference, cited in *Review and Herald* Supplement, Aug. 14, 1883.
2. Christian, *Fruitage of Spiritual Gifts,* pp. 53, 54.
3. *Review and Herald,* March 22, 1860. See p. 182 for a discussion of how the Seventh-day Adventist Church organized itself.
4. *Review and Herald,* Oct. 8, 1861.
5. *Ibid.*
6. On Jan. 5, 1978, the name was changed to *Adventist Review.*
7. *A Seal of the Living God* (New Bedford, 1849), p. 31.
8. *Review and Herald,* April 21, 1851. See also *Ibid.,* Feb. 28, 1856.
9. *Review and Herald,* Dec. 4, 1855.
10. This vision became Pamphlet No. 1 of the *Testimonies,* now found in *Testimonies,* vol. 1, pp. 113-126.
11. *Testimony for the Church* (No. 1, 1855), p. 8.
12. *Review and Herald,* Feb. 28, 1856.
13. *Ibid.,* Dec. 2, 1862.
14. *Ibid.,* Jan. 13, 1863.
15. *Ibid.,* Dec. 25, 1866.
16. *Review and Herald,* Sept. 29, 1868.
17. *Ibid.,* Feb. 15, 1870.
18. *Review and Herald,* Mar. 22, 1870.
19. *Ibid.,* Nov. 25, 1873.
20. *Ibid.,* May 12, 19, 26; June 2, 9, 1874.
21. *Review and Herald,* Aug. 14, 1883.
22. *Review and Herald* Supplement, Aug. 14, 1883. However, one year later, in a series of "maverick" articles for the church paper, G. I. Butler, still president of the General Conference, "meticulously argued that parts of the Bible were less fully inspired than other parts. Even though Butler himself did not abandon any essential characteristic doctrine, Ellen G. White in 1889 vigorously opposed his proposal, and it does not appear to have been openly adopted by any contemporary Seventh-day Adventist writer."—Mervyn Maxwell, "Brief History of Adventist Hermeneutics," *Journal of the Adventist Theological Society,* Autumn, 1993, p. 212.
23. Ibid.
24. *Selected Messages,* book 3, pp. 433-440.
25. *General Conference Bulletin,* June 1, 1913.
26. The last General Conference session she attended was in Washington, D.C., in 1909.
27. *Review and Herald,* Feb. 3, 1921.
28. *Ibid.,* Oct. 4, 1928.
29. *Adventist Review,* March 20, 1980.

Study Questions

1. How did Ellen White's contemporaries express their confidence in her authority?

2. What special significance do you see in the select committee's report in 1855 regarding their confidence in Ellen White and in her relationship to the Bible?

3. How do you explain the phrase, "progressive revelation"? Are there better ways to set forth the same idea? What are the dangers of misusing that phrase?

CHAPTER 38

Hermeneutics/7
1919 Bible Conference/History Teachers Council

"The 'pioneer position' urged that the writings could not be divided into 'inspired' and 'uninspired' sections, but seemed to have no real means of dealing with apparent discrepancies. The 'new view position,' with its emphasis upon context, offered a means of explaining those apparent discrepancies. Each side seemed to have additional concepts that could have been useful to the other. Sufficient opportunity for a dialogue seemed to be present."[1]

In 1919 a Bible Conference was held July 1-19, and a Teachers Council July 20-August 1. About sixty-five people attended these two meetings, not all present for both. About twenty-eight teachers are listed in attendance at the Council, representing fourteen colleges (2- and 4-year).[2]

Stenographers transcribed not only the lectures but also much of the ensuing discussions—a massive record of 2,494 pages. However, nearly half of these pages are duplicates, with the first copy totaling 1,308 pages. Of the 1,308 pages, about 1,100 are from the Bible Conference, the remainder from the Council.[3]

This material lay unnoticed in the General Conference archives until a year after the establishment of the General Conference Archives in 1983. Why were these records placed in the archives? The answer lies in the record itself. Many delegates talked freely, often in strong disagreement. Some would make comments that they would moderate after discussion. The judgment of many suggested that no possible good could come from publicizing the disagreements among leading Adventist thinkers over such colorful topics as "the Eastern question." Some believed that it would be "a rather hazardous thing to throw this out all over." Others wanted the material reduced about fifty percent and provided to the delegates only. Some wanted a synopsis sent to all church members, and others wanted nothing sent out.

After listening to the discussion, A. G. Daniells, president of the General Conference and chairman of the Bible Conference, said: "I sometimes think it would be just as well to lock this manuscript up in a vault, and have anyone who wishes to do so come there for personal study and research."[4]

The Locked-up Manuscript

It is more than interesting that the president's suggestion (which was eventually followed) was made subsequent to a spirited discussion regarding such subjects as the Eastern question and the Arian-Trinity controversy.[5] Unfortunately, some have used Daniells's statement to include the discussion on the authority and inspiration of Ellen White, a discussion that took place on July 30 and August 1, *two weeks after Daniells's suggestion "to lock up this manuscript."*

The two-day discussion in the Teachers Council on the role and function of Ellen White illuminated how Christians through the centuries, especially since the Reformation, have been in disagreement as to how God speaks through His prophets. One of the Adventist advantages is that Adventists lived very closely to Ellen White throughout her seventy-year ministry. They saw all aspects of her life and work. But even then, some Adventists strongly advocated the verbal inspiration position while others, more keenly aware of the process of revelation/inspiration, maintained the thought-inspiration position. *This fundamental contention lay at the bottom of the discussion in 1919.*

With W. E. Howell as chair of the Council, Daniells was asked to make the opening statement. He referred to his confidence in Ellen White even though he "had perplexities through the forty years" of his ministry, "but time has helped me to understand; and I have concluded that we do not see from the Lord's standpoint."

One of his concerns was the charge that he himself was a "doubter of the Testimonies" because he did not believe that they were verbally inspired.[6] He appealed to the teachers: "Oh, I would feel terribly to have this denomination lose its true, genuine, proper faith in this gift that God gave to this church in these messages that have come to us. I want that we shall stay by this clear through to the end."[7]

The Fruit of Ellen White's Ministry

Daniells declared that the "strongest proof" for the genuineness of the prophetic gift in Ellen White was its "fruits , . . . not in physical and outward demonstrations."[8] He went on to suggest how this "gift" should be taught to others. He would "begin with the beginning of this movement. At that time here was a gift to that individual, at the same time came this movement of the three-fold message. They came right together in the same year. That gift was exercised steadily and powerfully in the development of this movement. The two were inseparably connected, and there was instruction given regarding this movement in all its phases through this gift, clear through for seventy years."

He then reviewed how the fruit of Ellen White's writings had made the difference in the church's attitude toward the Bible and its study; in the church's commitment to evangelism, in this country and the world over; in the Adventist habit of unselfish support of this worldwide outreach; in its community help work; in its health and medical missionary programs, and in its "wholesome" educational philosophy. He concluded his talk with this challenge: "If that [recital of her impact on all areas of Adventist life] is not evidence of the source of this gift among us, then I do not know what would be evidence."

In reference to a question regarding Ellen White's relationship to the Bible, Daniells made it clear that it would be wrong to say that the "Spirit of prophecy [meaning Ellen White's writings] is the only safe interpreter of the Bible." After all, he said, what then would we do with people who become Adventists in other lands, "who have not seen a book on the Spirit of prophecy?"

Daniells spoke of his talks to ministerial meetings where he urged workers to study the Bible first and then to use "the Spirit of prophecy to enlarge our view. . . . The earnest study of the Bible is the security, the safety of a man."

On that point, W. W. Prescott and W. E. Howell added to Daniells's illustration as to how Ellen White's writings opened the deeper meaning of certain questions and texts that had troubled them.

Prescott then asked Daniells how Ellen White should be used to "settle historical questions." Daniells gave the proper answer: "Sister White never claimed to be an authority on history, and never claimed to be a dogmatic teacher on theology. She never outlined a course of theology. . . . She just gave out fragmentary statements, but left the pastors and evangelists and preachers to work out all these problems of scripture and of theology and of history."

Recalling the 1911 revision of *The Great Controversy,* he said that such work did not shake his faith but "there are men who have been greatly hurt by it, and I think it is because they claimed too much for these writings."

Regarding the conflicts between the King James Version and the appearance of more modern translations, Daniells responded that he did not "think Sister White meant at all to establish the certainty of a translation. . . . She used whichever version helps to bring out the thought she has most clearly."

The question relating to verbal inspiration arose again, to which he said: "I cannot camouflage in a thing like this. I have stood through it about forty years unshaken, and I think it is a safe position; but if I were to take the position that some do on the Testimonies, I would be shaken. I would not know where to stand."

Questions arose regarding Ellen White's counsel on health reform. Daniells's answer reflected the principles that Ellen White taught: "It is well known from the writings themselves and from personal contact with Sister White, and from common sense, that in traveling and in knowledge of different parts of the world, that the instruction was never intended to be one great wholesale blanket regulation for peoples' eating and drinking, and it applies to various individuals according to their physical condition and according to the situation in which they find themselves."

He went on to remind the group that "Sister White was never a fanatic, she was never an extremist. She was a level-headed woman. She was well-balanced. I found that so during a period of forty years of association with her."

W. E. Howell observed that those who use two positions of inspiration, one for the Bible and one for the writings of Ellen White, are in danger of making "extreme and radical positions." Yet, he also observed that the verbal-inspiration position seemed to be more prevalent among church members and many ministers, and that to correct this misunderstanding would take much wisdom.

C. L. Benson noted that letters had already arrived from members at home, wondering about the positions of the leaders of the General Conference. Benson voiced his fear that church members, being influenced by their local leaders would consider that those representing thought inspiration were "liberal." If history and Bible teachers taught what they had been hearing at the Council, "our schools are going to be at variance entirely with the field."

J. N. Anderson put the question clearly: "Can we hold something in the back of our head that we are absolutely sure about, and that most of the brethren stand with us on?—can we hold those things back and be true to ourselves? And furthermore, are we safe in doing it? Is it well to let our people in general go on holding to the verbal inspiration of the Testimonies? When we do that, aren't we preparing for a crisis that will be very serious some day? It seems to me that the best thing for us to do is to cautiously and very carefully educate our people to see just where we really should stand to be consistent Protestants, to be consistent with the Testimonies themselves, and to be consistent with what we know we must do, as intelligent men, as we have decided in these meetings."

The Core Issue

M. E. Kern probably got to the heart of the discussion more quickly than others. He asked how a man, in the same talk, could say "that we cannot depend on this historical data that was given in the Spirit of prophecy, and then assert his absolute confidence in the Spirit of prophecy and in the Testimonies." Then his central question: "What is the nature of inspiration? How can we feel and believe and *know* that there is an inconsistency there—something that is not right—and yet believe that the Spirit of prophecy is inspired?"

Kern, an educator, knew how difficult

it would be to explain all this to young people: "We may have confidence ourselves, but it is hard to make others believe it if we express this more liberal view [thought inspiration without a positive basis for confidence]. I can see how some might take advantage of this liberal view and go out and eat meat every meal, and say that part of the Testimonies is not reliable."

Kern pressed on: "Can we, either in the Bible or the Testimonies, play upon a word and lay down the law and bind a man's conscience on a word instead of the general views of the whole scope of interpretation? I do not believe a man can believe in the general inspiration of the Spirit of prophecy and still not believe that vegetarianism is the thing for mankind. I can understand how that testimony was written for individuals, and there are exceptions to it, and how Sister White in her human weakness could make a mistake in stating a truth, and still not destroy the inspiration of the Spirit of prophecy; but the question is how to present these matters to the people."

A few minutes later he said: "I wish we could get down to bedrock. I do not think we are there yet." He was seeking for the principle behind the way God deals with human prophets. He was asking that we should be looking at the message rather than the messenger, the content rather than the container. He believed that the consistency and coherence of the message is the basis for its integrity, not the human elements associated with certain details of the message.

G. B. Thompson seemed to be aiming at Kern's concern: "My thought is this, that the evidence of the inspiration of the Testimonies is not in their verbal inspiration, but in their influence and power in the denomination." He then related a remarkable incident. A year earlier, Ellen White had written a letter to him and A. G. Daniells, but had not mailed it until a few days prior to the Conference. When they received it, the letter described a meeting held in the church the night before! Daniells read the testimony at the Conference, and the audience of 3,000 was gripped with awe. Thompson spoke for many: "I was convinced that there was more than ordinary power in that document. . . . It carried the power of the Spirit of God with it."

But Kern felt that more needed to be said: "This question of verbal inspiration does not settle the difficulty. . . . She was an author and not merely a pen."

Dark Cloud of Verbal Inspiration

The Council participants were finding it difficult to see through the dark cloud of verbal inspiration that had enveloped many (perhaps most) of the church's ministers and teachers in 1919. The end result was a church membership, for the most part, that accepted Ellen White's writings without understanding the hermeneutical principles that Mrs. White herself had penned. As elsewhere in Christendom, verbal inspiration led to a sense of infallibility, either in the words of the Bible or in Ellen White's writings. Nothing seems to be more unnerving (to the verbal inspirationist) than to be told that Ellen White's words (or certain Biblical words or details) need to be understood in terms of "time, place, and circumstances." To speak in this way awakens insecurity and the cry of "liberalism."

Further complicating the 1919 event was the fact that W. W. Prescott had been given a major role in presenting many subjects. A brilliant scholar, an experienced administrator, a clear thinker in placing Christ at the center of Adventist theology—yet, it was Prescott who helped to promote the theory of verbal inspiration while he was president of Battle Creek College in 1893. Referring to that era, W. C. White wrote that Prescott's "forceful" position on the subject of inspiration led to "questions and perplexities without end, and always increasing."[9] Now, in 1919, White's observations became fulfilled prophecy

—the anguish of loyal believers in the ministry of Ellen White locked in divisive camps, calling each other "liberals" and "conservatives." The tone of discussion revealed deeply committed men and women all of whom thought they were protecting the messenger of the Lord—yet, in unhappy combat. White's prediction that the "perplexities" were "always increasing" extends to this day.

In Prescott's many remarks, he did his best to reveal his latest thinking after he had navigated out from underneath the verbal-inspiration cloud. No doubt some delegates at the Council were not prepared to accept readily his counsel, though now correct, in view of his previous positions on inspiration, his earlier "flirtation" with pantheism, and other matters.[10]

Near the end of the Council, Prescott bared his soul in relating his own experience in acknowledging that prophets did not write inerrantly, being dictated to by God. He said: "I did not throw up [out] the Spirit of prophecy, and have not yet; but I have had to adjust my view of things. I will say to you, as a matter of fact, that the relation of those writings to this movement and to our work, is clearer and more consistent in my mind than it was then. But still you know what I am charged with [that he was a "liberal" who was diminishing Ellen White's authority]. I have gone through the personal experience myself over that very thing that you speak of. If we correct it here and correct it there, how are we going to stand with it in the other places?"

Prescott recounted his experience with a General Conference leader who was reproved by Ellen White during the 1888 crisis and several times afterwards for his policies and attitudes. The leader wanted Prescott to help him "draw the line between what was authoritative and what was not." Prescott replied: "I will not attempt to do it, and I advise you not to do it. There is an authority in that gift here, and we must recognize it."

When Prescott was asked whether his "own findings must be your authority for believing and not believing," he replied, "You can upset everything by applying that as a general principle." Further questions were asked because he seemed to be equivocal regarding what he felt needed to be changed in Ellen White's writings [in the 1911 refinement of *The Great Controversy*] and his ringing endorsement of her authority. He responded: "I did not attack the Spirit of prophecy. My attitude has been to avoid anything like opposition to the gift in this church, but I avoid such a misuse of it as to set aside the Bible. I do not want anybody to think for a moment that I set up my judgment against the Spirit of prophecy."

A. G. Daniells summarized the two-day deliberations, defending his colleagues in the General Conference and suggesting a basis for common agreement: "I know that my associates have confidence right down on the solid platform of this whole question; and I know that if many of you had gone at this thing and experienced what we have, you would have passed through an experience that would have given you solid ground. You would have shaken a bit, and you are beginning to shake now, and some of you do not know where you are going to land. These questions show it. But that is not to say there is not a foundation. It *is* to say that you have not gone through the toils yet and got your feet on solid ground.

"I want to make this suggestion, because with all these questions we cannot follow one line of thought logically. We must use good sense in dealing with this whole question, brethren. Do not be careless with your words. Do not be careless in reporting or representing men's views."[11]

What Should We Learn From the 1919 Conference/Council?

(1) Some wonder why W. C. White was not present at the 1919 meetings. As a member of the General Conference Committee, he was automatically a dele-

gate and did receive the mimeographed invitation. Perhaps, after looking over the agenda, which included nothing on the work and relevance of Ellen White, he felt his time would be better spent in the Elmshaven office.[12] Working alone after his mother's staff had dispersed in 1915 (no budget allotted by the Trustees, not even provision for a letterhead), White felt pressure to finish compiling *Counsels on Health* to satisfy the requests from medical leaders. If anyone had been able to predict that two long days of discussion (that arose spontaneously) would have been devoted to his mother's prophetic role, "he doubtless would have made a greater effort to attend."[13]

W. C. White Not Present

W. C. White, the most valuable source person available, could have answered some of the questions more accurately, more constructively, than anyone else.[14] Perhaps, with his experience and communicative skills, he could have helped to focus more clearly the issues that were seriously dividing church leaders and laypeople at that time, and for years to come. That focus would have led to a careful, forthright examination of the facts regarding the work of a prophet in modern times. Cutting away mistaken ideas would have been painful for some, but the healing would have been quicker and longer lasting than the widening gap of confidence that followed the Conference/Council.

However, another aspect must be considered: For many church leaders, at the Conference and in the field, W. C. White was suspect, and had been for twenty years, as being one of the "liberals."[15] Why? Because he had been emphasizing that his mother's writings should always be understood in context with "time, place, and circumstances" determining their meaning and application. W. C. White, with Daniells, Wilcox, and later Prescott, represented those who were thought-inspirationists, though that term had not been used at that time.

Often at the heart of the controversy with Dr. J. H. Kellogg and A. T. Jones was the issue of how to interpret the statements of Ellen White. These two articulate leaders eventually used Mrs. White's writings only when they seemed to support their views. Part of Jones's attack on Daniells was based on Mrs. White's comments regarding the unreliability of General Conference leadership in 1897, and then charging that the same statements applied in 1906.[16] On other occasions, when they found difficulty with her writings, their response was that "someone" had told her wrong information. Often that "someone" was, in their mind, her son W. C. White.[17]

From 1919 to his death in 1937, W. C. White's contribution to the facts surrounding the prophetic ministry of his mother was enormously helpful.[18]

(2) Beneath the differences of the delegates (and many of the ministers and laypeople in the churches) over such agenda topics as the Eastern question, the Arian-Trinity controversy, the two covenants, the "daily" (Dan. 8:11-13), beginning and ending of the 1260 years, and the king of the north (Daniel 11), was the issue of how to interpret Ellen White. Accusations of disloyalty to her, of unfaithfulness to her authority by picking and choosing her writings as to what was inspired, of unsafe leaders leading the denomination down a fearful path without the guidance that she had given the denomination for seventy years—all such spirited words directed at General Conference officers and those among the teachers in the colleges who supported them did not bring out the best in people, on either side.

The Conference/Council was charged with tension the moment it opened. At stake, each side believed, was the authority of Ellen White. Each side further believed that on this issue would hang the future of the church.[19]

(3) Both sides, verbal- and thought-

inspirationists, had much of value to hold on to. But neither side saw the heart-truth for which the other was contending. Thus they missed the transcending, healing nature of the ellipse of truth.[20] Neither side saw clearly the biggest reason why the ministry of Mrs. White had made such an enormous impact on their lives, though each appealed to their own experience under her guidance as undeniable. Neither side could see clearly that her distinctive message, her coherent, integrating theological principles, were the foundation for her guiding concepts in education, health, mission, and the Adventist theological teachings.

The foundation principles, understood as the Great Controversy Theme,[21] were the reasons why the policies these leaders had followed were so effective. They had been living so close to the rapidly developing church and the equally rapid change in national and world conditions that most of them had not stepped back far enough to see the big picture. Both sides saw these undeniably wonderful results (in education, health, and rapid church growth) and they wanted to protect their divinely guided messenger from the use or misuse of her writings. Each side saw the other as the ultimate problem when they perceived what seemed to be a lack of appreciation for the gift of prophecy in their midst.

Downside of Verbal Inspiration

(4) But the downside of these two positions was played out in the lives of some of the most eloquent partisans. Many contributing influences affected Dr. John Harvey Kellogg but probably none was more crucial than his understanding of how revelation and inspiration works. The eventual drift of A. T. Jones and E. J. Waggoner, spiritual heroes of 1888 and the early 1890s, was largely caused by the same misunderstanding. Kellogg and Jones, especially, held to a rigid concept of virtual verbal inspiration without using the contextual principle for understanding Mrs. White's statements.[22]

(5) But some of those contending for thought inspiration found themselves on the other side of the slippery slope. Though they had a clearer grasp of how God speaks to the minds of prophets, few seemed to possess the inner core of Ellen White's message that provided the theological structure for her global contributions to theology, education, health, mission, etc.

As time passed, some of these otherwise able leaders had nothing to hang on to when they began to separate what was inspired from what was not. When they said that Ellen White could not be trusted in historical and medical matters, or even in administrative and theological issues —where would they stop? If Ellen White could not be considered an authority in these matters, how could she be considered authoritative in others?[23]

We do not know the motivation behind the written or public statements of either verbal- or thought-inspirationists. Generally, however, thought-inspirationists contended for the freedom to interpret Ellen White on the basis of sound hermeneutical principles—such as the application of time, place, and circumstances. Such sought the principle behind the policy. This approach had been best articulated by W. C. White in his remarks regarding the 1911 revision of *The Great Controversy.*[24] F. M. Wilcox, in a general way, at the Council, also asserted this coherent, integrating approach to the writings of Ellen White: "I would like to ask Brother Daniells if it could be accepted as a sort of rule that Sister White might be mistaken in details, but in the general policy and instruction she was an authority."[25]

Others who contended against the verbal-inspirationists did not accept, or perhaps did not understand, this larger, more constructive reasoning. The thought would be expressed, for whatever reason, "While I believe [that Ellen White is a prophet of God], I do not believe [that] all she writes and all she says is inspired; in other words, I do not believe in verbal inspiration."[26]

That kind of thinking, if not severely modified, is an open door through which many have walked away from the Adventist Church over the years. Such thinking leads to personal judgment as to what a "prophet" means and to personal judgment as to what is inspired and what is not. This is truly a slippery slope if there is not a prevailing, fundamental message to hold on to.

At least verbal-inspirationists knew, in their minds, how to hang on to authority—even if it might not have been for the right reasons. Those of this group (and there were many) who remained in the church as strong leaders in administration and evangelism, believed that they were the only ones left who could save the denomination from apostasy. They could point to many who tried to "reinterpret" Ellen White as examples of where such thinking would lead others—men such as the Ballenger brothers (A. F. and E. S.), J. H. Kellogg, A. T. Jones, W. A. Colcord, E. J. Waggoner, L. R. Conradi, and W. W. Fletcher.

Common to all these highly visible leaders who defected was their decision "that the Spirit of prophecy could be divided into 'inspired' and 'uninspired' portions. It seems relevant that, in most cases, those who began to make such determinations eventually lost confidence in the Spirit of prophecy."[27]

(6) Evidence that the Conference/Council did not appear to change anyone's mind is reflected in later comments. On one hand, A. G. Daniells wrote to W. C. White that "we stand together more unitedly and firmly for all the fundamentals than when we began the meeting."[28]

(7) On the other, J. S. Washburn, a highly visible representative of those who opposed Prescott and Daniells on their positions concerning the "daily," the Eastern question, etc., wrote an open letter to Daniells and the General Conference Committee, expressing the concern of many. In referring to "this so-called Bible Institute" where "teachers were undermining the confidence of our sons and daughters in the very fundamentals of our truth," he quoted "one of our most faithful workers" who said that the Institute "was the most terrible thing that had ever happened in the history of this denomination."[29]

(8) The issues that surfaced in the 1919 Conference/Council remain today, reflected in at least three of the four positions that divide Christians generally and Adventists specifically: (a) Those who believe that Biblical writers and Ellen White were inspired but were not given propositional truth; (b) Those who hold that Biblical writers and Ellen White received divinely dictated truth and that their messages were given as God wanted the writings to be read or heard: (c) Those who believe that the Bible and the writings of Ellen White are divinely inspired by God impressing thoughts on the prophets' minds who would then convey the message in the best language and thought frames at their disposal; (d) Those who believe that the Bible and the writings of Ellen White are generally inspired but their value is more pastoral than theological.

Endnotes

1. Bert Haloviak, "Background and Aftermath of the 1919 Bible and History Teachers Conference," an unpublished paper, 1979.
2. Robert W. Olson, "The 1919 Bible Conference and Bible and History Teachers Council," available from the E. G. White Estate.
3. *Ibid.*
4. Stenographic report of the 1919 Bible Conference and Bible and History Teachers Council, p. 912.
5. The Eastern question refers to the interpretation of the "king of the North" in Daniel 11. Most had been preaching strongly, especially in evangelism, that the "king" was Turkey; others believed that the "king" referred to the activities of the Papacy at the end of time; see Schwarz, *Light Bearers,* pp. 400-402.
6. See pp. 16, 120, 173, 375, 376, 421 for a discussion of

the difference between verbal inspiration and thought inspiration.

7. One of Daniells's most lasting contributions to this church was his book, *The Abiding Gift of Prophecy.*
8. As an example of such "demonstrations," Daniells referred to the story of Ellen White holding a "heavy Bible" on her outstretched hand. J. N. Loughborough records this miracle in his *Rise and Progress of Seventh-day Adventists* (pages 103, 104) and later in *The Great Second Advent Movement* (pages 236, 237) based on interviews he had with eyewitnesses of the event. Cursory readers of this discussion have mistakenly concluded that Daniells questioned the historicity of the event. They have missed Daniells's point, which he clarified later in the discussion when specifically asked whether he was discrediting the miracle or stating that he would not use such manifestations as a "proof" of inspiration. He replied, "No, I do not discount them nor disbelieve them; but they are not the kind of evidence I would use with students or with unbelievers. . . . I do not question them, but I do not think they are the best kind of evidence to produce." (*Spectrum*, vol. 10, No. 1, p. 37.)
9. *Selected Messages,* book 3, p. 454.
10. See pp. 120, 121, 204; Schwarz, *Light Bearers,* pp. 289, 294.
11. "The Use of the Spirit of Prophecy in Our Teaching of Bible and History, July 30, August 1, 1919," *Spectrum,* vol. 10, No. 1, pp. 27-57.
12. The list of topics to be discussed were: Person of Christ, Mediatorial Work of Christ, Nature and Work of the Holy Spirit, Two Covenants, Principles of Prophetic Interpretation, Eastern Question, Beast Power in Revelation, 1260 Days, United States in Prophecy, Seven Trumpets, Matthew Twenty-four. —Action taken by the Spring Council of the General Conference, 1919. D. E. Robinson, an editor at the Southern Publishing Association, attended the Bible Conference but apparently was not invited to the Teachers Council. Robinson, married to Ella White (Ellen White's eldest granddaughter), had worked with Mrs. White for about ten years as one of her secretaries and compilers. If anyone had known in advance that a two-day discussion of the ministry of Ellen White would follow, probably he would have been strongly urged to remain. He, along with W. C. White, would have contributed valuable information, countering some of the ill-informed statements made in that informal setting.
13. Bert Haloviak, in an unpublished paper, "In the Shadow of the 'Daily': Background and Aftermath of the 1919 Bible and History Teachers Conference," p. 5; Moon, *W. C. White and E. G. White,* p. 453.
14. W. W. Prescott's ambiguity, as sensed by some present, would have been clarified by W. C. White's presence and counsel.
15. For example, note the accusations by his brother Edson and echoed by followers of Dr. Kellogg in 1906—*Bio.,* vol. 6, pp. 62, 94-101, 155- 157; the harsh attack at the 1913 General Conference and Autumn Council, cited in Moon, *W. C. White and E. G. White,* pp. 340-342. Stephen Haskell's unsureness regarding W. C. White's role as the chief editor of his mother's writings was reflected in letters to both him and his mother in 1909. Haskell referred to "the experience that I have had," and challenged his younger colleague: "It is the dropping out of some of these things from what has been published in your mother's writings, and the changing of some things, that has been taken advantage of by the enemies of the truth and today is the cause of some of our best brethren losing confidence in you; because they think you change your mother's writings and call it 'editing.' Now I do not mean by this that you make changes in the thought, but in the wording and the reading of them."

    Later in the letter he recalled an experience "that put me to my stumps." A woman arose in a meeting where Haskell had announced that he would defend "your mother's writings from the Bible." The woman asked, "Can you prove from the Bible that a prophet ever had sons that changed the prophet's testimony, and called it editing?" Haskell answered in substance "that he could prove from the Bible that prophets had sons that did not always do right, and their not doing right tested the people. She sat down and said no more."—Moon, *W. C. White and E. G. White,* p. 361.
16. Haloviak, "In the Shadow of the 'Daily'. . .", p. 14. See page 396.
17. See *Selected Messages,* book 3, p. 63; *MR,* vol. 13, p. 122.
18. Moon, *W. C. White and E. G. White,* pp. 451-456.
19. Former General Conference president George I. Butler, in a letter written to A. G. Daniells, had foreseen the developing fissure between these two groups over conflicting interpretations of how to read Ellen White: "It is a terrible, terrible thing! And are we going into the conflict before us . . . the great and closing conflict, with two camps wrangling with each other, Arthur? I do not believe it is possible, unless we get this thing fixed up in some way, and union restored, to go on without being terribly crippled for years, and loss of many souls."—Haloviak, "In the Shadow of the 'Daily' . . .", p. 13.
20. See pp. 573-575.
21. See pp. 256-263.
22. Kellogg saw no "use of trying to explain what the Lord is doing, what the Lord says. The Lord says it as He wants to say it." "Report of the Work of the Sanitarium," Transcript, Dec. 28, 1905, Record Group 17, General Conference Report of the Work of the Archives. On a later occasion Jones told the Battle Creek congregation: "I have not a cent's worth of respect for any such plea as is made too often and especially of late years on 'Testimonies up-to-date'; as if a Testimony up-to-date is to take the place of all that ever went before it. Mahomet taught that doctrine as to his revelations—that the last revelation took the place of all that went before it. But God's revelation is not that way. God's revelation is truth, and is just as good today as it was a thousand years ago. It never gets out of date; and the last one that comes is not going to contradict, or vitiate, or set aside, or annihilate any that went before it. . . . No sir, the Bible is the Word of God. It is the same today as it was when Isaiah wrote it, when Amos wrote it, when Hosea wrote it, when Paul wrote it, and will be the same after the world is ended and gone. It is so with the Testimonies, too, as certainly as they are the truth of God."—Sermon at Battle Creek Tabernacle, Jan. 2, 1906, pp. 24, 25, Pamphlet Files. Both references cited in Haloviak, "In the Shadow of the 'Daily' . . .", p. 14.
23. This is where Prescott's presentations worried some of the 1919 delegates. As a question, probably C. L. Benson focused the issue best: "If there are such uncer-

tainties with reference to our historical position, and if the Testimonies are not to be relied on to throw a great deal of light upon our historical positions, and if the same is true with reference to our theological interpretation of texts, then how can we consistently place implicit confidence in the direction that is given with reference to our educational problems, and our medical school, and even our denominational organization? If there is definite spiritual leadership in these things, then how can we consistently lay aside the Testimonies or partially lay them aside when it comes to the prophetic and historic side of the message? And place these things on the basis of research work?"—*Spectrum*, vol. 10, No. 1, p. 46.

24. See p. 431; *Selected Messages*, book 3, pp. 433-440.
25. "Inspiration of the Spirit of Prophecy," *Spectrum*, vol. 10, No. 1, p. 53.
26. Letter from G. F. Watson to W. C. White, Dec. 15, 1913, cited in Moon, *W. C. White and E. G. White*, p. 411.
27. Haloviak, "In the Shadow of the 'Daily' . . .", p. 58.
28. Letter from A. G. Daniells, July 20, 1919, to W. C. White, White Estate correspondence files.
29. "An Open Letter to Elder A. G. Daniells and an Appeal to the General Conference," 1922, pp. 28, 29, J. S. Washburn Folder, General Conference Archives; both references cited in Haloviak, "In the Shadow of the 'Daily' . . .", p. 1.

Study Questions

1. What were the subjects at the Bible Conference that prompted A. G. Daniells to suggest that the minutes of the meeting should be "locked up" in the vault? Was the discussion on the writings of Ellen White part of that material?

2. What did Daniells declare to be the "strongest proof" for the genuineness of Ellen White's prophetic gift?

3. What were the fundamental issues that separated church leaders in 1919?

4. What are some lessons that should be learned from the 1919 Bible Conference/Council?

5. After studying the lessons to be learned from the 1919 Bible Conference, analyze how these lessons could help heal some of the divisions in the church today.

6. Can Ellen White help to resolve doctrinal divisions today?

CHAPTER 39

Understanding How the Books Were Written

"My words seem inadequate. I despair of clothing the truth God has made known concerning His great redemption, which engrossed to itself His undivided attention in the only-begotten Son of the Infinite One. The truths that are to last through time and through eternity, the great plan of redemption, which cost so much for the salvation of the human race, presenting before them a life that measures with the life of God—these truths are too full, deep, and holy for human words or human pen to adequately express."[1]

Ellen White's literary output totals approximately 25 million words or 100,000 printed pages—including letters, diaries, periodical articles, and books.[2]

Her writing habits, beginning with her teen-age years, were discussed on pages 108-120. She used editorial assistants, a practice employed by Biblical writers,[3] and, like Biblical prophets, wrote within the historical, social, and religious context of her time. She wrote with a nineteenth century accent, not that of modern times.[4]

Her wide reading habits helped her to flesh out the broad conceptual principles that she believed God wanted conveyed.[5] By the time of her death in 1915, her personal and office staff library consisted of approximately 1,400 volumes, which included more than 500 titles sold to her by one of her workers in 1913.[6]

Ellen White maintained a steady flow of letters, sermons, periodical articles, and books, especially after 1881. These materials were often reused in new formats. Sermons became periodical articles, and these articles, when reorganized and supplemented with new material, provided source material for books.

By reviewing the development of *Steps to Christ, The Desire of Ages,* and *The Great Controversy,* we will observe a pattern of how Ellen G. White books usually were created.

The Making of "Steps to Christ"

Usually printed in the 128-page edition, this 1892 volume was first produced by a nondenominational publisher[7] with the hope that it could be widely sold in America's bookstores. It was an instant success. Within six weeks of its initial printing, a *third* reprint had been issued, and within the first year, *seven* reprints.[8] Soon after the initial printing, the publisher printed the following advertisement: "It is not often that a publisher has the opportunity of announcing a third edition of a new work *within six weeks of the first issue.* This, however, is the encouraging fact in connection with Mrs. E. G. White's eminently helpful and practical work, *Steps to Christ.* If you will read this work, it will *ensure* your becoming deeply interested in extending its circulation. *Steps to Christ* is a work to guide the inquirer, to inspire the young Christian, and to comfort and encourage the mature believer. The book is unique in its helpfulness."[9]

Today, this religious classic has been published in more than 135 languages and circulated worldwide by the tens of millions.

Background of "Steps to Christ"

In the summer of 1890, *Patriarchs and Prophets,* the first volume in what would finally be called the Conflict of the Ages set, was released. Two years before, the revised and enlarged edition of *The Great Controversy* (eventually the fifth and last volume of the Conflict set) had been published. Work had begun on "The Life of Christ," which became *The Desire of Ages* (the third in the Conflict set). In addition, week after week Ellen White and her assistants prepared articles for the *Review and Herald, Signs of the Times,* and *Youth's Instructor.*

Then came a request for smaller books that could be sold in book stores or distributed by evangelists in their public meetings. Literature on the subject of conversion was especially needed.[10] Ellen White knew that this was the time for presenting in book form one of her favorite topics. She had spoken and written often, in simple, clear terms, about the steps sinners must take in finding their way to Christ. Now Marian Davis ("my bookmaker"[11]) was assigned the work of gathering from Mrs. White's diaries, manuscripts (published and unpublished), periodical articles, and previous books those materials that would make up the proposed chapters. With the materials before her, Mrs. White would often recognize that more was needed to fill out each chapter's thought. To meet this need and to provide necessary transitions, she would compose additional copy.

Marian Davis gathered materials and organized them (no small task) but did no writing. Ellen White did the writing and supervised the arrangement of her books. The work went slowly because of all her other writing and speaking commitments. In 1891 the manuscript was presented to a convention of ministers and teachers at Harbor Heights, Michigan, where it was read with great enthusiasm. At this meeting it was decided that the book should be called *Steps to Christ*. Further, it was strongly suggested that it be published by a nondenominational publishing house for wider circulation in the popular book stores—a proposal that Fleming H. Revell accepted gladly.

In 1896 the Review and Herald Publishing Association bought the copyright from Revell. After the copyright was transferred to Ellen White in 1908, she immediately assigned to the General Conference all rights in all languages other than English. Except for the Bible, *Steps* probably has been translated and printed in more languages and in greater number than any other book in history.

The first editions did not contain the present first chapter, "God's Love for Man." But after writing Manuscript 41, 1892, Ellen White quickly agreed that it would provide an appropriate beginning for the already best-seller.

A quick survey of the book reveals that it contains portions of earlier published materials from *Patriarchs and Prophets,* several volumes of the *Testimonies*, the *Review and Herald*, and the *Signs of the Times*.[12] In her broad reading, Ellen White had discovered insights and phraseologies from other authors that helped her to explain better the keen thoughts that she wanted conveyed. Obviously she felt that including certain expressions from these writers would strengthen her book.[13]

Over the years, some critics have put forth the claim that Fannie Bolton (one of Ellen White's editorial assistants for a few years[14]) had written *Steps to Christ* "in toto."[15] This allegation has been kept alive through various channels.[16] Obviously, it was impossible for the materials penned by Ellen White before 1890 to have been written by Miss Bolton, but the critics through the years have overlooked this basic fact.

Ellen White's Core Theme—the Title of One of Her Best-Known Books

Mrs. White's two-hour vision at Lovett's Grove, Ohio, in mid-March 1858, became known as the "Great Controversy vision."[17] In 1860 she stated that this vision repeated and amplified what she had been shown ten years earlier and that she was instructed to write out the vision in full.[18]

The broad outline of this vision became the first volume of *Spiritual Gifts* (1858).[19] Although others have written on the general subject of the "controversy" between good and evil, no other writer has unfolded the cosmic dimensions and the eternal consequences of the conflict between Christ and Satan as Ellen White has done.[20] The Great Controversy Theme presents a unique philosophy of history as well as a distinctive theological framework for Christian doctrine.[21]

In addition to the vision's panorama, Ellen White was given a warning that "Satan would make strong efforts to hinder me, but angels of God would not leave me in the conflict."[22] She soon learned what that warning meant. Before the Whites reached their Battle Creek home she experienced paralysis of her left arm and leg and was unable to speak. For weeks she could not feel any sensation in her hand, and not even cold water poured on her head. When trying to walk, she often fell. In this condition she began to write out the vision that ultimately became the book we know as *The Great Controversy Between Christ and Satan.*[23]

Three months later she learned in a vision what was behind this violent physical attack: "Satan designed to take my life to hinder the work I was about to write; but angels of God were sent to my rescue. . . . I saw, among other things, that I should be blessed with better health than before the attack at Jackson."[24]

During a general gathering of church members from May 21 to 24, 1858, Ellen White related some of the events she had seen in that vision and was now writing out. One day the group of 400 were enthralled with the "startling facts and vivid descriptions." When she reviewed the humiliation and suffering of Jesus, the audience was visibly moved, even audibly sobbing. She continued in the evening until ten o'clock! The audience then responded with a spontaneous testimony meeting.[25]

In September of 1858, this first of several revisions and expansions of the vision was published under the title, *The Great Controversy Between Christ and His Angels, And Satan and His Angels.* By 1864 the first expansion of this theme appeared as "Important Facts of Faith in Connection With the History of Holy Men of Old" in *Spiritual Gifts,* volume 3, and the first half of *Spiritual Gifts,* volume 4. This printing unfolded events from Creation to Christ's ascension.

The 1884 Edition of "The Great Controversy"

As the years passed and visions imparted further light on these great scenes, Ellen White believed that it was time to expand her earlier presentations of the great controversy. In the 1870s and 1880s she sketched out a four-volume series under the general title, *Spirit of Prophecy,* and the subtitle, *The Great Controversy,* with a further subtitle for each of the four books.[26] Volume 1 was expanded to become *Patriarchs and Prophets* (1890); Volume 2, the first 62 chapters of *The Desire of Ages;* Volume 3, the last part of *The Desire of Ages* (1898) and *The Acts of the Apostles* (1911); Volume 4, *The Great Controversy Between Christ and Satan* (1888).

The fourth volume of *Spirit of Prophecy*, published in 1884, introduced a new phase into Ellen White's writing ministry. Beginning with the destruction of Jerusalem, she continued the historical period through to the 1800s and into the future, ending with the establishment of the new earth after the destruction of evil. W. C. White noted that his mother's contribution to the 1884 revision of *The Great Controversy* was not only in the work of revision. He recalled, "Several times we thought that the manuscript of the book was all ready for the printer, and then a vision of some important feature of the controversy would be repeated, and Mother would again write upon the subject, bringing out the description more fully and clearly. Thus the publishing was delayed, and the book grew in size."[27]

Mrs. White wrote history, but not as a historian. She said in her introduction to the 1888 edition of *The Great Controversy* that she endeavored "to select and group together events in the history of the church in such a manner as to trace the unfolding of the great testing truths that at different periods have been given to the world."

Like a skilled author she stated the book's purpose: "To unfold the scenes of the great controversy between truth and error; to reveal the wiles of Satan, and the means by which he may be successfully resisted; to present a satisfactory solution of the great problem of evil, shedding such a light upon the origin and the final disposition of sin as to make fully manifest the justice and benevolence of God in all His dealings with His creatures; and to show the holy, unchanging nature of His law, is the object of this book."[28]

Adventist historian and college administrator Donald R. McAdams, after examining carefully certain sections of the various editions of *The Great Controversy,* concluded that Ellen White "placed predominant attention on her own day and the events of the future," and that about forty percent was historical.[29] His research reinforced Mrs. White's purpose for writing *The Great Controversy* (and the Conflict of the Ages series, generally): that it was "not conceived or developed primarily as a history . . . but rather as a book identifying the spiritual forces at work in history. . . . We must take *Great Controversy* for what it is and what it was intended to be, not a book simply to inform us about the past, not a book intended to be authoritative on the factual details concerning the activities of the Reformers, but a book written to put the Great Controversy in its proper perspective."[30]

Although the four volumes were written primarily for Seventh-day Adventists, church members soon began to lend them to their neighbors; some began to sell them to the general public. The response was remarkable. Published simultaneously in October 1884 by the Pacific Press and the Review and Herald in editions of five thousand copies each, the first printing on the west coast was sold out before the year ended. Fifty thousand copies of volume 4 had been distributed within three years.[31] The 1884 edition became the first Ellen White colporteur book in 1885.

This reception by the general public was a new day for Adventist publications. It also prompted Ellen White and her colleagues to think new thoughts about her books, especially those in the *Spirit of Prophecy* series. In 1887 C. H. Jones, manager of the Pacific Press, informed Mrs. White and her son, William, while they were in Europe, that after so many printings, new plates were needed.[32]

The 1888 Edition of "The Great Controversy"

Now was the time to examine the book in light of its appeal to the general public. Ellen White realized that the 1884 edition of *The Great Controversy* contained terms and some content that only Adventists in North America would completely understand. Also, while she was in Europe, 1885-1887, her mind had expanded with fresh insights into Reformation history as she visited sites in Italy, Switzerland, Germany, France, England, and Scandinavia.[33]

Another aspect that would help in the revision would be to use terms that could be translated easily into other languages. While in Basel, Switzerland, the Whites worked closely with the French and German translators of *The Great Controversy.* They discovered that many familiar English phrases were difficult to translate. In a letter to C. H. Jones, W. C. White wrote: "Mother has given attention to all of these points, and has thought that the book ought to be so corrected, and enlarged, as to be of the most possible good to the large number of . . . readers to whom it is now being offered. And she has taken hold with a remarkable energy to fill in some parts that are rather too brief."[34]

Responding to these requests, especially to one asking for more pages devoted to John Huss and Jerome, Mrs. White hastily prepared a handwritten manuscript of eighty-nine pages devoted to these two noble reformers, drawing heavily on Wylie's *History of Protestantism* for historical details. Before leaving for her last visit to Scandinavia, she left the manuscript with Marian Davis for editing.

Speaking later of his mother's development of those chapters on Reformation events, W. C. White wrote: "When we reached those chapters relating to the Reformation in Germany and France, the translators would comment on the appropriateness of the selection of historical events which Sister White had chosen, and in two instances which I remember, they suggested that there were other events of corresponding importance which she had not mentioned.

"When this was brought to her attention, she requested that the histories be brought to her that she might consider the importance of the events which had been mentioned. The reading of the history refreshed to her mind that which she had seen, after which she wrote a description of the event."[35]

Special attention was given to matters that Ellen White thought either should be deleted from the revised edition of *The Great Controversy* or be reprinted elsewhere. In 1911, reporting to the General Conference Council, W. C. White explained how his mother had always been conscious of selecting and adapting material to fit her various public audiences. When the time came to publish books for the general public, she believed that "the best judgment should be shown in selecting that which is best suited to the needs of those who will read the book."

Therefore, when the 1884 *Great Controversy* was being refined to meet the various kinds of people in America and other lands, about twenty pages of material that were "very instructive to the Adventists of America, but . . . not appropriate for readers in other parts of the world," were deleted.[36]

One such item was the first part of the chapter, "The Snares of Satan," wherein Ellen White described her view of Satan holding a council meeting with his angels as to how to mislead God's people. This material later was placed in *Testimonies to Ministers.*[37]

Why Some Materials Were Deleted

Some references to other churches were left out because Ellen White felt "that ministers of popular churches reading those statements would become angry and would array themselves against the circulation of the book."[38]

The frequent references to "I saw," "I was shown," etc., were omitted chiefly because the general public, unaware of her divine calling, would be distracted from the message of the book.

Mrs. White wrote the "Introduction" to the 1888 edition in May 1888, after she returned from Europe in 1887. In it she explained the distinctive purpose of the book and why she quoted from historians and others. She further informed her readers that she also included material from those who "were carrying forward the work of reform in our own time," no doubt referring especially to J. N. Andrews, Uriah Smith, and her husband James White.[39]

In developing the 1888 revised edition, she used additional materials from J. H. Merle D'Aubigné, J. A. Wylie, and others in fulfilling her purpose of tracing "the unfolding of the great testing truths" during the Protestant Reformation. In the interest of precision and convenience, some of their materials were quoted exactly, some were paraphrased, and some she summarized in her own words to provide background. At times, this historical background was used without specific credit, although the material was enclosed within quotation marks.

W. C. White recalled how his mother coordinated divine inspiration with historical sources: "The great events occurring in the life of our Lord were presented to her in panoramic scenes as also were the other portions of *The Great Controversy.* In a few of these scenes chronology and geography were clearly presented, but in the greater part of the revelation the flashlight scenes, which were exceedingly vivid, and the conversations and the controversies, which she heard and was able to narrate, were not marked geographically or chronologically, and she was left to study the Bible and history, and the writings of men who had presented the life of our Lord, to get the chronological and geographical connection."[40]

W. C. White stated further that Ellen White made no claim to being a "standard" by which all other historians were to be measured. Her purpose in quoting historians "was not to make a new history, not to correct errors in history, but to use valuable illustrations to make plain important spiritual truths."[41]

The 1911 Edition of "The Great Controversy"

With the hope of appealing to the general public, the 1888 edition included twenty-six full-page illustrations and twenty-six pages devoted to general notes and biographical notes.[42]

After twenty years of constant reprinting, the plates in both publishing houses were badly worn. Experience in selling the books to the general public suggested that the book should be reillustrated. Further consideration was given to historical quotations and to an appendix of references used.

When Ellen White studied the suggestions, she promptly responded, as she recalled after receiving her copy of the 1911 revised edition: "When I learned that *Great Controversy* must be reset, I determined that we would have everything closely examined, to see if the truths it contained were stated in the very best manner, to convince those not of our faith that the Lord had guided and sustained me in the writing of its pages."[43]

But the idea of "revising" a prophet's work raised many questions among Seventh-day Adventists, ministers and laypeople. Much of the concern arose because of an unclear understanding of how God communicates through His prophets.[44] The fact that Ellen White worked closely with the revisions helped to clarify the issue.[45]

On July 24, 1911, W. C. White wrote a letter to the managers of the two publishing houses and to the literature evangelism leaders in which he reviewed the refinements of the 1911 edition of *The Great Controversy* (some of which are noted above).[46] Among the alterations were: the improvement in noting historical references, especially in adding more modern historical sources that had even greater force, harmonizing spelling, punctuation, etc., with the other four volumes of the Conflict set, adjusting time references slightly in view of the passing of time, modifying some phrases to avoid giving offense (such as "Romish" to "Roman"), modifying some phrases in the interest of precision (such as "divinity of Christ" to "deity of Christ," "religious toleration" to "religious liberty," the rise and fall of the papacy in 538 A.D. and 1798, changed to "supremacy" and "downfall," instead of its "establishment" and "abolition"), changing slightly some passages that Roman Catholics had strongly disputed, by referring to references that are easily accessible to all.[47]

Ellen White was pleased with her copy of the 1911 revised edition of *Great Controversy.* In a letter to F. M. Wilcox, editor of the church paper, she wrote: "While writing the manuscript of 'Great Controversy,' I was often conscious of the presence of the angels of God. And many times the scenes about which I was writing were presented to me anew in visions of the night, so that they were fresh and vivid in my mind. . . . These changes I have carefully examined, and approved. I am thankful that my life has been spared, and that I have strength and clearness of mind for this and other literary work."[48]

One of the interesting sidelights to these revisions of *The Great Controversy* focused on its inappropriate use when used as the final authority on historical details. W. C. White wrote in 1912 that in relating to the general public, Adventists should use "references and quotations from those historians which will be accepted by the readers as authority." In other words, we should not use denominational publications as authority when dealing with people outside the church—it would be "a very poor policy."[49]

How "The Desire of Ages" Was Created

Except for the Bible, and perhaps *Steps to Christ*, this volume has become the favorite source of spiritual nourishment for hundreds of thousands, perhaps millions of people. Untold numbers have discovered in this book an authenticity that moved them to read other writings of Ellen White. Many thousands have testified that they were led to a saving relationship with Jesus Christ while reading this book. For these reasons, this book has been used extensively in proclaiming the good news of Jesus to youth and unchurched people.

Ellen White's interest in writing on the life of Christ began formally after her Lovett's Grove, Ohio, vision in 1858.[50] This "Great Controversy Vision" was first written out in *Spiritual Gifts,* volume 1, with more than fifty pages devoted to the life of Christ.

In 1876-1877 an enlarged narrative of this core vision was published as part of the four-volume series, *Spirit of Prophecy*. More than 640 pages were devoted to the life of Christ in volumes 2 and 3.

In the 1890s this material was expanded into three books, *The Desire of Ages, Thoughts From the Mount of Blessing,* and *Christ's Object Lessons.*

Need for editorial assistance. As discussed on page 109, Ellen White employed editorial help for several reasons: (1) assistants helped her to maintain a rigorous speaking and writing ministry; (2) assistants functioned as her copy editors;[51] (3) a chosen few, such as Marian Davis, were entrusted with book-making—the challenge of bringing together what Ellen White had written earlier on all aspects of the life of Christ.[52]

Need for enrichment of divine insights. Ellen White was a "great reader,"[53] a habit that helped to fill in her broad conceptual framework of God's love and His plan for the salvation of men and women. This enrichment has added to the descriptive force of *The Desire of Ages.*

In her introduction to *The Great Controversy* (published ten years prior to *The Desire of Ages*), she wrote that she employed the thoughts, and sometimes the words, of others because their statements provided "a ready and forcible presentation of the subject." She forthrightly noted that "specific credit" was not often given because she was not "citing that writer as authority." In other words, her use of the writings of others was not to focus on those writings as authoritative, as if proving a point. She used them to best convey her main point for writing: "to trace the unfolding of the great testing truths," past and present, and to cast light on "the conflict before us," all within the context of "the great controversy" between Christ and Satan.[54]

This kind of appreciation for the best thoughts of others to convey the fresh intent of the prophet's mind motivated Biblical writers.[55] For instance, John the Revelator borrowed forceful statements from noncanonical writers because they fit his overall purposes. He used them, not as authorities, but because their freshness supported his insights better than his own words could. When we understand Ellen White's overall purpose in her writings, we can see how her use of other books served her purpose.

When *The Desire of Ages* passed her final inspection as her best effort to unfold the purpose and manner of Christ's earthly ministry, the publishing house received a document that was "not a *replica* of another's work but rather a *customized* literary composition which reflects the particular faith and Christian hope she [Ellen White] was called to share with her fellow Adventists and the Christian community at large."[56]

An original work. The Desire of Ages is the product of creativity and selectivity, original and derived. Many authors write their books on blank pages, beginning with chapter one and continuing through to the end. As we noted in reviewing how *Steps to Christ* was written,[57] Ellen White and her editorial assistants used a method rarely available to other authors: they compiled from her earlier writings (diaries, manuscripts, articles) materials that would achieve the purpose of the next book. In that sense, *The Desire of Ages* was "derived," or produced from her previously written material.

It also was derived when one considers that Ellen White, as a prophet, received instruction from God. Her beloved Bible, especially the four Gospels, became the rich source for her thought framework. And at times from other favorite authors she derived fresh insights that helped her to provide descriptive color in fulfilling her theological purposes.[58]

Not a Scrapbook

But *The Desire of Ages* is not a "scrapbook" of choice devotional thoughts; Mrs. White remained in control of the final product. Not only did she approve all editorial adjustments, she provided the general scheme and the specific topics that unfolded that scheme. She maintained her independence and thus the "sources were her slaves, never her master."[59]

As one in control, Ellen White cast the mark of originality over *The Desire of Ages.*[60] One of her main skills, one of her literary "fingerprints," was her remarkable ability to be selective.[61] For example, whenever her sources used hyperboles and literary extravagances, whenever they strayed into curiosities or sideline thoughts, she avoided being diverted, but stayed with her own purpose for using that source.[62]

Further, using someone else's words does not imply that that person's thought is also adopted. Perhaps more biographies have been written about Jesus than any other person. Such authors generally use the same Biblical language. But a comparative study of these biographies quickly reveals that vastly different meanings are expressed with essentially the same words. The reverse is also true—the same meanings can be conveyed through different verbal expressions.[63]

Even more important than stylistic selectivity was Ellen White's ability to avoid the doctrinal errors that she perceived in her sources. It did not matter: regardless of her needs at the moment, (whether theological, devotional, narrative, etc.) she used her materials to *enhance* her theological thought, not to gather material to formulate her theological thought.[64]

Another "fingerprint" identifying the Ellen White style is "found in the proportion of commentary given to devotional, moral, or Christian appeals or lessons that usually appear at the end of a chapter.[65] Mrs. White's primary reason for writing was to lead her readers to Jesus, especially through making clearer what God is like. While working on *The Desire of Ages,* she wrote to her son, W. C. White, about the topics that "burden my mind, . . . the subjects of the life of Christ, His character representing the Father, the parables essential for us all to understand and practice the lessons contained in them."[66]

Endnotes

1. *Selected Messages*, book 3, p. 118.
2. See p. 108.
3. See p. 109.
4. See p. 111.
5. See p. 111.
6. Some of the books that Ellen White found helpful included *The Great Teacher* by John Harris (1870 ed.), *Life and Epistles of the Apostle Paul* by Conybeare and Howson (1851-52), *Old Testament Bible History* by Alfred Edersheim (1876-87), *The Life of Christ* by

William Hanna (1863), *Walks and Homes of Jesus* by Daniel March (1866), *The Life of Our Lord and Saviour Jesus Christ* by John Fleetwood (1844), *The Life and Times of Jesus the Messiah* by Alfred Edersheim (1883), *Night Scenes in the Bible* by Daniel March (1872), and *Elijah the Tishbite* by F. W. Krummacher (1848). The books in her library when she died are listed in "A Bibliography of Ellen G. White's Private and Office Libraries," compiled by Warren H. Johns, Tim Poirier, and Ron Graybill, Ellen G. White Estate, Third Revised Edition, April 1993.

7. Fleming H. Revell and Company, Chicago, Ill. The original edition contained only 12 chapters and 153 pages. See p. 445.
8. Tim Poirier, "A Century of *Steps*," *Adventist Review*, May 14, 1992.
9. *Bio.*, vol. 4, p. 36.
10. *Ibid.*, p. 11.
11. See p. 110.
12. *Steps to Christ*, pp. 9, 10—*RH*, Oct. 27, 1885; pp. 29-31—*RH*, Apr. 1, 1890; pp. 37-41—*Testimonies*, vol. 5, pp. 635-641; p. 49—*RH*, Nov. 2, 1886; p. 52—*RH*, Sept. 21, 1886; p. 80—*RH*, June 7, 1887; pp. 121-123—*RH*, Feb. 3, 1885.
13. In comparing the books in Ellen White's library with *Steps to Christ*, current evaluation has determined that approximately six percent of *Steps* may indicate literary indebtedness. Writers that she felt helpful include: Arthur, *Gold Foil;* Bickersteth, *A Treatise on Prayer;* John Harris, *The Great Teacher;* Daniel March, *Night Scenes;* Miller, *Silent Times* and *Week-day Religion;* Melvill, *Sermons;* Hannah Whitall Smith, *Christian's Secret;* Underwood, *God's Will Known and Done.* Certain words or phrases may have come from Cummings, *Sabbath Evening Readings*, and Houston, *Youthful Devotedness.*
14. See pp. 480-482.
15. *Bio.*, vol. 4, p. 250.
16. *The Gathering Call*, Sept. 1932, pp. 20, 21. For an examination of this charge, see F. D. Nichol, *Ellen G. White and Her Critics*, pp. 481-485.
17. For a description of the Lovett's Grove event, see *Bio.*, vol. 1, p. 368.
18. *Spiritual Gifts*, vol. 2, p. 270. See *Life Sketches*, p. 162. The broad outline of this important vision included (1) Lucifer's rebellion in heaven; (2) The fall of man and plan of salvation; (3) The ministry and sacrifice of Christ; (4) The early church and work of the apostles; (5) The great apostasy; (6) The reformation of the sixteenth century; (7) The Advent movement; (8) The first, second, and third angels' messages; (9) A firm platform; (10) The closing of the three messages; (11) Scenes connected with the Second Advent; (12) The Millennium; (13) The final eradication of sin.
19. Reprinted in *Early Writings*, pp. 145-295.
20. See p. 264, footnote 5 for a reference to H. L. Hastings, *The Great Controversy Between God and Man: Its Origin, Progress, and End* (1858).
21. See Index entry, Great Controversy Theme.
22. *Spiritual Gifts*, vol. 2, p. 270.
23. *Ibid.*, p. 272.
24. *Ibid.*
25. James White, *Review and Herald*, May 27, 1858.
26. 1. *The Great Controversy Between Christ and His Angels, and Satan and His Angels* (1870); 2. *Life, Teachings, and Miracles of Our Lord Jesus Christ* (1877); 3. *The Death, Resurrection, and Ascension of Our Lord Jesus Christ* (1878); 4. *From the Destruction of Jerusalem to the End of the Controversy* (1884).
27. *Selected Messages*, book 3, p. 442.
28. *The Great Controversy*, pp. xi, xii.
29. "Ellen G. White and the Protestant Historians," Revised, 1977, (an unpublished paper), p. 30.
30. *Ibid.*, pp. 230, 233.
31. *Bio.*, vol. 3, p. 249. Uriah Smith read the page proofs of volume 4 at a camp meeting with Ellen White in September and was deeply moved by the chapter, "The Time of Trouble," feeling every sentence was needed. Only a year before, he had taken issue with Mrs. White over events at Battle Creek College, events that ultimately affirmed Mrs. White's counsel.—*Ibid.*, p. 261.

    In November 1884, the General Conference "resolved" that "we hail with great pleasure the publication of volume 4, *The Great Controversy;* that, while we anxiously looked for it, expecting that it would give important information concerning the closing scenes of this world's history, we can freely say that it more than meets our most sanguine expectations; and that we earnestly urge all our people to read it carefully and prayerfully, to use all proper means to place it before the world."—*Review and Herald*, Nov. 25, 1884, p. 744.
32. Ten printings of five thousand each of volume 4, (*The Great Controversy*) had come from both the Pacific Press and the Review and Herald in less than four years—late 1884 to early spring, 1887.—*Ibid.*, pp. 434, 435.
33. See pp. 113, 114.
34. *Ibid.*, p. 437.
35. *Selected Messages*, book 3, p. 465. W. C. White recalled in 1905 a particular Sabbath experience in Basel when he was reading aloud to his mother Wylie's *History*, telling about Roman armies attacking much smaller bands of Bohemians—but beating a hasty retreat. Mrs. White interrupted him and told him of many things that were yet in the pages ahead, and about many things not even in the book. She said, "I never read about it, but the scene has been presented to me over and over again. I have seen the papal armies, and sometimes before they had come in sight of the Protestants, the angels of God would give them a representation of large armies, that would make them flee." W. C. White asked, "Why did not you not put that into your book?" His mother replied, "I did not know where to put it."— *Bio.*, p. 439.
36. *Selected Messages*, book 3, p. 439.
37. *Testimonies to Ministers*, pp. 472-475.
38. W. C. White, *Selected Messages*, book 3, p. 453. W. C. White deplored those who tried to find sinister reasons for the deletions and changes when they compared the 1888 edition with that of 1884: "Why will not our brethren study God's merciful dealings to us by imparting information to us by the Spirit of Prophecy in its beautiful, harmonious, and helpful features, instead of picking and criticizing and dissecting, trying to cut it up into little mechanical concrete blocks such as we buy for our children to play with and then ask somebody else to fit it together so that it will make a pattern that pleases them and leave out the particular parts of the pattern that they do not like?"—*Ibid.*

    "In our conversations with her regarding the truthfulness and the accuracy of what she had quoted from historians, she expressed confidence in the historians from whom she had drawn, but never would consent to the course pursued by a few men who took her writings as a standard and endeavored by the use of them to prove the correctness of one historian as against the correctness of another."—Letter from W. C. White to L. E. Froom, Feb. 18, 1932. Ellen G. White Estate Correspondence File.

39. *Ibid.,* p. 442.
40. Letter to L. E. Froom, Jan. 8, 1928, cited in *Selected Messages,* book 3, pp. 459, 460. Donald R. McAdams, in his article, "Shifting Views of Inspiration: Ellen G. White Studies in the 1970s," summarized Mrs. White's use of historical sources: "I believed when I wrote 'Ellen G. White and the Protestant Historians,' and still do, that the evidence is compatible with Ellen White's statements claiming inspiration regarding historical events and describing her use of Protestant historians. A belief that God revealed to Ellen White the activities of Christ and His angels and Satan and his angels in the great-controversy struggle, along with occasional flashlight views of historical events with explanations about the spiritual significance of those events, is compatible with the evidence. A belief that God showed Ellen White one historical scene after another making up the continuous historical narrative that appears in *The Great Controversy* is not."—*Spectrum,* March 1980, p. 34.
41. Letter from W. C. White to L. E. Froom, Feb. 18, 1932. Ellen G. White Estate Correspondence File.
42. *Ibid.*
43. Francis M. Wilcox, *The Testimony of Jesus* (Washington, D.C.: Review and Herald Publishing Association, 1934), pp. 115-117.
44. See pp. 16, 120, 173, 375, 376, 421.
45. The records of the 1911 revision of *The Great Controversy* rest in the White Estate headquarters office, Silver Spring, Maryland. Among these records is a large manila envelope marked, "Controversy Proofs Prepared for Mrs. E. G. White's Inspection and Approval." At the bottom of the envelope are the words, "All Approved."—Arthur White, *The Ellen G. White Writings* (Washington, D.C.: Review and Herald Publishing Association, 1973), p. 132.
46. *Selected Messages,* book 3, pp. 433-444.
47. *Ibid.* "When we presented to Mother the request of some of our canvassers, that there should be given in the new edition not only scripture references but also references to the historians quoted, she instructed us to hunt up and insert the historical references. She also instructed us to verify the quotations, and to correct any inaccuracies found; and where quotations were made from passages that were rendered differently by different translators, to use that translation which was found to be most correct and authentic. . . . In each case where there has been such a change, Mother has given faithful attention to the proposed substitution and has approved of the change. . . . If you hear reports that some of the work done on this latest revision was done contrary to Mother's wish or without her knowledge, you can be sure that such reports are false, and unworthy of consideration."—*Ibid.,* pp. 434-436.
48. Wilcox, *The Testimony of Jesus,* pp. 115, 116.
49. W. C. White to W. W. Eastman, Nov. 4, 1912, cited in *Selected Messages,* book 3, pp. 445-450.
50. See *Bio.*, vol. 1, p. 366.
51. "My heart is inexpressibly sad. . . . I am not a scholar. . . . I am not a grammarian."—*Selected Messages,* book 3, p. 90. "The rich current of thought takes possession of my whole being, and I lay down my pen, and say, O Lord, I am finite, I am weak, and simple and ignorant; Thy grand and holy revelations I can never find language to express."—*Ibid.*, p. 118.
52. See p. 110. After portions of the manuscript were ready for review, Ellen White would, at times, ask others outside of her editorial circle for their comments. In an 1876 letter to her husband, she wrote: "How will it do to read my manuscript to Elders [J. H.] Waggoner and [J. N.] Loughborough? If there is any wording of doctrinal points not so clear as might be, he might discern it (W., I mean)."—*Selected Messages,* book 3, p. 104.
53. James White, *Review and Herald,* June 21, 1881. See p. 111.
54. *The Great Controversy,* pp. x-xii.
55. See pp. 378-380.
56. Fred Veltman, "The E. G. White Research Project," p. 948.
57. See pp. 444. 445.
58. Current evaluation of Mrs. White's literary sources in *The Desire of Ages* suggests that at least twenty-three works were consulted. *Ibid.,* p. 934. For a list of these works and their usages in fifteen chapters selected at random, see the Veltman "Project."
59. Fred Veltman, "*The Desire of Ages* Project: the Conclusions," *Ministry,* Dec. 1990, p. 13.
60. "Ellen White could write. She obviously had the ability to express her thoughts clearly. She was not slavishly dependent upon her sources, and the way she incorporated their content clearly shows that she recognized the better literary constructions. She knew how to separate the wheat from the chaff."—*Ibid.,* p. 12.
61. See p. 112 for a discussion of a prophet's gift of selectivity in using source materials.
62. In concluding his research on *The Great Controversy,* Donald R. McAdams wrote: "One point remains. Does the acknowledgment of such borrowing deny the originality of Ellen White? Not at all. . . . Any honest critic must come away from a reading of *Great Controversy* impressed with the power of its message. I have not attempted to show the creative originality of *Great Controversy* in this study because it is a point that does not need to be proven, and because my purposes were necessarily quite different. But as one who has studied *Great Controversy* carefully I can testify to the originality of the book. . . . Ellen White, guided by the Holy Spirit, has created a book, which *in its entirety* cannot be missed [sic] for anything else but a work of unique power. . . . All that *Great Controversy* did for the early Advent believers it can still do for us. We must read it according to the purpose for which it was written and not damage its effectiveness by making claims for it that can only result in destroying the faith of many who might otherwise respond to its message."—McAdams, "E. G. White and the Protestant Historians," pp. 231-234.
63. Veltman, "Project," p. 907.
64. "The sections of the narrative where the work of God, of the angels, or of Satan and his angels, are described; where the great controversy motif is discussed; and passages of moralizing or devotional appeals occur; are more likely to contain Ellen White's independent comment than the narrative, historical, or Biblical portions of the text."—Veltman, "Project," p. 931. "Sources seem to be employed more often to provide background and descriptive comment than for devotional and evangelical content . . . . One is more apt to find Ellen White's independent comment in the moralizing or theologizing commentary."—*Ibid.,* p. 900. Dr. J. H. Kellogg, in his preface to Mrs. White's *Christian*

Temperance and Bible Hygiene (1890), noted: "The guidance of infinite wisdom is as much needed in the discerning between truth and error as in the evolution of new truths."—p. iv.

65. Veltman, "*The Desire of Ages* Project," p. 13. "It is among her devotional commentary and throughout her presentation of what I have called 'spiritual realities' that we are more likely to find her independent hand at work." Veltman did caution that his "research did not survey" all the possible sources in the nineteenth century and thus he could not "establish whether her apparent independence is owing to her originality or to the limits of our investigation."—*Ibid.*
66. *Selected Messages*, book 3, p. 116.

Study Questions

1. Why was *Steps to Christ* originally produced by a non-Adventist publisher?
2. What is the special significance of Ellen White's "Introduction" to *The Great Controversy,* especially in relationship to the issue of using secular sources?
3. How would you categorize the refinements made in the 1911 edition of *The Great Controversy*?
4. How do we know that the charge that Fannie Bolton wrote *Steps to Christ* is false?
5. Why did Ellen White employ editorial assistants?
6. Discuss how Marian Davis assisted Ellen White in the development of *The Desire of Ages*.
7. Trace the development of the Great Controversy story in various publications that unfolded out of the 1858 Lovett's Grove vision.
8. Why did opposition arise when it became known that the 1888 edition of *The Great Controversy* was to be refined in some respects in 1911?

CHAPTER 40

Understanding How the Books Were Prepared

"Sources seemed to be employed more often to provide background and descriptive comment than for devotional and evangelical content. . . . One is more apt to find Ellen White's independent comment in the moralizing or theologizing commentary."[1]

Some have wondered whether the expansion of Ellen White's original work on the life of Christ from approximately fifty small pages in *Spiritual Gifts*, volume 1, to the thousand or more pages in *The Desire of Ages*, *Christ's Object Lessons*, and *Thoughts From the Mount of Blessing* was due to an extensive use of other sources. After six years of study, Fred Veltman, the author of the research study on the literary sources in *The Desire of Ages*, concluded that there was "no evidence" that the enlarged commentary on the life of Christ was due "to a greater use of the sources." He readily saw that the broader treatment of the life of Christ—which included more narrative-incidents, combined with the greater accumulation of material written by Ellen White through the years from which the finished product was compiled—easily accounted for the increased number of pages.[2]

Another question some have raised relates to who did the "using" of other sources—Ellen White or her editorial assistants, including Marian Davis. The evidence reveals that Ellen White herself utilized the sources which were brought into her published writings. No evidence has been found that Marian Davis or other assistants were responsible for the materials Ellen White adapted from other religious writers.[3]

Ellen White maintained extensive diaries or journals. Not only did she (generally) keep daily records but often she amplified her thoughts, seemingly without any particular reason except to let her mind flow out on paper. These entries included both personal impressions and thoughts from her reading. At such times, without any attempt to organize under specific headings, Mrs. White copied or paraphrased those items from her extensive reading that she wanted to remember. From these journals her editorial assistants would gather material for periodical articles. As time passed, many of these early jottings became part of her published books.[4]

Some of these copied or paraphrased materials were used not only in her book production but in letters, sermons, and even in expressing herself better in her diaries. On rare occasions she used borrowed language to express thoughts directly impressed upon her in vision. To one accepting verbal inspiration, such borrowing in reporting a vision might be a problem, but not to one who recognizes that God's messengers relate inspired messages in words of their own choosing.[5]

W. C. White recalled that when his mother was actively engaged in preparing her Life of Christ "she had very little time to read. Previous to her work of writing on the life of Christ and during the time of her writing, to some extent, she read from the works of Hanna, Fleetwood, Farrar, and Geikie. I never knew of her reading Edersheim. She occasionally referred to [Samuel] Andrews, particularly with reference to chronology."[6]

Fred Veltman concluded that qualifying expressions such as "minimal borrowing," "wholesale borrowing," or references to percentage estimates are "relative and imprecise terms." He believed that those who use such terms are either attempting to dismiss "Ellen White's use of sources or are stressing the unusual amount of borrowing." Both emphases are misleading.[7] It is more accurate "to speak of her creative and independent use of her own writings and that of others than to minimize the amount of her borrowing."[8]

For those, however, who seek percentages of dependency, Veltman found that 31 percent of the sentences in the fifteen random chapters he studied, indicated at least one word or more of literary dependency.[9]

Deepening Insights by a Maturing Prophet

Truth does not change, but a person's appreciation for, and understanding of, truth does. Even prophets experience a deeper understanding of truth as time passes. In His humanity, "Jesus increased in wisdom and stature, and in favor with God and men" (Luke 2:52). When we study Peter's life, we have a clear picture of a maturing prophet after Pentecost.

In 1906 Ellen White testified that for "sixty years I have been in communication with heavenly messengers, and *I have been constantly learning* in reference to divine things, and in reference to the way in which God is constantly working to bring souls from the error of their ways to the light in God's light."[10] (Emphasis supplied.)

Mrs. White understood this human matrix through which the Word of God must pass in God's communication system.[11] In her Introduction to *The Great Controversy* she alerted readers to the "diversity" of Biblical writers, not only in style but in the unique insights of a writer who "grasps those points that harmonize with his experience or with his power of perception and appreciation."[12]

When Mrs. White spoke of "constantly learning," she was not thinking in evolutionary terms "that leaves God out of consideration, but rather a process of spiritual growth that is directly under the guiding hand of God."[13] The same principle of growth is emphasized throughout Christ's parables and the New Testament epistles.[14] The principle of growth underlies the wonder and excitement of the redeemed—the process begun on earth will be unending: "As knowledge is progressive, so will love, reverence, and happiness increase. The more men learn of God, the greater will be their admiration of His character."[15]

The principle of growth affected Ellen White's ministry in two ways: (1) Prophets can lead people only as fast as they can comprehend instruction.[16] This may mean that God will lead the prophet with His instruction only as fast as people would understand the prophet's message; or (2) God will speak to prophets only in terms that can be understood by the prophet. As prophets grow in knowledge, Christian discipline, and experience, their capacity to understand more about God's plans increases proportionately.

In reference to Ellen White's central theme—the great controversy story—we have found an expanding, more insightful unfolding of that theme from 1858-1911, through the various publications as noted above.[17] Something like a pencil sketch in 1858, the "theme-picture" was outlined in about 219 small pages. The picture was filled in with further details in the larger, 1,600-page, four-volume Spirit of Prophecy series. With the publication of the Conflict of the Ages series and its 3,757 pages, the sketch of 1858 had now become a four-color, 3-D rendition of the original story.

Do we find any evidence for the principle of growth in the mind of Mrs. White as she amplified the Great Controversy Theme from 219 small pages to the present 3,757 full pages? Much in every way. But the deepening insights are not in conflict with the original sketch in 1858, only the filling in of details. Readers can make the study for themselves by comparing how Mrs. White described key people and events in each of the three renditions—*Spiritual Gifts, The Spirit of Prophecy* four-volume series, and the Conflict of the Ages five-volume set.

For example, the expansion of thought, the filling in of details in *Patriarchs and Prophets* and *The Desire of Ages,* is dramatic. One senses no contradictions in the amplification; yet, the expansion is profoundly compelling.[18]

The expansion of insights is not merely a matter of descriptive details. Clearer theological insights are apparent. For example, emphasizing the readiness principle (see pp. 34, 282, 304, 311, 422) God seemed to wait until Seventh-day Adventists were ready for His prophet to speak more clearly about the deity of Christ. In both *Spiritual Gifts* and *The Spirit of Prophecy* set, little was said about the deity of Christ. But in *Patriarchs and Prophets* (1890) and *The Desire of Ages* (1898), Ellen White wrote clearly and in-depth regarding the eternal preexistence of Jesus.[19] This fresh emphasis became a distinct turning point for denominational thinkers on the deity of Christ.[20]

In her earlier writings, Ellen White reflected a prevailing Protestant understanding that emphasized God and His law in arbitrary, non-personal terms: if sinners are to be saved from the angry wrath of the Father, then Christ must die. The analogy of the courtroom (Judge) eclipsed the analogy of the family (Father). Although this early picture is correct in rough outline, both *Patriarchs and Prophets* and *The Desire of Ages* richly filled in the picture that added significant details to the traditional Christian interpretation of the atonement most often reflecting Calvinistic thought. To move from picturing an offended God, who needed to be placated, to a God who was willing to endure misunderstanding and deception in order for His creation to see the awful results of rebellion, is a magnificent unfolding in understanding the central issue in the great controversy.[21]

Ellen White's growth in knowledge regarding practical duties and God's patience in waiting for her to be ready to understand visions that would unfold additional truths may be demonstrated by the following examples. For years she agreed with other Adventists such as Joseph Bates that the Sabbath begins and ends at 6:00 P.M. In November 1855 she had a vision that affirmed John N. Andrews's Bible study on the previous Sabbath—that the Sabbath begins and ends at the setting of the sun.[22] In 1858 she wrote Stephen Haskell that he was inappropriate in making an issue over the use of pork. After her vision in 1863 she made clear that pork was indeed a prohibited article.[23]

Note that in neither case was Ellen White contradicting light given to her in vision. As she grew older, she grew in knowledge. Visions, from time to time, when God knew she was ready, confirmed her Bible studies in such a way that fellow Adventists were impressed with her spiritual authority.

What About Plagiarism?[24]

The legal aspect of the charge that Ellen White plagiarized was reviewed by Attorney Vincent L. Ramik of the law firm of Diller, Ramik and Wight, Washington, D.C. In his August 14, 1981 report, after spending more than 300 hours researching about 1,000 relevant cases in American legal history, he concluded that "Ellen G. White was not a plagiarist and her works did not constitute copyright infringement/privacy."[25]

Ramik observed: "Nowhere have we found the books of Ellen G. White to be virtually the 'same plan and character throughout' as those of her predecessors. Nor have we found, or have critics made reference to, any intention of Ellen White to supersede . . . [other authors] in the market with the same class of readers and purchasers."

Continuing, Ramik pointed out that Mrs. White "modified, exalted, and improved" the writings of others in an ethical, as well as legal, manner.[26]

Ramik came to his conclusions after many hours of reading Ellen White's books, as well as those used in her writing. Further, he read the material written by critics, from D. M. Canright to the present. He began his study with a prejudiced mind, due to certain newspaper articles of the late 1970s and early 1980s. But he turned 180 degrees after reading her own books, those of critics, and case law: "It was reading her *messages* in her writings that changed my mind. . . . I believe that the critics have missed the boat badly by focusing upon Mrs. White's *writings,* instead of focusing upon the *messages* in Mrs. White's writings. . . . Mrs. White moved me! I am a Roman Catholic; but, Catholic, Protestant, whatever—she moved me. And I think her writings should move anyone, unless he is permanently biased and is unswayable."[27]

When asked what he meant by "message," Ramik replied: "The message is what is crucial. The critic reads a sentence, and receives no meaning from it—he may, and often does, even take it out of context. But read the entire message. What is the author's intent? What is the author really saying—where the *words* come from is really not that important. What is the *message* of this? If you disregard the *message,* then even the Bible itself is not worth being read, in that sense of the word."[28]

In response to a question concerning the ethics of Mrs. White in using materials of others without publicly stating where she got them, Ramik responded, after noting some legal precedents: "Ellen White used the writings of others; but in the *way* she used them, she made them uniquely her own, ethically, as well as legally. And interestingly, she invariably improved that which she 'selected'! . . . She stayed well within the legal boundaries of 'fair use,' and all the time created something that was substantially greater (and even more beautiful) than the mere sum of the component parts. And I think the ultimate tragedy is that the critics fail to see this."[29]

Ramik found it interesting and "absurd" that, at times, critics charged Ellen White with plagiarizing books "that she publicly urged her readers to get . . . and read . . . for themselves."[30]

And yet questions remain. Has the church been silent until recently regarding Ellen White's use of sources? Has anyone deliberately been trying to hide the facts? Would it have been better to have known this information through the years? Does proving that Ellen White did not violate plagiarism laws settle all questions regarding her integrity and authority as a divinely used messenger?

Regarding the silence or hiding of facts, the record shows that the church through the years has attempted to convey the facts to its membership.[31] However, for various reasons, the information either did not get out effectively or it was received with indifference. As in most other areas, it is always easier to look back and fault others than it is to help resolve present concerns.

However, the record is not silent. At the 1899 General Conference session held at South Lancaster, Massachusetts, A. T. Jones summed up his remarks regarding Ellen White's method of writing: "There are statements that are true which God has led man to write. The Spirit of prophecy [as manifested in Ellen

White] picks out of surroundings that are not all true these gems of perfect truth, and sets them in the setting that is all true, so that they can shine in their own true luster."[32]

At the 1913 General Conference, W. C. White spoke clearly about many aspects of his mother's writing ministry, including how *The Desire of Ages* was written.[33]

W. C. White and Dores Robinson, representing the E. G. White Estate, tried to explain what we all see more clearly today. In a 1933 document, "Brief Statements Regarding the Writings of Ellen G. White," they wrote of how Mrs. White had been counseled by the Lord to seek out books that would provide "gems of truth tersely expressed." Further, she had "divine assurance that she would be guided in distinguishing the true from the false."

In fact, they told how Mrs. White "made no effort to conceal the fact that she had copied from other writers statements that exactly suited her purpose. And in her handwritten manuscripts, most of the passages that she had copied word for word, were enclosed in quotation marks." They then reviewed the printing process and noted: "The question arose, How shall these passages be handled? Much time would be required to study each passage and mark it consistently. The printers were waiting for copy, and the public were waiting for the book. Then it was decided to leave out quotation marks entirely. And in that way the book was printed."[34] We today would have given more attention to the use of quotation marks.[35]

Probably the lack of discussion among Seventh-day Adventists regarding Ellen White's indebtedness to certain literary sources was due, in part, to a lack of understanding of how inspiration worked, both in Bible writers and in the ministry of Ellen White. The prevailing concept among conservative Christians in the nineteenth century (as it is among many modern conservative Christians) was that prophets were verbally inspired and not thought inspired.[36] To think otherwise probably never occurred to most ministers and church members. But only an unconscious half step separates verbal inspiration from the greater error that "inspiration" means no human input—that the prophet speaks only "divine" words.

Another reason was that earlier Adventists were living with the prophet. They heard her speak often, followed her instruction at key intervals in the establishment of most denominational enterprises, and were greatly blessed with her "messages" contained in their periodicals.

Impact of Message

For those who listened with open minds and hearts, their confidence in her ministry constantly deepened. It never occurred to most that contemporary sources, at times, were adding literary force to her writings—the impact of her messages was too compelling for them to think about the mechanics of how the messages were, at times, put into words.

But what about those who, beside W. C. White, knew how the Spirit of prophecy worked with the human prophet in finding appropriate verbal vehicles? These leaders, admittedly few, knew that verbal inspiration without the inclusion of human research is a mental and spiritual straitjacket.

The issues that surfaced at the 1919 Bible Teachers Conference were fundamental, yet deeply divisive.[37] The same issues had divided the Christian church for centuries. The question was not whether Ellen White was authoritative. The problem surfaced when church members were divided as to how to understand her messages when she was not available to explain her statements, or when her literary sources, at times, were "discovered."

Church leaders in 1919 knew that most church members, including ministers and teachers, had learned through experience to trust the messages of Ellen

White—even though, at times, that trust was built on some unconscious variation of verbal inspiration. Knowing how divisive it was to discuss this subject even among Bible teachers and ministers, most leaders apparently hesitated to bring the whole church into the discussion. For the most part, they chose the "practical" way of putting their energies into evangelism and institutional development. The fruits of positive activity overshadowed the basic, even more "practical" question, of how prophets composed their human part in God's communication system.

Deception was not intended: the immediate issue was denominational unity. Pastoral concern for the quiet trust and confidence that church members had for the writings of Ellen White overshadowed the academic time bomb that quietly ticked behind the energetic evangelistic activity.

A Potential Problem Developing

But did not the option of being pastoral and practical set up church leaders for the potential charge of "cover-up"? By avoiding a clear, wholesome discussion of how revelation/inspiration works, did they not plant the time bomb that would burst within the Adventist Church in a future generation? When it is not made clear for generations that prophets do change with personal growth, that prophets do use other sources for bringing precision and force into their messages, rigid minds experience a terrifying awakening when the truth is brought forth. Assurance built on words and not the central message, begins to collapse.

The "cover-up" charge has affected church members in two ways: (1) Some who were avid supporters of their prophet have been shocked to learn that Ellen White used other sources in her messages. They have been shaken because they did not understand the process of revelation/inspiration. (2) People who were not committed to the basic messages of Ellen White have used her "borrowing" as one more "reason" to disregard her authority. This attitude is also the result of a misunderstanding of the revelation/inspiration process. Whenever anyone thinks in either/or terms, many other subjects besides the process of inspiration will be misunderstood—the eventual awakening will be frightening.[38]

What, then, do we know about Ellen White's use of literary sources?

Mrs. White read more widely, and enriched her writings with choice thoughts from her reading, more extensively than many were aware of.

For those who think in terms of verbal inspiration, "plagiarism" aims at the foundation of their confidence in inspired writings. For thought inspirationists, "plagiarism" is considered from other standpoints, such as intent, fair use, quality of selectivity, and ultimate originality of the author's contribution.

Mrs. White's use of literary sources is evident in almost all of her books.

Her literary sources enriched all phases of her writing, including historical and geographical details, theological concepts, and even insights into extra-Biblical matters such as activities of God, Satan, and the angels.

By promoting books by D'Aubigné, and Conybeare and Howson, it is obvious that Ellen White did not attempt to conceal her use of literary sources.

Master, Not the Slave

Ellen White used literary sources to amplify or to state more forcefully her own transcending themes; she was the master, not the slave, of her sources.

In her use of literary sources, Ellen White revealed her transcending ability to select those thoughts that harmonized with her theological principles while avoiding erroneous concepts. She did not copy wholesale or without discrimination. What she selected or did not select, and how she altered what she selected reveals the overriding purpose in her broad reading.

Mrs. White's main purpose in all her writings was to present a correct picture of God as seen through Jesus Christ so that the way of salvation was not only clear but winsome. All her writings must be seen in the light of her primary purpose.[39]

Ellen White's later writings, especially as the Conflict of the Ages series developed, were more complete than her earlier writings. Apparent discrepancies exist, as they do in the Bible, revealing the human touch—but the larger purpose is always clear.

Witnesses beyond number attest that in no case has anyone been misled by following Ellen White's counsel, when properly understood. Some may question the cogency of her reasoning at times that supports the counsel, but the counsel has always been sound.

Neither Marian Davis nor any other editorial assistant was responsible for inserting into Ellen White's writings material adapted from her reading.[40]

The charge that most of Ellen White's writings, especially the Conflict of the Ages series, have been copied from others is false and without merit.

A person should not lose confidence in either Biblical writers or Ellen White because they did not receive all of their words directly from visions. This may be difficult for those who have previously thought in verbal-inspiration terms or for any who have had a more narrow understanding of how God communicates with His prophets.

A prophet may quote from an uninspired source because of a certain insight that has particular value in enriching a prophet's message. However, the prophet's inspired purpose does not protect against possible error, such as in misstating a historical date.

What About Ellen White's Denials?

We have seen in this book many examples of the human element in God's communication system, both in the Bible and in the writings of Ellen White. We have also seen a few instances that are not readily explained.

Some have pointed to certain Ellen White denials regarding her use of contemporary sources as examples of duplicity. Others look at these examples in context and find Mrs. White void of deceit.[41]

Robert W. Olson, for twelve years director of the Ellen G. White Estate, summed up the focus on these denials by joining Fred Veltman's[42] conclusion: "It seems clear to me that Ellen White was worried over the danger of emptying the messages of their power through her dependence upon the writing abilities of others. . . . In my judgment it is basically this same burden of Ellen White's over the reception of her writings as messages from the Lord that led her not to fully disclose her dependence on literary sources."[43]

Olson listed ten alleged denials, or nonadmissions, made by either James or Ellen White—most of which presented no problem when seen in context.[44] He concluded his article: "In my opinion, she did not want her readers to be distracted from her *message* because of concentrating on her *method.* Undue attention to *how* she wrote might raise unnecessary doubts in some minds as to the authority of *what* she wrote. "If this is the correct explanation . . . let us not allow questions about methodology and inspiration to pull our focus away from the inspired communications God has sent us."[45]

Endnotes

1. Fred Veltman "*The Desire of Ages* Project," p. 900. Fred Veltman, Ph.D., a specialist in languages and source analysis, was chairman of the Religion Department of Pacific Union College, Angwin, California, when he was commissioned by the General Conference to research Ellen White's use of literary sources in writing *The Desire of Ages*. This project, spread over a period of almost eight years, involved the equivalent of five years of full-time work. Adventist colleges and universities throughout the world, as well as Ellen G. White Estate research centers, have received copies of the full report of this in-depth study.

2. *Ibid.*, pp. 873, 874, 940, 941.
3. *Ibid.*, pp. 896, 912; Veltman, *Ministry*, October 1990, p. 6; December, 1990, p. 14.
4. *Ibid.*, pp. 904, 944.
5. For an example of an occasion when she used the language of others to better express her thoughts in relating her visions, compare the following two sentences: *Testimonies*, vol. 3, p. 141 (1872): "I was shown that one great cause of the existing deplorable state of things is that parents do not feel under obligation to bring up their children to conform to physical law." "Parents are also under obligation to teach and oblige their children to conform to physical laws for their own sakes."—Larkin B. Coles, *Philosophy of Health* (Boston: Ticknor and Fields, 1855), p. 144. Ron Graybill, in his article, "The 'I saw' Parallels in Ellen White's Writings," wrote: "Consider, first of all what Mrs. White meant by the expression 'I saw' and 'I was shown.'. . . The terms . . . mean that Ellen White, in vision, either visually witnessed what she described or had the information explained to her orally. 'I saw' also can mean that she was led by the Holy Spirit to understand that certain concepts were true even apart from a vision. In any case, the expression always means that what was written was written under the inspiration of the Spirit of God."—*Adventist Review*, July 29, 1982.
6. *Selected Messages*, book 3, p. 459. In a letter to her children in 1885, Ellen White wrote: "Tell Mary to find me some histories of the Bible that would give me the order of events. I have nothing and can find nothing in the library here [Basel, Switzerland]."—*Ibid.*, p. 122.
7. Veltman, "Project," p. 913.
8. *Ibid.*, p. 948.
9. *Ibid.*, p. 941. "To deny her indebtedness . . . or to underplay their influence would . . . not be a fair assessment of the evidence. . . . But to stress the literary borrowing to such an extent that Ellen White's special contributions as a writer and as a messenger, for the content she wished to communicate, are severely downplayed or denied, is also in my opinion an inaccurate evaluation of the evidence."—*Ibid.*, p. 933.

   Since 1983, the White Estate has maintained an ongoing project to document passages in Ellen White's writings known to be verbally dependent upon a prior non-Ellen White and non-Biblical source. As of this writing, these are the titles with the highest percentages of known borrowing. (*The Desire of Ages* was not included in the study because it was included in the Veltman research.)

   Parallel Lines and Percentages

   The Great Controversy (in quotes), 3,241—15.11%
   The Great Controversy (uncredited), 1,084—5.05%
   Sketches From the Life of Paul, 1,185—12.23%
   Steps to Christ, 196—6.23%
   The Acts of the Apostles, 426—3.05%
   Faith and Works, 73—2.97%
   Testimonies, vol. 5, 638—2.82%
   Messages to Young People, 282—2.67%
   Patriarchs and Prophets, 543—2.28%
   Selected Messages, book 1, 235—2.03%
   Testimonies, vol. 4, 395—1.88%
   Prophets and Kings, 242—1.51%

   A complete report is available at the Ellen G. White Estate, Silver Spring, MD, U.S.A.
10. *Selected Messages*, book 3, p. 71.
11. See pp. 16, 120, 173, 375, 376, 421.
12. *The Great Controversy*, p. vi.
13. Alden Thompson, "Ellen White's Pilgrimage to Golgotha," *Adventist Review*, Dec. 24, 1981.
14. Mark 4:28; Heb. 5:12-6:1.
15. *The Great Controversy*, pp. 677, 678.
16. See pp. 34, 282, 304, 311, 422.
17. See pp. 445-450.
18. For one viewpoint of a growing prophet, see Alden Thompson, "From Sinai to Golgotha, I-V," *Adventist Review*, Dec. 3, 1981-Dec. 31, 1981; for reaction to this series and Thompson's response, see *Adventist Review*, July 1, 1982.
19. Christ "had ever stood at the right hand of the Father."—*Patriarchs and Prophets*, p. 38; "In Christ is life, original, unborrowed, underived."—*The Desire of Ages*, p. 530.
20. Compare the statements of Adventist belief in 1872 and 1980: 1872—"That there is one Lord Jesus Christ, the Son of the Eternal Father." 1980—"*The Son.* God the eternal Son became incarnate in Jesus Christ." "It was largely through the writings of Ellen G. White that the Trinitarian view finally prevailed."—*SDAE*, vol. 11, "Christology," pp. 352-354.
21. To move from the limited, conventional Protestant understanding of the plan of salvation as portrayed in *Spiritual Gifts*, vol. 1, pp. 22-28, to the larger view depicted in *Patriarchs and Prophets*, pp. 63-70, demonstrated the deepening, growing insights that Ellen White was capable of expressing. Deeper insights can be found in the chapters "Gethsemane" and "Calvary" in *The Desire of Ages*. Further, in periodical articles even more helpful concepts fill in the continuing refinement of that early 1858 salvation outline—for example: "What Was Secured by the Death of Christ," *Signs of the Times*, Dec. 30, 1889; "God Made Manifest in Christ," *Signs of the Times*, Jan. 20, 1890; "Inexpressible Joy," *Signs of the Times*, Dec. 22, 1914.
22. See p. 157.
23. See pp. 157, 158.
24. "Plagiarism is literary—or artistic or musical—theft. It is the false assumption of authorship: the wrongful act of taking the product of another's mind, and presenting it as one's own. . . . Plagiarism and infringement are not the same thing, though they overlap. Plagiarism covers a wider field; infringement involves more serious consequences. . . . There can be no plagiarism without the thief's posing as originator; infringement may occur even though proper authorship credit is given. . . .

    "However, where you select existing materials from sources open to everybody, and arrange and combine them in a new form, exercising study and discrimination in the process, and producing something new, you will be entitled to copyright protection on what you've created. . . .

    "First, there is no such thing as absolute, quintessential originality. Second, plagiarism and originality are not polar opposites, but the obverse and reverse of the same medal. Third, originality—as commonly understood—is not necessarily the hallmark of talent or the badge of genius."—Alexander Lindey, *Plagiarism and Originality* (New York: Harper & Brothers, Publishers, 1952), pp. 2, 5, 14.
25. *Adventist Review*, Sept. 17, 1981.
26. *Ibid.*
27. "There Simply Is No Case," *Adventist Review*, Sept. 17, 1981.
28. *Ibid.*
29. *Ibid.*

30. *Ibid.* Two years before the 1884 edition of *The Great Controversy* was published, Ellen White wrote in the church paper about a book she found helpful in her writing: "Provide something to be read during these long winter evenings. For those who can procure it, D'Aubigne's *History of the Reformation* will be both interesting and profitable. From this work we may gain some knowledge of what has been accomplished in the past in the great work of reform."—*Review and Herald,* Dec. 26, 1882. She highly recommended another book that she had read with profit: "*The Life of St. Paul* by Conybeare and Howson, I regard as a book of great merit, and one of rare usefulness to the earnest student of the New Testament history."—*Signs of the Times,* Feb. 22, 1883.
31. See pp. 118, 119 for two General Conference sessions that clearly reflected and printed the official position regarding the thought inspiration aspects of Ellen White's writings.
32. *General Conference Bulletin,* 1899, p. 112.
33. See pp. 450, 451; *General Conference Daily Bulletin,* June 1, 1913.
34. W. C. White and D. E. Robinson, "Brief Statements Regarding the Writings of Ellen G. White," August 1933, pp. 5, 10, 11. A copy of this pamphlet, included as an insert in the *Adventist Review*, June 4, 1981, may be obtained from the Ellen G. White Estate, Silver Spring, MD, U.S.A.
35. Many examples can be cited of nineteenth century writers "borrowing" liberally from others without crediting them with quotation marks. It seemed to be a common practice which led W. W. Prescott to write in his introduction: "All quotations in the notes taken from the Spirit of Prophecy were duly credited to book and page. The other quotations have been selected from many sources, but as they are not cited as authority, but are used merely for the expression of the thought, no credit has been given."—*The Doctrine of Christ* (Washington, D.C.: Review and Herald Publishing Association, 1920), p. 3. Even one of Ellen White's harshest critics, D. M. Canright, copied phrases and the title of his 1878 300-page book, *The Bible From Heaven*, from Moses Hull's 1863 182-page book, also called *The Bible From Heaven*. "The originals are not original. There is imitation, model and suggestion, to the very archangels, if we knew their history. The first book tyrannizes over the second. Read Tasso, and you think of Virgil; read Virgil, and you think of Homer; and Milton forces you to reflect how narrow are the limits of human invention. *Paradise Lost* had never existed but for its precursors; and if we find in India or Arabia a book out of our horizon of thought and tradition, we are soon taught by new researches in its native country to discover its foregoers and its latent but real connection with our Bibles."—Ralph Waldo Emerson, *Quotation and Originality, Complete Works* (London: George Rutledge & Sons, Ltd., 1883), Vol. 8, pp. 170-172, cited in Lindey, *Plagiarism and Originality,* pp. 14, 15.
36. See Index entry, Inspiration, verbal vs. thought.
37. See pp. 440, 441 for how the issues involved in both verbal and thought inspiration were addressed at the 1919 Bible Teachers Conference. The deep gulf at that time between equally committed men and women over these fundamental issues helps to explain why more effort was not made to educate Seventh-day Adventists generally regarding how the Spirit helped prophets to construct their messages.
38. In responding to those who are troubled when they become aware that Ellen White used source material, Alden Thompson wrote: "An additional assumption is also evident that has deep roots in the minds of conservative believers: true prophets do not change. If, then, in a weak moment, one discovers both *sources* and *change,* disillusionment and the 'cover-up' argument almost inevitably follows.

    "The 'cover-up' argument is clearly the most difficult for conservative believers to handle. But I am convinced that [the experience of such believers] provides some of the best evidence as to why there has been a necessary and well-intentioned 'cover-up' or, put in another way, why Ellen White and her assistants gradually—even reluctantly—revealed the human methods by which the prophet operated. Full disclosure would have led some to conclude that God was *'nonexistent in their program.'*

    "The Biblical precedent for a 'cover-up' was established by Christ Himself: 'I have yet many things to say to you, but you cannot bear them now' (John 16:12). Every parent and teacher can testify to the truth of that statement. Awareness and growth only can come gradually. For those who are inclined to think in stark either/or terms, any trace of humanity is enough to rob the Word of its divine credentials. In a community with just such inclinations, Ellen White emphasized that her message came from God, not man. To have done otherwise would have been a betrayal of her calling.

    "But as time went on, both she and the community came to the place where it was possible to understand more of the human element without denying the divine."—"The Imperfect Speech of Inspiration," *Spectrum,* June 1982.
39. "Sister White is not the originator of these books. They contain the instruction that during her lifework God has been giving her. They contain the precious, comforting light that God has graciously given His servant to be given to the world. From their pages this light is to shine into the hearts of men and women, leading them to the Saviour."—*The Publishing Ministry* (Washington, D.C.: Review and Herald Publishing Association, 1983), p. 354.
40. See p. 116.
41. "Ellen White sought to deceive no one. Thoughts, facts, and truths written by one person may be used by another without plagiarism. She made original applications of older material, while furnishing herself with thoughts and words of other books. She can hardly be reproached as a plagiarist, any more than the architect or sculptor can be censured as a copier of Christopher Wren or Michelangelo because he digs his marble from the same quarry, squares his stones by the same art, and unites them in columns of the same order. The freedom to adopt and adapt form the common property of scholars the world over. To use the arguments and follow the truths of other writers is by no means incompatible with originality. In fact, absolute originality is almost impossible.

    "No valid objection can be brought against Ellen White when she enlarges and clarifies her own ideas in the light of other men's works. To establish the charge of plagiarism, one must prove a deliberate attempt to use another's work to exalt oneself rather than the glory of God. Her whole purpose was the communication of truth, believing that whatever the source, the truth must be exalted and God glorified."—Edward Heppenstall, "The Inspired Witness of Ellen White," *Adventist Review,* May 7, 1987.

"Ellen White's statements about her sources taken as a whole clearly affirm a divine source and sometimes sound as if they would not allow for any literary borrowing. . . . This situation, I think, arises from the fact that the view of inspiration held by Mrs. White and her contemporaries presented her with a stark and over-simplified choice. . . . The choice was this: either her writings were all from God or all from Satan, and, given these two options, Mrs White honestly and justifiably chose to affirm that her writings were all from God. However, while it is true that her writings taken as a whole are all from God, there are elements found in those writings which came to her through human sources under the guidance of God's Spirit, a situation very similar to that observed in Scripture. And, thus Mrs. White's statements about her writings were not dishonest or deceptive, but they were incomplete in that respect. She simply didn't get into the mechanics of inspiration."—Ron Graybill, an unpublished manuscript, "Literary Work," November, 1981, pp. 22, 23.

42. See pp. 456, 457 for comments on Fred Veltman's *Full Report of the Life of Christ Research Project*, 1988.
43. Robert W. Olson, "Ellen White's Denials," *Ministry,* Feb., 1991.
44. *Ibid.*
45. *Ibid.*

Study Questions

1. Did Marian Davis draw on some material for *The Desire of Ages* that Ellen White had written previously?

2. What is meant by Ellen White's "creative use" of the writings of others?

3. If truth does not change, what is meant by a prophet's maturing insights?

4. What do you think was meant by "denominational unity" rather than "deception" being the primary motivation of church leaders who drew little attention to Ellen White's use of literary sources?

5. Analyze Attorney Ramik's conclusion that "the message is what is crucial."

8. How would you help others to understand how and why Ellen White at times used the writings of others?

SECTION VII

How to Evaluate Criticism

CHAPTER 41

Truth Still Makes One Free

"It is important that in defending the doctrines which we consider fundamental articles of faith, we should never allow ourselves to employ arguments that are not wholly sound. These may avail to silence an opposer, but they do not honor the truth. We should present sound arguments, that will not only silence our opponents, but will bear the closest and most searching scrutiny. . . . In meeting an opponent it should be our earnest effort to present subjects in such a manner as to awaken conviction in his mind, instead of seeking merely to give confidence to the believer."[1]

In a letter to A. G. Daniells, December 31, 1913, W. C. White referred to some of his mother's letters that were being misused: "Regarding the Fitzgerald letter and the Watson letter and other letters which may perplex us and others, it might be much easier to repudiate a few documents that perplex us, and say they were forgeries, but it is the truth that makes us free, and I do not know of any way in harmony with the law of God than to deal with these matters just as they are."[2]

To "deal with . . . matters just as they are" is precisely the aim of this book. Thus, we shall consider some of the charges, allegations, and insinuations that accompanied James and Ellen White during their lifetime (and ever since).. The charges and criticisms are generated by at least seven groups:

(1) Those who reject anyone who claims to be a modern prophet, including Ellen White.

(2) Those who fail to utilize basic, commonly accepted rules of interpretation as discussed in chapters 32 to 34. For example, to understand a letter written by Ellen White or one to her by a contemporary requires an understanding of the rules of interpretation. To read into the letter the reader's presuppositions often leads to faulty conclusions. Further, to read a letter of someone who is in conflict with Ellen White without a background of that writer's personal history and points of view will lead to faulty conclusions.

(3) Those who rely on rumors and hearsay with no documentary evidence for their allegations. Little credence should be given to information that exists only in the memory of an avowed critic of Ellen White.

(4) Those who see editorial changes in a prophet's writings and call them "suppressions."

(5) Those who are troubled by apparent literary dependency.

(6) Those who carry personal presuppositions about how a prophet should function. For example, they believe that prophets "should have full knowledge" from the start of their ministry; their predictions should be unalterable, their writings exempt from all errors, discrepancies, and mistakes, and never include uninspired sources. For them, prophets never express merely personal opinions in their writings.

(7) Those who accept Ellen White as an inspirational devotional writer but reject her theological ministry.

Differing Responses Depend on Circumstances and Attitudes

Dealing with those who have no personal experience with Ellen White's writings. From her earliest years, Ellen White was sympathetic and patient with those who opposed her, especially those who had strong convictions about spiritual gifts in modern times. Some of the opposition had seen the fanatical exercises of a few who claimed the prophetic gift, and thus feared all claims, even Ellen White's.[3] Others were opposed because they had been taught that the prophetic gift ended with John the Revelator on the Isle of Patmos.

In the summer of 1861 Mrs. White counseled that those who were "God's children" and yet "doubted the visions . . . should not be deprived of the benefits and privileges of the church." How were church members to relate to this group? She wrote: "Long patience and brotherly love should be exercised toward them until they find their position and become established for or against." However, "if they fight against the visions, . . . if they carry their opposition so far as to oppose that in which they have no experience, and feel annoyed when those who believe that the visions are of God speak of them in meeting, . . . the church may know that they are not right. . . . When professed believers in the truth oppose these gifts, and fight against the visions, souls are in danger through their influence, and it is time then to labor with them, that the weak may not be led astray by their influence."[4]

Avoid a controversial spirit. Ellen White counseled two approaches to the "quibbles of our opponents who deal in slander and misrepresentations": (1) the Nehemiah response—"I am doing a great work, so that I cannot come down. Why should the work cease while I leave it and go down to you?" (Neh. 6:3). Time devoted to "following the crooks and turns of dishonest opponents" is diverted from those "open to conviction [and] dying for want of knowledge"; (2) the direct response that should be "done promptly and briefly. . . . It is not the best policy to be so very explicit, and say all upon a point that can be said, when a few arguments will cover the ground, and be sufficient for all practical purposes to convince or silence opponents."[5]

Mrs. White often followed her own advice: "When errors come into our ranks we are not to enter into controversy over them. We are to present the message of reproof and then lead the minds of the people away from fanciful, erroneous ideas, presenting the truth in contrast with error."[6]

Gifts Are Self-Authenticating

Spiritual gifts are their own best evidence. All prophets have had to stand back and let their ministry speak for itself. In other words, rather than argue their own authenticity, they ignored critics and went about the work assigned to them. Jesus directed His hearers to observe His work: "If I do not the works of My Father, do not believe Me; but if I do, though you do not believe Me, believe the works, that you may know and believe that the Father is in Me, and I in Him" (John 10:37, 38).

While returning from Australia on the high seas late in 1900, Ellen White received a vision warning her of the danger of private interviews. Apparently some were using such interviews to advance their own agendas. The message was: "'Enter into no controversy. . . . I have a message for you to bear, and as this message is given to the people, it is not for you to try to make them believe it. This is not your work.'"[7]

During the 1904 pantheism crisis when subtle error had been endorsed by many church leaders, Mrs. White wrote: "Last night I woke at ten o'clock. . . . During that time the whole matter was laid open before me, and I was instructed that I must bear the testimony given me, and then leave matters with the Lord. It is not my work to try to make people believe the message given me. When the assertion is made, 'Someone has told her,' I am to make no response. On that point, the conflict is over for me."[8]

On some questions Ellen White was not to "answer Yes or No." Why? Because people would misconstrue her statements. She explained: They were "endangering their souls at times by listening to deceptive representations regarding the message that God has given me. Through many twistings and turnings and false reasonings on what I have written, they try to vindicate their personal unbelief. . . . They do not see clearly. Therefore I dare not communicate with them."[9]

Criticism Founded on a Misunderstanding of Revelation/Inspiration

Earlier we studied the deep differences that separated those who believed in verbal inspiration from those who believed in thought inspiration.[10] This difference of understanding has divided Biblical students for centuries; and it has caused division in the Seventh-day Adventist Church since its beginning, especially in understanding the ministry of Ellen White.

When church members do not agree on the basic rules of interpretation as discussed in chapters 32 to 34, it will be virtually impossible to agree on some subjects. *Many of the so-called charges of inconsistencies and of contradictions in the writings of Ellen White can be traced to differing rules of interpretation—virtually all of which are generated by a belief in some form of verbal inspiration.*

However, not all the charges against Ellen White were rooted directly in a limited view of inspiration. Some stemmed indirectly from a misunderstanding of inspiration, such as concerns for possible suppression of earlier material, her denial of literary dependence, and the supposed contradictions within her own works and/or with the Bible.

Criticism That Does Not Recognize That Prophets May Make Mistakes in Details

As we discovered, prophets at times misquote Scripture and make mistakes in minor details, such as dates and places.[11] For instance, Ellen White once wrote "Melbourne, NSW," instead of "Melbourne, Victoria."[12] Prophets are not infallible.[13]

Until one understands the nature of revelation/inspiration, any discrepancy in details appears to him/her as evidence of a lack of divine inspiration. From earliest times, discrepancies have appeared in prophetic writings. Anyone who says that discrepancies should not appear in Ellen White's writings does not understand how God speaks through prophets. Those who base their confidence in Matthew or Mrs. White on the fact that prophets never make mistakes are heading for disappointment, perhaps even complete loss of faith.

Unfounded Criticism Involving Ellen White Personally

The following charges have continued to be circulated even though they have been answered many times. Some of the earlier rumors were answered in *The Defense of Elder James White and Wife,* an 1870 pamphlet that was available at the publishing office. On the back page of the church paper, January 11, 1870, James had appealed: "Will those who know of things in the general course of Mrs. White and myself, during the period of our public labors, worthy of exposure, or unworthy of Christians and teachers of the people, be so kind as to make them known to the office immediately."

This notice was to help a committee composed of J. N. Andrews, G. H. Bell, and Uriah Smith complete their report regarding many harsh charges leveled against the Whites. What was the nature of those charges? That the Whites were dishonest, fraudulent, and covetous. The committee reviewed all the charges and showed them to be baseless.[14]

Often her colleagues would write about how Ellen White's presence would change the minds of those who had heard the "pure fabrications." J. H. Waggoner, in 1869, wrote: "Many who had never seen her had heard the foolish falsehoods circulated against her, and came with the full effect of them on their minds; but when they heard the plain, practical truths of the Bible, the pure principles of Christianity presented in the earnest and powerful manner in which she was aided by the Lord to speak them there, all these feelings were swept away."[15] But because most people even today hear only the charges, we will make a brief response to some of them.

Shouting, Prostration, Swooning, Creeping

From time to time the charge is made that Ellen White in her early years participated in the common excesses of certain Protestant groups in the 1840s. Methodist camp meetings and church services, especially, were known for their enthusiasm expressed in "shoutings," "swoonings," "prostrations," and "creepings."[16]

As a young Methodist, Ellen Harmon probably shared some of this enthusiasm. But after her divine calling, she soon was shown that some of these practices could tend toward fanaticism.

Soon after October 22, 1844, fanaticism increased among certain former Millerites, especially in the group that believed that Christ had indeed come to them spiritually on October 22, 1844. Ellen White recalled that some "thought it wrong to work. . . . Still others believed that the righteous dead had been raised to eternal life. . . . A few sought to cultivate a spirit of humility by creeping on the floor, like little children. Some would dance, and sing, 'Glory, glory, glory, glory, glory, glory,' over and over again. Sometimes a person would jump up and down on the floor, with hands uplifted, praising God; and this would be kept up for as long as half an hour at a time."[17]

In the first few months of her early ministry, Ellen Harmon, the timid teenager, had to contend with grown men who refused to work and crept like children: "I told them plainly that this was not required; that the humility which God looked for . . . was . . . a Christlike life, not . . . creeping on the floor. . . . God ordained that the beings He created should work. Upon this their happiness depends."[18]

All Ellen White knew about her new duties as God's messenger was to visit the former Millerites who still believed in the significance (though misguided) of October 22, 1844, and share her message of hope. In her divine assignment, where else would she go to find people who would even listen to her?[19]

Directed by God, she continued to attend such meetings during 1845, but no records portray her as a participant in these fanaticisms or excessive enthusiasms. However, in response to later charges against her, she wrote that she "never crept as a religious duty, and never sanctioned or gave the slightest encouragement to this voluntary humility." Further, she described those "very many instances where I was pressed and urged, wept over and prayed for by zealots to come to these manufactured tests and crosses. I utterly refused to submit my judgment, my sense of Christian duties, and the dignity we should ever maintain as followers of Jesus Christ, who were expecting to be translated to heaven by receiving the finishing touch of immortality."[20]

Gradually Mrs. White saw the danger of excessive enthusiasm in worshiping God. At Paris, Maine, in 1850, she saw in vision that spiritual "exercises were in great danger of being adulterated." How? By being orchestrated. "Therefore implicit confidence could not be placed in these exercises."

Her counsel continued: "I saw that we should strive at all times to be free from unhealthy and unnecessary excitement. I saw that there was great danger of leaving the Word of God and resting down and trusting in exercises. . . . I saw danger ahead."[21]

Various Effects of Menopause

Some have alleged that Ellen White's

open, or public, visions ceased after menopause, strongly suggesting a causal link between physiology and her visions. She herself dated menopause at 1869.[22] Even if her open visions stopped in 1869 or shortly thereafter, that could be sheer coincidence. However, people reported observing public visions in 1879, and the latest in 1884, as recalled by J. N. Loughborough at the 1893 General Conference session.[23]

No evidence exists to even intimate that public visions grew less frequent because of menopause; the real reason was that in later years one of the chief purposes for public visions was no longer needed. By the 1870s Ellen White's writings were widely published; her public witness to her divine call had been established in the experiences of many thousands of witnesses.[24]

Year-long Depression?

Ellen White was fifty-four years old when her husband died. They had been married thirty-six years. Rarely have married people endured so much together; rarely has a married couple accomplished so much of lasting significance. It is understandable that she felt that "the light of her home" had gone out when her husband, "the tired warrior," died.[25] At the funeral she spoke for ten minutes on the Christian's hope.[26]

Ellen White grieved, freely speaking of her aloneness. But she was never despondent. One week after the funeral she spoke for fifty minutes in the Battle Creek church "with great clearness of mind and strength of voice" on the uncertainty of life and the privileges of a Christian.[27] After a few months' rest in Colorado, she resumed her remarkable schedule of writing and speaking.

Charged With Profiting Financially

This charge arose early in Ellen White's ministry, and, in spite of full disclosure through the years, it is repeated occasionally. Critics judge her on the basis of what most other people would do with a successful writing career. But a quick look at her personal life style, including her proverbial frugality, her incessant giving and borrowing (on future royalties), and her investment in the education of many young people, should evoke admiration, not censure.[28]

Ellen White personally supported a staff of assistants. In addition, for many years she had to find money to loan to the publishing houses for the cost of typesetting, plate-making, and illustrating her books.

When she died, she was, according to the court's probate appraisal, $21,201.83 "in debt." In the last years of her life she devoted an enormous amount of office time to preparing new books and translating many of her previously published works. When these books were sold, the royalties paid off the liabilities with interest.[29]

Often related to charges that the Whites profited from their publications is James's letter to his wife about six months before his death: "We must get out certain books. . . . Our financial matters stand well, and there is wealth in our pens, if we will keep away from bustle and care and work, and use our pens. In this way we can leave something that will tell when we may be gone."[30] Usually when reference is made to "wealth in our pens," the last sentence is not quoted.

The Whites were generous, not selfish. In addition to his masterful literary skills and administrative abilities, James was an astute businessman. From his early years, long before he received wages, he provided for his growing family and acquired funds to establish periodicals and new church institutions with generous seed money. How? By selling Bibles, concordances, and other items wherever he went, and also buying and selling real estate. He did this for the same reason the apostle Paul made tents in Corinth (Acts 18:3).

Reflecting in 1888, Ellen White wrote:

"I do not begrudge a cent that I have put into the cause, and I have kept on until my husband and myself have about $30,000 invested in the cause of God. We did this a little at a time and the Lord saw that He could trust us with His means, and that we would not bestow it on ourselves. He kept pouring it in and we kept letting it out."[31]

Epilepsy and other physical trauma. The charge that Ellen White's visions were caused by temporal lobe epilepsy or psychomotor seizures was reviewed on pages 62, 63.

Oysters. The charges that Ellen White ate oysters were placed in context on pages 315, 316.

Ambivalent on meat-eating for most of her life. Mrs. White's health principles were explained on pages 310-317. After her health visions, she made it a policy to avoid flesh foods whenever possible. She gave freedom of choice to others, including members of her household.[32]

Israel Dammon's Trial

On Monday, February 17, 1845, Israel Dammon, one of the ex-Millerite leaders, was in court in Dover, Maine, for disturbing the peace.[33] The immediate occasion was a Saturday evening (February 15) gathering of approximately fifty people in the nearby town of Atkinson. Visitors had come from Exeter, Garland, and Orrington, all seeking some solace and meaning to their recent disappointment only four months past. The apparent leader for that evening was Israel Dammon from Exeter, a former sea captain.

Seventh-day Adventists are interested in this seemingly insignificant trial because, in the Saturday evening gathering, were young James White (23) and Ellen Harmon (17). Neither James nor Ellen was on trial, nor were they at the trial. They were incidentally mentioned by name, but they were not accused of any of the excesses that prevailed that Saturday evening.

What were James White and Ellen Harmon doing at that Atkinson gathering where crawling, rolling on the floor, "holy" kissing between sexes, emphasis on no-work, shouting, etc., were part of the events in that long evening?[34]

Shortly after her first vision in December, 1844, she was instructed to relate her vision to others, especially to disappointed ex-Millerites.[35] Her health was exceedingly poor; she was ravaged by tuberculosis, hardly able to walk, and "marked for the grave."[36] Not only was she timid by nature, she shrank from the bidding to relate her vision at a time when other visionaries were adding to the fanaticism of early 1845.[37]

But go she did—first to Poland, Maine, then to Orrington (where later she remembered first meeting James White), on to Garland, Exeter, Atkinson, and then home through Palmyra and Topsham. At Exeter, in Israel Dammon's home, Ellen had her next significant vision "of Jesus rising from His mediatorial throne and going to the holiest as Bridegroom to receive His kingdom."[38] This vision was most timely in that it helped certain ex-Millerites see beyond their "spiritualizing" of the October 22, 1844 event—that is, the Second Coming was not Jesus coming into their hearts and, thus, their religious experiences (fanaticisms) were not the validating witness of the Second Coming. These small groups were told not to allegorize or spiritualize away great Biblical truths—that God and heaven were indeed real, that the "holiest of all" was not in their hearts but in heaven where Jesus now functioned as High Priest and from which He would return with His angels in the real Second Coming.

Hearing all this from a very sick teenager, the "weakest of the weak," was not, at first, very compelling to many of those who thrived on their various interpretations of Scripture and their emotional experiences. Ellen White recalled that "a heavy burden rested upon me, from which I could not be free until I had related what had been shown me in regard to some fanatical persons who were present. I declared that they were deceived in thinking that they were actuated by the Spirit of God. My testimony was very displeasing to these persons and their sympathizers."[39]

Those Maine gatherings were specifically the places where God had sent Ellen Harmon, chiefly because "these shut-door advocates were the only ones who would listen to her."[40] She knew the commitment and devotion of these disappointed Millerites that had marked their fervor only a short time before, in 1843 and 1844. She wrote later: "These persons were our beloved brethren, and we were longing to help them. I went into their meetings. There was much excitement, with noise and confusion. . . . Some appeared to be in vision, and fell to the floor. Others were jumping, dancing, and shouting. They declared that as their flesh was purified, they were ready for translation. This they repeated again and again . . . . They had carried their strong ideas so far that they became a reproach to the precious cause of God. These sorely repented, and some were afterward among our most reliable men and women. But there were others who ever after walked in sadness."[41]

Such was the background for this Atkinson gathering where Ellen Harmon was bidden by God to relate her first vision of December 1844, (perhaps to relate also her second vision that came only days before the Atkinson meeting). Evidences of fanaticism were all around her. But her presence was in response to duty, not an endorsement of the group's behavior.

What should we make of the observation that Ellen Harmon encouraged some to be baptized that night or they would "go to hell"? We do not know if this was the interpretation made by hearers of what she actually said, or whether she used these words. At this time Ellen did not believe in hell as a place of "eternal fire."[42] If she said that unbelievers would be "lost," most Christians in that group would have interpreted that to mean that they were "going to hell—to eternally burning hell." From this record it seems apparent Ellen Harmon was a young soul-winner, reaching out for conversions after October 22, 1844.

What happened to Israel Dammon? The record indicates that Ellen White met Dammon at Garland, Maine, sometime later. In a letter to J. N. Loughborough in 1874, she mentioned Dammon and referred to the fanaticism in Maine as "a fearful stain . . . brought upon the cause of God which would cleave to the name of Adventist like the leprosy." She described how she bore a "testimony decidedly against it wherever we met it." Then she referred to Dammon and his group as being "in error and delusion." Dammon, she wrote, "had the most positive evidences that the visions were of God. He became my enemy only because I bore a testimony reproving his wrongs and his fanatical course which wounded the cause of God."[43]

No Sabbath Keepers at Atkinson

Did the Seventh-day Adventist Church begin amidst shouting, crawling, hugging, allegorizers of the Second Advent? Definitely not. No one at Atkinson was a Sabbath keeper, not even Ellen Harmon. No one that night understood the role of Jesus as High Priest. No one in Dammon's circle had the slightest concept of the Great Controversy Theme and its implications for them. The Dammon gathering was made up of disappointed Millerites who had not abandoned the Biblical doctrine of the Advent, even though they were groping their way through theological fog. The only person at that Saturday night meeting who had any light regarding God's plan for the future was Ellen Harmon.

Using the plan He had followed since our first parents left the Garden of Eden,

God had to start somewhere after the disappointment of October 22, 1844. He chose to work through the "weakest of the weak" to reach people where they were. Out of those experiences early in 1845 emerged a nucleus of Bible students who soon saw the dangers of emotion-dominated religion.

God gently started with the few who had not discarded their 1844 experience. Ever so patiently He led the few who would listen away from their many errors, such as Sunday sacredness, the extreme shut-door, "no-work" conviction, and emotional excesses in worship. Without the teaching, guiding intervention of the Spirit of prophecy working through Ellen White, clearly the Adventist witness of the 1840s would have been far different.

Endnotes

1. *Testimonies,* vol. 5, p. 708.
2. W. C. White to A. G. Daniells, Dec. 31, 1913, as cited in Moon, *W. C. White and E. G. White,* p. 412.
3. See p. 144.
4. *Testimonies,* vol. 1, pp. 326-329. "If persons are not settled in regard to the visions, they should not be crowded off. . . . Those who were, comparatively, strangers to the visions, have been dealt with in the same manner as those who have had much light and experience in the visions. Some have been required to indorse the visions when they could not conscientiously do so, and in this way some honest souls have been driven to take positions against the visions and against the body, which they never would have taken had their cases been managed with discretion and mercy."—*Ibid.,* p. 382. J. N. Andrews wrote in 1870 that all that was asked of prospective church members was that "they believe the Bible doctrine of spiritual gifts . . . [and] that they will candidly acquaint themselves with the visions of Sister White. . . . And those who occupy the ground are never denied all the time they desire to decide in this matter . . . [however, those who] have had opportunity to ascertain that fact, and to know it for themselves . . . spiritual gifts are manifestly a test that cannot be disregarded except at the peril of eternal ruin."—*Review and Herald,* Feb. 15, 1870.
5. *Testimonies,* vol. 3, pp. 36-39.
6. Letter 43, 1901, cited in *MR,* vol. 20, p. 307.
7. Ms 29, 1901, cited in *Sermons and Talks,* vol. 2, p. 151.
8. Manuscript 46, 1904, cited in *Sermons and Talks,* vol. 1, p. 348.
9. *Selected Messages,* book 1, pp. 29, 30.
10. See pp. 16, 120, 173, 375, 376, 421.
11. See p. 412. Matthew (in 27:9) mistakenly ascribed a quotation from Zechariah to Jeremiah; Luke (in 3:36) added a second Cainan to the list of the first twenty patriarchs, conflicting with Gen. 10:24; Stephen in Acts 7:14 said that Jacob's family numbered seventy-five at the time they entered Egypt, while Gen. 46:7 recorded seventy.
12. *Testimonies,* vol. 8, p. 158.
13. See p. 376.
14. *Bio.,* vol. 2, p. 284.
15. *Review and Herald,* Nov. 9, 1869. Unlike Ellen White's contemporaries, we do not have the privilege of going directly to the prophet for answers. In 1869 she wrote: "The lies of sheer malice and enmity, the pure fabrications of iniquity uttered and circulated to defeat the proclamation of truth, were powerless to affect the minds of those who were really desirous to know what is truth. I did not doubt for a moment but the Lord had sent me that the honest souls who had been deceived might have an opportunity to see and hear for themselves what manner of spirit the woman possessed who had been presented to the public in such a false light in order to make the truth of God of none effect."—Letter 12, 1869, as cited in *Bio.,* vol. 2, p. 276.
16. Everett Dick, "The Millerite Movement 1830-1845; Land ed., *Adventism in America,* pp. 22, 32. See Appendix A.
17. *Selected Messages,* book 3, pp. 370, 371.
18. *Life Sketches,* p. 86.
19. See Appendix K.
20. Letter 2, 1874, cited in *MR,* vol. 8, pp. 229, 230.
21. Ms 11, 1850, cited in *MR,* vol. 13, pp. 299, 300.
22. Letter 6, 1869, cited in MR, vol. 5, p. 393; *Bio.,* vol. 2, p. 72.
23. See p. 137.
24. See pp. 125-130.
25. Letter 9, 1881, cited in *MR,* vol. 6, p. 307; *Bio.,* vol. 3, p. 172 .
26. *Testimonies,* vol. 1, p. 110.
27. Uriah Smith's editorial, *Review and Herald,* Aug. 23, 1881.
28. See pp. 80, 81 for examples of her frugality and generosity.
29. See Nichol, *Critics,* pp. 516-530.
30. Letter from James to Ellen White, Feb. 7, 1881.
31. Letter 3, 1888, cited in Arthur White, *Messenger to the Remnant,* p. 123. Writing from Australia in 1897, Ellen White said: "I see so many things that must be done in order to make even a beginning, to raise the standard in these new fields. From every direction I hear the Macedonian cry for help, 'Come over and help us.' I also have calls to assist young people to attend school, and also to open primary schools in different locations, where the children may be educated. This is work that must be done. I wish to make some additions to *Christian Education,* and then if the Review and Herald wish to carry it, they can do so if they will pay me a small sum of royalty, to be invested in the education of many who cannot attend school and pay their own expenses. In Melbourne I bore the expenses of no less than fourteen. During the first term of the school in Cooranbong, I carried several through school, paying their board and school expenses."—Letter 7a, 1897, cited in *The Publishing Ministry,* p. 235.
32. Forgoing flesh food was a struggle for Ellen White. Understanding this struggle and the circumstances that made her resolves more difficult to achieve helps

everyone understand the process of Christian growth in themselves and others. See pp. 311-317.

33. Edited by Frederick Hoyt, a report of the trial, published first in the *Piscataquis Farmer,* March 7, 1845, appeared in *Spectrum,* August 1987.
34. The no-work belief was not necessarily prompted by laziness. For many, it was the logical consequence of believing that Christ had come to them personally on October 22, 1844, and that the millennium of rest had begun; thus, to plan for the future was a denial of their faith.
35. *Spiritual Gifts,* vol. 2, p. 35; *Life Sketches,* pp. 69-73. See Appendix K.
36. *Bio.,* vol. 1, p. 63.
37. Five women plus William Foy were known to be visionaries at that time and were mentioned as such in newspapers. See *Spectrum,* August 1987, p. 39.
38. Letter 3, 1847, cited in *Bio.*, vol. 1, p. 78.
39. *Life Sketches,* p. 73.
40. See Appendix K.
41. *Selected Messages*, book 2, p. 34. See Appendix A for examples of similar practices in various churches during the first half of the nineteenth century.
42. *Life Sketches,* pp. 48, 49.
43. Letter 2, 1874, cited in *MR,* vol. 8, pp. 236, 237. A signed statement by R. S. Webber, Feb. 9, 1891, said: "Israel Damon [sic] died October 27, 1886. For some time before his death he was in despair, or in a state of despondency, feeling that he was a lost man, as I was told by some of his brethren; and he would often say, 'I am a lost man.'"—Loughborough, *RPSDA,* p. 131.

Study Questions

1. In what seven general areas can almost all charges against, and criticisms of, Ellen White be placed?

2. What consequences often result when the process of revelation and inspiration is misunderstood?

3. What kind of mistakes do prophets occasionally make?

4. Why did Ellen Harmon go to gatherings where people were "jumping, dancing, and shouting" as part of their religious worship?

5. List some areas in church work as well as in personal matters in which Ellen White's counsel to use arguments that will "bear the closest and most searching scrutiny" is applicable.

6. Discuss the charge that the Whites profited financially from their church leadership.

7. Explain why you deny the charge that early Seventh-day Adventists belonged to groups that were known for crawling, shouting, hugging, etc., in their religious services.

CHAPTER 42

Criticism Involving Relationships With Other People

"The work of judging his brother has not been placed upon any man. 'Judge not,' the Saviour says, 'that ye be not judged; for with what judgment ye judge, ye shall be judged: and with what measure ye mete, it shall be measured to you again.' He who takes upon himself the work of judging and criticizing others, lays himself open to the same degree of judgment and criticism. Those who are ready to condemn their brethren, would do well to examine their own works and character."[1]

At times critics refer unfavorably to Mary Clough's contacts with the public press as if the Whites were seeking publicity and financial advantage for themselves. Mary, Mrs. White's young niece, worked with her aunt for about two years in the mid-1870s, and because of her exceptional editorial abilities prepared Ellen White's sermons for newspapers.

In James White's report on camp meetings in 1876 he lauded the favorable newspaper publicity "in nearly all parts of the United States" that he thought was worth more than ten thousand dollars. But some have missed the point of James's appreciation. He was not referring to the value of his wife's personal publicity. He stated specifically that it was the favorable exposure given to the Seventh-day Adventist Church, its "history, movement, and doctrine" that was valued at more than $10,000.[2]

James White's So-called "Cover-up"

James White is sometimes accused of a cover-up because of the following statement in the 1880 edition of *Life Sketches*: "Does unbelief suggest that what she writes in her personal testimonies has been learned from others? We inquire, what time has she had to learn all these facts? . . . And where is the person of superior natural and acquired abilities who could listen to the description of one, two, or three thousand cases, all differing, and then write them out without getting them confused, laying the whole work liable to a thousand contradictions? If Mrs. W. has gathered the facts from a human mind in a single case, she has in thousands of cases, and God has not shown her these things which she has written in these personal testimonies.

"In her published works there are many things set forth which cannot be found in other books, and yet they are so clear and beautiful that the unprejudiced mind grasps them at once as truth. . . . If commentators and theological writers generally had seen these gems of thought which strike the mind so forcibly, and had they been brought out in print, all the ministers in the land could have read them. . . . And if they are not to be found in print, and are not brought out in sermons from the pulpit, where did Mrs. W. find them? . . . She could not have learned them from books, from the fact that they do not contain such thoughts. . . . It evidently requires a hundred times the credulity to believe that Mrs. W. has learned these things of others, and has palmed them off as visions from God, than it does to believe that the Spirit of God has revealed them to her."[3]

In 1880 when James White's statement was printed, only a small fraction of his wife's works had been produced.[4] Examples of literary borrowing in her writings prior to 1880 are very few. To use James's statement today as if he were writing in 1915 (the year his wife died) regarding Ellen White's literary borrowings, is manifestly unfair.

After James's death, certain issues arose in Battle Creek wherein Ellen White acknowledged that she had letters from those distressed with the operation of the college. Further, she compared her situation to Paul's when he responded to circumstances in Corinth after receiving letters from some of its members. When Paul, "an inspired apostle," wrote his counsel, he responded on the basis of "the light which he had previously received . . . . The Lord had not given him a new revelation for that special time."[5]

When James White referred to "her published works," he said "there are many things set forth which cannot be found in other books. . . . They are new to the most intelligent readers and hearers." He did not claim originality for *all* her writings (that would be more than could be claimed for anyone, even Biblical writers![6]). He simply drew attention to those writings that were original, to those "gems of thought" that were "beautiful and harmonious which cannot be found in the writings of others." James White was neither ignorant nor dishonest.[7]

The Up-and-Down Experience of Fannie Bolton

The sad story of Francis (Fannie) E. Bolton would not be mentioned here except for the fact that critics still use her to cast a cloud over Ellen White's integrity. Shortly after 28-year-old Miss Bolton was baptized in early 1888, she was enthusiastically recommended to Ellen White for employment. Although she knew relatively little about Mrs. White before joining her staff, she worked, on and off, as a literary assistant for about seven years. The files contain a long exchange of letters between Mrs. White and Fannie Bolton, as well as other correspondence between Fannie and others until her death in 1926.[8]

Miss Bolton, a gifted writer with an artistic bent, seemed at first to be an ideal co-worker for Marian Davis.[9] Soon, however, difficulties arose. After a few months, Ellen White wrote about her concern for Fannie: "I want her to recover from this nervousness . . . and in order to do this she must take time to rest the brain that the nerves may not be completely out of tune like our old organ. . . . I want you to get waked up to this matter. Do not be a creature of impulse."[10]

Because of Fannie's nervous, unsettled temperament, Ellen White decided not to take her with her on speaking appointments: "Fannie is not the one to go with me [on trips]. It is too great a tax for her to take the discourses and to write them out. As soon as I came here they fastened upon her to get out articles for the paper, but after a little [time] I could not consent to it and again she feels so intensely that she becomes . . . much exhausted."[11]

Fannie Bolton's nervous weakness made her "utterly exhausted" when she prepared some of Ellen White's letters of reproof.[12] In addition, she thought that she could make the letters better by substituting her words for Ellen White's, leading Mrs. White to write: "I think Fannie feels that many of my expressions can be bettered, and she takes the life and point out of them."[13]

Not long after Fannie Bolton had been hired (June 1889), W. C. White, the overseer of Ellen White's editorial assistants, concluded that Fannie could do her best work elsewhere: "I believe that Sister Fannie Bolton is much better qualified for work on a journal like the *Pacific Health Journal,* for in this she would have more occasion for original work, and it would not demand the accuracy which our work on the *Signs* must have."[14]

Was Fannie Bolton instructed carefully about her role as an assistant? Was she familiar with the way prophets received divine revelations? Did she work from a background of verbal inspiration rather than thought inspiration?

In 1933 W. C. White and D. E. Robinson (another editorial supervisor) reviewed how she was instructed, emphasizing that "only Mrs. White's thoughts were to be used" and only "her own words as far as grammatically consistent in expressing those thoughts."[15]

Editing another's manuscripts was a pleasurable challenge to Marian Davis[16] but not for Fannie. She soon felt that she was burying her own talent in editing someone else's materials, and so she was released in 1891 to attend college at Ann Arbor, Michigan.[17] Shortly after Fannie was released, she wrote a warm, congenial letter to Ellen White which included: "Dear Sister White, forgive me [for] all; I know you do. I do love you, and thank you for all your many acts of love toward me."[18]

Five times Ellen White endured this pattern of confrontation and Fannie's confession of misrepresenting her, until Fannie finally left Mrs. White's employ in May 1896. On her ocean voyage returning to the United States from Australia, Fannie wrote: "I know your prayers will follow me. Thank you again for your patience and kindness and mercy to me. I go home with much lighter heart than I could have done before this."[19]

Fannie Bolton's Weaknesses

What should we make of all this? On one hand, many letters reveal both Ellen White's patience and concern for Fannie's welfare. On the other, documentation indicates that Ellen White did not avoid confrontation when Fannie's misrepresentations became apparent. Unfortunately, Fannie's confessions, candid and forthright as they were, did not change her weaknesses.

What were Fannie's weaknesses that were at the bottom of her "fitful, sky-rocket experience"?[20]

In an 1895 letter to Dr. J. H. Kellogg, Mrs. White wrote regarding Fannie: "She has a temperament that is high as the skies at one moment, and the next is deep down in proportion as she was up."[21]

As Fannie clearly confessed (1892), "I mourn over the hardness of my heart in so long centering my thoughts upon myself and looking critically upon others."[22] Part of her criticism was that Ellen White took all the credit for her books and articles "when those who worked up the matter were not recognized. . . . that [Fannie's] ideas were put into the books and papers, and yet sunk out of sight."[23] Her exaggerated claims as to how much she had "improved" the manuscripts with her own words became common talk in Australia. Sowing these seeds of untruth created discord and unrest, even among those who deeply valued Ellen White's writings. This imperiled the legitimacy and integrity of Mrs. White's ministry.[24]

Fannie's thirst for recognition and approval drove her to make many misrepresentations of how Ellen White's articles and books were prepared. At a time when few people seemed able to understand the difference between verbal and thought inspiration, misleading "inside" information bordered on betrayal.[25]

At the root of Fannie's problems, other than her nervous, flighty, disposition and desire to be recognized, was her treatment of Ellen White's writings as only a literary effort. Mrs. White wrote her in 1894: "In your mind they are too often placed on a level with common things; but the ideas, words, and expressions, which seem to you rather inferior, and which you regard as non-essential, may be the very things that should appear as they are, in their simplicity. . . . The writings given you, you have handled as an indifferent matter, and have often spoken of them in a manner to depreciate them in the estimation of others. . . . In changing, you would not improve, but would weaken and dilute with your supposed sparkling ideas."[26]

To Dr. J. H. Kellogg she wrote: "[Fannie] has represented my writings as being in need of taking all to pieces and doing up in another style. If this is the case the sooner I lay down my pen the better. The power of imagination is good, but when it leads to a highflown strain that only creates emotion, I do not care for it to be mingled with my work."[27]

After Fannie Bolton returned to Battle Creek, Dr. Kellogg wrote in 1897: "Miss Bolton looks thin and is extremely nervous and hysterical. She has done some writing for me but I have not been able to make use of it. What she writes seems to exhibit the hysterical, nervous character which she shows in her manner. I think she is sick."[28]

Mrs. S. M. I. Henry, nationally recognized temperance leader and a convert to the Seventh-day Adventist faith,[29] wrote to Ellen White in 1898 about her longtime friend, Fannie Bolton: "She has always been willful and impetuous, and she has never had training of any sort which would help her to correct these things, so they have grown with her growth. . . . I have, as you express yourself, sometimes been fearful that her mind was not exactly well balanced in these later years."[30]

Fannie Bolton's False Claims

By 1900 Fannie Bolton had become convinced that she had the gift of prophecy, and had created "something of a sensation" at Battle Creek. During this time, she returned to her malicious ways (no doubt due in part to her unbalanced mind that had become known to those who knew her well) and told of how years before she had written out testimonies to people, such as to A. R. Henry, after only a few points from Ellen White. Further, she "spoke rather contemptuously" about *The Desire of Ages,* saying: "Do you know that Marian Davis wrote the most of that book, and that I also wrote a portion of it?"[31]

When Marian Davis heard about Fannie's wild assertions, she wrote to G. A. Irwin, president of the General Conference: "It is reported that the writing of a testimony for a prominent man in Battle Creek [A. R. Henry] was entrusted to one of Sister White's former workers [Fannie Bolton], or that she was given matter for him, with instruction to fill out the points, so that the testimony was virtually her work.

"I cannot think that anyone who has been connected with Sr. White's work could make such a statement as this. I cannot think that anyone who is acquainted with Sr. White's manner of writing could possibly believe it. . . . For more than twenty years I have been connected with Sister White's work. During this time I have never been asked either to write out a testimony from oral instruction, or to fill out the points in matter already written. . . . From my own knowledge of the work, as well as from the statements of Sister White herself, I have the strongest possible ground for disbelieving that such a thing was done."[32]

In early spring, 1901, Miss Bolton wrote an open confession to "Brethren in the truth," in which she acknowledged her misunderstanding of the purpose of Mrs. White's prophetic ministry and of the "deadly work" her criticisms had caused.[33]

Fannie Bolton's later years were sad. She is quoted as saying that she "wrote *Steps to Christ* without any dictation or assistance from Mrs. White. It was her product, in toto, but was published as Mrs. White's production."[34] The claim was totally false.

Fannie Bolton was committed to the Kalamazoo State Hospital in February 1911, discharged one year later, and then recommitted in October 1924 for another year. She died at Battle Creek, Michigan, June 28, 1926. At the funeral, Fannie

Bolton's well-loved hymn, "Not I, but Christ," was sung.[35]

Influenced by Others?

Throughout her ministry Ellen White had to contend with those who asserted that she reflected the gossip and bias of others, not divine revelation. While her husband James was alive, her enemies accused him of being the dominant influence on her.[36] After his death, her son and counselor, W. C. White, was often accused of exercising inappropriate influence, even by his brother Edson.[37]

Ellen White responded to these charges, acknowledging the "unpleasant duty" to "reprove wrongs" but that she was "compelled by the Spirit of God" and not by other human beings.[38]

Struggles of Uriah Smith

In 1855, at the age of 23, Uriah Smith became editor of the church paper. His name remained on the editorial masthead until his death in 1903. Other than the Whites, not many have had more influence than Uriah Smith in developing Adventist thought. On two particular occasions he received warnings and pleadings from Ellen White to change his thinking and attitudes. The first occurred in 1882 while he was chairman of the board of Battle Creek College.[39] The second circumstance that called for direct intervention from Mrs. White was his militant relationship to A. T. Jones and E. J. Waggoner and their presentations at the General Conference session of 1888.

This usually gracious church leader had problems with these young and eloquent editors from the west coast. When Ellen White supported them, Smith was confused. Although he never fully capitulated to the emphasis on righteousness by faith as presented in 1888, nor to what he thought to be a change of position on the "law" in Galatians, his attitude became reconciled.[40] Not often do people other than the parties involved have the opportunity to read sensitive letters between two old friends, two friends in disagreement, as we do to when reading the interchanges between Ellen White and Uriah Smith.

Response to Physicians' Questions in 1906

For the most part, this interesting charge is contrary to fact; the rest of the charge is a misunderstanding. On March 30, 1906, during a troubled period in Battle Creek, the forces of Dr. J. H. Kellogg and A. T. Jones were arrayed against church leadership and, by association, against Ellen White. Mrs. White wrote a letter addressed "To Those Who Are Perplexed Regarding the Testimonies Relating to the Medical Missionary Work." The letter was specifically addressed to Drs. J. H. Kellogg, David Paulson, and W. S. Sadler, Elders A. T. Jones, G. C. Tenney, and Taylor, Judge Jesse Arthur, and about a dozen others. She wrote: "I was directed by the Lord to request them and any others who have perplexities and grievous things in their minds regarding the testimonies that I have borne, to specify what their objections and criticisms are. The Lord will help me to answer those objections, and to make plain that which seems to be intricate."[41]

The questions that arrived were, for the most part, sincere.[42] Many of them were caused by a faulty understanding of inspiration, expecting more from Ellen White than of Bible writers.[43]

How did Mrs. White and her staff respond? Between April and October, 1906, she wrote more than thirty letters dealing with the questions that had been sent her. In addition to these letters, four articles were published in the church paper relating to these questions.[44]

Accompanying the charge that she reneged on her "promise" to "answer these objections," was the citing of another vision she had on May 25, 1906, in which she was "directed by a messenger from heaven not to take up the burden of picking up and answering all the sayings and doubts that are being put into many minds."[45] Some have assumed that Ellen White used this vision as an excuse for not fulfilling her previous commitment.

The facts show that three-fourths of the letters written between April and October, 1906, were written *after* the vision of May 25. Ellen White and her assistants responded to those questions that could be answered with objective information; she did not promise that she would answer *all* the questions. She answered some, her assistants others. In responding to Dr. Charles Stewart, W. C. White wrote: "But that portion of the document addressed to her, which takes the form of an attack upon her integrity and her work, she will refer to her brethren to answer, because for many years she has been instructed that it is not any part of her legitimate work to answer the numerous and violent attacks which have been made upon her by her critics and the enemies of her work."[46]

Further, some questions can never be answered well enough to convince everybody. Some questions were "frivolous," some were "straw men." Ellen White appealed to the "elders of the Battle Creek church" to look beyond the human aspects of her writings to the message, to the content, not the container.[47]

She wrote: "In response to the enemy's work on human minds, I am to sow the good seed. . . . But those who are picking at straws had better be educating mind and heart to take hold of the grand and soul-saving truths that God has given through the humble messenger, in the place of becoming channels through whom Satan can communicate doubt and questioning. To allow images of straw to be created as something to attack, is one of the most unprofitable things that one can engage in. It is possible for one to educate himself to become Satan's agent in passing along his suggestions. As fast as one is cleared away, another will be proffered. . . . I have written something on the meaning of the words, 'I,' 'we,' and 'us,' in the *Testimonies.* This point is, as it were a man of straw, set up in the imagination of some who have been sowing tares."[48]

Areas of Concern Involving the Files of Ellen White's Writings

The "Z" file. In the White Estate vault there are 120 file drawers containing about 50,000 pages of typewritten documents. For several decades two of those drawers were commonly referred to as the "Z" file. While accessible to responsible researchers, these documents were segregated from the general file to remind the staff that they dealt with especially personal matters.

Over the years W. C. White and, later, Arthur L. White, placed in the "Z" file highly sensitive materials such as references to adultery and/or other difficult episodes that had potential to embarrass certain living individuals and family members. Ellen White counseled on several occasions against publishing the deficiencies of others, especially the leading workers: "The Lord by His power [through her writings] revealed the mistakes and errors that the brethren were committing, and those souls who had sincere love for God opened their minds and hearts to receive the light that was sent of God, and He forgave the mistakes they made, and through His great mercy cast their mistakes and errors into the depths of the sea. Now since God has thus covered their errors, who will presume to uncover them, and to present them to the world? Who has authorized anyone to present God's chosen, adopted children to the world, clothed in a robe of darkness?"[49]

Ellen White well knew the problems of misinformation caused by references removed from context.[50] She did her best to protect others who had been falsely accused or maligned. In a letter to a prominent minister, she laid out the problem clearly: "It is possible to relate that which has happened in connection with the past experiences of the people of God, and so relate it as to make their experience assume a ludicrous and objectionable appearance. It is not fair to take certain features of the work and set them apart from the great whole. A mixture of truth and error may be presented in so doing."

Continuing in that letter, she wrote: "You have made public the errors and defects of the people of God, and in so doing have dishonored God and Jesus Christ. I would not for my right arm have given to the world that which you have written. . . . You have given but a partial view; for you have not presented the fact that the power of God worked in connection with their labors, even though they made some mistakes. . . . God will charge those who unwisely expose the mistakes of their brethren with sin of far greater magnitude than He will charge the one who makes a misstep."[51]

The Board of Trustees in 1987 voted to discontinue this file and include all of its contents in the regular file. This decision was made in light of today's climate of research and the passage of time in relation to the principals mentioned in the file. Further, the Board has voted to publish all of Ellen White's available correspondence on a CD-ROM.

Endnotes

1. *Christian Leadership*, p. 59.
2. *Review and Herald*, Oct. 19, 1876.
3. *Life Sketches,* (1880 ed.), pp. 325-329. For whatever reason, when *Life Sketches* was reprinted in 1888, James White's statement was not reprinted.
4. In 1880 Ellen White's major works included *Testimonies* 1-29 (known today as *Testimonies,* vol. 1 and most of vol. 2), *Spiritual Gifts,* vols. 1-4; and *Spirit of Prophecy,* vols. 1-3. James White, in 1880, estimated that his wife had "five thousand pages of her writings in the field." Today, her published books total more than 20,000 pages, plus thousands of periodical articles in addition to thousands of additional pages in the form of letters and manuscripts.
5. *Testimonies,* vol. 5, p. 65.
6. See pp. 378, 379, 413.
7. See Tim Poirier's "Did James White Attempt a 'Cover-up' of Ellen White's Literary Borrowing?"—Ellen G. White Estate Document, August 15, 1985.
8. "The Fannie Bolton Story—A Collection of Source Documents (Updated, March, 1990)," Ellen G. White Estate, Washington, D.C.
9. See p. 110.
10. Letter 76, 1888, "The Fannie Bolton Story," p. 1.
11. Letter 66, 1889, *Ibid*., p. 2.
12. *Ibid.,* p. 8.
13. *Ibid.,* pp. 8, 9.
14. *Ibid.,* p. 2.
15. "It was explained to Miss Bolton, as was made clear to other workers who shared a part in the copying and correcting of Mrs. White's writings for publication, that the matters revealed to Mrs. White in vision were not a word-for-word narration of events with their lessons, but that they were generally flashlight or panoramic views of various scenes in the experiences of men, sometimes in the past, and sometimes in the future, together with the lessons connected with these experiences. . . .

    "Miss Bolton learned that the things revealed to Mrs. White were sometimes written out immediately after the vision, and that other things were not spoken of or written out till a long time afterward. . . .

    "In cases where paragraphs and sentences lost some of their power because of imperfect arrangement, Mrs. White's secretaries were instructed to make transpositions, leaving out what was clearly a repetition, when preparing matter for the printer. . . . It was made emphatic that only Mrs. White's thoughts were to be used, and also her own words as far as grammatically consistent in expressing those thoughts. In no case was the copyist given the privilege of introducing thoughts not found in Mrs. White's manuscripts."—*Bio.,* vol. 4, pp. 238, 239.
16. See p. 116.
17. "The Fannie Bolton Story," p. 29.
18. *Ibid.,* pp. 2, 3.
19. *Ibid.*, p. 71.
20. *Ibid.*, p. 53.
21. *Ibid.*, p. 59.
22. *Ibid.*, p. 5.
23. *Ibid.*, p. 23, 29.
24. Many were the confessions from Fannie regarding the spreading of doubt about the integrity of Ellen White's writings. In a lengthy letter in 1897 from Battle Creek, she wrote: "The personal testimonies that have seemed so harsh, so unkind, so unChristlike, now seem the most loving kindness. To think that God writes through you to me . . . why words cannot express my gratitude. That testimony I thought so cruel, is my treasure. Why have I persisted in being blind so long? . . . I meant to tell the truth; but the doubt, the suspicion, the magnifying of your literary faults and your editors' literary excellences, caused me to leave a false impression, because of my own false but to me real conception of matters. . . . As to the testimony you sent of my feelings, faults, errors, and ignorance of my attitude, I say it is true, true to the core."—*Ibid.,* pp. 83, 85, 86.
25. Fannie Bolton, later in 1901, spoke of her dissembling as "my rebellion."—*Ibid.*, p. 103.
26. *Ibid.*, pp. 20, 21.
27. *Ibid.*, p. 59.
28. *Ibid.*, p. 73.
29. See pp. 409, 517.
30. *Ibid.*, p. 89.
31. *Ibid.*, pp. 90, 91.
32. *Ibid.*, p. 91. The key word here is "testimony." Once, when she was sick, Mrs. White told Marian what to write about the law in Galatians, then signed the letter.
33. Anyone interested in Miss Bolton's thoughtful review of her relationship with Ellen White should read her entire statement of confession. At times, some have lifted paragraphs from this confession to challenge Mrs. White's own statements regarding her relationship with Fannie. In so doing they misrepresented Fannie Bolton

as well as Mrs. White. She referred to the damage that her criticisms had caused: "The influence of what I had told others . . . began its deadly work. One minister left the truth and spread far and wide my words of information, and great trial come [sic] upon the Australian brethren. . . . This work I have done among my brethren and some outsiders; but God has at last found me in a place where He could open the true principle upon which His work stands vindicated and infallible, and which eliminates all my objections, clears up my difficulties, and gives me a new gift for which to praise His glorious and terrible name. I now wish to make all the reparation possible in counteracting the influence I have disseminated. . . . I must say I was deceived in regard to myself. I did not know what was ruling me. I did it ignorantly and in unbelief."—"The Fannie Bolton Story," pp. 102-106.

34. *The Gathering Call,* Sept. 1932, pp. 20, 21. For an examination of this charge, see Nichol, *Ellen G. White and Her Critics,* pp. 481-485. See pp. 444, 445 for the background in writing *Steps to Christ*, noting that some of the text material was written before Miss Bolton joined Mrs. White's staff.
35. *Review and Herald,* Aug. 5, 1926.
36. *Selected Messages,* book 1, p. 26.
37. See *Bio.,* vol. 5, p. 335.
38. "God has been pleased to open to me the secrets of the inner life, and the hidden sins of His people. The unpleasant duty has been laid upon me to reprove wrongs and to reveal hidden sins. When I have been compelled by the Spirit of God to reprove sins that others did not know existed, it has stirred up the natural feelings in the hearts of the unsanctified. . . . Some are ready to inquire, Who told Sister White these things? They have even put the question to me, Did anyone tell you these things? I could answer them, Yes; yes, the angel of God has spoken to me. . . . For the future, I shall not belittle the testimonies that God has given me, to make explanations to try to satisfy such narrow minds, but shall treat all such questions as an insult to the Spirit of God. . . . He has laid upon me burdens of reproof that He has not given to any other one."—*Testimonies,* vol. 3, pp. 314, 315; see also *Ibid.,* vol. 5, pp. 65, 683-687. For a review of many of these charges that Ellen White was influenced by others in her testimonies, see Nichol, *Critics,* pp. 487-515.
39. Smith shared his frustrations with D. M. Canright who used these letters in his forthcoming attack on Ellen White. See Eugene F. Durand, *Yours in the Blessed Hope, Uriah Smith* (Washington, D.C.: Review and Herald Publishing Association, 1980), pp. 286-288.
40. *Ibid.,* pp. 252-269.
41. Letter 120, 1906, cited in *Bio.,* vol. 6, p. 90; see pp. 89-103 for a contextual study of this period.
42. For a review of some of the questions, see *Ibid.,* pp. 92-103.
43. See pp. 16, 120, 173, 375, 376, 421 for problems that arise when the concept of verbal inspiration controls one's study of inspired writings. For example, Ellen White wrote to young Dr. Paulson regarding his misunderstanding of how divine inspiration works in the writings of the prophet.—*Selected Messages,* book 1, pp. 24, 25.
44. *Review and Herald,* July 26, Aug. 9, 30, Sept. 6, 1906; information supplied by Tim Poirier, Ellen G. White Estate.
45. Manuscript 61, 1906, cited in the Paulson Collection, pp. 66-68.
46. Letter from W. C. White to C. E. Stewart, June 9, 1907. White Estate Correspondence File.
47. See pp. 26, 518.
48. Letter 244, 2906, cited in *MR,* vol. 12, pp. 87, 88. Ellen White answered this question regarding the occasional use of "I," "we," and "us," in her writings (some implying that others were influencing her) in a letter to Dr. C. E. Stewart, on June 13, 1906. See Spalding and Magan's *Unpublished Manuscript Testimonies,* (Graham, Wash.: Cornerstone Publishing, 1992), pp. 467-470.
49. Ms 27, 1894, cited in *MR,* vol., 5. pp. 286, 287. In that same 1894 manuscript, she also wrote: "Does it seem fitting that finite men, who have the benefit of their experience in order that they might be enabled to shun the mistakes and failures they may have made, and have had the blessing of the divine illumination these chosen men of God have received, so that they were enabled to overcome by the blood of the Lamb and the word of their testimony, should present these saints of God as though they were clothed in filthy garments? God forbid."
50. See pp. 394-405.
51. *MR,* vol. 5, pp. 283-286. See Letter 32, 1901, cited in *Bio.,* vol. 5, p. 48.

Study Questions

1. What was Fannie Bolton's job description when she worked for Ellen White?
2. What were Uriah Smith's theological problems in the late 1880s?
3. How did Ellen White and her staff respond to the questions asked by certain Battle Creek leaders allied with Dr. Kellogg in 1906?
4. What is meant by the "Z" File?
5. List the considerations that prompted the White Estate to create the "Z" File. Evaluate these concerns.
6. How can you answer the charge that James White "covered up" Ellen White's use of the writings of others?

CHAPTER 43

Predictions, Scientific Observations, and Unusual Statements

"The angels of God in their messages to men represent time as very short. Thus it has always been presented to me. It is true that time has continued longer than we expected in the early days of this message. Our Saviour did not appear as soon as we hoped. But has the Word of the Lord failed? Never! It should be remembered that the promises and the threatenings of God are alike conditional."[1]

One of the Biblical tests of a prophet is: "When a prophet speaks in the name of the Lord, if the thing does not happen or come to pass, that is the thing which the Lord has not spoken; the prophet has spoken it presumptuously; you shall not be afraid of him" (Deut. 18:20-22). On the other hand, the ability to make predictions is not necessarily a test of a prophet's credentials.[2] For example, Moses in the Old Testament and John the Baptist in the New Testament are not known for their predictions.

The word prophet suggests to modern minds the ability to make predictions. Ellen White never claimed to be a prophet because her work "includes much more than this name signifies."[3] The test of a prophet/messenger lies in another direction than to focus on the number of his or her predictions. Further, the principle of conditional prophecy must be taken into account. This applies to certain comments by Ellen White as it does to Biblical prophets.[4]

Various Civil War Statements

Some have charged that Ellen White made either unsubstantiated or false statements during the Civil War in the United States (1861-1865).[5] But when comparing careful historians of that period, her comments stand today as not only relevant but accurate. From the earliest days of the conflict, she saw clearly the hidden agendas behind the stated causes or objectives of the North.

Shortly after South Carolina seceded from the Union on December 20, 1860, even before the first shots were fired, Ellen White had a vision at Parkville, Michigan, on January 12, 1861. For the next few years she penned a continuing analysis of the motives and intrigue that characterized both Southern and Northern leaders. At that early date she was shown the naivete of the North, the rapid coalition of the Southern States, and the "terrible war" that would result, and the sober fact that families at that Parkville meeting would "lose sons in that war."[6]

On August 3, 1861, Mrs. White had another vision that revealed further aspects of the pro-slavery factions in the North, even in the highest levels of government. In fact, if everything was known, some leaders would be seen as traitors. She was given the reasons for the mysterious retreat of the Northern army at the first Battle of Manassas (Bull Run).[7]

Her vision on January 4, 1862, in Battle Creek, Michigan, provided the young Seventh-day Adventist Church with additional background and insights regarding the terrible conflict and its impending cost in lives and resources—a picture that no other people had at that early date.[8]

For these divinely given insights, Ellen White has been charged with being anti-Lincoln because, in the early years, he was more concerned about preserving the Union than with abolishing slavery. Because of the national fasts that were proclaimed invoking God to act on behalf of the North when they were more concerned about the rebellion against the Union than about the nefarious slave economy, Ellen White called such appeals to heaven "disgusting."[9]

Other charges are lifted out of context and made to appear contrary to fact. For example, note the reference to an alleged unfulfilled prophecy regarding England: "When England does declare war, all nations will have an interest of their own to serve, and there will be general war, general confusion."[10] When that sentence is read in context, within that same paragraph with all the other conditional statements regarding England, the sense changes from a prediction to a possibility. "If England does declare war . . . ."

On the previous page, Ellen White used the same grammatical construction: "When our nation observes the fast which God has chosen, then will He accept their prayers. . . ." Mrs. White was not making a prediction but a conditional statement. This use of "when" for "if" is a common English practice.

The charge is made that Ellen White thought that the Civil War was a sign that Jesus was about to return from heaven: "The signs of Christ's coming are too plain to be doubted. . . . All heaven is astir. The scenes of earth's history are fast closing. We are amid the perils of the last days."[10] First, those thoughts were not focused on the Civil War specifically but on the world in general. Commenting later on the war, she wrote: "Everything is preparing for the great day of God. Time will last a little longer, until the inhabitants of the earth have filled up the cup of their iniquity, and then the wrath of God, which has so long slumbered, will awake, and this land of light will drink the cup of His unmingled wrath."[12]

Time Is Short

Ellen White had the same urgency that compelled New Testament writers to say: "Knowing the time, that now it is high time to awaken out of sleep; . . . The night is far spent, the day is at hand" (Rom. 13:11, 12); "For yet a little while, and He who is coming will come and will not tarry" (Heb. 10:37, quoting Hab. 2:3, 4); and for Jesus Himself to tell John: "Surely I am coming quickly" (Rev. 22:20).

But since 1844, urgency has had a fresh time frame. Since 1844, Christ could have returned within the generation that saw the heavenly signs and that understood the impact of Christ's ministry in the Most Holy Place as the closing phase of His mediatorial work.[13]

From 1845 onward, Ellen White had strongly counseled against time-setting—a practice that some Millerite Adventists continued after 1844, including Joseph Bates up to 1851. Yet time had always been presented to her as "almost finished."[14]

One charge has been that in 1850 she insisted that Jesus would return "in a few months." The emphasis of the paragraph is on character preparation for the crisis of the last days: "Some of us have had time to get the truth and to advance step by step, and every step we have taken has given us strength to take the next. But now time is almost finished, and what we have been years learning, they will have to learn in a few months. They will have much to unlearn and much to learn again."[15]

In 1854 similar counsel was given to a

church beset with an adultery problem and neglect of children: "It is too late in the day to feed with milk. . . . Truths that we have been years learning must be learned in a few months by those who now embrace the third angel's message. We had to search and wait the opening of truth, receiving a ray of light here and a ray there, laboring and pleading for God to reveal truth to us. But now the truth is plain; its rays are brought together. . . . It is a disgrace for those who have been in the truth for years to talk of feeding souls who have been months in the truth, upon milk. . . . Those who embrace the truth now will have to step fast."[16]

These references to the apostle's admonition in Hebrews 5:12-16 have always applied to serious Christians, but never more than to those who believe they are proclaiming the messages of the three angels of Revelation 14. Obviously, some day there will be a "last generation." Ellen White links the sealing work of Revelation 7 and 14 with a people who have permitted the Holy Spirit to make them ready for God's seal.[17] This preparation should be the last-day Christian's highest priority. That urgency compelled Mrs. White to urge believers in "present truth" to learn and apply as much of this truth as fast as possible. Christians must mature in the truth and not remain babies who must be spoon-fed and given milk.

Some in 1856 Never to Die

At a Battle Creek conference on May 27, 1856, Ellen White was given a vision of "two ways" and what it means to travel in either: "They are opposite in character, in life, in dress, and in conversation." Then she made an observation that has intrigued church members for more than a century: "I was shown the company present at the conference. Said the angel, 'Some food for worms, some subjects of the seven last plagues, some will be alive and remain upon the earth to be translated at the coming of Jesus.'"[18]

For those present, these words were solemn. Three days after this vision, Clarissa M. Bonfoey, a close family friend of the Whites, died. At the time of the vision apparently she was in good health. But what should we think of this vision today? All who attended that conference have long been dead. Did Ellen White make a flawed prediction?

Understanding this 1856 prediction requires an understanding of the Biblical principle of conditional prophecy.[19] Those who trust the Biblical accounts of unfulfilled prophecy will have no difficulty understanding Ellen White's 1856 statement. She made frequent reference to the fact that God is not changing His mind about the timing of the Advent; His people have not fulfilled their part of the gospel commission.[20]

In 1901 she summed up her many references to the delayed Advent: "We may have to remain here in this world because of insubordination many more years, as did the children of Israel; but for Christ's sake, His people should not add sin to sin by charging God with the consequence of their own wrong course of action."[21]

Jerusalem Never to Be Rebuilt

Ellen White wrote in 1851 that "old Jerusalem never would be built up."[22] By itself, the statement looks unsustainable. But when the setting is reconstructed, we find Mrs. White counseling the growing Adventist group that both time-setting[23] and the "age-to-come" notion[24] were incompatible with Biblical truth. She emphasized that the Old Testament prophecies regarding the establishment of a Jewish kingdom in Palestine were conditional on obedience and forfeited by disobedience. Unfulfilled prophecies would be fulfilled to "true Israel" as unfolded in the New Testament text.

Thus the popular movement of the 1840s and 1850s to promote a Zionist state in Palestine was not a fulfillment of Biblical prophecy and not a quest in which Adventists should become involved. Her warnings and instruction were designed to turn the interest away from Palestine and toward the work God had opened up before them.

In a September 1850 vision she saw that it was a "great error" to believe that "it is their duty to go to Old Jerusalem, and think they have a work to do there before the Lord comes. . . ; for those who think that they are yet to go to Jerusalem will have their minds there, and their means will be withheld from the cause of present truth to get themselves and others there."[25]

Less than a year later, August 1851, she wrote with greater emphasis "that Old Jerusalem never would be built up; and that Satan was doing his utmost to lead the minds of the children of the Lord into these things now, in the gathering time, to keep them from throwing their whole interest into the present work of the Lord, and to cause them to neglect the necessary preparation for the day of the Lord."[26]

How did Ellen White's readers understand this statement? That there was no light in the popular "age-to-come" teaching, that there is no Biblical significance in the Jews returning to Palestine, that Jerusalem will never be rebuilt in a future millennial period. She was not talking about a possible political rebuilding of Jerusalem *but of a prophetically significant rebuilding of Old Jerusalem.* To continue to think that way, she emphasized, was to sink further into Satan's deceptions and away from present duty.[27]

Concern Over Unusual Statements

Prophetic writings occasionally contain statements that may not be easily understood. Peter once said that Paul had written "some things hard to understand, which those who are untaught and unstable twist to their own destruction" (2 Pet. 3:16).

Ignorant slave not to be resurrected. In 1858 Ellen White wrote that "the slave master would have to answer for the soul of his slave whom he has kept in ignorance. . . . God cannot take the slave to heaven, who has been kept in ignorance and degradation, knowing nothing of God, or the Bible, fearing nothing but his master's lash, and not holding so elevated a position as his master's brute beasts. But He does the best thing for him that a compassionate God can do. He lets him be as though he had not been."[28]

However, a few pages later she reported that she "saw the pious slave rise [in the resurrection] in triumph and victory."[29] In many places she referred to the terrible conditions imposed on slaves in the South, treated "as though they were beasts."[30] Nevertheless, she was equally emphatic that "many of the slaves had noble minds."[31]

In these statements Ellen White was distinguishing between the "pious" slave and the "ignorant" slave who knows "nothing of God." With prophetic insight she stated that the most compassionate act for a just God would be to let such slaves remain in their graves, not to be resurrected for judgment.

Some object to this statement because the Bible says that "all who are in the graves will . . . come forth" (John 5:28, 29). A few chapters later, John quoted Jesus: "And I, if I am lifted up from the earth, will draw all peoples to Myself" (John 12:32). Here we have two examples among many where Bible writers used all-inclusive language but with very definite restrictions. No one but Universalists argue that everyone, sooner or later, will be redeemed, regardless of character or desire. Not all people will be drawn to Jesus because not all are willing to be drawn!

Another example of a general, all-inclusive statement is John the Revelator's description of the Second Advent: ". . . every slave and every free man, hid themselves in the caves and in the rocks of the mountains, and said to the mountains and rocks, 'Fall on us and hide us from the face of Him who sits on the throne'" (Rev. 6:15, 16). Obviously, not all slaves and not all free men are going to be lost!

Prophets, as well as everyone else, use inclusive language at times, and most people understand the implied restrictions. The next question is, How does God deal with those who are neither among those "who have done good," or "those who have done evil" (John 5:29)? The best we can do is to join Abraham, the father of the faithful, and believe with confidence: "Shall not the Judge of all the earth do right?" (Gen. 18:25).

God's hand over a chart mistake. In 1850 Ellen White wrote that she "had seen that the 1843 chart was directed by the hand of the Lord, and that it should not be altered; that the figures were as He wanted them; that His hand was over and hid a mistake in some of the figures, so that none could see it, until His hand was removed."[32]

At first glance, one could wonder why God would want to hide a mistake! For those who begin with the presupposition that Jesus did not enter the closing phase of His mediatorial work in 1844, this Ellen White reference is ridiculed.

But those who have found meaning in these events, whether on earth or in heaven, also realize that God's ways are often unexplainable. Further, His ways are often cast in human language where circumstances that God permits are described as events that God causes. When the author of Exodus wrote of God's conversation with Moses, he portrayed God as the Agent who "hardened" Pharaoh's heart (Ex. 10:1). However, the same writer also wrote of Pharaoh's responsibility for hardening his own heart (Ex. 8:15, 32; 9:34).

We think of Biblical circumstances where knowledge was "withheld" from dedicated men and women. On the road to Emmaus, Jesus joined two devastated disciples but they did not recognize Him because "their eyes were restrained" (Luke 24:16). A few hours later, while eating with their traveling Companion, "their eyes were opened and they knew Him" (Luke 24:31). If their eyes had been "opened" prematurely while walking toward Emmaus, they would have missed a great experience that God wanted them to share.

For reasons that God alone can explain best, Biblical students in 1843 needed the experience of 1843-1844. Obviously God could have "stepped in" and guaranteed every date, every line of reasoning, when Fitch and Hale prepared their chart. But that kind of divine intervention has been rare throughout history. Permitting men and women to work through their problems, learning special lessons that would not have been experienced otherwise, seems to have been God's general plan.[33]

What would have happened if William Miller had preached the true significance of 1844? What kind of public response would he have received if he had proclaimed the truth about a change in Christ's ministry in the heavenly sanctuary, rather than to emphasize His imminent return? No one would have listened to him; no one would have been stirred to read the Bible. After the disappointment of October 22, a group of his followers restudied their Bibles to discover the real meaning of 1844, an interest that never would have developed if Miller had not focused their attention on the Bible and its prophecies prior to 1844.

Concern Over Ellen White's Scientific Statements

Attention has been called to statements that seem to show that Ellen White made grievous errors regarding scientific issues. Prophets are not called to update encyclopedias or dictionaries. Nor are prophets (or anyone else) to be made "an offender by a word" (Isa. 29:21). If prophets are to be held to the highest standards of scientific accuracy (every few years these "standards" change, even for the experts), we would have cause to reject Isaiah for referring to "the four corners of the earth" (Isa. 11:12) and

John for writing that he saw "four angels standing at the four corners of the earth" (Rev. 7:1).

Some point to the phrase, "As the moon and the stars of our solar system shine by the reflected light of the sun," charging that Ellen White was untrustworthy in scientific matters.[34] But most readers would recognize this use of "stars" for "planets of our solar system" as a non-technical description easily understood by laymen.

Some have declared Ellen White was in error when she allegedly said that she had visited a "world which had seven moons,"[35] and that the planets visited were Jupiter and Saturn. In point of fact, she never named the "world which had seven moons." But there is more to the story.

Less than three months after she and James were married in 1846, she had a vision at the Curtis home in Topsham, Maine, in the presence of Joseph Bates. Although Bates had seen Ellen White in vision on several occasions, he still had doubts about her prophetic gift; but through the Topsham vision he was convinced that "the work is of God."[36] James White reported that, in this vision, Mrs. White was "guided to the planets Jupiter, Saturn, and I think one more. After she came out of vision, she could give a clear description of their moons, etc. It is well known, that she knew nothing of astronomy, and could not answer one question in relation to the planets, before she had this vision."[37]

What was it that convinced Bates, the old sea captain and amateur astronomer, that Ellen White was "of God"? After the vision, she described what she had seen. Knowing that she had no background in astronomy, Bates said, "This is of the Lord."

Obviously, what Bates heard corresponded to his knowledge of what telescopes showed in 1846. Almost certainly this vision was given in Bates's presence to give him added confidence in Ellen White's ministry. If she had mentioned the number of moons that modern telescopes reveal, it seems clear that Bates's doubts would have been confirmed.[38]

Amalgamation

Critics have charged that Ellen White wrote in 1864 (and republished in 1870) that humans once cohabited with animals and that their offspring produced certain races that exist today. The statement reads: "But if there was one sin above another which called for the destruction of the race by the flood, it was the base crime of amalgamation of man and beast which defaced the image of God, and caused confusion everywhere. God purposed to destroy by a flood that powerful, long-lived race that had corrupted their ways before Him."[39]

No dictionary has ever used "amalgamation" to describe the cohabitation of man with beast. The primary use of the word describes the fusion of metals, the union of different elements such as in making tooth cements. Nineteenth-century usage included the mixing of diverse races.

Granted, her statement could appear ambiguous: Does she mean "amalgamation of man with beast" or "amalgamation of man and of beast"? Often, repetition of the preposition is omitted in similar construction.[40]

On two other occasions, Mrs. White used the word "amalgamation." She used it metaphorically, comparing faithful believers and worldlings.[41] And she used it to describe the origin of poisonous plants and other irregularities in the biological world: "Christ never planted the seeds of death in the system. Satan planted these seeds when he tempted Adam to eat of the tree of knowledge which meant disobedience to God. Not one noxious plant was placed in the Lord's great garden, but after Adam and Eve sinned, poisonous herbs sprang up. . . . All tares are sown by the evil one. Every noxious herb is of his sowing, and by his ingenious methods of amalgamation he has corrupted the earth with tares."[42]

Recognizing that Satan has been an active agent in the corrupting of God's plan for man, beast, plants, etc., we can better understand what Ellen White may have meant when she described the results of amalgamation. That which "defaced the image of God" in man and that which "confused the species [of animals]" has been the handiwork of Satan with the cooperation of humans. Such "amalgamation of man and [of] beast, as may be seen in the almost endless varieties of species of animals, and in certain races of men," becomes understandable.

Mrs. White never hinted of subhuman beings or any kind of hybrid animal-human relationship. She did speak of "species of animals" and "races of men" but not any kind of amalgam of animals with human beings.[43]

We recognize, however, that serious students of Ellen White's writings differ on what she meant by "amalgamation."[44] "The burden of proof rests on those who affirm that Mrs. White gave a new and alien meaning to the term."[45]

Volcanology

Some charge that Mrs. White's statements regarding the cause of volcanoes reflected the myths and fanciful thinking of age-old theories. Her writings contain eight relevant concepts[46] that have been debated since they first appeared in 1864.[47]

This list includes: (1) Formation of coal beds is linked to the Flood; (2) Coal produces oil; (3) Subterranean fires are fueled by the burning of both coal and oil; (4) Water added to the subterranean fires produces explosions, thus earthquakes; (5) Earthquake and volcanic action are linked together as products of these underground fires; (6) Both limestone and iron ore are connected with the burning coal beds and oil deposits; (7) Air is involved in the super heat; (8) Deposits of coal and oil are found after the subterranean fires have died out.[48]

Though similarities exist between Mrs. White's writings and John Wesley's famous sermon, "The Cause and Cure of Earthquakes" (1750), there are striking differences. Contrary to earlier authors, one finds no trace in Ellen White's writings of "eroding streams and violent winds; no vaulted cavities that collapsed and thus caused the Flood; no hollow caverns echoing with subterranean thunder; no fires fueled by underground stores of sulfur, naphtha, or niter. Viewed as a unit, her concept of subterranean fires is unique, and we search in vain to find it lent to her by a single human source."[49]

The next question, of course, is whether one can find scientific confirmation for her "unique" views regarding these violent natural phenomena. Many theories abound as to the causes of volcanoes and earthquakes, and the formation of oil and coal. Most earth scientists base their ideas on the plate-tectonic theory. Nothing in Ellen White's comments rules out that theory. Further, nothing in her writings states that all volcanoes are the product of burning coal fields or that all earthquakes are caused by subterranean fires. When she links earthquakes and volcanoes together, one immediately thinks of the Pacific Ocean "ring of fire" and its high potential for disasters from both.

However, notable scientists have confirmed Ellen White's observations. Otto Stutzer's *Geology of Coal* documented that "subterranean fires in coal beds are ignited through spontaneous combustion, resulting in the melting of nearby rocks that are classed as pseudo volcanic deposits."[50] Stutzer listed several examples of such activity, including "a burning mountain," an outcrop that "lasted over 150 years," and "the heat from one burning coal bed [that] was used for heating greenhouses in that area from 1837 to 1868."[51] Modern confirmation exists for the igniting of coal and oil with its sulfur constituent "seen around the eruptions of hot springs, geysers, and volcanic fumaroles."[52]

References to rocks "which overlie the coal have suffered considerable alteration because of the fires, being sintered and partly melted," correlate with Ellen White's statement that "rocks are heated, limestone is burned, and iron ore melted."[53] Further research in the western United States has produced conclusions and language very similar to Mrs. White's writings of a century earlier: "The melted rock resembles common furnace clinker or volcanic lava."[54]

One last charge has been that melted iron ore is not found in connection with burning coal and oil deposits. However, a United States Geological Survey paper records the discovery of hematite (an iron ore) that had been "formed in some way through the agency of the burning coal."[55]

The suggestion that Ellen White was indebted to existing sources for her scientific information is without merit, because some of this verification only became known many years after her death. Further, "It is much more unlikely that she resorted to the published ideas of contemporary Creationists on the subject, since their views were relics of wild cosmological speculations."[56]

Masturbation

Few topics have generated more ridicule from critics than Ellen White's statements regarding "self-abuse,"[57] "solitary vice,"[58] "self-indulgence,"[59] "secret vice,"[60] "moral pollution,"[61] etc. Ellen White never used the term "masturbation."

Her first reference to this subject appeared in a 64-page pamphlet, *An Appeal to Mothers*, April 1864, nine months after her first comprehensive health vision. Primarily devoted to masturbation, pages 5 to 34 were from her own pen; the remainder consisted of quotations from medical authorities.[62]

Ellen White did not say that all, or even most, of the potentially serious consequences of masturbation would happen to any one individual. Nor did she say that the worst possible degree of a serious consequence would happen to most indulgers.

Modern research indicates that Ellen White's strong statements can be supported when she is properly understood. The general view today, however, is that masturbation is normal and healthy and thus should be free from guilt feelings.

Two medical specialists have suggested that in "a zinc-deficient adolescent, sexual excitement and excessive masturbation might precipitate insanity,"[63] and "it is even possible, given the importance of zinc for the brain, that 19th century moralists were correct when they said that repeated masturbation could make one mad."[64]

Two professionals in the area of clinical psychology and family therapy have compared Ellen White's statements on masturbation with current medical knowledge.[65] Dr. Richard Nies defended Ellen White's general counsel on masturbation, making four main points: (1) Masturbation leads to "mental, moral, and physical deterioration. . . . It is not the stimulation, per se, that is wrong. It's what's going on in . . . [persons] when they're becoming self-referenced and self-centered." (2) Masturbation "breaks down the finer sensitivities of our nervous system. . . . It is not difficult to see in terms of the electrical mediation of our nervous system, how disease becomes a natural result of individuals who have placed their own gratification at the center of their being. . . . Disease is the natural result of this."

(3) Masturbation is a predisposition that can be "inherited and passed on and transmitted from one generation to another, even leading to degeneration of the race."

(4) In dealing with others, especially children, Ellen White's counsel lies in the direction of dealing with the conse-

quences, of showing them that we should be training for love and eternity, not self-gratification with its terrible consequences. Dr. Nies concluded his paper, "Self-gratification is synonymous with destruction."

Alberta Mazat observed that Ellen White's concern regarding masturbation was primarily on the mental consequences rather than the "purely physical act. She was more concerned with thought processes, attitudes, fantasies, etc." Mazat quoted Ellen White's references to the fact that "the effects are not the same on all minds," that "impure thoughts seize and control the imagination," and that the mind "takes pleasure in contemplating the scenes which awake base passion."

Mazat further noted that some may be embarrassed by Ellen White's strong statements regarding masturbation. However, many of Mrs. White's other statements also seemed "unrealistic and exaggerated before science corroborated them, for example, cancer being caused by a virus, the dangers of smoking, overeating, and the overuse of fats, sugar, and salt, to name a few. . . . It seems worthwhile to remind ourselves that medical knowledge at any point is not perfect."[66]

Phrenology

In one of the Whites' visits[67] to Dr. Jackson's health center, Dansville, New York, as part of the routine physical examination, Dr. Jackson made a phrenological "reading" of the heads of the two White sons, Willie and Edson.[68] This event was reported by Ellen White in a private letter. What was Mrs. White indicating by this phrenological examination? Was she contradicting her own counsel?

In 1862 she wrote that the power of evil works through "the sciences of phrenology, psychology, and mesmerism." Though "good in their place . . . they are seized upon by Satan . . . to deceive and destroy souls."[69]

In 1884 she repeated her warning: "The sciences which treat of the human mind are very much exalted. They are good in their place, but they are seized upon by Satan as his powerful agents to deceive and destroy souls. . . . The world, which is supposed to be benefited so much by phrenology and animal magnetism, never was so corrupt as now. Through these sciences, virtue is destroyed, and the foundations of Spiritualism are laid."[70]

What could Ellen White have meant by "they are good in their place"? Although phrenology is now considered quackery (and rightly so in certain aspects), students today must pause long enough to look at phrenology as scientists and physicians did in the nineteenth century. John D. Davies in his standard work on phrenology wrote: "In its own time phrenology, like Freudianism, was a serious, inductive discipline, accepted as such by many eminent scientists, doctors, and educators; its aberrations were the results not so much of charlatanism or credulity as of the limitations of early nineteenth century scientific method and medical techniques. However mistaken some of its anatomical deductions may have been, scientific it was in its determination to study the mind objectively, without metaphysical preconceptions. Its priority in this field is recognized in the histories of medicine and psychology, and many of its fundamentals are as commonplace today as they were radical a century ago.[71]

If a reader today is given only the absurd side of phrenology, as understood a century ago, and not the fundamental principles that are accepted today, then Ellen White's statements seem both naive and contradictory. Some of those principles teach that obedience to health laws (as interpreted by phrenology) would even reduce the effect of hereditary disease, that most physical problems originate in the mind and thus the mind and body must be treated as a unit, that controlling passion would give power to enhance moral virtues and intellectual capabilities.[72]

Critics suggest that Ellen White was deep into phrenology because she used terminology that phrenologists frequently used, such as "acquisitiveness," "cautiousness," "conscientiousness," and "benevolence." Other words that phrenologists freely used in "locating" certain characteristics in the brain included "secretiveness," "firmness," "causality," "self-esteem," "destructiveness," "parental love," "eventuality," "calculation," "hope," and "conjugally."

Was it possible for Mrs. White to write in terms of character development or the relationship between health and morals without employing commonly used words, even as we use them today? Referring to the impact of phrenology in the nineteenth century, Davies wrote: "Through lectures, societies, magazines, book and periodical articles, phrenological tenets were dinned into American ears until the appropriation of their peculiar vocabulary by fiction and popular speech made them familiar to everyone."[73]

But what about Ellen White's sons' receiving a phrenological examination? Mrs. White wrote: "Dr. Jackson gave an accurate account of the disposition and organization of our children. He pronounces Willie's head to be one of the best that has ever come under his observation. He gave a good description of Edson's character and peculiarities. He enjoined upon him outdoor exercise and not much study. I think this examination will be worth everything to Edson."[74]

No one would suggest that Ellen White understood all the mechanics and physiology of how the brain works; no one does today. Being a devoted mother, she was interested in anything that would help her to be a better mother. This routine examination at Dansville would be, at the most, interesting; in no way did it indicate that Ellen White espoused the philosophy of phrenology.[75]

Harm From Wearing Wigs

In the October 1871 issue of the *Health Reformer*,[76] Ellen White wrote of "hurtful indulgences" that militate against the highest interests and happiness of women. Among these "indulgences" she included wigs that, "covering the base of the brain, heat and excite the spinal nerves centering in the brain." As a result, she said, "many have lost their reason, and become hopelessly insane."

In the context of today's comfortable wigs, critics tend to ridicule this statement. But Mrs. White was referring to an entirely different product. The wigs she described were "monstrous bunches of curled hair, cotton, seagrass, wool, Spanish moss, and other multitudinous abominations."[77] One woman said that her chignon generated "an unnatural degree of heat in the back part of the head" and produced "a distracting headache just as long as it was worn."

Another *Health Reformer* article (quoting from the *Marshall Statesman* and the *Springfield Republican*) described the perils of wearing "jute switches"—wigs made from dark, fibrous bark. Apparently these switches were often infested with "jute bugs," small insects that burrowed under the scalp. One woman reported that her head became raw, and her hair began to fall out. Her entire scalp "was perforated with the burrowing parasites." "The lady . . . is represented as nearly crazy from the terrible suffering, and from the prospect of the horrible death which physicians do not seem able to avert."[78]

With reports such as this in the public press, it is easy to understand why Ellen White would warn women against the possible dangers of wearing wigs and trying to "keep pace with changing fashion, merely to create a sensation."[79]

What Drives Motivations

Only God can read motives as to why a person rejects the light of truth, whether it be reflected in the face and words of

Jesus Himself, or as presented through His prophets. Each individual has his or her own personal experience composed of circumstances that collectively are unique. No other person knows the configuration of those circumstances and thus is not capable of judging another's decision fairly. Yet a pattern has developed through the years that is shared by most critics.

In 1868 Uriah Smith wrote a brochure entitled "The Visions of Mrs. E. G. White—A Manifestation of Spiritual Gifts According to the Scriptures." Very few people worked more closely with James and Ellen White, or for a longer period of time. He reviewed the Biblical basis for spiritual gifts and listed the fruit of Mrs. White's ministry: (1) "They tend to the purest morality"; (2) "They lead us to Christ"; (3) "They lead us to the Bible"; (4) "They have brought comfort and consolation to many hearts"; (5) "They have never been known to counsel evil or devise wickedness."

Smith Addresses the Critics

Then Smith asked why objections arise against Ellen White: "We may emphatically ask the question which Pilate put to the Jews in reference to the Saviour, 'Why, what evil hath He done?'"

He proceeded to answer his question: "The first class is composed of those who believe, or did believe at the time their opposition commenced, the views held by Seventh-day Adventists, but in whom, or in someone with whom they sympathized, wrongs were pointed out and reproved by the visions. . . . The other class consists of those who are the avowed and open opponents of all the distinguishing views held by Seventh-day Adventists. Their opposition springs from a different motive from that of the first class. . . . They hate that system of truth with which the visions stand connected, and they attack the visions as the most sure and most effectual way of hindering the progress of that truth. In this they acknowledge the efficiency of the visions in advancing this work."

Smith summed up his description of the critics: "This covers the whole ground of the opposition; for we have never known any objection to arise which could not be traced to one or the other of these two sources."[80]

Presuppositions. Conscious or unconscious paradigms, or presuppositions, create intellectual grids that have blinded men and women since the first days this side of the Garden of Eden. Cain had his paradigm, into which his thinking must fit, and Abel had his. Copernicus and Galileo had to contend with the bitter atmosphere of hostile presuppositions among scholars in their day. Jesus and faithful believers have weathered rejection because the truth did not fit the expectations (the paradigms) of their contemporaries.[81]

Ellen White obviously had to contend with those who opposed her ministry. She could see that the reasons people gave for rejecting her work were not often the "true" reasons: "Sinful indulgences are cherished, the Testimonies are rejected, and many excuses which are untrue are offered to others as the reason for refusing to receive them. The *true* reason is not given. It is a lack of moral courage—a will, strengthened and controlled by the Spirit of God, to renounce hurtful habits."[82]

Mrs. White recognized the problem of presuppositions: "Some, hearing through the medium of their own prejudices or prepossessions, understand the matter as they desire it to be—as will best suit their purpose—and so report it. Following the promptings of an unsanctified heart, they construe into evil that which, rightly understood, might be a means of great good."[83]

Everyone knows the subtle tug of doubt. Everyone has had to contend with that tug. Doubt keeps one prudent in the face of the unknown. Doubt, however, can become the Maginot Line for the uncommitted; too often we allow doubt to become synonymous with calm reason and see it as the mark of intelligence. If we relate to the Spirit of God as we would to a telephone marketer, we are misusing reason.

Most people have observed the soundness of Mrs. White's warning: "Satan has ability to suggest doubts and to devise objections to the pointed testimony that God sends, and many think it is a virtue, a mark of intelligence in them, to be unbelieving and to question and to quibble. Those who desire to doubt will have plenty of room. God does not propose to remove all occasion for unbelief. He gives evidence, which must be carefully investigated with a humble mind and a teachable spirit, and all should decide from the weight of evidence."[84] "God gives sufficient evidence for the candid mind to believe; but he who turns from the weight of evidence because there are a few things which he cannot make plain to his finite understanding, will be left in the cold, chilling atmosphere of unbelief and questioning doubts, and will make shipwreck of faith."[85]

Believing in Ellen White's ministry is not a creedal matter. Nor is it akin to believing that Jesus was born in Bethlehem or that she was born in Maine. But it is similar to believing that Jesus is a believer's personal Saviour, which involves more than a mental commitment. Critics have found many "intellectually satisfying" reasons to dispute Biblical claims. Most often they are looking at the container, not the content. Or, they find "reasons" for rejecting Christ's call for self-denial and to follow Him in joyful obedience to the will of God.

Why? Because they are looking for a religion that their heart wants—"according to their own desires, because they have itching ears, they will heap up for themselves teachers; and they will turn their ears away from the truth" (1 Tim. 4:3, 4).

When one looks at the messenger's message, and not primarily at the limitations of the messenger, a distinctive and sturdy foundation is laid, safe enough to carry the "weight of evidence" that exists.

Endnotes

1. *Evangelism*, p. 645.
2. See p. 29.
3. *Selected Messages*, book 1, pp. 31-36.
4. See p. 272.
5. See pp. 158, 159. For a review of these charges, see Nichol, *Critics*, pp. 112-130.
6. *Bio.*, vol. 1, pp. 462-464.
7. *Testimonies*, vol. 1, pp. 264-268; *Bio.*, vol. 2, pp. 36-38.
8. *Ibid.*, pp. 253-260.
9. *Ibid.*, p. 258.
10. *Ibid.*, p. 259.
11. *Ibid.*, p. 260.
12. *Ibid.*, p. 363.
13. For a list of Ellen White statements regarding a delayed advent, see Herbert E. Douglass, *The End* (Mountain View, Calif.: Pacific Press Publishing Association, 1979), pp. 161-167.
14. Early Writings, pp. 58, 64, 67.
15. *Ibid.*, p. 67.
16. Ms 1, 1854, cited in *MR*, vol. 1, pp. 33, 34.
17. *Early Writings*, pp. 36-38, 44, 48.
18. *Testimonies*, vol. 1, pp. 131, 132.
19. See pp. 29, 30 for a discussion of this principle; see also Nichol, *Critics*, pp. 102-111.
20. See Douglass, *The End*, pp. 161-167.
21. *Evangelism*, p. 696.
22. *Early Writings*, p. 75. This sentence appears in the chapter, "The Gathering Time," which combined two visions and some additional lines. The first vision, Sept. 23, 1850, dealt with the "gathering time" of "Israel," the dates on the Millerite 1843 chart, the "daily," timesetting, and the error of going to Old Jerusalem. The second vision, June 21, 1851, focused on the third angel's message, timesetting, and Old Jerusalem's not being built up.
23. Many former Millerites were setting various dates for the return of Jesus, with 1850 and 1851 being the latest dates for the end of the 2300-day/year prophecy. Although Sabbatarian Adventists generally were immune from timesetting, Hiram Edson and Joseph Bates advocated 1850 and 1851, respectively. James White kept their views out of *Present Truth*, the *Advent Review*, and the *Review and Herald.*
24. Age-to-come exponents, led by Joseph Marsh, O. R. L. Crosier, and George Storrs, with several variations, believed that the Second Advent would usher in the millennial kingdom on earth during which time the world would be converted under the reign of Christ with the Jews playing a leading role. This group closely related to the Literalists (British Adventists) who had believed that in the 1840s the literal Jews would welcome their Messiah (Christ) in Palestine, thus fulfilling Old Testament prophecies with Jerusalem becoming Christ's capital during the millennium. The majority of

the Millerites had rejected this aspect of their Adventist theology, calling it Judaism. (See Josiah Litch, "The Rise and Progress of Adventism," *The Advent Shield and Review,* May 1844, p. 92, cited in *Seventh-day Adventist Bible Students' Source Book,* p. 513. The first defectors from early Seventh-day Adventists were H. S. Case and C. P. Russell who had, among other concepts, embraced the "age-to-come" theory. See *SDAE,* vol. 11, "Messenger Party," pp. 51, 52.

25. *Early Writings,* p. 75.
26. *Early Writings,* pp. 75, 76.
27. For background on the religious context of this topic concerning the rebuilding of Old Jerusalem, see Julia Neuffer, "The Gathering of Israel," (a pamphlet prepared by the Biblical Research Committee, General Conference of Seventh-day Adventists).
28. *Spiritual Gifts,* vol. 1, p. 193 (*Early Writings,* p. 276).
29. *Ibid.,* p. 206 (*Early Writings,* p. 286).
30. *Review and Herald,* Dec. 17, 1895.
31. *Ibid.*
32. *Early Writings,* p. 74. This chart, designed in 1842 by Charles Fitch, Congregational pastor, and Apollos Hale, Methodist preacher, was approved by the Millerites in their Boston General Conference of May, 1842. The chart's graphic symbols and time periods became a well-known trademark of Millerite preaching as they endeavored to simplify in an attractive manner the time prophecies focusing on 1843.—See Froom, *Prophetic Faith of Our Fathers,* vol. IV, pp. 538, 616.
33. See Matt. 11:25; Mark 4:33; John 16:12; 1 Cor. 3:2; Heb. 5:11-14.
34. *Education,* p. 14, (same statement, *The Desire of Ages,* p. 465).
35. *Early Writings,* p. 40. This vision was first described in the Broadside, *To those who are receiving the seal of the living God,* first published, Jan. 31, 1849.
36. *A Word to the Little Flock,* p. 21, cited in Nichol, *Critics,* p. 581.
37. *Ibid.,* p. 22. Ellen White wrote: "I was wrapped in a vision of God's glory, and for the first time had a view of other planets."—*Life Sketches,* p. 97; see also *Spiritual Gifts,* vol. 2, p. 83. No evidence exists that this is the same vision described in *Early Writings,* p. 40. See pages 144, 145.
38. Further information regarding this 1846 vision is found in Loughborough, *GSAM,* pp. 257-260. For a discussion of how Loughborough's memory of his conversation with Bates many years earlier fits into this memorable moment for Bates, see Nichol, *Critics,* pp. 93-101.
39. *Spiritual Gifts,* vol. 3, p. 64. "Every species of animal which God had created were preserved in the ark. The confused species which God did not create, which were the result of amalgamation, were destroyed by the flood. Since the flood there has been amalgamation of man and beast, as may be seen in the almost endless varieties of species of animals, and in certain races of men."—Page 75.
40. "We might speak of the scattering of man and beast over the earth, but we do not therefore mean that previously man and beast were fused in one mass at one geographical spot. We simply mean the scattering of man over the earth and the scattering of beasts over the earth, though the original location of the two groups might have been on opposite sides of the earth. In other words, the scattering of man and of beast."—Nichol, *Critics,* p. 308.
41. "Those who profess to be followers of Christ, should be living agencies, cooperating with heavenly intelligences; but by union with the world, the character of God's people becomes tarnished, and through amalgamation with the corrupt, the fine gold becomes dim." —*Review and Herald,* Aug. 23, 1892.
42. *Selected Messages,* book 2, p. 288.
43. We have no evidence that Ellen White read Alexander Kinmount's *Twelve Lectures on the Natural History of Man* (1839), pp. 152, 153, which gives us another example of how the word "amalgamation" was used in her lifetime: "Another specimen of the evil resulting from mixing science with religion, to the injury of both, may be seen in the argument for the amalgamation of the African and European races, on the ground of their being one family, both descended from Adam and Eve. . . . It belongs to science, and to the common instincts and feelings of mankind to say, whether there are not races of men so unlike in their temperaments as to prohibit, as nefarious and contrary to nature, the amalgamation of them."
44. For a contemporary review of the two interpretations, see Gordon Shigley, "Amalgamation of Man and Beast: What Did Ellen White Mean?" *Spectrum,* June 1982, pp. 10-19.
45. Nichol, *Critics,* p. 308.
46. See Warren H. Johns, "Ellen G. White and Subterranean Fires, Part 1," *Ministry,* August 1977, pp. 9-12.
47. *Spiritual Gifts,* vol. 3, pp. 79-80 (1864); see also *Spirit of Prophecy,* vol. 1, pp. 82, 83 (1870); *Signs of the Times,* Mar. 13, 1879; *Patriarchs and Prophets,* pp. 108, 109 (1890); Manuscript 21, 1902, cited in *Seventh-day Adventist Bible Commentary,* vol. 7, pp. 946, 947.
48. Johns, "Ellen G. White and Subterranean Fires, Part 1," *Ministry,* August 1977, p. 6.
49. *Ibid.*, p. 12.
50. Otto Stutzer, *Geology of Coal,* translated by Adolph Noe (Chicago: University of Chicago Press, 1940), pp. 309, 310, cited in *Ibid.,* p. 19.
51. Johns, "Ellen G. White and Subterranean Fires, Part 2," *Ministry,* October 1977, p. 20.
52. *Ibid.*
53. Stutzer, *Geology of Coal,* p. 310; *Patriarchs and Prophets,* p. 108, cited in Johns, "E. G. White and Subterranean Fires, Part 2," p. 20.
54. E. E. Thurlow, "Western Coal," *Mining Engineering,* 26 (1974), pp. 30-33, cited in *Ibid.,* p. 21.
55. G. Sherburne Rogers, "Baked Shale and Slag Formed by the Burning of Coal Beds," *U. S. Geological Survey Professional Paper,* 108-A (1918), cited in *Ibid.,* p. 21.
56. Johns, "E. G. White and Subterranean Fires, Part 2," p. 22. "The coal mines of Germany have become a veritable gold mine in a study of Ellen White's scientific declarations, indicating the intermingling of the divine and human in a unique way."— *Ibid.,* p. 22.
57. *An Appeal to Mothers,* p. 27; *Testimonies,* vol. 2, p. 470.
58. *Ibid.,* p. 5.
59. *Ibid.,* p. 18.
60. *Testimonies,* vol. 2, p. 391.
61. *Ibid.*
62. *Appeal to Mothers* was reprinted in 1870 as part of a larger work, *A Solemn Appeal Relative to Solitary Vice and Abuses and Excesses of the Marriage Relation.* A facsimile reprint appears in the Appendix to *A Critique of Prophetess of Health (E. G. White Estate).*

63. Carl C. Phieffer, Ph.D., M.D., *Zinc and Other Micro-Nutrients* (New Canaan, Ct.: Keats Publishing, Inc., 1978), p. 45.
64. David F. Horrobin, M.D., Ph.D., *Zinc* (St. Albans, Vt.: Vitabooks, Inc., 1981), p. 8.
65. Richard Nies, Ph.D., (Experimental Psychology, UCLA, 1964; equivalent Ph.D. in clinical psychology, including oral exam, but died during dissertation preparation), Lecture, "Give Glory to God," Glendale, Calif., n.d.; Alberta Mazat, M.S.W., (Professor of Marriage and Family Therapy, Loma Linda University, Loma Linda, Calif.), Monograph, "Masturbation," (43 pp.) Biblical Research Institute.
66. Mazat, Monograph, "Masturbation."
67. See p. 301.
68. Phrenology, regarded today as a pseudoscience, was the forerunner of modern psychology . . . [and] originated with Franz Josef Gall (1758-1828), a Viennese physician, who in 1790 became persuaded that localized mental faculties existed on the brain surface and skull."—George Reid, *A Sound of Trumpets*, pp. 85, 86. Along with his disciples, Johann Spurzheim, Gall circled Europe in lecture tours, ending up "as famous men" in Paris. Spurzheim, traveling later to England and America, coined the term, "phrenology," to describe his medical practice and "took America by storm." Ralph Waldo Emerson hailed Spurzheim as "one of the world's greatest minds. . . . Henry Ward Beecher preached phrenology from his pulpit; Horace Greeley published it in his New York *Tribune*; Horace Mann and Samuel G. Howe applied it to educational reform; and a bevy of literary figures endorsed it, including Walt Whitman, Edgar Allan Poe, and (with impish comments), Mark Twain."—*Ibid.*, pp. 86, 87.
69. *Testimonies*, vol. 1, pp. 290, 291.
70. *Signs of the Times*, Nov. 6, 1884 (*Selected Messages*, book 2, p. 352).
71. *Phrenology: Fad and Science—A Nineteenth Century American Crusade* (New Haven, Conn.: Yale University Press, 1971), pp. x, xi.
72. Reid, *A Sound of Trumpets*, p. 89.
73. Davies, *Phrenology: Fad and Science*, p. ix. An example of Ellen White's using a phrenology concept without the implications of phrenology philosophy: "When God has given us such a habitation, why should not every apartment be carefully examined? The chambers of the mind and heart are the most important. Then, instead of living in the basement of the house, enjoying sensual and debasing pleasures, should we not open these beautiful chambers and invite the Lord Jesus to come in and dwell with us?"—*Testimonies*, vol. 6, pp. 375, 376.
74. Dr. Jackson's examination report of Willie White's character may be found in *Manuscript Releases*, vol. 6, p. 346.
75. Notables who also had their "head" read include Hiram Powers, a sculptor; William Cullen Bryant; Theodore Weld; Arthur Tappan; John Greenleaf Whittier; and Clara Barton. See Reid, *A Sound of Trumpets*, p. 87.
76. *Health Reformer*, October 1871, pp. 120, 121.
77. *Ibid.*, July 1867,
78. *Ibid.*, January 1871.
79. *Ibid.*, October 1871.
80. *Witness of the Pioneers Concerning the Spirit of Prophecy* (Washington, D.C.: Review and Herald Publishing Association, 1981), pp. 33, 34.
81. See Appendix E as to how presuppositions determine a person's understanding of the shut-door issue.
82. *Testimonies*, vol. 4, p. 32; *Ibid.*, vol. 5, p. 675.
83. *Ibid.*, vol. 5, p. 695.
84. *Ibid.*, vol. 3, p. 255; *Ibid.*, vol. 5, p. 675. For a discussion of how presuppositions (or "theories") have driven Biblical scholarship in the past 200 years, see Paul A. L. Giem, *Scientific Theology* (Riverside, Calif.: La Sierra University Press, 1997), pp. 112-116.
85. *Ibid.*, vol. 4, pp. 232, 233; *Ibid.*, vol. 5, pp. 675, 676.

Study Questions

1. What is the key to understanding "conditional prophecy"?
2. How can Ellen White's statements regarding the "nearness" of the Advent be understood after many decades?
3. Under what conditions did Ellen White write that "Jerusalem never would be built up"?
4. How do you explain that God's hand covered a mistake in a prophetic chart?
5. What did Ellen White mean by her "amalgamation" statements?
6. About 40 statements exist wherein Ellen White stated that Jesus could have returned before she made those statements. Summarize why His return has not occurred.

CHAPTER 44

The Shut Door—A Case Study

"Clearer light came with the investigation of the sanctuary question. . . . When Christ passed from the holy to the most holy of the heavenly sanctuary, the door, or ministration, of the former apartment was closed, and the door, or ministration, of the latter was opened. Christ had ended one part of His work as our Intercessor, to enter upon another portion of the work; and He still presented His blood before the Father in behalf of sinners."[1]

Critics have called the "shut-door" issue "the darkest page in our denominational history,"[2] "the most serious error ever taught by Sister White."[3] On this question they have said that the "battles that have been fought . . . have not been mere exercises in academic hair-splitting."[4]

In 1885 General Conference president George I. Butler wrote: "Perhaps there has never been anything connected with the Advent movement that our enemies have tried harder to use to our reproach than the shut-door doctrine."[5] Yet, he could say: "When we understand all about the facts connected with the 'shut-door doctrine,' as it is called, we shall find nothing of which we need to be ashamed."[6]

More Than a Minor Footnote

The shut-door question is more than a minor footnote in the history of the Seventh-day Adventist Church. Connected with the shut-door issue is the validity of (1) the Millerite movement, especially the seventh-month message, (2) the significance of October 22, 1844, (3) the connection between the Sabbath and the sanctuary message, and (4) the relevance and integrity of Ellen G. White as a trustworthy messenger of God.

Critics contend that Ellen White, even until the early 1850s, held to the extreme "shut-door" notion. In so doing, they insist that she concurred with her husband, James, and Joseph Bates (among others), that probation had closed for all the world on October 22, 1844. Further, they point to several statements she made that suggest, in their opinion, that genuine conversions ceased on that date.

The crux of their argument is this: If Ellen White was wrong about the close of probation for the "wicked world" on October 22, 1844, then she was wrong about what happened on that date—that Jesus entered into the Most Holy Place in the heavenly sanctuary to complete His high priestly ministry.

Those who believe in the validity of Ellen White's position as to what happened on October 22 base their confidence on Biblical evidence and a careful reading of the original sources, connecting disputed passages with their various contexts. This chapter will look at all source documents that relate to the "shut-door" issue.

Recognition of Presuppositions

Both affirmers and critics work from presuppositions.[7] Everybody does. No thoughtful historian or theologian would say otherwise. Presuppositions determine the questions to be asked as well as the weight given to source materials. Presuppositions too often predetermine conclusions by finding "facts" that support the researcher's basic paradigm. The problem, however, is that most people consider themselves "objective" and "scientific," even while working from presuppositions (though often unconsciously).

How can one arrive at truth if differences of opinion arise from a different set of presuppositions? By first asking the God of truth to guide (John 16:13). Then, with the help of the Holy Spirit, one should examine (1) one's own presuppositions and (2) those of one's opponents. It is amazing how tempers cool when adversaries recognize each other's presuppositions.[8]

Essential Attitude of Truth Seekers

Unfortunately, people have differed regarding their understanding of God's will ever since Cain and Abel. But not even God will force love or compliance. Nor will He impose His presuppositions on another. He is willing to "reason" (Isa. 1:8) with men and women regarding the soundness of His will and the validity of their presuppositions. By the "weight of evidence" honest, humble people have gladly acknowledged the trustworthiness of their Creator Friend.

Those who choose to identify with God's plan of revealing truth must not only see His truth as a "whole"[9] but also reflect His spirit of graciousness. If not, His name is taken in vain, thus adding to the confusion, hurt, and satanic misrepresentation of His character that has prevailed for millennia.[10]

Ellen White pointed to one of the basic attitudes needed by those in the arena of opposing presuppositions: "True Christian love cherished in the heart and exemplified in the life, would teach us to *put the best possible construction upon the course of our brethren*. We should be as jealous of their reputation as of our own. If we are forever suspecting evil, this very fact will so shape their course of action as to produce the very evil which we have allowed ourselves to suspect. In this way, a great many difficulties are manufactured that otherwise would never have had birth, and brethren are often wronged by our being suspicious, free to judge their motives, and express our opinion to others in regard to their actions. That which one may be ready to construe into grave wrongs, may be no more than we ourselves are chargeable with every day."[11]

The underlying purpose of this book has been to join with the reader in searching for truth so that God's plan may be made so clear that no one will have cause to stumble. Most all historical research is limited at best. In fact, we have scanty resource material available on the "shut-door" issue. We have no opportunity to ask nineteenth-century participants what they may have meant regarding what has been recorded. Hence, one of the safest methods that fair-minded students have used to ascertain truth is to employ this basic principle: "*Put the best possible construction*" on differing points of view. In this way, a researcher's personal presuppositions are held in check.

Putting "the best possible construction" on an opponent's point of view not only enhances friendship but also may bring each party into a clearer understanding of the very truth each seeks.

Presuppositions of Critics

Because the shut-door issue would not have arisen without the charges of certain critics, we will first review the basic presuppositions of various critics. Though not all these points apply to all critics, the general paradigm is as follows:

• Ellen White was time-conditioned; that is, she was a prisoner of her time, largely dependent upon the concepts prevailing among her contemporaries. For example: she reflected the "shut-door" concepts of her husband and other Sabbatarian Adventists.[12]

• Ellen White and church leaders have not been forthright in dealing with the first seven or eight years of the public ministry of Ellen White and other "pioneers."

• Ellen White and early Adventist leaders were compelled to "open the door" in the early 1850s because of the growing interest in the Sabbath and sanctuary doctrines among those not involved in the 1844 experience.

• Ellen White's teaching on the atonement involving Christ's change of ministry into the Most Holy Place in 1844 is unBiblical, hence her role as a theological teacher is unacceptable. This presupposition perhaps underlies and drives all other presuppositions.

• If Ellen White's claim to be a divinely inspired writer is true, then her written words are either inspired or they are not. That is, from this verbal inspiration viewpoint, Ellen White would not be a prophet if she edited, deleted, or otherwise changed her previous statements.

In putting "the best possible construction" on the critics' concerns, affirmers must role-play and think through the "reasons" behind the critics' charges. The quiet sharing of one another's presuppositions will often eliminate the tensions caused by misperceptions.

Presuppositions of Affirmers

Presuppositions of affirmers are generally as follows:

• Ellen White was time-related, not time-conditioned.[13] However, on a continuum from time-related to time-conditioned, affirmers are not always at the same point. One of the weaknesses, for example, of most affirmers is that they place equal weight on both anachronistic statements and contemporary statements. Another weakness is that some affirmers have not always thoroughly studied the contemporary record.

• Ellen White, as all prophets, may not have fully understood all the implications of her visions at the time she received them. Through the years, affirmers have taken different positions on this point.[14]

• Ellen White's position on the shut door, after her first visions, was different from (1) other shut-door advocates and (2) from her husband's or Joseph Bates's understanding (at least before 1851); her developing clarity regarding evangelistic expansion led the Sabbatarian Adventists into their worldwide vision beginning in the early 1850s.[15]

• Affirmers are convinced that Ellen White's vision-messages are Biblically sound and time-urgent in the setting of the messages of the three angels of Revelation 14. Thus, her role as theological conceptualizer (always under the Biblical norm) can be safely followed.[16]

Reviewing the Record

What does the historical record reveal? In probing the contemporary sources for an understanding of the term, "shut door," we will examine, in order, (1) what Millerites believed regarding the shut door before 1844; (2) what they thought after 1844, noting that before another year would pass they would separate into two groups—Open-door Millerites and Shut-door Millerites; (3) the vision-messages of Ellen White as to how she understood the meaning of the shut door, the close of probation, etc., and 4) the thinking of Sabbatarian Adventists prior to 1852.

Millerites before 1844. Central to Millerite thinking after the 1830s was that the world would end in 1843-1844. The Bridegroom parable (the Matthew 25 parable that included the shut-door concept) was often used in connection with closing events. For all Millerites prior to October 22, 1844, the "shut door" symbolized the close of probation, the sealing of the saints, and immediate judgment by the coming Lord.[17]

Millerites after 1844. For a time after October 22, Millerites were stunned, disappointed, and confused.[18] Soon two main groups developed: (1) Open-door Millerites and (2) Shut-door Millerites. Open-door Millerites eventually repudiated the prophetic calculations that led to

October 22, 1844, and disavowed any significance to that date. (Some, however, continued to believe that Christ's coming was imminent and others continued to calculate and proclaim other dates for the visible return of Jesus.[19]) For a time, Shut-door Millerites generally maintained their confidence that both their time calculations and their message of Christ's return were correct,[20] even though they misunderstood *how* Christ would return.

Fanaticism within Shut-door Millerites. The extreme position that probation had closed for everyone on October 22, 1844, soon led many into fanaticism. This extreme group, within which were distinct variations, emphasized that Christ indeed came on October 22, not visually to the world but "spiritually" (that is, experientially) to believing Millerites who maintained their confidence in the validity of October 22. They were labeled "spiritualizers."[21] Believing that probation had closed (thus, fixing characters and destiny forever), some leaders advocated such practices as "no work" (to work would indicate a lack of faith that they were in their millennial rest), "creeping" even on the streets (to show their childlike humility as befitting those who belong to the kingdom of God—Luke 18:19), and eventually "spiritual wifery" (thus fulfilling the Biblical teaching that redeemed people will no longer be married—Mark 12:25).[22]

New View for Millerites[23]

When Ellen Harmon[24] described her Midnight Cry vision of December 1844, Millerites heard a distinctly new explanation for what happened on October 22, 1844[25]—Jesus was yet to come and probation had not closed for everyone. When little groups in Maine and Massachusetts heard this vision-story confirming their 1844 experience to be "the work of God," they also listened to Ellen Harmon's rejection of their prevailing fanaticisms and theological errors.[26]

Prior to this December Midnight Cry vision (only a few weeks after their great disappointment), Ellen Harmon, along with many other dismayed Millerites, had concluded that they had been in error—that is, the fulfillment of the 2300-year prophecy, the shut door of the Bridegroom parable, etc., were yet future.[27] This first vision convinced Ellen Harmon (with no hint of a general shut door for all the living on October 22, 1844) that God's people were at the beginning of new responsibilities, not at the end of all things.[28]

A few weeks later, Ellen Harmon had her second public vision, the Sanctuary-Bridegroom vision, at Exeter, Maine, February, 1845. At Exeter she, no doubt, had been relating her first vision to a group of Shut-door Adventists, along with reproof of their fanatical leaders and their incorrect teachings regarding their extreme shut-door position.[29]

First Connection Between 1844 and Heavenly Sanctuary

The Sanctuary-Bridegroom vision gave Ellen Harmon her first look at what happened in salvation-history on October 22, 1844, when Christ entered the Most Holy Place of the heavenly sanctuary.[30] In addition, it unfolded more clearly the principle of rejection—that, in addition to those who had either rejected or repudiated the light regarding the significance of 1844, a *third* group existed who had not yet seen clearly the choices available at that time.[31] Ellen Harmon described this group as "careless" people who had been "deceived"; that is, they had not consciously rejected the light of truth, and thus the possibility remained for them to accept the light if it were properly presented to them. *This third group provided the conceptual seeds for an enriched definition of the "shut door," that is, the door had not been shut on those who had not consciously rejected the light brought to the world in 1844.* In this vision there is no hint of a closed door for the whole world in 1844.[32]

Time of Jacob's Trouble

The *Time of Jacob's Trouble vision* in August 1845, saved some ardent, extreme shut-door advocates such as James White from another colossal disappointment. While Ellen Harmon was in Carver, Massachusetts, in August, James White, now 24 years of age, in nearby Fairhaven and Dartmouth, was proclaiming the imminence[33] of the Advent, one year after October 22, 1844.

After hearing Ellen Harmon's vision, James wrote a letter to a shut-door periodical describing the impact of her message: "Many were expecting the Lord to come at the 7th month [October], 1845. That Christ would then come we firmly believed."[34]

Continuing in that same article, he wrote: "At this time, Ellen was with the band at Carver, Mass., where she saw in vision, that we should be disappointed, and that the saints must pass through the 'time of Jacob's trouble,' which was future. Her view of Jacob's trouble was entirely new to us, as well as [to] herself."

Christ's Return Near, But Not Imminent

Part of the "newness" to James was that this 1845 vision unambiguously taught that Christ's return was not imminent, that significant events would yet take place on this earth. This vision seemed to have saved James from any further time calculations regarding the Lord's return, a common practice among some Millerite leaders.

This 1845 vision, so timely, so Biblical, evidently made a particularly profound impact on James as well as others. This August vision, coupled with her other visions and messages, provided a context of confidence as these early believers moved into fuller light yet to come. For them, Ellen Harmon could be trusted. Their experiences in connection with young Ellen's visions became a profound basis for confidence in her prophetic ministry.

Sabbath-in-the-Sanctuary Vision

The *Sabbath-in-the-Sanctuary vision (Halo of Glory vision)*, April 3, 1847,[35] focused on the last-day significance of the seventh-day Sabbath. With each successive vision, Ellen White laid down another brick in a coherent, integrated theological foundation. In this April 3 vision, the relationship was cemented between the sanctuary and the seventh-day Sabbath (the "shut door" and the Sabbath).

As in preceding visions, there is no hint of an extreme shut-door position. On the contrary, Mrs. White continued to lift the sights of her colleagues, as well as her own, as she relentlessly continued to open the door of missionary responsibilities: "I saw that God had children who do not see and keep the Sabbath. They had not rejected the light upon it." Here again, she applied the principle of rejection: Because the world was full of people who had not been introduced to the Sabbath truth, a vast mission field was waiting to be taught and warned. For her, *the door was not shut* to those (1) who had not understood clearly the Midnight Cry messages, or (2) who had not yet heard the Sabbath truth. Her reasoning? The door was always open to the repenting sinner who had not rejected the clear light of truth.

In a letter to shut-door advocate Eli Curtis, April 21, 1847, in response to his request for her views, Ellen White wrote that she "fully" agreed "on some points, but on others we widely differ."[36] She agreed on (1) two literal resurrections, 1,000 years apart, and (2) that the new earth appears only after the wicked are raised and destroyed at the end of the 1,000 years. She disagreed with him when he took the position that Michael had stood up (Dan. 12:1) in the spring of 1844, and that the time of trouble began at that time. Then she said: "The Lord has shown me in vision, that Jesus rose up, and shut the door, and entered the Holy of Holies, at the 7th month 1844." Further, she pointed out that the time of trouble when Michael stands up was yet future and would take place only after Jesus had finished His work in the Most Holy Place. She would elaborate on this connection in vision-messages to come. In other words, she and Eli Curtis disagreed fundamentally as to what happened on October 22, 1844, because she gave the term "shut door" a new definition.[37]

As far as we know, this was the first time Ellen White used the term, "shut door," in print. How did she use it? In the context of the sanctuary doctrine and specifically connected to the commencement of Christ's work in the Most Holy Place. She would elaborate on this connection in vision-messages to come. In other words, she and Eli Curtis disagreed fundamentally as to what happened on October 22, 1844.

Seal-of-God Vision

Ellen White did not write out her *Seal of God vision*, November 17-19, 1848.[38] However, while she was in vision at the Otis Nichols home in Dorchester, Massachusetts, Joseph Bates took notes of what she was saying. This vision stirred the Sabbatarian Adventist group, greatly widening their vision as to their tremendous missionary responsibility to proclaim the messages of Revelation 14's three angels.[39]

This vision described the events since 1844 as light breaking out "in the east," then "one light after another," as each new truth was "linked together; they cannot be separated"—all truths that were related to the sealing work. She also assured her hearers that "the time of trouble" had not broken out, even though some saw a possible fulfillment in the then current European unrest.

The most dramatic part of this vision was Ellen White's emphasis on publishing the "things that thou hast seen and heard" (that is, the salvation implications of the Sabbath as connected to the sanctuary doctrine and the sealing work). That challenge seemed, at first, to be staggering, almost beyond belief. But the prophet had spoken: The results of the publishing venture (that is, emphasizing the Sabbath as the seal of God connected with the sanctuary truth) would be like the "rising of the sun [as it] keeps on its course . . . but it never sets. . . . The rising is in strength and grows brighter and brighter."

Bates was so impressed with this vision that he asserted that the Sabbath truth should be published at once and sent to such places as France, Britain, Russia, and the Middle East.[40]

In context, this vision-promise was given to a handful of people only four years after their greatest disappointment. Obviously this small group of fewer than one hundred Sabbatarian Adventists had no idea of a worldwide program that would develop in the next fifty years. All they knew was that God had revealed to Ellen White that they were to begin publishing, with the means available, with the light they understood. Their confidence in this 21-year-old woman had been established during the previous three years—they would proceed.[41]

Holding-the-Winds Vision

Ellen White's *Holding-the-Winds vision*, January 5, 1849,[42] reemphasized her counsel given a few weeks earlier in Dorchester—that the various revolutions in Europe, both political and social, were not the "time of trouble" of Daniel 12, which was yet future.

She concluded this informative vision with further thoughts regarding the linkage between the holding of the winds (Revelation 7) and the sealing work (by implication, the close of probation). The winds would continue to be restrained by angels until God's people were sealed (that is, the return of Jesus was contingent on, among other factors, a people prepared for the sealing of God's name "written in their foreheads"—Rev. 7:3; 14:1). In this vision as in other messages, Ellen White emphasized that time was short, in spite of what they were beginning to understand as a "delay" in the Advent—that is, the Advent is contingent on when the sealing work would be finished.

Open-Door Vision

In her *Open Door vision*, March 24, 1849,[43] Ellen White provided further connections in the unfolding, step by step process of integrating vital truths that came to be known as "present truth," linkages such as: (1) "shut door" (i.e., validity of 1844) with the sanctuary truth; (2) Sabbath and the sanctuary truths "could not be separated"; (3) rise of spiritualism with the evils of Satan; (4) rise of hypnotism with the evils of Satan; (5) Paul's warning about "strong delusion" and "believe the lie" (2 Thess. 2:11, 12) applied to those ministers who were attacking the Sabbath and sanctuary truths.[44]

Here Ellen White emphasized her enriched understanding of the code word, "shut door."[45] The concepts of "shut door," the Sabbath, and the sanctuary truth (with its insights regarding Christ's work in the Most Holy Place) were "not [to] be separated." Frequently in this 1849 vision-message, she described Jesus as shutting the door of the Holy Place so that He could "open" His work in the Most Holy Place. In her graphic symbolism—one goes through the open door with Jesus after 1844, into the larger view that connects Christ's Most Holy Place ministry, the sealing work, and the time of His second coming.

The last sentence of this vision, however, has led critics to contend that Ellen White, even in 1849, held to the extreme shut-door notion—that probation had closed for all the world, except those who had held onto their 1844 experience: "My accompanying angel bade me look for the travail of soul for sinners as used to be. I looked, but could not see it; for the time for their salvation is past."[46]

Good interpretation connects any disputed passage with its contexts—first, its own letter or manuscript, and then the author's contemporary documents on the same subject. Even then, perhaps, no single interpretation of these two sentences will satisfy both the affirmers and the critics.

Affirmers generally find in earlier paragraphs the antecedents to the word *their* of this last sentence, that is: (1) to the non-Adventist pastors "who have rejected the truth"; (2) to those "professed Adventists who had rejected present truth"; (3) to new converts of the two previous ministers who "appeared to have been really converted . . . but if their hearts could be seen they would be as black as ever." In other words, among those involved in "false reformations" that went "from bad to worse" there was no "travail . . . for sinners as used to be." *For these false leaders and their unconverted "converts,"* as they continued their evil course, "the time for their salvation is past."[47]

Affirmers note further that Ellen White's messages for some time had been depicting, step by step, an opening door for evangelism for those who had not rejected the light of truth. The wider context for this disputed sentence, they feel, clearly explains what she did not mean.

"Present Truth" Article

Ellen White's article in *Present Truth,* September 1849, provided another example of the brick upon brick process by which she was helping to establish the rising foundation of a coherent, integrated theology. Her key points included: (1) that God's grace is sufficient to make Christians overcomers, (2) that character determines one's future, (3) that "what is done to rescue souls from the coming storm of wrath, must be done before Jesus leaves the Most Holy Place of the heavenly sanctuary," and (4) "that precious souls are starving, and dying for want of the present, sealing truth, the meat in due season; and that the swift messengers should speed on their way, and feed the flock with the present truth." *Here again we see no hint of a shut door or of a limited pool of prospects eligible for evangelism. Much to the contrary.*

Ellen White's cheery letter to the Hastings family, January 11, 1850, emphasized that "souls are coming into the truth, and soon the work will be all done. . . . I saw yesterday our work was not to the shepherds who have rejected the former messages, but to the honest deceived who are led astray. I saw the false shepherds would soon be fed with judgment. Let the truth come out everywhere we go. . . . Cheer up. There are better days coming."[48]

Here again the consistent understanding that Ellen White had had since 1845 is apparent—that there seemed to be no hope for the ministers who had either rejected or repudiated the 1844 truths, but there was hope for the "honest deceived." In this letter she reemphasized the principle of rejection that she reflected in her Bridegroom vision of February, 1845 when referring to the "careless" who had been deceived by Satan. When careless, deceived people "are led astray," the possibility exists that they may yet be led to see the truth and break with their deceptions.

Reviewing the Critics' Charges

For centuries, charges of inconsistencies and discrepancies have been made against the Bible.[49] Though explanations were offered as soon as the charges surfaced, many people, because of their presuppositions, continued to believe the charges. Yet, all charges, whether against the Bible or Ellen White, must be considered carefully and with due respect. Truth can afford to be open, frank, fair—and kind.[50]

Charge: Ellen White taught the extreme shut-door notion in her vision-messages. This accusation includes allegations such as: (1) Ellen White believed, from her vision-messages, that probation closed for everyone in 1844 (believers were saved and rejecters of the Millerite preaching were lost); (2) all "conversions" since 1844 were spurious.

Response: Records show that Ellen White grew in her understanding of the shut-door concept as God continued to unfold the truths relating to the significance of October 22, 1844. These records indicate that her vision-messages never taught that believers were "sealed" on that date. Nor did those messages teach that those who were not aware of the Millerite preaching, or those who had been honestly deceived by Satan, were "lost" on that date.

On the contrary, the same records reveal that from her earliest visions Ellen White enriched the shut-door concept, a position in direct conflict with other Shut-Door Millerites.[51] She taught that maintaining confidence in the Millerite calculations and the 1844 experience *did not automatically mean* that one had to believe that probation had closed for the whole world. Through her vision-messages she led the way into a Biblically based understanding of the events that occurred on October 22, 1844. Thus, for those who fully accepted young Ellen Harmon's early vision-messages, the "shut door" now became the *code word* for "validity of the 1844 message and experience" and the future-opening concept of Christ's change of ministry on October 22, 1844. This expanded understanding of the October 22 events soon became "present truth" for Sabbatarian Adventists.[52]

Ellen White's remarks regarding "conversions" by "false" teachers would apply to all such teachers from the beginning of time. Through the centuries, many have "felt saved" through unnumbered "plans" of salvation, whether in the mysticisms of ancient Babylon and Egypt, in the emotionally powerful preaching of many revivalists, or in the ecstasies of certain charismatic groups, past or present. Others have settled into a confidence that their reason and research have given them the "truth" about themselves and the universe. These "conversions," whether through feeling or reason, only God is able to judge as to personal motivations. But most will agree that rejecting truth is not the way to establish a saving relationship with God.

Charge: Ellen White and fellow Adventists have "covered up" her earlier, incorrect shut-door notions.

Response: At first glance, early critics had cause to ask questions—words here and there were deleted from later printings. Some of the first responses to this charge from later Adventist leaders did appear to be superficial, chiefly because not many people in later years had even seen the few, and not widely distributed, documents of the 1840s.[53] In fact, contemporary documents of the 1840s are more available today than they were to people in the 1840s! Further, no one in the 1840s could quickly access all the contemporary periodicals dealing with the shut-door subject as a modern student can; and few in the 1840s could access the private letters of Ellen Harmon-White and those of her contemporaries.

Whenever one role-plays, seeking to respond to the same challenges and conditions that young Ellen White faced, her responsibility to clarify earlier writings made in haste becomes clear and expected. Those few deletions or changes were *not made to change positions but to clarify them*—so that misunderstandings could be avoided. What else would a responsible author do, even a prophet?

No Evidence of Deception

No evidence exists that Ellen White (or anyone else) later tried to deceive her contemporaries into believing that she had not, after December 1844, taught the shut-door notion of the Turner-Hale group. For her contemporaries, it would have been a monstrous folly! Those early Adventists had learned through experience that they could trust Ellen White. If they had observed duplicity in "cover-ups," how could those same people trust her in the years to come when challenges arose that defied human wisdom? Those who had lived with her during the 1840s knew by experience how straightforward, how reliable, and timely her vision-messages were—from the beginning. To tamper with those vision-messages would have destroyed the unity of the small group of Sabbatarian Adventists. That group would not have survived long enough to be organized, any more than the early Christian church would have survived if founders had "covered up" the "fact" that Jesus was still in the grave.

Charge: Ellen White and her closest colleagues demonstrated their extreme shut-door notions from 1844 to 1852 by working only for Shut-door Millerites. (As we saw earlier, the Millerites were divided into Open-door and Shut-door Millerites.)

Response: Soon after her first vision, Ellen Harmon was instructed by the Lord to make her visions known. But to whom? The general population had already rejected the Millerite message, the general Christian world had scorned the premillennial emphasis of the Millerite message, the Open-door Millerites had repudiated the October 22 date and its significance—and only the Shut-door Millerites believed that something happened on that date. In fact, the Shut-door Millerites were the most nearly right people in the world! So she started where common sense and the Spirit of God led her. Further, many in "the little flock," which early Sabbatarian Adventists called themselves,[54] still held to the extreme shut-door positions and Ellen continued to lead them into unfolding truth.

No evidence exists that this approach to Shut-door Millerites caused a single person anywhere to be denied salvation.

Why didn't more Shut-door Millerites follow her fresh insight into the significance of 1844? Only God knows. But again to role-play, for Shut-door Millerites to follow the vision-messages of Ellen Harmon would mean to believe probation had not closed for the world on October 22, 1844. Further, it would mean that those who followed Ellen Harmon's leading would (1) understand why Christ went into the Most Holy Place, and (2) link the seventh-day Sabbath with the sanctuary message. All this may have been too much commitment for many Shut-door Millerites.

The additional reason why early Sabbatarian Adventists (barely one hundred by 1850) did not immediately launch aggressive evangelistic programs (as they began to do in the early 1850s) was that it took time for widely scattered early believers to establish their message. That early Adventists were able to formulate within a few short years a coherent theological message that would be "present truth" for everyone, Millerite or not, calls for admiration as well as amazement.

God did not ask them to launch out before He had made them ready. Without question, Ellen White's vision-messages and tenacity of spirit became the leading force in melding this small group into a world movement—all done within an amazingly short period of time.

Summary:

(1) Both affirmers and critics must deal fairly with all source materials available, not merely with those that fit their paradigms and presuppositions.

(2) During 1844 and 1845, Shut-door Millerites held a fairly uniform view that probation had closed for the world on October 22, 1844. Ellen White began to use this term as a code word for what happened in heaven on October 22, 1844, when Christ "shut" the door to the Holy Place and "opened" the door to the last phase of His atonement in the Most Holy Place.

(3) No source materials indicate that Ellen White or any of those who became Sabbatarian leaders engaged in the fanaticism associated with other shut-door advocates.

(4) No records prove that Ellen White believed that the door of mercy was shut on anyone in 1844, except for those who shut their own door by rejecting Bible truth—and only God could know those personal decisions. No records indicate that Ellen White repudiated any of her vision-messages.

(5) Source materials do not indicate that Ellen White in the early 1850s changed her mind and moved from an extreme shut-door position in the early 1850s because of changing circumstances. Early Sabbatarian Adventists were moving more aggressively in reaching out to the general public in the early 1850s, chiefly because it had taken a few years to formulate their message. *What would they have said to anyone regarding their reason for existing as a religious group much before 1850?* All this took time.

(6) The principle of rejection emphasizes the Biblical concept that (a) each person is responsible for his or her own salvation; (b) that no one is rejected by God until that person chooses to reject God; (c) that probation will not close for the world until all have settled into a habitual pattern of accepting light or rejecting it. This principle threads its way through all of Ellen White's vision-messages.

(7) Each successive vision revealed additional building material in the development of an integrated, consistent theological system that eventually became the "present" and distinctive truths of Seventh-day Adventists.

Endnotes

1. *Spirit of Prophecy*, vol. 4, p. 268.
2. W. W. Fletcher, *The Reasons For My Faith* (Sydney: William Brooks & Co., Ltd., 1932), p. 199.
3. Wallace D. Slattery, *Are Seventh-day Adventists False Prophets?* (Phillipsburg, N.J.: Presbyterian and Reformed Publishing Company, 1990), p. 29.
4. Dennis Hokama, *Adventist Currents*, July 1984, p. 26.
5. *Review and Herald*, Mar. 3, 1885.
6. *Ibid.*, Feb. 10, 1885.
7. See George Reid, "Another Look at Adventist Hermeneutics," *Journal of the Adventist Theological Society*, Spring, 1991.
8. See Appendix E: Basic Presuppositions Shared by Most Critics. (Appendices E-M are provided for this chapter in the general Appendix. For the best understanding of each subject, each appendix should be read when indicated in the body of the chapter.)
9. See pp. 256-263 for the development of the Great Controversy Theme.
10. See p. 257.
11. *Review and Herald*, April 15, 1880, italics supplied. See also *Mind, Character, and Personality*, vol. 2, p. 789; *MR*, vol. 19, p. 13.
12. See Appendix F: "Time-conditioned or Time-related."
13. Rolf Poehler used this distinction in his unpublished paper, "'. . . And the Door was Shut'—Seventh-day Adventists and the Shut-Door Doctrine in the Decade After the Great Disappointment," Andrews University, 1978.
14. See Appendix G: "Ellen White's Growing Understanding of Her Own Visions."
15. See Appendix H: "Ellen White Enriched the Term, 'Shut Door.'" During the 1840s, Ellen White used the term "shut door" in two ways, not in self-contradiction but with each way emphasizing a different, though complementary, point. The problem arises when no distinction is made between what "Shut-door" Millerites believed regarding the "shut door" and what Ellen White meant beginning with her first vision.
16. See Appendix I: "Ellen White Led the Way in Building a Biblical Message for the World." Beginning with her first vision Ellen White conceptually led the way in the development of a Biblically based coherency that eventually became the distinctive message of Seventh-day Adventists.
17. See Damsteegt, *Foundations*, pp. 42-44, 93-98. Damsteegt's *Foundations* is recognized as the most complete record of source materials available dealing with Millerite and Adventist thought from 1830-1874.
18. William Miller spoke for most: "We have done our work in warning sinners, and in trying to awake a formal church. God in His providence had shut the door; we can only stir one another up to be *patient;* and be diligent to make our calling and election sure." —*Advent Herald*, Dec. 11, 1844, cited in Damsteegt, *Foundations*, p. 106.
19. See Leroy Edwin Froom, *The Prophetic Faith of Our Fathers*, vol. 4, (Washington, D. C.: Review and Herald, 1954), pp. 838, 839.
20. Damsteegt, *Foundations*, pp. 104-115. Many shut-door advocates believed that Christ had indeed come spiritually. One of the first duties of young Ellen Harmon was to correct this error and point believers to the future and responsibilities yet to come.
21. The Albany group of Millerites referred to *all* who believed that something significant happened on October 22, 1844, as "spiritualizers." However, early Seventh-day Adventists labeled the extreme shut-door advocates "spiritualizers" because these "spiritualizers" believed that Jesus had indeed come, but only "to the hearts" of true believers.
22. Damsteegt, *Foundations*, pp. 114, 120-135; Schwarz, *Light Bearers*, pp. 55, 56. For example, Samuel Snow eventually thought he was Elijah the prophet (summer 1845). John Pearson, Jr. joined J. V. Himes (Open-door leader), and Enoch Jacobs went into Shakerism by April 1846.
23. See Appendix H: "Ellen White Enriched the Term, 'Shut Door.'"
24. On August 30, 1846, Ellen Harmon married James White.
25. An Advent Christian historian, Clyde E. Hewitt, wrote: "Not all of that minority of Adventists who believed in the October 22 date became fanatics. Nor did they spiritualize Christ's return. Some found instead an understanding of their great disappointment in a quite novel explanation. Miller, they argued, had been right in the *date*, but wrong in the *event*. . . . Out in western New York State on the morning of October 23 the local Adventist leader, Hiram Edson, after a lengthy prayer session with a few of those who had waited through the previous night with him, became convinced that the 'sanctuary' of Daniel 8:14 was in heaven. The prophecy did not refer to the earth but to the Holy of Holies in heaven itself. . . . To a small group of former Millerites this view of what had happened on October 22 seemed logical and, as buttressed with other arguments, often by scriptural analogy, convincing."—*Midnight and Morning* (Charlotte, N.C.: Venture Books, 1983), pp. 182, 183.
26. *Early Writings*, pp. 14-17; *Life Sketches*, pp. 64-68, 85-94; Damsteegt, *Foundations*, pp. 112, 120, 133; Schwarz, *Light Bearers*, pp. 63-65.
27. Letter to Bates, July 13, 1847; Manuscript 4, 1883, James White, *A Word to the Little Flock*, p. 22. (Cited in Nichol, *Critics*, p. 582 and George R. Knight, *1844 and the Rise of Sabbatarian Adventism* (Hagerstown, Md.: Review and Herald Publishing Association, 1994), p. 176.
28. Critics have charged that a one-sentence deletion in later publications of this vision belies the assertion that Ellen White did not believe in the extreme shut-door position after "viewing" her first vision. See Appendix J: "Response to Deletion of 'Wicked World.'"
29. *Life Sketches*, p. 73. Some have contended that this meeting and others with extreme Shut-door Adventists proves that Ellen White was also "one of them." For a discussion of why she attended these meetings with Shut-door Adventists, see Appendix K: "Why Ellen White Seemed to Reach Out Only to Shut-Door Adventists."
30. *Early Writings*, pp. 54-56.
31. The principle of rejection, in connection with the shut-door issue, meant that on October 22, 1844, those who consciously rejected truth closed their own door of probation—a principle that has been observed since sin entered the universe. For those who had not clearly heard the truth, the door of salvation had not been shut. The Biblical teaching is unambiguous: the door of salvation is always open to those who have not

consciously rejected the invitations of the Holy Spirit. God never arbitrarily closes the door of salvation on anyone; people close their own door of probation when they reject the Holy Spirit's promptings.

32. For how this vision broke new ground for the Shut-door Millerites, see Appendix I: "Ellen White Led the Way in Building a Theological Message for the World." Ellen White later said that her early visions corrected her previous error regarding October 1844, by revealing what Jesus did on that date. James White wrote on May 30, 1847, in *A Word to the Little Flock*, that "when she received her first vision, Dec. 1844, she and all the band in Portland, Maine, had given up the midnight cry, and shut door, as being in the past [that is, nothing significant happened on Oct. 22, 1844]. It was then that the Lord shew [sic] her in vision, the error into which she and the band in Portland had fallen." James White also reflected later that it was Ellen Harmon-White's visions that led emerging Seventh-day Adventists into the fuller light regarding the significance of October 22, 1844. —*Life Incidents* (Battle Creek: Seventh-day Adventist Publishing Association, 1868), pp. 204-209.
33. "Imminence" refers to a Second Coming that could happen at any moment in contrast to "nearness" which indicates that certain specific events must yet take place before Jesus returns, such as the Latter Rain, the Loud Cry, the Seven Last Plagues, etc. Seventh-day Adventists emphasize "nearness," not "imminence."
34. *Day Star,* Sept. 20, 1845, reprinted in *A Word to the Little Flock* (May 30, 1847), reproduced in Knight, *1844,* p. 171.
35. *Early Writings,* pp. 32-35; the description of this vision first appeared as a letter to Joseph Bates (April 7, 1847).
36. Eli Curtis was a contributor to *Day Dawn,* an extreme shut-door periodical of which O. R. L. Crosier was editor. This letter was reprinted in *A Word to the Little Flock,* cited in Nichol, *Critics,* pp. 571, 572, and Knight, *1844,* pp. 170, 171.
37. With so little source material available, no one can prove that what Ellen White meant in this April 21, 1847, letter was exactly what was in her mind in 1845. We can only reflect her growing divergencies from what was commonly held by others prior to this date.
38. Joseph Bates printed his notes of her comments during that vision in his *A Seal of the Living God,* cited, in part, in *Bio.,* vol. 1, p. 150.
39. "Sabbatarian" refers to Adventists who then worshiped on the seventh day of the week, differentiating them from "First-day" Adventists.
40. *A Seal of the Living God,* pp. 4, 35, 40, 45. Many years later Ellen White recalled this Dorchester vision and her words to her husband: "From this small beginning it was shown to me to be like streams of light that went clear round the world" (*Life Sketches,* p. 125). In 1887 she recalled that in her "very girlhood" [most probably before her marriage in 1846] she saw in vision that commandment-keeping believers in Jesus would be like "jets of light growing brighter . . . lighting the whole world."—*Review and Herald,* July 26, 1887.
41. Within the year, James White and company printed the first issue of *Present Truth,* July 1849, which later became the church paper, *Review and Herald,* one of the longest, continuously published religious journals in North America. It is now known as the *Adventist Review.*
42. *Early Writings,* pp. 36-38.
43. *Ibid.,* pp. 42-45, originally a letter to the Hastings family, March 30, 1849.
44. See Appendix I: "Ellen White Led the Way in Developing a Theological Message for the World."
45. For a discussion of how Ellen White enriched the term, "shut door," see Appendix H.
46. *Early Writings,* p. 45.
47. Damsteegt, *Foundations,* p. 154. It is more than interesting that Charles G. Finney, one of the leading evangelists in North America prior to 1850, wrote in 1845: "I have observed, and multitudes of others also I find have observed, that for the last ten years, revivals of religion have been gradually becoming more and more superficial. . . . There is very much less deep conviction of sin and deep breaking up of the heart."—Charles G. Finney, *Reflections on Revival* (Minneapolis, Minn.: Bethany Fellowship, 1979), p. 14.
48. Letter 19, cited in *MR,* vol. 19, p. 128.
49. See p. 16 for several examples.
50. See Appendix L: "Chief Charges Against Ellen White Regarding Shut-Door Issue and the Responses Through the Years."
51. See Appendix M: "The July 13, 1847, Letter to Joseph Bates."
52. "The 'Present Truth,' then, of this third angel's message, is, THE SABBATH AND THE SHUT DOOR." —Joseph Bates, *An Explanation of the Typical and Anti-typical Sanctuary* (New Bedford, Mass.: Press of Benjamin Lindsey, 1850), p. 14. Here Bates, as others, used the "shut door" code words for the sanctuary doctrine. See Ellen White's linkage in her Open and Shut Door Vision in 1849—*Early Writings,* pp. 42-45.
53. See Appendix L. For example, from the information available to him, J. N. Loughborough denied that any who later became Seventh-day Adventists had believed in the commonly understood notion of a "shut door" after the 1844 disappointment.
54. See Knight, *1844,* p. 165.

Study Questions

1. Why has the "shut-door" issue been called "the darkest page in our denominational history"?
2. What are the circumstances that drive the critics to charge that Ellen White believed, even after her first visions, that the door of salvation was closed to all in 1844?

3. How can it be affirmed that Ellen White's position on the shut-door is correct?

4. Why did it seem that Ellen White reached out only to the shut-door believers in her first two years of ministry?

5. How did Ellen White broaden the meaning of the "shut-door"? Include the circumstances under which she first used that term.

6. How did Ellen White's Sealing Vision (Jan. 5, 1849) set the tone for a key concept in the way Adventists think about the end times?

Continuing Relevancy of God's Messenger

CHAPTER

CHAPTER 45

Does Ellen White Measure Up?

"The golden rule for understanding spiritually is not intellect, but obedience. If a man wants scientific knowledge, intellectual curiosity is his guide; but if he wants insight into what Jesus Christ teaches, he can only get it by obedience. . . . Intellectual darkness comes through ignorance; spiritual darkness comes because of something I do not intend to obey. No man ever receives a word from God without instantly being put to the test over it. . . . Watch the things you shrug your shoulders over, and you will know why you do not go on spiritually."[1]

Does Ellen White measure up as a messenger bearing God's message in modern times? Does her seventy-year ministry warrant recognizing her as a divinely called messenger?

How did her contemporaries come to the conclusion that she was a prophet? Their experience becomes highly persuasive as we evaluate her credentials today. Why men and women since her death have come to this same conclusion is equally persuasive.

Applying Biblical Norms

The norms by which we measure Biblical prophets can easily be applied to Ellen White.

• Her teachings are in harmony with the Bible.[2] From the beginning to the end of her ministry, her counsel rings clear: "The Lord desires you to study your Bibles. He has not given any additional light to take the place of His Word. This light [her own ministry] is to bring confused minds to His Word, which, if eaten and digested, is as the lifeblood of the soul."[3]

Critics charge that Ellen White contradicts the Bible.[4] It may be that a few statements regarding a person or a date seem inconsistent with a Biblical text. But such discrepancies are insignificant. They merely are examples of the human element in the revelation/inspiration process, even as we observe discrepancies in the writings of certain Biblical prophets.[5]

The main issue is how well did she cut through the confusion and impasses of two thousand years and present to the modern world a full-orbed picture of the everlasting gospel? A fair review of her writings indicates that she united the basic concern of traditional conservatives with the heartfelt convictions of traditional liberals. In doing so, her theological message transcended the age-old stalemates that have caused divisions between churches and those within churches. Her main theological message transcends the limitations of the messenger. Her message is the basis for her claim to be God's messenger.[6]

• The fruitage of Ellen White's ministry becomes more compelling with the passing of time.[7] The test of time is a crucial test of a person's message. History books are full of leaders with great ideas in every field of knowledge; few of these people are even remembered today except for a possible footnote in a history book.

Scarcely one hundred believers in 1850, the Adventist movement has become worldwide, growing beyond ten million adherents. Non-Adventist observers, as well as Adventists, emphatically declare that Ellen White is a prime reason for this worldwide influence. Not just a preaching ministry, the Adventist Church sponsors the largest Protestant school system in the world. In addition, its medical program is internationally known, largely the product of Ellen White's nurturing.

These worldwide programs, including ADRA,[8] would never have reached their present achievements without the foresight and principles set forth by Ellen White. For example, Loma Linda University, with its internationally recognized School of Medicine, would not even exist had it not been for the vision and tenacity of Ellen White.

Unique Objectives

The distinctiveness of these programs lies not in the fact of their worldwide influence but in their unique objectives. Adventist schools and medical facilities are distinctive because of the carefully chiseled principles outlined by Ellen White, not because religious people imitate secular programs.

Further, Seventh-day Adventists today, because of principles set forth by God's messenger, are known as a giving people,[9] a longer-living, healthier people,[10] and a mission-oriented people.[11]

• Ellen White's consistent focus on Jesus as the center of both her spiritual life and her theological principles emphasizes how convincingly she cooperated with the "Spirit" of prophecy.[12] In hundreds of instances she emphasized the center of her own devotions and ministry: "The object of all ministry is to keep self out of sight, and to let Christ appear. The exaltation of Christ is the great truth that all who labor in word and doctrine are to reveal."[13] Her sermons uplifted Jesus as humanity's Source of peace and power.

Surprising as it may be for students of nineteenth-century religious movements, Ellen White left no monument to herself, no demand for adulation and the amenities that she surely deserved—characteristic of all Biblical prophets. Her life was driven by a sense of destiny wrapped up in her call to be God's messenger. She focused on making God better understood as she relayed to others His messages. Presenting Biblical truths as they are "in Jesus" was a favorite task.

One of the more practical tests of a prophet is found in the quality changes that the prophet's messages make in the lives of adherents. In reviewing the chief findings of the 1980 research done by the Institute of Church Ministry at Andrews University, we note that Seventh-day Adventists "who regularly study the writings of Ellen White are also more likely to be stronger Christians in their personal spiritual life and in their witness to their communities than those church members who don't."[14]

Ellen White Readers Read Bible More Than Others

Perhaps more significant than all the other characteristics of those who read the writings of Ellen White was the finding that "82 percent of the readers usually or always have daily personal Bible study, while only 47 percent of the nonreaders do." The difference of thirty-five percent was the largest relating to any question in the survey.

Adventists who read Ellen White place a higher value on Bible study than those who do not read her. Further, those who follow her counsel are the church's front-line sharers of the Good News that they continually receive from studying the Bible and her writings.

In other words, those who read Ellen White are those who best understand the mission and message of the Seventh-day Adventist Church.

Witness of Ellen White's Contemporaries

Ellen White's personal life was lived in full view of young and old. The acid test of people's integrity is whether they practice what they preach.

Young James White, an enthusiastic

Millerite Adventist in his early twenties, was much impressed with Ellen Harmon, a Portland teenager. In speaking of his first meeting with her, he recalled: "She was then a Christian of the most devoted type. And although but sixteen, she was a laborer in the cause of Christ in public and from house to house. She was a decided Adventist, and yet her experience was so rich and her testimony so powerful that ministers and leading men of different churches sought her labors as an exhorter in their several congregations. But at that time she was very timid, and little thought that she was to be brought before the public to speak to thousands."[15]

The consistency and integrity of Ellen White's personal relationships were subject to close scrutiny by her own family, her colleagues, and non-Adventists.[16] Her frugality and dedication of time and funds to missionary outreach are well known. Her generosity and commitment to duty are legendary. Her perseverance and courage, especially courage when standing alone, have prompted many to follow her example. Her humor and common sense relaxed many stressful situations.[17]

Convincing Integrity

Her associates would never have been convinced that her visions and counsel were of divine origin if she had been accused of immoral living.[18]

Ellen White's contemporaries on several continents came to the place in their institutional planning and various crises that they sought her counsel before making their decisions. Proven men and women, experienced in their several fields, learned to trust her judgment as she led her colleagues to principles that would help them solve their problems and enlarge their worldview.

This confidence was not a creedal belief imposed by church leaders. The leaders themselves were led to this confidence not by argument but by experience. At an 1857 Battle Creek conference of about two hundred and fifty Sabbath keepers, the "subject of the unity and gifts of the church . . . [was] presented which seemed to have a place in the hearts of the people. Many expressed themselves happy to see this subject taking its proper place in the church."

During this meeting, Ellen White read "a testimony for the church which was received as the voice of the Lord to His people." Someone proposed that the testimony be published and there was no opposition.[19] Mrs. White earned the confidence of her contemporaries by the integrity of her personal relationships as well as through the relevance of her messages.

The Witness of Uriah Smith

This kind of response happened from the earliest days of her ministry. Undaunted men like Joseph Bates became convinced through personal experience.[20] Strong-willed men who had their own Biblical viewpoints could have divided the early group of Sabbatarian Adventists before they even organized as a church. Uriah Smith, in a sermon delivered at the 1891 General Conference, recalled his own personal experience of forty years: "Our relation to it [ministry of Ellen White] is our relation to something which arose with this work, which has gone right forward with it, side by side, which has interwoven itself into and through it, and all about it, from the day this message began until this present hour."

Smith described the potential chaos of those early days when men and women "came with almost as many different views on some points as there were individuals . . . each one pressing his own individual ideas. Then the value of the Spirit of prophecy in connection with this work, again appeared. It pointed out the right course to pursue. And what was it? It was that the brethren should sink all their minor differences and their peculiarities of lesser importance, and unite in the one great movement of the third angel's message. These examples are merely an index of what it has done all the way along—guarding against giving up the truths of the past, and pointing the way to light and truth in the future."[21]

The Witness of Mrs. S. M. I. Henry

A well-known female leader, Mrs. S. M. I. Henry, was wary of the Testimonies and Ellen White, even after she became a Seventh-day Adventist. Why? Because of the "manner in which her [Mrs. White's] work was first brought to my notice."

But Mrs. Henry's own experience in grasping the purpose of Ellen White's ministry became self-authenticating. In her remarkable testimony called, "My Telescope," she said that she would "be willing to go back into my wheel chair if by doing so I could get another glimpse of the hitherto unseen, such as this has been to me. . . . This experience has given me confidence in this small body of people—new confidence in this organization. I do not believe that God would ever have given me to see the things that I have seen, and to feel what I have felt, and to see Him as I have seen Him in these circumstances, if there were not life and power in this organization to lift it up out of all shadows and doubts into the glory of His presence, and to carry it safely through."[22]

Unabated Confidence

Men and women who worked and interacted with Ellen White, receiving her private and public testimonies and trusting her advice on institutional development, voted an action at each session of the General Conference similar to this 1882 resolution: "That we express our unabated confidence in the Testimonies which have been so graciously given to this people, which have guided our ways and corrected our errors, from the rise of the third angel's message to the present time; and that we especially express our gratitude for Testimony No. 31, which we accept as a token of the care of God over us—an evidence that He has not forsaken us, notwithstanding our many backslidings."[23]

A. G. Daniells, president of the General Conference (1901-1922), perhaps knew Ellen White better than anyone else outside of her immediate family. In the 1919 Bible Conference[24] he outlined in an impromptu setting how he would teach the youth in the church and the general public about the veracity of Ellen White's claim to be a messenger for God.

He said he would begin "with the beginning of this movement," showing that Mrs. White and the Seventh-day Adventist movement "came right together in the same year," that her contribution "was exercised steadily and powerfully in the development of this movement," and that she and the movement "were inseparably connected."

Daniells then looked at the various phases of Adventist thought, including the Adventist attitude toward the Bible, toward world evangelism, toward rendering service to non-Adventists in community welfare work, toward health and medical service, and toward educational counsel. He emphasized that these worldwide programs, taken together, were "convincing evidence of the origin of this gift, and the genuineness of it."

Fidelity to Bible

Probably the greatest evidence underlying everything else Daniells said was Ellen White's fidelity to the Bible: "In all the other reformations that came up, the leaders were unable to rightly distinguish between all error and truth—the Sabbath day, baptism, the nature of man, etc.—and so they openly taught errors from this Book. But now, when we come to this movement, we find the wonderful power of discrimination on the part of the Spirit of prophecy, and I do not know of a single truth in this Book that is set aside by the Spirit of prophecy, nor a single Biblical or theological error that came down through the dark ages that has been fostered by the Spirit of prophecy and pressed upon the people that we have to discredit when we come to this Book."[25]

Ellen White's writings become compelling evidence of her divine credentials. Long before a reader knows anything about the author, her periodical articles and books have driven home the conviction that God was speaking through those pages.

Her Christ-centered writings become the vehicle for divine conviction. The experience of Francis D. Nichol, editor of the church paper for twenty-one years (1945-1966), was not uncommon. In the late 1890s, his young parents living "in a sparsely settled part of Australia," found a stray copy of the *Review and Herald.* Reading matter of any kind was scarce. One of the E. G. White articles "quickened their hearts" and they concluded: "The person who wrote this article seems to be inspired." While reading on, they wrote for more information about this singular writer. Soon they were members of the Seventh-day Adventist Church, a decision that opened up the future to their young son and to his own distinctive contribution to making others aware of this woman who "seems to be inspired."[26]

Ellen White's theological framework, known as the Great Controversy Theme, provided a distinctive coherence and insight to the plan of salvation. It transcends the various impasses that have separated Christians for centuries.

The Message Is Greater Than the Messenger

We have emphasized throughout these pages that the message is greater than the messenger, the content more important than the container.[27] Why? Because Ellen White's highest contribution to the church and thus to the world is a reclarification of the Bible's teaching on salvation. She has shown that all Biblical doctrines are interrelated, that to permit error on any doctrine is to invite confusion and incoherence to the entire theological system. For example, if one is confused on the nature of man, one is further confused on the nature of sin, the importance of health principles, and thoughts relating to the afterlife.

Without a knowledge of when and where sin originated, men and women have no clue as to how sin will ever be irrevocably dealt with. Without an understanding of the cosmic issues in the plan of salvation, human beings too often focus on themselves, working from self-oriented motives.

The history of the Christian church is littered with the casualties of theological warfare. Good people are not immune from theological error. For instance, the perils of objectivism, with the emphasis on God's sovereignty and man's relative passivity in the salvation process, have been defiantly met by the hazards of subjectivism, with the emphasis on human freedom exercised in feeling or reason. Each Christian group, whether among the different branches of Catholicism or the various Protestant denominations, represents either the objectivistic or subjectivistic emphasis. Or they are hopelessly confused with a mixture of both elements in their desire to be "balanced."

But Ellen White helped Seventh-day Adventist thinkers steer through the white-water theological rapids that have afflicted all other churches—not by introducing strange speculations and theological novelties but by introducing the big picture of God and His salvation plan that has been called the Great Controversy Theme.[28] When people look for the strongest reason, the most satisfying evidence, for developing confidence in Ellen White as God's messenger, many focus on her Great Controversy Theme as the bedrock on which all other evidence rests.

Erroneous Concepts Lead to Confusion

Visual examinations of a prophet in vision are compelling. Great philosophical systems undergirding educational or medical principles can be memorable and respected by both believers and others. An exemplary life of super energy in promoting an unselfish system of philanthropy and concern for the needy can be most convincing. But when critics point to human weaknesses and discrepancies in these various lines of evidence, confidence often turns to panic. If a believer recognizes a possible error in a prophet's memory, or in some factual detail, the thought arises that perhaps everything else one believes is in jeopardy. A compounding of the problem occurs when the believer has unconsciously believed that a prophet does not commit errors—that is, his or her words should stand as written.[29]

Perplexed believers, driven by an erroneous concept of revelation/inspiration,[30] then begin to reexamine those lines of evidence that they once thought comforting and secure. The arguments of the physical phenomena accompanying Ellen White's visions now become suspect because someone suggests that Satan could impersonate any physical manifestation. The undeniable record of educational and medical achievements throughout the world are then compared to Catholics, Lutherans, Mormons, and the thought arises that perhaps this "fruit" of Ellen White's ministry may not be especially distinctive.

Distinctive Theological System

In other words, if puzzled believers have not understood that one of the primary contributions of Ellen White lies in her distinctive theological system, they enter the slippery road that leads to a sense of betrayal and spiritual confusion. It is as if the well-ordered universe has suddenly lost its center with all its stars no longer in their traditional places in the night sky.

But with a calm and reasoned understanding of how the Great Controversy Theme transcends all the divisions and errors within Christianity, the believer is not disturbed by occasional factual errors and a prophet's literary indebtedness. Whenever Adventists allow other theological paradigms, or organizing themes, to determine the direction of any doctrine, division within the church is inevitable. Whenever Adventists prefer other theological systems to the Biblical framework found in Ellen White's writings, division within the church is predictable. Whenever Adventists downgrade Ellen White from being a theological authority to merely a nurturing mother, they reveal their own myopia, and mislead others.

Not to acknowledge what Mrs. White's contemporaries acknowledged through personal experience denies the facts of history. Further, such denials cut off the roots of coherency and distinctiveness in the Adventist message and its reason for existence. It leaves the Seventh-day Adventist Church without a chart or compass regarding its significance and purpose.

When Ellen White is kept in proper focus as God's messenger who has provided the world with the clearest understanding of the cosmic dimensions of the plan of salvation, the Adventist Church will be preserved from internal schism organizationally, and from confusion and disillusionment individually.

Keeping Mrs. White in focus will help church members navigate troubled theological waters so that a coherent, consistent Biblical picture of salvation can be offered to the world—a simple, clear, coherent Biblical message that will usher in the final test of these last days. John the Revelator referred to this last-day message as the "everlasting gospel" (14:6).

Understanding Ellen White's greatest contribution to the Adventist Church, as well as to the world, will give believers their strongest, safest, reasons for continuing to trust her as God's messenger.[31]

The Weight of Evidence

All divine revelation, by virtue of the

process, comes in a fallible package. Because the message comes in an imperfect container, God Himself invites us to weigh the evidence: "Come now, and let us reason together" (Isa.1:18).

When God invites us to reason with Him, He is not playing word-games: He truly appeals to our reasoning skills. Often Ellen White challenges the reader to recognize that sanctified reasoning powers are intended to make us "intelligent Christians." That means that Christians "are not requested to believe without evidence." In making this search for belief, "we must put away all skepticism, all exaltation of our own ideas. We must humble our hearts by repentance . . . praying for true enlightenment."[32]

God, true to His nature, does not coerce, compel, or force anyone to believe—He waits for men and women to respond to sufficient evidence. He will never "force faith."[33] Ellen White summarized it well when she said that although "God has given ample evidence for faith, He will never remove all excuse for unbelief."[34]

This respect for human responsibility flows out of God's arrangement for making human beings "in His own image" (Gen. 1:27). Love, respect, confidence, and any other human emotion involving trust cannot be forced or else it ceases to be what we seek for most. A trust or love that is forced is an oxymoron. Because God wants happy, convinced people, He does not play hide-and-seek; He makes sure that we have sufficient evidence amidst the possibilities of human error.

One of the surest signs of evil occurs when people "seek to compel the conscience" or when there is "the disposition to hurt and destroy those who do not appreciate our work, or who act contrary to our ideas." No matter what the motivation may be, force of any kind is the work of the evil one, not of Christ.[35]

However, in earlier chapters we have noted that presuppositions determine the way one weighs evidence. Presuppositions drive historians, scientists, and theologians to predetermined conclusions, often unconsciously. For this reason, paradigm shifts occur occasionally when researchers suddenly begin to see the same world through different lenses (Copernicus, Einstein, Pasteur, etc.). Those lenses are presuppositions that determine the way we look at evidence.[36] Self-evident "truths" are usually human constructs or paradigms that determine how a person weighs evidence.

For example, if one looks at the Bible as an anthology of Jewish history, and to references of God's interventions as myths by which believers interpret their religious experience, the message of the Bible as God's self-communication with men and women will never be understood. If miracles are ruled out because one does not believe in supernaturalism, one will never understand the stories in the four Gospels. Such events as the resurrection of Jesus will have to be explained in some contrived manner. If God does not personally intervene in the affairs of humanity, then surely Ellen White's claim to be His messenger cannot be taken seriously. And on it goes.

The epistemological principle set forth by Jesus runs through any research that requires moral response: "If anyone wants to do His will, he shall know concerning the doctrine, whether it is from God or whether I speak on My own authority" (John 7:17).[37] Built within men and women is the quest for autonomy, for believing what one wants to believe. Thus "all who look for hooks to hang their doubts upon, will find them. And those who refuse to accept and obey God's word until every objection has been removed, and there is no longer an opportunity for doubt, will never come to the light."[38]

Perfect Assurance Not Compatible With Faith

One of the most illuminating examples of presuppositions (bias, prejudice, etc.)

that drive a person contrary to the light of truth is the reaction of the religious leaders in Jerusalem to Jesus. After the resurrection of Lazarus, an undeniable fact with many witnesses, these leaders were even more determined to kill Jesus (John 11:47-57; Matt. 26:59, 60). Though these leaders were intelligent, they also were prejudiced. Jesus did not fit their presuppositions. He was a threat to their academic pronouncements. They were driven not by calm reason and an enlightened conscience, but by what they wanted to believe.

Men and women in every age have had to face the same questions that the Jews in Christ's day had to resolve. In the face of light, even in the presence of the God-man Jesus, the question of belief is more than a matter of reading undeniable scientific evidence, such as how much anything weighs or how fast an object is moving. For some questions, the answers can be beyond dispute and provide complete assurance.

But when Jesus gave His best answers and provided the best demonstration of truth, people still rejected Him. Why? For the same reason that people have rejected His prophets. The answer lies in a person's will to believe, in that secret, hidden mystery the Bible calls "faith." At its deepest point, faith is the response of love and appreciation, and neither can be intimidated or coerced—even in the face of "overwhelming" evidence. Think of Lucifer in heaven!

Thus Ellen White could say that "perfect assurance . . . is not compatible with faith. Faith rests not on certainty, but upon evidence. Demonstration is not faith."[39] That is, perfect assurance in spiritual matters does not happen as perfect assurance is reached in areas such as mathematics or laser measurements. Laboratory results are demonstrations, and no faith is required. But trusting God depends on factors other than observable, precise demonstrations.

Probably it has never been better said than when Mrs. White commented on an exchange Jesus had with religious leaders after He stated that any person who wills to know, shall know the truth (John 7:17): "The perception and appreciation of truth, He said, depends less upon the mind than upon the heart. Truth must be received into the soul; it claims the homage of the will. If truth could be submitted to the reason alone, pride would be no hindrance in the way of its reception. But it is to be received through the work of grace in the heart; and its reception depends upon the renunciation of every sin that the Spirit of God reveals."[40]

Three Basic Presuppositions That Hinder Acceptance

As we saw in chapters 41 to 43, the critical charges and allegations made against Ellen White generally rest on certain presuppositions by which critics judge the validity of her ministry:

1. Those who believe in some form of verbal inspiration often base their criticism or rejection on the change of a word or a questionable date.[41]

2. Those who are committed, consciously or unconsciously, to certain inadequate theological doctrines set forth by some Protestant reformers, reject key aspects of Ellen White's teachings on the plan of salvation. Those who do not believe that Christ has two specific phases as High Priest after His ascension will forthrightly dismiss her contribution to the Adventist doctrine of the sanctuary and probably her teaching ministry in general.[42]

3. Those who are uncomfortable with reproof of sin.[43] When a person falls into any one of these three categories, the usual response is the same as that given by those who do not accept the Bible as divine revelation—"It does not make sense to me." For those who are motivated by self-will and pride of opinion, to hear God's call to trust the message when the messenger makes human mistakes *does not make sense.*

For those who are so motivated, to hear that God calls for people to separate themselves from conventional theological understanding, to go against the tide of a vast array of conventional Bible students, *does not make sense.*

For those who are so motivated, to hear that God asks men and women to give up their pride of opinion, their security in always being "in command" of their lives, and their trust in status symbols by which they have established their "worth" and for which they are lauded, *does not make sense.*

For proud, independent sinners, the Beatitudes (Matt. 5) *do not make sense.* Nor does the invitation to "deny himself and take up his cross, and follow Me" (Mark 8:34) *make sense.*

To exchange for a new Master one's own desire to be the final judge as to what is best in life *makes sense* only after a person has capitulated to Christ. To see oneself for what he/she really is, is a fundamental, life-changing experience that leads a sinner to become a grateful, compliant son or daughter of God. *Only after this profound surrender to God's plans for one's life will God's plans make sense.*

In other words, it is contrary to an unbeliever's common sense to give up what seems to be human security to become a disciple of Jesus. That is why God gives us "supercommon sense" through His Holy Spirit as He puts us into that place where we "see" life correctly.

After the truth about ourselves and God's plan for us sinks in, everything else that God is trying to say to us *makes sense.* Then the *weight of evidence* makes sense. Only then does the weight of evidence seem equivalent to *common sense.*[44]

Truth "as it is in Jesus"

One of the simple tests that every person must use is Ellen White's focus: the truth must be presented "as it is in Jesus."[45] Did she live up to her challenge to others? She used this phrase in three ways:

(1) If Christians are to "stand firm" in the crises of life, "they must receive the truth as it is in Jesus. . . . Let the sinner behold Jesus as the way, the truth, and the life, and his soul will be open to receive the truth as it is in Jesus."[46] Ellen White dispelled all theological fog when she talked about this central truth: "The salvation of the soul, through faith in Christ, is the ground and pillar of the truth. Those who exercise true faith in Christ make it manifest by holiness of character, by obedience to the law of God. They realize that the truth as it is in Jesus reaches heaven, and compasses eternity."[47]

(2) Christians who teach others must "believe and teach the truth as it is in Jesus. Holiness of heart will never lead to impure actions."[48] Jesus set the example by reflecting His teachings in His life habits. Sound doctrine without the spirit of Jesus is not teaching truth "as it is in Jesus."

(3) Christians must present the gospel in all of its coherency and completeness. The problems that divide Christians in all churches are caused by each division seeing only parts of the gospel. Not seeing the completeness of the gospel leads to widespread resistance to obeying God's law as a basic component in the plan of salvation. Ellen White emphasizes that those who are "unacquainted with the laws of God's government . . . are unacquainted with the truth as it is in Jesus. . . . He that knows the truth as it is in the law, knows the truth as it is in Jesus; and if through faith in Christ he renders obedience to the commandments of God, his life is hid with Christ in God."[49]

Adventists have been known as "the people of the Book." Probably this description was more apt during the church's first one hundred years. Nevertheless, as the Institute of Church Ministry reported, Adventists today who habitually read Ellen White are also the Bible students of the church compared with those who do not read her regularly.[50] There is something about Ellen

White's messages that promotes faithful Bible study.

From another viewpoint, hundreds of thousands witness to the fact that Ellen White has made the difference in making theology accessible to the average church member. How else can it be explained that a large percentage of Adventists through the years have been actively involved in daily Bible study and conversant about theological subjects normally reserved for professional theologians?

Prediction of the End Times Never Contradicted

Contrary to all modern "prophets" who give their "ten best predictions" every January, or the perennial Nostradamuses who state their predictions so vaguely that they can be reinterpreted and "made to fit" as time passes, Ellen White's preview of closing events has never been contradicted by events.[51] Today's economic insecurity, political strife, social unrest, decline in moral values, New Age revival of spiritualism, and the worldwide interest in religious unity—all are an astonishing fulfillment of her predictions. For many years, some faulted Ellen White for overlooking Communism. They declared her eschatology outmoded. But now it is apparent that in following the Biblical outline, she was true to fact.

The weight of evidence that leads millions to trust the Bible in spite of its apparent discrepancies, less than perfect writers, etc., is the same kind of evidence that has led millions to trust Ellen White. If one is driven by presuppositions that supernaturalism is unreasonable or that literary borrowing is inappropriate for a prophet, then the Bible is rejected as a Word from the Lord. These same presuppositions hinder some from accepting Ellen White as God's messenger. Nevertheless, in spite of these objections, the Bible has survived—as has Mrs. White's ministry. Those who have been blessed by the Bible and the writings of Ellen White recognize the voice of God speaking to them. Human discrepancies are nonessential concerns when the purpose of Spirit of prophecy writings in any age are understood and realized in the life of believers.[52]

Young People Still Respond

Although Ellen White died in 1915, young people still respond to her writings with remarkable enthusiasm. She is still the catalyst and innovator for elementary school students as well as thoughtful collegians. Not only do youth sense her spontaneity, freshness, and call for courage in mastering tough personal circumstances, they sense her dynamic principles relating to career possibilities and personal achievement that would not even be considered without her prompting.

Further, youth join their mentors in sensing that not everything in institutional programs has been done well enough yet, that flexibility is necessary to meet changing circumstances—and they are emboldened by the same Ellen White that prompted skeptical men and women to build sanitariums and educational centers. Even today young people discover that Mrs. White is more than a reasonable, common-sense, spiritual leader. They discover that in some special way she still builds dreams, and ignites passions for the oppressed, no matter what may be the economic or social circumstances.

Adventist youth have discovered what her contemporaries discovered—no one can box up Ellen White. Just when people settle down with her, she surprises the conservatives with new responsibilities and new challenges. Liberals thrill with her call for action and flexibility and then are sobered by her appeal for commitment to the authority of revealed truths.

Many feel that the real Ellen White has been covered with conventional conservatism or liberal ridicule until she has become an unknown quantity—that is, somebody who won't go away but still somebody most people don't really know. The youth who seek out the real Ellen White are changed by what they find. They are the risk-takers of the present generation and the backbone of Adventism's future.

The weight of evidence has opened the eyes of modern Adventist youth to a brighter, more exciting future; without Ellen White, where else would they find meaning to the future and an insight as to how to make sense out of the present? Where else could youth go for a proven record of trustworthiness and a living sense of connecting with a messenger of God?

"Only an Instrument"

Ellen White had a deep awareness of her mission. Yet she kept a perspective that John the Baptist understood even in his bleakest moments. John's message to his contemporaries was often reflected in the experience of Ellen White: "He must increase, but I must decrease" (John 3:30).

In December 1886, Mrs. White was in Torre Pellice, Italy, holding evangelistic meetings. Miles Grant, an influential Advent Christian minister, followed her from America, determined to "expose" her "pretensions." On Friday evening, December 4, Grant held his meetings one floor above where Mrs. White was conducting hers—not a very good advertisement to the general public regarding Adventists from America!

Grant had done his best to gather up all the slander and animosity from those who had been reproved by Mrs. White. In addition, he had assembled a list of garbled statements that misrepresented Seventh-day Adventists. Knowing that in the time limits of only a few short hours at Torre Pellice she would not be able to "undeceive" the people, Mrs. White decided to ignore Grant; she determined to "keep right on seeking to speak the truth. . . . I long to have the people see the truth as it is in Jesus."

In her diary for that day, she wrote: "I am to do my duty. I am only an instrument in the hands of God, to do my part of the work in His love and fear. This truth will triumph, but when, where, and how is for the Lord to decide. These thoughts bring peace and trust and confidence to my soul."[53] Self-vindication and public argument with her opposers was not in her character.

Some non-Adventists have conjectured that without Ellen White Seventh-day Adventists would not have survived as they are known today. Kenneth L. Woodward, *Newsweek's* religion editor, observed: "If it [the Seventh-day Adventist denomination] loses its founding mother, the church may find that it has also lost its distinctive visionary soul."[54]

The Weight of Evidence

The weight of evidence points decisively to the trustworthiness of Ellen White's twin witness—her life and ministry. The integrity of her character was recognized by contemporaries, whether Adventists or not. The intense focus of her ministry in revealing the charm, reality, and power of Jesus was recognized by those within and without her church. Any attempt to accept either her life without her ministry, or her ministry without her life, seems irrational. As Edward Heppenstall put it: "It is impossible to place a high value upon her life and character and a low value upon her writings."[55]

The attempt by some to praise Ellen White for her devotional contributions but to deny her role as a theological messenger separates her life from her ministry. Her theological contribution is precisely the reason why Adventists have had an integrated world program of evangelism, education, and health ministries. It was her visionary insights into the everlasting gospel and God's plan for a world movement that inspirited a few hundred people to become the vanguard of a world movement.

Endnotes

1. Oswald Chambers, *My Utmost For His Highest* (Grand Rapids, Mich.: Discovery House Publishers, 1963), pp. 151, 152.
2. See pp. 417-420.
3. *Selected Messages,* book 3, p. 29.
4. See chapter 43.
5. See p. 16.
6. See pp. 26, 518.
7. The "fruit" argument is only one of many lines of evidence that support the validity and legitimacy of Ellen White's prophetic ministry. To rely on the "fruit" argument alone, one could also point to the worldwide activity of the Mormons or to the thousands who ascribe to Mary Baker Eddy their own fresh and salutary life experience. However, the "fruit" argument, joined with other evidences, is an argument that cannot be overlooked. For millions, this argument has been most persuasive.
8. ADRA, the acronym for Adventist Development and Relief Agency International (formerly SAWS; includes OFASA, and ASA). This humanitarian agency assists countries worldwide in development/emergency/disaster relief programs.
9. All contributions, 1995, worldwide, $1,332,781,946. (*GC Yearbook*, 1997, p. 4)
10. See pp. 330-336.
11. In 1995 the church was working in 207 countries, using 717 languages. It was operating 5,533 schools (from primary to university level); 56 publishing houses, printing in 229 languages; and operating nearly 600 health-care facilities, from small clinics and dispensaries to large city hospitals.
12. See p. 3.
13. *Selected Messages,* book 1, p. 156.
14. See *Ministry*, October, 1982, p. 10.
15. James White, *Life Sketches* (1880 ed.), p. 126.
16. At her death a well-known magazine reported: "She was absolutely honest in her belief in her revelations. Her life was worthy of them. She showed no spiritual pride, and she sought no filthy lucre. She lived the life and did the work of a worthy prophetess."—*The Independent* (New York), August 23, 1915, cited in *Bio.*, vol. 6, p. 444..
17. See p. 94.
18. Graham, *Co-founder,* p. 29.
19. *Review and Herald,* Nov. 12, 1857.
20. See p. 145.
21. *General Conference Daily Bulletin,* Mar. 14, 1891, p. 151. In 1868, Uriah Smith published a small brochure entitled, *The Visions of Mrs. E. G. White, A Manifestation of Spiritual Gifts According to the Scriptures.* In reviewing the fruit of her ministry, he wrote: "They lead to the purest morality . . . . They lead us to Christ. . . . They lead us to the Bible. . . . They have brought comfort and consolation to many hearts." Then he noted the "blindest prejudice, the intensest hate, and most malignant bitterness" aimed at Ellen White. Smith grouped these adversaries into two groups: "The first class is composed of those who believe, or did believe at the time their opposition commenced, the views held by Seventh-day Adventists, but in whom, or in someone with whom they sympathized, wrongs were pointed out and reproved by the visions. . . . The other class consists of those who are the avowed and open opponents of all the distinguished views held by Seventh-day Adventists. . . . They hate that system of truth with which the visions stand connected, and they attack the visions as the most sure and effectual way of hindering the progress of that truth." —Pages 6-10.
22. "My Telescope," *The Gospel of Health,* Jan. 1898.
23. *Review and Herald,* Dec. 26, 1882, p. 787.
24. See p. 435. See also pp. 409, 481.
25. *Spectrum* (May 1979), Vol. 10, No. 1, pp. 29, 30. In his later years, A. G. Daniells wrote: "In this present year of our Lord 1935, Mrs. White has been at rest twenty years, while I have been toiling on. I had had twenty-three years of direct observation of her lifework. Since her death I have now had twenty additional years for thoughtful reflection and study of that life and its fruits. Now, at an advanced age, with the constraint of expressing only sober, honest truth, I can say that it is my deep conviction that Mrs. White's life far transcends the life of anyone I have ever known or with whom I have been associated. She was uniformly pleasant, cheerful, and courageous. She was never careless, flippant, or in any way cheap in conversation or manner of life. She was the personification of serious earnestness regarding the things of the kingdom. I never once heard her boast of the gracious gift God had bestowed upon her, or of the marvelous results of her endeavors. She did rejoice in the fruitage, but gave all the glory to Him who wrought through her. I realize that these are grave statements, but they come from the deepest conviction and soundest judgment that I am capable of rendering. They are uttered in the sobering atmosphere of my last illness, as I face the Judge of all the earth, before whose presence I realize that I soon shall stand."—*The Abiding Gift of Prophecy,* p. 368.
26. *SDAE*, vol. 11, p. 179; Dedication page, Francis D. Nichol, *Critics.* About 1950 Nichol visited an aged leader of the Advent Christian Church (with a membership of fewer than 30,000 people), another denomination with roots in the Millerite movement. This leader, after reviewing the worldwide expansion of the Seventh-day Adventist Church, added: "Your men were more farsighted than ours and laid better plans." Nichol's reply: "No, our men were no wiser than yours, but we had a frail handmaiden of the Lord in our midst who declared that by visions from God she saw what we should do and how we should plan for the future."—Nichol, *Critics,* pp. 23, 24.
27. See pp. 26, 518.
28. See pp. 256-263, 344.
29. See *Adventist Review,* Mar. 22, 1990, for the experience of Pastor Ritchie Way who "felt betrayed and sick" after discovering that Ellen White, as all prophets, was not inerrant. In recovering his confidence in Ellen White, Pastor Way realized that he had been mistaken regarding how God works through prophets with human limitations. He now relies on two tests of a prophet that "Satan cannot duplicate": the "orchard" test—you can tell a tree by its fruit, and "the testimony of Jesus" test—does the claimant bear the "testimony" from Jesus and to Jesus?
30. See pp. 16, 120, 173, 375, 376, 421.
31. For an anthology of what prominent Seventh-day Adventists, past and present, have said about Ellen White's contribution to their lives, read Herbert E. Douglass, *What Ellen White Has Meant to Me* (Wash-

ington, D.C.: Review and Herald Publishing Association, 1973).
32. *Review and Herald,* Mar. 8, 1887.
33. "None are compelled to believe. God gives sufficient evidence that all may decide upon the weight of evidence, but He never has nor never will remove all chance [opportunity] for doubt, never will force faith." —Letter 12, 1868, cited in *Bio.,* vol. 2, p. 276. See also *Testimonies,* vol. 5, pp. 675, 676. For a discussion of how authority is established when one speaks of "inspiration" and "revelation," see Giem, *Scientific Theology*, pp. 68-86.
34. *The Great Controversy,* p. 527. "God never asks us to believe, without giving sufficient evidence upon which to base our faith. His existence, His character, the truthfulness of His Word, are all established by testimony that appeals to our reason; and this testimony is abundant. Yet God has never removed the possibility of doubt. Our faith must rest upon evidence, not demonstration. Those who wish to doubt will have opportunity; while those who really desire to know the truth, will find plenty of evidence on which to rest their faith."—*Steps to Christ,* p. 105.
35. *The Desire of Ages,* p. 487. "God does not compel men to give up their unbelief. Before them are light and darkness, truth and error. It is for them to decide which they will accept. The human mind is endowed with power to discriminate between right and wrong. God designs that men shall not decide from impulse, but from weight of evidence, carefully comparing scripture with scripture."—*Ibid.,* p. 458.
36. See pp. 374, 394, 549.
37. "Just as long as a door is open to receive the tempter's suggestions, difficulties will multiply. The hearts of those who will not come to the light are open to unbelief. If my time and strength are consumed upon such matters, this serves Satan's purposes."—*Selected Messages,* book 1, pp. 52, 53. See *Christ's Object Lessons,* pp. 34, 36, 59, 105, 110-112.
38. *The Great Controversy,* p. 527.
39. Letter 19d, 1892, cited in *The Ellen G. White 1888 Materials,* pp. 1029, 1030.
40. *The Desire of Ages,* p. 455; see *Testimonies,* vol. 8, p. 301.
41. See p. 470.
42. See p. 502.
43. "Disguise it as they may, the real cause of doubt and skepticism, in most cases, is the love of sin."—*Steps to Christ,* p. 111.
44. "In intellectual matters you can think things out, but in spiritual matters you will think yourself into cotton wool. If there is something upon which God has put His pressure, obey in that matter, bring your imagination into captivity to the obedience of Christ with regard to it and everything will become as clear as daylight. . . . The tiniest thing we allow in our lives that is not under the control of the Holy Spirit is quite sufficient to account for spiritual muddle, and all the thinking we like to spend on it will never make it clear. Spiritual muddle is only made plain by obedience. Immediately we obey, we discern. This is humiliating, because when we are muddled we know the reason is in the temper of our mind. When the natural power of vision is devoted to the Holy Spirit, it becomes the power of perceiving God's will and the whole life is kept in simplicity."—Chambers, *My Utmost for His Highest,* p. 190.
45. In Ellen White's published writings, she used the phrase, "the truth as it is in Jesus," hundreds of times.
46. *General Conference Daily Bulletin,* Jan. 28, 1893, p. 14.
47. *Review and Herald,* Sept. 17, 1895.
48. *Ibid.,* Nov. 10, 1885. "We are to present the truth as it is in Jesus, made fragrant and attractive by the grace and the courtesy that characterized the life of Christ. . . . Why do those who claim to be advanced in knowledge, make themselves objectionable, and bring the truth into disrepute? It is because the truth has not been permitted to sanctify their unholy dispositions. Those who misrepresent the truth are harsh, unsympathetic, and denunciatory."—*Signs of the Times,* Aug. 21, 1893. "And what course shall the advocates of truth pursue? They have the unchangeable, eternal Word of God, and they should reveal the fact that they have the truth as it is in Jesus. Their words must not be rugged and sharp. In their presentation of truth they must manifest the love and meekness and gentleness of Christ."—*Review and Herald,* Oct. 14, 1902.
49. *Ibid.,* June 17, 1890.
50. See footnote 14.
51. See pp 160-162.
52. Douglass, *What Ellen White Has Meant to Me,* Introduction, "How Confidence in a Book Is Born," pp. 10-21.
53. *Bio.,* vol. 3, pp. 335, 336.
54. *Newsweek,* Jan. 19, 1981.
55. Edward Heppenstall, "The Inspired Writings of Ellen G. White," *Adventist Review*, May 7, 1987.

Study Questions

1. What are the norms by which Biblical prophets are measured? How does Ellen White measure up when tested by these norms?
2. What impact do one's presuppositions have on the way a person weighs evidence?
3. Why does not God make truth so clear that no one could avoid making the right decision?
4. What are the basic reasons why some critics reject Ellen White's messages?

5. In what three ways did Ellen White use the phrase, "the truth as it is in Jesus"?

6. Apply the tests of a Biblical prophet to the ministry of Ellen White. Give examples for each test. Although the tests are cumulative, which test seems to be the most important to you?

7. List the evidences for Ellen White's special gifts that convinced early Adventists of her integrity. Not all were convinced for the same reasons. Give examples.

CHAPTER 46

She Still Speaks

"Whether or not my life is spared, my writings will constantly speak, and their work will go forward as long as time shall last. My writings are kept on file in the office, and even though I should not live, these words that have been given to me by the Lord will still have life and will speak to the people."[1]

On February 9, 1912, in her 85th year, Ellen White affixed her signature to her last will and testament.[2]

In essence, the will[3] created the Ellen G. White Estate, Inc., a self-perpetuating board of five members.[4] Its four-point task included disposition of her real property (such as personal goods and land), preservation of her manuscript files, printing of future compilations drawn from her writings, and supervision of the translation and publication of her books into other languages.

In 1937-38, following the death of W. C. White, her literary properties were moved from her Elmshaven home at St. Helena, California, to vaults and offices at the world headquarters of the Seventh-day Adventist Church in Washington, D.C. In the decades that followed, the Ellen G. White Board in cooperation with the General Conference set up eleven research centers in various world divisions of the church, plus branch offices at Andrews University in Berrien Springs, Michigan, and Loma Linda University, in California.[5] These centers contain copies of Mrs. White's letters and manuscripts, historical material relating to the church, and significant books and pamphlets not easily available elsewhere.

The Board has taken its responsibilities seriously. The original five-member Board worked together for nineteen years, "publishing ten posthumous compilations from Mrs. White's manuscript files, prepared and published a *Comprehensive Index* to her published books, sponsored a thorough indexing of the manuscripts, and, in counsel with the General Conference officers, arranged for the perpetuation of the trusteeship and close collaboration with top church leadership."[6]

Ellen G. White Board of Trustees

While the composition of the Board of Trustees (now numbering 15) has changed from time to time,[7] its mandate has remained clear: to make the writings of Ellen White available throughout the world in the most appropriate manner possible. Since 1934, when the Board made its first change of membership, it has authorized numerous compilations, including devotional books and a CD-ROM collection (*The Published Ellen G. White Writings on Compact Disc)* that "includes every known book, article, and pamphlet written by Ellen White during her 70-year ministry, as well as many thousands of pages that have been put into print from manuscripts unpublished at the time of her death in 1915." Also included on the disc is the six-volume *Ellen G. White Biography, Ellen G. White in Europe,* and the King James Version of the Bible. A summary of the scope of Ellen White's ministry and the development of her major publications is found in *Ellen G. White and Her Writings,* a small pamphlet that accompanies the disc.[8] All of Ellen White's published works are also available on the Internet.

E. G. White Board Release Policies

The various Ellen G. White-SDA research centers have clearly stated procedures to help access desired materials. Equally important is their responsibility to protect the materials from damage or loss.

Because research center personnel is limited, researchers desiring access to unpublished documents are encouraged to first consult the approximately 75,000 pages of published materials by means of the four-volume *Comprehensive Index* and the CD-ROM.

To avoid misplacement, research center personnel, not the researcher, retrieve and return requested documents to the file. Whenever scanning of specific years is necessary, an entire drawer or file of documents may be requested without individual documents being removed.

Provision exists for the researcher who may find it impossible to visit a center. Although centers do not maintain a "research by mail" program, the Permanent Loan Policy makes possible the help needed for special occasions. The center will supply specific letters or manuscripts (identified by the published reference), when requested, by mail. If the document requested has not yet been published in its entirety, a photocopy may be loaned, accompanied by a copy of the Permanent Loan Policy. For many reasons, continual requests for unpublished documents should be carried out in person at a center.

Research in unpublished Ellen G. White letters and manuscripts is permitted with the understanding that the Ellen G. White Estate has been mandated by Ellen White's will to maintain the publication rights for such documents. Consequently, the use of unpublished writings, as well as copyrighted materials in print, should conform to the provisions of the Copyright Code.

With the passage of time, and increased research needs, the release policy of the White Estate was changed from asking, "Why should it be published?" to "Why not publish it?" This eventually led to the decision to make all of Ellen White's letters and manuscripts available on CD-ROM.

The Value of Compilations

In her will, Ellen White authorized "the printing of compilations from my manuscripts."

Throughout her 70-year ministry, her daily agenda and prodigious writing schedule were phenomenal when compared to others, then and now (as we studied in chapter 11). She rarely had the leisure to devote consecutive weeks exclusively to writing a book from start to finish.[9] For many years she spent entire summers attending numerous camp meetings, speaking once or twice daily in almost continuous succession.[10] Many years she would be away from home for months. She traveled through Europe three times in two years, speaking almost every day, constantly holding interviews and writing personal testimonies.[11]

Throughout this ministry, she had little time to organize the various subjects scattered throughout these messages, most of which were either soon out of print, of limited circulation, or had never been published. Thus, it seems natural that at the end of her life she would want her messages to be made available in an organized manner. The most efficient procedure would be to classify these materials by subject and to make them available in systematic and balanced publications.

One of the chief benefits of a well-organized compilation (such as *Evangelism* or *Counsels on Diet and Foods)* is that readers are able to get a broad and balanced picture of what Ellen White said on a given subject. Everyone benefits when hitherto unpublished materials such as diaries, manuscripts, and sermons are accessed and properly integrated in such a compilation.

Nevertheless, questions always arise whenever anyone tries to "organize and systematize" the past. Why? Because no absolutely objective media reporter, historian, or theologian exists. To the degree that "experts" pursue their bias, no matter how intellectual their work may appear, to that extent their data may be suspect by someone. This potential weakness in any academic effort is greatly increased when compilers string together selected quotations to favor their personal views.

Danger of Compilations

Many privately issued compilations of Ellen White materials have been made through the years by individual compilers. Unfortunately, at times these compilations became verbal grenades that were tossed back and forth between compilers who disagreed as to what "Ellen White said."

The Ellen G. White Board has taken seriously its mandate to publish compilations that are accurate and helpful. Before work on a compilation begins, the corpus of Ellen White's writings on a given topic is gathered and examined. Every attempt is made to let the materials determine the emphasis Ellen White would give to various aspects of the topic. No authorized compilation is done by only one person working alone. The compiler presents his or her work to a small committee that reviews it for inherent integrity and faithfulness to Ellen White's intent. Then the compiler incorporates the committee's suggestions, and gives the manuscript to members of the Board for careful reading. Every effort is made to insure a complete and unbiased presentation of Mrs. White's mature teaching on the subject under consideration.

In using compilations, readers must always follow the simple rules of interpretation as they would with any written document.[12] But with compilations, added care should be taken not only to consider possible compiler bias but also other facts: (1) words evolve over the years; (2) time, place, and circumstances directly affect the meaning of words and applications of principles;[13] and (3) events are often reported differently by two or more people observing the same event.

In 1901 Ellen White had to confront the problem of compilations. A man was misusing the Bible by stringing together a series of texts to "prove" his claim that God had chosen Mrs. White to assume the place of Moses in modern spiritual Israel, and that he was to be her Joshua. She wrote: "'Yes,' I said, 'you have selected and put these scriptures together, but like many who have arisen as you have, you are wresting the Scriptures, interpreting them to mean thus and so, when I know they do not apply as you have applied them.

"'You, or any other deluded person, could arrange and have arranged certain scriptures of great force, and applied them according to your own ideas. Any man could misinterpret and misapply God's Word, denouncing people and things, and then take the position that those who refused to receive his message had rejected the message of God, and decided their destiny for eternity'. . . .

"Letters come to me entreating an answer; I know that many men take the testimonies the Lord has given, and apply them as they suppose they should be applied, picking out a sentence here and there, taking it from its proper connection, and applying it according to their idea. Thus poor souls become bewildered, when could they read in order all that has been given, they would see the true application, and would not become confused. Much that purports to be a message from Sister White, serves the purpose of misrepresenting Sister White, making her testify in favor of things that are not in accordance with her mind or judgment. This makes her work very trying."[14]

In 1906 Mrs. White recognized the continuing possibility that her writings could be wrongly used: "Those who are not walking in the light of the message, may gather up statements from my writings that happen to please them, and that agree with their human judgment, and, by separating these statements from their connection and placing them beside human reasonings, make it appear that my writings uphold that which they condemn."[15]

Are compilations valuable? Without question. Are there dangers inherent in compilations? Yes. And the warning always applies: If a quotation seems to portray an isolated viewpoint not represented in Ellen White's published works, be alerted to the need to get more of that quotation's context.[16]

Theological principles, for example, are founded on more than incidental paragraphs in a private letter. The principle of consistency must be applied. The greater mass of evidence should interpret the isolated, or infrequent, statement, not vice versa. Ellen White's advice is still indispensable: If there is a question on any subject, read her published books or let the weight of clear evidence, not the isolated statement, indicate her meaning and teaching. Readers must use ordinary common sense, enlightened by the Spirit, to discover the context and the principle involved, and be grateful for the full-orbed sweep that a good compilation provides.

Theological Principles Are Timeless

New truths do not make old truths obsolete. "Perceptions" of truth, however, change as fresh information is discovered or when presuppositions may be recognized as faulty. But two plus two will always equal four, and the fact that Christ was crucified and resurrected cannot be altered by "open and free discussion."

Truth, indeed, has been like the unfolding of a flower or the growth of a tree. Its organizing principle is embedded in its seed. Each stage of development shows new structure. The branches of the tree and the petals of the bloom are a natural unfolding of the unifying purpose of the original seed. Part of the flower's petals will not be daisy and part tulip. An oak tree trunk will not branch out with Ponderosa Pine limbs. Elements of truth are recognized by their coherence; in other words, truth in its development does not contradict itself.

Ellen White, as we have discovered, has been a guide for her fellow Adventists and those multiplied thousands who have found Christ through her writings. Her own 70-year experience reflected the reality of the constant unfolding of truth. Perhaps clearer than her contemporaries, she expressed this principle: "The truths of redemption are capable of constant development and expansion. . . . In every age there is a new development of truth, a message of God to the people of that generation. The old truths are all essential; new truth is not independent of the old, but an unfolding of it. It is only as the old truths are understood that we can comprehend the new."[17]

Thus, looking back, Ellen White saw how the stakes of truth were driven deeply into the Advent movement experience.[18] She looked ahead to the lengthening cords that were connected ever so securely to those stakes. She was a future-oriented leader, confident of the developing configuration of truth: "We have nothing to fear for the future, except as we shall forget the way the Lord has led us, and His teaching in our past history."[19]

Relevance

When considering the Adventist message and mission, the relevance of Ellen White for the present and future is as certain and as needed as the trunk is to the branch. For as long as the branch needs the trunk, so Adventists will continue to sense the security and strength found in her writings.[20] In 1907 she wrote: "Whether or not my life is spared, my writings will constantly speak, and their work will go forward as long as time shall last. My writings are kept on file in the office, and even though I should not live, these words that have been given to me by the Lord will still have life and will speak to the people."[21]

Relevance is a word that sums up the human need for personal meaning. But relevance often descends to mere desirability and convenience. Further, the appeal for relevance often supersedes the appeal for authority. If relevance is sought merely in a consensus of men and women who share common feelings, the lurking unease that longs for authority is unsatisfied.

Since Jesus is the Message-Giver and uses the best human messenger available for His purposes, the message is the important issue, regardless of when He sends the message, whether in the fifteenth century B.C., the first century A.D., or the nineteenth century A.D. "The testimony of Jesus" is always relevant.

During the spring and summer, throughout the Southland in the United States the sirens often blow and radio and TV stations go into special warning broadcasts, alerting people of an approaching tornado. Wise people know that they must take special precautions, even rushing into their underground shelters. They have learned to comply quickly. It does not matter if the warning is heard on a battery-powered radio that cost $25, a $2,000 digital TV, or from a wailing siren atop the fire station. The message is clear and only a fool would sit down and judge the fidelity of the message by evaluating the fidelity of the instrument by which it is delivered.[22]

A tornado warning is always relevant, even as is a prophet's message, especially the message of one who was sent to help prepare a people for a much greater storm than a seasonal tornado.

God's revelations through His prophets meet the desire for both relevance and authority. For those who accept the continuing messages of Ellen White through her writings, this blend of relevance and authority has become a living experience.

Endnotes

1. *Selected Messages*, book 1, p. 55.
2. At the time of her death her literary productions consisted of well over 100,000 pages: 24 books in current circulation; 2 book manuscripts ready for publication; 4,600 articles in the periodicals of the church; 200 or more out-of-print tracts and pamphlets; 6,000 typewritten manuscripts, aggregating approximately 40,000 pages; 2,000 handwritten letters, documents, and diaries, journals, et cetera.
3. Ellen G. White's will is reproduced in Appendix N.
4. The original members of the Ellen G. White Estate Board were A. G. Daniells, General Conference president; F. M. Wilcox, *Review and Herald* editor; C. H. Jones, Pacific Press Publishing Association manager; W. C. White, one of her two living sons; and C. C. Crisler, one of her secretaries.
5. Andrews University Branch Office (early 1960s); Loma Linda Branch Office (1976); EGW-SDA Research Centers in the following areas: Newbold College, England (1974); Avondale College, Australia (1976); Montemorelos University, Mexico (1978); River Plate University, Argentina (1979); SDA Theological Seminary, Philippines (1981); Helderberg College, South Africa (1983); Spicer Memorial College, India (1985); Brazil College, Brazil (1987); Adventist Seminary of West Africa, Nigeria (1990); Korean Sahmyook University, Korea (1992); Zaokski Theological Seminary, Russia (1995).
6. Schwarz, *Light Bearers*, p. 421.
7. With the demands upon them increasing steadily with the growth of the church and numerous constituencies to be represented, in 1950 the trustees increased the board's membership from five to seven and in 1958 amended the bylaws of the corporation to provide for a constituency and board of nine, seven to be life members and two to be elected for a term corresponding to that of General Conference elected personnel (originally four years, but now five). In 1970 the board was increased to 11; in 1980, to 13; and in 1985, to 15. The number of life members has been reduced to five to provide broader representation from various church entities. At quinquennial meetings the board also elects the secretary (now called director) and associate secretaries (directors), as well as officers of the corporation, as provided for in the bylaws.
8. "A Guide for Users," of *The Published Ellen G. White Writings on Compact Disc.*
9. See pp. 108-110.
10. For example, see *Bio.*, vol. 3, pp. 35-71.
11. *Ibid.*, pp. 287-384.

12. See chapters 33 and 34.
13. See pp. 394-397. In 1875, she declared: "That which can be said of men under certain circumstances, cannot be said of them under other circumstances." —*Testimonies,* vol. 3, p. 470.
14. *Selected Messages,* book 1, p. 44.
15. Letter 208, 1906, cited in "The Integrity of the Sanctuary Truth," a document available from the White Estate. See *Review and Herald,* Mar. 17, 1868.
16. "If you desire to know what the Lord has revealed through her, read her published works."—*Testimonies,* vol. 5, p. 696.
17. *Christ's Object Lessons,* p. 127.
18. "Let the aged men who were pioneers in our work speak plainly, and let those who are dead speak also, by the reprinting of their articles in our periodicals." —Manuscript 62, 1905, cited in "The Integrity of the Sanctuary Message." "We are to repeat the words of the pioneers in our work, who knew what it cost to search for the truth as for hidden treasure, and who labored to lay the foundation of our work. . . . The word given me is, Let that which these men have written in the past be reproduced."—*Review and Herald,* May 25, 1905.
19. *Life Sketches,* p. 196.
20. See Jack Provonsha, *A Remnant in Crisis,* pp. 49-60, 163-167.
21. Letter 371, 1907, cited in *Selected Messages,* book 1, p. 55.
22. Wood, "Toward an Understanding of the Prophetic Office," *Journal of the Adventist Theological Society,* Spring 1991, p. 28.

Study Questions

1. What were the four main responsibilities mandated to the Ellen G. White Estate Board of Trustees by Ellen White's will?

2. What is meant by a "self-perpetuating" board of trustees?

3. What is the chief purpose of the various compilations derived from Ellen White's writings?

4. List several ways now available to locate what Ellen White has written on certain subjects, such as (1) the Christian's responsibilities in helping the destitute; (2) the effect of a faulty diet on one's spiritual health; (3) the kind of people on whom God places His seal in the last days.

5. List the ways in which the unfolding of truth is similar to the development of a giant oak.

CHAPTER 47

Messenger and Message Inseparable

"Blessed are the dead who die in the Lord from now on. . . . that they may rest from their labors, and their works follow them" (Rev. 14:13).

As we have noted throughout this book, whenever God has spoken through His communication system, counterfeits soon followed. Satan is unceasing in his skill to follow through the door that truth opens. His messages are always appealing and believable because he knows how to appeal to the religiously inclined yet unconverted heart. He mixes truth with error, always in a way that appeals to human feeling and human authority rather than to a plain "Thus saith the Lord."

After the death of Ellen White, counterfeit messengers soon arose. In June 22, 1916, less than a year after Mrs. White died, Margaret Rowen in Los Angeles, California, claimed to have a vision. Her early "testimonies" had a superficial likeness to Mrs. White's testimonies. In addition to these "messages," the physical manifestations accompanying her visions were remarkably similar to those of Ellen White. "Both her followers, including several medical doctors, and skeptics agreed that these visions were supernaturally inspired. The question in dispute was: With which supernatural power did they originate?"[1]

Mrs. Rowen's attempt to usurp the role of "messenger" to the Adventist Church reached extraordinary lengths when she had a document "planted" in the Ellen G. White vault at Elmshaven, purporting to be a letter written by Mrs. White. This "letter" was intended to prove that she was Ellen White's designated successor. Even after this scandalous episode was exposed, her followers remained strongly supportive.

Rowen's specific but failed predictions culminated in her announcement that Jesus would return on February 6, 1925. This failed prediction caused many followers to wonder, but many accepted her explanation—that she had misunderstood how long it would take Jesus to travel from heaven to earth. Further elements in this strange story may be found in *Light Bearers to the Remnant,* including her attempt to murder her chief supporter and her jail time in San Quentin Penitentiary.[2]

We cite the Rowen story only to highlight the often captivating appeal of those who claim to have the prophetic gift. At any given time in the last few decades, at least a dozen people around the world have convinced others that they have been given the gift of prophecy. These include V. T. Houteff, Jeanine Sautron, and those supposedly receiving "thought messages."[3]

According to John the Revelator, Satan will be especially furious with last-day representatives of those "who keep the commandments of God and have the testimony of Jesus Christ" (Rev.12:17).

As we noted earlier (p. 3), "the testimony of Jesus" points to God's communication system whereby the Spirit of Christ inspires selected men and women with divine revelations pertaining to the plan of salvation.

Attempts to Make "Testimony of Jesus" of "None Effect"

Because of the nature of the great controversy, Satan hates the truth about God and how He plans to rescue men and women from Planet Earth. Consequently, he will do all his brilliant mind can devise to make "the testimony of Jesus Christ" of no effect. That should be expected.

Ellen White knew from experience and from divine instruction how Satan's tactics affected her ministry, and how he would operate in the future. In 1890 she wrote two letters:

"Satan is . . . constantly pressing in the spurious—to lead away from the truth. The very last deception of Satan will be to make of none effect the testimony of the Spirit of God. 'Where there is no vision, the people perish' (Prov. 29:18). Satan will work ingeniously, in different ways and through different agencies, to unsettle the confidence of God's remnant people in the true testimony."[4]

"There will be a hatred kindled against the testimonies which is satanic. The workings of Satan will be to unsettle the faith of the churches in them, for this reason: Satan cannot have so clear a track to bring in his deceptions and bind up souls in his delusions if the warnings and reproofs and counsels of the Spirit of God are heeded."[5]

How Satan Unsettles Confidence

If Satan's plan is to "ingeniously. . . unsettle . . . confidence," how does he do it?

Since the Garden of Eden, for reasons not always clear, a person's confidence in the truth about God has always been the special target of others who are not comfortable with divine authority. That is the way the cosmic controversy began, and that is the way it will end. To break down confidence in the trustworthiness of God and His gifted prophets has always been Satan's chief goal. How does he do his work? By subtle insinuations, out-of-context allegations, planted rumors, and exaggerated assertions borne out of an incident that often could be easily explained.[6]

We should expect that the same methods used by Satan to "unsettle" confidence in Moses, Elijah, Jeremiah, John the Baptist, or even Christ Himself, would be used with practiced precision on the ministry of Ellen White, or any future messenger from God.

When any issue arises today (or will yet arise between now and the return of Jesus), we should immediately ask: (1) If the allegation involves Ellen White as a person, what are *all* the facts? (2) If the question concerns her theological teachings, what is the theological or philosophical presupposition that underlies the questioner's (or "unsettler's") point of view?[7]

That difficult-to-understand technical questions and isolated points should arise in a writing ministry of 70 years is not surprising. Similar questions confront students of the Bible. Many people through the years have lost confidence in the Bible because of real or apparent difficulties.[8]

Why does this happen? Those who lose confidence often place more emphasis on the container than on its content, on the messenger rather than on his or her message. How does one focus on the content rather than the container, on the message rather than the messenger? How does one focus on Ellen White's message rather than on Ellen White herself?[9] By listening to her clear, prevailing message that illuminates the Bible's focus on the character of God as manifested in Jesus and about His simple plan to change rebels into restored sons and daughters. The message of genuine prophets is consistent, whereas their lives, although exemplary, may not be without flaws.

Even when a group accepts Ellen White as God's messenger, differences of opinion will exist as to how to apply her principles to present circumstances. However, an honest, shared commitment to divine authority warms the heart of those who differ; differences are not magnified to the point of open contention. Those who focus on the content, not the container, seek to draw near to those who differ; they emphasize the principles upon which they agree, and minimize their differences.

One other way that the writings of Ellen White (or the Bible) can be made "of none effect" is to *misuse* counsel. Some would call it the "woodshed rod" whereby the phrase, "Sister White said . . ." kindles deep resentment rather than appreciation.[10] Sadly, for many, both young and old, the "Testimonies" have suggested dread rather than blessing, a chill rather than warmth. Out of context and separated from intent, the writings of Ellen White can easily become a whip or club—just the opposite of her purpose when she wrote messages of warning and challenge to those who knew exactly the truth of what she was saying.

The best way to thwart Satan's attempt to make of "none effect" the ministry of Ellen White is to "listen" to her prevailing message about God's side in the great controversy, to read her published works[11] as the final statement as to what she believed on any given subject, to place every word that seems discouraging in its original context—and then to sit back and marvel at the coherency of a remarkable messenger whose ministry has accomplished such profound worldwide results.

Testing Contemporary Claims

Is it possible that another genuine prophet will appear in the Seventh-day Adventist Church before Christ returns? Adventists have never said that Ellen White is the complete fulfillment of such prophecies as Joel 2:28-32. Mrs. White herself was asked this question and responded that she had not been given any information on that subject.[12]

No one knows what God may think best regarding special leadership before the Advent. And no one knows in what manner a future prophet may fulfill his or her role. What we do know is that a church has the obligation to test the claim, as Paul has taught: "Do not quench the Spirit. Do not despise prophecies. Test all things; hold fast what is good. Abstain from every form of evil" (1 Thess. 5:19-22).

All the tests listed earlier must be applied to each claimant.[13] The highest test of all is to compare later prophets with the body of inspired writings of previous prophets.

Jesus made it clear that the church should expect the appearance of counterfeit prophets, especially in the last days before His return: "Then many false prophets will rise up and deceive many" (Matt. 24:11). No doubt very persuasive and believable claimants will arise. What makes them "believable"?

Counterfeiters don't print three-dollar bills. The purpose of the counterfeit is to appear as close to the original or the valid as possible. Satan knows this tactic well. His method has always been to cover error with much truth. Eventually, the error also becomes part of the truth in their minds.

Ellen White wrote to one who was confused about Anna Phillips's claim that she had received visions and messages: "Many things in these visions and dreams seem to be all straight, a repetition of that which has been in the field for many years; but soon they introduce a jot here, a tittle of error there, just a little seed which takes root and flourishes, and many are defiled therewith."[14]

Yes, another genuine prophet is possible. And yes, if such a prophet should arise, his or her credentials will meet the tests that every true prophet in God's communication system has met.

Another Church to Follow?

Occasionally the thought is expressed that "the Adventist ship is going through, no matter what!" Equally confident people say that "the church is Babylon" and a new organization must be formed to nurture "true believers." Both groups appeal to Ellen White for their authority. Here is another instance where careful study will avoid the unthinking optimism of some and the undue pessimism of others. Here again, without Ellen White modern church members would be adrift in their speculation.

Prophets, beginning with Moses, have always been identified with rebuke and reproof, as well as with encouragement and promise. People can read selectively and, depending on what they are looking for, they could consider Jeremiah or Isaiah either prophets of doom or of hope. Such may also be true with Ellen White.

She courageously pointed out to fewer than 3,000 fellow church members in 1856 that the Laodicean message (Rev. 3) applies to Seventh-day Adventists. That was very sobering to a people who saw themselves virtually alone in the world as those who "keep the commandments of God and have the faith of Jesus" (Rev. 14:12).

At the same time, she said very clearly that "God has invested His church with special authority and power which no one can be justified in disregarding and despising; for in so doing he despises the voice of God."[15]

Though she used strong language to describe the spiritual lethargy of the church, she was equally emphatic regarding its high destiny: "Has God no living church? He has a church, but it is the church militant, not the church triumphant. We are sorry that there are defective members, that there are tares amid the wheat. . . . Let all be careful not to make an outcry against the only people who are fulfilling the description given of the remnant people who keep the commandments of God, and have faith in Jesus. . . . God has a distinct people, a church on earth, second to none, but superior to all in their facilities to teach the truth, to vindicate the law of God."[16]

In the early 1900s, when certain forces within the church were attempting to deflect the church's message and mission, she steadied those who "listened" with courage and optimism: "We cannot now step off the foundation that God has established. We cannot now enter into any new organization, for this would mean apostasy from the truth."[17]

With a further look into the future, she wrote in 1908: "I am instructed to say to Seventh-day Adventists the world over, God has called us as a people to be a peculiar treasure unto Himself. He has appointed that His church on earth shall stand perfectly united in the Spirit and counsel of the Lord of hosts to the end of time."[18]

Revelation 3 depicts no last-day church beyond Laodicea, thus giving hope that some day many of them will repent, overcome, and fulfill God's plan for the last-day church (Rev. 3:18-21). No other subject for any church-related agenda, either for individuals or institutions, can be more urgent or important to implement.

The Final Shaking—a Prediction

One of Ellen White's unfulfilled predictions relates to future events. Key words that describe the forces that will focus on Seventh-day Adventists are "sifting" and "shaking."

Human beings have been sifted by trials and temptations ever since the Garden of Eden, but Ellen White foresaw a time prior to the close of probation when special circumstances will test and sift every Adventist. The special sifting is often called the "shaking" time. Sometimes she uses the term "shaking" to refer to the process[19] by which all church members will be tested; at other times she refers to the profound shaking that will prevail during the Seven Last Plagues.[20]

Some of the causes of the final shaking within the Adventist Church will be:

- Persecution from outside the church.[21]
- Erroneous doctrines within the church.[22]
- Prevailing worldliness caused by not having experienced "the love of the truth," or being "sanctified through obedience to the truth."[23]
- Resistance to the "straight testimony called forth by the counsel of the True Witness to the Laodiceans."[24]
- Specific rejection of the sanctuary doctrine involving the significance of the pre-advent judgment and the relationship between the cleansed sanctuary and cleansed people.[25]
- Rejection of the ministry of Ellen White.[26]

The impact of the shaking on Seventh-day Adventists will be enormous:

- Defections among church leaders.[27]
- Apostasies of ministers who have preached false doctrine.[28]
- The church will seem about to fall.[29]
- An impressive number of church members will leave.[30]
- New converts will take the place of the defectors.[31]
- Preparation for the crisis involves developing habits of enthusiasm, courage, and loyalty.[32]

Message and Messenger Inseparable

Robert S. Folkenberg, eighteenth president of the General Conference, summed up the convictions of many, past and present, when he wrote: "Without [the] invaluable contributions from the Spirit of Prophecy, I suspect the Seventh-day Adventist Church wouldn't even exist. From the earliest days of this movement, Ellen White's pen and voice have counseled, guided, and led God's people to a deeper level of spiritual experience, to higher standards of personal living, and to clearer concepts of truth."[33]

Dr. Jack Provonsha noted that without Ellen White there would be no Seventh-day Adventist Church today but he warned regarding the church's future. In reviewing the Adventist movement from its beginning, he asserted: "They had their Bible. But they had in large measure that other ingredient for a religious movement's vitality—the sense that they had been called by God and that He was in their movement! Had He not vouchsafed His presence with the gift of prophetic guidance? That made all the difference. Without such a sense at the beginning, there would not now even be a Seventh-day Adventist Church, at least one that made a great deal of difference to the world. The obvious corollary to this is that if that sense is ever lost, the church, even if it continues to exist institutionally, may no longer count where and in the way that it is supposed to count."

A few pages later, Dr. Provonsha wrote: "I have quoted liberally from Ellen G. White. I make no apology for this. She is my 'spiritual mother.' She has also been absolutely central to the life and thought of Adventism."[34]

Telling the story of the birth of Israel as a nation is impossible without reviewing the work of Moses, its prophet. How would one explain the Exodus without Moses? Or Mount Sinai? Or why Israel had to wander in the wilderness for forty years?

So it is impossible to tell the story of the Seventh-day Adventist movement without interweaving Ellen White's ministry in the affirmation of Biblical doctrine, in the building of a church organization strong enough to support a world church, and in the Moses-like messages of reproof and courage that helped to shape the character of the church. Without her today it is probable that the Adventist Church would be only a footnote in some history book of various religious groups in the nineteenth century.

Arthur G. Daniells, General Conference president from 1901-1922, lifted his pen in a plea to fellow church members not to follow the pattern of history: "It is possible to believe nominally in the gift of prophecy, to accept the messages of former prophets, and yet reject and oppose a contemporary messenger chosen of God to give instruction to His people. In Christ's day the words of the ancient prophets were read every Sabbath in their synagogues, yet the religious leaders rejected John the Baptist and crucified the Prophet who came direct from heaven—the greatest who ever appeared on earth. . . . It was Christ's rebuke of specific sins in their life that caused the Pharisees to reject His claim of being the Son of God. There is today, as there has always been in the past, a direct relation between the cherishing of some sin and a doubting of the messages of the Lord's chosen servants."[35]

To keep the Adventist ship on course as it heads toward harbor, the message that set its course must remain as unclouded and as effective as an ocean liner's compass and radar. And to keep the message relevant and meaningful, the Messenger who first framed the message must be listened to as the harbor pilot, especially as the ship enters the turbulence of the narrows, close to port.

"Therefore I have hewn them by the prophets" (Hosea 6:5, RSV).

"Believe in the Lord your God, and you will be established; believe his prophets, and you will succeed" (2 Chron. 20:20, RSV).

Endnotes

1. Schwarz, *Light Bearers,* p. 450.
2. *Ibid.,* pp. 450-452. See also Larry White, "Margaret W. Rowen, Prophetess of Reform and Doom," *Adventist Heritage,* Summer, 1979, pp. 28-40.
3. For more background on false prophetic claims since 1915, see Schwarz, *Light Bearers,* pp. 455, 456; J. R. Spangler, "The Gift of Prophecy and 'Thought Voices,'" *Ministry,* June 1986; Roger W. Coon, *Heralds of New Light,* (Nampa, Idaho: Pacific Press Publishing Association, 1987), pp. 24-26.
4. *Selected Messages,* book 2, p. 78.
5. Letter 40, 1890, in *Selected Messages,* book 1, p. 48.
6. See pp. 14, 34-36 for the limitations of prophets. See p. 457 for the maturing process all prophets experience. See p. 518 for a discussion of why believers focus on a prophet's message, rather than on the messenger. But confidence is often "unsettled" when negative, damaging stories are circulated, deliberately or impulsively—stories that cannot be checked adequately for one reason or another. These stories focus on the normal inadequacies of a maturing individual without placing the isolated incidents within the larger context and general tenor of that person's life. This kind of unfortunate "basis" for losing confidence in Ellen White is what we are concerned about when we discuss how Satan continues his attack on the ministry of the Spirit of prophecy.
7. A Wesleyan Methodist would obviously be contradicted by a Calvinist or Reformed theologian even though both declare that their motto is "The Bible and the Bible Only." (See p. 377.) Seventh-day Adventists expect disagreement from theologians who build their positions on different Biblical/philosophical principles.
8. See pp. 478-498 for a review of some charges and allegations that have been directed at Ellen White.
9. See pp. 256-263, 344 for a discussion of the Great Controversy Theme.
10. Paul B. Ricchiuti, *Ellen* (Mt. View, Calif.: Pacific Press Publishing Association, 1977) p. 132.
11. See *Testimonies,* vol. 5, p. 696.
12. *Bio.,* vol. 6, pp. 442, 443. See also p. 404.
13. See pp. 29-32.
14. *Selected Messages,* book 2, p. 87. For information on Anna Phillips, see *Bio.,* vol. 4, pp. 125-132.
15. *Testimonies,* vol. 3, p. 417 (1875).
16. *Testimonies to Ministers,* pp. 45, 58.
17. Manuscript 129, 1905, cited in *Selected Messages,* book 2, p. 390.
18. *Selected Messages,* book 2, p. 397. Ellen White stated this even though she recognized the larger principle of conditionalism. Organizations, as well as individuals, have not always continued to fulfill their responsibilities, and God could "no longer work with them. Others are then chosen to bear important responsibilities."
19. "We are in the shaking time, the time when everything that can be shaken will be shaken. The Lord will not excuse those who know the truth if they do not in word and deed obey His commands."— *Testimonies,* vol. 6, p. 332 (1900).
20. "Just as soon as the people of God are sealed in their foreheads—it is not any seal or mark that can be seen, but a settling into the truth, both intellectually and spiritually, so they cannot be moved—just as soon as God's people are sealed and prepared for the shaking, it will come."—Manuscript 173, 1902, cited in *SDABC,* vol. 4, p. 1161.
21. "The time is not far distant when the test will come to every soul. The mark of the beast will be urged upon us. Those who have step by step yielded to worldly demands and conformed to worldly customs will not find it a hard matter to yield to the powers that be, rather than subject themselves to derision, insult, threatened imprisonment, and death. . . . In this time the gold will be separated from the dross in the church."—*Testimonies,* vol. 5, p. 81. See also *The Great Controversy,* p. 608.
22. "When the shaking comes, by the introduction of false theories, these surface readers, anchored nowhere, are

like shifting sand. They slide into any position to suit the tenor of their feelings of bitterness."—*Testimonies to Ministers,* p. 112.

23. "Not having received the love of the truth, they will be taken in the delusions of the enemy; they will give heed to seducing spirits and doctrines of devils and will depart from the faith."—*Testimonies,* vol. 6, p. 401. "As the storm approaches, a large class who have professed faith in the third angel's message, but have not been sanctified through obedience to the truth, abandon their position, and join the ranks of the opposition." —*The Great Controversy,* p. 608.
24. "I asked the meaning of the shaking I had seen, and was shown that it would be caused by the straight testimony called forth by the counsel of the True Witness to the Laodiceans. This will have its effect upon the heart of the receiver, and will lead him to exalt the standard and pour forth the straight truth. Some will not bear this straight testimony. They will rise up against it, and this will cause a shaking among God's people." —*Testimonies,* vol. 1, p. 181.
25. "The enemy will bring in false theories, such as the doctrine that there is no sanctuary. This is one of the points on which there will be a departing from the faith."—*Evangelism,* p. 224. See *Ibid.,* pp. 221-225; *The Great Controversy,* pp. 423, 488; *Review and Herald,* Jan. 21, 1890; *Testimonies,* vol. 5, p. 575.
26. "One thing is certain: Those Seventh-day Adventists who take their stand under Satan's banner will first give up their faith in the warnings and reproofs contained in the Testimonies of God's Spirit."—*Selected Messages,* book 3, p. 84. See also *Ibid.,* pp. 48, 83; *Testimonies,* vol., 4, p. 211.
27. "Many a star that we have admired for its brilliance will then go out in darkness."—*Prophets and Kings,* p. 188. "Many will show that they are not one with Christ, that they are not dead to the world, that they may live with Him; and frequent will be the apostasies of men who have occupied responsible positions."—*Review and Herald,* Sept. 11, 1888. See also *MR,* vol. 13, pp. 379, 381.
28. "Many will stand in our pulpits with the torch of false prophecy in their hands, kindled from the hellish torch of Satan. . . . Some will go out from among us who will bear the ark no longer. But these cannot make walls to obstruct the truth; for it will go onward and upward to the end."—*Last Day Events,* p. 179. See also *Selected Messages,* book 3, p. 385; *MR,* vol. 7, p. 192.
29. "The church may appear as about to fall, but it does not fall. It remains, while the sinners in Zion will be sifted out—the chaff separated from the precious wheat. This is a terrible ordeal, but nevertheless it must take place."—*Selected Messages,* book 2, p. 380.
30. "The shaking of God blows away multitudes like dry leaves."—*Testimonies,* vol. 4, p. 89. "As the storm approaches, a large class who have professed faith in the third angel's message, but have not been sanctified through obedience to the truth, abandon their position and join the ranks of the opposition."—*The Great Controversy,* p. 608. "Soon God's people will be tested by fiery trials, and the great proportion of those who now appear to be genuine and true will prove to be base metal."—*Testimonies,* vol. 5, p. 136.
31. "The broken ranks will be filled up by those represented by Christ as coming in at the eleventh hour. . . . Large numbers will be admitted who in these last days hear the truth for the first time."—Letter 103, 1903, cited in *Last Day Events,* p. 182. See also *Early Writings,* p. 271; *Testimonies,* vol. 8, p. 41.
32. "When the religion of Christ is most held in contempt, when His law is most despised, then should our zeal be the warmest and our courage and firmness the most unflinching. To stand in defense of truth and righteousness when the majority forsake us, to fight the battles of the Lord when champions are few—this will be our test. At this time we must gather warmth from the coldness of others, courage from their cowardice, and loyalty from their treason."—*Testimonies,* vol. 5, p. 136.
33. *We Still Believe* (Pacific Press Publishing Association, Nampa, Idaho, 1994), p. 100.
34. Provonsha, *Remnant in Crisis,* pp. 11, 14.
35. Daniells, *The Abiding Gift of Prophecy,* p. 375.

Study Questions

1. What are the causes of the final "shaking" within the Adventist Church?
2. What criteria should we use to evaluate those who claim the prophetic gift?
3. What is meant by the admonition that we should focus on the message rather than on the messenger?
4. What are some of the ways by which the writings of Ellen G. White have been made of "none effect"?
5. Why are the Adventist message and its messenger (Ellen G. White) inseparable?
6. Why is it best, in looking at prophets in any age, to focus on the content of the messages rather than on the human container?
7. List the methods an angry Satan (Rev. 12:17) uses to destroy the influence of "the testimony of Jesus," which is "the spirit of prophecy" (Rev. 19:10).

Appendix

Appendix A

Camp Meetings in Early Nineteenth Century

The following description of early nineteenth-century camp meetings does not apply to all camp meetings at that time or later in the century. However, certain aspects of the camp meetings here described are often ascribed to events occurring in Ellen White's younger years.

In his autobiography Barton W. Stone, an outstanding revivalist in the first half of the nineteenth century, described camp meetings as he experienced them: "The bodily agitations or exercises, attending the excitement in the beginning of this century, were various, and called by various names;—as, the falling exercise—the jerks—the dancing exercise—the barking exercise—the laughing and singing exercises, etc.—The falling exercise was very common among all classes, the saints and sinners of every age and of every grade, from the philosopher to the clown. The subject of this exercise would, generally, with a piercing scream, fall like a log on the floor, earth, or mud, and appear as dead. Of thousands of similar cases, I will mention one.

"At a meeting, two . . . young ladies, sisters, were standing together attending to the exercises and preaching at the same time. Instantly they both fell, with a shriek of distress, and lay for more than an hour apparently in a lifeless state. Their mother, a pious Baptist, was in great distress, fearing they would not revive. At length they began to exhibit symptoms of life, by crying fervently for mercy, and then relapsed into the same death-like state, with an awful gloom on their countenances. After awhile, the gloom on the face of one was succeeded by a heavenly smile, and she cried out, 'precious Jesus,' and rose up and spoke of the love of God—the preciousness of Jesus, and of the glory of the gospel, to the surrounding crowd, in language almost superhuman, and pathetically exhorted all to repentance. In a little while after, the other sister was similarly exercised. From that time they became remarkably pious members of the church.

"I have seen very many pious persons fall in the same way, from a sense of the danger of their unconverted children, brothers, or sisters, of their neighbors, and of the sinful world. I have heard them agonizing in tears and strong crying for mercy to be shown to sinners, and speaking like angels to all around.

"The jerks cannot be so easily described. Sometimes the subject of the jerks would be affected in some one member of the body, and sometimes in the whole system. When the head alone was affected, it would be jerked backward and forward, or from side to side, so quickly that the features of the face could not be distinguished. When the whole system was affected, I have seen the person stand in one place, and jerk backward and forward in quick succession, their head nearly touching the floor behind and before. All classes, saints and sinners, the strong as well as the weak, were thus affected. I have inquired of those thus affected. They could not account for it; but some have told me that those were among the happiest seasons of their lives. I have seen some wicked persons thus affected, and all the time cursing the jerks, while they were thrown to the earth with violence. Though so awful to behold, I do not remember that any one of the thousands I have seen ever sustained an injury in body. This was as strange as the exercise itself.

"The dancing exercise. This generally began with the jerks, and was peculiar to professors of religion. The subject, after jerking awhile, began to dance, and then the jerks would ease. Such dancing was indeed heavenly to the spectators; there was nothing in it like levity, nor calculated to excite levity in the beholders. The smile of heaven shone on the countenance of the subject, and assimilated [sic] to angels appeared the whole person. Sometimes the motion was quick and sometimes slow. Thus they continued to move forward and backward in the same track or alley till nature seemed exhausted, and they would fall prostrate on the floor or earth, unless caught by those standing by. While thus exercised, I have heard their solemn praises and prayers ascending to God.

"The barking exercise (as opposers contemptuously called it) was nothing but the jerks. A person affected with the jerks, especially in his head, would often make a grunt, or bark, if you please, from the suddenness of the jerk. This name of barking seems to have had its origin from an old Presbyterian preacher of East Tennessee. He had gone into the woods for private devotion, and was seized with the jerks. Standing near a sapling, he caught hold of it, to prevent his falling, and as his head jerked back, he uttered a grunt or kind of noise similar to a bark, his face being turned upwards. Some wag discovered him in this position, and reported that he found him barking up a tree.

"The laughing exercise was frequent, confined solely with the religious. It was a loud, hearty laughter, but one *sui generis;* it excited laughter in none else. The subject appeared rapturously solemn, and his laughter excited solemnity in saints and sinners. It is truly indescribable.

"The running exercise was nothing more than that persons feeling something of these bodily agitations, through fear attempted to run away, and thus escape from them; but it commonly happened that they ran not far, before they fell, or became so greatly agitated that they could proceed no farther. I knew a young physician of a celebrated family, who came some distance to a big meeting to see the strange things he had heard of. He and a young lady had sportively agreed to watch over, and take care of each other, if either should fall. At length the physician felt something very uncommon, and started from the congregation to run into the woods; he was discovered running as for life, but did not proceed far till he fell down, and there lay till he submitted to the Lord, and afterwards became a zealous member of the church. Such cases were common.

"I shall close . . . with the singing exercise. This is more unaccountable than anything else I ever saw. The subject in a very happy state of mind would sing most melodiously, not from the mouth or nose, but entirely in the breast, the sounds issuing thence. Such music silenced everything, and attracted the attention of all. It was most heavenly. None could ever be tired of hearing it. . . .

"Thus have I [Barton Stone] given a brief account of the wonderful things that appeared in the great excitement in the beginning of this century [the 19th]. That there were many eccentricities, and much fanaticism in this excitement, was acknowledged by its warmest advocates; indeed it would have been a wonder, if such things had not appeared, in the circumstances of that time. Yet the good effects were seen and acknowledged in every neighborhood, and among the different sects it silenced contention, and promoted unity for awhile; and these blessed effects would have continued, had not men put forth their unhallowed hands to hold up their tottering ark, mistaking it for the ark of God."—Rhodes Thompson, ed., *Voices From Cane Ridge* (St. Louis: The Bethany Press, 1954), pp. 69-72.

Appendix B

Background to Exchange of Letters Between James and Ellen White in 1874

An exchange of letters between James and Ellen White in 1874 reveals honest confrontation between two lovers who had learned through the years to trust each other's integrity, even when dark hours came. What may have prompted this tense interchange?

By 1874 James had experienced four paralytic strokes, signals that his body was weary of the incessant demands of writing, traveling, planning, and administering a growing church and its chief institutions. Zeal and overwork were followed by depression, discouragement, and suspicion of others. Yet, in June 1874, he started another paper, *Signs of the Times*, on the Pacific coast. At this time he also was president of the Publishing Association (Battle Creek), editor of the church paper, *Review and Herald*, and nominally pastor of the Battle Creek church. Further, he was deeply involved in the development of a college in Battle Creek.

Gloom and depression followed his bold, expansive moves on the west coast. In spite of his periods of depression, he never questioned the authenticity and legitimacy of his wife's prophetic ministry. Earlier, on January 1, 1873, he had written out his attitudes toward her visions in a sixteen-page document, entitled, "A Solemn Appeal to the Ministry and the People." He wrote:

"I find that my wrongs have grown out of not being suitably affected by what God has shown my wife, especially what she has been shown of *my* dangers and wrongs. . . .

"I have never doubted the visions of Mrs. White. If a trial or temptation had for a moment come over my mind, as I did not, and could not, understand all, I at once fell back upon the vast amount of clear evidence in their favor, and there rested until all was made clear. But this statement applies more particularly to the first ten years of my experience relative to the visions, when many things were shown of the future history of the cause which time alone could explain. For the past ten years the visions have especially pointed out present duty, and all has appeared plain. . . .

"From the time of my first acquaintance with the one whom God has chosen to speak through to His erring people up to the time of the last vision, I have been cautioned from time to time of my danger of speaking, while under the pressure of a sense of the wrongs of others, in an unguarded manner, and using words that would not have the best effect on those I reproved.

"The Lord knowing the trials through which I was to pass, would prepare my mind to guard against the dangers to which I would be exposed. And had I been suitably impressed with His warnings, my usefulness would not have been marred from time to time by Satan's taking advantage of words that were not best selected. . . .

"I had a view of how terrible was the sin of those who profess to believe that God speaks to them through vision, yet from heedlessness receive no lasting impression when reproved, but go on as before, making no changes in those things wherein they are reproved. I felt that such a course was a fearful insult to the Holy Ghost, and that I was in a degree guilty of this sin."—Cited in *Bio.*, vol. 2, pp. 425-429.

But history repeated itself in the summer of 1874, even to a tense period between the Whites. The chapter, "The Prophet-Apostle Relationship," in *Bio.* vol. 2, pp. 425-445, lays out the circumstances and the forthright, frank letters they shared together. Loving confrontation, even when sharing the most candid observations, can be healthy and healing, if both parties first listen to the Lord's will. The months and years that followed these exchanges revealed the deep confidence and trust James and Ellen White continued to have for each other.

Appendix C

Excerpts from Robert Louis Stevenson's *Across the Plains* (1892)

"I suppose the reader has some notion of an American railroad car, that long, narrow wooden box, like a flat-roofed Noah's Ark, with a stove and a convenience, one at either end, passage down the middle, and transverse benches upon either hand. Those destined for emigrants on the Union Pacific are only remarkable for their extreme plainness, nothing but wood entering in any part into their constitutions, and for the usual inefficacy of the lamps. . . . The benches are too short for anything but a young child. Where there is scarce elbow-room for two to sit, there will not be space enough for one to lie. Hence . . . the company's servants have conceived a plan for the better accommodations of travelers. They prevail on every two to chum together. To each of the chums they sell a board and three square cushions stuffed with straw, and covered with thin cotton. The benches can be made to face each other in pairs, for the backs are reversible.

"On the approach of night the boards are laid from bench to bench making a couch wide enough for two, and long enough for a man of the middle height; and the chums lie down side by side upon the cushions with the head to the conductor's van and the feet to the engine. When the train is full, of course this plan is impossible, for there must not be more than one to every bench, neither can it be carried out unless the chums agree. It was to bring about this last condition that our white-haired official now bestirred himself. He made a most active master of ceremonies, introducing likely couples, and even guaranteeing the amiability and honesty of each. The greater the number of happy couples the better for his pocket, for it was he who sold the raw materials of the beds. His price for one board and three straw cushions began with two dollars and a half; but before the train left, and, I am sorry to say, long after I had purchased mine, it had fallen to one dollar and a half.

"[An] afternoon was spent in making up the train. I am afraid to say how many baggage-wagons followed the engine, certainly a score; then came the Chinese, then we [the single men], then the families, and the rear was brought up by the conductor in what, if I have it rightly, is called the caboose. The class to which I belonged was of course far the largest, and we ran over, so to speak, to both sides; so that there were more Caucasians among the Chinamen [Chinese], and some bachelors among the families. But our own car was pure from admixture, save for one little boy of eight or nine who had the whooping cough. At last, about six, the long train crawled out of the Transfer Station [at Council Bluffs] and across the wide Missouri river to Omaha, westward bound.

"It was a troubled uncomfortable evening in the cars. There was thunder in the air, which helped to keep us restless. A man played many airs upon the cornet, and none of them were much attended to, until we came to *Home, sweet home* [sic]. It was truly strange to note how the talk ceased at that, and the faces began to lengthen. I have no idea whether musically this air is to be considered good or bad; but it belongs to that class of art which may be best described as a brutal assault upon the feelings. Pathos must be relieved by dignity of treatment. If you wallow naked in the pathetic, like the author of *Home, Sweet Home,* you make your hearers weep in an unmanly fashion; and even while yet they are moved, they despise themselves and hate the occasion of their weakness. It did not come to tears that night, for the experiment was interrupted. An elderly, hard-looking man, with a goatee beard and about as much appearance of sentiment as you would expect from a retired slaver, turned with a start and bade the performer stop that 'damned thing.' 'I've heard about enough of that' he added, 'give us something about the good country we're going to.' A murmur of adhesion ran around the car; the performer took the instrument from his lips, laughed and nodded, and then struck into a dancing measure.

"There were meals to be had by the wayside . . . rarely less than twenty minutes for each; and if we had not spent many other twenty minutes waiting for some express upon a side track upon miles of desert, we might have taken an hour to each repast and arrived at San Francisco up to time. . . . Civility is the main comfort that you miss. Equality, though conceived very largely in America, does not extend so low down as to an emigrant. Thus in all our trains, a warning cry of 'All aboard!' recalls the passengers to take their seats; but as soon as I was alone with emigrants, and from the Transfer all the way to San Francisco, I found this ceremony was pretermitted; the train stole from the station without a note of warning, and you had to keep an eye upon it even while you ate. The annoyance is considerable, and the disrespect wanton and petty. . . .

"It had thundered on the Friday night, but the sun rose on Saturday without a cloud. We were at sea—there is no other adequate expression—on the plains of Nebraska. I made my observatory on the top of a fruit-wagon, and sat by the hour upon that perch to spy about me, and to spy in vain for something new. It was a world almost without a feature; an empty sky, and empty earth; front and back, the line of railway stretched from horizon to horizon, like a cue across a billiard board; on either hand, the green plain ran till it touched the skirts of heaven. Along the track innumerable wild sunflowers, no bigger than a crown-piece, bloomed in a continuous flower-bed; grazing beasts were seen upon the prairie at all degrees of distance and diminution; and now and again we might perceive a few dots beside the railroad which grew more and more distinct as we drew nearer till they turned into wooden cabins, and then dwindled and dwindled in our wake until they melted into their surroundings, and we were once more alone. . . .

"To cross such a plain is to grow homesick for the mountains. I longed for the Black Hills of Wyoming, which I knew we were soon to enter, like an ice-bound whaler for the spring. Alas! and it was a worse country than the other. All Sunday and Monday we traveled through these sad mountains, or over the main ridge of the Rockies, which is a fair match to them for misery of aspect. Hour after hour it was the same unhomely and unkindly world about our onward path; tumbled boulders, cliffs that drearily imitate the shape of monuments and fortifications—how drearily, how tamely, none can tell who has not seen them . . . and for sole sign of life, here and there a few fleeting antelopes; here and there, but at incredible intervals, a creek running in a canon [canyon]. The plains have a grandeur of their own; but here there is nothing but a contorted smallness. Except for the air, which was light and stimulating, there was not one good circumstance in that God-forsaken land." —Jensen, *The American Heritage History of Railroads in America,* pp. 130, 131.

Appendix D

A Partial List of Ellen G. White Visions

The following visions have been selected from approximately 2,000 dreams and visions. This selection was made of those visions that made a significant contribution to the development of Adventist theology and organization. Another list could be made solely of messages sent to individuals—messages that can be instructive to others who need similar counsel. (See *Comprehensive Index to the Writings of Ellen G. White,* vol. 3, pp. 2978-2984 for an extended list of Ellen White's published visions, noting time, place, and topic.)

1. (First vision) Portland, ME—December, 1844: Advent people on way to the Holy City (*Bio.*, vol. 1, pp. 55-59, 107; *Early Writings,* pp. 13-17; *Life Sketches,* pp. 64-68; *Testimonies,* vol. 1, pp. 58-61; Roger W. Coon, *The Great Visions of Ellen G. White* (Hagerstown, Md.: Review and Herald Publishing Association, 1992) pp. 15-23.

2. Exeter, ME—1845: Jesus and Father move to Most Holy Place in 1844 (*Bio.,* vol. 1, pp. 78, 79, 107; *Early Writings,* pp. 54-56).

3. New Hampshire—1845: Encouraged Washington Morse regarding Jesus entering Most Holy Place in 1844 to finish the atonement (*Bio.,* vol. 1, pp. 84-86; *Life Sketches,* pp. 77-79).

4. Portland, ME—1845: Glory of new earth (*Bio.,* vol. 1, pp. 88, 89; *Testimonies,* vol. 1, pp. 67-71).

5. Portland, ME—1845: Struck dumb, with the promise that in twenty-four hours she would speak; fifty Bible texts to give her encouragement (*Bio.,* vol. 1, pp. 90, 91; *Life Sketches,* pp. 88-90).

6. Carver, MA—1845: Jesus not to come until saints passed through "time of Jacob's Trouble," sparing Adventists another disappointment (*Bio.,* vol. 1, pp. 99, 100; *A Word to the "Little Flock,"* p. 22).

7. Randolph, MA—1845: Nearly four hours, her longest vision, revealing bad motives and sad future of the dissemblers; holding the Thayer family Bible while reciting texts that she pointed to without visually seeing the pages (*Bio.,*vol. 1, pp. 102-105; Coon, *Great Visions.,* pp. 25-37).

8. On ocean off MA—1846: Heavy storm, assured that her party would not die, refuting prevailing accusation that her visions came only under mesmeric power (*Bio.,* vol. 1, pp. 108, 109; *Early Writings,* pp. 23, 24).

9. Topsham, ME—Nov. 1846: Vision of "other planets" and "open space" that had profound effect on Joseph Bates (*Bio.,* vol. 1, pp. 113, 114; *Life Sketches,* pp. 97, 98).

10. Topsham, ME—Apr. 3, 1847: Heavenly sanctuary, a reality; confirmation of seventh-day Sabbath and its decisive role in the last days (*Bio.,* vol. 1, pp. 120, 121; *Early Writings,* pp. 32-35; Coon, *Great Visions,* pp. 39-48).

11. Dorchester, MA—Nov. 1848: Sealing work; duty to publish until "streams of light" are "clear round the world" (*Bio.,* vol. 1, pp. 150, 151; *Life Sketches,* pp. 125, 126)

12. Rocky Hill, CT—Dec. 16, 1848: Shaking of the powers of heaven; open space in Orion (*Bio.,* vol. 1, p. 154; *Early Writings,* p. 41).

13. Rocky Hill, CT—Jan. 5, 1849: Christ in Most Holy Place until plagues begin to fall (*Bio.*, vol. 1, pp. 154-156; *Early Writings,* pp. 36, 37).

14. Topsham, ME—Mar. 24, 1849: "Mysterious knocking in New York" to become more common (*Bio.,* vol. 1, pp. 159-161; Coon, *Great Visions,* pp. 49-61).

15. Oswego, NY—Jan. 10, 1850: *Present Truth* must continue and James White must "write, write, write" (*Bio.,* vol. 1, p. 172).

16. Oswego, NY—1850: Exposed dishonesty of county treasurer and gave confidence to the Patches (*Bio.,* vol. 1, pp. 174-176).

17. Oswego, NY—Aug. 24, 1850: Enhanced prediction of worldwide influence of spiritualism (*Bio.,* vol. 1, pp. 183, 184;

Early Writings, pp. 59, 60; Coon, *Great Visions,* pp. 49-61).

18. Camden, NY—June 21, 1851: Preaching of Advent should never make time a test (*Bio.,* vol. 1, p. 208; *Review and Herald,* July 21, 1851).

19. Rochester, NY—July 2, 1853: The *Review* should come out weekly; counsel to church groups in Michigan (*Bio.,* vol. 1, pp. 281, 282; *Early Writings,* pp. 93-96).

20. Oswego, NY—Feb. 1854: Beginning of comprehensive health message (*Bio.,* vol. 1, pp. 291, 292).

21. Oswego, NY—June 20, 1854: Prediction that "Messenger" party would soon be in disarray (*Bio.,* vol. 1, pp. 309-315).

22. Battle Creek, MI—Nov. 20, 1855: Confirmation of Sabbath from "even to even" (*Bio.,* vol. 1, p. 324; *Testimonies,* vol. 1, pp. 113-116).

23. Battle Creek, MI—May 27, 1856: The Two Ways plus the three groups in attendance—worms, plagues, and alive at Advent (*Bio.,* vol. 1, pp. 338, 339; *Testimonies,* vol. 1, pp. 127-140).

24. Round Grove, IL—Dec. 9, 1856: The Waukon, Iowa, crisis (*Bio.,* vol. 1, pp. 345-349; *Life Sketches,* pp. 160, 161).

25. Hillsdale, MI—Feb. 1857: First vision that included Advent believers in Laodicean message (*Bio.,* vol. 1, pp. 351, 352; *Testimonies,* vol. 1, pp. 141-146).

26. Battle Creek, MI—-Nov. 20, 1857: Graphic presentation of the "shaking" (*Bio.,* vol. 1, pp. 364, 365; *Testimonies,* vol. 1, pp. 179-184).

27. Lovett's Grove, OH—Mar. 14, 1858: The comprehensive Great Controversy vision with warning that Satan would try to greatly hinder Ellen White (*Bio.,* vol. 1, pp. 368-375; Coon, *Great Visions,* pp. 62-75).

28. Battle Creek, MI—late 1858: J. N. Andrews would develop a Bible study on tithing (*Bio.,* vol. 1, pp. 387-389).

29. Battle Creek, MI—June 3, 1859: Laodicean message not accomplished in a few months because it takes time to develop character (*Bio.,* vol. 1, pp. 407; *Testimonies,* vol. 1, pp. 185-187).

30. Battle Creek, MI—Dec. 23, 1860: Divine approval on organizational structure and name (*Bio.,* vol. 1, pp. 437, 438; *Testimonies,* vol. 1, pp. 210-216).

31. Parkville, MI—Jan. 12, 1861: Forecast of Civil War horror when most Americans thought otherwise; some families in audience would lose sons (*Bio.,* vol. 1, pp. 462-464; Coon, *Great Visions,* pp. 76-89).

32. Roosevelt, NY—Aug. 3-4, 1861: Church order, "straight chain of truth, harmonious connections," deficit in Methodist sanctification compared to Biblical sanctification, and the impact of the Civil War on the church (*Bio.,* vol. 1, p. 449; *Testimonies,* vol. 1, pp. 264-268, 326, 327).

33. Battle Creek, MI—Jan. 4, 1862: Renewed insight on the real issues in the Civil War and its protracted length (*Testimonies,* vol. 1, pp. 253-268).

34. Battle Creek, MI—Nov. 5, 1862: Situation regarding Moses Hull, a minister turned Spiritualist (*Bio.,* vol. 2, pp. 53-58; *Testimonies,* vol. 1, pp. 426-437).

35. Battle Creek, MI—1863: Counsel to young men and the Civil War draft (*Bio.,* vol. 2, pp. 49-52).

36. Battle Creek, MI—June 5, 1863: Satan works to lead ministers astray through unconsecrated wives (*Testimonies,* vol. 1, pp. 449-455).

37. Otsego, MI—June 6, 1863: Comprehensive health reform (*Bio.,* vol. 2, pp. 73-82; *Counsels on Diet and Foods,* pp. 481-484; Coon, *Great Visions,* pp. 90-107).

38. Rochester, NY—Dec. 25, 1865: Explanation for James's illness and how crisis would pass; how to prepare for "latter rain"; dangers of self-reliance in debating (*Bio.,* vol. 2, pp. 128-133; *Testimonies,* vol. 1, pp. 613-628).

39. Battle Creek, MI—Spring, 1867: Small portion of those who profess the truth will be saved (*Testimonies,* vol. 1, p. 608).

40. Battle Creek, MI—June 12, 1868: Remarkable counsel to several leaders; general comments about delay in Advent and how to prepare for it (*Testimonies,* vol. 2, pp. 156-199; *Bio.,* vol. 2, p. 245).

41. Battle Creek, MI—Aug. 1868: Heavily loaded wagons ascending a road that narrows; finally, only the cords: God holds the cords (*Bio.,* vol. 2, p. 247; *Testimonies,* vol. 2, pp. 594-597).

42. Adams Center, MI—Oct. 25, 1868. Lengthy vision covering many people, especially strong counsel to ministry who profess without growing Christian experience (*Testimonies,* vol. 2, pp. 411-439, 498-522).

43. Chicago, IL—July 6, 1870: Candid counsel to minister and wife who were spiritually unprepared for their duties (*Testimonies,* vol. 2, pp. 539-553).

44. Battle Creek, MI—Apr. 30, 1871: Call for divine/human cooperation in all things; *Testimonies* provided to direct attention to Bible; Adventists are walled with light (*Bio.,* vol. 2, pp. 317, 318).

45. Bordoville, VT—Dec. 10, 1871: Extended counsel on character preparation; health reform is a vital component in preparing a people to meet the Lord (*Bio.,* vol. 2, pp. 332, 333; *Testimonies,* vol. 3, pp. 39-98; 161-188; 202-221).

46. Santa Rosa, CA—April 1, 1874: Immense effectiveness of the press in proclaiming Adventist message; must take broader views—the whole world; deficiencies of ministers (*Testimonies,* vol. 3, pp. 434-467; *Bio.,* vol. 2, p. 408; *Life Sketches,* pp. 208-210).

47. Battle Creek, MI—Jan. 3, 1875: (Last vision accompanied by physical phenomena.) To ministers and publishing houses in foreign lands, especially Australia (*Testimonies,* vol. 3, pp. 468-471, 560-575; vol. 4, pp. 118-125, 227-254; *Life Sketches,* pp. 282, 283).

48. Rome, NY—Sept. 12, 1875: Strong appeal for literature evangelism (*Bio.,* vol. 2, pp. 480, 481; *Review and Herald,* Nov. 4, 1875).

49. Battle Creek, MI—Oct. 9, 1878: Reproved husband James orally for publicly conflicting with Uriah Smith over "king of the north" and Smith's belief that Armageddon was imminent; level of moral and intellectual culture expected at Battle Creek Sanitarium (*Bio.,* vol. 3, pp. 96, 97; *Testimonies,* vol. 4, pp. 306-383).

50. Battle Creek, MI—Oct. 23, 1879: Great day of God's judgment; book of the sins of those who profess the truth, with selfishness being the general heading (*Bio.,* vol. 3, pp. 122, 123; *Testimonies,* vol. 4, pp. 384-387; *Life Sketches,* pp. 241-246).

51. Battle Creek, MI—Nov. 23, 1879: Strong counsel to publishing houses; candid admonition to key leaders; Sabbath work, even in hospitals (*Bio.,* vol. 3, pp. 128, 129; *Testimonies,* vol. 4, pp. 449-462, 537-544).

52. Portland, OR—June, 1884: (Probably the last open vision) Brother Raymond, a dissembler with what he considered "new light," was seen as an example of how Satan works to unsettle confidence (*Bio.,* vol. 3, pp. 253-259; *Testimonies,* vol. 5, pp. 289-297; Letter 19, 1884, cited in *Selected Messages,* book 3, p. 86).

53. Basel, Switzerland—February, 1887: Concerning Canright changing ships from Adventist Church to one that will not reach the harbor (*Bio.,* vol. 3, pp. 360, 361; *Testimonies,* vol. 5, pp. 571-573;).

54. Healdsburg, CA—Summer, 1888: Unbelief and resistance to reproof (that had built up during her absence in Europe) which would make difficult her contribution at the General Conference in Minneapolis (*Bio.,* vol. 3, pp. 385, 386).

55. Minneapolis, MN—October, 1888: The resentful, divisive spirit of many revealed; even though most would not heed her messages, she must deliver them regardless (*Bio.,* vol. 3, pp. 404-410).

56. Salamanca, NY—Nov. 3, 1890: Worldly policy in Adventist institutions; wages and missionary spirit; council meeting regarding the philosophy of *The American Sentinel* (*Bio.,* vol. 3, pp. 464-469, 478-482, 487, 488; *Life Sketches,* pp. 319-330; *Selected Messages,* book 2, pp. 193, 194).

57. Melbourne, Australia—Dec. 1891: Comprehensive vision regarding publishing work in Australia, with personal testimonies for several, including Mr. and Mrs. Faulkhead (*Bio.,* vol. 4, pp. 50-56).

58. Napier, NZ—Apr. 9, 1893: Caution to A. T. Jones that there are conditions to justification and sanctification (*Selected Messages,* book 1, pp. 377-382).

59. Melbourne, Australia—Feb. 1894: Clear educational principles, especially the necessity to learn how to work (*Fundamentals of Christian Education,* pp. 310-327).

60. Granville, N.S.W.—July 29, 1894: Counsel to Battle Creek church, including the bicycle craze, appeal for Christlikeness; God will not do that which is human responsibility (*Testimonies,* vol. 5, pp. 48-80).

61. Cooranbong, N.S.W.—Nov., 1895: Southern work—we must not encourage blacks to work on Sunday (*Bio.,* vol. 4, p. 252; *The Southern Work,* pp. 66-71).

62. Cooranbong, N.S.W.—July, 1898: Counsel regarding the selection of Sydney for site of publishing house (*Bio.,* vol. 4, pp. 358-360).

63. Newcastle, N.S.W.—Dec. 23, 1898: Clear presentation of elements of salvation and the key to successful Christian life (*Bio.*, vol. 4, p. 373; *Review and Herald*, Apr. 11, 1899).

64. Cooranbong, N.S.W.—July 1899: Specific counsel regarding Avondale Health Retreat (*Bio.*, vol. 4, p. 439).

65. Cooranbong, N.S.W.—Jan. 1900: Counsel regarding erroneous theology ("Holy Flesh" error) and inappropriate worship practices (*Bio.*, vol. 5, pp. 101-108, 112, 113; *Selected Messages*, book 2, pp. 37-39).

66. Melbourne, Victoria—March 7, 1900: Strongly urged to return to America because she was "needed just now" (*Bio.*, 4, p. 454).

67. On board the *Moana*, Sept. 9, 1900: Counsel regarding her role in Battle Creek; on guard against private interviews, enter no controversies, simply to give messages (*Bio.*, vol. 5, p. 22).

68. Elmshaven, CA—Feb. 16, 1901: Appeal for excellence; counsel on manufacturing health food (*Testimonies*, vol. 7, pp. 127-131).

69. Elmshaven, CA—Apr. 30, 1901: Warning to Dr. J. H. Kellogg regarding overbuilding the new sanitarium (*Bio.*, vol. 5, pp. 153, 154).

70. Los Angeles, CA—Aug. 1901: Sanitariums should be established in southern California and away from cities (*Testimonies*, vol. 7, pp. 85, 86).

71. Elmshaven, CA—Sept. 26, 1901: Not the time to expand to China and India; build up American institutions and then workers would be better prepared (*Testimonies*, vol. 8, pp. 87-89).

72. Elmshaven, CA—Nov. 3, 1901: Work to be done in New York that will require fresh and creative methods; principles of effective evangelism spelled out (*Testimonies*, vol. 9, pp. 137-152).

73. Elmshaven, CA—Oct. 13, 1902: Retired areas in southern California where buildings could be bought for sanitariums at less than original cost (*Bio.*, vol. 5, p. 359).

74. Elmshaven, CA—Oct. 19, 1902: God countermanded Ellen White's counsel with a vision that saved the Southern Publishing Association (*Bio.*, vol. 5, pp. 189-193).

75. Oakland, CA—Mar. 30, 1903: Forthright counsel on coming "to our senses" and learning from the disastrous fires in Battle Creek (*Bio.*, vol. 5, pp. 244-246).

76. Elmshaven, CA—Summer 1903: Iceberg analogy and crucial counsel regarding how to handle the pantheism crisis (*Bio.*, vol. 5, pp. 300-306; *Selected Messages*, book 1, pp. 201-208).

77. Paradise Valley, CA—Summer, 1904: Selection of site for Paradise Valley Sanitarium and the confidence that water would be found by drilling (*Bio.*, vol. 5, pp. 362-367).

78. Washington, DC—May, 1905: Counsel to help A. T. Jones who did not see his danger (*Bio.*, vol. 5, p. 414).

79. Loma Linda, CA—Sept. 1, 1905: Ethnic groups must not separate into separate facilities (*Bio.*, vol. 6, pp. 47-51).

80. Loma Linda, CA—April 16, 1906: Buildings great and small fell to the ground, many lives lost, two days before San Francisco earthquake (*Bio.*, vol. 6, pp. 79-88; *Testimonies*, vol. 9, pp. 92-96).

81. Elmshaven, CA—Dec. 11, 1908: Counsel for the Mackins who believed that they had various spiritual gifts (*Bio.*, vol. 6, pp. 171-174).

82. Elmshaven, CA—July 5, 1912: Counsel regarding recreation, especially when "men and women, acting like children" seemed to forget their Christian responsibilities (*Bio.*, vol. 6, pp. 370-373).

Appendix E

Basic Presuppositions Shared by Most Shut-door Critics

The underlying issue that has divided critics and affirmers regarding the shut-door issue has been the question of what happened in heaven on October 22, 1844. Critics ask, If the atonement was completed on the cross, and Jesus went immediately into the Most Holy Place phase of His high-priestly ministry at that time, what would be the purpose of a second-apartment ministry?

To some degree, most all critics who assert that Ellen White held the extreme shut-door position prior to 1851/2 also reject the Biblical teachings that place significance on the 1844 date; that is, they do not find a change of ministry in the Bible and thus reject Ellen White's teachings on this subject. With that presupposition, it is only a half step toward rejecting Ellen White as a reliable theological teacher, especially in her vision-messages that taught the change of Christ's ministry in 1844.

Affirmers, on the other hand, believe that Ellen White not only received her vision-views from God, but led the way in a growing understanding of the Biblical teaching regarding the larger intent of the sanctuary doctrine. This viewpoint accepts the sanctuary doctrine as a further unfolding of the Great Controversy Theme wherein the universe is involved in the process of settling earth's rebellion—the process that culminates in the sealing of God's people in the final generation which, in turn, is linked to the completion of Christ's ministry in the Most Holy Place.

Thus, how one relates to the doctrine of the atonement immediately affects his/her understanding of: (1) the validity of the Millerite seventh-month movement; (2) the validity of the significance of October 22, 1844; (3) the connection between the Sabbath and the sanctuary message; (4) the meaning of "the third angel's message"; and (5) the validity of Ellen White as a trustworthy prophet.

In summary, if one presupposes that there is no Biblical significance to October 22, 1844, the next step is to conclude that Ellen White was in error, not only in interpreting Christ's high priestly ministry but also in identifying with certain shut-door positions prior to 1852.

If one presupposes, on the basis of many Biblical lines of support, that a significant event occurred on October 22, 1844, then Ellen White's vision-messages of the 1840s appear coherent, integrating, and understandable.

Further, if for other reasons one rejects the authenticity of Ellen White's role as God's messenger, then it would be difficult to attach credibility to her assertions in the 1840s. Presuppositions often drive the research; presuppositions often predetermine one's conclusions.

Appendix F

Time-conditioned or Time-related?

The distinction between being time-conditioned and time-related is, admittedly, one of degree. The difference is best observed when a person's position is placed on a continuum with time-relatedness on the far right and time-conditioned on the far left. Everyone is on that continuum, some more to the right or left than others.

Where one is placed on that continuum usually depends on the viewer's presuppositions. Presuppositions (most of the time unconsciously) determine both the questions asked and the source materials selected or ignored. Regarding Ellen White, two general, mutually exclusive viewpoints have been in conflict:

(1) Critics have tried to prove Ellen White's very strong dependence upon her contemporaries— that is, they see her far to the left on the "time-conditioned" side of the continuum. In so doing, they may not have fully recognized or understood how God through the centuries has chosen to reveal His messages through His prophets. They may not have fully appreciated how advanced Ellen White's theological concepts were, that she was not a prisoner of her times and limited to the notions of her contemporaries. Further, they believe that Ellen White and her colleagues were not forthright in reviewing the 1840s; that is, they believe that Mrs. White taught Biblical error, that her visions support this charge, and that she and her colleagues maintained a positive "cover-up" mode through suppressed documents and anachronistic, face-saving testimonies.

(2) Affirmers have largely resisted the "time-conditioned" approach and placed her to the right of the continuum's center—thus, recognizing her time-relatedness. However, though her advocates recognize that Ellen White was "time-related," they may not have fully recognized that God does not give His prophets an immaculately conceived mind, unconnected with the language, concepts, and social conditioning of their time. (That is, some advocates have placed her so far to the right that they deny any human limitations or contemporary influence.)

When prophets convey God's thoughts, they can process them only with the basic mental equipment they possess at the moment.[1] A prophet in the nineteenth century, for example, uses nineteenth century dictionaries or encyclopedias, not those of the twentieth century. Further, the conceptual framework that prophets use is not automatically changed by revelation so that the prophet immediately sees the whole picture intended in the vision. The full understanding of the vision may take time, long or short, as the prophet assimilates the new conceptual categories implicit in the vision. Prophets may describe the vision in conversation or in print, but the full understanding of what they said or wrote may take time.

For Ellen White, the words she used to describe her vision-thoughts had to be plugged into her own time-related frame of reference, out of which she began to see the far-reaching significance of the vision's implications. Such was the case when she saw in O. R. L. Crosier's article a good way to explain Biblically what she had seen in vision regarding Christ's change of ministry in 1844.[2]

In a similar way, God used Ellen White's earliest visions, among other purposes, to tap into the local shut-door groups led by Joseph Turner and Apollos Hale. If the vision had not used the Bridegroom analogy (a correct Biblical term then being used by Turner), she would not have found anyone, anywhere, who would have listened to her.[3] The unknown must be linked to the known if there is to be meaningful communication.

In other words, affirmers must take into account that Ellen White had to speak to her contemporaries in words and concepts that they both understood, or there would have been no communication. Leading others, step by step, from one viewpoint to another takes time, tact, patience—and a clear awareness of the *hearer's* conceptual framework.

The newer the thought, the longer it will take the prophet to understand its intent and how to convey its full message. For example, consider Ellen White's communication challenge while she was enlarging the term "shut door" (which had been used since 1844 as a code word indicating the "validity" of the Midnight Cry/1844 message). By the middle of 1846 the Sabbath doctrine had become clear to her after intensive Bible study. By April 3, 1847, now a Sabbathkeeper, she was conceptually ready to grasp the linkage between the sanctuary truth of her earlier visions and the seventh-day Sabbath. However, we find no hint that throughout this growing period after her first vision, she understood the "shut door" to mean that probation closed for everyone on October 22, 1844.

Thus, there should be agreement between critics and affirmers that the prophet's mental equipment, including thought categories, is in place *before* God's message comes.[4]

Ellen White had the essential qualities (equipment) God needed whereby His thoughts could be understood—equipment such as humility, openness to light, and willingness to submit to His leading. As time went on, God kept adding information that required a constant upgrading of her database to handle larger conceptions. Her mental files began to interconnect, developing a new and fresh understanding out of the basic thought forms of her day that continually fed into her mind through reading and conversations.

Thus, any attempt to draw time-lines in the 1840s as to when Ellen White moved from a "shut-door" belief to "open-door" convictions is fruitless and misguided. Beginning with her first vision in December 1844, Mrs. White led the way in breaking out of the limited beliefs of her contemporaries. She added an enriched meaning to shared code words, always surprising her closest colleagues with fresh, expansive thoughts relative to God's plan for this world. At the same time, we can observe her humanness, her time-related mental framework (with which she would naturally express herself) in the way she may have appeared to reflect certain aspects of the "closed door" that she later clarified to avoid misunderstanding. Not to use words that her hearers could identify with would have cut off all communication with those who held fast to the significance of 1844, not because she hesitated to offend them but because she had no other frame of reference with which to use language.

Footnotes

1. See p. 34.
2. In Ellen White's letter to Eli Curtis, April 21, 1847, she noted that "the Lord shew[ed] me in vision, more than one year ago, that Brother Crosier had the true light on the cleansing of the sanctuary, &c; and that it was His will that Brother C. should write out the view which he gave us in the *Day-Star,* Extra, February 7, 1846," (reproduced in Knight, *1844,* p. 171).
3. Damsteegt, *Foundations,* pp. 117-122.
4. Although not completely analogical, this would be like trying to run sophisticated software, requiring a

Pentium processor, on a computer with only a 286 or 386 CPU! With many programs, progressive system enhancements will be necessary to maintain or improve performance and/or productivity levels, but only as operator skills grow, creating an awareness of the need for, and benefits of, such upgrades. A powerful, high-end computer would be vastly underutilized if used only to write an occasional letter. However, when computer users begin to deal with increasingly complex and sophisticated graphical, multi-media material, they will definitely need the optimization and enhancement of all available resources.

Appendix G

Ellen White's Growth in Understanding Her Own Visions

Ellen Harmon White experienced the same growth patterns as do all men and women. Human beings understand concepts in a step-by-step process, starting early in life—a principle that Jesus and Paul well understood in their eagerness to teach new truth to their hearers.[1]

Young Ellen, it seems, did not fully understand, at first, all the implications of her earliest visions. She had to work with the mindset of her time as well as the mental equipment of a teenager. She freely admitted that the first vision dramatically reversed her understanding of what happened in 1844.[2] Later, she reflected on this phenomenon of not always understanding her own visions as soon as she received them: "Often representations are given me which at first I do not understand, but after a time they are made plain by a repeated presentation of those things that I did not at first comprehend, and in ways that make their meaning clear and unmistakable."[3]

Thus, assimilating all that was intended in her early vision-messages would take time for young Ellen as it did for her contemporaries—but each vision was seen to add brick after brick, plank after plank, girder after girder to the developing theological platform—bricks, planks, and girders that were new both to her and to her contemporaries.

Ellen Harmon White was led to see, step by step, what happened on October 22, 1844, that would be of great significance in the plan of salvation; this understanding had been seen in part (and fleetingly) by a few Bible students, such as O. R. L. Crosier. As she developed the meaning of the events seen in her first vision, and her mind became sensitive to the truths implicit in certain Biblical expositions of others, her theological insights not only completely changed the direction of her life but set the agenda for the Seventh-day Adventist movement. For example, she saw in Crosier's article certain Biblical themes that expressed well her broad outline of the significance of October 22, 1844. However, she also saw in Crosier and others, "Biblical" expositions that did not fit her broad vision-outline. Thus, the same Spirit that guided her in describing her visions was also guiding her in selecting those contemporary Biblical studies that reflected the core truths of her visions. This interaction with the Holy Spirit set the pace for the rest of her life: the same Spirit that revealed the visions was to help her differentiate between that which was faithful to her vision-messages and that which was unacceptable—even when looking at the same document.

When we review her vision-messages, we can trace this growth in understanding the theological framework that the Seventh-day Adventist Church would soon call "present truth," and the prophetic meaning of the messages of the three angels of Revelation 14.

1. *That first vision* (December 1844) *showed that the Seventh-month Movement was of God,* that God had led in the 1844 experience, that the significance of that experience would be a strong source of confidence for multitudes in the future, that those who stayed on the path to the City were those who kept their eyes on Jesus, who would keep them from stumbling as they traveled straight ahead toward the Holy City.

2. *Ellen Harmon's February 1845 vision revealed what happened in heaven when Christ entered the Most Holy Place in the heavenly sanctuary, and what happened on earth.* The "exceeding bright light" of the Millerite movement appeared to two groups "before the throne"—one "bowed down . . . deeply interested"; the other "stood uninterested and careless." Relatively "few would receive this great light." Many "resisted it," others were interested but grew "careless" and the light "moved off." Some "cherished it"

and joined the first group "bowed before the throne."

After the October 22 event when God the Father arose and went "into the holy of holies" and Jesus went "with Him," those "bowed down arose with Him." The "careless multitude" remained in "perfect darkness"; the once-believing Millerites still prayed to Jesus in the Holy Place but did not receive the breath of the Holy Spirit. As time passed, however, many who had joined the first group in following Jesus into the Most Holy Place, began to leave that group "one after the other" to rejoin those who believed nothing significant happened on October 22, 1844.[4] Obviously, in this vision the "door" had not been shut on those who were still making decisions regarding their spiritual commitments: probation does not close until people close their own probation.

3. Ellen Harmon's August 1845 vision stated that the return of Jesus would occur after certain events had taken place; that His return was *not imminent*, but *near*.

4. Her April 3, 1847 vision *focused on the significance of the seventh-day Sabbath, especially as linked with the sanctuary doctrine.* Ellen White further defined the Sabbath as a central issue in last-day events and foretold the tensions that would follow. In this vision, the door of salvation was still open to those who had not understood the gospel message in years past (for example, the Sabbath issue).

5. *In Ellen White's letter to Eli Curtis* (April 21, 1847) she laid more bricks in her developing theological structure by emphasizing the features of the two resurrections separated by 1,000 years. *For the first time* she mentioned "the shut door" *in its symbolic reference to Christ's entering the Most Holy Place in His final mediatorial work.*

6. Her November 17-19, 1848, vision associated the *significance of 1844 with the light that was breaking out,* a light that would rise as the morning sun *until all the earth would receive its message.* Further, this light would break out in its splendor and power through the publishing work—counsel that James White immediately began to implement.

7. *The Sealing vision* (January 5, 1849) enlarged the picture of last-day events. *Linkage between the holding of the winds (Rev. 7) with the sealing work and the close of probation emphasized the contingency of the second Advent;* that is, God will wait for a people on whom He can place His seal, His approval.

8. *The Open-door Vision* (March 24, 1849) *linked the "shut door" with the sanctuary doctrine and the significance of the Sabbath, and revealed that these truths "could not be separated."* Ellen White put in perspective the emergence of modern Spiritualism and hypnotism. She noted again the responsibility that ministers had who would prefer "strong delusion" rather than the truth about what Jesus is doing now. Here again, for her, the term, "shut door" was the code word for maintaining confidence in the significance of October 22, 1844.

9. Ellen White's article in *Present Truth* (September 1849) provided another example of the brick upon brick process by which she was helping to establish the rising foundation of a coherent, integrated theology. Her key points included: *God's grace is sufficient* to enable His people to be overcomers; habits form serious patterns, for good or ill; *when patterns of holiness or filthiness are so established that they are fixed forever, probation closes*; the sense of urgency rests on the inescapable fact that characters are being set daily, and Christ's return occurs when all characters are sealed or marked; and the door of opportunity is still open to those who are "starving" for "present truth."

Throughout the review of how Ellen White's theological structure developed, we see no hint of a shut door in 1844 to all the world. Much to the contrary! *Two facts should be obvious*: (1) Ellen White was never shown in vision that salvation had closed for the world on October 22, 1844; (2) from her first vision at the age of 17, she nurtured those early conceptual seeds that others saw better, as time passed, as the clear meaning of God's last-day message to a truth-starved world.

Footnotes

1. John 16:12; Mark 4:33; 1 Cor. 3:2; Heb. 5:11-14; Eph. 4:14, 15; 1 Pet. 2:2.
2. See p. 503.
3. *Selected Messages,* book 3, p. 56.
4. The last line of this vision is omitted in *Early Writings,* p. 56, for one of two reasons, or both—to save space to meet press requirements or because it repeats earlier sentiments.

Appendix H

Ellen White Enriched the Term "Shut Door"

During the 1840s Ellen White used the term "shut door" in two ways, not in self-contradiction but with each way emphasizing a different, though complementary, point. Most criticism arises because (1) these two separate concepts are often treated synonymously, and (2) no distinction is made between what Shut-door Millerites believed regarding the "shut door" and what Ellen White meant beginning with her first vision.

For her, the phrase "the shut door," on one hand became a code word that symbolized the validity and significance of the 1844 experience (thus agreeing with the Shut-door Millerites on that point). On the other, it was the code word for the sanctuary doctrine with its emphasis on Jesus leaving (shutting the door) His Holy Place ministry and beginning (opening the door) the second phase of His mediatorial work in the Most Holy Place.

However, critics maintain that the "shut door" term had *only one* meaning for Ellen White, as it did for Shut-door Millerites and, for a time, Sabbatarian Adventists: that the door of mercy had shut for everyone in 1844. With this presupposition, Ellen White's various comments during the 1840s sound confused and inconsistent. *When one recognizes that she used this term in two ways, Ellen White's writings unfold in a simple coherence.*

Furthermore, another distinction must be observed: When Shut-door Millerites used the term, "shut door," they automatically welded two thoughts: (1) if the 1844 message, including the date, was correct, it followed that (2) Christ had come, and that the door of mercy had shut. Any message that proposed a different understanding of that date would, for the Millerites, mean abandonment of any significance to their message and experience.

In other words, for Shut-door Millerites to retain confidence in the 1844 message meant automatically that one believed in the shut door for all on October 22, 1844—the two concepts were inseparable. Those who eventually repudiated their 1844 message and experience were called Open-door Millerites; those who held fast to their confidence that something significant happened in salvation history on October 22 were called Shut-door Millerites.

However, when Ellen White confirmed the validity of 1844 she was not stating that probation had closed as other shut-door advocates did (Turner, Hale, etc.). Her first vision separated this equation which seemed so logically compelling to the Shut-door Millerites. No longer did confidence in the 1844 message mean, at the same time, that one had to believe that probation had closed generally for the world. For Ellen White, the "door"of probation had not completely shut. Her first vision corrected the error of the extreme shut-door position.[1] In that vision the future for the affirmers of the 1844 experience was even more important than their past! They were not sealed yet! Ahead of them was an open road that would require further responsibilities before probation would close for them and others.[2]

Beginning with her first vision, Ellen White's understanding and enrichment involved in the term, "shut door," developed with further Bible study and vision-messages. To keep communication lines open with Shut-door Millerites (who were the most apt to listen to her), she indeed emphasized the "shut-door" concept as something never to be repudiated. But there was more, as she led them along as fast as God led her along.

Thus, it seems clear that anytime after December, 1844, when Ellen White referred to the "wicked world," or "salvation is past," etc., she was referring to those who had either knowingly rejected the messages of 1844 prior to October 22, or had repudiated that message after that date. Such people, in the noon-day awareness of truth, closed their own door of probation, as people continually do today, and will every day until all people are brought to final decision as to what to do with known duty in the light of truth.

Mrs. White did not use the term "shut door" to imply that God had automatically shut the door of mercy on October 22. She used it as a code word, not only to symbolize that *something* significant in salvation history had happened on that date but also for *what* happened on that date. The sanctuary doctrine of Christ's function as High Priest made it possible not only to confirm the change of ministry at the end of the 2300-year prophecy but also to explain that October 22 was not the Second Advent but the beginning of the antitypical day of atonement. The shut-door code word embodied both concepts.

For some Shut-door Sabbatarian Adventists between 1846-1850, that distinction was slowly grasped. But patiently, as occasions were provided, Ellen White tried to visit as many places as possible, almost a one-to-one evangelism, with her new insights. The few publications that did contain her developing messages were severely limited in their circulation, even by 1848. It simply took time to get into print even the few lines that reported her vision-messages—and then more time to get those pages around to the "scattered flock."

In her 1847 Halo of Glory vision[3] Ellen White clearly emphasized that she "saw that God had children who do not see and keep the Sabbath. They had not rejected the light upon it." Here again she applied the principle of rejection: only those who had decidedly rejected the light were in darkness, thus shutting their own door of salvation. But only God could know when people had shut their heart's door against further light. For Ellen White, the *door was not shut* to those (1) who had not understood clearly the Midnight Cry messages or (2) who had not yet heard the Sabbath truth. Her reasoning: The door was always open to the repenting sinner who responded to the clear light of truth.

In summary, Ellen White, from her first vision, taught that probation's door had not shut for everyone on October 22, 1844. However, she agreed with the Shut-door Millerites that *something significant* in salvation history did happen on that date. She disagreed with their interpretation of *what* had happened—thus rejecting their extreme shut-door position. By adding new truths to the teaching that the 1844 experience was valid, Ellen White led Sabbatarian Adventists into enriching their understanding of the shut-door code words. It *now meant* that (1) God had led in the 1844 movement, and (2) He was further leading as they walked through the open door into the sanctuary truths.

Footnotes

1. See pp. 503, 552.
2. See p. 552.
3. See pp. 504, 553.

Appendix I

Ellen White Led the Way in Building a Biblically-Oriented Message for the World

In the very early period (1844-1848), before even a nucleus of a dozen fellow believers was formed, before any published documents were available, Ellen Harmon was conceptually leading the way in developing the Biblically based coherency of what became the distinctive message of Seventh-day Adventists. This remarkable conceptual leadership and nurturing remained a fact of Adventist life till her death.

What were the steps by which Ellen Harmon White led contemporaries out of post-Disappointment confusion and despair?

1. Her first vision (December 1844) corrected the error held by those who had not repudiated their 1844 message and experience: the future was open, not closed, implying that a great work was yet to be done before Jesus returned.

2. Her February 1845 vision, only months after October 22, 1844, focused on what happened on that date: a great and final phase of Christ's mediatorial ministry had begun, resulting in further divisions among Millerites. Although this vision does not refer specifically to the shut door, one should recognize that for the "careless multitude" to be "in perfect darkness" does not necessarily mean that probation had closed for them. Further, "deceived" people could yet be "undeceived" by hearing truth in clear tones; for them, probation had not closed. Believers had a work to do.

3. Her August 1845 vision emphasized that Christ's return was not imminent: His return depended on certain events yet to take place, one further indication that there was much work to be done before probation would close.

4. Her April 1847 vision linked the seventh-day Sabbath with the sanctuary doctrine that she had opened up in her second vision: those two Biblical doctrines melded would provide the basis for the last-day urgency in the three messages of Revelation 14. A worldwide work was now beginning to stretch Sabbatarian Adventist minds.

5. Her letter to Eli Curtis (April 21, 1847) emphasized the two resurrections with the intervening 1000-year period. Here was the

first time (as far as we know) that Ellen White mentioned the shut door in her writings, though we can assume she had these concepts much earlier. She made plain that she used the term "shut door" as a symbolic reference to Christ's closing ministry in the Most Holy Place, begun on October 22, 1844. Thus, the code word "shut door" meant not only confidence in the validity of the 1844 message and experience, but also confidence in what Jesus is now doing, preparatory to His second coming.

6. Her fifth vision (November 1848) flung the door open to the vast, worldwide evangelical responsibilities resting on those with the "present truth" of the Sabbath-Sanctuary-Three Angels' Messages linkage.

7. Her Sealing vision (January 1849) further enlarged the global responsibilities of this small Adventist group by connecting the holding of the winds (Rev. 7) with the sealing work (and thus the close of probation). Here Ellen White unfolded the logic that the winds are being held, subject to the progress of the sealing work, thus recognizing the contingency of the second coming.

8. Her Open-Door vision (March 1849) linked even tighter the "shut door" with the sanctuary and Sabbath doctrines. She put into perspective (what then seemed highly unlikely) the last-day significance of modern spiritualism and hypnotism.

9. Her article in *Present Truth* (September 1849) emphasized the close correlation with the Biblical teaching that God's grace is sufficient to make His people overcomers, that their overcoming had much to do with their characters being fixed and thus the close of their probation. She further pictured a world of people "starving" for "present truth."

Each successive vision unfolded the truths already planted. Like steel beams of a building under construction, daily unfolding the architect's drawings, each vision added to the other, providing a clearer theological foundation for their soon-to-be grasped, expanding world message and mission.

Sometimes, to Ellen White's contemporaries, those steel beams formed a shape that wasn't expected, although altogether foreseen by the Architect. For example, she opposed the Shut-door Millerites by rejecting their "spiritual" second coming in favor of a literal Second Advent. By redirecting the eyes of the believers toward the heavenly sanctuary and Christ's work as High Priest in the Most Holy Place, she placed the believers in a totally different relationship to God's plan for this earth than seen heretofore. Against Joseph Turner's notion that Jesus had already been crowned King (a belief shared for a while by James White and Joseph Bates), Ellen White focused on Jesus as High Priest *who had not yet received His kingdom.*

It would have been too much to ask, then and now, to expect that Ellen White fully understood all the implications of her earliest visions. For her, it must have been a lonely venture with relatively few even welcoming her, never mind accepting her dramatically new concepts. Very few people were even aware of her first visions before 1846![1]

But Ellen Harmon-White pressed on. The shut/open door imagery turned the Adventist gaze upward and forward: greater events were yet to take place, greater than even the overwhelming impact of the 1844 message! Powerful doctrine? Yes! But Ellen White's fresh look into the heavens was also psychologically pivotal: although gratified that the Midnight Cry was God's light behind them lighting up the path ahead, they now were to turn their energies into the opening future as they cooperated with God's call in preparing believers for the "sealing work."

Whatever changes in belief and attitudes that were to come *anywhere* in the direction Seventh- day Adventists would eventually go, would be in response to Ellen White's relentless ministry to those relatively few who welcomed her. And the only places where she was even welcome were the shut-door believers, most of whom were either well into fanaticism or well into confusion and dismal discouragement. Without the vision-messages of Ellen White, no nucleus would have developed to even think in the direction of the distinctive message of the Seventh-day Adventist Church.

Footnote

1. Her first vision (December 1844) and the New Earth vision (December, 1845) were not published until in the *Day-Star,* January 24, 1846, then in "Little Remnant Scattered Abroad," April 6, 1846, and then in *A Word to the "Little Flock,"* May 30, 1847. Her Bridegroom vision was first published in the *Day-Star,* March 14, 1846.

Appendix J

Response to Deletion of "Wicked World"

When Ellen White's initial summary of her first vision (December 1844) was printed in a *Review and Herald* Extra, July 21, 1851, the following sentence was omitted: "It was just as impossible for them to get on the path again and go the City, as all the wicked world which God had rejected." Critics raise three questions: (1) What did Ellen White mean by "wicked world"? (2) Why was this sentence deleted in later printings, including page 15 in *Early Writings* (1882)? (3) Does not this deletion/suppression show that Ellen White tried to hide her "mistaken belief" of the 1840s?

Understanding what an author meant is usually discovered by considering the immediate context, the purpose of the document, and any later explanations. The disputed sentence first appeared in a letter that Ellen White wrote to the editor of *Day-Star* on December 20, 1845, about one year after receiving the vision she is describing in this letter. This letter was printed in the January 24, 1846, issue of *Day-Star.* It was reprinted in the broadside, *To the Little Remnant Scattered Abroad,* April 6, 1846, and later in *A Word to the "Little Flock"* May 30, 1847.

However, in the fourth appearance of this vision-message[1] the disputed sentence was omitted. In her brief introduction to this reprinted material, Ellen White wrote: "Here I will give the view that was first published in 1846. In this view I saw only a very few of the events of the future. More recent views have been more full. I shall therefore leave out a portion and prevent repetition."

In this statement Ellen White recalled for her colleagues that she had been led by God, step by step, for the past six years since December 1844—that the broad outline of her first vision had been in the process of being filled in by subsequent visions. With this formal reprinting of the Midnight Cry vision, Ellen White assumed the author's responsibility for making sure that her thoughts would be clearly understood. She edited out some repetition and one sentence that could be misunderstood. As any serious author would, she wanted to remove the possibility of misunderstanding.

Looking back from her vantage point in 1851, she realized that her young, inexperienced pen of December 20, 1845, did not express well what was only beginning to break through to her own mind at that time. In this first letter she tried to summarize in a few words a vision that took two hours to relate orally! Furthermore, *this first vision corrected her own thoughts.*[2] That is, she now saw that *probation's door had not shut on everybody* on October 22.

Those Millerites who accepted Ellen Harmon's explanation of her first vision now focused on the future, not only on the past. They began to think through the implications of that "straight and narrow path"[3] on which believers were yet to travel. Some of those shut-door travelers in 1844/45 would yet step off that path, and fall into the group below, characterized as those who had previously rejected the Midnight Cry message. This view, new to all, opened a slight crack in the door that all Millerites had proclaimed to be shut in 1844—a position held by most at the beginning of 1845.

A few months later, in February, 1845, Ellen Harmon indicated that the "careless multitude," though in "perfect darkness," were held by Satan's deceptions and that Satan was doing his best to "deceive God's children." Deceived people could be undeceived by seeing clearer light even as those with clear light could be deceived away from the truth.

Though not a contemporary source document in 1883, Ellen White wrote an extended reply to critics who charged that she had tried to suppress heretical teachings found in her first vision.[4] Part of her answer follows: "It is claimed that these expressions prove the shut door doctrine, and that this is the reason of their omission in later editions. But in fact they teach only that which has been and is still held by us as a people, as I shall show."

[In that reply she then developed the shut-door principle reflected in the Bible story.] In referring particularly to her first vision, she continued: "Those who did not see the light, had not the guilt of its rejection. It was only the class who had despised the light from heaven that the Spirit of God could not reach. And this class included, as I have stated, both those who refused to accept the message when it was presented to them, and also those who, having received it, afterward renounced their faith. . . . These two classes are brought to view in the vision—those who declared the light which they had followed a delusion, and the wicked of the world who, having rejected the light, had been rejected of God. No reference is made to those who had not seen the light, and therefore were not guilty of its rejection."

Obviously, the author's explanation in 1883 was *what she remembered to be the facts in 1844.* Critics may accuse her of a faulty memory but the facts are that *her memory does not conflict with the historical record.* Her explanation in 1883 faithfully reflected the unfolding of the seeds of truth inherent in the soil of her first visions. The fruit of later years is not in conflict with the terse, summarizing outline of a vision that first appeared as a short letter that was never meant to be published.[5] If Ellen White had known that her brief letter to Enoch Jacobs would be published and become a matter of great historical focus as time went by, she would have pondered how her words could be made so clear that they would not be misunderstood. But this short letter from a sick 18-year-old was not meant to be a carefully structured theological exposition. The teenager's letter summarized the central point of her vision: (a) the 1844 message and experience was valid and significant, (b) God had been in it, and He would lead the believers into the future, wherein their labors would now be devoted.

Ellen White could have been more precise in the description of her first vision, but Biblical writers also used hyperbole to emphasize their points. Note Genesis 6:12: "So God looked upon the earth, and indeed it was corrupt; for all flesh had corrupted their way on the earth." Not *all* flesh, for think of Noah and his family. Psalm 58:3: "Evil men go wrong all their lives; they tell lies from the day they are born." The *hyperbole* is obvious and the point is clear. "It will be more tolerable for Tyre and Sidon in the day of judgment, than for you. And you, Capernaum, who are exalted to heaven, will be brought down to Hades." *No one believes that Jesus meant that everyone in these cities was doomed, but the point is clear.* Many other examples exist throughout the Bible.

Young Ellen, overwhelmed, awed, and burdened with the divine assignment, began the journey on that December morning, 1844, that would turn the eyes of the faithful from the past to the future. She obviously did not understand fully where that road would lead her when she related her first vision. But even though she was confused by the Disappointment, that first vision opened the door of hope a crack as she saw a glimpse of the future. Not many weeks would go by before she would be further enlightened as to her duty to those who needed to hear the light that had changed her thinking and opened up the future for her.

In December 1845, what Ellen Harmon meant by the "wicked world" was different from what most others around her meant, including James White and Joseph Bates. When she wrote to Enoch Jacobs on December 20, 1845, she had already had the Bridegroom vision (February 1845) at Exeter, Maine. This second vision had helped her to further understand the grand salvation event of October 22. Ellen White saw that not everyone involved in the Millerite movement had fully settled the matter until after October 22. Nowhere in this vision does she relate specifically to the shut door.[6]

Here again we see Ellen White applying the principle of rejection, a principle that she may not have even understood to its fullest extent at that time.[7] But it does resonate with the statement of Marion C. Stowell who was in Paris, Maine, in the summer of 1845, *five or six months before* Ellen White wrote her first letter to the *Day-Star*: "During Miss Harmon's visit . . . I stated to her the particulars of a dear friend of mine whose father had prevented her attending our meetings; consequently she had not rejected light. She [Ellen Harmon] smilingly said, 'God never has shown me that there is no salvation for such persons. It is only those who have had the light of truth presented to them and knowingly rejected it.' Miss Harmon's reply coincided with my idea of a shut door, and in justice no other could be derived from it."[8]

For Ellen Harmon White, the door of mercy was not shut to those who had not understood clearly the Midnight Cry messages.

Footnotes

1. *Review and Herald*, Extra, July 21, 1851.
2. See p. 503.
3. Matt. 7:14, KJV. Printers misprinted "strait" (meaning "difficult") as "straight." "Because narrow is the gate

and difficult is the way which leads to life, and there are few who find it" (Matt. 7:14, NKJV).

4. *Selected Messages,* book 1, pp. 62, 63.
5. In her second published letter to Enoch Jacobs, March 14, 1846, she wrote: "My vision which you published in the *Day-Star* was written under a deep sense of duty, to you, not expecting you would publish it. Had I for once thought it was to be spread before the many readers of your paper, I should have been more particular and stated some things which I left out."
6. *Early Writings,* pp. 55, 56.
7. *Ibid.*
8. *Review and Herald,* April 7, 1885.

Appendix K

Why Ellen White Seemed to Reach Out Only to Shut-door Advocates

The immediate challenge for Ellen White after her first two major visions (December 1844 and February 1845) was to find an audience. *But who would listen to her?* Before six months elapsed after October 22, most Millerites had repudiated their time calculations that focused on that date—thus renouncing any validity to October 22, 1844. Further, they rejected all appeals to find significance in that day of great disappointment. Those who maintained the significance of October 22 were essentially the Shut-door Millerites. In addition to rejecting that viewpoint regarding October 22, the majority of the Millerites scorned the fanaticism of some Shut-door Millerites, including any activity generated by the several "prophetesses" among them.[1]

Thus it was to the Shut-door Millerites that young Ellen Harmon, the timid, eighty-pound, frail teenager, went on her first "missionary" journey—because they were the only Millerites who would listen to her. Her challenge was to break new ground for the Shut-door Millerites without violating their core conviction regarding the validity of Daniel's 2300-year prophecy ending on October 22, 1844.

Before Ellen Harmon's messages reached the Shut-door Millerites, *two notions were inseparable:* for Shut-door Millerites, the validity of the "shut door" (Matthew 25:10 or Luke 13:25), assumed and required the notion that probation had closed for the world on October 22. After young Ellen's visions, she retained the term "shut door" as "code words" for "validity" of the Midnight Cry, *but now with an added meaning*; instead of looking back only, she urged believers to look to the future for the significance of what happened in the heavenly sanctuary on October 22, 1844.

This contemporary religious "map" explains why Ellen Harmon went first to the Shut-door Millerites, such as those meetings in Exeter and Atkinson, Maine—groups where Israel Dammon was one of the leaders.[2] These groups welcomed her because of their mutually shared confidence in the validity of their Midnight Cry message and experience. What they soon learned was that Ellen White was trying to lead them away from "their" interpretation of the shut door to a "larger" understanding of the shut door; that is, while holding on to the validity of the Midnight Cry, they now must turn toward the opening future and accept God's unfolding truth regarding the whole truth of the Midnight Cry message and experience.

This understanding of the Millerite world of 1845 explains why the records of the period (scanty at best) seem to indicate that Ellen White dedicated her time to bringing good news only to shut-door advocates and their children. Who else would have listened to her?

This understanding also explains why only a few responded to her new direction. She had opened a view of the future that involved further commitments and a definite break with all Millerites, including Shut-door Millerites. If the latter agreed with Ellen White, they could no longer rest in the confidence that probation had "closed" favorably for them on October 22. No longer could they say, "Jesus has come to us spiritually," or "We are already saved!" First of all, many of them (the "no-work" group) would have to get a job and support their families, rather than continue to live off the alms of others. Some, of course, did respond and join the growing, vision-directed band.

To put Ellen Harmon White's personal challenge in focus we must try to imagine how enormously difficult it must have been even to get a hearing. She and her few supporters saw the doors shut to her messages when she declared the validity and significance of

October 22, 1844, *in terms of the sanctuary doctrine:* (1) they received the ridicule of the "wicked world" that had rejected the Millerites prior to October 22; (2) they received the scorn of the majority of those Millerites who repudiated the significance of the October 22 date; (3) they received the rejection of the extreme shut-door advocates because the sanctuary doctrine forced them to realize that the Advent was "near" but not "imminent"; (4) furthermore, all groups rejected Ellen Harmon because of the negative connotations concerning "visions," especially from an eighty-pound, emaciated, teenage girl. For most people, to claim the prophetic gift was the same as announcing some new foolishness. All this added up to a very unfavorable environment to launch a worldwide movement with last-day messages to truth-seeking men and women.

Something similar had happened in the beginning of the Christian church.[3] When Jesus sent forth His disciples, He sent them first to "the lost sheep of the house of Israel" (Matt. 10:6).[4] Why? For at least three reasons: (1) the disciples needed time to formulate their message; (2) the Jews would be the most logical people to talk to first; (3) and the disciples did not want to offend them by showing favor to "contemptible" Gentiles.

Given the circumstances facing Millerite Adventists after October 22, 1844—scorn, ridicule, disappointment, grave doubt regarding Biblical interpretation—time was needed to move from confusion and embarrassment to an understanding of "what happened." It would take time for those early Seventh-day Adventist pioneers to not only find a new Biblical base but to grasp its authenticity and distinctiveness—even as the post-resurrection disciples needed time.

Surely the post-resurrection disciples, in spite of their enthusiasm, wondered who would listen to them. For all that others knew, they were now worshiping a dead Teacher. How ridiculous, it seemed! Any talk of a resurrection of their Master would seem like a face-saving, forlorn exercise in futility! Who would believe them? For the disciples, it was not only reluctance to share their new insights; common sense dictated that they must go where people would be most apt to listen. Also, it would take time to formulate not only their message but their evangelistic approach.

How similar was the post-October 22, 1844 experience for disappointed Millerites! Little or no evidence exists, some point out, that Ellen White reached out to anyone outside their Shut-door Millerite circle. Neither is there any evidence that Ellen White *refused* to share her vision-messages with anybody who might be interested—regardless of that person's spiritual condition on October 22, 1844. How many outside this small circle would have listened to a sick, unschooled teenager proclaim in her early visions a totally new Biblical interpretation of what happened on October 22, especially when her message sounded like (to those working with the presupposition that Jesus completed the atonement on the cross without any further phases related to the Most Holy Place in heaven) "the most colossal, psychological, face-saving phenomenon in religious history"?[5]

But in a few short years, the vision-messages of Ellen White established a coherent, though new, theological grasp of salvation history, clear enough for her and her colleagues to speak convincingly to an increasing number of wary believers who did not want to go through another Disappointment.

Footnotes

1. Knight, *Millennial Fever,* p. 256.
2. See p. 474.
3. Similarities exist between the rise of Seventh-day Adventists and the launching of the early Christian church, including an enormous disappointment, a renewed search of the Scriptures to determine the meaning of the disappointment, and the guiding of the young group by prophetic ministry.
4. See Nichol, *Critics,* pp. 235, 236.
5. Donald Gray Barnhouse, "Are Seventh-day Adventists Christians?" *Eternity,* Sept. 1956.

Appendix L

Chief Charges Against Ellen White Regarding the Shut-door Issue and the Responses Through the Years

1. In 1862 W. H. Ball wrote to James White regarding what he thought was a problem in Ellen White's assertion that "the time for the salvation of sinners is past."[1] Ball thought that notion was unBiblical, to which Uriah Smith

responded in the *Review and Herald.*[2]

2. Elders Snook and Brinkerhoff, after defecting, charged in 1866[3] that Ellen White taught: that probation for sinners ended in 1844, that "conversions made since 1844 were all spurious," that she suppressed passages no longer held by the church, etc. Uriah Smith responded with editorials in the church paper between June 12 and July 31, 1866, and dealt with thirty-nine objections.[4]

3. In 1868 James White, in *Life Incidents,* admitted that early believers almost invariably assumed that "probation for sinners had closed." They moved from this extreme closed-door position by either (1) repudiating their confidence in 1844 or (2) following their new understanding in the sanctuary truth. Thus, when the sanctuary truth unfolded, many now realized that Christ as High Priest meant that mercy for sinners was still available.[5]

4. H. E. Carver, in 1870 (after joining Snook and Brinkerhoff's Marion Party), wrote *Mrs. E. G. White's Claims to Divine Inspiration Examined.*[6] In that book he recalled an 1865 conversation with James White and J. N. Loughborough. This conversation was remembered differently by Carver and Loughborough. Carver contended that early Adventists, including Ellen White, were involved in the "fanaticism of the shut door . . . in its extremest sense."

Carver remembered James White to have said: "Brother Carver, I will make an admission to you I would not make to a sharp opponent. Considering her youthfulness at the time, and her faith in the shut-door doctrine, and her association with those of the same faith, it should not be considered singular if these things should give a coloring to the vision not warranted by what she really saw."[7]

Loughborough recalled, in a letter to Uriah Smith,[8] that James White said: "'Brother Carver, I will make an admission to you, which, of course, I would not make in public to a sharp opponent. She did believe it. And so, as you know, did nearly all the Advent people. In her visions, she had views of an open as well as a shut door; and she did not at first distinctly understand what this open door meant. Many brethren opposed her views, because she told them there was an open door.

"After speaking of the vision in which mention is made of the shut door, given at Exeter, Maine, which vision, at this point, was the topic of conversation, Bro. White said, 'Considering her youthfulness, and her belief in the shut door, and the views of the Advent people, it would not have been considered very strange, if her vision had received a coloring, in writing it out.' I did not understand Bro. White, for a moment, to convey the idea that her views colored the vision, but that they did not; and that, for this reason: we had, in the same vision, what she saw about the open door, notwithstanding her vision of the open door was contrary to the faith of the Advent people at that time, and contrary to her own faith, before she had the vision.

"Still further, Bro. White went on to show that it was the visions that led them out of the extreme view of the shut door. Immediately after this vision, they labored for some who had made no profession before 1844, which was directly contrary to the practice of those who held the extreme view on the shut door. This vision was repeated at Oswego, N.Y., just before it was published in Saratoga; but instead of leading them to cease to labor for the unconverted, it led them to labor for those who are now Bro. and Sr. Patch of Minnesota.

"And I will here state, that, so far as I can learn from those who were living where this vision was given, instead of its leading them to the extreme shut-door view, it had the opposite effect, to lead those who received it, out of it."

Elder White's wording, as quoted by Carver, seems to contradict his own statement in "A Word to the 'Little Flock'"[9] when he forthrightly disagreed with the view that Ellen's "sentiments, in the main, are obtained from previous teaching, or study." Then James went on to show two incidents where Ellen Harmon's visions either corrected or presented views that were "entirely new to us, as well as herself."

In this conversation James White linked Ellen Harmon with the shut-door teaching as understood by all Shut-door Millerites that young Ellen shared until her first two visions.[10] In *Life Incidents,* 1868, he wrote: "That the door was shut. The clear light from the heavenly sanctuary that a door, or ministration, was opened at the close of the 2300 days, while another was closed at that time, had not yet been seen. And in the absence of light in reference to the shut and open door of the heavenly sanctuary, the reader can hardly see how those who held fast their Advent experience, as illustrated by the parable of the ten virgins, could fail to come to the conclusion that probation for sinners had closed.

"But light on the subject soon came, and then it was seen that although Christ closed one ministration at the termination of the 2300 days, He had opened another in the most holy place, and still presented His blood before the Father for sinners. . . . Was the door of mercy closed? This is an unscriptural expression, but, if I may be allowed to use it, may I not say that in the fullest sense of the expression the door of mercy was opened on the tenth day of the seventh month, 1844?"[11]

5. I. C. Wellcome, an Open-door Adventist and early chronicler for the Advent Christian denomination, wrote, in 1874, that the early Ellen White reflected the shut-door teachings that prevailed at the time of her first visions. However, he wrote that she changed her views as time passed, suppressing those earlier statements that she no longer believed.[12]

6. Miles Grant, also an Advent Christian spokesman and editor of *World's Crisis*, published in 1874 certain editorials that were expanded in his *The True Sabbath: Which Day Shall We Keep?*[13] Grant, leaning heavily on Carver's work, added a number of "witnesses" who supported the charge that Ellen White taught that no genuine conversions were made after 1844. This allegation is discussed in Appendix M.

7. Ellen White's long letter to J. N. Loughborough, 1874, was prompted by Grant's book. She responded: "I hereby testify in the fear of God that the charges of Miles Grant, of Mrs. Burdick, and others published in the *Crisis* are not true. The statements in reference to my course in forty-four are false. With my brethren and sisters, after the time passed in forty-four I did believe no more sinners would be converted. But I never had a vision that no more sinners would be converted. And am clear and free to state no one has ever heard me say or has read from my pen statements which will justify them in the charges they have made against me upon this point.

"It was on my first journey east to relate my visions that the precious light in regard to the heavenly sanctuary was opened before me and I was shown the open and shut door. We believed that the Lord was soon to come in the clouds of heaven. I was shown that there was a great work to be done in the world for those who had not had the light and rejected it. Our brethren could not understand this with our faith in the immediate appearing of Christ. Some accused me of saying that my Lord delayeth His coming, especially the fanatical ones. I saw that in '44 God had opened a door and no man could shut it, and shut a door and no man could open it. Those who rejected the light which was brought to the world by the message of the second angel went into darkness, and how great was that darkness.

"I never have stated or written that the world was doomed or damned. I never have under any circumstances used this language to anyone, however sinful. I have ever had messages of reproof for those who used these harsh expressions."[14]

8. G. I. Butler, president of the General Conference, urged the publication of *Early Writings* (1882) and wrote that it contained "the very first of the published writings of Sister White"; that it contained "all she has written for publication."[15] Butler was correct in that all known publications of the 1840s were included. He was not aware that *Christian Experience and Views* (1851), which was reprinted in *Early Writings*, did not include every statement found in earlier printings of the visions. (See Appendix J for a discussion of the alleged suppression, especially as it relates to the preface to *Early Writings.)*

9. Shortly after the 1882 appearance of *Early Writings,* A. C. Long reacted, in 1883, with *A Comparison of the Early Writings of Mrs. White With Later Publications.*[16] Long, apparently, was the first to show the missing sentences, comparing *Early Writings* and *Christian Experience and Views,* with the original documents. He believed that the deletions proved that Ellen White believed, after her first visions, that probation had closed, the door had shut, on October 22, 1844.

10. In response to Long, G. I. Butler and J. H. Waggoner wrote a 16-page Supplement to the *Review and Herald* of Aug. 14, 1883. One of their "most conclusive proofs"[17] was the testimony of Marion C. Stowell in a letter written on August 17, 1875: "During Miss Harmon's visit to Paris, Maine, in the summer of 1845, I stated to her the particulars of a dear friend of mine whose father had prevented her

attending our meetings; consequently she had not rejected light. She smilingly said, *'God never has shown me that there is no salvation for such persons. It is only those who have had the light of truth presented to them and knowingly rejected it.'* Miss Harmon's reply coincided with my idea of a shut door, and in justice no other could be derived from it." (Emphasis supplied.)

11. In 1883 Ellen White also responded to Long's charges: "For a time after the disappointment in 1844, I did hold, in common with the advent body, that the door of mercy was then forever closed to the world. *This position was taken before my first vision was given me. It was the light given me of God that corrected our error,* and enabled us to see the true position. I am still a believer in the shut-door theory, but not in the sense in which we at first employed the term or in which it is employed by my opponents.

"There was a shut door in Noah's day. . . . There was a shut door in the days of Abraham. . . . in Christ's day. . . .

"I was shown in vision, and I still believe, that there was a shut door in 1844. All who saw the light of the first and second angels' messages and rejected that light, were left in darkness. And those who accepted it and received the Holy Spirit which attended the proclamation of the message from heaven, and who afterward renounced their faith and pronounced their experience a delusion, thereby rejected the Spirit of God, and it no longer pleaded with them.

"Those who did not see the light, had not the guilt of its rejection. It was only the class who had despised the light from heaven that the Spirit of God could not reach. And this class included, as I have stated, both those who refused to accept the message when it was presented to them, and also those who, having received it, afterward renounced their faith. These might have a form of godliness, and profess to be followers of Christ; but having no living connection with God, they would be taken captive by the delusions of Satan. These *two classes* are brought to *view in the vision*—those who declared the light which they had followed a delusion, and the wicked of the world who, having rejected the light, had been rejected of God. No reference is made to those who had not seen the light, and therefore were not guilty of its rejection."[18]

12. In 1884, Ellen White wrote the fourth volume of *Spirit of Prophecy,* entitling a chapter, "An Open and a Shut Door,"[19] in which she again described the transition from the original shut-door-of-mercy concept to the one that places the shut door in the setting of the heavenly sanctuary; this chapter in 1888 was enlarged for *The Great Controversy,* pages 429-432.

13. Between February and April, 1885, G. I. Butler wrote ten articles for the *Review and Herald*, describing the events of the 1840s. He reviewed the shut-door charges, noting that they "have been repeated over and over, and some souls have been deceived and thrown into darkness thereby.

"For the sake of helping such and saving others from the same fate, we propose to sift these charges thoroughly and see what truth there is in them. We shall admit all the truth they contain, and expose the error. If this is God's truth, we can afford to be fair. If it will not bear the test of careful examination, and a full knowledge of the facts, the quicker those engaged in it hear the truth the better for them. . . .

"Nothing can ever be really gained by concealing any fact or by deception. . . . In saying this, however, we wish it to be understood that we have no idea that there was anything connected with the rise of this message which anyone should wish to conceal. . . ."[20]

Butler then reviewed the facts: (1) In common with most Millerites, most early Sabbatarian Adventists believed that their work for the world was finished; (2) Within six months the larger part of the Millerites had repudiated the 1844 movement as a mistake; (3) Those who were patient found light in the sanctuary truths; (4) Early Sabbath keeping Adventists had "much to say about a 'shut door' because they thus recognized the past movement as genuine in distinction from those Adventists who had given it up"; that those who repudiated the 1844 movement were "rejected of God." Up to 1851, they had much to say because "up to that time their efforts to proselyte were largely confined to those who had believed the advent doctrine in 1844; (5) "But [Sabbatarian Adventists] came to this understanding [grasping a world-wide work] gradually"; (6) "But their belief in the 'shut door doctrine' was *not* such as to forbid the salvation of those who had not rejected the first message, or those who had come to years of accountability since the passing of the time, for plenty of instances can be found where they worked for the salvation of such persons; (7) He produced twenty-one witnesses who lived through the 1840s and who verified that Ellen White never taught that probation had closed for everyone in 1844; (8) "That the vision of Mrs. E. G. White so often quoted is in perfect harmony with these positions"; (9) "Finally, that the Scriptures themselves are in perfect harmony with such a kind of shut door as this, and indeed, that various texts really teach the same thing."

Butler then injected his father's experience who embraced the "present truth" of the Sabbatarian Adventists in 1850 when the son was 16 years of age. After asking, "What kind of shut door did he believe in?" Butler quoted from a letter his father had written to the Whites. The letter appeared in the *Review and Herald,* January 1851: "Since I have been converted to the *shut door* and seventh-day Sabbath, I have been out in this town and some of the neighboring towns . . . to try to get off some of the prejudice from other minds which I so deeply felt on my own. . . . I have learned from conversation with others as well as from my past experience that the *shut door* has been *the great shoal* on which the Adventists [Millerites] have run their ship and foundered."

Butler described how his father, in referring to Millerites generally, spoke of "their contradictory positions on the messages, midnight cry, etc.," and their misunderstanding regarding the shut door: "'You see how all these have shunned the door. . . . They supposed the shut door would exclude from every degree of the Spirit of God all the unconverted having had *light* or *no* light, *young or old.* I think if this class could have the true shut door and the third angel's message set before them, some of them would see the true line of prophecy and rejoice again in the light. I have been striving to look up those who have not given up our past experience in these messages, and trying to show them what the sanctuary is and what the shut door is; that the sanctuary spoken of in Dan. 8:14 is being cleansed.'"

Then Butler said: "That father, in his view of the shut door, was at this time in perfect accordance with Brother and Sister White, we know by personal knowledge."[21]

14. D. M. Canright, after repeated troubles and reconciliations, made his final break with the church in 1887. He brought together all the major accusations of previous critics, including Snook, Brinkerhoff, Carver, Wellcome, Grant, and Long. He charged that Ellen White taught the shut door "in its very worst form." Canright's book, *Seventh-day Adventism Renounced After an Experience of Twenty-eight Years by a Prominent Minister and Writer of That Faith,*[22] was the most massive attack on the credibility of Ellen White in the nineteenth century, and probably was the strongest influence on later critics.

15. In 1887 Uriah Smith, the first to respond to Canright, listed Canright's charges that had been repeated for years, and then presented his denials.[23]

16. In a *Review* Extra, November 22, 1887, Uriah Smith and G. I. Butler again responded to Canright's assertions.

17. In 1905 J. N. Loughborough's revised edition of *Rise and Progress of Seventh-day Adventists* (1892) was published but retitled, *The Great Second Advent Movement.*[24] In this revised edition Loughborough added a chapter called, "The Shut Door." He reviewed again what he understood to be the facts of the 1840s, emphasizing that no Sabbatarian Adventists, including Ellen White, believed "that there was no more mercy for sinners." He too had his list of twenty-one witnesses supporting his positions.

18. D. M. Canright, in 1919, published his *Life of Mrs. E. G. White: Seventh-day Adventist Prophet: Her False Claims Refuted,* an extremely polemic book. His chapter on the shut-door issue occupied about one-fourth of the book.[25]

19. In 1925 M. E. Olsen's *A History of the Origin and Progress of Seventh-day Adventists* was published, but his treatment of the shut-door question was limited.[26]

20. W. A. Spicer recognized that "critics can find phrases to stumble over"; that early Adventist pioneers, at first, had limited, mistaken notions about their mission field; that Ellen White led the way in thinking through a clear message and mission, but he rejected the "ridiculous charge" that they believed that sinners could not be converted after 1844.[27]

21. A few years later, another former General Conference president, A. G. Daniells,

took a slightly different approach, contending that the pioneers did believe that probation had closed in 1844; even Ellen White "shared personally this view in common with those with whom she associated."[28] Then Daniells made an interesting distinction between Ellen White's "personal belief" and the "revelations" she received—that is, she never had a vision that probation had closed. Daniells believed that Mrs. White's visions implied a "clear scriptural position" which led the way for the pioneers. Two years later, when her 1874 letter to Loughborough was found in the White Estate files during the indexing of her thousands of letters, Daniells believed his positions were reaffirmed.[29]

22. However, W. A. Spicer was troubled, believing that Daniells's position gave away too much to the critics. He wrote another manuscript that was placed in both the General Conference files and Ellen G. White Estate files. One of his conclusions was that "our pioneers set forth the open door for sinners, all the way from 1844."[30]

23. During the 1930s the shut-door question became more than a North American issue. European leader L. R. Conradi left denominational leadership and, in the German language, wrote a strong polemic against the claims of Ellen White. His argument was basically a resurrection of Canright's charges.[31]

24. Also during the 1930s, an Australian leader, W. W. Fletcher, defected largely over his contention that nothing significant happened in 1844. His book, *The Reasons For My Faith,* focused on his view of the atonement and the related shut-door problem which he believed to be "the darkest page in our denominational history."[32]

25. In 1949 A. W. Spalding asserted that "Ellen Harmon's visions corrected those who maintained" that "there was no mercy for sinners" after 1844. But he clouded his position by including Ellen White with Joseph Bates and James White in his statement that "these three maintained the doctrine [shut-door] longer than most, until increasing light caused them to abandon it."[33]

26. F. D. Nichol was, perhaps, the most vigorous defender of Ellen White's legitimacy, especially in his 1951 book, *Ellen G. White and Her Critics.*[34] Devoting ninety-one pages to the shut-door issue, he responded to most of the charges that have been made since the middle 1860s. He amassed evidence that Ellen White did not have a vision that taught that probation had closed in 1844. Critics contend that Nichol lifted certain quotations out of their immediate context to serve his purpose. On balance, he seems to have mediated between the positions represented by Daniells and Spicer.

27. In 1971 Ingemar Lindén's doctoral dissertation, *Biblicism, Apokalyptik, Utopi,*[35] appeared with an updated version of previous criticism, this time with more historical documents available for scrutiny. In 1978, his *The Last Trump*[36] was published, followed by his *1844 and the Shut Door Problem*[37] in 1982. He charged church leaders with a coverup of the shut-door issue, and considered Nichol's *Critics* an inadequate treatment of the issue. Although he strongly accused denominational spokesmen of speaking "from preconceived viewpoints," many believe that Lindén's treatment of the shut-door issue is an example of presuppositions driving one's conclusions.[38]

28. In 1976 R. L. Numbers leaned heavily on Lindén's analysis and certain novel interpretations.[39]

29. In 1977 Gerard Damsteegt published his exhaustive review of the 1840s-1870s in *Foundations of the Seventh-day Adventist Message and Mission.*[40] Among other themes, Damsteegt focused on the shut-door issue, recognizing its connection with other core beliefs of Seventh-day Adventists. This book notes the seminal contribution of Ellen White's visions, the gradual transition in the meaning of the "shut door," and the clear evidence that Ellen White led the way in opening the future for those who understood the meaning of October 22, 1844.

30. It could be argued that with the publications of Lindén and Damsteegt, the clearest expressions of both the critic and the affirmer have been made. The arguments of Lindén and Damsteegt are mutually exclusive. Perhaps we have in these two scholarly presentations the flowering of two basic presuppositions in conflict.

Footnotes

1. Mar. 24, 1849, Open-door Vision, in *Christian Experience and Views,* 1851, and in *Early Writings,* p. 45.
2. *Review and Herald,* Jan. 21, 1862.
3. B. F. Snook and Wm. Brinkerhoff, *The Visions of E. G.*

White, Not of God (Cedar Rapids, Iowa: Cedar Valley Times and Book and Job Print, 1866).

4. "The Visions—Objections Answered," *Review and Herald,* June 12-July 31, 1866.
5. See pp. 168-216, 264-268.
6. Marion, Iowa: Advent and Sabbath Advocate Press, 1871, pp. 11, 12, 28-45. Photocopy in Pacific Union College Library.
7. *Ibid.*, p. 11.
8. *Review and Herald,* Sept. 25, 1866.
9. *A Word to the "Little Flock,"* p. 22 (1847).
10. See pp. 503, 552, 553 for an analysis of Ellen White's growing understanding of the doctrinal seeds planted in those first two visions.
11. *Life Incidents*, pp. 204-209.
12. Isaac C. Wellcome, *History of the Second Advent Message* (Boston: Advent Christian Publication Society, 1874), p. 406.
13. Miles Grant (Boston, Mass.: Advent Christian Publications, 1874).
14. Letter 2, 1874, cited in *MR,* vol. 8, p. 229.
15. *Review and Herald,* Dec. 26, 1882.
16. Reprint from the "Advent and Sabbath Advocate," Marion, Iowa, 1883. Pacific Union College Library.
17. *Review and Herald* Supplement, Aug. 14, 1883.
18. *Selected Messages,* book 1, pp. 59-73, emphasis supplied.
19. *Spirit of Prophecy,* vol. 4 (Oakland, Calif.: Pacific Press, 1884).
20. *Review and Herald,* Mar. 17, 1885.
21. *Review and Herald,* Mar. 31, 1885.
22. Chicago: Fleming H. Revel, 1889.
23. *Review and Herald* Extra, Nov. 22, 1889.
24. Washington, D.C.: Review and Herald Publishing Association, 1935.
25. Cincinnati: The Standard Publishing Company, 1919.
26. Washington, D.C.: Review and Herald Publishing Association, 1925.
27. *Review and Herald*, March 18-April 29, 1926.
28. *Review and Herald,* Feb. 6-27, 1930.
29. *Review and Herald,* Jan. 14, 1932.
30. A statement filed with the Secretary of the White Estate Board of Trustees by W. A. Spicer, p. 5— "Facts of Record vs Tradition," DF 434-a.
31. "Ist Frau E. G. White die Prophetin der Endgemeinde," Hamburg: Buchdruckerei Kroggel, 1933.
32. Fletcher, *The Reasons for My Faith,* p. 199.
33. Spalding, *Origin and History*, vol. 1, p. 162.
34. Nichol, *Critics,* pp. 161-252.
35. S. Ingemar Lindén, *Biblicism, Apokalyptik, Utopi,* Uppsala, 1971. Doctoral dissertation.
36. Lindén, *The Last Trump* (Frankfurt am Main: Peter Lang, 1978).
37. Lindén, *1844 and the Shut Door Problem* (Uppsala: Almqvist & Wiksell International, 1982).
38. "It is undeniable that, in spite of his efforts, his [Lindén] presentation shows considerable bias himself and is, at times, marked by superficiality and gross misinterpretation. . . . Lindén's superficial treatment of documents and his tendency to misrepresent the obvious meaning of primary sources can be demonstrated on various examples. . . . Since he is undoubtedly the ablest representative of the critics of SDA on the shut-door issue, it seems fair to say that, on the whole, they have been no less biased than their opponents, the SDA apologists, sometimes even surpassing them considerably through their unfriendly polemics. And the one serious scholarly attempt by one of the critics failed to prove that a truly objective and unbiased approach supports their far-reaching claims."—Rolf J. Poehler, "Shut Door Doctrine," unpublished paper, Andrews University, pp. 61-63.
39. Numbers, *Prophetess of Health,* pp. 26, 27, 35, 215.
40. Grand Rapids, Mich., William B. Erdmans Publishing Co., 1977.

Appendix M

The July 13, 1847, Letter to Joseph Bates

Modern critics point to this letter from Ellen White to Joseph Bates as the clearest evidence supporting the view that Mrs. White believed in the same shut-door understanding that prevailed among Shut-door Millerites, including Joseph Bates.[1]

The history of this letter is fascinating. In the twentieth century it first appeared as a first-page facsimile on page 104 of the 1915 edition of *Life Sketches.* At that time its purpose was merely to add a sense of history by showing an early letter in Ellen White's handwriting and then to note that the letter specified December 1844 as the date of her first vision. The significance of the letter was heightened when it was "re-discovered" by Ingemar Lindén while doing research in the White Estate vault in the 1960s.[2]

Nineteen-year-old Ellen White was at Gorham, Maine, eight months pregnant with her first child, when she wrote this letter to Joseph Bates on July 13, 1847, in response to his request for information. Bates wanted to know if, before her February 1845 vision, she had been aware of Joseph Turner's teaching regarding the significance of October 22.[3] On that date Turner, a prominent Millerite, believed that Christ had "come" as the Bridegroom to God the Father to receive His bride, the church—and that He would soon return to the earth as the Millerites had proclaimed.[4]

Ellen White responded that she was aware that one of Turner's papers was in her parents' home but said that she had not read it.[5] During December she was "very sick" and had "no interest in reading." After the December vision that had changed her mind about the validity of the 1844 message and experience, God had made it clear to her that she was "to deliver it to the band." She shrank from this challenge.

Hearing of a meeting in her parents' home that night, she hustled herself away to find seclusion in a friend's home—only to find Joseph Turner at that home. But she said nothing to him. Why? Because she feared that she would "come out against his views, thinking he believed with the rest." What did the rest believe? That the Millerites had been in error in teaching that there was any significance in October 22.

In distress all day, Ellen Harmon returned home after the meeting was over. Early the next morning, Turner stopped by, requesting that she "should tell him all that God had shown me in vision." Turner then said that her vision-message was essentially what he had related to the group in her parents' home the evening before. This was a great relief to the reluctant teenager. Because only a few attended that meeting, Ellen was asked to relate her vision at the next meeting where approximately sixty "confessed their error, and acknowledged their 7th month experience to be the work of God."[6]

Thus, Turner and Ellen Harmon, agreeing that the events associated with October 22, 1844, involved salvation history, were now able to restore confidence to hitherto disappointed Adventists. They disagreed, however, as to *what* happened on that date. Ellen Harmon's December vision did not relate to the Bridegroom topic although Turner, at that time, did use the Bridegroom analogy to explain what happened on that memorable date. The disagreement between Ellen and Turner over what the Bridegroom analogy meant in connection with October 22 was very clear after her Bridegroom vision at Exeter, Maine, a few weeks after their December meeting.

Continuing in the Bates letter, Ellen White next turned to a few highlights of her visit to Exeter "about the middle of February, 1845." The post-Disappointment Millerites were in confusion, often despair, most everywhere.[7] The Exeter group was no exception, for young Ellen remembered that "unbelief seemed to be on every hand."

As the meeting progressed, she recognized that "a division had risen in the band on the shut door." That is, confusion existed here as elsewhere (as it was in the Portland group before she helped to settle the matter in December 1844). During the confusion of the meeting, Ellen was given her Bridegroom vision wherein she "had a view of Jesus rising from His mediatorial throne and going to the Holiest as Bridegroom to receive His kingdom."[8] In relating this vision to the Exeter group, "they all said it was entirely new to them."[9]

The result? Ellen continued: "Most of them received the vision, and were settled upon the shut door." Further, she assured Bates: "I know the light I received came from God, it was not taught me by man."

Bates, the careful thinker, following closely each line in her letter, chose to put aside his earlier thoughts about a possible "borrowing" of her material from Turner. Her memory of that period was true to the facts as he had studied them. Comparing Turner's article in *The Advent Mirror* and Ellen White's description of the vision, one finds few essential thoughts in common, even as Bates concluded.[10]

But what did Ellen White mean by saying that the Exeter group was "settled upon the shut door"? Contemporary records, though few, help us to understand what she meant when she gave that group new light.

Her first vision, December 1844, emphasized that the Shut-door Millerite Adventists were wrong in believing that the "door was shut" on *all* people on October 22, 1844. Her Bridegroom vision, February, 1845, noted that many had been kept in ignorance by Satan's deceptions. Is it not possible for people in ignorance to break out of their deceptions when clear light is properly presented? No hint of a shut door on all unbelievers was mentioned in this vision.

On April 3, 1847, Ellen White received the Halo of Glory vision which she had described to Bates in her letter of April 7, ten weeks before this letter to him on July 13, 1847. Here she focused on the Sabbath, once more enriching the understanding of the shut-door issue. Again, no hint of a shut door on unbelievers.

On the contrary, Ellen White was most emphatic: "I saw that God had children who do not see and keep the Sabbath. They had not rejected the light on it. At the commencement of the time of trouble. . . . God's chosen all saw clearly that we had the truth, and they came out and endured the persecution with us."[11]

In the fuller description of this vision,[12] as presented in *A Word to the "Little Flock,"* these words were included (coming after the paragraph ending, "God's dear waiting saints"): "And if one believed, and kept the Sabbath, and received the blessing attending it, and then gave it up, and broke the holy commandments, they would shut the gates of the Holy City against themselves, as sure as there was a God that rules in heaven above."[13]

Here Ellen White spoke explicitly regarding her concept of the shut door. The principle of rejection[14] seems to have been clear to her ever since her first vision (although she no doubt experienced a growing understanding of how it applied in all circumstances.) In 1847 she unambiguously linked the shut-door concept (the close of probation) with willful rejection of Bible truth; that is, people shut their own doors and close their own probation.

On April 21, 1847 (less than eight weeks before her letter to Bates on July 13) Ellen White wrote to Eli Curtis, a strong shut-door Adventist, noting clearly what she understood the "shut door" to mean to her: "The Lord has shown me in vision, that Jesus rose up, and shut the door, and entered the Holy of Holies, at the 7th month 1844; but Michael's standing up (Dan. 12:1) to deliver His people, is in the future."[15]

For some time Ellen White had been connecting the code word, "shut door," with the sanctuary truth which completely redefined that phrase for Shut-door Millerites—a redefinition that many refused to accept. (They preferred to believe that, in some way, those who retained their confidence in the message of 1844 were already sealed.) For Ellen White in 1847, the code word, "shut door," meant that the message of 1844 was valid and that the most significant part of that message opened the door to a fresh, unfolding understanding of Christ's change of ministry in the heavenly sanctuary. The double emphasis on validity and Christ's change of ministry (in sanctuary terms) now functioned as the two sides of the same coin.

Such was the immediate context, the contemporary understanding of the Shut-door concept that Ellen White had in mind when she penned this July 30, 1847 letter to Joseph Bates. But there is no evidence that she had any different understanding in February 1845. A fuller understanding in 1847, no doubt, but nothing in the records remotely suggests that she had changed her mind during that two-year period. No records exist that suggest that she believed that only those who retained their confidence in the 1844 message and experience could be saved, all others remaining behind the door of mercy that was supposedly shut on October 22, 1844.

What exactly Bates was thinking after he received this July 13, 1847 letter may never be known, but what Ellen White meant, in her reference to the shut door, can be determined by contemporary documents.

Footnotes

1. Douglas Hackleman, "Picking the Shut-door Lock," *Adventist Currents,* July, 1984.
2. Lindén, *The Last Trump*, pp. 94-96. William C. White had quoted from this letter in a review of his parents' early ministry, in *Review and Herald,* Mar. 14, 1935, but with no reference to its shut-door implications.
3. Because no copies of the December 1844 issue of Turner's paper, *Hope of Israel*, now exist, it is not certain when Turner first taught his Bridegroom views. Those views were presented in the January issue (only issue) of his new paper, *Advent Mirror,* co-edited with Apollos Hale.
4. Bates had noticed a similarity between Ellen White's vision and Turner's views as implied in his own handwritten notes on her July 13, 1847, letter which suggested that he was aware of Turner's viewpoint from both the *Hope of Israel* and *Advent Mirror.*
5. Which issue of *Hope of Israel* was in the Harmon home in December 1844, is not known. It could have been any one of its earlier issues. For the December issue to be in the Harmon home prior to the incident Ellen White related in the Bates letter would seem unlikely, although it may have been in her home before the February vision.

6. "When she received her first vision, Dec. 1844, she and all the band in Portland, Maine, (where her parents then resided) had given up the midnight-cry, and shut door, as being in the past. It was then that the Lord shew[ed] her in vision, the error into which she and the band in Portland had fallen. She then related her vision to the band, and about sixty confessed their error, and acknowledged their 7th month experience to be the work of God."—James White, *A Word to the "Little Flock,"* p. 22, cited in Nichol, *Critics,* p. 582 and Knight, *1844,* p. 176.
7. See p. 39.
8. This vision was first printed in *Day-Star,* Mar. 14, 1846 and reprinted in *Early Writings,* pp. 55, 56.
9. Though Turner's interpretation of the Bridegroom analogy was probably well-known to that group, Ellen Harmon's view was "entirely new." This response would indicate that she not only did not "copy" Turner's viewpoint, but that her vision-message broke new ground in opening the "door" for a fresh look into the future and their new duties.
10. We do not find in Ellen White's description anything that refers to Jesus "coming as the King of glory" in 1844, or any references which "supposes the church to be the bride," or that those "who were ready have gone in with him to the marriage, and that the door is shut."
11. *Early Writings,* p. 33.
12. Bates himself, after receiving this April 7, 1847, letter, collaborated with James White in having it placed, along with two of Ellen White's earliest visions, in *A Word to the "Little Flock,"* on May 30, 1847. Connected to this printing of the Sabbath Halo vision, Bates added this recommendation: "I do not publish the above vision thinking to add or diminish from the 'sure word of prophecy.' That will stand the test of men and wreck of worlds! . . . It is now about two years since I first saw the author, and heard her relate the substance of her visions as she has since published them in Portland (April 6, 1846). Although I could see nothing in them that militated against the Word, yet I felt alarmed and tried exceedingly, and for a long time unwilling to believe that it was anything more than what was produced by a protracted debilitated state of her body.

    "I therefore sought opportunities in presence of others, when her mind seemed freed from excitement, (out of meeting) to question, and cross-question her, and her friends which accompanied her, especially her eldest sister, to get if possible at the truth. During the number of visits she has made to New Bedford and Fairhaven since, while at our meetings, I have seen her in vision a number of times, and also in Topsham, Me., and those who were present during some of these exciting scenes know well with what interest and intensity I listened to every word, and watched every move to detect deception, or mesmeric influence. And I thank God for the opportunity I have had with others to witness these things. I can now confidently speak for myself. I believe the work is of God, and is given to comfort and strengthen his 'scattered,' 'torn,' and 'pealed people,' since the closing up of our work for the world in October, 1844. The distracted state of lo, heres! and lo, theres! since that time has exceedingly perplexed God's honest, willing people, and made it exceedingly difficult for such as were not able to expound the many conflicting texts that have been presented to their view. I confess that I have received light and instruction on many passages that I could not before clearly distinguish. I believe her [Ellen White] to be a self-sacrificing, honest, willing child of God, and saved, if at all, through her entire obedience to His will.

    "At a meeting in Fairhaven, 6th of the last month, I saw her have a similar vision, which I then wrote down. It may be said that I send this out to strengthen the argument of my late work on the Sabbath. I do in the sense above stated. Respecting that work I entertain no fears. There is no scriptural argument to move it." —Cited in Nichol, *Critics,* p. 581, and Knight, *1844,* p. 175.
13. Reproduced in Nichol, *Critics,* p. 579 and Knight, *1844,* p. 174.
14. See p. 558 for a discussion of the principle of rejection.
15. *A Word to the "Little Flock,"* p. 11, cited in Nichol, *Critics*, p. 571 and Knight, *1844,* p. 170.

Appendix N

Last Will and Testament of Ellen G. White

IN THE NAME OF GOD, AMEN.

I, Ellen G. White, (widow) a resident of Sanitarium, Napa County, California, of the age of eighty-four (84) years, and being at the date hereof of sound and disposing mind and memory, and not acting under duress, menace, fraud or undue influence of any person whomsoever, do make, publish and declare this my last will and testament, in the manner following, that is to say:

FIRST: I direct that my body shall be interred with appropriate religious services of the Seventh-day Adventist Church, without undue ceremony or ostentation.

SECOND: I desire and direct that as soon as possible, payment shall be made of the expenses of my last sickness and funeral, and in order that no property belonging to my estate shall be disposed of or sold at a sacrifice, I earnestly request all my creditors to waive and relinquish their claims against my estate and accept payment thereof under the provisions, which I am hereinafter making, for the liquidation of their claims through the handling of my properties by trustees.

THIRD: I hereby give, devise, and bequeath to my son, James Edson White, now residing at Marshall, Michigan, the sum of Three Thousand Dollars ($3,000).

FOURTH: I hereby give and bequeath to my son, William C. White, now residing at Sanitarium, California, all my right, title and interest in the copyrights and book plates in all languages of the books entitled: *The Coming King* and *Past, Present and Future*, also all manuscripts (and right to publish the same) pertaining to the following books and proposed books:

Life Sketches of Elder James White and Ellen G. White
Life Incidents of Elder James White
Spiritual Gifts, Volumes 1-4
Facts of Faith
How to Live
Appeal to Youth
Experience of Ellen G. White in Connection with the Health Reform Movement Among Seventh-day Adventists
Story of Mrs. White's European Travels
Story of Mrs. White's Australasian Travels
Mrs. White's Letters to Mothers and Children
Youth's Life of Christ
The Southern Work
Education
Christian Education
Special Testimonies on Education
Bible Sanctification

Also, my personal library, and all manuscripts, letters, diaries, and writings not otherwise herein devised.

FIFTH: I hereby give, devise, and bequeath to William C. White, Clarence C. Crisler, Charles H. Jones, Arthur G. Daniells, and Frank M. Wilcox all the real property of which I may die seized or possessed, all my live stock and farm tools, and implements, all notes and accounts due to me and also all of my right, title, and interest in the copyrights and book plates in all languages of the following publications:

Desire of Ages
Patriarchs and Prophets
The Acts of the Apostles
Great Controversy
Early Writings
Testimonies for the Church Volumes 1-9 inclusive
Gospel Workers
Christian Temperance and Bible Hygiene
Christ's Object Lessons
Ministry of Healing
Steps to Christ
Mount of Blessing
Christ Our Saviour
Testimonies for Sabbath-school Workers
Manual for Canvassers
Special Testimonies

Also, my general manuscript file and all indexes pertaining thereto; also my office furniture and office library.

Together with all and singular, the tenements, hereditaments and appurtenances thereunto belonging, or in anywise appertaining in trust nevertheless for the uses and purposes hereinafter contained.

TO HAVE AND TO HOLD, the said real and personal property until said trustees, and their successors, upon the trust to enter into and upon and take possession of the said real estate and said personal property, to collect and receive the rents, issues and profits thereof, to manage and control said real and personal property, and to rent and lease the same, or any part thereof, to sell parts or portions of said real and personal property, excepting the book copyrights, for the purpose of re-investing the same in other real or personal property to be held under the same trust, and after paying all taxes, assessments, charges and encumbrances thereon and the expenses of repairing, administering, preserving and protecting the said real property and of handling said personal property, and publishing and selling said books and manuscripts and conducting the business thereof to distribute, pay over and apply the net proceeds from the rents and profits of said real property and from the business of publishing and selling said books and property in the manner following, that is to say:

(a) To pay over to my son, James Edson White,[1] annually, during his natural life ten (10) per cent of the net proceeds of said properties for his sole use and benefit, and upon his death to Emma L. White, his wife, during her natural life should she survive him.

(b) To pay over to my son, William C. White, annually for his sole use and benefit ten (10) per cent of the net proceeds of said properties during his natural life, and upon his death, to Ethel M. White, his wife, during her natural life should she survive him.

(c) To pay over annually to William C. White, Ethel M. White and Dores E. Robinson as trustees[2] five (5) per cent of the net proceeds of the said properties to be devoted to the education of my grandchildren, great grandchildren and other worthy individuals.

(d) The said trustees shall use the remainder of said net proceeds for the following purposes:

1. For the payment of creditors with accruing interest upon the principal indebtedness to the extent to which my creditors have agreed to relinquish their claims against my estate; such payments from said net proceeds to continue until all remaining indebtedness with interest has been fully paid.

2. If the entire remainder of said net proceeds from my said properties is more than sufficient to pay my said debts, with interest, in the manner in which my creditors shall agree to receive payment of their respective claims, then my said trustees shall use the over-plus for the improvement of the books and manuscripts held in trust by them, and herein provided; for the securing and printing of new translations thereof; for the printing of compilations from my manuscripts; for general missionary work of the Seventh-day Adventist denomination; for the support of mission schools, under the Negro Department of the Seventh-day Adventist General Conference; for the support of Mission Schools for the illiterate whites in the Southern States, Provided, however, that said trustees are hereby empowered and directed to sell my said real property or so much thereof as may be necessary to pay the following sums: to my granddaughter Ella May Robinson, now residing at Sanitarium, California, the sum of Five Hundred Dollars ($500); to my granddaughter, Mabel E. Workman, now residing at Loma Linda, California, the sum of Five Hundred Dollars ($500); to my faithful friend and helper, Sara McEnterfer, now residing at Sanitarium, California, the sum of Five Hundred Dollars ($500): to May Walling, now residing at Sanitarium, California, the sum of Five Hundred Dollars ($500); and to my faithful friend and helper Clarence C. Crisler, the sum of Five Hundred Dollars ($500).[3]

SIXTH: After the death of both James Edson White and his wife, my said trustees are hereby empowered and directed to apply the amount prescribed in subdivision (a) of paragraph FIFTH toward the discharge of any legal claims against the estate of said James Edson White, and then after the full discharge of such claims, the said amount mentioned in subdivision (a) shall be applied to the maintenance of the mission school for Negroes now conducted by the Negro Department of the Seventh-day Adventist General Conference.

SEVENTH: After the death of both William C. White and his wife, my said trustees are hereby empowered and directed to pay over to their surviving children, or grandchildren, if any, the respective amounts prescribed in subdivision (b) of paragraph FIFTH of this will; and if there be no children or grandchildren of my said son, then said respective amounts shall be devoted and used for the purposes set forth in subdivision (d) of said paragraph FIFTH of this will.

EIGHTH: Upon the termination of the trusts, or any of them, created and set forth in this will, from any cause whatsoever, I give, bequeath and devise all of the real and personal property mentioned in paragraph FIFTH or so much thereof as may from any cause be released or relieved from said trust to my said son, William C. White; or if he be not living, then to his heirs at law.

NINTH: My household furniture, dishes, carpets, pictures, photographs and clothing, I give and bequeath in equal parts to my sons, James Edson White and William C. White.

TENTH: All the rest, residue and remainder of my estate, real, personal and mixed, of which I may die seized or possessed, I give, bequeath and devise to my son, William C. White.

ELEVENTH: I hereby appoint William C. White and Charles H. Jones the executors of this my last will and testament, without bonds; and my executors are hereby authorized to sell any property of my estate without order of Court, and at either public or private sale, and with or without notice as the executors may determine.

I also direct that no bond be required of

any of the trustees named or their successors.

TWELFTH: If a vacancy shall occur for any reason among said trustees, or their successors, a majority of the surviving or remaining trustees are hereby empowered and directed to fill such vacancy by the appointment of some other fit person, and in the event that the majority does not agree upon the appointment, then such vacancy shall be filled by the Executive Committee of the Seventh-day Adventist General Conference; and the new trustee or trustees, so appointed shall have the same power touching the trust premises and in the execution of the trusts, herein contained, as the original trustees named herein.

THIRTEENTH: I hereby revoke all former wills by me made,

IN WITNESS WHEREOF, I have hereunto set my hand and seal this 9th day of February, 1912.

[Signed] ELLEN G. WHITE

Footnotes

1. Shortly after Mrs. White's death, Edson and William White, for a relatively modest consideration, relinquished all claims on this potential income.
2. The three trustees relinquished, without any consideration, all claims to this proposed educational fund.
3. These bequests were not paid until all creditors had been paid in full.

Appendix O

Comments of National Leaders in the Early 1860s Regarding Slavery Crisis

As documented in Lee Ellsworth Eusey, "The American Civil War: An Interpretation," a Master of Arts thesis, Andrews University, April 1965.

1. Alexander H. Stephens, vice-president of the Confederacy, told a Savannah audience on March 21, 1861, "that their revolution had thus far been accomplished without shedding a drop of blood—that the fear of a deadly collision with the Union they had renounced was nearly dispelled."—Horace Greeley, *The American Conflict,* I (Hartford, CT: O. D. Case, Co., 1866), pp. 437, 438.

2. "Let us make quick work. . . . A strong, active 'pull together' will do our work effectually in thirty days."—A *New York Times* editorial [between April 15 and July 21, 1861] quoted in Robert L. Dabney, *Life and Campaigns of Thomas J. Jackson* (New York: Blelock and Co., 1866), 210 n.

3. "If Abraham Lincoln is equal to the position he fills, this war will be over by January, 1862."—*Harper's Weekly,* May 4, 1861, p. 274 (re-issue).

4. "It is now recommended that you give legal means for making this contest a short and decisive one."—Abraham Lincoln, in a letter to Congress, July 4, 1861, cited in Carl Sandburg, *Abraham Lincoln, The War Years-I,* vol. 3 (New York: Charles Scribner's Sons, 1939), p. 290.

5. "Whatever war there is, may easily be made a war at sea,—a war of blockades,—a war having for its sole object the protection of American property and preservation of American commerce."—Editorial, *The New York Times,* Jan. 10, 1861.

6. In the fall of 1861, General William Sherman pressed Simon Cameron, war secretary, for 60,000 troops immediately and an additional 200,000 to meet future demands. Although this came nine months after Ellen White's Parkville vision, Sherman was criticized by the press as one mentally unbalanced. One month after this request, General Henry Halleck relieved Sherman of his command. But in the next four years, both Ellen White and General Sherman were proven to be the realists.—See William T. Sherman, *Memoirs of General T. Sherman,* I (New York: Appleton and Co., 1876, 2 vols.), pp. 203-205, 217.

7. [Lincoln] "like nearly everyone, cherished a hope that powerful advances in Virginia and down the Mississippi would end the fighting in 1862."—Allan Nevins, *War for the Union* (New York: Charles Scribner's Sons, 1959, 2 vols.), II, p. 5.

8. Following the capture of Fort Donelson the spirits of the North, including General Grant, ran high and "for a brief hour Northerners who saw what might be done believed the end near."—*Ibid.,* II, pp. 29, 76; James G. Randall, *Civil War and Reconstruction* (New York: D. C. Heath and Co., 1937), p. 281.

9. When Ellen White wrote her dire warnings in early 1862, after almost a year of fight-

ing, Northern cumulative casualties had reached only 5,498, Southern, 5,708. Before 1862 ended, the North had suffered 80,665 casualties, the South, 82,369—a frightful affirmation of Mrs. White's forebodings. See Eusey's Chart of Annual Forces and Casualties.

10. Mrs. White's dire warnings and vivid descriptions of forthcoming Civil War battles were often validated by eye witnesses. General U. S. Grant's *Memoirs* include: "This had been taken as a hospital, and all night wounded men were being brought in, their wounds dressed, a leg or an arm amputated as the case might require, and everything being done to save life or alleviate suffering. The sight was more unendurable than encountering the enemy's fire, and I returned to my tree in the rain. . . . I saw an open field, in our possession on the second day, over which the Confederates had made repeated charges the day before, so covered with dead that it would have been possible to walk across the clearing, in any direction stepping on dead bodies, without a foot touching the ground."—*Personal Memoirs of U. S. Grant* (New York: Charles L. Webster Co., 1885-1886, 2 vols.), I, pp. 349, 356.

11. Hope for a short end of the war was revived when Grant was given command of all the Northern armies in the spring of 1864. Horace Greeley wrote that "the strongly prevalent opinion of the loyal States, throughout the Spring of 1864, imported [spelled the hope] that Gen. Grant would make short work of what was left of the Confederacy."—Greeley, *The American Conflict,* II, p. 654.

12. But these hopes were quickly dashed when losses in Grant's army during the first twenty-eight days of the 1864 campaign against Richmond almost equaled Lee's total forces.—John B. Gordon, *Reminiscences of the Civil War* (New York: Charles Scribner's Sons, 1904), p. 294. "This costly and ineffective campaign of the new lieutenant general, from whom rapid success was expected, brought mourning to thousands of homes and discouragement to millions of hearts."—David S. Muzzey, *United States of America Through the Civil War* (New York: Ginn and Co., 1922), p. 587.

13. The combined Northern and Southern casualties [reporting far from complete] for 1864 amounted to 137,492, the all-time high.—*Ibid.,* n. 35.

14. Lincoln's Second Inaugural Address: "Neither party expected for the war the magnitude of the duration which it has already attained. Neither anticipated that the cause of the conflict might cease with, or even before, the conflict itself should cease. Each looked for an easier triumph, and a result less fundamental and astounding."—Sandburg, *War Years-IV,* vol. 6, p. 92.

15. "Finally, after four long years the destructive war machines ground to a stop. A supposed fracas had expanded during that time into the 'first of modern wars.' Warfare of attrition, of position, of siege, had dawned upon the world in America. Something akin to 'total war' had been sighted. White was certainly among the few, if there were any others, to have early 'sensed' what she called the 'reality' of the Struggle."—Eusey, "The American Civil War: An Interpretation," p. 23.

Appendix P

The Ellipse of Salvation Truth

Truth in any area of thought, whether in theology, philosophy, law, music, or education, must be understood in the form of an ellipse rather than a circle. An ellipse has two foci; a circle has one.

This means that truth is the sum total of its objective and subjective elements, the two foci in the ellipse. In music, for example, many find satisfaction primarily in objective elements such as harmony, unity, and order. Others seek music primarily for subjective reasons in that certain music expresses, or reflects, their feelings. Thus, one person may consider a particular piece of music as classical (Mozart) while another may classify it as expressionism (Beatles, rock, etc.). The point is that neither foci is the totality of truth. The human need for order, on the one hand, and the need for relevance and meaning, on the other, is the basic structure that truth is meant to satisfy.

In politics, we see the two focal points as socialism (collectivism) and free enterprise (democracy). In economics, the foci are Keynesian (government control) and free trade. In education, content-centered versus student-centered. In epistemology, idealism versus naturalism.

In theology, truth is the sum total of its objective and subjective elements. One focus is the emphasis on transcendence (revelation) and the other is immanence (human response, such as reason and feeling). To ignore the existence of the two foci in the theological ellipse makes the ellipse of truth into two circles. And the two circles have been arguing their particular point of view since Creation.

But Biblical truth unites the two circles within the ellipse of salvation. Thus, revelation with the authority of God's Word, meets our human need for meaning and relevance. Some call this interchange the objective, external Word meeting the subjective response of a person saying, "This truth is for me."

In other words, when someone appeals to the Bible as "truth" without an equal emphasis on personal meaning and relevance, we know that the ellipse has become two circles. On the other hand, when one appeals primarily to reason or feeling as the test of truth (human autonomy), we also know that the ellipse has become two circles.

Salvation truth binds together the objective will of God and the subjective "Yes" of a responsible (able-to-respond) person. Even as water cannot be divided between hydrogen and oxygen and remain water, so the objective and subjective elements of salvation cannot be divided and yet remain "salvation."

For example, grace fulfills its task only when men and women of faith respond. Likewise, pardon/forgiveness comes only to those who comply with its conditions such as a sincere desire for power to overcome the evil for which the pardon is sought.

All the divisions between various churches within Christianity, and between Christianity and other world religions, occur when the ellipse is ignored. When one of the foci becomes the "circle of truth," we surely have a heresy (a partial truth that becomes a whole error).

For example:

- An overemphasis on objective justification leads to human passivity, with faith becoming primarily a matter of mental assent to revelation. This often leads to a *careless* use of such phrases as "Jesus paid it all." Or "the atonement was completed on the cross," etc.
- An overemphasis on subjective sanctification leads to feeling and reason as the test of faith. This often leads a person to *minimize* the primary authority of God and to make predominant such words as, "It's not truth for me unless I feel it or until it makes sense to me." Or people may place primary weight on visual "evidence" such as faith healing, glossolalia (speaking in tongues), charismatic speakers, hugging, laughing, religious meetings, etc.
- An overemphasis on objective justification tends to make imputed righteousness the most important element in salvation.
- An overemphasis on subjective sanctification (imparted righteousness) tends to make human performance the basis of salvation.
- An overemphasis on Christ on the cross tends to eclipse the essential importance of Christ as our all-powerful Mediator/High Priest and/or to minimize the essential work of the Holy Spirit.
- Those who overemphasize free grace tend to seek assurance in the security of legal adjustments in heavenly books without understanding that repentance includes more than forgiveness. On the other hand, those who do not place proper emphasis on grace tend to seek their assurance in legalistic behavior. Neither group sees the larger picture of a gracious, forgiving Lord who extends His personal power to the penitent in the process of restoring sinners to be trusting, joyfully obedient children who will trust their Heavenly Father forever.

To sum up, to espouse and emphasize only one focal point in the ellipse, is to distort truth. Even though each focal point in the ellipse emphasizes truths worth dying for, arguments will never end until a person accepts the total picture of the truths emphasized in both foci. This understanding of truth is as inescapable as the joining of hydrogen and oxygen to make water.

The writings of Ellen White transcend the arguing circles of Methodists and Presbyterians, for example, (or the arguing circles of Christianity and Hinduism, from another viewpoint), by seeing truth as the embracing ellipse rather than a tug of paradoxes and eternal tensions.

Examples of how the ellipse works:

Soteriology

Law	**Gospel**
Doctrine ●	● **Experience**
Word	**Life**
Grace	**Faith**

Atonement

Cross	**Most Holy Place**
Victim ●	● **Priest**
Substitute/Example	**Intercessor/Enabler**

Soteriology

Justification by faith	*Sanctification by faith*
Pardon ●	● **Power**
Forgiven	**Cleansed**
For us	**In us, and through us**

Selected Bibliography

Abbott, George K. *The Witness of Science to the Testimonies of the Spirit of Prophecy*, revised edition. Mountain View, Calif.: Pacific Press Publishing Association, 1948. (Hereafter, PPPA)

Ahlstrom, Sydney. *A Religious History of the American People.* New Haven, Conn.: Yale University Press, 1972.

Anderson, Godfrey T. *Outrider of the Apocalypse*, Washington, D. C.: Review and Herald Publishing Association, 1971. (Hereafter, RHPA)

Baker, Delbert W. *The Unknown Prophet.* Washington, D. C.: RHPA, 1987.

Bates, Joseph. *Autobiography of Elder Joseph Bates.* Battle Creek, Mich.: Seventh-day Adventist Publishing Association, 1868.

Battistone, Joseph. *The Great Controversy Theme.* Berrien Springs, Mich.: Andrews University Press, 1978.

Bettmann, Otto. *The Good Old Days—They Were Terrible!* New York: Random House, 1974.

Bloom, Harold. *The American Religion.* New York: Simon & Schuster, 1993.

Branson, W. H. *In Defense of the Faith.* Washington, D. C.: RHPA, 1933.

Bull, Malcolm and Keith Lockhart. *Seeking a Sanctuary.* San Francisco: Harper & Row, 1989.

Canright, Dudley M. *Seventh-day Adventism Renounced.* New York: Fleming H. Revell Company, 1889.

Christian, Lewis H. *The Fruitage of Spiritual Gifts.* Washington, D. C.: RHPA, 1947.

Clark, Jerome. *1844.* (Three volumes.) Nashville, Tenn.: Southern Publishing Association, 1968. (Hereafter, SPA).

Coon, Roger. *A Gift of Light.* Washington, D. C.: RHPA, 1983.

____, *Ellen G. White and Vegetarianism.* Nampa, Idaho: PPPA, 1986.

____, *Heralds of New Light.* Nampa, Idaho: PPPA, 1987.

____, *The Great Visions of Ellen G. White.* Hagerstown, Md.: RHPA, 1992.

Cousins, Norman. *Anatomy of an Illness.* New York: W. W. Norton, 1979.

____, *Head First: The Biology of Hope.* New York: E. P. Dutton, 1989.

____, *The Healing Heart.* New York: Avon Books, 1984.

Damsteegt, P. Gerard. *Foundations of the Seventh-day Adventist Message and Mission.* Grand Rapids, Mich.: Eerdmans, 1977.

Daniells, Arthur G. *Christ Our Righteousness.* Washington, D. C.: RHPA, 1941.

____, *The Abiding Gift of Prophecy.* Mountain View, Calif.: PPPA, 1936.

Dayton, Donald W. and Robert K. Johnston, eds. *The Variety of American Evangelicalism.* Downers Grove, Ill.: Inter Varsity Press, 1991.

Delafield, D. A. *Ellen G. White in Europe, 1885-1887.* Washington, D. C.: RHPA, 1975.

Douglass, Herbert E. *The End.* Mountain View, Calif.: PPPA, 1979.

____, ed. *What Ellen White Has Meant to Me.* Washington, D. C.: RHPA, 1973.

Durand, Eugene F. *Yours in the Blessed Hope, Uriah Smith.* Washington, D. C.: RHPA, 1980.

Ellen G. White Estate. *I'd Like to Ask Sister White . . .* Washington, D. C.: RHPA, 1965.

Folkenberg, Robert S. *We Still Believe.* Nampa, Idaho: PPPA, 1994.

Froom, LeRoy E. *Prophetic Faith of Our Fathers.* Washington, D. C.: RHPA, 1950.

____, *The Conditionalist Faith of Our Fathers.* Washington, D. C.: RHPA, 1965.

Gaustad, Edwin, ed. *The Rise of Adventism.* New York: Harper & Row, 1975.

Gish, Ira and Harry Christman. *Madison: God's Beautiful Farm.* Mountain View, Calif.: PPPA, 1979.

Goldstone, S. Ross. *The Angel Said Australia.* Warburton, Victoria, Australia: Signs Publishing Company, 1980.

Gordon, Paul A. *Herald of the Midnight Cry.* Nampa, Idaho: PPPA, 1990.

____, *My Dear Brother M . . .* Nampa, Idaho: PPPA, 1997.

____, *The Sanctuary, 1844, and the Pioneers.* Hagerstown, Md.: 1983.

Graham, Roy. *Ellen G. White, Co-founder of the Seventh-day Adventist Church.* New York: Peter Lang, 1985.

Graybill, Ronald. *Mission to Black America.* Mountain View, Calif.: PPPA, 1971.

____, *E. G. White and Church Race Relations.* Washington, D. C.: RHPA, 1970.

Grotheer, William H. *The Holy Flesh Movement.* Florence, Miss.: Adventist Laymen's Foundation of Mississippi, Inc., n.d.

Haloviak, Bert. "In the Shadow of the 'Daily': Background and Aftermath of the 1919 Bible and History Teachers Conference," unpublished manuscript, November 1979.

____, "Pioneers, Pantheists, and Progressives," unpublished manuscript, June 1980.

Haynes, Carlyle B. *The Gift of Prophecy.* Nashville, Tenn.: SPA, 1931.

Hetzell, M. Carol. *The Undaunted: The Story of the Publishing Work of Seventh-day Adventists.* Mountain View, Calif.: PPPA, 1967.

Hewitt, Clyde E. *Midnight and Morning.* Charlotte, N. C.: Venture Books, 1983.

Holbrook, F. B., ed. *Issues in the Book of Hebrews.* Silver Spring, Md.: Biblical Research Institute, 1989.

____, ed. *Symposium on Revelation*, Book 1, Silver Spring, Md.: Biblical Research Institute, 1992.

Hook, Milton. "The Avondale School and Adventist Educational Goals." Doctoral dissertation, Andrews University, Berrien Springs, Mich., 1978.

Horn, Siegfried, ed. *Seventh-day Adventist Bible Dictionary*, revised edition. Washington, D. C.: RHPA, 1979.

Hudson, Winthrop S. *The Great Tradition of the American Churches.* New York: Harper & Row (Torchbooks), 1963.

Hyde, Gordon, ed. *A Symposium on Biblical Hermeneutics.* Washington, D. C.: Biblical Research Institute, 1974.

Jemison, T. Housel. *A Prophet Among You.* Mountain View, Calif.: PPPA, 1953.

Johns, Warren L. and Utt, Richard, eds. *The Vision Bold.* Washington, D. C.: RHPA. 1977.

Johnson, Carrie. *I Was Canright's Secretary.* Washington, D. C.: RHPA, 1971.

Johnson, Charles A. *The Frontier Camp Meeting.* Dallas, Texas: Southern Methodist University Press, 1955.

Kohn, Alfie. *No Contest.* Boston, Mass.: Houghton Mifflin Company, 1986.

Knight, George R. *Angry Saints.* Hagerstown, Md.: RHPA, 1989.

____, ed. *Early Adventist Educators.* Berrien Springs, Mich.: Andrews University Press, 1983.

____, ed. *1844 and The Rise of Sabbatarian Adventism.* Hagerstown, Md.: RHPA, 1994.

____, *Meeting Ellen White.* Hagerstown, Md.: RHPA, 1996.

____, *Myths in Adventism.* Washington, D. C.: RHPA, 1985.

____, *Reading Ellen White.* Hagerstown, Md.: RHPA, 1997.

____, *Millennial Fever.* Nampa, Idaho: PPPA, 1993.

Land, Gary, ed. *Adventism in America.* Grand Rapids, Mich.: Eerdmans, 1986.

____, *The World of Ellen G. White.* Washington, D. C.: RHPA, 1987.

Latourette, K. S. *A History of the Expansion of Christianity*, vol. 4. New York: Harper & Brothers, 1941.

Lesher, Richard. *Ellen G. White's Concept of Sanctification.* Doctoral dissertation, New York University, 1970.

Lewis, Richard B. *Streams of Light.* Mountain View, Calif.: PPPA, 1958.

Loughborough, John N. *The Great Second Advent Movement.* Nashville, Tenn.: SPA, 1905.

____, *Rise and Progress of the Seventh-day Adventists.* Battle Creek, Mich.: General Conference Association of Seventh-day Adventists, 1892.

Maxwell, C. Mervyn. *Tell It to the World.* Mountain View, Calif.: PPPA, 1976.

____, *Magnificent Disappointment.* Mountain View, Calif.: PPPA, 1994.

McArthur, Harvey K. and Robert M. Johnston. *They Also Taught in Parables.* Grand Rapids, Mich.: Zondervan Publishing House, 1990.

Moon, Jerry Allen. *W. C. White and Ellen G. White, The Relationship Between the Prophet and Her Son.* Berrien Springs, Mich.: Andrews University Press, 1993.

Neufeld, Don, ed. *Seventh-day Adventist Encyclopedia*, revised edition. Washington, D.C: RHPA, 1976.

Nichol, Francis D. *Ellen G. White and Her Critics*. Washington, D. C: RHPA, 1951.

____, *The Midnight Cry*. Washington, D. C: RHPA, 1944.

____, *Why I Believe in Mrs. E. G. White*. Washington, D. C.: RHPA, 1964.

Nichols, Thomas Low. *Forty Years of American Life: 1821-1861.* New York: Stackpole Sons, 1937.

Nissenbaum, Stephen. *Sex, Diet, and Debility in Jacksonian America.* Chicago, Ill.: The Dorsey Press, 1980.

Numbers, Ronald L. *Prophetess of Health.* New York: Harper & Row, 1976. Revised edition, Knoxville, Tenn.: The University of Tennessee Press, 1992

Numbers, Ronald L. and Jonathan M. Butler, eds., *The Disappointed.* Bloomington, Ind.: Indiana University Press, 1987.

Olson, A. V. *Thirteen Crisis Years.* Washington, D. C.: RHPA, 1981. (Reprint of *Through Crisis to Victory*, 1966.)

Olson, Robert W. *101 Questions on the Sanctuary and on Ellen White.* Washington, D. C.: Ellen G. White Estate, 1981.

Oosterwal, Gottfried. *Mission: Possible.* Nashville, Tenn.: SPA, 1972.

Osborn, Ronald E. *The Spirit of American Christianity.* New York: Harper & Brothers, 1958.

Paulien, Jon. *What the Bible Says About the End-Time.* Hagerstown, Md.: RHPA, 1994.

Peterson, Donald I. *Visions or Seizures: Was Ellen White the Victim of Epilepsy*? Nampa, Idaho: PPPA, 1988.

Provonsha, Jack. *A Remnant in Crisis.* Hagerstown, Md.: RHPA, 1993.

Rea, Walter T. *The White Lie.* Turlock, Calif.: M&R Publications, 1982.

Rebok, Denton Edward. *Believe His Prophets.* Washington, D. C.: RHPA, 1956.

Reid, George W. *A Sound of Trumpets.* Washington, D. C.: RHPA, 1982.

Ricchiuti, Paul B. *Ellen.* Mountain View, Calif.: PPPA, 1977.

Rice, George. *Luke, a Plagiarist?* Mountain View, Calif.: PPPA, 1983.

Rice, Richard. *The Reign of God.* Berrien Springs, Mich.: Andrews University Press, 1985.

Robinson, Dores Eugene. *The Story of Our Health Message.* Nashville, Tenn.: SPA, 1943.

Robinson, Ella M. *S. N. Haskell, Man of Action.* Washington, D. C.: RHPA, 1967.

Robinson, Virgil E. *James White.* Washington, D. C.: RHPA, 1976.

Schaefer, Richard A. *Legacy: The Heritage of a Unique International Medical Outreach.* Mountain View, Calif.: PPPA, 1977.

Schwarz, Richard W. "John Harvey Kellogg: American Health Reformer," Doctoral dissertation. University of Michigan, Ann Arbor, Mich., 1964.

____, *John Harvey Kellogg, M. D.* Nashville, Tenn.: SPA, 1970.

____, *Light Bearers to the Remnant.* Mountain View, Calif.: PPPA, 1979.

Shaw, Horace. "A Rhetorical Analysis of the Speaking of Mrs. Ellen G. White, A Pioneer Leader and Spokeswoman of the Seventh-day Adventist Church." Doctoral dissertation, Michigan State University, East Lansing, Mich., 1959.

Smith, H. Shelton, Robert T. Handy, Lefferts A. Loetescher. *American Christianity: An Historical Interpretation With Documents.* New York: Charles Scribners's Sons, 1963.

Spalding, Arthur W. *Origin and History of Seventh-day Adventists.* Washington, D. C.: RHPA, 1961.

Spicer, William A. *The Spirit of Prophecy in the Advent Movement.* Washington, D. C.: RHPA, 1937.

Steinweg, Virginia. *Without Fear or Favor.* Washington, D. C.: RHPA, 1979.

Teel, Charles W., Jr., ed. *Remnant & Republic.* Loma Linda, Calif.: Center for Bioethics, 1995.

Utt, Walter C. *A Mountain, a Pickax, a College.* Angwin, Calif.: Alumni Association of Pacific Union College, 1968.

Valentine, Gilbert M. *The Shaping of Adventism.* Berrien Springs, Mich.: Andrews University Press, 1992.

Vande Vere, E. K. *The Wisdom Seekers.* Nashville, Tenn.: SPA, 1972.

Wallenkampf, Arnold V. *What Every Adventist Should Know About 1888.* Washington, D. C.: RHPA, 1988.

Weeks, Howard B. *Adventist Evangelism in the Twentieth Century.* Washington, D. C.: RHPA, 1969.

Wellcome, Isaac C. *History of the Second Advent Message.* Boston, Mass.: Advent Christian Publication Society, 1874.

Wieland, Robert J. *The 1888 Message, an Introduction.* Revised and enlarged. Washington, D.C.: RHPA, 1997.

____, and Donald K. Short. *1888 Re-examined,* Revised and updated. Leominster, Mass.: The Eusey Press, 1987.

White, Arthur L. *Ellen G. White* (Six-volume biography). Washington, D. C.: RHPA, 1981-1986.

____, *Ellen G. White—The Human Interest Story.* Washington, D. C.: RHPA, 1972.

____, *The Ellen G. White Writings.* Washington, D. C.: RHPA, 1973.

____, *Messenger to the Remnant.* Washington, D. C.: RHPA, 1969.

White, James. *Life Incidents in Connection With the Great Advent Movement.* Battle Creek, Mich.: Seventh-day Adventist Publishing Association, 1868.

____, *A Word to the Little Flock.* Gorham, Maine: James White, 1847.

Whidden, Woodrow W. *Ellen White on Salvation.* Hagerstown, Md.: RHPA, 1995.

Wilcox, F. M. *The Testimony of Jesus.* Washington, D. C.: RHPA, 1934.

I

Index